THE URALIC LANGUAGES

Other works in the series

Forthcoming works in the series

THE URALIC LANGUAGES

EDITED BY
Daniel Abondolo

LONDON AND NEW YORK

First published 1998
by Routledge
2 Park Square, Milton Park, Abingdon, Oxon, OX14 4RN
270 Madison Ave, New York, NY1006

Reprinted 2006

Routledge is an imprint of the Taylor & Francis Group, an informa business

Typeset in 10.5/12 Times by Solidus, Bristol
Printed and bound in Great Britain by
The Cromwell Press, Trowbridge, Wiltshire

British Library Cataloguing-in-Publication Data

A catalogue record for this book is available from the British Library

Library of Congress Cataloging-in-Publication Data

   The Uralic languages / edited by Daniel Abondolo.
      (Routledge language family descriptions)
      Includes bibliographical references and index.
      1. Uralic languages.   I. Abondolo, Daniel Mario   II. Series.
   PH 14.U67   1997   96–29898
   494'.5—dc2l   CIP

ISBN10: 0-415-41264-1
ISBN13: 978-0-415-41264-3

Contents

List of Figures

List of Maps

List of Tables

List of Contributors

Daniel Abondolo, School of Slavonic and East European Studies, University of London, UK.

Sándor Csúcs, Hungarian Academy of Sciences, Budapest, Hungary.

Anu-Reet Hausenberg, University of Tallinn, Estonia.

Eugene Helimski, Russian State University for the Humanities, Moscow, Russia.

László Honti, Finno-Ugric Seminar, Groningen, The Netherlands.

Juha Janhunen, Department of Asian and African Studies, University of Helsinki, Finland.

Eeva Kangasmaa-Minn, Professor Emeritus, University of Turku, Finland.

László Keresztes, Institute for East European and Oriental Studies, University of Oslo, Norway.

Timothy Riese, Institute for Finno-Ugric Studies, University of Vienna, Austria.

Tapani Salminen, University of Helsinki, Finland.

Pekka Sammallahti, University of Oulu, Finland.

Péter Simoncsics, University of Budapest, Hungary.

Tiit-Rein Viitso, University of Tartu, Estonia.

Gábor Zaicz, Péter Pázmány Catholic University, Piliscsaba, Hungary.

Preface

In basic outline, this volume follows the model of previous works in the series, most particularly B. Comrie and G. C. Corbett (eds) *The Slavonic Languages* (London: Routledge 1993) and E. König and J. van der Auwera (eds) *The Germanic Languages* (London: Routledge 1994). Like those volumes, the present work focuses on the languages of a genetic unit, i.e. languages which can be said to be related to one another in that they have been shown to be later developments of an antecedent, putative, protolanguage. But whereas the Slavonic and Germanic groups are themselves genetic subdivisions of a much larger unit, namely the Indo-European family, with some 425 languages (Grimes 1996), the thirty-odd languages of the Uralic family have not been shown to be related to those of any other genetic grouping.

The total number of people who speak a Uralic language probably does not exceed twenty-five million. Compared with language families such as Indo-European, Semitic, Tibeto-Burman, or even Dravidian, the Uralic family may therefore be seen as small. On a global scale, however, twenty-five million speakers is a rather large number; the Algonkian family, for example, in North America, with a comparable geographic dispersion and number of languages, has only about 130,000 speakers.

Treatment of the present-day Uralic languages, plus one, Kamassian, whose last speaker died in 1989, is spread in this volume over fourteen different chapters. Of course, in a handbook of this size not every Uralic language can receive separate treatment in its own dedicated chapter. For the sake of compactness, for example, the nine or ten Saamic languages are handled in one overview chapter, which first outlines, from a historical perspective, the main isoglosses which distinguish these languages (and their dialects) from one another, then focuses on the synchronic description of one variety, the Eastern Enontekiö subdialect of the Finnmark dialect of North Saami. For similar reasons, the Fennic languages Ingrian, Votic, Livonian, Karelian, and Veps are treated together in a chapter which is primarily historical (Fennic); western readers in search of further detail concerning these languages may profitably consult Laanest 1982. In the case of languages with strong interdialectal cleavages, in particular Estonian, Khanty, and

Selkup, but to a degree in the Mari, Mordva, Komi, and Mansi chapters, as well, contributors have concentrated on one dialect, referring to other dialects only where this is helpful and unobtrusive. Some further information on the dialects thus sidelined may be found in the relevant historical chapters (Fennic, Permian, ObUgrian, and Samoyedic) and in the Introduction.

Throughout the volume, footnotes have been forborne and bibliography kept to a minimum, in keeping with series format. As a result, the presentation does not always make clear which of the ideas are the authors' own and which are transmitted; it is assumed that such information will not trouble specialists and would be of little interest to the general reader. Many general readers, though, will find that the bibliographical indications, particularly those of editorship and publisher, are often rather more sparse than those to which they are accustomed; this is not always a reflection of scholarly self-effacement but indicates the conditions under which the books were produced.

This book was prepared with many types of user in mind. The primary bias is synchronic, but there is also considerable treatment of the (pre)history of elements of each language and genetic subdivision. Therefore, those interested in diachrony, i.e. in change through time, will come by much general and specific information in this volume concerning the development of the Uralic languages, particularly in the nodal chapters on Saamic, Fennic, Permian, ObUgrian, and Samoyedic.

Those interested in finding out about a particular Uralic language will wish to proceed directly to the relevant language description chapter. These are in the form of brief sketches, and given the range of the material and of the theoretical backgrounds of the scholars recruited to cover it, it is inevitable that they vary somewhat in both style and content. All, however, strive for succinctness. The chapters are ordered on a geographical model and proceed roughly from west to east; thus, those interested in the geolinguistic context of a given language might usefully nose around in adjacent chapters. For example, after reading the Mordva chapter, the reader will find much that is instructively different or similar, from the typological perspective, in the chapters on Mari and Finnish. Parallel historical insights into Hungarian may be gained by a perusal not only of the ObUgrian chapter, but also of those on Permian and Samoyedic.

Typological comparatists, i.e. those interested in particular constellations of linguistic phenomena such as vowel inventories and harmony, consonant oppositions and gradation, negation, reflexive pronouns, loanwords, or the makeup of the noun phrase, will probably prefer to dip into various chapters as guided by cross-references and the subject index. Insofar as the diversity of the Uralic languages permits, the language description chapters follow a parallel design in order to facilitate such cross-linguistic checking.

Limits on space have meant that the Introduction cannot aspire to a balanced and critical survey of all topics, contentious or otherwise. It is written with the general reader in mind, and aims to provide basic background and to serve as an overture to some of the more prominent themes which crop up throughout the book; readers interested in gaining an overall impression of the Uralic language family should begin here. For further, and complementary, basic background reading, one might best begin with the far-reaching articles by B. Comrie and P. Sammallahti in Sinor 1988; with the compendious Hajdú 1992; and with Décsy 1965, which is concerned with Finno-Ugric only but is original and rich in insights. Historical and sociolinguistic perspectives on the Finno-Ugric languages and their speakers may be obtained from Haarmann 1974 and Taagepera (forthcoming). For the Samoyedic peoples and languages, the best overview is still Hajdú 1963. For a survey of the relatively insecure status of the languages spoken in the northern areas of the former Soviet Union, see Janhunen 1991.

Notes on Transcriptions and Other Apparatus

The default mode of presentation for language forms, even for languages with long-established orthographies, is phonemic; slant lines are therefore eschewed save where ambiguity would arise. Phonetic transcriptions, whether broad or narrow, are given in square brackets. In some instances, language data are presented on a more abstract plane, as well, in the form of a morphophonemic code. Such forms are given in majuscule and explained in the relevant chapters: see Finnish, Nganasan, and Hungarian.

Vowels are transcribed in accordance with the useful fiction of a three-tongue-height space, with basic **i e a o u** standing roughly for the vowel qualities of Spanish or Latin. These are supplemented by characters with dieresis, used to indicate a value of frontness or backness opposite to that of the plain symbol; thus **ü ö** are rounded *front* and **ï ë** are unrounded *back* vowels. A front (unrounded) low vowel is written **ä**, and the symbol **å** is used to render a back rounded low vowel. Phonologically distinct vowel length is rendered by doubled letters, e.g. **ii ïï üü uu**. Refinements and deviations from this usage are detailed *in situ*.

To simplify the typography of the transcription of consonants, palatalization is indicated uniformly by *j* superscript, e.g. **pʲ tʲ sʲ**, and separately from other feature diacritics, e.g. the palatalized pendant of hushing **š** is written **šʲ**. In most Uralic publications, it is traditional to combine such diacritics; thus what we write as **šʲ** here would be **ś**. Labialization is indicated in this volume by *w* superscript, e.g. **kʷ tʷ**. Affricates are transcribed either with their release component written superscript, e.g. **tˢ dᶻ**, or with unit symbols, e.g. **c ȼ**, depending on the phonology of the language concerned.

The orthographies of Hungarian, Finnish, and Estonian are used in an ancillary role in the chapters describing these languages. The writing systems of many of the Uralic languages spoken in Russia differ considerably in their use of Cyrillic; details will be found in the relevant chapters. For Nenets and Saami this book uses special writing systems, elaborated by the authors of the pertinent chapters in this book, which depart somewhat from the principles outlined above. It was deemed appropriate, in the light of the potential frailty of these languages, to cleave to these rather than to impose another system from outside.

Where relevant, forms are segmented insofar as the approach of the author and the type of transcription allow. Inflectional suffixes are preceded by hyphen, derivational suffixes by an equals sign, as in English *neighbour=hood-s*. The plus sign indicates the boundary between the members of a compound (*wind+fall*); ampersand signals reduplication (*willy&nilly*). Double hyphen precedes enclitics, e.g., *--kä*, Finnish *e-n--kä* 'and I don't', but follows a prefix, e.g., *em--* in Hungarian (orthography) *em--ez* 'this, (closer to speaker than *ez*)'. The glosses that accompany such forms have been designed to match them morpheme for morpheme: thus in the Mansi form *aasʲ-əm-nəl* FATHER-sl-abl, the root, meaning 'father', is *aasʲ*; the inflectional suffix *-əm* to its right is that of the first person singular (sl); and the inflectional suffix at the end of the form, *-nəl*, is the ablative. In keeping with common practice, full stop serves to link items that are separate in the metalanguage of the gloss, e.g. PRO.sl means 'first-person singular pronoun'.

Deviating from common practice, verb stems are glossed with the English third person singular present indicative form, e.g. (Erzya) Mordva *jarsa-* 'eats', contrast the infinitive *jarsa=ms* 'to eat' and the third person singular present form *jars-i* '(s)he eats'. For a list of abbreviations used throughout the book, see p. xxii.

Bibliographical Notes

There have been eight quinquennial international Uralist congresses since 1960. These have convened at venues rotating among Finland, Hungary, and the Soviet Union. With the exception of the first congress, they have been large events, and their proceedings, when published, usually run to several volumes. Thus, particular citations will have details such as '1B', meaning the second volume (B) in a subset of volumes.

No uniform convention of citation has emerged, but a widely used compromise writes *CXIFU*, where *C IFU* stands for *Congressus ... internationalis fenno-ugristarum* (with varying capitalization) and *X* stands for the number of the congress in question.

Perhaps out of piety, the first congress is referred to simply as *CIFU*, without the '1'. Details are as follows:

CIFU   *Congressus Internationalis Fenno-Ugristarum Budapestini habitus* 20.–24.IX.1960, Budapest.

C2IFU   P. Ravila, M. Kahla, A. Räisänen et al. (eds) (1968) *Congressus secundus internationalis Fenno-Ugristarum Helsingiae habitus*

23.–28.8.1965, Helsinki: Société Finno-Ougrienne.

C3IFU   P. Ariste, V. Hallap et al. (eds) (1975) *Congressus tertius internationalis Fenno-Ugristarum Tallinnae habitus* 17.–23.VIII.1970, Tallinn: Valgus.

C41FU   *Congressus quartus internationalis Fenno-Ugristarum Budapestini habitus* 9.–15. Septembris 1975, Budapest (I 1975, II 1980, III 1981).

C5IFU   *Congressus quintus Internationalis Fenno-Ugristarum*, Turku 20.–27. VIII. 1980, 1981.

C6IFU   È.A. Saveljeva and G.V. Fedüneva (eds) (1990) Материалы VI международного конгресса Финно-угроведов [Syktyvkar 24–30 July 1985], Vols I–II, Moscow: Nauka.

C7IFU   L. Keresztes et al. (eds) (1990) *Congressus septimus internationalis fenno-ugristarum*, Debrecen.

C8IFU   H. Leskinen et al. (eds) (1995) *Congressus octavus internationalis fenno-ugristarum*, Jyväskylä: Gummerus.

The following festschrifts are frequently cited:

Bereczki Festschrift	Domokos, P. and Pusztay, J. (eds) (1988) *Bereczki emlékkönyv (Bereczki Gábor 60. születésnapjára)*, Budapest: Faculty of Philosophy of the University of Budapest.
Hajdú Festschrift 1	Bereczki, G. and Domokos, P. (eds) (1983) *Urálisztikai tanulmányok (Hajdú Péter 60. születésnapja tiszteletére)*, Budapest: ELTE.
Hajdú Festschrift 2	Bakró-Nagy, M. Sz. and Szíj, E (eds) (1993) *Hajdú Péter 70 éves* [Festschrift for Péter Hajdú on the occasion of his 70th birthday], Linguistica. Series A, Studia et dissertationes 15 Budapest: MTA Nyelvtudományi Intézet.
Rédei Festschrift	Deréky, P., Riese, T., Bakró-Nagy, M., and Hajdú, P. (eds) (1992) *Festschrift für Károly Rédei zum 60. Geburtstag*, Studia uralica 6; Urálisztikai tanulmányok 3; Linguistica Series A, Studia et dissertationes 8, Vienna – Budapest: Institut für Finno-Ugristik der Universität Wien – MTA Nyelvtudományi Intezet.

References and Further Reading

Décsy, Gy. (1965) *Einführung in die finnisch-ugrische Sprachwissenschaft*, Wiesbaden: Harrassowitz.

Grimes, B. (ed.) (1996) *Ethnologue: Languages of the World*, Thirteenth (electronic) Edition.

Haarmann, H. (1974) *Die finnisch-ugrischen Sprachen. Soziologische und politische Aspekte ihrer Entwicklung*, Hamburg: Buske.

Hajdú, P. (1963) *The Samoyed Peoples and Languages*, Bloomington: Indiana University.
——— (1992) *Introduzione alle lingue uraliche*, translated and adapted by Danilo Gheno, Turin: Rosenberg & Seiler.
Janhunen, J. (1991) 'Ethnic death and survival in the Soviet north', *Journal de la Société Finno-Ougrienne* 83: 111–22.
Laanest, Arvo (1982) *Einführung in die ostseefinnische Sprachen*, Hamburg: Buske.
Sinor, D. (ed.) (1988) *The Uralic Languages: Description, History and Foreign influences*, Handbuch der Orientalistik 8/1, Leiden: Brill.
Taagepera, R. (forthcoming), *The Finno-Ugric Republics and the Russian State*, London: Hurst.

Acknowledgments

My first thanks go to my contributors, who not only furnished their chapters within deadlines but also often made thoughtful suggestions towards the improving of the volume as a whole. Thanks also go to colleagues who read various chapters and sections and made useful comments, most notably Peter Sherwood (University of London), Tapani Salminen (University of Helsinki), and Endre Tálos (University of Budapest). I owe a debt of gratitude to Jonathan Price, quondam senior editor at Routledge, for originally commissioning this volume, and sailing with me through helpful conversations concerning its form and content. I appreciate, and herewith thank, as well, all the other professionals at Routledge who helped me through the years, particularly Shân Millie, Louisa Semlyen, Seth Denbo, Denise Rea, and Sarah Hall. Special thanks go to Nicola Mooney, who typed swathes through more than half of this book, and to my copy-editor Judith Willson for her extraordinarily good-natured taking of pains.

My largest debt is owed to my teacher, Robert Austerlitz. He was the scholar who introduced me to the Uralic languages, and who first suggested that I teach a survey course on them. It was his teaching that most influenced my own thinking about language, and his encouragement and example that first got me started on the path that leads to this book. If these pages bear an editorial stamp, it is chiefly through my contact with him that that stamp was shaped.

July 1997
Daniel Abondolo
(editor) *The Uralic Languages*

List of Abbreviations

A	accusative	d	dual
A	adverbial	DD	definite declension
abe	abessive	def	definite
abl	ablative	desid	desiderative
abs	absolute	dn	denominal
acc	accusative	DN	Upper Demjanka
act	active	DT	Lower Demjanka
ade	adessive	du	dual
adj	adjective	dur	durative
adjsx	adjective-forming	dv	deverbal
	suffix	E	Erzya
adv	adverb	EE	Eastern Enontekiö
aff	affirmative	ela	elative
all	allative	EM	Eastern Literary
anaph	anaphoric		Mari
aor	aorist	enc	enclitic
app	approximative	ess	essive
Atl	Atlym	Eur	European
attrib	attributive	evid	evidential
B	Beserman	ext	extent
bot	botanical	Fe	Fennic (= 'Baltic
car	caritative		Finnic')
caus	causative	Fi	Finnish
cfv	comparative	FP	Finno-Permic
coll	collective	freq	frequentative
com	comitative	FU	Finno-Ugric
commis	commiserative	*FUF*	*Finnisch-ugrische*
cond	conditional		*Forschungen*
conj	conjunctive	FV	Finno-Volgaic
conneg	connegative	G	genitive
cx	case suffix	gen	genitive
D	dative	ger	gerund

ID	indefinite declension	mod	modal
id.	*idem*	Mr	Mari
IE	Indo-European	*MSFOu*	*Mémoires de la*
ill	illative		*Société*
imp	imperative		*Finno-Ougrienne*
impf	imperfect	N	nominative
ind	indicative	narr	narrative
ine	inessive	NdV	forms nouns from
inf	infinitive		verbs
ins	instrumental	nec	necessitative
inst	instructive	neg	negative
interr	interrogative	NF	North Fennic
intr	intransitive	Ni	Nizjam
ips	impersonal voice	nom	nominative
Irt	Irtysh	*NSK*	*Nykysuomen*
iter	iterative		*sanakirja*
J	Jugan	nsx	noun-forming suffix
Jk	Jukonda	O	Obdorsk
JSFOu	*Journal de la Société*	O	object
	Finno-Ougrienne	obj	object
K	Konda	obl	oblique
Kaz	Kazym	opt	optative
Kh	Khanty	ord	ordinal
KM	Middle Konda	OZ	Old Zyrian
KO	Upper Konda	P	partitive
kP	Komi-Permiak	P	Pelymka
Kr	Krasnojarsk	p	plural
KU	Lower Konda	part	participle
kY	Yaz'va Komi	partic	particle
kZ	Komi-Zyrian	pass	passive
L	Lozva	pejor	perjorative
lat	lative	perf	perfect
lim	limitative	pF	proto-Fennic
Lit	Literary	pFS	proto-Fennic-Saamic
lit.	literally	pFU	proto-Finno-Ugric
LM	Middle Lozva	plur	plural
LO	Upper Lozva	pM	proto-Mansi
loc	locative	Pn	Permian
LU	Lower Lozva	pO	proto-Ostyak
M	Moksha	PO	Yaz'va dialect of
MB	Middle Bulgarian		Zyrian
Md	Mordva	poss	possessive
M^E	Erzya Mordva	pOU	proto-ObUgrian
Mn	Mansi	pPN	proto-Permian

PR	predicate	sx	suffix
pred	predicative	Sy	Sygva
pres	present	SyG	syllabic gradation
pret	preterite	Syn	Synja
prf	perfective	T	Tavda
priv	privative	TČ	Čandyri
pro	pronoun	temp	temporal
prob	probabilitative	term	terminative
prol	prolative	TG	Gorodok
pros	prosecutive	TJ	Janyčkova
Ps	personal voice	tr	transitive
pS	proto-Saami	Tra	Tromagan
pU	proto-Uralic	trans	translative
pV	proto-Vogul	Trj	Tremjugan
pVo	proto-Votyak	*UAJb*	*Ural-Altaische*
px	person suffix		*Jahrbücher*
pZ	proto-Zyrian	*UEW*	*Uralisches*
refl	reflexive		*Etymologisches*
renarr	renarrative		*Wörterbuch*
RhG	rhythmic gradation	V	Vach
S	Saamic	V	verb
s	singular	VdN	forms verbs from
S	subject		nouns
Sa	Samoyedic	VH	vowel harmony
Sal	Salym	Vj	Vasjugan
sg	singular	VN	North Vagilsk
Sher	Sherkal	Vo	Votyak
Sib	Siberian	voc	vocative
sj	subjunctive	VR	verbal representation
S^N	North Saami	VS	South Vagilsk
So	Sosva	vsx	verb-forming suffix
SO	Upper Sysola	vx	verbal suffix
subj	subjective	WM	Western Mari
subl	sublative	Z	Zyrian

Map i   Uralic Idioms of the Volga Bend

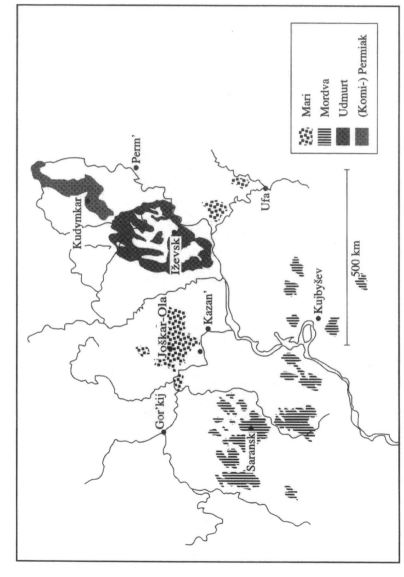

Source: Adapted from *Geographical Distribution of the Uralic Languages*, FU Society and Helsinki University, 1980.

Map ii   Komi

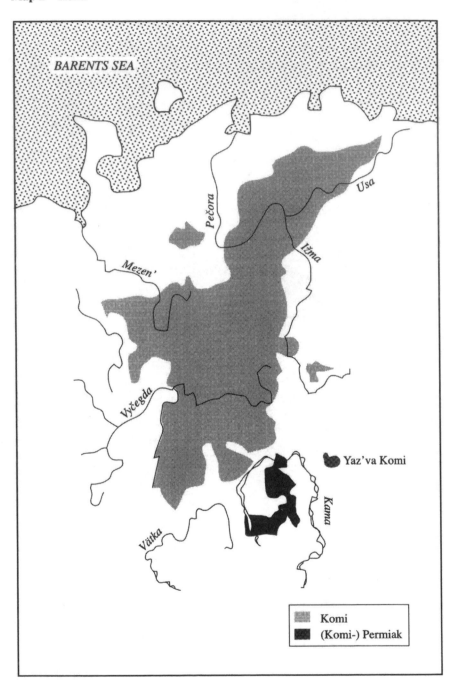

Source: Adapted from Haarmann 1974: 171–2.

Map iii ObUgrian

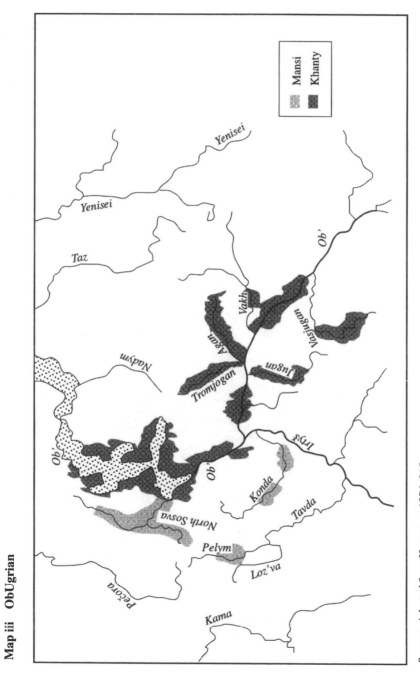

Source: Adapted from Haarmann 1974: 215.

Map iv   Samoyedic and ObUgrian (with Komi).

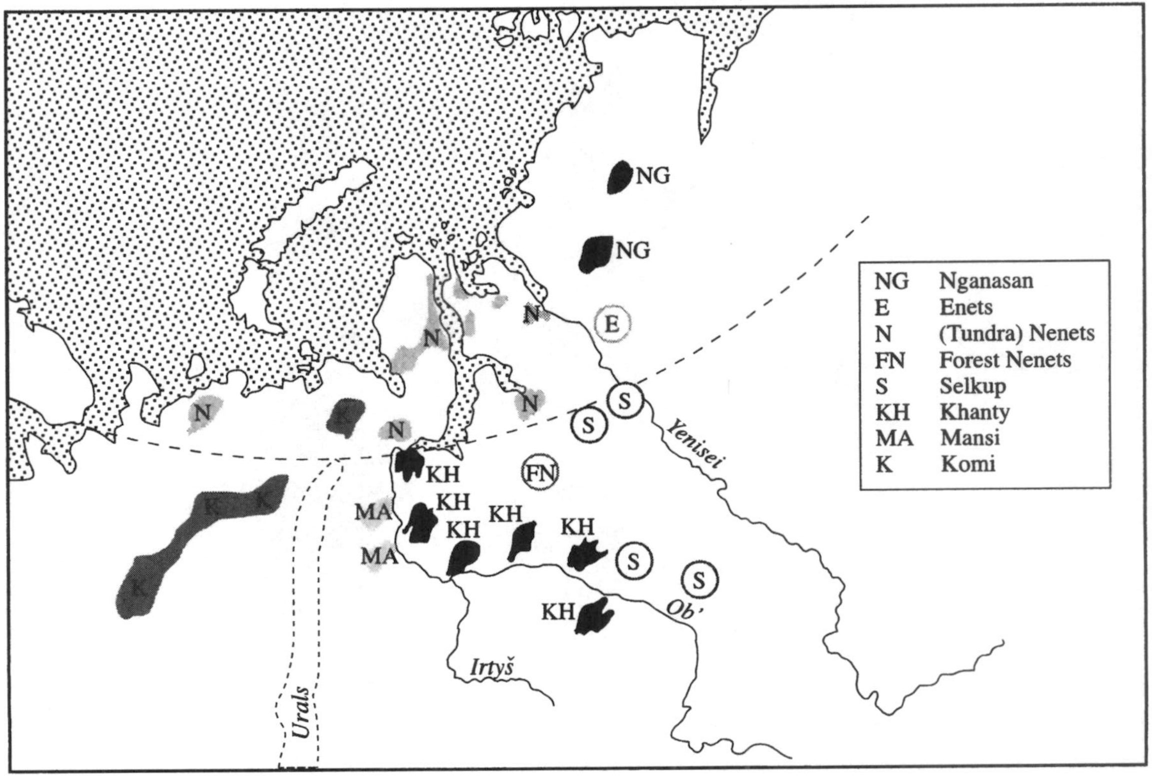

NG	Nganasan
E	Enets
N	(Tundra) Nenets
FN	Forest Nenets
S	Selkup
KH	Khanty
MA	Mansi
K	Komi

NG

NG

E

S

Yenisei

S

S

S

Ob'

N

N

FN

KH

KH KH

KH KH

KH KH

KH

KH KH

N

MA

MA

Irtyš

N

Urals

K

1 Introduction

Daniel Abondolo

The term 'Uralic' refers to the largest language family of northern Eurasia. This family consists of at least thirty languages, spoken in communities scattered over a vast area with western limits in Norway and Hungary and with eastern limits on the Taimyr peninsula and along the Yenisei and Ob' rivers of western Siberia. Their large number, and the considerable typological diversity of the phonology, morphology and even syntax of the Uralic languages make it impossible for this chapter to provide anything more than a brief survey of some of the more salient synchronic and historical features. The newer and older names for the languages and the names for their reconstructed ancestors are introduced below; the following sections treat phonology and morphology, from both a descriptive and a historical-comparative perspective; pp. 30–1 look briefly at some of the more common kinds of syncretism and suppletion in Uralic languages; syntax is broached on pp. 31–3; and the final section in this chapter gives a glimpse into Uralic vocabulary by presenting eight selected synonyms.

Good short general introductions to the Uralic languages are Janhunen 1992, Comrie 1988, and Austerlitz 1968. For a better understanding of the greater linguistic context, Comrie 1981b should be consulted; this book has good chapters not only on the Uralic languages but on 'Altaic' (Turkic–Mongolic–Tungusic) and Paleosiberian (Chukotko-Kamchatkan, Eskimo-Aleut, Yukagir, Ket, and Nivkh) as well.

Internal Subdivisions and Nomenclature; Possible External Connections

The locus from which these languages emanated, in other words: the proto-homeland of the speakers of the language from which all Uralic languages come, is unknown, but a relatively large and sparsely populated region at or near the southern end of the Ural mountains is likely. Some of the internal divisions of the Uralic language family are not entirely clear, but there is close to universal agreement within the profession that the primary chronological break was between Samoyedic on the one hand and Finno-Ugric on the other. The Samoyedic languages, spoken today chiefly to the east of the Urals, are thought to descend from a form of the Uralic protolanguage which spread

1

eastward, partly through the migration of its speakers, partly by pure linguistic expansion, and in the course of this separate existence developed its own traits and distinctive vocabulary. The population speaking proto-Samoyedic must have been quite small at first, and there is no reason to assume that it underwent any significant expansion before the dissolution of its linguistic unity, probably in the centuries immediately BCE. The bulk of the vocabulary which can be safely called common Samoyedic is surveyed in Janhunen 1977, which contains 650 root morphemes, of which only about 150 go back to proto-Uralic. This relatively small proportion makes it likely that the primary split of Uralic occurred at least six millennia ago, and possibly – given the sociological and demographic features of the early proto-Samoyedic population and the rate of change which these imply – much earlier (Janhunen 1992).

Many of the languages which resulted from the breakup of proto-Samoyedic have doubtless been lost without trace, but reports by European explorers from as early as the seventeenth century, and then by linguists beginning with Castrén 1854, have provided us with information about six distinct Samoyedic languages. Listed roughly from north to south, these are (older designations given in parentheses): Nganasan (Tavgy), Enets (Yenisei-Samoyed), Nenets (Yurak), Selkup (Ostyak-Samoyed), Kamass(ian), and Mator (Motor). The southernmost languages, Kamass and Mator, are now no longer spoken: Mator was replaced by Turkic idioms during the first half of the nineteenth century, and the fact that it is known at all today is because of intensive philological work done with word lists; the last Kamass speaker died in 1989. Of the more northerly languages, only Nenets is spoken by a relatively large number of people (some 27,000); Selkup, which has sharp dialectal divisions, has fewer than 2,000 speakers; Nganasan, some 600; and Enets, perhaps 100.

Compared with Samoyedic, the Finno-Ugric branch is and probably always was the larger, in terms of both absolute speaker numbers and internal subdivisions. At least one of these subdivisions must be quite old, dating back at least as far as the third millennium BCE. There is no universal agreement about the precise membership of the two groups which resulted from this first break within Finno-Ugric. As the name Finno-Ugric itself suggests, the traditional view since Donner 1879 has been that the two main subdivisions of this branch are:

1   a 'Finno-' sub-branch, which consists of Saamic (Lapp), Fennic (more commonly termed Baltic-Finnic), Mordva (Mordvinian), Mari (Cheremis), and the Permian languages Udmurt (Votyak), and Komi (Zyrian, Zyryene);
2   a 'Ugric' sub-branch, consisting of Hungarian and the ObUgrian (Ob-Ugric) languages, Mansi (Vogul), and Khanty (Ostyak).

Although basically correct, Donner's work was a false step, taken in haste by one whose forte was not the methodical side of historical-comparative linguistics (it was meant as a response to another, but intriguingly, mistaken publication of the same year by his rival, Budenz). The problem with Donner's subdivision lies not so much in its postulation of a primary divide between 'Finno-' and 'Ugric', as in the order of the subsequent subdivisions of the non-Ugric branch. Whereas Donner assumed that first Permian, then Mari-and-Mordva, and only then Saamic and Fennic had broken away, work since the 1970s comparing the Samoyedic branch with the Uralic family as a whole, but more particularly with the reconstruction of Fennic and Saamic, has led to a revision of this view. This revision sees Fennic and Saamic as forming a node of western peripheral languages, one which broke away from the rest of Uralic quite early, perhaps not long after the breakaway of Samoyedic; the Saamic–Fennic protolanguage itself had already begun to break up in the second half of the third millennium BCE (Sammallahti Saamic chapter 2, and 1984). Working with developments of the consonants in the Finno-Ugric languages, Viitso (1996) has now proposed a refinement to this revision, according to which the breakup of Finno-Ugric began in the west, with first Saamic–Fennic, then Mordva, then Mari, and finally Permian leaving the core. Expressed in terms of the conventional downward-growing ancestral tree, we would then have:

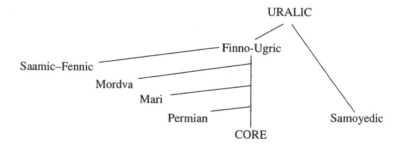

in which the 'core' is the linguistic cauldron from which 'Ugric' was to emerge.

As an alternative to the tree type of diagram, the meiotic amoeba model is useful for rendering transparent certain areal/typological zones (Sc = Saamic, Fe = Fennic, Mr = Mari, Md = Mordva, Pn = Permian, Hu = Hungarian, Kh = Khanty, Mn = Mansi, Sa = Samoyedic):

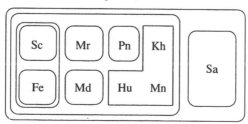

Whatever the cause of the split in the Saamic–Fennic node, there was a predictably uneven demographic result, with speaker populations living in climatically more clement areas expanding more quickly than, and eventually at the expense of, their northern linguistic relatives. The number of people speaking a Saamic language today is no more than about thirty-five thousand, while Fennic languages are spoken by more than six million. Within each branch the figures are no more evenly distributed: while Northern Saami has some thirty-thousand speakers, Akkala, Pite, and Ume Saami have next to no speakers left; while Finnish is spoken by about five million and Estonian by about one million, Veps, an eastern Fennic language with strong dialectal subdivisions, is spoken by some six thousand people in two non-contiguous regions of Russia, and Livonian, a western Fennic language, is spoken by fewer than forty. Treatments of the subdivisions and designations of Saamic and Fennic may be found in Chapters 2 and 3.

The next node to break free from the centre was the ancestor of Mordva, which survives today as two varieties called 'Erzya' and 'Moksha', with a combined number of speakers in excess of one million. The similarities and differences between Erzya and Moksha have frequently been exaggerated or minimized for extralinguistic reasons; it is in any case difficult to quantify divergence. What deserves to be emphasized is the fact that there has been extensive borrowing and cross-fertilization between the two main types of Mordva, resulting in Moksha dialects with heavy Erzya influence and vice versa.

Proto-Mordva may have separated from the core at roughly the same time as proto-Mari, but the idea, once widely-held, that there was a common Mordva–Mari protolanguage (so-called 'proto-Volgaic') is now out of favour. Mari is spoken by something between six and seven hundred thousand people. Accurate figures for numbers of speakers by dialect are not available, but if we divide the linguistic terrain into the traditional East–West split of dialect groups the overwhelming majority will then be classified as speaking a form of Eastern (or Meadow) Mari, and probably fewer than one hundred thousand speak Western (or Hill) Mari.

Taken together, Saamic, Fennic, Mordva and Mari may be seen as forming the western wing of the Uralic language family. That this wing must at one time have had even greater diversity may be deduced from ethnonyms known not only from Russian chronicles but also from the historian of the Goths, Jordanes (fourth century CE); particularly pertinent are the mysterious *Merja* and *Murom(a)*, peoples mentioned in connection with the ancestors of Mordva and Mari, usually as living to the west and north of the present-day Mordva and Mari Republics, i.e. closer to Moscow. Beside the shared innovations of the Saamic–Fennic node and retained inheritances from proto-Uralic, the western Uralic languages today show common traits which stem from two additional sources: common borrowings (e.g., from Baltic and Germanic) and areal (*Sprachbund*) convergence phenomena, such as the subtractive expressions for 'eight' and 'nine', e.g. *kAktA e-k-sä-n $^{(*)}$TWO NEG. VERB-PRES-3-DUAL 'two are not' = 'eight'. These geographical and areal factors should be seen against the background of intensive economic and political expansion, particularly in the ninth and tenth centuries, which involved the explosion of East Slavonic, the Varangian (Viking) conquests, and the re-immigration of western, probably mostly Fennic (cf. the people referred to in Russian chronicles as 'Chud'), Uralic speakers into what is now central western Russia.

The predecessor of the Permian languages, proto-Permian, was presumably the last to break away from what is here called the core. In its descendants one can see clearly the continuation of at least one drift feature already well underway in pre-Mordva and pre-Mari, namely the weakening of non-initial obstruents. For example, the intervocalic *-t- in the word for 'water', preserved nicely in the Finnish oblique stem *vete-* but voiced in Mordva (*ved^j*) and spirantized in Mari (*wüðə-*), has vanished entirely in the Permian languages, viz. Komi *va*, Udmurt *vu*. Permian symbiosis probably lasted well over two thousand years, from about the middle of the second millennium BCE to around the ninth century, when the forerunner of Komi began to take shape with the Permian expansion into the vast territory to the north of the putative Permian homeland between the Vyatka and Kama Rivers. That this expansion was no simple one-off departure, but rather a cyclical, back-eddying, centripetal as well as centrifugal, movement of people, goods, and language is suggested in Austerlitz 1985.

In Hungarian, but not in the ObUgrian languages, a similar sort of weakening took place; the Hungarian word for 'water' is (oblique stem) *vizä-*. The relative chronologies of obstruent weakening/voicing and of developments such as *nt > -d- in pre-Hungarian differ, however, from those of Permian, and the parallel development exemplified by cognates such as Komi *tëd-* = Hungarian *tud-* 'knows' is therefore evidence of secondary, areal contacts at best, and not of a genetic relationship between Hungarian and Permian closer than that between Hungarian and ObUgrian (Rédei 1988: 353–7). There must have been some early contact between speakers of pre-Hungarian and proto-Permian, however, to judge by the quantity and quality of correspondences between Hungarian and the Permian languages in the domains of morphological typology, both in root architectonics, predominantly (C)VC(C), and in inflection, seen particularly in the hypertrophic case systems discussed below; there are also lexical borrowings (e.g. the Hungarian words for 'bread', 'silver', and 'threshhold') and a few striking parallels in derivational morphology, e.g. the infinitive (Permian *-ni*, Hungarian *-ni* from a deverbal noun *=nA plus a lative suffix) and the suffix *=mVn, used to form decades, e.g. Hungarian =*vän*, Komi =*ïmïn* in *ötvän* = *vetïmïn* 'fifty'.

Similarities between Hungarian and Permian pale, however, when one compares Hungarian with the ObUgrian languages, Mansi and Khanty. The genetic node of these three languages, termed 'Ugric', has proven extremely difficult to reconstruct in convincing detail. The reasons for this difficulty flow from what has already been said above; we may summarize them as follows:

1   Hungarian, Mansi, and Khanty are the sole survivors of what is here seen as the core, i.e. most central and innovating region, of Uralic linguistic and cultural space; we would expect languages in such a central, innovating position to undergo relatively rapid changes, even upheavals, in their phonological and lexical makeup. Put another way: had we no records of Latin, Romance would be more difficult to reconstruct on the basis of French than of Romanian or Portuguese.
2   The period of Ugric symbiosis must have been fairly short. There is no overall agreement among scholars concerning the dating of the break-away of proto-Permian on the one hand and the separation of Hungarian out of Ugric on the other, but a safe estimate would place the former no earlier than the middle of the second millennium BCE, and the latter no later than its end, i.e. a period of five hundred years at the most. It is not uninteresting to note that some scholars have posited similar or even identical datings for the beginning of the independent existence of both Permian and Hungarian (e.g. Décsy 1965: 154, 169, 172, 183).
3   As vehicles of culture, both Hungarian and proto-ObUgrian suffered major blows in the form of radical restructuring of *genre de vie*: while speakers of proto-ObUgrian, in consequence of their migration east and north, were thrust back into a neolithic cultural frame, speakers of Hungarian underwent the reverse scenario, namely the accelerated modernization which attended their settling in central Europe. The effect on the shared lexicon has been catastrophic: in both cases, old discourse was replaced or transmuted, usually beyond recognition (but cf. Honti 1990).

Difficulties with the reconstruction of Ugric have been a stumbling block which has hindered progress throughout Uralic comparative linguistics, from the historical phonology to speculations concerning active/passive and transitive/intransitive in the verb, and such fundamental questions as the nature of the proto-Uralic noun phrase. Much further work within Ugric and Permian will be necessary before a useful assessment of competing hypotheses, including that offered here, can be made. For a range of other views on the internal organization of Uralic see Gulya (1975), Suihkonen (1987), Hajdú-Domokos (1987), and Salminen (1993).

The precise number of Uralic languages cannot be given, as this would require a good answer to the question, 'What is the difference between a language and a dialect?' (A facetious answer, but one worth pondering, is: 'A language is a dialect with an army and a navy'.) This question is one of the most important posed by linguistics, but like most such questions, linguistics alone cannot answer it: the question is entangled with extralinguistic factors such as nationality, identity, social strata, and other complex variables connected with the hierarchization and hieraticization of behavioural diversity. In any case answering it would lead into topics and further questions far afield from the subject of this book.

Nevertheless, it can be safely stated that some Uralic languages are dialectally much more fragmented than others. The richest in this regard are Selkup, Khanty, and Estonian, and in all of these cases the authors responsible for each of these languages have chosen to focus on one variety, with reference, where useful, to others. (The situation in Saamic is extreme and *sui generis*.)

Similarly, certain branches are richer in subdivisions than others, and limitations of space have meant that certain languages/dialects in such branches do not receive separate treatment. This is especially noticeable in the case of the peripheral branches, Fennic and Samoyedic; to compensate for the omission of separate chapters on e.g. Veps and Enets, nodal chapters are offered. There are nodal chapters on ObUgrian and Permian for somewhat different reasons: these chapters not only highlight the similarities and differences between the languages in these central sub-branches, but also introduce the reader to some of the difficulties involved in the reconstruction of their ancestor languages. The chapters on Hungarian and Finnish are also somewhat deviant: since numerous descriptions of these languages are readily available in English, these chapters aim to supplement such descriptions by focusing on aspects of these languages which are not so well known, particularly as they are relevant to Uralic typology and prehistory.

Attempts at proving external genetic connections of the Uralic languages have been numerous. It is of course not only possible but likely that some protoform of pre-Uralic broke away from some older genetic unit, but such a break would have had to take place long ago, and because of this, great time-depth enterprises which seek to demonstrate such a break are not likely to be convincing. In the case of comparing Uralic with Indo-European two kinds of difficulty arise. On the one hand, the gross divergences between proto-Uralic and proto-Indo-European morphological typology mean that there is an enormous gap to be bridged, in both form and function; on the other hand, the gross divergences between proto-Uralic and proto-Indo-European phonology make comparison too easy: because of the rich inventory of stops in proto-Indo-European, for any proto-Uralic root of the shape *CVC(V) there are a great many possible proto-Indo-European consonantal correspondents. For example, to a proto-Uralic root of the shape *kVt(V)- one could plausibly cite, as formally congruent, proto-Indo-European roots of the shapes *kVt-, *kVd-, *gVd^h-, *g^{h}Vd-, and *g^{h}Vd^h-, not to mention roots with initial labiovelars (e.g. *g^{w}Vt-), or laryngeals (e.g. *h$_1$Vd-), or with clusters with *s* (e.g. *skVt-), or with more complex phonotactics (e.g. *skVid-). The chances of finding a formal match between proto-Uralic and proto-Indo-European reconstructed roots are thus perilously good (for a cautious recent conspectus of Indo-European phonology and morphology see Beekes 1995).

At first glance, comparing Uralic with 'Altaic' would seem more promising on both morphological and phonological grounds, but here the comparative method runs into another kind of difficulty, one of its own making. ('Altaic' is a phylum, or stock, containing the language families Turkic, Mongolic, and Tungusic; many scholars also include Korean and Japanese.) The difficulty of comparing Uralic with 'Altaic' resides in the fact that what is called 'Altaic' is not a family in the strict sense being used here, i.e. in the sense that Uralic, Semitic, Tibeto-Burman, Japanese-Ryuku, or Eskimo-Aleut are families. The historical development of all of these families has been established, by means of the comparative method, to a degree of precision which is both predictive and productive. 'Predictive' means that given form X in language Y we can predict, on the basis of regular correspondences and credible courses of development, what the form of its cognate, form Z in related language W, will be. 'Productive' means that such predictions will either prove to be correct, buttressing and fleshing out the detail of the family's genetic integrity, or they will fail, forcing the investigator to rehone his or her tools and to ask different, perhaps more penetrating, questions about the family's internal relations. On this view, comparing Uralic genetically with 'Altaic' is a category mistake, akin to comparing the Florentine sonnet, say, with all of Provençal versification. For somewhat similar views, presented in greater detail, see Janhunen (1984), Doerfer (1984), and Austerlitz (1978); for an opposing view see e.g. Miller (1990). On the other hand, broadly conceived typological comparison of the belts and pockets of languages and language families which stretch across central and northern Eurasia has proven to be a fruitful exercise (Austerlitz 1980, Nichols 1992).

The only truly credible candidate for productive, predictive comparison with Uralic is Yukagir, a language most safely classified, at present, as an isolate, i.e. as having no proven linguistic relatives. Yukagir is spoken by about 300 people scattered in small groups in northeast Siberia, and is traditionally bundled, with other small families and linguistic isolates of central and northeast Siberia, into a grouping called 'Paleo-Siberian'. If Uralic is related to Yukagir, any superficial similarities between the two are unlikely to reflect an old, i.e. genetic, connection. The proof will have to come from analysis which goes much deeper, makes more daring hypotheses, and thereby incurs greater risks. Two such analyses stand out: Harms (1977), on morphosyntax, and Nikolaeva (1988), on historical phonology and morphology. Cogent as each of these two attempts is in some of its details, there are also important points at which they clash, such as the role and development of the genitive and its surrogates; perhaps further work will discover an answer which resolves the dissonance.

If Yukagir should prove to be related to Uralic, the protolanguage, 'proto-Uralo-Yukagir', will be at a temporal remove at the very edges of recoverability. With our present primitive understanding of the mechanisms of language change, such time-depth precludes, by implication, the detailed reconstruction of the type that has been possible for Uralic, and thus also precludes, *a fortiori*, any predictive–productive comparison further afield. For a parallel situation in far eastern Siberia, see Comrie 1980a.

Sound Systems

The default airflow initiation for all Uralic languages is pulmonic egressive. Long stretches of Finnish, however, are often spoken on an ingressive pulmonic airstream, with whisper replacing regular voice (Laver 1994: 170).

Word-stress falls on the first syllable in most languages, although certain languages (such as Estonian) are tolerant of stress on other syllables in foreign vocabulary. The most notable exceptions to this pattern are found in a belt of west–central languages (Moksha Mordva, Mari, all of Permian save Komi) and in Samoyedic. The precise nature of each exception is different: for example, stress may be fixed, as in West Mari or Nganasan, where it normally falls on the penult, or in Udmurt, where it falls on the last syllable; or it may be mobile, as in Permiak, where its position is governed by morphemic valence, or as in Moksha Mordva or Tundra Nenets, where its position is governed by vowel sonority or fullness. Stress position in Selkup is governed by both phonological and morphological factors.

Consonants

Three kinds of phonological opposition are widely exploited in the consonantal inventories of Uralic languages: quantity, voice, and palatalization. The distribution of distinctive quantity and voice is quite skewed, and to a large extent coincides with the core/periphery split: most languages are rich either in quantitative consonantal distinctions (e.g. Finnish, Estonian, or Selkup) or in voice distinctions (Hungarian, Permian). Voice is distinctive at the phonological, but not at the deepest morphonological levels of Tundra Nenets; the same is true of some Saamic languages, e.g. Northern Saami nominative singular *oabbá* 'sister', genitive singular *oappá*; note also that the difference in the intervocalic consonants is not simply one of voice but also of duration (see Saamic, Chapter 2). A parallel pattern, namely of short intervocalic voiceless, and long intervocalic voiced, stops, occurs in Enets (Tereščenko 1966: 440, Ristinen 1960: 42–3). In the core, i.e. non-borrowed and non-affective, vocabulary of Mordva and Mari, voiceless obstruents tend to occur in word-initial position or together in clusters, while their voiced counterparts tend to occur in non-initial positions, particularly after sonorants and before vowels, as in Erzya Mordva *kudo* 'house', *kurgo* 'month', *makso* 'liver', and their West Mari cognates *kuðə* (with [ð] ~ [d]), *körgə* (with [rɣ] ~ [rg]), and *mokš*. In Mordva and Tundra Nenets, such voiceless consonants as do occur intervocalically tend to be pronounced longer than their voiced counterparts, e.g. Erzya Mordva *koto* 'six' with short geminate [tt]. The opposition of voice is well established in Hungarian, partly because of the great number of loanwords from Turkic and Slavonic, but it is perhaps even more deeply rooted in Permian. Examples of miminal pairs are Hungarian *pap* 'clergyman': *bab* 'bean' (both Slavonic in origin), and Komi *kër* 'taste': *gër* 'plough' (both of which go back at least to proto-Permian, cf. Udmurt *korel*, *geri*).

Palatalization, along with its opposites, either lack of palatalization (as in Mordva) or velarization (as in Tundra Nenets), occurs in one form or another in all Uralic languages except Finnish. In Hungarian, palatalization survives as a morphonological process, but palatalized consonants have given way to a series of palatal consonants, probably as a result of areal (Danubian) convergence. In Tundra Nenets and Erzya Mordva, the palatalized consonants interact with vowels to produce limited kinds of vowel harmony; see pp. 17–18.

As far as place of articulation is concerned, most Uralic languages have their consonants distributed fairly uneconomically over five oral zones, namely (1) labi(odent)al, (2) dental, (3) post-alveolar/retroflex, (4) palatal, and (5) velar, as in Erzya Mordva, where the voiceless series are:

	1	2	3	4	5
Stops/affricates	p	t	č	t^j	k
Fricatives	(f)	s	š	s^j	(x)

with (f) and (x) restricted to interjections and recent loans. The opposition implied by the place-based classification of columns 2–3–4 is misleading, however, since the hissing/hushing distinction for central fricatives and affricates is widespread among the Uralic languages, and palatalization is commonly grafted onto either or both, e.g. Komi plain *s* v. hushing retroflex *š* v. hushing palatalized *š^j*, as in *sïla* 'fatty', *šïla* 'awl', *š^jïla* 'I sing'. In languages in which voice is distinctive, oral zones 2–3–4 can become rather crowded; for example, Udmurt distinguishes fifteen oral consonants in this region. On the other hand, the distinction between velar and postvelar (often called uvular) places of articulation appears to be limited to Selkup, although it may be nascent, and due to Selkup influence, in Surgut dialects of Khanty. This distinction is doubtlessly an import; it is typical of languages to the east of Uralic, including Ket, Yukagir, and the Chukotko-Kamchatkan group.

Other than this velar/postvelar (*k/q*) distinction, the chief deviations from the five-zone pattern are found in Finnish, which lacks columns 3 and 4, and in languages which have in addition to columns 1–5 either interdental fricatives (as in Saamic, and some Finnish dialects), or labiovelars (as in some Mansi, Khanty, and Selkup dialects, for example Tremjugan Khanty, with six nasals: columns 1–5 plus labiovelar *ŋ^w*).

Voicelessness in consonants which are normally voiced, i.e. nasals, laterals, and trills, is found in some varieties of Saamic and Khanty, and in Moksha Mordva. Bilabial *w* has been replaced with labiodental *v* in most languages, in keeping with the general western Eurasian trend (Austerlitz 1976), but *w* is still found sporadically, e.g. in Udmurt, Mansi, and Selkup;

not coincidentally, labialized obstruents are found in the latter two languages.

As far as non-oral, non-nasal consonants are concerned, the type usually reported for Uralic languages is glottal stop and related phenomena such as *stød* (in Livonian) and 'doubling' (in Finnish). Glottal stop is particularly important in the synchronic and diachronic morphophonologies of most Samoyedic languages; it is *in statu nascendi* in some dialects of Udmurt and Mari (for the latter, see Vasikova 1992).

Quantitative distinctions among the consonants are most readily understood in terms of history. As mentioned above, in Finno-Ugric languages nearer to the core, stops in weak position were weakened, i.e. they were either (1) voiced, or changed into (2) fricatives or glides, or (3) melted into the surrounding vocalism. In most of the peripheral Uralic languages, on the other hand, such stops either (4) persisted or, (5) were strengthened:

1   pU *witi 'water' > Erzya Mordva *ved^j*, *pilmitä 'dark' > Komi *pemïd*
2   pU *witi > Hungarian *viiz*, pFU *ikä 'year, age' > Erzya Mordva *ije*
3   pU *witi > Komi *va*, pU *pilmitä > Finnish *pimeä*
4   pU *witi > Selkup *üt*, Finnish *vete-en* 'water sIll', pFU *ikä > Finnish *ikä*
5   pFU *kaata 'tent, dwelling' > North Saami *goahti*, pFU *ikä > N Saami *ahki*

The fortition process seen in Saamic has parallels in Samoyedic, cf. the geminate pronunciation of non-weak obstruents in Tundra Nenets.

In Saamic, strengthened consonantisms like that of (5) were maintained when at the onset of open syllables, but were pronounced shorter when at the onset of closed syllables, yielding one kind of consonant gradation, e.g. Northern Saami sN *goahti* 'tent' << *kaa'tä, sG *goaði* << *kaatä-n. Parallel strengthening of geminates in weak position also occurred, with parallel shorter pronunciation before closed syllables (*-tt- > *-tt- ~ *-'t-). In Fennic, consonant gradation arose in reverse fashion, that is it arose through weakening (see Chapters 2 and 3), but the results were roughly the same. We may schematize the developments of single consonants (x), geminates (xx), and clusters (xy) in Saamic and Fennic as follows:

	Saamic		*Fennic*	
	Strong grade	Weak grade	Strong grade	Weak grade
*x >	xx	~	x	x	~	x/2
*xx >	x'x	~	xx	xx	~	x
*xy >	x'y	~	xy	xy	~	xy/2

where x'x and x'y stand for a strong geminate or cluster, and x/2 and xy/2 stand for weak consonants and clusters, the phonetic realization of 'strong' and 'weak' varying from language to language, and within each language, depending on (1) the segments involved and (2) their position in the word.

In many dialects of Fennic (Votic, Finnish, Ingrian and North Karelian), and in most dialects of Saamic, the two types of *xx* fell together, i.e. the strong grade of single consonants came to be identical with the weak grade of geminates. For a recent survey of Fennic gradation see Barbera 1993.

Another kind of consonant gradation arose in Nganasan, the northeastern-most Uralic language. Since Nganasan may constitute a sub-branch of its own within Samoyedic (Chapter 15), it is plausible that phonetic features of the protolanguage gave rise to both the far western (Saamic and Fennic) and the far eastern versions (Helimski 1996).

The historical background of the consonant systems found throughout Uralic is clear, in the main. We may reckon with a consonant system with the same broadly five-zone system as that of most present-day languages.

In addition, there seem to have been two further segments, usually written *δ, *δ^j. Disagreement and uncertainty about proto-Uralic consonants usually centre on the phonological status and phonetic nature of these, and *c^j and *x. Since Steinitz 1952: 37, the phonemic status of *δ and *δ^j has been questioned, and numerous suggestions have been made with an eye to dispensing with them; so far none has been deemed fully successful (e.g. Décsy 1969, Tálos 1983, Kazancev 1990, Abondolo 1990, Honti 1992).

Both cacuminal *č and palatal(ized) *c^j are commonly reconstructed as affricates, i.e. as having had delayed release, but it is equally possible that they were both normally realized as stops. While it is possible to reckon without *c^j, explaining correspondences which would derive from such a segment as affective variants of *s^j, it is more difficult to manage without setting up *x, which is little more than a cover symbol for various phonetic phenomena occurring in the syllable coda, most notably lengthening of the preceding vowel (or of the following consonant) in Finno-Ugric and vowel sequences in proto-Samoyedic (Sammallahti 1978).

By the time of proto-Finno-Ugric, the consonant system appears to fill out, in part, no doubt, because we have a greater number of reliable etymologies with which to work. Whatever their precise age, the new phonemes *š and *l^j may be reconstructed with some reliability by this stage. In general

Table 1.1   Proto-Uralic consonant system

	1	2	3	4	5
Glides	*w			*j	*x
Nasals	*m	*n		*n^j	*ŋ
Stops	*p	*t			*k
Affricates			*č	*c^j	
Fricatives		*s		*s^j	
Lateral		*l			
Trill		*r			

throughout the pU and pFU lexica as reconstructed the stops occur more frequently in strong (= word-initial) position, while the liquids and glides occur more frequently in weak (= word-final and syllable-final) position; thus pU *sala- 'steals, hides' has a canonic shape, whereas a stem with a shape such as *lVsV- would be doubly non-canonic (there are, in fact, no good pU or pFU roots reconstructed with such a shape). This distribution persists, *grosso modo*, in Mordva and Mari, as mentioned above. The relative age of medial clusters, geminates, and the distribution of (geminate) affricates complicate the picture, as does the role of affective vocabulary and loans.

Vowels

At least in the first syllable, vowel quantity, i.e. phonologically relevant distinctions in the durations of vowels, is characteristic of most Uralic languages. The chief exceptions are Erzya Mordva, with a five-vowel inventory *i e a o u*, and Permian, where quantity is either vestigial, as in the stress-assignment of Yaz'va Komi, or nascent, as in Ižma and Vym Komi, where *Vl has gone to VV before pause or a consonant, e.g. *soo* 'salt', *sol=an+teg* 'salt-box'. Note that in this book length is indicated by letter doubling, unless otherwise indicated. In Enets and Kamass, the status of vowel quantity is unclear.

Quantitative oppositions of vowels take two major typological forms in Uralic, and in most cases investigators are in accord concerning the nature of each system. The more widespread type is based on the opposition short v. long. In this type the vowel system is made up of two roughly equal sets of vowels whose primary difference is one of duration. Examples include Forest Nenets (Sammallahti 1974: 13), with five long and five short vowels (*i e u o a ii ee uu oo aa*), Finnish, with eight short (*i e ä u o a ü ö*) and eight long (*ii ee ää uu oo aa üü öö*) vowels, and Sosva Mansi with four short (*i a u o*) and four long (*ee aa uu oo*) vowels. The other type is based not only on quantity but on fullness of articulatory detail: systems of this type are said to contain full versus reduced vowels. What this means phonetically varies greatly from language to language, but in every case the short duration of a reduced vowel is intrinsic, whereas the duration of the full vowels is much more susceptible to conditioned variability. Full vowels usually outweigh their reduced counterparts, if not in absolute numbers, then at least in terms of the features needed to define their qualities. Examples of this type of system are Salym Khanty, with full *ii ee ää uu oo aa*, i.e. six vowels and three tongue heights, and reduced *e ä o a ö*, i.e. five vowels with two tongue heights; Hill Mari, with full *ii ee ää uu oo aa üü öö* and reduced ə ə̂, and Tundra Nenets, with one, or, in another interpretation (Janhunen 1993), three, reduced vowels opposed to eight (or six) non-reduced vowels.

Long vowels alternate paradigmatically, or are in skewed distribution, with diphthongs in many languages. An example of the former is *ie ~ ii, eä ~ ee, uo ~ uu, oa ~ oo* in North Saami, e.g. (orthographically) nominative singular *guolli* 'fish', genitive/accusative plural *gūliid*. An example of the latter is Finnish, where the long mid vowels *ee öö oo* occur in the first syllable chiefly in foreign or affective vocabulary, pre-Finnish *ee *öö *oo having gone to *ie üö uo* in that position, e.g. *tie* 'road', cf. Estonian *tee*. Diphthongs are prominent in the phonologies of many Fennic dialects, in Eastern and Western Mansi (Honti 1988: 150, Sammallahti 1988: 506), in Nganasan, in southwest Selkup dialects (Katz 1984: 41), and many dialects of Hungarian (Kálmán 1966: 40–1). The alternation of long vowels with their short counterparts is particularly characteristic of Hungarian and Southern Mansi; in Khanty, full and reduced vowels in the first syllable of certain stems alternate paradigmatically, e.g. *e ~ öö* in Vakh Khanty *jööŋətwəl* 'spins s3': *jeŋtii* 'spin!'

Turning to the qualitative distinctions among the vowels, we may safely say that the factors of tongue height, frontness v. backness, and lip rounding account for most systems. The smallest inventory, that of Erzya Mordva, was given above. Moksha Mordva elaborates on this with the addition of an *ä* and two schwas, one front (*ə*) and one back (*ə̂*); Hill (West) Mari has all these eight vowels plus front rounded *ü* and *ö*:

Moksha Mordva					Hill (West) Mari				
i		u			i	ü		u	
e		o	ə	ə̂	e	ö		o	ə	ə̂
ä	a				ä		a		

The vowel inventory of Meadow (East) Mari differs from that of West Mari in that it lacks *ä* and has only one reduced vowel (*ə̂*). The three mid vowels alternate with *ə̂*, the reduced vowel occurring chiefly in non-final position; this is analogous to the situation in Erzya Mordva, where non-first syllable *e* and *o* are largely recoverable from an abstract neutral vowel; see Chapter 6.

In first syllables, the vowel inventory of proto-Saamic was probably as follows:

*i		*u			
*e	*ë	*o	*ee		*oo
			*ää		*åå
				*aa	

where *ë represents a non-front unrounded mid vowel; see Lehtiranta 1989. Several varieties of Saamic developed front rounded vowels through anticipatory metaphony, e.g. proto-Saamic *koolee 'fish' > South Saami *guölie*, Inari Saami *küeli*; in some of the eastern Saamic languages (Ter, Skolt, and Akkala) back unrounded vowels have developed secondarily, e.g. proto-Saamic *moorë 'tree' > Skolt *muër*, Ter *mïrr* (where *ï* represents a non-front unrounded high vowel).

The classification of vowel types in the Saamic languages is further complicated by the feature tense/lax, which has been used, for example, to classify the vowels of Ter Saami in a manner reminiscent of the full/reduced dichotomy mentioned above. Compare the maximal vowel systems of Arjeplog Saami (adapted from Lehtiranta 1992: 73–6) and Ter Saami (adapted from Korhonen 1984: 316–20):

Arjeplog Saami				Ter Saami					
Short		Long		Tense			Lax		
i	u	ie	uo	ii	ïi	uu	ie	ïe	ï
e	o			ee		oo			
	å	aa	åå		aa		ea	oa	a

The development of bichromatic (= both front and rounded) vowels and of non-low achromatic (= neither front nor rounded) *ïë* in Saamic is probably the result, in part, of relatively recent areal convergence, with Norwegian, Swedish, and Finnish providing the impetus for bichromatic *ü* and *ö*, and Russian and Komi furnishing the adstratum for *ï* and *ë*. The non-front non-low unrounded vowels of Permian, on the other hand, appear to be older, and outside influences are not obvious. Both the Udmurt and the Komi literary languages have the seven-vowel system *i e u o ï ë a*, but the prehistory of these vowels is complex, and their lexical distribution in the present-day languages severely impedes, or even prevents, mutual comprehension. For example, Komi *ë* can correspond to any Udmurt vowel other than *i*, as in *sëp/sep* 'gall', *lëz/liz* 'blue', *sën/sën* 'tendon', *lëdž^j/luz^j* 'gadfly', *tëd-/tod-* 'knows', *këv/kal* 'rope'.

Thus far we have been looking at systems with three tongue heights, and this is the most common type in Uralic. In such systems, the presence of *ö* presupposes *ü*, and that of *ï* presupposes *ë*: note the maximal vowel inventory of Literary Estonian, with *ë* but no *ï*, and of Nganasan, with *ü* but no *ö*. However, some of the ObUgrian languages have vowel systems which lend themselves easily to a two-tongue height interpretation, such as Sosva Mansi and Nizyam Khanty, both with

i		u			uu		i	u		ee	uu
		o	ee			*i.e.*					
	a			aa	åå			a	o	aa	åå

Notice that such an interpretation dispenses with the feature [+/-back], since the specification for [+/- low] and [+/- round] is sufficient to identify all of the vowels (cf. Katz 1975: 55, where the Nizyam Khanty vowels *ee aa åå uu* are classified as [+ tense]). Very few Uralic languages distinguish more than three tongue heights, but a vowel system with four tongue heights has been proposed for proto-Permian, and the distinction between open mid *o* (as in *pon* 'end') and closed mid *ô* (as in *pôn* 'dog') in Upper Sysola Komi is thought to be a preservation. A synchronically similar and unexpected *ô* seems to exist in Enets (Mikola 1984). Other subsystems with four tongue heights have been reported for various dialects of Selkup and of Võru Estonian.

Probably no academic field is more contentious than the prehistory of the Uralic vowels, and this is not the place for a treatment in depth. What follows is merely a presentation of some of the high spots; for a brief but clear summary see Hajdú 1992: 175–88. It is important to bear in mind that throughout the history of research into this subject, the development of the vocalism of the first syllable has occupied centre stage, to the virtual neglect of syllables further into the word. But the second and third syllables must have been important, and in fact the vowel of the third syllable probably influenced that of the second, just as much as that of the second influenced the first. There are traces of vertical vowel alternations, i.e. alternations involving tongue height, in both the second and the third syllable of Uralic reconstructions; while the exact form and function of these alternations remains unknown, they appear to have been independently motivated. Apart from these alternations, the second and third syllables are generally seen as rather uninteresting, with a restricted vocalic repertoire: supposedly only two phonologically distinct vocalisms were possible, and proto-Uralic bisyllables will be referred to here as A-stems (with *a ~ *ä) and I-stems (with *i ~ *ï), according to the tongue-height of the second-syllable vowel.

The primary factor dividing opinion about proto-Uralic vocalism concerns quantity. According to the view that has been the most rigorously demonstrated, if not the most widely accepted, distinctive vowel length throughout Uralic is a secondary development. Scholars who work within such a framework set up a proto-Uralic vowel inventory with four high vowels (*i *ü *ï *u), two mid vowels (*e *o) and two low vowels (*ä *a); this view is most clearly presented in Sammallahti 1978 and Janhunen 1981b. Those who think phonemic quantity was present in the Uralic protolanguage form a smaller and more heterogeneous group: some, following Steinitz 1944, work with full v. reduced vowels in the protolanguage; others, following Itkonen 1939 and its sequelae, set up a quantitative distinction only for the mid vowels, and substitute long *oo for *ï; a third idea, first proposed by Tálos (1983) and then pursued by this writer (1996), posits a proto-Uralic vowel system with only two tongue heights, but with quantity as a feature applying to all vowels, at least in the first syllable of words with second-syllable vowels of equivalent tongue height. The protovocalism assumed by the most up-to-date compendium of Uralic etymology, the *UEW* (= *Uralisches Etymologisches Wörterbuch*), is a committee-like compromise which incorporates features of the Itkonen and Sammallahti approaches.

Uralic and Finno-Ugric protoforms set up or cited in this book are given in either the *UEW* or the Tálos (hereafter: 'two-tiered') system. The one is in most cases readily converted to the other: one must simply remember that *UEW* *e is seen, in the two-tiered system, as the equivalent of long *ää in

A-stems and of short *i in I-stems, and, in parallel fashion, *UEW* *o is the equivalent of long *aa in A-stems and of short *u in I-stems. Thus *UEW* *pesä 'nest' is, in two-tiered terms, *pääsä, while *UEW* *wete- 'water' is *witi; *UEW* *kota 'dwelling, tent' is two-tiered *kaata, and *UEW* *ko(nʲ)cʲV 'long' is *kunʲtʲï. The vowels reconstructed by the *UEW* as high and short are, in two-tiered terms, high and long, e.g. *UEW* *ku(nʲ)cʲe(-) 'urine, urinates' is two-tiered *kuunʲtʲï.

The two-tiered system seems to have two advantages over that used by the *UEW*. First, it assumes a vocalic inventory and chains of vowel development which better fit much of the current understanding of universals (cf., for example, Maddieson 1984: 128–30 on vowel length, vowel inventories, and vowel change). Second, the trajectories necessary to derive the vowel systems of all of the present-day Uralic languages, core as well as peripheral, are more believable, again in terms of what we now understand about universals, when the starting-points involve both tongue height and quantity. One example will have to suffice here: it is the fact that whereas *UEW* *e in A-stems (= two-tiered *ää) regularly gives proto-Mansi long vowels (*ää, *ii), *UEW* *e in I-stems (= two-tiered *i) regularly gives proto-Mansi short vowels (*i, *ä). For further argumentation and supporting evidence, the reader is referred to Tálos 1987 and Abondolo 1996; for a natural phonology background to many of the assumptions upon which the two-tiered system rests, see Donegan 1985. Approaches closer to the Itkonen–*UEW* type may be found in this volume, in the nodal chapters on ObUgrian and Permian.

High/low vowel alternations in non-initial syllables were mentioned above; the more well-known vowel alternation seen in non-initial syllables is of the horizontal, i.e. front v. back, variety; this is the Uralic type of vowel harmony, a widespread phenomenon in the world's languages. In Uralic, vowel harmony is reconstructed as occurring in roots, derived stems, and inflected forms; the vocalism of the root is always dominant, i.e. determines the frontness/backness of the vowels of attached suffixes. For example, the proto-Uralic locative suffix was presumably *-na when attached to a back-vocalic root such as *kala 'fish' (*kala-na), but *-nä when attached to a front-vocalic root such as *witi 'water' (*witi-nä): such twofold representations may be conveniently captured by the use of majuscule letters, e.g. *-nA for the locative suffix. The Hungarian forms *hålon* 'on fish' (<< *kala-na) and *viizen* 'on water' (<< *witi-nä) are thought to preserve this twofold representation, as are the Finnish analogues *kalassa* and *vedessä* (via *kala-s-na, *witi-s-nä). In some languages, vowel harmony has been extended to embrace the opposition rounded/unrounded, e.g. East Mari, where reduced *ə* is *ö* after front rounded vowels, *o* after back rounded vowels, and *e* elsewhere; or Hungarian, where the same three mid vowels may be recovered from an abstract vowel (or zero): *ö* after front rounded vowels, *e* after front unrounded vowels, and *o* elsewhere. In Mordva (and to a lesser, and lexically marked, degree, in Nenets) the consonants are involved in vowel harmony alternations, palatalized consonants occuring in front-prosodic, and non-palatalized in back-prosodic environments. Consonant alternations are also a side-effect of vowel harmony in Nganasan, where front/back and rounded/unrounded harmony combine to form four-way (*i ~ü ~ i̇ ~ u*) alternations. In Hungarian and Nganasan, vowel mergers in the first syllable have rendered the prosodic membership of many roots covert. On the other hand many Uralic languages, such as Saamic, Estonian, Permian, Selkup, and most ObUgrian dialects, have 'lost' vowel harmony through various combinations of (1) loss of the non-first-syllable vowel which would have shown the alternation, (2) neutralizations, through mergers, of front/back vowel distinctions, and (3) radical rotation of the first syllable vocalism.

Morphology

Nouns and Adjectives

Nouns were probably not morphologically distinct from adjectives in proto-Uralic, although the distribution of the comparative suffix *=mpV suggests that an adjective category may have been developing before the breakup of Finno-Ugric, cf. the *=mpa ~ =mpi* of Finnish *korkea=mpi* and the *=bb* of Hungarian *mågåšå=bb*, both 'higher'. The original function of *=mpV was almost certainly one of opposition, used primarily with deictics, cf. Erzya Mordva *ombo* and North Saami *nubbi* (< *muu=mpa) 'other'. In Saamic, morphology for distinguishing attributive from non-attributive adjectives has evolved, e.g. North Saami *dimis* 'soft (on the inside)', attributive form *dipma*. Otherwise, nouns and adjectives need not be considered separately on either morphological or syntactic planes; in what follows, therefore, the term 'nouns' will refer to both.

The three nominal categories common to all Uralic languages are case, number, and person. In the protolanguage, all three of these categories could be represented by a zero suffix, with the grammatical meanings 'unmarked for case' 'unmarked for number' and 'unmarked for person'; the last instance is traditionally called the nominative, but absolutive would be a better term. Proto-Uralic nouns thus differed sharply from verbs, which rarely, if ever, occurred with zero suffix.

Case

In proto-Uralic, the noun had at least two grammatical cases: an accusative *-m, which probably was used chiefly to mark the definite direct objects of finite verbs (i.e. verbs inflected for person), and a subordinative suffix *-n which functioned as a genitive/prenominalizer with nouns and as an adverb-formant with verbs. There were also at least three local cases, including a locative *-nA, a separative *tA ~ *-tI, and perhaps the latives *-k (and/or *-ŋ) and *-cʲ (and/or *-nʲ).

The local subsystems of the case paradigms of most of the present-day languages reflect a three-way spatial opposition, with stasis (locative) opposed to motion, and, within the motion subcategory, motion towards a target (various latives) opposed to motion away from a source (various separatives). A few languages have only one fully productive suffix for each spatial subtype, e.g. the three-member system of Sosva Mansi (locative:lative:ablative), but most have at least one more. In richer case systems, hypertrophy of the lative category is the norm.

Grammatical cases. With the exception of South Mansi, the core languages preserve little or no trace of the accusative *-m. It is unlikely, but just barely possible, that the Hungarian possessive suffixes s1 *-m*, s2 *-d* continue earlier sequences containing the accusative (< *-m-mV, *-m-tV). There is no trace of an accusative *-m in Khanty. In Permian, the vocalic accusative suffixes of certain personal pronouns (e.g. *-ë*, *-e* in the first-person singular pronouns Komi *men-ë*, Udmurt *mon-e*) are thought to be continuations of the stem-final vowel, protected by a final *-m which was eventually lost.

At and near the periphery, evidence for pU accusative *-m is fairly clear. South of Northern Saami, Western Saamic has denasalized reflexes, e.g. Lule Saami *goade-v* 'hut sA'. In Fennic, *-m > *-n in final position, and the *-m accusative thus fell together with the *-n genitive. Accusatives in *-n* are found throughout most of the present-day North Fennic dialects (see Chapter 3), and morphophonemic traces of a suffix at least similarly shaped may be found elsewhere in Fennic, e.g. weak-grade *nn* in Estonian *venna* 'brother sG', cf. strong-grade *nd* in the nominative singular *vend*. In Mordva, where there was a parallel, probably independent, syncretism of accusative and genitive, both of these cases are now marked with *-nʲ*, presumably after *m > n in final position and with analogical spread of the automatically palatalized variant in front-prosodic sequences; the details are not clear, however (see Chapter 6). There is no unambiguous reason to doubt that the accusative *-m* of Mari is a direct descendant of pU *-m. In Samoyedic, pU *-m is reflected clearly in Tundra Nenets, e.g. *myadᵒ-m* and Selkup, e.g. Taz Selkup *mååt-əm₂*, both 'tent sA'.

Accusative *-m in the branches of Uralic:

S	Mr	—	—	Sa
Fe	Md	—	Mn	

Despite its broader functional definition, the pU 'genitive' in *-n is slightly less well attested; it has vanished without trace in all four core branches:

S	Mr	—	—	Sa
Fe	Md	—	—	

Clear examples of the continuation of a pU *-n genitive are Finnish *vede-n*, Erzya Mordva *vedʲ-enʲ*, Meadow Mari *βüð-ən*, Taz Selkup *üt-ən₂* 'water sG'.

In languages with syllabic consonant gradation, a trace of earlier *-n lies in the morphophonemics of weak-grade forms such as Northern Saami *goaði* 'tent sG', cf. nominative singular *goahti*, Estonian *venna* 'sG' (homophonous with the accusative *venna* 'brother' cited above), and Nganasan, e.g. sG *kəðu* 'fingernail', cf. nominative *kətu*.

Local cases. The most clearly attested of the local cases is the locative *-nA. The descendants of this suffix still function as local cases in most languages, either alone, e.g. *-in* of Komi *ti̮-in* 'in a lake', or *-on* of Hungarian *tåv-on* 'on a lake', or combined with other morphemes, e.g. the *-na* of Tundra Nenets *-kᵒ-na* in *mya-kᵒ-na* 'tent sLoc', or the *sa* of *-ssa* in Finnish *talossa* (< *talo-s-na) 'in a house'. As a case suffix, Finnish *-nA* now functions chiefly as an essive ('functioning as a'), e.g. *sija+pää=tt=ee-nä* 'as a case suffix', but it still performs concrete spatial duties in postpositions and other closed sets of adverbs, e.g. *talo-n taka-na* HOUSE-G BEHIND-ess 'behind the house', *kotona* 'at home' (cf. *koti* 'home', *kota* 'Saami tent').

The separative *-tI (~ *-tA) is reflected in ablative forms such as Moksha Mordva *oj-dʲə* 'butter sAbl' and Fennic partitives such as Estonian *või-d* 'butter sP'. In Samoyedic, it occurs with the same co-affix as the locative, e.g. Tundra Nenets *mya-kø-dᵒ* 'tent sAbl', and in Fennic and Mordva it occurs with the same *-s- coaffix, e.g. the elative forms Moksha Mordva *kudə̂-stə̂* (< *kudə̂-s-tə̂) and Finnish *talo-sta* (< *talo-s-ta), both '(coming) out of the house'. In Mari, a trace of the separative remains in the *čʲ* at the ends of the postpositions *gə̂čʲ* and *dečʲ*, as in *pört gə̂č* '(coming) out of the house', *ješ-ə̂ž dečʲ* FAMILY-s3 FROM 'from his/her family'. It is also thought to survive in local-adverbial Permian cases such as the Komi transitive, e.g. *tuj vi̮v-ti* ROAD TOP-tr '(walking) along the road'. In Mari and in Saamic languages from North Saami north and eastwards, the initial *n* of the locative *-nA became *t* in case forms built with the co-affix *-s-; this sound change brought about a collision with separative forms, leading to syncretism in these Saamic languages, e.g. North Saami *dálus* 'in/out of a house', and, in Mari, spurring the formation of secondary postpositional constructions with *dečʲ* and *gə̂čʲ*. Proto-Samoyedic locative *-kø-na and ablative *-kø-t(ø) syncretized in Selkup, as well, but at the expense of the latter.

To judge by the number of different pU and pFU suffixes reconstructed for it, the lative category was the most used and differentiated in the proto-language. For example, the reconstruction of the Permian case system entails at least the proto-latives *-k, *-cʲ, and *-nʲ. The Permian egressive case suffixes (Komi *-šʲanʲ*, Udmurt *-išʲenʲ*) have been analysed as consisting, historically, of three lative suffixes in succession (Serebrennikov 1963: 63); this is probably incorrect – see Permian, Chapter 8 – but such a poly-morphemic background to a deictic is not impossible, cf. English *a-b-ove* from *ON+BY+ABOVE. The proto-Samoyedic dative *-ŋ presumably goes back to an earlier lative, as do the proto-Samoyedic coaffixes *-kø- and *-ntø(-). The *-s- coaffix of the secondary local cases of the western languages is also thought to have been originally a lative; according to this line of thinking, the -s- of the Finnish interior local cases (inessive -ssA < *-s-nA, elative -stA < *-s-tA, and illative *-sVn) is historically identical with the -s of such forms as *ulos* '(moving) towards the outside', cf. *ulko-na* '(located) outside'. Mordva uses this -s as its illative case (*kudo-s* 'into a house') but it also seems to have preserved lative *-nʲ (in reduplicated form in the dative/allative case, e.g. Erzya *kudo-nʲenʲ*), lative *-k (seen in the prolative case, e.g. *virʲ-ga* 'through a forest'), and lative *-ŋ (in the somewhat restricted lative case, e.g. *mastor-ov* 'to the ground').

The case system of the protolanguage was probably complemented by postpositions; these are discussed below (p. 23).

Number

Number in the protolanguage was marked with two different suffixes, but in all likelihood plurality was the salient semantic component of neither. One suffix, *-t, seems to have performed duties analogous to the absolutive (nominative) -Ø in the singular, but with additional meanings of definiteness and non-singularity. The other, *-j, functioned as a non-singular analogue both to the singular accusative *-m, marking certain direct objects, and to the singular genitive *-n, marking nouns in prenominal position (qualifiers, possessors). This *-j suffix also preceded further inflectional suffixes; whether case suffixes were so used is unclear, but the person suffixes must have occurred in such strings (Janhunen 1981a: 29).

The plural marker *-t is preserved as a suffix of nominal inflection only at or near the periphery. Note the nominative plural of 'tree': Taz Selkup *poo-t*, Sosva Mansi *jiw-ət*, Finnish *puu-t*, Moksha Mordva *šuft-t*. There is no reason to doubt that the glottal stop of the Nenets and Nganasan nominatives plural, e.g. Forest Nenets *pʲa-ʔ* 'trees' and Nganasan *muŋku-ʔ* 'forest' are also from this *-t; the Kamassian pluralizer - *ʔje ʔ- ~ -ʔjiʔ- ~ -ʔi* seems to have contained both *-t and *-j. New plural suffixes have replaced *-t in the noun paradigms of Mari (*pu-wlak*), Permian (e.g. Komi *pu-jas*), and Hungarian (*faa-k*), although Mari has preserved *-t in collectives formed from kinship terms and names, e.g. *awa-m-ət* MOTHER-sl-plur 'my mother and her associates'.

The other plural marker, *-j, now marks plurality of possession in Hungarian, e.g. *faa-i-m* 'my trees', cf. *faa-m* 'my tree'. In many Fennic languages it is used in all non-nominative cases, e.g. Finnish *pu-i-ssa* TREE-plur-ine 'in trees'; Estonian uses either *-t- or *-j-, e.g. *puudes/puis*. Plural genitive forms such as Finnish *kalojen* (< *kalo-j-δ-en < *kala-j-t-en) 'fishes pG' show that the two plural suffixes could co-occur in the west, as well; contrast the parallel (stylistically marked) *kala-i-n* 'fishes pG' < *kala-δ-en, Suhonen 1988: 309. In Nganasan and Nenets, *-j combined with stem-final vowels to produce complex vowel alternations.

In North Saami there is essentially no agglutinative plural formation; each case is different in singular and plural. This may been seen, for example, in the singular/plural forms of the North Saami word for 'name', *namma*, namely illative *namma-i/namma-i-de* (with singular *-j, plural *-i-tee-k), locative *nama-s/nama-i-n* (with singular *-st, plural *-ij-n). In sharp contrast is e.g. Arjeplog Saami, in which singular and plural forms of all local cases were kept distinct, cf. illative *namma-j/nama-j-ta*, inessive *nama-n/nama-j-n*, elative *nama-st/nama-j-st* (Lehtiranta 1992: 156).

Person

Person is a morphological category for nominals in most Uralic languages. The most widespread function is to express the person of the possessor, e.g. North Saami *áhččá-n*, Finnish *isä-ni*, Erzya Mordva *ťeťa-m*, East Mari *ačˣʲa-m*, Udmurt *ataj-e*, Hungarian *åpaa-m*, Nganasan *dʲesï-mə*, Forest Nenets *nʲeešaa-j/nʲeešaa-m*, Taz Selkup *äsä-mï*, all FATHER-s1 'my father'. A secondary, but quite widespread, use of the person suffixes is to indicate definiteness. The third- and second-person singular suffixes are most often recruited for this purpose, e.g. third person singular -(ï)s in Southern Permiak *gor-ïs kerku-šʲi-s mun-i-s* STOVE-s3 HOUSE-ela-s3 GOES-past-s3 'the stove went out of the house', second person singular -*ïd* in Komi *starik-ïd-lën pi-ïs* OLD.MAN-s2-ade SON-s3 'the old man's son'. Note also the use of the third person plural in Lipsha Mari *kok üðür-üšt-wlä* TWO GIRL-p3- plur 'two of the girls'.

In languages with relatively transparent nominal morphology, person suffixes generally follow a number suffix, e.g. Udmurt *pinal-jos-ï*, Hungarian *dʲärekä-i-m*, Taz Selkup *iija-ii-m(ï)*, all CHILD-plur-s1 'my children', although in some languages the reverse order is used to express associative plurals, e.g. Hungarian *åpaa-m-eek* FATHER-s1-assoc.plur 'my father and his friends'. Mari, which has one of the most transparent nominal morphologies in Uralic, permits both orders.

The position of person suffixes relative to that of case suffixes is more complex. There åre three patterns: (1) person before case, typical of Ugric; (2) case before person, typical of northern Samoyedic, Saamic, Fennic, and Erzya Mordva; and (3) mixed, i.e. both orders occurring in the same language. The languages which show mixed order do so in two different ways: in Mari, the order depends on the case, while in the Permian languages and in Moksha Mordva it depends on both case and person. For detailed discussions of the existing patterns, with diachronic interpretation, see Comrie 1980b and Honti 1995.

Other nominal categories which are expressed by means of suffixes include the definite declension in Mordva, the predestinative of northern Samoyedic, and the past and future clitics in Nganasan.

All present-day Uralic languages have postpositions, and we can assume that in the protolanguage there were already a number of nouns which were used primarily to specify spatial and temporal relations. The most clearly reconstructable of these are the antonyms pU *ïla 'space underneath' and *üli 'space above'. We can glimpse something of the pU noun phrase by comparing constructions such as Finnish *vede-n alla*, Tundra Nenets *jid°-h ngilna* 'under (the) water', in which the locational nouns *alla* and *ngilna* are fossilized old locatives of the pU locational noun *ïla and Finnish -*n*, Nenets -*h* are the genitive suffix. Whether the protolanguage had a true genitive case or not, some kind of subordinating suffix *-n probably optionally, but often, connected the two nouns in constructions of this sort.

In languages closer to the core, which have no genitive case, such postpositions most frequently take the nominative, e.g. Hungarian *åstål-Ø ålått*, Komi *piʒan-Ø ulïn*, Tremjugan Khanty *pȧsaan ïɫpïnȝ* 'under (a) table'. But the nominative is the norm in Mari and Mordva, as well, in spite of the fact that these languages have genitives inherited from pU *-n. In Fennic, many such forms occur optionally or exclusively as prepositions, e.g. Finnish (stylistically marked) *alla veden* 'under (the) water', and the genitive competes with the partitive, the partitive usually having the upper hand in prepositional constructions, e.g. Estonian *vee alla* (WATER-sG UNDER.loc) alongside *alla vett* (UNDER.loc WATER-sP) 'under (the) water'. This use of the partitive in Fennic is probably connected historically with the use of its cognate analogue in Mordva, the ablative, with certain postpositions, e.g. Moksha Mordva *sʲedʲi-də-ŋk baška* HEART-abl-p1 APART.FROM 'apart from our heart'. In Northern Saami both postpositional and prepositional constructions are common, and the lexical noun is always in the genitive.

Postpositions (and more rarely prepositions) often have more than one form, and these forms can be seen as making up small case paradigms, ranging from three to five members. In Mari, Hungarian, and ObUgrian, the most common type is the three-member set, and we may think of this as the basic Uralic minimum. Case suffixes which are often different from those of normal noun paradigms are used to distinguish stationary location from motion, and within the motion category, goal (latives) from source (separatives). Four-member sets are typical of Samoyedic, Mordva, Fennic (but not Estonian, which has three) and – historically – Saamic, i.e. of languages at or near the periphery. The present-day three-member sets of Saamic languages are the result of syncretism of case form and function (location and goal) or the loss of prolative forms. In the other three groups, the fourth member is synchronically a prolative ('moving along the expanse/length of X'), i.e. it is a further subdivision of the motion category. The Permian languages have evolved the richest postpositional case subparadigms, with the addition of the terminative category, for the *terminus post quem non* of motion.

Table 1.2 sets out the postpositions meaning 'behind, in back of' in a selection of Uralic languages.

The origins of the nouns used as postpositions are sometimes synchronically transparent, because an unbound doublet exists, e.g. Komi *piʒan vïl-ïn* 'on the table', *mu+vïv* (EARTH+TOP) 'surface of the earth'. More usually

Table 1.2   Selected Uralic postpositions 'behind, in back of'

	Stasis	Motion Source	Goal	Trajectory	Terminus
Hungarian	mögött	mögül	mögee		
Vakh Khanty	čönnə	čönčööγ	čönč(ää)		
Estonian	taga	tagant	taha		
Moksha Mordva	ftalə̂	ftaldə̂	ftalu	ftalga	
Forest Nenets	punnʲaana	puunʲaat	puunʲaaŋ	puunʲaamna	
Komi	sajïn	sajïšʲ	sajë	sajti	sajëdzʲ

they are old enough as to be invisible to the untrained eye, e.g. Hungarian *pištå* **mögött** 'in *back* of Pista', *pištå* **megjött** 'Pista came *back*' or can be recovered only by the comparative method, e.g. North Saami *čađa* 'through', a fossilized lative of the root found in Moksha Mordva *sʲedʲi*, Finnish *südämme-* 'heart'.

Personal pronouns. The reconstruction of the Uralic personal pronouns encounters difficulties specific to this word class. Like numerals or kinship terms, pronouns enter easily into analogical subpatterns which allow cross-infection. A further difficulty arises from the relatively small size of the proto-Uralic pronominal root, which was canonically monosyllabic (C)V(C). This contrasts sharply from the roots of denotatives, which were all bisyllabic (C)VC(C)V, though they probably alternated morphophonemically with (C)VC because of root-suffix sandhi.

It is therefore with great reservations that even the following imprecise indications are given. First- and second-person pronouns were distinguished by their initial consonant, which was *m in the first person, *t (? ~ *n) in the second. The initial consonant was followed by a vowel of indeterminate quality: s1 *mV, s2 *tV. In circumstances which are not clear, these syllables were extended by an element *nV or (in Hungarian and ObUgrian) *ŋ; whether these elements were derivational suffixes or were historically identical with local suffixes, perhaps serving in an ergative function, is unknown. Instead of the *nV-element, a plural suffix (*-k or *-t) could be added: p1 *mVk, p2 *tVk. There was also a dual, formed, perhaps, with an element *jn, viz. d1 *mVjn, d2 *tVjn.

The nominative forms of the axis-of-discourse personal pronouns of Arjeplog Saami, Tremjugan Khanty, and Forest Nenets are given here for comparison:

	s1	s2	d1	d2	p1	p2
AS	mån(na)	tån/tåtna	mååj(ah)	tååj(ah)	mij(ah)	tij(ah)
TK	mää	nöŋ	miin	niin	meŋ	neŋ
FN	manʲ	pit	maj/madʲii	pič/pičii	manʲa?	pita?

These samples present three degrees of uniformity in personal pronoun morphology, with the Saamic showing the most, and the Nenets the least, evidence of analogical levelling.

Root suppletion is found in the personal pronoun paradigms of Hungarian, Nenets, and Enets, e.g. the nominative and accusative forms of the first-person pronoun are Hungarian *een/änge-m*, Forest Nenets *manʲ/ša ʔ-j*, and of the second person singular, *tä/teege-d* and *pit/šaa ʔ-t* (*-m/-j* and *-d/-t* are first- and second-person suffixes). The accusative forms in Samoyedic seem to go back to an earlier **kit* (in ablaut to **kät*) 'face', and the *-ge-* of the Hungarian forms is perhaps from the same root (Helimski 1982: 88–94). In Fennic and Khanty, the personal pronouns use a special accusative suffix *-t*, as in the accusative forms of the first-person singular pronoun Finnish *minu-t*, Tremjugan Khanty *mään-t*. This *-t* is probably historically identical with the Hungarian accusative suffix *-t* which is used in most nominal forms (and optionally also in pronouns), e.g. *hålå-t* 'fish sA', *änge-mä-t*, cf. *änge-m* above.

The evidence for the Uralic third-person pronoun is not quite as clear, but it is probable that the protolanguage had a form **sF* (wherein F = front vowel) which had anaphoric properties at least. This pronoun, enlarged with various, usually nasal, suffixes, has clear reflexes in the peripheral Finno-Ugric languages, but if it occurs in Samoyedic it is only in the Selkup third-person singular pronoun *tëp*$_2$ (Hajdú 1990: 2–3). Examples from Finno-Ugric are North Saami and Mordva *son*, Finnish *hän*, Tremjugan Khanty *ɬeγʷ*, Sosva Mansi *taw*, Hungarian *öö*.

Reflexive pronouns have evolved separately in the various branches; the most widespread is seen in North Saami *iehča-*, Finnish *itse*, Udmurt and Komi *ačʲ*, a word which has been connected with the demonstrative pronouns based on **e-* and **cʲF*, but which is more likely originally to have been a noun meaning '(shadow) soul', cf. Sosva Mansi *is* 'shadow (of human); ghost'. Samoyedic, Selkup, and Nganasan use one root (e.g. Nganasan/Taz Selkup *ŋonə-nə/on-äk* 'I myself', *ŋonə-ntə/on-äntï* 'you (sg) yourself'), while Kamass and the Nenets languages use various words which are synchronically identical or doublets to words meaning 'body' or 'head', e.g. Kamass (*man*) *bos-pə* 'I myself', cf. *boš* 'body', a relatively recent bifurcation of a loan from Turkic (Joki 1952: 98–9; Hajdú 1990).

Demonstratives and other deictics. Proto-Uralic probably had a three-way system of demonstrative pronouns whose spatial extremes were built onto a base **t-*, with front vocalism (**tF*) corresponding to proximal reference, e.g. Finnish *tä=* in *tämä* 'this', and back vocalism (**tB*) corresponding to distal reference, e.g. Finnish *tuo* 'that'. Reflexes of these two pronominal bases may be found in all branches of Uralic; in some languages, one or the other has evolved into a third-person pronoun, replacing the earlier **sF* mentioned above, e.g. Estonian *tema*, East Mari *tudo* '(s)he/it', while in others they are now adverbs or have become otherwise fossilized, e.g. Udora Komi *tin* 'there', Hungarian *tee+tová* 'hesitant (< **'this way + that way'*).

The middle term of the three-way system has been reconstructed as *c^{j}F, i.e. *c^j plus a front vowel. The function of this pronoun is not quite clear: it may have been anaphoric; it may have referred to an area closer to the addressee; perhaps both uses existed side by side, as in Finnish *se* 'it, that (anaphoric)', *si-e-llä* 'there (anaphoric, or closer to addressee)'. In Mansi and Hungarian, all traces of *c^j= have been lost, but it survives in all forms of Khanty, e.g. Eastern Khanty *t^{j}ii(t)* 'this'. In Samoyedic it has survived as a demonstrative in Enets (*sed^{j}eo* 'that [one]') and developed into the third-person singular pronoun in Nganasan (*siti̇*).

Parallel to the paired set of front/back demonstratives with initial *t, which is well attested in all branches, there seems to have been another distal/proximal pronoun (or prefix?) pair *i- ~ *ä- 'this', *u- ~ *o- 'that', as in Hungarian *ä=z* 'this', *å=z* 'that', Sosva Mansi *an^j* 'now', Udmurt *otïn* 'there'. Neither pendant has a reflex in Saamic, and the back-vowel pendant has no reflex in Fennic or ObUgrian. Beside the poor distribution of the witnesses and the variety of functions, the scanty phonological substance of this reconstruction renders the etymology precarious.

At the heart of the demonstrative pronoun systems of the present-day languages is the simple two-term proximal/distal dichotomy, e.g. Finnish *tämä/tuo*, Erzya Mordva *t^{j}e/tona*, Hungarian *äz/åz* 'this/that'. Different languages elaborate on this in different ways: (1a) differentiation of the member which refers to remoteness, yielding two (or more) degrees of remoteness, e.g. late proto-Finnic *taa alongside *too (Laajavaara 1986), (1b) similar differentation of the member which refers to proximity, e.g. Vote *ka+se* 'this (closer to speaker than *se*), or (1c) both, e.g. Hungarian *äm--ä=z* 'this (closer to speaker than *ä=z*), *åm--å=z* 'that (further from speaker than *å=z*); (2) addition of the factor of visibility and/or concreteness, e.g. Vakh Khanty *tiimii* 'this (visible/concrete)', *t^{j}iit* 'this (non-visible/non-concrete)'; (3) addition of, and interaction with, anaphoric pronouns, as in Finnish, or Forest Nenets, where the distal/proximal pair is *čehaεj/čuhkii* and the anaphoric pronoun is *čihkii*. In Mari, where the reflex of the *c^{j}F pronoun is chiefly anaphoric, the asymmetry of the inherited *tB : *tF :: *c^{j}F system has been resolved with the analogous creation of a more remote anaphoric form *sade*, i.e. parallel to *tide/tudo* 'this/that' East Mari has *sede/sade* 'this/that (anaphoric)'. In a similar fashion, southern and eastern varieties of Khanty evolved back-vowel pendants to their reflexes of *c^{j}F, e.g. Vakh Khanty *t^{j}uut* 'that (non-visible/non-concrete)'.

The most complex systems of demonstratives are found in Saamic, where elaborations of types (1) and (3) both occur, as in Northern Saami:

Anaphoric	Demonstrative				
	Proximal		Distal		
	Near speaker	Near addressee	Far	Further	Further yet
dat	*dát*	*diet*	*duot*	*dōt*	*dūt*

Verbs

There is no one clear past-tense marker reconstructable for pU, and the original tense system may have been one similar to that found in Samoyedic, where the lexical, i.e. intrinsic, aspect of verb roots determines the semantic force of their finite forms. Thus an inherently non-perfective, stative verb such as 'lives' normally had present or non-past meanings, while a verb such as 'dies', with inherent punctual, perfective aspect, normally had past-tense meaning. Modifications to the basic temporal setting of a given verb were effected by means of derivational suffixes, e.g. '(s)he is (in the process of) dying' was expressed by appending a deperfectivizing suffix to the root.

It is perhaps from such derivational suffixes that the oldest attested past-tense suffixes evolved. These are pU *-s^j(A)- and pFU *-i-, distributed fairly widely across the Uralic or Finno-Ugric branches; although traditionally treated separately, it is possible that these two suffixes are historically identical (Helimski 1996: 40; on the suspect nature of intervocalic pU *-s^j-, see Abondolo 1990).

Distribution of past-tense *-s^j-:

— Mr? — Kh Sa
(Fe) Md? — Mn

Distribution of past-tense *-i-:

S Mr Pn Kh —
Fe Md Hu —

The representation of *-s^j(A)- in the western languages is either restricted (e.g. in Estonian, where it is limited to the negative verb) or controversial (it is thought to be reflected in certain Mordva past-tense forms, and in the inflection of the so-called 'second' conjugation verbs in Mari). The past-tense suffix *-i- is clearly preserved in forms such as Finnish *tul-i-n* 'I came', Mordva *ud-i-n^j* 'I slept' (cf. the corresponding non-past forms *tule-∅-n*, *uda-∅-n*), and may be reconstructed from the phonologies of forms such as East Mari *tol^{j}ə̂n* < *tolə̂-jə̂-n < pFU **tulï-i-n 'I came' (cf. nonpast *tola-m*), North Saami *gohččon* 'I called' < proto-Saamic *koc^{j}c^{j}åå-jë-m (cf. nonpast *gohčun*).

Most Uralic languages have gone on to enrich this simple tense system in diverse ways. In addition to the basic *past : non-past* opposition, many languages have evolved various kinds of future (either via the inflectioniza- tion of derivational material, as in Tavda Mansi or in Udmurt, or by means of auxiliary verbs, as in Hungarian (*fog-*) or Mordva (*karma-*). Different degrees of remoteness in past time may be expressed by compound-tense forms built with forms of a verb meaning 'is' or 'becomes', as in the pluperfect forms North Saami *le-dje-n boahtá-n*, Finnish *ol-i-n tul-lut* 'I had come'. In some languages the auxiliary verb has fused with the stem and become an inflectional suffix in its own right; the meaning is then most usually imperfective, e.g. Mordva second past *mor-ilʲ-inʲ* 'I used to sing'. Also usually imperfective are certain secondary past-tense forms of other lan- guages, in which the shortest inflected form of the auxiliary has become a frozen, uninflectable clitic, e.g. the West Mari third-person singular past-tense form of the verb 'is', *əlʲə*, when combined with the non-past finite form of the lexical verb, forms a past continuous tense: *tola-∅-m əlʲə* 'I was coming', cf. the synonymous, and morphologically parallel Udmurt *likt-isʲk-o val* and Hungarian (archaic and dialectal) *jöv-∅-ök vålå*. Convergence with Turkic is evident in all such constructions (Bereczki 1983: 218–21).

Another type of remoteness, but one not tied exclusively to time, is that of the inferential. This category goes under many different names (evidential, non-experiential, non-eyewitnessed, narrative, auditive) and is sometimes classified as a mood and not as a tense. In Estonian and Livonian it coincides with the quotative, i.e. it is the *ratio obliqua* analogue of the indicative (see Chapter 3); historically the Fennic quotative derives from a non-past participle *=wA. In the Permian languages and Mari the inferential category has been ascribed to Turkic, specifically Volga-bend, influence (Bereczki: 1983). The inferential here is usually classified as a tense; the forms derive historically from deverbal nominals (which evolved into past participles) in *=mA. In Mari, the syntagms classified as inferential are the same as the secondary, compound-tense forms mentioned above. Permian on the other hand has developed distinct, but defective finite inferential paradigms, e.g. Udmurt *so gïr-oz val* '(s)he used to plough (long ago)', *so gïr-oz vilem* '(they say that) (s)he ploughed; (s)he ploughed (as I remember)'. Finally, infer- entials are also present in Samoyedic, where their morphological implementa- tion is usually suffixal, cf. Selkup =NT- (probably historically identical with the non-past participle =NT-), Nganasan =HATU-.

Proto-Uralic had probably no more than two morphological moods, an unmarked indicative and an imperative in *-k(V)-. Tense and mood were thus in complementary distribution in the sense that the imperative knew no tense distinctions. By the Finno-Ugric stage, new mood markers, which marked unreal–conditional–desiderative sorts of modality, had begun to develop. In most languages, the reflexes of these markers are composites. For example, the Estonian conditional *-ksi-* is probably the continuation of a Proto-Fenno-

Saamic derivational complex *=(i)ks^ji-, seen in Finnish frequentatives; the Hungarian conditional -nee-/-naa- probably continues a suffix chain *-ne-i-, in which *-i- is the past-tense suffix mentioned above and *-ne- is the suffix seen in the Finnish potential (sata-ne-e RAINS-pot-s3 'it may rain') and the Mari desiderative (Hill Mari ələ-ne-žə LIVES-desid-s3 '(s)he would like to live'); the Finnish conditional -isi- (as in tul-isi-n 'I would come') consists of past-tense -i- preceded by the proto-Fenno-Saamic suffix *-ns^ji- seen in the North Saami potential -ž-/-žž-, -čč- e.g. bōđežan 'I may come'. As mentioned above, many Uralic languages have verb subparadigms with epistemic overtones, and these and other forms which refer to the speaker's knowledge or attitude about the predication and the utterance are often classified as moods, particularly in Samoyedic; cf. Tundra Nenets, with sixteen moods which cross-classify various kinds of evidential, obligational, and attitudinal modalities.

Most Uralic languages (but not southern Samoyedic or Hungarian) express negation by means of a negative (auxiliary) verb, usually with an irregular, suppletive, or defective paradigm. There is considerable variety in terms of which verbal categories are encoded on the negative auxiliary and which are encoded on the lexical verb; for a survey see Comrie 1981.

Most verb subparadigms show agreement for subject person, and in Mordva, Ugric, and Samoyedic, for certain features of a direct object, as well:

```
—    —    —    Kh  Sa
—    Md   Hu   Mn
```

The paradigms which encode information about the direct object are usually classified as belonging to 'objective' or 'definite' conjugations, the latter term being inspired by the fact that such forms are often associated with some kind of definiteness in the direct object, whether intrinsic or governed by the discourse or narrative. Since nouns in many languages have their own morphological means of expressing definiteness, the result can be redundant definiteness marking, as in Hungarian, where a noun phrase morphologically marked for definiteness (e.g. by means of person suffix or definite article) forces the selection of 'definite' suffixation on the verb. Other languages, however, for example Mordva, use indefinite and definite suffixation with both indefinite and definite direct objects to express a range of varieties of definiteness and aspect.

The definite conjugation is thought to have been nascent already in proto-Uralic; at this early stage probably no more than third-person objects were encoded, by means of the encliticization of the third-person/anaphoric pronoun *sF mentioned above. Southern Samoyedic, particularly Kamassian, has elaborated this primitive basis the least; Hungarian has developed full definite paradigms, with forms distinct from their indefinite analogues in most subject persons, and with a formal distinction between second- and third-person objects if the subject is first person singular. While the definite conjugations of the ObUgrian and northern Samoyedic languages do not distinguish object person, they do show number agreement, with varying syncretisms and degrees of obligatoriness. The definite conjugations of Erzya and Moksha Mordva are the richest in Uralic, in that they show agreement, albeit partial, with both person and number of the direct object.

Syncretism and Suppletion

From the typological point of view, it is conventional to think of the Uralic languages as agglutinating, i.e. as conforming to one degree or another to that broad linguistic type in which each grammatical category is represented, in the perceivable substance, by its own more or less immutable morpheme. For this classification to work, the definition of agglutination must be flexible enough to allow the qualification 'more or less', i.e. it must tolerate, or disregard, regular and phonetically banal (morpho)phonological alternations such as front/back and [+/−] rounded among the vowels, and assimilations of stricture-type or palatalization among the consonants. On the other hand we do not expect to find, in a language which we have classified as agglutinating, large amounts of either syncretism or suppletion. In fact, both of these phenomena are rather widespread in the Uralic languages. What follows is a brief sampling of some of the subtypes, beginning with syncretism and concentrating on the nominal paradigm.

In the nominal paradigm, there is often syncretism of case when person suffixes are involved, e.g. the Finnish sN (*käsi*) sG (*käden*) and pN (*kädet*) all syncretize in possessed forms such as *käteni* 'my hand(s) sNGpN'. Similarly, Komi -*a*- serves as both locative and lative in *ki-a-m* HAND-sIne/ sIll-s1 'in(to) my hand', contrast *ki-in* 'in a/the hand', *ki-ë* 'into a/the hand', and Selkup -*qä*- is locative, lative, and elative in *utoo-qä-k* HAND-sIne/sIll/ sEla-s1 'in(to)/out of my hand'. The reverse scenario, syncretism of person in certain case forms, also occurs in Selkup, e.g. sInstr *nomtïsä* 'with your/his (her/its) god', a form which syncretizes s2 with s3; contrast the nominative singular forms, in which the person forms remain distinct, viz. *nomlï* s2, *nomtï* s3 (d23 and p23 syncretize in parallel fashion).

Occasionally, syncretism of case is connected with non-singular number. For example in Nenets, which distinguishes nominative from genitive from accusative in the singular and plural paradigms of most nouns, there is a complete syncretism of these three grammatical cases in the dual: for 'tent' we have dNGA *myakᵒh*, contrast sN *myaq*, sG *myadᵒh*, sA *myadᵒm*. Selkup syncretizes the dative/allative with the illative in the non-singular, e.g. dD/Ill *nop-qıt-kinı* '(in)to two gods' contrast sD *nuu-nïk*, sIll *nom-tï*. In Finnish, the accusative syncretizes with the genitive in the singular, but with the nominative in the plural, in a manner reminiscent of the animate/inanimate accusatives of Russian. The reverse of this scenario, namely syncretism of number in certain cases, is more suspect on theoretical grounds. We may say that Northern Saami *beanan* 'as a dog/as dogs' is a syncretism of singular and plural essive; but such forms look more like derivation, i.e. they resemble adverbs, and the suppression of the number category is thus perhaps not particularly noteworthy. A striking example of number syncretism exists in the absolute declension of Mordva, where *all* non-nominative cases syncretize for number, e.g. sN *kudo* 'house' ≠ pN *kudot* 'houses', but spIne *kudoso* 'in a house/in houses', spIll *kudos* 'into a house/into houses', etc.

Syncretism of person in connection with non-singular number also occurs, e.g. in Sosva Mansi, where we have the syncretism of second and third persons dual when the stem is marked for dual number: *saali-ay-een* is 'two reindeer d23', but the singular paradigm distinguishes *saali-jin* 'the one reindeer of you two' from *saali-teen* 'the one reindeer of them two'; second and third dual forms can syncretize in the plural, as well. The reverse scenario, namely syncretism of stem number in connection with certain personal forms, is found in Mordva, e.g. Erzya Mordva *kudo-t* 'your (sg) house(s)'. Such syncretisms occurs in all personal forms save s1 and s3 in Erzya, cf. *kudo-m* 'my house', *kudo-n* 'my houses', *kudo-zo* 'his/her house', *kudo-nzo* 'his/her houses'. Even these distinctions break down in non-nominative cases, e.g. *kudo-so-nzo* 'in his/her house(s)'. Syncretism of person number may be seen in a form such as DN Khanty *xoottaat* 'houses sp3'; contrast the singular-stem forms *xootǝt* 'house s3' ≠ *xooteet* 'house p3'.

Suppletion of case suffix in the presence of person inflection, apart from that already seen in connection with such syncretic cases as Selkup *-qä-*, is rare. It does occur, however, in the dative of Tundra Nenets, which is (in the singular) *-nφ-h ~ tφ-h* when used without, but *-xφ-* when used with person suffixes, e.g. *mya-t°h* TENT-sD 'to a/the tent', *mya-k°-n* TENT-sD-s1 'to my tent'. The latter form illustrates the reverse suppletive type, that of person suffix in the presence of case, contrast *myad°-m* 'my tent', with *-m* instead of *-n* for s1. This type of suppletion is widespread in the peripheral languages, and may reflect an ancient state of affairs: it is probable that the nominal first-person suffixes in Fennic (e.g. Finnish *-ni*) and Saamic (e.g. North Saami *-m*) each reflect one of an earlier suppletive suffix-pair *-mi : *-ni, with the latter suffix occurring in oblique cases and/or when the possession was non-singular, a distinction still preserved sporadically in Mordva, cf. *kudo-m* 'my house', *kudo-n* 'my houses' cited above (Korhonen 1981: 233–6, 244). That the dichotomy *-mi : *-ni was the result of phonotaxis, with *-ni coming from an even earlier *-n-mi, has not been demonstrated to everyone's satisfaction, cf. Honti 1995: 59–61. The reverse scenario, namely suppletive number suffixes in the presence of person-marking, is seen in Hungarian (*faa-k : faa-i-m*, cited above) and ObUgrian, e.g. Vasjugan Khanty *kaat-ǝt* HOUSE – plur 'houses' : *kaat-laa-m* HOUSE – plur-s1 'my houses'.

Suppletion of case suffix in the presence of number inflection is also encountered. As mentioned above, the case suffixes for singular and plural nouns in North Saami differ to such a degree as to make the term suppletion seem inappropriate. Elsewhere in Uralic such suppletion is most usually centred on the formation of the genitive, accusative, or both, e.g. Finnish sG -N but pG -тEN, Forest Nenets *č^joon^ja-m* 'fox sA' but *č^joon^ji-i* 'fox pA'.

Syntax

The head noun is the centre of the typical Uralic noun phrase, in that it is followed by any inflectional suffixes and/or postpositions, and preceded by any modifying adjuncts. Agreement between head nouns and their adjuncts is fairly rare. Perhaps the most glaring exception is Finnish, e.g. *tuo-hon samaan iso-on rakennukse-en* THAT-ill SAME-ill BIG-ill BUILDING-ill 'into that same big building', but Hungarian has case and number agreement between demonstratives and their head, as in the synonomous *ud^jån+åb-bå å nåd^j eepüläd-bä* SAME+THAT-ill DEF. ART BIG BUILDING-ill 'into that same big building'. Agreement also occurs elsewhere, to varying degrees, especially in Saamic, Fennic, and northern Samoyedic.

Possession is expressed by the linking of noun phrases. In the peripheral languages, the possessor is put in the genitive and the possession is left unmarked, e.g. Finnish *lapse-n isä*, North Saami *máná áhčči*, Tundra Nenets *nyú-h nyísya*, Taz Selkup *iija-n ësï*, all '(the) child's father'. In the core languages, the possessor is marked in a variety of ways. Hungarian marks the possessor with zero, i.e. the nominative, or, less frequently, the dative (-nAk), and marks the possession with the third-person suffix, e.g. *å d^järmek(-näk åz) åp-jå* DEF.ART CHILD(-D DEF.ART) FATHER-s3 'the child's father', *åpaa-m-(nåk å) huug-å* FATHER-s1(-D DEF.ART) YOUNGER.SISTER-s3 'my father's younger sister'. Permian uses the adessive, with or without s3 marking on the possessed, e.g. Komi *mort-lën pi* 'MAN-ade BOY 'a man's son', Permiak *ëš=ëma-š^j mižik-vën d^jen^jga-jez* DISAPPEARS=inferential-plur MAN-ade MONEY-plur 'a man's money had gone missing', but marks the possessor with the ablative if the possessed is the direct object, e.g. Komi *kol^j--pë men-s^ji-m lov* LEAVES.imp PRO.s1-abl-s1 SOUL/LIFE 'spare my life!', cf. also Permiak *ëtik in^jka-viš^j gu-vviš^j šir-rez š^joj=ëma-š^j gos-Ø* ONE OLD.WOMAN-abl CELLAR-subl MOUSE-plur EATS=inferential-plur FAT-sN 'mice had eaten the fat in an old woman's cellar'. In the ObUgrian languages, the possessor is invariably in the nominative. The possessive relation may optionally be rendered explicit by placing the possessed in the third person, e.g. Pim Khanty *juuγ^w toj(-əł)*, Sosva Mansi *jiw tal^jx(-e)*, both TREE TOP(-s3) 'the top of the tree'. Mari also often marks the possession with the third-person suffix, even when the possessor is explicitly stated in its genitive form, e.g. *ača-m-ən üðər-žö* FATHER-s1-sG SISTER-s3 'my father's sister'. In Mordva, a complex system of degrees of definiteness marks the possessor with the definite or indefinite genitive, and the possessed in three different ways: with zero (as in the peripheral languages), with s3 (as in Mari), and with its definite declension, e.g. *kvart^jira-n^j keŋkš* FLAT-G DOOR '(the) door of (the) flat' *kvart^jira-n^j--t^j keŋkše-ze* FLAT-G-def DOOR-s3 'the door of the flat', *ejd^je-n^j avar^jd^jema--s^j* CHILD-G WEEPING--sNdef '(the) child's weeping'.

Possessive sentences, i.e. possessive constructions which involve verbs, are more complex, as is to be expected. Most Uralic languages lack a verb meaning 'has'; the notable exceptions are the ObUgrian languages and Nganasan, e.g. Cingali Khanty *taj-* in *taj-∅-kən pax-∅* HAS-past-d3 BOY-N 'they (two) had a son', Sosva Mansi *oon^js^j-* in *tas-∅ at oon^js^j-eey^w-əm* VESSEL-N NEG HAS-pres-s1 'I don't have a pot', and Nganasan *xon-* in *bənsə-gəj-∅ nï-j xon-tï-gəj* ALL-dual-N WOMAN-pA HAS-present. continuous-d3 'they both have wives'. However, normally to express something like '(s)he has a knife' the most widespread Uralic sentence-type uses a verb meaning 'exists', and marks possessor, possession, or both, with case and person suffixes. Mari and the Permian languages have the simplest construction: a verb meaning 'is/exists' (or its negative pendant) is added to a regular possessive noun phrase, e.g. *ača-m-ən üðər-žö ulo* 'my father has a sister', Komi *ta mort-lën vël-i-∅ kujim pi* THIS MAN-ade IS-past-s3 THREE SON 'this man had three sons'. In Saamic and Fennic, the possessor is marked with a local case rather than the genitive; thus the equivalents of the Komi example just given are North Saami *da-n olbmá-s le-ddji golbma bártni* THIS-G MAN-loc IS-p3past THREE BOY.-G, Finnish *tä-llä miehe-llä ol-i-∅ kolme poika-a* THIS-ade MAN-ade IS-past-s3 THREE BOY-sP. In Hungarian, suffixation of the dative becomes obligatory, e.g. *å feerfi-∅ haarom fi-å* DEF.ART MAN-N BOY-s3 'the man's three sons' but *å feerfi-nak haarom fi-å vol-t-∅* 'the man had three sons'. An overview of possessive sentences in Samoyedic in relation to nominal sentences as a whole may be gleaned from Katzschmann 1986.

While the study of syntax has steered most theoretical linguistics over the last few decades, relatively little progress has been made in our understanding of the Uralic sentence. Data-oriented surveys are rare: Tereščenko 1973 is limited to Samoyedic, Bartens 1979 to Mordva, Mari, and Udmurt, Wickman 1955 to direct-object marking, Rounds 1991 to Hungarian, Komi, and Finnish; only Koizumi 1994 attempts a syntactic overview of the entire family. The lag may be due, in part, to the enormity of the task of understanding the masses of morphophonology typical of most Uralic languages, some of which has been clarified only recently; but it is also doubtless due to the Anglocentricity, then Eurocentricity, of much of the early work in modern syntactic theory.

The archetypal Uralic sentence has often been characterized as 'SOV', but since subject and object noun phrases are regularly omitted in Uralic sentences it is probably more helpful to speak of '(T)FV', i.e. (optional) Topic(s)–Focus–Verb order. The Topic, if present, may be single, like 'death' in Hungarian (orthography) ^Ta halál-∅ ^Flevele-t ^Vhoz-∅-∅ DEATH-N

LETTER-A BRINGS-pres-s3 'death delivers a letter', or 'net' in Izhma Komi *kulem-ïs č'istej* 'the net is dry', or multiple, as in [T]*a fiatal zeneszerző* [T]*orvosának tanácsa ellenére* [T]*szombat reggel* [F]*Bécsbe* [V]*indult* '[T]the young composer [T]in spite of his doctor's advice [T]on Saturday morning [V]set off [F]for Vienna'. Focus may be shared; in this case the usual scenario is to place one of the focalized elements to the right of the verb, e.g. [F]*Így* [V]*írtok* [F]*ti* '[F]this is how [F]you [V]write', Izhma Komi [F]*č'eri-Ø* [V]*kïj-Ø-enïs* [F]*kulem-en* '[F]fish [V]they-catch [F]with a net'.

Vocabulary

Words for core, yet non-culture-specific, concepts across language families are most often compared in connection with attempts to determine, by means of various refinements of glottochronological method, the relative degree of closeness of relationship between languages and branches. No such purpose underlies the pilot presentation here, which aims merely to provide an introduction to the sorts of distributional patterns which occur. The patterns are of two basic types: retention or innovation.

Retention is a relative term: it can range from total, e.g. English *father* < Old English *fæder*, to vestigial, e.g. the *groom* of *bridegroom* < *guma* 'man'. Here we are interested more in the former extreme. We are also more interested, for the purposes of this exercise, in the fact that the Hungarian word for 'river' is *foj=oo*, i.e. historically the present participle of a verb *foj-* 'flows', than we are in the fact that the Hungarian reflex of the proto-Uralic word for 'river', reconstructed as *juka, lives on in potamonyms such as *Berettyó* < *bärek 'boggy grove alongside river' + *joo 'river'. As for innovation: in core vocabulary such as we are sampling here, innovation always implies replacement rather than new discourse. We may recognize two subtypes. An old word may be replaced with a loanword, e.g. English *table* (borrowed from French, and largely replacing Old English *bord*, but note vestigial, metonymic, retention in the phrase 'bed and board') or it may be edged out by another word and/or meaning drawn from the resources of the language, e.g. English *father-in-law* replacing Old English *sweoor*, or the expansion of the semantic sphere of *bread* (< *breead*) at the expense of that of *loaf* (< *hlaaf*).

There is no Uralic analogue to Buck (1949), which surveys the formal and semantic development of some 1,200 Indo-European synonyms. A great deal of formal detail, however, on 43 Uralic synonyms may be found in Veenker 1975.

As is to be expected, survival of both lexeme and sememe across the entire range of the family is rare. One such is the word for 'name' (S = Saamic, Fe = Fennic, Md = Mordva, Mr = Mari, Ud = Udmurt, Ko = Komi, Mn = Mansi, Kh = Khanty, Hu = Hungarian, Ng = Nganasan, En = Enets, Ne = Nenets, Sl = Selkup, Km = Kamassian, Mt = Mator):

		S	Fe	Md	Mr	Ud	Ko	Mn	Kh	Hu	Ng	En	Ne	Sl	Km	Mt
1	'name'	a	a	a	a	a	a	a	a	a	a	a	a	a	a	a

with clear reflexes in all of the daughter languages, e.g. Ume Saami *namma* = Finnish *nimi* = Erzya Mordva *ľem* = Hill Mari *ləm* = Udmurt *nʲim* = Sosva Mansi *nam* = Hungarian *neev* = Nganasan *nʲim* = Kamassian *nim*. It is possible that this word may have been borrowed into proto-Uralic from some form of proto-Indo-European, but its wide attestation throughout northern Eurasia points to more general, earlier, diffusion. Other good examples of a similar wide distribution across Uralic are the descendants of proto-Uralic *mïksa 'liver' and *ïla '(space) underneath'.

The type of distributional pattern shown by the words for 'hand' is fairly common, and has traditionally been seen as one of the better pieces of evidence in support of the idea that Samoyedic broke away from the rest of Uralic early, if not first:

		S	Fe	Md	Mr	Ud	Ko	Mn	Kh	Hu	Ng	En	Ne	Sl	Km	Mt
2	'hand'	a	a	a	a	a	a	a	a							
											b	b	b	b	b	b

Thus we have two sets of words for 'hand': one clearly Finno-Ugric, e.g. Ume Saami *giahta* = Finnish *käsi* (oblique stem *käte-*) = Erzya Mordva *kedʲ* = Hill Mari *kit* (oblique stem *kiðə-*) = Udmurt *ki* = Sosva Mansi *kaat* = Hungarian *keez* (oblique stem *käzä-*), all from proto-Finno-Ugric *käti; and the other Samoyedic, e.g. Nganasan *dʲütü* = Tundra Nenets *nguq* = Taz Selkup *utï* = Kamassian *uda*, from proto-Samoyedic *(j)uta. Other good examples of this sort of distribution are the words for 'stone' (proto-Finno-Ugric *kiwi, proto-Samoyedic *paj), 'cloud' (pFU *pilwi, proto-Samoyedic *tiâ) and the numerals from '3' to '6'.

Some Uralic etymologies point to innovation in a branch other than Samoyedic, e.g. the new word for 'fish' in Permian:

		S	Fe	Md	Mr	Ud	Ko	Mn	Kh	Hu	Ng	En	Ne	Sl	Km	Mt
3	'fish'	a	a	a	a			a	a	a	a	a	a	a	a	a
						b	b									

This word is 3b Udmurt *čʲorïg* = Komi *čʲeri*, with possible cognates referring to specific species in Saamic and ObUgrian. Other Permian innovations include the replacement of the pU word for 'bow', and of the proto-Finno-Ugric word for 'leg'.

A different kind of break in the distribution of an inherited Uralic lexeme may be seen in the descendants of *witi 'water':

		S	Fe	Md	Mr	Ud	Ko	Mn	Kh	Hu	Ng	En	Ne	Sl	Km	Mt
4	'water'	a							c							
			b	b	b	b	b			b	b	b	b	b	b

Even more than the word for 'name', the proto-Uralic word for 'water' looks as if it might be a loan from some proto-Indo-European idiom. Whatever the provenance of this word, within Uralic all daughter languages other than Saamic and Khanty have reflexes with expected form and with meaning intact, e.g. Finnish *vesi* (oblique stem *vete-*) = Erzya Mordva *ved^j* = Hill Mari *wət* (oblique stem *wəðə-*) = Udmurt *vu* = Sosva Mansi *wit* = Nganasan *bï?* (oblique stem *bïðə-*) = Kamassian *bü*. Judging by its shape alone, the Saamic word for water (4a), as seen in e.g. Ume Saami *tjaahtsee*, probably comes from some sort of hyponym which referred to water in one of its more forcible manifestations, e.g. 'flood' or '(sudden) thaw; freshet'; it has a possible cognate in Khanty, viz. Vasjugan Khanty *seeč* '(late-)summer flooding; rise in water-level'. The Khanty word for 'water' (4c), on the other hand, is a doublet to the inherited Finno-Ugric word for 'ice', e.g. Vasjugan Khanty *jeŋk* 'water' : *jööŋk* 'ice'.

It seems most likely that proto-Uralic had a word for 'tree' with initial *p-, but at our present state of knowledge very little else about this word may be reconstructed with certainty. The reflexes in Finno-Ugric point to a back vowel in the first syllable, e.g. 5b Finnish *puu* = Udmurt *pu* = Hungarian *få*; the front vocalism of some of the Samoyedic pendants, e.g. Forest Enets *pe*, is probably secondary, and points to lexically numerous compounds formed with this root as second member.

	S	Fe	Md	Mr	Ud	Ko	Mn	Kh	Hu	Ng	En	Ne	Sl	Km	Mt
5 'tree'	a		c				d	d		e					
	b		b	b	b			b			b	b	b	b	b

Whatever its precise original shape might have been, the proto-Uralic word for 'tree' has been replaced in four separate language zones. In Saamic (e.g. 5a Ume Saami *muarra*) and Nganasan (5e *muŋku*), the words for 'tree' are of unclear origin; these are not thought to be connected, but could represent different derivates of the same root. The Mordva word for 'tree', viz. 5c (Erzya) *čuvto* = Moksha *šuftə*, seems to be a generalization of a hyponym; its only cognates are in Fennic, e.g. Finnish *huhta* 'arable land won by felling of heavy timber in a forest'. The ObUgrian languages use reflexes of *jïxï, viz. 5d Sosva Mansi *jiw*, Vasjugan Khanty *juuɣ*; *jïxï also seems originally to have been a hyponym, in this instance with reference to some sort of conifer, e.g. Tundra Nenets *je*, Taz Selkup *čöö* 'pine'.

By contrast, the replacement of the proto-Uralic word for 'fire' has a focus:

	S	Fe	Md	Mr	Ud	Ko	Mn	Kh	Hu	Ng	En	Ne	Sl	Km	Mt
6 'fire'	a	a	a	a	a	(a)				a	a	a	a	a	a
						b									
							c	c	c						
							d	d							
							e									

The proto-Uralic word for 'fire', *tulï, has been replaced in the core languages except for Udmurt (*til*); in Komi, only vestiges of this root remain, e.g. *tïv* in *tïv* + *kërt* '(piece of) iron (*kërt*) for starting a fire'. Komi has a new word for 'fire', viz. 6b *bi*, with uncertain cognates (*UEW* 359–60). The Mansi word 6e *ulʲa*, known only in northern and eastern dialects, is also of obscure origin. The Ugric word for 'fire', 6c Hungarian *tüüz* = Pelymka Mansi *tååwt* = Tremjugan Khanty *tiiɣʷət*, is perhaps a taboo circumlocution (Abondolo 1996: 62). Taboo is probably also behind the ObUgrian use of one of the Finno-Ugric words for ' woman', *najï, as a cover-term for 'fire': 6d Sosva Mansi *naaj* = Tremjugan Khanty *nääj*; other meanings of this word include, beside 'sun', also 'beautiful/powerful woman; princess; queen (playing-cards)'; Hungarian *nådʲ* 'big, great' is probably cognate (Mészáros 1988).

In the most common expressions for 'white',

	S	Fe	Md	Mr	Ud	Ko	Mn	Kh	Hu	Ng	En	Ne	Sl	Km	Mt
7 'white'	a	a			c		e		h						
			b	b		d		g		i	i	i	i	i	i
				f				j				j			

Saamic and Fennic (7a) use derivates from front and back isotopes of an affective/imitative stem *wal=ke-/*wäl=ke- meaning 'shines, is bright', viz. North Saami *vielgat*, Finnish *valkoinen*, and words with related meanings ('bright', 'clear') seemingly built from a stem *wal- are found in Mordva and Mari. The Mordva and Mari words for 'white', however, are from another source. They are 7b Erzya Mordva *ašo* = Moksha Mordva *akšə̂* = Hill Mari *oš(ə)* = Meadow Mari *oš(o)*, with possible, but not very convincing, cognates in either Fennic (cf. Estonian *ahka* 'eiderduck', *hahk* 'grey') or Khanty (Southern Khanty *aaš* 'chalk, white clay'). The -*k*- of the Moksha form is thought to be the result of contamination with Turkic words meaning 'coin, money', or 'whitish', e.g. Kirgiz *akša*, from a root meaning 'white'. The Permian languages diverge from the foregoing and from each other, with at least three distinct words for white: Udmurt *tëdʲi*, Komi *jedžïd*, and Permiak *čʲočʲkëm* = Yaz'va Komi *čʲočʲkəm* = Izhma Komi *čʲočʲkem* = Vym Komi *čʲočʲkëm*. The last item, which means 'clean' in standard Komi, has a possible cognate in North Saami *čeaskát* 'to appear (snow-)white'; the other two Permian words for 'white' are of obscure origin, although *jedžïd* may be connected with a Permian word meaning 'raw; unripe (of berries)' (Komi *jëž*, Udmurt *jež*). The origin of Hungarian 7h *fäheer* is also unclear, as is that of the Khanty word seen in 7g Southern Khanty *näwə* 'white' = Tremjugan *neeɣʷi* 'bright grey (e.g. fox)'; this word may be a derivate of a verb root (proto-Khanty *nüüɣ- ~ *nääɣ-) meaning 'is (clearly) visible'. In Mansi and Samoyedic, terms for 'white' have evolved from words for 'ice', e.g. 7e Sosva Mansi *jaaŋk*, 7i Tundra Nenets *ser* = Taz Selkup *sërï*; this designation probably competed with and wholly or partially replaced a proto-Samoyedic synonym, *jekV, with descendants only in Nganasan and Selkup (7j). Another term for 'white', 7f *sajrëŋ*, is attested in non-northern dialects of Mansi.

The Uralic words for 'black' are even more disparate; a superficial scan turned up sixteen items:

		S	Fe	Md	Mr	Ud	Ko	Mn	Kh	Hu	Ng	En	Ne	Sl	Km	Mt
8	'black'	a		c		e	e		i	i		k		m		o
		b		d			g			j				l	n	
				f			h									
							p									

The only cognate terms are (8e) Permian (Udmurt = Komi *šëd*) and (8i), Hungarian *fäkätä* = e.g. Tremjugan Khanty *peɣtə*. Neither set has clear cognates elsewhere; the origin of Udmurt 8f *kïrš^j* is also unclear. The words in Saamic (e.g. Northern Saami *čáhppat*) are all derivates of a common Saamic root whose shape suggests affect; Finnish *musta*, too, represents a pan-Fennic formation to a root *muse-/*muhe- with affective (animal husbandry) undertones. The Mordva word, e.g. Erzya *rav(u)žo*, lacks a credible etymology; its initial *r*- looks foreign. Mari *šem* has Permian cognates meaning 'rust(s)', with formal difficulties (Udmurt *sïnem*, Komi *sim*); for the semantics, compare Erzya Mordva *čemen^j* 'rust' and its possible Fennic cognates, e.g. Finnish *hämä=rä* 'dark, unclear' (Keresztes 1986: 156). Mansi dictionaries report at least three words for 'black': one (8g *s^joras*) is obscure, another (8h *seeməl*) seems to have been built from the word for 'rust', borrowed from Komi; a third (8p *pit*), known from northern dialects only, is a loan from Khanty (cf. 8i). The range of etymologically unconnected words across Samoyedic is unusual; of eighty-seven core sememes examined by Helimski (1982: 129–33) only two ('black' and 'new') show such a spread, while twenty-nine (i.e. one-third) have uniform representations in all six Samoyedic idioms. The Samoyedic words include internal derivates such as 8j Nganasan *henko* and 8l Tundra Nenets *pøridyana* (the present participle of a stative verb meaning 'is black'), and a loan from Turkic (8n Kamassian *saaɣar*). The source of Selkup 8m *sääq* is obscure; the Mator item (8o) was probably a descendant of proto-Samoyedic *küntə 'smoke'. For a recent discussion of the relative chronology of the various types of Turkic in Samoyedic lexica see Helimski 1987, Janhunen 1989, and Helimski 1991.

References and Further Reading
Abondolo, D. (1990) 'Proto-Uralic without s-Laute: a distributional view', *C7IFU*, vol. III, pp. 80–85.
——— (1996) *Vowel Rotation in Uralic: Obug[r]ocentric evidence*, SSEES Occasional Papers no. 31, London: University of London.

Austerlitz, R. (1968) 'L'ouralien', in A. Martinet. (ed.), *Le Langage: Encyclopédie de la Pléiade*, Paris: Gallimard, pp. 1331–89.

—— (1976) 'Az európai [w] és [v] térben és időben', *Nyelvtudományi Közlemények* 76/2: 250–55 [= *Laziczius Festschrift*, ed. P. Hajdú].

—— (1978) 'On comparing Uralic with other language families', 455 *Finnougorskie narody i vostok – Trudy po vostokovedeniü (Oriental Studies)*, vol. IV, *Tartu Riikliku Ülikooli Toimetised = Acta et Commentationes Universitatis Tartuensis* pp. 119–30.

—— (1980) 'Language-family density in North America and Eurasia', *UAJb* 52: 1–10.

—— (1985) 'The Permian centre', in Советское Финно-Угроведение 21 = *C61FU, Texte der Plenarsitzungsvorträge*, pp. 99–109.

Barbera, M. (1993) *La gradazione baltofinnica*, London: Lothian.

Balázs, J. (ed.) (1983) *Areális nyelvészeti tanulmányok*, Budapest: Tankönyvkiadó.

Bartens, R. (1979) *Mordvan, tšeremissin ja votjakin konjugaation infiniittisten muotojen syntaksi*, MSFOu 170 Helsinki: Société Finno-Ougrienne.

Beekes, R.S.P. (1995) *Comparative Indo-European Linguistics. An Introduction*, Amsterdam: Benjamins.

Bereczki, G. (1983) 'A Volga-Kama-vidék nyelveinek areális kapcsolatai', in Balázs 1983, 207–36.

Buck, C.D. (1949) *A Dictionary of Selected Synonyms in the Principal Indo-European Languages: A Contribution to the History of Ideas*, Chicago: University of Chicago Press.

Castrén, M.A. (1854) *Grammatik der samojedischen Sprachen*, St Petersburg. Bloomington: Indiana University, Reissued 1966 as no. 53 of the Uralic and Altaic Series.

Comrie, B. (1980a) 'The genetic affiliation of Kamchadal: some morphological evidence', *International Review of Slavic Linguistics* 5: 109–20.

—— (1980b) 'The order of case and possessive suffixes in Uralic languages: an approach to the comparative-historical problem', *Lingua Posnaniensis* 23: 81–6.

—— (1981a) 'Negation and other verb categories in the Uralic languages', *C51FU*, vol. VI, pp. 350–55.

—— (1981b) *The Languages of the Soviet Union*, Cambridge: Cambridge University Press.

—— (1988) 'General Features of the Uralic Languages', pp. 451–77 in Sinor 1988.

Décsy, Gy. (1965) *Einführung in die finnisch-ugrische Sprachwissenschaft*, Wiesbaden: Harrassowitz.

—— (1969) 'Finnougrische Lautforschung', *UAJb* 41: 33–75.

Doerfer, G. (1984) 'Prolegomena zu einer Untersuchung der dem Tungusischen und Mongolischen gemeinsamen Wörter', *JSFOu* 79: 68–85.

Donegan, P. (1978) *On the Natural Phonology of Vowels*, PhD diss., Ohio State University, published 1985 in the series Outstanding Dissertations in Linguistics, ed. Jorge Hankamer, New York and London: Garland Publishing.

Donner, O. (1879) *Die gegenseitige Verwandtschaft der Finnisch-ugrischen Sprachen*, Helsinki.

Gulya, J. (1975) 'Gab es eine finnisch-ugrische Einheit?' *C31FU*, vol. I, pp. 87–92.

Hajdú P. (1990) 'Einiges über Fürwörter', *Linguistica Uralica* 1: 1–12.

—— (1992) *Introduzione alle lingue uraliche*, translated and adapted by Danilo Gheno, Turin: Rosenberg & Seiler.

Hajdú P. and Domokos P. (1987) *Die uralischen Sprachen und Literaturen*, Budapest: Akadémiai kiadó.

Harms, R.T. (1977) 'The Uralo-Yukaghir focus system: a problem in remote genetic relationship', in P. Hopper (ed.), *Studies in Descriptive and Historical Linguistics (Festschrift for Winifred P. Lehman)*, Amsterdam: Benjamins, pp. 301–16.

Helimski, E.A. (1982) Древнейшие венгерско-самодийские языковые параллели, Moscow: Nauka.

—— (1987) 'Two Mator-Taigi-Karagass vocabularies from the 18th century', *JSFOu* 81: 49–132.

—— (1991) 'On the interaction of Mator with Turkic, Mongolic, and Tungusic: a rejoinder', *JSFOu* 83: 257–67.

—— (1996) 'Proto-Uralic gradiation [recte: gradation]: continuation and traces', *C8IFU* vol. I, pp. 17–51.

Honti, L. (1984) *Chrestomathia ostiacica (Osztják nyelvjárási szöveggyűjtemény nyelvtani vázlattal és történeti magyarázatokkal)*, Budapest: Tankönyvkiadó.

—— (1988) 'Die ob-ugrische Sprachen', in D. Sinor (ed.) *The Uralic Languages: Description, History and Foreign influences*, Handbuch der Orientalistik 8/1, Leiden: Brill.

—— (1990) 'Ugrisches', *Linguistica Uralica* 16: 298–9.

—— (1992) 'Adalék a magyar *l ~* finn *t* megfelelésének és alapnyelvi előzményének magyarázatához,' in P. Deréky et al. (eds), *Festschrift für Károly Rédei zum 60. Geburtstag*, Vienna–Budapest: Finno-Ugric Institute of the University of Vienna–Department of Finno-Ugric, University of Budapest, Linguistics Institute of the Hungarian Academy of Sciences, pp. 209–13.

—— (1995) 'Zur Morphotaktik und Morphosyntax der uralischen/finnisch-ugrischen Grundsprache', *C8IFU* vol. I, pp. 53–82.

Itkonen, E. (1939) *Der ostlappische Vokalismus vom qualitativen Standpunkt aus mit besonderer Berücksichtigung des Inari- und Skoltlappischen, MSFOu* 79, Helsinki: Société Finno-Ougrienne.

Janhunen, J. (1977) *Samojedischer Wortschatz. Gemeinsamojedische Etymologien*, Castrenianumin toimitteita 17, Helsinki: Castrenianum.

—— (1981a) 'On the structure of Proto-Uralic', *FUF* 44: 23–42.

—— (1981b) 'Uralilaisen kantakielen sanastosta,' *JSFOu* 77/9: 219–74.

—— (1984) 'Altailaisen hypoteesin nykytila', *Virittäjä* 88: 202–7.

—— (1989) 'On the interaction of Mator with Turkic, Mongolic, and Tungusic', *JSFOu* 82: 287–97.

—— (1992) 'Uralic languages', W. Bright (ed.), *International Encyclopedia of Linguistics*, vol. IV, New York–Oxford: Oxford University Press, pp. 205–10.

—— (1993) 'Options for Tundra Nenets vowel analysis', in M. Bakró-Nagy and E. Szíj (eds), *Hajdú Péter 70 éves*, [= Linguistica Series A, Studia et Dissertationes, 15], Budapest: Linguistics Institute of the Hungarian Academy of Sciences, pp. 143–7.

Joki, A. (1952) *Die Lehnwörter des Sajansamojedischen, MSFOu* 103, Helsinki: Société Finno-Ougrienne.

Kálmán, B. (1966) *Nyelvjárásaink*, Budapest: Tankönyvkiadó.

Katz, H. (1975) *Generative Phonologie und phonologische Sprachbünde des Ostjakischen und Samojedischen*, Finnisch-Ugrische Bibliothek, Munich: Wilhelm Fink.

—— (1984) 'Selkupische Phonologie', in P. Hajdú and L. Honti (eds), *Studien zur phonologischen Beschreibung uralischer Sprachen*, Budapest: Akadémiai kiadó, pp. 33–46.

Katzschmann, M. (1986) *Nominal- und Esse-Satz in den samojedischen Sprachen*, Fenno-Ugrica, Hamburg: Buske.

Kazancev, D.E. (1990) 'К вопросу о реконструкции *δ и *δʲ в Финно-угорском праязыке', *Linguistica Uralica* 26: 180–87.

Keresztes, L. (1986) *Geschichte des mordwinischen Konsonantismus*, vol. II: *Etymologisches Belegmaterial*, Studia uralo-altaica 27, Szeged.

Koizumi, T. (1989) 'On the deictic function of Uralic demonstratives', *Uralica* 8:1–16.

——— (1994) *Uraru-go toogoron*, Tokyo: Daigaku Shorin (with English summary pp. 317–57).

Korhonen, M. (1981) *Johdatus lapin kielen historiaan*, Helsinki: Suomalaisen Kirjallisuuden Seura.

——— (1984) 'Zur zentralen Problematik der Terlappischen Phonologie', in P. Hajdú and L. Honti (eds), *Studien zur phonologischen Beschreibung uralischer Sprachen*, Budapest: Akadémiai kiadó, pp. 311–25.

Laajavaara, M. (1986) *Itämerensuomen demonstratiivit* vol. I, Helsinki: Suomen kirjallisuuden seura.

Laver, J. (1994) *Principles of Phonetics*, Cambridge: Cambridge University Press.

Lehtiranta, J. (1989) *Yhteissaamelainen sanasto*, MSFOu 200, Helsinki: Société Finno-Ougrienne.

——— (1992) *Arjeploginsaamen äänne- ja taivutusopin pääpiirteet*, MSFOu 212, Helsinki: Société Finno-Ougrienne.

Maddieson, I. (1984) *Patterns of Sounds*, Cambridge: Cambridge University Press.

Majtinskaä K.E. (1979) Историко-сопоставительная морфология Финно-угорских языков, Moscow: Nauka.

Mészáros, H.F. (1988) '*Nagy* szavunk eredetéről', in P. Domokos and J. Pusztay (eds), *Bereczki emlékkönyv (Bereczki Gábor 60. születésnapjára)*, Budapest: Faculty of Philosophy of the University of Budapest, pp. 277–82.

Mikola, T. (1984) 'Einige Probleme der enzischen Phonologie', in P. Hajdú and L. Honti (eds), *Studien zur phonologischen Beschreibung uralischer Sprachen*, Budapest: Akadémiai kiadó, pp. 29–32.

Miller, A. R. (1990) 'How dead is the Altaic hypothesis?', in B. Brendemoen (ed.), *Altaica osloensia*, Oslo: pp. 223–37.

Nichols, J. (1992) *Linguistic Diversity in Space and Time*, Chicago and London: University of Chicago Press.

Nikolaeva, I. A. (1988) 'Проблема урало-юкагирских генетических связей,' Автореферат: диссертация на соискание ученой степени кандидата Филологических наук, Moscow: Linguistics Institute, USSR Academy of Sciences.

Rédei, K. (1988) 'Geschichte der permischen Sprachen', pp. 351–94 in Sinor 1988.

Ristinen, E. K. (1960) 'Samoyed phonemic systems', unpublished PhD diss., Indiana University.

Rounds, C. (1991) 'Topicality and case marking in Hungarian, Komi and Finnish', unpublished PhD dissertation, Columbia University.

Salminen, T. (1993) 'Uralilaiset kielet maailman kielten joukossa', in T. Salminen (ed.), *Uralilaiset kielet tänään*, Snellman-Instituutti Series A, no. 13 (with English summary pages 103–105), Kuopio: Snellman-Instituutti, pp. 24–30.

Sammallahti, P. (1974) *Material from Forest Nenets*, Castrenianumin toimitteita 2 Helsinki: Castrenianum.

——— (1978) 'Über die Laut- und Morphemstruktur der uralischen Grundsprache', *FUF* 43: 22–66.

——— (1984) 'Saamelaisten esihistoriallinen tausta kielitieteen valossa' [with English summary] in J. Gallén (ed.), *Suomen väestön esihistorialliset juuret*, Helsinki: Suomen Tiedeseura, pp. 137–56.

——— (1988) 'Historical phonology of the Uralic languages, with special reference to Samoyed, Ugric, and Permic,' pp. 478–554 in Sinor 1988.

Serebrennikov, B. A. (1963) Историческая морфология пермских языков, Moscow: Publications of the Soviet Academy of Sciences.

Sinor, D. (ed.) (1988) *The Uralic Languages. Description, History and Foreign Influences*, Handbuch der Orientalistik 8/1, Leiden: Brill.

Steinitz, W. (1944) *Geschichte des finnisch-ugrischen Vokalismus*, Acta Instituti Hungarici Universitatis Holmiensis, Series B. Linguistica 2, Stockholm: University of Stockholm.

—— (1952) *Geschichte des finnisch-ugrischen Konsonantismus*, Acta Instituti Hungarici Universitatis Holmiensis, Series B, Linguistica 1, Stockholm: University of Stockholm, pp. 15–39.

Suhonen, S. (1988) 'Geschichte der ostseefinnischen Sprachen', pp. 288–313 in Sinor 1988.

Suihkonen, P. (1987) 'Suomensukuiset kansat väestötilastojen valossa', *Terra* 99/4: 209–32.

Tálos, E. (1983) 'Kép szöveg nélkül', in *Urálisztikai tanulmányok (Hajdú Péter 60. születésnapja tiszteletére)*, ed. G. Bereczki and P. Domokos, Budapest: ELTE, pp. 409–20.

—— (1987) 'On the vowels of proto-Uralic', in K. Rédei (ed.), *Studien zur Phonologie und Morphonologie der uralischen Sprachen, Akten der dritten Tagung für uralische Phonologie, Eisenstadt, 28. Juni–1. Juli 1984*, [= Studia Uralica 4], Vienna: Verband der wissenschaftlichen Gesellschaften Österreichs, pp. 70–80.

Tereščenko, N. M. (1966) 'Энецкий язык', in V. I. Lytkin et al. (eds), языки народов ссср, vol. III: Финно-угорские и самодийские языки Moscow: Nauka, pp. 438–57.

—— (1973) Синтаксис самодийских языков. Простое предложение, Leningrad: Nauka.

Vasikova, L. P. (1992) 'Аспирата ?, аффриката ŋk и сонант ŋ в горномарийском языке (к провблеме консонантизма в марийских языках', *Linguistica Uralica* 228: 120–5.

Veenker, W. (1975) *Materialien zu einem onomasiologisch-semasiologischen vergleichenden Wörterbuch der uralischen Sprachen*, Hamburger Uralistische Forschungen I, Hamburg.

Viitso, T.-R. (1996) 'On classifying the Finno-Ugric languages', *C8IFU*, vol. IV, 261–6.

Wickman, B. (1955) *The Form of the Object in the Uralic Languages*, Uppsala: Almqvist & Wiksells.

2 Saamic

Pekka Sammallahti

The Saami languages are spoken in an area stretching from Dalarna in central Sweden to the tip of the Kola Peninsula in Russia. All the Saami languages are fairly similar in structure and basic vocabulary. Although there are no wide linguistic boundaries, one can distinguish ten Saami languages which differ from one another at least to the same degree as the various Germanic languages. Peripheral dialects which lie on two different sides of a language boundary are normally close to one another in vocabulary, and this is why the Saami languages form a chain in which speakers of adjacent dialects understand one another rather easily. The more central dialects of adjacent Saami languages differ enough for mutual comprehension to require a fair amount of effort.

In the literature, the variants of Saami have been treated as dialects because of the regular correspondences in phonology and the similarity in basic vocabulary and grammar. Since six of the regional variants have independently standardized written forms, it is more justifiable to speak of separate languages. The remaining four varieties of Saami, which are generally held to fall outside the six main languages, are spoken by only a few older individuals.

It is customary to distinguish the following main varieties of Saami: (1) South Saami, (2) Ume Saami, (3) Pite Saami, (4) Lule Saami, (5) North Saami (also called Norwegian Saami), (6) Inari Saami, (7) Skolt Saami, (8) Akkala Saami (also called Babino Saami), (9) Kildin Saami, and (10) Ter Saami. Their territories are indicated on Map 2.1. The majority, as many as 75 per cent, speak North Saami and most of these, some 10,000 people, live in Norway (about 5,000 live in Sweden and about 2,000 in Finland). Ume, Pite, Akkala, and probably also Ter Saami are used mainly by older people. South, Inari, and Skolt Saami have about 300–500 speakers each. Kildin Saami is spoken by about 1,000 speakers, and the number of Lule speakers is about 2,000–3,000. The total number of Saami speakers is probably somewhat more than 20,000, i.e. in Finland 3,000; in Norway 12,000; in Russia 1,000; and in Sweden 7,000. All of these figures are estimates.

The orthographies of the standardized written languages are based on the Latin alphabet in South, Lule, North, Inari, and Skolt Saami, whereas Kildin now uses a variant of Cyrillic instead of the Latin-based alphabet used in the 1930s. South Saami orthography represents sounds in a manner closer to the orthographies of Swedish and Norwegian and so does that of Lule Saami, but to a lesser extent. The basis for North, Inari, and Skolt Saami orthography was laid by the Danish linguist Rasmus Rask at the beginning of the nineteenth century. As an amendment, in Inari and Skolt Saami double letters are used to indicate long vowels. There are also some additional letters for distinctive vowel and consonant qualities.

The Saami languages are most closely related to Fennic, a branch of Uralic of which Finnish has been Saami's neighbouring language since the breakup of the Fennic-Saamic protolanguage (also called Early Pre-Finnic) which began after the introduction of the Indo-European Battle-axe Culture on the coasts of Finland about 2500 BCE.

Saami differs from Fennic in a number of features. In phonology, the vowel system has undergone a radical reorganization whereas the consonant system has retained many older features, such as palatalized consonants, which were lost in Fennic as a consequence of the Indo-European contacts which ultimately helped bring about the disintegration of the Fennic-Saamic protolanguage. In morphology, Saami has retained the dual number in its personal pronouns, personal endings, and possessive suffixes, i.e. in all elements with the category person. Furthermore, Saami personal endings are different in the present and past tenses, and Saami lacks the external local cases which Fennic developed after the disintegration of the protolanguage. In Saami conjugation, most of the present-tense personal endings are based on earlier nominal derivational suffixes, a fact which suggests that the present-day symmetry of the Finnish personal endings developed in proto-Fennic, after the split from proto-Saamic. Saami declension seems to indicate that the plural local cases (illative, inessive, and elative) developed after the disintegration of the Fennic-Saamic protolanguage, and that the proto-language probably had only the grammatical and general local cases (essive and partitive) in the plural. Both branches of Fennic-Saamic have developed consonant gradation, but in Saami this morphonological phenomenon grew out of fortition processes (*kota 'hut sN' > North Saami goahti, *kota-n 'sG' > goaði) whereas in Fennic it is the result of weakening (*akka 'wife sN' > Finnish akka, *akka-n 'sG' > akan). A further difference is that Saami gradation entails all Saami consonants, whereas in Fennic only the stops alternate. The reorganization of the Saamic vowel system may be illustrated by the following examples (all reconstructed forms are p[roto-] F[ennic-]S[aamic]): *äjmä 'needle' > áibmi, *käti 'hand' > giehta, *appi 'father-in-law' > vuohppa, *kala 'fish' > guolli (*a sometimes > á, as in *vanča- 'walks' > vázzi-), *poŋi 'bosom' > buokŋa (*o sometimes is retained, as in *joki 'river' > johka), *kota 'hut' > goahti, *nōri 'young' > nuorra, *meni- 'goes' > manna- (*e sometimes > ie as in *velji > viellja), *kesä 'summer' > geassi, *kēli 'language' > giella, *puri- 'bites' > borra-, *kūli- 'hears' > gulla-, *süli 'lap' > salla, *kilpi 'shielding object' > galba, *pīri 'circle' > birra 'around'.

Western and Eastern Saami

The Saami languages may be divided into two main groups: (1) Western Saami languages (South, Ume, Pite, Lule, and North Saami) and (2) Eastern Saami languages (Inari, Skolt, Akkala, Kildin, and Ter Saami).

These two main groups are distinguished from one another by the fate of the proto-Saami consonant clusters *šʲt and *šʲk: in the Western languages the *šʲ has split into the consonant sequence /jh/, but not in the Eastern ones: '(river) rapids' in South Saami is *goejhke*, Ume *guajhkke*, Pite *guajhhka*, Lule *guojkka*, North Saami *guoika* (all with the cluster /jhk/), but Inari has *kuoškâ*, Skolt and Akkala have *kuõškk*, Kildin has *kuuššk* (orthographically: кӯшшк), and Ter Saami *kyyššk* (all with the cluster /šk/). The eastern coastal dialects of North Saami still had *šk* and *št* in the eighteenth century.

Another Eastern feature with traces in the west is *nž*-contraction, productive especially in diminutives: North Saami *lottáš* 'little bird', pN *lottážat* v. Inari Saami *loddááž*, pN *loddááh* (with contracted *áá* in the second syllable). The introduction of so-called prothetic stops in nasal geminates also largely coincides with this border (the exception is Sea Saami, a dialect of North Saami): in the west, original *mm, *nn, *nʲnʲ, *ŋŋ have changed into clusters beginning with a homotopic stop, e.g. North Saami *eadni* 'mother', sG *eatni* v. Inari Saami *enni*, sG *eeni* (/eeñi/), North Saami *bátni* 'tooth', sG *báni* v. Inari Saami *pääni* (/pääñi/), sG *pääni* (~ *päne*). Sea Saami has preserved the geminates: *jien'ne : jienne, bánne : báne*.

Western Saami

The Western Saami languages may be further subdivided into two groups: the southern group (South and Ume Saami) and the northern group (Pite, Lule, and North Saami). In the southern group, final sounds have usually been preserved in unstressed syllables, whereas the northern group has lost them: South *gåetesne* 'in the hut', Ume *gååtiesne* v. Pite *gååtien*, Lule *goaden*, North *goaðis*. As a consequence of consonant gemination after short stressed vowels, the southern group does not have short stressed syllables: South and Ume *johkesne* 'in the river' v. Pite and Lule *jågån*, North *jogas*. Furthermore, short stressed *i and *u have gone to the sequences /ij/ and /uv/ before single consonants in the southern group: North, Lule, and Pite *juhkat* 'to drink' v. Ume *jovhkkedh*, South *jovhkedh* (*u > /uv/); North *giðða* 'spring', Lule *gidá* v. Ume *gijđđe*, South *gijre* (*i > /ij/).

The Southern Group

The southern group of Western Saami consists of two languages: Ume Saami (in Sweden: the districts Ståkke and Maskaure in Arjeplog, Malå, Gran, and Ran in Sorsele, Umby in Tärna; Rana in Norway) and South Saami (all variants south of Ume Saami down to Idre in the Swedish province Dalarna).

Ume Saami has partial consonant gradation: *gååhtie* 'hut' (å = /o/), sG *gååtien* 'sG', *gååhtaje* 'sIll', *guutijne* 'pIne', whereas South Saami completely lacks gradation: *gåetie* 'hut', *gåetien* 'sG', *gåatan* 'sIll', *gåetine ~*

göötine 'pIne'. Furthermore, second-syllable long vowels have been reduced to short vowels in trisyllabic stress groups in South Saami, whereas Ume Saami has retained them: compare the underlined segments of South *gåetẹsne* v. Ume *gååtiẹsne* 'hut sIne', South *bearkọsne* v. Ume *bierkọesne* 'meat sIne', South *maanẹste* v. Ume *maanạste* 'child sEla' (second-syllable *a* = /aa/).

South Saami has two main dialects: the northern (or Åsele) dialect (in Sweden: Vapsten in Tärna, Vilhelmina and Frostviken; in Norway: Vefsn, Grane, Hattfjelldal, Bindal, and Namdal), and the southern (or Jämtland) dialect (in Sweden: Hotagen, Offerdal, Kall, Skalstugan, Undersåker, and Härjedalen; in Norway: Meråker and the area between Snåsa and Verdal). The northern second-syllable diphthong *oe* (= /uo/ << *å̄) corresponds to southern *a* (= /aa/): Åsele *aahkoe* v. Jämtland *aahka* 'grandmother'. The infinitive suffix is *-dh* in the north and *-jh* in the south: Åsele *båetedh* v. Jämtland *båetijh* 'to come'. Final *-m* has been retained in the south but changed to *-b* in the north: Åsele *båatab, guelieb* v. Jämtland *båatam* 'I come', *gueliem* 'fish sA'.

The Northern Group

The northern group of Western Saami is divided into two branches, North Saami (Torne, Finnmark, and Sea Saami) and the western subgroup (Lule and Pite Saami).

In North Saami the labial stop in the clusters *BD, *Bž^j, *pc, *pč^j, *ps, *pš^j, and *pt has become velar (G, K; in Finnmark and Sea Saami *G has subsequently gone to a fricative *v*): North *dovdat* (Torne *dogdah ~ dogduoh*) 'to recognize' v. Lule *dåbddåt*; North *gokčat* 'to cover' v. Lule *gåbttjåt* (~ *gåpttjåt*). There are some conspicuous morphological differences between North Saami and the western subgroup. The North Saami locative corresponds to western inessive and elative: Pite *gååtien*, Lule *goaden* 'in the hut', Pite *gååtiest*, Lule *goades* 'from the hut' v. North *goađis* 'in/from the hut'. In the western subgroup, the negative verb has retained the old present-tense and past-tense forms, whereas North Saami uses the original present-tense forms in both functions: Pite *ij bååtie* and Lule *ij boade* '(s)he does not come', Pite *ittjij bååtie* and Lule *ittjij boade* '(s)he did not come' v. North *ii boađe* 'does not come' and *ii boahtán* 'did not come'. Furthermore, the genitive and accusative singular forms have syncretized in North Saami, but the western subgroup has retained the distinction: Pite *gååtie* 'hut sG', *gååtiev* 'hut sA', Lule *goade* 'hut sG', *goadev* 'hut sA' v. North *goađi* 'hut sG/A'. In all these features, North Saami patterns with the Eastern Saami languages, while Lule and Pite agree with the South.

North Saami is divided into the following main dialects: Torne Saami, Finnmark Saami and Sea Saami (the northern coast from Fisher Pensinsula to Troms, except the Porsanger Fjord).

Torne Saami has second-syllable short /u/ (< proto-Saami *u) in third-person singular present-tense forms of *u*-verbs, with ensuing monophthongization in the first syllable, e.g. *čirro* '(s)he cries' (phonologically /čiirru/ ~ /čiirro/; elsewhere with a long vowel from earlier *åå: *čierru*, phonologically /čierruu/). Torne Saami agrees here with the languages further southwest. The locative singular ending is *-n* in Torne, whereas Finnmark and Sea Saami have *-s(t)*: Torne *gielan* 'in the snare' v. Finnmark/ Sea Saami *gielas*. Sea Saami has retained old nasal geminates which have gone to clusters in Torne and Finnmark: Sea *bánni* ~ *bánne* 'tooth', *biem'mu* ~ *biem'mo* 'food', and *jieŋŋa* 'ice' v. Finnmark and Torne *bátni*, *biebmu*, *jiekŋa*. Sea Saami agrees here with the Saami languages further to the east.

Torne Saami has four subdialects: the Finnish Wedge dialect (Western Enontekiö in Finland and adjacent areas in the west between Skibotnelva, Gálggojávri and Nordreisa in Norway); the Karesuando dialect (Könkämävuoma and Lainiovuoma districts in Sweden, Lyngen and Balsfjord in Norway); the Jukkasjärvi dialect (the districts Saarivuoma, Talma, Rautasvuoma, and Kaalasvuoma in Sweden, and the areas around Vågsfjord and Ofotfjord in Norway); and the Kaitum dialect (the districts Norrkaitum and Mellanbyn in Sweden).

In Jukkasjärvi and Kaitum, the plural locative ending is *-s* instead of the *-n* in the rest of North Saami: Jukkasjärvi/Kaitum *dáis váriis* 'in these mountains' v. Karesuando/Finnish Wedge *dáin váriin*. In Karesuando, the monophthongal variants *ee* and *oo* of proto-Saami *ea and *oa have been rediphthongized into *ie* and *uo*: Karesuando *buohten* 'I came' and *giessen* 'I pulled' v. *boohten* and *geessen* in the rest of North Saami. Corresponding to *a* in Kaitum, Jukkasjärvi and Karesuando have *e* before following *j* and *v*: *geikuot* 'to tear' v. Kaitum/Finnish Wedge *gaikut*. Kaitum and Finnish Wedge have /ii/ and /uu/ in the second syllable corresponding to standard-language *i* and *u*, whereas Jukkasjärvi and Karesuando have /ie/ and /uo/: Kaitum/ Finnish Wedge *aski* 'lap' and *viessu* 'house' v. Jukkasjärvi/Karesuando *askie* and *viessuo*. The Kaitum dialect has been regarded as a dialect of Lule Saami because of lexical similarities, but structurally it belongs to North Saami. Furthermore, the Finnish Wedge dialect agrees with West Finnmark Saami in that proto-North Saami *GD and *Gž^j (from proto-Saami *mD and *mž^j) have gone to /vt/ and /vč/, respectively: Karesuando *dogduoh* 'to recognize', *vuogdieh* 'to sell', *lágžie* 'strap', Jukkasjärvi *dogdat*, *vuogdiet*, *lágžie*, Kaitum *dogdat*, *vuogdit*, *lágži* v. Finnish Wedge *dovdah*, *vuovdih*, *lávži* (and standard *dovdat*, *vuovdit*, *lávži*). Jukkasjärvi, Karesuando and Finnish Wedge have generally lost the opposition between /c/ and /č/ and between the corresponding voiced affricates /z/ and /ž/, e.g. Karesuando /oaz'zuoh/ 'to obtain', /vaaz'zieh/ 'to walk', Finnish Wedge /oaž'žuuh/, /vaaž'žiih/, standard *oažžut*, *vázzit*.

Finnmark Saami has two dialect groups: western dialects (Eastern Enontekiö, Northern Sodankylä, and part of Inari in Finland; Kautokeino and Alta in Norway), and eastern dialects (Utsjoki and part of Inari in Finland, and Karasjok, Porsanger, and Tana in Norway).

Corresponding to western intervocalic *b* and *g*, the eastern dialects have fricatives or zero: western *stobus* 'in the house', *logan* 'I read' v. eastern *stovus* (~ *sto'us*), *loγan* (~ *lo'an*). In the eastern dialects, stressed single vowels have been lengthened before relatively short consonants: /juhken/ 'I drank' v. /juuhken/ 'I dealt' in the west, but /juuhken/ for both in the east. The western dialects have a phonological opposition between long and short geminates, while the eastern ones have transferred the difference onto the vowels: western /kol'lii/ 'gold', /kollii/ 'gold sG' v. eastern /kollii/ : /koollii/ (~ /kollii:/ with secondary stress on the second syllable; in some eastern idioms /kollii/ for both).

The western subdivision of the northern group of Western Saami is divided into two languages: Lule Saami and Pite Saami.

In Pite Saami, the extensive metaphonic alternations in stressed vowels depend mainly on the second syllable vowel; only /i/ and /u/ (and, in some dialects, /aa/) do not participate in metaphonic alternations. In Lule Saami, stressed vowel alternations are dependent on the quantity of the following consonant centre and the following vowel, and only the low diphthongs take part. In Pite Saami, stressed *a* has gone to *i*, and *å* (= /o/) has gone to *u* before *i* or *u* in the next syllable: *mannat* 'to go' v. *minniv* 'I went', *bårråt* 'to eat' v. *burriv* 'I ate'. In Lule Saami, the clusters *kt*, *ktj*, *ks* and *ksj* (*tj* = /č/, *sj* = /š/) participate in qualitative gradation, whereas in Pite they have quantitative gradation only: Lule *tjakta* 'autumn sN', *tjavtav* 'sA' v. Pite *tjakttja* : *tjaktjav*. The Lule Saami qualitative alternations *bb:pp*, *dd:tt*, *gg:kk*, *dts:tts*, *dtj:ttj*, *bbm:bm* (= /b'm/:/pm/), *ddn:dn*, *ggn':gn'* (= /g'ŋ/:/kŋ/) correspond to Pite quantitative alternations *p'p:pp*, *t't:tt*, *k'k:kk*, *t'ts:tts*, *t'tj:ttj*, *p'm:pm*, *t'n:tn*, *k'n':kn'*: Lule *gádde* 'shore sN' : *gáttev* 'sA', *biebbmo* 'food sN' : *biebmov* 'sA' v. Pite *gaat'tie* : *gaattiev*, *biep'muo* : *biepmuov*.

Lule Saami is divided into the following dialects: northern (Sörkaitum, Sirkas, and Jåkkåkaska districts in Sweden, Tysfjord in Norway), southern (Tuorpon district in Sweden), and forest dialects (Gällivare and Serri forest Saami districts in Sweden).

In the northern dialect, second-syllable *á* is labialized by first-syllable *å* : northern *jåhttåt* (= /jot'toot/) 'to start' v. southern and forest *jåhttát* (= /jot'taat/). The forest dialects have the alternation *a~e* in stressed positions: northern and southern *mannat* 'to go' : *manniv* 'I went' v. forest *mannat* : *menniv*.

Pite Saami is divided into three dialects: northern (the district of Luokta-Mavas in Sweden), central (the district of Semisjaur-Njarg in Sweden), and southern (the district of Svaipa in Sweden).

Long (or double) *aa* alternates with *ee* before second-syllable *u* and *i* in the central and southern dialects, but not in the north: northern *vaassiet* 'to go by' : *vaasij* 'it went by' v. central and southern *vaassiet* : *veesij*. The southern dialects have *r* where the northern and central dialects have *đ*: southern *åårriet* 'to sleep' v. central and northern *ååđđiet*.

Eastern Saami

The Eastern Saami languages fall into two groups: the mainland group (Inari, Skolt, and Akkala Saami), and the peninsular group (Kildin and Ter Saami).

The weak grades of the single sibilants, affricates, and *k have been geminated in the mainland group but not in the peninsular group (in Inari Saami, the geminates have been secondarily shortened in certain positions), Inari *keesist* (old language *keezzist* with the voiced sibilant /z/) 'summer sLoc', Skolt and Akkala *kʹie'zzest* v. Kildin and Ter *kie'zest*, Inari *ivveest* 'year sLoc', Skolt *ee'jjest* ~ *ii'jjest*, Akkala *ii'jjest* v. Kildin and Ter *y'gest*. The mainland group has replaced the reflexes of non-contracted *u with those of *ā̄: Inari *kuárrum* 'sewing' and '(having) sewn', Skolt *kuärram* 'idem', but Kildin куаррам 'sewing' (phonologically: /koarram/) v. кӯррма (phonologically: /kuurrma/) 'having sewn'.

The Mainland Group

The mainland group consists of two branches: Inari Saami (Inari of Finland), and the Skolt group. The most conspicuous of the several features which distinguish Inari Saami from the Skolt group (Skolt and Akkala Saami) are the following:

1   In Inari Saami, the strong grade of the single stop *k* (as well as other instances of *k*) has gone to *h*, and the weak grade to *v*, e.g. Inari *juuhâ* 'river' : *juuvvâst* 'sLoc' v. Skolt and Akkala *jokk* : *jooɣɣâst*.
2   Skolt and Akkala have lost final unstressed vowels whereas Inari has preserved them as a rule, e.g. Inari *kyeli* 'fish', *tullâ* 'fire', *áldu* 'reindeer cow' v. Skolt and Akkala *kue'll*, *toll*, and Skolt *äldd*, Akkala *aldd*.
3   Second-syllable *ā̄ has lost its lip-rounding and fallen together with *a* in Skolt and Akkala but not in Inari, e.g. Inari *kuárrum* 'having sewn' v. Skolt *kuärram*, Akkala *koarram* ~ *koarrmõnž̌*. Skolt and Akkala share this feature with the peninsular group, but it seems to be a relatively recent innovation because it has also affected certain secondary cases in the mainland group, in which *ā̄ goes back to *u as in Inari *kuárrum* < *koaȓāmă < proto-Saami *koaȓumă[nž̌ʲă]. The now-extinct idioms of the mainland group further south in Sodankylä, Savukoski, and Kuolajärvi (Salla) also had the rounded vowel.
4   Skolt and Akkala Saami have tongue-height alternations which Inari lacks, e.g. Inari *kuullâđ* 'to hear' : *kulá* '(s)he hears' v. Skolt and Akkala *kuullâ(d)* : *kooll*, Inari *siirdij* '(s)he moved' : *sirdá* '(s)he moves' v. Skolt and Akkala *sii'rdi* : *serdd*.

The Skolt group is divided into two languages: Skolt Saami, and Akkala Saami (the former villages Babino and Yokostrov on Imandra Lake, north of Kandalaksha). Akkala has preserved the nasal-plus-stop/affricate clusters, whereas Skolt Saami has denasalized them (*nd* > *dd*, *mb* > *bb*, *ŋg* > *gg*, *nȼ*

> *çç, nž̌* > *ž̌ž̌*), e.g. Akkala *lå'ndd* 'bird' v. Skolt *lå'dd*, Akkala *soa'mbb* 'stick' v. Skolt *suä'bb*, Akkala *čuâŋgga* 'to stick' v. Skolt *čuâggad*. In this Skolt Saami agrees with the Saami languages further west, Akkala with the languages further east. Denasalization spread east across the North/Inari Saami border after the acquisition of Christian names and terminology, probably in the sixteenth or seventeenth century, cf. North *ándagassii*, Inari *addâgâs* 'pardon' < Finnish *anteeksi*.

Skolt Saami has two main dialect groups, northern, and southern. In the northern group, *b* has turned into *v* in the clusters *bd* and *bž*, but not in the southern group, e.g. Neiden *tovdâd* 'to know', Paatsjoki *tovddâd* v. Suonikylä – Nuortijärvi *tobddâd*. In the southern group, final *g* has gone to *γ* after sonorants in weak-grade clusters, but the northern group has preserved the stop: Neiden *ålggas* '(going) out', Paatsjoki *ålgas* v. Suonikylä ~ Nuortijärvi *åålγas*. The southern group has preserved the second-syllable contracted vowel *u* but it has gone to *â* in the northern dialects, e.g. Neiden *poåc'câ*, Paatsjoki *puoc'câ* 'reindeer pN', v. Suonikylä – Nuortijärvi *puõc'cu*. The northern group has preserved the dual in conjugation but the southern group has only singular and plural, e.g. Paatsjoki *mõõnij* '(s)he went', *mõõnin* 'the two of them went', *mõ'nne* 'they went' v. Suonikylä *mõõni* '(s)he went', *mõ'nne* 'they (two or more) went'.

The northern group of Skolt Saami consists of two dialects: Neiden (Neiden in Norway, now extinct), and Paatsjoki (Paatsjoki, Petsamonkylä, and Muotka villages in the former Petsamo area, moved over to Nellim, Finland, after the Second World War). The Neiden dialect had the marker *-k* in the nominative plural of nouns, whereas the Paatsjoki dialect has zero: Neiden *kuelek* 'fish pN' v. Paatsjoki *kue'l*. The Neiden dialect agrees here with North Saami, from which the feature was probably borrowed.

The southern group of Skolt Saami is divided into two dialects: Suonikylä (in the southern Petsamo area, now in Sevettijärvi, Finland), and Nuortijärvi-Hirvasjärvi dialect (around Lake Nuortijärvi and south of it in the former villages Nuortijärvi [Notozero] and Hirvasjärvi [Girvasozero]). Nuortijärvi-Hirvasjärvi has the stop *d* instead of the Suonikylä fricative *đ*: Suonikylä *vue'đđed* 'to sleep' v. Nuortijärvi *vue'dded*, Hirvasjärvi *vue'dde*. Instead of the word-final voiced sibilants *z* and *ž* found in Suonikylä, Nuortijärvi-Hirvasjärvi has unvoiced *s* and *š*: Suonikylä *kõrrâz* 'hard pN' v. Nuortijärvi-Hirvasjärvi *kõrrâs*, Suonikylä *sä'mmlaž* 'Saami' v. Nuortijärvi-Hirvasjärvi *sä'mmlaš*.

The Peninsular Group

The peninsular group consists of two languages: Kildin (in the former villages of Kildin, Voroninsk, Varsina, Maselga, Lovozero, Lyavozero; the inhabitants have been transferred mainly to Lovozero), and Ter (in the former villages of Yokanga, Lumbovsk, Ponoy, Sosnovka and Kamensk, now scattered on the Kola Peninsula). The main differences between these two languages rest on

Map 2.1   Varieties of Saamic

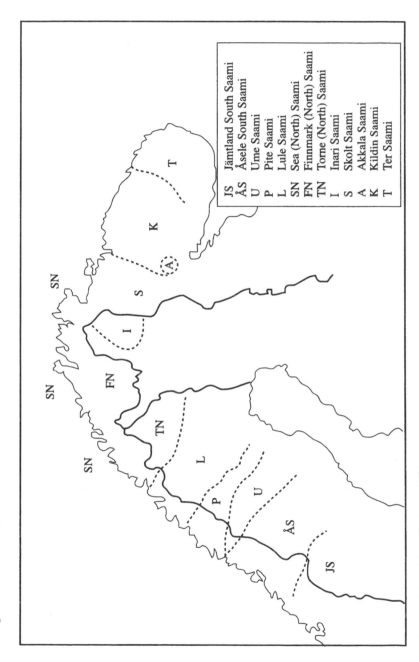

JS	Jämtland South Saami
ÅS	Åsele South Saami
U	Ume Saami
P	Pite Saami
L	Lule Saami
SN	Sea (North) Saami
FN	Finnmark (North) Saami
TN	Torne (North) Saami
I	Inari Saami
S	Skolt Saami
A	Akkala Saami
K	Kildin Saami
T	Ter Saami

Source: Adapted from Korhonen 1981.

vowels. In Ter, the reflexes of *uo have lost their lip-rounding, but not in Kildin: Kildin *kuu'ddõ* 'they left' v. Ter *kïï'd'dõ*, Kildin *kuõda* 'I leave (it)' v. Ter *kiõdam*. In Ter the reflexes of short stressed *o and *a do not alternate, whereas in Kildin they show qualitative and quantitative alternation: Kildin *mõõnnõ* 'to go' : *mânn* '(s)he goes' v. Ter *mânni* : *mânna*, Kildin *poorrô* 'to eat' : *pårr* '(s)he eats' v. Ter *porri* : *porra*. Here, Kildin agrees with Skolt and Akkala, where first-syllable *i and *u alternate, as well.

The Saami languages have largely the same basic vocabularies. For the Swadesh basic list of one hundred words, the average percentage of shared vocabulary is over 80 per cent, and neighbouring languages share over 90 per cent of this basic vocabulary, as a rule. Vocabulary pertaining to the environment, kinship, and traditional means of livelihood is largely the same in all Saami languages. The most important lexical differences stem from transitions in meaning and use of traditional vocabulary and from recent loanwords which have been acquired in Northern and Inari Saami from Finnish, in the South, Ume, Pite, and Lule Saami from Scandinavian languages, and in Skolt, Akkala, Kildin, and Ter Saami from Russian.

Map 2.1 represents the situation at the end of the nineteenth century and the beginning of the twentieth century, when administrative measures had only minimal impact on Saami life. From the beginning of the present century, speakers of North Saami have moved southwest as far as Arjeplog in the Pite Saami area. In Finland, the Skolt Saami from the Petsamo area were resettled north and east of Lake Inari as a consequence of the ceding of Petsamo to the Soviet Union after the Second World War. In Russia (at that time the Soviet Union), the Hirvasjärvi and Akkala Saami were moved to Yona kolkhoz, roughly half way between their old winter villages. The speakers of Kildin Saami have been concentrated in Lovozero where they are in the minority (they make up one-quarter of the population). The Nuortijärvi Saami dispersed in different directions when the Tuuloma hydroelectric power station was built and (Lake) Nuortijärvi became a regulated reservoir. They now live mainly in Murmansk and Lovozero. A few families have been able to stay in the Verxnetulomskij kolkhoz in their traditional area.

Phonology

General Organization

Saami words are composed of one or more stress groups containing at least one stressed syllable which can be followed by one or two (or in rare cases three) unstressed syllables. A word with more than three syllables therefore consists of more than one stress group. As a rule, odd-numbered syllables are stressed.

The stressed syllable nucleus is called the *vowel centre* and the consonants between it and the next syllable nucleus are called the *consonant centre*. The first unstressed nucleus is called the *latus*, and the consonants between it and the next unstressed nucleus are called the *consonant margin*. The following unstressed nucleus (the third of the stress group) is called the *vowel margin*. Final consonants are called the *finis*, and initial ones the *initium*. In a stress group, only the vowel centre is obligatory.

The trisyllabic word **vuojašan** 'I drive around' is thus divided into positions as follows:

Initium	Vowel centre	Consonant centre	Latus	Consonant margin	Vowel margin	Finis
v	**uo**	**j**	**a**	**š**	**a**	**n**

The word *viehkalattan* 'I am about to run off' contains two stress groups; the initium of the non-initial stress group is called by a special name, *limes*, because of phonological restrictions: /v - ie - hk - a - /l - a - tt - a - n. Normally, a stress group contains two syllables. If a word has an uneven number of syllables (i.e. is *imparisyllabic*), the final syllable is the last of a trisyllabic stress group, e.g. /v - ie - hk - a -/l - a - dd -a -m -e 'being about to run off'. In some cases, the initial stress group is monosyllabic and the word has two consecutive stressed syllables, e.g. /oa - m/b - ea - ll - e 'female cousin'.

The Vowels
The eastern Enontekiö subdialect of the Finnmark dialect of North Saami (henceforth: EE) has five basic short vowels, /i e a o u/, e.g. /ihte/ 'they appeared', /te/ 'then', /mana/ 'go!', /oca/ 'seek!', /kula/ 'listen!', (= standard language *ihte, de, mana, oza, gula*). These five vowels can be combined into double (long) vowels (written double in this presentation) and diphthongs: /ii ee aa oo uu/, e.g. /tiihten/ 'I knew', /keessen/ 'I pulled', /paahcen/ 'I stayed behind', /poohten/ 'I came', /juuhken/ 'I divided' (= standard *dihten, gessen, báhcen, bohten*, and *juhken*), and /ie ea oa uo/: /tiehko/ 'there', /reahka/ 'sledge', /oassii/ 'part', /tuokko/ '(going) that way' (= standard *diehko, reahka, oassi, duokko*).

The diphthongs and the double vowel /aa/ can be stressed on their first or second component. The vowel combinations with first-member stress are phonetically of greater duration than those with second-member stress. In the phonological transcription, vowel combinations with stress on their second member will be indicated by means of a following ´: /ie' ea' uo' aa' oa' uo'/, e.g. /maa'hte/ '(does not) know how to', /tuo'kko/ '(does not) get tangled', /oa'ste/ 'buy!', /kea'se/ 'pull!', /vie'rro/ 'foreign' (= standard with *e̦, o̦, a̦ máhte, duokko̦, oastte̦, gease̦, vierro̦-*; note such oppositions as /tuokko/ '[going] that way' v. /tuo'kko/ '[does not] get tangled'). The *central* nucleus (normally the first syllable) may contain all of the possibilities mentioned. The *lateral* nucleus (normally the second syllable) can have neither second-member stressed vowel combinations nor diphthongs (i.e., only /i e a o u ii aa uu/ occur). The *marginal* nucleus (normally the third syllable) has no vowel combinations (in fact only /i e a u/ occur).

As a rule, the stressed single vowels go back to vowels which were short in proto-Saami: /pirraa/ 'around' < *pïřă, /kullaah/ 'to hear' < *kulăɒēk, /mon'nii/ 'egg' < *moňē and /nammaa/ 'name' < *nămă (orthographically *birra, gullat, monni, namma*). Before consonant centres of quantity III (see p. 58), the short vowels /i/ /e/ /u/ and /o/ can also derive from proto-Saami diphthongs; in these cases, there is a historically high vowel (*i or *u) in the second syllable: /kir'ten/ 'I endured' < *kieřɒim (infinitive /kier'tah/), /ted'den/ 'I pressed' < *teaňɒim (infinitive /tead'diih/), kus'ken 'I touched' < *kuoškim (infinitive /kuos'kah/), /kor'tnʲon/ 'I climbed' < *koařŋum (infinitive /koar'tnʲuuh/); orthographically *girden, dedden, gusken,* and *gorgŋon.*

The double vowel /aa/ goes back to proto-Saami long *ā: /aaj'pmii/ 'triangular needle' < *ājmē (standard: *áibmi*), and the diphthongs /ie/, /ea/, /uo/ and /oa/ derive from proto-Saami diphthongs *ie, *ea, *uo and *oa: /kiehka/ 'cuckoo' < *kieǩă (standard *giehka*), /keassii/ 'summer' < *keaṡē (standard *geassi*), /kuollii/ 'fish' < *kuolē (standard *guolli*), /toarruu/ 'fight' < *toařō (standard *doarru*).

The vowel combinations with stressed second member derive from cases in which a long vowel in the second syllable has been shortened: /čaa'le/ 'write!' < *čʲālēk (standard *čále*), /kea'se/ 'pull!' < *keasēk (*geasẹ*), poa'ɖan/ 'I come' < *poaɒām (*boaɖán*), /kie'ltte/ 'deny!' < *kielɒēk (*gieldde̦*), /kuo'tte/ 'carry!' < *kuonɒēk (*guotte*). These combinations are phonetically of less duration than the corresponding combinations with stress on their first member, e.g. /čaa'le/ [čʲàle] 'write!' v. /laave/ [làve] 'he used to' (standard *čále* and *láve*). This shortening has affected certain morphological categories, such as the present connegatives and second-person singular imperatives, most modifier components in compound words (/vaarrii/ 'hill' + /čoh'ka/ 'top' combining as /vaa'rre+čoh'ka/ 'hilltop', standard *várrečohkka*), and some textually frequent word forms such as /poa'ɖan/ 'I come' alongside unshortened /poaɖaan/, standard *boaɖán*, oa'ččon/ 'I get' alongside unshortened /oaččuun/, standard *oaččun*. It is also fairly common in unstressed positions. The shortened second-syllable vowels are identical with the original short vowels, resulting in oppositions such as /soaɖan/ 'I fight' v. /poa'ɖan/ 'I come' (standard *soaɖan* and *boaɖán*).

The background of the proto-Saami stressed vowels and their development into the present-day Eastern Enontekiö dialect is shown by the following examples (pFS = proto-Fenno-Saamic, pS = proto-Saami, EE = Eastern Enontekiö. The forms given in brackets under 'standard' are in Konrad Nielsen's orthography [KN = Nielson 1932–62]):

By and large, the pFS old low (*a and *ä) and long mid (*ē and *ō) vowels have developed into long vowels, while pFS high vowels (*ī, *i, *ū, *u, *ü)

Table 2.1 Background and development of the proto-Saami stressed vowels

PFS			> pS		> EE		Standard
*ū	*kūli-	'hears'	> *u	*kulă-	> /u/	/kullaa-/	gulla- (gullâ-)
*u	*puri-	'bites'	> *o	*poř ă-	> /o/	/porraa-/	borra- (borrâ-)
[*o(-i)	*joki	'river'	> *o	*jokă	> /o/	/johkaa/	johka (jokkâ)]
*i	*nimi	'name'	> *ă	*năm̀ă	> /a/	/nammaa/	namma (nâmmâ)
*ü	*süli	'bosom'	> *ă	*sălằ	> /a/	/sallaa/	salla (sâllâ)
*e(-i)	*meni-	'goes'	> *ă	*mănằ	> /a/	/manna-/	manna- (mânnâ-)
*ī	*pīri	'circle'	> *i	*piř ằ	> /i/	/piirraa/	birra (birrâ)
*a	*kala	'fish'	> *uo	*kuol̀ē	> /uo/	/kuollii/	guolli (guolle)
	*kala-na	sEss	>	*kuol̀ēnē	> /uo/	/kuolliin/	guollin (guollen)
	*kala-mi	sl	>	*kuol̀ēmă	> /uo/	/kuollaan/	guollán (guollam)
	*kala-sin	sIll	>	*kuol̀ān	> /uo/	/kuollaaj/	guollái (guollai)
	*kala-j-ta	pP	>	*kuolijᴅē	> /uu/	/kuulijh/	gūliid (gūliid)
*o(-i)	*kosŋi-	'touches'	>	*kuos̀ŋă-	> /uo/	/kuos'ka-/	guoska- (guos'kâ-)
	*kosŋi-j-i-m	past sl	>	*kuos̀ŋim	> /u/	/kus'ken/	gusken (gus'kim)
*ō	*vōli-	'whittles'	>	*vuol̀ă-	> /uo/	/vuolla-/	vuolla- (vuollâ-)
	*vōli-i-i-m	past sl	>	*vuol̀im	> /uu/	/vuullen/	vūllen (vūllim)
*o(-a/o)	*kota	'hut'	> *oa	*koat̀ē	> /oa/	/koahtii/	goahti (goatte)
	*kota-j-ta	pP	>	*koaᴅijᴅē	> /oo/	/koođijh/	gǒđiid (gǒđiid)
*ä(-ä/o)	*äjmä	'needle'	> *ā	*ājmē	> /aa/	/aaj'pmii/	áibmi (ai'bme)
[*a(-a/o)	*akka	'wife'	>	*āh̀kē	> /a/	/ah'kaa/	áhkká (ak'ka)]
*e(-ä/a/o)	*kesä	'summer'	> *ea	*keas̀ē	> /ea/	/keassii/	geassi (gæsse)
	*kesä-j-tä	pP	>	*keasijᴅē	> /ee/	/keesijh/	gēsiid (gēsiid)
	*kejno	'way'	>	*keaj̀nā	> /ea/	/keaj'tnuu/	geaidnu (gæi'dno)
	*kejno-j-ta	pP	>	*keajnōjᴅē	> /ea/	/keajnnuujh/	geainnuid (gæinoid)
	*kejno-ŋsʲi	diminut.	>	*keaj̀nun	> /ee/	/keejnnoš/	gēinnoš (gēinuš)
	*kejno-sin	sIll	>	*keajnunž̀ʲă	> /e/	/kej'tnuj/	geidnui (gei'dnui)
*ä(-i)	*käti	'hand'	> *ie	*kiet̀ă	> /ie/	/kiehta/	giehta (giettâ)
	*käti-sin	sIll	>	*kiet̀in	> /ii/	/kiihtij/	gīhtii (gīttii)
*ē	*kēli	'language'	>	*kiel̀ă	> /ie/	/kiella/	giella (giellâ)
	*keeli-sin	sIll	>	*kiel̀in	> /ie/	/kiella/	gīllii (gīllii)
[*e(-i)	*sʲelki-	'clear'	>	*čʲielɢă-	> /ie/	/čielkkas/	čielggas (čielgâs)

have developed into short vowels. The pFS short mid vowels (*e and *o) have developed into long vowels before second-syllable low vowels. There is an asymmetry in the development of pFS *e and *o before second-syllable short vowels (pFS *o-i > proto-Saami *uo-ă, but pFS *e-i > proto-Saami *ă-ă), the reason for which is not clear; there are also some exceptions (enclosed in square brackets in Table 2.1) which tend towards symmetrical development. The development of the proto-Saami vowels in the other Saami languages is complex and cannot be gone into here; some of the changes leading to the present-day languages and dialects have already been referred to in the introductory section.

The main course of development of the vowels of the second syllable may be inferred from Table 2.1. Complications arise, however, from the fact that vowels of the third syllable influenced the development of vowels in the second syllable. Third-syllable mid proto-Saami *ë (which became proto-Saami *ă) caused the descendents of pFS *a and *ä to remain low (> proto-Saami *ā), preventing them from fronting (proto-Saami *ē), but causing pFS *o to develop into proto-Saami *u instead of regular proto-Saami *ā. These second-syllable vowels, in turn, influenced the vowels of the first syllable: proto-Saami diphthongs went to monophthongs before second-syllable *i and *u. Vowel contractions are complex processes with ample morphological conditioning; only some cases (in which intervocalic *s and *j go to zero) have been included in the table. In the West Finnmark dialect group to which EE belongs, there is a lengthening of second-syllable *ă to /aa/ after a relatively short first syllable, thus coinciding with the regular reflex of proto-Saami *ā: proto-Saami *tolă 'fire' > /tollaa/, proto-Saami *jokă 'river' > /johkaa/, proto-Saami *kulăm 'I hear' > /kulaan/, proto-Saami *năṁă 'name' > /nammaa/ (standard *dolla, johka, gulan, namma*).

Consonants

The system of consonant phonemes of EE is characterized by the extensive use of the opposition of voice.

Extensive use of the voice opposition is typical of all Saami idioms, but North Saami has some pairs which are not normally found in others, e.g. M:m, N:n, L:l, R:r, J:j, t:đ. The West Finnmark dialects, Eastern Enontekiö among them, lack /ŋ/, because prevocalic /ŋ/ > /nʲ/. The standard language has ŋ: *maŋŋil* 'afterwards', EE /maanʲnʲiil/. Preconsonantal ŋ in forms such as *máŋga* 'many' is a variant of /n/: /maanˈka/. The consonants /tʲ dʲ g z ž lʲ/ occur only as geminates of the consonant centre, e.g. /aadʲˈdʲaa/ 'grandpa', /pealʲˈlʲii/ 'ear'.

The distribution of the consonants is highly skewed; there are severe restrictions on their occurrence everywhere except in the consonant centre, i.e. in initial, final, marginal and liminal positions. In these positions the voice opposition is generally neutralized (only the unmarked members occur), palatalization is restricted, and, in initial and final position, the dental

Table 2.2   Consonant phonemes of Eastern Enontekiö

	Bilabial	Labiodental	Interdental	Post-dental	Alveolar	Palatalized	Pre-palatal	Velar	Laryngeal
Nasals									
Voiced	m			n		nʲ			
Unvoiced	M			N					
Stops									
Voiced	b			d		dʲ		g	
Unvoiced	p			t		tʲ		k	
Affricates									
Voiced				z		ž			
Unvoiced				c		č			
Fricatives									
Voiced		v	đ				j		
Unvoiced		f	ŧ	s		š	J		h
Liquids									
Voiced				l	r	lʲ			
Unvoiced				L	R				

fricatives are lacking (/đ/ is found intervocalically). The consonants /m n nʲ p t k c č v f s š j h l r/ can occur in initial position, plus the clusters /sp st sk sm sn snʲ sl sr šnʲ šl/. In marginal position only /p k c č m n v s š đ j h l/ occur, plus the clusters /st sk št rt rs lt lk lm jk jm jn jđ jst/. In final position, labials, palatalized consonants, and velars are lacking; the only consonants occurring here are /t n s š l j h/, plus the clusters /rs rh lh jn js jh/.

The Consonant Centre
The consonant centre is rich in oppositions and morphophonemic alterna-tions. Grade alternation and shortening have already been mentioned. Other alternations affecting the phonology of the consonant centre are strengthen-ing, lengthening, and secondary shortening. Grade alternation has doubled original single consonants before originally open syllables, e.g. pFS *kala 'fish' : *kalan 'sG' : *kalana 'sEss' : *kalasin 'sIll' > EE /kuollii/ : /kuolii/ : /kuolliin/ : /kuollaaj/ (standard *guolli* : *guoli* : *guollin* : *guollái*), pFS *men(i)täk 'to go' : *menim 'I go' : *menijim 'I went' > EE /mannaah/ : /manaan/ : /mannen/ (standard *mannat* : *manan* : *mannen*). In certain cases, these geminates have developed into secondary clusters: pFS *kota 'hut' >> EE /koahtii/, pFS *sōni 'sinew' >> EE /suotna/. Historically, the strong grade originates in an extra subglottal pulse in the consonant centre; with time, the strong grade of the single consonants became phonetically identical with the weak grade of the geminate consonants by way of *-V$_(\cdot)$C$_(\cdot)$CV- > *-VC$_(\cdot)$CV-, where '$_(\cdot)$' denotes a pulse boundary (there are dialects in which this merger has not occurred). In original geminates and clusters, the strong grade is manifested as an extra subglottal pulse within the consonant centre before

originally open syllables, making the strong grade longer than the corresponding weak grade: /pas'te/ 'spoon' : /paste/ 'sG', k̇ol'lii/ 'gold' : /kollii/ 'sGA',
in broad phonetic transcription with pulses marked: [pas₍s₍te] v. [pas₍te] and
[kol₍l₍lì] v. [kol₍lì] (more commonly, notations such as [paš̌te] v. [paste] have
been used). In consonant clusters beginning with a voiced consonant, the final
component of a weak grade cluster has been geminated: /vaal'taan/ 'takes
perf.part' v. /vaalttaaan/ 'I take'; contrast /kuos'kah/ 'to touch' : /kuoskan/ 'I
touch' (standard *váldit, válddán, guoskat, guoskkan*).

There are three contrasting quantities in qualitatively identical EE consonant
centres: /kol'liis/ 'gold s3 sN' : /kolliis/ 'gold s3GA' : /oliis/ 'at, near' (standard
gol'lis : *gollis* : *olis*, KN *gol'les* : *golles* : *olest*), /čaal'liih/ 'writer pN' : /čaalliih/
'to write (inf)' : /čaaliih/ 'to make X write (s2pres/imp)' (standard *čál'lit* : *čállit*
: *čálit*, KN *čal'lek* : *čallet* : *čalet*). The longest possible quantity, which
historically is in most cases the strong grade of original geminates and clusters
and is written with ' in phonological transcription (and in the somewhat
modified standard orthography of this chapter) is called grade III: /čuol'pma/
'knot', /ah'kuu/ 'grandmother', /kuos'sii/ 'guest', /seal'kii/ 'back', /vis'tii/ 'flat
(standard *čuolbma, áhkku, guos'si, sealgi, visti*). Quantity II normally represents (1) the *weak* grade of geminates and clusters and (2) the *strong* grade of
original single consonants. Examples of (1): /čuolmma/ 'knot sGA', /aahkuu/
'grandmother sGA', /kuossii/ 'guest sGA', /sealkkii/ 'back sGA', /vistii/ 'flat
sGA'; examples of (2): /koahtii/ 'hut', /oassii/ 'part', /kiella/ 'language',
/suotna/ 'sinew' (standard *čuolmma, áhku, guossi, sealggi, vistti, goahti, oassi,
giella, suotna*). Quantity I is the weak grade of original single consonants: /koađ
ii/ 'hut sGA', /oasii/ 'part sGA', /kiela/ 'language sGA', /suona/ 'sinew sGA'
(standard *goađi, oasi, giela, suona*).

Strengthening is a process whereby the reflexes of originally single
consonants equal quantitatively the strong grade of original geminates, i.e.
where original simplex consonants go not to grade II, but to grade III. In North
Saami, strengthening occurs when a consonant belonging to the stem or
derivational suffix is lost, e.g. /sul'loh/ (standard *sul'lot*) 'islands' < proto-
Saami *suol̇luk < mid proto-Saami *sōl̇uj-ëk < pFS *saloj-i-t, /juoh'kii/
(*juohkki*) 'one who deals' < proto-Saami *juok̇kē < pFS *jaka=ja. If the lost
consonant was part of an inflectional suffix strengthening did not occur, e.g.
/juuhken/ (*juuhken*) 'I dealt' < proto-Saami *juok̇im < < pFS *jaka-j-i-m
(infinitive *juohkit*).

Lengthening from quantity II to quantity III occurs before second-syllable
long vowels (/ii aa uu/) when the first syllable contains a short vowel (/i a o
u/) and also, if the resulting lengthened consonant centre does not equal the
strong grade of an original geminate or cluster, a high diphthong (/ie uo/).
Where the strong grade of a single consonant is a cluster beginning with /h/
or a geminate other than /pp tt tʲtʲ kk cc čč/, lengthening results in a consonant
centre equal to the strong grade of original clusters or geminates: /jah'kii/
'year' : /jakii/ 'year sGA' (standard *jahki* : *jagi*), /pal'luu/ 'fear' : /paluu/ 'fear

sGA' (standard *ballu : balu*), /joh'taa/ '(s)he travels' : /jođaan/ 'I travel' (standard *johtá : jođán*; cf. cases with strengthening such as /joh'taa/ '(s)he starts to travel' : /joh'taan/ 'I start to travel', standard *johttá : johttán*). In the remaining cases, the lengthened consonant centre shows quantity III but does not equal the strong grade of original geminates and clusters. The phonological opposition between lengthened and unlengthened sequences rests on secondary lengthening of second-syllable *ă to /aa/ in EE (the normal reflex being /a/): /loniis/ 'ransom' : /lot'naasah/ 'pN' as opposed to /sonaas/ 'shrunken' : /sotnaasah/ 'pN' (standard *lonis : lotnásat* v. *sonas : sotnasat*). Similarly, from /lod'dii/ 'bird' is formed a diminutive /lot'taaš/ but from /pod'da/ 'short time' we have /pottaaš/ (standard *loddi, lottáš, bodda, bottaš*); from /čal'pmii/ 'eye' we have diminutive /čalm'maaš/, contrast /čalmmaas/ 'reticulum' (standard *čalbmi, čalmmáš* v. *čalmmas*).

A *secondary shortening* in the consonant centre from quantity III to quantity II may occur if the second-syllable long vowel undergoes secondary shortening. Normally there is an accompanying overall shortening of the long elements (of vowel combinations and of the consonant centre in quantity III) in the stress group: /vuol'kaa/ > /vuo'lka/ '(s)he goes' (standard *vuolgá*), /aal'kaa/ > /aa'lka/ '(s)he begins' (standard *álgá*), /saah'taa/ > /saa'hta/ '(s)he might' (standard *sáhttá*), /peas'taa/ > /pea'sta/ '(s)he lets', /šad'daa/ > /šadda/ '(s)he grows' (standard *šaddá*), /jah'kii/ 'year' > /jahke+peallii/ 'half-year' (standard *jahki, jahkebealli*), /čat'naa/ > /čatna/ '(s)he ties' (standard *čatná*). Quantities II and I are not affected by shortening: /kuollii/ 'fish' > /kuo'lle+piv'tuu/ 'fishing' (standard *guolli, guollebivdu*). Vowel combinations with stressed second member which occur in these cases are shorter than those with stressed first member, e.g. /raahta/ 'rattle' v. /saa'hta/ '(s)he might' (standard *ráhta, sáhttá*).

As a result of the various processes affecting consonant centre quantity, the following phonological quantitities may be posited for EE clusters beginning with a voiced consonant:

Cluster	EE example	Gloss	Standard
/l'k/	/vuol'kaan/	'having left'	*vuolgán*
/lk/	/vuo'lka/ (~ /vuol'kaa/)	'(s)he leaves'	*vuolgá*
/lkk/	/vuolkka/	'departure'	*vuolgga*
/lk'k/	/vuolk'kaan/	'I leave'	*vuolggán*

This four-way set of quantitative oppositions is possible for the following clusters (cited in unshortened strong grade): /m'p n't n'č n'k đ'k đ'p v't v'č v'k v'l v'L v'r j'l j'r j'k j'p j't j's j'v j'L j'M j'N l'j l'k l'p l't l's l'f l'v l'j l'š l'č/.

EE grade alternation also affects *consonant quality*. A weak-grade single consonant alternates with a strong-grade cluster (standard-language forms given in brackets)

- if the consonant goes back to a proto-Saami stop or affricate, e.g. /koahtii/ 'hut' : /koađi/ 'sG' (*goahti : goađi*), /kiehpa/ 'soot' : /kiepa/ 'sG' (*giehpa : gieba*), /čiehka/ 'corner' : /čieka/ 'sG' (*čiehka : čiega*), /paahciih/ 'to stay' : /paacaan/ 'I stay' (*báhcit : bázán*), /paahčiih/ 'to shoot' : /paačaan/ 'I shoot' (*báhčit : bážán*).
- if the consonant goes back to a proto-Saami nasal, and the initium does *not* contain a nasal consonant: /liepma / 'broth' : /liema/ 'sG' (*liepma : liema*), /suotna/ 'sinew' : /suona/ 'sG' (*suotna : suona*), /potnʲaah/ 'to wind' : /ponʲaan/ 'I wind' (*botnjat : bonjan*), /jietnʲa/ 'ice' : /jienʲa/ 'sG' (*jiekŋa : jieŋa*), and (proto-Saami *-j- >) -j- alternates with -tʲtʲ-, e.g. /vuotʲtʲa/ 'butter' : /vuoja/ 'sG' (*vuodja : vuoja*).

Voiceless weak-grade double stops and affricates alternate with voiced strong-grade geminates : /nub'bii/ 'second' : /nup'pii/ 'sG' (*nubbi : nuppi*, KN *nub'be : nubbe*), /lod'dii/ 'bird' : /lot'tii/ 'sG', /cag'gii/ 'support' : /cak'kii/ 'sG', /vaaz'ziih/ 'to walk' : /vaaccaan/ 'I walk' (*vázzit : váccán*), /oaž'žuuh/ 'to acquire' : /oaččuun/ 'I acquire' (*oažžut : oaččun*), /aadʲ'dʲaa/ 'grandfather' : /aatʲtʲaa/ 'sG' (*áddjá : ádjá*).

Clusters consisting of a nasal preceded by a voiced stop in the strong grade have a voiceless stop in the weak grade: /caab'miih/ 'to beat' : /caapmaan/ 'I beat' (*cábmit : cápmán*), /ead'nii/ 'mother' : /eatnii/ 'sG' (*eadni : eatni*), /poad'nʲii/ 'husband' : /poatnʲii/ 'G' (*boadnji : boatnji*), /tuod'nʲah/ 'to patch' : /tuotnʲan/ 'I patch' (*duogŋat : duokŋan*).

Strong-grade clusters with initial /k/ alternate with weak-grade clusters with initial /vh/ before a stop or affricate, but with /v/ before sibilants which are doubled, e.g. /cik'cuuh/ 'to pinch' : /civh'cuun/ 'I pinch' (*cikcut : civccun*), /kok'čah/ 'to cover' : /kovhčan/ 'I cover' (*gokčat : govččan*), /ruok'tuu/ 'home' : /ruovh'tuu/ 'sG' (*ruoktu: ruovttu*), /suok'sa/ 'maggot' : /suovssa/ 'sG' (*suoksa : suovssa*), /tik'šuuh/ 'to tend' : /tivš'šuun/ 'I tend' (*dikšut : divššun*).

Weak-grade clusters with a final nasal geminate alternate with strong-grade clusters with a stop-plus-nasal combination. The initial component may be /j/, /l/, or /v/: /čal'pmii/ 'eye' : /čalm'mii/ 'sG' (*čalbmi : čalmmi*), /oaj'tniih/ 'to see' : /oajnnaan/ 'I see' (*oaidnit : oainnán*), etc.

In some clusters, the difference between strong and weak grades lies mainly in the *location of the syllable boundary*. Some of these clusters begin with /r/ and end in a nasal: /paar'tnii/ 'son' : /paartnii/ 'sG', phonetically [pàrɟᵉₜnì] : [pārₜnì] (standard *bárdni : bártni*), /čor'pma/ 'fist' : /čorpmaa/ 'sG' (*čorbma : čorpma*), /koar'tnʲuuh/ 'to climb' : /koartnʲuun/ 'I climb' (*goargŋut : goarkŋun*). Others have /h/ as an internal segment, begin with /j/, /l/, /m/, /n/, /r/, or /v/, and end in a stop or affricate: /paaj'hkii/ 'place' : /paajhkii/ 'sG', phonetically [pàjɟᶜʰkì] : [pāʲɟₖì] (*báiki : báikki*), /aaj'hcah/ 'to notice' : /aajhcan/ 'I notice' (*áicat : áiccan*), /peal'hkiih/ 'to scold' : /pealhkaan/ 'I scold' (*bealkit : bealkkán*), /pol'htuuh / 'to root up' :

/polh'tuun/ 'I root up' (*boltut : bolttun*), /paar'htii/ 'mishap' : /paarhtii/ 'sG' (*bárti : bártti*), /kum'hpe/ 'wolf' : /kumhpe/ 'sG' (*gumpe : gumppe*). The latter group contains the following clusters (given in strong grade): /m'hp n'hk n'hc n'hč j'hp j'hk j'ht j'hc v'hp v'hk [v'ht] l'hk l'hp l'ht l'hc l'hč r'hp r'hk r'ht r'hc rh'č/.

The Relationship Between Marginal and Final Consonants
Morphonological alternations cause *marginal consonants* to become *final consonants*; this in turn causes numerous neutralizations. When they become word final, marginal stops and /đ/ are all replaced by /h/ (before absolute pause phonetically [ht]), e.g. /paavhčakih/ 'to hurt' : /ij paavhčah/ 'does not hurt' (*bávččagit : ii bávččat*, i.e. in this pair /k/~/h/ is orthographically <g> ~ <t>), /nuorapuh/ 'younger pN' : /nuorah/ 'sN' (*nuorabut : nuorat*), /viel'kađah/ 'white pN' : /viel'kah/ 'sN' (*vielgadat : vielgat*). Marginal /m/ is replaced by /n/ when final: /ealliimis/ 'sLoc' : /ealliin/ 'sN' (*eallimis : eallin*). Marginal affricates are replaced by corresponding sibilants when final: /lot'taačah/ 'little bird pN' : /lot'taaš/ 'sN' (*lottážat : lottáš*), /smiirecih/ 'to chew the cud' : /ij smiires/ 'does not chew the cud' (*smirezit : ii smires*). Marginal clusters beginning with a voiceless consonant are replaced by a single consonant when in final position; marginal clusters consisting of a voiced consonant plus a stop replace the stop with /h/ when final, examples: /vuo'jestih/ 'to drive a little' : /vuo'jes/ 'drive a little! (s2 imp)' (*vuojestit : vuojes*), /peeroštih/ 'to care' : /ij peeroš/ 'does not care' (*beroštit : ii beroš*), /jaamaalkih/ 'to faint' : /ij jaamaalh/ 'does not faint' (*jámálgit : ii jámál*), etc.

Notes on the Historical Background
A few additional remarks will supplement the consonant development implicit in the previous sections.

From a qualitative point of view, the Saami consonant stock is fairly conservative. Proto-Fennic-Saamic palatalization has been preserved, e.g. pFS *nʲōli 'arrow' > EE /nʲuolla/ (standard *njuolla*), pFS *minʲä 'daughter-in-law' > EE /manʲ'nʲii/ (*mannji*), pFS *punʲi- 'twists' > EE /potnʲaa-/ (*botnja-*), pFS *sʲilmä 'eye' > EE /čalp'mii/ (*čalbmi*), pFS *küsʲi- 'asks' > EE /kahčaa-/ (*gahča-*), pFS kunsʲi 'urine'> EE /kož'ža/ (*gožža*), pFS *kosʲki 'river rapids' > proto-Saami *kuošʲšʲkǎ > EE /kuoj'hka/ (*guoika*). So has pFS *ŋ, as a rule (but in EE and other West Finnmark dialects it has gone to /nʲ/ prevocalically), e.g. pFS *jäŋi 'ice' > North Saami *jiekŋa*, EE /jietnʲa/, pFS *jäŋkä 'bog' > proto-Saami *jeaŋɢē > EE /jeag'gii/ (standard *jeaggi*), but cf. pFS *joŋsi 'bow' > proto-Saami *juoksǎ > EE /juok'sa/, standard *juoksa*.

Some shifts have occurred, however. The post-alveolars (the probably somewhat retroflex sibilant *š and affricate *č) have changed into dentals (and pFS *š thus fell together with pFS *s), e.g. pFS *viči 'new snow' > proto-Saami *vǎčǎ > EE /vahcaa/ (*vahca*), pFS *künči 'nail' > proto-Saami *kǎnnɢǎ > EE /kaz'za/ (*gazza*), pFS *nʲočka 'depression' > proto-Saami *nʲoacckē > EE /nʲoas'kii/ (*njoaski*). In consonant clusters, the following major changes occurred after the split of proto-Fennic-Saamic:

pFS		proto-Saami	EE example (standard in brackets)
*ns	>	*ss	*kansa 'folk' > /kuos'sii/ *(guos'si)*
*sj, *šj	>	*šš	*pošjo 'bottom' > /poaš'šuu/ 'innermost part of hut' *(boaš'šu)*
			*osja 'horsetail (plant)' > proto-Saami *oašʲšʲē >> EE hoaš'ša *(hoaš'ša)*

Also, pFS *k > proto-Saami *v before *j, *l, and *nʲ, e.g. pFS *saknʲa 'hole (in ground)' > EE /suov'tnʲii / 'grazing-hole' *(suovdnji)*, pFS *vakja 'wedge' > Lule Saami *vuovjje*.

Morphology

General Features

The morphological mechanisms in Saami are phonological alternation, suffixation, compounding, and encliticization. Suppletion and reduplication are rare. Some oppositions rest on suffixes: North Saami *boahtá* '(s)he comes' v. *boahtán* '(having) come'. Others rest on stem phonology: North Saami *boaðán* 'I come' v. *boahtán* '(having) come'. Still others rest on both: North Saami *goahti* 'tent' v. *gōðiin* 'in tents'.

In general, distinctions tend to be made towards the centre of the word (the vowel and consonant centre), with corresponding reductions in other positions. Proto-Fennic-Saamic can be reconstructed as a purely agglutinative language with no or very little morpheme interaction. Already in proto-Saami, grade alternation, contractions, and, to some extent, metaphony, had brought about a shift towards fusional instead of agglutinative morphology. After the proto-Saamic stage, metaphony of stressed-syllable vowels and reduction of unstressed positions have made the original morphemes and the boundaries between them less and less transparent.

Saami suffixes may be divided according to their positional privileges into three types: *markers* (for mood, tense, and number), *inflectional suffixes* (for case, possessor, and person), and *derivational suffixes* (for modification of meanings and recategorization, i.e. shifts in part of speech). Derivational suffixes are attached directly to stems to form new stems, markers come after derivational suffixes, and inflectional suffixes come after markers (*clitics* come after inflectional suffixes). In compounds, the last constituent is the head, and those preceding it are modifiers.

Saami is the only Finno-Permic language to have a distinct dual number. The Saami dual is restricted to morphology with personal reference, viz. the personal pronouns (North Saami *mun* 'I', *moai* 'the two of us, we two', *mii* 'we (more than two); the personal suffixes of verbs (North Saami *bōhten* 'I came', *bōđiime* 'we (dual) came', *bōđiimet* 'we (plur) came'), and the possessive suffixes (North Saami *goahtán* 'my tent', *goahtáme* 'the tent belonging to the two of us', *goahtámet* 'the tent belonging to us (plur)'.

Inflection

Inflection is of two basic types: declension (for nouns, adjectives, numerals, and pronouns) and conjugation (for verbs). Most adjectives have a special attributive form (e.g. *duojár lea čeahppi* 'the craftsman is skilful' v. *čeahpes duojár* 'skilful craftsman'), the categorization of which is not clear. The morphology of attributive forms is irregular and thus typical more of derivation than inflection; it is not a clear-cut derivational category, on the other hand, for there are a substantial number of adjectives which lack a special attributive form yet which function as attributives in the same way as attributive forms, e.g. *nieida lea nuorra* 'the girl is young', *nuorra nieida* 'young girl'.

Declension

Nouns, adjectives, numerals, and pronouns are inflected for number, case, and possession. It is customary to distinguish between absolute declension (possession not indicated) and possessive declension. There are two numbers, singular and plural. The cases in standard North Saami and most dialects are seven: N[ominative], G[enitive], A[ccusative], Ill[ative], Loc[ative], Com[itative], and Ess[ive]. For nouns and most pronouns, genitive and accusative singular are identical in form, and hence the term genitive/accusative is used. In numerals higher than *okta* 'one', the accusative singular is identical with the nominative singular, while the genitive singular matches the genitive/accusative singular forms of nouns as far as morphonology is concerned (e.g. *guokte* 'two', sA *guokte*, sG *guovtti*; cf. *luokta* 'bay', sGA *luovtta*).

Genitive and accusative plural are identical in the standard language and in most dialects. The essive has the same form in the singular and the plural. Some North Saami dialects add the abessive to the list of cases, but in most dialects this case has been replaced with a postpositional construction (genitive + the postposition *haga*).

The demonstrative pronouns have historical singular and plural prolative case forms (*duokko* 'that way over there', *duoigo* 'about that way over there') but synchronically these are adverbs, together with other local expressions based on the stems of demonstrative pronouns (*duohko* '[going] over there', *duoppe* 'over there').

The possessive suffixes refer to first, second, and third person in singular, dual, and plural. Possessive forms for the nominative plural (first persons only) occur, rarely, in a vocative-like function. Possessive suffixes normally come after case endings, except in the comitative plural where they precede the case ending *-guin*.

Stems may be classified into the following groups: parisyllabic, imparisyllabic, and contracted. Examples of inflection are given below (for

Table 2.3 Absolute declension

	Singular	Plural	Singular	Plural	Singular	Plural
Parisyllabic						
N	guolli	guolit	giehta	gieđat	beaivváđat	beaivváđagat
GA	guoli	gūliid	gieđa	gieđaid	beaivváđaga ~ beaivváđat	beaivváđagaid
Ill	guollái	gūliide	gīhtii	gieđaide	beaivváđahkii	beaivváđagaide
Loc	guolis	gūliin	gieđas	gieđain	beaivváđagas	beaivváđagain
Com	gūliin	gūliiguin	gieđain	gieđaiguin	beaivváđagain	beaivváđagaiguin
Ess	guollin		giehtan		beaivváđahkan	
Imparisyllabic						
N	beana	beatnagat	oalis	oallásat	cielus	cīllosat
GA	beatnaga ~ beatnat	beatnagiid	oallása ~ oallás	oallásiid	cīllosa ~ cīllos	cīllosiid
Ill	beatnagii	beatnagiidda	oallásii	oallásiidda	cīllosii	cīllosiidda
Loc	beatnagis	beatnagiin	oallásis	oallásiin	cīllosis	cīllosiin
Com	beatnagiin	beatnagiiguin	oallásiin	oallásiiguin	cīllosiin	cīllosiiguin
Ess	beanan		oalisin		cielusin	
Contracted stems						
N	jalŋŋis	jalgŋát	boazu	bohccot		
GA	jalgŋá	jalgŋáid	bohcco	bohccuid		
Ill	jalgŋái	jalgŋáide	bohccui	bohccuide		
Loc	jalgŋás	jalgŋáin	bohccos	bohccuin		
Com	jalgŋáin	jalgŋáiguin	bohccuin	bohccuiguin		
Ess	jalŋŋisin		boazun			

Table 2.4   Possessive declension: *guos'si* **'guest'**

		Singular	Dual	Plural
sN	1	guos'sán	guos'sáme	guos'sámet
	2	guos'sát	guos'sáde	guos'sádet
	3	guos'sis	guos'siska	guos'siset
sGA	1	= sN	= sN	= sN
	2	goussát	goussáde	goussádet
	3	guossis	guossiska	guossiset
pIll	1	gūssiidasan	gūssiidasame	gūssiidasamet
	2	gūssiidasat	gūssiidasade	gūssiidasadet
	3	gūssiidasas	gūssiidasaske	gūssiidasaset
pCom	1	gūssiidanguin	gūssiideameguin	gūssiideametguin
	2	gūssiidatguin	gūssiideatteguin	gūssiideattetguin
	3	gūssiidisguin	gūssiideaskkaguin	gūssiideasetguin

parisyllabic: *guolli* 'fish', *giehta* 'hand, arm', *buođđu* 'dam', *beaivvádat* 'sunshine'; for imparisyllabic: *beana* 'dog', *oalis* 'groove in bottom of ski', *cielus* 'abuse'; for contracted stems: *jalŋŋis* 'tree stump', *boazu* 'reindeer'. When not evident from the standard orthography, double vowels are indicated with a macron, e.g. ū; quantity III in the consonant centre is indicated with ', e.g. s's.

The sLoc, sIll, sCom, Ess, pGA, and pLoc possessive forms are built by combining the stems:

sLoc	guossist-
sIll	guos'sás-
sCom	gūssiin-
Ess	guos'sin-
pGA	gūssiid-
pLoc	gūssiin-

with the suffixes (standard orthography ẹ, ọ, ạ written here as E, O, A):

	Singular	Dual	Plural
1	-an	-eame	-eamet
2	-at	-eatte	-eattet
3	-is	-easkka	-easet

Note the following morphophonological alternations of vowels in lateral position (second syllable): *i ~ á* (with pFS *i in the next syllable: *guos'si ~ guos'sán* < *kansa ~ *kansami) and *u ~ o* (with pFS *i in the next syllable:

cielus ~ cīllosat, buoḍḍu 'dam' ~ *būḍḍon* 'my dam' < pFS *paδo ~ *paδomi). Before marginal preconsonantal /j/ (orthographic *i*) pFS *a/ä has gone to proto-Saami short *i, which monophthongizes the first-syllable diphthong, e.g. pFS *kala-j-ta > proto-Saami *kuolijᴅē > North Saami *gūliid*). The second-syllable *i*, *u*, and *á* of the illative singular forms *gīhtii*, *būḍḍui* and *guollái* are the results of contraction (of pFS *-isi-, *-osi-, and *-asi-), as are the short *o* (and *u* before *i* = /j/) in the declension of *boazu* (from pFS *-oji-); before a lateral short *i*, *e*, *o*, and *u*, first-syllable diphthongs are monophthongized (uo > ū/u, oa > ō/o, ie > ī/i, ea > ē/e; the short variants occur before consonant centre quantity III).

Case endings: Historically, the genitive and accusative singular have syncretized after the loss of the final nasals (pU *-n for the genitive and pU *-m for the accusative). The illative singular has acquired the secondary case ending -*i*, originally the marginal stem consonant in *j*-stems (e.g. *boazu*, proto-Saami sN *poazōj, sIne *poaccustē < pFS *počoj-i-sta, sIll *poaccujin < pFS *počoj-i-sin); the original illative suffix has merged with the stem by contraction (e.g. pFS *käti-sin > proto-Saami *kietin > North Saami *gīhtii*; illative singular forms without the secondary ending -*i* have also been attested).

The locative singular (in older orthographies with the ending -*st* as in the possessive declension) continues the former inessive and elative, which are preserved as separate cases in the idioms southwest of North Saami (pFS inessive *-sna/*-snä and elative *-sta/*-stä, in which *-s- was originally a lative element attested also in Mordva and Mari, and *-na/*-nä as well as *-ta/*-tä continue original general local cases. The suffix *-na/*-nä and probably also *-ta/*-tä are of pU origin, from a pU locative *-na/*-nä and an ablative *-ti.) The syncretism in the locative of North Saami and the Eastern Saami languages is due to loss of the final vowel followed by denasalization of the final *n* in the inessive ending (proto-Saami *-snē > *sn > -*st*), after which the merger spread from this central case to more peripheral parts of the grammar and vocabulary where the phonetic conditions did not obtain. The merger therefore also occurred in the plural, in the possessive declension, and in adverbs, where there were no phonetic grounds for the change (e.g. *olgun* '[being] outside; [coming] from outside', contrast Lule *ålggon* 'outside' v. *ålggot* 'from outside'. At least in part, an analogical explanation is valid for the merger of the genitive and accusative, too.

The comitative singular goes back to pFS *-jna/*-jnä, which is originally the essive case of a possessive *j*-adjective (the *j* is ultimately the same as the pU plural oblique case marker *-j-). Inari Saami, Lule Saami and most of Fennic presuppose a pFS form *-jni yielding proto-Saami *-jnă; *-ni may be an old variant of *-na/*-nä.

The essive ending -*n* goes back to the pU locative *-na/*-nä.

In trisyllabic stems with grade alternation (cf. *oalis* in the paradigms above) and in contracted stems, the consonant centre is in the weak grade in the essive (as in *oalisin, jal ŋŋisin, boazun*). In these cases, the vocalic stem is secondary; it is based on the analogy of the trisyllabic stems without grade alternation, i.e. old vocalic stems, and the second syllable was originally closed, causing the weak grade. Consonantal stems have been attested in (now extinct) Sodankylä Saami, and in Lule Saami essives such as *bálgen* (from *bálges* 'path'), stem-final *-s* has been assimilated into the essive ending *-n* (*-s-n > *-n*), just as the inessive ending *-n* goes back to earlier *-sn (< pFS *-sna/*snä).

The plural marker *-t*, used in the nominative (*-k* in the old orthographies, < proto-Saami *-k < pFS *-t, cf. the *-t* s2 ending in the verb which similarly < proto-Saami *-k < pFS *-t) goes back to pU *-t, as does the plural marker *-i- (phonologically /j/ < *-j-) in the oblique cases. The genitive plural of *guolli* 'fish' was written *gūlii* in Konrad Nielsen's orthography; its merger with the accusative plural (written *gūliid* in KN; cf. present-day pGA *gūliid*, proto-Saami pG *kuolij and pA *kuolijᴅē) in North Saami is at least partly based on analogy with the singular, where the merger is due to phonetic development, both proto-Saami sG *kuolēn and sA *kuolēm giving North Saami *guoli*. Ultimately, the accusative plural ending goes back to the Uralic partitive/ablative ending *-ti; Saami, Fennic, and Mordva presuppose at least pFV *-ta/*-tä: *gūliid* < proto-Saami *kuolijᴅē < pFS *kalajta).

The illative plural endings *-de* (as in *guliide, gieđaide, bohccuide*) and *-dda* (as in *beatnagiidda, oallásiidda*) are obscure. In North Saami, they seem to be based on the accusative plural ending (pFS partitive *-ta/*-tä) to which the pFS illative ending *-sin was attached. Intervocalic *s went to zero, as in other illatives, and contraction produced (1) the vowel *i in marginal position, yielding *e* in the present-day language: pFS *-j-ta-sin > proto-Saami *-j-ᴅin > *-de*; some dialects have added the same *-i* that appears in the illative singular, yielding *guliidii* instead of standard *guliide*; and (2) the vowel *ā in lateral position (secondarily shortened to present-day A: pFS (-j-ta-sin > proto-Saami *-j-ᴅān > -ddA.) South Saami, however, points back to pFS *-ta/*-tä without any additions, e.g. *gieriehtsidie* 'into the sledges'), but here we probably have a secondary syncretism of the illative plural with the accusative plural due to the narrow phonological difference between the two. The comitative singular, the essive, and the inessive plural have coincided in South Saami in the same way. Inari Saami points back to proto-Saami *-j-ᴅăn: pIll *kieđááid* v. pA *kieđâid* of *kietâ* 'hand', as well as some relict forms in Lule Saami (e.g. *ejduda* 'away' instead of *ädojda). There seems to be no clear way to reconcile these conflicting reconstructions. The morphology suggests that the illative plural might have developed relatively late in proto-Saami.

The locative plural now covers the functions of the former elative and inessive, but the loss of the morphological opposition in the plural is not due to phonological development but to analogy with the singular. The functions of the elative were transferred to the inessive (in Finnmark Saami, Sea Saami, and the Finnish Wedge and Karesuando dialects, and in all Eastern Saami idioms) or to the elative (the Kaitum and Jukkasjärvi dialects of Torne Saami). The locative plural ending in the standard language goes back to the pU locative *-na/*-nä, preceded by the plural marker. In Kaitum and Jukkasjärvi, the case ending is -s (gūliis, gieđais instead of standard gūliin, gieđain), continuing the proto-Saami elative *-stē. The incongruity between the inessives singular and plural, with the singular a reflex of proto-Saami *-snē but the plural continuing *-nē, suggests that they developed during proto-Saami. The elative plural also bears other signs which suggest late development: in pFS, the suffixation of *-sta/*-stä to the plural marker *-j- would have been possible only with an epenthetic vowel, producing **käti-j-i-stä; this, in turn, would have yielded the contracted proto-Saami form **kieťistē, and not the *kieₚäjstē reconstructed on the basis of Lule, Pite, Ume, and South Saami forms. In addition, the South Saami elative shows an unassimilated plural marker -j- whereas in the inessive, the plural marker is assimilated to the illabial stem vowel: pIne gietine v. pEla gietijste from giete 'hand'. On the whole, the interior local cases illative, inessive, and elative plural seem to have developed during proto-Saami. This means that the symmetry between the singular and the plural declension in, say, Fennic and Mordva does not date back to their common protolanguage.

The comitative plural (gūliiguin, gieđaiguin) has developed from a phrase consisting of the genitive plural plus the word guoibmi 'companion'. The genitive plural has similar functions in all Saami languages; it is also used as a comitative plural in Lule Saami.

In the present-day Saami idioms, the partitive is a regular case in Eastern Saami only (e.g. Inari čiččâm alged 'seven sons', with the partitive alged from alge 'son', used with numerals higher than six), but there are relict cases in Western Saami as well, and even examples of the partitive as a regular case in old Ume Saami texts. The partitive goes back to the same pFS *-ta/*-tä as that seen in the accusative plural ending.

As a whole, Saami declension suggests a pFS system with no specific local cases in the plural. The singular had the following pFS cases: the grammatical cases nominative (zero ending: North Saami guolli, giehta), connective (= genitive/instructive) (*-n: North Saami guoli, gieđa), and accusative (*-m: North Saami guoli, gieđa); the general (or abstract) local cases translative (*-ksi, of Finno-Volgaic origin > proto-Saami *-ssä: in North Saami adverbs, e.g. davás 'to the north', dálvvás 'for the winter'), essive (-na/*-nä: North Saami essive guollin, giehtan, and also adverbs like olgun 'outside'), partitive (*-ta/*-tä: in North Saami adverbs, e.g. oapmet 'as of old'), and abessive (*-ptak/*-ptäk, of Uralic origin: in Lule Saami pronouns, e.g. dabdá 'without it', in North Saami adverbs like gahperahttá 'without a cap' and postposition/ adverb haga ~ taga 'without'); the specific local cases illative (*-sin: North Saami guollái, gihtii with a secondary ending -i), inessive (*-sna/*-snä: North Saami locative guolis, gieđas, Lule Saami guolen, giedan), and elative (*-sta/ *-stä: North Saami locative guolis, gieđas, Lule Saami guoles, giedas). The plural had the following cases: grammatical cases nominative (which probably acted as the case of the plural object as well; plural marker *-t: North Saami *guolit, gieđat*) and connective (plural marker *-j: North Saami genitive plural, KN *gūlii, gieđâi*, modern *gūliid, gieđaid*); and general local cases partitive (*-j-ta/ä: North Saami accusative plural *gūliid, gieđaid*) and essive (*-j-na/ä: North Saami locative plural *gūliin, gieđain*).

The possessive suffixes. The possessive suffix system has undergone radical simplification in North Saami. The proto-Saami system is shown below (Table 2.5).

The singular suffixes had no number marker. The dual marker was *-n. The plural marker was *-k, which goes back either to pU *-t or to the *-k attested in Mordva and Hungarian. The pFS system was isomorphic with the proto-Saami one, the differences being due solely to sound changes such as pFS *ns > proto-Saami *ss, pFS *i > proto-Saami *ă, pFS *a/ä > proto-Saami *ē.

In North Saami, the phonological differences between the three series has been lost. The first- and second-person plural suffixes are attached analogically to the same kinds of stems as the singular and dual suffixes: *guollán* 'my fish', *guolláme* 'the fish of us two' (instead of *guollama), and *guollámet* 'our (plur) fish' (instead of expected *guollimat). The suffix vowel *e* in *guolláme(t)* was obtained from lateral positions (e.g. *beatnageamet* 'our dog'), where it is regular in the plural and third-person suffixes. In later positions, the expected suffix vowel would have been *a* in the first and second person dual, not the attested *e* (*beatnagama instead of *beatnageame* 'the dog of us two', and *beatnagatta instead of *beatnageatte* 'the dog of you two'). Here, too, the plural suffixes (*beatnageattet*, etc., with regular *e*) served as the basis for analogy. In central positions, the second-person dual and plural suffixes have irregular geminate -*tt*- in the nominative instead of expected single -*đ*- (e.g. *beatnageattet* 'your (plur) dog', instead of expected *beatnageađet); the geminate -*tt*- is regular, however, in the genitive and other oblique cases (proto-Saami possessive suffixes d2 *-nᴅăn and p2 *nᴅēk), on

Table 2.5   Proto-Saami possessive suffix system

		Singular	Dual	Plural
sN	1	*-mă	*-mă-n	*-mē-k
	2	*-ᴅă	*-ᴅă-ɴ	*-ᴅē-k
	3	*-sē	*-sē-n	*-sē-k
sA	1	*-mă	*-mă-n	*-mē-k
	2	*-mᴅă	*-mᴅă-n	*-mᴅē-k
	3	*-msē	*-msē-n	*-msē-k
pN and other cases	1	*-nă	*-nă-n	*-nē-k
	2	*-nᴅă	*-nᴅă-n	*-nᴅē-k
	3	*-ssē	*-ssē-n	*-ssē-k

which the analogical change was based. In the same central positions, the third-person dual and plural suffixes have irregular single -s- in the oblique cases instead of expected geminate *-ss-, e.g. *beatnageaset* 'their dog', *goađisteaset* 'in their hut' instead of *beatnageasset, *goađisteasset. The single -s- in the nominative singular, which has served as the basis for the analogical change, is regular.

Present-day North Saami has only a single series of possessive suffixes with slightly different forms for the different stress positions (after a stressed and after an unstressed vowel). The original nominative plural forms have disappeared in North Saami (proto-Saami pN *niejᴅănă 'my daughters' v. sN *niejᴅămă 'my daughter'); the genitive/accusative plural forms are used instead, in vocative functions only, e.g. *nieiddaidan!* 'my daughters!' The plural illative has the case ending -das-/-ddás- (e.g. *gieđaidasan* 'into my hands', *beatnagiiddásan* 'to my dogs') peculiar to North and parts of Lule Saami but not attested elsewhere. It consists of the partitive (pFS *-ta/ä) plus illative (pFS *-sin) suffixes. The North/Ume Saami third-person dual suffix -ska/-skka (*guossiska* 'the guest of them two') is secondary; its origin is not clear. Its use in declension may be based on an analogy with its use in conjugation, or vice versa (*manai* 'he went' : *manaiga* 'they two went' parallel to *guossis* 'his/her guest', *guossiska* 'the guest of them two'). The vowel points back to proto-Saami *ā (< pFS *a/ä), but this may be due to the analogical influence of the corresponding present-tense suffix -ba/-ba (< pFS *pa/ä+n) in verbs.

Pronouns. Pronouns show by and large the same morphology as nouns, but with the architectonic distinction that pronouns may also have monosyllabic stems whereas nouns are bisyllabic or longer. Some representative paradigms are given in Table 2.6.

In the paradigm of monosyllabic stems, the essive ending is reduplicated (*danin, manin, dūnin*). The interrogative *mii* 'what' has separate forms for genitive (*man*) and accusative (*maid, man*); the accusative form *man* is used mainly for definite referents. The illative singular in monosyllabic stems has retained the s of the suffix and therefore does not show contraction (*dasa,*

Table 2.6   Sample pronoun paradigms: 'it', 'what', 'who'

	'It' Singular	Plural	'What' Singular	Plural	'Who' Singular	Plural
N	dat	dat	mii	mat	gii	geat
G	dan	daid	man	maid	gean	geaid
A	dan	daid	maid, man	maid	gean	geaid
Ill	dasa	daidda	masa	maidda	geasa	geaidda
Loc	das	dain	mas	main	geas	geain
Com	dainna	daiguin	mainna	maiguin	geainna	geaiguin
Ess	danin		manin		geanin	

Table 2.7   Sample pronoun paradigms: 'you', 'someone'

	'You' Singular	Dual	Plural	'Someone' Singular	Plural
N	don	doai	dii	soameş	soapmásat
G	dū	dudno	dīn	soapmása	soapmásiid
A	dū	dudno	dīn	soapmása	soapmásiid
Ill	dutnje	dutnuide	didjiide	soapmásii	soapmásiidda
Loc	dūs	dudnos	dīs	soapmásis	soapmásiin
Com	duinna	dudnuin	dīnguin	soapmásiin	soapmásiiguin
Ess	dūnin	dudnon	dīnin	soamisin	

masa, geasa). The personal pronouns have initial *m-* in the first person (*mun~mon, moai, mii*), *d-* in the second (*don, doai, dii*), and *s-* in the third (*son, soai, sii*). The dual personal pronouns originally had bisyllabic stems in the nominative as well (*monōj, *tonōj, *sonōj < pFS *munoj etc.), but these were reduced to monosyllabic forms in Inari, North, and Lule Saami (North *moai, doai, soai*; cf. Skolt *måna*, etc.). After initial *m-*, nasal geminates were retained (*mun*, illative *munnje*; *moai*, genitive/accusative *munno*). In the dual and plural of the personal pronouns, some cases show plural morphology (*doai*, illative *dudnuide*; *dii*, illative *didjiide*, comitative *dīnguin*). The palatalized /nʲ/ in illative singular *munnje, dutnje, sutnje* has met with no satisfactory explanation; the fact that Skolt, Kildin, and Ter have non-palatalized nasals (Skolt *mu′nne, tu′nne, su′nne*) could indicate that there was innovation in the west. The illative plurals *midjiide, didjiide, sidjiide* have acquired a secondary illative plural morphology; original forms were based on the illative singular suffix, with contraction in the second syllable (proto-Saami *mijin, *tijin, *sijin < pFS *me-j(-i)-sin etc. > Finnish *meihin* 'to us' etc.); Inari Saami has expected *mijjân, tijjân, sijjân*, Lule Saami has *midjij, tidjij, sidjij* with the secondary (singular) illative suffix *-j*.

The reflexive pronoun (sN *ieš*, pN *ieža*, stem *iehča-*) is inflected with obligatory possessive suffixes in the oblique cases, e.g. sGA *iehčan/iežan* 'my own', *iežat* 'your own', sCom *iežainis* 'with him/herself', Ess *iehčanis* 'by him/herself', pA *iežaideaset* 'themselves'. The illative and locative singular have suppletive stems based on the adverbs *ala* 'onto the top' and *alde* 'on the top', e.g. *alccesan* (~ *alccen* ~ *allasan*) 'to myself' (where *c* is an irregular, and *s* a regular, reflex of the singular illative case ending *-s-*), *alddán* 'with/from myself'.

Conjugation
The verb is conjugated for two voices (active and passive, the latter used mainly to avoid expressing the agent, whether transitive or intransitive), four moods (indicative, conditional, potential, and imperative), two tenses (plus two compound ones), three numbers, and three persons. There are also a

Table 2.8 Sample verb paradigms

	Negative verb	leat 'to be'	oaddit 'to sleep'	muitalit 'to tell'	gul'lot 'to be heard'
Indicative					
Present					
s1	in	lean	oaḍán	muitalan	gul'lon
s2	it	leat	oaḍát	muitalat	gul'lot
s3	ii	lea	oaḍḍá	muitala	gul'lo
d1	ean	letne	ōḍče	muitale(tne)	gul'loje(tne)
d2	eahppi	leahppi	oaḍḍibeahtti	muitaleahppi	gul'lobeahtti
d3	eaba̧	leaba̧	oaḍḍiba	muitaleaba̧	gul'loba
p1	eat	leat	oaḍḍit	muitalit	gul'lot
p2	ēhpet	lēhpet	oaḍḍibēhtet	muitalēhpet	gul'lobēhtet
p3	eai	leat	ōḍčet	muitalit	gul'lojit
Past					
s1	—	ledjen	ōḍḍen	muitalin	gul'lojin
s2	—	ledjet	ōḍḍet	muitalit	gul'lojit
s3	—	le(a)i	ōḍii	muitalii	gul'lui
d1	—	leimmȩ	ōḍiimȩ	muitaleimmȩ	gul'luime
d2	—	leiddȩ	ōḍiidȩ	muitaleiddȩ	gul'luide
d3	—	leigga̧	ōḍiiga̧	muitaleigga̧	gul'luiga
p1	—	leimmet	ōḍiimet	muitaleimmȩt	gul'luimet
p2	—	leiddet	ōḍiidet	muitaleiddet	gul'luidet
p3	—	ledje	ōḍče	muitale(dje)	gul'loje(dje)
Conditional					
s1	—	livččen	oaḍášin	muitalivččen	gul'lošin
s2	—	livččet	oaḍášit	muitalivččet	gul'lošit
s3	—	livččii	oaḍášii	muitalivččii	gul'lošii

Table 2.8 (Continued)

	Negative verb	leat 'to be'	oađđit 'to sleep'	muitalit 'to tell'	gul'lot 'to be heard'
d1	—	livččiime	oađáŝeimmẹ	muitalivččiime	gul'lošeimmẹ
d2	—	livččiide	oađáŝeidde	muitalivččiide	gul'lošeidde
d3	—	livččiiga	oađáŝeigga	muitalivččiiga	gul'lošeigga
p1	—	livččiimet	oađáŝeimmẹt	muitalivččiimet	gul'lošeimmẹt
p2	—	livččiidet	oađáŝeiddet	muitalivččiidet	gul'lošeiddet
p3	—	livčče	oađáŝe(dje)	muitalivčče	gul'loše(dje)
Potential					
s1	—	leaččan	ōđežan	muitaleaččan	gul'ložan
s2	—	leaččat	ōđežat	muitaleaččat	gul'ložat
s3	—	leažžá	ōđeža	muitaleažžá	gul'loža
d1	—	ležže	ōđeže(tne)	muitaležže	gul'lože(tne)
d2	—	leažžabeahtti	ōđežeahppi	muitaleažžabeahtti	gul'ložeahppi
d3	—	leažžaba	ōđežeaba	muitaleažžaba	gul'ložeaba
p1	—	leažžat	ōđežit	muitaleažžat	gul'ložit
p2	—	leažžabēhtet	ōđežēhpet	muitaleažžabēhtet	gul'ložēhpet
p3	—	ležžet	ōđežit	muitaležžet	gul'ložit
Imperative					
s1	allon	lēhkon	ōđđon	muitalēhkon	gul'lojēhkon
s2	alẹ	leagẹ	oađẹ	muital	gul'lo
s3	allos	lēhkos	ōđđos	muitalēhkos	gul'lojēhkos
d1	al'lu	leahkku	oađ'đu	muitaleahkku	gul'lojeahkku
d2	al'li	lahkki	oađ'đi	muitalahkki	gul'lojeahkki
d3	alloska	lēhkoska	ōđđoska	muitalēhkoska	gul'lojēhkoska

Table 2.8 (Continued)

	Negative verb	leat 'to be'	oaddit 'to sleep'	muitalit 'to tell'	gul'lot 'to be heard'
p1	allot	lēhkot	ōđđot	muitalēhkot	gul'lojēhkot
p2	allet	lēhket	ōđđet	muitalēhket	gul'lojēhket
p3	alloset	lēhkoset	ōđđoset	muitalēhkoset	gul'lojēhkoset
Non-finite forms					
Infinitive		leat, leahkit	oaddit	muitalit	gul'lot
connegatives:					
indic.pres		leat	oadE	muital	gul'lo
conditional		livčče	oađáše	muitalivčče	gul'loše
potential		leačča	ōđeš	muitaleačča	gul'loš
imperative		leage	oađe	muital	gul'lo
Second imperative		lēhko	ōđđo	muitalēhko	gul'lojēhko
Action		leahkin	oađđin	muitalan	gul'lon
Action essive		leame(n)	oađđime(n)	muitaleame(n)	gul'lome(n)
Action locative		leames	oađđimis	muitaleames	gul'lomis
Gerund		leagedēttiin	oađedēttiin	muitalēttiin	gul'lodēttiin
Present participle		leahkki	oađ'đi	muitaleaddji	gul'lojeaddji
Perfect participle		lean, leamaš	oađđán	muitalan	gul'lon
Verb abessive		leagekeahttá	oađekeahttá	muitalkeahttá	gul'lokeahttá
Verb genitive		—	oađi	muital	gul'lo
Supinum	ama'n, -t, -s, -me, -de, -ska, -met, -det, -set				

number of non-finite forms classifiable according to their syntactic roles as infinitives, participles, and gerunds. Verb stems are bisyllabic or longer, with two exceptions: *leat* 'to be' and the negative verb.

The endings have different forms according to position. There are vocalic stems ending in *a*, *i*, or *u* (parisyllabic), consonantal stems (imparisyllabic), and contracted stems, which have both a parisyllabic vocalic stem (ending in *á*, *e*, or *o*) and a consonantal stem (ending in *-j-*). Sample paradigms for North Saami are given in Table 2.8.

Personal endings and tense marking. The first and second persons singular have the same personal endings in both tenses, and the third person has zero (the *-a* final in *muitala* is, at least historically, the stem vowel). First person *-n* < proto-Saami *-m < pU *-m, cf. the *m-* of *mun* 'I'; second person -t < proto-Saami *-k < pFS *-t < pU *-t, cf. the *d-* of *don* 'you'.

The remaining persons have true personal endings in the past tense, but in the present tense use endings based on deverbal nominals (agentives). The nominal suffixes on which the present-tense forms are based are as follows:

* From pFS *=ja/ä (probably < pU *=j or *=ja/ä, a *nomen agentis*) were built
  the first person dual, e.g. *manne* 'we two go' < pFS *meni=jä-n, with the dual marker *-n;
  the third person plural, e.g. *mannet* 'they (all) go' < pFS *meni=jä-t, with the pU plural marker *-t.
* From pFS *=pa/ä (< pU *pa/ä, another *nomen agentis*) were built
  the second person dual, e.g. *mannabeahtti* 'you two go', probably < pFS *meni=pä-tä-n, with the pU non-singular second-person ending *-ta/ä and the dual marker *-n;
  the third person dual, e.g. *mannaba* 'they two go' < pFS *meni=pä-n;
  the first person plural, e.g. *mannat* 'we (all) go' < pFS *meni=pä, i.e. without a marker for number;
  the second person plural, e.g. *mannabehtet* 'you go' < pFS *meni=pä-tä-t, or possibly, but on conflicting evidence, without the plural marker, i.e. *men=pä-tä.

The present-tense dual and plural second-person endings presuppose a reduplication of the personal ending in proto-Saami (mid proto-Saami d2 *mënë-ʙā-tā-ᴅā-n and p2 *mënë-ʙā-tā-ᴅā-k) with subsequent contraction of unstressed *-(t)ā-ᴅā- in the dual but for some reason – perhaps because there was no final consonant closing the syllable – not in the plural.

In the past tense, the personal endings (the third persons had zero originally) were attached to a stem built with the past-tense marker *-j-, resulting in contraction when the *-j-* was intervocalic (in the first and second persons singular and the third person plural). Examples: *mannen* 'I went' < pFS *meni-j-i-m, *mannet* 'you went' < pFS *meni-j-i-t, *manne* 'they (all) went' < proto-Saami *mănin, with unexpected final *-n instead of *-k < pFS *meni-j-i-t, all with the epenthetic vowel *-i- to the right of the past-tense marker. The remaining past-tense forms are without contraction: *manai* '(s)he went' < pFS *meni-j, *manaime* 'we two went' < pFS *meni-j-mi-n, *manaide* 'you (two) went' < pFS *meni-j-ti-n, *manaimet* 'we (all) went' < pFS *meni-j-mä-t, *manaidet* 'you (all) went' < pFS *meni-j-tä-t. The plural marker may have been not *-t, but *-k, as suggested by Mordva (*palatamk* 'we kiss') and Hungarian (*várunk* 'we wait'). The past third person dual has the secondary ending -ga/-gga, peculiar to the Western Saami languages. In the east (Inari and some dialects of Skolt), the forms point back to a somewhat more regular pFS form *meni-j-n-i-n > proto-Saami *mănăjnăn (note, however, the reduplicated dual marker *n*), yielding *moonááin* 'they (two) went' in Inari Saami. Similar forms have also been attested in some North Saami idioms of the nineteenth century, e.g. Varanger Sea Saami *suhtaina* 'they (two) got angry'. The origin of the suffix *-ga/-gga* (proto-Western Saami *-Gā) is not clear.

In the imperative, the suffix of the first person singular and all third-person suffixes are identical with the corresponding possessive suffixes, and the first-person plural and dual suffixes are the same as in the present indicative. The second person singular is zero (the original suffix *-k as in *mana!* 'go!', < pU *meni-k, was the old imperative marker). The second person dual and plural show the Uralic non-singular second person ending *-ta/ä and the number markers *-n (dual) and *-t or *-k (plural). Unlike the corresponding present indicative forms, these lack the old agentive suffix *=pa/ä.

In Lule, Pite, Ume, and South Saami, the negative verb has separate tense forms (e.g. Lule *ittjiv ~ idtjiv* 'I did not', *ejma* 'we did not') used with the indicative connegative (e.g. Lule *ittjij boade* '(s)he did not come', contrast synonymous North *ii boahtán*, built with the perfect participle.) The affricate in *ittjiv* (South *idtjim* etc.) goes back one way or the other to the pU past-tense marker *-sʲ(a/ä)- seen in South Estonian *esin*, Nenets *nyídømcyᵒ* 'I did not'; Saami presupposes pFS *-nsʲ-, but if there is a sporadic lengthening of the consonant centre as suggested (*-žʲ- > *-žʲžʲ-) the more regular pFS *-sʲ- can be reconstructed.

The compound tenses, perfect and pluperfect, are formed with the copula and the perfect participle: *lean boahtán* 'I have come', *ledjen boahtán* 'I had come'. The conditional and the imperative have a compound perfect only: *livččen boahtán* 'I would have come', *lēhkos boahtán* 'may (s)he have come'. The potential on the other hand has both perfect and pluperfect, at least in some dialects: *leažžá boahtán* '(s)he might have come', pluperfect *leaččai boahtán*; such dialects also have past potential forms for the copula. For more complex temporal reference, even double perfects and pluperfects are used, e.g. *lei leamaš boahtán* '(s)he had come already on an earlier occasion', see p. 79.

Mood markers. Stem-formation in the *imperative* is based on the following pFS imperative markers:

1   *-ō- used in first and third persons in parisyllabic stems, e.g. d1 *mannu* 'let us (two) go' < proto-Saami *măṅōn, s3 *mannos* 'let him/her go' < proto-Saami *măṅōsē;

2   *-k used in the second person singular, e.g. *mana* 'go!' < proto-Saami *mănăk;

3   *-k̇ō- used in the first and third persons of imparisyllabic stems, e.g. *oahpistēhkos* 'may (s)he guide' < proto-Saami *oahpēsteak̇ōsē;

4   *-k̇ē- used in the second person dual and plural in parisyllabic stems, e.g. d2 *oahpisteahkki* 'guide! (you two)' < proto-Saami *oahpēsteak̇kēn < mid proto-Saami *ăppāstākāᴅān, p2 *oahpistēhket* 'guide! (you lot)' < proto-Saami *oahpēsteak̇ēᴅēk;

5   *-∅ used in the second person dual and plural in parisyllabic stems, e.g. d2 *manni* 'go! (you two)' < pss *măṅṅēn, with a contracted vowel from earlier *-ăᴅē- in the second syllable, and subsequent gemination of the central consonant, p2 *mannet* 'go! (you lot)' < proto-Saami *măṅăᴅēk.

Of these five manifestations of the imperative marker, those based on *-k and *-k̇ē- are clearly the oldest and go back directly to pU *-k and *-ka/ä. The rounded vowel of *-k̇ō- is probably due to Fennic influence, cf. Finnish *antako-on* 'may (s)he give'. Of those without the stop *k, at least *-ō- seems to have arisen, through *fausse coupe*, from forms containing the stop; this left the vowel *ō, which replaces the stem vowel, to fulfil the function of imperative marker. The resulting forms were thus of the canonic type for Saami, viz. parisyllabic. As for Ume, Pite, Lule, and North Saami, the forms with *-∅ seem to have an analogical history in the Western Saami languages, although they are usually thought of as having the personal endings attached directly to the stem.

The *potential* marker -ž-/-žž-, -čč- (*bōđežan* 'I may come' from *boahtit* 'to come', *muitaleaččan* 'I may tell' from *muitalit* 'to tell') goes back to proto-Saami *-nžʲă- and ultimately to pFS *-nsʲi- (> proto-Fennic *-nʲsʲi- + *-j- > late proto-Fennic *-jsi- > the Finnish conditional marker -*isi-*). It may have the same origin as the nominal diminutive suffix of the same pFS shape (*=nsʲi).

The *conditional* has two markers. For North and Eastern Saami it is proto-Saami *-kčʲi- (in which the *i is originally a contracted vowel containing the past-tense marker *-j-), yielding North Saami forms such as *oađášin* 'I would sleep' and *muitalivčč̌en* 'I would tell'. For western North Saami and to the south of it (overlapping with -*ši*-/-*včče*- in West Finnmark), the marker consists of the present-tense marker *-k (probably also found in the present-tense connegative) and the contracted past-tense stem of the copula (proto-Saami *li-, proto-Saami infinitive *leaᴅēk). Thus we have western North Saami *oađálin* 'I would sleep' (< proto-Western Saami *oaδávlim; in North Saami this type is confined to parisyllabic stems). A complete conditional form of the copula may also be suffixed, e.g. North Saami *oađálivčč̌en* 'I would sleep', Lule Saami *guláluluv* (~ more frequently, the compound *luluv gullat*) 'I would hear'. The marker *-kč^{j}i-* is identical with the conditional marker *-ksi-* found in Estonian (*tuleksin* 'I would come'); it seems to have originally been identical with a continuative suffix, cf. pFS *-(i)ks^{j}i- > North Saami =*aš-* (*vuojašit* 'to drive along' form *vuodjit* 'to drive'), Finnish =*(e)ksi-* (*kanneksia* 'to carry around', from *kantaa* 'to carry'). Instead of the compound perfect with the conditional morpheme (*livččen boahtán* 'I would have come') an equivalent construction consisting of a past-tense form of the copula plus the infinitive is also used (*ledjen boahtit*).

Voice. The Saami *passive* differs from most passives in that its main function is not so much to topicalize the patient as it is to submerge the agent (or logical subject) of the action expressed by the verb, and is accordingly used with intransitive as well as transitive verbs, e.g. *el'lojuv'vui* 'life went along, people lived' from *eallit* 'to live'). Some scholars hold that the Saami passive belongs to the realm of derivation and not to that of inflection.

The marker is *-(oj)uv'vo(j)-* in North Saami, e.g. *dolvojuv'vot* 'to be taken somewhere' (from *doalvut* 'to take, lead'), *muitaluv'vot* 'to be told' (*muitalit* 'to tell); such forms are conjugated like *gul'lot* 'to be heard', cf. above. Historically, the passive marker contains two elements. The first element, proto-Saami *-ujă- (from earlier *-ōjë-) may originally have been a frequentative suffix; or it may historically be the same as the second element, proto-Saami *-uovă- (from pFS *-ov(i)-), which was originally a reflexive suffix. Cognates for the reflexive suffix are known from Mordva (*-v-* in Erzya *n^{j}eja=v-oms* 'to be seen', *n^{j}eje-ms* 'to see'), from Mansi (Vogul; *-w-* in *totawe* 'he is brought'), and Hungarian, where it survives as the labiality in reflexive suffixes, e.g. *ü* in *épül-ni* 'to be built'.

Nominal forms of the verb. The *infinitive* marker *-t* (e.g. *oađđit* 'to sleep') goes back to proto-Saami *-pēk. It is historically identical with the marker of the Finnish first infinitive (*saa-da* 'to get', *juos-ta* 'to run'), with largely the same functions. Both go back to pFS *-tak/*-täk, which consists of the pU deverbal noun suffix *=ta/ä plus lative *-k, itself possibly of pU vintage. The *connegatives* (of the verb *oađđit* 'to sleep': indicative *oađe̬*, conditional *oađáše*, potential *ōđeš*, imperative *oađe̬*) ended in the proto-Saami suffix *-k which was probably the same as the element found in the second person singular imperative (< pU *-k). Note that in the negative imperative, mood is encoded in the negative verb. The *second imperative* (*lēhko*, *ōđđo* etc.) exhibits the same stem and has, accordingly, the same history as the third person imperative. The *action* forms, e.g. nominative *čállin* in *áhči čállin girji* FATHER.sG WRITES.ACTIO BOOK 'a book written by father' are based on the pU deverbal action noun suffix *=ma/ä, to which the essive (*čállimin* 'when writing') and locative (*čállimis* 'from writing') suffixes were attached. The *gerund*, e.g. *muitalēttiin* 'while telling', is based on the pU deverbal noun suffix *=nta/ä plus the comitative suffix *-jan/ä (cf. declension, above).

The *present participle* (*boahtti* 'comer, one who comes', with a contracted lateral vowel, from *boahtit* 'to come') has acquired verbal features but is originally clearly a derivational rather than a true conjugational form in Saami. Its suffix goes back to pFS *=ja/ä, cf. Finnish *tuli=ja* 'comer' from *tule-* 'comes') and is probably of pU origin. The *perfect participle* (*mannan* 'gone', from *mannat* 'to go', *dolvon* 'taken', from *doalvut* 'to take, lead', *lean ~ leamaš* 'been', from *leat* 'to be') has the marker -*n* (-*maš* occurs in *leamaš* only, but there is evidence for an older -*m*, and eighteenth-century -*maž* in North Saami bisyllabic stems). This -*n* goes back to proto-Saami *-mă or, with the diminutive suffix, *-mă-nž^{j}ă. Proto-Saami *-mă-nž^{j}ă, in turn, goes back to pFS *-mi-ns^{j}i (cf. Finnish *mene-mi-se-*, the oblique stem of *meneminen* 'the act of going', from *mene-* 'goes'). In pFS *-mi-ns^{j}i, the *-mi is of Uralic origin and *-ns^{j}i is the diminutive suffix.

The *supinum* of the negative verb (*aman* 'lest I do', *amat* 'lest you do', etc.) takes the infinitive as its argument: (*amas gahččat* 'lest it fall, so that it does not fall'); functionally it resembles the infinitive of other verbs. Its marker is -*ma-*, which is identical with the marker of the proto-Saami perfect participle *-mă(nž^{j}ă), and occurs only with personal suffixes attached. In some dialects, the *supinum* has evolved into a conjunction, *amas*, which occurs with finite negative constructions such as *amas ii gahča* 'so that it will not fall'.

The *verb abessive* and *genitive* are gerunds: *oađekeahttá* 'without sleeping', *oađi* 'by sleeping'. The former derives from the abessive of a deverbal noun formed with the pFS suffix *=kka/ä. The latter originally had the marker *-n (preserved in South and Inari Saami), which has similar functions in Finnish (cf. the second infinitive instructive *kantaen* 'by carrying', probably from pFS *kanta-ta-n) and Mari (e.g. *kanden* 'by carrying'). It seems to derive from the pU connective suffix *-n (with more specific functions such as genitive, instructive, lative, and dual, all expressing different kinds of connectivity).

Word Formation

Derivation

Derivation is possible both within and across part-of-speech category boundaries. A substantial number of stems are inflectible as both nouns and verbs without any derivational operations, e.g. *biegga(-)* 'wind; (the wind) blows'. There are also highly productive derivational suffixes which operate only within a given category. The diminutive suffix, for example, which is all but obligatory after *unna/uhca* 'little', is restricted to nominals (*boazu* 'reindeer', *unna bohccoš* 'little reindeer', *guolli* 'fish', *unna guoláš* 'little fish'). In parallel fashion, there are causative, frequentative/continuative, diminutive, and momentaneous suffixes which are restricted to deverbal derivation, e.g. *vuodjit* 'to drive', *vuojihit* 'to make X drive', *vuojašit* 'to keep driving', *vuojestit* 'to drive a little'. The use of frequentative/continuative (often with conatory nuances) and momentaneous verbal derivatives is normal, even obligatory, whenever they are available and appropriate in relation to the act to be described by the verb; this makes their use close, if not equivalent, to an aspectual system.

A highly productive instance of cross-category derivation is the system of deverbal nouns (e.g. action nouns with -*n/-pmi* and -*muš* such as *oađđin* 'sleeping' and *oađđimuš* 'having to sleep', and actor nouns such as *oađˈđi* 'sleeper') and denominal adverbs such as *fūnet* 'badly' (from *fuotni* 'bad'), *njōzet* 'slowly' (from *njoahci* 'slow'). There are also some productive derivational suffixes borrowed from Fennic such as the deverbal adjective ending =*meahttun* 'not X-ing', from Finnish =*maton/=mätön*, e.g. North Saami *duhtameahttun* 'dissatisfied' from *duhtat* 'to be satisfied'), and the denominal adjective ending =*laš* 'belonging to or having X', from Finnish =*llise-*, e.g. North Saami *soajálaš* 'wingèd', from *soadji* 'wing'.

Most derivational suffixes have different forms after stressed and unstressed vowels. Thus the causative is -*h*- to the right of the unstressed second syllable in *vuojihit* 'to make X drive', from *vuodjit* 'drives', but -*htt(i)*- to the right of the stressed third syllable in *muitalahttit* 'to make X tell', from *muitalit* 'tells'; both -*h*- and -*htt(i)*- continue pFS *=tta/ä-. Similarly the frequentative is -*d*- in *vuojadit* 'to swim around', from *vuodjat* 'to swim', but -*dd(a)*- in *muitaladdat* 'to keep telling', from *muitalit* 'to tell'; both -*d*- and -*dd(a)*- continue pFS *=(i)nti-.

The most common derivational suffixes, marked with equals (=) sign, are exemplified briefly in the paragraphs that follow.

1   *Deverbal nouns* may be subclassified into broad functional/semantic categories as nouns denoting

(a) the act itself: *oađđi=n* 'sleeping', *muitalea=pmi* 'storytelling' (< pU *=ma/ä); *barg=u* 'work' (*bargat* 'to work'), < pFS *=o, perhaps from a Finno-Volgaic *=v); *goarru=muš* 'having to sew' (*goarrut* 'to sew'), < Fennic *=mus/*=müs; *bávkk=as* 'banging' (*bávkit* 'to bang'), < pFS *=iš;

(b) the actor: *oađˈđi* 'sleeper', *muital=eaddji* 'storyteller' (< pFS *=ja/ä < pU *=jV); *sōlo=n* 'one who is eager to pick his/her teeth' (*soallut* 'to pick one's teeth'), < proto-Saami *=njă;

(c) instrument: *loavdda* (sG *loavda=ga*) 'tent-cloth' (*loavdit* 'to cover the tent'), *golgad=at* (sG *golgad=aga*) 'drift-net' (*golgadit* 'to fish with a drift-net'), < pFS *=ik); *vuojá=n* 'vehicle' (*vuodjit* 'to drive') < proto-Saami *=njă; *vuoidd=as* 'ointment' (*vuoidat* 'to smear'), < pFS *=iš; *jeara=ldat* 'question' (*jearrat* 'to ask'), < proto-Saami *=lᴅăk < pFS *=l=ta/ä=ik;

(d) result: *juog=us* 'section' (*juohkit* 'to divide'), < pFS *=oksi < Finno-Volgaic *=w(i)ksi; *čála* (sG *čálla=ga*) 'writing' (*čállit* 'to write'), < pFS *=ik;

(e) object: *vuošš=us* 'something to be cooked' (*vuošˈšat* 'to cook') , <

pFS *=oksi < Finno-Volgaic *=v(i)ksi; *borra=muš* 'food' (*borrat* 'to eat'), < Baltic-Fennic *=mus/*=müs;

(f) place : *njuova=hat* 'butchering place' (*njuovvat* 'to butcher'), < proto-Saami *=ttăk < pFS *=tta/ä- < pU *=kta/ä + pFS *=ik;

(g) conditions: *oainn=ádat* 'seeing' (*oaidnit* 'to see'), < proto-Saami *=ānoăk < pFS, pU *=nta/ä + pFS *=ik.

2 *Denominal nouns*: the chief subdivisions are

(a) diminutive: *guolá=š* 'little fish' (*guolli* 'fish'), < pFS *=nsʲi;

(b) property: *guhkk=odat* 'length' (*guhkki* 'long'), < pFS *=oti < *-vōti + *=ik; *allat=vuohta* 'height' (*allat* 'high'), < proto-Fennic *=vōti;

(c) material: *báni=s* 'material for tooth of a rake' (*bátni* 'tooth'), < pFS *=ksi < Finno-Volgaic *=ksi;

(d) person: *suopmẹ=laš* 'Finn' (*suopma* 'Finnish'), < Fennic *=la/äise-;

(e) group: *golmma=s* 'group of three' (*golbma* 'three'), < proto-Saami *=s < pFS, Finno-Volgaic *=ksi;

(f) order: *njealjá=t* 'fourth' (*njealljẹ* 'four'), < proto-Saami *=noă < pFS *=nti < pU *=mta/ä;

(g) conditions: *balvv=ádat* 'cloudy weather' (*balva* 'cloud'), < proto-Saami *=ānoăk < pFS, pU *=nta/ä + pFS *=ik.

3 *Deverbal adjectives*:

(a) negation: *duhta=meahttun* 'dissatisfied';

(b) inclination: *soddj=il* 'flexible' (*sodjat* 'to bend [intr]'), < mid proto-Saami *=(jā)=lā < pFS *=ja/ä + *=la/ä; *čīrro=las* 'apt to cry' (*čierrut* 'weeps'), < proto-Saami *=lăs < pFS *=la/ä + *=iš; *suhtte=š* 'quick-tempered' (*suhttat* 'to get angry'), < proto-Saami *=ičʲčʲē < pFS *=ja/ä + pFS *=cʲcʲa/=cʲcʲä;

(c) susceptibility: *jugahahtti* (*juhkat* 'to drink'), < proto-Saami *=tteaìtē < pFS *=tta/ä- + *=ja/ä < pU *=kta/ä + *jV.

4 *Denominal adjectives*:

(a) lack: *guolẹ=heapmẹ* 'fishless' (*guolli* 'fish'), < pFS, pU *=pta/ä + *ma/ä;

(b) negation: *buhtis=meahttun* 'unclean' (*buhtis* 'clean'), < Fennic *=ma/äto/ön;

(c) abundance: *geaðgá=i* 'stony' (*geaðgi* 'stone'), *vuddji=i* 'rich in fat' (*vuodja* 'fat, oil') < mid proto-Saami *=ŋă < pFS, pFU *=ŋa/ä (> Finnish =*va/ä*);

(d) character: *jahká=saš* 'yearly' (*jahki* 'year'), < proto-Saami *=sănž̌ʲă < pFS *=si=nsʲi; *(guhkes)juolgg=at* '(long-)legged' (*juolgi* 'leg'), < proto-Saami *=(a)ŋGă < ? pFS *=ŋki;

(e) comparativity: *guhki=t* (sG *guhki=bu*) 'longer' (*guhkki* 'long'), < proto-Saami *=mBē < pFS, pU *=mpa/ä;

(f) superlativity: *guhki=mus* 'longest', < pFS *=moksi.

5   *Deverbal verbs*:
   (a) causative: *goaru=h-it* 'to make X sew' (*goarrut* 'to sew'), < pFS
       *=tta/ä- < pU *=kta/ä-; *nohkka=d-it* 'to put X to sleep' (*nohkkat* 'to
       fall asleep'), < proto-Saami *=Dē- < pFS, pU *=ta/ä-; *buori=d-it* 'to
       make X better' (*buorránit* 'to become better'), < proto-Saami
       *=mDǎ- < pFS *=m=ta/ä- < pU *=mi- + *=ta/ä-;
   (b) reflexive: *basa=d-it* 'to wash oneself' (*bassat* 'to wash X'), < proto-
       Saami *=nDǎ- < pFS *=nti-; *geassá=d-it* 'to withdraw (intr)' (*geassit*
       'to draw'), < proto-Saami *=Dǎ- < pFS *=ti-;
   (c) reciprocal: *dovdda=d-it* 'to know one another' (*dovdat* 'to know'), <
       proto-Saami *=nDǎ- < pFS *=nti-; *oaidn=al-it* 'to see each other'
       (*oaidnit* 'to see'), < proto-Saami *=ǎlǎ- < pFS *=ili-;
   (d) momentaneous: *čolga=d-it* 'to spit once' (*čolgat* 'to spit'), < proto-
       Saami *=Dē- < pFS *=ta/ä- < pU *=ta/ä-; *njuik=e-t* 'to jump once'
       (v. *njuikut* 'to jump many times'), < mid proto-Saami *=ǎjǎ- < pFS
       *=iji-; *bávk=al-it* 'to bang once' (v. *bávkkuhit* 'to bang again and
       again'), < proto-Saami *=ǎlǎ- < pFS *=ili-;
   (e) subitive: *borra=l-it* 'to eat quickly' (*borrat* 'to eat'), < proto-Saami
       *=lē- < pFS, pU *=la/ä-; *njuike=st-it* 'to jump quickly' (*njuiket* 'to
       jump once'), < proto-Saami *=stē- < pFS *=šta/ä-; *jávkk=ih-it* 'to
       disappear quickly' (*jávkat* 'to disappear'), < proto-Saami *=ēttē- <
       pFS *=tta/ä- < ? pU *=kta/ä-; *bárgg=ád-it* 'to cry out' (*bárgut* 'to
       cry'), < proto-Saami *=ānDǎ-;
   (f) frequentative: *láhp=ad-it* 'to lose (many objects)' (*láhppit* 'to lose'), <
       proto-Saami *=(ǎ)nDǎ- < pFS *=(i)nti-; *čohkán=adda-t* '(many) sit
       down' (*čohkánit* 'to sit down'), < proto-Saami *=ǎnDǎ- < pFS *=inti;
       báhč=al-it 'to shoot (many times)' (*báhčit* 'to shoot'), *čoaskudallat* 'to
       cool (many objects)' (*čoaskudit* 'to cool [one object]'), < proto-Saami
       *=ǎlǎ- < pFS *=ili-; *luodd=u-t* 'to keep splitting' (luddet 'to split
       once'), < proto-Saami *=ō- < ? pFS *=o-; *geas=aš-it* 'to be pulling at
       leisure' (*geassit* 'to pull'), < proto-Saami *=ǎčʲčʲǎ- < pFS *=(i)ksʲi-;
   (g) continuative: *čučČo=d-it* 'to be standing' (*čuoǧǧut* 'to stand'),
       loga=d-it 'to be reading' (*lohkat* 'to read'), < proto-Saami *=(ǎ)nDǎ
       < pFS *=(i)nti-; *bargg=ild-it* 'to work at leisure' (*bargat* 'to work'),
       < proto-Saami *=ēlDē-;
   (h) diminutive: *atte̜=st-it* 'to give a little' (*addit* 'to give'), < proto-Saami
       *=stē- < pFS *=šta/ä-;
   (i) conative: *bokt=al-it* 'to try to wake X up' (*boktit* 'to wake X up'), <
       proto-Saami *=ǎlǎ- < pFS *=ili-; *ōčČo=d-it* 'to try to obtain' (*oažžut*
       'to obtain'), *ribadit* 'to try to wrench' (*rihpat* 'to wrench'), < proto-
       Saami *=(ǎ)nDǎ- < pFS *=(i)nti;
   (j) inchoative: *lohkagoahtit* 'to begin to read' (*lohkat* 'to read'), < proto-
       Saami *=Goatē- < pFS, Finno-Volgaic *=kata-/*=kätä-; *buol'lát* 'to
       catch fire' (*buollit* 'to burn'), < mid proto-Saami *=jë̄- < ? pU *=j-.

6   *Denominal verbs*:

(a) causative: *nama=h-it* 'to name' (*namma* 'name'), <pFS, pU *=kta/ä-;

(b) translative: *buorrá=n-it* 'to become better' (*buorre̞* 'good'), < proto-Saami *=mă- < pFS, pU *=mi-; *buoid=u-t* 'to become fat' (*buoidi* 'fat'), < proto-Saami *=ō- < pFS *=o-; *bealje̞h=uvva-t* 'to become deaf' (*bealje̞heapme̞* 'deaf'), < proto-Saami *=uoʹvă- < pS *=ovi-;

(c) essive: *bodnj=á-t* 'to be twisted' (*botnji* 'a twist'), < proto-Saami *=āšʲă-;

(d) instrumental: *niibbá=st-it* 'to use a knife' (*niibi* 'knife'), < proto-Saami *=stă- < ? pFS *=šti-;

(e) sensive: *fasttá=š-it* 'to consider ugly' (*fasti* 'ugly'), < proto-Saami *=čʲčʲă- < pFS *=ksʲi-.

7   *Denominal adverbs*:

(a) state: *ráiggi-l* 'with a hole' (*ráigi* 'hole'), < proto-Saami *=lᴅē < pFS *=l(a/ä) + *=ta/ä); *muohtanaga* 'with snow on it' (*muohta* 'snow'), < proto-Saami *=năɢăn < mid proto-Saami *=nāɢën < pFS, pU *=na/ä + pFS, pU *=k + (-i-) *-n;

(b) reciprocity: *giehta=laga* 'hand in hand' (*giehta* 'hand'), < proto-Saami *=lăɢăn < pFS *=li- + pFS, pU *=k- + (-i-) *-n~*-j;

(c) manner: *čeahpi=t ~ čēhpe̞=t* 'skilfully' (*čeahppi* 'skilful'), < proto-Saami *=ktē < pFS *=kta/ä < Finno-Volgaic *=kta/ä.

Compounding

Compounding is confined almost exclusively to nominal bases. Examples:

muorra 'wood' + *bihttá* 'piece'
muorrabihttá 'piece of wood'

láibi 'bread' + *váibmil* 'fond'
láibe̞váibmil 'fond of bread'

várri 'hill' + *čohkka* 'top'
várre̞čohkka 'hilltop'

rukses 'red [attrib]' + +*nierat* 'having X cheeks'
ruksesnierat 'red-cheeked'

eatni 'mother sG' + *giella* 'language'
eatnigiella 'mother tongue'

golmma 'three sG' + +*jahkásaš* 'X number of years old'
golmmajahkásaš 'three-year-old'

ovda+ 'fore-' + *juolgi* leg, foot'
ovdajuolgi 'foreleg'

čađa 'through' + *čuovgi* 'shining'
čađačuovgi 'transparent'

vuoste̞+ 'which is against' + *biegga* 'wind'
vuoste̞biegga 'headwind'

eahpe̞+ 'un-' *čielggas* 'clear'
eahpe̞čielggas 'unclear'

bealli 'half' + +*mielat* 'having an X
mind'
beallẹmielat 'mad'

The verb base +*njaddit* 'to taste like X', which does not occur independently, takes as its modifier component substantives or adjectives in the attributive form: *guollẹ+njaddit* 'to taste like fish' (*guolli*), *njuoska+njaddit* 'to taste raw' (*njuoska*, attributive form of *njuoskkas* 'raw'). The deverbal inchoative suffix =*goahtit* comes close to being a verb base: *manna=goahtit* 'to begin to go' (*manna* 'to go').

Calquing on Scandinavian constructions has produced some verbs which occur with an adverb modifier, e.g. *bajásgeassit* 'to educate' (*bajás* 'up' + *geassit* 'to pull', cf. Norwegian *oppdra*).

Syntax

Syntactic relations are expressed by morphological means (e.g. case-marking, derivational endings) and, – mostly within noun phrases – by word order. The ordering of main constituents (subject, verb, object, adverb) is guided largely by pragmatic principles. The basic order is SVO, as in *áhčči* (S) *oinnii* (V) *Niillasa* (O) 'father saw Nils', *mátki* (S) *lea* (V) *guhkki* 'the journey is long ~ it is a long journey'. However, infinitival and participial constructions tend towards the order SOV, e.g. *ii diktán mu dan* (O) *oaidnit* (V) 'did not let me see it', with *dan* 'it' coming before *oaidnit* 'to see'. In South Saami, SOV is the rule in finite cases as well: *dah* (S) *maanah* (O) *utnieh* (V) 'they have children'. Noun phrase constituents generally have a modifier–head order, e.g. *dát nuorra olmmái* 'this young man'.

The subject is not an obligatory constituent. First- and second-person verb forms do not require a subject pronoun, and third-person pronouns are optional in subordinations, e.g. *oidnen Biera* 'I saw Peter', *oidnetgo Biera?* 'did you see Peter?', *go Biera bōđii, de muitalii, ahte* ... 'when Peter came, he said that ...' Formal subjects are not required in cases like *arvá* 'it is raining', *lea čoaskkis* 'it is cold', although they often do occur, as a result of Scandinavian influence, e.g. *dat lea čoaskkis*.

Questions begin with the focalized phrase. Thus we have **gos** *don boađát?* '**where** do you come from?', with the question word *gos* '(from) where?' in initial position (in the reply, the adverb which supplies the information is in normal final position, e.g. *mun boađán* **váris** 'I come **from the hills**'. In *oidnetgo don Biera?* 'did you see Peter?' it is the verb that is focalized; note the question marker -*go* and compare the simple declarative *mun oidnen Biera* 'I saw Peter', with regular SOV order. Answers repeat the focalized question word of a yes/no question, with appropriate modifications concerning personal reference and other deixis, e.g. – *oidnetgo Biera?* – *oidnen* '– did you see Peter? – yes', and supply the appropriate information in others, e.g. – *gos don boađát?*

–*Anáris* '– where do you come from? – Inari', with the answer in the locative case in keeping with the question word *gos*.

On the other hand, if we take the morphosyntactic properties of the head to be diagnostic, then a head–modifier (or base–argument) order may be seen in numeral constructions (with numerals higher than *okta* 'one') and in verb complexes. For example, if the noun phrase *golbma dálu* 'three houses' acts as a subject in the sentence *golbma dálu ledje buollán* 'three houses had burned down', *golbma* 'three sN' is the head and *dálu* 'house sG' modifies it: *golbma ledje buollán* 'three had burned' is syntactically acceptable whereas **dálu ledje buollán* is not. The same holds for the verbal predicate in the sentence *mun ledjen boahtán* 'I had come': *ledjen* is the base to which the participle *boahtán* is an argument. Noun phrases are insoluble as a rule, i.e. they cannot be intersected by noun-phrase-external elements (verb or sentence modifiers).

Unlike noun phrases, *verb complexes* such as compound tenses and moods or other constructions consisting of a finite and a non-finite form cannot be considered to constitute a phrase in the same narrow sense: their components tolerate intervening elements and their order is not strict. They receive the same analysis as other combinations of finite and non-finite verb forms: the non-finite form is subordinated to the finite one and represents a separate predicate. For some verbs, such as *sáhttit* 'may' or *leat* 'be' (as copula), the subordination has no distinct label because other arguments are not possible, e.g. *sáhtán vuolgit* 'I may leave', *lean vuolgán* 'I have left', *ledjen vuolgit* 'I would have left'. For others, the non-finite form may function as an object (e.g. *mun máhtán vuodjat* 'I can swim', cf. *mun máhtán dárogiela* 'I can [speak] Norwegian') or as an adverbial (*manan čohkkát* 'I go and sit', cf. *manan stohpui* 'I go into the house'; *ledjen vázzimen* 'I was walking', cf. *ledjen stobus* 'I was in the house').

South Saami can have purely nominal predicates: *Laara saemie* 'Lars is a Saami', *dihte báeries* '(s)he is old', *Piere gåetesne* 'Peter is in the hut'. Some cases have also been attested in Ter Saami: *aa'jtte si'zn saa'hpliŋg* 'there was a mouse (*saa'hpliŋg*) in the store house (*aa'jtte si'zn*)'. In North Saami, the perfect participle *leamaš* can be used alone as a predicative verb without a finite form: *dat leamaš dōn geahčen gili* '(s)he has been to the other end (*dōn geahčen*) of the village'.

Morphological Marking

The case of subject and predicative noun phrases is the nominative: *áddjá* (S) *boahtá* 'grandpa is coming', *dát mátki* (S) *lea oalle guhkki* (PR) 'this journey is fairly long', *soappit* (S) *ledje guhkit* (PR) 'the sticks were long'. The object of most verbs is in the accusative: *oidnen ádjá* (O) 'I saw grandpa' (sN *áddjá*). In South Saami, there are also plural nominative objects, originally used, it seems, with indefinite referents: *aehtjie* (S) *treavkah* (O) *dorjeme* 'father has made (a pair of) skis'.

There are also a number of verbs which take arguments cognitively equivalent to objects (i.e. which are not predicates or adverbials or other circumstantial modifiers) but which are put in cases other than the accusative. Examples include *liikot* 'to like', which takes objects in the illative (*mun liikon birgui* 'I like meat'), *ballat* 'to fear', which takes the locative (*dat ballá guovžžas* 'he is afraid of the bear'), and *hilbošit* 'to tease', which takes the comitative (*mánát hilbošedje ádjáin* 'the children teased grandpa'). These have been called rection adverbials and, recently, objects.

The first argument of habitive constructions, corresponding to the subject in many languages, is in the locative, the second in the nominative, and the verb is the existential *leat*: *Lásses lea beana* LARS-loc IS.s3pres DOG 'Lars has a dog'. In South Saami, the first argument is in the genitive instead of a local case, e.g. *Laaran bienje* 'idem' (note the zero copula), or the transitive verb *utnedh* 'to have' is used, e.g. *Laara bienjem åtna* LARS accusative HAS-s3pres; this construction is also found in Ume, Pite, and Lule Saami. The second argument in *Lásses lea beana* has been analysed as a predicative; the first can be seen as a special kind of subject. The same regards also the first argument of existential sentences, which is normally in the locative: *gárddis ledje ollu bohccot* 'there were many reindeer (*bohccot*) in the corral (*gárddis*)'.

The agent of causative verbs and of verbs ending in *-halla-* is in the illative, e.g. *Biera goaruhii Birehii gápmagiid* 'Peter had Berit sew him some shoes', *Máhtte borahalai beatnagii* 'Matthew was (unfortunate enough to get) bitten by a dog' (*beatnagii* is sIll of *beana* 'dog').

The adverbial is marked by special derivative endings (cf. p. 83) and by a number of cases. Chief among these are:

- the genitive, as in *dat boahtá dōn beaivve* '(s)he comes **the day after tomorrow**', *áddjá veallá soggái čalmmiid* 'grandpa is lying **with his eyes** (*čalmmiid*, pG of *čalbmi* 'eye') towards the wall (*soggái*, sIll of *soggi* 'the space nearest the wall');
- the illative, as in *mii manaimet **Anárii*** 'we went to Inari', *dat báhce **Avvilii*** 'they stayed in Ivalo';
- the locative, as in *Máhtte bōðii **Láhpọluobbalis*** 'Matthew came **from Láhpọluoppal**';
- the comitative, as in *mun vuoján **dainna biilain** Roavẹnjárgii* 'I shall drive **that car** to Rovaniemi';
- the essive, as in *ii galgga **bassin** bargat* 'one should not work on a Sunday' (impersonal third person singular in *ii galgga* 'one should not').

A number of postpositional constructions are also possible, e.g. *bus'sá njuikii **beavddi ala*** 'the cat jumped **onto the table**', *mii leimmẹt joga alde* 'we were **on the river**'.

In noun phrases, a noun attribute is in the genitive, e.g. *ádjá soabbi* 'grandpa's stick' (sN *áddjá* 'grandpa'), *beavddę vuolde* 'under the table' (sN *beavdi* 'table'), and an adjective attribute is in the attributive form, if available, e.g. *čeahpęs duojár* 'a skilful craftsman' (*čeahppi* 'skilful'). Some attributes are in (partial) congruence with their head; they will be dealt with in the section on the noun phrase, below.

Noun Phrase
Pronoun attributes, genitive attributes, numerals, and adjectival attributes come before the noun: *dát soabbi* 'this stick', *ádjá soabbi* 'grandpa's stick', *guoktę soappi* (sG; see below) 'two sticks', and *guhkęs soabbi* 'a long stick'. If several of them are present, their order is that these examples: *dát ádjá guhkęs soabbi* 'this long stick of grandpa's', *dát ádjá guoktę guhkęs soappi* 'these two long sticks of grandpa's'. Constructions corresponding to postpositional ones in other languages are of the genitive/attributive type in Saami, e.g. *várę vuollái* '(going) under the hill', *borgga siste* 'in a snow flurry': the adverb/postposition is in the morphological form required by the syntactic function and is thus, by definition, the head of the phrase.

The demonstrative pronouns, the numerals, and certain indefinite pronouns expressing an approximate number (e.g. *moaddę* ' a couple') stand in partial congruence with the noun. In constructions with numerals higher than '1' and those with indefinite pronouns like *moaddę*, the head (in italics in Table 2.9) is the numeral or pronoun in the nominative singular and the noun in the rest of the cases.

The constructions with the relative interrogative pronouns *mii* 'which' and *gii* 'who' behave in a similar manner but here the noun is the modifier in the nominative plural (formally: the accusative plural), as well.

There are also a restricted number of modifiers which are placed after the head. Especially common is the relative clause, which is connected to its correlate by the relative pronouns *mii* 'which', *gii* 'who', *goabbá* 'which

Table 2.9   Sample noun phrases, illustrating distribution of case and number

	Singular 'this house'	Plural 'these houses'	Singular 'three houses'	Plural 'three pairs of skis'
N	*dát* dállu	dát *dálut*	*golbma* dálu	golmmat *sabehat*
G	dán *dálu*	dáid *dálūid*	golmma *dálu*	golmmaid *sabehiid*
A	dán *dálu*	dáid *dálūid*	golbma *dálu*	golmmaid *sabehiid*
Ill	dán *dállui*	dáidda *dálūide*	golmma *dállui*	golmmaide *sabehiiddą*
Loc	dán *dálus*	dáin *dálūin*	golmma *dálus*	golmmain *sabehiin*
Com	dáinna *dálūin*	dáiguin *dálūiguin*	golmmain *dálūin*	golmmaiguin *sabehiiguin*
Ess		dánin *dállun*	golbman *dállun*	(not used)

Note: Also, sN *moaddę* dálu 'a couple of houses', sG moatti *dálu*, sA moaddę *dálu*, sIll moatti *dállui*, etc., like *golbma* dálu.

Table 2.10   Noun phrases with relative/interrogative pronouns

	Singular 'which house'	Plural 'which houses'	Singular 'which priest'	Plural 'which priests'
N	*mii* dálūid	*mat* dálūid	*gii* báhpaid	*geat* báhpaid
G	man *dálu*	maid *dálūid*	gean *báhpa*	geaid *báhpaid*
A	man *dálu* (maid *dálūid*)	maid *dálūid*	gean *báhpa*	geaid *báhpaid*
Ill	man *dállui*	maiddA *dálūide*	gean *báhppii*	geaiddạ *báhpaide*
Loc	man *dálus*	main *dálūin*	gean *báhpas*	geain *báhpain*
Com	mainna *dálūin*	maiguin *dálūiguin*	geainna *báhpain*	geaiguin *báhpaiguin*
Ess	manin *dállun*		geanin *báhppan*	

(of two)', *guhte* 'who', and *guhtemuš* 'which (of a specific set)', e.g. *dat olbmot, mat manne sisa* 'those people who went in' (*mat* pN of *mii*); *dat vielppis, goabbá lea stuorit* 'the one of the two puppies that is bigger'. Among other post-modifiers are the infinitive (*mūs ii leat dilli **vuordit*** 'I do not have time **to wait**'), postpositional constructions (*dat lea muitalus ovtta nieidda **birra*** 'it is a story **about** a girl'), the partitive locative (*mun dovddan ovtta dū vieljain* 'I know one **of your brothers**'), and probably also specifier nouns agreeing with their head in case (*mūs lea okta gilo **vuodja*** PROs1.loc IS.s3pres ONE. sN KILO.sN BUTTER.sN 'I have a kilo of **butter**').

Negation
The negative verb is combined with the connegatives to express negation in the present tense. The negative verb has the same form for indicative, conditional, and potential, and the main verb carries the mood marker (indicative is zero). Examples of the indicative: *it boaḍẹ* 'you do not come', *it leat* 'you are not'. Conditional: *it boaḍáše* 'you would not come', *it livčče* 'you would not be'. Potential: *it bōḍeš* 'you may not come', *it leačča* 'you may not be'. In the imperative, the mood marker is encoded in the negative verb: *alẹ boaḍẹ* 'do not come', *alẹ leagẹ* 'do not be'. The second imperative, itself a connegative, is used with third-person forms of the negative verb: *allos bōhto* 'let him/her not come', *alloset bōhto* 'let them not come', *allos lēhko* 'let him/her not be'. The indicative past is expressed by the main verb in the perfect participle: *it boahtán* 'you did not come', *it lean ~ it leamaš ~ it leamašlean ~ it leamašan* 'you were not'. The compound tenses are negated in a manner analogical to that of the copula: *it leat boahtán* 'you have not come', *it lean boahtán* 'you had not come', *it livčče boahtán* 'you would not have come', etc.

   Negation normally concerns the verb constituent and has therefore the entire sentence as its scope. There are, however, ways to narrow the scope down to a single constituent: *mun ožžon dan, in fal Niillasis, muhto Iŋggás* 'I got it not from Nils but from Inga'. In participial and infinitival constructions, the matrix verb will be negated even though the scope of the negation is the embedded sentence: *dat ii lohkan bierggu nohkat* 'he said that meat does not run out' (*ii lohkan* 'did not say', *bierggu* 'meat sA', *nohkat* 'to run out, to be finished').

Participial and Infinitival Constructions

Embedded sentences can be represented by constructions with the embedded verb in a non-finite form. The action essive is used with verbs of direct observation to indicate the present tense, e.g. *dat ōinnii báhpa boahtimen* '(s)he saw the clergyman coming'. With other verbs, the infinitive is used for the same purpose, e.g. *dat jáhkká báhpa diehtit vástádusa* '(s)he believes that the clergyman knows the answer, (s)he believes the clergyman to know the answer'. The past tense of the embedded sentence is expressed by the perfect participle, e.g. *dat ōinnii báhpa boahtán* '(s)he saw that the clergyman had come', *dat jáhkká báhpa diehtán vástádusa* '(s)he believes that the clergyman knew the answer, (s)he believes the clergyman to have known the answer'.

The nominative subject and nominative predicate of an unembedded sentence go into the accusative case when their constituents are embedded: *Joavnna logai daid olbmuid* (S; pA) *leat čeavláid* (PR; pA) 'John said that those people are haughty', contrast unembedded *dat olbmot* (S; pN) *leat čeavlát* (PR; pN) 'Those people are haughty'. If the subject of the embedded sentence is co-referential with the subject of the matrix sentence, it is replaced by the reflexive pronoun (*iehča-*) in these constructions, e.g. *Joavnna logai iežas diehtán vástádusa* 'John said that **he** (= John) knew the answer'.

Co-ordination and Subordination of Sentences

The co-ordinating conjunctions, all from or via Fennic, are *ja* 'and', *sihke — ja* '(X) as well as (Y)', *juogo — dahje* 'either X or Y', *vai* 'or (in questions)', *muhto* 'but'. Examples: *válddE gáffala ja niibbi* 'take a fork and a knife', *daga dola ja vuošša gáfe* 'make a fire and make some coffee', *boahtágo eadni vai áhčči* 'will father or mother come?', *mun čurvon, muhto don it gullan* 'I shouted, but you didn't hear'. In negated cases, co-ordination can also be expressed with the enclitic *--ge* attached to the negative verb, e.g. *mun in leat oaidnán inge gullan* 'I haven't seen or heard'.

Subordination can be expressed with a number of conjunctions: *ahte* 'that' (< Finnish *että*), *go* 'when, that' (< Finnish *kun*), *goas* 'when' (< Finnish *konsa*), *juos* (cf. Finnish *jos*), *vai ~ vuoi* 'in order to', *amas* (in some dialects) 'lest, in order that not', *vaikko* 'even though' (< Finnish *vaikka*). Subordinated sentences can have many different functions, e.g. subject: *buorre lei, go bōhtet* 'it was good that you came'; object: *mun diedán, ahte Niillas boahtá* 'I know that Nils is coming'; adverbial: *mun boadán, go don dáhtut* 'I shall come when you ask (me to do so)'. Indirect questions are subordinated as subjects (*ii leat čielggas, boahtágo Niilas* 'it isn't clear whether Nils will come') or objects (*mun in diede, boahtágo Niilas* 'I don't know whether Nils will come').

In subordinated reported speech, the pronouns for the first person are replaced by those of the third, e.g. *dat logai, ahte son áigu njuovvat sávzza* '(s)he said that (s)he will butcher a sheep', *dat logai munnje, ahte soai vuolgiba bajás joga* '(s)he said to me that we (*soai* 'they [dual]') would go up river'. Reported speech is often indicated by the particles *gul* (indicating citation of someone else's statement, e.g. *logai, ahte son ii gul dieđe* '[s]he said that [s]he does not know') or, rarely and in the eastern dialects only, *jat* (indicating citation of one's own statement).

Lexicon

The North Saami lexicon is expanding rapidly as a result of more or less conscious development. Because of the large number of word stems and the rich system of word formation, new words are based mostly on traditional stems and endings, often replacing even recent loanwords. Thus the neologism *dáidda* 'art' (based on *dáidu* 'knowing how') has supplanted the Scandinavian loan *koansta* (from Swedish *konst*), used as late as the 1980s and practically the only word for this concept in the 1970s. The largest North Saami dictionary to date contains about 35,000 entries and is far from exhaustive.

Of the traditional vocabulary, slightly fewer than 600 words have cognates in other Uralic languages. Of these, approximately 100 date from proto-Uralic, e.g. *vuoni* 'mother-in-law', *vuohppa* 'father-in-law', *goaski* 'senior maternal aunt', *čeahci* 'younger paternal uncle', *mannji* 'daughter-in-law', *gálojeatni* 'sister-in-law', *nađđa* 'shaft', *suhkat* 'to row'.

About 160 words date from pFU, e.g. *eahki* 'senior paternal uncle', *vuovdit* 'to sell', *áhčči* 'father' (augmented from proto-Saami *ăčʲē > Kildin аджь), *vuodjit* 'to drive', *lohkat* 'to count', *liepma* 'broth', *njuovvat* 'to flay'. About 60 words may be ascribed to the Finno-Permian phase, e.g. *áddjá* 'grandfather', *astat* 'to have time', *juohkit* 'to divide', *gáma* 'shoe', *gođđit* 'to knit', *boazu* 'reindeer', *boarti* 'bark vessel'; roughly another 60 words have cognates in the Volgaic languages, e.g. *máksit* 'to pay', *gahčat* 'to ask', *gealdit* 'to draw (bow), to cock (trigger)', *mealli* 'rudder', *sadjit* 'to hone', *fanas* 'boat'.

Finally, Saami shares about 200 words with Fennic, e.g. *áhkku* 'grandmother', *čiehkat* 'to hide', *juoigat* 'to sing in the Saami way', *gal'let* 'to visit' *gietkka* 'cradle', *viellja* 'brother', *vuordnut* 'to take an oath', *joddu* 'net', *geaidnu* 'way', *goarrut* 'to sew', *lávži* 'rein', *lohti* 'wedge', *bassat* 'to wash', *seakti* 'bait', *dohppa* 'sheath'.

Alongside old inherited vocabulary there are about 800 common Saami word stems, over 600 of which are without etymology, e.g. *atnit* 'to use', *bivvat* 'to keep warm', *coagis* 'shallow', *časkit* 'to strike', *čáhppat* 'black', *čiekčat* 'to kick', *dálkkas* 'medicine', *garvit* 'to dodge', *gáhččat* 'to hurry', *heavdni* 'spider', *jalŋŋis* 'tree stump', *jorrat* 'to spin', *láhppit* 'to lose', *mánná* 'child', *nagir* 'sleep', *njivli* 'slime', *ohca* 'bosom', *oakti* 'rain shower', *ravgat* 'to fall', *sarrit* 'blackberry', *šiehttat* 'to make an agreement', *uhcci* 'small', *váldit* 'to take'. About 100 of the 800 are Scandinavian or Germanic loanwords, e.g. *áiru* 'oar', *bárru* 'wave', *dápmat* 'to tame', *gáica* 'goat', *eallju* 'zeal', *gussa* 'cow', *luovOs* 'loose', *mánnu* 'moon', *návli* 'nail', *riekkis* 'ring', *sávza* 'sheep', *vievssis* 'wasp', and about 150 are borrowed from Finnish, e.g. *áigi* 'time', *báiki* 'place', *dávda* illness', *easka* 'recently', *giitit* 'to thank', *ihtit* 'to appear', *joavdat* 'to arrive', *lávlut* 'to sing', *mearra* 'sea', *neav'vu* 'advice', *oahppat* 'to learn', *reahkut* 'to howl', *suhttat* 'get angry', *šaddat* 'to be born', *vašši* 'hatred'.

In addition to the bulk of Scandinavian and Finnish loanwords (there are several thousands of each), there are the following layers of borrowings:

1   Old Indo-European loanwords shared with several, mostly western Finno-Ugric languages. There are about twenty of these, e.g. *oarbbis* 'orphan', *čoarvi* 'horn', *čohkut* 'to comb', *čuohti* 'hundred', *veahčir* 'hammer', *goahti* 'hut, teepee, tent', *dahkat* 'to do', *geassi* 'summer'.

2   Baltic loanwords, shared mainly with Fennic. There are over twenty of these; examples are *leaibi* 'alder', *suolu* 'island', *luokta* 'bay', *jávri* 'lake', *luossa* 'salmon', *guoibmi* 'companion', *vuos'si* 'pot handle', *lasta* 'leaf'. Some are not shared with Finnish, e.g. South Saami *saertie* 'heart (as food)', indicating that there were also direct contacts with Baltic speakers.

3   Old Germanic loanwords shared mainly with Fennic. There are more than twenty, e.g. *gierdat* 'to endure', *bassi* 'sacred', *soallut* 'to pick one's teeth', *buoidi* 'fat', *roavgu* 'skin rug', *ruovdi* 'iron', *guos'si* 'guest', *vuotta* 'shoelace', *lahttu* 'member'. Some independent loans (e.g. *luoikat* 'to borrow') indicate direct contacts with Germanic-speaking populations.

4   Russian loanwords. There are hundreds of recent Russian loans in Skolt, Kildin, Akkala, and Ter. Some Russian words have spread, via Finnish and Karelian, further west, e.g. *dárru* 'Norwegian', *rádji* 'border', and *gistta* 'glove' have found their way down to South Saami. In addition, North Saami has the following words of Russian origin: *šávká* 'cap', *spīre* 'beast of prey (< зверь)', *iskat* 'to try', *šibit* 'domestic animal', *ohpit* 'again'.

From among the textually most frequent 100 words in North Saami (comprising about 60 per cent of the spoken-language texts in the corpus measured) 11 words (i.e. 3 per cent) do not have an etymology outside Saami, e.g. *boahtit* 'to come', *buot* 'all', *váldit* 'to take', *bidjat* 'to put', *orrut* 'to dwell'. Over 40 per cent of the word stems in the texts was covered by those most common core words which have an etymology connecting them with other Uralic languages (52 in number, e.g. the negative verb, the personal pronouns, nouns like *áhčči* 'father', *bealli* 'half', *eallu* 'herd', *beana* 'dog', *olmmoš* 'human being', *siida* 'village', and verbs like *galgat* 'to have to', *vuolgit* 'to leave', *gullat* 'to hear', *eallit* 'to live'). There were 37 loanwords among the top 100 words, comprising 14 per cent of the texts in the corpus, e.g. *ja* 'and', *ahte* 'that', *vel* 'still', *áigi* 'time', *juo* 'already' from Finnish, *lávet* 'to have the habit of' from Scandinavian. Some items of the core vocabulary which were thought to have no etymologies have recently been shown to be Germanic loans, e.g. *oaidnit* 'to see', *gávdnat* 'to find', perhaps also *váldit* 'to take'. In any event, the 600 or so word stems shared with other Uralic languages still bulk largest in any Saami text.

North Saami Text
From Hans Aslak Guttorm: *Iešnjárgga šiljut.*

A: text in standard orthography, segmented; B: morpheme-by-morpheme gloss; C: English translation.

A1. beatnaga-t--ge	bahkke=st-edje		veagal
B1. DOG-pN--ENC	FORCES.ONE'S.WAY=SUBIT-p3past		FORCIBLY

olbmu-i-d	julgg-i-id	gaskka	vistá-i.
PERSON-plur-gen	LEG-plur-gen	BETWEEN	HOUSE-sIll

A2. Lemet	doabu-i	beatnagi-i-d	ma-n
B2. *CLEMENT*	GRABS-s3past	DOG-plur-acc	WHICH.ONE-sA

niská-i,	ma-n	seaibá-i	fáhti-i	ja
NECK-sIll	WHICH.ONE-sA	TAIL-sIll	CATCHES-s3past	AND

bálkesti-i	uksa+lanja	olggos.	A3. beana	lienju-i
THROWS-s3past	DOOR+CHINK.sG	OUT	B3. DOG	WHINES-s3past

go	Lemet	čeabehi-i		čárvi-i.
WHEN	*CLEMENT*	*NECK/THROAT*-sIll		SQUEEZES-s3past

C1. The dogs, too, forced their way between people's legs into the house. C2. Clement grabbed the dogs, caught one by the neck, the other by the tail and threw them out of the door. C3. The dog whined when Clement grabbed its throat.

References and Further Reading
Abercromby, J. (1895) 'The earliest list of Russian Lapp Words', *JSFOu* 13/2: 1–10.
Äimä, F. (1918) *Phonetik und Lautlehre des Inarilappischen*, vols I–II, MSFOu 42, 43, Helsinki: Société Finno-Ougrienne.
Bartens, H.-H. (1980) *Die Verwendung von Potential und Konditional im Lappischen*, MSFOu 177, Helsinki: Société Finno-Ougrienne.
Bartens, R. (1971) 'Zur Kongruenz des lappischen Adjektivattributs', *FUF* 39: 31–40.

—— (1972) *Inarinlapin, merilapin ja luulajanlapin kaasussyntaksi*, MSFOu 148, Helsinki: Société Finno-Ougrienne.

—— (1978) *Synteettiset ja analyyttiset rakenteet lapin paikanilmauksissa*, MSFOu 166, Helsinki: Société Finno-Ougrienne.

Bergsland, Kn. (1945) 'L'alternance consonantique date-t-elle du lapon commun?', *Studia septentrionalia* 2: 1–53.

—— (1946) *Røros-lappisk grammatikk*, Series B43, Oslo: Instituttet for sammenlignende kulturforskning.

—— (1962) 'The Lapp dialects south of Lappland', in *Commentationes Fenno-Ugricae in Honorem Paavo Ravila*, MSFOu 125, Helsinki: Société Finno-Ougrienne, pp. 27–39.

—— (1967) 'Lapp Dialectal Groups and Problems of History', *Lapps and Norsemen in Olden Times*, Series A26, Oslo: Instituttet for sammenlignende kulturforskning, pp. 32–53.

—— (1968) 'The Grouping of Lapp Dialects as a Problem of Historical Linguistics', in *C2IFU* vol. I, Helsinki: pp. 77–85.

—— (1973) 'Simplification of the Finno-Ugric Transcription: Lapp', in L. Posti and T. Itkonen (eds), *FU-transkription yksinkertaistaminen*, Castrenianumin toimitteita 7, Helsinki: Castrenianum, pp. 45–67.

Collinder, Bj. (1938) *Lautlehre des waldlappischen Dialekts von Gällivare*, MSFOu 74, Helsinki: Société Finno-Ougrienne.

—— (1949) *The Lappish dialect of Jukkasjärvi*, Skrifter utgivna av K. Humanistika Vetenskaps-Samfundet i Uppsala 37/3, Uppsala: K. Humanistika Vetenskaps-Samfundet i Uppsala.

Genetz, A. (1891) *Kuollan Lapin murteiden sanakirja ynnä kielennäytteitä*, Bidrag till kännedom af Finlands natur och folk, Utgivna av Finska Vetenskaps Societeten 50, Helsingfors: Finska Vetenskaps-Societeten.

Grundström, H. (1946–54) *Lulelappisches Wörterbuch*, auf Grund von K. B. Wiklunds, Björn Collinders und eigenen Aufzeichnungen ausgearbeitet von Harald Grundström, Series C1, Schriften des Instituts für Mundarten und Volkskunde in Uppsala, Uppsala: Instituts für Mundarten und Volkskunde.

Halász, I. (1885–96) *Svéd-lapp nyelv*, vols I–IV, Budapest: Ugor füzetek.

Hansegård, N. E. (1965) 'Sea Lappish and Mountain Lappish', *JSFOu* 66/6: 1–91.

—— (1967) *Recent Finnish Loanwords in Jukkasjärvi Lappish*, Acta Universitatis Upsaliensis, Studia Uralica et Altaica Upsaliensia 3, Uppsala: University of Uppsala.

Hasselbrink, G. (1965) *Alternative Analyses of the Phonemic Systems in Central South-Lappish*, Indiana University Uralic and Altaic Series 49, Bloomington: Indiana University.

—— (1981–85) *Südlappisches Wörterbuch*, vols I–III, Schriften des Instituts für Mundarten und Volkskunde in Uppsala, Series C4, Uppsala: Instituts für Mundarten und Volkskunde.

Itkonen, E. (1939) *Der ostlappische Vokalismus vom qualitativen Standpunkt aus mit besonderer Berüksichtigung des Inari- und Skoltlappischen*, MSFOu 79, Helsinki: Société Finno-Ougrienne.

—— (1946) *Struktur und Entwicklung der ostlappischen Quantitätssyteme*, MSFOu 88, Helsinki: Société Finno-Ougrienne.

—— (1949) 'Beiträge zur Geschichte der einsilbigen Wortstämme im Finnischen', *FUF* 30: 1–54.

—— (1954) 'Über die suffixalen Labialvokale im Lappischen und Ostseefinnischen', in *Scandinavica et Fenno-Ugrica, Studier tillägnade Björn Collinder den 22 juli 1954*, Stockholm: Almqvist & Wiksell, pp. 183–91.

—— (1960) *Lappische Chrestomathie mit grammatikalischem Abriss und Wörterverzeichnis*, Apuneuvoja suomalais-ugrilaisten kielten opintoja varten 7, Helsinki.

—— (1968) 'Zur Frühgeschichte der lappischen und finnischen Lokalkasus', in *C2IFU* vol. I, pp. 202–11.

—— (1969) 'Über einige Formen der dritten Person in der lappischen Konjugation', *FUF* 37: 98–117.

—— (1972) 'Über das Objekt in den finnisch-wolgaischen Sprachen', *FUF* 39: 153–213.

—— (1973) 'Zur Geschichte des Partitivs', *FUF* 40: 278–339.

—— (1986–91) *Inarilappisches Wörterbuch*, vols I–IV, Lexica Societatis Fenno-Ugricae 20, Helsinki: Société Finno-Ougrienne.

Itkonen, T. I. (1958) *Koltan- ja kuolanlapin sanakirja*, vols I–II, Lexica Societatis Fenno-Ugricae 15, Helsinki: Société Finno-Ougrienne.

Itkonen, T. (1973) 'Lisiä erään lapin vokaaliston ongelmaan', in *Commentationes Fenno-Ugricae in Honorem Erkki Itkonen*, MSFOu 150, Helsinki: Société Finno-Ougrienne, pp. 75–120, German summary pp. 120–24.

Koivulehto, J. (1992) 'Germanisch-lappische Lehnbeziehungen', in L. Honti, S.-L. Hahmo, T. Hofstra, J. Jastrzebska, and O. Nikkilä (eds), *Finnisch-ugrische Sprachen zwischen dem germanischen und dem slavischen Sprachraum*, Amsterdam – Atlanta, GA: Rodopi, pp. 55–95.

Korhonen, M. (1967) *Die Konjugation im Lappischen, Morphologisch-historische Untersuchung*, vol. I: *Die finiten Formkategorien*, MSFOu 143, Helsinki: Société Finno-Ougrienne.

—— (1969) 'Die Entwicklung der morphologischen Methode im Lappischen', *FUF* 37: 203–362.

—— (1974) *Die Konjugation im Lappischen, Morphologisch-historische Untersuchung*, vol. II: *Die nominalen Formkategorien*, MSFOu 155, Helsinki: Société Finno-Ougrienne.

—— (1981) *Johdatus lapin kielen historiaan*, Helsinki: Suomalaisen Kirjallisuuden Seura.

Kuruč, Rimma (1985) (ed.), Саамско-русский сиоварь, Moscow: Russkij Äzyk.

Lagercrantz, E. (1923) *Sprachlehre des Südlappischen nach der Mundart von Wefsen*, Bulletin 1, Kristiania: Kristiania Etnografiske Museum.

—— (1926) *Sprachlehre des Westlappischen nach der Mundart von Arjeplog*, MSFOu 55, Helsinki: Société Finno-Ougrienne.

—— (1929) *Sprachlehre des Nordlappischen nach den seelappischen Mundarten*, Bulletin 3, Oslo: Oslo Etnografiske Museum.

—— (1939) *Lappischer Wortschatz*, vols I–II, Lexica Societatis Fenno-Ugricae 6, Helsinki: Société Finno-Ougrienne.

Lehtiranta, J. (1989) *Yhteissaamelainen sanasto*, MSFOu 200, Helsinki: Société Finno-Ougrienne.

Nesheim, A. (1942) *Der lappische Dualis mit Berücksichtigung finnisch-ugrischer und indo-europäischer Verhältnisse*, Oslo: Norwegian Academy of Sciences.

Nickel, K. P. (1990) *Samisk grammatikk*, Berlings: Universitetsforlaget.

Nielsen, K. (1932–62) Lappisk ordbok – Lapp Dictionary, vols I–IV, B17, Oslo: Instituttet for sammenlignende kulturforskning.

Posti, L. (1953) 'From Pre-Finnic to Late proto-Finnic', *FUF* 31: 1–91.

Qvigstad, J. K. (1893) *Nordische Lehnwörter im Lappischen*, Christiania Videnskabs-Selskabs Forhandlingar for 1893 no. 1, Oslo: Christiana Videnskabs-Selskab.

Ravila, P. (1932) *Das Quantitätssystem des seelappischen Dialekts von Maattivuono*, MSFOu 62, Helsinki: Société Finno-Ougrienne.

Ruong, I. (1943) *Lappische Verbalableitung dargestellt auf Grundlage des*

Pitelappischen, Uppsala Universitets Årskrift 1943, 10, Uppsala: University of Uppsala.

Sammallahti, P. (1977) *Norjansaamen Itä-Enontekiön murteen äänneoppi*, MSFOu 160, Helsinki: Société Finno-Ougrienne.

────── (1984) 'The Phonology of the Guovdageaidnu Dialect of North Saami', in B. Brendemoen, E. Hovdhaugen, and O. H. Magga (eds) *Riepmočála: Essays in Honour of Knut Bergsland. Presented on the Occasion of his Seventieth Birthday*, Oslo: Norvus Forlag, pp. 136–47.

────── (1989a) *Sámi-suoma sátnegirji. Saamelais-suomalainen sanakirja*, Ohcejohka: Jorgaleaddji.

────── (1989b) 'A linguist looks at Saami Prehistory', *Acta Borealia* 2: 3–11.

Sammallahti, P., and J. Mosnikoff (1991) *Suomi-koltansaame sanakirja. Lää'ddsää'm sää'nke'rjj*, Ohcejohka: Girjegiisá.

Schlachter, W. (1958) *Wörterbuch des Waldlappendialekts von Malå und Texte zur Ethnographie*, Helsinki: Lexica Societatis Fenno-Ugricae 14.

Sköld, T. (1961) *Die Kriterien der urnordischen Lehnwörter im Lappischen*, vol. I, Skrifter utgivna av institutionen für Nordiska språk vid Uppsala universitet 8, Stockholm: Almquist & Wiksell.

Wiklund, K. B. (1891) *Laut- und Formenlehre der Lule-Lappischen Dialekte*, Göteborgs Kongl. Vetenskaps och Vitterhets Samhälles Handlingar, Ny Tidsföljd 25, Stockholm: Göteborgs Kongl. Vetenskaps och Vitterhets Samhälles.

3 Fennic

Tiit-Rein Viitso

The Fennic branch of the Uralic family is a dialect continuum that is usually divided into seven languages: Livonian, Estonian, Votic, Ingrian, Finnish, Karelian and Veps. A Lude language has sometimes been extracted from Karelian as an eighth language, but Ludes identify themselves as Karelians. Estonian (one million speakers) and Finnish (five million speakers) are discussed in separate chapters in this volume. The remaining Fennic languages have become languages of bilingual minorities in their traditional territories; they are Votic (25 speakers), Ingrian (300 speakers), Karelian (62,500 speakers) and Veps (6,000 speakers) in Northwest Russia, and Livonian (15 native speakers) in Latvia.

Livonian

Livonian (*liivõ keel*^{j}, *raandakeel*^{j} 'coast language'), as spoken in Kurland, is relatively homogenous. Three dialects, West, Central and East Livonian, differ from each other only slightly. The poorly attested dialect of historical Livonia, spoken to the north of the lower reaches of Daugava River, became extinct in the nineteenth century.

There has been literature in Livonian since the translation of the Gospel according to Matthew into Western and Eastern Livonian in 1863 and the publication of the same gospel in a Central-and-Eastern Livonian compromise language in 1880. In the 1920s a new orthography was elaborated. The Livonian literary language was annihilated with the Soviet occupation of Latvia. Most Livonians were forced to leave their homeland (Līvõd Rānda); they now live scattered among other nations. Not until 1989 were a few booklets published once again in Livonian and efforts begun to revive the language.

Livonian is the most innovative Fennic language. The chief characteristic features of Livonian are:

Two distinctive lexical tones: the level tone and the glottalized/laryngealized one (or *stød*; often from *h; indicated in this chapter as $^+$);

Gradation of both historically long and short stressed syllables with short vocalism;

Long and short falling diphthongs ùo: ^{u}o, ìe: ^{i}e;

Map 3.1   Fennic: North/South and East/West Divisions

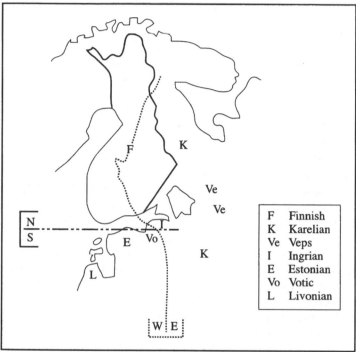

F	Finnish
K	Karelian
Ve	Veps
I	Ingrian
E	Estonian
Vo	Votic
L	Livonian

Source: Adapted from Itkonen 1980.7, as reproduced in Szíj 1990: 154.

Rising diphthongs and triphthongs that can occur in up to five tone and
quantity patterns, e.g. $k^u o^i g i_D$ 'ships', $k^u o^+ i g \partial$ 'ship (sP)', $l^u o i m \partial$ 'warp
(sP)', $t u^+ o i g \partial z$ 'birchbark', *lùoima* 'warp (sNG)', $a^i g à$ 'edge (sNG)', $a^+ i g \partial$
'edge (sP)', $a i g \partial$ 'time, weather (sP), *àiga* 'time, weather (sNG)', $l \varrho^+ \varrho i g i$
'asunder';
Delabialization of the p[roto-]F[ennic] labial front vowels;
Reminiscences of metaphony;
The contrastive behaviour of bisyllabic *à-* and *a*-stems vis-à-vis *ù-*, *ì-* and
∂-stems in inflectional paradigms;
The dative case;
Near-complete loss of the external local cases.

Estonian

Estonian (*eesti keel*, older style: *maakeel*) is spoken mainly in Estonia.
Translations of scripture into Estonian date from 1535. Alongside the North
Estonian literary language (formerly called the Tallinn language) the South
Estonian literary language (the Tartu language) was used in Southeast Estonia

from the first half of the seventeenth up to the second half of the nineteenth century; the degeneration of the Tartu language began with the publication of the Bible in North Estonian in 1739.

Estonian dialects are usually classified into three main groups: (1) Northeastern coastal dialect, (2) North Estonian (consisting of the Insular, Western, Central and Eastern dialects), (3) South Estonian (including the Mulgi, Tartu, and Võru dialects). This classification, however, is incompatible with data from the other Fennic languages; accordingly, a classification into five main groups is to be preferred: (1) Coastal, (2) Northeast, (3) East, (4) North and (5) South Estonian. With the exception of the Coastal and Northeast groups, all Estonian dialects contrast three syllabic quantities in stressed syllables. The North Estonian literary dialect has assimilated and superseded almost all other Estonian dialects.

Coastal Estonian, spoken on the southern coast of the Gulf of Finland, was originally closer to the Finnish dialects than to any other dialect group of Estonian. Coastal Estonian never had the back unrounded vowel *ë*.

Northeast and East Estonian, together with Votic proper, stem from one protodialect; they share the merger *o > *ë in about twenty stems and the assimilation *st > ss; Northeast Estonian has been influenced by Coastal and, later, by North Estonian. East Estonian was influenced first by South and later by North Estonian.

South Estonian probably split directly from proto-Fennic. In some cases it has retained pF (and even proto-Uralic) *cʲ, e.g. *latʲsʲ* 'child' < *lapcʲi, *katʲsʲ* 'two' (< *kakcʲi < *kakti), *küüɒʲzʲ* 'nail, claw'. On the other hand, it has undergone the characteristic changes *kti > *kcʲi > *tʲsʲi, *kt > *tt after the vowel of the first syllable.

Votic

Votic (*vadʲdʲaa čeeli, maačeeli*) is presently spoken in coastal villages of Vaipooli, Northwest Ingermanland, east of the mouth of the Luga River. Vaipooli Votic was the westernmost dialect of Votic proper. Votic proper has usually been divided into West and East Votic. West Votic was a dialect chain (Vaipooli, Pontizõõ, Mäči, Orko) characterized by loss of word-final -ɢ (< *-k) and -h, which were still retained in East Votic; on the other hand, West Votic had preserved word-final -n in the first-person singular suffix of the verb (similarly to non-South Estonian), whereas in East Votic the loss of -n was total (as in South Estonian and Livonian). Other dialects of Votic were Kukkuzi on the eastern bank of the Luga River, which became extinct in the 1980s, and Krevin. The Krevin dialect was spoken by descendants of Votic war prisoners who were moved to the vicinity of Bauska, Latvia, about 1445 by the Teutonic Order. Krevin became extinct in the nineteenth century and is very poorly attested. There was never a Votic scripture.

Votic proper probably separated from East and Northeast Estonian around

1000 CE. In Votic proper, pF *k has gone to *č before front vowels.

Kukkuzi Votic never had the vowel *ë. On the other hand, both Votic proper and Kukkuzi have merged *ps and *ks into *hs* ~ *hz* and, similarly to Northeast and East Estonian, have assimilated *st to an *ss which is susceptible to gradation (*ss* ~ *s*) in .Votic proper and Kukkuzi. Kukkuzi Votic was originally a North Fennic dialect that was first influenced by Votic proper and later by Lower Luga Ingrian.

Ingrian

Ingrian, or Izhor (*ižoran keeli*, earlier also *karjalan keeli*) may have had five dialects resulting from dialect split, with the possible exception of Lower Luga Ingrian, which may well have developed on the basis of a Votic proper or Kukkuzi Votic substratum. Lower Luga Ingrian is spoken along the Rosona River in Estonian Ingermanland (still annexed by Russia) and on both banks of the lower reaches of the Luga River; Soikkola Ingrian is spoken on the Sojkino peninsula; Hevaha Ingrian is spoken in the vicinity of the Koltuši River. The Upper Luga, or Oredež, dialect, spoken inland, became extinct in the 1970s. The North Ingrian that was spoken by the Orthodox population north of the Gulf of Finland has been Fennicized and probably served as the substratum for the Äyrämöinen dialect, traditionally classified as a form of Southeast Finnish. An attempt to create an Ingrian literary language was made in 1932–7.

Finnish

Finnish (*suomen kieli*) is spoken mainly in Finland, Sweden, and Ingermanland.

Finnish dialects have been traditionally classified into West Finnish (Southwest Finnish, Southern Transitional, Häme, South Pohjanmaa, Central and North Pohjanmaa, Deep North) and East Finnish (Savo and Southeast Finnish). This classification seems somewhat oversimplified: West and Southeast Finnish as groups are too heterogeneous and should rather be divided into separate groups.

Karelian

Karelian consists of North (or Viena), South, Aunus (or Olonec) and Lude Karelian.

North Karelian is spoken in North Karelia. South Karelian is a scattered set of dialects, some few of which are spoken in Karelia, but most of which are spoken in outlying parts of the Tver', St Petersburg and Novgorod regions of Russia, to which Karelians moved after 1617. The outlying regions are Tihvinä, Vessi (Ves'egonsk), Valdai, Tolmaččuu, and Djorža. Aunus (Karelian), called *livvin kieli*, is spoken in Southwest Karelia. Lude (Karelian), called *l^jüüd^jin kiel^ji*, is spoken in Karelia in a strip east of Aunus and South Karelian. Lude is a dialect chain that can be divided into North, Central, and Kuudärv dialects.

North and South Karelian (*karjalan kieli*) are often called Karelian proper. North Karelian, however, is in fact more properly a dialect close to East Finnish which has undergone strong South Karelian influence. Similarly, Aunus and Lude are dialects that were first close to Veps but later have undergone different degrees of South Karelian influence. In any case, Kuudärv Lude has remained closest to Veps.

The first written document in Karelian is a spell from the eleventh century, written on birchbark and found in Novgorod. Attempts to create Karelian scripture date from the nineteenth century. In 1804 books containing St Matthew's gospel and some Orthodox prayers were published in both South and Aunus Karelian. In 1820 a St Matthew' for Tver' Karelians was published. Until the October Revolution, mostly Orthodox literature and a few primers were published. Under Soviet power Karelians in Karelia were first taught the Finnish literary language. In 1931–7 a new literary language based on the Tolmaččú dialect was created for Karelians of the Tver' region; this used Latin script. In 1938–9 in both Karelia and the Tver' region a new variant of Karelian was introduced: this was a mixture of South and Aunus Karelian and used Cyrillic script. A massive Russification of Karelians as well as of other small peoples began after 1940; since 1989, attempts to revive different Karelian dialects have been made in Karelia. A primer and some other school books have been prepared in Aunus Karelian. Some South and Lude Karelian has been taught at some schools although there are no school books. A project of creating a literary language for North Karelians has even been started and a primer has been printed despite the closeness of North Karelian to Finnish.

Veps

Veps is the easternmost Fennic language. It is spoken in two different areas: (1) on the southwestern coast of Lake Onega in Karelia and (2) in the northeast of the St Petersburg region and the northwest of the Vologda region of Russia. Since 1989 efforts have been made by Vepsians to have the two Veps territories united under their own administration; these efforts have met with resistance on the part of the administration of the St Petersburg region.

Veps has been classified into North, Central, and South Veps. North Veps (*l^jüd^jikel^j*) is the closest to Lude and may have been influenced by its former, now Russianized, Lude neighbours. South Veps and Central Veps (*bepsan kel^j*) make up a dialect continuum in which South Veps is the most innovative dialect and the northern dialects of Central Veps share some features with North Veps and with Lude Karelian. For Central and South Veps, scriptures based on Central Veps existed in 1931–7. In 1991 three books for Veps children, including a primer, were published.

Classification of the Fennic Dialects

The Fennic languages have been considered to be so closely related with the Saamic languages that a common ancestor has been set up for both groups. This putative common ancestor is usually called Early Proto-Fennic rather than the more logical proto-Fennic-Saamic. Fennic and Saamic are doubtless close to one another: they have been neighbours for several millennia; they both have Scandinavians and Russians as their neighbours; there has been a continuous Finnish and Karelian expansion into Saamic territories and at the same time the Saamic languages have been influenced by Fennic. If Saamic and Fennic have split from a proto-Fennic-Saamic, the split is connected with the massive introduction of Baltic and Germanic borrowings into Fennic.

Since the work of E. N. Setälä, the Fennic languages have usually been divided on the basis of their most important dialects into North(east) Fennic (= Finnish, Ingrian, Karelian, Veps) and South(west) Fennic (= Livonian, Estonian, Votic) This classification exploits such innovations as *e > *ë in words with back vocalism and *ns > s in South Fennic. This classification ignores some crucial facts, namely that (1) both Estonian and Votic include dialects, namely Coastal Estonian and Kukkuzi Votic, which should be classified as being of North Fennic origin and (2) unlike North Fennic, which really can be treated as a group, South Fennic is not simply more heterogeneous than North Fennic but rather a blanket term for different non-North-Fennic groups which have formed, over time, various *Sprachbunds* in which North Estonian has usually been the dominating dialect. In short, what can be classified are not the Fennic languages, but the Fennic dialects.

The main linguistic subgroups of Fennic, i.e. Livonian, South Estonian, Maa and North Fennic, can be described in terms of the Stammbaum model, i.e. as resulting from divergence from proto-Fennic, cf. Figure 3.1.

Recent studies have revealed that several important innovations, e.g. *cj >> *s and *s > *h intervocalically after a non-initial syllable, and *š > *h, *ti > *si, which earlier were ascribed to proto-Fennic, in fact occurred after it, but during a period when common innovations were still possible, i.e. in Common Fennic.

Livonian, alongside numerous innovations, also has some important characteristic archaic features. For example, it has preserved (1) the contrast of pF *ktt : *kt via *htt : *ht > ⁺tt : ⁺d as in the partitive and illative singular forms of the numerals *ükti 'one' and *kakti 'two', and (2) the former stem

Figure 3.1   Main historical groupings of Fennic

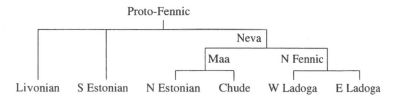

vowel *-a of several nominals that have elsewhere shifted to *e-stems (e.g.
Fennic *jarva/*järve- 'lake' from Baltic, cf. Lithuanian *jaurà*). Livonian is
also the only Fennic language in which there are distinct affirmative and
negative imperative s2 forms of the verb, at least for bisyllabic *a*-stems such
as *anta- 'to give'. Schematically:

	Livonian	S Estonian	N Estonian	Finnish	Veps
1	kǫǫ⁺ttə̂ : kǫǫ⁺də̂	kaìte⁻ : kaȉtè	kaȟt(e) : kaȟte	kahta : kahteen	kaht : kahthe
2	jǫǫra : pN jǫǫrad	järʲvʲ : järv̌e?	jaȓv : jäȓveᴅ	järvi : järvet	dʲärʲv : dʲärʲved
3	aanda : alà aȟd(ə̂)	aȟna? : annᶐi? (< *anna? ei?)	aȟna : ärà aȟna	anna : älä anna?	anda : ala anda

South Estonian has, characteristically, (1) *tʲsʲ* from the pF cluster *pcʲ (as
in *lapcʲi 'child'); (2) *tʲsʲ* < *kcʲ (< *kt before *i), as in *kakcʲi < *kakti '2';
(3) *tt* or *ᴅ* from *kt, when not followed by *i (as in *näktü 'seen' [impersonal
perfect participle]) (4) unmarked present indicative s3 forms instead of forms
ending in *-pi* (e.g. *anta instead of *antapi 'gives'):

	S Estonian	Livonian	N Estonian	Votic	Finnish	Veps
1	latʲsʲ	läp̌š	laȵs	lahsi	lapsi	lapsʲ
2	katʲsʲ	kaȟš	kaȟs	kahsi	kaksi	kaksʲ
3	nättü	nä⁺ädə̂ᴅ	näȟtuᴅ	nähtü	nähtü	nähtu
4	aȟᴅ	aandaʙ	aȟnaʙ	annaʙ	antaa	andab

Dialects of the Neva group have characteristically (1) the diphthong *ei
corresponding to Livonian and South Estonian *ai* in a set of words, e.g. *heinä
v. *haina 'hay'; (2) the vowel *e corresponding to Livonian and South
Estonian *ä in another lexical set, e.g. *selkä v. *sälkä 'back'; (3) *e instead
of *ë in the stem *metsä v. *mëtsa 'forest'; (4) *s* instead of the affricate *cʲ
as a reflex of *t in the earlier sequence *nti, e.g. *künsi v. *küncʲi (both from
*künti) 'nail, claw':

	N Estonian	Votic	Finnish	Veps	Livonian	S Estonian
1	heìn	einä	heinä	hein ~ hiin	àina	haìn
2	seʲlɢ	selčä	selkä	sʲelʲg	säälga	sälɢ
3	meìs	meccä	metsä	mʲets	mëȟsà	mëȉs
4	kü:üz	čüüsi	künsi	kʲünʲzʲ	kiinʲtš	kü:üᴅʲzʲ

The Neva group in turn may be broken down into North Fennic and Maa. North Fennic has several characteristic innovations, e.g. *sesar > *sisar 'sister' (Finnish, Lower Luga Ingrian, North Karelian *sisar*, Soikkola and

Figure 3.2   North Fennic innovations

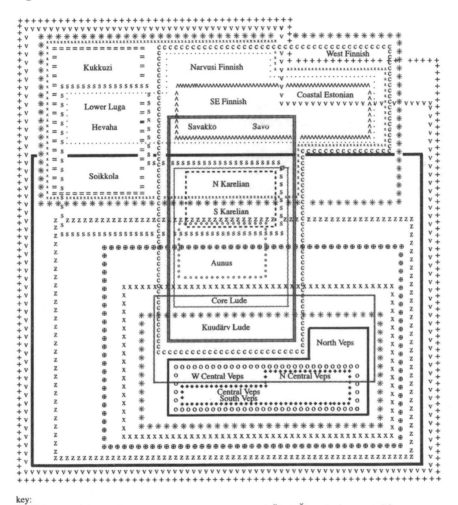

key:

++   *-iten in genitive plural
vv   *e > *ö in nominative of pluralic personal pronouns
* *   (*seppä :) *sepän, *sepä (: *sepän)
xxx   *l̆k *r̆k >> l r in e-stems and in words with front vocalism
cc   breaking of the Proto-Fennic *ō, *ö, *ē
···   *str > tr ~ dr
ʍ   breaking of the secondary *ō and ē from *oko, *eke etc.
≡   breaking of *ā and ǟ
ss   *st > ss in the weak degree
▬   *str > *sr

─   *–p̆i > *–b̆i > –u/–ü in present s3 forms
--   allative ⇒ adessive
zz   *p *t *k *s š > b d g z ž in voiced environments
°°   *l̆k *r̆k >> l l rr
⊞⊞   *is *iz > iš iž; *VisC > VšC
xx   *v > b word-initially
─   *j >dʲ ~ gʲ word-initially and postconsonantally
**   (1) *–bi > –b in present s3 forms; (2) syncopation
─   shortening of *ō *ā *ō̄ *ǟ *ē̄
oo   shortening of *ū *ü *i
♦♦♦   *pp *tt *kk > p t k everywhere

Hevaha Ingrian *sizar*, South, Aunus, and Lude Karelian and Veps *sizar*) and
*o > *ö in non-first syllables of words with a front vocalism of the first syllable.
Dialects of the Maa group are characterized by several Maa innovations such as
*o > *ë in more than ten stems (e.g. *oppi- > *ëppi- 'learns'), and also by
innovations shared with Livonian and South Estonian, e.g. *e > *ë in words with
back vocalism, *o > *ë and *ns > *(V)s (e.g. North Estonian *maazikkaz*, Votic
Proper *maazikaz*, Livonian *mǫǫšʲkɜz* 'strawberry'). One common feature of
various Maa dialects and a part of the South Estonian dialect is the use of the
stem *maa 'country, land' for the identification of one's own group, cf. Estonian
mâke:el 'Estonian language', *mârahvaz* 'the Estonian people', Votic proper
maačeeli 'Votic language'.

The Maa group may itself be subdivided into North Estonian and the
Chude group (East Estonian, Northeast Estonian, and Votic proper). There is
in East and Northeast Estonian a very strong, but difficult to pinpoint, North
Estonian superstratum and similarly in Votic there are Ingrian and Finnish
superstrata; the precise identification of characteristic and common features
is therefore often difficult. In any event, in North Estonian there has been the
change *ë > o in some stems, cf. *kord* 'time, turn' (< *kërta < *kerta), and
in Chude the change *o > *ë has occurred in about twenty stems.

The interrelations of dialects of North Fennic are complex: cf. Figure 3.2,
which considers twenty-one types of innovation. Contemplation of Figure 3.2
gives rise to various kinds of speculation. Most probably, North Fennic split
first into two groups: into East Ladoga, which voiced *p *t *k *s into *b *d
*g *z in voiced environments, and West Ladoga, which merged the weak
members *p̆p *ťt *ǩk of the gradational pairs *pp : *p̆p, *tt : *ťt, *kk : *ǩk
with *p *t *k that alternated with their weaker variants *p̆ *ť *ǩ (or *β *δ *γ).
Voicing of voiceless single obstruents in East Ladoga cannot be considered
a late Russian influence because it was the voicing that prevented the spread
of the West Ladoga merger to South and Aunus Karelian.

Phonology

Stress

In all Fennic dialects a few words (mostly conjunctions) are usually
unstressed, a few are often unstressed, and most words have the primary stress
on the first syllable. Quadrisyllabic and longer words have secondary stresses
on odd non-final syllables, i.e. there is a tendency towards trochaic stress
patterning, cf. Estonian *maɒala:male* 'lower (sAll)', *maɒala:masse* 'lower
(sIll)'.

The tendency towards trochaic stress is counteracted by certain derivational
suffixes that attract secondary stress, i.e. there is a morphologically bound
secondary stress, e.g. Estonian *pĕɢenemi:ne* 'escaping', Finnish *pakenemi:nen*.
In addition, in Finnish and Votic, and locally also in North Estonian,

quinquesyllabic and longer words with a short third and a long fourth syllable have their secondary stress on the fourth syllable, e.g. Finnish *todelli:sen* 'real (sG)' : *todellise:ssa* 'real (sIne)'. In short, secondary stress is not fixed. In some Finnish dialects there are cases of historically motivated secondary stress, namely, of cases in which the stress has remained fixed on a formerly odd syllable even after the syncopation of the vowel of the original second syllable as in Eurajoki Southwest Finnish *muur.mi:s* (< *muurami:sa 'in cloudberries (pIne)': *kuarmis* (< *kuormisa 'in loads (pIne)'), or after the rise of a new second syllable because of epenthesis, cf. Kuhmalahti Häme *kulumassa:pa* (with secondary second syllable *u*, < *kulmassa:pa 'in the corner (sIne)' v. *kuluma:ssapa* 'being worn out', with original second-syllable *u*.

In negative North Setu varieties of Võru Estonian, fusional negation suffixes (from the old negation verbs *ei?* 'not [non-past]' and *eš* 'not [past]') regularly attract the primary stress, so that a short initial syllable of a bisyllabic form lacks stress, and otherwise the initial syllable receives a secondary stress, e.g. *eläi?* 'I do not live', *elä:äš* 'I did not live'.

Quantity

In pF only vowel quantity was distinctive: there were both short and long monophthongs. Most Fennic dialects have preserved the distinction of short and long vowels, but as a result of diphthongization the number of long vowels may be reduced considerably. Central and South Veps deviate in that in these varieties all long vowels have merged with their short counterparts; South Veps then evolved a new set of long monophthongs, formed as a result of (1) assimilative monophthongization of diphthongs in non-initial syllables, rarely in initial syllables, and of (2) assimilative vocalization of syllable-final or word-final *l, e.g *kuudaan^j e* < *kuldain^j e* < pF *kultainen* 'golden'.

With the exception of the Finnish dialects of Finland, the contrast of single and geminate consonants has evolved into two series of consonants. In Livonian, South Karelian, Aunus Lude and Veps, single obstruents became voiced in voiced environments; geminate obstruents remained voiceless and, for various different reasons, at least a part of them was degeminated into voiceless single obstruents. In most Central Veps dialects and in South Veps, all geminate consonants were degeminated. Moreover (and again with the exception of the Finnish dialects of Finland, where all geminates are degeminated as a side-product of apocopation) former geminates have in similar cases been rendered by final consonants different from those that come from former single ones.

In most Fennic dialects original closedness of posttonic syllables has caused the weakening of single and geminate stops on the boundary of that and the preceding syllable, e.g. *sepa : *sep̌än 'neuk sN:sG', *seppä : *sep̌pän 'smith sN:sG'. This process and alternation is called radical gradation. In Livonian a similar weakening of geminate stops arose, but for more complicated reasons. In Votic, Finnish, Ingrian and North Karelian the weak grade of geminates merged with the strong grade of singles, e.g. *seppä: *sepän, *sepä: *sep̆än); cf. Figure 3.2. In South, North, and East Estonian the alternations of geminate stops were reinterpreted as alternations of heavy and light long syllables and were generalized to all long stressed syllables; in Livonian they were generalized to long stressed syllables with no long monophthongs. Later, syllabic weight was re-interpreted as an internal property of long stressed syllables that was retained even after the former conditions for the rise of distinctive syllable weight were changed. Accordingly in Estonian grammars three syllabic quantities are distinguished: Q1 refers to short stressed syllables, Q2 to light long stressed syllables, and Q3 to heavy long stressed syllables. Syllables of Q1 and Q2 are obligatorily followed by at least one unstressed syllable, except in some subdialects of Võru Estonian where some verb forms of Q2 have lost the unvoiced vowel of the second syllable, e.g. North Setu *sööz^j ?* 'eat (conditional)', *nuᴅ^j z^j* 'being sucked'.

Tone

Tone was non-distinctive in proto-Fennic. In Livonian a contrast of level (or slightly rising) tone and *stød* (or laryngealized tone) was developed either as a result of the change of preconsonantal and certain cases of intervocalic *h into a tonal feature or as a concurrent feature of gemination of weak single consonants in contrast to original geminate consonants that occurred with a level tone. In South, North, and East Estonian tone can be polarized in connection with the distinction between weak and strong long syllables: in comparison to syllables of Q3, syllables of Q2 have a pitch contour with a delayed peak.

Vowels

The pF vowel system is reconstructed as having, symmetrically, eight short and eight long monophthongs in the first syllable but only seven short monophthongs in non-first syllables:

First syllable				Non-first syllables			
*i	*ü		*u	*i	*ü		*u
*e	*ö		*o	*e			*o
*ä		*a		*ä		*a	
*ii	*üü		*uu				
*ee	*öö		*oo				
*ää		*aa					

In proto-Fennic the existence of the back/front pairs *u : *ü, *o : *ö, and *a : *ä in first syllables, and of *u : *ü and *a : *ä in non-first syllables provided the basis for a partial vowel harmony. The distribution of vowels in non-first syllables of proto-Fennic was regulated by the following rules: (1) *o *i *e could occur in any non-first syllable; (2) *ü and *ä occurred in a non-first syllable only if not preceded in the word by a syllable containing any of the vowels *u *o *a; (3) *u and *a occurred in a non-first syllable only if not preceded in the word by a syllable containing any of the vowels *ü, *ö *ä, but even then if a syllable containing *o intervened.

Some of the changes in the vowel systems of Fennic languages have tended to elaborate vowel harmony, e.g., (1) the split *o > *o : *ö in non-first syllables in North Fennic; (2) the split *e > *ę : *e in non-first syllables in Veps; (3) the split *e > *ë : *e in Livonian, South Estonian, and Maa (in South Estonian, ë in the first and ę in non-first syllables are allophones of the same phoneme). On the other hand other changes, such as the rise of syllabic quantity and tone distinctions in the first syllable in Livonian and Estonian, and the rise of CV-harmony (i.e., the congruence of consonant and vowel palatality v. non-palatality) in Veps, have often led to the loss of vowel harmony. The youngest speakers of North Veps often ascribe the feature of palatality not to front vowels but to the palatalized consonants which accompany them. These and some other changes have yielded a considerable variation of vowel correspondences and alternations in the first syllables in different Fennic dialects; for an overview see Tables 3.1 and 3.2. Another consequence has been a considerable reduction of the vowel system of non-first syllables in Livonian and North Estonian.

The syllable-quantity distinctions of Livonian and Estonian, the breaking of initial components of diphthongs in Livonian, and assimilations have been sources of the great variability of polyphthongic systems in Fennic; see Table 3.3. The monophthongization of long monophthongs (Table 3.2) and contractions following the loss of intervocalic consonants have been other sources of

Table 3.1 Proto-Fennic short monophthongs and their reflexes

	WLi	*ELi*	*Maa*	*NEsWSa*	*NF*
*u	u/ū	u/ū	u	u	u
*o	ᵘo/ùo i/ī o	ᵘo/ùo ǭ/ǭ ë/ëë o	o ë	o ö	o
*a	a/ā̊ o	a/aa ǭ o	a	a	a
*ü	i/ī	i/ī	ü	ü	ü
*ö	ⁱe/ie e/ē	ⁱe/ie e/ē	ö	ö	ö
*ä	ä/ā̈ e/ē	ä/ā̈ e/ē	ä	ä	ä
*i	i/ī	i/ī	i	i	i
*e|F	ⁱe/ie e/ē	ïe/ie e/ē	e	e	e
*e|B	i/ī	ë/ē	ë	ö	e

Notes: WLi = West Livonian, ELi = East Livonian, NEsWSa = West Saareman dialects of North Estonian, NF = North Fennic. F = front vocalism, B = back vocalism. In Livonian, a reflex standing left from a slash occurs in a gradationless form or in the strong degree and one standing right from a slash occurs in the weak degree. Paired reflexes alternate regularly.

Table 3.2 Proto-Fennic long monophthongs and their reflexes

pF	ELi	EsSV	NEs	EEs	VoP	Fi	EFiSa	SKa	CSVec
*ū	ū	ú/ū	ú/ū	ú/ų̄	ū	ū	ū	ū	u
*ō	ùo	ú̯/ō ó/	ó/ō	ú̯/uŏ	ō	uo	uo	uo	o
*ā	ǭ	á/ā	ā/ā	uà/uǎ	ā	ā	oa	ua	a
*ǖ	ī	ú̈/ǖ	ú̈/ǖ	üì/ų̈̄	ü	ü	ǖ	ü	ü
*ȫ	ìe ē	ú̯̈/ȫ	ö́/ȫ	ú̯̈/üŏ̈	ȫ	üö	üö	üö	ö
*ǟ	ǟ	ǽ/ǟ	ǽ/ǟ eà/eǎ	ià/iǎ	ǟ	ǟ	eä	iä	ä
*ī	ī	í/ī	í/ī	í/į̄	ī	ī	ī	ī	i
*e|F	ìē ē	í/ē	é/ē	í/iě	ē	ie	ie	ie	e
*e|B	ē̄	í/ē̄	é/ē̄	eè/oě	ę̄	ie	ie	ie	e

Notes: ELi = East Livonian, EsSV = South Võru dialects of Estonian, NEs = North Estonian, EEs = East Estonian, VoP = Votic proper, Fi = Finnish, EFiSa = Savo dialects of East-Finnish, SKa = South Karelian, CSVec = Central and Southern Veps. F = front vocalism, B = back vocalism. In Estonian, a reflex standing left from a slash occurs in a syllable of Q3 and one standing right from a slash occurs in a syllable of Q2.

the multitude of diphthongs in various Fennic dialects.

In Livonian and in most of the Estonian dialects there has been a reduction in the number of vowels occurring in non-first syllables. North Estonian dialects usually have only the vowels *u a i e* in that position. In Livonian the

Table 3.3 Proto-Fennic diphthongs and their reflexes

pF	ELi	NEs	EEs	VoP	WFi	NVeK
*ou	où/ō	ëù/ëŭ	ëù/ëë	ëu	ou	ū
*au	où/ō	aù/aŭ	aù/ā	au	au	ū
*iu	iù/ìu	iù/iŭ	iù/iŭ	iu	iu	üu
*eu	ëù/ē̄	ëù/ëŭ	ëù/	ëu	eu	üü
*eü	ⁱeù/ìe	eì/eĭ	eì/ē	eü	öü	üu
*äü	äù/ā̈	äì/äĭ	äì/äĕ /ā	äü	äü	äu
*öü	ⁱeù/ìe	öì/öĭ	öì/ȫ	öü	öü	üu
*ui	uì/ùi	uì/uĭ	uì/oě	ui	ui	ui
*oi	ᵘoì/ùoi ǫì/ǫ̀i ëì/ëi	oì/oĭ oè/oě ëì/ëĭ	oì/oě /ō ëì/ëĕ	oi ëi	oi	oi
*ai	aì/ài /ǭ	aì/aĭ aè/aĕ	aì/aĕ /ā	ai	ai	ai
*öiIV	eì	ëì/ëĭ	eì/eĭ	ei	öi	ī
*äi	eì/ē̄	äì/äĭ äè/äĭ	äì/äĕ /ā	äi	äi	äi
*e|F	eì/ē̄	eì/eĭ	eì/ē	ei	ei	ī
*e|B	ëì/ē̄	eì/ëĭ		ëi	ei	ī

Notes: ELi = East Livonian, NEs = North Estonian, EEs = East Estonian, Vop = Votic proper, WFi = West Finnish, NveK = North Veps. B = back vocalism, F = front vocalism, V = verb. In Livonian and Estonian, a reflex standing left from a slash occurs in the strong degree and one standing right from a slash occurs in the weak degree.

same four vowels occur after a short first syllable, but after a long first syllable of the weak degree ə̂ *a i* occur, and in other non-first syllables only ə̂ and *i* occur. Voiceless vowels occur in non-first syllables of some Fennic dialects, e.g. in Setu South Estonian, Ingrian, and West Finnish.

In Livonian, South, North, and East Estonian, and Veps, an earlier final vowel (except **a/*ä* in Livonian) has been regularly apocopated both in bisyllabic words with a long first syllable (Livonian ukš, Estonian uk̇s, Veps uksʲ < *uksi 'door') and in longer words. In Djorža South Karelian, final vowels of all disyllabic and longer words have been apocopated. In the same dialects, except Livonian, the vowel of an open short second syllable in a trisyllabic or a longer word has regularly been syncopated if the first syllable was long (e.g. Estonian tütre, Veps *tʲütʲrʲen* < *tüttären 'daughter' [sG]).

Consonants

In Common Fennic after *ti > *si and after the rise of *h there were probably thirteen consonants, viz.

*m	*n			*ŋ
*p	*t			*k
			*s	*h
*v	*ð	*j		
	*l			
	*r			

Several innovations have led to the rise of new consonant series, viz. (1) the shift of single obstruents to voiced *b d g z*, which triggered a partial or total degemination of geminates in Livonian and East Ladoga (cf. Figure 3.1); (2) apocopation, to different extents, in all Fennic dialects that has led, in all dialects save Livonian, Central and South Veps, and Finnish, to the rise of a long consonant series from those geminate consonants that had preceded the apocopated vowel; (3) the fusion of a consonant with a following *j that yielded a series of long palatalized consonants in Votic, Lude, and North Veps; (4) the assimilative influence of front vowels, most usually *i, on preceding consonants, especially dentals, together with the subsequent apocopation or syncopation of the vowel; these processes that have given rise to a parallel contrastive series of palatalized consonants in Livonian, Estonian (except Northeast and Coastal Estonian), Savo Finnish, Karelian and Veps; in Võru Estonian all consonants except ? and *j* may be palatalized.

In Votic proper *k has shifted to *č before front vowels (*käsi > *čäsi* 'hand'); in some dialects *g has similarly shifted to *dž*. In Aunus, Lude, and Veps, *s* and *z* have shifted to *š* and *ž* when preceded by *i*; in North and South Karelian under similar conditions *s* and *z* have shifted to *sʲ* and *zʲ*; elsewhere they have gone to *š*. In Livonian and South and East Estonian, fusion of postvocalic *i* with a following dental has yielded a palatalized dental (or palatalized $š^j$ in Livonian), e.g. South Estonian *naaz^j e?* 'women', Livonian *laaš^j ka* 'lazy'.

The weakening of single stops initial in posttonic unstressed syllables within the framework of radical gradation, and the subsequent loss of the reflexes of the weakened stops, have led to an increase of homophonous forms and to contractions that have altered word structure, e.g. Estonian *luGù* 'story': pN *lo:oᴅ* (< *luǩot) and *lo:oᴅ* 'islet': pN *lo:oᴅ* (< *loŏtot).

The weakening of syllable-initial single stops after unstressed syllables within the framework of suffixal gradation, and the further loss of weakened stops, has triggered various assimilations and contractions that have radically changed the structure of non-first syllables everywhere in Fennic except Veps. The loss of intervocalic *h in Livonian, Estonian, Votic and Finnish has had a similar effect.

Morphology

From the typological point of view, the Fennic dialects range across an extensive gamut, from the quasi-agglutinative North Fennic and Votic to the fusional Livonian and Estonian, where as many as five paradigmatic forms can be different suffixless stem allomorphs.

Nominal Inflection

All Fennic languages have at least three grammatical cases (nominative, genitive, partitive) and a number of adverbial cases, for the most part in both singular and plural; proto-Fennic had at least ten adverbial cases.

The nominative singular is unmarked. The nominative plural ends in a pluralizer (-t, -d, -ᴅ or, in Võru Estonian, -? < *-t) or is unmarked (*-t has gone to zero in Mulgi and in Tartu South Estonian).

The genitive singular has retained its ending (*-n) in North Fennic and lost it elsewhere. The genitive plural had the ending *-ten in North and East Estonian, West Finnish, and probably in Livonian, and the ending *-iten (> *-ťen) elsewhere; *-iten contained two pluralizers, *-i- and *-t.

Both the partitive singular (*-ta) and the partitive plural (*-ita) have undergone changes of various kinds and exhibit a great variety of case formatives and fusional effects in Fennic.

The pF adverbial cases include (the uppercase letters A E U render the front/back harmonic pairs ä/a e/e⁼ ü/u):

three interior local cases (illative *-sen, inessive *-snA, elative *-stA);
three exterior local cases (allative *-len, adessive *-lnA, ablative *-ltA);
the translative (*-ksi), the essive (*-nA), the instructive (*-in), the comitative
    (*-ine-) and the abessive (*-ttAk).

In Common Fennic, the illative and adessive endings underwent certain phonetic changes: *-sen > *-hen, *-lnA > *-llA. The suffix *-hen has been lost in Livonian, Estonian, and Votic. The change *-snA > *-hnA occurred in

South Estonian (with reflexes -*hn*, -*h*, or -*n*); a similar change in South Pohjanmaa West Finnish is either a reminiscence of the same period or an analogical change. The change *-len > *-llen in at least Estonian, Votic, Ingrian and Finnish was at least partly in analogy to the new form of the adessive ending, *-llA. North and South Karelian have merged the illative with the inessive, and the allative with the adessive. In Aunus, Lude, and Veps, the elative and the ablative have merged with the inessive and the adessive; secondary elative and ablative endings have often been formed on the basis of the inessive and adessive endings and the postposition *päin 'in the direction of'. The essive as a case has been lost in Livonian and in South, East, and most of North Estonian (but was reintroduced into the literary language). The instructive and especially the comitative have become non-productive in all Fennic dialects; new comitative endings have appeared in Estonian and Votic (from the former postposition *kans(s)a), and in Lude and Veps (from the postposition *kera). Livonian has a dative in -*n* or -*ən* (*amà viilʲa ìeb lapˋstən* 'all the property remains to [the] children'); Livonian has also merged the translative and the comitative into an instrumental case and uses the exterior case forms only for some toponyms and certain lexicalized and adverbialized forms. Some Finnish Karelian, Ingrian and Votic pronouns have an accusative case form. Veps dialects have several secondary case forms that result from fusion of former case forms and postpositions.

Verb Inflection
The Fennic verb has finite and non-finite forms. Finite forms can be characterized in terms of person and number, voice, aspect, mood and tense. Non-finite forms include participles, infinitive, gerund and supines.

Finite Form Categories
Fennic distinguishes two numbers: singular and plural, and three persons. The proto-Fennic finite verb had at least two voices (personal and impersonal), two aspects (affirmative and negative), four moods (indicative, conditional, imperative and potential) and four tenses (present, imperfect, perfect, and pluperfect; the perfect and pluperfect were composites).

Proto-Fennic had the following personal endings: s1 *-n (< *-m), except in the imperative, which had no s1 form; s2 *-t, except in the imperative, where the second person singular had no personal ending; p1 *-mV and p2 *-tV, with diverse pluralizers in different dialects added in the indicative, the conditional, and the potential probably only later, e.g. Võru Estonian -*mEʔ*, East Votic -*mmAG*, Hevaha Ingrian -*mmAn*, Central Veps -*mAi*.

The third-person singular forms had the personal ending *-sen in the imperative; this same ending also occurs in the reflexive conjugation of Aunus, Lude, and Veps and in certain South Estonian verbs. Otherwise, the s3 forms have no personal ending: in South Estonian, many s3 forms in the present indicative are entirely unmarked, and elsewhere the s3 forms come from those ending in *-pi (< *-pA) from the present participle suffix *-pA;

all other s3 forms end in a tense or mood suffix shared with other forms. The p3 ended in the imperative in *-set (> *-het); elsewhere the tense or mood suffix was simply followed by the pluralizer *-t, in the present indicative after the suffix *-pA, i.e. *-pA-t.

The s1 ending has been lost in Livonian, South Estonian, and East Votic. Later, the Livonian unmarked s1 forms were replaced mostly by s3 forms. Perhaps already in proto-Fennic, the p1 and p2 suffixes assimilated to the preceding present-tense suffix: *-k-me- > *-mme-, *-k-te- > *-tte; later the suffix *-tte- and often also the suffix *-mme- became generalized to other p1 and p2 forms.

Corresponding to the six forms that make up the personal voice there was an *impersonal* voice in proto-Fennic. From a transformational perspective, we could say that a predicate verb in any of the three persons, singular or plural, could be replaced by a special impersonal form that contained (1) the impersonal suffix *-tA- or *-ttA-, (2) an imperfect or a mood suffix and, (3) in the indicative and the imperative, the ending *-sen. The corresponding nominal or infinitive subject was simultaneously removed. Such impersonalization is still possible in all tenses and moods in all Fennic languages except Livonian, e.g. Estonian *kaks me:est maɢavaᴅ konìserᴅil* 'two men are sleeping at the concert' >> *konìserᴅil maɢattakse* 'one sleeps at the concert'. Note that in the latter case the sentence has no formal subject. Võru Estonian also has a *passive*: a transitive clause with the predicate verb in a personal form of the present or imperfect indicative can be made passive by transforming the object into a subject and replacing the active predicate verb with the corresponding passive verb. The s3 passive forms are homophonous with the corresponding impersonal forms, while other forms have the usual endings.

The negative forms in Fennic have been formed by means of an auxiliary negation verb *e- (inflected in the indicative) or a prohibitive verb *elä-/älä-/ala-* (inflected in the imperative) followed by the main, or lexical, verb in the appropriate tense or mood form. In Livonian, South, and East Estonian, and locally in Insular Estonian, the negation verb also has imperfect forms (used only in the indicative mood) and followed by the main verb indicative mood stem. Elsewhere the negation form has only the present-tense forms; these are followed in the present indicative by the main verb indicative mood stem (see below), and in the imperfect by the preterite participle. Both models have parallels in other Finno-Ugric languages.

The indicative mood has two tenses. The present is built with the suffix *-k-. The imperfect is built with the suffix *-i-, except in the negation verb, where the imperfect suffix was *-s(i)-, cf. Livonian s3 i^+z, South Estonian *ess*. The conditional mood marker comes from *-ksi- in Livonian, and in South, North, and East Estonian, and from *-isi- in Votic and North Fennic, with the exception of Coastal Estonian, where the suffix *-iksi-* of monosyllabic and *e*-stems is thought to be the result of contamination. Although *-ksi- and *-isi-are sometimes treated as suffixes of different origin, this -*iksi*- may well be identical with their common protoform. The potential in *-ne- has been preserved mainly in North Fennic. The imperative has the markers *-k in s2, *-kA- in p2, and *-ko- in s3, p3 and the impersonal. The s2 imperative marker has been preserved as *k* only in East Votic and Hevaha Ingrian.

Livonian and Estonian have two additional moods, the quotative (or narrative) and the jussive. These are *ratio obliqua* analogues of the indicative and imperative moods and in Livonian are more or less obligatory.

Non-finite Form Categories

Proto-Fennic had four participles: the present personal in *-pA, the preterite personal in *-nUt, the present impersonal in *-tApA/*-ttApA, and the preterite impersonal in *-tU/*-ttU. Participles occurred as attributes, as predicatives, and as components of composite perfect and pluperfect forms built with the present and imperfect forms of the auxiliary verb 'is'. In Livonian the impersonal participles have become passive participles. Participles are inflected as nominals. In several dialects the preterite participle suffixes have contaminated one other: there has been either loss of the final *t of the personal participle or a spread of this *t to the impersonal participle.

Infinitives built with the suffix *-tAk served as both subjects and objects. All Fennic dialects have at least one gerund built with the suffix *-tesnA (originally the inessive of the infinitive) that functions as an adverbial indicating a simultaneous action. Supines are verbal adverbs, formed by means of the suffix*-mA- plus a case suffix, e.g. illative *-mAsen, inessive *-mAsnA, ablative *-mAstA, translative *-mAksi, abessive *-mAttAk.

Syntax

All Fennic languages are SOV languages. In contrast to most other Uralic languages adjectives, participles, and some pronouns in the role of attribute agree with their head noun in case and number. In Võru Estonian and in Veps the negation verb often follows the main verb.

Vocabulary

The Common Fennic vocabulary contains (1) stems inherited from earlier stages (protolanguages) which continue proto-Uralic, and derivates built from these stems; (2) stems of unknown origin; (3) stems borrowed from various ancient Indo-European languages into pF or Common Fennic, viz. ancient Baltic, Germanic, and Slavonic borrowings; (4) stems borrowed into Fennic from known contact languages, chiefly Swedish borrowings into Finnish and, to a lesser extent, into Estonian; (5) Low and High German borrowings into Estonian and Livonian, Latvian borrowings into Livonian and, to a considerably lesser extent, into Estonian; (6) Russian borrowings (on a massive scale) into Karelian, Veps, Votic, Ingrian and, to a lesser extent, into other languages.

Turning to the oldest borrowings, there are about 400 loans from Baltic (however, fewer than 200 of these are absolutely certain, e.g. *kirves 'axe', *heinä/*haina 'hay', *järvi/*jarva 'lake', *tüttär 'daughter', *šampas 'tooth'); about 500 loans from Germanic (e.g. *lampas 'sheep', *kana 'hen', *pelto 'field', *laiva 'boat, ship', *kuninkas 'king', *kurkku 'throat'); about 10 borrowings from Slavonic (e.g. *hauki 'pike', *vilja 'property; crop', *širti 'log, pole'). Baltic and Germanic borrowings include a number of terms relating to agriculture and technology, but also topographic, somatic, and kinship terminology. The flow of Germanic loanwords must have been continuous. There was a long time interval, though, between the Baltic and Latvian borrowings and between the oldest Slavonic and Old Russian borrowings.

References and Further Reading

Ariste, P. (1968) *A Grammar of the Votic Language*, Bloomington–The Hague: Indiana University: Mouton.

Hofstra, T. (1985) *Ostseefinnisch und Germanisch. Die Lehnbeziehungen im nördlicher Ostseeraum im Lichte der Forschung seit 1961*, Groningen: Drukkerij van Denderen B.V.

Kettunen, L. (1913) *Lautgeschichtliche Untersuchung über den kodaferschen Dialekt*, Helsinki: Société Finno-Ougrienne.

—— (1914) *Lautgeschichtliche Darstellung über den Vokalismus des kodaferschen Dialekts*, Helsinki: Société Finno-Ougrienne.

—— (1938) *Livisches Worterbuch mit grammatischer Einleitung*, Helsinki: Société Finno-Ougrienne.

—— (1960) *Suomen lähisukukielten luonteenomaiset piirteet*, Helsinki: Société Finno-Ougrienne.

Laanest, A. (1982) *Einführung in die ostseefinnische Sprachen*, Hamburg: Buske.

Posti, L. (1942) *Grundzüge der livischen Lautgeschichte*, Helsinki: Société Finno-Ougrienne.

—— (1954) 'From Pre-Finnic to Late Proto-Finnic: studies on the development of the consonant system', *FUF* 31: 1–91.

Suhonen, S. (1988) 'Geschichte der ostseefinnischen Sprachen', in D. Sinor (ed.), *The Uralic Languages: Description, History and Foreign Influences*, Handbuch der Orientalistik 8/1, Leiden: Brill, pp. 288–313.

Vaba, L. (1990) 'Die baltischen Sondernentlehnungen in den ostseefinnischen Sprachen', in *Itämerensuomalaiset kielikontaktit*, Helsinki: Valtion Painatuskeskus, pp. 125–39.

Viitso, T.-R. (1978) 'The history of Finnic õ of the first syllable', *Sovetskoe finno-ugrovedenie* 14: 18–106.

Viks, Ü. (1992) *A Concise Morphological Dictionary of Estonian*, vol. I. *Introduction and Grammar*, Tallinn: Estonian Academy of Sciences, Institute of Language and Literature.

4 Estonian

Tiit-Rein Viitso

Estonian (native name from the nineteenth-century *eesti keel*, formerly *maakeel*) is spoken by about 1 million Estonians, mainly in Estonia but also in Russia (mainly by descendants of resettlers of the end of the nineteenth century), and in Sweden, Canada, the United States, and Australia (mainly by refugees from Nazi and Soviet terror and by their descendants). There have been some South Estonian enclaves also in Latvia and in Russia; the Leivu enclave in Ilzene and the Lutsi enclave in Ludza, Latvia, did not become extinct until the twentieth century.

Estonian has traditionally come into contact with Finnish in the north and in the northeast, with Ingrian and probably Votic in the northeast, with Russian in the east, with Latvian in the south, with Livonian in the southwest and with Swedish in the west. From the thirteenth century until 1939 a sparse German population has lived in Estonia (16,000 in 1939) and approximately from the same time up to 1944, a small Swedish population (8,000 in 1939), this latter concentrated along the northwest coast and on Vormsi and Ruhnu islands. Mostly beginning from the second half of the seventeenth century there has been on the west coast of Lake Peipsi, on the east bank of the Narva River south from Estonian Ingermanland, and in eastern Setumaa a Russian population, at present about 150,000 descendants of 80,000 persons in 1939, and about 450,000 Russian-speaking Soviet colonialists who arrived in Estonia in 1944–88.

Dialects

Estonian dialects have usually been classified into three groups: (1) Northeast Coastal; (2) North Estonian, including (a) the Insular, (b) Western, (c) Central and (d) Eastern dialects; and (3) South Estonian including (a) Mulgi, (b) Tartu and (c) Võru dialects. For the purposes of this chapter both the traditional North and Northeast Coastal groups are reclassified into two groups, so Estonian is considered to consist of five main groups: (1) North, (2) East, (3) Northeast, (4) Coast, and (5) South Estonian. South Estonian, in particular its southeasternmost Võru dialect has been poorly understood by speakers of other Estonian dialects. The Võru dialect remained uninfluenced by North Estonian until the second half of the nineteenth century and its easternmost Russian Orthodox group, called Setus, were administratively united with other Estonians only in the course of Estonia's War of Liberation in 1919. South Estonian probably stems directly from proto-Fennic. Coast Estonian was originally a North Fennic dialect and probably close to East Finnish; Northeast and East Estonian were originally closer to Proper Votic than to North Estonian.

As a result of the high general level of literacy already achieved by the nineteenth century, and of the prestige of education and educated speech and of several other, historical, factors, the former dialects have been almost completely absorbed by standard (North) Estonian. Only Võru South Estonian is to some extent still actively used, although rarely by children.

Literary Estonian

The first recordings of Estonian names date from the beginning of the thirteenth century, the earliest running texts date from the sixteenth century, and the first (partial) book was printed in 1535. This was a catechism written by Simon Wanradt in North Estonian or in the Tallinn language and translated into Estonian by Johann Koell. In the southeastern part of Estonia, namely in the territory of Tartu and Võru South Estonian, another literary language, usually referred to as the Tartu language, was used at least as early as the seventeenth century. The first North Estonian grammar (*Anführung zu der Esthnischen Sprach*, 1637) was written by Heinrich Stahl (1600–57), and the first South Estonian grammar was written by Johann Gutsleff in 1648. Both literary languages were developed first by clergymen of German origin in the framework of the Lutheran ideology of making the Scriptures understandable and available to anyone and in one's native language. From the 1720s calendar books and books on health care were printed. In 1766 the first Estonian journal, the weekly *Lühhike öppetus* ... began to be published by the physician E. P. Wilde in North Estonian. In 1806 the first attempt was made to issue an Estonian newspaper in the Tartu language: *Tarto-ma rahwa Näddali leht*. The retreat of the Tartu literary language, however, had begun already in the eighteenth century, after Anton Thor Helle (1683–1748) had published his North Estonian grammar (*Kurtzgefaßte Anweisung zur Ehstnischen Sprache*, 1732) and especially after the Bible was translated into North Estonian under the supervision of Helle and published in 1739. The decline of South Estonian as a literary standard was completed in the second half of the nineteenth century.

From the 1820s more and more Estonians took part in developing the literary language; especially influential was Otto Wilhelm Masing (1763–1832). Masing published several educational books on fundamentals of Christianity and on secular subjects, such as the educational calendar series *Marahwa Kalender* (1823–6); he initiated the tradition of North Estonian newspapers with his weekly *Marahwa Näddala-Leht* (1821–5) and was first to discuss several complex problems of Estonian pronunciation and orthography. Masing was the first to notice and to write the Estonian vowel *ë* (‹õ›). From 1840, the physician and writer Friedrich Reinhold Kreutzwald (1803–82), made significant contributions in creating the new medicinal, chemical, and geographical terminology that he used in his textbooks and popularized writings on health care and general knowledge. With the rapid rise of the national movement in the 1860s, Estonian began to develop from being a rural language into a universal and unified national language. From the 1870s Finnish became an important source of lexical borrowing and served as a model for word formation. The grammar published by Karl August Hermann in 1884 put an end to several long-lasting disputes in the fields of pronunciation and morphology and Ado Grenzstein's Estonian dictionary (*Eesti Sõnaraamat*, 1884), which was the first dictionary addressed directly to Estonians, included 1600 neologisms and international words. Extremely fruitful for literary Estonian was the activity in the years between 1910 and 1940 of two competing schools of language development: those advocating language innovation (*keeleuuendus*), headed by Johannes Aavik (1880–1973), and those in favour of more moderate language regulation (*keelekorraldus*), headed by Johannes Voldemar Veski (1873–1968). Veski's activities include his participation in the compiling of the Estonian orthographic dictionary (*Eesti keele õigekirjutuse-sõnaraamat*, 1918), his role as co-ordinator in the preparation of more than thirty terminological dictionaries, and his work as chief compiler of the Estonian orthoëpic dictionary, *Eesti õigekeelsuse-sõnaraamat* (1925–37), with about 130,000 lexemes; all this work formed a firm basis for the literary standard.

Orthography

Estonian orthography has passed through the following states of development:

1 Estonian was at first written inconsistently, on the model of Low German and Latin orthography, until the second quarter of the seventeenth century.

2 Estonian was subsequently written on the model of High German orthography, using most of the letters of the Latin alphabet, especially under the influence of Heinrich Stahl.

3 There followed the Old Orthography, first applied by Bengt Gottfried Forselius in his primer (1684); this orthography dispensed with the letters ‹c›, ‹f›, ‹q›, ‹x›, ‹y›, and ‹z›, distinguished between *ä* and *e*, but still followed the Swedish and German method of distinguishing between short and long vowels in open initial syllables by doubling the consonant after a short vowel. As a result, word-pairs such as *samma* [samà] 'the same' and *sama* [sa:ama] 'to get' were distinguished, but intervocalic single and geminate consonants were not disinguished: e.g. the spelling *warras* rendered ambiguously both [varàz] 'thief' and [vařraz] 'rod'.

4   The New, or so-called 'Finnish' orthography was first proposed for Estonian by the Finn A. J. Arwidsson (1822); it was then recommended by Eduard Ahrens (1803–63) in the first edition of his grammar (*Grammatik der Ehstnischen Sprache Revalschen Dalektes* I, 1843) and first applied in Gustav Heinrich Schüdlöffel's booklet *Toomas Westen, Lapo rahwa uso ärataja Norra maal* (1844), and then in the second and full edition of Ahrens's grammar (1853). In this orthography, short and long vowels are written by means of one and two vowel letters, respectively; similarly, intervocalic single and geminate consonants are written by means of one and two consonant letters. The New Orthography resembled preceding orthographies in not reflecting the distinctive palatalization of dental consonants and the distinctive syllabic quantity of long syllables (with one exception: the two syllabic quantities of long syllables which have a short monophthong followed by a strong intervocalic geminate stop or *šš* are indicated by writing the shorter v. longer geminates by means of one v. two consonant letters).

The Alphabet

The Estonian alphabet includes the letters ‹a b d e f g h i j k l m n o p r s š z ž t u v õ ä ö ü›; note the aberrant position of ‹z› (and ‹ž›). The letters ‹f z ž› occur only in late borrowings. Similarly the letters ‹b d g› at the beginning of a word are a sign that the word is a late borrowing; in all vocabulary, initial ‹b d g z ž› stand for strong voiceless consonants [p t k s š], elsewhere they stand for weak voiceless consonants [ʙ ᴅ/ᴅʲ ɢ z zʲ ž]. The letters ‹p t k š› stand for strong voiceless consonants; intervocalically they render short geminates [p̆p t̆t/t̆ʲt k̆k š̆š] when they follow a short monophthong in a stressed syllable, and for the most part they render long geminates [p:p t:t k:k š:š] when they follow a long monophthong or a diphthong in a stressed syllable; they represent a geminate of ambiguous length when they follow the vowel of an unstressed syllable. The letter ‹s› stands for the strong voiceless sibilant [s] at the beginning of a word, at the beginning of a consonant cluster, and after an obstruent; it stands for a weak voiceless sibilant [z/zʲ] intervocalically, at the end of a cluster when preceded by a sonorant consonant, and after a vowel at the end of a word. In rendering foreign names borrowed from languages using Latin scripts, Estonian orthography follows the source strictly.

The letter ‹õ› stands in standard Estonian for a mid or, if of Q3 (see below), optionally an upper mid unrounded back vowel.

Phonology

The Syllable

A syllable in Estonian contains at least one vowel optionally preceded by 1–3 consonants and optionally followed by 1–4 consonants. Except in the word `praegu 'now' (‹ *para aikoihen), an initial consonant cluster in a first syllable signals that the word is descriptive, borrowed, or both. Stressed syllables may be either short or long. A short stressed syllable has one single short monophthong, optionally preceded by consonants; a long stressed syllable ends in a consonant, long monophthong or diphthong. Stressed syllables distinguish three syllabic quantities, Q1, Q2 or Q3: see pp. 119–21.

Stress

In words which have stress, the primary stress is usually on the first syllable; some interjections, e.g. *aitäh* [aittähh] 'thanks', and a number of borrowings have the primary stress on a non-first syllable, e.g. *idee* [idê] 'idea', *militaristlik* [mi:littaristlik] 'militarist' (adj)' (primary stress underlined, secondary stress marked with colon). There is a strong tendency towards trochaic stress-patterning, and to dactylic word-final stress groups if the trochaic patterning cannot be applied; as a result, secondary stresses are usually on odd syllables counting from the stressed syllables: *vallandatavate-legi* [vallanDa:ttava:ttele:Gi] 'even to ones being discharged', *kõnelesime* [kënele:zime] 'we spoke'; this tendency is counteracted by certain derivational affixes that attract the secondary stress: *elajalik* [elajali:k] 'beastly', *kõnelemise* [kënelemi:ze] 'of speaking (sG)'.

Quantity

In all forms of Estonian except Coastal and Northeast, quantity is distinctive on two levels. First, the *segmental* quantity correlation SHORT v. LONG holds for vowels and consonants. In standard Estonian all vowels in primarily stressed syllables and most consonants (at least after short monophthongs of primarily stressed syllables) have both short and long counterparts. Second, there exists in stressed syllables a tripartite correlation of distinctive syllabic quantities, usually referred to as quantity 1, quantity 2, and quantity 3 (hereafter Q1, Q2, and Q3). This correlation is based (1) on the contrast of SHORT and LONG stressed syllables, and (2) on the contrast of LIGHT and HEAVY stressed syllables:

			Syllable length	Syllable weight
Syllabic quantity	Q1		short	light
	Q2		long	
	Q3			heavy

A stress group, a stem, a suffix, or a word consisting of one stress group can be referred to as one of Q1, Q2, or Q3 depending on the quantity of its stressed syllable.

   A stressed syllable is short and, hence, of Q1, if it ends in a short monophthong, e.g. the *e* of *elu* [elù] 'life'; otherwise the stressed syllable is long. A heavy stressed syllable, or a syllable of Q3, can compose a stress group on its own, e.g. *puu* [pû] 'tree'. A light syllable can compose a stress group only when followed by at least one unstressed syllable; nevertheless both light and heavy stressed syllables can be followed by at most two unstressed syllables. Below, in words written in the conventional orthography, all light syllables of Q1 and Q2 are marked with an acute accent (´) and heavy syllables of Q3 with the grave accent (`).

A syllable of Q2 has a full-long monophthong, a diphthong both components of which are short, or ends in one or two short consonants or the short initial component of a geminate, e.g. ´*piinad* [piinaD] 'pains', ´*saate* [saàtte] 'you (plur) get', ´*auto* [aŭtto] 'car', ´*naeris* [naĕriz] 'rape (bot)', ´*enne* [enne] 'omen', ´*salgas* [salGaz] 'in the band', ´*kaarte* [kaartte] 'arch (pG)', ´*heinte* [heĭntte] 'hay (pG)'. Note that except for some foreign proper names, the co-occurrence of a long monophthong or a diphthong with a geminate obstruent in a word with a syllable of Q2 is restricted (1) to genitive plural forms of some nouns and (2) to the second-person plural present-tense forms of monosyllabic vocalic verb stems, both of which have the suffix *-te*.

A syllable of Q3 has an overlong monophthong, a long diphthong, or a long consonant or long consonant cluster, cf. `*piinad* [pi:inad] 'you (sing) torment', `*saate* [sa:atte] 'transmission (sG)', `*autu* [aùttu] 'dishonest', `*naeris* [naèriz] '(s)he laughed', `*kallas* [kallaz] 'it poured', `*enne* [enne] 'before', `*salgas* [salGaz] '(s)he disavowed', `*kaarte* [ka:artte] 'card (pP)'. Syllables of Q3 may have a more complicated structure than light long syllables, e.g. clusters consisting of three or more consonants (`*tursk* 'cod', `*vintskleb* '(s)he rolls about'); the occurrence of certain diphthongs is restricted to syllables of Q3, e.g. `*kaotus* [kaottuz] 'loss'.

Estonian has both short and long vowels and consonants (or geminates) co-occurring with long vowels and consonants (or geminates) in syllables of different types, and Estonian words are frequently, even usually,

Figure 4.1   Homomorphemic monophthong and stop sequences

Q1 lagì[1]	makkì[2]	makki[3]	mak[4]
Q2 māgi[5]	màkki[6]		
Q3 mágĭ[7]	måkkì[8]		mág[9] mák[10]

Key: 1 ´*laGi* 'ceiling', 2 ´*maki* 'tape recorder (sG)', 3 `*makki* 'tape recorder (sP)', 4 `*makk* 'tape recorder', 5 ´*maagi* 'ore (sG)', 'magician (sG)', 6 ´*Maacki* 'Maack (sG)', 7 `*maagi* 'magician (sP)', 8 ´*maaki* 'ore (sP)', `*Maacki* 'Maack (sP)', 9 `*maag* 'magician', 10 `*maak* 'ore', `*Maack* 'Maack'.
Note: In this figure and in Figure 4.2, special diacritics are used to indicate relative duration of segments. Listed (with the vowel *a*) in order of increasing quantity, these are ă a à ā̀ ā á̄ â.

Figure 4.2   Monophthong and stop sequences conditioned by the morpheme boundary

mak̆₍ki[1]

Q3   mắɢ₍ki[2]   mắk̆₍ki[3]

    mâɢi[4]   mâk̆ke[5]

Key: 1 ˋmakki 'even a/the tape recorder', 2 ˋmaagki 'even a/the magician', 3 ˋmaakki 'even the ore', ˋMaackki 'even Maack', 4 ˋmaagi 'even the country', 5 ˋmaake 'country (diminutive)'.

polymorphemic. As a result, Estonian has a complex system of quantitative patterns, especially because of complicated sequences of monophthong plus obstruent: cf. Figures 4.1 and 4.2 (note that in a morpheme, a long or geminate resonant occurs only after a short monophthong).

Tone

In addition to the features sketched above, the contrast of Q1, Q2, and Q3 is usually supported by differences in the position of the peak of pitch in the stressed syllable: a syllable of Q1 has a prevailingly rising pitch, followed by a short fall, a syllable of Q2 has a rising-falling pitch and a syllable of Q3 has a level or a falling pitch, sometimes preceded by a short rise.

Vowels

Monophthongs

In first, primarily stressed syllables of native words, Standard Estonian has short and long monophthongs of nine qualities:

i	ü		u
e	ö	ë	o
ä		a	

In standard orthography, all long monophthongs are written double; they can occur in syllables of both Q2 and Q3. The vocalism of non-first syllables is restricted to four short monophthongs: *i*, *e*, *a* and *u*.

In several dialects, the number of long monophthongs has been reduced as a result of the breaking (diphthongization) of long monophthongs. In West Saaremaa and East Hiiumaa the system of short monophthongs has been reduced as a result of the merger of *ë* and *ö*; this merger is somehow related to the labialization of long monophthongs *ëë > œœ and *aa > åå.

First syllable   Non-first syllable

i	ü		u	ii	üü	uu		i		u
e	ö		o	ee	öö	oo		e		
ä		a		ää	œœ	åå			a	

In South Estonian, the number of long monophthongs is the highest in Võru South Estonian, where the characteristic long upper mid monophthongs *iiᵛ*, *üüᵛ*, *uuᵛ* and high back unrounded *ïïᵛ* occur only in syllables of Q3, and *ëë* never occurs in syllables of Q3. In the Räpina and North Setu subdialects of Võru, the vocalism of non-first syllables is the richest found in an Estonian dialect:

First syllable

Q1				Q2				Q3			
i	ü	ï	u	ii	üü		uu	ii	üü	ïï	uu
								iiᵛ	üüᵛ		uuᵛ
e	ö	ë	o	ee	öö	ëë	oo	ee	öö	ëë	oo
ä		a		ää		aa		ää		aa	

Non-first syllable

i	ü		u
e	ö	ë	o
ä		a	

Diphthongs

Diphthongs in standard Estonian end in *u*, *o*, *a*, *e*, or *i*. All diphthongs occur in syllables of Q3; diphthongs ending in *u* and *i* (and a few others) also occur

Figure 4.3   Standard Estonian long monophthongs and diphthongs

	u	o	a	õ	ü	ö	ä	e	i
u	uu²	[uo²]	[ua]					[ue]	ui²
o	ou²	oo²	oa					oe²	oi²
a	au²	ao	aa²					ae²	ai²
õ	õu²	õo	õa	õõ²				õe²	õi²
ü		[üo]	[üa]		üü²			[üe]	üi²
ö			öa			öö²		öe	öi²
ä	äu²	äo					ää²	äe²	öi²
e	[eu²]	eo	ea²					ee²	ei²
i	iu²	[io]	[ia]					[ie]	ii²

Note: The index number 2 indicates that the sequence occurs in addition to syllables of Q3 also in syllables of Q2. Diphthongs that occur only in borrowings are given in brackets. The vowel *ë* is here written with <õ>.

in syllables of Q2, cf. Figure 4.3. In non-first syllables of native words, only the diphthongs *ui, ai,* and *ei* occur; in such cases *i* is either a pluralizer or belongs to the superlative suffix *-im*.

In Estonian dialects which have vowel harmony there are also diphthongs ending in *ü*, viz. *öü, äü, eü*. In Coastal, Northeast and northernmost North Estonian dialects, as a result of the breaking of long monophthongs, the diphthongs *uo, ie,* and *üö* occur instead of the *oo, ee,* and *öö* of standard Estonian; in East Estonian such breaking was limited to long mid vowels of Q3.

Consonants

In standard Estonian eighteen consonant qualities are phonemic:

v			j	
f				h
	s	sʲ	š	
p	t	tʲ		k
m	n	nʲ		ŋ
	l	lʲ		
	r			

The orthography does not distinguish the palatalized dentals from the unpalatalized ones, and writes ŋ as <n>. Long intervocalic and long postvocalic final consonants are written double in syllables of both Q2 and Q3, with the exception of long intervocalic stops and long *š* in syllables of Q2 and after a vowel other than a short monophthong, even in syllables of Q3. The short and weak voiceless stops are written with <b d g>.

Consonant palatalization in standard Estonian and in most Estonian dialects is manifested phonetically as a weak palatalization of the initial part of a denti-alveolar consonant or the presence of a very short *i*-coloured transition between the vowel of the stressed syllable and the following consonant; in view of this, any system of transcription (including the traditional FU ones) in which consonant palatalization is indicated by an acute accent written above or after the consonant letter is somewhat misleading. Thus the pronunciation of the 'phonetically' written *kulʲlʲ* for `*kull* 'hawk' is actually [ku'll]. When occurring after original long non-high back vowels, such transitions have developed into vocalic segments in Insular and locally also in West North Estonian, e.g. *laes* for *klaas* 'glass'. In Võru South Estonian, where consonant palatalization is manifested as the thorough palatalization of a consonant or a consonant cluster and a word-final palatalized consonant receives a *j*-coloured terminal part, almost all consonants can be palatalized, cf. *vašʲk* 'calf' : *vašʲkʲ* 'copper'. Coastal and Northeast Estonian and Hiiumaa North Estonian have no palatalized consonants.

Consonant clusters in Estonian consist of from two to five consonants.

Most clusters occur only after the vowels of the syllables with primary stress. The occurrence of certain clusters depends on the preceding long or short vocalism and on syllable quantity. Clusters beginning in a weak voiceless stop *b d g* never follow a short vocalism of a syllable of Q3. Several clusters, among them biconsonantal clusters ending in a resonant and all clusters with *s* after a weak stop, always contain a morpheme boundary or have arisen as a result of vowel syncope (`küünlad 'candles', cf. ´küünal 'candle'; `kaablid 'cables', cf. `kaabel 'cable', `võrd'len 'I compare', `kuld'ne 'golden': sG `kuld'se.

Morphophonological Alternations
Estonian is typologically more inflecting than agglutinating. It has numerous morphophonological alternations, most of which, however, occur in a certain restricted set of stems.

Gradation
Gradation in Estonian includes (1) quantitative gradation of long stressed syllables, whereby Q3 in the strong grade alternates with Q2 in the weak grade, and (2) qualitative gradation, whereby an initial weak stop of the second syllable, or *t* and *k* in the strong grade, are lost, assimilated or weakened into *v* or *j* in the weak grade. Quantitative gradation is reflected in the orthographical alternations <pp : p>, <tt : t>, <kk : k>, <šš : š> after a short vocalism (note that *p, t, k,* and *š* after a short vocalism render short geminates) and <p : b>, <t : d>, <k : g>, <ss : s> after a long vocalism or a resonant; there are also cases of quantitative gradation which are not reflected in the orthography. For qualitative gradation, *t* and *k* occur in the strong grade only after the consonants *s* and *h*.

Although in most cases of gradation the strong grade is historically primary, gradations are classified on synchronic morphological grounds into (1) weakening and (2) strengthening gradations. For weakening gradations, the nominative and partitive singular forms of nominals and the *da*-infinitive form of verbs are in the strong grade whereas the genitive singular form of nominals and the first-person singular form of the present indicative are in the weak grade; for strengthening gradation the distribution of grades is the reverse, cf.:

'Weakening' gradation:

Strong grade	Weak grade
sN ´nägu 'face', sP ´nägu	sG `näo
sN `jalg 'foot', sP `jalga	sG ´jala
sN `välk 'lightning', sP `välku	sG ´välgu
sN `vill 'wool', sP `villa	sG ´villa
sN `keel 'tongue', sP `keelt	sG ´keele
inf ´siduda 'to tie'	s1pres `seon
inf `anda 'to give'	s1pres ´annan

'Strengthening' gradation:

Weak grade	Strong grade
sN ´tahe 'will', sP ´tahet	sG `tahte
sN ´võti 'key', sP ´võtit	sG `võtme
inf ´õmmelda 'to sew'	s1pres `õmblen
inf ´ärgata 'to wake up'	s1pres `ärkan
inf ´kallata 'to pour'	s1pres `kallan

Note that nominal stems with weakening gradation have their partitive singular in the strong grade and are either (1) monosyllabic and marked with the case ending -tt (after a short monophthong) or -t (elsewhere) or (2) bisyllabic and for the most part morphologically unmarked. Stems with strengthening gradation have their partitive singular in the weak grade; it is bisyllabic and marked with the case ending -t. For both weakening and strengthening gradation all partitive plural forms of nominals and all supine illative forms of verbs are in the strong grade.

Alongside cases of an easily recognizable single-stop mutation, qualitative gradation is also defined as characterizing certain types of nominals in which a single stop *t in the strong-grade forms has undergone several changes so that it has been eliminated in most or all environments, e.g.

	sN	sP	sG	sIll	pG	pP	Gloss
1	´käsi	`kätt	`käe	`kätte	´käte	´käsi	'hand'
2	`uus	`uut	´uue	`uude	´uute	`uusi	'new'
3	`õõs	`õõnt	´õõne	`õõnde	´õõnte	`õõsi	'cavity'
4	`vars	`vart	´varre	`varde	´varte	`varsi	'shaft'

In such cases, the sequence *ti has become *si in the sN and pP forms and undergone apocope in the sN forms of (2), (3), (4). In addition, in the sP and pG forms earlier stem-final *t fused with case-ending-initial *t to yield new case endings. The short single stop has been geminated after a short monophthong in first illative forms as seen in stem-types (2)–(3); however, in these types the stop d has been treated as belonging to the case ending. These new sP, sIll and pG endings occur e.g. in the following paradigm where quality gradation did not originally occur:

5	`keel	`keelt	´keele	`keelde	´keelte	`keeli	'tongue'

Vowel Apocope

In bisyllabic nominal stems with a long first syllable and weakening gradation and in most trisyllabic stems the stem vowel is apocopated in the nominative singular, cf. sN `sepp 'smith', sP `seppa, sG ´sepa; sN `ring 'circle', sP `ringi, sG ´ringi; sN ´jumal 'god', sP ´jumalat, sG ´jumala.

Vowel Syncope
In nominals with strengthening gradation, the vowel of the second syllable, present in weak-grade forms, is syncopated in strong-grade forms, cf. ´tütar 'daughter': sG `tütre; `kümme 'ten': sG `kümne; `katel 'kettle': sG `katla; ´ainus 'single': sG `ainsa; ´mõtelda 'to think': `mõtlen 'I think'. Syncope also occurs in nominals which have a bisyllabic stem of Q3 that ends in a resonant or, in a-stems, in the sibilant s, e.g. `ankur 'anchor': sG `ankru; `tähtis 'important': sG `tähtsa.

Stem-vowel Alternation
In addition to alternations conditioned by apocope or syncope of a stem vowel, there also occur the stem-vowel alternations *i ~ e* and *u ~ o*.

Bisyllabic nominals with a short first syllable have the stem vowel *i* in the nominative singular instead of the stem vowel *e*, which is present in most case forms, cf. ´tuli 'fire': sG ´tule, sEla ´tulest; ´nimi 'name': sGP ´nime; ´mägi 'hill': sG `mäe, sP ´mäge.

For bisyllabic stems with qualitative gradation the stem vowels *u* and, after a long first syllable, the *i* of strong grade forms alternate with stem vowels *o* and *e* of those weak-grade forms that have lost the single stop *d* or *g*, cf. ´tigu 'snail': sG `teo; ´tegu 'deed': sG `teo; ´lugu 'story': sG `loo; `pood 'shop' : sP `poodi : sG `poe; `saagida 'to saw' : `saen 'I saw'.

Lowering of Short High Vowels
As a result of the loss of *b d g* in weak-grade forms, the short high vowels *i u ü* of the first syllable are lowered to the mid vowels *e o ö* before *o, a*, and *e*, e.g. `oad 'beans' (´uba 'bean'), `põab 'cuts the hair' (´pügada 'to cut the hair') `seon 'I bind' (´siduda 'to bind').

-ne : -s(e) Alternations
The suffix alternation *-ne* (sN): *-s-* (sP): *-se(-)* (elsewhere) occurs in adjectives, in the ordinal numerals *esimene* 'first', *teine* 'second' and in nouns (in complex suffixes such as *=lane, =line, =mine*), cf. `sakslane 'a/the German': sP `sakslast : sG `sakslase.

Gemination in the First Illative (Illative-1)
In bisyllabic nominal stems with a short first syllable the intervocalic consonant is geminated in the illative-1 singular or the 'short' illative, e.g. ´veri 'blood': `verre 'into the blood', ´udu 'fog': `uttu 'into the fog'. See Nominal Inflection, p. 127.

se-Syncopation in Illative
A postvocalic stem-final *se*-sequence is optionally syncopated before the illative ending *-sse* in a trisyllabic stem of Q3 or in a quadrisyllabic stem, e.g. `rasku`sesse ~ `raskusse, ´juma´lusesse ~ ´juma´lusse, ´ini´mesesse ~ ´ini´messe from `raskus 'difficulty', ´jumalus 'deity', ´ini´mene 'man, human being'.

Plural Stem Formation

In monosyllabic vocalic stems ending in a long monophthong other than *üü* or *ii*, the long monophthong is shortened before the pluralizer -*i*-, e.g. `puu 'tree': pP `puid, `soo 'swamp': pP `soid, `töö 'work': pP `töid, i`dee 'idea': pP i`deid.

For a set of bisyllabic vocalic stems with a short first syllable or with weakening gradation the so-called *stem plural* is possible: in such cases the vowel is replaced by another vowel, mostly in the partitive plural, but also in other plural case forms according to the following scheme:

u > *e*, e.g. `võrk 'net', sP `võrku, pP `võrke;
i > *e*, e.g. `värv 'colour', sP `värvi, pP `värve;
e > *i*, e.g. `järv 'lake', sP `järve, pP `järvi;
a > *u*, after first-syllable *a(a)*, *i(i)*, *õ(õ)*, *ei*, or *äi*, and after *lj* after first-syllable *e* or *ä*, e.g. *kala* 'fish', pP *kalu*; `vaal 'whale', sP `vaala, pP `vaalu;
a > *i*, except after *j*, after first-syllable *e*, *ä*, *ö* or *ü*, or if there is *o(o)* or *u(u)* in the preceding long first syllable, e.g. `koer 'dog', sP `koera, pP `koeri;
a > *e* after *j* and *i* if there is an *o*, *u*, or *ü* in the first syllable or if there is an *o* or *u* in the preceding short syllable, e.g. *ori* 'slave', sP `orja, pP `orje.

Morphology

Nominal Inflection

In Estonian as elsewhere in Fennic, nominals, i.e. nouns, adjectives, numerals and pronouns, are mostly inflected in number and case.

There are in Estonian fifteen nominal cases, in both singular and plural. Three are grammatical cases, namely nominative (N), genitive (G), and partitive (P); the remaining twelve are adverbial cases, namely illative-1 (Ill-1) (sometimes called 'additive'), illative-2 (Ill-2), inessive (Ine), elative (Ela), allative (All), adessive (Ade), ablative (Abl), translative (Trans), terminative (Term), essive (Ess), abessive (Abe), and comitative (Com).

In a departure from tradition, here Ill-1, from the proto-Fennic illative in *-hen, which is in modern Estonian morphologically unmarked (except for monosyllabic vocalic singular stems, where it has the endings -*ha*, -*he*, -*hu*), is treated separately from the innovative Ill-2, (the 'long' illative) in -*sse* or -*de*. The 'short' illative cannot be formed from several structural types of nominal stems; the 'long' illative is used instead, including adjectival attributes of nouns in Ill-1. Nevertheless, when there exist in a paradigm both a 'short' and a 'long' illative form, the former one can be replaced by the interrogative pronoun `kuhu 'where to', whereas the corresponding 'long' form can be replaced by the pronoun `millesse 'in(to) what'; the choice between these two forms is not free, but depends rather on verb government. Thus, for example, it is possible to say `lähen `sõja`väkke 'I go into the army', `lähen `kooli 'I go to school', `võtan

Figure 4.4 Interrelations of case forms of weakening stems: *jalg* 'foot'

	Singular	*de*-Plural	Stem plural	*e*-Plural
N	` jalg	´ jala **d**		
P	` jalga	` jalga **sid**	` jalgu	
I11-1	` jalga		` jalgu	
G	´ jala	` jalga **de**		` jalg **e**
I11-2	´ jala **sse**	` jalga **desse**		
Ine	´ jala **s**	` jalga **des**	´ jalu **s**	` jalg **es**
Ela	´ jala **st**	` jalga **dest**	´ jalu **st**	` jalg **est**
All	´ jala **le**	` jalga **dele**	´ jalu **le**	` jalg **ele**
Ade	´ jala **l**	` jalga **del**	´ jalu **l**	` jalg **el**
Abl	´ jala **lt**	` jalga **delt**	´ jalu **lt**	` jalg **elt**
Tr	´ jala **ks**	` jalga **deks**	´ jalu **ks**	
Term	´ jala **ni**	` jalga **deni**	´ jalu **ni**	
Ess	´ jala **na**	` jalga **dena**		
Abe	´ jala **ta**	` jalga **deta**	´ jalu **ta**	
Com	´ jala **ga**	` jalga **dega**		` jalg **ega**

`kätte 'I take in the hand', ´pistan ´suhu 'I stick into the mouth', `kostab `kõrva 'it sounds in (one's) ear', `kostab `kõrvu 'it sounds in (one's) ears', but one cannot say *´lähen ´sõja`väesse, *´lähen `koolisse, *´võtan `käesse, *´pistan `suusse, *`kostab `kõrvasse, *`kostab `kõrva`desse. Note that one uses the 'long forms' in constructions such as `suhtun ´vaenu´likult ´sõja`väesse 'I have a hostile attitude

Figure 4.5 Interrelations of case forms of strengthening stems: *hammas* 'tooth'

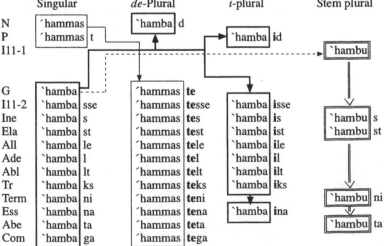

	Singular	*de*-Plural	*i*-plural	Stem plural
N	´ hammas	` hamba **d**		
P	´ hammas **t**		` hamba **id**	
I11-1				` hambu
G	` hamba	´ hammas **te**		
I11-2	` hamba **sse**	´ hammas **tesse**	` hamba **isse**	
Ine	` hamba **s**	´ hammas **tes**	` hamba **is**	` hambu **s**
Ela	` hamba **st**	´ hammas **test**	` hamba **ist**	` hambu **st**
All	` hamba **le**	´ hammas **tele**	` hamba **ile**	
Ade	` hamba **l**	´ hammas **tel**	` hamba **il**	
Abl	` hamba **lt**	´ hammas **telt**	` hamba **ilt**	
Tr	` hamba **ks**	´ hammas **teks**	` hamba **iks**	
Term	` hamba **ni**	´ hammas **teni**		` hambu **ni**
Ess	` hamba **na**	´ hammas **tena**	` hamba **ina**	
Abe	` hamba **ta**	´ hammas **teta**		` hambu **ta**
Com	` hamba **ga**	´ hammas **tega**		

towards the army', *see `puutub `käesse* 'it concerns the hand'. As a result of the restricted functions of Ill-1, many nominals have no Ill-1 form for semantic reasons. On the other hand, in this chapter the illative in *-de*, often held to be a 'short' illative, since it has been abstracted from certain Ill-1 forms (cf. `õõnde* from `õõs* 'cavity', sG *õõne*, where the *-de* was originally a part of the stem), is treated as different from Ill-1. The illative in *-de* is beginning to replace the illative in *-sse* in bisyllabic stems whose stem vowel *e* follows a resonant preceded by a long vocalism, cf. `keelde* and `keelesse* from `keel* 'tongue; language'.

Apart from Ill-1, the remaining eleven adverbial cases of Estonian (Ill-2, Ine, Ela, All, Ade, Abl, Trans, Term, Ess, Abe and Com) can be formed by adding a case ending to the genitive singular form to yield the singular form, and to the genitive plural form to yield the plural form. In addition, the common genitive plural form can be formed by adding the ending *-de* or *-te* to the genitive singular form (this is not the case for most pronouns). Among the grammatical cases, the nominative singular (sN) and genitive singular (sG) are always unmarked, while the partitive singular (sP), partitive plural (pP), and genitive plural (pG) have several endings or, in the cases of the sP and pP, may be unmarked; see Figures 4.4 and 4.5.

Plural Formation
There are several types of plural stem formation. The most common is the so-called *de*-plural, based on the plural genitive form. This is the only method available for nominals which take only the ending *-sid* in the plural partitive; for nominals taking the pP ending *-id* the *i*-plural is also possible. For many nominals having in their partitive singular an unmarked bisyllabic form, the stem plural is possible alongside the *de*-plural . In such cases the stem vowel of the plural stem is different from that of the singular stem according to the general scheme given under Plural Stem Formation, p. 127.

The different types of plural formation have different stylistic values and the stem plural, in particular, is subject to several restrictions, causing complicated alternations and homophony.

Case Formation
Nominative, genitive, partitive, and illative-1 forms are often distinguished only by stem alternations that can be present also in morphologically marked case forms. A noun can have from one to six stem allomorphs. The interrelation of stem allomorphs in the paradigm depends also on the deployment of weakening v. strengthening gradation; see Figures 4.4 and 4.5.

Comparative and Superlative of Adjectives
Adjectives take the comparative suffix *-m* in the nominative singular and *-ma(-)* in other case forms; the suffix regularly follows the usual stem vowel (transparent in sG forms) for *u-*, *i-*, and *e*-stems and for trisyllabic *a*-stems and bisyllabic *a*-stems of Q3. In bisyllabic *a*-stems of Q2, the stem vowel *a* is

Table 4.1   Comparative and superlative of adjectives

sN	pP	Comparative	Superlative	Gloss
´rahulik	´rahu`likke	´rahu`likum	´rahu`likem	'peaceful'
´nüri	´nürisid	´nürim	`kõige ´nürim	'dull'
´sinine	´siniseid	´sinisem	´siniseim	'blue'
`uhke	`uhkeid	`uhkem	`uhkeim	'proud'
`suur	`suuri	´suurem	´suurim	'big'
´madal	´madalaid	´madalam	´madalaim	'low'
´rikas	`rikkaid	`rikkam	`rikkaim	'rich'
`must	`musti	´mustem	´mustim	'black'
`laisk	`laisku	`laisem	`kõige `laisem	'lazy'
´vana	´vanu	´vanem	´vanim	'old'
`kena	`keni	`kenam	`kenim	'nice'

regularly replaced by *e*, in stems of Q1 this is a rarer feature. The adjective `hea 'good' has the suppletive comparative form *parem* 'better'. The superlative suffix is *-im* in the nominative singular and *-ima* in other case forms; its occurrence is regular for adjectives having the plural partitive form ending in *-id* or *-i* and in derivatives built with *=ik* and *=lik*; the superlative suffix is *-em* and *-ema*.

Alongside the suffixal superlatives for all comparable adjectives an analytical superlative form consisting of the sequence `kõige plus the comparative grade form is possible; `kõige is the genitive singular form of `kõik 'all'.

The adjectives ´alumine 'lower', ´ülemine 'higher', `pealmine 'upper, higher', ´esi´mene 'first, foremost, front', ´viimane 'latter, recent', ´tagu´mine 'back', ´väli´mine 'outer, opposite from inside', ´äärmine 'outer, farther from the middle' have no comparative grade forms but may have the analytical superlative grade forms.

Numerals

The Estonian underived cardinal numerals and their patterns of declension are shown in Table 4.2.

The corresponding ordinal numerals are mostly derived from the genitive singular stem; in the course of derivation the vowel *e* is substituted for the stem vowel *i* of certain cardinal numerals. The ordinal *kolmas* 'the third' is exceptional in that it adds the derivational suffixes to the stem vowel *a* instead of *e*. The ordinals *esimene* 'the first' and *teine* 'the second' are suppletive.

The formation of the cardinal numerals from 11 to 19 is based on subtraction, e.g. `üks`teist`kümmend '11' (i.e. 'one of the second ten'), `kaks-`teist`kümmend '12', where `kümmend is an otherwise obsolete partitive form of *kümme* '10'; the corresponding ordinals are ´ühe`teist`kümnes and `kahe-`teist`kümnes. The cardinal numerals for tens, hundreds, thousands, millions etc. are based on multiplication, but with singular morphology, e.g. `kaks

Table 4.2   Cardinal numerals

	sN	sG	sP	sIll-2
0	`null	´nulli	`nulli	`nulli
1	`üks	´ühe	`üht(e)	`ühte
2	`kaks	´kahe	`kaht(e)	`kahte
3	`kolm	´kolme	`kolme	`kolme
4	´neli	´nelja	`nelja	`nelja
5	`viis	´viie	`viit	`viide
6	`kuus	´kuue	`kuut	`kuude
7	´seitse	´seitsme	´seitset	´seitsmesse
8	´kaheksa	´kaheksa	´kaheksat	´kahek`sasse
9	´üheksa	´üheksa	´üheksat	´ühek`sasse
10	´kümme	`kümne	´kümmet	`kümnesse
100	´sada	´saja	´sadat	´sajasse
1,000	´tuhat	´tuhande	´tuhandet	´tuhan`desse
10^6	`miljon	`miljoni	`miljonit	`miljo`nisse
10^9	`miljard	`miljardi	`miljardit	`miljar`disse

Table 4.3   Ordinal numerals

	sN	sG	sP	Ill-2	pG
1	´esimene	´esimese	´esimest	´esi`messe	´esi´meste
2	´teine	´teise	`teist	`teise	´teiste
3	´kolmas	´kolmanda	´kolmandat	´kolman`dasse	´kolman´date
4	´neljas	´neljanda	´neljandat	´neljan`dasse	´neljan´date
8	´kaheksas	´kahek´sanda	´kahek´sandat	´kahek´sandasse	´kahek´sandate
1,000	´tuhandes	´tuhan´denda	´tuhan´dendat	´tuhan´dendasse	´tuhan´dendate
10^6	`miljones	`miljo´nenda	`miljo´nendat	`miljo´nendasse	`miljo´nendate

´sada '200', `kaks ´tuhat '2,000', `kaks `miljonit '2,000,000'. Teens, tens, and hundreds make compounds, and their declension pattern in cases other than nominative, genitive, and partitive differs from that of numerals for thousands, millions etc., e.g.:

	12	200	2,000
sN	`kaks`teist(`kümmend)	`kaks´sada	`kaks ´tuhat
sG	´kahe`tcist(`kümne)	´kahe´saja	´kahe ´tuhande
sP	`kaht`teist(`kümmend)	`kaht´sada	`kaht(e) ´tuhat
sIll	´kahe`teist`kümnesse	´kahe´sajasse	`kahte ´tuhandesse
sIne	´kahe`teist`kümnes	´kahe´sajas	´kahes ´tuhandes

With the exception of the informal fractional numerals `pool 'half' and

ˋveerand 'quarter', simple fractional numerals, i.e. denominators, are derived on the analogy of ordinal numerals by means of the suffix =ndik, e.g. ´kahendik 'a half'; ´kolmandik 'a third' ´neljandik 'a quarter'. Fractional numerals with numerators are inflected similarly to cardinals for thousands, millions, etc. e.g.

	One-third	Two-thirds
sN	ˋüks ´kolmandik	ˋkaks ˋkolmanˋdikku
sG	´ühe ´kolmanˊdiku	´kahe ´kolmanˊdiku
sP	ˋüht(e) ´kolmanˋdikku	´kaht(e) ´kolmanˋdikku
sIll	ˋühte ´kolmanˋdikku	´kahte ´kolmanˋdikku
sIne	´ühes ´kolmanˊdikus	´kahes ´kolmanˊdikus

Table 4.4   Personal pronouns

	1	2	3
Singular			
N	´mina ~ ma	´sina ~ sa	´tema ~ ta
G	´minu ~ mu	´sinu ~ su	´tema ~ ta
P	ˋmind	ˋsind	´teda
Ill-2	ˋminusse ~ ˋmusse	ˋsinusse ~ ˋsusse	´temasse ~ ˋtasse
Ine	´minus ~ mus	´sinus ~ sus	´temas ~ tas
Ela	´minust ~ must	´sinust ~ sust	´temast ~ tast
All	´minule ~ ˋmulle	´sinule ~ ˋsulle	´temale ~ ˋtalle
Ade	´minul ~ mul	´sinul ~ sul	´temal ~ tal
Abl	´minult ~ mult	´sinult ~ sult	´temalt ~ talt
Trans	´minuks	´sinuks	´temaks
Term	´minuni	´sinuni	´temani
Ess	´minuna	´sinuna	´temana
Abe	´minuta	´sinuta	´temata
Com	´minuga ~ muga	´sinuga ~ suga	´temaga ~ taga
Plural			
N	´meie ~ me	´teie ~ te	´nemad ~ nad
G	´meie ~ me	´teie ~ te	´nende
P	ˋmeid	ˋteid	ˋneid
Ill-2	ˋmeisse	ˋteisse	ˋnendesse ~ ˋneisse
Ine	ˋmeis	ˋteis	´nendes ~ ˋneis
Ela	ˋmeist	ˋteist	´nendest ~ ˋneist
All	ˋmeile	ˋteile	´nendele ~ ˋneile
Ade	ˋmeil	ˋteil	´nendel ~ ˋneil
Abl	ˋmeilt	ˋteilt	´nendelt ~ ˋneilt
Trans	ˋmeiks	ˋteiks	´nendeks ~ ˋneiks
Term	´meieni	´teieni	´nendeni
Ess	´meiena	´teiena	´nendena
Abe	´meieta	´teieta	´nendeta
Com	´meiega	´teiega	´nendega

Personal Pronouns

Personal pronouns have, in addition to the so-called long forms, short forms, most of which usually occur in unstressed positions. In the singular the first- and second-person short pronouns have two stems, one of which occurs only in the nominative, viz. *ma* 'I' and *sa* 'thou'; the other stems, *mu(-)* and *su(-)*, occur elsewhere, except in the partitive, translative, terminative, essive and abessive; similarly, instead of the third-person plural forms of the illative, inessive, elative, allative, adessive, and ablative, forms exploiting the partitive stem `nei- or (in monosyllabic forms also unstressed) nei- can be used. This stem has been borrowed from the paradigm of the demonstrative plural pronoun `need 'these'. In the plural, the first and second persons have the short forms *me* 'we' and *te* 'you' only in the nominative and the genitive; contrast the third person, where the short stem form *ta* occurs in several case forms.

Possessive Pronoun

The possessive pronoun is *oma* (substitutable by ˈkelle? 'whose?'), e.g. ˈjutusta ˈoma ˈlastest! 'tell about your children!'; contrast the adjective *oma* (substitutable by ˈmilline? 'which?', but not by ˈkelle) as in ˈma ei ˈräägi ˈomadest ˈini ˈmestest 'I do not speak about (my) own people', where ˈoma agrees with the following noun in case and number (elative plural).

Reflexive Pronoun

The reflexive pronoun 'self' has a suppletive paradigm. Sample forms:

	Singular	Plural
N	ˈise	ˈise
G	ˈenese ~ `enda	ˈeneste ~ `endi
P	ˈennast ~ `end	ˈennast ~ `endid
Ill-2	ˈene`sesse ~ `endasse	ˈenes`tesse ~ `endisse
Ine	ˈeneses ~ `endas	ˈenestes ~ `endis

Demonstratives

The underived demonstrative pronouns of Estonian are `see 'this', `too 'that', ˈsama 'same'. Of the two demonstrative/locative pronouns, most Estonians manage with just the first, *see* 'this' which, like the personal pronouns, has both long and short forms, the latter normally unstressed. Historically, the genitive plural form and all long forms have been borrowed from the paradigm of the third-person plural pronoun *nemad*. The other demonstrative/locative pronoun, `too 'that', is characteristically used by South Estonians. Its declension is entirely analogous to that of `see, e.g. sG ˈtolle, sP ˈtoda, pN `nood, pG ˈnonde, pP ˈnoid. The pronouns `see and `sama are inflected as shown in Table 4.5.

Demonstrative pronouns form compounds with one other, e.g. `see ˈsama 'the same', `too ˈsama 'that same (one)'.

Table 4.5　Demonstrative pronouns

	Singular	*Plural*	*Singular*	*Plural*
N	`see	`need	´sama	´samad
G	´selle	`nende	´sama	´samade
P	´seda	`neid	´sama	´samu
Ill	´sellesse ~ `sesse	`nendesse ~ `neisse	´samasse	´sama`desse
Ine	´selles ~ ses	`nendes ~ `neis	´samas	´samades
Ela	´sellest ~ sest	`nendest ~ `neist	´samast	´samadest
All	´sellele	`nendele ~ `neile	´samale	´sama´dele
Ade	´sellel ~ sel	`nendel ~ `neil	´samal	´samadel
Abl	´sellelt ~ selt	`nendelt ~ `neilt	´samalt	´samadelt
Trans	´selleks ~ seks	`nendeks ~ `neiks	´samaks	´samadeks
Term	´selleni	`nendeni	´samani	´sama´deni
Ess	´sellena	`nendena	´samana	´sama´dena
Abe	´selleta	`nendeta	´samata	´sama´deta
Com	´sellega	`nendega	´samaga	´sama´dega

There is also a set of demonstrative adjectives formed from demonstrative pronouns either by derivation or compounding, e.g. ´selline 'such', `see-´sugune 'such', ´sama´sugune 'of the same kind', `see´samane 'the same'. The demonstrative adjective `nii´sugune 'such, of that kind', is formed from the adverb `nii 'so, in this way'. The demonstrative adjectives are inflected on the model of ´selline and `see´sugune:

	Singular	Plural	Singular	Plural
N	´selline	´sellised	`see´sugune	`see´sugused
G	´sellise	´selliste	`see´suguse	`see´suguste
P	´sellist	´selliseid	`see´sugust	`see´suguseid
Ill	´selli`sesse	´sellis`tesse ~ ´sellis`eisse	`see´sugu`sesse	`see´sugus`tesse ~ `see´sugu`seisse

Interrogatives and Relatives

Estonian has the interrogative/relative pronouns `kes 'who', and `mis 'what', both of which are usually inflected in the singular; they are inflected in the plural for special emphasis. The pronoun `kumb 'which (of the two)' inflects in the singular or the plural depending on the singularity or plurality of the two sets under selection, e.g. `kumb `king 'which one of the two shoes' and `kummad `kingad 'which (pair) of the two pairs of shoes'. The pronouns `kes, `mis, and `kumb are inflected as follows:

	Sg	Plur	Sg	Plur	Sg	Plur
N	`kes	`kes	`mis	`mis	`kumb	`kummad
G	`kelle	`kellede	´mille	´millede	`kumma	`kumbade
P	`keda	`keda	´mida	´mida	`kumba	`kumbi
Ill	`kellesse	`kelle`desse	´millesse	´mille`desse	`kumba	`kumba`desse

There are also interrogative/relative adjectives meaning 'which', namely `milline, `mis `sugune, both formed from the pronoun `mis, and the adjective *mäherdune*, which is sometimes used in informal style.

Another set of interrogatives and relatives are case forms of the stem *ku-*, e.g. illative-1 `kuhu '(to) where', inessive `kus 'where', `kust 'from where', `kuhuni 'as far as where', essive `kuna 'when'. These forms occur in appositional compounds with several postpositions, e.g. `kuhu`poole 'towards what, in which direction', `kus`pool 'in which direction', `kust`poolt 'from which direction', `kust`kaudu 'which way, through which point', `kust`peale 'beginning from which point or time', `kust`saadik 'up to which point or time'. The same stem also occurs in the interrogative/relative `kuidas 'how, in which way', e.g. `kuidas sa tead? 'How do you know?') and in the interrogative/relative `kui 'how', e.g. `kui vana 'how old' and the conjunction `kui 'when; if'.

Indefinite and Negative Pronouns

The pronouns `keegi 'somebody; nobody', `miski 'something; nothing', `mingi 'a, some; no' and `kumbki 'either; neither (of two)' `ükski 'at least one; none' are indefinite in affirmative sentences and either indefinite or negative in negative sentences. Example: `keegi ei `sulgenud `välis`ust means, depending on the context, either 'somebody has not closed the outer door' or 'nobody closed the outer door'. The pronouns `keegi and `miski are inflected only in the singular, `mingi (pG *mingite*, pP `mingeid), `kumbki and `ükski are inflected in both singular and plural. Sample singular forms:

sN `keegi	`miski	`mingi	`kumbki	`ükski
sG `kellegi	`millegi	`mingi	`kummagi	`ühegi
sP `kedagi	`midagi	`mingit	`kumbagi	`ühtki ~ `ühtegi
sIll `kelles`segi	`milles`segi	`mingisse	`kumbagi	`ühtegi

When used as negative pronouns, the negative character of the pronouns can be emphasized by means of the preposed word `mitte, e.g. `mitte `keegi. The compound adjective `mingi`sugune carries negative meaning only when preceded by the word `mitte; otherwise it has the meaning 'a, some'.

Some pronouns are purely indefinite, e.g. `mõni 'some', `kõik 'all', `muu 'else' and `iga 'any, every', `emb`kumb 'either this or that'. Sample forms:

	Sg	Plur	Sg	Plur	Sg	Plur	Sg
N	`mõni	`mõned	`kõik	`kõik	`muu	`muud	`iga
G	`mõne	`mõnede	`kõige	`kõigi ~ `kõikide	`muu	`muude	`iga
P	`mõnd(a)	`mõnesid	`kõike	`kõiki	`muud	`muid	`iga(t)
Ill	`mõnda	`mõne`desse	`kõike	`kõigisse	`muusse	`muudesse	`igasse

Verb

The Estonian verb has (1) finite forms, which occur only as predicates or as the auxiliary components of complex predicates, and (2) non-finite forms, which occur (a) in complex predicates in combination with a finite form (past participles), (b) similarly to adjectives as attributes and predicatives (participles), (c) as adverbials (supines and gerunds), (d) as subjects and objects (infinitives).

Simple Finite Forms

Finite forms can encode voice, mood, tense, aspect, person and number.

Of the two voices, the personal voice (Ps) is indicated by person and number suffixes (s1 -n, s2 -d, p1 -me, p2 -te, p3 -d) that are obligatory in the indicative mood and optional in the conditional. Subject pronouns and nouns can be omitted when the finite form has a personal ending. There are no person or number suffixes in the quotative and jussive moods. The markers of the impersonal voice (Ips) are -a-, -da-, and -ta- in the affirmative present indicative, -da(-) and -ta(-) in the conditional, quotative, and jussive moods and in the negative present indicative, and -d- and -t- in the imperfect tense of the indicative mood.

Mood in Estonian includes the indicative, conditional, imperative, quotative and jussive. The indicative mood is used when the speaker affirms or denies the occurrence or non-occurrence of a situation or an action (*sa kõnnid liiga kiiresti* '**you walk** too quickly'). The conditional mood is used to express the speaker's opinion that a situation or an action should or should not have occurred, or would or would not occur, under certain conditions (*kõnniksin aeglasemalt kui oleks soojem* '**I would walk** more slowly if it were warmer') or that the occurrence or non-occurrence of a situation or an action is obligatory or preferable (*räägiksin nüüd tõtt* '**I should tell** the truth now'). The imperative mood expresses the speaker's request, order, or prohibition to the listener(s), e.g. *minge mõlemad koju!* 'you both **go** home!') or the speaker's suggestion to the listener(s) that a joint action be undertaken, e.g. *võidelgem lõpuni!* '**let us fight** to the finish!'). The quotative mood is used when the speaker wants to point out that (s)he is not responsible for the veracity of a statement, but is only an intermediator or reporter, e.g. *sa ostvat maja* 'you **are (reported to be) buying** a house'. The jussive mood expresses either that the listener(s) should convey the request, order, or prohibition to a third party (*tulen kell viis, Mari oodaku mind!* 'I'll come at five o'clock, **let** Mary **be waiting** for me!') or that one is compelled by someone to do (or not to do) something (*meie lugegu nüüd iga senti!* 'we **should be counting** every cent now!').

There are simple, i.e. non-compound affirmative present- and imperfect-tense forms and complex, i.e. compound, perfect and pluperfect forms in the indicative mood and simple affirmative present- and past-tense forms in the conditional and quotative moods; there are also corresponding compound forms for the non-compound past conditional and quotative. There are in addition to the non-compound present-tense forms of the imperative and jussive moods also compound perfect forms. All compound tense forms contain a finite form of the auxiliary verb `olla 'to be' and a personal or an impersonal past participle.

The *affirmative* is characterized by (obligatory or optional) personal endings in the personal indicative and conditional mood forms and by special tense suffixes in the impersonal indicative mood forms. The *negative* has characteristic complex forms: (1) in the indicative, conditional, and quotative moods, a specific negative form, which is marked only for voice and mood or tense, and the preposed negation particle *ei*, and (2) in the imperative and jussive moods, a personal form preceded by the appropriate form of the defective prohibition verb (s2imp `ära, p1imp `ärgem ~ `ärme, p2imp `ärge and jussive `ärgu).

In the imperative, there is no first-person singular form, and the former third-person form has been generalized in most dialects (including the standard language) to all persons to render an indirect order or a forced action or situation, thus yielding a new mood, the jussive. The second-person singular form is unmarked, the second-person plural form has the suffix -*ge*/-*ke*, and the same suffix occurs in the rarely used formal first-person form, which has the unique personal ending -*m*. In informal style the first-person plural form of the present indicative is used instead of the imperative mood form; however, in contrast to the negative forms of the indicative mood, the first-person plural forms retain their personal ending when forming complex negative forms with the informal first-person prohibition verb form `ärme, e.g. `ärme `ootame 'let us not wait', `ärme `läh(e)me 'let us not go', contrast the formal equivalents `ärgem `oodakem and `ärgem `mingem and the morphologically unmarked negative present indicative forms *me ei* `oota 'we do not wait', `me ei `lähe 'we do not go'.

With the exception of the imperative mood, the finite-form voice, mood, and tense suffixes in the affirmative (aff) and negative (neg) are as presented in Table 4.6.

Non-finite Forms
Non-finite forms include participles, the supine, the infinitive and the gerund, as set forth in Table 4.7. Participles and the supine may be either personal or impersonal, e.g. `valvav `mees 'a/the guarding man' and `valvatav `mees 'a/the man who is being guarded', `valvanud `mees 'a/the man who has guarded', `valvatud `mees 'a/the man who has been guarded'. Present participles function like adjectives, and are inflected in case and number. Past participles, in addition to their use as attributes or predicatives, can compose complex tense forms built with finite forms of the verb 'to be', namely the perfect and pluperfect indicative, past conditional, past quotative and perfect imperative, e.g.

Table 4.6 Voice, mood, and tense markers in finite forms

Mood and tense		Indicative Present	Imperfect	Conditional Present	Imperfect	Quotative Present	Imperfect	Jussive Present
Ps aff	s3	-b	-i, -is, -s	-ks	-nuks	-vat	-nuvat	-gu, -ku
	p3	-va-	-i, -si-	-ks(i-)	-nuks(i-)	-vat	-nuvat	-gu, -ku
	s12, p12	—	-i, -si-	-ks(i-)	-nuks(i-)	-vat	-nuvat	-gu, -ku
Ps neg		ø	-nud	-ks	-nuks	-vat	-nuvat	-gu, -ku
Ips aff		-akse -dakse }	-di	-daks	-duks	-davat	—	-dagu
		-takse	-ti	-taks	-tuks	-tavat	—	-tagu
Ips neg		-da	-dud	-daks	-duks	-davat	—	-dagu
		-ta	-tud	-taks	-tuks	-tavat	—	-tagu

Table 4.7   Infinite form markers

Infinite forms		Personal			Impersonal	
Participle	present	-v	-ev		-dav	-tav
	past	-nud			-dud	-tud
Supine	illative	-ma			-dama	-tama
	inessive	-mas				
	elative	-mast				
	translative	-maks				
	abessive	-mata				
Infinitive		-a	-da	-ta		
Gerund		-es	-des	-tes		

1   *Kütt on haavanud hunti* 'A hunter has wounded the wolf'.
2   *Hunti on haavatud* 'One has wounded the wolf'.
3   *Hunt on haavatud* 'The wolf is wounded'.

Sentences (1) and (2) have predicates in the perfect indicative and an object (*hunti*) in the partitive singular; sentence (3) has the predicate *on* in the present indicative and the subject *hunt* in the nominative singular, *haavatud* being a predicative complement.

Supine forms function as adverbials, with various case forms expressing intentions or attempts at doing something, ongoing states and activities, goals, etc., for example, illative *ˈlähen ˈmalet ˈmängima* 'I'm going (somewhere) to play chess', *ˋhakka ˈlugema!* 'start reading!', inessive *ˈolin ˋklubis ˈmalet ˈmängimas* 'I was in the club playing chess', elative *ˈtulen ˈmalet ˈmängimast* 'I come from playing chess', translative *ˈoled ˋliiga ˈvana ˈvaletamaks* 'you are too old for lying', abessive *ˈära ˋlahku ˋmaksˋmata* 'don't leave without paying!' The impersonal supine is used only with the indicative and conditional verb forms *ˋpeab* 'must' and *ˋpeaks* 'should': *ˋseda ˋpeab ˋsöödama* 'one must eat it', *ˋseda ˋpeaks ˋsöödama* 'one should eat it'. As the illative form of the personal supine is always in the strong grade, it has been the traditional citation form for verbs in Estonian dictionaries.

Infinitives serve as subject (*ˈlugeda on ˋmeeldiv* 'reading is pleasant') or object (*ˈeelisˈtame ˈoodata* 'we prefer to wait'). Gerunds are adverbials which indicate a parallel action or process (*ˈoodates ˋrongi ma ˈlugesin* '(while) waiting for the train, I was reading').

In certain constructions the use of the illative supine or of the infinitive depends on the predicate verb, cf. *ta ˋpeab ˋootama* 'he must wait', *tal ˈtuleb ˈoodata* '(s)he (adessive) has to wait'.

Verbal Nouns
Most Estonian grammars include in the verb paradigm two (de)verbal nouns which are inflected in both case and number. These are the *nomen agentis* in =*ja* and the *nomen actionis* in =*mine*, e.g. `sööja 'eater', `söömine '(the act of) eating'. In fact, *nomina actionis* belong to a more complicated system of actor and undergoer nouns that has resulted from a split of the former past participles, cf. `sööja 'eater (unspecified for time)', ´söönu 'one who has or had eaten (previously)', `söödu 'something or someone that has been eaten (previously)'. In certain petrified phrases, *ja*-derivatives behave like present participles but remain unspecified for time, e.g. `haukuja `koer 'a/the dog that has the habit of barking (a lot)' and `haukuv `koer 'a/the dog that is (= just happens to be) barking'.

Verb Inflection
Like nominal inflection, verb inflection is complicated by extensive suffix and stem alternation, neither of which is entirely predictable.

   As an example of verb inflection the paradigm of the verb `sööta 'to feed' is presented below; it represents verbs with weakening gradation.

   Infinite forms are as follows:

Participles	Personal: present `söötev, past `söötnud
	Impersonal: present ´söödetav, past ´söödetud
Supine	Personal: ill `söötma ine `söötmas ela `söötmast trans `söötmaks abe `söötmata
	Impersonal: ill ´söödetama
Infinitive	`sööta
Gerund	´söötes

Table 4.8   Sample verb paradigm, indicative: `sööta 'to feed'

	Present	Imperfect	Perfect	Pluperfect
Affirmative				
s1	´söödan	`söötsin	´olen `söötnud	´olin `söötnud
s2	´söödad	`söötsid	´oled `söötnud	´olid `söötnud
s3	´söödab	`söötis	`on `söötnud	´oli `söötnud
p1	´söödame	`söötsime	´oleme `söötnud	´olime `söötnud
p2	´söödate	`söötsite	´olete `söötnud	´olite `söötnud
p3	´söödavad	`söötsid	`on `söötnud	´olid `söötnud
Ips	´söödetakse	´söödeti	`on ´söödetud	´oli ´söödetud
Negative				
Ps	`ei `sööda	`ei `söötnud	`ei ole `söötnud	`ei ´olnud `söötnud
Ips	`ei ´söödeta	`ei ´söödetud	`ei ole söödetud	`ei ´olnud ´söödetud

Table 4.9   Sample verb paradigm, conditional: ˋsööta 'to feed'

	Present	Past	
Affirmative			
s1	´söödaks(in)	ˋsöötnuks(in)	´oleks(in) ˋsöötnud
s2	´söödaks(id)	ˋsöötnuks(id)	´oleks(id) ˋsöötnud
s3	´söödaks	ˋsöötnuks	´oleks ˋsöötnud
p1	´söödaks(ime)	ˋsöötnuks(ime)	´oleks(ime) ˋsöötnud
p2	´söödaks(ite)	ˋsöötnuks(ite)	´oleks(ite) ˋsöötnud
p3	´söödaks(id)	ˋsöötnuks(id)	´oleks(id) ˋsöötnud
Ips	´söödetaks	´söödetuks	´oleks ´söödetud
Negative			
Ps	ˋei ˋsöödaks	ˋei ˋsöötnuks	ˋei ´oleks ˋsöötnud
Ips	ˋei ´söödetaks	ˋei ´söödetuks	ˋei ´oleks ´söödetud

Table 4.10   Sample verb paradigm, imperative: ˋsööta 'to feed'

	Present Affirmative	Negative	Perfect Affirmative	Negative
s1	—	—	—	—
s2	´sööda	˝ära ´sööda	´ole ˋsöötnud	˝ära ´ole ˋsöötnud
s3	—	—	—	—
p1	ˋsöötkem	˝ärgem ˋsöötkem	´olgem ˋsöötnud	˝ärgem ´olgem ˋsöötnud
p2	ˋsöötke	˝ärge ˋsöötke	´olge ˋsöötnud	˝ärge ´olge ˋsöötnud
p3	—	—	—	—

Table 4.11   Sample verb paradigm, quotative and jussive: ˋsööta 'to feed'

	Present Affirmative	Negative	Perfect Affirmative	Negative
Quotative				
Ps	ˋsöötvat	ˋei ˋsöötvat	ˋsöötnuvat	ˋei ˋsöötnuvat
Ips	´sööde´tavat	ˋei ´sööde´tavat	—	—
Jussive				
Ps	ˋsöötku	˝ärgu ˋsöötku	´olgu ˋsöötnud	˝ärgu ´olgu ˋsöötnud
Ips	ˋsööde´tagu	˝ärgu ´sööde´tagu	´olgu ´söödetud	˝ärgu ´olgu ´söödetud

Adverbs

Adverbs modify (1) a verb (`jookse `ruttu 'run quickly'), adjective ('liiga `noor 'too young') or an adverb ('väga `ruttu 'very quickly') or (2) a clause: these are the interrogative/relative adverbs.

The most frequent interrogative/relative adverbs are `kuhu '(to) where', `kus 'where', `kust 'from where', `millal 'when', `kunas 'when', `kuidas 'how', and `miks 'why'.

Local adverbs often have three case forms, one lative, one locative, and one separative, depending on the direction of the verb's action, e.g. `koju '(to) home', `kodus 'at home', `kodunt 'from home'; `alla, `all, `alt 'down'; `üles, `üleval, `ülevalt 'up'; `ette, `ees, `eest 'before'; `taha, `taga, `tagant 'behind'; `siia, `siin, `siit 'here'; `sinna, `seal, `sealt 'there'; `sisse, `sees, `seest 'in'; `välja, `väljas, `väljast 'out'. Others are not inflected, e.g. `ära 'away'.

The most frequent temporal adverbs are `nüüd 'now', `praegu 'now', `kohe 'immediately', `pärast 'after(wards)', `siis 'then', `varsti 'soon', `ammu 'long ago', `hiljuti 'lately', ('üks)`kord 'once', `äsja 'not long ago', `just 'just', `vara 'early', `hilja 'late', `eile 'yesterday', `täna 'today', `homme 'tomorrow', `mullu 'last year', `tänavu 'this year', `hommikul 'in the morning', `päeval 'in the daytime', `õhtul 'in the evening', `öösel ~ `öösi 'at night'.

Adverbs of manner are most often built with the suffixes =sti or =lt, and have special comparative forms in =mini and superlative forms in =imini, e.g. `kiiresti ~ `kiirelt 'quickly', `kiire `mini 'more quickly', `kiirei `mini 'most quickly'. The adverb `palju 'many; much' has suppletive comparative and superlative forms, viz. `enam or `rohkem 'more' and `enim ~ `kõige `enam or `kõige `rohkem 'most'. Some adverbs of manner have two case forms, one occurring with verbs which indicate a change into a state, the other occurring with verbs which indicate being in a state, e.g. (läheb) `pilve '(it becomes) cloudy': (on) `pilves 'it is cloudy'.

Postpositions and Prepositions

Prepositions and postpositions modify nouns in various case forms; many are identical with adverbs. Like adverbs, several local or orientational prepositions and postpositions have as many as three case forms. There are more postpositions than prepositions.

Some words act as both prepositions and postpositions, e.g. `läbi, `üle, `ümber, `mööda, usually with a difference in meaning, (`läbi `puu 'through the tree', `puu `läbi 'through the fault of a tree'; `üle `silla 'across the bridge', `silla `üle 'about the bridge'), less often with only stylistic overtones ('ümber `sõrme ~ `sõrme `ümber 'around the finger', `mööda `teed ~ `teed `mööda 'along the way').

Nouns governed by prepositions are in the genitive (with the prepositions `alla 'below, beneath', `läbi 'through', `üle 'above; across, beyond', `ümber 'round, around) and in the partitive (with `enne 'before', `ligi 'close to', `piki 'along', `keset 'in the middle of', `mööda 'along', `peale 'after', `pärast 'after', `vastu 'against'). The terminative occurs with `kuni 'until', the abessive with `ilma 'without', and the comitative with (`ühes) `koos 'together with'.

Postpositions govern nouns in the nominative (the postposition läbi 'along, throughout, as in `päev `läbi 'all day long'), the genitive (`järgi 'according to', `kaudu 'by way of', `kaupa 'by', as in `kahe `tosina `kaupa, 'by two dozens'), `jooksul 'during', `kestel 'in the course of', `korral 'in case of', `paiku 'about', as in `kella `ühe `paiku 'at about one o'clock', `pärast 'because of', and for most orientational postpositions, e.g. `vastu 'against, to(wards); in exchange for', `vastas 'beyond'. The postpositions `peale 'beginning with', and `saadik 'up to' govern the elative.

Conjunctions

The most frequent conjunctions are *ja* and *ning* 'and', *ehk* and *või* 'or', *aga*, *vaid*, *ent* and *kuid* 'but', `ainult 'only', *ega* 'nor', *kui* 'if; as', `nagu 'as', `kuigi 'although', *et* 'that', *sest* 'because, for', *kuna* 'while, as, for', `ometi 'still', `siiski 'still, however, nevertheless', `nii`siis 'hence, thus', `nii(`hästi) ... *kui (ka)* 'both ... and', *kas ... või* 'either ... or', `ei ... `ega 'neither ... nor'.

Syntax

Word Order and Sentence Types

In a clause, S[ubject], V[erb], O[bject], P[redicate], and A[dverbial] usually build the following patterns: (1) SV, (2) SVO, (3) SVP, (4) SVA, (5) SVAO, (6) AVS, (7) AV, (8) AVP, (9) AVA, (10) OV, (11) OVA, (12) AVO, as exemplified below.

1   Tähe-d sära-vad. '(The) stars are shining.'
    STAR-plur SPARKLE-p3

2   Tüdruk müü-b lilli. 'A/the girl sells flowers.'
    GIRL SELLS-s3 FLOWER.pP

3   Lapse-d on väikese-d. 'The children are small.'
    CHILD-plur IS.s3 SMALL-plur

4   Kutsika-d ol-i-d aia-s. 'The puppies were in the garden.'
    PUPPY-plur IS-past-plur GARDEN-ine

5   Ma lahuta-n tulu-st kulu-d. 'I delete the expenses from the income.'
    PRO.s1 DELETES-s1 INCOME-cla EXPENSE-plur

6   Koera-l ol-i-d kutsika-d. 'The dog had puppies.'
    DOG-ade IS-past-plur PUPPY-plur

    Aia-s kasva-b lilli. 'There are flowers growing in the garden.'
    GARDEN-ine GROWS-s3 FLOWER.pP

7   Välja-s mürista-b. 'It is thundering outside.'
    OUTSIDE-ine THUNDERS-s3

8   Varvas-te-l hakka-s külm. '(The/his/her . . .) toes began to feel cold.'
    TOE-plur-ade BEGINS-past COLD

    Tänava-l ol-i külm. 'It was cold on the street.'
    STREET-ade IS-past COLD

    Võõras-te-l tule-b lahku-da. 'Strangers have to leave.'
    STRANGER-plur-ade COMES-s3 LEAVES-inf

9   Me-i-l lähe-b hästi. 'We are doing well.'
    PRO.p1-sAde GOES-s3 WELL

10 Sin-d pete-t-i. 'You were deceived.' (= 'One has deceived you.')
    PRO.s2-sP DECEIVE-ips-past

11 Rahvas-t pee-ta-kse rumala-ks. 'People are held (to be) foolish.'
    PEOPLE-sP HOLDS-ips-pres FOOLISH-trans

12 Õun-te-st saa-da-kse mahla. 'One gets juice out of apples.'
    APPLE-plur-ela GETS-ips-pres JUICE.sP

Patterns 6–9 represent existential clauses, 10–12 impersonal clauses. In patterns 1–5, the verb agrees with the subject in person and number; in patterns 7–9 verbs are in the singular, in 10–12 in the impersonal mood. Pattern 6 includes both sentences in which the verb agrees with the subject in person and number and sentences with singular verbs and partial subject (i.e. with the subject in the partitive case).

    In the main, word order in a clause depends not on subject v. object, i.e. grammatical, relations, but rather on topic (what is assumed) v. focus (the central component of the comment on the topic). The topic normally occupies clause-initial position, and the focalized element either occupies clause-final position or attracts the strongest sentence stress in the comment. Thus sentence 5 can be reordered into *tulust ma lahutan kulud* 'from the income I delete the expenses' topicalizing the word *tulust* 'from the income'. Similarly, in *kulud ma lahutan tulust* 'as for expenses, I am deleting them from the income' the word *kulud* 'expenses' has been topicalized and *tulust* has been focalized.

Subject
A subject noun is in either the nominative or the partitive case. The subject noun is in the singular or plural partitive (1) when the predicate verb is in the third person singular and the subject noun, usually in final position, refers to an indefinite amount (´metsas on `loom-i FOREST-ine IS.s3pres ANIMAL-pP 'there are animals in the woods') or (2) when the clause, with predicate verb

in the third person singular and with the subject noun in final position, is negated (*'metsas 'ei ole 'hunt-e* 'there are no wolves in the woods'). Otherwise the subject noun is in the nominative. A subject noun in the partitive is called a partial subject; one in the nominative is called a total subject.

Object
Usually an object nominal is in the partitive: *ema 'ostis 'leiba* MOTHER BUYS-s3past BREAD.sP 'mother bought some bread', *kas sa 'suudled mind?* 'do/will you kiss me?'). An object nominal is in the nominative or genitive only when it denotes a definite quantity in an affirmative clause whose predicate verb is either in distinctively perfective aspect or is a transitive verb with a final adverbial: *'ema 'ostis 'leiva* 'mother bought the bread', *kas sa 'suudled mu 'surnuks?* 'will you kiss me to death?' Note that in the first of these two sentences, the genitive singular object *'leiva* permits three interpretations of the clause: (1) 'I bought one loaf of (rye) bread'; (2) 'I bought all the bread that was available', and (3) 'I bought the amount of bread mentioned earlier'. An object nominal in the partitive is usually called a partial object; one in the nominative or genitive is called a total object.

A singular nominal, including the first- or second-person singular pronoun, as a total object, is in the genitive if the clause is affirmative, the predicate verb is personal and not in the imperative or jussive mood. A singular nominal, except the first- or second-person pronoun, as a total object, is in the nominative if the predicate verb is impersonal or in the imperative or jussive mood. The total object case of plural nominals is the nominative plural; only the first- and second-person pronouns are in identical conditions in the partitive plural.

Measure Adverbials
Much like objects, these occur in the nominative, genitive, and often in the partitive, depending on the morphological form of the predicate verb. Examples: *'olin 'kodus 'terve 'nädala* (sG) 'I was at home a whole week', *'ole kodus 'terve nädal!* (sN) 'be at home a whole week!', ma ei *'olnud 'kodus 'tervet 'nadalat* (sP) 'I was at home (but) not for a whole week'; cf.*ma ei 'olnud 'kodus 'terve 'nädal* (sN) 'I was not at home for a whole week'.

Lexicon
In addition to the lexicon inherited from proto-Fennic and its daughter protolanguages, Estonian has borrowings from both Low and High German, from Estonian Swedish, Finland Swedish, and Sweden Swedish, from Old and Modern Russian, from Latvian, and from Finnish. German was the most significant source of loans from the thirteenth century until 1940, and it was via German that the greater part of the international lexicon entered Estonian. To this day, borrowing patterns of international lexical stock of Latin and Greek origin follow to a great extent those used when borrowing took place

via German, although from the 1920s the original source languages have been taken into account more carefully. Finnish has been a significant source of loans since the 1870s.

Low German was influential up to the sixteenth century. After the Reformation the local German noblemen and bourgeoisie began to shift to High German, and with this shift the local standard form of High German (so-called *Baltendeutsch*) became the main source of borrowings. In many cases it is impossible to distinguish between borrowings from Low and High German on the one hand and between those from Low German and Sweden Swedish on the other. There are about 770–850 borrowings from Low German (e.g. *aabits* 'primer', *haamer* 'hammer', *ingel* 'angle', *kants* 'fort', *kee* 'necklace', *kirik* 'church', *klooster* 'monastery', *kool* 'school', *käärid* 'scissors', *köök* 'kitchen', *kühvel* 'shovel', *küün* 'barn', *munk* 'monk', *mölder* 'miller', *müür* 'stone wall', *naaber* 'neighbour', *ohver* 'victim', *orel* 'organ', *pann* 'pan', *pihtida* 'to confess', *pott* 'pot', *preili* 'Miss', *proua* 'Mrs', *pööning* 'attic', *raad* 'city council', *raatus* 'town hall', *ruum* 'room', *röstida* 'to roast', *röövel* 'robber', *veerida* 'to spell', *vorst* 'sausage', *ämber* 'bucket'), and about 490–540 borrowings from High German (e.g. *kamm* 'comb', *kett* 'chain', *kirss* 'cherry', *loss* 'palace', *pirn* 'pear; electric bulb', *sink* 'ham', *vürts* 'spice; flavouring') including about 60 Baltic German borrowings (e.g. *kutsar* 'coachman', *redel* 'ladder', *sirel* 'lilac', *porgand* 'carrot'). Loan translations from German are no less important.

There are 100–150 borrowings from Swedish (e.g. *hiivata* 'to heave', *iil* 'blast of wind', *moor* 'old woman', *norss* 'smelt', *plika* 'girl', *riik* 'state', *räim* 'Baltic dwarf herring', *säng* 'bed', *tasku* 'pocket').

Except in Setu and the other easternmost dialects which have been in contact with Russian from as early as the Old Russian period, borrowing from Russian began in earnest after 1710, when Russia first engulfed Estonia. In literary Estonian there are about 300–350 Russian loans, including both archaisms and Sovietisms (e.g. *kapsas* 'cabbage', *majakas* 'lighthouse', *morss* 'fruit juice', *munder* 'uniform', *puravik* 'boletus', *riisikas* 'milk mushroom', *tassida* 'to carry').

Borrowings from Latvian began to appear in Estonian in the eighth century. There are about 30–45 in literary Estonian (e.g. *kauss* 'bowl', *kõuts* 'tomcat', *lääts* 'lentil', *nuumata* 'to fatten [tr]', *sõkal* 'chaff', *viisk* 'bast shoe').

There are about 800 Finnish loans in Estonian. These are mostly derived stems built to roots which the two languages have in common, such as *annus* 'portion', built to *anda* 'gives'; cf. the synonymous Finnish *annos*, built from Finnish *anta-*. There are also about 100 Finnish-origin stems which were new to Estonian, such as *aare* 'treasure', *julm* 'brutal', *jäik* 'stiff', *mugav* 'comfortable', *rünnata* 'to attack', *sangar* 'hero', *säilida* 'to preserve', *tehas* 'factory'.

Since the 1920s Estonian has taken on terminology from English and French, usually following the example and pattern of other languages

(German, Russian, or Finnish); there is also direct borrowing from English.

Estonian also has a few direct borrowings from other non-Indo-European languages, e.g. *jaana+* in *jaanalind* 'ostrich', and *koi* 'stingy' from Hebrew, *velmata* 'to revive (tr)' from Mordvin, *nulg* 'spruce' from Mari.

From 1913, about 55 artificial roots have been created *quasi ex nihilo*, mainly by Johannes Aavik, e.g. *eirata* 'ignores', *küülik* 'rabbit', *laip* 'corpse', *lünk* 'gap, lacuna', *meenuda* 'to come into one's mind', *mõrv* 'murder', *mürsk* 'missile', *nentida* 'states', *nõme* 'ignorant', *range* 'strict', *relv* 'weapon', *taunida* 'to condemn', *veenda* 'to convince'.

(Northern Literary) Estonian Text

A1–3: text in orthography; B1–3: transcription (primary stress is underlined, secondary stress is marked with colon); C1–3: morpheme-by-morpheme glosses; D1–3: free translation.

A1	laeva	võis	siiski	põletada,
B1	laèva	vëì-s-Ø	si:i--ki	pële=tta:-Da
C1	SHIP.sP	CAN-past-s3	THEN--EVEN	BURNS=VdeV-inf

kuid	ainult	ühel	päeval	aastas,	kui
kuìD	aìnult	ühe-l	päèva-l	àsta-z	kui
BUT	ONLY	ON ONE	ON DAY	IN YEAR	WHEN

päikesering	oli	jõunud	oma
päikkeze+rìŋG	ol-ì-Ø	jëùD-nuD	omà
SUN.sG+CIRCLE	IS-past-s3	REACHES-past.part	OWN.sG

haripunkti.	A2	suveharjaks
(h)arì+Bu:ŋkti	B2	suvè+(h)a:řja-ks
RIDGE+POINT.sIll-l	C2	SUMMER.sG+RIDGE-sTrans

nimetati	seda	päeva.	A3	see
nime=tta:-ťt-i	se-Dà	päèva	B3	sê
NAME=VdeV-imp-past	THIS-sP	DAY-sP	C3	THIS

on	nüüdne	jaaniõhtu.
on	nü:üD=ne	jaanʲi+ëhtu
IS.s3pres	NOW=ADJdeADV	JOHN-sG+EVE

D1 One could nonetheless burn a ship, but only on one day in the year, when the sun had reached its apogee. D2 This day was called the summer peak. D3 It is the contemporary St John's Eve.

References and Further Reading

Erelt, M., Kasik, R., Metslang, H., Rajandi, H., Ross, K., Saari, H., Tael, K., Vare, S. (1993–5) *Eesti keele grammatika*, vols I–II. Tallinn: Eesti Teaduste Akadeemia Eesti Keele Instituut.

Hasselblatt, C. (1992) *Grammatisches Wörterbuch des Estnischen* (Veröffentlichungen der Societas Uralo-Altaica 35), Wiesbaden: Ural-Altaic Society.

Kasik, R. (1996) *Eesti keele sõnatuletus*, Tartu Ülikooli eesti keele õppetoali toimetised 3. Tartu.

Raag, R. (1997) *Elementär estnisk satslära* FU Läromedel 22. Uppsala: Uppsala universitet, Finsk-ugriska institutionen.

Raun, A. and Saareste, A. (1965) *Introduction to Estonian Linguistics*, Wiesbaden: Harrassowitz.

Rätsep, H. (1978) *Eesti keele lihtlausete tüübid*, Emakeele Seltsi Toimetised 12, Tallinn: Valgus.

Saareste, A. (1958–63) *Eesti keele mõisteline sõnaraamat*, (*Dictionnaire analogique de la langue estonienne*, vols I–IV), Stockholm: Kirjastus Vaba Eesti.

Tauli, V. (1973–83) *Standard Estonian Grammar*, vols I–II, Acta Universitatis Upsalensis; Acta Uralica et Altaica Upsalensia 8, Uppsala: University of Uppsala and Almquist & Wiksell.

Valgma, J. and Remmel, N. (1968) *Eesti keele grammatika (Käsiraamat)*, Tallinn.

Viks, Ü. (ed.) (1992) *A Concise Morphological Dictionary of Estonian*, vol. I: *Introduction and Grammar*, Tallinn: Eesti Teaduste Akadeemia, Keele ja Kirjandnse Instituut.

Wiedemann, F. J. (1869) *Ehstnisch-deutsches Worterbuch*, St Petersburg.

5 Finnish

Daniel Abondolo

Finnish (native name: *suomi*) is the first language of some four and a half million people in Finland (roughly 95 per cent of the population), and of approximately half a million people living in Sweden, Norway, Estonia, and Russia. Census statistics show a steady decline in native speakers of Finnish in Russia, from about 60 per cent of 92,000 declaring themselves Finns in 1959 to about 35 per cent of 67,000 in 1989 (Künnap 1992). There are also significant pockets of speakers in the United States and Canada, chiefly around the Great Lakes; the emigratory surge to these countries was at the turn of the nineteenth and twentieth centuries.

Contemporary standard Finnish is a northern Fennic language with both western and eastern features. It is northern by virtue of isoglosses such as the third-person pronoun *hän* instead of **tämä* (as in Estonian *tema*), and *-i-* in *sisar* 'sister' instead of **ë* (as in Estonian *sõsar*). It is both western and eastern in that it combines

1 western Finnish dialect features such as =U- detransitivizers (as opposed to eastern reflexives in =kse-, which are available to speakers of the standard language, to varying degrees according to education and interests, from poetic tradition) with
2 eastern features such as neutral *kesä* 'summer', *ilta* 'evening' (as opposed to western *suvi*, *ehtoo*, which are stylistically charged synonyms).

The complexity of nominal inflection, much of which centres on the formation of the genitive plural, is in part a consequence of east/west dialect amalgamation (Laakso 1991: 53).

As a Fennic language, Finnish is peripheral and it is therefore not surprising that it has preserved many archaic features from proto-Uralic. On the other hand its high degree of agglutinativity (compared with, say, that of North or South Estonian, or Saamic) may suggest innovation as well as conservatism, and 'the choice of Finnish as the Finno-Ugric prototype may have impeded progress in the field' (Austerlitz 1993: 29).

Good short sketches are Austerlitz 1968: 1336–47, Branch 1987, and Karlsson 1992.

Table 5.1   Finnish vowel phonemes

Short			Long			
i	ü	u	ii	üü	uu	High
e	ö	o	ee	öö	oo	Mid
ä	a		ää		aa	Low
−	+	−	+	−	+	Rounded
−	−	+	+	−	−	+	+	Back

Phonology

Vowels

Finnish has eight short and eight long vowel phonemes; see Table 5.1.

The orthography writes the vowels as given above, except that the high front rounded vowels are written ⟨y⟩ and ⟨yy⟩.

Vowel length is distinctive in all positions. If we assume that proto-Uralic had no distinctive vowel length, then in Finnish the short vowel *ö* and all the long vowels are ultimately of secondary origin in all positions, although the length of first-syllable *uu* in some words is quite old. In native vocabulary, long vowels in first syllable are most commonly the result of contraction after the loss of a p(F)U consonant, e.g *-ŋ-* in *riihi* 'drying house' (Komi *riniš*) and *jää* 'ice' (North Saami *jiekŋa*) and *-x-* in *kuusi* 'spruce' (< pU *kaxsï, cf. Nganasan *kuo* < proto-Samoyedic *kaât).

In the first syllable, both *ö* and *öö* signal affect (*hölmö* 'fool', *jörö* 'peevish', *pöönä* 'coffee bean [folksy, jocular]') or relatively recent borrowing (*köli* 'keel', cf. Swedish *köl*; *köngäs* 'precipitous waterfall', cf. North Saami *geavŋŋis*) or proper-name status (*Töölö*, a northwestern suburb of Helsinki). First-syllable *ü*, on the other hand, seems to continue pU *ü in five or six words, e.g. *syli* '(space between) outstretched arms; lap; womb' < pU *süli 'arms; lap' (Janhunen 1981b).

Vowel Harmony and Morphophonemic Code

Within root morphemes and any suffixes attached to them, the mixed occurrence of front rounded with back vowels is restricted. In general, words with a front rounded vowel in their first syllable have no back vowel in subsequent syllables, and words with a back vowel in their first syllable have no front rounded vowels in subsequent syllables; thus *koulussa* 'in a school' and *väylässä* 'in a channel' occur, but forms such as *koulussä, *koulyssä and *väylussa do not. Non-rounded front vowels mix with all other vowels, e.g. *perunassa* 'in a potato', *pirussa* 'in a devil', *kielessä* 'in a language'.

The restrictions on the occurrences of vowels, and the front v. back variants of suffixes such as the *-ssa* v. *-ssä* 'in' of forms such as the examples cited above, permit the use of a morphophonemic code which writes Finnish vowels with only five symbols, I E A O U, and marks certain morphemes as front-prosodic with a prosodemic symbol, e.g. front-prosodic #SAVU *sävy* 'nuance' v. unmarked, back-prosodic SAVU *savu* 'smoke'. To compress the discussion and to render much of the morphology explicit, this chapter presents Finnish forms using a morphophonemic code devised by Robert Austerlitz (Austerlitz 1964, 1965, 1967, 1983). The elements of this code are set out in Figure 5.1; for the synchronic readings and the historical background of τ, Q, and X, see p. 154.

Root morphemes containing only the front unrounded vowels I and/or E are assumed to be prosodically front, with the exception of the singular partitive forms of MERE *meri* 'sea' and VERE *veri* 'sea', which are back-prosodic, viz. MERE-τA *mer-ta*, VERE-τA *ver-ta*.

In foreign vocabulary, violations of this distribution abound, e.g. *volyy-mistä* 'from/concerning volume'; such forms must be written in code with modulations of prosody, e.g. VOL#UUMI-STA; cf. Hungarian #NU^{b}ANS [nüäns] 'nuance'. But even in native vocabulary, the picture is quite complex if derived stems are considered: derivational suffixes behave differently from inflectional suffixes, and the degree of transparency of a given derivate is difficult to assess. For example, the nominalizer =U is front *y* when attached to #KASKE- 'commands', yielding #KASKE=U *käsky* 'command', but *u* when attached to ISKE- 'strikes', yielding *isk=u* 'blow', and there is in general a kind of vertical gradient according to which the more open the front vowel in a root, the more likely it is to trigger front readings of derivational suffixes. On the other hand, we have #NIITTA=U *niitty* 'meadow', from #NIITTA- 'mows'; contrast *niitto* '(a) mowing', with back *o* in spite of the front prosody of the root to which it is attached. This latter pair of forms illustrates a widespread distributional pattern which is the result of the relative newness of *ö* as a phoneme. See Karlsson 1983: 98–104, with literature.

In addition to the base vowel units I E A O U, it is useful to work with an operator □, which copies the vowel to its left. In the most frequent occurrence of this operator, the first vowel to the left of □ is immediately adjacent. If this adjacent vowel is high or low, the result is a long vowel, e.g. PU□ *puu* 'tree', #SA□ *sää* 'weather'; if it is mid vowel, the result is a vowel sequence equivalent to a high-to-mid diphthong of appropriate frontness/backness and lip-rounding, e.g. SO□RA *suora* 'straight', #PO□RA *pyörä* 'round', TE□RA *tiera* 'lump of snow and ice which adheres to the bottom of a shoe or a horse's hoof', #KE□RA *kierä* 'not straight'. The sequences EE and OO also occur in the first syllable, but are rare in native non-affective vocabulary; examples are foreign SOOLO *soolo* 'solo', slang #ROOKI *rööki* 'cigarette', and TEERI *teeri* 'black grouse'.

If the first vowel to the left of □ is not adjacent, the result is vowel copy, e.g. PU□-X□N *puu-hun* 'into a tree'; for more examples see the illative case and the discussion of X and Q (pp. 154–5).

Table 5.2 Finnish consonant phonemes

	1	2	3	4	5
Nasals	**m**	**n**		ŋ	
Stops, -v	**p**	**t**		**k**	ʔ
Stops, +v	b	d		g	
Fricatives, +v	**v**			**h**	
Fricatives, -v	f	**s**	š		
Lateral		**l**			
Trill		**r**			
Glide		**j**			

Note: Non-marginal phonemes are given in bold. –v = voiceless, +v = voiced. Columns correspond to places of articulation: 1 = bilabial (nasals and stops) or labiodental (fricatives), 2 = dental (but *d* is more usually alveolar, and the default pronunciation of *s* is somewhat retroflex), 3 = palato-alveolar (and hushing), 4 = dorsovelar (*h* is glottal prevocalically), 5 = glottal.

Consonants

The consonant phonemes of Finnish are set out in Table 5.2. The orthography writes the consonants as given in the table, with two exceptions: ŋ, which only occurs intervocalically and long, is written ‹ng›; and ʔ is not written at all.

The difference between the vowel *i* and the glide *j* may usually be recovered from the morphemic shape, e.g. #OLIU *öljy* 'oil' but OLE=IO *olio* 'being'. The voiced stops *b* and *g* and the fricatives *f* and *š* are restricted to foreignisms and slang; some, especially older, speakers do not have some or all of these, and use *p*, *k*, *(h)v*, and *s* instead. The phonemes *d*, ŋ, and ʔ, on the other hand, occur frequently in native non-affective vocabulary, and thus may be seen as belonging to the core inventory of phonemes (Karlsson 1983: 64–6). In a morphophonemic analysis such occurrences are predictable, however, and the first two can be unambiguously recovered, via a process called gradation (outlined below), from morphophonemic T and N, e.g. RATA-N *rada-n* 'track sG', ONKE-N *ongen* [oŋŋen] 'fish hook sG'. The

Figure 5.1 Finnish morphophonemes and operators

```
          M  N
 I    U   P  T  K
 E    O   V  S  H
    A        L
             R


    □        X  Q
             τ
```

Note: After Austerlitz 1967. For the operators Q X τ □, see text.

glottal stop *?* is only one of a range of phonetic phenomena which may emerge from the relatively abstract morphonemic operator Q; see below. Instances of standard-language *d* which arise from morphophonemic T have considerable dialectal variation, including [w], [v], [j], [l], [r], and [ð].

Consonant length is distinctive for *m n p t k s l r j* intervocalically; prevocalically to the right of nasals and liquids, length is distinctive for *p t k s*. In intervocalic consonant clusters of two, the first consonant is pronounced with (non-distinctive) greater duration. See Karlsson 1983: 104–29 for details on surface consonant distribution.

Gradation
With certain systematic exceptions, the stops P T K are all converted to less fortis counterparts, called weak grade, when they occur in the onset of a non-initial closed syllable within the word, provided that syllable contains a single vowel or vowel-*i* sequence. These less fortis counterparts are briefly specified below, using the suffixation of the genitive singular suffix (-N) as a sample conditioning environment (for more detailed treatments of Finnish consonant gradation, see Fromm 1982: 49–56, Austerlitz 1967: 24):

1   The geminate sequences PP TT KK are read as single P T K, e.g. KORPPI-N *korpin* 'raven sG', TATTI-N *tati-n* 'boletus sG', TA□KKA-N *taakan* 'hearth sG'. This subtype is called quantitative gradation, as distinct from the remaining types, called qualitative.

2   Intervocalically, T is read as *d*; P is read as *v*, as is K in the sequence UKU; in other intervocalic positions, K surfaces as a variety of prosodic and glottalic transitional phenomena, including lengthening of the preceding vowel, e.g. TAIKA-N *taian* [taiiʲjan] 'magic sG', and whispery and/or creaky voice. In three morphemes, K exceptionally surfaces as zero in the weak grade: AIKA *aika* 'time', POIKA *poika* 'boy', and OIKO- 'straight' as in OIKO-SSA *ojossa* 'outstretched; fixed (of bayonets)'. T is also read as *d* in the cluster HT, which is a by-product of KT in a few core words: see Numerals, p. 168.

3   P T K assimilate fully to a nasal to their left, e.g. SAMPE-N *samme-n* 'sturgeon sG', KANTE-N *kanne-n* 'lid sG', HANKE-N *hange-n* [haŋŋe-n] 'thick snow-cover'.

4   To the right of L and R, P is read as *v*; T assimilates fully to these consonants (e.g. KORPE-N *korve-n* 'backwoods sG', PARTA-N *parra-n* 'beard sG'). To the right of L, R, and H, K surfaces either as zero (e.g. #NALKA-N *nälä-n* 'hunger sG') or, before E, as *j* (e.g. #IALKE-N *jälje-n* 'trace, track sG'). In some words, K in the cluster HK is resistant to gradation, e.g. #SAHKO-N *sähkö-n* 'electricity sG'.

Note that word boundary and syllable boundary need not coincide, e.g. VAHINKO-N+ILO DAMAGE/MISFORTUNE-G+JOY *vahingonilo* [vahiŋŋonilo] '*Schadenfreude*'.

Exceptions to gradation may be classified as morphological or lexical. Systematic morphological exceptions are found in (1a) forms inflected for person (see below); (1b) the readings *t* and *tt* for τ in the genitive plural (see below), as well as in certain deictics, e.g. *sitten* 'then' : *siten* 'thus'; (1c) the sP and pG of nominals derived with =ISE, and the first infinitive, perfect active participle, and third-person imperative forms of phonaesthemic-affective verbs derived with =ISE, e.g. VALKO=ISE-τA *valkoista* 'white sP', VIKISE-τAQ *vikistä?* 'to squeal/squeak/peep'; (1d) forms in which a vowel sequence ending in *i* arises from the suffixation of an -I-, with cancellation of an underlying vowel to the left of this -I-, formulaically VV-I-, e.g. #TARKEA -I-SSA *tärkeissä* 'important pIne', HAMPAX-I-SSA (> HAMPA[☐] -I-SSA >) *hampaissa* 'tooth pIne', contrast #IARKE-I-SSA-☐N *järjissään* 'in his/her senses (s3pIne)'. Systematic lexical exceptions are (2a) certain formal types of proper noun, which have only quantitative gradation (Austerlitz 1979, Vesikansa 1989a: 293–5); (2b) acronymic and stump-word abbreviations, e.g. *alko* 'Finnish state-run alcohol retail outlet', *sapo* 'secret police' < *sa(la)+ po(liisi)*; (2c) slang, nursery, and otherwise affective vocabulary such as *rööki* 'a smoke', *pupu* 'bunny', *töpö* 'short (of tails)'; (2d) unassimilated foreign-isms, including *auto* 'car'.

Consonantal Morphophonemic Operators
These are Q, τ, and X, all entities which are more abstract than the fifteen morphophonemes I E A O U P T K M N V S H L R. Q, τ, and X differ from the vocalic operator ☐ (introduced on p. 151) in that they can function as consonants and thus can close a syllable, thereby triggering gradation.

The operator Q occurs only in morpheme-final position, and has a number of non-segmental realizations. In prepausal position, it is realized as a glottal stop or as relatively short duration of the preceding vowel, e.g. second person singular imperative ISTU-Q [istu?], [istŭ] 'sit!', ANTA-Q [anna?] 'give!' To the left of most inflectional suffixes, Q is realized as ☐, e.g. HUONEQ-N *huoneen* 'room sG'. It assimilates partially or wholly to the initial consonants of words and enclitics to its right, usually with transitional stretches of creaky and/or breathy voice. In traditional descriptions, this phenomenenon is usually called coda (*loppu-*) or onset (*alku-*) 'doubling' (*kahdennus*), i.e. *loppukahdennus, alkukahdennus*, after its acoustically most salient feature, the increased duration of the oral segmental consonant of the following morpheme; see Karlsson 1983: 348–50. The presence of Q in certain, especially inflectional, morphemes, varies dialectally, and the behaviour of the Q in the allative case suffix -LLEQ deviates slightly from the pattern outlined here; see pp. 157–8.

Tau, i.e. the operator written here as τ, occurs in both root and suffixal morphemes. It behaves like T except that it alternates, under circumstances which are morpheme-specific, not only with *d* but also with zero (and, in the genitive plural, with *tt*). For examples, see the partitive (-τA) and genitive plural (-τEN) suffixes of the nominal, and the infinitive suffix (-τAQ) of the verb.

X occurs both morpheme-final and suffix-initial. In morpheme-final position, X is read as *s* at word-end and before τ, as □ elsewhere, e.g. #AKEX *äes* 'plough', sP #AKEX-τA *äes-tä*, sG #AKEX-N *äkee-n*. For further examples see the discussion of nominal and verbal X-stems. X may also be used to capture the suffix-initial *s* ~ *h* alternation which characterizes the illative suffix, q.v.

Historical Background of the Consonants
Relatively minor changes in the consonantal inventory of proto-Fennic separate Finnish from the rest of the Fennic languages. On the other hand the proto-Fennic consonantal inventory deviates sharply from that of proto-Saamic, putatively its closest congener; the sole shared Saamic–Fennic innovation in the realm of the consonants is the merger of pU *δ^j- and *t- into *t- (Viitso 1996: 262). The major proto-Fennic innovations were the loss, through merger, of the palatalized apicals *n : *n^j > *n*, *l : *l^j > *l*, and *s : *s^j (and *c^j) > *s*, and the merger of initial *š- and *č- (yielding Finnish *h-*) and non-initial *t and *č (yielding Finnish *t*). Finnish non-initial *h* has at least eight sources (Hakulinen 1961: 36–8).

In considering the development of the Finnish consonants, it is important to distinguish four kinds of position: (1) root-initial, (2) central, i.e. the position between the first and second syllables, (3) marginal, i.e. the position between the second and third syllables, and (4) final position. Whereas proto-Fennic consonants in initial position (apart from the affricates) remained intact in terms of constriction type, consonants in the other positions underwent different types of weakening. In central position, stops were pronounced shorter, or even as fricatives, when their following syllable was closed (syllabic gradation); this positionally determined, morphologically conditioned alternation is the source of Finnish consonant gradation as seen in e.g. PATA-N *pada-n* 'pot sG'. In marginal position a similar, but not identical, kind of weakening occurred, regardless of the openness of the following syllable (rhythmic gradation); this positionally determined process led to allomorphy of the kind seen in the Finnish partitive, e.g. *maa-ta* 'land sP' (< *maa-ta, with *-t- in central position) v. *pata-a* 'pot sP' (< *pata-ta, with *-t- in marginal position). In final position, *k and (*š >) *h became ʔ, and *m became *n*. Massive analogical levelling has covered up most of the traces of rhythmic gradation in Finnish; for the distinction syllabic v. rhythmic, rather than the traditional root v. suffixal, gradation, see now Helimski 1996. An overview of the development of consonants in central position in Finnish and North Saami is given in tabular form by Korhonen (1981: 189–92).

A few sample forms and cognates will illustrate some of the developments sketched above (S^N = North Saami, M^E = Erzya Mordva). Finnish *syks=y* 'autumn' < pFU *sʲüksi > S^N *čakča*; Finnish *sül(=)i* '(outstretched) arms; lap' < pU *süli > S^N *salla*; Finnish *kynne-ssä* < *künti-s-nä , M^E *kenče-se* < *kinči-s-nä '(finger)nail, claw sIne', with root from pFU *künči > S^N *gazza*; Finnish *kala-a* 'fish sP' < pFU *kala-ta > M^E *kal-do* 'fish sAbl'; Finnish *vene?* 'boat sN' < *wini=ši > S^N *fanas*; *venee-t* 'boat pN' < *wini=ši-t > S^N *fatnasa-t*; Finnish *nido-?* 'stitches together s2imp' < *nʲiδa=i-k, M^E *nʲedʲa-k*, S^N *njađe*.

The functions of the operator Q correspond to the various positional and combinatory fates of *k and *š (as in NITO-Q *nido-?* and VENEQ *vene?* 'boat', above) in morpheme-final position. Tau (τ) is simply a morphonologically different sort of T, in terms of history: one which was susceptible to weakening by rhythmic gradation. The operator X is a multiple, covering phenomena related to the prehistory of both *s* and *t* in marginal position.

Inflection

Nominals

As is to be expected in a language without agreement classes, the distinction noun v. adjective in Finnish is mainly a semantic and distributional/syntactic one. Even the comparative suffix (=MPA) can be attached to stems with noun, usually spatial, reference, e.g. RANTA=MPA-NA   SHORE=cfv-ess *ranne=mpa-na* 'closer in to the shore'. A few nominals which are semantically and syntactically adjective-like are morphologically deviant in that they are uninflectible: PIKKU *pikku* 'little', ENSI *ensi* 'next (in sequence)', VIIMEQ *viime?* 'last/most recent (in sequence)', ERI *eri* 'separate, distinct, different', KOKO *koko* 'whole, entire', IOKA *joka* 'each, every'.

Finnish nominals are inflected for number, case, and person. As in most Uralic languages, zero (-Ø-) encodes singular (or non-plural) number, absence of person, and nominative case.

Nominal plural forms are built with the suffix -T (in the nominative) and -I- (elsewhere; but see the discussion of the genitive plural, p. 160f.). Along with the meaning 'more than one' the suffix -T encodes a pragmatic/textual component of definiteness or knownness; this is not true of -I-. Examples: TALO-Ø *talo* 'house', pN TALO-T *talo-t* 'the (definite/defined set of) houses', pIne TALO-I-SSA *talo-i-ssa* 'in (the) houses'. The greatest area of morphophonemic complexity in Finnish nominal inflection centres on operations triggered by the plural suffix -I-; see pp. 159–62.

The case suffixes are attached to the right of the number suffix. There are twelve cases, and in the analysis offered here, each case suffix has only one underlying form, except the genitive, which has distinct singular and plural suffixes. The twelve cases may be divided into four groups as follows:

Table 5.3   Four-by-three matrix of Finnish cases

	Stasis	*Source*	*Goal*
Grammatical	-Ø	-N/-τEn	(see text)
Semi-grammatical	-NA	-τA	-KSE
Local interior	-SSA	-STA	-X□N
exterior	-LLA	-LTA	-LLEQ

1   Three purely grammatical cases: N[ominative] -Ø, G[enitive] (singular -N, Genitive plural -τEN), and A[ccusative], with various suffixes borrowed from other cases;

2   Three semi-grammatical cases: Ess[ive] -NA, P[artitive] -τA, and Trans[lative] -KSE;

3   Three interior-local cases: Ine[ssive] -SSA, Ela[tive] -STA, Ill[ative] -X□N;

4   Three exterior-local cases: Ade[ssive] -LLA, Abl[ative] -LTA, and All[ative] -LLEQ.

Following Austerlitz 1968: 1338 (cf. Fromm 1982: 71) we may think of the Finnish cases as they are set out in Table 5.3, i.e. in terms of a four-by-three matrix defined by function and reference (grammatical v. spatial) on the one hand, and the trichotomy stasis :: motion away : motion towards on the other.

Grammatical case marking is complicated by the fact that nouns have no dedicated accusative suffix. In the singular, nouns use -N (homophonous with the genitive) if the finite verb is inflected for person, and with active participles; they use -Ø (homophonous with the nominative) otherwise, e.g. if the governing verb is impersonal or the first infinitive. Plural nouns use -T (homophonous with the plural nominative) for all instances of the accusative. The cardinal numerals use -Ø. Both singular and plural personal pronouns have a dedicated accusative suffix -T, with a probable cognate in Khanty. Figure 5.2 is an attempt at capturing the interaction of some of the grammatical, syntactic, and aspectual factors at play in suffix selection for the nominative, accusative, genitive and partitive cases. Notice that the partitive stands out as being the only case to have its own suffix, not shared with any other case. For subject-marking types 1 and 2, see Syntax, p. 176.

Many grammarians also recognize three adverbial cases: Abe[ssive] =TTA, Inst[ructive] =(I)N, and Com[itative] =INE-, e.g. Fromm 1982: 84–5, Karlsson [2]1979: 133. As their name implies, the status of the adverbial cases is not entirely solid; they are of restricted distribution and stylistically charged.

The E final in the translative suffix is read as *i* when in word-final position, e.g. SAMMAKKO-KSE *sammakoksi* 'frog sTrans, = turned into a frog'. The Q final in the allative suffix is regularly glottal stop [ʔ] when word-final

Figure 5.2   Finnish grammatical case marking

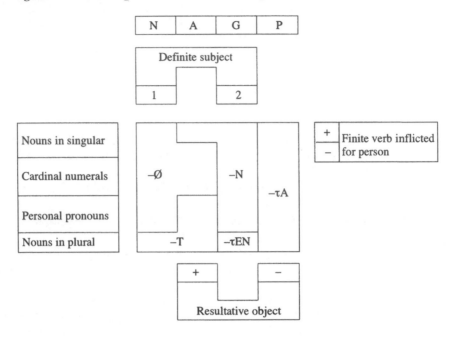

(#HULLU-LLEQ *hylly-lle?* 'shelf sALL'), but is cancelled before person suffixes; see p. 159. In the illative suffix -X□N the X is read as *s, h,* or zero, and the element □ is read as simple vowel copy, *ee,* or *ii,* depending on the surrounding segments and (in part) on the stem-type involved; see stem-types, pp. 159–63. The τ of the genitive plural suffix -τEn, like all instances of τ, is susceptible to cancellation, i.e. alternates with zero; it is unique, however, in allowing the parallel readings *d* and *tt* in forms built with the plural suffix -I-, e.g. OSA=STO-I-τEN *osastoiden/osastoitten* 'department pG', and in resisting gradation in sequences such as that of MERE-τEN *merten* 'sea pG'; see Austerlitz 1983.

The semi-grammatical cases stand somewhere between the local cases and the grammatical ones; their original spatial meanings are still evident in their use with postpositions and other deictics.

The personal forms chiefly denote possession. They are built with the suffixes (s1) -NI, (s2) -SI, (sp3) -NSA(Q) ~ -□N, (p1) -MME(Q), and (p2) -NNE(Q), and are attached in agglutinating fashion to the right of any number and case suffixes, with two exceptions:

1   the functions of the genitive and accusative singular and of the nominative plural are filled by the nominative singular. Thus TALO-SI is not only sN, but also sG, sA, and pN of 'house s2'.

2   the Q final in the allative suffix -LLEQ, and the N final in the illative
suffix -X□N, are read as zero before person suffixes. Examples: #ISA-
LLEQ-NI *isä-lle-ni* 'father s1 sAll', LAUKKU-X□N-SI *laukku-u-si* 'bag
s2 sIll'.

Recall that person suffixes are a systematic exception to gradation, e.g.
KOTI-NNE(Q) *kotinne(?)* 'your home'.

The element (Q) final in most person suffixes has a varied distribution
across the dialects; axis-of-discourse forms without Q, and third-person forms
with Q, are probably the more common; see the section on history, pp. 167–8.

The variant -□N of the sp3 suffix is usual to the right of case suffixes that
end in a vowel (including the allative, which loses its Q to the left of all person
suffixes, including -□N, yielding the sequence *-lle-en*). Further examples:
TALO-SSA-MME *talo-ssa-mme* 'house p1 sIne', LAPSE-I-LLE-NNE *laps-
i-lle-nne* 'child p2 pAll'.

Inflection Types
At the most abstract level, all nouns inflect according to only one type. At the
other extreme, we have the descriptive acribie of the *Nykysuomen sanakirja*
(*NSK*), the Finnish Academy dictionary, wherein eighty-two non-compound
nominal inflection types are distinguished (*NSK* 1: xi–xvi; re-analysed and
annotated in Tuomi [2]1980: 525–39). To make the discussion tractable, here
we distinguish the following basic types: (1) long-vowel stems; (2) stems in
final E; (3) mutating stems (in final A and I); (4) consonant stems (in final Q,
X, and τ); and (4) stable stems (in final U, O, and E^2). It is a fruitful exercise
to compare Karlsson 1982: 203, who also distinguishes five basic types, but
with quite different limits and memberships (Karlsson uses the nominative
singular as his point of departure, rather than a Pāṇini-like abstraction, as here
or in Eliot 1890).

1 Long-vowel Stems
In accordance with the rules stated above, many of these are written as having
□ as their second member. All Finnish monosyllabic nouns belong to this
type; there are about fifty such roots, if alongside core vocabulary such as
PU□ *puu* 'tree, wood' and TE□ *tie* 'road' we include letter-names such as
VEE [vee] '(the letter) v'. There are also some twenty-odd bisyllables, none
native, e.g. VAPA□ *vapaa* 'free' (< Slavonic), FILE□ *filee* 'filet'. Sympto-
matic of this type is the reading of τ as *t* in the partitive singular, e.g. VAPA□-
τA *vapaa-ta* 'free sP'.

To the left of the plural suffix -I-, final □ is cancelled: MA⌀-I-τA *ma-i-ta*
'land pP', SO⌀-I-τA *so-i-ta* 'bog pP'. The only other source of inflectional
complexity involves the allomorphy of the illative suffix -X□N. When
attached to monosyllables, the X is read as *h* and the □ is read as a copy of
the first vowel to its left, e.g. MAA-X□N *maa-han* 'land sIll'; when attached
to bisyllables, -X□N is read as *-seen* (optionally *-hen* to the right of E□) in

the singular, and *-hin* or *-siin* in the plural: VAPA□-X□N *vapaa-seen* 'free sIll', FILE□-X□N *filee-seen/filee-hen* 'filet sIll', VAPA⊘-I-X□N *vapa-i-siin/ vapa-i-hin* 'free pIll'.

2 E-stems

The E final in all E-stems is read as *i* in the citation form (= sN); E-stems thus formally resemble I-stems in any dictionary which does not indicate inflectional type. Any T penultimate in an E-stem is read as *s* to the left of *i*, whether this *i* is from underlying E (VETE-∅ *vesi* 'water') or from the pluralizer -I- (VETE-I-SSA *vesissä* 'water pIne'). There are some 230 E-stems, some of which date back to p(F)U and many of which are textually frequent. The chief variables which produce the NSK subtypes are:

2a   the cancellation v. persistence of stem-final E to the left of the partitive suffix (-τA);
2b   the order of preference for parallel forms emerging from dual output of variable 2a;
2c   double (-I-τEN) or single (-τEN) plural-marking in the pG;
2d   the application v. non-application of assimilation rules to the essive suffix (-NA).

An example of the first type of variable is provided by the words *ovi* 'door' and *suoni* 'vein': *ovi* has sP *ove-a*, with persistence of stem-final E (OVE-ⅠA), but *suoni* has sP *suon-ta*, with deletion of E (SUONE-τA). The deletion v. cancellation of stem-final E in such circumstances is connected with the nature of the consonant(ism) which precedes it: if this is a single dental (N T S L R), the E is cancelled, witness *suon-ta* and VETE-τA *vet-tä* 'water sP', KUUSE-τA *kuus-ta* 'spruce sP', NUOLE-τA *nuol-ta* 'arrow sP', and NUORE -τA *nuor-ta* 'young sP'. In eight words (*NSK* types 32 and 33), E is also cancelled to the right of H, e.g. LOHE-τA *loh-ta* 'salmon sP'; this behaviour reflects the apical origins of H in most if not all of these words. Note also M > *n*, obligatory in textually frequent LUME-τA *lun-ta* 'snow sG', optional in rarer TUOME-ⅠA *tuome-a*, TUOME-τA *tuon-ta* 'chokecherry (tree)'.

The second type of variable arises in the formation of the sP of stems ending in E preceded by a cluster whose second member is S; the *NSK* lists ten such stems (types 45–50), and reports that E-deletion is optional for all but two of them, viz. LAPSE-τA *las-ta* 'child sP' and VEITSE-τA *veis-tä* 'knife' (note the concomitant cancellation of P and T). The remaining eight stems have parallel partitives singular, with various preferences, e.g. SUKSE-ⅠA *sukse-a* is favoured over SUKSE-τA *sus-ta*, both 'ski sP'; with UKSE-τA *us-ta*, UKSE-ⅠA *ukse-a*, both 'doorway sP' the order of preference is reversed.

The third variable reflects the prehistory of the pG suffix -τEN, in which the initial τ was originally a plural marker. The τ in this suffix behaves uniquely in that it resists gradation in forms such as the stylistically charged

VETE-τEN *vetten* 'water pG' (historically: *wete-te-n) alongside secondary, and normal, VETE-I-τEN *vesien*.

The fourth variable is relevant to the language of verbal art, in which forms resulting from E-deletion and assimilation such as NUORE-NA > *nuorra* 'young sEss' are possible.

Certain E-final derivational suffixes are characterized by their own morphophonemic operations:

(a) In nominals formed with =(I)SE, the S is read as *n* in the nominative singular, and the nominative is marked with a suffix -N, e.g. NA=ISE *nainen* 'woman' (cf. the section on numerals, p. 168);

(b) In nominals formed with =NTE, which forms ordinal numerals, the N is cancelled in the sP, e.g. VIITE=NTE-τA *viidettä* 'fifth sP'.

(c) Stems built with =UUTE shift this suffix to =UUKSE to the left of the -I- plural suffix, e.g. SUURE=UUTE *suuruus* '(large) size', sG SUURE =UUTE-N *suuruude-n*, pG SUURE=UUKSE-I-τEN *suuruuks-i-en*.

(d) In the perfective active participle, =NUτE, the sequence Uτ is read as E$^{\square}$ to the left of all suffixes except the sP, e.g. SAA=NUτE-N *saaneen* 'that has acquired sG'.

About forty-five E-stems owe their somewhat deviant paradigms to the presence of a τ, e.g. OLUτE *olut* 'beer', sG OLUτE-N *olue-n*. In most cases, the sequence UτE is synchronically a derivational suffix, e.g. PILVE=UτE *pilvyt* 'little cloud (poetic)'.

3 Mutating Stems End in Either I or A

I-stems are of two basic types: those which form their pG with -τEN (*NSK* 4) and those which use both -τEN and -I-τEN (*NSK* 5 and 6). Stems of the latter type are all at least trisyllabic. In all I-stems, the stem-final I is read as *e* to the left of the plural suffix -I-, e.g. pP RISTI-I-τA *riste-j-ä* 'cross pP'.

The chief variables which produce the NSK subtypes of A-stems are the mutation or cancellation of the stem-final vowel. To the left of the plural suffix -I-, stem-final A is normally either (a) read as if O (i.e. *o* or *ö*, depending on prosody), or (b) it is cancelled. The conditions which determine which, if either, of the two operations *a* or *b* is to apply to a given string are multiples which involve the interaction of syllable-count, front v. back prosody, the consonant(ism) immediately preceding the stem-final vowel, homophonic pressure, and the reading of τ in the pG (Karlsson 1982: 282–6 is a concise account, with a slightly different approach; see also Tuomi ²1980: 530, notes 6 and 7).

For example, the A final in LO$^{\square}$LA *luola* 'cave' is cancelled to the left of plural -I- regularly, i.e. in accordance with a rule which prescribes such cancellation in bisyllables with a labial vowel in the first syllable: LO$^{\square}$LA -I-τA *luol-i-a* 'cave pP'. The Λ final in #KESA 'summer' is also deleted to the left of plural -I-, again regularly, but this time in accordance with a rule which prescribes such cancellation in all front-prosodic bisyllables. The A final in SO□LA 'salt' is not cancelled, even though there is a labial vowel in its first syllable (SO□LA-I-ɪA *suoloja* 'salt pP'), thus avoiding a homophonic clash with SO□LE-I-ɪA *suol-i-a* 'intestine pP'.

A further, more precious, example may be drawn from the I-stems. The *NSK* distinguishes the paradigms of *paperi* 'paper' (*NSK* 5) and *banaali* 'banal' (*NSK* 6) ostensibly because in the pG of the latter, the non-cancellation of τ produces forms which are stylistically neutral: we have both PAPERI-ɪEN and bANA□LI-ɪEN giving *paperi-en* and *banaali-en*, but only *papere-i-den* (PAPERI-I-τEN) is given as neutral, while the parallel *banaale-i-den* (bANA□LI-I-τEN) is given in brackets.

Certain A-final derivational suffixes are characterized by their own morphophonemic operations:

(a) The A final in the comparative suffix =MPA is read as *i* in the nominative singular, e.g. KORKEA=MPA *korkeampi* 'taller', cf. sG KORKEA=MPA-N *korkeamma-n*. Stem-final A in bisyllables is read as *e* before this suffix, e.g. VANHA=MPA *vanhempi* 'older' (cf. *vanha* 'old');

(b) The A final in the superlative suffix =IMPA is read as zero in the nominative singular, and the resulting impermissable final sequence *MP is read as *n*, e.g. KORKEA=IMPA *korkein* 'tallest', cf. sG KORKEA=IMPA-N *korkeimma-n*. Before the τ of the sP, final MPA is read as *n*, e.g. KORKEA=IMPA-τA *korkein-ta*;

(c) The morphophonemic behaviour of the privative suffix =TTOMA is the same, mutatis mutandis, as that of the superlative, e.g. ONNE=TTOMA *onneton* 'unlucky, unhappy', sG ONNE=TTOMA-N *onnettoma-n*, sP ONNE=TTOMA-τA *onneton-ta*.

4 Consonant-final Stems end in Q, X, or τ

The inflectional peculiarities of Q-stems all flow from the properties of Q, outlined above. The sequence Q–τ, which arises in the partitive singular, is read *tt*, e.g. SATA=EQ-τA *sadetta* 'rain sP'. The X final in X-stems surfaces as *s* before the zero of the sN and the τ of the sP, but as □ elsewhere, e.g. sN HAMPAX *hammas* 'tooth', HAMPAX-N *hampaa-n* 'tooth sG', HAMPAX-τA *hammas-ta* 'tooth sP'. Tau occurs final in very few words, of which only #KEVAτ *kevät* 'spring' is frequent; its behaviour is identical to that of X, except that it is read as *t* where X is read as *s*, e.g. #KEVAτ-N *kevää-n* 'spring sG', #KEVAτ-τA *kevät-tä* 'spring sP'.

A few Q-stems and X-stems are synchronically monomorphemic, e.g. HUONEQ *huone?* 'room', VIERAX *vieras* 'guest, foreign-', but most are derivates built with the productive suffixes =EQ, e.g. #PEITTA=EQ *peite?* 'cover(ing)', cf. #PEITTA- 'covers', SATA=EQ *sade?* 'rain', cf. SATA- 'it rains', =IAX, e.g. ANTA=ELE=IAX *antelias* 'generous', cf. ANTA=ELE-

'gives on several occasions', and =KKAX, e.g. LAHIA=KKAX *lahjakas* 'gifted', cf. LAHIA *lahja* 'gift'.

5   Stable Stems Exhibit no Stem-final Morphophonemic Peculiarities

To this class belong all stems ending in U, O, or E^2; in all, easily over 6,000 items. Examples are SATU 'fairy tale', #OLIU *öljy* 'oil', OLE=IO *olio* 'being', #HOLMO *hölmö* 'fool', and fAdE^2 *fade* 'father (slang)'. The class represented by this last item is fast growing; it contains neologisms such as ALE^2 *ale* 'sale, period of lower prices' and slang.

To the class of stable stems could also be assigned unassimilated foreignisms which end in an underlying consonant other than Q or X, such as SLALOM *slalom*, NAILON *nailon* 'nylon', or SANSKRIT *sanskrit*. These stems append an *i* for all of their inflected and derived forms built with consonant-initial suffixes, e.g. NAILONi-STA *nailonista* 'nylon sEla'.

To give an idea of the sorts of variety which are concealed by the morphophonemic lumping outlined above, Table 5.4 sets out the singular and plural genitive, partitive, and illative forms of thirty-two subvariants of the five stem types outlined above. The lexical examples are a slight reduction of the set chosen by Sammallahti (1989) for his concise presentation of Finnish nominal inflection types. The forms are given in morphophonemic code, with operations indicated as follows: (1) cancellation of an underlying segment is indicated by solidus, e.g. E, Í; (2) segments which undergo other changes (e.g. gradation; T > s to the left of *i*) are left unmarked. Vowel harmony is not indicated, nor are the readings of □ or X□, save where these serve to distinguish multiple surfacings, as in *korkeihin/korkeisiin* 'high pIll'.

Postpositions and Prepositions

These are for the most part spatial nouns with defective paradigms. Postpositions often use the semigrammatical suffixes, or variants of these, with spatial meaning, e.g. TAKA-NA BACK.SPACE-ess *takana* 'behind', TAKA-ʈA *takaa* 'from behind', TAKA-KSE-Q *taakse?*BACK.SPACE-translat 'to behind'.

There are about thirty nouns of this type: most are used as postpositions in neutral styles, but can also be used prepositionally in poetic or other marked language, e.g. VETE-N ALLA WATER-G UNDER *vede-n alla* 'under (the water)', ALLA VETE-N *alla veden* 'under (the) water (poetic)'. Neutral as prepositions are *ennen* 'before', *ilman* 'without', *paitsi* 'besides, except', *vasten* 'against', all of which govern the partitive, e.g. *vasten seinä-ä* 'against the wall'. The partitive is in fact the default case for prepositions, and the genitive for postpositions, e.g. *keskellä lattia-a*, *lattia-n keskellä* 'in the middle of the floor', but there are also a few nouns which take one or the other case in both positions, e.g. *läpi seinä-n, seinä-n läpi* 'through the wall', *kohti seinä-ä, seinä-ä kohti* 'towards the wall'.

Table 5.4 Subvariants of Finnish nominal inflection types

Sammallahti (1989: 503–4)

no.	sN	sG	sP	sIll	pG	pP	pIll	Gloss
1	VALA=O *valo*	VALA=O-N *valon*	VALA=O-tA *valoa*	VALA=O-X□N *valoon*	VALA=O-I-tEN *valojen*	VALA=O-I-tA *valoja*	VALA=O-I-X□N *valoihin*	light
6	OSA=STO *osasto*	OSA=STO-N *osaston*	OSA=STO-tA *osastoa*	OSA=STO-X□N *osastoon*	OSA=STO-I-tEN *osastojen*; OSA=STO-I-tEN *osastoiden*	OSA=STO-I-tA *osastoja*; OSA=STO-I-tA *osastoita*	OSA=STO-I-X□N *osastoihin*	department
2	RISTI *risti*	RISTI-N *ristin*	RISTI-tA *ristiä*	RISTI-X□N *ristiin*	RISTI-tEN *ristien*	RISTI-I-tA *ristejä*	RISTI-I-X□N *risteihin*	cross
5	PAPERI *paperi*	PAPERI-N *paperin*	PAPERI-tA *paperia*	PAPERI-X□N *paperiin*	PAPERI-tEN *paperien*; PAPERI-I-tEN *papereiden*	PAPERI-I-tA *papereja*; PAPERI-I-tA *papereita*	PAPERI-I-X□N *papereihin*	paper
3	KALA *kala*	KALA-N *kalan*	KALA-tA *kalaa*	KALA-X□N *kalaan*	KALA-I-tEN *kalojen*	KALA-I-tA *kaloja*	KALA-I-X□N *kaloihin*	fish
4	KOIRA *koira*	KOIRA-N *koiran*	KOIRA-tA *koiraa*	KOIRA-X□N *koiraan*	KOIRA-I-tEN *koirien*	KOIRA-I-tA *koiria*	KOIRA-I-X□N *koiriin*	dog
9	OMENA *omena*	OMENA-N *omenan*	OMENA-tA *omenaa*	OMENA-X□N *omenaan*	OMENA-I-tEN *omenien*; OMENA-I-tEN *omenoiden*	OMENA-I-tA *omenia*; OMENA-I-tA *omenoita*	OMENA-I-X□N *omeniin*	apple
10	KULKE=IA *kulkija*	KULKE=IA-N *kulkijan*	KULKE=IA-tA *kulkijaa*	KULKE=IA-X□N *kulkijaan*	KULKE=IA-I-tEN *kulkijoiden*	KULKE=IA-I-tA *kulkijoita*	KULKE=IA-I-X□N *kulkijoihin*	wanderer
11	SOLAKKA *solakka*	SOLAKKA-N *solakan*	SOLAKKA-tA *solakkaa*	SOLAKKA-X□N *solakkaan*	SOLAKKA-I-tEN *solakoiden*; SOLAKKA-I-tEN *solakkoiden*	SOLAKKA-I-tA *solakoita*; SOLAKKA-I-tA *solakkoja*	SOLAKKA-I-X□N *solakoihin*; SOLAKKA-I-X□N *solakkoihin*	slender
12	KORK=EA *korkea*	KORK=EA-N *korkean*	KORK=EA-tA *korkeaa*; KORK=EA-tA *korkeata*	KORK=EA-X□N *korkeaan*	KORK=EA-I-tEN *korkeiden*	KORK=EA-I-tA *korkeita*	KORK=EA-I-X□N *korkeihin*; KORK=EA-I-X□N *korkeisiin*	high
13	ISO=MPA *isompi*	ISO=MPA-N *isomman*	ISO=MPA-tA *isompaa*	ISO=MPA-X□N *isompaan*	ISO=MPA-I-tEN *isompien*	ISO=MPA-I-tA *isompia*	ISO=MPA-I-X□N *isompiin*	larger

Table 5.4 (Continued)

Sammallahti (1989: 503–4)

no.	sN	sG	sP	sIll	pG	pP	pIll	Gloss
32	#SIS-A=IMPA *sisin*	#SIS-A=IMPA-N *sisimmän*	#SIS-A=IMPA-tA *sisintä*	#SIS-A=IMPA-X□N *sisimpään*	#SIS-A=IMPA-I-tEN *sisimpien* #SIS-A=IMPA-tEN *sisinten*	#SIS-A=IMPA-I-tA *sisimpiä*	#SIS-A=IMPA-I-X□N *sisimpiin*	innermost
26	OSA=TTOMA *osaton*	OSA=TTOMA-N *osattoman*	OSA=TTOMA-tA *osattomaa*	OSA=TTOMA-X□N *osattomaan*	OSA=TTOMA-I-tEN *osattomien*	OSA=TTOMA-I-tA *osattomia*	OSA=TTOMA-I-X□N *osattomiin*	portionless
14	MA□ *maa*	MA□-N *maan*	MA□-tA *maata*	MA□-X□N *maahan*	MA□-I-tEN *maiden*	MA□-I-tA *maita*	MA□-I-X□N *maihin*	land
15	SO□ *suo*	SO□-N *suon*	SO□-tA *suota*	SO□-X□N *suohon*	SO□-I-tEN *soiden*	SO□-I-tA *soita*	SO□-I-X□N *soihin*	bog
16	VAPA□ *vapaa*	VAPA□-N *vapaan*	VAPA□-tA *vapaata*	VAPA□-X□N *vapaaseen*	VAPA□-I-tEN *vapaiden*	VAPA□-I-tA *vapaita*	VAPA□-I-X□N *vapaisiin*	free
18	OVE *ovi*	OVE-N *oven*	OVE-tA *ovea*	OVE-X□N *oveen*	OVE-I-tEN *ovien*	OVE-I-tA *ovia*	OVE-I-X□N *oviin*	door
19	TOIME *toimi*	TOIME-N *toimen*	TOIME-tA *toimea* TOIME-tA *tointa*	TOIME-X□N *toimeen*	TOIME-I-tEN *toimien* TOIME-tEN *toinen*	TOIME-I-tA *toimia*	TOIME-I-X□N *toimiin*	function
20	KU□SE *kuusi*	KU□SE-N *kuusen*	KU□SE-tA *kuusta*	KU□SE-X□N *kuuseen*	KU□SE-I-tEN *kuusien* KU□SE-tEN *kuusten*	KU□SE-I-tA *kuusia*	KU□SE-I-X□N *kuusiin*	spruce
21	LUME *lumi*	LUME-N *lumen*	LUME-tA *lunta*	LUME-X□N *lumeen*	LUME-I-tEN *lumien*	LUME-I-tA *lumia*	LUME-I-X□N *lumiin*	snow
22	*KATE *käsi*	*KATE-N *käden*	*KATE-tA *kättä*	*KATE-X□N *käteen*	*KATE-I-tEN *käsien*	*KATE-I-tA *käsiä*	*KATE-I-X□N *käsiin*	hand
23	*KUNTE *kynsi*	*KUNTE-N *kynnen*	*KUNTE-tA *kynttä*	*KUNTE-X□N *kynteen*	*KUNTE-I-tEN *kynsien*	*KUNTE-I-tA *kynsiä*	*KUNTE-I-X□N *kynsiin*	claw, nail
24	KAKTE *kaksi*	KAKTE-N *kahden*	KAKTE-tA *kahta*	KAKTE-X□N *kahteen*	KAKTE-I-tEN *kaksien*	KAKTE-I-tA *kaksia*	KAKTE-I-X□N *kaksiin*	two
25	*KUTKE=IME *kytkin*	*KUTKE=IME-N *kytkimen*	*KUTKE=IME-tA *kytkintä*	*KUTKE=IME-X□N *kytkimeen*	*KUTKE=IME-I-tEN *kytkimien* *KUTKE=IME-tEN *kytkinten*	*KUTKE=IME-I-tA *kytkimiä*	*KUTKE=IME-I-X□N *kytkimiin*	coupling

Table 5.4 (Continued)

Sammallahti (1989: 503–4)

no.	sN	sG	sP	sIll	pG	pP	pIll	Gloss
27	NA=ISE *nainen*	NA=ISE-N *naisen*	NA=ISE-tA *naista*	NA=ISE-X□N *naiseen*	NA=ISE-I-tEN *naisien* NA=ISE-tEN *naisten*	NA=ISE-I-tA *naisia*	NA=ISE-I-X□N *naisiin*	woman
28	#tANIKSE *jänis*	#tANIKSE-N *jäniksen*	#tANIKSE-tA *jänistä*	#tANIKSE-X□N *jänikseen*	#tANIKSE-tEN *jänisten* #tANIKSE-I-tEN *jäniksien*	#tANIKSE-I-tA *jäniksiä*	#tANIKSE-I-X□N *jäniksiin*	hare
29	OHUtE *ohut*	OHUtE-N *ohuen*	OHUtE-tA *ohutta*	OHUtE-X□N *ohueen*	OHUtE-I-tEN *ohuiden*	OHUtE-I-tA *ohuita*	OHUtE-I-X□N *ohuihin/ohuisiin*	thin
30	VIITE=NTE *viides*	VIITE=NTE-N *viidennen*	VIITE=NTE-tA *viidettä*	VIITE=NTE-X□N *viidenteen*	VIITE=NTE-I-tEN *viidensien*	VIITE=NsE-I-tA *viidensiä*	VIITE=NsE-I-X□N *viidensiin*	fifth
31	OLE-NUtE *ollut*	OLE-NUtE-N *olleen*	OLE-NUtE-tA *ollutta*	OLE-NUtE-X□N *olleeseen*	OLE-NUtE-I-tEN *olleiden*	OLE-NUtE-I-tA *olleita*	OLE-NUtE-I-X□N *olleihin/olleisiin*	been
34	#ISA=UUTE *isyys*	#ISA=UUTE-N *isyyden*	#ISA=UUTE-tA *isyyttä*	#ISA=UUTE-X□N *isyyteen*	#ISA=UUKSE-I-tEN *isyyksien*	#ISA=UUKSE-I-tA *isyyksiä*	#ISA=UUKSE-I-X□N *isyyksiin*	paternity
33	VIERAX *vieras*	VIERAX-N *vieraan*	VIERAX-tA *vierasta*	VIERAX-X□N *vieraaseen*	VIERAX-I-tEN *vieraiden*	VIERAX-I-tA *vieraita*	VIERAX-I-X□N *vieraisiin*	guest
35	VENEQ *vene?*	VENEQ-N *veneen*	VENEQ-tA *venettä*	VENEQ-X□N *veneeseen*	VENEQ-I-tEN *veneiden*	VENEQ-I-tA *veneitä*	VENEQ-I-X□N *veneihin/veneisiin*	boat

Most postpositions and prepositions can take person suffixes as well, e.g. ALLA-SI *allasi* 'under you', VE□RE-X□N-NI *viereeni* 'to next to me'.

Historical Background of Suffixes

Both plural suffixes probably date back to pU, when they had essentially the same distribution and function as in present-day Finnish (Janhunen [1981a: 30] classifies their ancestors as plural case suffixes, pN *-t and pGA *-j).

The historical background of the case suffixes is also for the most part clear. As for the grammatical cases, the use of the zero-case form to mark certain direct objects as well as subjects is in all likelihood an inheritance from pU. The genitive/accusative suffix -N is a merger of those two cases as inherited from pU, namely *-n and *-m.

Two of the semigrammatical cases were originally local suffixes. The partitive, attested also in Saamic, Mordva, Mari and Samoyedic, continues a pU separative *-tA (~ *-tI). The essive continues pU locative *-nA; alone or in combination with co-affixes, it has cognates in all Uralic languages. The translative is of disputed origin: it may be identical with the derivational suffix =(U)KSE; it may be a composite of two latives, *-k and *-s; it may even be related to the predestinative of Nganasan, Nenets, and Enets, cf. Janhunen 1989.

The present-day Finnish local cases are composites, built by the addition of primary case suffixes to the elements *l (exterior cases) and *s (interior cases). The lines along which these elements developed is not known with precision, and their age and origin is disputed. In purely mechanical terms, however, the lines of descent of the Finnish inessive, elative, adessive and ablative cases are obvious, viz. *-s-nA > -SSA, *-s-tA > -STA, *-l-nA > -LLA, *-l-tA > -LTA, whatever the origins and original functions of *s and *l might have been. The Finnish illative is clearly a composite of two latives, one (*-s) with cognates in Saamic, Mordva, and Mari, the other (*-n ~ *-nʲ) of uncertain distribution across FU (Kangasmaa-Minn 1973); this particular combination, *-sVn, is known only from Fennic and Saamic. The geminate LL of the allative suffix -LLEQ arose via analogy with the adessive; the Q final in this suffix corresponds to *n* in Finnish dialects and in the Mari pendant *-lan*.

The set of Finnish possessive suffixes is a merger of two parallel sets used in nominative v. oblique-and-plural in proto-Fennic. For example, whereas the s2 suffix -SI, now used in all cases, continues a proto-Fennic s2 suffix (*-te) which was used only in the nominative, the suffixes of the first and third person singular, -NI and -NSA(Q), continue proto-Fennic suffixes which originally were not used in the nominative:

Proto-Fennic	s1	s2	s3	Finnish	
Nominative	*-me				
		*-te >		-SI	s2
			*-sA		
Non-nominative	*-ne >			-NI	s1
		*-nte			
			*-nsA >	-NSA(Q)	s3

As mentioned above, there is considerable dialectal variation concerning the auslaut of all person suffixes save those for first and second person singular; the axis-of-discourse variants with final Q continue an old pluralizer, either *-k (as in Mordva p1 -mok; cf. Korhonen 1981: 244) or *-t (as in Selkup p1 -mit; cf. Janhunen 1981a: 32). The origin of the (Q) final in the third person suffix(es) is disputed; see Fromm 1982: 87, with literature.

Numerals
Each of the first ten non-derived cardinal numerals deviates slightly from canon in shape, morphophonemic behaviour, or both:

1	#UKTE	*yksi yhte-*	6	KUUTE	*kuusi kuute-*
2	KAKTE	*kaksi kahte-*	7	#SEITSEMA	*seitsemän seitsemä-*
3	KOLME(Q)	*kolme(?) kolme-*	8	KAKTE=KSA	*kahdeksan kahdeksa-*
4	#NELIA	*neljä*	9	#UKTE=KSA	*yhdeksän yhdeksä-*
5	VIITE	*viisi viite-*	10	#KUMMENE	*kymmenen kymmene-*

The numeral for '3' has a parallel stem KOLMA= used in derivation; this final E~A alternation is found in only two other words, SO□ME *Suomi, suomi* 'Finland; Finnish (language)' ~ SO□MA=LAISE *suomalainen* 'Finnish' and RO□TSI *Ruotsi, ruotsi* 'Sweden; Swedish (language)' ~ RO□TSA=LAISE *ruotsalainen* 'Swedish'. Nominal stems with shapes resembling VIITE and KUUTE (i.e. long vowel plus T plus E) exist, but they are lexically and textually rare. The cluster -*lj*- is unusual between mid and low vowel, as in *neljä*. Outside of poetic vocabulary, the abstract sequence KT is read as *ht* (~ *hd* in weak grade) only in the numerals '1' and '2' (and in '8' and '9', which are based on them), and in the infinitives of the only front-prosodic two verbs that end in the sequence KE, #NAKE-τAQ *nähdä* 'to see' and TEKE -τAQ *tehdä* 'to do'. The words for '7' to '10' take a nominative case suffix -N unique to them and to nominals formed with the derivational suffix =ISE.

Above '10' there are the roots SATA *sata* '100', TUHANTE *tuhat* '1,000' (note NTE > *t*, sG is TUHANTE-N *tuhannen*), and MILIOONA *miljoona* 'million', bILIOONA *biljoona* '(US) billion', MILIARDI *miljardi* '(UK) billion', etc. Teens are formed with +TOISE-τA, the sP of TO□=ISE *toinen* 'other (of two)', e.g. #NELIA+TO□=IS-τA *neljätoista* '14'. Decades are noun phrases with the partitive of '10' as second member, e.g. KAKTE

#KUMMENE-τA *kaksikymmentä* '20', and hundreds and thousands are formed in similar fashion, e.g. VIITE TUHANTE-τA *viisituhatta* '5,000'.

For the ordinals, see E-stems, p. 161. Fractions are formed by the addition of =KSE to the ordinal stem, e.g. KOLMA=NTE-KSE *kolmannes* '(one) third', sG KOLMA=NTE=KSE-N *kolmannekse-n*.

Pronouns

There are personal pronouns for all three persons, singular and plural; sample forms are set out in Table 5.5. All personal pronouns have front prosody, but the stems for the first and second persons singular (#MINA #SINA) have back-vowel oblique stems (MINU- SINU-). The plural pronouns p1 ME, p2 TE, p3 HE inflect in a manner identical to that of the plural noun paradigm, except in three cases: the nominative lacks the plural suffix -T, and the accusative, partitive, and genitive case suffixes are attached to a plural stem extended with -TA. The s3 pronoun inflects like any E-stem of comparable shape, except in the nominative, where its final E is cancelled: #HANE *hän* '(s)he'. In colloquial speech, allegro s1 and s2 forms without the IN sequence are the norm, e.g. nominative s1 #MA *mä*, genitive s2 SU-N *sun*, and the third-person personal pronouns are often replaced by the anaphoric pronouns SE and NE, qq.v.

Apart from their use in contrasting or focalizing emphasis, the personal pronouns are normally used only in non-nominative forms, with one exception: third-person pronouns always, and, in casual speech, axis-of-discourse pronouns usually, are used as verb subjects, e.g. *hän/se kuuli-Ø* '(s)he heard', *m(in)ä kuul-i-n* 'I heard', *me o-n men=ty* 'we went'.

The genitive forms of the third-person pronouns are used to indicate a possessor other than the salient actor (usually = the subject) in a sentence; if the personal pronoun #HANE is used, the noun indicating the possession bears the third-person suffix, e.g. *hän/se sö-i-Ø häne-n voi+leivä-nsä/se-n voi+leivä-n* '(S)he₁ ate his/her₂ sandwich', contrast *hän/se sö-i-Ø voi+leivä-nsa* '(S)he₁ ate his/her₁ sandwich'.

Table 5.5 Sample Finnish personal pronoun forms: s1#M(IN)A ~ MINU-, p2 TE(-I(-TA)-), s3 #HANE

	s1	p2		s3
N	#MINA	TE		#HANE
	minä	*te*		*hän*
A	MINU-T		TE-I-TA-T	#HANE-T
	minut		*teidät*	*hänet*
P	MINU-τA		TE-I-τA	#HANE-τA
	minua		*teitä*	*häntä*
Ine	MINU-SSA		TE-I-SSA	#HANE-SSA
	minussa		*teissä*	*hänessä*

The reflexive pronoun is ITSE(Q), oblique stem ITSE- *itse(?)* 'self'. It takes case and person (but not plural) suffixes like a regular noun, e.g. s1sP ITSE-*t*A-NI *itseäni*, p2All ITSE-LLEQ-NNE *itsellenne*.

Finnish has a three-way demonstrative system, with distal TO$^\square$ *tuo*, proximal #TA=MA *tämä*, and anaphoric-neutral SE *se*. The inflection of all three of these words deviates from that of the noun in that their plural paradigms are based on stems with initial N, viz. NO$^\square$ *nuo*, #NA=MA *nämä*, NE *ne*. The proximal pronoun is also deviant in that it contains the morpheme =MA only in forms which would otherwise be monosyllabic, viz. sNG and pN. The anaphoric-neutral pronoun SE exhibits the uniquely deviant vowel alternation E ~ I ~ I$^\square$, with E occurring in sNG and pN, I$^\square$ in the interior local cases, and I elsewhere. In casual speech, the anaphoric-neutral pronoun is used instead of the third-person personal pronouns. In addition, it has two different but related functions: in casual speech as a premodifier in the noun phrase (e.g. *se poika*), it indicates a kind of definiteness, cf. Sulkala and Karjalainen 1992: 269; in more formal style, it is an explicit indicator of cataphora, and marks a following relative clause as restrictive, e.g *se nainen, joka tul-i-0 hoitaa=ma-an laps-i-a* PRO.NEUT WOMAN-N PRO.REL COMES-past-s3 CARES.FOR=inf3-ill CHILD-plur-P 'the woman that came to look after the children'; both constructions have exact parallels in Swedish (with *den/det*; cf. Andersson 1994: 288).

It is instructive to consider the paradigms of the demonstrative pronouns in conjunction with the deictic adverbs, which similarly distinguish distal, proximal, and anaphoric-neutral spheres. These adverbs do not distinguish interior from exterior location; the distal forms are formally identical with the exterior cases of the corresponding demonstrative pronoun, but the proximal and anaphoric-medial forms use a lative suffix -NTEQ *-nne?* not known from the noun paradigm, as well as stem-extending morphemes, -KA- (proximal) and -KE- (anaphoric-medial), e.g. #TA-KA-LLA *täällä*, #SE-KE-LLA *siellä*. The stem-extender -KA- also occurs, e.g., in the deictic adjective *tä=kä=lä=inen* 'local, of this place'.

The deictic adverbs (in italics) and sample forms of the demonstrative pronouns may be found in Table 5.6.

Interrogative and relative pronouns overlap, in part. KU=KA ~ KE(NE)-*kuka* 'who?' is only rarely used as a relative pronoun, but MI=KA *mikä* 'what?; which' is common in both roles. There is also a dedicated relative pronoun, IO=KA *joka*. The distribution of the =KA element in these words is similar to that of =MA in the proximal pronoun in that it occurs only in forms which would otherwise be monosyllabic, but the suffix order is the reverse, e.g. sG MI-N=KA *minkä* 'of what?, of which' (contrast sG #TA=MA-N *tämän* 'of this'). The plural nominative is formed with -T, as in the noun paradigm, e.g. KE-T=KA *ketkä* 'who (plur)?' Interrogative deictics are built to MI, e.g. MI-SSA *missä* 'where?', MI-NTEQ *minne?* 'whither?', MI=LL-OIN *milloin* 'when?', MI-KSE *miksi* 'why?'

Table 5.6   Demonstrative pronouns and deictic adverbs

	Proximal pronoun	Deictic adverb	Anaphoric-medial pronoun	Deictic adverb	Distal pronoun	Deictic adverb
N	tä=mä		se		tuo	
G	tä=mä-n		se-n		tuo-n	
P	tä-tä		si-tä		tuo-ta	
Ine	tä-ssä	tä-ä-llä	sii-nä	si-e-llä	tuo-ssa	tuo-lla
Ela	tä-stä	tä-ä-ltä	sii-tä	si-e-ltä	tuo-sta	tuo-sta
Ill	tä-hän	tä-nne?	sii-hen	si-nne?	tuo-hon	tuo-lle?
Ade	tä-llä		si-llä		tuo-lla	
Abl	tä-ltä		si-ltä		tuo-lta	
All	tä-lle?		si-lle?		tuo-lle?	

Indefinite and negative pronouns and deictic adverbs are built with the enclitic --(KA)[□]N, which is added to inflected interrogative pronoun bases (the longer form is used after consonants), e.g. sN KU=KA--[□]N *kukaan*, sP (E-I) KE-ᴛA--[□]N *(ei) ketään* 'no one', sG (E-I) KENE-N--KA[□]N *(ei) kenenkään* 'nobody's', (E-I) MI-SSA--[□]N *(ei) missään* 'nowhere'. There are also specifically indefinite pronouns, IO=KIN *jokin* 'some (one/thing)', which inflects like MI=KA, and the compound IO+KU *joku* 'some (one/ thing)', both of whose members inflect, e.g. sAde IO-LLA+KU-LLA *jollakulla* 'some (one/thing)'.

Verb Inflection
Finnish verbs can be inflected for either tense or mood, and for person. The tense/mood suffix attaches directly to the stem; in non-imperative forms, the tense/mood suffix is followed by the person suffix.

The tense/mood suffixes are -Ø- (present indicative), -I- (past indicative), -NE- (potential), -ISI- (conditional), and, in the imperative, -Q (second person singular) ~ -KAA(-) (first and second persons plural) ~ -KO- (third person; there is no s1 imperative form). The person, i.e. subject, suffixes are s1 -N, s2 -Ø (imperative) ~ -T (elsewhere), s3 -[□] (present and potential) ~ -Ø (past and conditional) ~ -[□]N (imperative), p1 -MME, p2 -TTE, p3 -VAT (~ -[□]T in the imperative). There is also a subparadigm of impersonal inflection, used when the subject is unknown or to avoid stating the subject explicitly; see below.

Both past-tense -I- and the second I of conditional -ISI- continue a past-tense morpheme which probably evolved from a verbal noun in proto-Uralic. The IS of conditional -ISI- has an exact analogue in proto-Saamic *-nʲ(d)zʲ- (Korhonen 1981: 251–2) and was homophonous, if not identical, with the antecedent of the diminutive nominalizer seen in Finnish =ISE. At least the -Q form of the imperative dates back to proto-Uralic, as well. Potential -NE- has certain cognates in Mari, Mansi, and Hungarian, and possible cognates in all of Samoyedic save Nganasan. The person suffixes are of either pronominal origin (axis-of-discourse forms) or continue verbal nouns (third person -□ < *-wV, rhythmic weak grade of the non-perfective active participle =PA; cf. p3 -VAT < *=wV-t, with *t* plural). The long consonants initial in p1 -MME and p2 -MME are thought to continue bimorphemic sequences *-k-mV-, *-k-tV- in which *-k- was a present-tense marker.

The *NSK* and its progeny (e.g. Tuomi [2]1980) distinguish forty-five patterns of verb inflection. Most of the variation is due to stem-final morpho-phonemics triggered by the past-tense suffix -I- (cf. the effects of plural -I- in nominal inflection, above). Examination of Table 5.7 will reveal that similar, but not identical, rules govern the behaviour of the verbal analogues of the nominal stem-types; for an exhaustive and systematic overview see Austerlitz 1965. Specifically, beside stable stems there are E-stems, A-stems, and long-vowel stems; there is also a rich and varied vein of X-stem verbs, many but not all of which are built with a synchronically segmentable suffix, such as factitive =X or inchoative =EXE. Notice that the X of the former behaves differently from the X of the latter, e.g. *salasi* '(s)he kept concealed' but *vanheni* '(s)he grew old'. Notice, also, that segmentation of such suffixes often leaves the analyst with a bound lexical morpheme, e.g. KATKE= of KATKE=X- 'breaks'; such morphemes, which have been called themes (Austerlitz 1976, Abondolo 1988), are a by-product of segmentation so ruthless as to resemble internal reconstruction. They deserve further scrutiny nonetheless.

Impersonal forms are built with the discontinuous morphemes -TA ... -□N (present tense) ~ -τTA ... □N (all other tenses and moods); tense/mood suffixes are sandwiched between the two components, e.g. impersonal past SANO=τTA-I-□N *sanottiin* 'it was said, people said', impersonal imperative SANO-τTA-KO-□N *sanottakoon* 'let it be said', impersonal present SANO-TA-∅-□N *sanotaan* 'it is said, people say', impersonal conditional SANO-τTA-ISI-□N 'it would be said, people would say'. To the left of the impersonal morpheme a stem-final A is read as *e* (cf. the comparative, p. 162), e.g. impersonal potential ANTA-τTA-NE-□N *annettaneen* 'it might be given, people might give'. The prehistory of these forms is obscure in its details.

In casual speech, impersonal forms usually replace first-person plural personal forms, e.g. *me men-t-i-in* = *me men-i-mme* 'we went'.

Negative forms are built with the negative auxiliary E-, which is inflected for person but not for tense/mood; the tense/mood of the construction is encoded on the lexical verb, with suffixation as follows: present -Q (the so-called connegative, which is formally always identical with the s2 imperative), past =NUτE (i.e. identical with the perfect active participle), conditional -ISI-Q, potential -NE-Q. The negative auxiliary has deviant third-person forms, viz. s3 E-I *ei*, p3 E-IVAT *eivät*. Examples, using the verb EHTI- 'has enough time for X': E-N EHTI-Q *en ehdi?* 'I don't have time', E-I EHTI-ISI-Q *ei ehtisi?* '(s)he wouldn't have enough time',

Table 5.7 Subparadigms of sample Finnish verbs

	s1 Present	s3 Past	s3 Conditional	s3 Imperative	Perfective active participle	Past impersonal	Infinitive 1
SANO- says	SANO-N *sanon*	SANO-I-∅ *sanoi*	SANO-ISI-∅ *sanoisi*	SANO-KO-□N *sanokoon*	SANO=NUtE *sanonut*	SANO=tTA-I-□N *sanottiin*	SANO-tAQ *sanoa?*
MUISTA- remembers	MUISTA-N *muistan*	MUISTA-I-∅ *muisti*	MUISTA-ISI-∅ *muistaisi*	MUISTA-KO-□N *muistakoon*	MUISTA-NUtE *muistanut*	MUISTA-tT-A-□N *muistettiin*	MUISTA-tAQ *muistaa?*
#TIETA- knows	#TIETA-N *tiedän*	#TIETA-I-∅ *tiesi*	#TIETA-ISI-∅ *tietäisi*	#TIETA-KO-□N *tietäköön*	#TIETA-NUtE *tietänyt*	#TIETA-tT-A-□N *tiedettiin*	#TIETA-tAQ *tietää?*
KAIVA- digs	KAIVA-N *kaivan*	KAIVA-I-∅ *kaivoi*	KAIVA-ISI-∅ *kaivaisi*	KAIVA-KO-□N *kaivakoon*	KAIVA-NUtE *kaivanut*	KAIVA-tTA-I-□N *kaivettiin*	KAIVA-tAQ *kaivaa?*
SALLI- permits	SALLI-N *sallin*	SALLI-I-∅ *salli*	SALLI-ISI-∅ *sallisi*	SALLI-KO-□N *sallikoon*	SALLI-NUtE *sallinut*	SALLI-tTA-I-□N *sallittiin*	SALLI-tAQ *sallia?*
VOI- is able	VOI-N *voin*	VOI-I-∅ *voi*	VOI-ISI-∅ *voisi*	VOI-KO-□N *voikoon*	VOI-NU-tE *voinut*	VOI-tTA-I-□N *voitiin*	VOI-tAQ *voida?*
IO□- drinks	IO□-N *juon*	IO□-I-∅ *joi*	IO□-ISI-∅ *joisi*	IO□-KO-□N *juokoon*	IO□-NUtE *juonut*	IO□-tTA-I-□N *juotiin*	IO□-tAQ *juoda?*
TUNTE- senses	TUNTE-N *tunnen*	TUNTE-I-∅ *tunsi*	TUNTE-ISI-∅ *tuntisi*	TUNTE-KO-□N *tuntekoon*	TUNTE-NUtE *tuntenut*	TUNTE-tTA-I-□N *tunnettiin*	TUNTE-tAQ *tuntea?*
NOUSE- rises	NOUSE-N *nousen*	NOUSE-I-∅ *nousi*	NOUSE-ISI-∅ *nousisi*	NOUSE-KO-□N *nouskoon*	NOUSE-sUtE *noussut*	NOUSE-tTA-I-□N *noustiin*	NOUSE-tAQ *nousta?*
TULE- comes	TULE-N *tulen*	TULE-I-∅ *tuli*	TULE-ISI-∅ *tulisi*	TULE-KO-□N *tulkoon*	TULE-IUtE *tullut*	TULE-tTA-I-□N *tultiin*	TULE-tAQ *tulla?*
#NAKE- sees	#NAKE-N *näen*	#NAKE-I-∅ *näki*	#NAKE-ISI-∅ *näkisi*	#NAKE-KO-□N *nähköön*	#NAhE-NUtE *nähnyt*	#NAKE-tTA-I-□N *nähtiin*	#NAKE-tAQ *nähdä?*
SALA=X- keeps X secret	SALA=X-N *salaan*	SALA=X-I-∅ *salasi*	SALA=X-ISI-∅ *salaisi*	SALA=X-KO-□N *salatkoon*	SALA=X-NUtE *salannut*	SALA=X-tTA-I-□N *salattiin*	SALA=X-tAQ *salata?*
KATKEX- breaks (intr)	KATKEX-N *katkean*	KATKEX-I-∅ *katkesi*	KATKEX-ISI-∅ *katkeaisi*	KATKE=X-KO-□N *katketkoon*	KATKEX-NUtE *katkennut*	KATKEX-tTA-I-□N *katkettiin*	KATKEX-tAQ *katketa?*
VANHA=EXE- ages	VANHA=EXE-N *vanhenen*	VANHA=EXE-I-∅ *vanheni*	VANHA=EXE-ISI-∅ *vanhenisi*	VANHA=EXE-KO-□N *vanhetkoon*	VANHA=EnE-NUtE *vanhennut*	VANHA=EtE-tTA-I-□N *vanhettiin*	VANHA=EtE-tAQ *vanheta?*
VALITSE- chooses	VALITSE-N *valitsen*	VALITSE-I-∅ *valitsi*	VALITSE-ISI-∅ *valitsisi*	VALITSE-KO-□N *valitkoon*	VALITSE-NUtE *valinnut*	VALITSE-tTA-I-□N *valittiin*	VALITSE-tAQ *valita?*

E-T EHTI=NUτE *et ehtinyt* 'you didn't have time'. Prohibitives, i.e. negative imperatives, are formed with the prohibitive auxiliary #ALA. The s2 prohibitive is formed by simple combination of this auxiliary stem with the connegative of the lexical verb, e.g. #ALA UNOHTA-Q *älä unohda?* 'don't (s2) forget'. The p2, s3 (and impersonal), and p3 prohibitives are built with #AL-KAA, #AL-KO-□N, and #Al-KO-□T respectively, and combined with a prohibitive connegative verb form made with the suffix -KO, e.g. #AL-KAA UNOHTA-KO *äl-kää unohta-ko* 'don't (p2) forget!', #AL-KO-□N UNOHTA-KO *äl-kö-ön unohta-ko* 'let him/her not forget!', #AL-KO-□N UNOHTA-τTA-KO *äl-kö-ön unohde-tta-ko* 'may it not be forgotten, let people not forget', #AL-KO-□T UNOHTA-KO *äl-kö-öt unohta-ko* 'let them not forget!'.

Compound tenses and moods of personal forms of the verb are constructed with the perfective active participle and the auxiliary OLE- 'is' (LIE- in the potential), e.g. s1 perfect OLE-N TULE-NUτE *olen tullut* 'I have come', s1 past conditional OLE-ISI-N SAA-NUτE *olisin saanut* 'I would have gotten'. Example of negative compound constructions: E-N OLE-ISI-Q EHTI=NUτE *en olisi? ehtinyt* 'I wouldn't have had time'. Impersonal compound tenses and moods use the perfective passive participle, the finite verb standing in the third person singular, e.g. O-N #IARKE=STA-τTU, i.e. IS-s3 INTELLI-GENCE=vsx-perf.pass.part *on järjestetty* 'one has organized, people have organized', E-I OLE-Q MENE-τTU, i.e. NEG.VERB-s3 IS-CONNEG GOES-perf.pass.part *ei ole[m] menty* 'one didn't go, people didn't go'.

Infinitives and Participles
The non-finite forms of the verb are illustrated here with forms of the verbs MENE- 'goes', TAPA=X- 'meets', and TAPPA- 'kills'.

We may distinguish at least four infinitives:

1   First infinitive -τAQ, whose final Q descends from a lative: MENE-τAQ *mennä?*, TAPA=X-τAQ *tavata?*, TAPPA-ίAQ *tappaa?*.

2   Second infinitive -τE-, which occurs in instructive (-N) and inessive (-SSA) forms, both with gerundive functions, e.g. MENE-τE-N *mennen*, TAPA=X-τE-SSA *tavatessa*, TAPPA-ίE-SSA *tappaessa*. A stem-final E that is not cancelled is read as *i* to the left of this suffix, e.g. TUNTE-ίE-SSA *tuntiessa*.

3   Third infinitive =MA, which occurs in numerous cases, including the nominative: MENE=MA *menemä*, TAPA=X=MA *tapaama*, TAPPA=MA *tappama*. A form built with person suffixes to the plural adessive of a derivate of this stem is sometimes called the fifth infinitive, e.g. (OLE -I-N) TAPPA=MA=ISE-I-LLA-NI *(olin) tappamaisillani* 'I was about to kill'. The third infinitive is also used suppletively as perfective passive participle in attributive constructions with explicit agents: see Syntax, p. 177.

4   =MISE, which is a fully declinable verbal noun: MENE=MISE *menemi-nen*, TAPA=X=MISE *tapaaminen*, TAPPA=MISE *tappaminen*.

The four participles are most succinctly presented in terms of a matrix which distinguishes perfective v. non-perfective and active v. passive:

	Perfective	Non-perfective
Active	=NUτE	=VA (~ =PA)
Passive	=τTU	=τTAVA

The non-perfective passive participle is historically a composite consisting of the non-perfective active suffix =VA added to the impersonal stem.The alternate =PA of the non-perfective active participle is a strong-grade relict of rhythmic gradation alternations; its use in the present-day standard language is restricted, e.g. #KAU=PA *käypä* as in *käy=pä hinta* 'going price' parallel to #KAU=VA, as in *koulu-a käy=vä* 'attending school' and lexicalizations such as #SUO=PA *syöpä* 'cancer', cf. #SUO=VA *syövä* 'eats nonperf.act.part'. Sample participial forms: MENE-NUτE *mennyt*, TAPA=X-NUτE *tavannut*, TAPPA-NUτE *tappanut*; MENE=VA *menevä*, TAPA=X=VA *tapaava*, TAPPA=VA *tappava* MENE-τTU *menty*, TAPA=X=τTU *tavattu*, TAPPA=τTU *tapettu*; MENE-τTAVA *mentävä*, TAPA=X=τTAVA *tavattava*, TAPPA=τTAVA *tapettava*. Note stem-final A > e to the left of =τTU and =τTAVA, and compare the impersonal (p. 172).

The N initial in the perfective active participle assimilates to dentals which become stem-final through the cancellation of final E, e.g. NOUSE-NUτE *noussut*, cf. NOUSE-□ *nousee* 'rises s3', PURE-NUτE *purrut*, cf. PURE-□ 'bites s3'.

The non-perfective passive participle often expresses necessity or obligation, e.g. LUKE=τTAVA KIRIA *luettava kirja* 'book which must/should be read'.

Syntax

The noun phrase is centred on a head nominal, which has optional modifiers before it, after it, or both. Quantifiers and adjectives, including demonstratives and other pronominal adjectives, and other noun phrases in the genitive, are all premodifiers. Examples: *joku toinen henkilö* 'some other person', *tuo mielenkiintoinen ihminen* 'that interesting person'. Premodifiers may themselves be preceded by modifiers such as (1) adverbs, e.g. *hyvin* 'very', *aivan* 'quite', as in *tä=mä aivan uusi kaupunki* 'this quite new city', or (2) subordinated adjectival modifiers in the genitive, as in *sellainen tumma-n ruskea takki* THAT.KIND DARK-G BROWN JACKET 'that kind of dark-brown jacket', or (3) adverbial expressions governed by the premodifer, such as the partitive of bested comparison, e.g. *minu-a vanhe=mpi mies* PRO.s1-P

OLD=cfv MAN 'a man older than I'. This last type is especially frequent with participle premodifers, e.g. *tä-ssä kaupungi-ssa asu=va säveltäjä* 'a composer living in this city'. In general, premodifiers agree with their head in number and case, e.g. *tä-ssä aivan uude-ssa kaupungi-ssa* THIS-ine QUITE NEW-ine CITY-ine 'in this quite new city', *kaikk-i-in nä-i-hin kaupunke-i-hin* ALL-plur-ill THESE-plur-ill CITY-plur-ill 'to all these cities', *kaik-i-ssa Euroopa-n ma-i-ssa* ALL-plur-ine EUROPE-G LAND-plur-ine 'in all the countries of Europe'; there are, however, a few invariable modifiers, most notably *ensi* 'next', *viime(?)* 'last', *joka* 'each (and every)', *koko* 'whole', *eri* 'various', *pikku* 'little', e.g. *koko kahde-n miljardi-n asukkaa-n aluee-lla* WHOLE TWO-G MILLIARD-G INHABITANT-G AREA-ade 'in the region of the entire two thousand million inhabitants'.

Postmodifiers are normally in the partitive, and refer to some larger scope of which the head is a part or the measure, e.g. *kymmene=s maaliskuu-ta* TEN=ord MARCH-P 'the tenth of March', *lasi olut-ta* GLASS BEER-P 'a glass of beer'. Numerals over '1' and a few other quantifiers (such as PUOLE *puoli* 'half') function as head when they are in the nominative or accusative (both marked with -∅, cf. p. 157); the items counted are then postmodifiers and so stand in the partitive, e.g. *kolme-∅ lasi-a* THREE GLASS-P 'three glasses (subject or direct object)'; such constructions may be chained, e.g. *puoli-∅ tunti-a puhet-ta* HALF-N HOUR-P SPEECH-P 'a half hour of (e.g. recorded) speech'. In cases other than nominative and accusative, numerals function as premodifiers, and accordingly agree with their head in case; number is usually formally singular, however, e.g. *kahde-n erillise-n otokse-n tapaukse-ssa* TWO-G SEPARATE-G SAMPLING-G CASE-ine 'in a/the case of two separate samplings'.

A traditional European subject/object approach is unable to come to grips with the Finnish sentence, since not only subject/object case-marking, but also (1) verbal aspect, (2) topic/focus, and (3) kinds and degrees of definiteness of both subject and object are expressed by a combination of case-selection, constituent order, subject-predicate number agreement, and lexical valence. All of these factors therefore should ideally be treated together. Thus the nominative case normally marks a definite subject (type 1 in Figure 5.2), and the accusative normally marks a resultative object, as in the sentence *romppu-∅ sisältä-ä presidenti-n puhee-n* CD-N CONTAINS-s3 PRESIDENT-G SPEECH-A 'the CD contains the president's speech', with S[ubject]-V[erb]-O[bject] order. (On resultative objects and the verbs which attract and produce them, see Karttunen 1975). An indefinite subject is normally in the partitive, as in the sentences *levy-ssä o-n puhet-ta* DISK-ine IS-s3 SPEECH-P 'there is (some e.g. recorded or transcribed) speech on the disk', and *levy-ssä o-n puhe-i-ta* DISK-ine IS-s3 SPEECH-plur-P 'there are (some e.g. recorded or transcribed) speeches on the disk', both with A[dverbial]-V-S order; note the lack of number agreement in the latter, so-called existential, sentence. VS order is typical of sentences with indefinite subjects, but topicalization moves even an indefinite subject into preverbal position, e.g. *puhet-ta o-n levy-ssä* 'as for speech, there's some on the disk'; contrast the neutral S-V-A order of *puhe-Ø o-n levy-ssä* 'the speech is on the disk'. The constituent orders S-O-(A-)V and O-S-(A-)V occur as a by-product of focalization, e.g. *Jussi-Ø tämä-n hevose-n markkino-i-lta ost-i-Ø* JUSSI-N THIS-A HORSE-A MARKET-plur-abl BUYS-past-s3 'it was **Jussi** who bought this horse at the market', *tämä-n hevose-n Jussi markkino-i-lta ost-i-Ø* THIS-A HORSE-A JUSSI-N market-plur-abl BUYS-past-s3 'it was **this horse** that Jussi bought at the market' (Heinämäki 1976).

The actor in constructions built with modal verbs is usually marked with the genitive (subject type 2 in Figure 5.2), and any resultative singular noun direct object of such a construction is marked with -Ø, thereby syncretizing with the nominative, e.g. *opettaja-n täyty-y kirjoitta-a? kirja-Ø* TEACHER-G IS.NECESSARY-s3 WRITES-inf1 BOOK-A 'the teacher must write the/a book'. The genitive is also used to mark the agent in constructions made with the third infinitive, e.g. *opettaja-n kirjoitta=ma-ssa kirja-ssa o-n virhe-i-tä* TEACHER-G WRITES=inf3-ine BOOK-ine IS-s3 ERROR-plur-P 'there are mistakes in the book written by the teacher'.

Finite-verb clauses can be linked by simple parataxis, by co-ordinating or subordinating conjunctions, or by enclitics such as --KA, e.g. *Minä e-n ole-?, e-n--kä halua-? ol-la?, ni-i-den jouko-ssa* PRO.s1 NEG.VERB-s1 IS-conneg NEG.VERB-s1--enclitic WANTS-conneg IS-inf1 PLUR.PRO.NEUT-plural-pG GROUP-ine 'I am not, nor do I want to be, among them', or --KO, which marks both direct and indirect questions, e.g. *kyse? e-i ole-? sii-tä, pääse-e--kö puol=ue? hallit=ukse-en* QUESTION NEG.VERB-s3 IS-conneg PRO.NEUT-ela MANAGES.TO.ARRIVE-s3--question.particle HALF=nsx CONTROLS=nsx-ill 'the question is not whether the party will get into government'. (There are also enclitics which express the speaker's attitude towards the utterance or the speech situation, or which invite the collocutor to concur; in casual speech, enclitics often form chains of up to three members.) Verbal nominals often express the equivalent of clauses, as mentioned above under case-marking; one further example: *hän käv-i-Ø Helsingi-ssä vuon-na 1984 pyyde-tty-ä-ni hän-tä tule=ma-an* PRO.s3 COMES.AND.GOES-past-s3 HELSINKI-ine YEAR-ess 1984 ASKS-perf.pass.part-s1 PRO.s3-P COMES=inf3-ill '(s)he came to Helsinki (temporarily) in 1984 when I asked her/him to (come)'.

Lexicon

Dialectal and folklore resources provide Finnish with a huge range of synonyms and affective-phonaesthemic vocabulary. Many domains of the Finnish lexicon are characterized by synonymic differentiation which appears rich in a European context, e.g. three words for 'or' (*tai* = Latin *aut*, *eli* = Latin *vel*, plus *vai*, used in questions; similarly, three words for 'and'); kinship terms (*eno* 'maternal uncle' : *setä* 'uncle'); verbs of disappearing; and verbs of possibility/sufficiency; on this last, see Flint 1980, which discusses a network of forty-five such verbs in detail. Besides calquing and outright borrowing, there is also a productive urban source of new lexical material, namely slang (Waris 1973, Anttila 1975, Karttunen 1989); nursery language also produces new stems and stem architectonics (e.g. Austerlitz 1960). Crisscrossing these sources is the mechanism of derivation: the Finnish lexicon bristles with words formed with one or more derivational suffixes. Because of the sometimes imprecise boundaries between derivation and inflection on the one hand, and between derivation and compounding on the other, it is difficult to determine the precise number of derivational suffixes productive in Finnish. Nevertheless, about fifty-five nominal-forming suffixes may be found in Vesikansa 1978: 22–90; note that this number far exceeds the number of nominal inflectional suffixes, which is less than thirty even if we include the comparative and superlative as inflectional categories. Words formed with derivational suffixes number in the tens of thousands, and the derivational profiles of Finnish have not yet received a treatment which is both systematic and exhaustive (but see Vesikansa 1978 and Cannelin 1932); here we have room for only a small sample.

Prominent among suffixes which derive nominals is =EQ, which originally formed nomina instrumenti, but is now a factotum nominalizer, e.g. KOKE =EQ *koe* 'test', cf. KOKE- 'tests, tries; earlier: checks fish-traps'. Currently names of instruments tend to be made with =URI (~ =ERI ~ =ORI in foreign items), =IME and =KKEQ, e.g. PRINTT=ERI '(computer) printer', cf. PRINTT=AX- 'prints (from a computer document)', NOSTA=URI *nosturi* 'crane', NOSTA=IME *nostin* 'lever', both from NOSTA- 'raises', #SAATA =IME *säädin* 'regulator', cf. #SAATA- 'regulates', SULA=KKEQ *sulake* 'fuse', cf. SULA- melts'; PALVELE=IME *palvelin* '(computer) server' from PALVELE- 'serves', cf. PALVELE=IA *palvelija* 'servant', with =IA (below). Other deverbal nominals are formed with =O and =U, e.g. MENE=O *meno* 'going, course', cf. MENE- goes', LAULA=U *laulu* 'song', cf. LAULA- 'sings', #KASKE=U *käsky* command, order', cf. #KASKE- 'commands'. Nomina actoris are formed with =IA, e.g. LAULA=IA *laulaja* 'singer', KOKE=IA *kokija* 'fish-trap checker' (note stem-final E > *i*, as in the second infinitive). There is also =TTARE, from which some designations of women are made, e.g. RUNO=TTARE *runotar* 'poetess', cf. RUNO *runo* 'poem', KUNINKAX=TTARE *kuningatar* 'queen', cf. KUNINKAX *kuningas* 'king'. Locational nouns are made with =MO, e.g. KORIAX=MO *korjaamo* 'repair shop', cf. KORIAX- 'repairs', #KEITTA=MO *keittämö* 'cookery', cf. #KEITTA- 'cooks'. Some of the more common suffixes which form denominal nominals are =SE, =ISE, =ISA, =LLISE, and =LAISE, e.g. KOKE =EQ=LLISE *kokeellinen* 'experimental', KALA=SE *kalanen* '(little) fish', KALA=ISE *kalainen*, KALA=ISA *kalaisa*, both 'abounding in fish', LAULA =U=LLISE *laulullinen* 'musical, vocal', #KASKE=U=LAISE *käskyläinen* 'subordinate, servant'. Abstract nouns are formed primarily with =U□TE, e.g. LAULA=U=LLIS=U□TE *laulullisuus* 'musicality, songfulness', VAPA◫= U□TE *vapaus* 'freedom', cf. VAPA□ *vapaa* 'free'.

Verbs are formed from verbs with some twenty different suffixes, used alone or in combination. The result is an abundance of forms which express a range of aspectual/Aktionsart distinctions and degrees of (in)transitivity, or better: exocentric v. endocentric orientation (traditional terminology in this area is especially infelicitous; see Austerlitz 1982). For example, from the inherently exocentric ('transitive') root #NAKE- 'sees' (s3 *näke-e*) is formed, by means of the suffix =U-, the less exocentric stem #NAKE=U- 'is visible' (s3 *näky-y*); attaching the 'transitivizer' =TTA- to this stem produces the more exocentric #NAKE=U=TTA- 'shows' (s3 *näyttä-ä*). To this stem the 'frequentative' =ELE- may be added, yielding #NAKE=U=TTA=ELE- 'displays, shows, portrays (a part on stage)' (s3 *näyttele-e*). As is typical, there are also nominal derivates made from each of these verb stems, e.g. #NAKE=O *näkö* 'sight', #NAKE =U=ISE=UUTE *näkyisyys* 'showiness', #NAKE=U=TTA=MO *näyttämö* 'theatre, arena', #NAKE=U=TTA=ELE=IA=TTARE *näyttelijätär* 'actress'.

Loanwords are known to have come into Fennic, then Finnish primarily from Germanic, Baltic, Slavonic and Saamic languages. The relative chronology of these language groups as sources is disputed; some investigators claim to have found reflexes of Indo-European laryngeals in words borrowed into pre-Fennic. For a review of the debate, see Helimski 1995.

Among the old loanwords which can be ascribed with certainty are SAIRAX *sairas* 'ill' and RENKAX *rengas* 'wheel', from Germanic *saira-z, *xreŋga-z (cf. English *sore, ring*); HAMPAX *hammas* 'tooth', #HEINA *heinä* 'hay', #TUTTARE *tytär* 'daughter' (and its derivational suffix pendant =TTARE, mentioned above), from Baltic; and AHRAIME *ahrain* (dialect *atrain*) '(forked fishing-spear)', RISTI *risti* 'cross', and PAPPI *pappi* 'clergyman', from (Old) Russian. Examples of words borrowed from or via Saamic are POUNU *pounu* 'large tussock in a bog, especially in Northern Finland', SEITA *seita* 'striking topographical feature with traditional religious significance for the Saami', and KAAMO(S+), as in *kaamo(s+aika)* (AIKA *aika* 'time') 'sunless period in midwinter in the north of Finland', this last ultimately from Norwegian *skam(tid)*.

Finnish Text

Taken from p. 170 of H. R. Nevanlenna, 'Suomalaisten juuret geneettisen merkkiominaisuustutkimuksen valossa', in J. Gallén (ed.) (1984) *Suomen väestön esihistorialliset juuret*, Helsinki: Suomen Tiedeseura, pp. 157–74.

A: text in orthography (but phenomena associated with Q are indicated with ?); B: morphophonemic code; C: morpheme-by-morpheme gloss of B; D: paraphrase of C; E: fairly free translation.

A1 Suomenruotsalaisten
B1 SO☐ME-N+RO☐TSA=LAISE
  -τEN
C1 Finnish-G+Swedish=adj-pG
D1 of Finland Swedish

väestöelementtien
#VAKE=STO+ELEMENTTI-
ιEN
PEOPLE=coll+ELEMENT-pG
of population elements

vaikutuksesta
VAIKKUTTA=UKSE-STA
INFLUENCES=NdV-ela
about influence

suomalaisiin
SO☐MA=LAISE-I-☐N
Finnish=adj-plur-ill
on Finns

on
OLE-N
IS-s3
it is

vaikea
VAI.KEA
DIFFICULT
difficult

juuri
IUURI
(particle)
actually

mitään
MI-τA--☐N
WHAT?-sP--enc
anything

sanoa?
SANA=O=ιAQ
WORD=vsx-inf
to say

koska
KOSKA
BECAUSE
because

suomalaiset
SO☐MA=LAISE-T
Finn=adj-pN
the Finns

ilmeisesti
ILMEISE=STI
OBVIOUS=adv
obviously

ovat
OLE-VAT
IS-p3
have

vaelluksensa
VAELTA=UKSE-
NSA
WANDERS-NdV-
pGsp3
of their wanderings

eri
ERI

VARIOUS
various

vaiheissa
VAIHEQ-I-SSA

STAGE-plur-ine
in stages

vastaanottaneet
VASTA-X☐N+OTTA-
NUτE-T
AGAINST+TAKES-
perf.act.part.-pN
(they have) taken on

runsaasti
RUNSAX=STI
AMPLE=adv
amply

germaanista
GERMAAN=ISE-τA
German=adj-sP
Germanic

ja
IA
AND
and

skandinaavista
SKANDINAAV=ISE-τA
Scandinav=adj
Scandinavian

geenistöä.
GEENI=STO-τA
GENE=coll-sP
genetic material

A2 Edellä
B2 ETE=LLA
C2 FORE-ade
D2 earlier

jo
IO
ALREADY
()

mainitsin,
MAINITSE-I-N
MENTIONS-
past-s1
I mentioned

että
#ETTA
THAT

that

suomalaiset
(= B1)
(= C1)

the Finns

eivät
E-IVAT
NEG.VERB-
p3
have ———

ole?
OLE-Q
IS-conneg

not

havaittavissa
HAVAITSE=τTAVA-I-SSA
PERCEIVES=nonperf.
pass.part-plur-ine
in perceivables

olevissa	määrin	siirtäneet
OLE=VA̸-I-SSA	#MAARA̸=IN	#SIIRTA-NUτE-T
IS=nonperf.act.part-plur-ine	MEASURE=instr	TRANSFERS-perf.act.part-pN
in beings	to degree(s)	(they have not) transferred

näihin	omia	piirteitään	ja
#NA-I-X□N	OMA̸-I-τ̸A	PIIRE̸=TA̸=EQ-I-τA-□N	(= B1)
THESE-plur-ill	OWN-plur-P	CIRCLE=VdN=NdV-plur-P-sp3	(= C1)
to these (latter)	own	their traits	and

erikoisuuksian.
ERI=KO.ISE̸=U□KSE̸-I-τ̸A-□N
VARIOUS=adj=nsx-plur-P-sp3
their peculiarities

E1 It is difficult to say anything, actually, about the influence of Finland–Swedish elements of the population on the Finns, because at various stages of their wanderings the Finns have obviously taken on a great deal of Germanic and Scandinavian genetic material.
E2 I have already mentioned earlier that the Finns have not transferred to these latter, to any degree which is perceivable, their own traits and peculiar features.

References and Further Reading

Andersson, E. (1994) 'Swedish', in E. König and J. van der Auwera, (eds), *The Germanic Languages*, London: Routledge, pp. 271–312.

Anttila, R. (1975) 'Affective vocabulary in Finnish: an(other) introduction', *UAJb* 47: 10–19.

Austerlitz, R. (1960) 'Two nascent affective suffixes in Finnish?', in *American Studies in Uralic Linguistics*, edited by the Indiana University Committee on Uralic Studies, Indiana University Publications Uralic and Altaic Series 1, Bloomington: Indiana University, pp. 1–5.

——— (1964) *Finnish Reference Grammar*, Bell and Howell Microfilm Editions.

——— (1965) 'Zur Statistik und Morphonologie der finnischen Konjugationstypen', in A.V. Isačenko (ed.), *Beiträge zur Sprachwissenschaft, Volkskunde und Literaturforschung* [Steinitz-Festschrift], Berlin: Akademie-Verlag, pp. 39–43.

——— (1967) 'The distributional identification of Finnish morphophonemes', *Language* 43/1: 20–33.

——— (1968) 'L'ouralien', in A. Martinet (ed.), *Le langage*, Encyclopédie de la Pléiade no. 25, Paris: Gallimard, pp. 1331–87.

——— (1976) 'Stem-types and segmentability in Finnish', *Texas Linguistic Forum* 5: 13–20. [= Papers from the *Translatlantic Finnish Conference*, ed. Robert T. Harms and Frances Karttunen]. Austin: Department of Linguistics, University of Texas.

——— (1979) 'The morphology and phonology of Finnish given names', in I. Rauch and G.F. Carr (eds), *Linguistic Method: Essays in Honor of Herbert Penzl*, Janua

linguarum, Series Maior, 79, The Hague: Mouton, pp. 299–306.
———— (1982) 'Finnish derivational profiles', Språkhistoria och språkkontakt i Finland och Nord-Skandinavien. Studier tillägnade Tryggve Sköld, den 2 November 1982. Language History and Language Contact in Finland and Northern Scandinavia ... dedicated to Tryggve Sköld, Acta Regiæ Societatis Skytteanæ 26: Umeå, pp. 1–9.
———— (1983) 'Partitive, infinitive, passive, and genitive plural in Finnish', UAJb 55: 81–91.
———— (1993) 'Agglutination, demography, Finnish, Turkic', in M. Sz. Bakró-Nagy and E. Szíj (eds), Hajdú Péter 70 éves [Festschrift for Péter Hajdú] Linguistica, series A, Studiae et Dissertationes 15, Budapest: MTA Nyelvtudomány intézet.
Branch, M. (1987) 'Finnish', in B. Comrie (ed.), The World's Major Languages, London: Croom Helm and London: Oxford University Press, pp. 593–617.
Cannelin, K. (1932) Finska språket. Grammatik och ordbildningslära, Helsingfors.
Collinder, B. (1960) Comparative Grammar of the Uralic Languages, Stockholm: Almqvist & Wiksell.
Eliot, C. N. E. (1890) A Finnish Grammar, Oxford: Clarendon Press.
Fromm, H. (1982) Finnische Grammatik, Heidelburg: Winter.
Hakulinen, L. (1961) Structure and Development of the Finnish Language, Indiana University Publications, Uralic and Altaic Series 3, Bloomington – The Hague: Indiana University and Mouton.
Heinämäki, O. (1976) 'Problems of basic word order', in N. E. Enkvist and V. Kohonen (eds), Reports on Text Linguistics: Approaches to Word Order, Publications of the Research Institute of the Åbo Akademi Foundation No. 8, Åbo: Åbo Akademi, pp. 95–106.
Helimski, E. (1995) 'Сверхдревние германизмы в прибалтийско-финских и других финно-угорских языках. История плоблемы в краткой аннотированной и комментированной библиографии', in V.A. Dybo et al. (eds), Этноязыковая и этнокультурная история Восточной Европы, Moscow: Indrik, pp. 3–37.
———— (1996) 'Proto-Uralic gradation [sic]: continuation and traces', C8IFU, vol. I, pp. 17–51.
Janhunen, J. (1981a) 'On the structure of Proto-Uralic', FUF 44: 23–42.
———— (1981b) 'Uralilaisen kantakielen sanastosta', JSFOu 77: 219–74.
———— (1989) 'Samojedin predestinatiivisen deklinaation alkuperästä', JSFOu 82: 298–301.
Kangasmaa-Minn, E. (1973) 'Genetiv und Lativ, Adjektiv und Plural', Folia Fenno-Ugrica 8 [FUF 40], Turku: Finno-Ugric Institute of the University of Turku, pp. 74–87.
Karlsson, F. (1983) Suomen kielen äänne- ja muotorakenne, Porvoo: Söderström.
———— (1992) 'Finnish', in W. Bright (ed.), International Encyclopedia of Linguistics, vol. 2, New York–Oxford: Oxford University Press.
Karttunen, K. (1989) 'Stadi on hervoton pleisi', in Vesikansa 1989b, pp. 148–64.
Karttunen, L. (1975) 'On the syntax of the word paljon in Finnish', C3IFU, vol. I, pp. 227–35.
Korhonen, M. (1981) Johdatus lapin kielen historiaan. Helsinki: Suomalaisen Kirjallisuuden Seura.
Künnap, A. (1992) 'Die uralischen Völker nach den Angaben der sowjetischen Volkszählungen 1959–1989', Linguistica Uralica 28: 50–54.
Laakso, J. (ed.) (1991) Uralilaiset kansat. Tietoa suomen sukukielistä ja niiden puhujista, Porvoo–Helsinki–Juva: Söderström.

NSK = *Nykysuomen sanakirja*, ed. M. Sadeniemi et al. (1951–61), six volumes, Porvoo–Helsinki: Söderström.

Sammallahti, P. (1989) 'Suomagiela nomeniid ja vearbbaid sojahus. Deataleamos sojahantiippaid ovdamearkahámit. Nomenat ja numerálat', in P. Sammallahti (compiler), *Sámi-Suoma sátnegirji/Saamelais-suomalainen sanakirja*, Ohcejohka (Utsjoki): Jorgaleaddji, Appendix B (pp. 503–4).

Sulkala, H. and Karjalainen, M. (1992) *Finnish*, Descriptive Grammars Series, London: Routledge.

Tuomi, T. (1980) *Suomen kielen käänteissanakirja. Reverse Dictionary of Modern Standard Finnish*, Suomen Kirjallisuuden Seura Toimituksia 274, Helsinki: Finnish Literature Society.

Vesikansa, J. (1978) *Johdokset*, Nyksuomen oppaita No. 2, Porvoo: Söderström.

—— (1989a) 'Etunimet', in Vesikansa 1989b, pp. 276–95.

Vesikansa, J. (ed.) (1989b) *Nykysuomen Sanavarat*, Porvoo–Helsinki–Juva: Söderström.

Viitso, T.-R. (1996) 'On classifying the Finno-Ugric languages', *C8IFU*, vol. IV, pp. 261–6.

Waris, H. (1973) *Työläisyhteiskunnan syntyminen Helsingin Pitkänsillan pohjoispuolelle*, Helsinki: Weilin & Göös.

6 Mordva

Gábor Zaicz

Approximately thirty-five per cent of Mordva speakers, i.e. roughly 350,000 people, live in the Autonomous Mordva Republic in Russia. Here the two primary ethnic and linguistic subgroupings, the Erzya and the Moksha, are represented in about equal numbers. But Mordva speakers make up only about one-third of the population of their own republic, the greater part of the population consisting of Russians; Tatars and Chuvash also live there. Outside of the Mordva Republic proper, Mordvas live in the Penza, Nižnij-Novgorod, Simbirsk, Orenburg and Saratov regions; in the Chuvash, Tatar, and Baškir Autonomous Republics; in the zone between the Volga and the Belaja Rivers; in Siberia, and in Central Asia. Diaspora Mordva speakers live scattered from Ukraine to Vladivostok and Sakhalin.

In terms of numbers, Mordva speakers today occupy third place in the Uralic family, after Hungarian and Finnish. Owing to the sparse settlement pattern of much of the population, however, the demographic figures show a diminishing tendency. Compared with the 1959 census, the 1989 census statistics show a drop from 1,211,000 to 1,073,000 speakers in Russia (88.6 per cent). For the former Soviet Union as a whole, the drop is slightly greater: from 1,285,000 to 1,154,000 (89.8 per cent). What is more, the percentage of Mordvas who considered Mordva to be their native language dropped from 77.8 per cent in 1970 to 72.6 per cent in 1979, and continued to fall, to 67.1 per cent, in 1989. Although the official view recognized two distinct literary languages, Erzya and Moksha, national census figures do not make the distinction; it has been estimated that the Erzya make up some 65 per cent of the ethnic total.

From the standpoints of linguistics, ethnography, and physical anthropology, Mordva speakers may be divided into two groups: in Mordvinia proper, those living around the eastern branch of the Sura River are called Erzya, while a western group living in the valley of the Moksha River are called Moksha (two other ethnic groups, the Karatay and Terjuxan, no longer use Mordva). The two main dialect groups, Erzya and Moksha, differ chiefly in their phonology; subdialects of both Erzya and Moksha also differ chiefly in their phonology, but also, to a lesser degree, in their morphology (for Erzya dialects see Ermuškin 1984: 6–27; for Moksha: Feoktistov 1966: 219–20, 1975: 258–60; for an overview and classification of subdialects: Keresztes 1990: 14–18).

The following introduction to the grammar and lexicon of Mordva is based on the Erzya literary standard, but with reference, where pertinent, to the Moksha literary standard and to non-literary dialects as well. Unless otherwise specified, therefore, Erzya forms will not be marked; the abbreviations E[rzya] and M[oksha] signal forms cited for purposes of comparison.

The ethnonym *mordvin, mordva*, like E *mirde*, M *mirdä* 'man, husband' (Rédei 1986:53) is presumably a loan from proto-Indo-Iranian *mr̥tá-* 'human', borrowed into proto-Mordvin as *murta (> *murda > *morda). The *v* of modern Russian мордвин, collective мордвà, is secondary; compare Moskva < Old Russian Mŏský. The self-designation may have been *morda in common Mordva, but this term was ousted by the tribal names E *erźa* and M *mokšă*.

Phonology

Consonants

Literary standard Erzya has twenty-eight consonant phonemes (Rédei 1984: 209). This figure includes the marginal *f* and *x*, which occur only in recent (mostly Russian) loans: cf. E *fabrika*, dialect *kvabrika* 'factory', E *kolxoz*, dialect *kolkoz* 'kolkhoz'. Northern Erzya dialects have, in addition, the velar nasal *ŋ* where the literary standard has innovated a *v*, e.g. E *kov*, dialect *koŋ* 'moon' (< pU *kuŋe).

The consonant inventory of literary standard Erzya is set out in Table 6.1.

Allophonic variation is the result of environment, as follows: (1) palatalization of bilabials, labiodentals, and velars to the left of front vowels; (2) *n* is realized as velar [ŋ] the left of the velar stops *k* and *g*; (3) *v* is often [w] before consonants and at word-end; and (4) the sibilants *s*, *š*, and *sʲ* are often realized as the corresponding voiced affricates when to the right of *n*, *nʲ*, *r* and *rʲ*. Examples: *pe* [pʲe] 'end', *venč* [vʲenč] 'boat'; *kenkš* [kʲeŋkš] 'door', *pango* [paŋgo] 'mushroom'; *čuvto* [čuwto] 'tree', *kev* [kʲew] 'stone'; *kumanža* ~

Table 6.1   Consonant inventory of literary standard Erzya

	Bilabial	Labiodental	Dental	Alveolar	Palatal	Velar
Nasals	m		n		nʲ	
Voiceless stops	p		t		tʲ	k
Voiced stops	b		d		dʲ	g
Voiceless fricatives		f	s	š	sʲ	x
Voiced fricatives		v	z	ž	zʲ	
Affricates			c	č	cʲ	
Laterals			l		lʲ	
Tremulants			r		rʲ	
Glide					j	

[kumanǯa] 'knee', *erzʲa* ~ [erʲǯʲa] 'Erzya Mordva'.

Within the morpheme, length is non-distinctive. In intervocalic position, the voiceless stops and fricatives show a slightly greater duration, e.g. the *tʲ* of *vetʲe* 'five' is phonetically half-long [vetʲe]. Phonologically long consonantisms occur only at morpheme boundaries, e.g. *vedʲ-tʲe* [vetʲtʲe] 'water sAbl'.

The present-day Erzya consonant system differs from that of proto-Mordva chiefly by virtue of the new phonemes *f* and *x*, which have taken root under the influence of Russian. Present-day Moksha, on the other hand, shows more significant innovations: the literary language has five additional phonemes, the voiceless laterals [ɫ ɫʲ], the voiceless tremulants [R Rʲ], and the voiceless palatal fricative [ç], which we shall write *L Lʲ R Rʲ J*. What is more, palatalized *šʲ žʲ* and *čʲ* are phonemes in some Moksha dialects. All eight of these additional phonemes may be present in Erzya dialects which have been subjected to strong Moksha influence.

Correlations of Palatalization and Voice

In literary Erzya, the correlation of palatalization extends to eight pairs of consonants: *t : tʲ, d : dʲ, n : nʲ, s : sʲ, z : zʲ, c : cʲ, l : lʲ, r : rʲ*. The correlation of voice also entails eight pairs: *t : d, tʲ : dʲ, p : b, k : g, f : v, s : z, š : ž, sʲ : zʲ*.

Consonant Distribution

In word-initial position in core (= non-borrowed, non-affective) vocabulary normally only the unvoiced members of the [+/-] voiced pairs occur, i.e. *b d dʲ g z ž zʲ* occur word-initially primarily in loanwords and in onomatopoeic/ affective items. Relatively rare in this position are the newer phonemes *f* and *x* and the voiceless affricates *c* and *cʲ*. Clusters of two or three consonants, in which the first consonant is a stop or sibilant, are not uncommon, e.g. *prʲa* 'head', *skal* 'cow', *kšnʲi* 'iron', *šna-* 'praises', *štapo* (dialect: *štrapo*) 'naked; only'.

All consonant phonemes occur in word-internal position. Here a great variety of clusters occur, consisting of two to five consonants. Both the architectonics and the morphophonemics of such clusters are highly complex; they await a thorough and systematic study. A pilot study of twenty-three three-member clusters (Rédei 1984: 214–18) revealed that they always contain at least one liquid or sibilant. Four-member clusters usually begin with a liquid or nasal, e.g. *karʲske* 'shoelace', *vanʲsʲtʲnʲe-* 'defends (freq)'. Clusters of five are much rarer; examples are *karks-t-ne* BELT-plur-def 'the belts'. In Moksha, clusters may contain as many as six consonants.

Word-finally, *p b g f x c* are extremely rare, occurring only in the most recent loans. Traditionally, a paragogic *a* has been added to Russian loans ending in *b, g*, or in a cluster alien to Mordva, e.g. *stolba* 'pillar', *luga* 'meadow', *tʲeatra* 'theatre' (< Russian). Often in bisyllabic and polysyllabic words the literary language has a voiced consonant where dialects have the voiceless analogue, e.g. *tarvaz* 'sickle', *r^jivez^j* 'fox', *tarad* 'bough' (dialect: *tarvas*, *r^jives^j*, *tarat*). Word-final clusters are also quite common: Rédei (1984: 218–21) found twelve types of two-membered clusters and nine types of three-membered clusters. Four-membered clusters occur only through concatenation of morphemes. Examples: *koms^j* 'twenty', *kan^js^jt^j* 'hemp', *alks-t* 'beds'.

The stops are unaspirated. Palatalization is more prominent in Moksha than in Erzya.

Vowels
The literary language and most dialects have five vowels:

	Front	Central	Back
High	i		u
Mid	e		o
Low		a	

There are no diphthongs. The back rounded vowels *u* and *o* show little allophonic variation, but the front unrounded *i* and *e* have backed variants when to the right of distinctively non-palatalized consonants (*t d n s z c l r*), e.g. *sin^j* [sïn^j] 'they', *sen^j* [sën^j] 'blue'; contrast *s^jin^jd^je-* 'breaks X' (with [i]), *s^jen^jks* 'heron' (with [e]). The phoneme *a* has a fronted allophone [ä] when to the left of any palatalized consonant, e.g. *a er^javi* [ajer^jäv^ji] 'it isn't necessary/allowed'.

In Erzya dialects which have been under Moksha influence there can be a phonemic *ä* and a phonemic reduced vowel *ə*, as well. The Moksha literary language has a rectangular system with schwa (*i e ä u o a ə*).

We may reckon with a similar system, enriched by a front/back schwa pair *ə/*ə̂, in the first syllable of the later stages of proto-Mordva (cf. Bereczki 1988: 319, 321), and in the earlier stages of proto-Mordva there was certainly a high front rounded *ü, as well. A high vowel (*i *u *ü) in the first syllable followed by a low vowel (*a *ä) in the second syllable triggered a stress-shift (from first to second syllable), followed by reduction (and usually loss) of the first-syllable vowel, e.g. (stressed vowels underlined) *usk<u>a</u>l > *ə̂sk<u>a</u>l > EM sk<u>a</u>l 'cow', *kürs<u>ä</u> > *kərz<u>ä</u> > EM *kši* 'bread'. In Erzya, the reduced vowels of non-first syllables have been replaced by full vowels, e.g. *juž<u>ə̂</u> > *jož<u>ə</u> > *jožo* 'skin', *kilmə > *kelmə > *kel^jme* 'cold'. In Moksha, the reduced vowel developed from any full vowel in unstressed position.

Vowel Correlations and Distribution
Erzya has the smallest vowel inventory in the Uralic family. Even so, many oppositions are not heavily exploited. Of the high vowels, for example, *u* does not occur in word-final position in core vocabulary and *i* occurs there only in suffixes. Both high vowels are in fact frequent only in the first syllable. It is

thus not surprising that it is the vowels *e o a*, which are free of such distributional restrictions, which are the most common (Veenker 1981: 46).

Vowel sequences occur only in loans, e.g. *nʲeušto* 'really?' (< Russian) or, occasionally, as the result of loss of an intervening consonant, e.g. *raužo* 'black' < *rawužo.

Further examples illustrating vowel distribution and canonic shapes: *azoro* 'lord', *inʲzʲej* 'raspberry', *tʲelʲe* 'winter', *kuvaka* 'long', *molʲ-i* '(s)he goes', *srazu* 'at once'(< Russian).

Morphophonology

Morpheme Architectonics

Perusal of Erzya texts has uncovered eighteen shapes for nominal, thirteen for verbal stems; with suffixes the pattern is the reverse, viz. eleven verb-suffix shapes but only five shapes for nominal suffixes; the distribution is roughly identical in Moksha (Keresztes 1990: 30–1). According to Cygankin (cited in Raun 1988: 100), the most typical Erzya morpheme shapes are as follows: V, VC, VCC, CV, CVC. As an illustration, here are examples of (1) the vowel-initial nominal stem types and (2) the consonant-initial verbal suffix types:

1   VC *ej* 'ice', VCV *ašo* 'white', VCVC *ozʲaz* 'sparrow', VCVCV *uzʲerʲe* 'hatchet', VCCV *ekše* 'cool', VCCVC *irʲdʲes* 'rib', VCCVCC *ejkakš* 'child', VCCCVC *ukštor* 'maple';
2   C -*k* (s2 imperative), CV -*do* (p2 imperative), CC -*zt* (p3 optative), CVC -*nʲek* (p1 first past), CCV =*vto-* (transitivizer), CVCV =*zʲeve-* (inchoativizer), CVCC -*sink* (p2 subject, sp3 object), CCCV =*kšno-* (frequentativizer).

Mordva is rich in morphophonological alternations. What follows is no more than a sketch based on the available literature (Cygankin 1980: 31–43, Rédei 1984: 225–9, Keresztes 1990: 31–7).

Stem Variants

All verbs and nouns have both consonant-final and vowel-final variants, to which suffixes attach according to various rules (Nadjkin 1981). Which variant is selected depends in part on the stem itself (i.e. is lexical) and in part on the suffix to be attached. Thus the third-person singular first past tense suffix -*sʲ* is always added to the vowel-stem of verbs ending in *a*, e.g. *jarsa-* 'eats', *jarsa-sʲ* '(s)he ate'; but it is added to the vowel stem of *udo-* 'sleeps', and to the consonant-stem of *kado-* 'leaves (tr)', giving *udo-sʲ* '(s)he slept', but *kad-sʲ* '(s)he left'. Somewhat parallel circumstances exist in the morphology of the nominal, where certain suffixes tend to require consonant stems, and some stems even lose their last syllable before certain morphemes, e.g. *pando* 'hill', inessive *pand-so*, illative *pand-s*, plural *pand-t*; *pilʲge* 'leg', inessive *pil'g-se*, illative *pil'g-s*, plural *pil'g-t'; s'el'me* 'eye', inessive *s'el'm-se*, illative *s'el'm-s*, plural *s'el'(m)-t'*, note also *s'el'+ved'* 'tear (EYE +WATER)'.

Certain suffixes always attach to the consonant stem, e.g. the third person singular present -*i*, e.g. *jarsa-* 'eats', *jars-i* '(s)he eats', *udo-, ud-i* '(s)he sleeps', *kado-, kad-i* '(s)he leaves'. Others always attach to the vowel stem, e.g. genitive -*n'* added to *moda* 'earth', or *s'el'me* 'eye' gives *moda-n'*, *s'el'me-n'*. Attaching such suffixes to consonant-final nouns such as *oš* 'city', *vir'* 'forest' triggers epenthesis: *oš-on', vir'-en'*.

Suffix Variants

The most salient type of suffixal allomorphy is determined by the front/back prosody of the stem; stem prosody, in turn, depends on the presence/absence of palatalization of stem-final consonants and the identity and order of vowels. For example, the vowel of the inessive suffix is *e* in *piče-se* '(Scotch) pine (ine)', but *o* in *moda-so* 'earth (ine)'; the (indefinite) plural suffix is non-palatalized -*t* in *oš-t* 'cities' and *paks'a-t* 'fields', but palatalized -*t'* in *vir'-t'* 'forests' and *vel'e-t'* 'villages'. As these examples show, suffixal allomorphy may entail front/back vowels (usually *e/o*), plain v. palatalized consonants (e.g. *t/t'*), or both, as in the ablative forms *paks'a-do, vel'e-d'e*. There is also automatic alternation of voice in cases such as ablative *oš-to* 'from a city'; in addition to such voiced/voiceless allomorphy, the prolative suffix (-*ka ~ -ga*) has a variant -*va* which occurs after vowel stems: *oš-ka* 'by way of the city', *ked'-ga* 'by the hand', *moda-va* 'along the ground'.

Other Sandhi Phenomena

Word-internally there is voice assimilation in which voicelessness moves from right to left; this type of voice assimilation devoices voiced stops and sibilants when the morphology places voiceless consonants to their right, e.g. *ked'* 'hand' with voiced [d'], but *ked'-se* with voiceless [t'] ([ket'së]). Further examples with 'hand': illative *ked'-s* [ket's], plural *ked'-t'* [ket't'], and the derivative *ked'=ks* [ket'ks] 'bracelet'. In parallel fashion, from the root *čalga-* 'treads on (tr)' is formed a frequentative *čalg=s'e-* [čalks'e]. The official orthography is somewhat inconsistent in rendering these assimilations; for example, 'bracelet' is written кедькс (not indicating the assimilation), while 'tramples on' is written чалксе-, with the letter к indicating the voice assimilation. In nominal stems ending in *n* or *n'* these nasals may assimilate to the plural suffix, e.g. *loman'* 'human being', plural *lomat'-t'* (~ *loman'-t'*).

There is also voice assimilation in which voice moves from left to right; in this type of assimilation, a non-distinctively voiced consonantism at the end of a morpheme causes the initial consonantism of the next morpheme to be voiced. This type of voice assimilation operates not only within the word but also across word boundaries, i.e. in the compound or phrase, e.g. *tolban'd'a* 'campfire' (compound of *tol* 'fire' and *pan'd'a* 'bed'), *ejz'uro* 'icicle' (compound of *ej* 'ice' and *sʲuro* 'horn'), *erzʲa=nʲ kelʲ* [erzʲaŋʲgʲelʲ] 'Erzya language'. Word-internal examples: *nʲilʲ-tʲano* (with [lʲdʲ]) 'we swallow', *čav-tan* (with [wd]) 'I strike you'. The orthography renders this type of assimilation only in compounds, i.e. not in phrases or within inflected forms.

A few more examples will illustrate and expand upon the rules outlined above. We have voice assimilation (*dʲ* > *tʲ*) in abessive *kedʲ-tʲeme* [tʲtʲ] 'without hand(s)'; assimilation of voice and palatalization (*dʲ* > *t*) in inessive *kedʲ-se* ([ttˢ], phonemically /kecce/; more careful pronunciations with [tʲtʲˢ] also exist); and automatic replacement of voiced with voiceless in the middle of a cluster (**ndl* > *ntl*) in frequentative *kunt=lʲe-* 'keeps grasping', from *kunda-* 'seizes'.

Vowel and Consonant Harmony

The p(F)U harmony of vowels within the stem has been fairly well preserved in Mordva: roughly 80 per cent of the inherited word stock of Mordva has either front or back vocalism, preserving the original frontness or backness inherited from p(F)U; in the remainder, front and back vowels occur mixed, usually because of secondary effects caused by consonants, e.g. *usʲke* 'wire' with front *e* due to the *sʲ*. Borrowed and onomatopoeic vocabulary naturally show a higher proportion of mixed-vowel words, e.g. *cʲelkovoj* 'rouble', *pocʲerʲdʲe-* 'drips'.

Vowel harmony in suffixes is a different matter. Whereas in Moksha most suffixes have only one harmonic shape, in Erzya over twenty have front v. back variants (Zaicz 1993). The vocalism of these suffixes adjusts to the prosody of the last stem vowel; the most common pair of alternants is *o ~ e*, e.g. *kudo-so* 'in a house', but *pirʲe-se* 'in a garden', *tol-oz-onzo* 'into his/her fire' but *kelʲ-ez-enze* 'into his/her language'.

Alongside this kind of rudimentary vowel harmony Erzya has evolved a kind of consonant harmony. Suffixes with initial apical consonants (but not *s*) show an alternation plain ~ palatalized according to the prosody of the stem to which they are attached, e.g. *kal* 'fish', dative *kal-nenʲ* and plural *kal-t*, but *kalʲ* 'willow', dative *kalʲ-nʲenʲ* and plural *kalʲ-tʲ*. The vocalism of *piks* 'rope' is front, but the distinctively non-palatalized *s* final in this stem selects the non-palatalized alternants, dative *piks-nenʲ* and plural *piks-t*; contrast *virʲ* 'forest' with *virʲ-nʲenʲ*, *virʲ-tʲ*.

Stress

Erzya stress is free and non-distinctive with regard to grammar and lexicon. This means that any syllable of a word such as *varakanʲtʲenʲ* 'raven (dat)' or *sʲimemazo* 'drinking (s3)' may be given accentual prominence indifferently, and that the unstressed syllables are pronounced fully, with unreduced vowels. In general, compound words are stressed on the first syllable of their components, e.g. k̲i̲lʲej+bu̲lo 'birch grove'; first-syllable stress in non-compound words is also quite common. Moksha deviates sharply in this regard, placing a strong stress on the first full vowel of the word (Paasonen 1903: 114–19).

In recent Russian loanwords, stress follows the Russian pattern in both Erzya and Moksha.

Morphology

Nominals

Types of Nominal, and Nominal Stem-types
We may treat as nominals all stems which take declensional suffixes: nouns, adjectives, numerals, and pronouns. The citation form for Mordva nominals is the nominative singular, e.g. *moda* 'earth', *vir^j* 'forest', *sir^{j}e* 'old', *od* 'new; young', *vejke* 'one', *koms^j* 'twenty', *s^{j}e* 'that, it', *mon* 'I'. Nominals whose citation form ends in a consonant take an epenthetic vowel, *e* or *o* depending on prosody, before certain suffixes, e.g. the genitive *-n^j*: *vir^j-en^j*, *od-on^j*, *koms^j-en^j*, *mon^j-s^j-en^j* (*mon-s^j* 'I myself').

Both Erzya and Moksha distinguish indefinite from definite forms of the nominal. The development of the definite declension was already well underway in common Mordva, and complemented the older, inherited dichotomy of plain v. possessive declension; examples of this three-way distinction are *vir^j-se* 'in a forest', *vir^j-sen^{j}t^j* 'in the forest', *vir^j-sen^j* 'in my forest'.

Noun Declension
Indefinite and definite paradigms. With certain syncretisms noted below, Erzya declension distinguishes two numbers, singular and plural. It has become standard practice to list eleven or twelve cases for the Erzya indefinite paradigm, and ten or eleven cases for the definite (Wiedemann 1865: 42, Bubrix 1947: 17, Collinder 1957: 232, Cygankin 1980: 220, Keresztes 1990: 56). The discrepancies in case-counts are due to the inclusion or exclusion of the lative case in the indefinite, and of the translative case in the definite paradigm.

In the I[ndefinite] D[eclension], the opposition singular : plural is neutralized in all cases except the nominative, e.g. sN *kudo* 'house', pN *kudo-t* 'houses', spEla *kudo-sto* 'out of a house ~ out of houses'. The ID pN suffix *-t* continues the pU plural suffix **-t*. In the D[efinite] D[eclension], the illative and dative/allative cases syncretize, e.g. ID dative/allative *vir^j-n^{j}en^j* 'to a forest', illative *vir^j-s* 'into a forest', but DD *vir^j-en^{j}t^{j}en^j* '(in)to the forest'.

The forms of the DD are distinguished from those of the ID by *-s^j* in the nominative singular, *-t^j* in the genitive/accusative, and *-n^{j}t^j* in the other cases of the singular; in the plural the definiteness marker is *-n^{j}e/-ne*. These morphemes all derive from demonstrative pronouns (cf. Finnish *se* 'it, that', *ne* 'those', *tä-* 'this'); the *-n^j-* in the sequence *-n^{j}t^j-* probably continues the pU genitive **-n*. Synchronically, it is no simple matter to derive the DD from an agglutinating analogue made up of these definiteness markers and the case suffixes of the ID, and no such segmentation is essayed here.

Besides the forms given in Table 6.2 for singular and plural inessive, elative, illative, prolative, and ablative (and singular comparative) there exist parallel constructions built with the noun in the definite genitive plus the postposition *ez* (~ *ej* before *s*) in the appropriate case, e.g. DD sProl *vir^j-gan^{j}t^j* or *vir^j-en^{j}t^j ez-ga* 'through the forest'.

Taxonomy and historical background of the case suffixes. The nominative, genitive/accusative, and dative/allative are chiefly grammatical in function and thus differ clearly in function from the local cases. The nominative marker is zero, as generally in Uralic. The suffix *-n^j* represents a merging of two originally distinct cases, pU genitive *-n and pU accusative *-m. In the definite declension in front-prosodic environments there occurred palatalization (*-n-t > *-n^j-t^j) and assimilation (*-m-t > *-m-t^j > *-n^j-t^j); these forms then generalized to non-front environments, and the *-n^j-* element invaded the indefinite paradigm as well. The *-n^{j}en^j* suffix of the dative/allative (*-nen^j* after distinctively non-palatalized consonants, e.g. *panar-nen^j* 'shirt [dat/all]') is the result of a reduplication of an old lative in *-n^j.

The local cases may be classified according to their concrete spatial reference into two subclasses, interior (inessive, elative, and illative) and exterior (ablative, lative, and prolative). Interior cases refer to more intimate contact than exterior cases.

Historically, the interior cases are all built with a putatively lative suffix *-s known also from Cheremis, Fennic, and Saamic. The Mordva inessive *-se* ~ *-so* continues a suffix chain reconstructed as *-s-nA, cf. the fossilized inessive adverb *on-sne* 'in a dream', and *n*-allomorphs such as *vaz-ne* 'calf (ine)', attested in Erzya dialects. The elative *-ste* ~ *-sto* consists of the same *-s plus a separative suffix *-tV which dates back to pU. The illative *-s* is the *-s suffix alone; contrast its intervocalic *-z-* allomorph (*kudo-z-onzo* 'into his/her house') with the *-s-* of the inessive (< *-ss- < *-sn-) in the same phonotaxis (*kudo-s-onzo* 'in his/her house').

Turning to the exterior cases, we find the same pU *-tV separative occurring alone in the ablative *-do* (with allomorphs *-d^{j}e -de -to -t^{j}e -te* in keeping with vowel and consonant harmony), e.g. *ver^{j}giz-de* 'wolf (abl)', *oš-to* 'city (abl)', *venč-t^{j}e* 'boat (abl)', *piks-te* 'rope (abl)'. The prolative, which is *-ga* to the right of voiced consonants, *-ka* to the left of voiceless consonants, and *-va* to the right of vowels, continues a common Mordva suffix *-kV; this suffix no doubt contains pU lative *-k. The somewhat rare lative suffix *-v*, which has Erzya dialect reflexes *-ŋ* (in back-prosodic contexts) and *-j* (in front-prosodic contexts) and is represented in Moksha by *-u* ~ *-i* ~ *-v*, continues a nasal variant of the same *-k lative.

The translative, abessive, and comparative may be seen as semi-grammatical, i.e. half way between the local cases and the pure grammatical cases nominative, genitive/accusative, and dative/allative. The translative may

Table 6.2 Selected Erzya nominal paradigms: *moda* 'earth', *virʲ* 'forest'

	Indefinite		Definite singular		Definite plural	
sN	moda	virʲ	moda-sʲ	virʲ-esʲ	modatʲ-nʲe	virʲtʲ-nʲe
pN	moda-t	virʲ-tʲ				
G/A	moda-nʲ	virʲ-enʲ	moda-nʲtʲ	virʲ-enʲtʲ	modatʲ-nʲenʲ	virʲtʲ-nʲenʲ
Dat/All	moda-nʲenʲ	virʲ-nʲenʲ	moda-nʲtʲenʲ	virʲ-enʲtʲenʲ	modatʲ-nʲenʲenʲ	virʲtʲ-nʲenʲenʲ
Ine	moda-so	virʲ-se	moda-sonʲtʲ	virʲ-senʲtʲ	modatʲ-nʲese	virʲtʲ-nʲese
Ela	moda-sto	virʲ-ste	moda-stonʲtʲ	virʲ-stenʲtʲ	modatʲ-nʲeste	virʲtʲ-nʲeste
Ill	moda-s	virʲ-s	moda-nʲtʲenʲ	virʲ-enʲtʲenʲ	modatʲ-nʲes	virʲtʲ-nʲes
Prol	moda-va	virʲ-ga	moda-vanʲtʲ	virʲ-ganʲtʲ	modatʲ-nʲeva	virʲtʲ-nʲeva
Abl	moda-do	virʲ-dʲe	moda-donʲtʲ	virʲ-dʲenʲtʲ	modatʲ-nʲedʲe	virʲtʲ-nʲedʲe
Lat	moda-v	virʲ-ev	—	—	—	
Trans	moda-ks	virʲ-ks	(moda-ksonʲtʲ)	(virʲ-ksenʲtʲ)	(modatʲ-nʲeks)	(virʲtʲ-nʲeks)
Abe	moda-vtomo	virʲ-tʲeme	moda-vtomonʲtʲ	virʲ-tʲemenʲtʲ	modatʲ-nʲevtʲeme	virʲtʲ-nʲevtʲeme
Cfv	moda-ška	virʲ-ška	moda-škanʲtʲ	virʲ-škanʲtʲ	modatʲ-nʲeška	virʲtʲ-nʲeška

well be simply a concatenation of two of the old lative suffixes already mentioned, viz. *-k and *-s; or its history may be more complex, involving a connection with a pU noun-forming derivational suffix *=ks. Cognates of the Mordva abessive suffix are usually seen as adjective-forming derivational suffixes (compare Finnish *pää=ttömä-n* with Mordva *pe-vt͡ʲeme-nʲ*, both genitives of HEAD+ABESSIVE); here again we most probably have to deal with an old suffix-string, namely *=ptV plus *=mV. The comparative seems to be a string of two diminutive derivational suffixes, *=š and *=kA.

In Moksha there is a thirteenth ('causative') case, built with *-nksë*, which has its origin in the inessive of a postposition *inksë* meaning 'on account of'.

Secondary and tertiary declension. Metadeclensional forms may be obtained by attaching definiteness strings such as sN -*sʲ*, sGA -*nʲtʲ*, sDAll -*nʲtʲenʲ* to most already-inflected case forms. Thus to the indefinite inessive form of *moda* 'earth, ground', *moda-so*, one can add the definite sN ending -*sʲ*, yielding *modasosʲ* 'that which is in the ground', the definite inessive ending -*sonʲtʲ*, yielding *modasosonʲtʲ* 'in that which is in the ground', and so on. Each of the eleven definite case strings can be added to forms inflected for at least six of the cases (genitive, inessive, elative, translative, abessive, comparative). Such metaforms are built to genitive bases by the addition of a reduplicative: sN -*sʲesʲ*, sG -*sʲenʲtʲ*, sDAll -*sʲenʲtʲenʲ*, and so on, e.g. secondary lative form of the genitive *virʲ-enʲ-sʲesʲtʲenʲtʲ* 'out of that of the forest'.

Parallel to secondary forms such as the secondary inessive *moda-so-sʲ* cited above there exist tertiary, essentially synonymous, forms in which the -*sʲesʲ* (-*sʲenʲtʲ*, -*sʲenʲtʲenʲ*, etc.) endings are added to an inflected form augmented by -*nʲ*-, e.g. sN *moda-so-nʲ-sʲesʲ*, sG *moda-so-nʲ-sʲenʲtʲ* (Erdődi 1968: 233).

Possessive declension. Alongside, and in complementary distribution with, the definite declension Erzya has forms which indicate the person and number of the possessor and, in the first and third person singular nominative, also the number of the thing possessed.

The literature reckons with eight to nine distinct case forms for the Erzya possessive declension (Wiedemann 1865: 52, Cygankin 1980: 201, Keresztes 1990: 196). The possessive suffix always follows the case suffix in Erzya, e.g. *virʲ-ste-nʲek* FOREST-ela-p1 'out of our forest(s)'. In Moksha, where distinct possessive forms for genitive/accusative and dative/allative have evolved, as well, the possessive suffix precedes the markers of those cases, and the number of the possession can be distinguished, e.g. M *valʲmä-zʲë* WINDOW-s1sgposs 'my window', *valʲmä-nʲë* WINDOW-s1plurposs 'my windows', *valʲmä-zʲë-nʲ* WINDOW-s1sgposs-gen/acc 'of my window', *valʲmä-nʲë-nʲ* WINDOW-s1plurposs-gen/acc 'of my windows', *valʲmä-zʲ-tʲi* WINDOW-s1sgposs-dat/all 'to my window', *valʲmä-nʲë-nʲdʲi* WINDOW-s1plurposs-dat/all 'to my windows'. In cases beyond the dative/allative even Moksha cannot distinguish possession number.

Table 6.3   Selected Erzya possessive declension subparadigms, nominative: *moda* 'earth, ground', *vir^j* 'forest'

Possessor	Possession in Singular	Plural	Possession in Singular	Plural
s1	moda-m	moda-n	vir^j-em	vir^j-en^j
s2	moda-t		vir^j-et^j	
s3	moda-zo	moda-nzo	vir^j-eze	vir^j-enze
p1	moda-nok		vir^j-en^jek	
p2	moda-nk		vir^j-enk	
p3	moda-st		vir^j-est	

Table 6.4   Selected Erzya possessive declension subparadigms, s3, p1: *moda* 'earth, ground', *vir^j* 'forest'

	Third person singular Singular possession	Plural possession	First person plural	
sN	moda-zo		spN	vir^j-en^jek
pN		moda-nzo		
Ine	moda-so-nzo		vir^j-se-n^jek	
Ela	moda-sto-nzo		vir^j-ste-n^jek	
Ill	moda-z-onzo		vir^j-ez^je-n^jek	
Prol	moda-va-nzo		vir^j-ga-nok	
Abl	moda-do-nzo		vir^j-d^je-n^jek	
Trans	(moda-ks-onzo)		(vir^j-ks-en^jek)	
Abe	moda-vtomo-nzo		vir^j-t^jeme-n^jek	
Cfv	moda-ška-nzo		vir^j-ška-nok	

The Erzya possessive suffixes all go back ultimately to the pU personal pronouns, with roots *mV, *tV, and *sV for first, second, and third persons. Plurality of thing possessed, where expressed (e.g. *kudo-n* 'my houses'), is expressed by means of a reflex of a p(F)U pluralizer *-n-. The p1 and p2 suffixes (*-nok* ~ *-n^jek*, *-nk*) contain a reflex of another p(F)U pluralizer *-k; the *-nk* of the second person plural may have spread analogically from a specifically plural-possession form *-ntVk (Bereczki 1988: 325).

Adjectives: Declension, Comparison, and Superlative
The morphology of adjectival declension is identical with that of the noun, but adjectives are ordinarily inflected only when they function syntactically as nouns, e.g. *kona kudoson^jt^j er^jat, odson^jt^j il^ji taštoson^jt^j* 'in which house do you live, **in the old (one)** or **in the new (one)**?'. Adjectives in predicate position are inflected for number to agree with nouns, e.g. *čuvtoš^j pokš* 'the tree is big', *čuvtne pokšt* 'the trees are big'. In attributive position adjectives

are not normally inflected either for case or for number, e.g. *paro moda* 'good ground', genitive *paro moda-n^j* 'of good ground(s)', plural nominative *od kudo-t* 'new houses', inessive *od kudo-so* 'in a new house, in new houses'. The only exception is the optional, and rare, plural nominative agreement of attributes with their animate heads, e.g. *par-t loman^j-t^j* GOOD-plur HUMAN.BEING-plur 'good people'.

Comparison is achieved not by means of a comparative suffix, but simply by placing the bested member of the comparison into the ablative, e.g. *c^{j}ora-do pokš* BOY-abl BIG 'bigger than a boy'. The thing than which something is 'Xer' must be specified, or at least referred to with the ablative of the demonstrative pronon *s^{j}e*: *s^{j}e-d^{j}e pokš* IT-abl BIG 'bigger'. Various superlatives may be formed, by (1) repetition of the root, with the first instance in the ablative and usually with the enclitic *-jak*, e.g. *pokš-to(-jak) pokš* 'biggest'; (2) more commonly, by preposing one of the particles *s^{j}ex(-t^{j}e)* (< Russian 'of all'), *samaj* (< Russian 'the very'), *pek* (< Tatar 'very') or *ves^{j}eme-d^{j}e* 'than/of all', e.g. *s^{j}ext^{j}e pokš* 'biggest', *ves^{j}emed^{j}e pokš* 'biggest of all'. Dialects also use the particle *en^j* (cf. standard Erzya *in^{j}e* 'big' < pU *enä 'big, much'.

A kind of excessive superlative is formed by threefold repetition, e.g. *pokš, pokš di pokš* (*di* 'and' < Russian) 'the very biggest'.

Declension of Numerals and Pronouns

Numerals used attributively remain uninflected, and their head is usually put in the plural, especially if the sole or last numeral is from 2 to 10, e.g. *kavto či-t^j* 'two days', *kolon^{j}gemen^j n^{j}il^{j}e kal-t* 'thirty-four fish', *kavkson^{j}gemen^j vejkse umar^j-t^j* 'eighty-nine apples', *s^{j}ado ije-t^j* 'a hundred years'. The head stands in the singular, however, after numerals ending in *ve(jke)* '1', e.g. *kodgemen^j vejke celkovoj* 'sixty-one roubles', and after the compound numerals which constitute the teens, twenties, and (optionally) the hundreds, e.g. *koms^j+vet^{j}e=je kudo* TWENTY+FIVE=sx HOUSE 'twenty-five houses', *s^{j}is^{j}em+s^{j}ad-t či* SEVEN+HUNDRED-plur DAY '700 days'.

When used as nouns, the numerals decline in the same way as nouns, in both indefinite and definite paradigms, e.g. inessive *vejke-se* 'in one', DDsN *vejke-s^j* 'the one', DDsIne *vejke-se-n^{j}t^j* 'in the one', DDpIne *kavto-t^j-n^{j}e-sen^{j}t^j* 'in the two'.

Ordinals, formed with the suffix *=c^{j}e*, are similarly declined, e.g. *n^{j}il^{j}e=c^{j}e-se* 'in a fourth', *s^{j}ado=c^{j}e-se-n^{j}t^j* 'in the hundredth'. 'First' and 'second' are built to suppletive roots: *vas^{j}en^{j}c^{j}e*, *omboc^{j}e*. There are also collective numerals built with *=n^{j}e* followed by possessive suffix, e.g. *kolmo=n^{j}e-st* 'the three of them (*-st* p3)'.

Interrogative and relative pronouns decline in the same way as nouns, e.g. genitive indefinite *kona-n^j* 'whose', p3 *kona-st* 'which of them?', DDpN *mez^j-t^j-n^{j}e* 'which ones?', *mez^{j}e-m ul^j-i* WHAT?-s1 EXISTS-s3pres 'what do I have?' The personal pronouns, however, deviate in that their oblique case-

Table 6.5 Selected Erzya pronominal paradigms

	PRO.s3 '(s)he'	Possessive.PRO.s3 'his/hers'		REFLEX.PRO.s3 'him/herself'
N	son	sonʲ-sʲesʲ	~ son-zesʲ	esʲ
G/A	son-ze	sonʲ-sʲenʲtʲ	~ son-zenʲtʲ	esʲ-enze
Dat/All	sonʲ-enze	sonʲ-sʲenʲtʲenʲ	~ son-zenʲtʲenʲ	esʲ-tʲenze
Ine	sonʲ-senze	sonʲ-sesenʲtʲ	~ son-zesenʲtʲ	esʲ-senze
Ela	sonʲ-stenze	sonʲ-stesenʲtʲ	~ son-stesenʲtʲ	esʲ-stenze
Ill	sonʲ-zenze	sonʲ-zesenʲtʲ	~ son-zesenʲtʲ	esʲ-senze
Prol	sonʲ-ganzo	sonʲ-ganʲtʲ	~ son-ganʲtʲ	esʲ-kanzo
Abl	sonʲ-dʲenze	sonʲ-dʲenʲtʲ	~ sonʲdʲenʲtʲ	esʲ-tʲedʲenze
(Trans	sonʲ-ksenze	sonʲ-ksenʲtʲ	~ son-ksenʲtʲ	esʲ-ksenze)
Abess	sonʲ-tʲemenze	sonʲ-tʲemenʲtʲ	~ sonʲtʲemenʲtʲ	csʲ-tʲemenze
Cfv	sonʲ-škanzo	sonʲ-škanʲtʲ	~ son-škanʲtʲ	esʲ-eškanzo

forms end in redundant person markers, e.g. *monʲ-se-nʲ* PRO.s1.obl-ine-s1 'in me', *sonʲ-se-nze* PRO.s3.obl-ine-s3 'in him/her'. There is also a possessive pronoun, e.g. *sonʲ-sʲesʲ* (~ *son-zesʲ*) 'his/hers'. The forms of the third-person singular personal and possessive pronouns are set out in Table 6.5 along with the s3 paradigm of the reflexive pronoun.

The Verb

Verb Stems
The citation form of Mordva verbs is an infinitive built with *-ms*. The vowel-final stem of a Mordva verb may be found by shearing off this ending, e.g. *jarsams* 'to eat', vowel stem *jarsa-*; *jarsavtoms* 'to feed', vowel stem *jarsavto-*; *jarsʲnʲems* 'to eat (freq)', vowel stem *jarʲsʲnʲe-*. The consonant-final stem is obtained by lopping off the last vowel, e.g. *jars-*, *jarsavt-*, *jarʲsʲnʲ-*. The chief source of morphonological complications in Mordva conjugation lies in stem-suffix sandhi, and the situation is not clarified by the fact that the final vowel of some stems is intrinsic (i.e. we might do better to segment *jarʲsʲnʲe-ms*) while that of others is epenthetic (i.e. *jarsavt-oms*). On Mordva verb stems in general see Nadjkin 1981.

Conjugation
Mordva conjugation is exceptionally rich in morphological entities, morpho-nological rules, and paradigmatic categories (Abondolo 1982: 11–23). The primary category distinction is that of indefinite v. definite forms, e.g. indefinite *kund-an* 'I catch', definite *kunda-tan* 'I'll catch you'.

Use of the definite conjugation presupposes (1) that the verb is transitive, (2) that there is a definite direct object, explicit or implied, and (3) that the aspect is perfective. The full definite paradigm evolved during the separate life of Mordva, but the core around which it formed is probably much older.

Table 6.6   Schematic for Mordva verb: tense and mood suffixes

Mood	Tense	Mood suffix	Tense suffix	Person suffixes
indicative	present/future	(-Ø-)	(-Ø-)	present
	past 1	(-Ø-)	-i-, -sʲ	past
	past 2	(-Ø-)	-i-lʲ-	past
conditional	present/future	-inʲdʲerʲa-		present
	(past	-inʲdʲerʲa-		past)
conjunctive	present/future	-vlʲ-		past
conditional/ conjunctive	present/past	-inʲdʲerʲa-vlʲ-		past
desiderative	past	-ikselʲ-		past
optative	present/future	-zo- ~ -ze-		present
imperative	present/future	—	-k ~ -t ~ -tʲ (s2)	
			-do ~ -dʲe (p2)	

Crisscrossing the definite/indefinite distinction is that of affirmative/ negative. Negative verb forms are built in some tenses/moods with negative particles, in others with a negative verb; compare *a kund-an* 'I don't catch', *ezʲ-i-nʲ kunda* 'I didn't catch', *a kunda-tan* 'I won't catch you', *ezʲ-i-tʲinʲ kunda* 'I didn't catch you'.

The Mordva grammars of the twentieth century all distinguish seven moods, all of which maintain the definite/indefinite distinction, at least in dialects (Keresztes 1990: 45–50; contrast Serebrennikov 1967: 202).

Tense is distinguished in only two of the moods, the indicative and the conditional. The indicative distinguishes three tenses: present, and first and second past. The present-tense indicative could be said to be marked by double zero, -Ø- for indicative and -Ø- for present, e.g. *sod-Ø-Ø-an* 'I know'; for the sake of simplicity such zeros will not be indicated in cited forms. The past-tense markers are -i- (~ -sʲ in the third person) for the first past, -ilʲi- for the second past, e.g. *sod-i-nʲ* 'I knew', *soda-sʲ-Ø* '(s)he knew', *sod-ilʲi-nʲ* 'I used to know'. The structure of affirmative finite verb forms is set out in Table 6.6.

When used as predicates, noun phrases and adverbs are also conjugated; only second past-tense (and not first past-tense) forms occur, and, since no direct object is involved, only indefinite person markers, e.g. *kudo-so-nzo* 'in his/her house', > *kudo-so-nzo-lʲ-inʲ* 'I was in his/her house'. Table 6.9 sets out the present and second past-tense forms of a verb, an adjective in the nominative, and an inessive noun phrase.

In the present tense of the indefinite conjugation, the singular first (-n < *-m) and second (-t) person suffixes continue the pU personal pronoun roots *mV, *tV, cf. the present-day Erzya personal pronouns s1 *mon*, p1 *minʲ*, s2 *ton*, p2 *tinʲ*. The third-person singular suffix -i is homophonous with the present participle (see below), cf. *lomanʲ kand-i* 'the person is carrying',

Table 6.7 Erzya conjugation: person suffixes: present tense

	Indefinite conjugation Present tense	Definite conjugation					
		Object					
		s1	s2	s3	p1	p2	p3
Subject							
s1	-an	—	-Tan	-sa	—	-Tadiz^j	-sin^j
s2	-at	-samak	—	-sak	-samiz^j	—	-sit^j
s3	-i	-samam	-Tanzat	-si	-samiz^j	-Tadiz^j	-sin^{j}z^{j}e
p1	-Tano	—	-Tadiz^j	-sin^{j}ek	—	-Tadiz^j	-sin^{j}ek
p2	-Tado	-samiz^j	—	-sink	-samiz^j	—	-sink
p3	-it^j	-samiz^j	-Tadiz^j	-siz^j	-samiz^j	-Tadiz^j	-siz^j

Note: (T = t t^j d d^j, according to morphonology)

Table 6.8 Erzya conjugation, person suffixes: first past tense (with past-tense morphemes -i-, -s^j-)

	Indefinite conjugation First past tense	Definite conjugation					
		Object					
		s1	s2	s3	p1	p2	p3
Subject							
s1	-i-n^j	—	-i-t^{j}in^j	-i-ja	—	-i-d^{j}iz^j	-i-n^j
s2	-i-t^j	-i-mik	—	-i-k	-i-miz^j	—	-i-t^j
s3	-s^j-Ø	-i-mim	-i-n^{j}z^{j}it^j	-i-z^{j}e	-i-miz^j	-i-d^{j}iz^j	-i-n^{j}z^{j}e
p1	-i-n^{j}ek	—	-i-d^{j}iz^j	-i-n^{j}ek	—	-i-d^{j}iz^j	-i-n^{j}ek
p2	-i-d^{j}e	-i-miz^j	—	-i-nk	-i-miz^j	—	-i-nk
p3	-s^j-t^j	-i-miz^j	-i-d^{j}iz^j	-i-z^j	-i-miz^j	-i-d^{j}iz^j	-i-z^j

kand=i loman^j 'carrying people, people who carry'. The *-t(-)* which figures in the plural forms continues the pU pluralizer *-t. The second components of both first and second person plural also descend from pronominal forms (*-Tano* < *ta-mok, *-Tado* < *ta-tok). Negation in the present tense is carried out by the particle *a*, e.g. *a mor-an* 'I don't sing', *son a mor-i* '(s)he doesn't sing'; this particle probably descends from the base of the pFU negative verb *e- ~ *ä- (with metaphony *e/ä > * a in *e wole- >> *avol^j* 'isn't').

The present tense could more properly be termed a non-past, since it often refers to the future. There are also compound futures built with the present tense of the verb *karma-* 'begins' and the *-mo/-me* infinitive of the main verb, e.g. *karm-an mora-mo* 'I shall sing, I'm going to sing', *a karm-an mora-mo* 'I'm not going to sing'.

The first past tense is built with two different tense-suffixes, *-s^j-* in the third

Table 6.9 Erzya indefinite and predicative conjugation: *kand(o)-* 'takes, brings', *mazi(j)* 'beautiful', *oš-so* 'in a city'

	kand(o)-	*mazi(j)*	*oš-so*
Present tense			
s1	kand-an	mazij-an	oš-s-an
s2	kand-at	mazij-at	oš-s-at
s3	son kand-i	son mazi(j)	son oš-so
p1	kand-tano	mazi(j)-tʲano	oš-so-tano
p2	kand-tado	mazi(j)-tʲado	oš-so-tado
p3	sinʲ kand-itʲ	sinʲ mazij-tʲ	sinʲ oš-so-tʲ
Second past tense			
s1	kand-ilʲ-inʲ	mazi-lʲ-inʲ	oš-so-lʲ-inʲ
s2	kand-ilʲ-itʲ	mazi-lʲ-itʲ	oš-so-lʲ-itʲ
s3	son kand-ilʲ-Ø	son mazi-lʲ-Ø	son oš-so-lʲ
p1	kand-ilʲ-inʲek	mazi-lʲ-inʲek	oš-so-lʲ-inʲek
p2	kand-ilʲ-idʲe	mazi-lʲ-idʲe	oš-so-lʲ-idʲe
p3	sinʲ kand-ilʲ-tʲ	sinʲ mazi-lʲ-tʲ	sinʲ oš-so-lʲ-tʲ

person and *-i-* in the axis of discourse. Both go back to suffixes reconstructed for proto-Uralic (*-j, *-sʲ). The palatalization of the initial consonants (*-nʲ -tʲ -dʲ*) of the person markers is due to the *-i-* past-tense suffix to their left. In the first past tense, negation is carried out by the negative verb *ezʲ-*, e.g. *ezʲ-i-nʲ mora* 'I didn't sing'. Historically, forms such as *ezʲ-i-nʲ* are twice marked for past tense, because the *zʲ* final in the negative verb descends from the pU past-tense suffix *-sʲ-*. It is possible that this sibilant suffix was originally used only with the negative verb, then spread to the affirmative paradigm (e.g. *kand-sʲ-Ø*) to avoid homophonic clash with the present tense (*kand-i*).

The second past tense, which is lacking in Moksha, refers to events in the past which either lasted long or habitually recurred. Its suffix, *-ilʲ-*, developed out of the verb *ulʲe-* 'is'; thus *son mor-ilʲ-Ø* '(s)he used to sing' is homophonous with the past-tense predicative form of the present participle *mor=i* 'singer', i.e. equals '(s)he was a singer'. Negation is performed by the *a* particle: *a mor-ilʲ-inʲ* 'I didn't used to sing, I wasn't in the habit of singing'.

Most of the person markers of the definite conjugation represent combinations of the pU personal pronoun stems *mV *tV *sV, e.g. *-samam*, as in *kunda-samam* '(s)he'll catch me', continues third-person *sV plus a reduplicated first-person marker *mV. Details are spelled out in Bereczki (1988: 329).

The suffix of the conditional, *-inʲdʲerʲa-*, is historically a combination of two morphemes. The first component, *-inʲ-*, is perhaps a reflex of the pU conditional/potential morpheme *-ne-*. The second component continues pre-Erzya *tʲerʲa-*, a verb stem meaning 'tries, attempts' which survives in dialects to this day (cf. tʲerʲavto-id.). Sample forms: *mor-inʲdʲerʲ-an* 'if I sing', *son* *mor-in^j d^j er^j a-j* 'if (s)he sings'; note the deviant morphophonology *a-i > aj*, and contrast present-tense *a-i > i*, as in *mor-i* '(s)he sings'. (Past-tense forms of the conditional exist in dialects; examples: *mor-in^j d^j er^j -i-n^j* 'if I sang', *sin^j mor-in^j d^j er^j -es^j -t^j* 'if they sang'.) Negation is by means of the *a* particle, e.g. *a mor-in^j d^j er^j -an* 'if I don't sing'.

The conjunctive suffix *-vl^j-* (*-vol^j ~ vel^j* in final position) is historically a combination of a verb-forming derivational suffix *=v-* plus the second past-tense marker mentioned above, and as such is structurally reminiscent of the Tatar conjunctive (Bereczki 1988: 328). In more recent years conjunctive forms are reinforced by the particle *bu* (< Russian бы), e.g. *mora-vl^j-in^j (bu)* 'I would sing, I would have sung', *son mol^j e-vel^j-Ø (bu)* '(s)he would go, (s)he would have gone'. The negative conjunctive is built with the first past-tense forms of the negative verb *avol^j-*, e.g. *avol^j-i-n^j mora* 'I wouldn't sing, I wouldn't have sung'.

The suffix of the conditional/conjunctive, *-in^j d^j er^j avl^j-*, developed from the concatenation of the two mood markers just discussed, e.g. *mor-in^j d^j er^j avl^j-it^j* 'if you were to sing, if you had sung'. Similar sorts of unlikely hypotheses and unreal conditions may also be expressed by the simple conjunctive plus the enclitic *--gak* (*~ --kak ~ --jak*), e.g. *mora-vl^j-it^j --kak* 'if you were to sing, if you had sung'. Negation: *a mor-in^j d^j er^j avl^j-it^j* 'if you ..'

The desiderative is formed with *-iksel^j-*. This, too, is a composite suffix: the first element is identical with the (rarer) *=iks* variant of the first present passive participle *=viks*, which historically contains the translative suffix *-ks*; the remainder (*el^j*) descends from the verb 'is'. Thus *mor-iksel^j-in^j* 'I wanted to sing' is etymologically something like *'I was leaning-towards-becoming (= translative) a singer". The negative desiderative is formed with desiderative forms of the negative verb *avol^j-*, e.g. *avol^j-ksel^j-in^j mora* 'I didn't want to sing'.

The optative suffix (*-zo ~ -ze*) derives from a person marker: it is historically identical with the third-person possessive suffix (*kudo-zo* 'his/her house'). The optative originally had only third-person forms, and to the present day these forms are textually the most frequent. Its main use is as a suppletion to the imperative, e.g. *son mora-zo-Ø* 'may (s)he sing', *mora-z-an* 'let me sing', but second-person forms also occur, e.g. *mora-z-tano* 'may you (plur) sing'. Negative forms are built to the negative verb *il^j a-*, e.g. *il^j a-z-an mora* 'let me not sing', *il^j a-zo-Ø mol^j e* 'may (s)he not go', etc.

The imperative has only second-person forms. In the singular, *-k* and its post-consonantal variants *-t/-t^j* continue the pU imperative suffix **-k*. The suffix (*-do ~ -d^j e*) of the plural imperative forms is historically identical with the second component of present-tense *-Tado*, i.e. it is of pronominal origin (pU second person **tV*). Sample forms: *mora-k* 'sing!', *mora-do* 'sing [plur]!', *čav-t* 'strike!', *čavo-do* 'strike [plur]!', *t^j ej-t^j* 'do!', *t^j eje-d^j e* 'do [plur]!'. Commands are often mitigated and/or made more intimate by the use of various enclitics such as *--(j)a(k)*, *--jat*, *--ka*, *--t^j a*, e.g. *kund-t--a(ja)* 'carry

(, please)!', *ašt'e-d'e--jak* 'wait [plur] (a minute!)'. The negative imperative (= prohibitive) is built with the negative verb *il'a-*; the bare stem serves in the singular, e.g. *il'a mora* 'don't sing!'. Further examples: *il'a--ka mora* 'please don't sing', *il'a-do t'ej* 'don't [plur] do'.

Derivation

Mordva has rich resources for the production of both nominals and verbs, and only a small sampling of the most important suffixes can be presented here. Derivation may stay within part-of-speech categories (cf. English *strong* > *strongish*) or cross (cf. English *strong* > *strength, strength* > *strengthen*).

Formation of Nominals

Here are the more productive Erzya nominal-forming suffixes:

=c'e forms ordinals from names of integers, e.g. *kolmo=c'e* 'third'. This suffix continues pU demonstrative base *c'e (> Mordva s'e 'that, it').

=či forms abstracts, e.g. *šumbra* 'healthy' > *šumbra=či* 'health'. From *kečä 'frame, (circular) form' (cf. Finnish *kehä* 'ring, periphery', Mordva *či* 'sun').

=ka forms nouns from adjectives and vice versa, e.g. *r'iz'an'a* 'sweet-and-sour' > *r'iz'an'a=ka* 'sorrel', *at'a* 'Dad' > *at'a=ka* 'male'; note also *=aka*, which forms nominalizations from verbs, e.g. *pišt'e-* 'goes without' > *pišt'=aka* 'wretch'. Probably (also next *=ke*) from pU *kkV.

=ke forms diminutive nouns and lends nuances to adjectives, e.g. *mekš* 'bee' > *mekš=ke* 'little bee', *ordakš* 'sensitive' > *ordakš=ke* 'capricious'.

=ks forms metonymic/metaphoric nouns from nouns, e.g. *sur* 'finger' > *sur=ks* 'ring', *piz'ol* 'rowanberry' > *piz'ol=ks* 'rowan bush'. Co-occurs with *=či (vide supra)*, as in *jalga* 'friend' > *jalga=ks=či* 'friendship'. Also forms result nouns and agentives from verbs, e.g. *jovta-* 'narrates', *jov=ks* 'story'. From pU* *=ks*.

=ma and *=mo ~ =me* form *nomina actionis* and *instrumenti* from verbs, e.g. *lovno-* 'reads' > *lovno=ma=* '(act of) reading', *iza-* 'harrows' > *iza=mo= 'harrow'. From different configurations of a pU nominal-forming suffix *=mV.

=n' forms adjectives from nouns, e.g. *erz'a=n'* 'Erzya [adj]', *kev* 'stone' > *kev=en'* 'made of stone'. Historically identical with the pU genitive *-n.

=n'e (~ =ne); *=in'e* form diminutives from nominals, e.g. *n'ur'ka* 'short' > *n'ur'k=in'e* 'short, little', *kal* 'fish' > *kal=ne* 'little fish'. Descends from a pU nominalizer *=nA.

=pel' forms nouns from verbal nominals, e.g. *jarsa=mo* 'eating' > *jarsa=mo =pel'* 'food'. Sometimes held to be a compound-formant rather than a derivational suffix (cf. the noun *pel'* 'half').

=pulo forms collectives from nouns, e.g. *tumo* 'oak' > *tumo=pulo* 'oak grove'. Sometimes held to be a compound-formant rather than a derivational suffix (cf. the noun *pulo* 'tail; shaft; plait').

$=v \sim =j$ forms adjectives from nouns, e.g. *var^{j}a* 'hole' > *var^{j}a=v* 'full of holes', *pit^{j}n^{j}e* 'price' > *pit^{j}n^{j}e=j* 'expensive'. The *j*-variant favours environments with front, the *v*-variant environments with back, prosody. From pU *=ŋ.

Formation of Verbs
Here are the more important suffixes which make verbs from verbs:

$=do- \sim =d^j e$ makes intransitives and mediopassives into factitives, e.g. *eže-* 'warms up (intr)' > *ež=d^{j}e-* 'warms up (tr)'. This suffix may be related to the suffix $=to-$ ($\sim =t^j e-$), which has the opposite effect, e.g. *stroja-* 'builds' > *stroja=to-* 'is built'. Perhaps from pU *=ttV.

$=do- \sim =d^j e-$ makes momentaneous verbs, e.g. *vačka-* 'stacks in a pile' > *vačko=d^{j}e-* 'strikes'. Probably cognate with the Mari frequentative-formant $=edë-$.

$=kšno- \sim =kšn^j e-$ makes iteratives, e.g. *kekše-* 'conceals', > *kekše=kšn^{j}e-* 'keeps hiding'. A combination of a pFV *=ks and of $=no$ (see below).

$=l^j e-$ makes frequentatives and duratives, e.g. *korta-* 'speaks' > *kort=l^{j}e-* 'converses'. Continues a pU *l frequentative.

$=no \sim =n^j e$ makes frequentatives and duratives, e.g. *lovo-* 'counts' > *lov=no-* 'reads'. Probably a continuation of a pU frequentative/durative suffix with *nt; cf. Moksha $=nd-$, e.g. M *vanë-* 'looks' > *vanë=ndë-* 'looks around'.

$=s^j e-$ makes frequentatives and duratives, e.g. *jaka-* 'goes, walks' > *jak=s^{j}e-* 'comes and goes, wanders about'. May be from p(F)U *=s^j ~ *=c^j.

$=v-$ makes reflexives and mediopassives, e.g. *čav-* 'strikes' > *čavo=v-* 'is smashed'; this suffix has clear cognates in Saamic, Fennic, Mansi and Hungarian (< pU *=w).

$=vt- \sim =vt^j-$ makes factitives and causatives, e.g. *ara-* 'stands (intr)' > *ara=vt-* 'stands (tr)'; this suffix continues a suffix-string, either *=k=tV- or *=p=tV-, with wide but not entirely clear distribution across Uralic.

$=z^j ev-$ makes inchoatives, e.g. *pel^j-* 'is afraid' > *pel^{j}e=z^{j}ev-* 'becomes frightened'. Perhaps a combination of a pFU momentaneous suffix *=s^j with the reflexive/mediopassive $=v-$ mentioned above.

These suffixes, mostly of p(F)U (*=t, *=j, *=k, *=l + *=tv, *-m) or pFP ([*=k +] *=kt, [*=nt] *=s^j) origin, make verbs from nominals:

$=d- \sim =d^j-; = ta-$ make instructives ('provides with X'), e.g. *onks* 'measure' > *onks=ta-* measures'; *s^{j}orma* 'writing; epistle' > *s^{j}orma=d-* 'writes'.

$=gad- \sim =kad-$ ($\sim =lgad-$ after vowels) (< *kad-* 'leaves') makes translatives from adjectives and nouns, e.g. *ašo* 'white' > *ašo=lgad-* 'turns white', *lapš* 'flat' > *lapš=kad-* 'becomes flat'.

$=gavt- \sim =kavt-$ ($\sim =lgavt-$ after vowels) makes causative analogues to the preceding, e.g. *ašo=lgavt-* 'makes white', *lapš=kavt-* 'makes flat'.

=ija- makes translatives from nouns ('becomes X-y'), e.g. *sal* 'salt' > *sal=ija-* 'becomes salty'.

=ld- makes colour statives, e.g. *piže* 'green' > *piže=ld-* 'is green'.

=m- makes translatives from nouns and adjectives, e.g. *čuvto* 'tree; wood' > *čuvto=m-* 'becomes stiff'; *čevtʲe* 'soft' > *čevtʲe=m-* 'becomes soft'.

=nza- makes multiplicatives from numerals, e.g. *kolmo* 'three' > *kolmo=nza-* 'trebles', *nʲilʲe* 'four' > *nʲilʲe=nza-* 'quadruples'. A combination, perhaps, of the genitive *-n with pFP *=sʲ. Note also = *nʲzʲa* in *pelʲenʲzʲa-* 'becomes cloudy' (*pelʲ=enʲ* 'cloudy').

It is also not uncommon for related nominal and verb stems to be homophonous, e.g. *čapo* 'groove', *čap(o)-* 'cuts out', *kalado* 'torn, worn out', *kalad(o)-* 'is ruined, collapses'.

Non-finite Verb Forms

Mordva is unusually rich in non-finite verb forms. Literary Erzya distinguishes twelve forms: three infinitives, three present participles, three perfect participles, and three gerunds. These are set out in Table 6.10; rarer functions and forms are given in brackets.

Negation is rendered by the particles *a*, *avolʲ*, and *apak*; their distribution is determined by both structural and functional factors. Thus, for example, *avolʲ* is used for contrastive negation of the infinitive: *avolʲ mora-ms, a kištʲe-ms* 'not to sing, but/rather (*a* < Russian) to dance', cf. *a mora-ms* 'to not sing'; *avolʲ moramodo kortatano, a lʲijado* 'we're not talking about singing, but/ rather (we're talking about) something else', *a moramodo kortatano* 'we're talking about not singing'. Negative participles are formed with *apak* and the bare verb stem, or with *avolʲ* and the suffixed form, e.g. *apak mora moro ~ avolʲ mora-zʲ moro* 'song not sung'.

The participles are often used as nouns; *=icʲa* then indicates the agent (more rarely *=i*, *=j*) as in *pidʲ=icʲa* 'cook' (*pidʲe-* 'cooks'), *čar=i* 'wheel' (*čara-* 'turns'), *čenga=j* 'vodka' (*čenge-* 'burns'), and *=st* (*~ =t ~ =vt*) indicates the result of the action, e.g. *kan=st* 'burden' (*kando-* 'carries'), *poč=t* 'flour' < *počodo-* 'pours out'. The nominal-forming deverbal suffixes *=ks*, *=ma*, and *=mo/=me* are also participial in origin.

Adverbs and Postpositions

Adverbs and postpositions are often built with non-productive suffixes from non-productive nominal stems. These stems usually have a spatial meaning, and may function as both independent adverbs and postpositions, e.g. *ikelʲe* 'in front (of)', *udalo* 'in back (of)', *tombalʲe* 'on the far side; beyond'. Possessive suffixes are also used, e.g. *sʲkamo-n* 'by myself, I (am) alone', *sʲkamo-t* 'by yourself, you (are) alone', *sʲkamo-nzo* ' him/herself, (s)he (is) alone'; *malaso-n* (*~ monʲ malaso*) 'next to me', *langso-t* (*~ tonʲ langso*) 'on you', *ekšne-nze* (*~ sonze ekšne*) 'behind it/him/her'.

The case forms of postpositions and adverbs often distinguish the static

Table 6.10   Erzya non-finite verb forms

	Primary function/meaning	Negative built with	Example	Origin
Infinitives				
=mo ~ =me	nominative of nomen actionis	—	mora=mo 'singing', n^jeje=me 'seeing'	pU *=mV
=m-s	illative	a, avoľ	mora=ms, 'to sing', n^jeje=ms 'to see'	
=mo-do ~ =me-d^je	ablative	a, avoľ	mora=modo 'from singing', n^jeje=med^je 'from seeing'	
Present participles				
=i(=c^ja)	non-past *nomen agentis*	a (avoľ)	mor=ic^ja 'singer', mor=i loman^j 'singing person'	*=jA + *=c^j
=viks	passive non-past, passive potential	a (avoľ)	mora=viks 'being sung, singable'	*=w + transl
=ma	passive necessive	a	mora=ma 'which must be sung'	pU *=m
Perfect participles				
=z^j	perfect agent (intransitives) or patient (transitives)	apak, avoľ	mora=z^j 'sung', kulo-z^j 'dead'	pU *-s^j-
=n^j	perfect passive participle (folkloristic)	(apak)	mora=n^j 'sung'	pU *-n
=vt ~ =vt^j	agentive passive participle	(apak)	mora=vt 'sung' n^jeje=vt^j 'seen'	pFU *=kt
Gerunds				
=msto ~ =mste	anterior, simultaneous	avoľ	mor=amsto, 'singing' n^jeje=mste 'seeing'	=mo/e + Ela
=z^j	simultaneous	avoľ, apak	mora=z^j 'singing'	perf.part
=do	simultaneous (not productive)	avoľ	s^jť^ja=do 'standing'	? perf.part *=do < pFU *-t ?

from the dynamic, and within the dynamic, source from goal (e.g. *ikeľe* 'in front' : *ikeľev* 'to the front' : *ikeľd^je* 'from the front'), but there are many postpositions and adverbs that occur in only one case form, as well. Further examples of adverbs built from noun and adjective bases: *či-ť* 'in the daytime', *či-n^jek&ve-n^jek* '(by) day and (by) night', *ťeľ-n^ja* 'in winter', *kudo-n^jek* 'along with all the people of the house', *par-s^jť^je* 'well'; from pronominal bases: *koso* 'where?', *ťese* 'here', *kosto* 'whence?', *ťeste* 'hence', *kozon^j*, *kov* 'whither?', *ťezen^j*, *ťej* 'hither', *kuva* 'along where?', *t'ija* 'along here', *koda* 'how?', *is'/t'a* 'like this', *meks* 'why?', *s'eks* 'for that reason'; postpositions: *ez'ems* 'instead of', *karšo* 'opposite', *mejl'e* 'after'; *alo* 'under', *aldo* 'from under', *alov* 'to under', *alga* '(moving) along beneath'; *pel'e* 'next to', *pel'd'e* 'from next to', *pel'ev, pel'ej* 'towards the side of'. Most postpositions occur with their noun in the nominative (e.g. *ez'ems, alo*) or the genitive (e.g. *karšo, pel'e*); a few take the ablative (e.g. *mejl'e, ikel'e*).

Most other modifiers and conjunctions are of more recent (Russian) origin. Examples: *da* 'yes', *vot* 'look', *--lji* '(question particle)', *daj(t'e)* 'come on!', *ved'* '(invites agreement on part of collocutor)', *i, di* 'and', *a* 'but (rather)', *el'i* 'or', *što(bu)* '(in order) that', *but'i* 'if', *xot'* 'although'.

Syntax

Simple Sentences

Order of Constituents

The rich formal morphological apparatus of Mordva allows constituent order to fulfil semantic, logical, pragmatic and stylistic functions rather than grammatical ones. Thus a four-member sentence, with S[ubject], O[bject], A[dverbial complement] and V[erb] may occur with any of the theoretically possible twenty-four orders. The basic rule is: topic(s) to the head of the sentence, focalized element immediately before the finite verb; a focalized verb must therefore stand sentence-initial. Suprasegmentals complicate the picture. A few examples: *t'et'am kundas' kalt is'ak* (SVOA) 'it's my father who caught fish yesterday', *t'et'am kalt kundas' is'ak* (SOVA) 'as for what my father caught yesterday, it was fish', *t'et'am kalt is'ak kundas'* (SOAV) 'as for my father's catching fish, it was yesterday that he did that', *t'et'am is'ak kundas' kalt* (SAVO) 'as for my father, it was yesterday that he caught fish', *kalt is'ak kundas' t'et'am* (OAVS), 'as for fish, it was yesterday that my father caught them', *kundas' kalt is'ak t'et'am* (VOAS) 'my father *did* catch fish yesterday'.

The order SVO is textually preponderant; it derives from an earlier SOV, which ceded ground under foreign (Russian) influence.

Within the noun phrase, the order of elements is fixed: modifier must precede modified. Examples: *er'an keven' od kudoso* 'I live in a new house made of stone', *er'an od keven' kudoso* 'I live in a new stone house', *Mordovija-so kas-it' piče=n', čovor'a=z' di l'istvennoj vir'-t' MORDVINIA*-ine GROWS-p3pres CONIFER=adj, MIXES=past.part AND LEAFY FOREST-pN 'In Mordvinia there grow coniferous, mixed, and deciduous forests'.

Main Clause

Relation of Subject to Predicate
We may abstract – somewhat artificially – the subject and predicate from the rest of the sentence in order to examine their interaction more closely.

The subject is most usually a noun or pronoun, though adjectives and verbal nominals (participle, infinitive) may also serve. The predicate may be nominal or verbal. Both verbal and nominal predicates occur in all persons and tenses. Examples: *varaka-sʲ sʲimev-sʲ* 'the crow drank itself full', *jakšamo tʲelʲe-sʲ, psʲi kize-sʲ* COLD WINTER-def HOT SUMMER-def '(the) winter is cold, (the) summer is hot', *ton cʲora-m-at* PRO.s2 SON-s1-s2pres 'you are my son', *tonavtʲnʲicʲa-tʲ-nʲe udalo-t, učitʲelʲ-esʲ stolʲ ekšse* PUPIL-plur-def IN.BACK-p3 TEACHER-def TABLE BEHIND 'the pupils are at the back, (and) the teacher is behind the table', *sʲkamo-lʲi-nʲ, kijak ezʲ sa* ALONE-past2-s1 NO.ONE NEG.VERB.s3past COMES 'I was alone, no one came', *tinʲ ombocʲe-tʲ-nʲe-tʲado* PRO.p2 OTHER-pN-def-p2pres 'you (plur) are the seconds'.

When functioning as subject, toponyms appear in the definite, e.g. *Saransko(je)sʲ Mordovija-nʲ stolʲica* 'Saransk is the capital of Mordvinia', as do personal names when focalized, e.g. *Nʲina-sʲ sa-sʲ* 'it was Nina who came'.

Normally, subject and predicate agree in person and number.

Object-marking, Modality, and Negation
Determinacy of the object is indicated by the choice of definite or indefinite conjugation of the verb. The moods reflect different stances towards the reality of the event expressed by the predicate: indicative and imperative for the relatively real, optative for what is not real but wished for, e.g. *son molʲeze* 'let him/her go, (s)he can/may go'. The other four moods all refer to more or less unreal circumstances. The conditional refers to conditions or hypotheses, e.g. *molʲinʲdʲerʲan* 'if I go' in *molʲinʲdʲerʲan bazarov, lʲišme raman* 'if I go to market I'll buy a horse'. The conjunctive implies possibility or desirability, e.g. *son palavolʲ (bu)* '(s)he might kiss/might have kissed'; it also occurs frequently in compound sentences, e.g. *isʲak molʲevlʲinʲ umarʲs, a tʲeči a molʲan* 'yesterday I might have gone/might have felt like going berrying, but I'm not going today'. The conditional-conjunctive refers to contrary-to-fact conditions, e.g. *son palinʲdʲeravolʲ* 'if (s)he were to kiss (but [s]he won't), if (s)he had kissed (but [s]he didn't)'. In a compound sentence: *ulʲinʲdʲerʲavlʲitʲ ton lomanʲ, pelʲenze carstvam maksovlʲija tʲetʲ* 'if you were/had been a (real) human being, I would give/would have given you half my kingdom'. The desiderative covers desired but non-occurring events in the past, e.g. *son palikselʲ* '(s)he would have liked to kiss (but didn't)'.

Negation of the verbal predicate in the indicative (present, second past, future), the conditional, and the conditional-conjunctive is carried out by the particle *a*. Conjugated forms of the negative verb are used in the first past (*e-*), and in the conjunctive and desiderative (*avol-*); conjugated forms of the prohibitive verb (*ilʲa-*) are used in the imperative and optative. Negation of nominal predicates is normally effected with *a* or *avolʲ*. Examples: *a lomanʲ* '([s]he/it is) not a person', *a/avolʲ pokš* '([s]he/it is) not large', *a lamo* '(it is) not a lot', *a erʲavi* '(it is) not necessary/allowed'; *avolʲ atʲa* '(he is [still]) not an old man', *avolʲ sirʲe* '([s]he/it is) not old', *avolʲ isʲtʲa* 'it isn't like this'. Non-existence is expressed in Erzya with the particle *arasʲ*, which is also used for categorical denials (*avolʲ* is used to express doubt). Examples: – *tonʲ ulʲ-i sʲemija-t?* – *arasʲ, mon apak urʲvaksto* PRO.s2 EXISTS-s3pres FAMILY-s2 NOT.EXIST PRO.s1 NEG.PARTIC MARRIES 'do you have a family?' 'No, I haven't married/am unmarried'; – *tink ulʲ-i ruzonʲ+erzʲanʲ valks?* – *arasʲ, ruzonʲ+erzʲanʲ valks minʲek arasʲ, vesʲe tʲiraž-osʲ mije=zʲ* PRO.p2 EXISTS-s3pres RUSSIAN-ERZYA DICTIONARY NOT.EXIST, WHOLE PRINTRUN SELLS=part 'do you have a Russian–Erzyan dictionary?' 'No, we don't have a Russian–Erzyan dictionary; the entire print run is sold out'; – *ton umok uš uč-at monʲ ej-se?* – *avolʲ, mon s-i-nʲ vetʲe minuta-do ikelʲe* PRO.s2 LONG.TIME ALREADY WAITS-s2pres PRO.s1.gen/acc IN-loc NEG.PART PRO.s1 ARRIVES-past1-s1 FIVE MINUTE-abl BEFORE 'have you been waiting for me long?' 'No, I arrived five minutes ago'; – *kijak s-i-lʲi?* – *tʲese kijak arasʲ. kijak ezʲ sakšno. tʲeči konastkak ezʲ sakšno* NO.ONE ARRIVES-s3pres--interr.part   HERE NO.ONE NOT.EXIST NO.ONE NEG.VERB.s3past1 COMES TODAY WHO-p3--part NEG.VERB-s3past1 COMES 'is anyone coming?' 'No one is here. No one came here. Not one of them came today'; *a merʲ-an karšo val—gak* NEG.PART SPEAKS-s1pres AGAINST WORD-part 'I'll not say a word against him/her/it'.

Direct Objects

An indefinite direct object is normally in the nominative indefinite, but the ablative is often used with non-count nouns. If the verbal aspect is imperfective, the indefinite forms are used even if the direct object is definite. Examples: *lʲišme ram-i-nʲ* HORSE-ID.sN BUYS-past1-s1 'I bought a horse', *lovnan jovtʲnʲema* READS-s1pres STORY-ID.sN 'I'm reading a story', *varaka-sʲ karma-sʲ kajsʲe-me kevnʲe-tʲ* CROW-DDsN BEGINS-s3past1 THROWS-inf PEBBLE-pN 'the crow began to throw pebbles', *jars-an jam-do, sʲim-an vedʲ-tʲe* EATS-s1pres SOUP-abl DRINKS-s1pres WATER-abl 'I eat soup, I drink water', *skal-osʲ tʲikše(-dʲe) pornʲ-i* COW-def.sN GRASS(-abl) CHEWS-s3pres 'the cow eats grass'.

A definite direct object is normally in the definite declension, and usually in the genitive/accusative, although the inessive is also used. Generally, the definiteness of the direct object is echoed by definite conjugation forms on the finite verb or personal suffixes on the infinitive. Personal names count as indefinite in Erzya, definite in Moksha. Examples: *tʲe lʲišme-nʲtʲ tʲetʲa-m ram-izʲe* THIS HORSE-DDgen/acc FATHER-s1 BUYS-s3s3past1 'my father bought this horse (as for this horse, it's my father who bought it)', *nʲej-an lʲišme-nʲtʲ/lʲišme-se-nʲtʲ* SEES-s1pres HORSE-DDgen/acc *or* HORSE-ine-def 'I see the horse', *cʲora-sʲ nʲe-inʲzʲe tʲejtʲerʲ-tʲnʲe-nʲ* BOY-DDN SEES-s3p3past GIRL-DDplur-gen/acc 'the boy saw the girls', *katka, užo, kiska--sʲ karm-i saje-me-tʲ* CAT WATCH.OUT DOG-DDsN WILL-s3pres CATCHES-inf-s2 'watch out, cat, the dog will catch you'.

Adverbial Complements
These are expressed with inflected nominal and postpositional phrases, as well as with infinitives. The definite and indefinite declensional forms are identical from the syntactic perspective. The cases refer primarily to space (dat/all, ine, ela, ill, prol, abl, lat) and time (dat/all, ela, ill, prol, occasionally nom and gen/acc), but they also encode indirect object (dat/all), instrument (ine), cause (abl, trans), measure and other adverbial categories (abl, cfv). For details see Wiedemann 1865: 33–47, Kolädenkov and Zavodova 1962: 106–57, Erdődi 1968: 209–14, Cygankin 1980: 159–78, Keresztes 1990: 73–5. Examples: *kardaz-so aštʲe-sʲ vedʲ marto kuvšin* YARD-ine EXISTS-s3past1 WATER WITH JUG 'in the yard was a jug of water', *pilʲge-m kev-s tomb-ija* FOOT-s1-sN STONE-ill HITS-s1s3past1 'I hit my foot on a stone', *molʲ-an kavto vajgelʲbe-tʲ* GOES-s1pres TWO VERST-pN 'I'm walking two versts', *cʲokov mazi=ste mor-i* NIGHTINGALE BEAUTIFUL=adv SINGS-s3pres 'the nightingale sings beautifully', *varaka-nʲtʲ-enʲ a koda sʲime-ms* CROW-def-dat/all NEG.PART HOW DRINKS-inf 'the crow didn't manage to drink at all', *ram-i-nʲ knʲiga sʲado-ška cʲelkovoj-dʲe* BUYS-past1-s1 BOOK-sN HUNDRED-cfv RUOBLE-abl 'I bought a book for about a hundred ruobles', *služ-an učitʲelʲ-ks velʲe-se* SERVES-s1pres TEACHER-trans VILLAGE-ine 'I serve as a teacher in a village'. The tridimensional use of the elative, illative, and inessive local cases is one of the more archaic features of Mordva, e.g. *bazar-sto kalacʲ ram-i-nʲ* MARKET-ela LOAF-sN BUYS-past1-s1 'I bought a loaf at (lit. from) the market', *požarnʲik-esʲ lʲepija-sʲ kačamo-s* FIREFIGHTER-sN SUFFOCATES-s3past1 FIRE-ill 'the firefighter suffocated in (lit. into) the fire', *sʲive-dʲe kaj-imim kudo-sto* COLLAR-abl THROWS-s3s1.past1 HOUSE-ela '(seizing me) by (lit. from) the collar (s)he flung me from the house'. There are also verbs and nominals which govern the inessive or the ablative, e.g. *karta-so nalʲkse-tano* CARD-ine PLAYS-p1pres 'we're playing cards', *mora-mo-do melʲe-m molʲ-sʲ* SINGS-inf-abl FEELING-s1 GOES-s3past1 'I don't feel like singing any more', *bocʲka-sʲ pešksʲe vina-do* BARREL-def.sN FULL WINE-abl 'the cask is full of wine'.

Attributive Constructions
Nominals and participles may serve as attributes. Qualitative and quantitative attributes are unmarked; possessive attributes are in the genitive/accusative. The formal distinction is not always clear, however, because many qualitative

adjectives are formed with a suffix (=*n^j*) which is homophonous with that of the genitive. If the possessor attribute is definite, the possession may stand in either the appropriate possessive or definite-declension form, e.g. *n^j er^j-en^j t^j kuvalmo-zo/kuvalmo-s^j ez^j s^j ato* BEAK-def.sG LENGTH-s3/LENGTH-def.sN NEG.VERB.s3past1 IS.SUFFICIENT 'the length of the beak wasn't sufficient'.

Further attributive examples: *Mordovija-va čud^j-it^j kavto pokš l^j ej-t^j: Sura di Mokša* Mordvinia-prol FLOWS-p3pres TWO BIG RIVER-pN *SURA* AND *MOKŠA* 'two great rivers flow through Mordvinia: the Sura and the Moksha', *vejkin^j e, večkeviks c^j ora-zo kulo-s^j* SOLE LOVES-part SON-s3 DIES-s3past3 'his/her only beloved son died', *kšn^j i-n^j izamo-t^j n^j e čuvto-n^j = s^j e-t^j-n^j ed^j e par-t* IRON-abl HARROW-pN-def WOOD-abl-sec.def-pN-def GOOD-pN 'iron harrows are better than those (made) of wood', *mez^j e t^j e: kšn^j i-n^j vad^j r^j a kojme il^j i vad^j r^j a kšn^j i-n^j kojme?* WHAT... 'what is this: a good iron spade or a good spade made of iron?', *vir^j čir^j e-se er^j z^j a=n^j c^j ora-s^j pen^j g-t^j ker^j-i* FOREST EDGE-ine ERZYA=adj BOY-def.sN BILLET-pN CHOPS-s3pres 'at the edge of the forest an Erzyan boy is chopping wood', *varaka-n^j t^j s^j imema-zo sa-s^j* CROW-gen THIRST-s3 ARRIVES-s3past1 'the crow became thirsty'.

The existential verb *ul^j-* is used in possessive sentences; the possessor stands in the genitive and the possession takes the pertinent possessive suffix. Examples: *mon^j ul^j-i alaša-m* PRO.s1.gen EXISTS-s3pres HORSE-s1 'I have a horse', *mon^j ul^j-it^j mazij(-t^j) pac^j a-n* PRO.s1.gen EXISTS-p3pres BEAUTIFUL(-pN) SCARF-plurposs.s1 'I have beautiful scarves', *učit^j el^j-en^j t^j ul^j=n^j e-s^j vad^j r^j a kudo-zo* TEACHER-gen EXISTS=freq-s3.past1 BEAUTIFUL HOUSE-s3 'the teacher used to have a beautiful house'.

Constructions with Verbal Nouns

Constructions built with verbal nouns are common Mordva equivalents of subordinate clauses. Those built with *infinitives* mainly express object or goal clauses, e.g. *učit^j el^j-es^j mer^j-s^j tonovt^j n^j e-ms vad^j r^j a-sto* TEACHER-def.sN SAYS.s3.past1 STUDIES-inf GOOD=adv 'the teacher said to (= said that we/they/you/one, etc. should) study well', *son sov-i obeda-mo* PRO.s3 ENTERS-s3pres HAS.DINNER-inf '(s)he goes in to have dinner'. Those built with *participles* serve as qualifiers, e.g. *is^j=en^j sajez^j od^j ir^j va-s^j pek mazij* YESTERDAY=adj CATCHES=part BRIDE-DDsN VERY BEAUTIFUL 'the bride who got married yesterday is very beautiful', *sodav=t loman^j-es^j t^j eči aras^j el^j* KNOWS=part PERSON-DDsN TODAY NOT.EXISTS-s3.past2 'the person whom they (we, people) know wasn't (there) today', *kado=viks t^j eve-n^j t^j son ez^j-iz^j e pr^j ado* LEAVES=part WORK-DDsGA PRO.s3 NEG.VERB-s3s3.past1 FINISHES '(s)he didn't finish the work that was left'. Those built with *gerunds* serve the same function as clauses of manner or temporal clauses, e.g. *an^j s^j ak ojms^j e=z^j lamo a t^j ejat* ONLY RESTS=ger MUCH NEG.PART DOES-s2pres 'if you only rest, you don't do much', *t'eve-n' apak pr'ado a er'av-i ojms'e-ms* WORK-GA NEG.PART FINISHES NEG.PART IS.ALLOWED-s3pres RESTS-inf 'if you don't finish the work, you can't rest'.

Compound Sentences

Co-ordinate clauses form compound sentences either asyndetically, e.g. *ved'- es' keped'ev-s', varaka--s' s'imev-s'* 'the water rose, the crow drank its fill', or with a conjunction, e.g. *kardaz-so ašt'e-s' kuvšin,* **no** *ved' ul'=n'e-s' an's'ak potmakske-se-n't'* 'in the yard was a jug, **but** there was water only at its very bottom'.

Subordinate clauses are normally linked by means of conjunctions, e.g. *son n'e-iz'e r'ivez'-en't', kona-s' sal-iz'e saraz-on't'* '(s)he saw the fox, which (had) stole(n) the hen', *a sodan, z'ardo s-i meke-v* 'I don't know when (s)he'll come back'. Such subordination, often effected by means of conjunctions of Russian origin (e.g. *što* 'that', *but'i* 'if', *xot'* 'although'), is spreading at the expense of equivalent constructions built with verbal nouns.

Lexicon

Layers of the Lexicon

Mordva roots belong to three main etymological classes, each accounting for about 30 per cent of the lexicon: inherited, innovated, and borrowed. The rest of the root inventory (about 10 per cent) is without etymology. Textual frequency is more difficult to assess, but a glimpse is provided by the text given at the end of this chapter: of the twenty-nine words occurring in this text, fourteen are inherited (three times each: *varaka* 'crow', *ved'* 'water'; twice: *a* 'NEGATIVE PARTICLE'; once each: *sa-* 'comes', *koda* 'how', *n'er'* 'beak', *son* 'PRO.s3', *karma-* 'begins', and probably *sato-* 'is sufficient'), nine are Mordva innovations (*s'ime=ma* 'drinking', *s'ime-ms* 'to drink' and *s'imev-* 'drinks one's fill', from *s'im-* 'drinks'; *marto* 'with', from *mar* 'hill, heap'; *ul'=n'e-* 'is FREQ', from *ul'-* 'is'; *potm=aks=ke* 'the very bottom/ inside', from *potmo* 'inside part'; *kaj=s'e-* 'throws around, flings', from *kaja-* 'throws'; *kev=n'e* 'pebble', from *kev* 'stone' and *keped'e=v-* 'rises' from *keped'-* 'lifts'); five are loans (*kuvšin* 'jug', three times, and *no* 'but' once, both from Russian; and *kardaz* 'courtyard', from Baltic), and only one is without clear etymology (*ašt'e-* 'exists').

Inherited vocabulary is, in turn, of various ages, and may date back to Finno-Volgaic, Finno-Permic, Finno-Ugric, or proto-Uralic. At each of these levels, a given word may be an internal innovation or a loan. Prominent among the former are onomatopoeic or affective-descriptive vocabulary such as Erzya *puva-* 'blows', which probably continues a proto-Uralic word of onomatopoeic origin (*puwV-, *puɣV-, cf. Nenets *pū-* 'id'), and other items such as *načko* 'damp' (Finno-Ugric *n'ačkV, cf. Kazym Khanty *n'ašax* 'raw'), *tard'e-* 'stiffens' (Finno-Permic *tara 'stiff', cf. Komi *tur=d-* 'stiffens with cold'), and *piz^je-* 'rains' (Finno-Volgaic *pis^(j)a- 'drips', cf. Finnish *pisa=ra* 'drop').

Iranian and Indo-Iranian Loans

The oldest loans which can be traced into various stages from proto-Uralic to Finno-Volgaic are those from (Indo-)Iranian; Rédei (1986: 94–5) counted roughly forty such items, e.g. *mije-* 'sells', a word dating back to Uralic *miγe-* 'gives', itself a loan from Indo-Iranian; *t^jeje-* 'does', which dates back to FU *teke-*, an Indo-Iranian or early Iranian loan. Other examples include *sal* 'salt', which can be traced back as far as Finno-Permic *salV, *ažija* 'thill' (< FP *ajša), *sazor* 'younger sister' (< FP *sasare), *uz^jer^j* 'axe' (< Finno-Volgaic *was^jara). Mordva *paz* 'god' and *tarvaz* 'sickle' lack cognates in Uralic, but their reconstructed shapes (FP *pakase, *tarwase) suggest that they were borrowed from some form of early Indo-Iranian; similarly, *s^jeja* 'goat' (< FP or FV *s^jaka or *s^jawa) looks like an old Iranian word. Other Mordva words with probable Iranian backgrounds are *kšn^ji* 'iron' and *sir^jn^je* 'gold'; their antecedents may have been borrowed from a form or forms of Old or Middle Iranian into Finno-Volgaic (*kürtänä, *sern^jä); Mordva *pango* 'mushroom' is more difficult to date, since its reconstructum (*pankV) may reflect FU or FV age. If a Mordva word of putative Iranian origin has a pendant in Mari, as well, it is difficult to determine whether we have to deal with joint or separate borrowing, e.g. Moksha *c^jongə* 'island', Erzya *pušto* 'pap, mush', *s^jija* 'silver'.

Other Indo-European Connections

Contacts with speakers of Tocharian may lie behind the antecedent of Mordva *us^jke* 'wire' (< pU *was^jke '(a type of metal)'); the word for 'salt', *sal*, also, may stem from Tocharian and not Iranian.

Evidence for contacts between speakers of (Uralic) Finno-Volgaic and (Indo-European) Baltic may be found in items such as +*kirda* '-fold; -times' (FV *kerta, cf. Saami *geardi*), *kšna* 'strop' (FV *šišna, cf. Finnish *hihna*), and *t^jejt^jer^j* 'daughter' (FV *tüktäre, cf. Finnish *tytär*). The Mordva word for the elm (*ukso*), on the other hand, may ultimately be of either Baltic or Iranian origin; *sazor* 'younger sister' has also been considered as Baltic, and not Iranian, in origin.

Semantic Fields

An analysis of 566 inherited Mordva roots revealed the following breakdown according to semantic fields: nature, flora, fauna 186; actions 124; dwellings, clothing, meals, transport, tools 112; parts of the body 55; properties 45; kinship 23; spatial orientation 17; religion 4 (Zaicz 1988: 402; see also Mosin 1985).

Loans into Common Mordva

The most important groups of loanwords from other languages into Common Mordva are Iranian, Baltic, Turkic, and Russian (Serebrennikov 1965:

242–56). Besides these, however, there must also have been many other donor languages which are now no longer spoken and of which we have no trace. Furthermore, there is some small but compelling evidence of contact with speakers of East Germanic: *pondo* 'pound', and there is certain evidence of later (eighteenth-century) contact with German speakers who settled in the Volga area, e.g. *kept^jer^j* 'linden bark basket', *pur^je* 'mead'. Loans from Baltic may have travelled via Muroma or Merja (two extinct west Uralic languages), and some older Turkic loans may have come into Mordva via Mari.

Much of the vocabulary shared by Mordva and Mari may have been borrowed separately into the two languages from and via unknown donors. Examples include *arvo* 'honey dissolved in water', *embel^j* 'carpenter's plane', *lav* 'dandruff' (East Mari *lëgë*), *s^jn^jaro* 'that much', and *žaba* 'child'. All layers of the borrowed lexicon of Mordva await an up-to-date reworking, including both those words which have been borrowed directly and those which have entered Mordva via Turkic and Russian mediation; Mordva calques based on Turkic and Russian models should also be re-examined. The groundwork for such undertakings lies ready in the recently published dictionary by Paasonen (1990–96).

Iranian Loans
Old and Middle Iranian loanwords which entered Common Mordva more or less directly are usually classified under the labels Scythian, Sarmatian, and Alanic. Relatively certain members of this layer are E *al^ja* M *al^jä* 'young man', E *kan^js^jt^j* M *kan^jf* 'hemp', EM *loman^j* 'human being', EM *maraz^j* 'elm (E), maple (M)', E *pit^jn^je* M *pit^jn^jə* 'price', E *ser^ja* M *s^jär^jə* 'acorn', E *tirdaz* 'thrush', E *vasta* 'spouse', E *vir^jes* M *värəs* 'lamb'; the list could be doubled with the inclusion of controversial examples. Iranian influence was not limited to the lexical sphere; according to E. Lewy, a great deal of the definiteness-marking and agreement phenomena of Mordva may be attributed to Iranian interference, altering Mordva typologically to resemble more inflecting types of languages such as (Iranian) Ossetian (Stipa 1973: 10).

Baltic Loans
These seem to be roughly equal to the Iranian elements in number, but it is often difficult to determine the time and trajectory of the borrowing: E *kardaz* '(court)yard', E *l^jen^jge* M *l^jen^jgə* 'linden bark', E *l^jija* M *l^jijä* 'other', E *mukoro* M *məkər* 'buttocks', E *panst* M *pandəz* 'bridle', E *pejel^j* M *pejəl^j* 'knife', E *pur^jgin^je* 'thunder', E *simen^j* M *s^jimən^j* 'root; tribe', E *suro* M *surə* 'millet', E *tor* '(ritual) knife; rod (used at weddings)', E *t^jožon^j* M *t^jožän^j* 'thousand'.

Turkic (Tatar and Chuvash) Loans
Quite a few dozen Middle Bulgarian (= Old Chuvash) loans entered especially southern, i.e. pre-Moksha, dialects of Mordva during the heyday of the Volga Bolgar Empire (seventh century CE). Only a few of these Chuvash

words persist into the present-day literary languages; examples are E *ajira* M *aj(ə)ra* 'cold, biting wind', E *kenʲdʲal* M *kelda* 'bedbug', E *komolʲa* M *komlʲä* 'hops', E *kšumanʲ* M *kušma* 'radish', E *sʲirʲtʲ* M *sʲirʲək* 'elm, ash', E *sʲukoro*, M *cʲukər* 'a kind of pie'.

With the thirteenth century came the Tatar invasions, and Tatar loans succeed Chuvash loans in Mordva. On (western) Mordva territory the predominant form of Tatar to exert an influence were the western, primarily Mišer, dialects; to the east, where Mordva speakers had settled beyond the Volga, Kazan Tatar and Bashkir were the main influences.

Mišer–Mordva contacts were a two-way street: many Mordva words were borrowed into Mišer, as well. A more striking example of the depth of Mordva–Turkic contact is the ethnic and linguistic duality of the Karatay Mordva, who are descendants of Mordva speakers but who now speak Tatar. The Moksha Mordva in the south were more directly influenced by Tatar contact, as is witnessed by Tatar loans found only in Moksha and not in Erzya, e.g. M *aru* 'clean', *cʲebärʲ* 'good', *ezna* 'brother-in-law', *isa* 'willow', *konak* 'guest', *osal* 'evil', *ucʲəz* 'cheap'; there are also a few words with the opposite distribution, e.g. E *tolkun* 'wave', *ucʲa* 'spine', *ulov* 'the deceased'. If we count all lexical items including obsolete words and words with limited dialectal distribution, the number of Tatar loans into Mordva exceeds one thousand: for example, Tatar loans beginning with *k-* in Paasonen 1990–96 number close to one hundred. As for the present-day literary languages, there may well be a hundred in Moksha and roughly half that many in Erzya. Among the Tatar loans of the core vocabularies of the Mordva literary languages are (both Erzya and Moksha unless otherwise indicated): *ajdʲa-* 'drives', *alaša* 'horse', E *ajgor* M *ajgər* 'stallion', *ulav* 'car; team of horses', E *paksʲa* M *paksʲä* 'meadow', E *emež* M *iməž* 'fruit, berry', E *parʲcʲej* M *paRʲcʲi* 'silk', *cʲora* '(young) man', *cʲotmar* 'cudgel', *čavka* '(jack)daw', *kurka* 'turkey', *jarmak* 'money; coin', E *karšo* M *karša* 'opposite', E *pek* M *päk* 'very'. Chuvash and Tatar influence today is quite limited and affects only a few dialects. The enormously challenging task of sorting out the chronology and the linguistic–geographical and phonological detail of the older Turkic loans in Mordva still awaits an appropriately trained researcher.

Russian Loans

There are no Common Slavonic elements in Mordva, and lexical evidence from Old Russian is scant and uncertain; tentative candidates for the latter loan status include *rozʲ* 'rye' and *rašta-* 'increases (in number)'. Russian–Mordva contacts were close in the eleventh and twelfth centuries, but the best evidence for such contacts is in the influence exercised by Mordva on non-northern Russian dialects (*cokanie* and even *akanie*; see Stipa 1973: 13–24). In subsequent centuries Mordva provided many Russian place names in the Vyatka area.

From the thirteenth to the sixteenth century Russian influence on Mordva rivalled that of Tatar; from the seventeenth to the nineteenth it surpassed it; and in the twentieth century Russian influence became exclusive. All linguistic levels were affected: the adoption of /f/ and /x/ phonemes, the spread of the correlation of palatalization, the use of conjunctions (borrowed from Russian) and the resulting shifts in sentence structure, all originated in Russian. Towards the end of the twentieth century not only Russian dialects but also the Russian literary standard played an important role. In the realm of the lexicon this influence has swollen into a mass of several thousands of words. A short sampling from literary Erzya might include *bednoj* 'poor', *narodnoj* 'folk-', *rodnoj* 'domestic', *glavnoj* 'chief', *životnoj* 'animal', *ščastlivoj* 'happy, fortunate', *ves^jola* 'merry', *brat* 'brother', *nuc^jka* 'grandchild', *gos^jt^j* 'guest', *soldat* 'soldier', *jaguda* 'berry', *z^jorna* 'seed', *kalac^ja* 'loaf', *vina* 'wine, vodka', *stol^j* 'table', *stul* 'chair', *škap* 'armoire', *z^jerkala* 'mirror', *škola* 'school', *t^jetrad^jka* 'notebook', *kn^jiga* 'book', *pera* 'pen', *pomoc^j* 'help', *ol^ja* 'will; freedom' *robota-* 'works', *stroja-* 'builds', *poluča-* 'gets', *otveča-* 'answers', *r^jisova-* 'sketches', *raz* '+times' (competing with the very early Baltic loan *kirda* from the Finno-Volgaic age), *tišča* 'thousand' (replacing the earlier Baltic loan *t^jožon^j*). Present-day Mordva technical vocabularies and the vocabularies of the natural and social sciences consist, with very few exceptions, of Russian loan elements combined and extended on Russian models.

Words of Internal Origin

Onomatopoesis accounts for several hundred items, including verbs such as *buldordo-* 'murmurs, bubbles', *c^jaxa-* 'neighs', *c^jimbel^jd^je-* 'flashes', *c^jir^jn^je-* '(piglet) squeals', *gl^jonkod^je-* 'drinks in a noisy fashion', *karno-* 'claws', *korča-* 'slurps', *pot^ja-* 'sucks' (~ *pot^je* 'female breast'), *tr^jonkad^je-* 'thumps' (~ *tr^jonk* 'sound of thumping') and barnyard and other animal calls such as *kšu+kšu* 'shoo!' and *kuko* 'cuckoo'.

Less affective vocabulary has been regularly made by the processes of derivation and compounding. *Derivation* was broached on pp. 202–4; here we list a few more (Erzya) examples: from *al* 'lower (part)' is derived *alks* '(feather-)bed', and from *ava* 'mother' are derived *avaks* 'female (animal)', *avakš* 'female (bird)', and *avavt* 'mother-in-law'. The word for 'lock', *panžoma*, is derived from the verb *panžo-* 'opens'; the word for 'splits', *lazo-*, is derived from the noun for 'plank', *laz*. Further examples: *jamks* 'millet' (*jam* 'soup'), *s^jel^jmukš-t* 'eyeglasses' (*s^jel^jme* 'eye'), *kever^je-* 'rolls away' (*kever^j* 'round'), *s^jormav* 'multi-coloured' (*s^jorma* 'writing; embroidery').

Compounding may be co-ordinative or subordinative. Examples of the former are verbs such as *kišt^je-+mora-* 'has fun' (DANCES+SINGS), *l^jis^je-+sova-* 'comes and goes' (EXITS+ENTERS), *kuz^je-+valgo-* 'swings' (RISES+FALLS), *šl^ja-+narda-* 'washes up' (WASHES+WIPES), *s^jt^ja-+pra-*

'lives'(STANDS.UP+FALLS), *vidʲe-+soka-* 'farms' (SOWS+PLOUGHS) and nouns such as *ponks-t+panar-t* 'linen' (TROUSERS+SHIRTS), *ejkakš* 'child' (CHILD+CHILD), *suks-t+unža-t* 'vermin' (WORM+BUG). Mitigative verbs are built by combining the lexical verb with the verb root *tʲeje-* 'does', e.g. *aštʲe-+tʲeje-* 'stands around (ineffectually)' (*aštʲe-* 'stands'), *jarsa-+tʲeje-* 'eats away at' (*jarsa-* 'eats').

Most subordinative compounds are of the order X+Y, i.e. are simple combinations of two root morphemes, e.g. *inʲevedʲ* 'sea' (*inʲe* 'big' + *vedʲ* 'water'), *kirʲgaparʲ* 'throat' (*kirʲga* 'neck' + *parʲ* 'basin'), *modamarʲ* 'potato' (*moda* 'earth' + *marʲ* 'apple'). Some morphophonemics may be involved, with varying degrees of productivity, e.g. *u ~ i* in *odirʲva* 'bride' (*od* 'young' + *urʲva* 'daughter-in-law'), *me ~ Ø* in *sʲelʲvedʲ* 'tear' (*sʲelʲme* 'eye' + *vedʲ* 'water'). Collocations involving the genitive of the modifier are best treated as syntagms (and the orthography writes them as two words), e.g. *ije-nʲ ška* 'season (YEAR'S TIME)', *prʲa-nʲ šnamo* 'self-praise (HEAD'S PRAISE)', *šanžav-onʲ koct* 'cobweb (SPIDER'S WEAVING)'.

Quite a few dozen derivates and compound constructions which are now extinct may be found in eighteenth-century sources; the semantic fields of religion, government, societal structure, and law predominate, and conscious neologizing was probably the cause in most cases. Examples include *čudʲi vedʲ* 'river (FLOWING+WATER)', *inʲazoro(-nʲ) erʲamo* 'Russia; the State, the Tsardom (BIG.LORD'S+LIFE)', *jovtʲlʲicʲa* 'prophet (STORYTELLER)', *kovonʲ val* 'calendar (MONTHLY+WORD)', *lʲija kelʲicʲa-t* 'pagans (OTHER/FOREIGN LANGUAGE'D.ONES)', *paz-onʲ urʲe* 'angel (GOD'S +SERVANT)', *pukšturdi* 'soldier (ONE.WHO.CAUSES.[CANNON].TO. FIRE)', *šačmo pelʲ* 'family (TRIBE+PART)', *vesʲe lomatʲ* 'world (ALL-+PEOPLE)'.

Erzya Mordva Text
A: text in transcription, segmented; B: morpheme-by-morpheme gloss; C: close translation; D: freer translation;
nomsx = derivational suffix which forms nominals; vbsx = derivational suffix which forms verbs.

A1 varaka-nʲtʲ   sa-sʲ   sʲime=ma-zo   A2 kardaz-so
B1 CROW-DDsG COMES-s3past1 DRINKS=nomsx-s3 B2 YARD-ine
C1 the crow's   it came   its thirst   C2 in yard

aštʲe-sʲ   vedʲ   marto   kuvšin,   no   vedʲ-esʲ
STANDS-s3past1 WATER   WITH   JUG   BUT WATER-sNdef
it stood   with——   water   jug   but   the water

kuvšin-sen^jt^j	ul^j=n^je-s^j	potm=aks=ke-se	A3 varaka-n^jt^jen^j
JUG-DDine	IS=freq-s3past1	INSIDES=nomsx- =nomsx-ine	B3 CROW-DDdat
in the jug	it was	at the very bottom	C3 for the crow

a	koda	s^jime-ms:	a	sat-i
NEG.PART	HOW?	DRINKS-inf	NEG.PART	IS.SUFFICIENT-s3pres
no	way	to drink	not	it is enough

n^jer^j-eze	A4 son	karma-s^j	kaj=s^je=me	=kuvšin-en^jt^jen^j
BEAK-s3	B4 PRO.s3	BEGINS-s3past1	THROWS= freq-inf	JUG-DDdat
its beak	C4 it	began	to throw	into the jug

kev=n^je-t^j	A5 ved^j-es^j	keped^je=v-s^j
STONE=nomsx-plur	B5 WATER-DDsN	RAISES=vbsx-s3past1
pebbles	C5 the water	it rose

varaka-s^j	s^jime=v-s^j
CROW-DDsN	DRINKS=vbsx-s3past1
the crow	it drank its fill

D1 The crow became thirsty. D2 In a courtyard stood a jug with water, but the water was at the very bottom. D3 There is no way for the crow to drink: its beak isn't (long) enough. D4 It began to throw pebbles into the jug. D5 The water rose, the crow drank its fill.

References and Further Reading

Abondolo, D. (1982) 'Verb paradigm in Erźa Mordvinian', *Folia Slavica* 5: 11–24.

Bereczki, G. (1988) 'Geschichte der wolgafinnischen Sprachen', in D. Sinor (ed.), *The Uralic Languages. Description, History and Foreign Influences*, Handbuch der Orientalistik 8, Leiden: Brill, pp. 314–50.

────── (1994) *Grundzüge der tscheremissischen Sprachgeschichte*, vol. I, Studia Uralo-Altaica 35, Szeged: Universitas Szegediensis de Attila József nominata.

Bubrix, D.V. (1947) Эрзя-мордовская грамматика. Минимум, Saransk: Mordovian State Publishers.

Budenz, J. (1877) 'Moksa- és erza-mordvin nyelvtan', *Nyelvtudományi Közlemények* 13: 1–134.

Collinder, B. (1957) 'Mordvin', in *Survey of the Uralic Languages*, Stockholm: Almqvist & Wiksell, pp. 227–46.

Cygankin, D.V. (1980) (ed.) Грамматика мордовских языков. Фонетика, графика, орфография, морфология, Saransk: Mordovian State University.

Erdődi, J. (1968) *Erza-mordvin szövegek (magyarázatokkal, nyelvtani vázlattal és szótárral)*, Budapest: Tankönyvkiadó.

Ermuškin, G.I. (1984) Ареальные исследования по восточным финно-угорским

языкам (Эрзя-мордовский язык), Moscow: Nauka.
Feoktistov, A.P. (1966) 'Мордовские языки', in V.I. Lytkin et al. (eds), Языки народов СССР 3, Финно-угорские и самодийские языки, Moscow: Nauka, pp. 172–220.
—— (1975) 'Мордовские языки', in V.I. Lytkin et al. (eds), Основы финно-угорского языкознания 2, Прибалтийско-финские, саамский и мордовские языки, Moscow: Nauka.
Keresztes, L. (1987) *Geschichte des mordwinischen Konsonantismus*, vol. I, Studia Uralo-Altaica 27, Szeged: Universitatis Szegediensis de Attila József nominata.
—— (1990) *Chrestomathia Morduinica*, Budapest: Tankönyviadó.
Kolädenkov, M.N., and Zavodova, R.A. (eds) (1962) Грамматика мордовских (мокшанского и эрзянского) языков, I: Фонетика и морфология, Saransk: Mordovian Book Publishers.
Mosin, M.V. (1985) Финно-угорская лексика в мордовских и прибалтийско-финских языках (Семантический анализ), Saransk: Mordovian State University.
Nadjkin, D.T. (1981) 'Основа глагола в мордовских языках, Автореферат' [unpublished Ph.D. thesis], Tartu: Tartu State University.
Paasonen, H. (1903) *Mordvinische lautlehre*, Helsingfors: Finnische Literaturgesellschaft.
—— (1990–6) *Mordwinisches Wörterbuch*, compiled by K. Heikkilä; edited and published by M. Kahla, vols I–IV, Helsinki: Société Finno-Ougrienne.
Raun, A. (1988) 'The Mordvin language', in D. Sinor (ed.), *The Uralic Languages. Description, History and Foreign Influences*, Handbuch der Orientalistik 8, Leiden: Brill, pp. 96–110.
Rédei, K. (1984) 'Phonologische Analyse des Erza-Mordwinischen', in P. Hajdú and L. Honti (eds), *Studien zur phonologischen Beschreibung uralischer Sprachen*, Budapest: Akadémiai Kiadó, pp. 209–30.
—— (1986) *Zu den indogermanisch-uralischen Sprachkontakten*, Wien: Verlag der Österreichischen Akademie der Wissenschaften.
Serebrennikov, B.A. (1965) 'История мордовского народа по данным языка', in B.A. Rybakov et al. (eds), Этногенез мордовского народа, Saransk: Mordovian Book Publishers.
—— (1967) Историческая морфология мордовских языков, Moscow: Nauka.
Stipa, G. J. (1973) *Mordwinisch als Forschungsobjekt*, Napoli: Istituto Universitario Orientale.
Veenker, W. (1981) 'Zur phonologischen Statistik der mordvinischen Schriftsprachen', *UAJb* (*Neue Folge*), vol. I: 33–72.
Wiedemann, F.J. (1865) *Grammatik der ersa-mordwinischen Sprache nebst einem kleinen ... Wörterbuch*, St. Petersburg: Commissionäre der Kaiserlichen Akademie der Wissenschaften.
Zaicz, G. (1988) 'A mordvin lexika ősi elemei', in P. Domokos and J. Pusztay (eds), *Bereczki emlékkönyv*, Budapest: Humanities Faculty of the University of Budapest, pp. 397–402.
—— (1993) 'Hangrend és illeszkedés a mordvinban', in M. Sz. Bakró-Nagy and E. Szíj (eds), *Hajdú emlékkönyv*, Budapest: Humanities Faculty of the University of Budapest, pp. 427–32.

7 Mari

Eeva Kangasmaa-Minn

The Mari (older name: Cheremis) language is spoken in Central Russia around the middle stretch of the Volga and in scattered areas in the east towards the Urals. There exists a Mari Autonomous (Soviet) Republic (now, Republic of Mari El) extending to both sides of the river. The Volga is also a dialect boundary: the Mari on the western, hilly side speak *kur∂k mari* or Hill Mari those on the low eastern shore speak *ol∂k mari* or Meadow Mari.

Only about one half of the Mari live in their own republic. A large concentration of the Mari population is found in the Bashkir Republic, around the city of Ufa. The Mari in the Bashkir area call themselves *üpö mari*; they speak far eastern variants of Meadow Mari dialects, a fact which indicates that they have wandered eastwards from the left bank of the Volga.

The Mari are very unevenly distributed: in their own republic they comprise less than one-half of the population (323,009 or 48.3 per cent in 1989) and are outnumbered by Russians. Speakers of Mari tend to live in rural areas, while the cities, most notably the capital Joškar Ola, are almost completely Russian. In addition, small numbers of Tatars and Chuvash live among the principal nationalities. In Bashkiria the number of Mari was reported in the 1989 census as 106,793. Together with the Mari living in scattered settlements in neighbouring districts, the number of Eastern Mari was 160,000 in 1970. Since the Soviet census in 1989 registered altogether 670,277 persons of Mari nationality, the proportion of the Mari living outside their own republic is about one-third (Lallukka 1990: 112–24).

The Mari have long been settled in the area, but toponyms indicate that they once lived to the west of their present-day habitations. They are mentioned in the Jordanes Chronicle (551) by the name of Sremnisc, together with their close relatives the Merens. The latter name seems to be a Latinization identical with the present-day self-designation *mari*. The areas which the Mari have inhabited have also been home to Chuvash and Tatar. The Chuvash built a large and flourishing commercial empire which spread over central and southern Russia and far into the Balkans. The Tatars arrived somewhat later, with Genghis Khan, and overthrew all political opponents in the region. After the Russians had freed themselves from Tatar supremacy they began to invade the area around the middle stretches of the Volga, thus establishing dominance over the earlier inhabitants. The Mari people and language continued to live side by side with Turkic peoples and languages.

219

It was not until the twentieth century, and especially under the Soviet regime, that the Russification of Mari culture began in earnest. Material conditions and educational standards were improved, but at a cost: a decrease in the usefulness, cultivation, and prestige of the native language. Only in the villages, and there only at the elementary level, was education carried out in Mari; all higher education was in Russian. The Mari have retained, nevertheless, a sense of their cultural uniqueness and of the value of their native language, perhaps better than any other central Finno-Ugric group.

The Mari language was first adapted to literary use by missionaries who translated parts of the gospels into the Western (Hill) Mari dialect.

From the beginning, there were two literary languages, one based on Western (Hill), one on Eastern (Meadow) Mari. The two varieties are more or less mutually understandable, the differences consisting mainly in the inventory and distribution of the vowels and in certain discrepancies in vocabulary. The phonetic structure of Eastern Mari is somewhat simpler than that of the Western type, a fact which has tended to favour it as the more or less official language of Mari culture.

The Mari people have a rich body of folklore and now a flourishing literature, as well. Their interest in their ethnic and national heritage is evident in the text fragment included at the end of this chapter, a fragment taken from a literary journal, celebrating the achievements of the ethnologist and folklore collector Timofei Evseev.

Phonology

(Literary) Eastern Mari has nineteen consonant and eight vowel phonemes.

Consonants

Distribution

The unvoiced stops *p t k* occur in all positions, i.e. word initially: *koklašte* 'among', *tuδ ən* 'his/hers', *pal ə̂me* 'known'; medially after both voiced and unvoiced sounds: *koklašte*, *žap ə̂št ə̂že* 'in his/her time', *ške šotan* 'as a matter of fact'; and word-finally: *kal ə̂k* 'people', *surt* 'farm', *žap* 'time'. The voiced counterparts to the stops, written here as *b/w d g*, present some allophonic complications. In earlier days it was sufficient simply to state that the phonemes in question occurred as voiced fricatives except after homotopic nasals, when they assumed the quality of voiced stops. In a compromise with phonetic transcription these phonemes were written as β δ γ, since the fricative allophones occurred far more frequently than the stop allophones. Nowadays, however, the velar and dental fricatives are usually replaced by stops in all positions and I see no controversy in writing them as such, i.e. as *d g*. For the sake of consistency, the labial should also be written with *b* in all environments; but for the sake of clarity in this chapter, *w* and *b* will be used according to the more common pronunciation. This practice parallels

Table 7.1   Consonant phonemes of Eastern Mari

	Phonemes					*Cyrillic equivalents*			
Unvoiced stops	p	t		k		п	т		к
Voiced counterparts	b/w	d		g		б/в	д		г
Affricate			č					ч	
Unvoiced s(h)ibilants		s	š				с	ш	
Voiced s(h)ibilants		z	ž				з	ж	
Nasals	m	n	nʲ	ŋ		м	н	нь	н
Laterals		l	lʲ				л	ль	
Trill		r					р		
Glide			j					й	

Western Mari has four additional phonemes:

		tʲ				ть	
f			x	ф			x
	c				ц		

Of these the palatalized *tʲ* and the two voiceless spirants, velar *x* and builabial or labio-dental *f*, occur in Chuvash loanwords; the dental affricate *c* is found in native words, as well.

that of the literary language, which uses the Cyrillic letters ‹г› and ‹д› for velar and dental, but two different graphs for the corresponding labial phoneme: ‹б› after *m*, as in комбо *kombo* 'goose' and ‹в› elsewhere: лувит *luwit* 'fifteen'. This graphic discrepancy is due to a skew in distribution, which is itself due, in turn, to phonetic history. Mari *g* and *d* represent the p(F)U stops *k and *t in voiced environments, but the voiced labial represents a merger of two p(F)U consonants: *p in voiced (and, *a fortiori*, non-initial) environments, e.g. *rəwəž* 'fox' (cf. Finnish *repo* of *revo-n+tule-t* 'aurora borealis') and *w in both medial and initial positions, cf. *luwit* 'fifteen' (Finnish *viite* 'five') and *waštər* 'maple' (Finnish *vaahtera*). This fact accounts for the differences in distribution: whereas *g* and *d* occur only word-medial after a vowel or a voiced consonant; their labial counterpart is found not only word-medially but word-initially as well. Therefore I have followed the principle adopted in the literary language and have throughout this chapter used the character *b* for the historical allophone after *m and the character *w* elsewhere, even for a *w* which has developed from an earlier *p.

Examples of the occurrences of *g*, *d*, and *b/w*: *šoga* '(s)he stands', *tudən nergen* 'about him', *kundeməse*, 'hailing from the X region', *lombo* 'Prunus padus', *kuwa* 'old woman', *wer* 'place', *luwit* 'fifteen'.

The hushing affricate *č* has a voiced allophone [ǯ] after *nʲ*. It is not marked in script and is lexically rare. Example: *šinʲčem* 'I know'.

Morphophonemic Alternations

The occurrence of voiced v. voiceless consonant phonemes is largely conditioned by their phonetic environment. In principle, unvoiced stops, affricates, and sibilants change into their voiced counterparts in voiced environments and vice versa. Thus the voiced fricatives *g* and *d* become voiceless stops before voiceless consonants. Example: *ludšowlaklan* 'to the readers', derived from the verb *ludem* 'I read' (pronounced [luðem]), is pronounced [lutšowlaklan]. In the postpositional construction *awa deč posna* MOTHER FROM SEPARATE 'without mother', the initial voiced *d* of the postposition *deč* 'from' has developed from a *t*: cf. the historically related locational noun *ter-*, *tor-* 'proximity'.

Further examples of the alternation between the two series: *kið-ân* 'hand sG', *kit-kâč* 'from the hand', *jol-gâč* 'from the foot', *kit-še* 'his/her hand', *jol-žo* 'his/her foot'.

However, certain suffixes do not observe this basic rule, but remain unaltered in all environments, e.g. the verbal noun suffix =šV (*lut=šo* 'reader') retains its *š* even after a voiced consonant: *tol=šo* 'one who is coming'. There are also several derivational suffixes in which a *t* remains unaltered after an *l* or *r*, e.g. *pualtem* 'I thresh', *nörtem* 'I make wet', but not after a nasal: contrast *pöremdem* 'I make wet'.

It follows from the morphophonemic rule given above that voiced fricatives/stops and voiced sibilants do not form clusters with voiceless consonants. Certain types of consonant cluster may occur word-finally, especially those consisting of *š/l/r* + t (*surt* 'village', *wošt* 'through') but medial clusters which become final through morphology lose their first or second member in most cases, e.g. *kočkam* 'I eat', *koč* 'eat!'; *šinčam* 'I sit', *šič* 'sit!' Word-finally, voiced stops/fricatives are automatically replaced by their voiceless counterparts: compare the long and short forms of the present third person singular negative verb in *ogeš nal ~ ok nal* '(s)he does not take'.

Vowels

Eastern Mari vowels:

					Cyrillic equivalents			
i	ü		u		и	ÿ		у
e	ö	â	o		е	ö	ы	о
		a					a	

Western Mari has, in addition, the phonemes

ə	ӹ
ä	ä

Eastern Mari vowel alternations (allophonic representations in brackets):

Non-final syllables		Final syllable	
First	Non-first	Non-word-final	Word-final
o u	i e u o a ậ	ậ	o
ö ü	i e ü ö [ä] [ə]	[ə]	ö
a ậ e i	i e u o a ậ	ậ	e

Figure 7.1 Western Mari palatal attraction

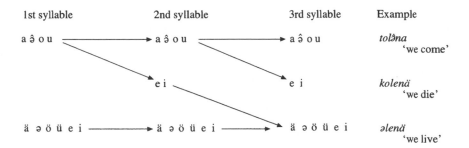

The presentation of the vowel phonemes would ideally use three dimensions, since there are three phonological contrasts:

1 Full v. reduced, the latter being written ậ. Literary Hill Mari distinguishes two reduced vowels, ậ and â (fronter) ə; some Western Mari dialects distinguish four reduced vowel qualities.
2 Front v. back. Front are *e i ö ü* (and *ə ä* in Western); *a o u ậ* are back.
3 Labial v. illabial, i.e. *o ö u ü* v. *a e i ậ (ə ä)*.

Distribution
All vowel phonemes occur in all syllables, but with restrictions imposed by the morphophonemic alternations outlined below. In Eastern Literary Mari (henceforth: EM), the back non-high vowels *a* and *ậ* have front variants if the first syllable has *ö* or *ü* (in dialects, also after *e* and *i*); these allophones are not indicated in the orthography. In the Western Mari (henceforth: WM) literary language non-first-syllable *ä* and ə are similarly not indicated in writing, but here they are phonemes, not allophones, since they occur in the first syllable, as well: *näleš* '(s)he takes' (EM *naleš*), *təŋ* 'beginning' (EM *tüŋ*).

Morphophonemic alternations. Mari has two different types of vowel alternation, each morphophonemically conditioned. The first type is rooted in the fact that the first vowel in a word rules structurally over the following in subsequent syllables. This so-called *vowel harmony* is typical of several Uralic, as well as of Turkic and Mongolic languages. Vowel harmony in these languages is usually an alternation, in corresponding structural entities, of back with front vowels, of rounded with unrounded vowels, or of both. The second type of vowel alternation is based on the contrast between reduced v. full vowels and is characteristic of the Eastern dialects.

In EM the contrast back : front, labial : illabial and reduced : full cannot be dealt with separately. The WM vowel system is ruled by palatal attraction and the situation is both more logical and more complex than the eastern one.

In EM, palatal prosody prevails through the word only if the first vowel in the word is front rounded *ö* or *ü*, i.e. then only front vowels (or front-vowel allophones) occur in the rest of the word. If there is a back vowel in the first syllable then there will be only back vowels and/or the phonetically front, but phonologically neutral vowels *e* and/or *i* in subsequent syllables. The alternation of full v. reduced occurs in morpheme-final syllables. An *ə* in this syllable remains reduced if a further suffixal morpheme is attached but otherwise it is converted to a full mid vowel. The quality of this full vowel is determined by that of the first preceding full vowel in the (non-compound) word: (1) if this vowel is unrounded, *ə* > *e*; (2a) if it is rounded and front, *ə* > *ö*, but (2b) if it is rounded and back, *ə* > *o*. Examples: *təl̬əze* 'moon', *təl̬əzə-šte* 'in the moon', *šör* 'milk', *šör-žö* 'its milk', *lud=šo* 'reader', *lud=šə-n* 'reader's', *kaj=še* 'walker', *kaj=šə-lan* 'to a walker'. (The conditions for this alternation are not uniform across the subdialects, and in some dialects the alternation is triggered by some suffixes and not by others.)

The situation in WM is of special interest. Since here the occurrence of back v. front vowel depends on the phonetic quality of the vowel in the preceding syllable, a word may change sides, as it were, in the middle of its structure: compare *tolənam* 'we seem to have come' with *kolenäm* 'we seem to have died'. On the other hand, labial harmony is weak or nonexistent in WM and there is no alternation between reduced and full vowels. The great frequency and perseverance of the reduced vowels obscure the phonological patterns of WM; it is perhaps partly due to this fact that the EM varieties have established themselves as the primary basis for the standard language.

Word stress is non-phonemic. In EM it falls on the last phonologically full vowel, e.g. *olma̱* 'apple' but *mu̱no* 'egg' (phonologically /munə́/), *mu̱nə́-n* 'of an egg'. If a word contains only reduced vowels, the stress falls on the first syllable, e.g. *tə̱l̬əzə́-m* 'moon (accusative)'. In WM stress usually falls on the penult, even if it contains a reduced vowel and the following syllable has a full vowel, e.g. *ə̱štäš* 'to sweep'; there is lability, however, if such a penult is preceded by full vowel, e.g. *wäškə̱ktäš* 'to hurry', but *wä̱škəmäš* 'haste' (Alhoniemi 1985: 15–40).

Morphology

Morpheme Classes

Mari words can be monomorphemic, but most contain at least two morphemes. Morphemes fall into three classes: bases, suffixes, and enclitics. A *base* is a morpheme that can appear alone as a monomorphemic word, or as the first member of a polymorphemic word. Any sequence of a base plus one or more affixes which, in its morphological functions, is equivalent to a base, is a *stem*.

A *suffix* is a morpheme which occurs only in connection with a base or a stem, i.e. bound in a polymorphemic word. Suffixes fall into three classes: derivational, inflectional, and enclitic.

A *derivational* suffix is one which when added to a base or stem forms a polymorphemic word that in its morphological functions is equivalent to a monomorphemic word. The morphological class (part of speech) of a derived word is determined by the derivational suffix occurring last in it. An *inflectional* suffix is one which when added to a base or stem indicates the syntactic function of the form in question. Derivational suffixes precede inflectional ones, with one exception: the adjective-formant =*sǝ̂*, e.g. *Morko kundemǝ̂=se* 'hailing from the district of Morko' can occur to the right of local case suffixes, e.g. *puš-ǝ̂š=so jeŋ* BOAT-ine-adj.sx PERSON 'the person in the boat'. *Enclitics* are bound morphemes that may occur last in any word, regardless of morphological category.

There are a few suffixes which hover between the categories of case suffix and enclitic, e.g. the comitative -*ge* (see below).

Morphological Categories
We may classify Mari bases into three groups according to their susceptibility to suffixation: nouns, which take case suffixes; verbs, which take tense/mood suffixes; and particles, which do not take suffixes (these are usually petrified case forms of non-productive nouns).

Nominal Inflection
Nominal inflection extends to nouns, pronouns, and numerals. Adjectives are declined only when they function syntactically as nouns; they are declined in neither attributive nor predicative position.

Case forms. As indicated above, the boundaries between case suffixes, derivational suffixes, and enclitics are far from clear-cut. The number of cases reported by various grammarians therefore varies considerably. Wichmann (^{2}1923: 8) gives the number as 13, as does Collinder (1957: 124), but Sebeok-Ingemann list 8 (1956: 33–41), and Alhoniemi has 10 (1985: 44–5). Native grammarians usually list 7, e.g. Savatkova and Učaev (1956: 803).

In Table 7.2 below, noun inflection is illustrated by five stems: *kol* 'fish', *wer* 'place', *wüt* 'water', *muno* 'egg', and *paša* 'work'.

The non-marginal cases may be divided into two basic groups: nominative, accusative, and genitive are purely *grammatical* cases, i.e. they indicate syntactic role and have no semantic content. The rest of the non-marginal cases are in the broadest sense *local* cases, since they can contain a semantic indication of locality.

Table 7.2   Eastern Mari noun inflection

	kol 'fish'	*wer* 'place'	*wüt* 'water'	*muno* 'egg'	*paša* 'work'
N	kol	wer	wüt	muno	paša
A	kolǝm	werǝm	wüdǝm	munǝm	pašam
G	kolǝn	werǝn	wüdǝn	munǝn	(pašan)
D	kollan	werlan	wütlan	munǝlan	(pašalan)
Ine	(kolǝšto)	werǝšte	wüdǝštö	munǝšte	pašašte
Lat	(koleš)	wereš	wüdeš	muneš	pašaš
Ill	(kolǝš[ko])	werǝš(ke)	wüdǝš(kö)	munǝš(ko)	pašaš(ke)
(Abl	kolleč	werleč	wütleč	munǝleč	pašaleč)
Marginal cases:					
Mod	kolla	werla	wütla	munǝla	pašala
Com	kolge	werge	wüδǝge	munǝge	pašage
(Car	kolde	werde	wütte	munǝde	olmade)

Note: Textually less frequent forms in brackets; see text.

Within the local-case subsystem a three-way distinction is maintained, as is characteristic of Uralic languages: static location *in* a place is distinguished from motion *to* (GOAL) and motion *from* a place (SOURCE). The inventory of cases recruited to serve this trichotomy is lopsided: there is only one static case, the inessive, and only one source case, the ablative, but there are as many as four goal cases. The functions of the lative and the illative overlap somewhat; the former seems to designate a more permanent change of place or condition than the latter (Alhoniemi 1967: 320–1).

Another factor crisscrosses the categories of case, namely that of animacy. The nominative and accusative are commonly used by all nouns, but genitive, dative, and ablative are common only with nouns which refer to animates, while inessive, lative, and illative occur more frequently with inanimates. Deviations from this basic pattern do occur; for example, the inanimate *paša* 'work' occurs in the dative in a construction such as *pašalan kaja* 'goes (to look) for work'. The lative of animates is not uncommon in utterances indicating a change into a state, e.g. *kugužan üdǝžǝm* **wateš** *nalǝn* 'he took the king's daughter **as a wife**'.

In dialects, the ablative *-leč* is quite common as a marker of the bested member of comparisons, e.g. *mü-leč tutlo* HONEY-abl SWEET 'sweeter than honey'.

In addition to the core case forms there exist a few *marginal* cases which may also be classified as declension. Most prominent among these are modal *-la*, comitative *-ge*, and caritive *-de*. These suffixes have a somewhat restricted distribution, and forms built with them therefore resemble petrified adverbs; on the other hand their meaning is not so clear-cut as to suggest that they be termed adverbial modifiers as such.

Modal *-la* (sometimes called the comparative) has lative undertones in constructions such as *mar-la ojla* 'speaks Mari', but is decidedly adjectival (and derivational) in a construction such as *totar=la solэk* 'Tatar scarf'. In yet a third role, the modal suffix is tacked on to illative forms, thus resembling an enclitic, e.g. *jal muča-škэ-la kaja* VILLAGE END-ill-mod GOES 'goes to the end of the village'; the sequence *-škэ-la* is treated as a single suffix (the 'approximative') by some grammarians (e.g. Bereczki 1990: 32, 39).

The comitative quite commonly has an inclusive meaning, e.g. *maskan kum igэge satašenэt* BEAR-gen THREE CHILD-com GOES.ASTRAY-past2-p3 'the bear went astray with its three cubs'. The caritive, e.g. *jol-de* 'without legs', contrasts not with the comitative but with the adverbial genitive, as in *jol-эn košt-eš* '(s)he/it goes on foot'; an example is *trupka-de kuze il-em* TOBACCO.PIPE-car HOW? LIVES-s1pres 'How (can/will) I live without (my) pipe?'.

The above-mentioned functional gaps in the somewhat lopsided local case system are smoothed over with the help of postpositions. The most important of these are historically petrified case forms built from non-productive local nouns with obsolete declensional suffixes. Among the more important are *gэč*, with various separative meanings, e.g. *pört gэč lektaš* 'to come *out of* the house' and *de-*, with fossilized forms *deč(эn)* 'from', *den(e)* 'with, at, by', *deran* 'at', *deke* 'to'. From the point of view of declension, the most important function of *de-* is supplying animate concepts with the means of expressing their locational relations, e.g. *jolmaš deč serэš* 'a letter (serэš) **from** a friend', *oza kuwaž deke* '(coming back) **to** the old woman (who is their) owner (*oza*)'; the form *den* also serves to link noun phrases, e.g. *maska den pire* BEAR WITH WOLF 'a bear and a wolf'.

Pronouns have a limited declension when used as head words.

Number and Person. There are two numbers, singular and plural, and three persons, first, second, and third. The singular and plural person markers are s1 *-(e)m*, s2 *-(e)t*, s3 *-(э)ž(э)*, p1 *-na*, p2 *-da*, p3 *-(э)št*; the *-e-* element of the s1 and s2 suffixes is dropped after a stem-final *a*. The distribution of the various allomorphs of the third-person suffixes is also largely phonologically conditioned.

In the genitive and accusative, person markers precede the case suffix, in the local cases they follow it; in the dative the order varies. Cf. Table 7.3.

A kind of generic, non-personal plural may be expresssed by the p3 suffix, e.g. *šüšpэk-эšt mura er dene* NIGHTINGALE-p3 SINGS-s3pres MORNING AT 'nightingales sing in the morning', note also *tosešэšt ulo kazde jeŋэn* FRIEND-p3 EXISTS EVERY HUMAN-gen 'every person has his/her friends'.

There are also several dedicated plural markers, occurring with different distributions in different dialects. Chief among these in eastern dialects is *-wlak*, e.g. pD *lud=šo-wlak-lan* 'to readers'. This suffix may be a loan from Tatar, where it is a noun meaning 'cattle'; or it may be related to Mordva *velʲe* 'village' and Saami *valvi* 'pack (of wolves, dogs)'. Its position in

Table 7.3 Selected Eastern Mari possessive declension forms: animate noun *kol* 'fish'

	Nominative	Genitive	Accusative	Dative
s1	kolem	kolemə̂n	kolemə̂m	kolemlan
s2	kolet	koletə̂n	koletə̂m	koletlan
s3	kolə̂žo	kolə̂žə̂n	kolə̂žə̂m	kolə̂žlan
p1	kolə̂na	kolə̂nan	kolə̂nam	kolə̂nalan
p2	kolə̂da	kolə̂dan	kolə̂dam	kolə̂dalan
p3	kolə̂št	kolə̂štə̂n	kolə̂štə̂m	kolə̂štlan

Table 7.4 Selected Eastern Mari possessive declension forms: inanimate noun *pört* 'house'

	Nominative	Accusative	Dative	Inessive	Lative	Illative
s1	pörtem	pörtemə̂m	pörtlanem	pörtə̂štem	pörtešem	pörtə̂škem
s2	pörtet	pörtetə̂m	pörtlanet	pörtə̂štet	pörtešet	pörtə̂šket
s3	pörtšö	pörtšə̂m	pörtšə̂lan	pörtə̂štə̂žö	pörtešə̂že	pörtə̂škə̂žö
p1	pörtna	pörtnam	pörtlanna	pörtə̂štə̂na	pörtešna	pörtə̂štə̂na
p2	pörtta	pörttam	pörtlanda	pörtə̂štə̂da	pörtešta	pörtə̂škə̂da
p3	pörtə̂št	pörtə̂štə̂m	pörtə̂štlan	pörtə̂štə̂št	pörtešə̂št	pörtə̂škə̂št

relation to person and case suffixes is rather labile. In the nominative, it can either precede or follow the person marker, e.g. *olma-m-wlak* or *olma-wlak-em* 'my apples', and in the grammatical cases both orders, person–number and number–person, are possible again, e.g. *joltaš-em-wlak-ə̂m* FRIEND-s1-plur-acc, *joltaš-wlak-em(-ə̂m)* FRIEND-plur-s1-acc 'my friends (acc)'. In local cases, besides these two orders, there also exists a third order, number–case–person, e.g. *olma-wlak-ə̂št-em* APPLE-plur-ine-s1 'in my apples'. The only restrictions operating in trisuffixal sequences with local cases seems to be that the plural marker cannot come last, and that the case marker cannot come first. Other, distributionally more restricted, plural suffixes in EM are *-la*, used mainly with nouns which designate places (e.g. *ola-la* 'cities'; see also Derivation, p. 234), and *-mə̂t*, which is used with (chiefly human) animates and forms inclusives, e.g. *awa-mə̂t* 'mother and her associates'.

A singular form often designates a plural conception; depending on the situation *kol* can refer to one fish or to many. There are also syntactic means of expressing plurality, viz. a noun in the singular followed by a verb in the plural: *kol ijat* FISH SWIMS-p3pres 'fish(es) swim', contrast *kol ija* FISH SWIMS.s3pres 'a fish swims' and the example with *šüšpǝk-ə̂št* 'nightingales' cited above. In sum, the category of number is *in statu nascendi* in Mari, and is highly pragmatic.

As in many Uralic languages, referents (usually body parts) normally occurring in pairs are encoded morphologically as singulars, e.g. the unmarked meaning of *kit* is '(the two) hands/arms'. Disambiguation therefore specifies the marked meaning 'one hand/arm', which is expressed by means of the word *pel* 'half', e.g. *pel+kid=an* HALF+ARM=adj 'one-armed'.

The second- and third-person singular person markers also act as indicators of definiteness, thus functioning as article surrogates, e.g. *užeš kugužan+üdâr-âm. kugužan+üdâr-et mâgâra* 'he sees a princess (*kugužan+üdâr-âm*, sA). **The** princess (*kugužan+üdâr-et*, s2; lit. your princess) is weeping.'

Verb Inflection
Finite forms. There are two conjugations, called *em* and *am* conjugations after their first-person singular present indicative endings. The precise mechanics of the development of these two inflectional patterns – discernible in most forms, both finite and non-finite – have not been adequately explained. In all probability the difference is due to the conspiracy of several factors, phonetic, morphological, and functional. In this chapter, the membership of a verb stem to one conjugation or another will be indicated by stem-final â: presence of this segment indicates the *em*-conjugation class; its absence indicates the *am*-conjugation.

There are three moods: indicative, desiderative, and imperative. The indicative has a present/future, i.e., non-past, tense as well as two past tenses. The other two moods have no tense oppositions. The indicative and the desiderative distinguish three persons, singular and plural, while the imperative has only second- and third-person (singular and plural) forms.

These finite forms are set out in Table 7.5.

The primary difference between the two past tenses is neither grammatical nor lexical/aspectual but rather pragmatic. The first past refers especially to states and events which the speaker has personally witnessed, while the second past is more or less a record of what has been or happened without any emphasis on the speaker's attitude towards the truth value of the utterance; the second past might be called a 'non-witnessed past' ([Kangasmaa-] Minn 1960: 116–7). In many contexts this pragmatic opposition is neutralized, i.e. the two tenses are interchangeable.

The first past derives historically from the pU past-tense markers *-i- (in the *am* conjugation) and *-sʲ- (in the *em* conjugation). The former is discernible in Mari only as morphophonemics: stem-suffix sandhi (e.g. p1 present *ludâna*, p1 first past *lutna*), palatalization of stem-final *n* and *l* (as in *nalʲe* '(s)he took) and the s2 suffix variant -*č* (as in *tolʲ-oč* 'you came'). The second past is historically a construction consisting of the gerund and the present-tense forms of *ulam* 'is', except in the third person singular, where the

Table 7.5   Eastern Mari finite verb forms

	nalam 'I take'	*kodem* 'I leave (tr)'
Indicative		
Present/future (non-past)		
s1	nalam	kodem
s2	nalat	kodet
s3	naleš	koda
p1	nalə̂na	kodena
p2	nalə̂da	kodeda
p3	nalə̂t	kodat
First past		
s1	naľʲə̂m	kodə̂šə̂m
s2	naľʲə̂č	kodə̂šə̂č
s3	naľʲe	kodə̂š
p1	naľʲna	kodə̂šna
p2	naľʲda	kodə̂šta
p3	naľʲə̂č	kodə̂št
Second past		
s1	nalə̂nam	kodenam
s2	nalə̂nat	kodenat
s3	nalə̂n	koden
p1	nalə̂nna	kodenna
p2	nalə̂nda	kodenda
p3	nalə̂nə̂t	kodenə̂t
Desiderative		
s1	nalnem	kodə̂nem
s2	nalnet	kodə̂net
s3	nalneže	kodə̂neže
p1	nalnena	kodə̂nena
p2	nalneda	kodə̂neda
p3	nalnešt	kodə̂nešt
Imperative		
s2	nal	kodo
p2	nalza	kodə̂za
s3	nalže	kodə̂žo
p3	nalə̂št	kodə̂št

gerund occurs alone. This reflects the fact that these forms (e.g. *nalə̂n*, *koden*) were originally nominal predicates in which the present-tense copula is zero.

The third person plural imperative is the only finite verb form which is homophonous in both conjugations. In the main, the *am* conjugation is characterized by the occurrence of consonant stems and reduced vowel, the *em* conjugation by vowel stems, both full and reduced. The axis-of-discourse personal endings coincide with the person markers which are attached to nouns. The third-person endings of the indicative paradigms differ from those seen in the noun, having developed from verbal nouns or tense stems.

The primary auxiliary verbs *ulam* 'is' and *lijam* 'becomes' have slightly divergent paradigms and functions. Both are conjugated as regular *am* verbs (but note the *u ~ ə̂* metaphony in the first past of *ulam*), and there is also a special s3 present form *ulo* used in existential/local and possessive constructions, and a special nominal form *ulmaš* used for the s3 in the second past. The two verbs are interchangeable in many contexts, but the present of *lijam* often refers to the future and sometimes expresses change. Besides their use in the present tense, *ulam* functions chiefly as an auxiliary and *lijam* chiefly as an independent verb, but there are deviations in various dialects. The 'regular' s3 present-tense form *uleš* is textually quite rare (Kangasmaa-Minn 1969b: 7). The simple (finite) forms of *ulam* and *lijam* are set out in Table 7.6.

Another auxiliary is the negative verb *o-*, which has a defective and heterogeneous paradigm. In the present tense it has the present-tense marker *-k* (~ *-g-*) and conjugates like an *am* verb; in the first past its stem is *ə̂-* (~ zero) and it conjugates like an *em* verb. The negative second past is a compound form, consisting of the gerund plus forms built from the present-tense of the negative verb plus the *ə̂l* variant of the verb 'is'. The negative verb never stands alone but always together with the connegative of the main (lexical) verb. The connegative is always homophonous with the s2 imperative. The negative counterpart of *ulo* 'exists, *il y a*' is *uke*, a noun of perhaps Turkic origin which meant something like 'non-existence'; this form also functions as a sentence-substitute in the answer 'no'.

There is no formal category of passive voice in Mari. Passive meaning is achieved by means of syntactic constructions and certain derivational elements.

Non-finite forms. Verbal nouns play an important role in Mari sentence structure. They are formed with various derivational suffixes, often combined with case endings. Actually their status as members of the verb paradigm is

Table 7.6   Eastern Mari primary auxiliaries *ulam* 'is' and *lijam* 'is, becomes'

	Present	First past	Second past	Desiderative	Imperative
s1	ulam, lijam	ə̂lʲə̂m, lijə̂m	ulə̂nam, lijə̂nam	ulnem, lijnem	—
s2	ulat, lijat	ə̂lʲə̂č, lijə̂č	ulə̂nat, lijə̂nat	ulnet, lijnet	—, li
s3	ulo, liješ	ə̂lʲə̂, lije	ulmaš, lijə̂n	ulneže, lijneže	—, liže
p1	ulna, lijə̂na	ə̂lʲna, lijna	ulə̂nna, lijə̂nna	ulnena, lijnena	—
p2	ulda, lijə̂da	ə̂lʲda, lijda	ulə̂nda, lijə̂nda	ulneda, lijneda	—, liza
p3	ulə̂t, lijə̂t	ə̂lʲə̂č, lijə̂č	ulə̂nə̂t, lijə̂nə̂t	ulnešt, lijnešt	—, lizə̂št

Table 7.7   Eastern Mari negative verb

	Present	First past	Second past	Desiderative	Imperative (= prohibitive)
s1	o(gə̂)m + C	(ə̂)šə̂m + C	G + omə̂l	ə̂nem + C	—
s2	o(gə̂)t + C	(ə̂)šə̂č + C	G + otə̂l	ə̂net + C	it + C
s3	ok ~ ogeš + C	ə̂š + C	G + ogə̂l	ə̂než + C	ə̂nže + C
p1	o(gə̂)na + C	ə̂šna + C	G + onal	ə̂nena + C	—
p2	o(gə̂)da + C	ə̂šta + C	G + odal	ə̂neda + C	ida + C
p3	ogə̂t + C	ə̂št + C	G + ogə̂tə̂l	ə̂nešt + C	ə̂nə̂št + C

Note: C = connegative; G = gerund.

dependent on their syntactic roles, since most non-finite verb forms may also occur as ordinary deverbal nominal derivatives.

Verbal nouns represent embedded sentences and as such may take their own arguments, both objects and adverbials. The verbal noun is fitted to the structure of the matrix sentence and occurs as a noun dependent on the governing (matrix) verb. The number of forms belonging to this category varies from dialect to dialect; EM recognizes two infinitives, four participles, and five gerunds. These are:

1a Infinitive =*aš*: *kodaš* 'to leave', *nalaš* 'to take'. This form is homophonous in the two conjugations. It is therefore unfortunate that it is the citation form, since the conjugation must then be given separately.
1b Necessive infinitive =*man*: *kodə̂man* 'must leave', *nalman* 'must take'.
2a Active participle =*šə̂*: *kodə̂šo* 'leaver', *nalše* 'taker'.
2b Passive participle =*mə̂*: *kodə̂mo* 'left; act of leaving', *nalme* 'taken; act of taking'.
2c Future participle =*šaš*: *kodə̂šaš* 'which must be left', *nalšaš* 'which must be taken'.
2d Negative participle =*də̂mə̂*: *kodə̂də̂mo* 'not left', *naldə̂me* 'not taken'.
3a Affirmative gerund –*n*: *koden* 'leaving', *nalə̂n* 'taking'.
3b Negative gerund =*de*: *kodə̂de* 'without leaving', *nalde* 'without taking'.
3c Simultaneous gerund =*šə̂-la*: *kodə̂šə̂la* 'while leaving', *nalšə̂la* 'while taking'.
3d Anterior gerund =*mek(ə̂)*: *kodə̂meke* 'having left', *nalmeke* 'having taken'.
3e Posterior gerund =*meške*: *kodə̂meške* 'until leaving', *nalmeške* 'until taking'.

The morphological makeup of many of these non-finite forms is fairly transparent, and still other deverbal nouns might be invoked as members of this category, e.g. *naldə̂mašə̂n* 'without taking' might be analysed as the stem 'takes' plus a string of semi-productive nominalizers *(mə̂, =aš)* and case suffix variants (caritive, genitive).

Derivation
Derivational suffixes serve to make new words from words already existing in the language. Some suffixes attach only to nominal stems, others only to verb stems, but the greatest number attaches to both. Derivation may remain within a part-of-speech category (noun > noun, verb > verb) or cross from one category into another (noun > adjective, noun > verb, verb > noun, etc.).

We may thus distinguish six types of derivational suffix according to the parts of speech before and after the derivational process (N = nominal):

1   N/V > N, e.g. *=mə̂* in *pükšer=me* HAZEL=mə̂ 'hazel bush' and *palə̂=me* KNOWS=mə̂ 'known';
2   N > N, e.g. *lə̂* in *lüm=lö* NAME=lə̂ 'famous';
3   V > N, e.g. *=em* in *kuč=em* SEIZES=em 'handle';
4   N/V > V, e.g. *üšt=al-* BELT=al- 'puts a belt on X', *mur=al-* SINGS=al- 'hums a tune';
5   N > V, e.g. *joškar=gə̂-* RED=gə̂- 'becomes red';
6   V > V, e.g. *kalas=kalə̂-* TALKS=kalə̂- 'chats'.

Derivational suffixes which do not alter the grammatical status of a word have instead a modifying influence. Modifying nominal meanings include collectives, abstracts, and diminutives, e.g. *pükš* 'hazelnut' plus *=er* > *pükš=er* 'hazel (tree)', *šoŋgo* 'old' plus *=lâk* > *šoŋgə̂=lâk* 'old age'. Modifiers within the verb category indicate the Aktionsart, or quality of the event, producing frequentative, momentaneous, or durative derivates, e.g. *pu-* 'gives' plus *=edə̂* > *pu=edə̂* 'distributes', *kuštə̂-* 'dances' plus *=altə̂-* > *kušt=altə̂-* 'dances (once)'. As types (1) and (4) above illustrate, the same suffix may operate as both modifier within a category and transformer from one category to another.

Noun-forming Suffixes
The textually most frequent noun-forming suffixes have already been listed in connection with the non-finite verb. All also form nouns from nominal stems, at least to a degree:

=aš as an infinitive suffix enjoys 100 per cent productivity. It also occurs in combination with other suffixes, e.g. **=šə̂=aš > =šaš* (future participle) and **mə̂=aš > =maš*, the *nomen actionis*: *nal=maš* 'the act of taking'. It is productive and thus lexically frequent added to nouns, e.g. *parnʲa* 'finger' > *parnʲaš* 'thimble', *šorə̂k* 'sheep' > *šorə̂kaš* 'lamb', *tə̂lze* 'moon, month' > *tə̂lzaš* 'one month long'.
=šə̂ added to verb stems forms the active participle (see above). The same (or

a homophonous) suffix occurs (with an *-m-* element) in the formation of
ordinal numerals, e.g. *n∂l* 'four' > *n∂l∂mše* 'fourth'.
=*m∂* added to verbs makes passive participles and names of actions.
Occasional denominal derivates are found referring to individuals within
a collective, e.g. *pükšerme* 'hazel bush'.
=*∂š* forms nouns from both nominal and verb stems, e.g. *kut* 'long', *kut∂š*
'length', *peled-* 'blooms', *peled=∂š* 'flower'.

Among derivational suffixes which operate only within the nominal
category are those which form adjectives from nouns or vice versa. The most
productive of the former type is =*an*, e.g. *lüm* 'name' > *lüm=an* 'having X
name', *jük* 'voice' > *jük=an* 'loud'. Another productive adjective-formant is
=*l∂*, originally borrowed from Chuvash together with its stem, e.g. *tamle*
'sweet' (cf. *tam* 'taste'), but now productive with native words as well, e.g.
lüm=lö 'famous'. The suffix =*s∂* is unusual in that it can be added to adverbs
or nouns which are already inflected for case. It thus may render the
equivalents of spatial and temporal subordinate clauses, e.g. *wüd-∂št∂=sö* 'the
one which is in the water'; there is no parallel in Mordva. Purely denominal
suffixes which form nouns from adjectives are rarer, but there is non-
productive =*t* (e.g. *kelge* 'deep', *kelg∂=t* 'depth'); compare the =*∂š* mentioned just above, and the weakly productive =*er*, which forms collectives
and phytonyms (see p. 233), may be seen in a formation such as *t∂g∂d=er*
'shrub' (*t∂g∂de* 'small, delicate') or the neologism *tošter* 'museum' (*tošto*
'old').

Collective-forming suffixes, in particular, abound, and may even be used
in combination, e.g. *kož* 'spruce' > *kož=er* 'spruce grove', *kož=la*, *kož=er=la*
'forest', similarly *pünčö* 'pine', > *pünč=er* 'pine grove' > *pünč=er=la* 'pine
forest'; this =*la* is historically identical with the pluralizer mentioned above,
p. 228.

There are also a few adjective-to-adjective derivations. These may have a
syntactic function, e.g. =*(g)e*, which forms predicatives from colour words,
e.g. *sar* 'yellow', *sar=e* 'yellow (pred)', *joškar* 'red (attrib)', *joškar=ge* 'red
(pred)' as in *sar saska*, *joškar saska* 'yellow flower(s), red flower(s)' and
saska sare, *joškarge* 'flowers are yellow and red', or they merely mitigate
semantically, e.g. =*alge* in *kande* 'blue' > *kand=alge* 'blueish', and =*rak* in
joškar=g∂=rak 'reddish'.

Verb-forming Suffixes
Most verb-forming suffixes belong unswervingly to one of the two conjugations; deverbal verb formation may therefore entail a switch from one
conjugation to another, e.g. the *em*-conjugation verb *tügan∂-* 'wears out
(intr)' becomes an *am*-conjugation verb when mitigating/momentaneous =*al-*
is added: *tügan=al-* 'wears out a little'. There are in fact about a dozen verb
pairs of which the transitive member belongs to the *em*-conjugation and its

intransitive counterpart belongs to the *am*-conjugation, e.g. *kod-em* 'I leave (tr)', *kod-am* 'I remain', *woz-em* 'I drop, let fall', *woz-am* 'I fall'. The origin of this duality is uncertain, and the degree to which it might reflect an ancient distinction is highly controversial. Whatever its pedigree, it is also seen in some deverbal derivational suffixes, e.g. reflexive/passive-forming =*alt-*, which produces *am*-conjugation verbs like *šarn=alt-eš* 'is remembered, comes to mind', and momentaneous-forming =*altә-*, which produces *em*-conjugation verbs like *šarn=alt-a* '(s)he remembers it, calls it to mind, mentions it'. Whatever the original difference between the two conjugations, it is not to be sought in transitivity alone, for there is ample counter-evidence, e.g. *kol-am* 'I hear' and *kol-em* 'I die'.

Among suffixes which form verbs from both nominal and verbs are:

=*tә-* (=*dә-* to the right of nasals). This forms factitives from nominals, e.g. *lüm* 'name' plus =*dә-* > *lüm=dә-* 'names', *joškar* 'red' plus =*tә-* > *joškar=tә-* 'makes X red'. As a deverbal suffix it changes intransitive and reflexive verbs into transitive ones, and builds causatives, e.g. *pur-* 'enters' > *pur=tә-* 'lets in'. It is extremely common to the right of the productive translative denominal verb suffix =*em-*, e.g. *poro* 'good' > *por=em-* 'becomes better' > *por=em=dә-* 'cajoles, wins over (earlier: heals)'.

=*әktә-* also makes factitives from nominals, e.g. *kәlme* cold' > *kәlmә=ktә-* 'makes X cold'. As a deverbal suffix it builds causatives, e.g. *šoč-* 'is born' > *šoč=әktә-* 'gives birth to X', *kuә-* 'weaves' > *ku=әktә-* 'makes X weave'.

=*al-* builds denominal instructives, e.g. *upša* 'cap' > *upš=al-* 'puts on cap' (> *upš=al-tә-* 'puts cap on X'). Used deverbally this suffix has a diminutive, hypocoristic meaning. In keeping with this type of affect, it may occur reduplicated, e.g. *murә-* 'sings' > *mur=al-*, *mur=al=al-* 'hums to oneself, sings a little'.

Suffixes which create verbs exclusively from nominals are many, but most are no longer productive. The chief productive suffixes are:

=*em-*, mentioned above in connection with =*tә-* (~ =*dә-*), e.g. *molo* 'other' > *mol=em-* 'changes (intr)';

=*lanә-*, as in *kokte=lanә-* 'doubts, is of two minds', from *kok(tә=)* 'two, dual', cf. *koktәte* 'in twain';

=*aŋ-*, as in *pu=aŋ-* 'grows stiff/numb', from *pu* 'wood, tree', *kumd=aŋ-* 'widens (intr)', from *kumda* 'wide'.

There is also a non-productive =*gә-* (~ =*kә-*), which may be related historically with =*aŋ-*, e.g. *kudәr* 'curl(s)' > *kudәr=gә-* 'becomes curly'. The formation of a verb such as *šuldәraŋ-* 'becomes wingèd' (*šuldәr* 'wing', *šuldə̂r=an* 'wingèd') is not entirely clear: is the *ŋ* at the end of this stem a variant of *=aŋ-* and/or *=gə̂-* ?

Among the suffixes which create verbs exclusively from nominals, reflexive/passive-forming *=alt-* and momentaneous-forming *=altə̂-* were mentioned above. To these we may add the still somewhat productive *=(e)št(ə̂)-*. Note the conjugational ambiguity; it is difficult to determine whether we are dealing here with one suffix or two, since the meaning is sometimes frequentative, e.g. *ruə̂-* 'chops; fells (trees)' > *ru=ešt-* 'chops repeatedly' and sometimes (though less often) momentaneous, e.g. *törg-* 'jumps' > *tör=štə̂-* 'jumps once/suddenly'. Numerous frequentatives are built with the no longer productive suffix *=edə̂-*, e.g. *nal=edə̂-* 'keeps taking' (from *nal-* 'takes'); the meaning of these derivates, as with frequentatives generally, is often connected with multiple object complements, e.g. *puə̂-* 'gives' > *pu=edə̂-* 'gives to many, distributes'.

Enclitics
If we restrict to the class of clitics only those elements which lack any grammatical or semantic implications, we are left with very few examples. Only *--at* and *--ak* qualify; the former is especially frequent. Examples: *iktə̂t jeŋ--at uke* 'there is not even one person', *tudə̂-m--ak užə̂m* PRO.s3-acc--enc SEES.s1past1 'It was (s)he that I saw'. The enclitics act as emphasizers and can be attached to verbs as well as to nominals, e.g. *kol=en--at kolt-ə̂nə̂t* DIES=ger--enc FINISHES-p3past2 'they certainly did die'.

A few case suffixes, e.g. comitative *-ge* and modal *-la*, occasionally function as enclitics, and the comparative/adjective-formant *=rak* may also behave in this way. The temporal/modal conjunction *gə̂n* (~ *kə̂n*) 'if, when; (evidential)' hovers between being an enclitic and an independent word.

Syntax
A great many gaps in the morphological system of Mari are conspicuously smoothed over with the help of syntactic constructions. It is therefore difficult, and perhaps counterproductive, to keep the two categories strictly apart. The problem is clear from both the nominal and verbal side.

Noun Phrases
Noun phrases consist of a single noun, optionally preceded by another noun or by an attributive phrase (see p. 237). The noun may also be followed by a postposition; this construction is treated in the next section.

Postpositional Phrases
These consist of a noun or pronoun followed by a postposition. Postpositions are nouns with local meanings and defective paradigms, the forms often being built with non-productive case suffixes. The postpositional phrase has the syntactic function of a case, the adjunct noun acting as a stem and the

postposition (local noun) acting as a case ending. Adjunct nouns – which could more accurately be termed conjuncts – normally stand in the nominative, even if they refer to animates; pronouns are in the genitive. Examples: *jeŋ-že-wlak kokla-šte* PERSON-s3-plur INTERSTICE-ine 'among the people', *tudȘ-n nergen* PRO.s3-gen ABOUT 'about him/her/it'. The textually most frequent postpositions, *gȘč* and the various forms *den(e)*, *deč*, *deran*, *dek(e)* – all fossilized inflections of a noun *ter, which survives as an independent word *tür* 'edge, border' – were presented in the morphology section, p. 227 (Kangasmaa-Minn 1966: 38).

Attributive Phrases
These may be simple, i.e. consist simply of a noun head preceded by an adjective (*lümlö jeŋ* 'famous person') or by an adjective which is itself modified by an adverb (*peš lümlö jeŋ* 'a very famous person'). Adjectival attributes are not declined; there is often no difference between a noun and an adjectival attribute, e.g. in *mari kalȘk* 'Mari people' *mari* designates both individual ('a Mari') and quality ('pertaining to Mari').

As indicated in Morphology, p. 226 the genitive is used to mark the animate owner in possessive constructions. The possession is then usually, but not necessarily, marked with the appropriate person marker: *kugȘža-n üdȘr(-žö)* 'the Tsar's daughter'. An inanimate noun adjunct appears in the nominative, and there is no marking on the head noun (*kurȘk jol* HILL FOOT 'foot of the hill'). Animate noun adjuncts also occur in the nominative, and the use of the genitive to mark inanimate noun adjuncts has begun to spread in the present-day language, but the original distinction is still discernible (Kangasmaa-Minn 1966: 255).

Attributive phrases may also be complex, i.e. consist of two or more noun phrases joined. For example, the two noun phrases *mari kalȘk* 'Mari people' and *lümlö jeŋ* 'famous person' may be joined by placing the head of the first, or subordinate, noun phrase in the genitive and attaching the third-person singular suffix to the head of the second phrase, viz. *mari kalȘk-Șn lümlö jeŋ-že* 'a famous person of the Mari people'. Attributive and postpositional phrases can co-occur: *Mari kalȘk-Șn lümlö jeŋ-že-wlak kokla-šte* 'among the famous persons of the Mari people'.

Comparative and Superlative Phrases
The comparative phrase is special in that in it the adjunct noun is in a local case: the bested member of the comparison stands in one of the source cases, separative *-deč* or ablative *-leč*, depending on dialect. The adjective which expresses the quality by which the comparison is made may take the suffix *=rak*, but is just as often unmarked. The literary language favours *-deč*; an example is therefore *waštar kue-deč kugu(=rak)* MAPLE BIRCH-sep BIG(=cfv) 'the maple is taller than the birch'.

The superlative is usually formed with *en*, a loan from Tatar: *en alama* 'worst' (*alama* 'bad').

Verb Phrases
These contain a finite verb form in connection with another verb form, either finite or non-finite.

Compound Tense Forms
The finite verb paradigm is augmented by two types of compound verb forms. One type, built with the negative verb, was presented in the section on morphology. In this section we turn to the other type, namely compound tenses built with the auxiliary *ul-* 'is'.

There are four compound tenses, the first and second imperfect and the first and second perfect. All four tenses refer to the past. These four tenses are the products of combining the present and second-past forms of the main verb with the first and second past-tense forms of the auxiliary:

		Auxiliary verb	
		Past 1	Past 2
Main verb	Present	Imperfect 1	Imperfect 2
	Past 2	Perfect 1	Perfect 2

Both the imperfects translate in the same way, e.g. imperfect 1 *kodǝm ǝlʲe*, imperfect 2 *kodǝm ulmaš* are both English 'I was leaving'. The functional difference between the two constructions parallels the formal difference: first v. second past in the auxiliary. The use of these two tenses is the same as the use of the first and second past in general, i.e. they are more or less interchangeable, but the first past refers especially to events the speaker has personally experienced. The same is true of the two perfect tenses: *koden ǝlʲe* (perfect 1) and *koden ulmaš* (perfect 2) both translate as '(s)he had been leaving', and the choice of the auxiliary is more or less a pragmatic one.

The Mari compound tenses are built on two subsequent predications, as are the corresponding categories in other languages. But in Mari there are formally two kinds of compound tense, built on two different principles. In the first, person-marking occurs on the auxiliary. Recall that the second past is itself a complex tense, at least historically: it consists of the main verb in the gerund plus the present-tense personal forms of the verb 'is', *ul-*. In some dialects the ingredients are still synchronically transparent in the plural, e.g. *nalǝn ulna* corresponding to literary *nalǝnna*, both 'we have taken'.

The periphrastic imperfects and perfects are built on the reverse principle, i.e. person-marking occurs on the main verb, not on the auxiliary. The main finite verb, on which are encoded person and tense, is the underlying predication, while the auxiliary merely relates the event to a point in time, that is to the past.

The negative periphrastic imperfects and perfects are a sequence of three verbs: person is marked on the negative verb, time (present or second past) is marked on another verb – these two taken together form the lower predication – and the third verb, the auxiliary, stands for the upper predication and relates the verb process to present or past, e.g. first imperfect *ok kodo ə́lʲe* NEG.VERB-s3(pres) LEAVES-conneg IS-(s3)past '(s)he was not leaving', second perfect *nal=ə́n o-na-l ul=maš* TAKES=ger NEG.VERB-p1past(2) IS=*nomen.actionis* 'we had not been taking'. The same system operates in the desiderative mood, e.g. second imperfect desiderative *kodə́-ne-da ul=maš* 'you (plur) would like to be leaving', negative first imperfect desiderative *ə́-ne-ž nal ə́lʲe* '(s)he would not like to be taking'. The desiderative lacks periphrastic perfects.

Indicative periphrastic perfects and imperfects sometimes have decidedly moralizing overtones, e.g. second imperfective *nalə́nam ulmaš* 'I should have been taking' (Kangasmaa-Minn 1976).

Adverbial Complements and Converbs
Verb phrases consisting of a finite verb together with a verbal nominal may be divided into several subgroups according to both the nominal form used and to the inner cohesion of the construction.

The infinitive in =*aš* is found in causal contexts; the finite verb usually designates locomotion or change, e.g. *mal=aš woz-eš* SLEEPS-inf DESCENDS-s3pres 'goes to bed', *kol kuč=aš kaj-a* FISH SEIZES-inf GOES-s3pres '(s)he goes to catch fish'. The infinitive also serves as complement to a few modal verbs such as *töčə́-* 'tries', *tüŋal-* 'begins', *lij-* 'becomes, is permitted', *kül-* 'is necessary', e.g. *kol kuč=aš töč-a* '(s)he tries to catch fish', *mur=aš kušt=aš tüŋal-enət* 'they began to sing (and) dance', *nal=aš lij-eš?* 'Is it permitted to take (this)?', *mündə́r mod=aš kaj=aš o-g-ə́t küštö* FAR PLAYS-inf GOES-inf NEG.VERB-pres-p3 COMMANDS-conneg 'they don't allow one (me, us) to go far to play', *tudə́-m tunə́kt=aš kül-eš* PRO.s3-acc TEACHES-inf IS.NECESSARY-s3pres '(s)he must be taught'.

The gerund in =*n* is widely used in verb phrases. It is the usual form of the verb complement with a variety of verbs having vague semantic content such as *moštə́-* 'is able', *ončə́-* 'looks, tries', *kert-* 'is able' as in *mo-m ə́šte=n mošt-et* WHAT?-acc DOES=ger IS.ABLE-s2pres 'what can you do?', *ojle=n onč-a* '(s)he tries to speak', *tudə́-m ə́šte=n kert-am* 'I can do that'.

But the most important function of the *n*-gerund is its uses in converb constructions. These consist of one or more gerunds followed by a finite verb form; the semantic core of the construction may reside in a converb, in the finite verb, or in both. The following more common types may be distinguished:

1   The event indicated by the gerund is simultaneous with that of the finite verb, e.g. *oksa mure=n tol-eš ta šüške=n kaj-a* MONEY SINGS=ger COMES-s3pres AND WHISTLES=ger GOES-s3pres 'money comes singing and goes whistling'.

2   The event indicated by the gerund occurs before that of the finite verb, e.g. *nuno male=n kə̂nʲel-ə̂t* 'after sleeping, they get up'. Note that the order of the gerunds need not necessarily match the order of events, e.g. *maska kaza-m kuče=n tol-ə̂n kaj-a* BEAR GOAT-acc SEIZES=ger COMES=ger GOES-s3pres 'the bear comes, catches the goat, and goes'.

3   The converb construction may convey aspectual information about the event, stressing its duration or its punctuality. In such cases the semantic content is borne by the gerund, while the aspect is specified by the lexical choice of the finite verb. Verbs used for this purpose are somewhat colourless and simple in meaning, and their number is limited – there may be as many as forty. Imperfective, continuous action is conveyed by finite verbs such as *šogə̂- 'stands'*, e.g. *ojə̂rtemaltše wer-ə̂m nal=ə̂n šog-a* DISTINGUISHED PLACE-accusative TAKES=ger STANDS-s3pres 'will always have a distinguished place'. Various kinds of perfective aspect are expressed by finite verbs designating actions such as beginning, finishing, finding, leaving, sending, readying, reaching, and going or coming, e.g. *kas tene ola-ške tol=ə̂n šu-eš* EVENING AT CITY-ill COMES=ger REACHES-s3pres '(s)he will arrive in town in the evening', *jöralt(=ə̂n) kaj-enə̂t ta kole=n--at kolt-enə̂t* FALLS.DOWN(=ger) GOES-p3past2 AND DIES=ger--enc SENDS-p3past2 'they fell down and died' (the bare stem of *am*-verbs, as *jöralt-* here, may function as the gerund in converb constructions) (Bartens 1979: 143–9).

Simple Sentences
In Mari, predication is based on a noun or a verb.

Noun-based Predication
Nominal predication sets two nouns against one another. The borderline between them is marked by the copula, which in the present indicative third person singular is zero; in other persons, tenses, and moods, verb forms based on both *ul-* 'is' and *lij-* 'becomes' occur. Examples: *šoŋgo ul-at* 'you are old', *kuwa šoŋgo* 'the woman is old', *kuwa šoŋgo ul=maš* 'the woman was old'. It is not the absence (zero) of the copula that makes the sentence a nominal one; the nominality lies in the fact that the copula is merely a peg on which to hang person, tense, and mood markers.

On the other hand *lij-eš* (s3pres) does occur; but *kuwa šoŋgo lij-eš* is 'the woman grows old'. This approach recognizes another, dynamic type of nominal sentence alongside the static statement 'the woman is old'. The system of two verbs 'to be' is discernible in most Finno-Ugric languages, but the functions of the two verbs have become tangled; in Mari, too, they are not clearly differentiated, and there is much dialectal variation. In fact, *lij-* may be found in static sentences, as well, especially in those referring to the past; recall that standard EM has second-past forms of *lij-* in suppletion for the defective paradigm of *ul-*. On the other hand, *ul-* cannot replace *lij-* when notions of futurity or change are involved (Kangasmaa-Minn 1969b: 6).

Verb-based Predication
When built on a verb form the sentence structure presupposes the co-occurrence, actual or implied, of a noun in a local case form. There are several subtypes:

The *possessive sentence* is most akin to nominal-based predication. It is built on a verb characteristically found in localizing connections but occurring without a local adverbial. The verb most often is *ul-* 'is, exists', with its special third-person singular present indicative form *ulo* and *uke* as its negative counterpart; the verb always stands in the third person. The possessor is an animate noun in the genitive case, and the thing possessed usually has the person marker implicated by the genitive, e.g. *mənʲ ən kok üdər-em ulo* PRO.s1gen TWO DAUGHTER-s1 EXISTS.s3pres 'I have two daughters', *ergə-n imnʲə-že uke* BOY-gen HORSE-s3 NOT.EXIST.s3pres 'the boy does not have a horse', *memnan ul-maš pört-na* 'we had a house', *lud=šo-wlak-ən knʲiga-že (~ knʲi-ga-št) uke* 'the readers do not have a book'; as the last example shows, the third person singular marker (*-že*) often appears instead of the third person plural (*-št*) if the owners possess one thing together, or all of them one thing each.

A possessive relation is not necessarily static; it can involve loss and gain, as well. An animate genitive is found in constructions such as *tudə-n jümə-že šu-eš* PRO.s3-gen THIRST-s3 ARRIVES-s3pres '(s)he becomes thirsty', *nunə-n šoč-ən üdər-že* PRO.p3-gen IS.BORN-s3past2 DAUGHTER-s3 'a girl was born to them', *jeŋ-ən jom-ən oksa-že* PERSON-gen GETS.LOST-s3past2 MONEY-s3 'a (wo)man lost his/her money'.

Static possessive constructions are reminiscent of nominal-based predications inasmuch as they may occur without the verb 'is': *ergə-n imnʲə-že*, when representing a sentence, may be translated as 'the boy has a horse'. The possessor noun need not be present; the person marker, encoding the possessor, then achieves syntactic significance: *imnʲə-že ulo* '(s)he has a horse', *üdər-em uke* 'I do not have a daughter', *jüm-em šu-eš* 'I become thirsty'.

Locational predication consists of a verb and a local adverbial, usually a noun in one of the local cases or followed by a postposition. The verb may be transitive or intransitive; the occurrence of a direct object does not affect the basic locational structure of the utterance. A *static* verb presupposes an adverbial in the inessive or locative, e.g. *Mari kalək-ən lüm=lö jeŋ-že-wlak kokla-šte ... T. Jewsejew ... šog-a*, 'T. Jewsejew stands among the famous persons of the Mari people' in which *šog-a* 'stands', as a static verb, requires an adverbial in a static case form, here the postpositional phrase *jeŋ-že-wlak kokla-šte* 'among persons', with the inessive ending *-šte*. An example with a static transitive verb is *tudə-m m(ə)lande ümbal-ne kijə=kt-em* PRO.s3-acc GROUND SURFACE-at LIES=caus-s1pres 'I keep him/her lying on the ground'. As in possessive constructions, the third-person singular present indicative *ulo* may be omitted in simple statements such as *üdᵊr pörtᵊ̂-štö* 'the girl is in the house'; such constructions do not represent nominal sentences, since an adverbial modifier is present.

A *dynamic* predication requires adverbials in separative and/or in lative or illative cases, or in postpositional phrases with appropriate, i.e. goal or source, functional endings. The verb designates motion of some kind, e.g. (separative) *surt-šo gᵊ̂čᵊ̂n lekt=ᵊ̂n kajat* HOUSE-s3 FROM EXITS=ger GOES-p3pres 'they leave his house'; (lative) *kö-n ter-eš šinč-at* WHO?-gen SLEIGH-lat SITS.DOWN-s2pres 'into whose sleigh do you sit?'; (illative) *kož pügelme wol=en woz-eš ik meraŋᵊ̂n wuj-ᵊ̂škᵊ̂-žo* SPRUCE CONE DESCENDS=ger FALLS.s3pres ONE HARE-gen HEAD-ill-s3 'a spruce-cone, falling, hits a hare on the head', *me čotl-ena pušeŋgᵊ̂-m ᵊ̂lᵊ̂kšᵊ̂-š* PRO.p1 ESTEEMS.p1 TREE-acc LIVING-ill 'we consider a tree a living thing'; (illative) *wara pop memnan ergᵊ̂-lan lüm-ᵊ̂m pu-a* 'then the priest gives a name to our son'.

Complex Sentences
Apart from relatively recent borrowings Mari has few conjunctions; coordination and subordination of simple finite sentences is accordingly rare. Instead, utterances are linked together with the help of non-finite verb forms.

Nominalization
This is the process whereby a verb is converted, by derivational morphology, into one of the non-finite forms introduced above, p. 232. This non-finite verb form, together with its arguments, is then embedded into the framework of the matrix sentence, and any elements which the two sentences share are deleted. We have already met with an example of a gerund serving as a simple embedding, in which the subject is the same in both embedded and matrix sentences, viz. *oksa mur=en tol-eš* 'money comes singing', a compression of *oksa mur-a, oksa tol-eš* 'money sings, money comes'. Even a nominal sentence can be nominalized: *mᵊ̂j-ᵊ̂n mo jeŋem(-ᵊ̂m) šinčᵊ̂m-et šu-eš--gᵊ̂n* PRO.s1-gen WHAT? PERSON-s1-acc KNOWS=pass.part-s2 ARRIVES-s3pres--IF 'if you want to know what kind of person I am' shows a nominal predication (*mᵊ̂nʲ mo jeŋ* 'I am what kind of person') embedded as a direct object (-*ᵊ̂m*, optional to the right of s1 -*em*-) into the matrix sentence *šinč=ᵊ̂m-et šu-eš--gᵊ̂n* 'IF YOUR KNOWING IS WANTED >> if you want to know'.

A nominalized possessive phrase is a genitive attribute with its head; the relation is transparent since the same case – the genitive – occurs in both constructions: embedding *ergᵊ̂-n ulo imnʲᵊ̂-že* 'the boy has a horse' into *imnʲe kudal-eš* 'the horse is running' gives *ergᵊ̂-n imnʲᵊ̂-že kudal-eš* 'the boy's horse is running'.

Locational embeddings are the most complex because many functional elements may be involved: subject, object, one or more adverbials plus adjectival attributes and modal adjuncts. The subject of the embedded sentence stands in the nominative or the genitive, the object in the nominative or the accusative, and the local adverbials in the appropriate case forms. All the non-finite forms mentioned in the morphology section may occur. Examples: *kugәza ušә̂-že kaj=en šog-a* OLD.MAN MIND-s3 GOES=ger STANDS-s3pres 'the old man stands stupefied', *pәrәs už-әn maska-n kü tarwәltә̂=mә̂-m* CAT SEES-s3past2 BEAR-gen STONE MOVES=pass.part-acc 'THE CAT SAW THE BEAR'S STONE-MOVING >>> the cat saw the bear move the stone', *možә̂č tәj šinč-et mәj-әn kušan kol=šaš-em tožo* MAYBE PRO.s2 KNOWS-s2pres PRO.s1-gen WHERE? DIES=fut.part-s1 ALSO 'maybe you know where I'm going to die, as well?', *er-la pazar-ә̂š mij=dә̂=maš-la--rak lij=әn ojl=en kodo* MORNING-mod MARKET-lat GOES=car= *nomen.actionis*-mod--enc IS=ger SPEAKS=ger REMAINS-s3past1 '(S)HE REMAINED SAYING BEING SOMEHOW-WITHOUT-GOING TO MARKET NEXT-MORNING >>> '(s)he persisted in saying that (s)he would somehow not be going to market the next morning' (Kangasmaa-Minn 1969c).

Co-ordination and Subordination

Besides nominalization and embedding, Mari also uses the locational postposition *den* as a co-ordinator between equal members, as in the riddle *pire den maska waš onč-at* WOLF AT BEAR MUTUALLY LOOKS-p3pres 'the wolf and the bear look at one another'. Since the verb *onč-at* is in the third person plural we may take *den* here to be a conjunctive element. (The answer to the riddle is *törza den opsa* 'window and door').

An enclitic can sometimes link two co-ordinated clauses, e.g. *ik kana mәj čodra-š mij-ә̂šә̂m--ak peš šuko pirә̂-m už-ә̂m* ONE TIME PRO.s1 FOREST-lat/ill GOES-s1past1--enc VERY MANY WOLF-acc SEES-s1past1 'once when I went into the forest I saw many wolves'. An enclitic *--kә̂n ~ --gә̂n* added to the finite verb at the end of an utterance marks a temporal or conditional clause: *meraŋ waške ošem-eš--kә̂n, lum waške tol-eš* HARE EARLY WHITENS-s3pres–enc SNOW EARLY COMES-s3pres 'if the hare becomes white early, there will be an early snow'.

Finite relative clauses do occur in Mari; they usually refer to a determinative pronoun in the main clause, as in *kö dene il-et, tudә̂-n dečә̂n kojә̂š-ә̂m pog-et* WHO AT LIVES-s2pres, PRO.s3-gen FROM CHARACTER-acc GATHERS-s2pres 'you get your character from the person with whom you live'. This type of relative clause also appears in rather early translations, e.g. in that of the Gospel according to St Matthew, edited by J.F Wiedemann in a Hill (= Western) Mari dialect: *mar-lan kej-enet sedä ketsä jakte, kuda-že-n Noi pur=en poš-ška* MAN-dat GOES-p3past2 THAT DAY UNTIL, WHICH-s3-loc *NOAH* ENTERS-s3past2 ARK-ill 'they married (= went to man) until the day on which Noah entered the Ark'.

Lexicon

Three chronological layers are clearly discernible in the Mari lexicon. The basic vocabulary is Uralic or Finno-Ugric in origin; this is followed by a thick layer of Turkic (Tatar and Chuvash) loans; and on top are the Russian loanwords, which are the easiest to detect.

At first glance the Turkic element seems to predominate; this reflects the high lexical frequency of the Turkic loans in Mari. Words of (F)U origin, on the other hand, have been in the language longer and thus tend to have more derivates; for this reason, but also because they designate primary concepts, words of (F)U origin have a higher textual frequency in most everyday texts. The semantic fields covered by words of (F)U origin include nature, the body, primitive *genre de vie*, and basic feelings and actions.

An inventory of the word roots occurring in the text at the end of this chapter gives representative results. If we discount proper names, there are forty-five words in total. Fifteen roots of (F)U origin account for twenty-one occurrences : occurring twice are *mari* 'Mari' (an old loan from IE to FU), *ške* 'self', and *lüm* 'name', which is of Uralic pedigree; the root *lu-*, with an original meaning of 'counts', occurs three times in the text (in *lud=šo* 'reader', *lu+wit* 'fifteen', and *kok+lu* 'twenty'). The remainder occur once each: Uralic *kok* 'two', *wit* 'five', *tide* 'this', *tudo* 'that', *ilǝ-* 'lives', and *kodǝ-* 'leaves'; Finno-Ugric *ij* 'year', *šog-* 'stands', *wij* 'strength', *tüŋ* 'base', *ǝštǝ-* 'finishes, does'. Of Turkic origin (or mediation) are *ojǝr-* 'divides', *samǝrǝk* 'mostly', *šagal* 'a little', *palǝ-* 'knows', *ojlǝ-* 'speaks', *šǝmlǝ-* 'studies', *kundem* 'region', *pǝtartǝ-* 'finishes', *gǝna* 'only', *nergen* 'about, concerning', *dokan* (hypothetical/conditional sentence particle), *suap* 'reward for good deeds' and *kalǝk* 'people' (both < Tatar < Arabic), *žap* 'time' (< Chuvash < Arabic), *šot=an* 'intelligible, clear' (< Chuvash < Russian), possibly also *nal-* 'takes' and *jüla* 'way', altogether seventeen occurrences. Two of the words, *jeŋ* 'person' and *woz-* 'writes', cannot be assigned a sure etymological classification. Only the sentence particles *a* and *wet*, used together in the transitional collocation *a wet* 'anyway', and the pan-European *kultur* are direct Russian loans.

Even more striking evidence of strong Turkic influence is provided by the morphology. Of Turkic origin is the moderative/comparative suffix/enclitic *--rak*, as are (perhaps) the pluralizer *-wlak* and the modal suffix *-la*. There are also a number of derivational suffixes which Mari shares with Chuvash and/or Tatar. These originally entered Mari along with the roots to which they were attached, but were then abstracted and functionalized, becoming parts of the Mari derivational machinery. According to the degree to which these morphemes have been freed from their Turkic roots they may be classified into two broad types: those that appear only in words of Turkic origin and those that occur attached to native roots as well. Only the latter qualify as borrowed suffixes in the strict sense; among them are the *=le ~ =lö ~ =lo* , as in *lüm=lö* 'famous' which originally occurred only in Chuvash loans such as in the above-mentioned *tam=le* 'sweet'. Borrowed suffixes often are connected more loosely with the stem than their native counterparts, cf. *-wlak*, *=sǝ*, *--rak* and the abstract suffix *=lǝk* (from Chuvash), which can be added even to finite verb forms, e.g. *kül-eš=lə̂k* 'necessity' (*kül-eš* 'it is necessary', a third person singular present-tense form). Among borrowed verb-forming suffixes is the iterative *=kalə̂-*, originally occurring only in Chuvash borrowings, e.g. *jamdə̂l=kalə̂-* 'prepares repeatedly', but available now for (F)U roots, as well: *lüj=kalə̂-* 'shoots repeatedly' from *lüjə̂-* 'shoots'.

Canonic Shapes for Non-borrowed Vocabulary

Compared with its putative original structure, the inherited Uralic and Finno-Ugric lexical stock of Mari is well worn. Original I-stems and most A-stems have lost their final vowel, e.g. *lüm* 'name' < *nime, cf. Erzya Mordva *lʲem*, Finnish *nimi*; *kok* 'two' < *kakta < *käktä, cf. Mordva *kavto*, Finnish *kahte-*; *kol* 'fish' < *kala, cf. Mordva *kal*, Finnish *kala*. Some original A-stems which had a rounded vowel in the first syllable have preserved their final vowel, e.g. *kudo* '(summer) cooking-house' < *kota, cf. Mordva *kudo*, Finnish *kota* 'Saami tent', (Northern) Saami *goahti* 'tent'; *lümö* 'glue' < *δʲümä, cf. Finnish *tymä*; *šiže* 'autumn' < pFU *s⁽ʲ⁾üksʲV, cf. Erzya Mordva *sʲoksʲ*, Finnish *syksy*, Saami *čakča*.

On the other hand, Mari has preserved Uralic consonant oppositions fairly well. The most characteristic changes are the following: (1) intervocalic *-k- has gone to *-j* or zero, e.g. *ij*, WM *i* 'year', cf. Finnish *ikä* 'age', Saami *jahki* 'year'; (2) there is no clear evidence of original geminates *-pp- *-tt- *-kk-; (3) the s(h)ibilants *s *sʲ *š have all regularly fallen together into *s*, save in certain positions in certain eastern dialects; (4) stops and sibilants have become voiced in voiced environments.

Many Turkic loanwords have taken on canonic shapes in Mari; for example, word-initial voiced stops and sibilants have become voiceless, as in Far Eastern *pagə̂t* 'time', from Tatar *bayə̂t*. The voiceless velar fricative *x*, more or less at home in WM (*xala* 'town', from Chuvash), was lost in such older loans into EM (*ola* 'town, city'), but has entered with Russianisms such as *xarakteristika*, which also has Russian stress.

Chuvash loanwords have been responsible for the reintroduction of *s* and the high frequency of *l* and *r*, even in clusters: *jorlo* 'lazy', *sorla* 'sickle', but these are features which are not unknown in native vocabulary, as well. Because of structural parallels between Uralic and Turkic, foreign influence is not always easy to ascertain. Russian elements on the other hand are very easily recognized. Russian loanwords refer to technical and political concepts and they are usually pronounced as strictly in accordance with Russian phonology as possible. Despite the rich resources within Mari to coin new vocabulary, for political reasons most twentieth-century neologisms have been Russian, often down to the last suffix; thus for example 'railway station' is *železobetonnə̂j sooružěnij*, defined in a Mari–Russian dictionary (Asylbaev 1956: 116) as 'železobetonnə̂j sooružěnij'.

Literary Eastern Mari Text

From *Kugarnʲa*, 31 January 1992.

A: text in phonological transcription, segmented; B: morpheme-by-morpheme gloss; C: close English translation; D: free English translation.

adj = 'adjective-forming suffix'; =vb = 'verb-forming suffix'; =nom = 'nominal-forming suffix'

A1.marij	kalâk-ân	lüm=lö	jeŋ-že-wlak	kok=la-šte
B1.Mari	PEOPLE-gen	NAME=adj	PERSON-s3-plur	TWO-=nom-ine
C1.Mari	people's	famous	persons	among

Morko	kundem=âse	Az+jal		marij
(toponym)	REGION=adj	(toponym)+VILLAGE		MARI
Morko	region's	Azjal		Mari

ške	šot=an	ojâr=t=em=alt-še	wer-âm	nal=ân
SELF	SENSE=adj	DIVIDES=vb=act.part	PLACE-acc	TAKES=ger
own	clear	distinct	place	oc-

šog-a	A2. samârâk	lud=šo-wlak-lan		tide
STANDS-s3pres	B2. MOSTLY	READS=act.part-plur-dat		THIS
-copies	C2. mostly	to readers		this

lüm	šagal	palâ=me	dokan	A3. tud-ân
NAME	A.LITTLE	KNOWS=pass.part	*(hypothesis)*	B3. PRO.s3-gen
name	little	known	IT MAY BE	C3. of him

nerge-n	pât=ar=t=âš	lu+wit	kok+lu
ABOUT-loc	FINISHESvb=nom	TEN+FIVE	TWO+TEN
on the subject	last/most recent	fifteen	twenty

ij-la-šte	gâna	ojl=aš	woz=aš	tüŋ=al-ân-ât
YEAR-plur-ine	ONLY	SPEAKS-inf	WRITES-inf	BASE=vb-past2-p3
in years	only	to speak	to write	they have begun

A4. a	wet	T. Jewsejew	ške	žap-âštâ-že	kultur-âm
B4. BUT	LO	T.J.	SELF	TIME-ine-s3	CULTURE-acc
C4. In an event		T.J.	in his own time		culture

wij=an=ŋ=d=m=aš-(š)te	ilə̂=š+jüla-m
STRENGTH=adj=vb=vb=nom=nom-ine	LIVES=nom-+WAY-acc
in making strong	way of life

šə̂mlə̂=m=aš-(š)te	kugu	suap-ə̂m	ə̂št=en	kod-en
STUDIES=nom=nom-ine	BIG	BENEFIT	MAKES=ger	LEAVES-s3past2
in studying	great	benefit	he	left behind

D1. Among the famous personages of the Mari people Timofej Evseevich Evseev, from the village of Azjal in the district of Morko, stands out in his own class, taking a glorious place. To many readers this name may well be unknown. Only in the last fifteen or twenty years have people started to talk and to write about him. In any event, in his era T. Evseev had great merit in strengthening culture and studying folkways (i.e. in doing cultural and ethnographic research).

References and Further Reading

Alhoniemi, A. (1967) *Über die Funktionen der Wohin-Kasus im Tscheremissischen*, MSFOu 142, Turku: Société Finno-Ougrienne.
—— (1985) *Marin kielioppi*, Helsinki: Société Finno-Ougrienne. [*Hilfsmittel für das Stadium der finnisch-ugrischen Sprachen X*].
—— (1993) *Grammatik der tscheremissischen (Mari) Sprache*, Hamburg: Helmut Buske Verlag.
Asylbaev, A. A., et al. (1956) Марийско-русский словарь, Moscow: Gosudarstvennoe Izdateljstvo inostrannyx i nacionaljnyx slovarej.
Bartens, R. (1979) *Mordvan, tšeremissin ja votjakin infiniittisten muotojen syntaksi*, MSFOu 170, Helsinki: Société Finno-Ougrienne.
Bereczki, G. (1990) *Chrestomathia ceremissica*, Budapest: Tankönykiadó.
—— (1992) *Grundzüge der tscheremissischen Sprachgeschichte*, vol. II, Studia uralo-altaica 34, Szeged: Attila József University.
Collinder, B. (1957) *Survey of the Uralic Languages*, Stockholm: Almqvist & Wiksell.
—— (1960) *Comparative Grammar of the Uralic Languages*, Stockholm: Almqvist & Wiksell.
Galkin, I.S. (1964) Историческая грамматика марийского языка, vol. I, Yoshkar-Ola: n.p.
—— (1966) Историческая грамматика марийского языка, vol. II, Yoshkar-Ola: n.p.
Isanbaev, N.I. (1978) 'Общее и отличительное в составных глаголах марийского и поволжско-тюрских языков', Вопросы Марийского Языка, Yoshkar-Ola, pp. 59–90.
Itkonen, E. (1962) 'Beobachtungen über die Entwicklung des tscheremissischen Konjugationssytems', MSFOu 125, Helsinki: Société Finno-Ougrienne, pp. 85–125.
Ivanov, I.G. (1975) История марийского литературного языка, Yoshkar-Ola.
—— (1981) Марий диалектологий, Yoshkar-Ola.

[Kangasmaa-]Minn, E. (1956) *Studies in Cheremis*, vol. IV: *Derivation, International Journal of American Linguistics* vol. 22/2 = [Publication 2 of the Indiana Research Center in Anthropology, Folklore, and Linguistics] Indiana University Slavic and East European Series, Bloomington, Indiana University, I: vii + 99 pp.

—— (1960) 'The So-Called Past Tenses in Cheremis', in *American Studies in Uralic Linguistics*, Uralic and Altaic Series I, edited by the Indiana University Committee on Uralic Studies, Bloomington: Indiana University, pp. 93–120.

Kangasmaa-Minn, E. (1966) *The Syntactical Distribution of the Cheremis Genitive*, vol. 1, I, MSFOu 139, Turku: Société Finno-Ougrienne.

—— (1969a) *The Syntactical Distribution of the Cheremis Genitive*, vol. II, MSFOu 146, Helsinki: Société Finno-Ougrienne.

—— (1969b) 'Types of Nominal Sentence in Cheremis', *JSFOu* 70: 1–12.

—— (1969c) 'Über die Nominalisierung des Satzes im Tscheremissischen', Göttingen: *Symposion über Syntax der uralischen Sprachen*, pp. 118–28.

—— (1976) 'Les rapports temporels dans le système verbale du tschérémisse (mari)', *Études Finno-Ougriennes* 13.

Lallukka, S. (1990) *The East Finnic Minorities in the Soviet Union*, Annales Academiae Scientiarum Fennicae, series B 252, Helsinki: Finnish Academy of Sciences.

Savatkova, A. A., and Uchaev, Z. (1956) 'Краткий грамматический очерк марийского языка', pp. 793–863 in Asylbaev 1956.

Sebeok, Th. A., and Ingemann, F.J. (1961) *An Eastern Cheremis Manual*, Indiana University: Uralic and Altaic series 5, Bloomington: Indiana University.

Sebeok, Th. A., and Raun, A. (eds) (1956) *The First Cheremis Grammar (1775): A Facsimile Edition*, Chicago.

Serebrennikov, B.A. (1960) Категории времени и вида в финно-угорских языках пермской и волжской групп, Moscow.

—— (1961a) Современный марийский язык. Морфология, Yoshkar-Ola.

—— (1961b) Синтаксис сложного предложения, Yoshkar-Ola.

Wichmann, Y. (^{2}1923) *Tscheremissische Texte mit Wörterverzeichnis und grammatikalischen Abriss*, Hilfsmittel für das Studium der finnisch-ugrischen Sprachen 5, Helsinki: Société Finno-Ougrienne.

8 Permian

Timothy Riese

Much has been written about the meaning and origin of the word 'Permian'. The controversy began in the nineteenth century and to this date no one explanation has found general acceptance. Here there is space for only a very brief survey of the various theories. It is advisable to begin with the facts and then proceed to the hypotheses.

The word 'Permian' is used today to designate a subgroup of the Uralic language family which is composed of the Komi (Zyrian) and Udmurt (Votyak) languages, both spoken in the northeastern part of European Russia. It is a scholarly designation, not having been taken from the languages in question; these do not have a native expression denoting 'Komi + Udmurt' or 'Udmurt + Komi'. The word can be traced back philologically to the Russian Перемь ~ Пермь, forms which occur in medieval Russian chronicles. At first, the word was used to designate certain territories, not a people or language. The first territory in question was the area of the lower course of the Dvina River (near the present-day city of Arkhangelsk, on the White Sea), the second was the area very roughly bounded by the Urals in the east and the Pechora, Vychegda, and Kama Rivers on the north, west, and south. This latter territory was incorporated into the Russian Empire in 1478. 'Greater Perm' lay on and about the area of today's Komi Republic. The word 'Permian' (пермский) was used for the non-Russian inhabitants of this territory, for the most part Zyrians, both before and for some time after its annexation to the Russian realm. Later the Russians began to use the appellation 'Zyrian'. Since the nineteenth century 'Permian' has been in use in scholarly writing to designate not only the Zyrians, but also their close linguistic relatives, the Udmurt.

There is much evidence which points to the Russian 'Perm' being ultimately identical with the 'Bjarma-Land' of old Scandinavian sagas. This 'Bjarma-Land' can be located on the Kola Peninsula and the southern shores of the White Sea, i.e. an area approximately corresponding to the first territory called 'Perm' by the Russians. The inhabitants of this area, the 'Bjarmians', were certainly not Zyrians, but rather Karelians, who very likely had intensive trade contacts with the Zyrians farther to the east. The fabled wealth of 'Bjarma-Land' cannot have been due to the richness of the land itself, but to the trade routes running through it and connecting Scandinavia, via the upper Kama/Zyrian territory, with the Bulgarian Empire on the lower Kama and

Volga. Even if 'Perm' and 'Bjarma' are accepted as being etymologically identical, this does not solve the problem of the origin of the word. For this, several theories have been offered, the most widespread being the following three:

1   It is of Zyrian origin. The Komi word *parma* '(certain kind of) wooded mountain ridge' has been advanced in this regard.
2   It is of Baltic-Fennic origin. A hypothetical **perä+maa* 'back country, hinterland' has been much discussed.
3   It is of Scandinavian origin. Under this theory, it is regarded as cognate with Germanic *berm-, *barm- (cf. English *brim*), meaning 'border; shore'.

Of these theories the first and second still have their supporters, but the third is perhaps in the (shaky) ascendancy.

At this point it is necessary to clarify the question as to how many Permian languages there actually are. The traditional view is that there are two: Komi and Udmurt. In the Soviet Union, however, the official line spoke of three: Komi-Zyrian, Komi-Permyak, and Udmurt. The question is, therefore, whether Komi-Zyrian and Komi-Permyak constitute two separate languages or are dialects of the same language.

Since the 1920s two separate literary languages, differing from one another in no significant way, have been in use: Komi-Zyrian for the Zyrians in the Komi Republic, and Komi-Permyak for the Zyrians in the Komi-Permyak Autonomous Region to the south of the Komi Republic. The Soviet official line maintained that these two literary forms are distinct, separate languages and that the people speaking them constitute distinct, separate nationalities. Consequently, they were treated separately in censuses. The question as to whether the Komi-Permyak constitute a separate nationality or are a part of the Komi people as a whole can be answered only by the Komi-Permyak themselves. National affiliation is a subjective matter which cannot be determined by outsiders.

Linguistic affiliation, on the other hand, is objective and can be judged just as capably by non-Komi-Permyak as by the Komi-Permyak themselves. There is no doubt that dialectal differences exist between Komi-Zyrian and Komi-Permyak. These differences are, however, much smaller than the differences between the dialects of most western European languages and are by no means so large as to justify speaking of two distinct languages. The opinion that we are dealing with two separate languages has never been accepted outside the Soviet Union and presumably there would have been much more debate on this matter within the Soviet Union had citizens not had to fear the consequences of deviation from the official line.

Why, then, was a separate literary form, Komi-Permyak, created in the 1920s? Why was not the literary Zyrian language adopted for all Zyrian-speaking territories, as would have been more expedient? One reason is administrative unimaginativeness. In addition to the above-mentioned dialectal differences, the Komi-Permyak are separated from the Komi-Zyrians by a swath of Russian-populated territory and have traditionally belonged to a different administrative unit. Another reason is idealism. One must bear in mind the linguistic policy of the early years of Soviet power, a policy for the most part highly beneficial to the speakers of smaller minority languages. New literary languages were created and the opportunity of using them in education, publication, and other cultural pursuits was provided. In several cases, however, the authorities went too far and fostered the creation of two literary languages where one would have sufficed, thus splitting a nationality into two segments. It has been maintained that this was no coincidence and had the purpose of weakening minority languages *vis-à-vis* Russian (*divide et impera*), but it is not felt to be necessary to impugn the efforts of the language reformers of the 1920s, which were undoubtedly laudable to a high degree. On the other hand, there is no doubt that the existence of two literary forms for one language has served to estrange the Komi-Permyak from the Komi-Zyrians and has made the struggle of both groups for linguistic development and survival all the more difficult.

The following data are taken from various censuses conducted in the Soviet Union. It should be noted that in the censuses of the Soviet era citizens were asked to report their ethnic nationality as well as the language they considered to be their mother tongue. Due to the widespread language shift of the last few decades (usually, minority language > Russian) the reported mother tongue is very often not the language of the citizen's ethnic group, i.e. many people may feel that they are Komi or Udmurt (and not Russians, Tatars, etc.), but give their mother tongue not as Komi or Udmurt, but (in the great majority of these cases) as Russian. In the following statistics the word Zyrian is, unless otherwise indicated, used to mean Komi-Zyrian *and* Komi-Permyak.

The number of people identifying themselves as Zyrians and Votyaks has risen in every census in this century, but at a pace much slower than that of other peoples of the CIS. Indeed, the word stagnation would now seem more appropriate than growth. The growth rate of the last decade was a mere 0.2 per cent (Zyrian) and 0.5 per cent (Votyak).

Nationality affiliations:

	Zyrians	Votyaks
1939	422,300	606,300
1959	431,128	624,800
1989	496,579	746,793

Of even more interest are the linguistic data of the censuses, which purport to tell us how many people actually speak these languages. These statistics present a gloomy picture: in the past few decades the actual number of speakers has been slowly but steadily decreasing. In 1989 a total of 360,000 people declared Zyrian, and 520,000 declared Votyak, to be their mother tongue. The language-retention rate expressed in percentages of Zyrians/Votyaks with Zyrian/Votyak as their mother tongue, is particularly revealing:

	Komi-Zyrian	Komi-Permyak	Votyak
1959	89.3	87.6	89.1
1970	82.7	85.8	82.6
1979	76.2	77.1	76.4
1989	70.4	70.1	69.6

Language retention can also depend on (1) whether the Zyrians/Votyaks live in their ethnic administrative areas, (2) whether they live in a rural or urban area, and (3) sex.

1   The percentage of Komi-Zyrians living in the Komi Republic remained stable throughout the twentieth century (1926: 84.5 per cent; 1989: 84.5 per cent). Approximately two-thirds of the Komi-Permyaks still live in the Komi-Permyak Autonomous Region. The percentage of Votyaks living in the Udmurt Republic has declined somewhat (1926: 78.5 per cent; 1989: 66.5 per cent). That residence in these areas is conducive to the retention of the native language is borne out by the figures. In 1989, 74.3 per cent of the Zyrians in the Komi Republic spoke Zyrian, and 75.7 per cent of the Votyak living in their administrative region spoke Votyak, as their mother tongue. The slightly higher retention rate is due, *inter alia*, to the possibilities of using Zyrian and Votyak to some extent in education, the press, and other cultural pursuits, possibilities which are not normally available outside the republics in question.
2   Zyrians and Votyaks have traditionally been rural peoples. The language retention rate is also consistently higher among those still residing in the countryside as opposed to those who have moved to urban centres, which uniformly have an overwhelming Russian-speaking majority.
3   The number of women retaining Zyrian and Votyak as their mother tongue has always been 3 to 4 percentage points higher than that of men.

The cause for the decline in the number of Zyrian/Votyak speakers has thus not been a decrease in the numbers of Zyrians/Votyaks, but a steadily accelerating linguistic assimilation of Zyrian/Votyak > Russian. What have been the major causes of this switch-over?

1   The prestige of Russian. Russian is the language identified with modern-day society, with progress. Zyrian and Votyak on the other hand have to some extent come to be identified with a rural, antiquated way of life. A good command of Russian became imperative in the past few decades for anyone wishing to rise in Soviet society.

2   Loss of compact Zyrian/Votyak territories. While still existing, the size and numbers of areas where Zyrian/Votyak is spoken almost exclusively have been steadily shrinking. Previously, large-scale ethnic contact, intermingling, and assimilation took place only in urban areas or on the fringes of a large, relatively homogeneous Zyrian or Votyak area. Now, a much greater proportion of the Zyrian and Votyak peoples live in the 'fringe' areas, and the rural exodus affecting all peoples of the CIS has also led many Zyrian and Votyaks to (Russian-speaking) urban centres. There has also been an influx of Russians and other nationalities into traditional Zyrian and Votyak territories. This is readily evident from the percentages of Zyrians and Votyaks in the total number of inhabitants of the Komi and Udmurt Republics. Whereas in the 1920s the Zyrians and Votyaks made up about 90 per cent of the population of their respective republics, this figure has now plummeted to (1989) 23 per cent in the Komi Republic, 58 per cent in the Komi-Permyak Autonomous Region, and 30.9 per cent in the Udmurt Republic. The offspring of the now commonplace ethnically mixed marriages are overwhelmingly raised as Russian speakers.

3   Decline in the use of Zyrian/Votyak in education and the press. The decade following the Bolshevik Revolution saw a rapid upswing in the use of Zyrian and Votyak in education and print. An effort was made to provide all Zyrian and Votyak children who lived in their respective republics with the opportunity of being educated in their native tongue – if not for their complete schooling then at least for the first years of primary education. Ever since the 1950s, however, the opportunities for education in Zyrian and Votyak have been gradually whittled away, until now the great majority of Zyrian and Votyak children are educated exclusively in Russian, their native tongue being at most an optional subject. An interesting survey has shown that rural Zyrians prefer to speak Zyrian, but to read and write in Russian. It does not need to be stressed that being educated in Russian is highly conducive to linguistic assimilation. It was not until the 1920s that Zyrian and Votyak began to be used extensively in printed media. The number of books in these languages has, however, declined steeply in the past few decades. This development has also been detrimental to the fostering and development of Zyrian and Votyak.

What are the prospects now for the Permian languages? Will there still be speakers of Zyrian and Votyak fifty years hence, or will the process of assimilation result in complete Russification? It can safely be said at the present moment that the situation is serious, but not yet hopeless. The fall of the Soviet regime and the weakening of central power have brought about the possibility that the Permian peoples will be able to determine their own affairs as regards education, the press, and other cultural activities. The situation is, however, still extremely volatile, making predictions quite hazardous. It is also a question of what Permians themselves want and what efforts they are willing to make to achieve their goals. If a concentrated effort is made now, a great deal can be done to offset the weakening of the language which has set in over the recent past. If a strengthening of national consciousness were to come about, one which results in a renewal of school education in the Permian languages and a new upswing in the use of Zyrian and Votyak in the press and in local government, the future of these languages would be assured.

Proto-Permian

After the westward migration of the ancestors of the Finno-Volgaic (= western Finno-Permic) peoples, a group of Finno-Ugrians (or Finno-Permians, if we assume that Ugric had already broken away) remained in the area of the Kama and Vyatka Rivers, to the east of the Volga. It has been estimated that this separation took place about 2000 BCE. Those remaining became the ancestors of the Zyrians and Votyaks and are referred to as proto-Permians. The language they spoke is called proto-Permian (pPN). During the long pPN period the language underwent far-reaching changes involving all linguistic domains. These changes produced a separate language quite distinct from its congeners. Proto-Permian later evolved into two separate languages after the ancestors of the present-day Zyrians began migrating northwards in the eighth and ninth centuries CE. We have no written records of pPN, and all our statements about it are therefore hypothetical. Studies of pPN are based on the evidence provided by present-day Zyrian and Votyak, older written records of these languages, by other Uralic languages, and by loanwords in and from other languages, related and unrelated. Of particular interest are the Middle Bulgarian and Iranian loanwords in pPN.

The present-day Permian languages are relatively closely related. That they are related is obvious not only to linguists, but also to naïve native speakers. The areas of identity and similarity extend to all subsystems of language structure. Mutual intelligibilty over any significant stretch of discourse is, however, not possible.

Old Zyrian (OZ) and the Yaz'va Dialect of Zyrian (PO)

In the following sections of this chapter linguistic examples will be cited from both Old Zyrian and the Yaz'va dialect of Zyrian.

Old Zyrian

By 'Old Zyrian' is meant the language of the earliest texts in Zyrian. These date from the fourteenth century and are based on the Lower Vychegda (VU) dialect of that time. It does *not* mean an older stage of Zyrian from which all the modern dialects evolved.

Yaz'va Dialect

This dialect, also known as East Permian, is spoken by 3–4,000 people in the northeastern portion of the Perm' Oblast. It diverges markedly from other Zyrian dialects and is especially noteworthy in that it has preserved a number of features that have been lost elsewhere. Of particular interest are the vowel and stress systems of PO. The creation of a separate literary language would have been more justified in the case of PO than in the case of Komi-Permyak, but this was not essayed because of the small number of speakers.

Phonology

In what follows, I shall attempt a survey of the phonological structure of the Permian languages. The main emphasis will be on historical development, i.e. p[roto-]U[ralic]/p[roto-]F[inno-]U[gric] > pPN > Z[yrian] and Vo[tyak]. Only a succinct review of the most important historical processes will be provided; details lie in the literature listed.

The Consonant System

Initial Consonants
Our point of departure is, for the sake of simplicity, the consonant system of proto-FU. This system is generally accepted, while of course being hypothetical and still subject to debate.

Clearly the main difference between pFU and pPN is the appearance, in pPN, of voiced analogues for most of the pFU obstruents. About one-sixth of inherited pFU words appear with voiced initial obstruent in pPN.

The bilabial glide *w- of pFU developed into pPN labiodental v-. A new, i.e. secondary, w- arose in initial position (> *u̯ô- > wô-) in pPN from the diphthongization of the pPN vowel *ô.

Table 8.1   The pFU initial consonant system

	Labials	Dentals	Alveolars	Palatals	Palatovelars
Nasals	*m	*n̥		*nʲ	
Stops	*p	*t			*k
Affricates			*č	*cʲ	
Fricatives		*s, *δ?	*š	*sʲ, *δʲ	
Glides	*w			*j	
Liquids		*l	*r	*lʲ	

Table 8.2   The pPN initial consonant system

	Labials	Labiodentals	Dentals	Alveolars	Palatals	Palatovelars
Nasals	*m		*n		*nʲ	
Voiceless stops	*p		*t		(*tʲ)	*k
Voiced stops	*b		*d		(*dʲ)	*g
Voiceless affricates				*č	*cʲ	
Voiced affricates				*ǯ	*ɟʲ	
Voiceless fricatives			*s	*š	*sʲ	
Voiced fricatives			*z	(*ž)	*(zʲ)	
Glides	(*w)	*v			*j	
Liquids			*l	*r	*lʲ	

pFU *δʲ > pPN *lʲ (Permian offers no good evidence for initial pFU *δ).

The consonants given in brackets (w, tʲ, dʲ, ž, zʲ) are of late pPN origin and probably played only a peripheral role in the consonant system of that time.

The initial consonant system of the present-day Permian languages is almost identical with that of pPN. The Permian languages are thus quite conservative in this respect.

Secondary pPN *w- > Zyrian/Votyak v-, w-, or zero, depending on dialect.

pPN *r- > Votyak ǯ- or ɟʲ- depending on the frontness/backness of the following vowel in pre-Votyak.

Initially, tʲ-, dʲ-, ž-, and zʲ- are still among the least frequent phonemes of the Permian languages.

The following examples illustrate these three-stage developments. Unless otherwise indicated, the stages are pFU > pPN > Zyrian and Votyak.

1   pFU *p- > pPN *p-/*b- > Zyrian/Votyak p-, b-
    *piŋe 'tooth' > *piŋ > Z/Vo pinʲ
    *perä 'back part' > *bär > Z bër Vo ber

Table 8.3   The Zyrian/Votyak initial consonant system

	Labials	Labiodentals	Dentals	Alveolars	Palatals	Palatovelars
Nasals	m		n		nʲ	
Voiceless stops	p		t		tʲ	k
Voiced stops	b		d		dʲ	g
Voiceless affricates				č	cʲ	
Voiced affricates				ǯ	ɟʲ	
Voiceless fricatives			s	š	sʲ	
Voiced fricatives			z	ž	zʲ	
Glides		v			j	
Liquids			l	r	lʲ	

2 pFU *t- > pPN *t-/*d- > Zyrian/Votyak t-, d-
   *tälwä 'winter' > pPN *tOl > Z tëv Vo tol
   *tarV 'proximity' > pPN *dôr > Z dor= Vo dor

3 pFU *k- > pPN *k-/*g- > Zyrian/Votyak k-, g-
   *käte 'hand' > pPN *ki > Z/Vo ki
   *kinče 'nail, claw' > pPN *gUži > Z giž Vo giži̇̈

4 pFU *m- ≡ pPN *m- ≡ Zyrian/Votyak m-
   pFU *maɣe 'land, earth' > pPN *mu > Z/Vo mu

5 pFU *n- ≡ pPN *n- ≡ Zyrian/Votyak n-
   pFU *nejδe 'girl, daughter' > pPN *nUl > Z nïv Vo nïl

6 pFU *nʲ- ≡ pPN *nʲ ≡ Zyrian/Votyak nʲ-
   pFU *nʲële 'arrow' > pPN *nʲÔl > Z nʲëv Vo nʲël

7 pFU *č- > pPN *č-/*ǯ- > Zyrian/Votyak č-, ǯ-
   pFU *čiŋ 'fog; smoke' > pPN *čUŋ > Z/Vo čïn
   pFU *čačV '(a sort of) bed' > pPN *ǯôǯ > Z ǯoǯ 'cellar' Vo ǯïǯ+ol 'space
   under bed'

8 pFU *cʲ- > pPN *cʲ-/*ʒʲ- > Zyrian/Votyak cʲ-, ʒʲ-
   pFU *cʲäŋkV- 'breaks' > pPN *cʲêg- > Z cʲeg- Vo cʲig-
   pFU *cʲerV 'grey' > pPN *ʒʲor > Z ʒʲor Vo ʒʲar, both 'dawn'

9 pFU *w- > pPN *v- ≡ Zyrian/Votyak v-
   pFU *wete 'water' > pPN *va > Z va Vo vu
   later pPN *w- (generally) > Zyrian/Votyak v-
   pFU *oδe 'year' > early pPN *ô- > late pPN *wô- > Z vo Vo va

10 pFU *s- > pPN *s-/*z- > Zyrian/Votyak s-, z-
   pFU *soja 'arm, sleeve' > pPN *sôj > Z soj Vo suj
   pFU *sorV '(sort of) plant' > pPN *zÔr > Z zër 'oats' Vo zër 'Bromus
   secalinus'

11 pFU *š- ≡ pPN *š- ≡ Zyrian/Votyak š-
   pFU *šiŋe=re 'mouse' > pPN *šUr > Z/Vo šïr

12 pFU *sʲ ≡ pPN *sʲ- ≡ Zyrian/Votyak sʲ-
   pFU *sʲata 'hundred' > pPN *sʲô > Z sʲo Vo sʲu

13 pFU *j- ≡ pPN *j- ≡ Zyrian/Votyak j-
   pFU *jäŋe 'ice' > pPN *ji ~ *jÔ > Z ji Vo jë

14 pFU *l- ≡ pPN *l- ≡ Zyrian/Votyak l-
   pFU *luwe 'bone' > pPN *lU > Z/Vo lï

15 pFU *lʲ- ≡ pPN *lʲ- ≡ (Zyrian?)/Votyak lʲ-
   pFU *lʲekkV 'tight, narrow' > pPN *lʲôk > Vo lʲuk=ï+

16 pFU *δʲ- > pPN *lʲ- ≡ Zyrian/Votyak lʲ-
   pFU *δʲëme 'Prunus padus' > pPN *lʲÔm > Z/Vo lʲëm

17 pFU *r- ≡ pPN *r- > Zyrian r-, Votyak ǯ-, ʒʲ-
   pFU *rekkV 'mush, grits' > pPN *rôk > Z rok Vo ʒuk
   pFU *repä=cʲV 'fox' > pPN *rVpVcʲ > Z ručʲ Vo cʲicï̇

Non-initial Consonants

In the Finno-Ugric languages it is of great importance to differentiate between the development of consonants in initial and non-initial position, as these developments can differ greatly. As will be seen below, in the development of the Permian consonants the nasals and the liquids show no great difference due to position, but the obstruents (stops, affricates, and fricatives) show a strong divergence. Whereas the consonant development of p(F)U > pPN > Zyrian/Votyak is remarkably conservative with regard to initial position, in non-initial position great changes took place, drastically altering the shape of pPN words.

The stock of pFU non-initial consonants was larger than that of initial consonants. In addition to all the initial consonants treated on p. 257 the following consonants could occur in non-initial (primarily intervocalic) position: (1) *-ŋ-, *-δ-, *-γ-; (2) intervocalic geminate stops *-pp-, *-tt-, *-kk-; (3) many consonant clusters at the border between the first two syllables.

In the present-day Permian (literary) languages the stock of non-initial consonants is identical with that of the initial consonants. This state of affairs dates back to late pPN. In the following survey the intermediate stage of pPN can be omitted, as in most cases there was no major change between pPN and Zyrian/Votyak.

The following examples illustrate the development of non-initial consonants, pFU > Zyrian/Votyak.

Intervocalic position:

1 pFU *-p- > Zyrian/Votyak Ø
   pFU *kopa 'skin, bark' > pPN *ku > Z/Vo *ku*
2 pFU *-t- > Zyrian/Votyak Ø
   pFU *sʲata 'hundred' > pPN *sʲô > Z *sʲo* Vo *sʲu*
3 pFU *-k- > Zyrian/Votyak Ø
   pFU *joke 'river' > pPN *ju > Z *ju* Vo *ju+*
4 pFU *-pp- > Zyrian/Votyak -p-
   pFU *säppä 'gall (bladder)' > pPN *säp > Z *sëp* Vo *sep*
5 pFU *-tt- > Zyrian/Votyak -t- (in some words, with secondary palatalization *t* > *tʲ*)
   pFU *witte 'five' > pPN *vit > Z *vit* Vo *vitʲ*
6 pFU *-kk- > Zyrian/Votyak -k-
   pFU *rekkV 'mush, grits' > pPN *rôk > Z *rok* Vo *čuk*
7 pFU *-m- ≡ Zyrian/Votyak -m-
   pFU *sʲëme 'fish scale' > pPN *šʲÔm > Z/Vo *šʲëm*
8 pFU *-n- ≡ Zyrian/Votyak -n-
   pFU *sëne 'vein' > pPN *sÔn > Z/Vo *sën*
9 pFU *-nʲ- ≡ Zyrian/Votyak -nʲ-
   pFU *kunʲa- 'shuts eyes' > pPN *kUnʲ- > Z *kunʲ-* Vo *kïnʲ-*

10 pFU *-ŋ- ≡ pPN *-ŋ- > Zyrian -nʲ-, -n-, -m- Votyak -ŋ- -nʲ-, -n-, -m-
    (Depends on dialect and vocalic environment. In general: in front-vocalic
    surroundings *-ŋ- > -nʲ-, in back-vocalic surroundings *-ŋ- > -n- or,
    particularly in the neighbourhood of rounded vowels, > -m-. Some Votyak
    dialects retain -ŋ-.)
    pFU *piŋe 'tooth' > *piŋ > Z/Vo pinʲ
    pFU *päŋe 'head' > pPN *poŋ > Z pom/pon Vo pum/puŋ
11 pFU *-č- > Zyrian/Votyak -č-, -ǯ̌-, -š-, -ž̌-
    pFU *mučV '(sort of) illness' > pPN *mUž > Z/Vo miž̌
    pFU *kečä 'ring, circle' > pPN *kUč > Z/Vo kič̌
12 pFU *-cʲ- > Zyrian/Votyak (various sibilants or affricates)
    pFU *repä=cʲV 'fox' > Z rucʲ Vo ǯ̌icï
13 pFU *-w- > Zyrian/Votyak Ø
    pFU *luwe 'bone' > pPN *lU > Z/Vo lï
14 pFU *-δ- > Zyrian/Votyak -l-, -Ø
    pFU *sʲüδä=mV 'heart' > pPN *sʲVlVm > Z sʲëlëm Vo sʲulem
    pFU *wiδV=mV 'marrow' > pPN *vêm > Z vem Vo vim
15 pFU *-δʲ- > Zyrian/Votyak -lʲ-
    pFU *wuδʲe 'new' > pPN *vUlʲ > Z/Vo vilʲ
16 pFU *-s- > Zyrian/Votyak -z-
    pFU *pesä 'nest' > pPN *poz > Z poz 'nest' Vo puz 'egg; scrotum'
17 pFU *-sʲ- > Zyrian/Votyak -zʲ-
    pFU *kusʲV 'twenty' > pPN *kUzʲ > Z/Vo kïzʲ
18 pFU *-š- > Zyrian/Votyak -ž-
    pFU wanša 'old' > pPN *vôž > Z važ Vo vuž
19 pFU *-j- ≡ Zyrian/Votyak -j-
    pFU *woje 'adipose tissue' > pPN *vÔj > Z vïj Vo vëj
20 pFU *-γ- > Zyrian/Votyak -Ø-
    pFU *maγe 'land, earth' > pPN *mu > Z/Vo mu
21 pFU *-l- ≡ Zyrian/Votyak -l-
    pFU *kola- 'dies' > pPN *kul- > Z/Vo kul-
22 pFU *-lʲ- ≡ Zyrian/Votyak -lʲ-
    pFU *elʲV 'wet' > pPN *ulʲ > Z ulʲ Vo ilʲ
23 pFU *-r- ≡ Zyrian/Votyak -r-
    pFU *wire 'blood' > pPN *vir > Z/Vo vir

We may summarize the major developments among the non-initial
intervocalic consonants as follows: (1) the oral stops went to zero, as did *-w-
and its velar analogue *-γ-; (2) the nasals, liquids, and the palatal glide *-j-
usually remained unchanged; (3) the affricates partially lost their stop
components, sometimes acquiring voice; (4) the intervocalic fricatives
voiced, *-s- *-sʲ- *-š- > *-z- *-zʲ- *ž-; (5) the interdental fricatives merged
with the laterals, *-δ- *-δʲ- > *-l- *-lʲ-.

Consonant Clusters

Approximately seventy different consonant clusters have been reconstructed for p(F)U, with roughly an additional twenty for Finno-Permic. Although there are not always Permian reflexes for these combinations, we still have some sixty-five clusters to account for. Here I shall do no more than illustrate the developments of the main types of clusters.

Development of the clusters is of two basic types: retention or simplification. Simplification, usually the loss of one element, was much the more frequent.

1   pFU clusters of two stops: pFU *-pt- was simplified to Z/Vo -t-; *-kt- most frequently gave the alternation k ~ kt-.
    pFP *saptV=rV 'currant' > pPN *soter > Z setër Vo suter
    pFU *käktä 'two' > pPN *kUk(t-) > Z kïk Vo kïk(t-)
2   pFU stop plus sibilant: in this combination, the stop was lost in pPN.
    pFU *mekše 'bee' > pPN *môš > Z/Vo muš
    pFU *kipsV 'leg hide' > pPN *kUS > Z kïs
3   pFU sibilant or affricate plus stop: retention of the cluster is possible, but not uniform.
    pFU *musⁱke- 'washes' > pPN *mUš̯k- > Z miš̯k- Vo miš̯k-
    pFU *kusⁱka 'dry' > early pPN *kôsʲ > late pPN *kwôsʲ > Z kosʲ Vo kwasʲ
4   pFU nasal plus stop: the nasal went to zero; the stop was subsequently voiced.
    pFU *kumpa 'wave' > pPN *gUb= > Z gib= 'ripples', Vo gib=ed 'dungheap'
    pFU *lamte 'low(lands)' > pPN *lud > Z/Vo lud
    pFU *cʲäŋkV- 'breaks' > pPN *cʲêg- > Z cʲeg- Vo cʲig-
5   pFU fricative, glide, or liquid plus stop: both retention and simplification occurred, but the latter was more frequent. The fricatives *δ *δʲ and the glides *w *j disappeared more readily than the liquids, which proved to be somewhat more resilient.
    pFU *pilwe 'cloud' > pPN *pil > Z piv Vo pilʲ=em
    pFU *kertV '(sort of) wild duck' > pPN *gord=a > Z gorda Vo gurdo

Development of Consonantism after Proto-Permian

Although in various dialects a number of minor changes have taken place since the breakup of Permian unity, there has been only one change of major importance. This change involves the phoneme l which, depending on the dialect, has either (1) remained unchanged or (2) developed wholly or partly into v, w, or zero.

In Zyrian the dialects may be classified into four groups according to the development of pPN *l:

1   *l remains unchanged;
2   *l > v (or w) in all positions;
3   *l > v in non-prevocalic position within the word;
4   *l > zero in non-prevocalic position within the word; the preceding vowel
     is lengthened.

We may use variants of Common Zyrian lol 'soul; breath' and the suffixes
-tëg 'without' and -ën 'with' to illustrate these developments:

	1	2	3	4
Word-initial, Word-final	lol	vov	lov	loo
Preconsonantally	loltëg	vovtëg	lovtëg	lootëg
Intervocalically	lolën	vovën	lolën	lolën

In the Zyrian literary languages the l ~ v alternation (type 3) is the accepted
norm. In the majority of Votyak dialects as well as in the literary language l has
proven to be stable (type 1), but in some dialects (e.g. Shoshma) we find changes
and alternations similar to those seen in Zyrian (literary Votyak nïl 'girl', nïltek
'without a girl', nïlez 'girl (acc)'; Shoshma dialect nïw, nïwtek, nïwez).

The Vowel System

Vowels of the First Syllable
The development of the vowel system in the Permian languages has been the
subject of a great deal of study and of even more debate. There are few topics
more controversial within the field of Finno-Ugric linguistics than that of
vowel history, and the Permian vowels form one of the most contested parts
of the whole.

It seems to be a linguistic universal that vowels adjust to their phonological
surroundings more than do consonants and similarly, that vowels are more
susceptible to change than consonants. That consonants tend to be more stable
than vowels is well illustrated by the present-day Finno-Ugric languages, since
the differences between dialects are made up to a large part by differences in the
vowels and not by differences in the consonants. Although many problems
remain unsolved, a relatively high degree of consensus has been reached in the
field of Finno-Ugric consonant history. The major points of Permian consonant
history are similarly relatively free of controversy: research being carried out
now in this field is directed at details, not at basic questions.

With the vowels, on the other hand, the situation is quite different. While
it is possible to speak of prevailing theories in this field, nothing approaching
a consensus on consonant development has been reached. Views vary on the
reconstructed pU, pFU, and pPN vowel systems.

Scholars who work on p(F)U vowel history have made much use of the concept of 'key' languages, assuming that one or more languages have retained the original vowel system to a much greater extent than others. Whereas at one time a commonly held theory spoke of the inherent conservativeness of the East Cheremis and East Ostyak vowel systems, today most researchers are more inclined to regard the vowel system of Baltic-Fennic as having preserved better the original character of the pFU vowel system. Whether this is correct or not, this theory automatically entails not only a comparative regularity of vowel correspondences between Baltic-Fennic and Permian, but also a comparative irregularity of vowel correspondences between Permian and pFU. Such a starting point for the examination of the Permian vowels therefore makes a description of their development all the more difficult.

This chapter cannot essay a comparison, or even a survey, of the various theories regarding the diachrony of the Permian vowels. Instead, the best-known and perhaps most widely accepted theory, that connected with the names Itkonen, Lytkin, and Rédei, will be briefly presented. The order of stages will be descendent rather than ascendent, with each stage becoming more hypothetical and subject to query. We may number the stages thus: (1a) Zyrian < proto-Zyrian, (1b) Votyak < proto-Votyak; (2) proto-Zyrian and proto-Votyak < pPN; (3) pPN < pFU.

As noted above, the consonant systems of both Zyrian and Votyak (literary languages) are identical. Interestingly enough, the same is true for their vowel inventories. The seven vowel phonemes of literary Zyrian and Votyak are shown in Figure 8.1.

Of relevance here are also the dialects with divergent vowel systems. For Zyrian, these are above all Yaz'va (PO) and (to a lesser extent) Upper Sysola (SO). Old Zyrian (OZ) as attested in medieval texts also plays an important role in the research of Zyrian vowel diachrony. Votyak is on the whole somewhat more uniform in this connection, but the Beserman (B) dialect and the southwest (SW) dialects diverge somewhat and must be taken into account. The Yaz'va vowel system is shown below. (R = rounded, UR = unrounded.)

Figure 8.1   Zyrian and Votyak vowel inventory (literary languages)

	Unrounded		Rounded
High	i	ï	u
Mid	e	ë	o
Low		a	
	Front		Back

	Front		Back	
	UR	R	UR	R
High	i	u̇		u
Close-mid			ө	
Open-mid	e	ȯ		o
Low			a	

Corresponding to (literary) Zyrian *o* Upper Sysola Zyrian has two vowel phonemes, a relatively closed (high) *ô* and a more open (lower) *o*. For present-day Zyrian *o* and *e*, Old Zyrian had two vowel phonemes each, closed and open *ô*, *o*, and *ê*, *e*.

Corresponding to literary Votyak *ï*, *ë*, and (pPN *ô* >) *u* Beserman has *Øë*, *e*, *Ø* and southwestern dialects (such as Shoshma) have *ë*, *u̇*, *ȯ*.

It must be emphasized that the precise phonological nature of several of the above-mentioned phonemes is controversial (e.g. PO ө) and subject to varying interpretation, a fact which makes historical analysis all the more difficult. It must furthermore be noted that although the vowel systems in the literary Permian languages are identical, cognates in the two languages do not necessarily, indeed do not often, show the same vowels. As will be shown below, there are important correspondences between Zyrian and Votyak, but also a great number of minor correspondences and exceptions.

Zyrian < proto-Zyrian (pZ)

OZ	SO	PO	Z Lit	<	pZ
a	a	a	a	<	*a
o	o	o	o	<	*o
ô	ô	u	o	<	*ô
u	u	u/u̇	u	<	*u
ë	ë	ȯ	ë	<	*O
ë	ë	u̇	ë	<	*Ô
ï	ï	ө	ï	<	*u̇
e	e	e	e	<	*e
ê	e	i	e	<	*ê
i	i	i	i	<	*i

The reconstructed vowel system for pZ is thus:

*i	*u̇		*u
*ê	*Ô		*ô
*e	*O		*o
		*a	

The development from pZ to literary Zyrian, which represents the majority of present-day dialects, is thus characterized by delabialization (*ù > ï), merger (*o, *ô > o and *e, *ê > e), or both (*O, *Ô > ë). There is a good possibility that the distinction between the pairs *o/*ô, *O/*Ô, *e/*ê was not so much tongue height as a difference in tenseness/laxness.

Votyak < proto-Votyak (pVo)

B	SW	Vo Lit		pVo
a	a	a	<	*a
ø	ù	u	<	*ô
u	u	u	<	*u
o	o	o	<	*O
e	ȯ	ë	<	*Ô
ø	ø	ï	<	*ù
e	e	e	<	*ä
e/o	e/o	e/o	<	*e
i	i	i	<	*i

The vowel system of proto-Votyak is thus:

*i	*ù	*u
	*Ô	*ô
*e	*O	
*ä		*a

The developments from proto-Votyak to literary Votyak are not as regular as those of pZ > Zyrian and are thus less compelling. There are examples of raising (*ô > u, *ä > e), delabialization (*Ô > ë, *ù > ï), partial labialization (*e > e/o) and backing (*O > o).

The Development of pZ and pVo from pPN

The following four tongue-height vowel system has been reconstructed for pPN:

*i	*U	*u
*ê	*Ô	*ô
*e	*O	*o
*ä	*a	

In pZ, pPN *ä merged with its rounded neighbour *O to give the pZ vowel system. In the development from pPN to pVo on the other hand neighbouring *e and *ê merged as pVo *e, and pPN *u and *o (not *ô !) merged as pVo *u. That *u and *o underwent a merger, rather than *u and *ô, could be an indication that the difference between these vowels was one of tenseness/laxness rather than tongue height, as in the case of pZ mentioned above.

Examples illustrating the development of the vowels in pPN > Zyrian and Votyak:

Z/Vo correspondence

pPN *baŋ 'face' > Z *ban* Vo *bam*	a/a
pPN *poz 'nest' > Z *poz* Vo *puz*	o/o
pPN *lôl 'breath, soul' > Z *lov* Vo *lul*	o/u
pPN *juk 'pile' > Z *juk* Vo *juk*	u/u
pPN *tOl 'winter' > Z *tëv* Vo *tol*	ë/o
pPN *šʲÔm 'fish scale' > Z *šʲëm* Vo *šʲëm*	ë/ë
pPN *lUmi 'snow' > Z *lïm* Vo *lïmï*	ï/ï
pPN *säppä 'gall (bladder)' > Z *sëp* Vo *sep*	ë/e
pPN *pelʲ 'ear' > Z *pelʲ* Vo *pelʲ*	e/e
pPN *zer 'rain' > Z *zer* Vo *zor*	e/o
PPN *vêž 'green' > Z *vež* Vo *vož*	e/o
pPN *vir 'blood' > Z *vir* Vo *vir*	i/i

The Development from Proto-Finno-Ugric to Proto-Permian
The vowel system usually proposed for pFU is this:

*i	*[ü]		*u
*e		*ë	*o
*ä		*a	

Many attempts have been made to derive the pPN vowel system (and its descendants, the pZ and pVo systems) from pFU, but hitherto the task has proven well nigh insurmountable. One is juggling here with three reconstructed levels of vowel diachrony, and thus far no one has succeeded in reconciling the widely accepted pFU reconstructed inventory with a pPN reconstruction. A survey of the etymological material reveals that most pPN vowels have at least two pFU forebears. To list only the most frequent reflexes:

pPN		pFU	pPN		pFU
*ä	<	*ä, *e	*Ô	<	*e, *o
*a	<	*ä, *e, *a	*U	<	*ü, *u
*o	<	*ä, *e	*e	<	*e, *i
*ô	<	*a, *e, *o	*ê	<	*ä, *i
*u	<	*a, *o	*i	<	*i
*O	<	*ä			

Given this many major reflexes (not to mention the many minor ones), the chasm between pFU and pPN has not been bridged. What has been possible in the case of the consonants seems still out of reach in the case of the vowels. In conclusion, one is tempted to believe that either (1) a satisfactory theory accounting for the basic outline of pFU > pPN vowels diachrony will never be found, or (2) such a theory would involve considerable rewriting of what most now assume to be true for p(F)U and pPN.

Vowels Beyond the First Syllable
In the preceding section only the vowels of the first syllable were discussed. It is typical for the Finno-Ugric languages that not all the vowels occurring in the first syllable can occur in other syllables, or that some occur with less frequency. In present-day Zyrian, for example, the vowels *o*, *u*, and *e* occur only rarely in non-first syllable. For pFU only *e and *a/*ä (the distribution being dictated by vowel harmony) are usually reconstructed for non-first syllables.

The attentive reader will already have noted the drastic shortening of words which occurred in the transition from pFU to pPN: among the examples given above are pFU *käte 'hand' > pPN *ki; pFU *šiŋere 'mouse' > pPN *šUr. These two examples illustrate one of the most common fates to befall a non-first vowel, namely annihilation. The other possibility was raising of the non-first syllable *e and *a/*ä to a high vowel, probably *i, with allophones. This high vowel was in turn lost in Zyrian, but retained in most Votyak dialects (as *i* or *ï*). Further examples of annihilation:

pFU   *soja 'arm, sleeve' > pPN *sôj > Z *soj* Vo *suj*
pFU   *säppä 'gall (bladder)' > pPN *säp > Z *sëp* Vo *sep*
pFU   *piŋe 'tooth' > *piŋ > Z/Vo *pin^j*

Examples of raising (with later loss in Zyrian):

pFU   *lume 'snow' > pPN *lUmi > Z *lïm* Vo *limï*
pFU   *kinče 'nail, claw' > pPN *gUži > Z *giž* Vo *gižï* (with pPN *U < pFU *[ü])

Vowel Harmony
Unlike many other Finno-Ugric languages Permian has no vowel harmony. In p(F)U it was certainly present, but in a rudimentary form. In some Finno-Ugric languages it has developed into a mechanism which pervades the phonology; in others it has waned away. The massive vowel changes in the first syllable and the wholesale reduction and loss in the second eradicated vowel harmony already in pPN, and it has not sprung up anew in either Zyrian or Votyak.

Stress
In p(F)U stress was probably non-distinctive. It is also probable that stress tended to fall on the first syllable. We can assume the same for proto-Permian.

In the present-day languages the stress systems are different and form one of the major distinguishing factors between Zyrian and Votyak.

Zyrian

In most Komi-Zyrian dialects stress is non-distinctive and the tendency is to stress the first syllable. Stress in the Komi-Permyak dialects is more fixed: certain grammatical endings are accented, others are not. The system in these dialects is not entirely uniform. In the Yaz'va dialect (PO) we find a unique stress system. In general, the first non-high vowel in polysyllabic words is stressed, but in inflected words with a high vowel in their monosyllabic stem this high vowel either loses or retains its stress in the inflected form depending on its history. The high vowel retains the stress if it developed from a pZ non-high vowel, as in the case of PO i < pZ *ê, u < *ô, or ù < *Ô, e.g.

pPN *tôš 'beard' > Zyrian Lit *toš*, PO *tuš*, instrumental *tu̠š-θn*

but if the high vowel continues a pPN high vowel, then the stress moves to the right in accordance with the general rule, e.g.

pPN *purt 'knife' > Zyrian Lit *purt*, PO *purt*, instrumental *purt-θ̠n*

In Votyak, the stress falls on the last syllable except in certain grammatical forms. This accentuation pattern, so atypical of the Finno-Ugric languages, is certainly due to the influence of the neighbouring Tatar language. In both Tatar and Votyak the imperative forms of the verb form an exception to the general rule in that they are accented on the first syllable.

Morphology

Both Permian languages are typically agglutinative in that their word stems are normally not subject to change when inflected and every semantic element is expressed, as a rule, with a single morphological element. Words which contain several semantic elements are thus built up out of morphological elements of the same number. For example, the Zyrian equivalent of Latin in *silv-īs* 'in forests' is *vër-jas-in*, with separately encoded plural (*-jas-*) and local case (*-in*).

Declension

This section briefly treats number, case, and the possessive suffixes.

Number

In addition to singular and plural, for p(F)U a dual is also postulated. This ancient dual is not to be found in Permian. The p(F)U plural markers *-t, *-i- are similarly absent (the plural morpheme *-n will be mentioned below, under possessive suffixes). In pPN a new plural suffix evolved from the pPN noun *jOsV 'limb; joint; people, folk'. This word survives in both Zyrian and Votyak both as an independent noun (Zyrian *jëz* 'people, folk; joint', Votyak *joz* 'limb, joint; contemporary') and as a plural suffix (Zyrian *-jas*, Votyak *-jos* ~ *-os*). The suffix occurs in all cases of the plural, including the possessive forms, e.g. Z/Vo *ki* 'hand', plural nominative Zyrian *ki-jas*/Votyak *ki-os*, plural dative Zyrian *ki-jas-lï*/Votyak *ki-os-lï*, dative plural third person singular ('to his/her hands') Zyrian *ki-jas-ïs-lï*/ Votyak *ki-os-ez-lï*.

Case
Both Permian languages are characterized by a relatively large number of cases: in the Komi-Zyrian and Komi-Permyak literary languages the number is usually held to be seventeen; in Votyak it is fifteen. The discussion to follow briefly treats eighteen case suffixes; in Zyrian, the adverbial is not generally viewed as being a case, and in Votyak the first and second prolatives are usually regarded as one case, although historically they are distinct.

		Zyrian	Votyak
1	Nominative	(zero)	(zero)
2	Accusative	zero, -ës, -ë	zero, -e, -(j)ez
3	Genitive	-lën	-len
4	Genitive/Ablative	-lïsʲ	-lesʲ
5	Dative	-lï	-lï
6	Approximative	-lanʲ	-lanʲ
7	Inessive	-ïn	-ïn
8	Elative	-ïsʲ	-ïsʲ
9	Illative	-ë	-(j)e
10	Terminative	-ëɕʲ	-ozʲ
11	Instrumental	-ën	-(j)en
12	Egressive	-šʲanʲ	-(ï)šʲen
13	Caritive	-tëg	-tek
14	Prolative 1	-ëd	-(j)eti
15	Prolative 2	-ti	-ti
16	Adverbial	-ja, -ji	-ja
17	Consecutive	-la	—
18	Comitative	-këd	—

The Permian case suffixes fall into two main historical groups, primary and secondary. The latter group may be further subdivided into those suffixes which are built with the co-affix *-l- and those suffixes which are the result of combining two case suffixes.

Primary case suffixes: (2) the *accusative*, from pU *-m. The *m* has been lost, and its role has been taken up by the stem-final vowel. In the forms Zyrian -ës, Votyak -ez the element s/z is identical with the third-person singular suffix; see below. (7) the *inessive* continues the pU locative *-nA. (8) the *elative*: it is very likely that this suffix is identical with the homophonous *nomen possessi* derivational suffix, e.g. Komi-Permiak vër=is^j 'forest spirit', derived from vër 'forest' with the suffix =is^j 'belonging/pertaining to X'. The -t- element found in the Votyak non-final variant of the elative (e.g. gurt-is^{j}t-id 'out of your house') can be traced back to the pU ablative *-tA. (9) the *illative*, from pU lative *-k:. After the k was lost, its role was assumed by the stem-final vowel, as in the accusative. (10) the *terminative* continues pU lative *-c^{j}V. (11) the instrumental probably continues the pU genitival/adjectival suffix *-n. (14) the first prolative continues pU ablative *-tA.

Secondary case suffixes built with *-l-: the (3) genitive, (4) genitive/ablative, and (6) approximative cases are innovative formations combining a coaffix *-l- with the descendents of pU *-nA, pPN elative *-s^j, and a pU lative *-n^j. The Permian dative (5) and consecutive (17) cases are the result of a bifurcation; both go back to coaffix *-l- plus the descendant of a pU lative *-k.

Other secondary case suffixes: (12) in Zyrian, the egressive combines the elative -s^j with the reflex of pU lative *-n^j; in Votyak the second component seems to be an allomorph of the inessive case. (13) The caritive is probably a combination of the pU caritive suffix *=ttA plus the pU lative *-k, but the retention of the final k is irregular. (15) the second prolative continues a pFU locative *-ttV plus pFU lative *-j. (16) the adverbial is a combination of some p(F)U lative or locative suffix with lative *-k, but the details are unclear. (18) the comitative is probably a k-coaffix with locative meaning (cf. the Cheremis comitative -ke ~ -γe) plus the first prolative.

Possessive Declension
As in most of Uralic, in the Permian languages personal suffixes are used to indicate possession. The basic inventory is set out below:

	Zyrian	Votyak
s1	-ë(j)	-e, -ï
s2	-ïd	-ed, -ïd
s3	-ïs	-ez, -ïz
p1	-nïm	-mï
p2	-nïd	-t/dï
p3	-nïs	-s/zï

In the singular the systems of the two languages are close to identical (the -j in the Zyrian s1 is a secondary element, of diminutive/vocative origin). It is in the plural that the two systems diverge. For pPN a different system has

Table 8.4   Proto-Permian possessive suffixes

	Possession in singular	*Plural*
s1	*-mV	*-nV-mV
s2	*-tV	*-nV-tV
s3	*-sV	*nV-sV
p1	*-mV-k	*-nV-mV-k
p2	*-tV-k	*-nV-tV-k
p3	*-sV-k	*-nV-sV-k

been reconstructed, in which plurality of the possession was expressed by a suffix *-n- (known from several related languages), and plurality of the possessor was marked with the pFP pluralizer *-k. The basic building-blocks of this reconstructed system are the pU personal pronouns of the first, second, and third persons, *me, *te, and *se.

This reconstruction is continued intact in the singular forms of the present-day Permian languages (in the first person singular -m was lost in most cases and its role was assumed by the preceding vowel). Zyrian plural possessive suffixes such as p1 -nïm are the continuation of the pPN singular system with plural possession, i.e. the marker of plurality of the possession came to mark plurality of the possessor. In Votyak on the other hand the suffixes of analogous function (e.g. -mï) continue the old pPN plural suffixes with singular possession. The loss of word-final vowels is regular, as is the retention of the vowel before a consonant which was later lost, as in Votyak -mï < *-mV-k.

The general rule (from which there is a certain amount of deviation) for the order of possessive and case suffixes in both Zyrian and Votyak is that primary case suffixes precede, and secondary case suffixes follow, the possessive suffixes. Examples: the terminatives of 'his/her house' are Zyrian kerka-ëȼʲ-ïs, Votyak korka-ozʲ-az; the datives of 'his/her daughter' are Zyrian nïl-ïs-lï, Votyak nïl-ez-lï.

Conjugation
The conjugational systems of Zyrian and Votyak resemble one another to a great degree, but not to the extent that their declensional systems do. The following remarks will concentrate on the differences more than on the many similarities.

Number of Conjugational Patterns
In p(F)U as well as later in pPN there was only one conjugational pattern. This is still the case in Zyrian. In Votyak, however, a major change has come about: historical phonetic changes have caused verbs originally ending in a certain common derivational suffix to be conjugated in a different way from other verbs. This suffix, pre-Votyak *=al-, was originally a frequentative formant,

but this meaning is now no longer obvious in most cases. The *l* element of this suffix now appears only in intervocalic position, while the *a* has been preserved in all positions. The stem-final vowel is now synchronically diagnostic: if it is *ï*, the verb is of the first conjugation; if it is *a*, the verb is of the second conjugation (the synchronic stem is most easily obtained from Votyak dictionary citation forms by lopping off the infinitive suffix *-nï*). The most important differences between the two conjugations are the presence or absence of the *-a(l)-* sequence, and the fact that the primary past-tense suffix *-i-* shows up only in the first person singular of second-conjugation verbs (*vera-j* 'I said'), while it runs through the entire paradigm of first-conjugation verbs (*mïn-i* 'I went', *mïn-i-d* 'you went', *mïn-i-z* '(s)he went', etc.).

Tense
Proto-Permian had four non-compound tenses: present, past, perfect (= auditive, narrative), and future. The present was marked with zero. The suffix of the past tense was *-i-*, inherited from pU. The suffix of the perfect was historically identical with that of the past participle, from pU *=mA*. The future tense was morphologically distinct only in the third person; this is still the case in present-day Zyrian: *munë* '(s)he goes', *munënï* 'they go'; *munas* '(s)he will go', *munasnï* 'they will go'. Otherwise, present and future forms syncretized.

Zyrian has retained the old pPN tense system. The perfect (auditive, narrative) is used only in second and third persons and the future is restricted to the third person. This system has been augmented by a number of secondary, periphrastic tenses, built for the most part with the verb *vël-* 'is'.

In Votyak, on the other hand, the tense system has undergone restructuring. Once again a frequentative suffix is to blame: the derivational suffix *=s^jk* came to function as a present-tense marker. This morpheme now occurs in the first and second persons of the present-tense paradigm, e.g. *mis^jk-is^jk-o* 'I am washing', *das^ja-s^jk-odï* 'you (plur) are preparing'. The future tense, originally formally distinct only in the third person, now came to differ from the present tense in all persons, i.e. alongside the original distinction between *mis^jk-e* '(s)he washes' and *mis^jk-oz* '(s)he will wash' there arose the new and parallel distinction between *mis^jk-is^jk-o* 'I am washing' and *mis^jk-o* 'I shall wash'. With the auditive perfect (used in all persons), Votyak thus has four full basic tenses; like Zyrian, it also has a number of secondary, periphrastic tenses, built with the invariable past-tense forms *val* and *vïlem*.

Mood
Proto-Permian had only two moods, indicative and imperative, the pU conditional (built with *-ne-*) having vanished without trace. In Votyak a new conditional mood has arisen secondarily. Synchronically, the suffix is *-sal-*. Historically, it is the result of fusion of the gerund (*=sa*) with the past-tense auxiliary *val* mentioned above, thus the syntagm *mïnï=sa val* became

restructured as the finite form *mïnï-sal* 'I would go; I would have gone'. In Zyrian, the category conditional is either expressed by the indicative plus the particle *(v)es^j-kë* or implicit in the context.

Personal Endings

Nearly all personal endings figuring in the Permian conjugational system can be traced back to the personal pronouns *me *te *se or are ultimately identical with an old participial suffix. The Zyrian and Votyak systems are quite similar and the deviations are in most cases of easy explanation. The sole major discrepancy is found in the Zyrian s2 ending *-n*, e.g. *muna-n* 'you go', *mun-i-n* 'you went'. The Votyak pendant, *-d* (as in *minis^jkod* 'you go', *mïnid* 'you went'), is the expected reflex (< pU *te, the second-person singular pronoun). Thus far no explanation for this anomaly has found general acceptance. NB: in both Zyrian and Votyak we find *-d* as the s2 suffix in the nominal paradigm. It is true that we find the same s2 ending *-n* in the ObUgrian languages, but this does not solve the problem.

Negative Verb

Like most Uralic languages, both Permian languages make use of a special verb of negation. In this verb, which is defective, are encoded number and person of the subject as well as tense. Following the negative verb the stem of the main, lexical verb, is used.

In both Zyrian and Votyak the negative verb has fewer distinct forms than there are grammatical person-and-number distinctions. Syncretism of subject number is avoided by suffixation on the lexical verb, e.g. Zyrian *oz mun* '(s)he does not go', *oz mun-nï* 'they do not go', Votyak *ëd mïnï* 'you (s.) didn't go', *ed mïne(le)* 'you (plur.) didn't go'. For the full paradigms, see pp. 315, 292.

The stem of the negative verb can be traced back to the pU negation morpheme *e~*ä. The past-tense forms seen in Permian developed from this stem plus the past-tense suffix *-i-.

Syntax

The Permian languages are traditionally left-branching, i.e. determining or modifying elements precede the elements determined/modified. In terms of word order this means adjective precedes noun, noun precedes postposition, possessor precedes possession, and – very generally speaking – direct object precedes verb. Traditional Permian sentence structure seems not to have differed from that of other Uralic languages, which in turn is for all practical purposes identical with that of the typologically similar Turkic, Mongolic, and Tungusic languages. One salient feature of this language type is the nearly complete lack of relative pronouns and conjunctions; this lack, in turn, entails a lack of subordinate clauses. Sentence subordination could, of course, be made plain enough through mere juxtaposition and context, but the more usual way to express what (Indo-)European languages typically express with subordinate clauses was by means of deverbal nominal and adverbial constructions: participles, infinitives, gerunds, *nomina actionis*, using the usual nominal case and person suffixes. The Permian languages possess a richly developed store of such deverbal constructions, the greater part of which goes back to pPN.

So much for the traditional picture. The past decades have seen the rapid advance of the 'Indo-European' model of sentence extension via subordinate clauses, the catalyst being chiefly Russian. Today all Permian literary languages use a goodly number of both subordinating and co-ordinating conjunctions, many of which have been been borrowed from Russian, e.g. и 'and' > Z/Vo *i*, но 'and, but' > Z/Vo *no*, будто 'as if' > Z *bïťťë*, Vo *budto*, etc. The interrogative pronouns 'who' and what' (Zyrian *kod*, *mïj*; Votyak *kin*, *ma*) are nowadays also used as relative pronouns, this use involving the employment of case and plural suffixes on the pattern of Russian который and что. Zyrian *mïj* 'what' is also used as a subordinating conjunction; cf., once more, Russian что.

Russian influence on Permian sentence structure is by no means new; it has simply become more marked in recent years. What Hungarian underwent in the Middle Ages is now occurring in Zyrian and Votyak, namely a radical restructuring of traditional sentence patterns.

Contacts with Other Languages

Proto-Permian and its daughter languages have come into contact with a number of other languages, and these contacts have left their traces in present-day Zyrian and Votyak. These traces are clearest in the lexica, but they can also be demonstrated in the domains of phonology, morphology, and – as we have seen in the previous section – syntax. The discussion below is limited to a brief survey of the loanword strata to be found in Permian.

Base Vocabulary of Proto-Permian

The basic lexical stock of pPN was dominated by words inherited from pU, pFU, and pFP and enriched by loanwords, mostly from branches of Indo-European, adopted prior to pPN. Non-borrowed vocabulary included items such as p(F)U *nʲë(ë)le 'arrow' > pPN *nʲÔl > Z *nʲëv* Vo *nʲël*, pFU *säppä 'gall (bladder)' > pPN *säp > Z *sëp* Vo *sep*.

In addition, we can identify an important layer of pPN words which are not demonstrably inherited or borrowed. Examples are pPN *ker 'log, beam' (Z *ker*, Vo *kor*), *dUž 'membrane' (Z *dïš*, Vo *dïž*), *gÔrd 'red' (Z *gërd*, Vo *gord*), *bOsʲti- 'takes' (Z *bosʲt-*, Vo *basʲtï-*).

Proto-Permian had strong contacts with Iranian languages and a number of Iranian loanwords in pPN have been identified, e.g. *amVȼV 'ploughshare' (Z *amïsʲ*, Vo *amezʲ*; cf. present-day Persian *amaaȼ*), *das 'ten' (Z/Vo *das*; cf. present-day Ossetian *däs*).

Of equal importance for pPN were the contacts with Middle Bulgarian

(MB, an earlier stage of the branch of Turkic from which present-day Chuvash descends); these contacts began approximately in the eighth century. This stratum of Turkic loanwords, the earliest in the Permian languages, can be distinguished from later Turkic loanword strata, both later Middle Bulgarian and later Tatar, by their distribution (the oldest MB loans are found in both Zyrian and Votyak, later ones only in Votyak – and possibly Komi-Permyak) and by means of phonetic criteria. For example, Votyak *bam*, Zyrian *ban* 'face' are from pPN *baŋ < MB *bäŋ ~ *beŋ, but Votyak *murjo* 'chimney' is a later loan from Chuvash, and Votyak *azbar* 'courtyard' is from Tatar.

Zyrian Particulars
The move northwards which gave rise to the separate Zyrian nation and language also determined which languages would be sources for new loans. Through loss of direct contact Zyrian could no longer borrow directly from MB, or later from Tatar, but as Zyrian settlements spread to the north, west, and east, they came into contact with Baltic-Fennic languages such as Karelian and Veps, with Nenets, and with the ObUgrian languages. The number of loans from these languages is not great and they are to a large extent restricted to the Zyrian dialects spoken farther to the northwest (Baltic-Fennic contacts), the north (Nenets), and the northeast (ObUgrian). Nonetheless, some of these loanwords have spread to all areas of Zyrian, e.g. *joma* 'witch' < Baltic-Fennic *jumala* 'god', *ľampa* 'ski' < Nenets *lampa*, *jaran* 'Samoyed; northerner' < Ostyak (cf. Southern Ostyak *jaran*) or Vogul (cf. Northern Vogul *jåårən*).

Of much greater importance for Zyrian are the loans from Russian. The contacts between Zyrians and Russians began long before the conversion of the former to Christianity, and the flow of loans grew with the passing of the centuries. One can distinguish between an older stratum of loans adopted by various dialects and adapted to some extent to the Zyrian sound system (e.g. *visʲt* 'news' < north Russian *vʲisʲtʲ*, *gïrnjicʲ* 'pot', cf. Old Russian гърньць) and more recent loans, adopted in greater numbers, which preserve more closely the sound qualities of the original.

Votyak Particulars
Three languages shaped the vocabulary of Votyak: Middle Bulgarian, Tatar, and Russian. These are also the three peoples under whose hegemony the Votyak have lived to the present day.

Unlike the Zyrians, the Votyaks remained within the sphere of Middle Bulgarian culture until the Golden Horde put an end to that kingdom. Accordingly, there are many more Bulgarian loans in Votyak than there are in Zyrian. Examples: *busï* 'field' (cf. Chuvash *pusă*), *kuno* 'guest' (cf. Chuvash *xăna*), *uksʲo* 'money' (cf. Chuvash *ukśa*).

Until the fall of Kazan in 1552 the Votyaks formed a part of the territories subject to the Tatars, and there are many Tatar loanwords in Votyak to attest to this. Not all such loans are found in all Votyak dialects or used in the literary language; many are restricted to dialects spoken in areas close to, or co-territorial with, Tatar. Examples: *batïr* 'hero(ic)' (cf. Tatar *batïr*), *gine* 'only' (cf. Tatar *genä*), *taza* 'healthy, strong' (cf. Tatar *taza*).

In the sixteenth century the Tatars were supplanted by the Russians as rulers of the Votyak territories. As in the case of Zyrian, one can distinguish an older and a younger layer of Russian loans. The older loanwords took part in Votyak-specific sound changes, e.g. *ukno* 'window' < Russian окно, *dusko* 'board' < доска. In the nineteenth and twentieth centuries Votyak has been inundated by Russian loanwords which for the most part have retained their original shape.

References and Further Reading

Csúcs, S. (1990) *Chrestomathia votiacica*, Budapest: Tankönyvkiadó.
Lallukka, S. (1990) *The East Finnic Minorities in the Soviet Union*, Helsinki: Suomalainen Tiedeakatemia.
Lytkin, V.I. (1961) Коми-язьвинский диалект, Moscow: Academy of Sciences of the Soviet Union.
―――― (1964) Исторический вокализм пермских языков, Moscow: Nauka.
Lytkin, V.I., and E.S. Gulaev (1970) Краткий этимологический словарь коми языка, Moscow: Nauka.
Rédei, K. (1978) *Syrjänische Chrestomathie. Mit Grammatik und Glossar*, Studia Uralica 1, Vienna: Finno-Ugric Institute of the University of Vienna.
―――― (1988) 'Geschichte der permischen Sprachen', in D. Sinor (ed.) *The Uralic Languages: Description, History and Foreign Influences*, Handbuch der Orientalistik 8/1, Leiden: Brill, pp. 351–94.
―――― (1988–91) (ed.) *Uralisches etymologisches Wörterbuch*, Budapest: Akadémiai kiadó.
Serebrennikov, B.A. (1963) Историческая морфология пермских языков, Moscow: Nauka.
Uotila, T.E. (1933) *Zur Geschichte des Konsonantismus in den permischen Sprachen*, Helsinki: Société Finno-Ougrienne.

9 Udmurt

Sándor Csúcs

In the 1989 Soviet census 747,000 people declared themselves to be of Udmurt nationality; of these approximately 70 per cent (thus *c.* 520,000 people) speak the language of their ancestors.

Two-thirds (*c.* 500,000) of the Udmurt (older name: Votyak) live in the Udmurt Republic (Udmurtia), which is located between the Vyatka and Kama Rivers and forms a part of the Russian Federation. The area of Udmurtia is 42,000 km^2, its population is 1.6 million; its capital is the industrial city Izhevsk, with 635,000 inhabitants. The Udmurt are thus a minority within their own republic. (Breakdown by nationality: Udmurt 31 per cent, Russian 59 per cent, Tatar and other 10 per cent.) The distribution of the Udmurt population is not homogeneous: their proportions are greater in villages than in the cities. So for example 16.5 per cent of the population of Izhevsk is Udmurt, but in Alnasi province the Udmurt make up more than 80 per cent. This disproportion is characteristic of language use, as well. Generally in the villages 95 per cent of the Udmurt population speak their mother tongue, while in the cities the proportion is considerably lower. This state of affairs is partly due to the fact that in urban schools no provision for education in Udmurt was provided under the Soviet system.

Approximately 100,000 Udmurt live in the neighbouring republics of Bashkiria and Tatarstan, and in the Vyatka (Kirov) and Perm' regions. These Udmurt have lived in the same places for several centuries, almost exclusively in villages, and have in general preserved their language skills well. The proportion of mother-tongue speakers here is between 80 and 90 per cent.

The remaining roughly 150,000 Udmurt live in scattered settlements in the former Soviet Union, chiefly in towns. This dispersion occurred during the Soviet period; the motivation to move was to lessen economic hardship. Among this population the proportion of mother-tongue speakers has fallen to 40–50 per cent. With time, the majority will probably become completely Russified.

At least 90 per cent of the Udmurt are bi- or trilingual. The second language is generally Russian, the third Tatar. Udmurt who live in Tatarstan and Bashkiria speak Tatar as their second or third language. There is great variety in the degree of competence in the second and third languages; factors include place of residence, amount of schooling, occupation, age, social and societal status and family circumstances. The young and the intelligentsia speak Russian perfectly, but when communicating with one another consciously strive to use their mother tongue. In the countryside in everyday situations Udmurt is spoken, but at official functions Udmurt speak Russian even among themselves. It will be interesting to observe to what degree the political events of the early 1990s will influence language use.

Russian and Udmurt are quite distinct from one another, but I have occasionally witnessed the mixture of the two. In one instance, I was with the head of a kolkhoz in his office. He was a native speaker of Udmurt; we were discussing the kolkhoz. The person accompanying me was posing the questions, and our host duly tried to reply in his native language; but he kept slipping into Russian or, at least, mixing Russian expressions and sentences into his speech. The difficulty was caused by the fact that he had acquired the habit of dealing with official matters, in his office, in Russian or Tatar, and not in Udmurt. On many occasions I have observed conversations among students or teachers in which extensive code-switching to Russian occurred (phrases, half-sentences, proverbs). Such code-switching is usual whenever the subject-matter is better expressed in Russian.

Between Udmurt dialects there are no significant differences. The syntactic and morphological systems are nearly identical across the entire linguistic area. The phonemic systems of the central dialects of Udmurtia are identical with each other and with that of the literary standard. The only real deviation is in the distribution of phonemes, e.g. the cacuminal affricates (č and ǯ) occur word-internally only in the central dialects, while other dialects and the literary standard have the corresponding fricatives.

Common Udmurt *ï* has reduced, retracted, and lowered variants in the northern and southern dialects. This feature is also typical of the dialects spoken outside Udmurtia, i.e. to its west, south, and east, chiefly in the two Turkic republics. These dialects are often lumped together as a 'peripheral' group. Their shared isoglosses are word-internal -ŋ- and the retention of proto-Udmurt *Ô and *ù, see pp. 263–4. In some peripheral dialects a new (front open unrounded) *ä* phoneme has arisen through Tatar influence. Strong Tatar influence in these dialects is evident in other domains, as well.

The lexicons of the various dialects differ only in non-central domains. Regionalisms are usually deviant only in form or in meaning, but true regionalisms do occur, e.g. *madʲïnï* 'sings ~ 'tells', *mumï* ~ *anaj* 'mother'. It is not uncommon for one dialect to borrow a Russian word, and another dialect to borrow a synonymous word from Tatar, e.g. *zavod* (from Russian) ~ *arberi* (from Tatar), both 'stuff, rubbish'. Often both words are at home in the literary lexicon.

Dialectal peculiarities thus present little or no obstacle to mutual comprehension. This is not least due to the fact that the literary standard, which is taught in schools and used in the media, is a felicitous alloy of the dialects, based on the central dialects but amply enlarged by northern and southern features which are not strongly divergent.

The development of literary written Udmurt began in the eighteenth century, but Udmurt-language publications did not begin to appear until the middle of the nineteenth century.

Before the 1917 revolution the demand for the development of a unified Udmurt literary language did not arise. Publications were written in the local dialect, but the small interdialectal differences meant that – as far as material circumstances allowed – these works were theoretically able to become common intellectual property for the entire Udmurt population.

During the 1920s there was lively debate over questions of orthography. As elsewhere, among the Udmurt, too, there arose the idea of switching to the Latin alphabet. Numerous articles on this question appeared, but there had been no tradition of the use of Latin letters in writing Udmurt (linguistic transcriptions aside), nor was the cultural milieu favourable for such a solution. The idea was thus more or less definitively rejected. The use of Cyrillic on the other hand had an extensive tradition: since the eighteenth century, every Udmurt publication that appeared in Russia was in Cyrillic. A second debate arose among Udmurt writers and linguists over the question of how Cyrillic was to be implemented. One camp wanted to develop their own orthography, based on Cyrillic letters, but adapted and augmented to accord with Udmurt phonology; the opposing camp argued for the importation not only of the letters, but of Russian orthographic principles, as well. The latter side won the argument. This led to the adoption of the entire Russian alphabet along with many of its orthographic rules. In this system, which is valid to this day, the three Udmurt affricates and one Udmurt vowel which Russian lacks are indicated by Cyrillic letters with diacritical marks ӵ = $\check{c}$, ӝ = $\mathcal{\'g}$, ӟ = $\check{\mathcal{g}}$, ӧ = $\ddot{e}$). A further diacritical letter, ӥ was introduced to write the vowel i when this sound was preceded by a distinctively non-palatalized consonant, i.e. after t, d, n, l, s, z (the letter with the analogous function in the Komi alphabet is і). Thus нӥ = ni, but ни = $n^{j}i$, and ми represents mi, because m has no distinctively palatalized pendant. It would be more consistent, and technically simpler, if the distinctively palatalized consonants were uniformly indicated with the aid of the soft sign (ь); this solution is already employed at word-end and before the vowel $i̇$ (written ы). A further oddity of the present-day orthography is the practice of preserving the Russian spelling of recent Russian loanwords intact, e.g. 'dictionary' is written словарь in spite of the fact that Udmurt has no palatalized r^{j} phoneme.

A good feature of the orthography, and a vital one, is its ability to distinguish unambiguously every Udmurt phoneme – albeit with the aid of a somewhat complex system of rules.

This is not the place to go into the history of the Udmurt language, but a brief listing of important innovations and retentions will be of use. Prominent phonological innovations include the development of the voiced : voiceless opposition among the obstruents, the simplification of the vowel system, and the large-scale erosion of the ends of words. As a result of these changes, present-day Udmurt is morphophonemically straightforward, a mainstream agglutinating language with very few stem or suffix alternations.

A prosodic innovation is the shift of the word stress, partly as a result of Tatar influence, to the last syllable.

The main morphological innovations are the hypertrophic case system and the development, in the verb, of future and conditional paradigms.

Against the background of all these innovations one should mention that Udmurt, like Komi, has retained the older proto-FU distinctions among the s(h)ibilants and affricates, as well as the system of personal suffixes. The extensive use of verbal nominals, including that of asyndetic sentence-linking, is perhaps also a retention.

Phonology

Consonants

The velar nasal (*ŋ*), which probably belonged to the inventory of proto-Udmurt, has been lost in all save certain peripheral and southern dialects. The post-alveolar affricates *č*, *ǯ* have (apico)retroflex articulations.

The status of the sound written *w* in the table is problematic. This sound occurs in three contexts:

1   Word-initially before the vowel *a* in about twenty words, e.g. *wan^j* 'exists'. This is a dialectal phenomenon; the literary standard has *van^j*.
2   After word-initial *k* in a few dozen words, e.g. *kwala* 'family shrine', *kwin^j* 'three'. This phenomenon is characteristic of the entire language.
3   Word-internally and word-finally after vowels in the Shoshma dialect (older name: Malmizh-Urzhum).

Table 9.1   The Udmurt consonant system

	1	*2*	*3*	*4*	*5*	*6*
Nasals	m		n		n^j	(ŋ)
Voiceless stops	p		t		t^j	k
Voiced stops	b		d		d^j	g
Voiceless affricates				č	č^j	
Voiced affricates				ǯ	ǯ^j	
Voiceless fricatives		v	s	š	š^j	(x)
Voiced fricatives			z	ž	ž^j	
Laterals			l		l^j	
Rhotic			r			
Glides	(w)				j	

Note: Places of articulation: 1 bilabial, 2 labiodental, 3 (apico)dental, 4 post-alveolar, 5 palatal, 6 (palato)velar.

The salient characteristic feature of the Udmurt consonant system is the presence of the correlations of voice and palatalization. Nine consonant-pairs participate in the correlation of voice, eight in that of palatalization. In fact, only four consonants take part in neither correlation; these consonants may be thereby defined as peripheral (*v, j, m, r*).

There are no long consonant phonemes, but geminates do arise at morpheme boundaries, often as the result of assimilation, e.g. *ač̆ č̆ini* 'to look', *liktilʲlʲam* 'they came'.

With the exception of *ŋ*, all consonants may occur initial, final, and medial in the word; certain consonants are rare, however, in certain positions. So for example the palatal stops *tʲ* and *dʲ* are quite rare in word-initial position in the literary standard and in the majority of the dialects, as are the post-alveolar/ cacuminal affricates in word-internal position.

Clusters of two consonants are not uncommon in word-internal and word-final position; clusters of three also occur, e.g. *murtli* 'to a person'. In clusters of three, one of the consonants is usually a liquid.

Vowels

The literary language and the majority of the dialects have the same seven-vowel system, one shared with Komi:

	Front	Back Unrounded	Rounded
High	i	ï	u
Mid	e	ë	o
Low		a	

The *e* is open-mid [ɛ], especially in word-final position; the *o* is pronounced quite far back.

In suffixes, there are no examples of *ë*; *u* is rare; and *o* occurs only in certain verb suffixes (e.g. *mïno* 'I shall go') and in the noun plural suffix *-(j)os*.

Certain dialects have vowel systems which differ from that given above. There are also combinatory variants of the above-listed vowels.

Vowel sequences are rare, and occur usually at morpheme boundaries, e.g. *korka-os* HOUSE-plur 'houses'.

Stress

The stress is of the quantitative-dynamic type and generally falls on the last syllable. A stressed syllable is approximately 1.5 times as long as an unstressed one. Unstressed vowels do not undergo reduction.

In certain verb forms, stress location distinguishes meaning: *silé* '(s)he stands', *síle* 'stand! (plural imperative)'; *verá* '(s)he speaks', *véra* 'speak! (singular imperative)'. As these examples illustrate, in imperative forms the stress falls on the first syllable. Initial-syllable stress also characterizes negative verb forms (e.g. *ud mįniš^jke* 'you [plur] do not go') and reduplicative adjectives and adverbs (e.g. *gọrd&gord* 'very red').

Certain adverbs and pronouns (with first component *og-*, *olo-*, *no-*, *kot^j-*) and certain affective-onomatopoeic words have free stress, i.e., in these cases stress placement depends on expressive and logical features of the utterance.

Morphophonemics

Deletions and Additions

Vowel syncope. Certain stems show syncope of their last vowel (usually *ï*) when a vowel-initial suffix is added. Adjacent to the syncopating vowel is always at least one liquid or nasal. Examples: *turïn* 'hay', *turnanï* 'to mow'; *polïs* 'oar', *polsanï* 'to row'; *kotïr* 'circle', *kotres* 'round'.

Paragogic consonants. Certain stems show a paragogic consonant to the left of vowel-initial suffixes. The consonant is always one of the set *k t m*. Examples: *n^jules* 'forest', *n^julesk-ïn* 'in the forest', but *n^jules-mï* 'our forest'; *in* 'sky', *inm-ïn* 'in the sky'; *kïk* 'two', *kïkt=eti* 'second'.

Hiatus-blocker j

A *j*-glide is epenthesized in the literary standard between a stem-final vowel and certain vowel-initial suffixes (*e*-initial suffixes, the adjective-formant *=o*, and the verb-formant *=a[l]-*). Examples: kuno-e > *kunoje* 'my guest', ukš^jo=o > *ukš^jojo* 'moneyed', gubi=al- > *gubijal-* 'goes mushroom-picking' (from *kuno* 'guest', *ukš^jo* 'money', and *gubi* 'mushroom'). In dialects, *j*-epenthesis is more widespread.

Assimilation

Assimilation of voice, general

In a sequence of two obstruents C_1C_2, C_1 adjusts in voicing to match C_2. This assimilation is not indicated by the orthography. Examples: *pereš^j* 'old', comparative *perež^j=gem* 'older'; *lud* 'meadow', prosecutive *lut-ti* 'along the meadow'; *gož=ja-nï* 'to write', *goš=tï-nï* 'to write down'.

Adaffrication

The dental stops *t* and *d* melt into, and lengthen, the stop element of the affricates *č^j* and *ǯ^j* when these immediately follow, e.g. *kut* 'sandals', *kutč^janï* [c:ᶜ] 'to pull on (one's) sandals'; *lïd* 'number', *lïdǯ^jinï* [ɟːᶻ] 'to count'.

Assimilation of voice, special

This assimilation affects only the possessive suffixes. The initial consonant of the second-person suffixes is *t* or *d*, and that of the third-person suffixes is *s* or *z*, in assimilation to the preceding consonant. (To the right of vowels *d z* occur.) Notice that the direction in which this assimilation operates is the reverse of that of general assimilation, above. Examples: *val-de* 'your horse (acc)', *eš-te* 'your friend (acc)', *val-zï* 'their horse', *eš-sï* 'their friend'.

Inflectional Morphology

Nominals (including postpositions, see p. 293) and verbs take inflectional suffixes as detailed in the sections immediately following. Conjunctions, particles, onomatopoeic words and interjections do not inflect.

Nominals

The noun (and in certain instances the adjective and numeral) distinguishes the following categories: number, case, and person (= possessor). All three categories are indicated by suffixes.

In terms of their stem structure, Udmurt nouns are unusually straightforward. With very few exceptions, all nouns belong to a single, unvarying, declension-type.

Number

The singular is unmarked; stated in terms of the orthography, the suffix of the plural is *-jos* to the right of consonants, *-os* to the right of vowels (*j*-epenthesis is regular to the left of the *-os* suffix.) Examples: *korka* 'house', *korka-os* [korkaj<u>os</u>] 'houses'; *bekčʲe* 'barrel', *bekčʲeos* [bekčʲej<u>os</u>] 'barrels'; *murt* 'human being', *murt-jos* 'people'; *derem* 'shirt', *derem-jos* 'shirts'.

The plural suffix also functions as a collective marker, e.g. *mumï* 'mother', *mumï-os-ïz* MOTHER-plur-s3 'mother and her relatives/associates'.

Case

There are fifteen cases. Every noun is declinable, but according to recent grammars nouns which designate animates do not take local cases (inessive, illative, elative, transitive, egressive) and usage with the approximative and terminative fluctuates. Observation in the field shows that these cases are

Table 9.2   Absolute declension, singular: *val* 'horse', *busï* 'field'

Nominative	-∅	val	busï
Genitive	-len	vellen	busïlen
Ablative	-lešʲ	vallešʲ	busïlešʲ
Dative	-lï	vallï	busïlï
Accusative	-∅, -(j)ez	valez	busïjez
Instrumental	-(j)en, -ïn	valen	busïjen
Abessive/Caritive	-tek	valtek	busïtek
Inessive	-ïn	—	busi-in
Elative	-ïšʲ	—	busi-ïšʲ
Illative	-(j)e	—	busïje
Approximative	-lanʲ	vallanʲ	busïlanʲ
Egressive	-ïšʲenʲ	—	busi-ïšʲenʲ
Transitive	-([j]e)ti	—	busïjeti
Terminative	-ožʲ	—	busïožʲ
Adverbial	-ja	valja	busïja

in fact used with animates, but in non-local meanings, e.g. *dišetiš^j-in uža* TEACHER-ine WORKS.s3pres '(s)he works as a teacher'.

The *j*-initial allomorphs occur to the right of vowels. Nouns referring to places and ending in *a*, most notably *korka* 'house', take vowelless variants of the local suffixes, e.g. inessive *korka-n*, elative *korka-š^j*, illative *korka-Ø*.

A closed set of nouns (chiefly body-part and kinship designations) take the -*in* allomorph of the instrumental, e.g. *ki-in* 'by hand'. Another closed set take -*i* in the illative, e.g. *n^julesk-i* 'into the forest'.

The transitive variants -*eti* ~ -*ti* appear to be in free variation.

The zero-accusative is used with indefinite direct objects. For further information concerning the uses of the cases see Syntax, pp. 295 and 297–9.

For the most part, *plural case forms* are built by adding to the stem the plural suffix followed by the same case suffixes as those used in the singular, e.g. abessive/caritive *val-jos-tek* 'without horses', approximative *busï-os-lan^j* 'towards the fields'. In a few cases, however, the case suffixes have different forms in the plural:

Singular accusative	val-ez	busï-jez
Plural accusative	val-jos-tï	busï-os-tï
	val-jos-ïz	busï-os-ïz
Singular instrumental	val-en	busï-jen
Plural instrumental	val-jos-ïn	busï-os-ïn
Singular illative	—	busï-je
Plural illative	—	busï-os-ï
Singular transitive	—	busï-jeti
Plural transitive	—	busï-os-tï

The variants of the plural accusative (e.g. *valjostï, valjosïz*) are in free variation in the literary standard (the former is characteristic of northern, the latter of southern and peripheral dialects).

The shape of the instrumental suffix in the plural (-*in*) means that plural inessive and instrumental cases have syncretized (e.g. *busï-os-in*).

Possessive Forms

The allomorphic distribution is fairly straightforward: *j*-variants to the right of vowels, *j*-less variants elsewhere. There are, however, exceptions, e.g. *ku-e* 'my skin'.

All singular possessives with initial *e* have variants with *ï* which are used with a closed set of nouns, most of which designate body parts, kinship, or (periods of) time, e.g. *jïr-ï* 'my head', *mïlkïd-ïz* 'his/her mood', *lul-ïd* 'your soul', *tusbuj-ïz* 'his/her exterior', *dïr-ï* 'my time', *nunal-ïz* 'his/her day', *nïl-ïd* 'your daughter', *nïl-ïn-ïm* 'with my daughter'. Not all words belonging to these semantic areas follow the rule, however, e.g. *jïrš^ji-je* 'my hair'.

Table 9.3   Possessive paradigm: possession in singular

	s1	*s2*	*s3*
Nominative	-(j)e, -ï	-(j)ed, -ïd	-(j)ez, -ïz
Genitive	-e/ïlen	-e/ïdlen	-e/ïzlen
Ablative	-e/ïlï	-e/ïdlï	-e/ïzlï
Dative	-e/ïleš^j	-e/ïdleš^j	-e/ïzleš^j
Accusative	-me	-te, -de	-se, -ze
Instrumental	-e/ïnïm	-e/ïnïd	-e/ïnïz
Abessive/Caritive	-e/ïtek	-e/ïdtek	-e/ïztek
Inessive	-am	-ad	-az
Illative	-am	-ad	-az
Elative	-ïš^jtïm	-ïš^jtïd	-ïš^jtïz
Egressive	-ïš^jenïm	-ïš^jenïd	-ïš^jenïz
Transitive	-e/ïtim	-e/ïtid	-e/ïtiz
Terminative	-ož^jam	-ož^jad	-ož^jaz
Adverbial	-e/ïja	-e/ïdja	-e/ïzja

Table 9.4   Possessive paradigm: possessor in plural

	p1	*p2*	*p3*
Nominative	-mï	-tï, -dï	-sï, -zï
Genitive	-mïlen	-t/dïlen	-s/zïlen
Ablative	-mïleš^j	-t/dïleš^j	-s/zïleš^j
Dative	-mïlï	-t/dïlï	-s/zïlï
Accusative	-mes	-t/des	-s/zes
Instrumental	-enïmï	-enïdï	-enïzï
Abessive/Caritive	-mïlan^j	-t/dïlan^j	-s/zïlan^j
Inessive	-amï	-adï	-azï
Illative	-amï	-adï	-azï
Elative	-ïš^jtïmï	-ïš^jtïdï	-ïš^jtïzï
Egressive	-ïš^jenïmï	-ïš^jenïdï	-ïš^jenïzï
Transitive	-etimï	-etidï	-etizï
Terminative	-ož^jamï	-ož^jadï	-ož^jazï
Adverbial	-mïja	-t/dïja	-s/zïja

Examples of the *s/z* and *t/d* alternation (special assimilation, above): *busï-dï* 'your (plur) field', *gurt-tï* 'your (plur) village', *pud-de* 'your foot (acc)', *gurt-se* 'his/her village (acc)'.

The order of case and person suffixes is of two types. In the first type, the person suffix precedes the case suffix. This is the order in the genitive, accusative, dative, ablative, abessive/caritive, adverbial, and approximative cases. Example: *val-ed-tek* 'without your horse'. The reverse order, i.e. case before person, occurs in the remaining cases, e.g. *busï-jeti-d* 'along your field'.

The only striking allomorphy among the case and person suffixes which results from their co-occurrence is in the accusative (*-me, -t/de, -s/ze, -mes, -t/des, -s/zes*), the inessive/illative (*-am, -ad, -az, -ami̇, -adi̇, -azi̇*), and the elative (*-iš̌ʲt-* instead of *-iš̌ʲ*).

Plurality of possession is expressed by the ordinary plural suffix *-(j)os* followed by the possessive suffixes as set out above, with the following stipulations. Initial *i̇* is always used, and never initial *e*, in both possessive suffixes and in the instrumental case suffix; the transitive suffix is *-ti̇*. Examples: *val-jos-i̇* HORSE-plur-s1 'my horses', *pi-os-i̇z-li̇* SON-plur-s3-dat 'to his/her sons', *val-jos-i̇n-i̇mi̇* HORSE-plur-ins-p1 'with our horses', *uram-jos-ti̇-z* STREET-plur-transitive-s3 'along its streets'.

The possessive forms are used primarily to express possessive relations in both narrow and broad senses of the term, e.g. *mi̇nam tir-e* PRO.s1 gen AXE-s1 'my axe', *č̌ʲagi̇reš̌ʲ š̌ʲin-jos-i̇z* BLUE EYE-plur-s3 'his/her blue eyes', *korka-len ʎipet-ez* HOUSE-gen ROOF-s3 'the roof of the house', *ni̇l-i̇z-len ni̇l-i̇z* DAUGHTER-s3-gen DAUGHTER-s3 'his/her daughter's daughter', *so-len mi̇lki̇d-i̇z* PRO.s3-gen MOOD-s3 'his/her mood', *pinal-jos-len ki̇rǯʲan-zi̇* CHILD-plur-gen SONG-p3 'the children's song', *ni̇l-len č̌ʲeber-ez* GIRL-gen BEAUTY-s3 'the girl's beauty'.

The first-person singular suffix is also used in affectionate forms of address, e.g. *iž̌ʲ, iž̌ʲ gi̇di̇k-e, nuni̇ka-je, č̌ʲeber-e* 'sleep, sleep, my dove, my child, my beauty'.

The second- and third-person singular suffixes are also used to express definiteness or determinedness. Second-person forms are rarer in this function, and seem to have affective overtones, e.g. *vati̇š̌ʲk-i-z šundi̇-jed teʎ š̌ʲër-i̇* CONCEAL.refl-past-s3 SUN-s2 FOREST BEHIND-ill 'the (dear) sun has hidden behind the forest'.

There is widespread use of the third-person singular suffix (*-ez*) as a stylistically more or less neutral means of marking definiteness. It functions much as the definite article in Hungarian or English, e.g. *guž̌dor vi̇l-i̇n turi̇n-ez č̌ʲeber* CLEARING SURFACE-ine GRASS-s3 BEAUTIFUL 'the grass in the clearing is beautiful'. It can be added not only to nouns, but also to fully declined nouns, thereby rendering them both definite and susceptible to further declension, e.g. *gurt* 'village', genitive *gurt-len* 'of the village', with added s3 *gurt-len-ez* 'that of the village', metagenitive *gurt-len-ez-len* 'of that of the village', metainessive *gurt-len-az* 'in that of the village'.

Adjective

The adjective is formally not distinct from the noun, but it has morphological and syntactic properties peculiar to it.

Chief among these is *comparison*. The absolute degree is unmarked; the comparative is built with *=ges* (or *=gem*, in free variation). Example: *kuž̌ʲ* 'long', *kuž̌ʲ=ges/kuž̌ʲ=gem* 'longer'. The *superlative* is built with the help of particles or by means of reduplication, e.g. *pič̌ʲi* 'small', *samoj pič̌ʲi-jez* 'the smallest ones'; *tuž kuž^j* 'longest' (*tuž* 'very'); *š^jëd* 'black', *š^jëd&š^jëd* 'blackest', *vil^j* 'new', *van^jmiz-leš^j vil^j* EVERYTHING-abl NEW 'newest (= than everything new)'.

Plurality in the predicate adjective is indicated by the suffix *-eš^j*, e.g. *kišet liz* 'the cloth is blue', *kor-jos kuž^j-eš^j no zëk-eš^j* 'the beams are long and thick'.

Most Udmurt adjectives can be used as adverbs with no change in form (*umoj* 'good; well'). The meaning of some adverbs (e.g. *kema* 'for a long time') can be intensified by means not unlike that of the superlative (*kema-leš^j no kema* 'long, long ago; the very longest time ago').

Numerals

Numerals used as quantifiers in noun phrases do not decline or otherwise agree with the head; the head is usually in the singular, occasionally in the plural, e.g. *so tue t^jamïs kion kut-em* PRO.s3 THIS.YEAR EIGHT WOLF CATCHES-s3perf '(s)he caught eight wolves this year', *tačite vit^j vorgoron-jos č^jorïga-nï košk-i-zï* THIS EVENING FIVE MAN-plur FISHES-inf DEPARTS-past-p3 'this evening five men went fishing'.

Used as nouns, the numerals can be fully declined, in both absolute and possessive declensions. In compound numerals only the last number is declined.

Ordinals are formed with the suffix *=eti*, e.g. *n^jil=eti klass* 'fourth class'. The definite (i.e. s3) forms of ordinals are also declined, e.g. *kwin^jm=eti-jez-len* 'of the third'.

Fractions are formed with *=mos*: *vit^j=mos* '(one-) fifth', *ukmïs=mos* '(one-) ninth', *kwin^j kwat^j=mos* 'three-sixths'.

Approximate number is expressed either with the word *og* or the adjective-forming suffix *=o*, e.g. *og vit^j=ton murt* 'about fifty people', *das=o minut-jos* 'about ten minutes'.

Pronouns

Personal Pronouns

The personal pronouns distinguish nine cases; they lack the inessive, illative, elative, transitive, terminative and egressive cases.

The declension of the third-person pronoun is analogous to that of the noun.

Reflexive Pronouns

Three similar but distinct roots figure in the paradigm of the Udmurt reflexive pronoun. These are *as-*, *aš^j-*, and *ač^j-*. The first root (*as-*) also occurs uninflected in the meaning '(one's) own', e.g. *as nïl-ï* 'my own daughter', and with postpositions, e.g. *as dor-az* 'at his/her own home'.

Table 9.5   Udmurt personal pronouns: singular

	s1	*s2*	*s3*
Nominative	mon	ton	so
Genitive	mïnam	tïnad	solen
Ablative	mïnešʲtïm	tïnešʲtïd	solešʲ
Dative	mïnïm	tïnïd	solï
Accusative	mone	tone	soje
Instrumental	monen(ïm)	tonen(ïd)	soin
Abessive/Caritive	montek	tontek	sotek
Adverbial	monja	tonja	soja
Approximative	monlanʲ	tonlanʲ	solanʲ

Table 9.6   Udmurt personal pronouns: plural

	p1	*p2*	*p3*
Nominative	mi	ti	soos
Genitive	miⱡam	tiⱡad	sooslen
Ablative	miⱡešʲtïm	tiⱡešʲtïd	sooslešʲ
Dative	miⱡem(lï)	tiⱡed(lï)	sooslï
Accusative	miⱡemïz	tiⱡedïz	soosïz
	miⱡemdï	tiⱡeddï	soostï
Instrumental	miⱡemïn	tiⱡedïn	soosïn
	miⱡenïmï	tiⱡenïdï	
Abessive/Caritive	mitek	titek	soostek
Adverbial	mija	tija	soosja
Approximative	milanʲ	tilanʲ	sooslanʲ

Table 9.7   Udmurt reflexive pronouns: singular

	s1	*s2*	*s3*
Nominative	ačʲim	ačʲid	ačʲiz
Genitive	aslam	aslad	aslaz
Ablative	aslešʲtïm	aslešʲtïd	aslešʲtïz
Dative	aslïm	aslïd	aslïz
Accusative	asme	aste	asse
Instrumental	asenïm	asenïd	asenïz
Abessive/Caritive	ačʲimtek	ačʲidtek	ačʲiztek
Adverbial	ačʲimja	ačʲidja	ačʲizja
Approximative	ačʲimlanʲ	ačʲidlanʲ	ačʲizlanʲ

Table 9.8   Udmurt reflexive pronouns: plural

	p1	*p2*	*p3*
Nominative	ašʲmeos	ašʲteos	ašʲseos
Genitive	ašʲmelen	ašʲtelen	ašʲselen
Ablative	ašʲmelešʲ	ašʲtelešʲ	ašʲselešʲ
Dative	ašʲmelï	ašʲtelï	ašʲselï
Accusative	ašʲmemïz	ašʲtedïz	ašʲsezïz
	ašʲmedï	ašʲtedï	ašʲsezï
Instrumental	ašʲmemïn	ašʲtedïn	ašʲsezïn
	ašʲmeosïn	ašʲteosïn	ašʲseosïn
Abessive/Caritive	ašʲme(os)tek	ašʲte(os)tek	ašʲse(os)tek
Adverbial	ašʲme(os)ja	ašʲte(os)ja	ašʲse(os)ja
Approximative	ašʲme(os)lanʲ	ašʲte(os)lanʲ	ašʲse(os)lanʲ

Other Pronouns

Reciprocal pronouns are built by attaching the appropriate plural personal suffixes to reduplicated *o(dï)g* 'one': *og&og-mï-lï* 'to one another (of us)', *og&og-en-ïmï* 'with one another (of us)', *og&og-dï-tek* 'without each other (of you [plur])', *og&og-zes* 'each other (of them [acc])'.

With the exception of the definite forms *ta--iz* and *so--iz* 'this/that particular, precisely this/that, this/that very', the *demonstrative* pronouns are not inflected when used attributively. Example: *ta udïs-in* THIS REGION-ine 'in this region'. The inflection of *taiz* and *soiz* is identical with that of nouns, and when used as attributes these words agree with their head, e.g. *ta--iz knʲiga* 'this very book', *taiz-tek knʲiga-tek* 'without this very book', *ta-os-ïz knʲiga-os* 'these very books'.

When used independently, all the demonstrative pronouns are declined. Their paradigm follows that of the nominal closely, but there are deviations, e.g. *ta-je* 'this (acc)' (cf. *mon-e* 'me'). Other demonstrative pronouns are *tače* 'like this', *siče* 'like that', *tamïnda* 'this much', *somïnda* 'that much'.

The *interrogative* pronouns are also used as *relative* pronouns. The most important are *kin* 'who', *ma(r)* 'what, which', *kud(iz)* 'which', *kiče* 'what kind', *kënʲa* 'how much'. Apart from a few deviations (e.g. *kin-e* 'whom') they decline like nouns, e.g. *kin-lï* 'to whom', *kin-en* 'with whom'. Plural personal suffixes may be used with *kud*, e.g. *kud-mï* 'which of us'.

Indefinite, negative, and general (universal, indifferent) pronouns are formed, in the main, from the interrogative pronouns. Both absolute and personal declension are frequent. Examples: *kin+ke*, *olo+kin* 'someone', *no+kin*, *nʲe+kin* 'no one', *kotʲ+kin* 'anyone, no matter who', *kotʲ+ma(r)* 'anything, no matter what', *no+kin-mï* 'none of us', *no+mïr-dï* 'nothing of yours (plur)'. Others include *muket* 'other', and *vanʲ(mïz)*, *bïdes* 'all', inflected: *vanʲ-dï* 'all of you (plur)'.

The addition of the suffix *-na* forms numeric pronouns; they are always inflected for person. Examples: *og-na-m* 'I alone', *kïk-na-dï-lï* 'to you two'.

Verb

Conjugation: Finite Forms
The finite verb paradigm distinguishes the categories of mood, tense, number, and person.

Stem-types and conjugations. The citation form in Udmurt dictionaries is the infinitive, whose suffix is *-nï*. Lopping off this suffix gives us the verb stem, which always ends in either *ï* or *a*. Two conjugations may be distinguished, the first conjugation (*ï*-stems) and the second conjugation (*a*-stems). Suffix allomorphy presented below will be labelled with I and II accordingly. The stem-final *ï* of first-conjugation verbs is deleted whenever a vowel-initial suffix is attached.

Mood and tense. Tense and mood are in complementary distribution. There are three moods: indicative, imperative, and conditional. The indicative mood distinguishes four tenses: present (*vetliš^jko* 'I go', *turnaš^jko* 'I mow'), future (*vetlo* 'I shall go', *turnalo* 'I shall mow'), primary past (or preterite: *vetli* 'I went', *turnaj* 'I mowed'), and secondary past (or perfect: *vetlem* '(s)he has gone', *turnam* '(s)he has mowed'). The primary past refers to activities in the past without reference to their completion or to any result. The secondary past refers to the result of activities in the past, events which are often not directly witnessed. The suffix of the primary past is *-i-* in the first conjugation, *-a-* in the second conjugation. The suffix of the secondary past is *-(e)m*, which is preceded in the first person, and in the second and third persons plural, by other morphemes of derivational origin. The *-(e)m* suffix is historically identical with that of the perfect participle, see below.

The segmentation of the present and future morphemes is not synchronically transparent.

All four simple tense-forms may combine with *val* 'was/been' and *vilem* 'has been, was (evidently)' to form *compound* tenses. These tenses express durativity or habitual activity, e.g. *so gïr-e val* PRO.s3 PLOUGHS-s3pres BEEN '(s)he was ploughing', *so gïr-oz* (s3fut) *val* '(s)he used to plough (long ago)', *so gïr-oz vilem* '(they say that) (s)he ploughed; (s)he ploughed (as I remember)', *mïn-em val* GOES-past2 BEEN '(s)he had (already) gone (evidently)'. Dialectal use of such compound tenses varies considerably and awaits further investigation.

The suffix of the *imperative* is zero in the singular. First-conjugation verbs optionally lose their final *ï* if this is preceded by a single consonant. Examples: *vetlï* 'go!', *gïr(ï)* 'plough!', *vera* 'speak!' The second-person plural imperative is formed with *-e(le)* (I)/*-le* (II), e.g. *mïn-e* 'go! (plur)', *kïrǯ̌a-le* 'sing! (plur)'. Commands and suggestions directed to other persons are expressed with the future tense; outside the axis of discourse, the particle *med*

Table 9.9   Finite affirmative forms of the verb

	First conjugation mïni̯- 'goes'	Second conjugation daš^ja- 'prepares'
Indicative mood		
Present		
s1	mïniš^jko	daš^jaš^jko
s2	mïniš^jkod	daš^jaš^jkod
s3	mïne	daš^ja
p1	mïniš^jkom(ï)	daš^jaš^jkom(ï)
p2	mïniš^jkodï	daš^jaš^jkodï
p3	mïno	daš^jalo
Future tense		
s1	mïno	daš^jalo
s2	mïnod	daš^jalod
s3	mïnoz	daš^jaloz
p1	mïnom(ï)	daš^jalom(ï)
p2	mïnodï	daš^jalodï
p3	mïnozï	daš^jalozï
Primary past		
s1	mïni	daš^jaj
s2	mïnid	daš^jad
s3	mïniz	daš^jaz
p1	mïnimï	daš^jamï
p2	mïnidï	daš^jadï
p3	mïnizï	daš^jazï
Secondary past		
s1	mïniš^jkem	daš^jaš^jkem
s2	mïnem(ed)	daš^jam(ed)
s3	mïnem(ez)	daš^jam(ez)
p1	mïniš^jkemmï	daš^jaš^jkemmï
p2	mïnil^jl^jam(dï)	daš^jal^jl^jam(dï)
p3	mïnil^jl^jam(zï)	daš^jal^jl^jam(zï)
Imperative mood		
s2	mï̤n(ï)	da̤š^ja
p2	mï̤ne(le)	da̤š^jale
s3	me̤d mïnoz	me̤d dašal^joz
p3	me̤d mïnozï	me̤d dašal^jozï
Conditional mood		
s1	mïnïsal	daš^jasal
s2	mïnïsal(ïd)	daš^jasal(ïd)
s3	mïnïsal(ïz)	daš^jasal(ïz)
p1	mïnïsalmï	daš^jasalmï
p2	mïnïsaldï	daš^jasaldï
p3	mïnïsalzï	daš^jasalzï

must also precede the verb, e.g. *med užal-oz* 'let him/her work'.

The *conditional* suffix is *-sal-*. The first person singular is zero, and the second- and third-person suffixes may be omitted; syncretism of singular forms is thus possible. Example: dïši-sal(-ïz) '(s)he would study, (s)he would have studied'.

Some negative verb forms are built with the negative verb (*u-* in the present in future, *ë-* in the primary past, *e-* in the imperative), others with negative particles (*ëvël* in the secondary past, *ëj* in the conditional) or the negative suffix *=mte* (in the secondary past, in free variation with the use of the particle *ëvël*).

Tables 9.9 and 9.10 set out the complete finite paradigms of *mïnï-* 'goes' and *dašʲa-* 'prepares'. Brackets are used to indicate parallel forms which seem to differ at most stylistically in the standard language.

Alongside the completely regular factotum verb *luï-* 'is, becomes, happens; is able, is possible; exists' there is also a constellation of suppletive forms which express pure existence: present *vanʲ* 'exists', primary past *val*, secondary past *vïlem*, negative present *ëvël* 'there isn't'. These forms inflect for neither person nor number.

Verbal Nominals
Infinitive (*-nï*) is used with auxiliary verbs and as a substitute for final clauses with verbs of motion, e.g. *potizï ara-nï* 'they went out to harvest'.

Participles function as both attributes and predicates (see Syntax, p. 299).

The *imperfective active participle* (*=iśʲ* I/*=śʲ* II), e.g. *vetl=iśʲ* 'going', *vera=śʲ* 'speaking' forms many nouns, e.g. *dišet=iśʲ* 'teaching, teacher'. It has its own negative form, built with *=tem*, e.g. (from *dišʲt-* 'is brave') *dišʲt=iśʲ=tem* 'timid'.

The *perfect participle* (*=em* I/*=m* II) renders passive meanings with transitive verbs and resultative meanings with intransitive verbs. Examples: *gïr=em busï* 'ploughed field', *tone vaj=em murt gurt-az košk-iz* PRO.s2acc BRINGS=perf.part HUMAN HOUSE-s3ill DEPARTS-s3past1 'the person who brought you went home', *lïkt=em kišnomurt* ARRIVES=perf.part WOMAN 'the woman who has arrived'. This suffix also forms many nouns, e.g. *kul=em* 'death (*kulï-* 'dies'), *uža=m* 'work' (*uža-* 'works'). It has its own negative form, *=mte*, e.g. *kutï=mte kion* 'a wolf which has not been caught'.

The *necessitive participle* (*=ono* I/*=no* II) expresses the necessity of carrying out an action, e.g. *esker=ono už* 'a matter which must be investigated', *kora=no pu* 'a tree which must be felled'. Its negative form is *=on=tem* I/*=n=tem* II and expresses impossibility, e.g. *bïdest=on=tem už* 'work that is impossible to carry out', *čʲida=n=tem pëšʲ nunal* 'an unbearably hot day'.

The *potential participle* (*=mon* I/II) is the affirmative analogue to the preceding (*=(o)n=tem*), e.g. *gïrï=mon pijaš* 'a young man capable of ploughing', *gïrï=mon intï* 'a place which can be ploughed'.

Table 9.10   Finite negative forms of the verb

	First conjugation mïnï- 'goes'	Second conjugation dašʲa- 'prepares'
Indicative mood		
Present		
s1	u-g mïnišʲkï	u-g dašʲašʲkï
s2	u-d mïnišʲkï	u-d dašʲašʲkï
s3	u-g mïnï	u-g dašʲa
p1	u-m mïnišʲke	u-m dašʲašʲke
p2	u-d mïnišʲke	u-d dašʲašʲkïe
p3	u-g mïno	u-g dašʲalo
Future tense		
s1	u-g mïnï	u-g dašʲa
s2	u-d mïnï	u-d dašʲa
s3	u-g mïnï	u-g dašʲa
p1	u-m mïne(le)	u-m dašʲale
p2	u-d mïne(le)	u-d dašʲale
p3	u-g mïne(le)	u-g dašʲale
Primary past		
s1	ë-j mïnï	ë-j dašʲa
s2	ë-d mïnï	ë-d dašʲa
s3	ë-z mïnï	ë-z dašʲa
p1	ë-m mïne(le)	ë-m dašʲale
p2	ë-d mïne(le)	ë-d dašʲale
p3	ë-z mïne(le)	ë-z dašʲale
Secondary Past		
s1	mïnišʲkïmte(je)	dašʲašʲkïmte(je)
	ëvël mïnišʲkem	ëvël dašʲašʲkem
s2	mïnïmtejed	dašʲamtejed
	ëvël mïnem(ed)	ëvël dašʲam(ed)
s3	mïnïmte(jez)	dašʲamte(jez)
	ëvël mïnem(ez)	ëvël dašʲam(ez)
p1	mïnišʲkïmtemï	dašʲašʲkïmtemï
	ëvël mïnišʲkemmï	ëvël dašʲašʲkemmï
p2	mïnilʲlʲamte(dï)	dašʲalʲlʲamte(dï)
	ëvël mïnilʲlʲam(dï)	ëvël dašʲalʲlʲam(dï)
p3	mïnilʲlʲamte(zï)	dašʲalʲlʲamte(zï)
	ëvël mïnilʲlʲam(zï)	ëvël dašʲalʲlʲam(zï)
Imperative (prohibitive)		
s2	en mïn(ï)	en dašʲa
p2	en mïne(le)	en dašʲale
s3	medaz mïn(ï)	medaz dašʲa
p3	medaz mïne(le)	medaz dašʲale

Conditional mood

s1	ëj mïnïsal	ëj dašasal
s2	ëj mïnïsal(ïd)	ëj dašasal(ïd)
s3	ëj mïnïsal(ïz)	ëj dašasal(ïz)
p1	ëj mïnïsalmï	ëj dašasalmï
p2	ëj mïnïsaldï	ëj dašasaldï
p3	ëj mïnïsalzï	ëj dašasalzï

The inessive of the perfect participle expresses resultative predicates, e.g. *busï' gïr=em-ïn* 'the field is (in a) ploughed (state)', *turïn turna=m-ïn* 'the hay is (in a) cut (state)'.

Gerunds express cause and result as well as various temporal relations (simultaneity, anteriority, duration).

The *=sa* gerund expresses simultaneity or anteriority, e.g. *š^jerekja=sa vetl-e* LAUGHS=ger GOES-s3pres '(s)he walks laughing'. This gerund occurs frequently in compound verbs, see below.

The *=tek* gerund is the negative of the *=sa* gerund, e.g. *veraš^jki=tek puk-e* '(s)he sits without speaking'.

General temporal relations are expressed with the *=ku-* gerund, which may also take personal suffixes. Examples: *ǯeg ara=ku tuž pëš^j val* RYE HARVESTS=temp.ger VERY HOT EXISTED 'at rye-harvest time it was very hot', *bertï=ku-m* 'when I returned'.

The *=toǯ^j* gerund refers to the *terminus post quem non*, e.g. *žad^jï=toǯ biž^j-iz* TIRES-term.ger RUNS-s3past1 '(s)he ran until (s)he was exhausted'.

The *=mon* gerund, homophonous with the potential participle, means something like 'in a manner such that X can be Y'd, -ably', e.g. *vala=mon ver-az* 'he spoke intelligibly' (*vala-* 'understands'), *lidǯ^jï=mon gožt=em-ïn* 'it is (in a) legibly written (state)'.

Further gerundive forms are made from the perfect participle by adding the instrumental and elative case suffixes, e.g. *bërd=em-en-iz nomïr vera-nï u-g bïgatï'* WEEPS=perf.part-ins-s3 NOTHING SAYS-inf NEG.pres-s3 IS.ABLE 'what with his/her weeping it is impossible to say anything', *Ol^još kopa= m-iš^j dugd-iz* ALYOSHA DIGS=perf.part-ela CEASES-s3past1 'Alyosha ceased digging'.

Postpositions

These may be classed morphologically as either segmentable, e.g. *ul-ïn* 'under', *ul-iš^j* 'from under', *ul-e* 'to under' (cf. *ul* 'lower part') or unsegmentable, e.g. *ponna* 'for'. Personal suffixes are attached to the postposition, not to its head, e.g. *ukno ul-am* WINDOW UNDER-s1ine 'under my window'.

The head is usually in the nominative, but there are exceptions, e.g. *tonen seren* PRO.s2ins BECAUSE 'on account of you'.

Derivational Morphology

Formation of Nouns

Some of the more important noun-forming suffixes in the literary standard are =*lïk*, which build abstracts (*zem* 'truth', *zem=lïk* 'justice', *muskït* 'moist', *musk= ït=lïk* 'moisture'), =*č^ji*, which builds names of occupations (*vuz* 'item for sale', *vuz=c^ji* 'merchant', *argan* 'accordion', *argan=č^ji* 'accordionist'), =*es* (implements and body parts: kut- 'grasps', *kut=es* 'threshing-rod', *urd* 'rib', *urd=es* 'side'), =*on* I/=*n* II (abstracts: *veraš^jkï*- 'converses', *veraš^jk=on* 'conversation'), =*et* (objects, results: *l^jukï*- 'divides', *l^juk=et* 'part, piece'), =*em* I/=*m* II (abstracts; = perfect participle: *pïžï*- 'roasts', *pïž=em* 'roast, joint').

Formation of Adjectives

These include =*o* (roughly 'having X': *jël* 'milk', *jël=o skal* 'milk cow', *kužïm* 'strength', *kužm=o* 'strong'; this suffix has a mitigating effect when added to intensive reduplicated adjectives, e.g. *gord* 'red', *gord&gord* 'very red', *gord=o&gord=o* 'reddish'), =*tem* (privatives: *vu* 'water', *vu=tem* 'waterless', *šud* 'happiness', *šud=tem* 'unhappy'), =*es* (makes adjectives and nouns from nouns, adverbs, and onomatopoeics: *š^jerem* 'laughter', *š^jerem=es* 'funny', *ul-lan^j* 'downward', *ul-lan^j=es* 'declivity', *žingïr* 'ting-a-ling', *žingr=es* 'small bell').

Formation of Verbs

Verbal derivation is extensive, and permits nuanced differentiation in the expression of the type and manner of the action as well as the relation of actor to action.

The following suffixes make verbs from verbs: =*lï*- (regular, repetitive action: *gïrï=lï*- 'ploughs regularly, is always ploughing, ploughs and ploughs', *kuštï*- 'throws out/away', *kuštï=lï*- 'throws around a lot, keeps flinging'), =*l^jl^ja*- (with similar function: *loba*- 'flies', *loba=l^jl^ja*- 'flits about', *vera*- 'says', *vera=l^jl^ja*- 'keeps saying, regularly/always says'), =*tï*- (causatives and factitives: *uža*- 'works', *uža=tï*- 'makes [someone] work'), =*iš^jkï*- (~ =*skï*) I/=*š^jkï*- II (reflexives, mediopassives, and reciprocals: *diš^ja*- 'dons', *diš^ja=š^jkï*- 'gets dressed', *č^jupa*- 'kisses', *č^jupa=š^jkï*- 'kiss one another', *dišetï*- 'teaches', *dišet=skï*- 'learns'), =*emjaš^jkï*- I/=*mjaš^jkï*- (devalues or questions the quality or validity of the action: *uža=mjaš^jkï*- 'pretends to work; works away (ineffectually) at').

Other verb-forming suffixes include =*ï*- (*zor* 'rain', *zor=ï*- 'rains', *viž* 'bridge', *viž=ï*- 'crosses'), =*a*- (*n^jim* 'name', *n^jim=a*- 'names', *jig&jig* 'knock-knock', *jig=a*- 'knocks, hits'), =*ma*- (*gord* 'red', *gord=ma*- 'makes X red', *vož^j*- 'holds, contains', *vož^j=ma*- 'waits'), =*mï*- (*iz* 'stone', *iz=mï*- 'petrifies', *vil^j* 'new', *vil^j=mï*- 'is renewed', *viž^j=tem* 'stupid', *viž^j=tem=mï*- 'becomes stupid/stultified'), =*dï*- (*vï^j=dï*- 'renews, reconstructs'), =*tï*- (*gož* 'line, mark', *gož=tï*- 'writes').

The Morphology of Compounding

Nominal compounds may be co-ordinative, e.g. *s̄ʲëdales+lïz* 'dark blue (DARK+BLUE)', *ulino+vilino* 'one-storey house (roughly: DOWNSTAIRS +UPSTAIRS)' or subordinative, e.g. *pës̄ʲ+kïl* 'typhus (HOT+ILLNESS)', *vajo+biž* 'swallow (DOUBLE+TAIL)'. Dvandva compounds also occur, e.g. *ïm+nïr* 'face (MOUTH+NOSE)', *anaj&ataj* 'parents (MOTHER &FATHER)'.

Co-ordinative verb compounds may consist of paired verbs, e.g. *šudï-nï&s̄ʲerekja-* 'has fun (PLAYS&LAUGHS)', or of NOUN+VERB syntagms, e.g. *kur+ač̄č̄ï-* 'suffers (BAD/EVIL+SEES)'.

Subordinative verb compounds, so-called 'double verbs' (they are in fact verb complexes built with the *=sa* gerund), are extremely common. The semantics of the two verbs meld to create complex aspectual/semantic shadings. Examples: *kora=sa bïdtï-* CUTS=ger FINISHES 'fells (perfective)', *žua=sa bïrï-* BURNS=ger PERISHES 'burns down completely', *peḡǯʲï=sa koški-* ESCAPES=ger DEPARTS 'gets away safely'.

Another type of compound verb is built from recent Russian loans. In this construction, the Russian verb is put in the (Russian) infinitive and the Udmurt factotum verb *karï-* 'does' is added, e.g. *diktovatʲ karï-* 'dictates'.

Syntax

Nominal Constructions

In attributive constructions modifier precedes modified. Besides adjectives, modifiers may be deictics, numerals, nouns, and participles; participles may have, in turn, their own complements. Examples: *tëdʲï derem* 'white shirt', *siče čʲorïg* 'such a fish', *ukmïseti klass* 'ninth class', *pu korka* 'wooden house', *lulo gondïrez kutïmon pëjšuras̄ʲ* 'hunter capable of catching a live bear'.

Attributive adjectives stand before the noun they modify and do not generally agree with it, either in number or in case, e.g. *lïz kišet-jos-tek* 'without blue cloths'. Exceptionally there is plural agreement; the adjectival plural suffix is again *-es̄ʲ*, e.g. *kuž̄ʲ-es̄ʲ no zëk-es̄ʲ kor-jos uram-ïn kïlʲlʲo* 'long and thick beams lie in the street', *veras̄ʲkis̄ʲtem-es̄ʲ vorgoron-jos* 'silent (non-speaking) men'. Adjectives with the s3 definiteness-marker are declined as nouns, whether alone or in noun phrase apposition, e.g. *vilʲ-ez-lï* NEW-s3-dat 'to the new (one)', *jegit-jos-ïn-ïz nïl-jos-ïn* YOUNG-plur-ins-s3 GIRL-plur-ins 'with the young ones, with girls', *bur-ïn-ïz s̄ʲinm-ïn-ïz* RIGHT-ins-s3 EYE-ins-s3 'with his right eye'.

In the possessive construction the possessor stands either in the genitive or (if the possession is the direct object) in the ablative. The possession takes person suffixes. Examples *dišetïs̄ʲ-len knʲiga-os-ïz* TEACHER-gen BOOK-plur-s3 'the teacher's books', *gurt-len pum-ïz* 'the end of the village', *muž^jej-leš^j jurt-se tupat=jano* MUSEUM-abl BUILDING-s3acc RENO-VATES=nec.part 'the museum building has to be renovated'. If the possessor is encoded by a personal pronoun, this stands in the genitive: *so-len vïn-ïz* 'his/her younger brother'; the pronoun may also be omitted (*vïn-ïz*). Furthermore, invariable *as* or the inflected reflexive pronoun may be used instead: *as pi-jez-lï* 'to his/her own son', *aslad korka-jed* 'your own house'.

Two other constructions which border on the possessive are simple juxtaposition (*ǯ̌ek kuk* 'the leg of the table (TABLE LEG)', *korka ës* 'the door of the house (HOUSE DOOR)', used with inanimates, and the use of the elative to mark the place where something belongs or comes from (*jag-ïš^j pužïm-jos* 'pines from/of the forest', *magaž^jin-ïš^j vitrina-ïn* 'in the shop window').

Subjects and Predicative Constructions

Any nominal can function as subject. The subject is usually in the nominative, with or without personal/determinative suffixes: *pi turna* 'the boy is mowing', *soos turnalo* 'they are mowing', *pimï dišetske* 'our son is studying', *badǯ̌ïm-ez pi-je zavod-ïn uža, pič^ji-jez kolxoz-ïn* ELDER-s3 SON-s1 FACTORY-ine WORKS.-s3pres, SMALL-s3 KOLKHOZ-ine 'my older son works in a factory, my younger son in a kolkhoz'. Paired subjects go into the instrumental, e.g. *nïl-ïn pi-jen gorod-e košk-i-zï* GIRL-ins BOY-ins CITY-ill DEPARTS-past1-p3 'the boy and girl went to the city'.

A special form of subject is marked with a case suffix (most commonly elative or genitive) *followed* by the plural suffix *-jos*; this construction is used to express a collectivity of people from a certain place or group: *otïn kutsa-š^jk-o kolxoz-ïš^j-jos* THERE THRESHES-p3pres KOLKHOZ-ela-plur 'people from the kolkhoz are threshing there', *aš^jme-len-jos gïron-zes bïdest-i-zï* PRO.REFLEX.p1-gen-plur PLOUGHING-s3acc FINISHES-past1-p3 'our lot have finished the ploughing'. The infinitive can also function as subject: *til^jed-ïn uža-nï tuž kapč^ji* PRO.p2-ins WORKS-inf VERY EASY 'working with you (plur) is very easy'.

In impersonal constructions the logical subject stands in the dative: *Kol^ja-lï dišetiš^j dor-ï mïn=ono lu-i-z* KOLYA-dat TEACHER NEAR-ill GOES= nec.part IS-past1-s3 'Kolya had to go to the teacher'.

Predicates are of two basic types: verbal and nominal. Verbal predicates agree with their subject in number and person, and express the modality and relative time of the action. The conditional mood is used to convey desirability or contingency, e.g. *ti dor-ï vetlï-sal-mï* 'we would (like to) go to you(r place)', *so-leš^j kïlzïš^jkï-sal-zï--ke, nomïr ëj luï-sal* PRO.s3-abl LISTENS-cond-p3--IF NOTHING NEG HAPPENS-cond 'if they had listened to him/her, nothing would have happened'. Commands and prohibitions are expressed directly by the imperative: *košk-ele tatïš^j* '(you plur) go away from here', *en mïn* 'don't go!', *nïl-lï vera, med pïr-oz korka-Ø* GIRL-dat SAYS-s2imp PARTICLE ENTERS-s3fut HOUSE-ill 'tell the girl to go into the house'.

We may classify not only nouns, adjectives, numerals, and adjectives, but also adverbial complements as nominal predicates. Examples: *viznan nʲër kuʐʲ* 'the fishing rod is long', *so dišetiŝʲ* '(s)he is a teacher', *mi doriŝʲen čʲupčʲi šur kiďok-ïn* PRO.p1 FROM *CHEPCHA* RIVER DISTANT-ine 'the Chepcha River is far from us', *so knʲiga-jez lïdʒʲ=ono* 'this book must be read'.

Present-tense forms of the nominal predicate take zero copula, e.g. *ton udmurt--a* 'are you Udmurt?', *mon tatïn ŝʲër murt* PRO.s1 HERE STRANGER HUMAN 'I am a stranger here'. In the past tense, indeclinable *val* is used for all persons and numbers: *tïnad brat-ed soku stuďent val* 'your (older) brother was a student then', *tolon bert=ono val* 'yesterday it was necessary to return (home)'. In other tenses or to express change of state, the copula and factotum verb *luï-* is used: *mïnam brat-e agronom lu-oz* 'my (older) brother is going to be an agronomist', *zor ber-e omïr čʲilkït lu-i-z* RAIN AFTER-ill AIR CLEAN BECOMES-past1-s3 'after the rain the air became clean'.

Pure existence is expressed by the indeclinable particle *vanʲ*: *ta gurt-ïn odig motor nïl vanʲ* 'there is a beautiful girl in this village'; non-existence is expressed by indeclinable *ëvël*: *kanfet ëvël, sakar ëvël, ma-in ben čʲaj ju-omï* SWEETS NOT.EXISTS SUGAR NOT.EXISTS WHAT-ins INDEED TEA DRINKS-p1pres/fut 'there isn't any sweet, there isn't any sugar, with what shall we drink tea?'.

Udmurt lacks a possessive verb corresponding to English 'has', and *vanʲ* (negative: *ëvël*) is used instead, e.g. *aŝʲme-len tros uʐaŝʲ-jos-mï vanʲ* PRO.REFLEX.p1-gen MANY WORKER-plur-p1 EXISTS 'we have many workers', *pi-je-len kosťum-ez ëvël* SON-s1-gen SUIT-s3 NOT.EXISTS 'my son has no suit'.

Direct Objects

The direct object can be in the nominative or the accusative. The general rule is that indefinite objects stand in the nominative (-∅) , e.g. *gožtet-∅ gožto* 'I'll write **a letter**', *vumurt so abï-lï ŝʲote majtal-∅* 'the water-spirit gives that old woman (some) soap', *nʲulsekaŝʲjos gondïr-∅ kutiľľam* 'the hunters have caught **a bear**', while definite direct objects stand in the accusative: *ʒeg-ez oktïsa bïdtïmï inʲi* 'we've already gathered in **the rye**', *ta gazet-jos-tï ček vile pon* 'put **these newspapers** on the table'. Direct objects marked with person/definite suffixes always count as definite; the nominative personal forms are therefore never used as direct objects. Examples: *baŝʲte majtal-ze* '(s)he picks up **his/her soap**', *kin so tïpï-jez pogïrtoz, so-lï nïl-me ŝʲot-o, šu-em eksej* WHO THAT OAK-acc FELLS-s3fut PRO.s3-dat DAUGHTER-s1acc GIVES-s1pres/fut SAYS-past2 TSAR 'whoever fells that oak, to that one I shall give **my daughter**, said the Tsar', *aʐʲtem-leŝʲ umoj uʐam-ze en vitʲi* LAZY-abl GOOD WORK-s3acc PROHIB.VERB-s2 AWAITS 'don't wait for **the good work** of a lazy person, i.e. don't expect good work from a lazy (person)'. The infinitive, too, can serve as direct object: *tros mediŝʲkod leŝʲtï-nï* 'you want **to accomplish** a lot'.

Adverbial Complements and the Use of the Case Suffixes

Adverbials are either independent, like ǯ́eč́ 'well': so ǯ́eč́ leš́t-e '(s)he does it well', gerunds, or formed from nominals with case suffixes or postpositions. Here there is space for only a brief survey of some of the more important adverbial uses of the cases.

Ablative expresses motion away from X, origin, cause: *Petrov* **mašina-leš́** *palensk-i-z* 'Pterov jumped **away from the machine**', *stal-leš́ kuso leš́t-o* 'they make scythe[s] **of steel**', *šunït-leš́ lïmï suna* 'the snow melts **from the heat**'. It is also used to mark the superlative member of a comparison (*šundï-leš́ jugït* 'brighter **than the sun**') and with certain verbs (*kaban-leš́ val u-g kiškaš́kï* 'a horse isn't afraid **of a hayrick**').

Dative is most frequently used to indicate the indirect object, as in *eš-e-lï kn^jiga š́ot-i* 'I gave a book **to my friend**', *nene-lï jurttï-nï* 'to help **mother**', but it can also express intended time-span (*nunal-lï* 'for a day'), objective (*Ol^ja* **vu-lï** *mïn-e* 'Olya goes **for water**'), or result (*č́aš́-i-z, kiž́pu-ez šelep-lï përmït-i-z* 'lightning struck (it), the birch turned **into (a piece of) kindling**'.

Caritive/abessive expresses the lack of something: *mumï-tek&bubï-tek kil^j-i* 'I was left **without mother or father**'.

The *adverbial* case indicates accordance with something, whether temporal or qualitative: *plan-ja* 'according to plan', **užam-ja** *milkïd č́utskïl-i-z* '**during/in the course of the work** the mood became more cheerful', *tus-sï-ja no soos og&og-zï-lï kel^jš-o* 'they resemble one another **in their appearance**, as well'.

Instrumental is used both for instrumental proper (**kač́i-jen** *vandï-nï* 'to cut **with scissors**', *š́ulm-ïn-ïm šediš́ko* 'I feel (it) **with my heart**') and for accompaniment (**Pedor-en** *uža-mï* 'we worked **with Pedor**').

Approximative indicates drawing near to a place or approximation in time: *nil* **sur-lan^j** *biž́-i-z* 'the girl ran **towards the river**', **gužem-lan^j** *ož́ï lu-i-z* 'this happened **towards summertime**'.

Inessive refers to location within or on a place (*gurt-ïn* 'in a village', *busï-os-ïn* 'in the fields'), to point in time (*vit^j=eti č́as-ïn* FIVE=ord.num HOUR-ine 'at five o'clock'), or to state, as in **dïšetiš́-ïn** *uža* '(s)he works **as a teacher**'.

Illative refers primarily to movement towards a place (*Petrov* **kanava-je** *uš́-i-z* 'Petrov fell **into the canal**'), but also to points in time (*arn^ja nunal-e* 'on Sunday'), *č́ït-jos-ï* 'evenings, every evening', *šundïjo nunal-jos-ï* 'on sunny days'.

Elative refers primarily to movement from a place (**busï-ïš́** *bert-e* '(s)he comes back **from the field**'), but is also selected by certain verbs, e.g. *van^j-ze so-je ti šed^jt-odï ta* **kn^jiga-ïš́** 'you (plur) will find all this **in this book**'.

Transitive indicates trajectory, i.e. route traversed or aperture franchised, e.g. **ulč́a-jeti** *avtobus košk-i-z* 'the bus drove **along the street**', *so* **ukno-jeti** *uč́ke val* '(s)he was looking (out) of **the window**'.

Terminative indicates the point in space or time beyond which something does not proceed, e.g. *arama-ož̌ⁱ biž̌ʲ-i-mï* 'we ran **as far as the grove**', *ǯ̌ït-ož̌ⁱ uža-zï* 'they worked **until evening**'.

Egressive indicates the reverse of the terminative, i.e. the spatial or temporal starting-point: *Iževsk-iš̌ⁱen pojezd-en mïn-i-mï* '**From Izhevsk**, we went by train', *siž̌ʲil-iš̌ⁱen* '(starting) from autumn'.

Major Constituent Order

In neutral sentences the subject is in the first part of the sentence, the predicate is at the end, and any direct object and adverbial complements stand somewhere in between, e.g. *Mixajlov važ̌ʲ č̌ʲukna ik užaš̌ⁱjos dorï liktiz* MIKHAILOV EARLY MORNING DULY WORKERS TO WENT 'so, early in the morning M. went to the workers'. Deviation from this neutral order is the rule, however, particularly (but not exclusively) in interrogative and exclamatory sentences. Factors include position in the discourse, communicational roles, sentence-types, and logical stress (emphasis).

Constructions with Verbal Nominals

Verbal nominals (infinitive, participles, gerunds) which function as complements may take complements of their own; they then are functionally equivalent to subordinate clauses. The nature of the subordination may be temporal, causal, or other. A sentence can contain more than one such construction, e.g. *gorod-iš̌ⁱ tolon likt=em inž̌enʲer, už-ze lïmšor-ož̌ⁱ bïdestï =sa, gurt-e benž̌ʲin-lï košk-i-z* CITY-ela YESTERDAY ARRIVES=perf. part ENGINEER WORK-s3acc NOON-term COMPLETES=ger TOWN-ill PETROL-dat DEPARTS-past1-s3 'the engineer who came from the city yesterday, having finished his work by midday, left for town to get petrol'.

Here are some further examples of verbal nominal constructions. With infinitive: *ta už-ez ǯ̌og bïdestï-nï ponna, tros kuž̌ïm kule luoz* THIS WORK-acc QUICK FINISHES-inf FOR, MUCH ENERGY NECESSARY IS.s3fut 'much energy will be necessary in order to finish this work'. With participles: *š̌ʲërpala úč̌ʲkiz no **urobo dorin siliš̌ⁱ adʲamijez** adǯ̌ʲiz Oleksan* 'Oleksan looked to his side and saw **the man who was standing next to the waggon** (WAGGON NEXT.TO STANDING MAN)', ***vuko-iš̌ⁱ bert=em Oddo** val-ze jusk-e* '**Oddo, having returned from the mill** (MILL-ela RETURNS-=past.part *ODDO*) unharnesses his horse', ***pinal-jos kosk=em ber-e**, tatïn mëzmït lu-i-z* '**after the children left** (CHILD-plur DEPARTS=past.part AFTER-ill) it became boring here'. With gerunds: ***nunalbït š̌ʲekït mešok-jos-tï ǯ̌utja=sa žadʲ-i-z** Mikvor Pedor* '**lifting heavy sacks all day** (ALL.DAY HEAVY SACK-plur-acc LIFTS=ger) P. M. became tired', *ma **šuï-nï todï=tek**, so palensk-i-z* '**not knowing what to say** (WHAT SAYS-inf KNOWS=neg.ger), (s)he left', ***pi-me dišetskï-nï nuï-ku-m** vedra duren kiš̌ⁱt=em kadʲ zor-i-z* '**when I took my son to be taught** (to his lesson; SON-s1acc TEACHES-inf TAKES=temp.ger-s1) it was raining as if poured from a bucket (BUCKET FROM POURED AS)', ***ton nʲulesk-i vuï=tož̌ⁱ** so gurt-az* *lu-oz inʲi* 'by the time you get into the forest (PRO.s2 FOREST-ill ARRIVES-term.ger) (s)he will be home already'.

Compound Sentences

Compound sentences may be further subdivided into co-ordinate and subordinate types. In the following examples the conjunctions and relative pronouns are highlighted. Co-ordinate examples: *kwažʲ zoriz* **no**, *turïn vožektiz* 'the rain fell, **and** the grass grew green', *gužem nunaljos kužʲešʲ luo,* **a** *ujjos vakčʲiješʲ* 'summer days are long, **while/but** the nights are short', *šutetskono val* **no**, *dïr ëvël* 'one ought to rest, **but** there isn't time', *umme ušʲinï ug luï:* **to** *punïos uto,* **to** *jegitjos kïrǯalo* 'it is impossible to fall asleep: **either** the dogs are barking **or** the young people are singing'. Subordinate examples: *ton važʲ valad,* **kin** *luono tïnïd* 'you learned early **who** you should become', **kïtïn** *tolon gïridï,* **otïn** *ik vožʲmano luodï* '**where** you ploughed yesterday, **there** you must wait', **kuke** *šunït luiz,* **soku** *čʲorïganï mïnomï* '**when** it has become warm, [**then**] we shall go fishing', *pinal-jos korka-n ëvël* **dïr-ja**, *mon knʲiga lïdǯʲ-išʲk-o* CHILD-plur HOME-ine NOT.EXIST TIME-adv PRO.s1 BOOK READS-pres-s1 '**when** the children aren't home I read a book', **kinlen** *praktikajez badǯʲïm,* **solen** *užez* **no** *volʲït mïne* '**(s)he who** has (had) a lot of practice [**that person**] has his/her work go smoothly', *adʲamilen kïče šʲulmïz,* **sïče** *ik užez* **no** '**as** a person's heart is, **so** too is his/her work', *už bordï kutskid* **ke**, *soje odno ik bïdestïnï tïršï* '**if** you have started to do something, try to finish it as well'.

There are also asyndetic compound sentences of both types, e.g. *brigadaos šʲežʲïzes gine oktïsa&kaltïsa vuizï, vïlʲišʲ zorïnï kutskiz* 'the brigades had just finished bringing in the oats, it began to rain', *juž vïlti valen vetlizï, sokem so jun val* 'they went by horse over the snowcrust, so firm was it'.

Indirect Discourse

Declarative, interrogative, and exclamatory sentences are reported by means of the conjunction *šuïsa* (i.e., the *sa*-gerund of *šuï-* 'says'): *vara veraz, so vanʲmïz šʲarišʲ todiz šuïsa* VARA SAYS-s3past1 PRO.s3 EVERYTHING ABOUT KNOWS-s3past1 SAYS=ger 'Vara said that she knows about it all', *kulʲto vorttomï šat šuïsa, purga kenez pužej-lešʲ juaz* SHEAF DELIVERS.p1fut PERHAPS SAYS=ger, *PURGA* MRS *PUŽEY*-abl ASKS-s3past1 'Mrs Purga asked Puzhey whether we might perhaps send sheaves'. As these examples show, the subordinate clause may stand before or after the main clause.

Imperatives are rendered indirectly by means of the future forms of the verb, preceded by the particle *med*. As in other forms of indirect discourse, the subordinate clause ends with *šuïsa*, e.g. *čʲeberšur-išʲ kalïk-ez vičʲak-se tatčʲï med ulʲlʲalozï šuïsa, pop kos-e ČEBERSUR*-ela PEOPLE-acc ALL-s3acc HITHER PARTIC DRIVES.p3fut SAYS=ger PRIEST COMMANDS-s3pres 'the priest orders that they drive all the people from Čebersur here'.

Lexicon

Architectonics

Loanwords
Native roots have a relatively simple structure. Two vowels occur adjacent
normally only at morpheme boundaries. Consonant clusters of two normally
occur only root-internal and root-final; in the latter case one of the consonants
is a resonant. Examples: *iz* 'stone', *gu* 'pit', *uno* 'many', *bur* 'good', *bord*
'wall', *tïlï* 'feather', *gondïr* 'bear'. Onomatopoieic words typically show
(partial) reduplication, e.g. *žingïr&žangïr* 'ting-a-ling'.

Older Loans
Older loanwords do not deviate formally from native canonic shapes. There
is a Chuvash layer (the Udmurt paid tribute to the Chuvash from the tenth to
the thirteenth century), e.g. *ara-* 'harvests', *arnʲa* 'week', *buskelʲ* 'neighbour',
ukšʲo 'money'. There is also a later layer of Tatar loanwords dating from the
thirteenth century. Four to five hundred Tatar loans entered common Udmurt,
and even more into many dialects. Examples: *batïr* 'fearless; hero', *kijar*
'cucumber', *uram* 'street', *jemïšʲ* 'fruit', *adʲami* 'person', *alda-* 'cheats,
deceives', *bujol* 'paint'. Tatar loans continue to flow into peripheral dialects
of Udmurt to the present day.

Russian Loans
The consonants *f*, *x*, and *c* occur only in recent loans, mostly from Russian
(*cement, fabrika* 'factory', *xirurg* 'surgeon'). In earlier Russian borrowings,
these sounds were replaced by *p*, *k*, and *č*, e.g. *porma* 'form', *kalera* 'cholera',
ulča 'street'.

More recent loans also retain initial consonant clusters, e.g. *dvorec*
'palace'; in earlier borrowings such clusters were either syncopated or
rendered medial by prothesis, e.g. *durug* 'suddenly' < вдруг, *ižʲver* 'wild
animal' < зверь.

Northern groups of Udmurt speakers had already come into contact with
Russian during the Tatar reign, but the great upsurge in Russian influence
began after 1552, when the Udmurt came under Russian domination and the
numbers of Russian colonists began to increase. By 1917 some six to eight
hundred Russian loans had been borrowed into Udmurt; some of these were
used only in translations of religious literature, however.

After 1917 writers and scholars worked to create an Udmurt literary
language. Thorough language renewal and hundreds of neologisms would be
necessary if Udmurt was to be a useful and supple instrument in all the new
social, economic, and cultural domains of life. The outstanding author Gerd
Kuzebaj and like-minded contemporaries began this work with enthusiasm,
but the 1930s and Stalinism put an end to their activity. Only a few neologisms

managed to take root, e.g. *vir+ser* 'artery (BLOOD+VEIN)', *nʲimtul=tem* 'anonymous (NAME.AND.PATRONYMIC=LESS)', *kïl+ož* 'debate (LANGUAGE+WAR)'.

Udmurt Text

A text in the literary language, written by the prominent linguist V. I. Keljmakov. Adapted from Csúcs (1990: 71).

A: Cyrillic orthography; B: Latin transcription, segmented; C: morpheme-by-morpheme gloss; D: word-by-word English translation; E: freer English translation.

A1. Ужме	быгатамея	умойгес	быдэсъяны
B1. už-me	bïgat=em-e-ja	umoj=ges	bïdesja-nï
C1. WORK-s1acc	KNOWS=NdV-s1-adv	GOOD-cfv	ACCOMPLISHES-inf
D1. my work	according to my ability	better	to carry out

турттӥсько,	угось	тодӥсько,	озьы	гинэ
turtt-iš^jko,	ugoš^j	tod-iš^jko,	ož^jï	gine
STRIVES-s1pres	PARTIC	KNOWS-s1pres	THUS	ONLY
I strive	after all	I know	thus	only

калыкелы	зеч	лесьтыны	быгато	шуыса
kalïk-e-lï	ȼ^ječ^j	leš^jtï-nï	bïgat-o	šuï=sa
PEOPLE-s1-dat	GOOD	BUILDS-inf	IS.ABLE-s1fut	SAYS=ger
my people	good	to build	I shall be able	[end quotation]

A2. Удмурт	калык	азьланяз	но	кылзэ
B2. udmurt	kalïk	až^j-lan^j-az	no	kïl-ze
C2. UDMURT	PEOPLE	FORE-app-s3ine/ill	AND	LANGUAGE-s3acc
D2. Udmurt	people	in the future	both	its language

но	культуразэ	мед	утёз	шуыса
no	kul^jtura-ze	med	ut^j-oz	šuï=sa
AND	CULTURE-s3acc	PARTIC	FOSTERS-s3fut	SAYS=ger
and	its culture	in order that	it fosters	[end quotation]

тыршисько	A3. Оскисько	лыктӥсь
tïrš-iš^jko	B3. osk-iš^jko,	lïkt=iš^j
STRIVES-s1pres	C3. BELIEVES-s1pres	COMES=pres.part
I strive	D3. I believe	coming

выжыосмы	но	та	удысын	тыршыса
viži-os-mï	no	ta	udïs=ïn	tïrši=sa
GENERATION-plur-p1	AND	DEM.PRO	AREA-ine	STRIVES=ger
our generations	as well	this	in area	diligently

ужалозы
užal-ozï
WORKS-p3fut
they will work

E1. I try to do my work to the best of my ability, because I know that this is the only way I shall be able to do my people good. E2. I work hard to ensure that in future the Udmurt people foster their language and culture. E3. I believe that future generations, too, will work diligently in this area.

References and Further Reading

Alatyrev, V.I. (1970) (ed.) Грамматика современного удмуртского языка. Синтаксис простого предложения, Izhevsk: Izdateljstvo Udmurtiä.

——— (1983) 'Краткий грамматический очерк удмуртского языка', in V.M. Vaxrušev (ed.), Удмурт-ӟуч словарь, Moscow: Russkij Äzyk.

Csúcs, S. (1970) 'A votják nyelv orosz jövevényszavai I.–II.', Nyelvtudományi Közlemények 72: 323–62 and 74: 27–47.

——— (1979) 'A votják-tatár nyelvi kapcsolatok és történeti hátterük I.–II.', Nyelvtudományi Közlemények 81: 365–72 and 82: 135–48.

——— (1988) 'Die wotjakische Spache', in D. Sinor (ed.) The Uralic Languages: Description, History and Foreign Influences, Handbuch der Orientalistik 8/1, Leiden: Brill, pp. 131–46.

——— (1990a) Chrestomathia votiacica, Budapest: Tankönyvkiadó.

——— (1990b) Die tatarischen Lehnwörter des Wotjakischen, Budapest: Akadémiai kiadó.

Décsy, G. (ed.) (1967) The First Votyak Grammar, Indiana University Uralic and Altaic Series 81, Bloomington: Indiana University.

Kelmakov, V.K. (1981) Образцы удмуртской речи, Izhevsk: Izdateljstvo Udmurtiä.

——— (1990) Образцы удмуртской речи 2, Izhevsk: Udmurtskij Institut IJaL.

Munkácsi, B. (1896) A votják nyelv szótára. Lexicon linguae votiacorum, Budapest: Magyar Tudományos Akadémia.

Munkácsi, B. and Fuchs, D.R. (1952) Volksbräuche und Volksdichtung der Wotjaken, MSFOu 102, Helsinki: Société Finno-Ougrienne.

Perevošikov, P.N. (ed.) (1962) Грамматика современного удмуртского языка. Фонетика и морфология, Izhevsk: Udmurtskoe knižnoe izdateljstvo.

Stipa, G. (1960) Funktionen der Nominalformen des Verbs in den permischen Sprachen, MSFOu 121, Helsinki: Société Finno-Ougrienne.

Suihkonen, P. (1990) Korpustutkimus kielitypologiassa sovellettuna udmurttiin, MSFOu 207, Helsinki: Société Finno-Ougrienne.

Vaxrušev, V.M. (ed.) (1956) Русско-удмуртский словарь, Moscow.

Vaxrušev, V.M., Zaxarov, V.N. and Kalinin, L.I. (eds) (1974) Грамматика современного удмуртского языка. Синтаксис сложного предложения, Izhevsk: Izdateljstvo Udmurtiä.

Vikár, L. and Bereczki, G. (1989) Votyak Folksongs, Budapest: Akadémiai kiadó.

Wichmann, Y. (1893) *Wotjakische Sprachproben*, vol. I, Helsingfors: Druckerei der Finnischen Literatur-Gesellschaft.

—— (1901) *Wotjakische Sprachproben*, vol. II, Helsingfors: Druckerei der Finnischen Literatur-Gesellschaft.

—— (1903) *Die tschuvassischen Lehnwörter in den permischen Sprachen*, Helsingfors: Société Finno-Ougrienne.

—— (1954) *Wotjakische Chrestomathie mit Glossar*, Helsinki: Société Finno-Ougrienne.

Wichmann, Y., Uotila, T.E., and Korhonen, M. (1987) *Wotjakischer Wortschatz*, Helsinki: Société Finno-Ougrienne.

10 Komi

Anu-Reet Hausenberg

Komi, together with Udmurt, make up the Permian group of the Uralic language family. Since ancient times speakers of Komi have lived in the Vychegda basin and along rivers on the upper reaches of the Kama.

History has divided Komi into three dialect groups. The Komi-Zyrian dialects are spoken in the northern part of the area, while the Komi-Permyak and the Yaz'va groups dominate in the southern part. Some linguists treat the Komi-Zyrian and the Permyak groups as separate languages. As the name 'Komi' is often applied to the Zyrians only, this may cause misinterpretation of statistics.

According to the 1989 census there were 344,519 Zyrians and 152,060 Permyaks in the Soviet Union. 84.5 per cent of the Zyrians (291,542 people) live in the Komi Republic (capital Syktyvkar). The average density of the population is 3 people per km^2, but the actual distribution is rather uneven. The Zyrian-dominated villages are situated along rivers. Of the population of the Republic (1,263,000 in 1989) 954,000 are urban, but of these only about 15 per cent are ethnic Zyrians.

Outside the Republic relatively compact Zyrian settlements exist on the Kola Peninsula and in western Siberia. A major exodus (mostly from the Izhma basin) took place in the second half of the nineteenth century.

The administrative territory of the Permyaks, the Komi-Permyak National Okrug (capital Kudymkar), is part of the Perm' Oblast. Unfortunately about 14,000 Permyaks remained outside the Okrug when it was created; they live in separate villages in the neighbouring region. There are also some small Permyak settlements in western Siberia which date from the second half of the nineteenth century. The socio-political situation renders official statistics concerning the Permyaks scarce and not very reliable.

Speakers of the Yaz'va dialect live east of the Permyaks on the banks of the Vishera and the Yaz'va Rivers. In the 1960s the number of Yaz'va speakers was estimated at 4,000.

Dialectal Variation

The present-day variants of the Komi language reflect the impact of natural factors as well as migrations and contacts – both a result of the language's linguo-geographic position in the centre of the Finno-Ugric area. Watersheds, dense forests, and bogland have favoured differentiation. Prolonged settlement alongside related tribes, however, has supported parallel developments and led to lexical borrowing. The ancient trade routes which traverse the original Komi homelands used to connect Scandinavia with Siberia and the South. The Komi themselves were enterprising merchants, setting up contacts with several distant peoples. Different reasons forced the Komi to migrate to smaller and more remote rivers and to more sparsely populated areas. This brought about a mixing of dialects and a distortion of dialect borders. The most heterogeneous area nowadays is situated near the Vychegda and the Pechora. According to documents it was in the sixteenth and seventeenth centuries that the Upper Vychegda region received many new settlers from the Udora, Vym', and Lower Vychegda regions, and later on from the basins of the Sysola and Luza Rivers. The Komi settlement of the Pechora basin began at the end of the seventeenth century, the settlers coming mostly from the banks of the Sysola, Vym', and Mezen', and from the Upper Vychegda.

It is traditionally emphasized that differences among the Komi dialects are insignificant, as most of them are the result of phonological development (among them: variation in the reflexes of a syllable-final *l*, depalatalization of d^j and t^j, variation in Anlaut glide phenomena and in suffixal vowels). While this statement is true of the Zyrian dialects, the greater Komi area is divided by differences in word stress as well as in morpheme inventories and morpheme-assignment (e.g., the number and functional load of the cases, cf. Baker 1985: 50–115). The three-way dialectal division mentioned above, i.e. a division into Komi-Zyrian (kZ), Komi-Permyak (kP) and Yaz'va (kY) varieties, is based primarily on administrative and territorial principles, and finds linguistic support only in isoglosses which concern word stress. In kZ, stress is free; in kP, it is morphological; in kY, it is phonological.

The isogloss lines do not coincide with administrative boundaries. The southern Zyrian and Permyak groups are linked via the language pockets in the Kirov Oblast (the Upper Kama subdialect) on the one hand, and via the Upper Vychegda and Upper Lup'ya subdialects on the other. Even the Yaz'va dialect, despite its notable idiosyncrasies, is linked to the southern Permyak group via the highly divergent On' subdialect.

The main criterion underlying the traditional division of the Zyrian dialects is the varied representation of original syllable-final *l*. In fact, however, the *l*-phenomenon could just as well be treated as an argument for a linguistic continuum, as it links the southern Zyrian dialects with the Permyak and Yaz'va groups. South of the Vychegda, proto-Komi **l* is generally manifested as *l* in all environments. The periphery is characterized by phonetic instability of *l*, the occurrence of *l* or its surrogates (*w*, *v*, Ø, *l* ~ *v* alternation) being environmentally conditioned (see Phonology, p. 309). Dialectal variation seen as a linguistic continuum within the whole Komi area has been described by Baker (1985).

History and Present-day Status of the Literary Standards

The oldest written records of the Komi language date from the fourteenth century and are connected with the (self-)Christianization of the Komi. The northern territories, with their relatively sparse population and rich natural resources, had interested Russian colonists as early as the tenth century. From the twelfth to the fifteenth century the Komi paid tribute first to the feudal state of Novgorod, then to the Principality of Moscow, until their territory was finally annexed to Russia. State power was to be reinforced by Christianity.

One of the most enthusiastic missionaries was Stefan Khrap, the first bishop to the Zyrians, called St Stefan of Perm' since 1383. He devised an alphabet that has been described as a combination of Ancient Greek, Aramaic, and Old Slavonic letters with Komi owners' marks (*pas*). The so-called Old Komi writing system was used to some extent until the seventeenth century; later linguistic monuments use Cyrillic. Only 225 words of Old Komi writing, fragments of religious texts, have been preserved to this day (Lytkin 1952). The development of a literary standard began after the 1917 socialist revolution, together with efforts to create an independent national state. But as the Zyrians and the Permyaks had been separated geographically by that time, they were subjected to administrative separation as well. In 1921 the Komi (Zyrian) Autonomous Oblast (the later Komi Autonomous Soviet Socialist Republic) was formed within the Russian Federation, and in 1925 the Komi-Permyak National Okrug was established in the Perm' Oblast. The cleavage was further sharpened by different literary standards. The Zyrian version was based on the Syktyvkar dialect, a natural transitional dialect. Permyak literary norms, on the other hand, are not based on any one natural dialect. Especially striking is the adoption of the *l ~ v* alternation from literary Zyrian. Such official differentiation has contributed to a further weakening of the Komi language in its struggle for existence.

Subsequent developments are the result of Soviet language and national policies. In 1940 the Zyrians still constituted an ethnic majority of about 80 per cent on their own territory. Their language enjoyed official status as the language of national affairs. Beginning in the 1950s, however, there was a marked rise in Russification. The growing intensity of exploitation of the natural resources of the Komi lands brought with it an influx of aliens, mostly ethnic Russians. According to the 1989 census the proportion of Zyrians in the Komi Republic had decreased to 23.3 per cent. The industrial regions are dominated by aliens, while the Komi prevail numerically in the villages on the Udora, Sysola, Izhma and Upper Vychegda Rivers (Lallukka 1990: 125–35). This means, of course, that there is a great asymmetry in Komi–Russian bilingualism: only 1.2 per cent of the local Russians can speak Komi. This bilingualism is on its way to the second phrase: the Komi language has been ousted from business management, services, and other non-domestic spheres. The prognosis for coming generations is not good, for Komi is spoken less and less at home, as well. Only 39 per cent of urban Komi speak Komi at home, and no more than 3 per cent use Komi at work (Napalkov et al. 1990). The abolition of national schools has, in turn, limited the use of literary Komi. For example, about 60 per cent of the rural population between the ages of eighteen and sixty who speak Komi and Russian about equally fluently, prefer to use Komi in speech only, while Russian is preferred for reading and writing, since schooling in literary Komi has not been sufficiently systematic (Rogačev 1984).

Although the Permyaks have retained ethnic numeric prevalence (60 per cent) on their own territory, their language enjoys even fewer rights. Only the most recent changes in national policy have enabled the local intelligentsia to begin the work of restoring the vernacular culture.

Phonology

Phonemes
Standard literary Komi has thirty-three segmental phonemes, seven vowels, and twenty-six consonants. The *vowels* are differentiated by frontness/ backness, tongue-height, and +/– lip-rounding. To describe the Komi vowel system it suffices to use four distinctive features: high, low, back, and front. The Yaz'va system differs substantially.

Literary Komi   Yaz'va-Komi

i	ï	u		i	ü		u
e	ë	o		e	ö	ө	o
	a				a		

In the literary standard, only back vowels are rounded, whereas in dialects one may find also labialized $ï^ø$ and $ë^ø$. In the Yaz'va dialect, however, there are front rounded *ü* (indicated by various scholars as *u̇*, *ɯ*, and *ÿ*) and *ö* (*ȯ*, ̥ɜ) instead of back unrounded vowels. The role of non-low back unrounded vowels is filled by a reduced vowel written here as *ө*. According to Lytkin (1961: 24–6) this vowel is to be placed somewhere between *a* and *o*, but the system would lead one to expect a high back (unrounded) vowel (Rédei 1978: 67–8). In the first syllable it is always unstressed, corresponding to Old Komi and Zyrian *ï*. In non-initial syllables Yaz'va *ө* can correspond to any Zyrian vowel.

The literary standard has non-distinctively short vowels. However, in those dialects which have undergone *l > Ø, the preceding vowel may be lengthened, e.g. Ižma *tuusoo* 'vernal', *pukooni̇* 'to sit', *og vetlii̇* 'I don't walk' (cf. literary standard *tuvsov*, *pukavni̇*, *og vetli̇v*).

Vowel combinations may occur at morpheme boundaries, e.g. *va-i̇n* 'in water', *kerka-i̇s^j* 'out of the house', *nu-a* 'I am taking (something somewhere)'. In dialects a long vowel may develop in such contexts via assimilation, e.g. *una-an* (< *una-ën*) 'many', *baba-as* (< *baba-ïs*) 'his wife'.

The initial syllable may contain any vowel. In non-initial syllables rounded vowels are rare. In non-foreign vocabulary, *e* never occurs in the non-initial syllable of stems. The inflectional suffixes, if they have a vowel at all, usually have one of the back unrounded ones (*ï, ë, a*). (In some dialects, *ï* > *i* and/or *ë* > *e* in suffixes.) Thus, in texts the unrounded back vowels are the most frequent.

Consonants are distinguished not only by place and manner of articulation but also by correlations of voice and of palatalization (see Table 10.1).

The sounds here transcribed as *c, f,* and *x* occur only in relatively recent Russian loans and are not (yet) part of the Komi core phonemic inventory. (In older loans they had been replaced by *s, p,* and *k*.)

All consonants except *l* and *v* may occur in any position. The occurrence of *l* and *v* is restricted by their position and phonetic environment. The literary standard and those dialects which, like the literary standard, have the *l ~ v* alternation, do not have *l* in word-final position as there *l* > *v* has occurred: *vëv* 'horse', *vël-ën* 'with a horse'. Word-internally *v* occurs only as a substitute for a pre-consonantal *l*: *vëv=tëg* 'horseless' Morpheme-internal *v* is not characteristic of genuine Komi words. In the In'va subdialect of kP, *l* has been ousted by *v* in all positions.

There is no quantitative opposition in Komi. Long consonants may occur at morpheme boundaries, however, either through accidental adjacency or because of word-internal or word-external sandhi, e.g. *mïšʲšʲï-* 'washes self', cf. *mïšʲkav-* 'washes (tr)'; [koššor] (< *kos šor*) 'dried-up creek'; *lïdʲdʲï-* 'reads' (morphophonemically lïd=jï-). In kZ, morpheme-initial *j* is assimilated to a preceding palatalized consonant, in kP to any preceding consonant: kZ *kanʲ-nʲas* 'cats' (morphophonemically kanʲ-jas), kP *rïtʲtʲalnas* 'in the evenings' (morphophonemically rït=ja=l-na-s).

Table 10.1   **The consonant system of Komi**

	1	*2*	*3*	*4*	*5*	*6*
Nasals	m		n		nʲ	
Voiceless stops	p		t		tʲ	k
Voiced stops	b		d		dʲ	g
Voiceless affricates			(c)	č	čʲ	
Voiced affricates				ǯ	ǯʲ	
Voiceless fricatives		(f)	s	š	šʲ	(x)
Voiced fricatives		v	z	ž	žʲ	
Laterals			l		lʲ	
Rhotic			r			
Glide					j	

Note: Places of articulation: *1* bilabial, *2* labiodental, *3* (apico)dental, *4* post-alveolar, *5* palatal, *6* (palato)velar

Consonant clusters occur word-initial only in onomatopoeic and late Russian loans, e.g. *žborgï-* 'purls', *drug* 'friend'. Word-finally one finds consonant clusters of the following types: (1) liquid plus stop/sibilant: *kol'k* 'egg', *purt* 'knife', *gërd* 'red', *pors^j* 'pig', *gorš* 'throat'; (2) fricative plus *t* (kZ only): *kost* 'interval', *bos^j t-Ø* 'take', *suv=t-Ø* 'stand up! (tr)' (with *v < l*). This type of cluster occurs mostly astride a morpheme boundary and to the left of the imperative, which is zero. The cluster does not occur in kP or kY, where *t > Ø* in this position.

Word-internal consonantisms occur at morpheme boundaries, e.g. *un=ǯik* 'more', *ët+mëdar* 'both'. In theory, any two consonants may be adjacent, but with the following restrictions. In clusters of three the first consonant is always either a liquid or a fricative, e.g. *vorslï-* 'plays', *bërd-nï* 'to weep', *gort=sa* 'domestic', *vëvtjï-* 'covers'. Note also that there are no combinations of liquids or fricatives alone.

In texts the ten most frequent consonants are, in descending order, *s, n, d, k, j, l, v, t, m, s^j* (Veenker 1982: 436).

Orthography

Both of the Komi literary standards now use the Cyrillic alphabet, with modifications as detailed below.

Palatalization is indicated either by я, е, ё, ю, и, or ь to the right of the relevant consonant. A non-palatalized consonant is written with а, э, о, у, or i following.

The Komi-specific vowels *ï, ë* are indicated by ы, ö. Two of the Komi affricates (*c, č^j*) are written with simple ц, ч. The remaining affricates are rendered by digraphs: *č* = тш, *ǯ* = дж, *ǯ^j* = дз. The transcription-systems used by various scholars are summarized by Rédei (1978: 65–8).

In 1935–8 an attempt was made to adopt the Latin alphabet, but as in the case of other Soviet minorities the effort was suppressed.

Stress

Komi word stress varies across the dialects. In kZ word stress is free, i.e. one may stress any syllable without changing word meaning. The first syllable usually exhibits a slight prominence. In southern kZ dialects stress is in part morpheme-bound.

In kP, word stress is morphological: it differentiates morphemes and parts of speech. Stress never falls on inflectional suffixes, whereas certain derivational suffixes are always stressed. Example: *ol=ëm* 'life', *ol-ëm* '(s)he lived' (Batalova 1975: 81–123).

Yaz'va word stress is phonological: it is dependent on the etymological quality of the vowels involved. The non-high stem-vowels *a e ö o* are always stressed; *ə* is never stressed. Whether or not the high vowels *i ü u* are stressed depends on further conditions (they are each the result of a merger; Lytkin (1961: 33–4); see Permian, Chapter 8 of this book).

The phonetic character of kZ stress is more pitch-based, while that of kP and kY stress has been characterized as dynamic.

Morphophonology
Due to historical sound changes most non-borrowed Komi roots are monosyllabic. The most common type of root is CVC; VC, CV, VC_1C_2, CVC_1C_2 occur more rarely. A longer stem suggests foreign origin or the presence of a latent derivational suffix. The most common syllable structure types are CV and CVC. The basic shapes for bound morphemes are V, C, VC, CV, CVC, all of which can be combined into longer chains. Variation in both free and bound morphemes is for the most part phonologically conditioned:

1   Regular stem variants arise through the *l* ~ *v* alternation. Before a suffix beginning with a consonant, stem-final *l* > *v*, whereas before a vowel the *l* remains, e.g. *vël-ën* 'with a horse', *vëv=tëg* 'horseless'. This rule does not apply to onomatopoeic words, e.g. *kolskï-* 'smacks'; *n^javzï-* 'miaows', *n^javëst-* 'miaows once', nor does it apply to adjectives derived with the suffix =*ov* (~ =*ëv*), e.g. *lëz=ov-ës^j* 'bluish (plur)'.
2   Certain stems show syncopation of the vowel in their final syllable when certain vowel-initial derivational suffixes are attached: *gëtïr* 'wife', *gëtr=as^j-* 'gets married', but *gëtïr=a* 'married'.
3   Certain, chiefly nominal, stems show a paragogic consonant to the left of vowel-initial suffixes. The consonant, always one of the set *j k t m*, is only partly predictable on the basis of the synchronic phonology. Examples: *bïg* 'foam', *bïgj=a* 'foamy'; *lok-* 'comes', *lokt-i-s* '(s)he came'; *mës* 'cow', *mësk-ën* 'with a cow'; *š^jin* 'eye', *š^jinm-iš^j* 'out of the eye'. This phenomenon is for the most part restricted to kZ; in kP it is quite rare.
4   In dialects, variants of bound morphemes follow their own idiodialectal phonotactic rules, giving rise, for example, to alternations such as *ë* ~ *e*, *ï* ~ *i*, or *d* ~ *t* in suffixes. There may also be sporadic deviation, however, in both derivational and inflectional suffixes; in several dialects, vowel harmony at an earlier stage of the language has been replaced by secondary assimilation, resulting in allomorphs which are difficult to classify (cf. the Upper Vychegda forms in Table 10.2).

The stem variants of the personal and reflexive pronouns and of certain verbs are conditioned morphologically. The plural of the personal pronouns and the ordinals for 'first' and 'second' are suppletive.

Morphology

Noun Declension
The morphological categories encoded in the Komi noun are number, case, and person. Person is associated with both possession and definiteness.

Table 10.2   Noun declension paradigms (after Baker 1985: 66, 111)

	Permyak	Zyrian (standard)	Zyrian (Upper Vychegda)	Yaz'va
Nominative	-Ø	-Ø	-Ø	-Ø
Genitive	-vën	-lën	-len	-lan
Ablative	-viš^j	-lïš^j	-liš^j	-liš^j
Dative	-vë	-lï	-li	-lɵ
Accusative	-Ø, -ës	-Ø, -ës	-Ø, -(e/a/o/ë)s	-Ø, -ɵs
Instrumental	-ën	-ën	-(e/a/o)n	—
Comitative	-kët	-këd	-ked	-kɵt
Abessive	-tëg	-tëg	-teg	-tɵg
Consecutive	—	-la	-la	-la
Inessive	-ïn	-ïn	-(i/a/o/u)n	-ɵn
Elative	-ïš^j	-ïš^j	-(i/a/o/u)š^j	-iš^j
Illative	-ë	-ë	-e/a/o/Ø	-ɵ
Approximative	-van^j	-lan^j	-lan^j	-l^jan^j
Egressive	-š^jan^j	-š^jan^j	-š^jan^j	-š^jan^j
Prosecutive	-ët^j	-ëd	-(e/a)d	-ɵt
Transitive	—	-ti	-ti	—
Terminative[1]	-ëǯ^j	-ëǯ^j	-(e/a/o/ë)ǯ^j	-ɵǯ^j
Terminative[2]	-vi	—	—	—
Superessive	-vïn	—	—	—
Superlative	-vë	—	—	—
Sublative	-viš^j	—	—	—
Perlative	-vët^j	—	—	—
Superterminative	-vëǯ^j	—	—	—
Comparative	-š^ja	—	—	—

The category of number has two representations: singular (unmarked) and plural. The marker for plural varies across the dialects: kZ -jas (~ -jës), kP -(j)ez, -e, kY -jɵz.

The number of cases is fifteen for Yaz'va, seventeen for kZ, and twenty-four for kP. The plural suffix precedes the case morpheme, e.g. č̌oj-jas-këd 'with sisters'. For an example of the variation of case morphemes across the principal dialects see Table 10.2. It should be noted here that the consecutive case is absent only in southern kP dialects, and that the comparative in -š^ja occurs in southern kZ dialects as well.

Postpositions are functionally akin to case suffixes. They come after the noun in its basic (sN) form and can be complemented by plural and case suffixes of their own, in which case they resemble the second members of compounds, e.g. pïzan vïv TABLE SURFACE 'the surface of the table', pïzan vïl-in TABLE SURFACE-ine 'on the table', pïzan vïv-jas-in TABLE SURFACE-plur-ine 'on the tables'. In southern kP dialects the development of postpositions into case suffixes is synchronically evident (Baker 1985: 175–201).

The association of certain nouns with certain case suffixes seems to be influenced by animacy. Animate nouns tend to take -*ës* in the accusative, and their use of the illative, inessive, elative and terminative is restricted. The transitive and prosecutive forms do not occur, their functions being carried out by postpositions. Usually an inanimate noun takes the instrumental and not the comitative suffix. At the same time, it must be noted that there is no one-to-one correspondence between natural and grammatical animacy. Thus 'cow' can be inanimate, e.g. *nʲëbi mës-Ø* 'I bought a cow'; cf. *ad́d́a mort-ës* (with accusative -*ës*) 'I see a man'.

The personal (possessive) suffixes are: s1 -*ëj*, s2 -*ïd*, s3 -*ïs*, p1 -*nïm*, p2 -*nïd*, p3 -*nïs*. Plurality of the possession is indicated by means of the regular pluralizer -*jas*: *vok-ïs* 'his/her brother', *vok-jas-ïs* 'his brothers'.

The s1 suffix may also perform a vocative function. The singular second- and third-person suffixes indicate definiteness more often than possession, e.g. *lun-ïs gaža* 'the day is merry'. The s2 suffix -*ïd* tightens the sphere of reference closer to the collocutors, while s3 -*ïs* is neutral in this respect.

As a rule, the personal suffix precedes the case suffix, but in some cases the positions are reversed. In the inessive and illative, the case endings have fused with the possessive suffix, resulting in a syncretism: *gort-am* 'in(to) my house', *gort-anïs* 'in(to) their house'.

The personal suffixes may, in certain syntactic functions, be attached to the adjective (to mark definiteness). They may also be attached to certain pronouns and verbal nouns, and participate in the formation of collective and emphatic pronouns.

Pronominal Declension

Komi pronouns may be divided according to their function into prosub-stantives, proadjectives, and pronumerals. The prosubstantives (or pronouns proper) are generally declined in the same way as nouns. Personal and reflexive pronouns exhibit deviant stem allomorphy, however, and certain cases are formed differently from their nominal analogues. Examples: *me* 'I', accusative *menë*, ablative *menśʲïm* (kP *menčʲim*); *mi* 'we', accusative *mijanës*, ablative *mijanlïśʲ*. For the third person plural the kZ dialects offer the following variants: *naja* ~ *najëzda* ~ *nijëzda* ~ *nijë* ~ *nija* ~ *nïa* ~ *nïda* ~ *nʲida* ~ *nʲidajas* ~ *sijajas* ~ *sijëzda* ~ *ënžajas*.

The functions of possessive pronouns are performed by the nominative, genitive, and ablative forms of the personal pronoun and the genitive and ablative of the reflexive pronoun, e.g. *menam jort* PRO.s1-gen FRIEND 'my friend', *as-la-nïm kerka* SELF-gen-p1 HOUSE 'our own house'. The reflexive stem *as* also denotes the neutral 'one's own', as in *as kerka dor-ïn* 'near one's own house'.

The reciprocal pronouns *ëta+mëd*, *mëda+mëd* 'each other' take both case and personal suffixes; only the second member is declined, e.g. *mëda+mëd-ïśʲ* 'from each other', *mëda+mëd-nïs-li* 'for one another of them'.

Demonstrative pronouns serve to distinguish between the closer (*tajë* 'this', *tačëm* 'such') and the more distant (*sijë*, *sečëm*). Both sets can take the emphatic proclitic *e--*, e.g. *e--tajë* 'this (one) here', *e--sičëm* 'like that (one) there'. When functioning as substantives they may take suffixes for plural and case, but not for person, e.g. *ta-ïn* 'in this one', *tajë-jas-lën* 'of these'.

Interrogative and relative pronouns may stand for nouns (*kod ~ kodi* 'who', *mïj* 'what'), adjectives (*kučëm*, *mïj+ᵍama* 'what kind of') and numerals (*kïmïn*, *mïjta*, *mïj mïnda* 'how many'). The interrogative pronoun *kod(i)* (kY *kin*) is declined, and can take personal suffixes, e.g. *kod-nïd* 'which of you?', *kod-ïs tajë-jas pi-iᵍ* WHO-s3 THIS-plur BOY-ela 'which of these boys?', kY *kin-køt* 'with whom?'. In dialects one may meet variants such as *kin ~ kinʲ ~ këd* 'who', *këda* 'what kind of', *muj ~ mëj* 'what?', and others.

Negative pronouns are formed by means of the negative particle *nʲ(e) ~ nʲi*, e.g. *nʲe+kod* 'nobody', *nʲ+ëtʲi(k)* 'not one' (*ëtʲik* 'one'), *nʲe+kodnan* 'not a single one'. In substantival function, they are declined, and *nʲe+kod(nan)* may also take a personal suffix, e.g. *nʲe+kodnan-nïm* 'none of us'.

Indefinite pronouns are formed by means of the particles *--kë* and *=ᵍurë*. The latter forms a lexical unit with the pronoun, e.g. *kod=ᵍurë-lï* 'to someone'. The former particle, on the other hand, is attached as a loose enclitic to the right of any inflectional suffix, e.g. *kod-lïᵍ--kë* 'from someone', and even to the right of a postposition, e.g. *kod+vïl-ë--kë* 'onto someone'.

Totalizing pronouns (inter alia *bïd* 'every(one)', *stav* 'all') may be declined if in substantival function. *Stav* may also take personal suffixes, e.g. *stav-nam* (s1 instrumental) 'I wholly', *stav-nïm* 'we all'.

Comparative and Superlative

Adjectives may be put into comparative and superlative grades. The comparative is formed with a suffix *=ǯïk* (kP *=žïk*, kY *=ǯïk ~ =ǯig*). The superlative is most commonly constructed by means of preposed *med* or *med-ᵍa* (the latter is written separately), e.g. *med+jon*, *med-ᵍa jon* '(the) strongest'. The superlative may also be formed by means of a reduplicative construction with the elative: *jon-iᵍ jon* STRONG-ela STRONG, roughly: 'the strongest of the strong'. The negative comparative is built by adding the comparative suffix to the negative particle *abu*, e.g. *abu=ǯïk miǯʲa* 'less beautiful'. Occasionally, comparatives may be formed from adverbs or even from verbs, e.g. *voǯʲ* 'early', *voǯ=ǯïk* 'more early', *ëni o-g=ǯïk viᵍliØ* NOW NEG-s1=cvf AILS-conneg 'I am less (often) ill now' (Coates 1982).

Verb Conjugation

The finite paradigm of the verb distinguishes the grammatical categories of person, number (singular v. plural), tense (present v. various pasts), mood (indicative, imperative), and +/– AFFIRMATIVE. The endings are predominantly syncretic, and simultaneously encode several grammatical meanings. There is little stem/suffix allomorphy, except that stems which have an *ï*

Table 10.3   Zyrian (kZ) verb conjugation, with a few relevant kP and kY variants: *mun-* **'goes'**

	Affirmative	*Negative*
Indicative		
Present tense		
s1	mun-a	o-g mun-Ø
s2	mun-an	o-n mun-Ø
s3	mun-ë	o-z mun-Ø
p1	mun-am (kY mun-a̲mө)	o-g(ë) mun-ëj
p2	mun-annïd/ad (kY mun-a̲tө)	o-n(ë) mun-ëj (kP o-dë mu̲n-ë)
p3	mun-ënï (kY mun-ө̲nөs)	o-z mun-nï (kY o-z mun-ni̲s)
Future tense (= present, except:)		
s3	mun-as	
p3	mun-asnï (kP mun-asë)	
Imperfect		
s1	mun-i	e-g mun-Ø
s2	mun-i-n	e-n mun-Ø
s3	mun-i-s, mun-i-Ø	e-z mun-Ø
p1	mun-i-m (kY mun-i̲-mө)	e-g(ë) mun-ëj
p2	mun-i-nnïd (kY mun-i̲-tө)	e-n(ë) mun-ëj (kP e-d[ë] munë)
p3	mun-i-snï (kY mun-i̲-nis, kP mun-i-së)	e-z mun-nï (kY i-z mun-ni̲s)
Perfect		
—	—	—
s2	mun-ëmïd	abu mun-ëmïd (kY o̲bө mun-ө̲m[a])
s3	mun-ëm(a)	abu munëm(a) (kY o̲bө mun-ө̲m[a])
—	—	—
p2	mun-ëmnïd	abu munëmnïd (kY o̲bө mun-ө̲maš^j)
p3	mun-ëmaëš^j	abu munëmaëš^j (kY o̲bө mun-ө̲maš^j)
Pluperfect		
s1	mun-ëma vël-i	abu mun-ëma vël-i//e-g vëv mun-ema
s2	mun-ëmïd vël-i(-n)	etc.
s3	mun-ëm(a) vël-i	etc.
p1	mun-ëmaëš^j vël-i(-m)	etc.
p2	mun-ëmnïd vël-i(-d)	etc.
p3	mun-ëmaëš^j vël-i(-nï)	etc.
Imperative		
s2	mun-Ø	e-n mun
p1	mun-amë(j)	o-g(ë) mun-ëj
p2	mun-ë(j)	c-në mun-ëj

before the infinitive suffix -nï lose this ï before a vowel-initial suffix, e.g. vetlï-nï 'to go', vetl-a 'I go', vetl-ënï 'they go', vetlï-Ø 'go!'

The negative forms are built by means of either a negative verb or a negative particle. For the system see Table 10.3.

The perfect and pluperfect 'tenses' refer more to point of view than to time. Formally, they are compound, consisting of the present tense of the finite verb plus a form of the verb vëv- 'is', either the past-tense form vël-i or the perfect participle vël=ëm. Examples: me bïd+lun sï-lï vël-i nʲëb-a kalbas PRO.s1 EVERY+DAY PRO.s3-all IS-s3past BUY-s1pres SAUSAGE 'every day, I used to buy him a sausage', buxta-ë uš̑-ë vël-i nʲe+i ̑čïd šor BAY-ill FALL-s3pres IS-s3past NOT+BIG BROOK 'a small brook fell into the bay', këž̑ajka-ïs vël=ëm nokš̑-ë pač̑ dor-ïn MISTRESS-s3 IS=past.part BUSIES.SELF-s3pres STOVE SIDE-ine 'the mistress was busying herself near the stove'. The context often implies inferentiality, i.e. that the events being reported were not directly witnessed. In addition, various shadings of Aktionsart have been observed (Serebrennikov 1960: 58–82).

Non-finite Verb Forms

The *Infinitive* is formed with the suffix -nï. In dialects it may co-occur with plural, comparative, and personal suffixes, e.g. Lower Vychegda ju-nï-nïm koš̑m-ë DRINKS-inf-p1 GETS.DRY-s3pres 'we want to drink', puktïš̑= išt-nï-jas-te ots=išt-e PLANTS=momentaneous-inf-plur-s2 HELPS=momen-taneous-s3pres '(s)he is having a go at helping (us) plant them' (note the use of the s2 suffix; cf. p. 313). According to Ludykova (1984: 173–7) there is a second infinitive, namely the verbal derivatives built with =m(=ëm), which functions in a manner analogous to the Baltic-Fennic supine. Traditionally the =m(=em) derivatives are classed along with the other productive deverbal derivatives; this approach emphasizes the importance of the semantics of each verb, and the productivity of the suffix – it may be attached to all verbs (Fedjuneva 1985: 66–9). Unlike the derivatives, which are fully declined like ordinary nouns, the =m(=ëm) verbal nouns occur in the singular only, and they take only a few case suffixes (elative, consecutive, illative). Examples: dugd-i-s jëkt=ëm-iš̑ʲ CEASES-past-s3 DANCES=verbal.noun-ela '(s)he ceased (from) dancing', vuč̑-i-s š̑ʲil=ëm-ë BEGINS-past-s3 SINGS= verbal.noun-ill '(s)he began to sing'.

Participles are formed by means of the suffixes =iš̑ʲ (present imperfective passive), =an (present perfect passive), =ëm (perfect active/passive), and =tëm (negative perfect active/passive). This traditional list has been extended by Cypranov (1987: 17) to include a participle built with =mën, which expresses the extent of the action, e.g. ëč̑ʲč̑ʲïd lomtï=mën pes ONCE HEATS=ext.part FIREWOOD 'enough firewood to heat up (the oven) once', murt=sa kïv=mën gëlës BARELY HEARS=ext.part VOICE 'a barely audible voice'.

Verbal adverbs, or *gerunds*, express time relations between actions. Simultaneity is indicated by forms built with =ëmën, =sën, and =ig (kY =ki

~ =*k*), precedence by forms built with =*mišʲt(ën)* ~ =*mišʲ*; and succession by forms built with =*tëǯʲ*. The suffix of the negative gerund is the same as the nominal abessive case, viz. =*tëg*. The simultaneous gerund suffix =*ig* usually occurs in the instrumental or illative case and with personal suffix, e.g. *leǯʲǯʲ=ig-a-s* DESCENDS=ger-ill-s3 'when (s)he descended/descends'

Derivation

The formation of the comparative of the adjective, and of verbal nouns and participles, has been discussed on p. 314 because they are regular formations typical of their word classes. True derivational suffixes, by contrast, are not regular in this sense: they do not associate with all members of their word class.

Most of the noun-forming suffixes are unproductive. Having once formed nouns from both nominal and verbal stems, they have now ceased to participate in active derivational processes. They are characterized by sporadic variation of their vocalic component (all are of the shape VC). Examples: *kulʲ=ëm* ~ *kulʲ=em* ~ *kulʲ=im* ~ *kulʲ=ïm* 'spawn' (*kulʲ-* 'spawns'), *ǯʲetër* ~ *ǯʲetʲïr* 'currant', *asïv* ~ *asuv* 'morning' (cf. *aski* 'tomorrow'). They are also characterized by a motley semantic structure, involving a great deal of synonymy, e.g. *kiš=ed* ~ *kiš=an* ~ *kiš=as* 'clothes', *ǯʲoj=an* ~ *ǯʲoj=ëd* ~ *ǯʲoj=ëm* ~ *ǯʲoj=ëb* 'food' (Fedjuneva 1985: 43–50, 60–61, 116–17).

Two groups of derivational suffixes are productive in the formation of nominals:

1   the deverbal suffixes =*išʲ* and =*an*. The first forms agents, the second forms nouns referring to actions, means, and objects. Examples: from *gër-* 'ploughs', *gër=išʲ* 'ploughman', *gër=an* 'ploughing'; from *ǯʲoj-* 'eats', *ǯʲoj=an* 'food'; from *šïr-* 'cuts', *šïr=an* 'scissors';
2   secondary nominal suffixes which have developed from independent words and can be attached to most word classes. The most productive representatives of this group are from *lun* 'day' and *tor* 'piece'. Examples: *bur=lun* 'goodness' (contrast the syntagm *bur lun* 'Good day!'), *pov=tëm=lun* 'fearlessness' (*pov-* 'fears', *pov=tëm* 'fearless'), *ëtkodʲ=lun* 'similarity' (*ëtkodʲ* 'similarly'), *vuzal=an=tor* 'article for sale' (*vuzav-* 'sells', =*an* participle), *em=lun* 'property, something extant' (*em* 'exists').

Komi verbs can be derived from nouns by means of suffixes (including zero), but also from other verbs. Phonaesthemic themes enter into constructions with auxiliary verbs to form onomatopoieic verbs. Of the primary verb-forming suffixes the most productive are =*m*, =*t*, =*šʲ*, =*l*, =*(ë)d*, =*al*, and =*iš(t)*. More frequently, however, one meets compound suffixes consisting of two to four primary suffixes chained together. Most suffixes (and all suffix chains) are polysemantic. Thus =*t* and =*(ë)d* express causativity and factitivity, =*l*, =*al*, =*ïl*, =*ïvl*, =*lïvl*, =*lal* express durativity and frequentativity, =*š͡ʲ*, =*ž͡ʲ*, =*ǯ͡ʲ* express inchoativity, reflexiveness, or simple non-transitiveness. Examples: *lebav-* 'flies', *lebž͡ʲï-* 'takes off', *lebž͡ʲïvlï-* 'takes off repeatedly', *lebtï-* 'raises', *lebtav-* 'raises slowly', *lebtïštï-* 'raises a little'.

Compounding and Reduplication

Komi compounds are formed by the juxtaposition of word stems. They are distinguishable from analogously built syntagms by the fact that the meaning of a compound differs from the mechanical sum of the meanings of its components. Most such compounds are nouns, e.g. *paš͡ʲ+këm* 'clothes (FUR.COAT+FOOTWEAR)', *š͡ʲin+va* 'tears (EYE+WATER)', *č͡ʲunʲ+kič͡* 'ring (FINGER+HOOP)', *kad+kolast* 'period (TIME+INTERVAL)'. Since the semantic shift is not always obvious the borderline between a compound and a syntagm may be indistinct. The orthography tends to follow tradition rather than semantics.

Compounding is surpassed in productivity by reduplication and paired words. Paired words may be found in practically all word classes, formed from associative-metonymic, antonymous, or synonymous stems; often the difference between such reduplicatives and their simplices is one of emphasis only.

The components of paired words denoting collectives may have an =*a* suffix: *č͡ʲoj=a&vok=a* SISTER=a&BROTHER=a 'sister and brother', *mam=a&zon=a* 'mother and son', *vël=a&mësk=a* 'cattle (HORSE&COW)', *lun&voj* 'day and night', *nïr&vom* 'face (NOSE&MOUTH)', *bër-ë&voǯ͡ʲ-ë* 'here and there (BACK-ill&FORTH-ill)', *pu-nï&pežav-nï* 'to cook and bake', *pïr-nï&pet-nï* 'to go in and out (ENTERS-inf&EXITS-inf)', *lun&lun* 'from day to day', *mat-ïn&mat-ïn* 'very close', *aj=tëm&mam=tëm* 'without father and mother', *š͡ʲoj=an&ju=an* 'food and drink'. In onomatopoeic pairs the stem may vary considerably: *gïma&gama + kïv-nï* 'to rattle' (*kïv-* = 'gives off sound'), *tur&bar šu-nï* 'to speak hurriedly and indistinctly' (*šu-* 'says'), *tërli&mërli* 'nonsense', *lʲigi&lʲogi* 'staggering(ly)'.

Syntax

Komi syntax shows many Uralic traits as well as innovations that are mostly due to Russian influence. Many aspects of the field still await systematic exploration.

The Noun Phrase

In a sentence the Komi noun phrase may function as subject, object, adverbial or predicate. The head of the noun phrase may be a noun or pronoun, an infinitive, a substantized adjective or a numeral. The head may take an attribute from any nominal subclass, e.g. *bur nïv* 'good girl', *tajë knʲiga* 'this book', *kïk pi* 'two boys', *gër=tëm mu* 'unploughed land'. As a rule the attribute precedes its head and does not agree with it: *gaža lun-jas* 'merry days', *bur niv-jas-ën* 'with good girls'. A noun following a numeral is always in the singular, varying only in case, e.g. *vit pi-li* 'for five boys'. There are no prepositions. Before a postposition the noun is usually in its basic (sN) form.

An attribute, in turn, may be preceded by members of various word classes, e.g. *lïm jёǧïd dёra* 'snow-white shirt', *ručʲ kodʲ muder niv* FOX LIKE CLEVER GIRL 'a girl clever like a fox', *Ëlʲёk Oponʲ kerka din jolʲ ËLJËK OPONJ* HOUSE BASE BROOK 'brook near the house of Ëlʲёk Oponʲ'. A noun attribute denoting a possessor precedes adjectival attributes and is put in the genitive, or, sometimes, in the ablative, e.g. *ur-jas-lёn kuǯʲ gёn=a bež-jas-nïs* SQUIRREL-plur-gen LONG HAIR=adj TAIL-plur-p3 'the long-haired tails of the squirrels', *badʲ-lïsʲ murtsa na pet=ёm posnʲidʲik da nerinʲik kor-jas* WILLOW-abl BARELY YET EXITS=perf.part SMALL AND TENDER LEAF-plur 'the small and tender just-opened leaves of the willow'.

Extensions of a noun phrase may also come after the head; in this position they agree with the head in number and case. The plural morpheme in this construction is *-ёsʲ*. Appositions also agree with the head. Examples: *vaj-Ø te, Varuk, nʲanʲ-te, ǯёskïd-ёs da pёsʲ-ёs* BRING-imp PRO.s2 *VARUK* BREAD-s2acc TASTY-acc AND WARM-acc 'Vera, will you bring some bread, tasty and warm'; *naje, važ kodʲ vesʲel-ёsʲ da kïpïd-ёsʲ* PRO.p3 OLD LIKE GAY-plur AND MERRY-plur 'they, gay and merry as before …'; *kёǯʲajn-ïs šu-i-s sï-li, Lïsko-lï* MASTER-s3 SAYS-past-s3 PRO.s3-all *LÏSKO*-all 'the master said to him, to Lïsko …'.

The Verb Complex
In a sentence the verb complex functions as a predicate. A predicate may be (1) a simple verbal predicate consisting of finite (including compound) forms of the verb, (2) a compound verbal predicate consisting of finite verb forms and an infinitive, or (3) a nominal predicate consisting of a copula and a noun.

The finite predicate agrees with the grammatical nominative subject in number and person. In generic-personal and impersonal sentences the third-person singular form is used: *zer-ё* 'it's raining', *pemd-i-s* 'it was getting dark', *mort-ïd ёd bïd+tor verm-as vёčʲ-nï* HUMAN-s2 PARTICLE ANYTHING IS.ABLE-s3fut DOES-inf 'Man can do anything, after all'. If a quantifier phrase is functioning as subject, the verb form depends on the *genus verbi* (active or passive) and the animateness of the subject: sentences with an active verb and animate subject prefer the plural form of the predicate verb, and in the opposite case the singular is preferred, e.g. *ёkmïs mort vol-i-snï* NINE HUMAN COMES-past-p3 'nine people came', *sočʲčʲ-i-s kïk kerka* BURNS.INTR-past-s3 TWO HOUSE 'two houses burned down'.

Modal verbs, verbs which denote the beginning or ending of an activity, and several verbs of perception and cognition form the predicate in combination with an infinitive: *sijë dugd-i-s šʲerav-nï* '(s)he stopped laughing', *dʲetʲina-jas zavodʲit-i-snï velëčʲčʲi-nï* 'the boys began to do their homework'. The traditional infinitive may be replaced by the verbal noun in =*ëm* (see under verbal nouns, p. 316), e.g. *dugd-i-s majšašʲ=ëm-išʲ* '(s)he stopped worrying', *për-i-Ø busit=ëm-ë* 'it started drizzling'. In the case of the modal verbs *požʲ-* 'is possible; is permitted', *kov-* 'is necessary', *lo-* 'is obliged' and others, the subject is in the dative: *menïm kol-ë mun-nï* PRO.s1-dat IS.NECESSARY-s3pres GOES-inf 'I must go', *sï-lï požʲ-ë mun-nï* '(s)he is allowed to go'.

In the function of the copula in a nominal predicate we find the finite forms of the verb 'is', *vëv-* (~ *lo-*). In the present affirmative, however, the copula is zero: *lun-ïs žar* 'the day is hot', *lun-ïs lo-ë žar* 'it's going to be a hot day'. The place of the predicate can be filled by a noun, adjective, numeral, pronoun, or participle. Examples: *Viktor Savin vël-i-Ø bur artist-ën* 'V. S. was a good actor (NB *-ën* instrumental)', *povodʲdʲa-ïs vež=la=šʲ=an=a* 'the weather is changeable', *pu-jas lo-i-nï kerka sud=ta-ëšʲ nʲin* TREE-plur BECOME-past-p3 HOUSE HEIGHT=adj-plur ALREADY 'the trees have grown as tall as the house', *sijë vël-i-Ø këkjamïs=ëd* '(s)he was the eighth'.

The copula of a nominal predicate agrees with the subject in person and number, while a predicative agrees with the subject in number. The plural of a predicate noun is formed by means of *-jas*; other word classes take *-ëšʲ*. Examples: *nʲolʲ=nan-nïm morjak-jas* FOUR=collective-p1 SAILOR-plur 'we four are sailors', *tuj-jas bur-ëšʲ* 'the roads are good', *mu-jas vël-i-nï gër=tëm-ëšʲ* 'the fields were unploughed'.

The modality of a sentence is modified by modal words, verb semantics, and their corresponding sentence structures. Komi has several verbs which denote psycho-physiological reactions; in sentences containing these verbs, the experiencer is put in the accusative, genitive, or dative, e.g. *menë kïz=ëd-ë* PRO.s1-acc COUGHS=causative-s3pres 'I feel like coughing', *Mišë-lën vun-i-Ø šʲoj=ëm-ïs MIŠË*-gen IS.FORGOTTEN-past-s3 EATS-verbal.noun-s3 'Misha forgot to eat', *menïm o-z užʲ=šʲi-Ø* PRO.s1-dat NEG.PRES-s3 SLEEPS=intr-conneg 'I don't feel sleepy' (Ievleva 1984: 5–9).

Passive, durative, and continuative meanings are conveyed by certain past-tense forms of the verb. Repetition of a verb form also emphasizes the intensity or duration of an activity, and for the same purpose a particle or certain non-finite forms of the verb may be used: *vot sijë šʲïl-i-s--kë i šʲïl-i-s* 'oh, how (s)he sang!', *jëz-ïs žu=ëmën žu-ë* 'what a crowd!' (*žu-* 'buzzes, swarms').

Negation is conveyed by a negative verb (present tense stem *o-*, past tense and prohibitive *e-*) or one of the negative particles *abu, nʲe, nʲi*. In sentence negation the negative verb immediately precedes the main verb; emphatic negation is expressed by using the negative verb or particle before the focus: *pišʲmë-së e-g me giž* LETTER-s3acc NEG.PAST-s1 PRO.s1 WRITES 'it wasn't I who wrote the letter', *sï-lën lo-i-Ø nʲe ëtʲi, a das mës* PRO.s3-gen BECOMES-

past-s3 NOT ONE BUT TEN COW '(s)he got not one, but ten cows'. Double
negation occurs if a sentence contains both a negative verb (expressing sentence
negation) and a negative pronoun, adverb, or an emphatic negative particle: *najë
nʲi+nëm o-z šu-nï* PRO.p3 NOTHING NEG.PRES-p3 SAYS-conneg.plur
'they don't say anything', *sï-lën nïv nʲi pi abu* PRO.s3-gen DAUGHTER NOT
SON NOT.EXISTS '(s)he has neither daughter nor son'.

Simple Sentence

An ordinary Komi sentence consists of a subject and a predicate, with their
extensions, the usual order being S[ubject] P[redicate] O[bject] A[dverbial].
But any other order is possible, constraints applying only within the phrase.
Only the position of the nominal predicate after the subject is fixed: *kerka ïǯïd*
'the house is big' (contrast the noun phrase *ïǯïd kerka* 'big house').

   Closer observation reveals certain regularities in the relations obtaining
between other sentence constituents. If a sentence begins with an adverb, the
predicate precedes the subject: *sijë kad-šʲanʲ kolʲ-i-Ø kïžʲ vo* 'since this time
passed twenty years'; *tëdlï=tëg kolʲ-i-Ø vo* 'a year passed unnoticed' (contrast
vo kolʲ-i-Ø tëdlï=tëg 'the year passed unnoticed'). An infinitival subject
normally precedes the predicate, and an infinitival object usually follows it,
e.g. *kër-ën mun-nï vël-i-Ø lëšʲïd* 'to go by reindeer was pleasant', *tan požʲ-ë
i čʲeri vugrav-nï* 'here it is permitted even to fish'. Deviant word order is
usually caused by discourse structure. A focused element is usually brought
nearer to the beginning of the sentence, and new information moves towards
the sentence's end. Examples: *pukal-a me gort-ïn* SITS-1pres PRO.s1
HOME-ine 'I'm sitting at home', *pu-së e-g me përëd-Ø* 'as for the tree (*pu-së*),
it wasn't I who felled it', *me vok-lïšʲ bošʲ-t-i vilʲ knʲiga* 'I took a new book
from brother', *vok-šʲanʲ pišʲmë lokt-i-s* 'a letter has come from brother'.

   In writing, the focus may be raised into prominence by means of word-
order, sometimes also with the emphatic particles (*në, žë, inter alia*). In
speech, prominence is primarily achieved prosodically: the focused element
receives greater stress and has distinctive intonational profiles.

   Prosodic means play an important role in illocutionary meanings, as well.
Although there are grammatical means to distinguish various functional types
of sentence, the participation of distinctive stress and intonation is obligatory.
An imperative sentence, for example, is formed either by means of the
imperative form of the verb or by special particles, but a command can also
be expressed as a statement (*te vo-an as kad-ë* 'you will come on time'). An
interrogative sentence is usually formed with a question word such as *mïj*
'what?' as in *mïj te-këd lo-i-s* 'what happened to you?' or with a particle, e.g.
--ë in *o-z--ë sijë tëd* 'doesn't (s)he know?' But a question can be implied
purely by intonation, so that the stress falls on the focused word. In writing,
the actual focus can be discerned only from the answer, e.g. if the focus of
– *te gazet-së nʲëb-i-n?* 'did you buy a newspaper?' is on 'did you buy' (*nʲëb-
i-n*), an affirmative answer will be – *da, nʲëb-i* 'yes, I did (I bought)'. If on

the other hand the focus is on 'you' (*te*), the answer will be – *da, me* 'yes, it was I (who bought the paper)'.

Non-simple Sentence

Co-ordination between the components of a compound sentence can be expressed either by purely prosodic means (intonation, pause) or by co-ordinating conjunctions such as *i, da, daj* (< *da + i*), *nʲi*. Examples of the latter: *mïjtëm ozïrlun tani, i stavïs vešʲšërë kujlë* 'so many riches here – **and** all lying about useless', *uǯavnï dugdim, daj zermis* 'we stopped working **and** it started raining', *nʲi mort. vuǯër nʲekën e-z tïdav, nʲ e-z kïv neʲkučëm šï* **NEITHER** HUMAN SHADOW NO.WHERE NEG.PAST-s3 IS.VISIBLE-conneg **NOR** NEG.PAST-s3 IS.AUDIBLE NO.KIND.OF SOUND 'not a soul could be seen anywhere, not a sound could be heard'. Usually the conjunction stands at the beginning of the clause, but the contrasting particle --*a* can be added to the end of the clause only: *bur jëz-lï prazdnʲik talun--a, mi so uǯalam* GOOD FOLK-dat HOLIDAY TODAY-whereas PRO.p1 BEHOLD WORKS.-p1pres 'good people have a holiday today, but we are working', *kučëma bi-ïs ëtʲi voj-ën pašʲkal=ëma, tërït na nʲemtor e-z vëv--a* HOW FIRE-s3 ONE NIGHT-ins SPREADS.INTR-evid, YESTERDAY STILL NOTHING NEG.PAST-s3 IS--whereas 'how the fire has spread in one night, even though yesterday there was still nothing'.

Subordination is expressed by conjunctions and relating words. Most of the subordinators which relate subclauses to the main clause are of pronominal origin, though some are borrowed. The position of a subclause depends on the semantics as well as on the structure of the sentence as a whole. As a rule the subclause comes after the main clause and begins with a subordinator, e.g. *vot i mëvpala ëni, **mïjla** me oli* 'here I am thinking now, (wondering) **why** I have lived', *a kodi sïïšʲ miža, **mïj** këjdïsïs abu?* 'but who is at fault **that** there is no seed?' On the other hand the subordinators *da* and *si* always stand at the end of their subclause, e.g. *peʲuk roz buras rozjalë **si**, bur ruǯʲëg voas* '**if** the rowan blossoms bloom well, there will be a good harvest', *tajë knʲigasë me tenïd šʲeta, lidʲdʲa **da*** 'I'll give this book to you **when** I have read it through'.

The conditional clause usually precedes the main clause. The relating particle --*kë* never stands at the beginning of its subclause; rather, it follows the first (rarely the second) component, e.g. *ez--**kë** šog vël, gaž eg tëdë* 'if there had not been sorrow, I would not have experienced joy', *jen--**kë** šʲias, tekëd loam šudajasën* 'if God (*jen*) will, we shall be happy with you'.

The subclause of indirect speech is analogous to any other subordinated clause. Which subordinator is selected depends on the character of the message: a statement has *mïj*, a command or wish has *med(ïm)*, and an indirect question uses the same words as a direct question (e.g. *kučëm* 'which, what kind?', *kïmïn* 'how many?'), e.g. *Stepan čëktis, **med** vičʲčʲišʲasnï* 'Stephan ordered **that** they should wait', *Nadʲa jualis, **kučëm** knʲiga nʲëbnï*

'Nadya asked **which** book to buy'. Indirect yes/no questions are built with the interrogative particle *--ë*, e.g. *ič'ët'ik Pedër jualis, nʲëbis--ë dʲedïs sïlï piščalʲsë* 'little Peter asked **whether** Grandfather had bought him the rifle'.

Instead of a subordinate clause one often finds a non-finite construction, functioning as subject, object, attribute, predicate, or adverbial. Examples: (subject) *mun=ïšʲ-jas pukšʲ-i-snï piž-ë* GOES-part-plur SITS-past-p3 BOAT-ill 'those who were leaving sat down in the boat'; (object, adverbial) *stav-së vël-i dašʲt=ëma bur=a dumišt=ëmën* ALL-s3acc IS-s3past PREPARES-evid GOOD=adv CONSIDERS=gerund 'one had prepared everything, everything having been well considered'; *šʲižʲim ar-ës tïrt=ëǯʲ na me-në mamë škola-ë mëdëd-i-s* SEVEN YEAR-acc FILLS-perf.part YET PRO.s1-acc MOTHER SCHOOL-ill SENDS-past-s3 'already before I was seven my mother sent me to school'; *zerkalë voǯʲ-ïn čʲužëm-së kosëd=ig šu-i-s* ... MIRROR FRONT-ine FACE-s3acc DRIES=gerund SAYS-past-s3 'drying his face before the mirror, he said ...'

Lexicon

The basic word-stock consists mostly of monosyllabic roots with the structure CV(C), rarely VC. Examples: *va* 'water', *ki* 'hand', *vo* 'year', *šʲin(m-)* 'eye', *vir* 'blood', *jem* 'needle', *ručʲ* 'fox', *kïk* 'two', *ur* 'squirrel', *ov-* 'lives', *ju-* 'drinks', *mun-* 'goes', *vaj-* 'brings'. The same structure is typical of early loans, but here bisyllabic roots begin to turn up, as well. The oldest layer of loanwords comes from various Iranian languages, of which the following is a sampling: *das* 'ten', *dom-* 'tethers', *idëg* 'angel', *nʲebëg* 'book', *purt* 'knife', *zarnʲi* 'gold'.

The contacts between the Permyaks and the Volga Bulgars are reflected in the Komi lexicon by a few dozen words such as *gob* 'mushroom', *ban* 'face', *čʲarla* 'sickle', and *šʲorkni* 'turnip'. The northwestern Komi dialects have borrowed from Baltic-Fennic, while the northern dialects have taken most of their reindeer-breeding vocabulary from the Nenets.

The greatest number of loans comes from Russian. The earliest have a typical Komi structure, but in more recent loans even foreign sounds are retained.

The non-borrowed word-stock has developed and grown richer by means of derivation and compounding, and *belles-lettres* have served as a channel for the dissemination of regionalisms. Further examples of word-formation: *bïdmëg* 'plant' < *bïdm-* 'grows'; *rëdmanlun* 'fertility' < *rëdm-* 'bears fruit'; *lomtas* 'fuel' < *lomt-* 'heats'; *kïrïmpas* 'signature (*kïrïm* 'hand' + *pas* 'sign')'. These methods have also been used for creating new terminology, e.g. *nʲimtan* 'nominative' < *nʲimt-* 'names', *nïrpïr šu=šʲ=an* 'nasal sound' (*nïr* 'nose' + *pïr* 'through'; *šu=šʲ-* '(re)sounds (intr)', *=an* participle; "pronounced through the nose"), but for the most part vernacular creations retreat before terms borrowed from Russian. The result is a pidgin well exemplified by a sentence taken from a university handbook: *Sostavnëj skazujemëj podľ ežašč'ëj-këd sëglasujt=ëm* COMPOUND PREDICATE SUBJECT-com AGREES=perf. part 'agreement of a compound predicate with the subject', in which all morphemes are Russian save the suffixes of the comitative and the negative participle.

Komi Text
Sysola dialect. Adapted from Rédei (1978: 110).

A: text in phonological transcription, segmented; B: morpheme-by-morpheme gloss; C: word-by-word English translation; D: freer English translation.

car = caritative; egr = egressive.

A1. drug	šʲinm-ë	ušʲ-i,	va
B1. SUDDENLY	EYE-ill	FALLS-s3past	WATER
C1. suddenly	into (my) eye(s)	it fell	water

pïčk-a-s	tïdal-ë	pašʲ=tëm	mort,
MIDST-ine-s3	IS.VISIBLE-s3pres	CLOTHING=car	HUMAN.BEING
in its middle	can be seen	naked	person

abï	va+vel	dor-a-s	a	va
NOT.EXIST	WATER+SURFACE	EDGE-ine-s3	BUT	WATER
not	water's surface	at	but	water

pïčk-a-s.	A2. sijë	vël-i	tïdal-ë	toľkë
MIDST-ine-s3	B2. PRO.s3	IS-s3pret	IS.VISIBLE-s3pres	ONLY
in its middle	C2. it	was	is visible	only

sitan-šʲanʲ-ïs	vel+dor	čʲašʲt-ïs,	šʲin-së
BUTTOCKS-egr-s3	UPPER+EDGE	PART-s3	EYE-s3acc
from its buttocks	upper body	its/the part	its eye(s)

kunʲ=ëma,	jur+šʲi=tëm,	nïr=a	vom=a
SHUTS.EYES-s3perf	HEAD+HAIR=car	NOSE=adj	MOUTH=adj
it had shut (evidently)	bald	with a nose	with a mouth

peľ=a	i	kïrïm-jas-ïs	bok	kužʲa
EAR(S)=adj	AND	HAND/ARM-plur-s3	SIDE	ALONG
with ear(s)	and	its hands/arms	side	along

nʲužĕd=ĕma-ĕšʲ	A3. me	viǯʲĕd-i	sij-ĕs
STRETCHES=perf.part-plur	B3. PRO.s1	WATCHES-s1past	PRO.s3-acc
were stretched	C3. I	I watched	it

zel	dïr
VERY	LONG.TIME
very	for long

D1. Suddenly I saw it: a naked person was visible in the water, not at the surface, but in the water. Only its upper body was visible, from the buttocks (up); it had its eyes closed and was bald, (but) it had nose, mouth, and ears, (and) its arms were stretched along (its) side(s). I watched it for a long time.

References and Further Reading

Baker, R. (1985) *The Development of the Komi Case System: A dialectological investigation,* MSFOu 189, Helsinki: Société Finno-Ougrienne.

Batalova, R.M. (1975) Коми-пермяцкая диалектология, Moscow: Nauka.

Bátori, I. Sz. (1967) 'Wortzusammensetzung und Stammformverbindung im Syrjänischen mit Berücksichtigung des Wotjakischen', unpublished Dr. Phil. thesis, University of Göttingen.

Bubrix, D.V. (1949) Грамматика литературного коми языка, Leningrad: University of Leningrad.

Černyx, V.A. (1981) Глагольное словообразование в коми языке, автореферат кандидатской диссертации, Tartu: n.p.

Coates, J.G. (1982) 'The -джык comparative suffix in contemporary Komi usage', *Transactions of the Philological Society,* Oxford.

Cypanov, E.A. (1987) Морфология причастий в коми языке, автореферат кандидатской диссертации, Tartu: n.p.

Fedjuneva, G.V. (1985) Словообразовательные суффиксы существительных в коми языке, [An SSSR, Komi filial, Institut jazyka, literatury i istorii,] Moscow: Nauka.

Ievleva, T.M. (1984) Синтаксис глагола в коми языке (связь глагола с подлежащим и допонением), автореферат кандидатской диссертации, Moscow: n.p.

Kneisl, M. (1978) *Die Verbalbildung im Syrjänischen,* Veröffentlichungen des Finnisch-Ugrischen Seminars an der Universität München, Serie C: Miscellanea. Band 9. Munich.

Lallukka, S. (1990) *The East Finnic Minorities in the Soviet Union: An Appraisal of the Erosive Trends,* Suomalaisen tiedeakatemian toimituksia, Sarja B, 252, Helsinki: Finnish Academy of Sciences.

Ludykova, V.M. (1984) 'Сказуемое с m-овым инфинитивом в коми языке' Sovetskoe Finnougrovedenie 20, 3: 173–7.

Lytkin, V.I. (1952) Древнепермский язык, Moscow: Academy of Sciences of the Soviet Union.

——— (1961) Коми-язьвинский диалект, Moscow: Academy of Sciences of the Soviet Union.

Manova, N.D. (1976) Сложноподчиненные предложения в коми языке в историческом освещении (основные типы), автореферат кандидатской диссертации, Moscow: n.p.

Napalkov, A.D., Popov, A.A., Smetanin, A.F., and E.A. Cypanov (1990) 'Осуществление начионально-языковой политики в условиях Коми АССР', in Komi кыв öнія олöмын = Проблемы функционирования коми языка в современных условиях, Syktyvkar.

Rédei, K. (1978) *Syrjänische Chrestomathie. Mit Grammatik und Glossar*, Studia Uralica 1, Vienna: Association of Austrian Learned Societies.

Rogačev, M.B. (1984) 'Билингвизм сельских коми (социологический аспект)', in Взаимодействие финно-угорских и русского языков, Syktyvkar.

Serebrennikov, V.A. (1960) Категории времени и вида в финно-угорских языках пермской и волжской групп, Moscow: Academy of Sciences of the Soviet Union.

Stipa, G. (1960) *Funktionen der Nominalformen des Verbs in den permischen Sprachen*, MSFOu 121, Helsinki: Société Finno-Ougrienne.

—— (1970) 'Impersonalia im Syrjänischen', in *Symposion über Syntax der uralischen Sprachen 15–18 Juli 1969 in Reinhausen bei Göttingen, Abhandlungen der Akademie der Wissenschaften in Göttingen*, Philologisch-historische Klasse 3/76, Göttingen.

Veenker, W. (1982) 'Zur phonologischen Statistik der syrjänischen Sprache', *Études Finno-Ougriennes* 15: 435–45.

11 ObUgrian

László Honti

The common ancestor of the ObUgrian languages, proto-ObUgrian, was spoken after the breakoff of Hungarian (roughly, in the first half of the second millennium BCE) and before the split into proto-Vogul (Mansi) and proto-Ostyak (Khanty) (roughly, in the first centuries CE).

This long period of independent existence – nearly two millennia – distinguishes proto-ObUgrian clearly, in terms of cladistic status, from branches which diverged more recently, such as Permian or Fennic. The resulting enormous divergences and independent innovations in p[roto-] O[styak] and p[roto-]V[ogul] make it extremely difficult to reconstruct the history of proto-ObUgrian and its daughter languages. Although Ostyak and Vogul share a good stock of inherited root and suffixal morphemes and common syntactic features, each of them also shows features which are characteristic of it alone, or which are present in it to a higher degree than in the other, and in many instances the same or similar aims are achieved by different, historically unrelated, means, as in the case of the different Ostyak and Vogul passive morphemes. As a result of these differences, over the years various scholars have called into question the validity of setting up a proto-ObUgrian node, a proto-Ugric node, or both. One aim of this chapter is to make clear why this author cannot share such views.

However it must be noted that a full and clear outline of the prehistory of either of the two ObUgrian languages is yet to be written. Many questions of detail remain unresolved, and the following presentation will accordingly contain lacunae and some unevenness of emphasis. An appendix at the end of the chapter summarizes the key ObUgrian and Ugrian shared features.

Internal Divisions of Vogul

Most conservative from the phonological point of view were the southern dialects of Vogul, which at the beginning of the twentieth century were still spoken along the T[avda] River. To this group belong those of the villages Janyčkova (TJ), Čandyri (TČ), and Gorodok (TG); all these forms of Vogul are now extinct.

The eastern group of Vogul dialects includes those forms spoken along the Konda River and its tributary, the Jukonda (Jk). These are the dialects of

Vogul spoken by people living along the Lower Konda (KU), Middle Konda (KM), and Upper Konda (KO).

To the western group of dialects belong North Vagilsk (VN), South Vagilsk (VS) and those which were spoken along the Lower (LU) and Middle (LM) L[ozva] and the P[elymka] Rivers. It appears that this dialect group no longer has any speakers living.

The northern group, which served as basis for the Vogul literary language, is made up of the following dialects: Upper Lozva (LO), So[sva], Sy[gva], and Ob'.

Internal Divisions of Ostyak

Among the Ostyak dialect groups it is the eastern that is the most conservative from the phonological point of view. The eastern group consists of the far-eastern pair of dialects V[ach] and Vasjugan (Vj), often cited together (VVj) because of their genetic closeness, and the dialects of the Surgut region, including Tremjugan (Trj), Pim, and J[ugan]. The Sal[ym] dialect may also be classified as eastern, although it is in certain respects transitional between the eastern and southern groups.

The southern group consisted of dialects spoken along the Irt[ysh] River. Best-known among these are the Upper (DN) and Lower (DT) Demjanka, K[onda], and Kr[asnojarsk] dialects. It appears that no speakers of these dialects remain.

To the northern group belong the Sherkal (Šer), Kaz[ym], and Syn[ja] dialects, as well as, to the south, the Atl[ym] and Ni[zyam] dialects, although these two latter show southern morphological features. The O[bdorsk] dialect, spoken around present-day Salexard, preserves well the vowel system of

Figure 11.1   Vogul and Ostyak dialect groups

Vogul dialect groups   Ostyak dialect groups

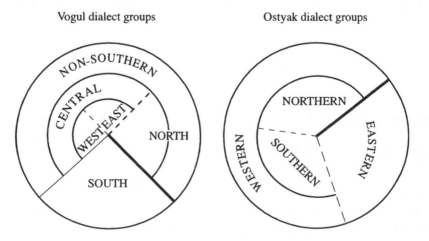

proto-West Ostyak, but is somewhat deviant among the northern group because of innovations in its consonantism.

In what follows, I shall survey the developments which brought about the present-day Ostyak and Vogul dialects from their protolanguages chiefly upon the basis of material cited from two Vogul, and two Ostyak, dialects: the phonologically conservative T Vogul and VVj Ostyak on the one hand, and the innovative So Vogul and Kaz Ostyak on the other.

The Phoneme System of Proto-ObUgrian

Vowels

We must distinguish the vowel systems of first and non-first syllables.

The development of the vowels of the first syllable in the ObUgrian languages was investigated and written up in detail by W. Steinitz (1950, 1955). He also attempted to reconstruct the vocalism of the first syllable of their common ancestor; writings on this subject have been published in part (1989), but parts still remain in manuscript. There are serious problems with Steinitz' assumptions, however, and I have found it necessary to attempt a revision of his views (see Honti 1980, 1982a, 1983b for details).

For Steinitz (n.d.), the proto-ObUgrian (pOU) vowel inventory was identical with that of proto-Ostyak (pO), with the exception that pOU probably lacked *öö: see Table 11.1.

My own reconstruction differs primarily along structural, quantitative, lines. Instead of Steinitz' full/reduced dichotomy, I propose a system of long v. short vowels, with roughly equal membership in the two quantitative classes: see Table 11.2.

I thus set up a three-way opposition among the short front unrounded vowels (*i : *e : *ä) where Steinitz had only *e. Whereas Steinitz reckoned with a split of his *e in pOU which led to the correspondences pV *i = pO *e on the one hand and pV *e = pO *e on the other, I set up respectively pOU *i and *e/*ä for these correspondences. Similar considerations have led me to propose two tongue-heights for the short back vowels *u and *o. Steinitz'

Table 11.1 pOU/pO vocalism according to Steinitz

	Front		Back		
	–R	+R	–R	+R	
Full	*ii	*üü	*ï	*uu	High
	*ee	(*öö)		*oo	Mid
	*ää	*œœ	*aa	*åå	Low
Reduced	*e	*ö	*a	*o	

Table 11.2 pOU vocalism according to Honti

	Front −R	+R	Back −R	+R	
Long	*ii	*üü	*ïï	*uu	High
	*ee	*öö		*oo	Mid
	*ää		*aa		Low
Short	*i	*ü		*u	High
	*e	(*ö)		*o	Mid
	*ä		*a		Low

*åå and *œœ are unnecessary for a reconstruction of pOU, since they are allophones of Steinitz' *aa and *oo on the one hand, and of *öö and *ää on the other.

On the way to pV, the pOU non-high vowels merged, such that e.g. *oo and *aa became *aa. Some pOU long vowels shortened in pV, probably in connection with syllable structure, e.g. long *uu became short *u in the closed syllable of pOU *juust- 'rewards' > pV *just-, but remained long in the open syllable pOU *kuu/ïïrəγ 'bag' > pV *kuurəγ. On the other hand, shortening probably also occurred in connection with the quantity of the vowel of the second syllable, cf. the short *u of pV *tulʲaa 'ring' from pOU *θuuδʲ(VVj).

In pO, *o and *a became *å, and *ö and *ä became *œ, sporadically (but usually in the neighbourhood of velar consonants). Non-low pOU long vowels became low in pO if the vowel of the second syllable was stem-final.

The following examples are meant to illustrate these and other regular developments of the pOU vowels of the first syllable:

> Proto-ObUgrian

*ïï   *nʲïïlV 'arrow' >
      pV *nʲëëlV > T nʲeel, So nʲaal
      pO *nʲaal > VVj nʲaal, Kaz nʲååł

*uu   *θuup 'oar' >
      pV *tuup > T toop, So tuup
      pO *łuup > V luw, Vj juw, Kaz łǫp

*oo   *θoopəs 'net-needle' >
      pV *taas > T taas 'small stick'
      pO *soopəs > VVj sawəs, Kaz sǫpəs

*aa   *aač 'sheep' >
      pV *aaš > So åås
      pO *aač > VVj aač, Kaz ååš

*ii   *θiiləγtə- 'mixes' >
      pV *tiiləγtə- > T tilt-, So teeləγt-
      pO *łiiləγtə > V liiləγtə-, Vj iiləγtə-, Kaz łiłət-

*ee *meel= 'warm' >
    pV *määl= >T *määl=iit*; So *maal=tip* 'thaw'
    pO *meeļək > VVj *meeļək*, Kaz *meeļək*

*ää *äämpV 'dog' >
    pV *äämpV > T *äämp*, So *aamp*
    pO *äämp > VVj *äämp*, Kaz *aamp*

*üü *čüüŋk 'fog' >
    pV *šiiŋʷkʷ > T *šiikʷ*, So *seeŋʷkʷ*
    pO *čuuɣ > VVj *čüüɣ*, Kaz *šiw*

*öö *ööŋkV 'mother' >
    pV *ääŋʷkʷV > T *üŋ⁽ʷ⁾*, So *aaŋʷkʷ*
    pO *ääŋki > VVj *ääŋki*, Kaz *aaŋki*

*u *θuɣ 'summer' >
    pV *tuj > T *toj*, So *tuji*
    pO *łoŋ > V *loŋ*, Kaz *luŋ*

*o *jokət- 'comes' >
    pV *joɣət- > T *jokt-*, So *joxt-*
    pO *joɣət- > VVj *joɣət-*, Kaz *joxət-*

*a *taɣ= 'reindeer hide' >
    pV *taw=əlʲ > T *tawəlʲ*, So *towl* 'skin, leather'
    pO *taɣ=ta > Kaz *taxti* 'reindeer hide'

*i *θiɣəl- 'flies' >
    pV *tiɣl- > T *täwl-*, So *tiɣl-*
    pO *łeɣəl- > V *leɣ əl-*, Vj *jeɣ əl-*

*e/*ä *jeɣ/*jäɣ 'father' >
    pV *jäɣ > T *jüw, jäw*, So *jiɣ*
    pO *jeɣ > VVj *jeɣ*, Kaz *jiw*

*ü *θükəs 'autumn' >
    pV *tükəs > T *tüks*, So *takʷəs*
    pO *söɣəs > VVj *söɣ əs*, Kaz *sus*

*ö *θöɣ '(s)he, it' >
    pV *täw > T *täw, tüw*, So *taw*
    pO *łöɣ > V *löɣ*, Vj *jöɣ*, Kaz *łuw*

In non-first syllables, the vowel inventory of pOU was as follows:

	Front	Back
Long	ii	ïï
	ää	aa
Short	ə	ə̂

This system persisted, virtually unchanged, into pV and pO.
  Front/back *vowel harmony*, inherited from proto-Uralic, survived into only

some of the ObUgrian dialects: southern Vogul and eastern Ostyak. Elsewhere it perished, a victim of various vowel shifts and mergers. For example, contrast the T Vogul form-pair *min^j-ii* '(s)he goes' : *kart-ёё* '(s)he pulls' (front/back suffix-alternants *ii : ёё*) with the corresponding So Vogul forms *min-i, xart-i* (phonetically front, phonologically neutral *i* in the suffix of both forms). Similarly, we have VVj Ostyak front-vocalic *äämp-äm ~ iimp-əm* 'my dog' v. back-vocalic *kaat-am ~ kuut-ə̂m* 'my house', but Kaz Ostyak *aamp-əm, xåå̂t-əm*.

Word Stress
In pOU, as in the present-day ObUgrian languages, word stress was probably on the first syllable, except when displaced by sentence stress (emphasis).

Consonants
When non-initial, p(F)U *w became *γ in proto-Ugric (Honti 1985b: 150), e.g. pFU *kiwe 'stone' >> VVj Ostyak *kööγ*.

The non-palatalized p(F)U sibilants *s and *š merged in proto-Ugric to *θ, which subsequently, after the breakup of pOU, developed into pV *t and pO (secondary) *ɬ.

In the inventory below, the reconstructed voiceless lateral fricatives *ɬ and *ɬ^j replace the traditional *δ and *δ^j. It is more convincing to reckon with *ɬ and *ɬ^j through pOU, after which in early pV they became approximants (*ɬ > *l, *ɬ^j > *l^j), and in pO *ɬ > *l but *ɬ^j> *j; later in pO, a new *ɬ arose, from *θ (Honti 1992).

w		j	γ	γ^w
	θ			
	ɬ	ɬ^j		
	s		š	
		c^j	č	
p	t		k	
m	n	n^j	ŋ	
	l	l^j		
	r			

As is clear from the inventory, in pOU, as in pV and pO, there was a correlation of palatalization affecting non-obstruent coronals (1 : l^j, n : n^j, ɬ : ɬ^j).

In pOU, *w was restricted to word-initial position, while *γ, *γ^w, and *ŋ did not occur word-initial. The etymological data indicate that *ɬ was also restricted to non-initial position.

There was only one labialized consonant in pOU: *γ^w. This segment was lexically quite rare, but occurred invariably in first-person plural possessive and verb suffixes.

The pOU sibilants *s and *š are not the descendants of p(F)U *s and *š (which merged as pOU *θ, see above), but are rather the result of a split, and date back to early proto-Ugric, when the depalatalization of p(F)U *sʲ had begun. This depalatalization started first in those *sʲ-initial words which had a following *j or a palatalized consonant, i.e. we may assume simple dissimilation *sʲ > *s. In other environments, *sʲ became *š.

The following examples may serve to illustrate the main developments of the consonants from pOU to the daughter OU languages:

Proto-ObUgrian

*w-	*wuuɫəm ~ *wuuɫmV 'dream; sleep' >	
	pV *uulmV >	T *oоləm*, So *uuləm*
	pO *wuuləm ~ *waaləm >	VVj *wuuləm*, Kaz *wuuɫəm* 'dream', VVj *aaləm*, Kaz *ǫǫɫəm* 'sleep'
*j	*jokət 'comes' (see above)	
*-γ(-)	*θuγ 'summer' (see above)	
*-γʷ(-)	*jeγ-Vγʷ ~ *jäγ-Vγʷ 'our father' >	
	pV *jäγ-Vγʷ >	T *jüw-əw, jäw-əw*, So *jiγ-əw*
	pO *jeγ-əγʷ >	V *jeγ-öγ*, Vj *jeγ-əw*, Kaz *jiw-əw*
*θ	*θuγ 'summer' (see above)	
*-ɫ(-)	*weeɫəm 'marrow' >	
	pV *wääləm >	T *wäl əm*, KU KM *wæcæləm*, VS *waaləm*, VN P *waləm*, LU LO So *waaləm*
	pO *weeləm >	VVj *weeləm*, Trj J *wäɫəm*, DN Kø Ni *weetəm*, O *weeləm*
*ɫ̓ʲ	*ɫ̓ʲïïm(V) 'Prunus padus' >	
	pV *lʲïïmV >	T *lʲeem*, KU *lʲaam*, KM KO *lʲëëm*, VS VN P LU LM *lʲeem*, LO So *lʲaam*
	pO *jååm >	VVj *jååm*, Trj J *joom*, DN Ni *juum*, Kaz *jǫǫm*
*s	*sïïmV 'fish scale' >	
	pV *sïïmV >	T *sëëm*, So *saam*
	pO *saam >	VVj *saam*, Kaz *sååm*
*š	*šim 'heart' >	
	pV *šim >	T *šäm*, So *sim*
	pO *sem >	VVj *sem*, Kaz *sam*
*cʲ	*cʲäärəγ- 'hurts' >	
	pV *cʲäärəγ- >	T *cʲärk-*, So *sʲaariγ-*
	pO *cʲäärəγ- ~ *cʲœœrəγ- >	Kaz *sʲaari-*, Trj *tʲeerəγ-*

*č	*čüüŋk 'fog' (see above)	
*p	*piiθ- 'cooks, boils' >	
	pV *piit- >	T *piit-*, So *peet-*
	pO *pääł- >	Vj *pääl-*, Kaz *paał-*
*t	*taγ- 'reindeer hide' (see above)	
*k	*kööγ 'stone' >	
	pV *käw >	T *küw*, So *kaw*
	pO *kööγ >	VVj *kööγ*, Kaz *keew*
*m	*meel= 'warm' (see above)	
*n	*nïïpət- 'drifts, floats' >	
	pV *nïït- >	So *naat-*
	pO *naapət- >	VVj *naawət-*, Kaz *nǫǫpət-*
*nʲ	*nʲïïlV 'arrow' (see above)	
*ŋ	*čüüŋk 'fog' (see above)	
*l	*luuntV 'goose' >	
	pV *luuntV >	T *loont*, So *lu(u)nt*
	pO *låånt >	VVj *låånt*, Kaz *łǫǫnt*
*lʲ	*lʲüük- 'reviles' >	
	pV *lʲüük- >	So *lʲuuk-*
	pO *lʲœœγət- >	VVj *lʲœœγət-*, Kaz *łʲaawət-*
*r	*rüγət- 'mixes' >	
	pV *räwət- >	T *rüwt-*, So *rawt-*
	pO *röγət- >	VVj *röγət-*, Kaz *ruwət-*

The Development of the Vogul Phonemic System

Vowels
Once again we must distinguish developments in first from those in non-first syllables.

Proto-Vogul vowels of the first syllable are shown in Table 11.3. This inventory is the author's own departure from that proposed by Steinitz (1955).

In southern Vogul, we must reckon with the following changes: (1) *ii > *ee* to the left of *r; (2) *ïï > *ee* to the right of *j or a palatalized consonant,

Table 11.3   pV vowels of the first syllable

	Front		Back		
	–R	+R	–R	+R	
Long	ii	üü	ïï	uu	High
	ää		aa		Low
Short	i	ü	ï	u	High
	ä		a	å	Low

but otherwise *ïï fell to *ëë*; (3) *üü, which was quite rare, merged with *ü; (4) *uu > *oo* and *u > *o*.

In the other three dialect groups *aa went to *oo (So. *åå*) and *ii went to *ee* in non-palatal environments; *ïï fell to *aa*, merging with the *aa* from *ää. For examples, see the material assembled above.

In non-initial syllables, the vocalic inventory of pOU survived intact into pV; the front/back opposition of the reduced vowels (*ə : *ə̂) became neutralized, however.

In southern Vogul, high vowels fell (*ii > *ee*, *ïï > *ëë*); in the north, *ii and *ïï fell together as *e*; it is possible that there was a phonemic quantitative distinction *e : ee*.

Some Vogul non-initial vowel inventories:

	Tavda		Sosva
Long	ee	ëë	i
	ää	aa	e
			a
Short	ə		ə

Consonants

In some dialects of pV, *k and *ŋ frequently, and *γ always, became labialized when adjacent to rounded vowels; *γ thus merged with the already extant but rare *γ^w. When such labialization occurred, the rounded vowel itself became unrounded. All instances of *γ^w eventually became *w*.

Among the laterals, the opposition fricative : approximant was neutralized in favour of the latter, yielding *ɫ, *l > *l, *ɫʲ, *lʲ > *lʲ. By pV, pOU *č had lost its stop component (> *š).

The pOU fricative *θ became *t.

The consonant inventory of pV is set forth below:

w		j		γ	γ^w
	s		š		
		cʲ			
p	t	tʲ		k	k^w
m	n	nʲ		ŋ	ŋ^w
	l	lʲ			
	r				

With the breakup of pV, in northern and most eastern dialects *s and *š merged as *s*. The palatalized pV affricate *cʲ lost its stop component (*cʲ > sʲ) in all dialects except those of the south, where it persisted as an affricate, particularly in syllable-initial position.

Table 11.4   pO vowels of the first syllable

	Front		Back		
	–R	+R	–R	+R	
Full	ii	üü	ïï	uu	High
	ee	öö		oo	Mid
	ää	œœ	aa	åå	Low
Reduced	e	ö	a	o	

The Development of the Ostyak Phonemic System

In the first syllable, pO distinguished full v. reduced vowels (Steinitz 1950: 2): see Table 11.4.

Apart from sporadic changes in a few words, the vowel inventory of VVj Ostyak preserves the pOU distribution. The journey from pOU to Kaz Ostyak is much more complicated: we may sketch it in ten steps.

In proto-Western Ostyak, two major developments occurred:

1 *œœ became *oo when adjacent to *k or *ŋ, but otherwise unrounded to *ää;
2 *öö unrounded to *ee*, and *üü unrounded to *ii*.

The transition from proto-Western to Kaz Ostyak involved the following changes:

3 to the left of pO *w, *k, or *ŋ, *o > *u, then*ö > *o; elsewhere *ö > *e and *o remained;
4 to the right of *w, *e became *u, unless adjacent to *j, in which case it became *i; otherwise it became *ä;
5 *ïï became *ii*, while *uu and *ii underwent an uncompleted split, with *ii > *ii*, *ee*, and *uu > *uu, *oo. At this stage, the first-syllable vowel inventory must have been *ii *uu *ee *oo *ää *aa *åå *e *a *o;
6 the quantitative opposition was then neutralized among the high vowels, such that *uu x *u > u and *ii x *i > i;
7 to the right of *w, *i rounded to *u;
8 the full back mid rounded vowel *oo became slightly fronted to $ǫǫ$;
9 *aa rounded to *åå*, and *a rounded to *o* (but *a remained *a* to the left of x and $ŋx$);
10 finally, the depleted slots were replenished by the changes *ää > *aa* and *ä > *a*.

The resulting first-syllable vowel inventory for Kaz Ostyak was therefore as follows:

Full		Reduced		
ee	ǫǫ	i	u	Non-low
aa	å̊å	a	o	Low
–R	+R	–R	+R	

For examples, see the etymological material assembled in previous sections.

The pO vowel system in non-initial syllables was preserved intact into VVj. The origin and morphophonemic behaviour of the passive suffix (-*uj*-) of the first and second persons remains unclear, however.

In the predecessor to the western dialects the front/back harmonic opposition was destroyed. First, each of the phoneme-pairs *ii and *ïï, *aa and *ää merged at the expense of the marked members, yielding *ii and *aa. Later, the quantitative pair *ii and *i merged as *i, and *e to the left of *j became *i. The resulting non-initial inventory in Kaz Ostyak was thus only *ee aa i e.*

Consonants
From pOU to pO, the most important consonant changes occurred among the coronals.

1   The pOU palatalized voiceless lateral fricative *ɬʲ became *j in pO, while *ɬ became *l. After this change, pO soon acquired a new *ɬ:
2   pOU *θ became pO *ɬ, e.g. pOU *θïïnV 'new' became pO *ɬaan.

The change *θ > *ɬ was blocked (2a) when *θ occurred in word-initial position and there was an *s later in the word. In this environment, total assimilation took place, i.e. *θ-s > *s-s, e.g. pUgric *θüγsV 'autumn' > pOU *θükəs > pO *söγəs, cf. pV *tükəs (Honti 1974: 369–70, 1986b: 262; cf. also Collinder 1960: 96).

The cacuminals (*ṇ *ḷ) are the result of a secondary development within pO: they originally occurred as allophonic variants when adjacent to the (non-distinctively) cacuminal affricate *č, then spread, beginning with affective and descriptive vocabulary, to other positions, where they became phonemic (Itkonen 1961: 58–9).

The consonant inventory of pO is set out below:

Glides	w		j		γ	γ^w
Central fricative		s				
Lateral fricative		ɬ				
Affricates			cʲ	č		
Stops	p	t			k	
Nasals	m	n	nʲ	ṇ	ŋ	
Lateral approximants		l	ḷʲ	ḷ		
Other		r				

Table 11.5 Consonant systems of VVj and Kaz Ostyak

Vach/Vasjugan				Kaz					
w		j	γ		w		j		
	s					s	sʲ	š	x
			č						
p	t	tʲ		k	p	t			k
m	n	nʲ	ṇ	ŋ	m	n	nʲ	ṇ	ŋ
	l	ļʲ	ḷ			ɬ	ɬʲ	ḷ	
	r					r			

The systems of the modern dialects are the results of the following developments:

3   The laterals *ɬ and *l merged everywhere: in VVj as *l* (except in initial position in Vj, where *ɬ > *j > *j* ~ *Ø*), in the Surgut group and in Kaz as *ɬ*, in all other dialects as *t*. In somewhat parallel fashion, (3a) *ļʲ > *ļʲ* in VVj Syn O, *ļʲ* in Surgut and Kaz, and *tʲ* in Sal Irt Atl Ni Šer.
4   The labialized velar glide/approximant *γʷ remained only in Trj; it became *y* in Vach, *w* elsewhere.
5   *γ remained more or less unchanged in the eastern dialects, changed (partly) to *ŋ* in southern dialects, and was replaced by *w*, *j*, and *x* in northern dialects.
6   *č remained unchanged in eastern dialects, and changed (partly) to *š* in southern dialects. *cʲ lost its fricative release to become *tʲ* in the east and south; it became *sʲ* in the north. In Kaz, both affricates lost their stop component: *č > *š*, *cʲ > *sʲ*.

Further detail may be found in Honti (forthcoming).

Morphophonology
There were in all likelihood alternations involving various kinds of cluster simplification at morpheme boundaries, much as in the present-day OU languages, such as *ṇč+C → *ṇC ~ *čC.

Proto-Ugric had a class of verbs which I shall term *unstable stems*. In these verbs, longer stems ending in the glides *γ, *w, or *j alternated with shorter, vowel-final stems which lacked these semi-consonants. The majority of unstable stems were inherited from p(F)U, e.g. pFU *sewe- 'eats' > pUgric *θewV- > > POU *θiiγ(V)- > pV *tii- ~ *tiij- ~ *tiiγ- (> T *tii- ~ *tääj-*, So *tee- ~ *teeγ- ~ *taaj-*) and pO *ɬii(γ)- (> V *lii- ~ *liiγ-*, Vj *ii- ~ *iiγ-*, Kaz *ɬee- ~ *ɬeew-*); for details see Honti (1985a: 51–4; 1987). It is not clear whether each unstable stem had two or three variants, i.e. whether more than one distinct final consonant could be distinctive in any given paradigm. In all Vogul dialects except T, three variants are attested: the *w*-variant (< *γ) is used in the present indicative (the picture here is somewhat clouded, because the present-tense morpheme is also -γ-/-w-), the *j*-variant is used in the imperative, the passive, and with certain derivational suffixes, and the vowel-final variant is used in the past tense and the conditional. Examples from Sosva Vogul: *teeγ-əm* 'I eat', *taaj-ən* 'eat!', *tee-s-əm* 'I ate', *wiγ-əm* 'I take', *woj-ən* 'take!', *wi-s-əm* 'I took'; compare Tavda Vogul *tii-m*, *tääj-ən*, *tii-s-əm* and *ü(w)-m*, *üj-ən*, *ü-s-əm*. In proto-Ostyak unstable stems had two variants: a consonant-final stem, which occurred with the past tense built with *-∅- and with certain derivational suffixes, and a vowel-final stem which occurred elsewhere. The consonant of consonant-final stems was *j if the stem began with a labial consonant, *γ if it began with a coronal (no unstable stems began with a velar consonant), i.e. a kind of core/peripheral dissimilation was at work, e.g. pO *me- ~ *mej- 'gives' but *łii- ~ *łiiγ- 'eats'. Examples from the daughter dialects: Vach *me-s-əm* 'I gave', *mej-ää* 'give!', *lii-s-əm* 'I ate', *liiγ-ää* 'eat!', cf. Kazym *ma-s-əm*, *mij-aa*, *łee-s-əm*, *łeew-aa*.

There was also a class of *thematic* verbs in pOU, characterized by the alternation of a low vowel, *aa or *ää, with zero in the second syllable; in some thematic stems, the vowel of the first syllable alternated, as well. It is difficult to interpret historically the evidence for thematic verbs: there are just under thirty in T Vogul, and more than fifty in Ostyak, but only nine are attested in both languages. An example is pOU *kolaa- ~ *kaal- 'dies' >pV *kalaa- ~ *kaal-, pO *kalaa- ~ *kool-; for details see Honti (1982a: 83, 104–7).

Rich systems of vowel alternations, occurring in both inflectional paradigms and derivational profiles, are attested in eastern Ostyak dialects and in all Vogul dialects save the northern ones. These alternations may have originated partly in analogy to those of the thematic verbs, partly as a result of independent developments (Honti 1983b).

In Vogul we must distinguish between two basic types of alternation. One is dependent on syllable structure, with long vowels tending to occur in open, and short vowels tending to occur in closed syllables, e.g. T *kääləw* 'rope', plural *kälkət*. In the other type of alternation, long first-syllable vowels followed by high vowels in the second syllable (e.g. long *ää* in *wäärii* '[s]he does, will do') alternate with their short pendants when followed by non-high vowels (e.g. short *ä* in *wäreem* 'I [will] do', *wäräänt* '[s]he does').

In proto-Ostyak, a system of vowel alternations arose in derivational profiles such as *wuuləm* 'dream' ~ *aaləm* 'sleep', both derived from the verb *alaa- ~ *ool- 'sleeps'. The historical background of these alternations has not yet been satisfactorily explained, but they must in part be connected with the fact that there was an incomplete shift of pOU long high vowels to long low vowels in early pO, e.g. VVj *tiin*, Kaz *tin* 'price' ~ VVj *tään*, Kaz *taan* 'bride-price', cf. KU So Vogul *tiin* 'price'. In many cases the vowel of the root word and that of its derivate are indications of a particular pO vowel alternation, and we may associate particular derivational suffixes with particular alternations. Thus for example roots with original long high vowels show long low-vowel alternants when the momentaneous/pusillanimous suffix *=əɣ/ə̂ɣ is attached, as in Trj *kiit-*, Kaz *kit-* 'sends', Trj *käätəɣ-*, Kaz *kati-* 'sends for a bit', VVj *küül-* 'gets up', *kǽǽləɣ-* 'gets up for a little while'. The reverse distribution occurs in verbs formed with the momentaneous suffix *=tə/tə̂, namely roots with original long low vowels show high-vowel alternants when this suffix is attached, e.g. VVj *maas-*, Kaz *måås-* 'is necessary; loves', VVj *muustə̂-*, Kaz *mǫǫstə-* 'appeals'.

In eastern Ostyak dialects, an elaborate system of vowel alternations has evolved in both verb inflection and in the nominal possessive paradigm. Forms showing the alternations have not completely supplanted the older, non-alternating forms, with the result that there is much superabundance and many parallel forms are attested, in different degrees and in different lexical items, across the dialects. In VVj, for example, the first-person singular form of *äämp* 'dog' is either *äämpääm* or *iimpəm*. High vowels optionally replace low ones in parallel fashion in the formation of the imperative and of the past tense built with *-Ø*, e.g. V *lääwətləm* 'I feed', *lääwtää* or *liiwtää* 'feed!', *lääwtəm* or *liiwtəm* 'I fed'.

Morphology

The categories of the nominal are number, case, and person (possession). The verbal categories are number, mood, tense, genus, and person (subject and object). In order to compress the discussion, pertinent reference to syntactic phenomena is incorporated in the presentation of the morphology.

Number

Proto-OU distinguished three morphological numbers: singular, plural, and dual. The morpheme of the singular was Ø; plural and dual each had a range of markers, depending on the lexical and grammatical category of the word in which they occurred.

A dual-marker *-n may be seen in the sequence *iin known from the forms of the dual personal pronoun: *miin 'we two' (> pV pO *miin), *niin 'you two' (> pV pO *niin), *θiin 'they two' (> pV *tiin, pO *ɬiin), compare the corresponding singular pronouns pV *ääm, pO *mää(n) 'I' and pV *näɣ, pO *neɣ 'you (sg)'. No corresponding plural morpheme can be isolated in the plural personal pronouns, pV *mään, pO *meŋ 'we', pV *nään, pO *neŋ 'you (plur)', pV *tään, pO *ɬeŋ 'they'.

Another dual marker, *ɣ or *ɣʷ, may be seen in nouns (1) as the dual marker in the non-possessive paradigm, (2) as a marker of duality of possession, and (3) in verbs, as a marker of duality of the direct object. The category dual has vanished from the morphology of T Vogul. Otherwise, Vogul dialects have *-ɣ-*.

In Ostyak the dual marker is formally more substantial: the *-ɣ-* is followed either by *-n-* (in case 1) or *-l-* ~ *-ɬ-* ~ *-t-* (in cases 2 and 3), e.g. VVj *weeli-ɣ ən* 'two reindeer', *kaat-kə̂n* 'two houses', V *küür-əγl-ääm* AXE-dual-s1 'my two axes', Vj *kaat-kə̂l-aam* HOUSE-dual-s1 'my two houses', V *tuu-l-ə̂γl-aam* BRINGS-pres-dO-s1 'I'm bringing them (2)', Vj *we-l-əγl-ääm* TAKES-pres-dO-s1 'I'm taking them (2)'.

The *-γ-* in all of the above-cited manifestations descends from the proto-Uralic dual marker. The *-n-* of *-γən-* is identical to the dual marker found in the personal pronouns. The *-l-* of *-γəl-* is perhaps related to the Fennic toponym-formant *=la/=lä*, which in Karelian dialects has developed into a pluralizer. In south Ostyak dialects, the number marker of the possessive declension came to mark the number of the direct object of finite verbs, as well: see below.

The *plural* marker of the non-possessive nominal paradigm is *-(ə)t* in Vogul, *-(ə/ə̂)t* in Ostyak. The marker of plural possession and the marker of plurality of the direct object of finite verbs is *-aan-/-ään-* in Vogul, *-l-* in Ostyak. Examples: So Vogul *kʷol-t* 'houses', *kʷol-aan-əm* HOUSE-plur-s1 'my houses', V Ostyak *äämp-ət* 'dogs', *küüri-l-ääm* AXE-plur-s1 'my axes', *kaat-l-aam* 'my houses', *tuu-l-l-aam* BRINGS-pres-pO-s1 'I bring them', Vj Ostyak *we-l-l-ääm* 'I take them'. The *n* of the Vogul plural marker may be related to the *n* initial in the plural demonstrative pronouns of Fennic, e.g. Finnish *nämä* 'these', cf. *tämä* 'this'.

In certain dialect groups, particularly western Vogul and western Ostyak, the paradigms marking possession and direct object have undergone considerable simplification.

Person
Both nouns and verbs were inflected for person in pOU. In the nominal paradigm, person correlated mainly with possessor; the verb paradigm could encode information about both subject and direct object.

Person was encoded in combination with number, and in most cases the morphemes involved correspond clearly to the pertinent personal pronouns, as is consistent with their putatively agglutinative p(F)U prehistory. There are three exceptions, however: (1) non-singular second-person subjective and passive suffixes reflect an older form of the personal pronoun (see below); (2) the suffix of the first person plural cannot be connected with any pronominal base; and (3) in some dialects, the suffix indicating third-person singular subject and definite singular direct object is not of pronominal origin (see p. 342–3). In proto-Vogul, the marker for third-person plural possessor and plural direct object was *-aanə̂l-/-äänəl-*, a form which arose through analogy (Honti 1983d).

The OU second-person pronouns deviate from the rest of Uralic in having not initial *t, but rather initial *n, e.g. the s2 pronoun is T Vogul *nuw, näw*, So Vogul *naŋ*, VVj Ostyak *nöŋ*, Kaz Ostyak *naŋ*, contrast Hungarian or Komi *te*, Mordva or Udmurt *ton*, Finnish *sinä* (< *tinä), Selkup *tan*. Hajdú (1985; 1987: 241) has suggested that the OU pronouns are the result of an

Table 11.6 pOU personal pronouns and person suffixes

	Personal pronoun	Verb suffixes		Nominal (possessive) suffixes
		Subject	Object	
s1	*ääm, *mää		*-(V)m	*-(V)m
s2	*näγ, *neγ		*-(V)n	*-(V)n
s3	*θöγ	*-Ø	*-(V)θ, *-θ(V)	*-(V)θ, *-θ(V)
d1	*miin		*-miin	*-miin
d2	*niin		*-niin, *-tən	*-niin, *-tən
d3	*θiin	*-γ	*-θiin	*-θiin
p1	*määŋ, *mään		*-(V)γʷ	*-(V)γʷ
p2	*nääŋ, *nään		*-(V)n(Vn)`	*-(V)n(Vn)
p3	*θVVŋ, *θVVn	*-(V)t	*-(V)θ(Vn)	*-(V)θ(Vn)

assimilation (*tVn > *nVn) that pre-dates pOU; evidence of *t*-initial pronouns may be found scattered in the morphology, however, such as the d2 suffixes which continue pOU *-tən/-tə̂n, as in Vj Ostyak *ööγi-tən* 'the daughter of you two', Vj Ostyak *we-l-ətən* TAKES-pres-d2 'you two take', and the p2 suffixes which continue pOU *-təγ/-tə̂γ, as in Vj Ostyak *we-l-təγ* 'you (plur) take' (Hajdú 1966: 132–3, Honti 1984: 38).

Table 11.6 sets out reconstructions for the personal pronouns and person suffixes of pOU; to conserve space, only front-vocalic pendants are given.

This system survived largely into pV, with modifications as outlined above; the Vogul dialects show varying degrees of person syncretism, especially s2-d2-p2 and d2-d3-p2. See also the section on object marking, p. 347 ff.

In the proto-Ostyak system, a geminate sequence *ɬ-ɬ arose in certain forms of the possessive and objective paradigms; this was simplified to *-ɬ-,

Table 11.7 pV personal pronouns and person suffixes

	Personal pronoun	Verb suffixes		Nominal (possessive) suffixes
		Subject	Object	
s1	*äm		*-(V)m	*-(V)m
s2	*näγ		*-(V)n	*-(V)n
s3	*täγ	*-Ø	*-ii, *-tii	*-ii, *-tii
d1	*miin		*-miin	*-miin
d2	*niin		*-niin	*-niin
d3	*tiin	*-əγ	*-iin, *-tiin	*-iin, *-tiin
p1	*mään		*-(ə)γʷ	*-(ə)γʷ
p2	*nään		*-(ə)n(ən)	*-(ə)n(ən)
p3	*tVVn	*-(ə)t	*-VVnəl	*-VVnəl

Figure 11.2   Proto-Ostyak personal pronouns and person suffixes

	Personal pronoun	Verb suffixes			Nominal (possesive) suffixes	
		subj cj	sO	dpO	dual/plur	singular
s1	*mää(n)	*-(V)m	*-iim	*-ääm		*-(ii)m
s2	*nöŋ	*-(V)n	*-iin	*-ään		*-(ii)n
s3	*łöγ	*-θ		*-(ə)ł/-łii		
d1	*miin	*-mən	*-imən	*-äämən		*-(ii)mən
d2	*niin	*-tən		*-äänən		*-tən
d3	*łiin	*-γən		*-łən		
p1	*meŋ	*-γ^w	*-iγ^w	*-ääγ^w		*-iiγ ^{w}
p2	*neŋ	*-təγ	*-(ə)tən	*-ään *		*-(ə)tən
p3	*łəγ	*-(ə)t	*-iił	*-ääł		*-iił

Note: subj cj = subjective (= indefinite) conjugation.

e.g. pO *ööγi-γəł-ł > *ööγi-γəł > V Ostyak *ööγiγəl* 'his/her two daughters'. The Ostyak dialects tend to syncretize the same categories as Vogul (see Figure 11.2 above).

Cases

Noun Declension
Six noun cases can be reconstructed for pOU (cf. Riese 1992: 387): alongside the nominative in zero (-∅) there were

Accusative	*-m(V)	Ablative	*-(V)l
Locative I	*-naa/-nää	Lative I	*-(V)γ
Locative II	*-taa/-tää	Lative II	*-(V)j

Lative I probably already also functioned as a translative ('turning into/treated as X'). Beside these case suffixes there were also three postpositional forms, lative *nääj, comitative *näät, and ablative *nääl, built from a pronominal base. These had begun to agglutinate on to their head noun in pOU; in present-day Ostyak may be found traces of their use both as postpositions and as suffixes.

The number of cases in the noun paradigms of the various Vogul and Ostyak dialects varies greatly: while T Vogul had seven and Sosva Vogul has six, the easternmost dialects of Ostyak have ten or eleven, while northern Ostyak dialects such as Kazym have only three.

Table 11.8   Case suffixes

	Ostyak Kaz	Ostyak Vach/Vasjugan	Vogul Tavda	Vogul Sosva
Nominative	-∅	-∅	-∅	-∅
Accusative	—	—	-m, -mee/-mëë	—
Dative/lative	-aa	-ää/-aa	-n, -nää/-naa	-n
Locative	-ən, -nii	-nə/-nə̂	-t, -tää/-taa	-t
Ablative	—	-ö(ö)γ/-o(o)γ	-nääl/-naal	-nəl
Comitative	—	-näät/-naat	-näät/-naat	—
Instrumental	—	-(t)ə/-(t)ə̂	-(t)əl	-(t)əl
Translative	—	-əγ/-ə̂γ	(ə)w	-əγ
Approximative	–	-(ää)pää/-(aa)paa	–	–
Abessive	—	-ləγ/-lə̂γ	—	—
Comparative	–	-nïŋï(t)/-niŋi(t)	—	—
Distributive	—	-təltää/-tə̂ltaa	—	—

The case suffixes of our four sample ObUgrian languages are set out in Table 11.8 for comparison.

The zero *nominative* is a continuation of the proto-Uralic state of affairs. The *m-accusative* of southern Vogul is also of Uralic origin; it is attested in eastern Vogul dialects as well, but there is no trace of it in Ostyak.

The functions of the three primary spatial cases – dative/lative, locative, and ablative – are performed, in Ostyak and Vogul, by morphemes which are not historically connected. Thus the Ostyak *dative/lative* suffixes are not connected with those of Vogul. The Vogul suffixes developed either from a Ugric postposition *nää (Liimola 1963: 91–5, 120–3) or from a pronominal base which functioned as a postposition (Riese 1992: 381); the origin of the Ostyak *-ää/-aa lative is obscure.

The Ostyak and Vogul *locative* suffixes are also unrelated. The *t* of the Vogul suffixes date at least from Ugric times; cognate elements are attested in fossilized adverbs in Ostyak. The *n* of the Ostyak locatives is inherited from proto-Uralic. The vocalic components of both the Vogul and the Ostyak locatives are obscure.

Finally, there is the *ablative*. The function of this case is carried out in Vogul by a suffix which derives from the same postposition seen in the dative/lative (*nää), but with an ablative suffix *l* which dates back to at least Ugric times (Liimola 1963: 66). In western dialects, the ablative has taken on the function of indicating the (partial) direct object (Liimola 1963: 43–4). In Ostyak, the ablative is expressed by means of a range of morphemes (suffixes in the east and south, e.g. V *-ööγ/-ooγ*, DN *-eewə*, postpositions in the Surgut group and in the west, e.g. Pim *iiwəɫ*, Kaz *eewəɫ*) which probably all go back to a spatial noun of the shape *Vγ^w, with or without case suffixes (Rédei 1977: 208–9, Honti 1984: 61).

Note that the less central cases, comitative, instrumental, and translative, continue common pOU ancestors. The *comitative*, known as a suffix in Vogul only in the south, and in Ostyak only in the east, derives from the base *nää plus the *t*-locative mentioned on p. 344. It also survives in one western Ostyak dialect, Sherkal, as a postposition occurring with person suffixes, e.g. Šer *maa naataaŋeem* 'with me', *naŋ naataaŋeen* 'with you (sg)', *tuw naataaŋeet* 'with him/her' (*DEWOS*: 1023).

In the Vogul *instrumental* suffix -*(t)Vl*, the *l* element derives from an ablative suffix dating from the Ugric period. The *t* of the longer variant, -*təl*, is identical with the *t*-locative mentioned above; this is also the origin of the *t* in the Ostyak suffix (Liimola 1963: 100–101, 117–18).

The *translative* suffix derives from a lative *-γ in both ObUgrian languages (Liimola 1963: 129–30); this *γ is also attested in adverbs with its original lative function (Liimola 1963: 176).

At least the easternmost dialects of Ostyak innovated the *approximative* case, which like the dative/lative indicates lative motion, but in a more general direction. The shorter form cited above (-*pää/-paa*) is presumably identical with a homophonous emphatic particle; the longer variant (-*ääpää/-aapaa*) is a compound of this particle with the dative/lative suffix. We may assume that the particle was originally used with lative deictics, e.g. *nuu-γ-paa* 'upwards', then spread to other contexts, e.g. *kaat-aa-paa* 'towards the house' (Honti 1984: 62).

The comparative is another eastern Ostyak innovation. It derives from the postposition *niiŋət, with (spatial) ablative meaning – cf. Trj *mää niiŋteem* 'from me', Vj *tii=m-ääl niiŋət seem=ləγ* IS.BORN=past.part-s3 FROM/ SINCE EYE=LESS '(s)he has been blind since birth' (*DEWOS*: 1006; Honti 1982b: 111–12; 1984: 65, 83).

The distributive, also limited to Ostyak, is clearly a compound, but its prehistory is unclear. The Ostyak abessive is also of obscure origin.

Declension of Personal Pronouns

The case systems of Vogul and Ostyak personal pronouns are for the most part identical with those of their nouns, and there is no reason to suspect that the situation was any different in pOU.

Apart from minor differences (such as the lack of translative, and of course of distributive, forms in Ostyak) the main difference between the nominal and pronominal paradigms in both ObUgrian languages may be seen in the formation of the accusative. In Vogul the relevant personal suffix is attached to an oblique variant of the pronoun base, e.g. K *niina-n* 'you two (acc)'. The base may occur alone, e.g. T *änää-m* 'me', or reinforced (T *änää-m-mii* 'id.'); metathesized forms are also attested (T *ämään, ämäänmii* 'id.'). Examples from So Vogul: *aanə-m* 'me', *naŋə-n* 'you (sA)', *meen-men* 'us two'. In the northernmost dialects of Ostyak, the accusative of personal pronouns is built in the same way, e.g. Kaz *man-eem* 'me'; elsewhere in Ostyak, the suffix *-t* is used, e.g. V *mään-t* 'id.'. The divergences evidenced by the pronominal paradigms of the various Ostyak dialects are so great as to prevent the reconstruction of the pO system; the pOU system is thus completely out of reach.

Verb Inflection

Tense

The ObUgrian languages have two non-compound tenses, past and present. In pOU, the morpheme of the present tense was *-γ-, zero, or possibly both; both p(F)U past-tense markers, *-j- and *-sʲ- (> pOU *-s-) were used.

Vogul and Ostyak form their respective present tenses using similar strategies, but with different materials. In most Vogul dialects the most widely used present-tense marker consists of a vowel plus a -γ- which, in western and southern dialects, undergoes sandhi (consonant gemination, vowel lengthening) with preceding and/or following segments; this γ is perhaps a continuation of the pFU present-tense morpheme *-k-. Another present-tense marker, *-i-*, attested in e.g. the Sosva s3 form *ool-i-Ø* LIVES-pres-s3 '(s)he/it lives', may be a reflex of the pFU deverbal nominalizer *=jV (e.g. Finnish *opetta=ja* 'teacher', from *opetta-* 'teaches'). In some dialects, many forms of the subjective conjugation contain both present-tense markers combined synchronically into one, e.g. So *min-e(e?)γ-əm* 'I go' < *min-iiγ-əm < *min-əj-γ-əm, while forms of the objective conjugation contain *-i-* alone, e.g. So *tot-i-l-əm* 'I bring it'. In the passive paradigm, a variant of the γ-less present-tense marker is used, e.g. So *tot-a-w-em* 'I am brought; (it) is brought to me'. In southern Vogul at the beginning of the twentieth century, these present-tense markers were used to refer to future and momentaneous events; ongoing events were indicated by means of different, historically derivational, suffixes, notably *-äänt-/-aant-* and *-(ää/aa)l-*, e.g. T *minʲiim* 'I shall go', *minʲäänteem* 'I am going (now)'.

A somewhat similar adaptation was made in Ostyak, where the present-tense markers of the present-day dialects (Surgut and Kaz *-ɬ-*, Sal, Southern, Ni, and Šer *-t-*, VVj Ber O *-l-*) all descend from a frequentative derivational suffix *=l. In the easternmost dialects this *l*-marker was preceded, in the third person singular, by an element *-pää/-paa, yielding a suffix sequence *-w-əl* > *-wəl*, e.g. Vj *we-wəl-Ø* '(s)he takes'; the sequence *wə(l)* then spread to the s2 and p3, e.g. *menwən* 'you (sg) go', *menwəlt* 'they go'; contrast *men-l-əm* 'I go'. This *-pää/-paa was originally a deverbal nominalizer; a parallel development may be seen in the Finnish third-person present-tense forms, viz. *mene-e* '([s]he) goes' < *mene=pä 'goer', *mene-vät* '(they) go' < *mene=pä-t 'goers'.

The pU past-tense morpheme *sʲ (> *-s-*) survives in both ObUgrian languages, e.g. So Vogul *min-əs-Ø*, VVj Ostyak *men-əs-Ø* '(s)he went'. The other inherited past-tense morpheme is pFU *-j-, attested only in Ostyak, where it melted into the preceding stem-final vowel. The result has been interpreted synchronically as a linking vowel, and the descriptive grammars therefore refer to a zero past-tense (or 'perfect') morpheme, e.g. VVj *men-Ø-əm* 'I went' opposed to *men-s-əm* 'I was going' and *men-l-əm* 'I am going'. Only the eastern dialects use both past tenses; to the west, either -Ø- (southern dialects and Nizyam) or -s- (Šer Kaz Ber O) is used. In Vach and Vasjugan Ostyak two additional tenses evolved, the so-called 'historic perfect' (-γääs-/-γaas-) and the 'historic imperfect' (-γääl-/-γaal-), e.g. *men-γääs-əm*, *men-γääl-əm* 'I went'; the function of these tenses has not been clarified.

Mood

We can be certain that Proto-ObUgrian had the three following moods: indicative (*-Ø-), imperative (*-Ø-), and conditional (*-nVγ-). Although the morphemes for indicative and imperative were both zero, the two moods did not syncretize, because the indicative occurred only with tense markers, while the presence of the imperative zero precluded tense-marking.

The indicative morpheme is still zero in both ObUgrian languages. The imperative, on the other hand, has evolved along distinct paths. In Vogul, zero still marks the imperative, i.e. the person suffixes are attached directly to the stem; in this Vogul contrasts with all other Uralic languages, all of which have either a distinct imperative morpheme, distinct person suffixes characteristic of the imperative paradigm, or both. Number syncretism characterizes the northern Vogul imperative, e.g. *min-ən* serves as singular, dual, and plural 'go!'

In Ostyak, the imperative morpheme is reflexes of *-ää/aa- in the s2 subjective, *-ii-/-ïï- elsewhere, e.g. V *tuuγ-aa-Ø* 'bring (some[thing])!', *tuuγ-ïï-tân* 'you two bring (some[thing])!; you (dual or plur) bring (something or someone definite)', *tuuγ-ïï-Ø* 'bring (something or someone definite)!', *tuuγ-ïï-γl-aa* 'you (sg) bring them (dual)!'.

The pU conditional/optative morpheme was preserved in Vogul. We may reconstruct pV *-nəγ^w-, the reflexes of which (T *-nëë-/-nee-*, So *-nəw-*) occur in complementary distribution with tense morphemes, e.g T *min^j-nee-m*, So *min-nəw-əm* 'I would go'. In Ostyak the categories of conditional and optative are expressed by means of various participles, often in conjunction with particles.

Marking of the Direct Object

As in many other Uralic languages, the pOU verb encoded information, in its morphology, about the direct object. This information included indications of definiteness and number (as in Nganasan or Nenets), but not of person (as in Mordva, or, in part, Hungarian). Forms which indicate a 'definite' direct object are usually called the *objective*, or *definite*, conjugation. The material makeup of the morphemes which indicate definiteness varies from language to language, except in the case of the third-person singular subject forms, where the morpheme signalling a definite object derives from a third-person pronoun (in eastern Ostyak dialects, this morpheme stems from a demonstrative pronoun). The marking of definiteness elsewhere in the Ostyak and Vogul paradigms, and the marking of object number throughout, is so highly heterogeneous that the reconstruction of the pOU objective conjugation is wellnigh impossible.

In non-southern Vogul dialects, definiteness of the direct object is indicated by -*l*- if the subject is first or second person, but by -*t*- if the subject is third person; secondary developments have altered this picture in southern Vogul, where -*t*- came to be used in past-tense forms, and -*l*- was used elsewhere. The -*t*- or -*l*- element is followed by morphemes which indicate whether the (definite) object is singular (sO), dual (dO), or plural (pO); these morphemes are historically identical with those which indicate the number of possessions (cf. above). In both instances the -*t*- is historically identical with the third-person marker (see above). The vocalic element which follows this -*t*- is of unknown origin and function (Liimola 1963: 222). To the right of consonants, only this vocalic element normally survives: compare -*te* in Sosva *tot-i-te* '(s)he brings (sO)' with -*e* in *tot-i-an-e* '(s)he brings (pO)'. Further examples: Sosva *tot-i-an-əm* 'I bring (pO)', *tot-s-an-e* '(s)he brought (pO)', *tot-nəw-te* '(s)he would bring (sO)', *tot-nəw-aγ-e* '(s)he would bring (dO)'; Tavda *tat-ëë-l* '(s)he brings (sO)', *tat-ëë-l-aan-əm* 'I bring (pO)', *tataa-s-t-aan-ëë* '(s)he brought (pO)', *tat-n-ə̂ə̂l* '(s)he would bring (sO)'.

In proto-Ostyak, as in non-southern Vogul, the primary split in the morphology of the objective conjugation was along the feature [+/-] axis-of-discourse. In forms with a third-person subject, definiteness of the direct object was marked by an ending which derived from the third-person pronoun, while in forms with first-and second-person subjects, the subject person suffix was preceded by a full vowel, *ïï/ii if the (definite) object was singular, *aa/ää if dual or plural. Much analogical levelling has occurred in the modern dialects; for details, see Honti (1976; 1983c; 1984: 38–46). Unlike Vogul, the Ostyak objective conjugation forms for axis-of-discourse subjects have the same morphemic schema as those of the corresponding non-objective forms, viz. STEM-TENSE/MOOD-PERSON. The difference lies in the vowel to the left of the person suffix: in the non-objective forms this vowel goes back to pO *ə̂/ə, in the objective forms to *ïï/ii ~ *aa/ää. Examples: VVj *tuu-l-ə̂m* 'I bring (something, someone)', *tuu-l-iïm* 'I bring (sO)', *tuu-l-ə̂γl-aam* 'I bring (dO)', *tuu-l-l-aam* 'I bring (pO)'.

In southern Ostyak dialects, the position of the dual and plural (definite) object markers moved from the left of the subject person-marker suffix (STEM-TENSE/MOOD-dO/pO-PERSON) to its right (STEM-TENSE/MOOD-PERSON-dO/pO). The identity of these number-marking suffixes changed, as well: the new scheme used the same number suffixes as those of the non-possessive nominal paradigm, e.g. older Kr *seeŋk-Ø-eeγ ət-aam*

STRIKES-past-dO-s1 was gradually being replaced by *seeŋk-∅-eem-ɣən* STRIKES-past-s1-dO, both 'I struck (past) (dO)'; the corresponding forms with plural object were *seeŋk-∅-ət-aam* STRIKES-past-pO-s1 and *seeŋk-∅-eem-ət* STRIKES-past-s1-pO. This shift probably occurred in stages; for a reconstruction, see Honti 1983c.

Genus Verbi
Both Vogul and Ostyak know the distinction between active and passive. The active is unmarked; if it is to be assigned a morpheme, that morpheme is zero (-∅-). The passive is marked differently in the two ObUgrian languages. In Vogul the morpheme is -*w*-, which goes back to a proto-Uralic derivational suffix (*=w) which built reflexives. In Ostyak the passive is marked by -*Vj*-, in which the *j*-element is thought to descend from another pU reflexivizer (*=j). The use of the passive is widespread in both Vogul and Ostyak, and we may therefore assume that the category was present in pOU, even though its formal expression in the daughter languages is effected by morphemes of different origin.

In VVj and Surgut Ostyak, the vowel of the passive marker is invariably [+ BACK] in the first and second persons, regardless of the frontness or backness of the stem to which it is attached; in the third person, on the other hand, this vowel reflects the harmonic pO pair *aaj/ääj, e.g. V *tuu-l-uuj-əm* 'I am brought; to me is brought', *tuu-l-ïï* (< *tuu-l-aaj) '(s)he is brought; to him/her is brought', Vj *we-l-uuj-əm* 'I am taken; from me is taken', *we-l-ii* (< *we-l-ääj) '(s)he is taken; from him/her is taken'.

Derivational Morphology
Vogul and Ostyak have rich derivational morphologies, and many of the individual derivational suffixes go back to shared pOU morphemes, often with p(F)U backgrounds (Ganschow 1965; Sauer 1967). Here we shall restrict our attention to the morphemes which form verbal nouns.

The forms of the *infinitive* in the various Vogul dialects are quite diverse, but certainly must go back to something like pV *-ŋʷkʷe. The full form of this morpheme persisted, for the most part, in northern dialects, while elsewhere there was loss of at least the vowel, and often of one or the other of the consonants, e.g. Sosva *tee-ŋkʷe*, Pelymka *tee-x*, LM *tee-xʷ*, Tavda *tii-ŋ*, all 'to eat'. The origin of the Vogul infinitive suffix is unclear. Gombocz (1898) thought it to be a combination of the present participle (=*n*-) plus the translative ending -*ɣ*; while this is plausible functionally (cf. the formation of the Ostyak infinitive, below), it does not explain the labiality of the infinitive morpheme. It is in any case likely that the translative morpheme was somehow involved: variants of this suffix similar to that of the infinitive may be found in adverbs, as well (Liimola 1963: 193–4).

In proto-Ostyak the infinitive morpheme was *-taa/-tää; in the Surgut dialects, this base was extended with the translative, yielding e.g. Trj -*taaɣə/*

-tääyə (cf. the Finnish infinitive from *-ta-k/-tä-k). The pO infinitive morpheme was probably one and the same as that of the present participle; the forms subsequently diverged in most dialects, yielding distinct verbal nominals. Thus in Vach Ostyak we have the infinitive *lii-tää* 'to eat' distinct from the present participle *lii-tə* 'eating', but in Kaz Ostyak both forms are *łee-ti*; cf. Sauer (1967: 96, 102).

In the Vogul dialects the morpheme of the *present participle* derives from a different suffix, consisting of *n* plus a vowel, and related, *inter alia*, to the infinitive suffixes of Hungarian and Permian, e.g. T *tii-nii*, So *tee-ni*, both 'eating'.

Both Vogul and Ostyak form their *past participle* with reflexes of pOU *=Vm, a suffix of proto-Uralic origin, e.g. T Vogul *tašaam*, So Vogul *tååsam* 'dry' = Trj Ostyak *sasâm*, Kaz Ostyak *sosəm* 'hard, tough', the past participles of pV *tašaa- = pO *sasaa- 'dries/becomes dry'. In addition, both languages have a gerund which is clearly related to this *=Vm, cf. T Vogul *tatëëləm* '(while/by) bringing', So Vogul *nomim* '(while/by) thinking'. The Ostyak pendant, which had a high/low vowel alternation in pO (*=maan/mään ~ *=mïïn/=miin), is clearly compound, and perhaps dates from the Ugric period (Kispál 1968: 272). Examples: Vj Ostyak *poot=mïïn-* '(while/by) running', Kaz *łaawəł=maan* '(while/by) leading'.

Syntax

Both ObUgrian languages have preserved, by and large, the dominant pU constituent order SOV, e.g. Sosva Vogul *taw aan-əm waay-te* s3.PRO s1.PRO.acc SEES.pres-s3sO '(s)he sees me', Vasjugan Ostyak *nii jeləw potʲiiŋkaa jååt=kəl-wəl* WOMAN NEW SHOE BUYS=refl-s3pres 'the woman buys (a pair of) new shoes (for herself)'. Also of Uralic age is the tendency to put nouns in the singular when they are modified by numerals over 'two', e.g. Vach Ostyak *lääwət aal* SEVEN YEAR 'seven years', Sosva Vogul *saat eet* SEVEN NIGHT 'seven nights'. The dual is usually used with 'two' e.g. Pim Ostyak *käät kåår-yən* TWO MALE.REINDEER-dual 'two reindeer', So Vogul *kit aayi-iy* 'two girls'.

Both Vogul and Ostyak use the *mihi est* (it is to me) possessive construction, e.g. Vj Ostyak *men-nə wal-wəl mååsʲnʲaalʲïï* s1.PRO.loc IS/EXISTS-s3pres PURSE 'I have a purse', but each has also innovated its own verb meaning 'has', e.g. Sosva Vogul *tas at oonʲsʲ-eey-əm* CONTAINER NEG HAS-pres-s1 'I don't have anything to put it in', Tromagan Ostyak *iimii jek-kən ääŋkee-yən taj-əł-Ø* WOMAN FATHER-dual MOTHER-dual HAS-pres-s3 'the woman has a father and mother'.

In both Vogul and Ostyak, constructions with verbal nouns frequently correspond to subordinate clauses in other languages. The verbal nouns usually take person suffixes and either case suffixes or postpositions, e.g. Pim Vogul *kääm+min=n-äät wujəl šïm-tə nëëkəs-w-əs-Ø* OUTWARDS+

GOES=pres.part-s3 WHEN HEART-loc PECKS-pass-past-s3 'when (s)he went out, (s)he felt a pang in his/her heart', Vj Ostyak *kuuj-əl lüüγt=əm piïr-nə nii meγ+uuj ḷææk-ööγ iilən+jöγil-wəl* HUSBAND-s3 EXITS=past.part AFTER-loc WOMAN EARTH+SPACE.UNDER PATH-abl FORWARD +GOES-s3pres 'after her husband had gone out, the woman went along the underground passage'.

The widespread use of the passive in both Vogul and Ostyak suggests that it is an ObUgrian innovation. Ostyak has innovated ergative constructions, common especially in the eastern dialects; see (Kulonen 1989: 297–302).

Lexicon

The ObUgrian languages inherited a considerable number of words and stems from earlier phases of their Uralic past. The *UEW* reports just over 700 Vogul, and just under 800 Ostyak words of p(F)U or proto-Ugric origin. Most of these words belong to the core of the lexicon, and are thus liable to wide derivation, so that a substantial percentage of the Ostyak and Vogul lexicons are made up of non-borrowed vocabulary.

We have no reliable data concerning the period after the breakup of Ugric unity. In all probability the speakers of pOU had intensive contacts with the aborginal populations of western Siberia, but of the genetic and linguistic affiliations of these people we know next to nothing. It is natural, but intellectually sterile, to suppose that some of the unetymologized Ostyak and Vogul vocabulary stems from such contacts.

After the breakup of pOU, speakers of pV and pO took vocabulary from speakers of Iranian languages in roughly the fourth to sixth centuries CE (Korenchy 1972), e.g. Vogul T *iisərəm*, KU KO Pim *eesərəm*, KM *eesərmə*, VS VN LU *jeesərəm*, LO So *eesarma* '(feeling of) shame' < Middle Iranian **äfsärm*, cf. Avestan *fšarəma-*, Middle Persian *šarm*; Ostyak Kr *käärt*, Ni *kaartə*, Kaz *kaarti*, O *kurti* 'iron' < Middle Iranian **kart* (? **kärt*), cf. Avestan karəta- 'knife', Modern Persian *kaard*; Ostyak V *looγər*, Vj *jooγər*, Trj *łaγə̂r*, DN Kr Ni *taxər*, Kaz *łaxər*, O *laxər* 'armour, mail (shirt)' < Middle Iranian **zγar-* 'armour', cf. Ossete *zγar, zγär*, Afghan *zγarah* 'chain-mail armour'.

About thirty loanwords into Ostyak attest to contacts with speakers of various kinds of Tungus before the twelfth century CE (Futaky 1975), e.g. VVj *jææŋ*, Trj J *jeeŋʷ*, DN Ko *jooŋ*, Ni Šer Kaz Syn *jaaŋ*, O *jooŋ* 'ten' < Tungus **joan ~ *joon*.

Most loans taken into Vogul and Ostyak during the past millennium are borrowings from Komi, Tatar, Samoyedic (chiefly Nenets, to a lesser degree Selkup), and Russian. From Komi comes, for example, the word for 'bread': Vogul KU KM KO *nʲæænʲ*, VS VN *nʲänʲ*, Pim *nʲinʲ*, LU *nʲenʲ*, LO So *nʲaanʲ* and Ostyak VVj Trj J DN *nʲäänʲ*, Ni Šer Syn *nʲaanʲ*, O *nʲäänʲ* are all from Komi *nʲanʲ* (which, together with its homophonous Udmurt cognate, was originally a loan from Iranian). Also from Komi (and also ultimately Iranian) is the word for 'paper; writing': Vogul KU KM KO VS VN Pim LU *neepǝk*, LO So *neepak* and Ostyak VVj Trj *niipiik*, J *niipeek*, DN Ko Kr *neepaak*, Ni Šer Kaz Syn O *neepeek* are all from Komi *nʲebëg ~ nebëg* 'book, paper; birchbark with property marks'.

Example of loanwords from Tatar: T Vogul *aacʲǝw*, KU VN *oosʲǝɣ*, DN Ostyak *aatʲǝ* 'sour', cf. Tatar *ačy* 'sour'; T Vogul *jarmaa*, KU KO *joormǝ*, KM *joorǝm*, Pim LU *jorǝm*, DN Ostyak *jaarmaa*, Ko *jäärmää* 'grits', cf. Tatar *jarma* '(barley) grits'. From Nenets: LO Vogul *xoopt*, So *xååpt*, Šer Ostyak *xååptǝ*, Kaz *xååpti*, O *xaapti* 'castrated reindeer', cf. Nenets *xabt°* 'id.', LO Vogul *poorxa*, So *poorxa*, Ni Kaz Ostyak *påårxa* 'parka' < Nenets *parka* 'id.'. From Russian: T Vogul *pop*, KM KO VN Pim *pup*, LO So *puup*, V Ostyak *pååp*, *pååw*, Trj *poop*, Ko Kr Ni *puup*, Kaz *pǫǫp*, O *poop* 'priest' from Russian поп, T Vogul *rümkää*, KU KM KO LU *rümkǝ*, P *rumkǝ*, So *rumka*, DN Ostyak *ruumkaa*, DT *rüümkaa*, Kr Ni O *ruumka* 'whisky glass' < Russian рюмка.

Loan relations have long existed between northern Vogul and northern Ostyak on the one hand, and (to a lesser extent) between eastern Vogul and southern Ostyak on the other, for example LO So Vogul *aapsʲi* 'younger brother' is a loan from Ostyak, cf. Kaz Syn Ostyak *aapsʲi*, O *ääpsʲi* 'id.' as is northern Vogul *kaat* 'idol', cf. Ni Šer Ostyak *kaat*, Kaz *kaałt*, O *käält* 'protective spirit'. Loans in the other direction include Kaz Ostyak *xašap*, O *xasap* 'midge-proof tent', from northern Vogul, cf. So *xašap*, and Šer Ostyak *aamtʲikee*, Kaz *aamaamsʲi* 'riddle' < LO Vogul *aamsʲi*, cf. So *aamǝsʲ* (ultimately from Tatar *ämälči*).

Appendix

In order to supplement the picture given in the main body of this chapter, in the two sections below I list briefly the most important features shared by (1) the ObUgrian and (2) the Ugric languages. The presentation is based chiefly on Honti 1979.

ObUgrian Shared Features

1   The names of the teens (11–19) in northern, western, and eastern Vogul and in western Ostyak were based on the model 'X (and) lying ten', e.g. So Vogul *kit+xujp+luw*, Kaz Ostyak *kat+xosʲ+jaŋ* both TWO+LYING-+TEN '12' (Honti 1986a: 199).

2   Widespread use of the passive.

3   In passive sentences, marking of the agent with a morpheme containing *n*. The suffixes which perform this function in the modern ObUgrian languages are of different origin: in Vogul, it is the lative -*n(aa/ää)*, which derives from a Ugric postposition *nää-, while in Ostyak it is the locative (< pO *-naa/-nää, from a pU locative). But the occupation of the Vogul 'lative' slot by -*n(aa/ää)* is secondary. What happened is this: in pOU, the locative in *-nV served to mark agents in passive sentences. *Qua* locative,

this suffix was lost in proto-Vogul, where it was replaced by the newer, probably Ugric, locative *-ttV. The potential homophonic clash with the pV lative may have helped to oust the old locative; in any event, the -*n* which marks passive agents in Vogul is now synchronically a lative.

4   In both ObUgrian languages there is a copula-like verb which is phonologically similar, but unrelated, to the verb 'is': T Vogul *aas-*, So *åås-*, VVj Ostyak *was-*, Kaz *wǫǫs-* 'is someone or something' (*DEWOS*: 1630–1) ≠ T Vogul *aal-*, So *åål-*, VVj *wal-*, Kaz *wǫǫ̯-* 'is, exists, lives' (*DEWOS*: 1577–80).

5   In both Ostyak and Vogul, the instrumental marks the object in sentences with benefactive force; the benefited participant is put in the accusative, if there is one available. Thus alongside Trj Ostyak *ɫääjəm määnteem mej-ee* AXE s1.PRO.dat GIVES-imp.s2sO 'give me the axe!', there is also the benefactive *ɫääjəm-äät mään-t mej-ää* AXE-ins.fin s1.PRO.acc GIVES-imp.s2, roughly 'endow me with the axe!'

Ugric Shared Features
1   In proto-Ugric, the sibilant (*s) and shibilant (*š) inherited from p(F)U fell together and changed into *θ; the resulting gap began to be re-filled, in proto-Ugric, by the depalatalization *sʲ > *s.

2   Already in proto-Ugric, *k had markedly different allophones in front-vocalic versus back-vocalic environments. The result was the development, albeit separately in each of the three Ugric languages, of *k > x (> *h-* in Hungarian) in back-vocalic words. In Vogul, this change was restricted to the northern and Lower Konda dialects; in Ostyak, it was restricted to the western (= southern plus northern) dialects.

3   Non-initial p(F)U *w changed to *γ in proto-Ugric. This *γ subsequently reverted to *w* (> *v* in Hungarian) in certain dialects and in certain environments. For details, see Honti 1985b. Examples: pFU *tälwä 'winter' (the source of Finnish *talvi*) gave proto-Ostyak *teləγ > VVj Ostyak *teləγ*, pU *luwe 'bone' (the source of Finnish *luu*) gave pOU *luγ > pV *luw (> So *luw*), pO *loγ (> VVj *loγ*), pFU *kiwe 'stone' (the source of Finnish *kivi*) gave pOU *kööγ > pV *käw (> So *kaw*), pO *kööγ (> VVj *kööγ*), pFU *kewδe (or perhaps better: *kewɫe) 'rope' (the source of Finnish *köysi*) gave (with metathesis) pOU *kööləγ > pV *kʷääləγ (> So *kʷaaliγ*), pO *kööləγ (> Ni *keetə*, Kaz *keeɫ*).

4   The sequence-type p(F)U lateral plus *m (i.e. *lm, *ɫm, *ɫʲm; in more traditional formulation *lm *δm *δʲm) yields parallel results in the three Ugric languages.

5   In certain words, the Ugric languages have preserved evidence of an original high back unrounded vowel (*ï), as in the word for 'arrow': Hungarian *nyíl* (with í < *ï), pV *nʲïïl, pO *nʲaal (with *aa* < *ïï); contrast Finnish *nuoli*.

6   In the word for '3', Hungarian and Vogul have changed internal *-l- to

-r- (Hungarian *három*, So Vogul *xuurəm*). Contrast Finnish *kolme* – and VVj Ostyak *kåålâm*.

7   The gerundive suffixes of Hungarian (=*ván*/=*vén*) and Ostyak (*=maan/ =mään ~ *=mïïn/=miin) point to Ugric origin.

8   A new set of local suffixes, based on the pronominal base *nä-, evolved in proto-Ugric.

9   It is virtually certain that the ablative suffix -*l* is not older than Ugric.

10 Proto-Ugric innovated a derivational suffix which formed momentaneous verbs, *=pp(V)-. Cf. Hungarian *áll-* 'stands', (fifteenth-century Hungarian) *áll=ap-* 'stops', So Vogul *sʲalt-* 'enters', *sʲalt=ap-* 'enters suddenly', Jugan Ostyak *nʲaxt-* 'sneezes', *nʲaxt=ip-* 'sneezes once'.

11 Also of Ugric origin are the Hungarian denominal verb-formant =*h*- and its ObUgrian pendants.

12 The Hungarian and Vogul formulation of the caritive suffix is probably of Ugric origin (but see also Itkonen 1992).

13 The non-attributive form of the numeral 'two' is of parallel structure in the three Ugric languages, viz. STEM+dual: Hungarian *kettő* (< *kätəγ), So Vogul *kitiγ*, VVj Ostyak *käätkən*, cf. the attributive forms *két*, *kit*, *käät*.

14 The long front rounded vowel of the Hungarian third-person singular pronoun, *ő*, reflects the loss of an earlier *=ŋ suffix which is still attested in Ostyak and Vogul.

15 The possessive and verbal suffixes marking the first person plural are to be reconstructed as 'rounded vowel plus *k' in proto-Ugric (Honti 1985a: 75–6).

16 The Hungarian word for 'flea', *tetű*, descends from a form derived with the same compound derivational suffix as in pO and pV (Honti 1985b: 153).

17 The =*kály* element of Hungarian *harkály* 'woodpecker' is an Ugric derivational suffix-chain.

18 The development of the class of unstable verb stems appears to date from the period of common Ugric (Honti 1985a: 50–52, 77–8; 1987).

19 The Ugric languages show a tendency to use distinct suffixes in the formation of certain types of exocentric adjectival compounds depending on whether the attributes are alienable (Hungarian =*s*, northern Vogul =*ŋ*) or inalienable (Hungarian =*ú/ű*, northern Vogul =*p*). (Kálmán 1983.)

20 The order of suffixes in nominal inflection is identical in the three Ugric languages: STEM + PERSON SUFFIX + CASE SUFFIX for nouns, STEM + CASE SUFFIX + PERSON SUFFIX for postpositions.

21 In all three Ugric languages, postpositions reflect three-way deixis.

22 In all three Ugric languages, coverbs play an important role in the lexical, aspectual, and pragmatic domains.

23 Ugric preserves the pU dichotomy of subjective v. objective conjugation (Honti 1990a).

24   Hungarian *iafia* 'descendants (of someone)' appears to be a copulative (*'daughter-s3+son-s3') compound of Ugric origin.

25   The Ugric languages have a considerable number of shared inherited vocabulary items (Honti 1979: 13–18). Among these, certain types invite special attention, such as the vocabulary and even phraseology of equiculture and the shared self-designation Hungarian *magy=ar* 'Hungarian' = So Vogul *maanⁱsʲi* 'Vogul'.

26   The Hungarian collocation *kenyere-t keres-* 'earns [literally: seeks] one's bread (= living)' is a taboo-motivated euphemism which may be retraced to the Ugric period (Honti 1990b).

References and Further Reading

General
Collinder, B. (1960), *Comparative Grammar of the Uralic languages*, Stockholm: Almqvist & Wiksell.
DEWOS = Steinitz 1966–93.
Ganschow, G. (1965), *Die Verbalbildung im Ostjakischen*, Ural-Altaische Bibliothek 13, Wiesbaden: Harrassowitz.
Gombocz, Z. (1898) 'A vogul infinitivus', *Nyelvtudományi Közlemények* 28: 127–8.
Hajdú, P. (1966) *Bevezetés az uráli nyelvtudományba*, Budapest: Tankönyvkiadó.
——— (1985) 'Personalbezeichnungen für die 2. Person im Uralischen', Советское финно-угроведение 1: 1–8.
——— (1987) 'Die uralischen Sprachen', in P. Hajdú and P. Domokos, *Die uralischen Sprachen und Literaturen*, Budapest – Hamburg: Akadémiai kiadó – Buske Verlag, pp. 23–450.
Honti, L. (1974) 'Etimológiai adalékok', *Nyelvtudományi Közlemények* 76: 369–78.
——— (1976) 'Az osztják személyjelölő szuffixumok történeti áttekintése', *Nyelvtudományi Közlemények* 78: 71–119.
——— (1979) 'Characteristic features of Ugric languages (Observations on the question of Ugric unity)', *Acta Linguistica Academiae Scientiarum Hungaricae* 29: 1–26.
——— (1980) 'Milyen volt az obi-ugor alapnyelv teljes magánhangzórendszere?', *Nyelvtudományi Közlemények* 82: 172–90.
——— (1982a) *Geschichte des obugrischen Vokalismus der ersten Silbe*, Bibliotheca Uralica 6, Budapest: Akadémiai kiadó.
——— (1982b) 'A szalimi osztják nyelvjárás hang- és alaktanának ismertetése', *Nyelvtudományi Közlemények* 84: 91–119.
——— (1983a) 'Zur ugrischen Lautgeschichte (Beiträge zur relativen Chronologie einiger Lautwandel in den ugrischen Sprachen)', *Acta Linguistica Academiae Scientiarum Hungaricae* 33: 113–22.
——— (1983b) 'Ablautartige Vokalwechsel in den obugrischen Sprachen', *FUF* 45: 25–45.
——— (1983c) 'Alanyi és tárgyas igeragozás a demjankai osztják nyelvjárásokban', in G. Bereczki and P. Domokos (eds), *Urálisztikai tanulmányok (Hajdú Péter 60. születésnapja tiszteletére)*, Budapest: ELTE, pp. 173–8.
——— (1983d) 'A harmadik személyt jelölő szuffixumok a vogulban', *Nyelvtudományi Közlemények* 85: 349–55.

—— (1984) *Chrestomathia ostiacica*, Budapest: Tankönyvkiadó.
—— (1985a) 'Széljegyzetek instabil tövű igéink történetéhez', *Nyelvtudományi Közlemények* 87: 49–87.
—— (1985b) 'Ősmagyar hangtörténetei talányok (Ugor hangtörténeti és etimológiai jegyzetek)', *Magyar Nyelv* 81: 140–55.
—— (1986a) 'Szláv hatás a magyar számnévszerkesztésben?', *Nyelvtudományi Közlemények* 88: 196–207.
—— (1986b) 'A vogul *s* és *š* alapnyelvi előzményei', *Nyelvtudományi Közlemények* 88: 258–63.
—— (1986c) 'Er soll mit Begrüßung geschrieben werden!', *Finnisch-Ugrische Mitteilungen* 10: 155–63.
—— (1987) 'Lautgeschichte, Etymologie, historisch-vergleichende Morphologie (ein gemeinsamer Type von Stammalternation im Ugrischen)', in E. Lang and G. Sauer (eds), *Parallelismus und Etymologie, Studien zu Ehren von Wolfgang Steinitz anläßlich seines 80. Geburtstags*, Linguistische Studien, Reihe A, Arbeitsberichte 161/II, Berlin: Akademie der Wissenschaften, pp. 187–93.
—— (1990a) 'К проблеме возникновения объектного спряжения угорских языков', in G.V. Fedjüneva (ed.), Материалы VI международного конгресса финно- угроведов, Moscow: Nauka, vol. 2, pp. 211–14.
—— (1990b) 'Ugrisches', *Linguistica Uralica* 16: 298–9.
—— (1992) 'Adalék a magyar *l* ~ finn *t* megfelelésének és alapnyelvi előzményének magyarázatához', in P. Deréky et al. (eds), *Festschrift für Károly Rédei zum 60. Geburtstag*, Studia uralica 6; Urálisztikai tanulmányok 3; Linguistica Series A, Studia et dissertationes 8, Vienna–Budapest: n.p., pp. 209–14.
—— (forthcoming) 'Geschichte des obugrischen Konsonantismus', in L. Honti and M. Sz. Bakró-Nagy (eds), *Uralische lautgeschichtliche Studien*, Budapest.
Itkonen, E. (1961) 'Suomalais-ugrilaisen kantakielen äänne- ja muotorakenteesta', in E. Itkonen, *Suomalais-ugrilaisen Kielen- ja historiantutkimuksen alalta*, Tietolipas 20, Helsinki: Suomalaisen Kirjallisuuden Seura, pp. 48–84.
Itkonen, T. (1992) 'Ugrilaisten kielten karitiivista', in P. Deréky et al. (eds), *Festschrift für Károly Rédei zum 60. Geburtstag*, Studia uralica 6; Urálisztikai tanulmányok 3; Linguistica Series A, Studia et dissertationes 8, Vienna–Budapest: n.p., pp. 221–37.
Kálmán, B. (1983) 'A szerves és szervetlen kapcsolat egyik kifejezése az ugor nyelvekben', in G. Bereczki and P. Domokos (eds), *Urálisztikai tanulmányok (Hajdú Péter 60. születésnapja tiszteletére)*, Budapest: ELTE, pp. 193–205.
—— (1988) 'The history of the Ob-Ugric languages', in D. Sinor (ed.), *The Uralic Languages: Description, History and Foreign influences*, Handbuch der Orientalistik 8/I, Leiden: Brill, pp. 395–412.
Sz. Kispál, M. (1966) *A vogul igenév modattana*, Budapest: Akadémiai kiadó.
—— (1968) 'Über einige Fragen der ugrischen Verbalnomina', in P. Ravila (ed.), *Congressus Secundus Internationalis Fenno-Ugristarum ... Pars I, Acta Linguistica*, Helsinki: Societas Fenno-Ugrica, pp. 267–72.
Kulonen, U.-M. (1989) *The Passive in Ob-Ugrian*, MSFOn 203, Helsinki: Société Finno-Ougrienne.
Liimola, M. (1944) 'Zu den wogulischen Personalpronomina', *FUF* 28: 20–56.
—— (1963) *Zur historischen Formenlehre des Wogulischen*, vol. I. *Flexion der Nomina*, MSFOu 127, Helsinki: Société Finno-Ougrienne.
Rédei, K. (1977) 'Szófejtések', *Nyelvtudományi Közlemények* 79: 201–16.
—— (1988) (ed.) *Uralisches etymologisches Wörterbuch*, vols. I–II, Budapest–Wiesbaden: Akadémiai Kiadó–Harrassowitz.
Riese, T. (1992) 'Zur Entwicklung des Kasussystems im Wogulischen', in P. Deréky

et al. (eds), *Festschrift für Károly Rédei zum 60. Geburtstag*, Studia uralica 6; Urálisztikai tanulmányok 3; Linguistica Series A, Studia et dissertationes 8, Vienna–Budapest: n.p., pp. 379–88.

Sammallahti, P. (1988) 'Historical phonology of the Uralic languages', in D. Sinor (ed.), *The Uralic Languages: Description, History and Foreign Influences*, Handbuch der Orientalistik 8/1, Leiden: Brill, pp. 478–554.

Sauer, G. (1967) *Die Nominalbildung im Ostjakischen*, Finnisch-Ugrische Studien 5, Berlin: Akademie-Verlag.

Steinitz, W. (1950) *Geschichte des ostjakischen Vokalismus*, Berlin: Akademie-Verlag.

—— (1955) *Geschichte des vogulischen Vokalismus*, Berlin: Akademie-Verlag.

—— (1966–93): *Dialektologisches und etymologisches Wörterbuch der ostjakischen Sprache*, Berlin: Akademie-Verlag.

—— (1989) *Ostjakologische Arbeiten*, vol. III: *Texte aus dem Nachlaß*, Budapest–Berlin: Akadémiai Kiadó–Akademie-Verlag.

—— (n.d.) (unpublished essays and notes by Wolfgang Steinitz on the history of ObUgrian vocalism).

UEW = Rédei 1988.

Zsirai, M. (1933) *Az obi-ugor igekötők*, Értekezések a Nyelv- és Széptudományi Osztály körébol, 26/3, Budapest: Magyar Tudományos Akadémia.

Contacts

Futaky, I. (1975) *Tungusische Lehnwörter des Ostjakischen*, Veröffentlichungen der Societas Uralo-Altaica 10, Wiesbaden: Harrassowitz.

Hajdú, P. (1990) 'Einiges über Fürwörter', *Linguistica Uralica* 26: 1–12.

Joki, A.J. (1973) *Uralier und Indogermanen*, MSFOu 151, Helsinki: Société Finno-Ougrienne.

Kálmán, B. (1960) *Die russischen Lehnwörter im Wogulischen*, Budapest: Akadémiai Kiadó.

Korenchy, É. (1972) *Iranische Lehnwörter in den obugrischen Sprachen*, Budapest: Akadémiai kiadó.

—— (1981) 'Iranian contacts during the period of Ugric division', in G. Ortutay (ed.), *C4IFU*, vol. III, Budapest: Akadémiai Kiadó, pp. 70–76.

Kulonen, U.-M. (1990) 'Das Nord-, Süd- und Ostobugrische: Syntaktische Unterschiede und Übereinstimmungen', in L. Jakab, L. Keresztes, A. Kiss and S. Maticsák (eds), *C7IFU*, vol. IB, Debrecen: Congress Committee, pp. 139–145.

Liimola, M. (1971) 'Zur Kasuslehre der Vach- und Vasjugan-Mundart der ostjakischen Sprache', *JSFOu* 71: 3–24.

Rédei, K. (1970) *Die syrjänischen Lehnwörter im Wogulischen*, Uralic and Altaic Series 109, Budapest–Bloomington–The Hague: Akadémiai Kiadó–Indiana University–Mouton.

Riese, T. (1984) *The Conditional Sentence in the Ugrian, Permian, and Volgaic Languages*, Studia Uralica 3, Vienna: Verband der wissenschaftlichen Gesellschaften Österreichs.

Steinitz, W. (1980) *Ostjakologische Arbeiten*, vol. IV: *Beiträge zur Sprachwissenschaft und Ethnographie*, Budapest–Berlin: Akadémiai Kiadó–Akademie-Verlag.

Toivonen, Y.H. (1956) 'Über die syrjänischen Lehnwörter im Ostjakischen', *FUF* 31: 1–169.

Vértes, E. (1967) *Die ostjakischen Pronomina*, Uralic and Altaic Series 74, Budapest–Bloomington–The Hague: Akadémiai Kiadó–Indiana University–Mouton.

12 Khanty

Daniel Abondolo

Khanty (older name: Ostyak) is a complex chain of dialects spoken by people who live in a vast, roughly L-shaped area along the Ob', the lower Irtysh, and tributaries. According to the most recent figures (1989 census), there are some 22,000 speakers of Khanty; of these, 62.9 per cent were native speakers (i.e. *c*. 14,000). Khanty speakers make up about 1 per cent of the population of the Khanty–Mansi Autonomous Okrug (Künnap 1993: 86).

From a historical-typological perspective, Khanty presents with a rather odd amalgam of central and peripheral Uralic features. Like Permian and Hungarian, Khanty has lost the proto-Uralic accusative *-m, but like Saamic and Samoyedic, it has preserved traces of the proto-Uralic reflexivizer *=j. Khanty is the only Finno-Ugric language in which proto-Uralic *ð^j has merged fully with *j in all positions – the regular development in proto-Samoyedic. The closest congener of Khanty is almost certainly Mansi, but many of the Khanty/Mansi shared features could be *Sprachbund* convergence phenomena, and many aspects of their putative protolanguage, proto-ObUgrian (most critically, the vocalism) have not been reconstructed in fully convincing detail (Abondolo 1996: 7–15). Some of the mystery of the morphophonemics of the present-day Khanty dialects is a result of our ignorance of this aspect of Khanty (and ObUgrian) linguistic prehistory.

Dialects

On both historical-phonological and syntactic-typological grounds, these may be broken into two major groupings, East v. West. The East group further subdivides into (1) the Far Eastern dialects V(ach) and Vasjugan (Vj), and (2) the Surgut group, which includes Jugan, Malij Jugan, Pim, Likrisovskoe, Tremjugan (Trj), and Tromagan (Tra); for the difference between these last two varieties, see pp. 362–4. The Vartovskoe dialect is transitional between the Surgut and the Far Eastern dialects. There is also a Sal(ym) dialect, which some see as transitional between the major East and West groupings, but which probably is better classified with the southern subgroup of the western group.

The West group subdivides into North and South subgroups. Clearly southern are the Demjanka (DN DT) dialects and Konda, Cingali, and

Krasnojarsk. Clearly northern are the O(bdorsk) dialect and the Ber(jozov) subgroup, consisting of the Synja, Muzhi, and Shurishkar dialects, and, to the south, Kaz(ym). Transitional between North and South are the Sher(kal) and Ni(zyam) dialects.

Reliable population figures for the various dialects are not available. Perhaps two-thirds of Khanty speakers use a northern dialect, the remaining third being speakers of one of the eastern forms; southern Khanty is probably no longer used.

Selected dialect isoglosses are set out in Figure 12.1. The table has been designed to dramatize the fact that the periphery, i.e. far northwest Obdorsk and far southeast Vj and V, is in several respects more conservative than the centre, but also that there are pockct retentions just short of the periphery, such as the *ł* of Kazym and the Surgut group. The western innovation *k- > *x-* before back vowels may be seen as convergence with northern and some eastern Mansi dialects, where the same change took place, e.g. (in the word for 'three') Pelymka (western) Mansi *kuurᶔm*, v. Lower Konda (eastern) and Sosva (northern) Mansi *xuurᶔm* = Tremjugan Khanty *koołᶔm* v. Obdorsk Khanty *xoolᶔm* = Nizyam Khanty *xuutᶔm*. The -*r*- of all Mansi dialects in this word is probably an example of an earlier convergence, namely of proto-Mansi and proto-Hungarian, cf. Hungarian *haarom*.

Vowel harmony of the palatovelar (i.e. front/back) type is found in the easternmost dialects: Vach, Vasjugan, and some of the Surgut group. Example: Vach *kööγ-ääm* 'my stone', *kuul-aam* 'my fish'. Since Southern Mansi dialects also had vowel harmony it is assumed that vowel harmony in east Khanty is a retention from at least proto-ObUgrian times.

Vowel inventories vary greatly from dialect to dialect, with the largest in the east and the smallest in the north. As in most Uralic languages, and in keeping with the principles of vowel harmony, the full vowel inventory occurs only in the first syllable of the word, the vocalism of non-first syllables being severely restricted in every Khanty dialect, regardless of whether it has retained

Figure 12.1   Selected Khanty dialect isoglosses

	O	Ber	Kaz	Sher	Ni	Irt	Sal	Trj	Vj	V
VH				-					+	
*kB-			x-				k-			
*cⱼ			sⱼ				tⱼ			
-s- past			+			-		+		
*ł-		1-	ł-		t-			ł-	j-	1-
*l		1	ł		t			ł		1
*aa	aa		åå			oo		åå		aa

Note: VH = vowel harmony, B = back vowel. For dialect abbreviations, see text.

vowel harmony. As in all Mansi dialects, the vocalism of all Khanty dialects is characterized by a quantitative opposition, termed in Ostyakology full v. reduced; full vowels will be transcribed here as long, i.e. written geminate. Examples of minimal pairs: Vach *kööt* 'hand', *köt* 'distance'; *seem* 'eye', *sem* 'heart'; *jool* 'sorcery', *jol* 'border'; *saart* 'pike (fish)', *sart* 'interstice'.

Sample Inventories

A relatively rich system is that of Vach Khanty, in the far southeast, with nine (or eleven, Katz 1975: 78–81) full, and four reduced vowels:

ii	üü	ïï	uu			
ee	öö		oo	e	ö	o
ää	(œœ)	aa	(åå)			a

Contrast Obdorsk, in the far northwest, with only six and three, respectively:

ii		uu		
ee		oo		o
ää	aa		ä	a

The smallest system is found in Nizyam, Sherkal, and Berëzovo:

	uu	i		u
ee				o
	aa	åå		a

This inventory is identical with that of Sosva Mansi, which is spoken directly to the west. At least two waves of rotation have shuffled the lexical distribution of the vowels of these two idioms, with the result that for each vowel in Nizyam Khanty there are two, equally regular, correspondents in Sosva Mansi. For example, Nizyam Khanty *ee* corresponds to Sosva Mansi *a* in *seem/sam* 'eye', *keew/kaw* 'stone', *teeŋkər/taŋkər* 'mouse', and *weet-/al-* 'kills', but to Sosva Mansi *aa* in *weetəm/waaləm* 'marrow', *eewə/aayi* 'daughter', *keej/kaaĺ* 'female (animal)', and *teep-/laap-* 'has enough room to fit'. In parallel fashion, Nizyam Khanty *aa* corresponds to Sosva Mansi *aa* in *aamp/aamp* 'dog', *paaw/paak^w* 'pine cone', *ńaarə/ńaar* 'raw', and *šaaš/saans* 'knee', but to Sosva Mansi *ee* in *ńaatəm/ńeeləm* 'tongue', *taaŋkə/leeŋən* 'squirrel', *aaŋən/eeŋən* 'chin', and *paat-/peet-* 'cooks, boils'; parallel patterns hold for the rest of the vowels, the regular Nizyam Khanty/Sosva Mansi correspondences being *i/ee* and *i/i*, *o/u* and *o/o*, *uu/o* and *uu/åå*, *åå/åå* and *åå/uu*, *u/uu* and *u/u*, *a/i* and *a/a*.

In Vach, Vasjugan, and the Surgut dialects, many nouns and verbs undergo stem-vowel alternations in their paradigms, e.g. Trj *kååt* 'house', *kuut-əm* 'my house'. The same, as well as other, alternations underlie many processes of (now no longer productive) derivation, e.g. Trj *käär* 'bark', *kiir* 'snowcrust'; *jäŋʷkʷ* 'ice', *jeŋk* 'water'; *kæt* 'hand', *kät=əɬ* 'bear's forepaw'. The reconstruction of the vowel system of proto-Khanty (and thus of proto-ObUgrian) is complicated by these alternations, whose extent in both space and time is hotly disputed.

Consonants
In all Khanty dialects distinctive voice is marginal or non-existent. On the other hand all Khanty dialects have the correlation of palatalization to some degree. For example, Vach Khanty has *t ≠ tʲ, n ≠ nʲ, l ≠ lʲ* and Kazym Khanty has *s ≠ sʲ, n ≠ nʲ, ɬ ≠ ɬʲ*. (The Surgut dialects and Kazym Khanty have plain and palatalized voiceless lateral fricatives.) Most Khanty dialects have retroflex consonant phonemes: parallel with the hushing non-palatalized *č* and/or *š* which are well established in e.g. Mansi, Komi, and Hungarian, we find in e.g. Vach, Vasjugan, and Kazym a retroflex lateral (written here *ḷ*) and a retroflex nasal (*ṇ*). Minimal pair from Vach: *liis* '(snare for trapping birds)', *ḷiis* 'slack, not tight'. The Surgut dialects distinguish labialized v. plain velars (as in Sosva Mansi); these are in perhaps all cases the result of transfer of the feature of labiality from the preceding vowel, e.g. Trj *jaɣʷëɬ* 'bow' < *joɣëɬ; cf. Vach *jooɣël*.

Morphology of the Noun: Case Suffixes
The number of cases varies considerably from dialect to dialect. Vach, in the far east, has ten cases; Obdorsk, in the far north, has three. All dialects distinguish singular, dual and plural forms of both possessor and possessed; non-possessed nouns also have three numbers. For example: Nizyam Khanty *xååp* 'boat' has these non-possessed forms:

	Singular	Dual	Plural
N	xååp	xååp-ŋ̂ən	xååp-ə̂t
Lat	xååp-a	xååp-ŋ̂ən-a	xååp-ə̂t-a
Loc	xååp-na	xååp-ŋ̂ən-na	xååp-ə̂t-na

Examples of possessed forms: *xååp-eem* 'my boat', *xååp-ŋə̂t-aam* 'my (two) boats', *xååp-t-am* 'my (3 or more) boats', *xååp-eemə̂n* 'the boat of us (two)', *xååp-ŋə̂t-ə̂mə̂n* 'the (two) boats of us (two)'. Person suffixes precede case suffixes, e.g. *xååp-eem-na* 'in my boat'.

Khanty verbs observe essentially the same categories as Mansi verbs, viz. (1) definite v. indefinite direct object; (2) within the category 'definite', number (sg/dual/plur) is distinguished; (3) there is also a so-called 'passive'. Thus in Vach we have e.g. (*-l-* is the present-tense morpheme) *tuu-l-ə̂m* 'I bring', *tuu-l-i̇-m* 'I bring it/him/her', *tuu-l-ə̂ɣlaa-m* 'I bring them (two)', *tuu-l-laa-m* 'I bring them (3+)', *tuu-l-uuj-ə̂m* 'I am brought; X is brought to me'. These are the same five distinctions made by Sosva Mansi, but with different material.

Whereas all known Mansi dialects have distinct suffixes for present and past tense, Khanty presents a more complex picture: northern dialects have an -s- past-tense morpheme, southern dialects (and Nizyam) have a Ø past-tense morpheme, and Vach, Vasjugan, and most Surgut dialects have both.

Sketch of Tremjugan/Tromagan Khanty

Tremjugan (Trj) and Tromagan (Tra) Khanty are two varieties within the Surgut subgroup which differ in time rather than in space: Tromagan is now spoken where Tremjugan was in the nineteenth century, along a tributary of the Ob' which is called *torəm jaɣ^wən* 'sacred river' by Trj/Tra speakers (Csepregi 1993: 59). Because of the sparseness of available material, data from both varieties will be adduced in the sketch which follows, with the two temporal variants (Trj or Tra) marked only when it is crucial to the discussion; data from other dialects is also adduced for purposes of contrast, or when an appropriate Trj/Tra example is lacking.

Segmental Inventory
Vowels. In the first syllable, Trj/Tra Khanty has a vowel inventory of thirteen terms, with nearly equal membership in the two quantitative classes.

In non-first syllable, Tremjugan Khanty had six full vowels, front *ii ee ää* and back *ïï ëë aa*, and two reduced vowels, front and back schwa: *ə ə̂*. In Tromagan Khanty, the front/back opposition has been neutralized in favour of the unmarked members; fieldworkers report only *ii ee aa ə*. This neutralization has eliminated vowel harmony from the phonology: contrast Tremjugan *wååjə̂ɣ*, Tromagan *wååjəɣ* 'animal'. Throughout this chapter, only the unmarked forms will normally be cited, with the understanding that in earlier, i.e. Tremjugan, instantiations there was also the corresponding front or back analogue.

Notes on Pronunciation
The phonetic realization of *ää* is more central than front; since the last century, this phoneme has been moving back, in the wake of *åå*, which developed from earlier *aa (** in the table). The reduced vowels classed here as mid are usually pronounced as close mid. The duration of the low reduced vowels often approaches or equals that of the full lows; the primary acoustic cue is then vowel colour (Csepregi 1993: 60).

Table 12.1   First-syllable vowel inventory of Trj/Tra Khanty

	Full				*Reduced*			
High	ii		ïï	uu				
Mid	ee			oo	e	ö		o
Low	ää		**	åå	ä	œ	a	
Rounded	–	+	–	+	–	+	–	+
Back	–		+		–		+	

Full vowels may be pronounced short, especially in non-first syllables.

Within the non-compound word, stress is never distinctive, and is normally on the first syllable, but may move to the second syllable under certain circumstances (Honti 1988: 176). Secondary stress has been perceived on non-final odd syllables, e.g. *sä″m+jenk-kə´ɬ-aam* EYE+WATER-dual-s1 'my tears'. There is evidence that stress on subsequent syllables within the noun phrase is forbidden, e.g. *nʲuur ooɣ=əp* BARE HEAD=ED 'bald', cf. *wer=əŋ wäänʲm=əp* BLOOD=adj CHEEK=ED 'rosy cheeked'.

Consonants and consonant sandhi. The Trj/Tra Khanty consonant inventory distinguishes three places of apical articulation: a dental, a palatalized, and a cacuminal series, in rather uneconomical fashion. This three-way opposition is phonetically at its purest among the nasals. Affricate pronunciation characterizes the palatalized obstruent usually; it characterizes the cacuminal obstruent always, except before the apical fricatives *ɬ* and *s*.

Nasals	m	n	nʲ	ṇ	ŋ	ŋʷ
Stops	p	t	tʲ		k	kʷ
Affricate				č̣		
Non-lateral fricatives		s			ɣ	ɣʷ
Lateral fricatives		ɬ	ɬʲ			
Lateral approximant				ḷ		
Glides	w		j			
Trill		r				

The bilabial approximant or glide *w* and the labialized velar fricative or approximant *ɣʷ* are probably to be subsumed under one phoneme.

Both the palatalized and the cacuminal consonants continue proto-Khanty segments, where the palatalized consonants are of proto-Uralic origin, and all the cacuminals save *č* seem to be proto-Khanty innovations. A pre-Surgut innovation is the transfer of labiality from a preceding vowel to a following velar (*k ɣ ŋ*); this has given rise to an opposition between plain and labialized velars, e.g. *ḷeekʷ* 'ring', cf. Vach *ḷœœk*. Note also *-aŋ- in *ɬaŋaaɬ* '(s)he enters', but *-oŋ- in *ɬaŋʷ* '(s)he entered'. These two velar series contrast to the right of the two vowels which are each the result of a merger of one rounded with one unrounded pre-Surgut vowel: first-syllable *a* (ultimately from *ï) and *ii* (from *üü), e.g. *ɬaɣʷï* 'knot in a bough or in split wood' : *laɣï* 'wave', *piiɣʷəɬ* 'heart (of the bear; a taboo word; cf. Vach *püüɣəl* 'fishing-line') : *piiɣəɬ* 'patch on boat' (cf. Katz 1975: 88–9). Another Surgut innovation, but one shared with Kazym Khanty in the west, is the fricativization of the proto-Khanty plain and palatalized laterals, *l > ɬ and *lʲ > ɬʲ, the cacuminal *ḷ* alone remaining an approximant.

When adjacent to *k ɣ ŋ*, the voiced velar fricatives *ɣ* and *ɣʷ* are automatically replaced by the corresponding stops *k* and *kʷ*, e.g. *ɣ-ɣ > k-k* in *jek-kən ääŋkee-γən* FATHER-dual MOTHER-dual 'father and mother' (cf. *jeγ* 'father', *ääŋkii* 'mother'), *γʷ-k > kʷk* in *lakʷ kiinʲɬ̣ää* 'compared to a horse' (cf. *laγʷ* 'horse'). Stem-final γ goes to *k* before the adjective-forming suffix =*əŋ*, e.g. *wæk=əŋ* 'strong' (cf. *wæγ* 'strength').

There is left-to-right assimilation among the distinctively D(ental), P(alatal), and C(acuminal) consonants such that C+D > CC and P+D > PP if the second consonant is an obstruent, e.g. *poč-* 'rakes together' plus the infinitive suffix *-taayə* yields *poččaayə* (with longer duration in the closed phase, not in the release), and the infinitive of *ɬ̣ååɬ̣-* 'stands' is *ɬ̣ååɬ̣ɬ̣aayə*. The sequence *č-ɬ* yields [tɬ] because of the unreleased pronunciation of *č* before *ɬ*, e.g. [tɬ] in *koč-ɬ-eem* 'I tune it (musical instrument), I swaddle it (child in cot)'.

Morphology

Architectonics
Monomorphemic nouns tend to be of the shape (C)VC(C) or (C)VC(C)ə(C), i.e. with at most one full vowel, and that in the first syllable. Apart from nouns ending in *ïï/ii*, which continues a proto-Khanty diphthong whose components more often than not straddled a morpheme boundary, deviance from this canon usually signals a loanword or affect, e.g. *järnaas* 'shirt' (a loan from Komi), *nʲeeγʷreem* 'child'. Consonant clusters in initial position seem to be excluded, even in fairly recent loans such as *poruunt* 'one of several small pieces of wood used as a guide in hollowing out a boat' (< Russian dialect *šprunt*, cf. standard *špunt*, from German *Spund*). Final clusters are always homotopic, and their second member is always a stop or affricate, e.g. *mp*, *rt*, *ņč*, *ŋk*. In triconsonantal clusters which arise through the concatenation of morphemes, the middle consonant is cancelled, but its voicelessness is transferred to the latter portion of the preceding segment, e.g. perfect *kenč=∅ -əm* 'I was hunting, looking for' : present *ken[ᴺ]-ɬ-əm* 'I'm hunting, I'll hunt'. Stems of the shape (C)VC(C)əC syncopate the schwa before vowel-initial suffixes, e.g. *kaaḷəγ* 'nephew': *küḷγ-əm* 'nephew s1', *jöntəγ* 'bowstring', *jön[ᴺ]γ-əɬ* 'bowstring s3', *kiimpəḷ* 'unevenness in bark of birch; individual scale of cedar cone' : s3 *kiim[ᴹ]ḷ-əɬ*.

Further examples of each shape: (C)VC(C): *čuunč* 'flea', *äämp* 'dog', *nääŋk* 'larch', *såårt* 'pike (fish)', *kåår* 'male (animal)', *aγʷ* 'current', *ɬ̣aγʷ* 'thin ice', *koos* 'star', *kor* 'swampy place'. (C)VC(C)ə(C): *panə* 'string', *ååləŋ* 'tip', *äpəɬ* 'smell', *muuγəɬ* 'liver', *nʲääɬəm* 'tongue', *nʲoorəm* 'swamp', *kååləp* 'net', *kæjəγ* 'female (animal)', *ooγəɬ* 'sandbank on river'.

Ablaut
We may distinguish two types of ablaut series. In the first, the high full vowels alternate with their low and mid counterparts in the following sets: *ii ~ ää, ii ~ ee; uu ~ åå, uu ~ oo*. This type occurs widely in both nouns and verbs, in

both derivation and inflection. Examples from nominal inflection: *mååγ* 'beaver' : *muuγ-əm* 'beaver s1', *äämp* 'dog' ~ *iimp-əm* 'dog s1', *ḷeek^w* 'ring': *ḷiik^w-əm* 'ring s1', *ooγ* 'head' : *uuγ-əm* 'head s1'. In verbs, *åå* alternates with *ïï* in the imperative: *kåånt-* 'picks up' : *kïïnm-ee* 'pick it up!' and in derivation, e.g. *ḷååḷəm-* 'steals' : *ḷïïḷm=əγt-* 'approaches stealthily'; the *åå* ~ *ïï* alternation also occurs in at least one noun, namely *kååḷəγ* 'nephew' : *kïïḷγ-əm* 'nephew s1'.

The second type is restricted to verbal inflection. Here the ablaut involves the reduced sets *ä ~ e* and *a ~ o*, e.g. *wäḷ-Ø-eem* 'I killed it' : *weḷ-ee* 'kill it!', *kaḷaa-ḷ* '(s)he is dying' : *koḷ-Ø* '(s)he died'. As mentioned above, the roundedness of *o* or *ö* is transferred to a following velar, giving rise to alternations such as *ḷaŋ-aa-* 'enters' ~ *ḷaŋ^w* '(s)he entered', *äγ^wəḷ-* 'believes', s2 imperative *äγḷ-ää*; there are also analogical levellings.

The age of the various kinds of ablaut found in Khanty is one of the most hotly disputed questions in Uralic historical and comparative linguistics; opposing views may be viewed in Honti (1982: 18–23) and Katz (1987–8).

Nominal Paradigms

Nominal Stem Types
Two nouns have irregular stem allomorphy: *koo* 'man', with a stem *kuu(j)-* in certain inflected forms, e.g. *kuuj-əm* 'my husband'; and *nee ~ niiŋ-* 'woman', e.g. *niiŋ-ət* 'women'.

Number
Singular is marked with zero (*Ø*); dual is -*γ*ən (-*γ*əḷ- before person suffixes); plural is -*t* (-*ḷ*- before person suffixes). Consonant-final stems epenthesize schwa before -*t*, and schwa-final stems show a final low full vowel before both -*t* and -*γ*ən. Examples: sN *äγ^wii* 'daughter', dN *äγ^wii-γ*ən, pN *äγ^wii-t*; sN *kååt* 'house', dN *kååt-γ*ən, pN *kååt-ət*; sN *taγtə* 'piece', dN *taγtaa-γ*ən, pN *taγtaa-t*. Stem-final *ii* vacillates: it either remains (as in dN *äγ^wii-γ*ən above) or changes to *ee*, e.g. *ääŋkee-γ*ən 'mother dN'.

Person
The person suffixes are s1 -*(V)m*, s2 -*(V)(n)*, s3 -*ḷ*, d1 -*mən*, p1 -*γ^w*, p3 -*iiḷ*, all others (i.e. d23p2) -*iin*. Sample forms may be found in Table 12.2.

Stem-suffix Sandhi
To the left of person suffixes with an initial consonant, stem-final schwa > *aa*, e.g. *panaa-ḷ* 'string s3', *taγtaa-γ^w* 'piece p1'. To the left of person suffixes with initial *ii*, all final stem-final vowels are cancelled, e.g *pan-iiḷ* 'string p3', *wäḷ-iin* 'reindeer d23p2'. But the chief locus of allomorphy in person inflection is to be found in the first and second persons singular, where there is a complex pattern of vowel alternation which is reminiscent of vertical vowel harmony, and which is captured here as (V). When attached to vowel-

Table 12.2   Number and person suffixes of a Trj/Tra Khanty noun (all nominative forms): *kååt* 'house'

Possessor in	Possession in	1st person	2nd person	3rd person
Singular				
	Singular	kuut-əm	kuut-ən	kuut-əɬ
	Dual	kååt-ɣəɬ-aam	kååt-ɣəɬ-aa	kååt-ɣəɬ-Ø
	Plural	kååt-ɬ-aam	kååt-ɬ-aa	kååt-əɬ-Ø
Dual				
	Singular	kuut-mən	kuut-iin	kuut-iin
	Dual	kååt-ɣəɬ-əmən	kååt-ɣəɬ-ən	kååt-ɣəɬ-ən
	Plural	kååt-ɬ-əmən	kååt-ɬ-ən	kååt-ɬ-ən
Plural				
	Singular	kuut-əɣ^w	kuut-iin	kuut-iiɬ
	Dual	kååt-ɣəɬ-əɣ^w	kååt-ɣəɬ-ən	kååt-ɣəɬ-aaɬ
	Plural	kååt-ɬ-əɣ^w	kååt-ɬ-ən	kååt-ɬ-aaɬ

final stems, suffixes with initial (V) have zero vowel; stem-final *ii* then changes to *ee* and schwa changes to *aa*, e.g. *wäɬee-m* 'reindeer s1' (*wäɬii* 'reindeer'), *panaa-m* 'string s1' (*panə* 'string'). When attached to consonant-final monosyllabic stems, (V) is read (1) as a full low vowel, if the root vowel is a reduced vowel; (2) as *ee* (< *ii *ïï), if the root vowel is a high full vowel; and (3) as schwa, if the root vowel is a low full vowel; in this last case the low vowel ablauts to its high full counterpart. Examples of these three types are (1) *paɣ-aam* 'son s1', *mäɣ^{w}ɬ-ääm* 'breast s1', *kör-aam* 'foot s1'; (2) *kuuɬ-eem* 'fish s1', *ɬiiɬ-eem* 'breath s1'; (3) *kuut-əm* 'house s1' (*kååt* sN), *iimp-əm* 'dog s1' (*äämp* sN). Some kinship terms behave as if they belonged to class (3), e.g. *uup*: *uup-əm* 'my father-in-law', *jeɣ-əm* 'my father'. Roots with more than one syllable fluctuate.

The *(n)* final in the second person singular suffix is realized as *n* when followed by a case suffix or a postposition, as zero otherwise. Both the debilitation of this *n* and the lowering of the vowel to its left are Surgut innovations (Honti 1984: 46).

Case

Case suffixes come after any number or person suffix. Following tradition, we shall call the morphologically unmarked (-*Ø*) case the nominative, even though absolutive would be a better name. There are no other dedicated grammatical cases, the remaining nine being either local (locative -*nə*, lative -*aa*, approximative -*naam*, ablative -*ii*) or more abstract, i.e. adverbial (instructive -*aat*, comitative -*naat*, abessive -*ɬəɣ*, expletive -*ptii*, translative -*ɣə*). There is also a suffix -*iin* which forms temporal adverbs from time words such as *ɬoŋ* 'summer', e.g. *ɬoŋ-iin* 'in the summer(time)'. Certain other case suffixes, now extinct, are fossilized in deictics, e.g. separative -*ɬ* in *to-ɬ*

Table 12.3   Selected Trj/Tra noun number and case forms: *kååt* 'house'

	Singular	Dual	Plural
N	kååt	kååt-γɔn	kååt-ət
Lat	kååt-aa	kååt-γən-aa	kååt-ət-aa
App	kååt-naam	kååt-γən-naam	kååt-ət-naam
Loc	kååt-nə	kååt-γən-nə	kååt-ət-nə
Abl	kååt-ii	kååt-γən-ii	kååt-ət-ii
Inst	kååt-aat	kååt-γən-aat	kååt-ət-aat
Com	kååt-naat	kååt-γən-naat	kååt-ət-naat
Trans	kååt-γə	kååt-γən-γə	kååt-ət-γə

'from there'; see p. 370. There is also a distributive suffix *-təłtaa* which occurs with some postpositions and with numerals. Abessive plural, and expletive dual and plural forms are not attested. For sample forms, see Table 12.3.

Suffix order is invariably person + case, as in Mansi and Hungarian, e.g. *ääŋkee-m-nə* MOTHER-sl-loc, *łuuł-əł-ii* MOUTH-s3-abl, *ont-əł-nə* INTERIOR-s3-loc '(thought) to him/herself'. Such bisuffixal forms appear to be relatively rare, however.

Postpositions, Preverbs, and Gerund
The true postpositions are nouns with defective paradigms and distributions. Some have only one form, with fossilized, synchronically opaque morphology, e.g. the intrinsically lative *močə* '(to) as far as', e.g. *łåår tom=pii peetə močə* LAKE THERE=adj SHORE AS.FAR.AS 'as far as the opposite/far shore of the lake'. Most, however, occur with at least one, and usually two or more synchronically segmentable local suffixes attached, e.g. lative *pïïr-aa* 'to behind' : locative *pïïr-nə* 'behind, after' : distributive *pïr-əłtaa* 'from behind'; this is especially true of postpositions formed with the suffix =*pii*, e.g. locative *ïïł=pii-nə* 'under' : lative *ïïł=pij-aa* 'to underneath' : ablative *ïïł=pii-jii* 'from under', cf. *ïïł+päŋʷkʷ* 'lower teeth'. It is probably impossible to draw a sharp outer perimeter around the class of postpositions, since many nouns can enter into ad hoc postpositional constructions, e.g. *kiim* 'extent' in *łuuł-eem kiim-nə jeŋk-nə łååłʲ-łʲ-əm* MOUTH-s1 EXTENT-loc WATER-loc STANDS-pres-s1 'I'm standing in water up to my mouth'.

Postpositions are defective distributionally, i.e. they are syntactically bound, in that they always occur either with a head noun or with person suffixes. Nouns are usually in the nominative, e.g. *łåånʲrʲ-∅ köt-nə* SNOW-sN INTERSTICE-loc 'in the snow', *pełəŋ ont-naam* CLOUD INTERIOR-app 'into (the) cloud'. In most Khanty postpositions, person suffixes precede case suffixes just as in the inflection of fully productive nouns, e.g. *köt-iin-nə* INTERSTICE-d2-loc 'between the two of you', *iiłp-eem-aa* SPACE.IN.FRONT-s1-lat 'to in front of me'. Here Khanty patterns with

Mansi (e.g. North Mansi *xal-anel-t* INTERSTICE-p3-loc 'between them') but not with Hungarian, where the order is case suffix + person suffix (*köz-t-ük* INTERSTICE-loc-p3 'between them'). In Khanty, only a very few older postpositions show the reverse order, e.g. Synja Khanty *naŋ xosʲ-aj-ən* PRO.s2 SPACE.BESIDE-lat-s2 'to beside you', cf. the isomorphic and synonymous Hungarian *hoz-zaa-d*.

Another special subclass of adverb is the set of preverbs, which are adverbial, usually lative, particles such as *nok* 'up', *ïïɬ* 'down', *uutə* '(up) on to shore from the water; (up) inland from the shore', *niik* '(down) to the shore from inland; (down) from a smaller river to a larger one', *jakʷə* 'back, home, back home'. Preverbs create loose compounds which are semantically and/or aspectually distinct from their simplices, e.g. *wär-* 'does, makes, puts' : *ïïɬ wär-* 'buries', *kiiɬ-* '(a)rises' : *nok kiiɬ-* 'stands up'. Their normal place is immediately before the verb, but a negative particle usually intervenes, e.g. *toyə ääɬ tääɬiiɬiittən* 'don't (d2) drag me into it', cf. *toyə tääɬ-* 'drags thither'. From the lexico-cultural and syntactic point of view the Khanty preverbs are most closely akin to those of Mansi, but there are close parallels in Hungarian and even, in terms of aspect, in Estonian and Livonian, as well. See Sauer 1992 for a review of the literature and a discussion of preverbals from pronominal bases.

For the gerund, see p. 376.

Comparison

There is no comparative suffix. In Trj/Tra Khanty, the bested member of a comparison is marked with a postposition borrowed from Komi, e.g. *wäɬii ɬayʷ kiinʲtʲää nʲ ååyəɬ* REINDEER HORSE COMPARED.TO SHORT 'a reindeer is shorter than a horse'. In Vach and Vasjugan Khanty the bested member is marked with the postposition *niiŋiit (niiŋa)*, e.g. Vj *looy mees+niiŋə ooyər* HORSE COW+niiŋə VALUABLE 'a horse is more valuable than a cow'.

Pronouns

The case inventory of the personal pronouns differs from that of nouns in two key points: (1) they have a dedicated accusative form, built with the suffix *-(aa)t*, and (2) there are no distributive and expletive case forms. Several of the cases show deviant formations: (1) all oblique cases other than the locative and ablative are formed by the addition of an element =*tii* (with regular alternant =*təj-* before vowel-initial case suffixes), and in the first-person singular pronoun (only!) this element is followed by the first-person singular suffix, resulting in the sequence =*t-eem*; (2) to the right of this =*tii*, the lative/ dative suffix is zero; (3) the ablative is formed by the addition of an element +*niiŋt-* (cognate with the postposition used in VVj in comparative constructions mentioned above) followed by the appropriate person suffix.

The personal pronouns also have intensive forms, especially in far eastern and southern dialects (Honti 1984: 72–3).

Table 12.4   Paradigms of selected Trj personal pronouns

	PRO.s1	PRO.s2	PRO.d3
N	mää	nöŋ	łiin
A	mään-t	nöŋaa-t	łiinaa-t
Lat/Dat	mään-t-eem	nöŋaa-tii-Ø	łiinaa-tii-Ø
App	mään-t-eem-nääm	nöŋaa-tii-naam	łiinaa-tii-naam
Loc	mää-nə	nöŋ-nə	łiin-nə
Abl	mää-niiŋt-eem	nöŋ-ŋiiŋt-ee	łiin-niiŋt-iin
Com	mään-t-eem-näät	nöŋaa-tii-naat	łiinaa-tii-naat
Instr	mään-t-eem-äät	nöŋaa-təj-aat	łiinaa-təj-aat
Trans	mään-t-eem-γə	?	łiinaa-tii-γə
Abe	mään-t-eem-łəγ	?	?

Personal pronouns are used solely for emphasis (foregrounding, contrast). Paradigms of three sample pronouns are set out in Table 12.4.

Demonstrative Pronouns and Other Deictics

The eight demonstrative pronouns distinguish concrete/visible (with the consonantal frame *t--m*) v. abstract/invisible (with initial *tʲ-*), near (with *-ee-*, *-ii-*) v. far (with *-o-*, *-uu-*), and independent v. attributive forms (with and without final *-ii, -t*):

Figure 12.2   Trj/Tra Khanty demonstrative pronouns

	Independent	Attributive	Independent
near	t|eem|ii	t|eem	tʲ|ii	tʲ|ii|t
far	t|om|ii	t|om	tʲ|uu	tʲ|ii|t

	Concrete/Visible	Abstract/Invisible

The 'independent' forms can be used attributively, as well, and the 'invisible' category includes anaphora. Examples: *tom päłək-nə* THAT SIDE-loc 'on that side', *tʲuu łåår-aa tʲe ät-Ø-Ø* THAT LAKE-lat BEHOLD! ARRIVES-perf-s3 'and sure enough, (s)he arrived at that (previously mentioned) lake', *teemii toγʷən man=ma-ł tååγii* THIS THITHER GOES=past.part-s3 PLACE 'this is the place where (s)he went by'.

Other deictics include spatial adverbs built from the stems *te-* for near, and *to- ~ tåå-* for far reference, with suffixation of *-t, -ł,* and *-γə(-naam)* indicating stasis, motion from, and motion towards the location referred to:

	Stasis	Motion from	Motion to	Motion towards
Near	te-t	te-ł	te-γə	te-γə-naam
Far	to-t	to-ł	tåå-γə	tåå-γə-naam

There are also variants with palatal initial, e.g. *t'ee-naam* 'in this direction', and modal deictics such as *t'ee(γə)nə* 'in this way'. 'Now' is *iit*, 'just now; in a moment (French *tout à l'heure*)' is *iin*, 'then' is *t'uut-nə*.

Interrogative and *indefinite pronouns* are few. Most are built to the inherited interrogative stems *ko-* and *me-* with fossilized suffixes similar or identical to those of the demonstrative pronouns. Thus corresponding to *tot/tet* 'there/here' is *kot* 'where?', to *toł/teł* is *koł'(t'aa)* 'whence?', to *teγə/tåågə* is *koł (močə)* 'whither?' Further examples: 'who?' is *kojaγii*, 'what?' is *meγ*ʷ*ii*, 'someone' is *kojiikaam*, and 'something' is *metääłii*. 'How' is *kołnə*; 'what?' is *kotə*; 'when?' is *kuuntə*. (Note: constituent order seems to be decisive in such minimal pairs as *men-ł-ən kuuntə* 'when you go' : *kuuntə men-ł-ən* 'when are you going?').

The numeral *ej* 'one' and the noun stem *koo ~ kuu(j)-* 'man' serve as the base for individuative pronouns such as *ej+kuuj-mən* ONE+MAN-d1 'one of the three of us'.

Negative pronouns are also built with *ej*, e.g. *ej+metääłii-p(ə)* 'nothing'.

The synchronically monomorphemic cardinal numerals are:

1	*ej*	6	*kuut*
2	*käät*	7	*łääpət*
3	*ko(o)łəm*	8	*n'iiłəγ*
4	*n'ełə*	9	*jerjeeŋ*ʷ/*iirjeeŋ*ʷ
5	*wät*	10	*jeeŋ*ʷ

20	*koos*
100	*sååt*
1,000	*t'orəs*

'9' is from *ej+ör.t-jeeŋ*ʷ (*)ONE-SHORT.OF-TEN (Honti 1984: 77). Other cardinals are formed by (1) addition, with the particle *-örəkk(ə)-*, e.g. *jeeŋ*ʷ*-örəkk-ej* '11', (2) multiplication, e.g. *koołəm+jeeŋ*ʷ '30', (3) subtraction, with the element *iir* (cf. '9', above), e.g. *iir+sååt* '90', and (4) combinations of these, e.g. *iir++jeeŋ*ʷ*+sååt* '900, i.e. one (hundred) less than ten hundred', *jeeŋ*ʷ*+örəkk+iir+jeeŋ*ʷ '19, i.e. ten plus one (unit) less than ten'. Note also *n'iił+sååt* '80'. The roots meaning '100' and '1,000' are Iranian loans; the origin of '10' is obscure. The word for '20' is a core innovation shared with Mansi, Hungarian, Permian, and perhaps Mordva, and built to a root meaning '(hu)man', cf. *koo* 'man'. The word for '8' is either related to the Hungarian word *n^jălaab* 'bundle (originally, of hides)' or – less likely – is an eroded, ablauted, dual of '4'. Multiplicatives are formed with the suffix *=paa(/ää)* or by compounds built with the roots *pïï/iič* or *pïïɣ ǝr*, e.g. *kiit=pää* 'twice', *kootǝm pïïɣ ǝr, kootǝm pïïč* 'three times'.

Ordinal numerals are formed from the cardinals more or less regularly with the suffix *=mǝ/ǝt*, e.g. *n^jet=mǝt* 'fourth', *wät=mǝt* 'fifth', *kuut=mǝt* 'sixth', *tääpǝt=mǝt* 'seventh', *n^jïïtǝɣ=mǝt* 'eighth'. 'Third' is either *kootǝmmǝt* or *kuutmǝt*. 'First' is *ååtǝŋ* (also 'tip, beginning'); 'second' is *kiimǝt* < *kiit=mǝt. The translative of ordinals forms ordinal multiplicative temporal adverbs, e.g. *kiimǝt-kǝ* 'for a second time'. Fractions with the denominator 'two' are made with *päļǝk* 'half'; the others consist of the formula (numerator = cardinal) + (denominator = ordinal) + *jökään* 'part'.

Verb Conjugation
Khanty verb finite forms distinguish two moods (indicative and imperative) and, depending on dialect, from two to five tenses. Conditional, optative, and conjunctive moods are constructed with the help of particles and/or deverbal nominals; see p. 375. As in Mansi and Northern Samoyedic, different sets of person suffixes, traditionally termed definite (or subjective) v. definite (or objective) conjugations, refer to the definiteness v. indefiniteness, of the direct object, as well as to its number (singular v. non-singular) or its absence (the so-called passive). Tremjugan had three tenses: present *-t-*, past *-∅-*, and perfect *-s-*; in Tromagan, the *-s-* perfect seems to have been lost. The far eastern dialects Vach and Vasjugan have innovated two additional tenses, *-ɣääl-* and *-ɣääs-*, with discourse functions. The rest of the Khanty dialects, like Tromagan, have only one past tense: southern dialects and Nizyam have no perfect, and the dialects from Sherkal north have no simple past. Futurity is expressed by means of derivation, e.g. inchoative *=ɣt-*, or with syntagms of infinitive plus inceptive verbs such as *je-* or (in western dialects) *pit-*, both 'begins' (Honti 1984: 49–50).

Tremjugan/Tromagan Conjugation
As in all Khanty dialects, three formal classes of verbal stem types may be distinguished: the closed sets of thematic and unstable stems, and the open set of regular stems (Honti 1984: 35–6). The thematic stems show an alternation of stem-final *aa* (in the infinitive and present tense) ~ ∅ (elsewhere), e.g. *tot(aa)-* 'melts', *kot(aa)-* 'leaks'. Most stems with *a* in their longer alternant show an ablaut with *o* (or its prosodic equivalent, *aŋ^w*, see Consonants, p. 363) in their shorter form; examples are *kataa- ~ kot-* 'dies', *pančaa- ~ ponč-* 'ripens', *ataa- ~ ot-* 'sleeps', *sasaa- ~ sos-* 'dries (intr)', *kanaa- ~ kon-* 'adheres', *taŋaa- ~ taŋ^w-* 'enters'. Other such roots keep the *a* in all forms, e.g. *tat(aa)-* 'gets/makes wet', *pan(aa)-* 'places, lays'. Unstable stems also have longer and shorter stem alternants; in this case the longer forms have an additional *j* (if the initial consonant is a labial) or *ɣ^w* (otherwise) in imperative, perfect, and most derived forms. Examples include *we(j)-* 'takes', *me(j)-* 'gives, endows', *wuu(j)-* 'sees',

nii(γ^w)- 'is visible', *łii(γ^w)-* 'eats', and *tuu(γ^w)-* 'brings'. Note also the bifurcated pair *jö(γ^w)-* 'comes', *je(γ)-* 'begins'.

Both thematic and unstable stems have lexical counterparts in Mansi, but the prehistory of both the phonology and the morphology of these stem types is still unclear (for thematic stems, see Honti 1982: 104–8).

Makeup of Indicative Mood Forms

The suffix of the indicative mood is -∅-, added directly to the stem. Only the indicative mood has morphologically distinct tenses. A tense suffix is added to the right of the indicative suffix -∅-, and is itself immediately followed by a person suffix from one of three series, termed traditionally after their agreement properties with direct objects indefinite, singular definite, and non-singular definite. Alternatively, the tense suffix may be followed by the passive suffix *-oo(j)-* ~ *-ii-*, which is then followed by a suffix from the passive series. The different pre-zero allomorphs of the passive suffix (*-oo-* in the second-person singular, *-ii-* in the third person singular) reflect the different histories of these person suffixes: s2 -∅ reflects a recent loss of final *n in Surgut, while s3 -∅ dates back to proto-Khanty and beyond. The Khanty passive suffix is notorious in the literature for its back rounded vocalism, a vocalism which is not only immune to vowel harmony but overturns the front vocalism of a word, e.g. back *uu*...*ə* after *e*...*ää* in Vasjugan historic perfect *we-γääl-uuj-əm* TAKES-hist.perf-pass-s1 'I was taken (long ago)'. The staunch back-roundedness of its vowel is due to its recency: it is the analogically levelled outcome of earlier diphthongs (*aj, *äj) in which the *j element continues a Uralic reflexive morpheme known from Saamic and Samoyedic, as well (Honti 1984: 52).

The person suffixes of the Khanty passive series are similar to, but not identical with, those of the indefinite series. They are most different from those of the singular definite series, a state of affairs which parallels that found in Tundra Nenets, where the paradigmatic analogue of the passive is the reflexive conjugation (cf. Ostrowski 1983: 17).

The person suffixes of the four series are set out in Figure 12.3 (the -γ suffix variant in the third person singular occurs only in the perfect tense, and is obligatory only with verbs in final *ii-* ~ *əj-*, e.g. *åårəj-∅-əγ* 'it broke', stem *åårii-*). From a glance at the table it is obvious that with the exception of the suffixes which mark a second person singular subject, all subject classes syncretize to one degree or another, and there is even syncretism of subject person (e.g. *-ttən* can be second or third person dual, as well as second person plural).

A more protracted examination of Figure 12.3 will reveal that the first and third person subject classes are mirror images of one another in terms of the failure to syncretize (see Figure 12.4). The singular first person has a dedicated suffix for non-singular definite objects (*-aam*), but the non-singular first person does not: first person dual *-mən* and plural *-əy^w* encode not only

Figure 12.3   Trj/Tra Khanty indicative verb suffixes

		Passive	Indefinite object	Definite object Singular	Definite object Non-singular
S	s1	-əm	-əm	-eem	-aam
U	s2	-∅	-ən	-ee	-aa
B	s3	-ɣ	-ɣ	-təɣ	-∅
J	d1	-mən	-mən	-təmən	-mən
E	d2	-ttən	-ttən	-ttən	-ən
C	d3	-ɣən	-ɣən	-ttən	-ən
T	p1	-əɣ^w	-əɣ^w	-təɣ^w	-əɣ^w
	p2	-təɣ	-təɣ	-ttən	-ən
	p3	-t	-t	-iił	-aał

Figure 12.4   Selected verbal person suffixes in Trj/Tra Khanty

	Subject First singular	Subject First dual, plural	Subject Third singular	Subject Third dual, plural
Passive	-əm	-mən, -əɣ^w	-θ	ɣən, -ət
Indefinite	-əm	-mən, -əɣ^w	-θ	ɣən, -ət
Non-singular definite	-aam	-əɣ^w	-θ	-ən, -aał
Singular definite	-eem	-təmən, -təɣ^w	-təɣ	-tən, -iił

non-singular definite object, but also indefinite and passive. With the third person the reverse is the case: it is the non-singular third person which has a dedicated suffix for non-singular definite objects (dual third-person subject -ən, plural third-person subject -aał), while in the singular third-person non-singular definite objects are encoded by -∅, which also marks agreement in the passive and indefinite series.

This symmetry is perhaps part of the explanation for the singular definite suffixes which Trj/Tra has innovated, distinct from those of other Khanty dialects, viz. d1 -təmən, p1 -təɣ^w; these suffixes were built with the addition of a -t- element to the template of s3 definite singular -təɣ, which has a pendant in VVj.

Sample conjugational forms are given in Table 12.5.

Table 12.5   Present-tense indicative forms of Tromagan *pan-* 'puts, places'

Object type	Subject person 1	2	3
Singular subject			
Indefinite	pan-ɬ-əm	pan-ɬ-ən	pan-əɬ-Ø
Singular	pan-ɬ-eem	pan-ɬ-ee	pan-ɬ-ətəɣ
Dual	pan-ɬ-əɣəɬ-aam	pan-ɬ-əɣəɬ-aa	pan-ɬ-əɣəɬ-Ø
Plural	pan-ɬ-əɬ-aam	pan-ɬ-əɬ-aa	pan-ɬ-əɬ-Ø
Passive	pan-ɬ-ooj-əm	pan-ɬ-oo-Ø	pan-ɬ-ii-Ø
Dual subject			
Indefinite	pan-ɬ-əmən	pan-ɬ-əttən	pan-ɬ-əɣən
Singular	pan-ɬ-ətəmən	pan-ɬ-əttən	pan-ɬ-əttən
Dual	pan-ɬ-əɣəɬ-əmən	pan-ɬ-əɣəɬ-ən	pan-ɬ-əɣəɬ-ən
Plural	pan-ɬ-əɬ-əmən	pan-ɬ-əɬ-ən	pan-ɬ-əɬ-ən
Passive	pan-ɬ-ooj-mən	pan-ɬ-oo-ttən	pan-ɬ-ii-ɣən
Plural subject			
Indefinite	pan-ɬ-əɣ^w	pan-ɬ-ətəɣ	pan-ɬ-ət
Singular	pan-ɬ-ətəɣ^w	pan-ɬ-əttən	pan-ɬ-iiɬ
Dual	pan-ɬ-əɣəɬ-əɣ^w	pan-ɬ-əɣəɬ-ən	pan-ɬ-əɣəɬ-aaɬ
Plural	pan-ɬ-əɬ-əɣ^w	pan-ɬ-əɬ-ən	pan-ɬ-əɬ-aaɬ
Passive	pan-ɬ-ooj-əɣ^w	pan-ɬ-oo-təɣ	pan-ɬ-aa-t

Note: Adapted from data courtesy of M. Csepregi.

Imperative

It is useful to distinguish primary (second-person active), secondary (non-second-person active), and tertiary (all passive) imperative forms. Only southern and eastern dialects have secondary and tertiary imperative forms. In primary and secondary imperative forms, the suffix of the imperative is (1) *-ää/aa-* with the indefinite s2 suffix *-Ø*, (2) *-Ø-* with the definite s2 suffix *-ee*, and (3) *-ii-* (~ *-əj-*) elsewhere; see Figure 12.5.

The secondary imperative forms consist of stem plus imperative suffix (as given above), followed by the regular indicative suffixes, followed by the enclitic *--äät/aat*, which also occurs as a free sentence particle meaning 'let('s)!'. Thus 'let me feed' is FEEDS-imp-s1--enc *ɬiipt-ii-m-Ø--aat*, 'let him/her feed' is FEEDS-imp-s3--enc *ɬiipt-əj-Ø-Ø--aat*, and 'let them (2) feed them (2)' is FEEDS-imp-d3dO--enc *ɬiipt-ii-γ əɬ-aaɬ--aat*. The function of non-singular first-person adhortatives is usually filled by ordinary indicative forms.

Tertiary imperatives are formed by means of a suffix *-moos- ~ -muus-* and the enclitic *--aat*. Between these two morphemes stand the indefinite verb suffixes, e.g. *ɬääpət-muus--əm--aat* 'let me be fed', except in the third person plural, where the person marker is unexpectedly *-ää-*. The provenance of the suffix *-moos- ~ -muus-* is also unknown (Honti 1984: 49).

Figure 12.5   Trj/Tra Khanty primary imperative suffix sequences

		Indefinite	Definite		
			Singular	Non- singular	
				Dual	Plural
s2		-ää-∅	-∅-ee	-iiɣəɬ-ää	-ii-ɬ-ää
d2		-ii-tən	-ii-tən	-ii-ɣəɬ-ən	-ii-ɬ-ən
p2		-ii-təɣ	-ii-tən	-ii-ɣəɬ-ən	-ii-ɬ-ən

Nonfinite Verb Forms
It is difficult to distinguish infinitive from present participle in proto-Khanty, and the two categories are scarcely distinct in Trj/Tra, where they are built with =taa (with an optional longer form, built with the translative suffix: =taa-ɣə) and =tə (before person suffixes: =taa), respectively. There is also a past participle built with =(ə)m(ə) ~ =(ə)maa-, and a conditional participle =ŋaa.

The infinitive functions as a complement to verbs of motion and to modals, e.g. (*kenč-taa >) kenč=aa(-ɣə) men-ɬ-əm 'I'm going hunting'. The participles are often used adjectivally, e.g. wååjəɣ waɬ=tə tååɣii WILD.REINDEER LIVES=pres.part PLACE 'place where the reindeer lives'. An agent can be encoded as a person suffix, as well, e.g. toɣ^w-ən men=maa-ɬ tååɣii THERE-loc GOES=past.part-s3 PLACE 'place where s3 has gone'. The past participle is also frequently used with passive meaning; in this case the agent is normally in the nominative if the participle is used attributively, and in the locative if it is used predicatively: nääj ɬiiɣ^w=əm tååɣïï FIRE EATS= past.part PLACE 'a place which has been consumed by fire', Kazym Khanty xojaat-ən waant=əm 'seen by someone' (Honti 1984: 57). However, the locative sometimes marks the agent when the participle is used attributively, as well, e.g. Vasjugan Khanty apaa-l-nə̂ mej=mää waɣ FATHER-loc GIVES=past.part MONEY 'money given by his father'.

Both present and past participles can have temporal reference. The past participle refers to past or previous time, as in wej=maa-ɣə kääsaa-ɬ-əm TAKES=past.part-trans DOUBTS-pres-s1sO 'I doubt that it was taken', kör=əŋ wååj toɬ men=maa-ɬ LEG=GED ANIMAL THENCE GOES= past.part-s3 'after the reindeer had gone from there'. With person and various case suffixes, the past participle constructs equivalents to subordinate clauses, e.g. tääsəŋ-kə̂ je=tää-näät taj-ee RICH-trans BECOMES=pres.part-approx HAS-s2sOimp 'keep it until you become rich!' Compounded with the noun kiim 'extent', the present participle forms constructions which refer to ability, e.g. ɬååɬ^j=t^jə+kiim taj-ɬ-əm STANDS=pres.part + EXTENT HAS-pres-s1 'I can stand', ɬååɬ^j=t^jə+kiim entəm 'I/you/(s)he can't stand'.

The conditional participle, used almost exclusively with person suffixes attached, renders the equivalent of a finite verb plus the adverbial kuuntə̂ 'when/if', e.g. *men-ŋa-ł* GOES=cond.part-s3 'if (s)he goes', cf. *men-əł-Ø kuuntə* GOES-pres-s3 'if (s)he goes'. It is also used with postpositions.

The negative participle usually has imperfective aspect. It is made with the suffix =*ləy*, which is formally identical with that of the abessive case of the nominal paradigm. Examples: *łoŋ-iin pååt=ləy töły-iin pååt=ləy* SUMMER-temp FREEZES=neg.part WINTER-temp FREEZES=neg.part '(remaining) unfrozen winter and summer', *kæł kooł=ləy koo* WORD/ LANGUAGE HEARS=neg.part MAN 'obtuse man'. Unlike its nominal analogue, the negative participle frequently occurs with person (and case) suffixes, e.g. *wał=ləy-aam-nə men–Ø-Ø* IS=neg.part-s1-loc GOES-perf-s3 '(s)he went while I was not (t)here'.

There is also a gerund, i.e. a verbal adverb, formed with full productivity from verbs by means of the suffix =*miin*. It takes neither case nor person suffixes. Examples: *naɣ*ʷ*łiip=miin łååł–Ø-Ø* LEANS=ger STANDS-pres-s3 '(s)he stands leaning', *nʲeeɣ*ʷ*reem łääpət=miin änə=mtə-ł-əm* CHILD.nom FEEDS=ger BIG=vsx-pres-s1 'I raise the child by feeding (it)', *puut jeŋk-əł keeɣ*ʷ*ər=miin tərəm–Ø-Ø* POT WATER-s3 BOILS=ger STOPS-perf-s3 'the water in the pot boiled away (until it was all evaporated)'.

Non-finite verb forms frequently combine to form complex noun phrases, e.g. GERUND + INFINITIVE + PARTICIPLE in *pååt=miin päɣ*ʷ*=taayə wär=tə łäät-nə* FREEZES=ger BURSTS=inf STARTS=pres.part TIME-loc 'when X is about to burst, it's so cold = when it's very cold'. For more examples, see Syntax, below.

Syntax

The Use of the Cases
The use of case suffixes in Khanty to mark the participants in actions and events is most easily understood not in syntactic terms of subject and object, but rather in semantic terms of agent and patient. There are three basic sentence types, active, ergative, and passive:

1   In active sentences, the agent is in the nominative; any patient noun is also in the nominative, but a patient pronoun is in the accusative (-*t*); the verb takes active (i.e. non-passive) suffixes.
2   In ergative sentences, the agent is in the locative (-*nə*); the patient is marked as in active sentences, and the verb takes active suffixes.
3   In passive sentences, the patient is marked as in active sentences, and any agent is marked as in ergative sentences; the verb takes passive suffixes.

The NP agents of passive sentences can be, but are not typically, omitted; the passive nature of a sentence is in any case clear from the passive morphology of the verb. A noun-phrase subject, i.e. the agent of active and the patient of passive sentences, can also always be omitted if it is clear from the context; subject person and number are in any case encoded on the verb. Since the only formal difference between active and ergative sentences is the marking of the subject, it is perhaps prudent to work with the hypothesis that the active/ergative distinction is neutralized in sentences without explicit NP subjects. Note that such neutralization never occurs with direct objects: objects known from the context are normally omitted from a sentence, but they are then always encoded formally on the verb.

Ergative sentences are most frequent when the agent is in the third person (Honti 1984: 94), but overall they are decidedly rare (Kulonen 1991: 189–91), and this has hindered attempts at elucidating their function. The choice of one sentence type over another seems to be discourse-driven, i.e. narrative salience and speaker's point of view are leading factors. In terms of topic-focus grammar we may simplify, with Gulya (1970: 80–3), and say that whereas the definite-object suffixes on the verb signal that the direct object is known, ergative (i.e. locative) case-marking on the subject signals that the subject is known. In terms of functional sentence perspective we may simplify by saying that while passive sentences focalize the patient, and active sentences, *ceteris paribus*, are neutral with regard to focus, in ergative sentences neither the patient nor the agent is singled out, but the subjecthood of the agent is highlighted. It has been claimed that both the subjects and the objects of ergative sentences tend to be relatively high on the animacy and intentionality hierarchies; this is a tendency only, however, and not a rule, as shown by the examples given below.

The following are examples of each subtype as outlined above:

1a Active sentence, definite (singular-object) verb: *kïïnt-əmən-Ø nöŋ kïïnm-ee* BACKPACK-d1-sN PRO.s2 PICKS.UP-s2sOimp 'you pick up our backpack!'

1b Active sentence, indefinite verb: *kajm-əł-Ø nok ken-ł-əm* GRAZING.AREA-s3-sN UP SEEKS-pres-s1 'I'll look for its grazing area'; *kïïnt-Ø kïïnm-aa* BACKPACK-sN PICKS.UP-s2imp 'pick up the backpack'.

2   Passive sentence: *wänəp-Ø kuuł-nə raŋkałtał-Ø-ii-Ø* HOOK-sN FISH-loc NIBBLES-pres-pass-s3 'the hook is being nibbled by a fish'; *(jey-əm-nə) pästaa-yə äärjał-Ø-oo-Ø* (FATHER-s1-loc) SWIFT-trans CREATES-perf-pass-s2 'you were created swift, my father made you swift when he created you'; *koo-nə mej-Ø-ii-Ø* MAN-loc GIVES-perf-pass-s3 'the man gave (some[thing])'.

3a Ergative sentence, definite (singular object) verb: *kuuł-nə wänəp nʲałʲ= łʲaayə wär-Ø-təy* 'the fish is beginning to bite at the hook', *łöyʷ-nə körə-ł-Ø toyə oyʷərkəmtə-Ø-təy* PRO.s3-loc LEG-s3-N THITHER STRIKES.INVOLUNTARILY-perf-s3sO '(s)he bumped her leg against it'.

3b   Ergative sentence, indefinite-object verb:Vasjugan Khanty *räät-nə mään-ää me-s-Ø* OLD.MAN-loc PRO.s1-lat GIVES-perf-s3 'the old man gave me (something)' (cited by Kulonen 1991: 193).

Although passive sentences of the classic type, i.e. in which the agent and patient have syntactic roles opposite to those of their active-sentence counterparts, are frequent, e.g. *äämp-nə por-s-ooj-əm* DOG-loc BITES-past-pass-s1 'I was bitten by a dog', cf. Vach *por-s-iim nʲiilm-əm* BITES-past-s1sO TONGUE-s1-sN 'I bit my tongue', passive sentences with intransitive verbs, especially statives and locomotives, are also quite common, e.g. *juuɣʷ-nə änm-Ø-ii-Ø* TREE-loc GROWS-perf-pass-s3 'a tree was growing', *mää-n ɬïɬ=məɣt-Ø-oo-Ø* PRO.s1-loc APPROACHES.STEALTHILY-perf-pass-s2 'I sneaked up on you'.

The picture is only slightly complicated by the fact that for many verbs the ends are expressed by the means, i.e. they take direct objects in the instructive, e.g. *kuuɬ-aat wänəp=ɬ-əɬ-əm* FISH-inst ANGLES-pres-s1 'I'm angling for fish', *rääk-aat ɬääɣɬəksə-ɬ-Ø* GRUEL-inst WAITS.AROUND-pres-s3 '(s)he's waiting for gruel'. This use of the instructive is probably connected with its appearance in benefactive constructions (see below).

Comitative and Instructive
The comitative is used to express accompaniment, e.g. *tʲe iimii-naat waɬɬəɣən* '(s)he lived with that/the woman'. Both comitative and instructive are used as instrumentals, but the instructive has an additional nuance: with ditransitive verbs it also expresses alienability from the agent (to the benefit of the patient, if there is one). Examples: comitative/instrumental *jaɣʷəɬ ååɬəŋ-naat paɣʷəɬ-taa wär-Ø-ii-Ø* BOW TIP-com POKES-inf BEGINS-pres-pass-s3 '(s)he began to poke with the tip of (his/her) bow', instructive *tom nʲaɣʷə-jaat tʲii ɬääpət-ɬ-ən* THERE/THEN MEAT-inst BEHOLD FEEDS-pres-s2 'then you'll feed (someone) with meat', *mää nöŋ-aat me-ɬ-əm jem järnaas-aat* PRO.s1 PRO.s2-acc GIVES-pres-s1 GOOD SHIRT-inst 'I'll give you a good shirt (I'll endow you with a good shirt)' (see Honti 1984: 63, 96).

Noun Phrase
The members of noun phrases show no agreement, except that number may optionally be expressed formally on the head noun in noun phrases which contain a numeral higher than *ej* '1', e.g. *käät nʲeeɣʷreem(-ɣən)* TWO CHILD(-dual) 'two children', *wät wont(-ət)* FIVE HIGH.FOREST(-plur) 'five wooded ridges'.

Unmodified nouns are co-ordinated by simple juxtaposition (see below), or, if they share one or more semantic components, by putting both in the dual, e.g. *siiɣʷəs-ɣən körək-kən* OSPREY-dual EAGLE-dual 'an osprey and an eagle'.

Noun phrases can be linked in two basic ways. One type of linkage forms possessive constructions; in these, the possessor is unmarked, and the possessed is optionally in the third person, e.g. *torəm ääj pay(-əɬ)* GOD YOUNG SON(-s3) 'God's young(est) son'. In the other type of linkage, the two nouns are simply juxtaposed, e.g. *lakʷ kååt* HORSE HOUSE 'stable', *poom kååt* HAY HOUSE 'house made of hay'. In Tremjugan Khanty, if the first noun was inflected for case or even followed by a postposition, the two nouns were linked with the attributivizing particle -γə, e.g. *ej ɬär-nə-γə kååt-ət* ONE ROW-loc-γə HOUSE-plur 'houses in a row', *juuyʷ ont-ii-γə ḷeekʷ* FOREST INTERIOR-abl-γə PATH 'a path (leading) out of the forest'. It is not clear whether or not this construction is now extinct, but in Tromagan a noun in the locative can function as an attribute to a second noun, e.g. *ťåårəs-nə jeŋk-aa* SEA-loc WATER-lat 'into the sea water' (Honti 1984: 87).

Direct-object Marking
The formal encoding, onto the verb, of semantic and pragmatic features of the direct object was outlined in the verb morphology section above. We may summarize the deployment of this agreement system briefly as follows. A direct object may be indefinite; or it may be definite, either intrinsically (unique global entities, e.g. the sky, names, deictics, nouns with person suffixes) or by virtue of its occurrence earlier in the discourse. In active and ergative sentences, this definiteness may optionally be encoded on the finite verb. If the definiteness is encoded, the non-singular number of the direct object may optionally be encoded, as well. (Note: in northern dialects number agreement with non-singular objects is obligatory for definite verbs.)

For sentences with definite direct objects there are thus three scenarios, A, B, and C:

		A	B	C
1	Definiteness encoded on verb	–	+	+
2	Non-singular number encoded	0	–	+

Nominal and Adverbial Predicates
Sentences with nominal predicates display a range of formal alternatives.

1   In sentences with non-past reference, a nominal predicate in the nominative case may combine with the copula *wos-*, which has no tense inflection and is zero in the third person, e.g. (*mää*) *tälaaŋ wos-əm* 'I'm healthy', (*ɬöɣʷ*) *tälaaŋ* '(s)he's healthy'.
2   A nominal predicate in the translative case may combine with the copula *waɬ-*, which takes tense markers and is otherwise fully inflected, e.g. the synonymous (*mää*) *tälaaŋ-kə waɬ-ɬ-əm*, (*ɬöɣʷ*) *tälaaŋ-kə waɬ-ɬ-ø*.

3   Contaminations of types 1 and 2 are also attested, e.g. Vasjugan *mää morək-kə was-əm* 'I'm healthy' (Honti 1993: 138).

In all cases, number agreement between subject and predicate is the norm, e.g. *pak-kəɬ-aam ääj-γən* 'my two sons are young'. Existential sentences can also have zero verb, e.g. *kåånəŋ-nə oγ^wər wont* SHORE-loc TALL FOREST 'on the shore there is a tall forest'.

Sentences with adverbial predicates are characterized by optional number agreement between subject and predicate. The regular nominal number suffixes are then added to the case form, e.g. *miin kååt-naa-γən* PRO.d2 HOUSE-loc-dual 'we two are in the house', contrast non-predicative *kååt-γən-nə* 'in two houses', with the reverse suffix order.

Major Constituent Order
Within the simple declarative or interrogative sentence, the neutral major constituent order seems to be SOV, no matter whether the sentence is active, ergative, or passive. Sentences can be co-ordinated or subordinated by simple juxtaposition or by means of conjunctions such as *pään* 'and' or clitics such as *--pə*. As is to be expected, topics are normally at the beginning of clauses, and the place for focus is immediately before the verb, as in *nöŋ äγ^w-e-Ø jem-γə taj-ɬ-e, mään-t wååjəγ ɬəγ-ɬ-ən* PRO.s2 DAUGHTER-s2-sN GOOD-trans HAS-pres-s2sO, PRO.s1-acc MISTREATS-pres-s2 'you love your daughter, (but) me you mistreat' or *nöŋ kiim=ə koo-nə kotə wär-ɬ-ii-Ø* PRO.s2 EXTENT=adj MAN-loc WHAT? DOES-pres-pass-s3 'what can a man like you do?'

Negation and Prohibition
Negation of constituents or of the sentence as a whole is effected by the negative particle *entə*, e.g. *entə taj-ɬ-əm* 'I don't have any'. Existence is negated with *entəm*, e.g. *ɬäŋ^wk^wər entəm* 'there is no mouse'. Prohibition is expressed with the modal negative particle *ääɬ* plus the imperative, e.g. *teem rïït-aa ääɬ ɬeɬ-aa* THIS BOAT-lat DON'T SIT-s2imp 'don't sit in this boat'; Trj Khanty had distinct prohibitive forms in all persons and numbers, e.g. third person singular passive prohibitive *ääɬ åårəj-əj--aat* 'may it not break' (Honti 1984: 89).

Substitutes for Subordinate Clauses
Equivalents to the subordinated sentences of other languages are regularly constructed with the help of verbal nouns; many of these have been illustrated above in the section on non-finite verb forms. Here, two more examples will illustrate the principle underlying this type of construction.

1   Equivalents to 'if/when' clauses can be built as noun phrases with the locative of *ɬäät* 'time' as head, modified by the participle of the main verb. The participle, in turn, may have its agent explicit, e.g. *teγ^wət*

päγ^wəm=tə ɬäät-nə FIRE GIVES.OFF.SPARKS=pres.part TIME-loc 'when/if a/the fire gives off sparks'.

2   Another type of subordinate clause-equivalent, a temporal one, is made up of the past participle (plus any explicit agent) plus a postposition such as *piïr-nə̂* 'after', e.g. *iikii soočm=ə̂m piïr-nə̂* OLD.MAN LEAVES= past.part BEHIND-loc 'after the old man left'.

Alongside the noun-phrase substitutes for subordinate clauses, in Trj/Tra Khanty we may distinguish at least two kinds of parallel construction involving finite verb forms: (1) conditionals, which merely state conditions, built with *kuuntə̂* 'if/when', e.g. *men-ɬ-əm kuuntə̂* GOES-pres-s1 'if I go', *ɬ̵eeγ^wət-ɬ-ətən kuuntə̂* ARGUES-pres-d2 IF 'if you two are going to argue', and (2) conjunctives, which refer to contrary-to-fact states and actions, built with the particle *oɬəŋ*, e.g. *oɬəŋ men-ɬ-əm* 'I would go'.

Lexicon

The nature of Khanty (and Mansi) traditional poetic devices has created lexica which are particularly rich in synonyms (e.g. Sherkal *šaŋk* : *måås* 'sweat') and parallel words, both natural (Sherkal *tiləs^j* 'moon': *xatl* 'sun') and cultural (Sherkal *taapət* 'seven' : *xuut* 'six'). The vocabulary pertaining to the bear and the bear festival, as well as to other spiritual matters, further supplements the basic lexical stock with a large array of secret words and taboo paraphrase.

The lexical stock is also enlarged by processes of derivation, only a small sampling of which can be touched upon here.

Deverbal Derivation

In addition to the fully productive non-finite forms treated above, both nominals and, to a rather greater extent, verbs are formed from verbs. Among the most common verb-forming suffixes are the frequentative/multi-objectival =ɬ- and =nt-, e.g. *äγ^wət-* 'cuts', *äγ^wət=ɬ-* 'cuts into many pieces', *kooɬ-* 'hears', *kooɬ=ənt-* 'listens, obeys', the inchoative =m-, e.g. *keeγ^wər-* '(water) boils (intr)', *keeγ^wr=əm-* '(water) begins to boil', the transitivizer/ causative =t-, e.g. *keeγ^wər=t-* 'cooks (tr)', and the momentaneous/ pusillanimous/repetitive =γ-, e.g. *kiiɬ-* 'rises', *keeɬ=əγ-* 'gets up for a little while; gets up usually; makes a short side-trip'. Often two or more suffixes share a root morpheme which does not occur otherwise (synchronically; cf. Hungarian and Finnish *themes*), e.g. *påås=ə̂m-* 'drips once' : *påås=əγ-* 'drips repeatedly', *söj=əm-* 'spits once' : *söj=əγ-* 'spits repeatedly'.

Verb-forming deverbal suffixes occur in clusters and chains at least as frequently as they do singly. For example, alongside the simple derivates *keeγ^wər=t-* and *keeγ^wr=əm-* mentioned above there is also *keeγ^wr= əm=əɬ=tə-* 'brings to the boil'. Further examples: *ɬaŋ-* 'enters', *ɬaŋ=əɬ=t-* 'causes (animals or people) to enter'; *wäɬ-* 'kills', *wäɬ=ii=ɬ-* 'kills on several occasions'; *uus=ii=p-* 'yawns once', *uus=ii=ł-* 'yawns (repeatedly)', *uus=ii=p=əγ=əł-* 'yawns a little'.

With the exception of the non-finite verb forms treated above, deverbal nominal derivation is sparse and unproductive. Historically, many nouns are secondary formations built from verb stems with =*pə*, =*əp*, =*əs* and their combinatory variants =*pəs* and =*psə*, e.g. *aγ^w-* 'flows', *aγ^w=əs* 'lower stretch of a river', *łiiγ^w-* 'eats', *łiiγ^w=pəs* 'food'.

Denominal Derivation

Suffixes which form verbs from nominals are for the most part homophonous with their deverbal counterparts, e.g. *tółəγ* 'winter', *tółγ=əm-* 'it begins to be winter', *łoŋ* 'summer', *łoŋ=ət-* 'it is/will be summer', *wänəp* 'fish-hook', *wänəp=ł-* 'angles'.

Denominal nominals, on the other hand, are both lexically and textually frequent. Particularly salient are the suffixes =*əŋ* and =*pə̂* ~ =*ə̂p*, which build *nomina possessoris* and bahuvrihi compounds, respectively, e.g. *kuuł=ə̂ŋ* 'rich in fish', *ej+säm=əp* ONE+EYE=adj 'one-eyed'. The frequent use of these suffixes is due, in part, to their role in the formation of circumlocutions, e.g. *körə=ŋ* 'having legs' (*körə* 'leg'), *körə=ŋ wååjəγ* 'deer (leggèd animal)', *oγ^w ər körə=p ot* LONG LEG=adj THING '(taboo word for) wolf', but also because of their role in the formation of parallel lines of verse in traditional Khanty verbal art, e.g. (recited, i.e. not sung, version; from Csepregi 1995: 272): *sïïs=əŋ wååjəγ kow jem sïïs-əł/märə=ŋ wååjəγ kow jem märə-ł* 'the long(-lasting) good persistence of the persistent animal/the long(-lasting) good perseverence of the persevering animal'. There are also secular circumlocutions, many of which are areal calques, e.g. 'mirror' is *wään^j əm sååł=ii waγ* FACE IS.JUST.VISIBLE=adj METAL, with parallels in Mansi and Selkup (Austerlitz 1990: 50).

Khanty (with Mansi) deviates from the Uralic norm in having a verb which means 'to have', e.g. Trj *taj(aa)-* ~ *toj-*, Sosva Mansi *oon^j s^j-*. Neither verb has a credible etymology, but it is likely that each is a separate borrowing during a period of bi- or multilingual convergence with an autochthonous language or languages now lost.

Loanwords

It is difficult to distinguish loans from Iranian languages into proto-Khanty after the breakup of ObUgrian from those borrowed into proto-ObUgrian and subsequently lost in Mansi. An example of the former is probably *pent* 'path'; this item was also borrowed into Komi (cf. *pad+vež* 'crossroads') and Germanic. With all due caution one can speculate, on the basis of the number and distribution of Iranian loans in the two ObUgrian languages, that Iranian–Mansi contacts were more intensive, longer lasting, or both, than Iranian–Khanty contacts. If there is truth in such a speculation, it is echoed in the fact that the number of well-distributed Komi loans is greater in Khanty than it is in Mansi (Toivonen, Rédei); from this Salminen (1989: 19) has inferred that at the time of contact with Komi speakers, speakers of pre-Khanty lived to the north of speakers of pre-Mansi. Examples of loans acquired by both Khanty and Mansi from or via Komi include *iinäär* 'saddle' (acquired by proto-Permian from a Turkic language of Chuvash type), and the northern and eastern words for 'cow', e.g. Obdorsk *mus*, Trj/Tra *mäs* (originally an Iranian loan into proto-Permian). Komi loans attested only in Khanty include not only words limited to western dialects, such as Obdorsk *korti*, Kazym *karti* 'iron' or to southern dialects, such as Demjanka *puuš* 'sieve' (cf. Yaz'va Komi *puž*), but also widely distributed items such as Trj and Demjanka *mečƏk*, Obdorsk *mazƏx* 'fist' (cf. Lower Vychegda Komi *mižik* 'punch'), Vach *riimƏk*, Nizjam *rimƏx* 'dark (cf. Komi *rëm* 'dark(ness)').

The question of the age and extent of contacts between speakers of Khanty and various Tungus languages remains open; possible Tungus loans are *ajƏ* 'luck', *siiγ(=)Ət* 'short brook between lakes', and *iiɬeem* 'shame, shyness' (Futaky 1975; Katz 1977).

From Turkic languages come, e.g., Vasjugan *jaarmaa* 'barley grits' and Demjanka *muuγƏt* 'haycock'. A Turkic word for 'cow' was the source of the word found in southern Khanty, e.g. Demjanka *sayƏr* (the word is also attested in non-northern Mansi dialects). Note also *jääm* 'posting station'(via south Khanty as early as the twelfth century, and ultimately from Chinese, perhaps through Mongolic, see Futaky 1992: 18–20 and Clauson 1972: 933). From Ket: *kåånƏŋ* '(edge of) river bank'.

Loans from Tundra Nenets are most numerous in the northern dialects of Khanty (and Mansi); the Khanty Surgut group has had closer contacts with speakers of Forest Nenets (Sal 1976: 336). An example of a Selkup word borrowed into (eastern) Khanty is (Taz) Selkup *aqsiɬ* '(mushroom)', cf. Vach *axsƏɬ*, Trj/Tra *aks=Əŋ*.

Russian loans began to enter Khanty in the seventeenth century. The first and strongest impact was on southern and western dialects, and Russian contacts have always been most intensive here, e.g. Krasnojarsk *suťnʲiik* 'onion' (< чеснок), Nizjam *ruupuutaa*, Kazym *roopaataa* 'work' < работа, Nizjam *äsʲťenää*, Demjanka *sťenää* 'wall' < стена, but many old loans have a wide distribution across the dialects, e.g. Demjanka, Trj *äärƏnt*, VVj *äärƏn*, Nizjam *äärŋƏ*, Obdorsk *äärƏn* 'debt' < аренда 'lease'. In terms of semantic fields, older Russian loans in Khanty resemble Latin loans into Old High German (cf. *Mauer* 'wall', *Tisch* 'table', *Zwiebel* 'onion'); more recent, especially Soviet, loans resemble twentieth-century English loans into French or Hungarian.

Tromagan Text
Excerpted from Honti 1984: 165.

A: segmented text, in transcription; B: morpheme-by-morpheme gloss; C: periphrase; D: metaphrase (free translation).

A1 iikii-Ø   taj-əł-Ø,   iimii-Ø   wej-Ø-Ø
B1 OLD(ER).MALE- HAS-pres-s3 OLD(ER).FEMALE TAKES-perf-s3
   sN
C1 an older male   he has,   a woman   he took
   relative

A2 iimii-Ø   jek-kən   ääŋkee-γən   taj-əł-Ø
B2 OLD(ER).FEMALE FATHER-dual MOTHER-dual HAS-pres-s3
C2 (his) wife   father-   and-mother   she has

A3 uup-əł + iikii-nə   ääŋk=aaγtə=miin
B3 FATHER.IN.LAW-s3 + OLD(ER).MALE-loc   NAGS=ger
C3 by his father-in-law   naggingly

kołə   taj-ł-ii-Ø   A4 näm=t–Ø-ii-Ø
always   HAS-pres-pass-s3   B4 NAME=vsx-perf-pass-s3
always   he is had   C4 he is called

seγ+jeŋk=ii   looγʷtʲaa=Ø   kon-Ø
BURBOT+WATER=adj SPLASHES=pres.part BELLY-sN
burbot soup   splashing   belly,

łäärəγ+jeŋk=ii   looγʷtʲaa=Ø   kon-Ø
RUFFE+WATER=adj   SPLASHES=pres.part BELLY-sN
ruffe soup   splashing   belly.

A5 nom=s-əł-aa   entə   joγʷət-əł-Ø
B5 THINKS=NdeV-s3-lat NEG.PART ARRIVES-pres-s3
C5 to his mind   it doesn't   come

D1 He has a father-in-law, (because) he has taken a wife. D2 His wife has a father and a mother. D3 He is constantly being nagged by his father-in-law. D4 He is called burbot-soup-belly, ruffe-soup-belly. D5 He doesn't like it.

References and Further Reading

Abondolo, D. (1996) *Vowel Rotation in Uralic: Obug[r]ocentric Evidence*, SSEES Occasional Papers no. 31, London: School of Slavonic and East European Studies.
Austerlitz, R. (1958) *Ob-ugric metrics: The Metrical Structure of Ostyak and Vogul Folk-Poetry*, Folklore Fellows Communications 174, Helsinki: Finnish Academy of Sciences.

—— (1990) 'Contact, space, history', *C7IFU*, vol. IB (Sessiones plenares et symposia), pp. 47–54.

Clauson, G. (1972) *An Etymological Dictionary of Pre-thirteenth-century Turkish*, Oxford: Clarendon.

Csepregi, M. (1993) 'Az összeférhetetlen egér (Tromagani osztják mese)', in M. Bakró-Nagy and E. Szíj (eds), *Hajdú Péter 70 éves* [= Festschrift on the occasion of P. Hajdú's seventieth birthday], Linguistica Series A, Studia et dissertationes 15, Budapest: Hungarian Linguistics Institute, pp. 59–64.

—— (1995) 'Surgutin hantien karhulaulujen kielenpiirteitä', *C8IFU*, vol. IV, pp. 271–8.

Futaky, I. (1975) *Tungusische Lehnwörter des Ostjakischen*, Veröffentlichungen der Societas Uralo-Altaica 10, Wiesbaden: Societas Uralo-Altaica.

—— (1992) 'Etymologische Beiträge zu den obugrisch-russischen Sprachbeziehungen I', in L. Honti et al. (eds), *Finnisch-ugrische Sprachen zwischen dem germanischen und dem slavischen Sprachraum. Vorträge des Symposiums aus Anlaß des 25-jährigen Bestehens der Finnougristik an der Rijksuniversiteit Groningen 12–15 November 1991*, Amsterdam–Atlanta: Rodopi, pp. 17–24.

Ganschow, G. (1962) 'Zur Frage des reduzierten Auslautsvokals im Ostostjakischen', *UAJb* 34: 4–7.

Gulya, J. (1966) *Eastern Ostyak Chrestomathy*, Indiana University Uralic and Altaic Series 51, Bloomington: Indiana University.

—— (1970) 'Aktiv, Ergativ und Passiv im Vach-Ostjakischen', in W. Schlachter (ed.), *Symposion über Syntax der uralischen Sprachen 15–18 Juli 1968 in Reinhausen bei Göttingen*, Göttingen: pp. 80–83.

Haarmann, H. (1974) *Die Finnisch-ugrischen Sprachen: Soziologische und politische Aspekte ihrer Entwicklung*, Hamburg: Helmut Buske.

Honti, L. (1982a) *Geschichte des obugrischen Vokalismus der ersten Silbe*, Bibliotheca Uralica 6, Budapest: Akadémiai kiadó.

—— (1982b) 'Vergleichende Analyse der Phonologie der nördlichen Mundarten der obugrischen Sprachen', *FUF* 44: 11–22.

—— (1984) *Chrestomathia ostiacica*, Budapest: Tankönyvkiadó.

—— (1988) 'Die ob-ugrische Sprachen, II.: die Ostjakische Sprache', in D. Sinor (ed.) *The Uralic Languages: Description, History and Foreign Influences*, Handbuch der Orientalistik, 8/1, Leiden: Brill.

—— (1993) 'A névszói állítmány alaktana az osztjákban', in M. Bakró-Nagy, and E. Szíj (eds), *Hajdú Péter 70 éves* [= Festschrift on the occasion of P. Hajdú's seventieth birthday], Linguistica Series A, Studia et dissertationes 15, Budapest: Hungarian Linguistics Institute, pp. 135–42.

Katz, H. (1975) *Generative Phonologie und phonologische Sprachbünde des Ostjakischen und Samojedischen*, Finnisch-Ugrische Bibliothek 1, Munich: Wilhelm Fink.

—— (1977) Review of Futaky 1975, *Nyelvtudományi Közlemények* 79: 1–2, 444–9.

—— (1987–8) Review of Honti 1982, *Néprajz és Nyelvtudomány*, Acta Universitatis Szegediensis de Attila József nominatae 31–2, pp. 251–61.

Korenchy, É. (1972) *Iranische Lehnwörter in den obugrischen Sprachen*, Budapest: Akadémiai kiadó.

Kulonen, U.-M. (1989) *The passive in Ob-Ugrian*, MSFOu 203, Helsinki: Société Finno-Ougrienne.

—— (1991) 'Über die ergativischen Konstruktionen im Ostostjakischen', *JSFOu* 83: 181–201.

Künnap, A. (1993) 'Siperian uralilaiset kielet tänään', in T. Salminen (ed.), *Uralilaiset kielet tänään*, A-sarja 13, Kuopio: Snellman-Instituutti, pp. 85–8.

Ostrowski, M. (1983) *Zur Nomen:Verb-Relationierung im Wogulischen, Jurakischen und Jukagirischen*, Arbeiten des Kölner Universalien-Projekts 51.

Rédei, K. (1970) *Die syrjänischen Lehnwörter im Wogulischen*, Research Center for Language Sciences, Uralic and Altaic Series 109, Bloomington–The Hague: Indiana University–Mouton.

Sal, É. (1975) 'Über die Stammendvokale im Ostostjakischen', *C3IFU*, vol. I, pp. 674–6.

—— (1976) 'Лексика', chapter (pp. 332–9), with bibliography compiled by É. Sal, J. Gulya, and E.I. Rombandeeva (pp. 339–41) in V.I. Lytkin, K.E. Majtinskaä and K. Rédei (eds), Основы финно-угорского языкознания. Марийский, пермские и угорские языки, Moscow: USSR Academy of Sciences.

Salminen, T. (1989) 'Classification of the Uralic languages', in R. Grünthal, S. Penttinen and T. Salminen (eds.), *IFUSCO 1988: Proceedings of the Fifth International Finno-Ugrist Students' Conference, Helsinki, 22–26 May 1988*, Castrenianumin toimitteita 35, Helsinki: Snellman-Instituutti.

Sauer, G. (1968) 'Nominalstämme auf *-a/*-ä im Ostjakischen', *C2IFU*, vol. I, pp. 459–61.

—— (1992) 'Zur Verbalpräfigierung im Ostjakischen', in P. Deréky, et al. (eds), *Festschrift für Károly Redei zum 60. Geburtstag*, Studia Uralica 6, *Urálisztikai tanulmányok* 3, Linguistica Series A, Studia et dissertationes 8, Vienna–Budapest: Institut für Finno-Ugristik der Universität Wien – MTA nyelvtudományi intézet, pp. 399–402.

Schlachter, W. (1970) *Symposion über Syntax der uralischen Sprachen 15–18 Juli 1968 in Reinhausen bei Göttingen*, Göttingen.

Steinitz, W. (1950) *Geschichte des ostjakischen Vokalismus*, Berlin: Akademie-Verlag.

Terëškin, N.I. (1981) Словарь восточно-хантыйских диалектов, Leningrad: Nauka.

Toivonen, Y.H. (1956) 'Über die syrjänischen Lehnwörter im Ostjakischen', *FUF* 32 1–169.

In addition, the following are invaluable lexical sources:

DEWOS = Steinitz, W., et al. (1996–93) *Dialektologisches und etymologisches Wörterbuch der ostjakischen Sprache*, Berlin: Akademie Verlag.

KT = Karjalainen, K. F. (1948) *Ostjakisches Wörterbuch*, bearbeitet und herausgegeben von Y. H. Toivonen, Lexica societatis Fenno-ugricae 10, vols I and II, Helsinki: Société Finno-Ougrienne.

13 Mansi

László Keresztes

History of the Investigation into Mansi

The first written attestation of Mansi is in the form of personal names, found sporadically in Russian chronicles. Interest in the Mansi language dates from the eighteenth century, when travellers from various lands (Messerschmidt, Strahlenberg, Fischer, Schlözer, Klaproth, Pallas) began to report vocabulary they had collected. This early lexical evidence is both linguistically naïve and of great philological importance; it must be used, therefore, with linguistic judiciousness and acumen.

The first investigator to visit the Mansi for the express purpose of collecting linguistic and ethnographic data was Antal Reguly (1819–58; fieldwork 1843–4). At that time about fifty Mansi still lived west of the Urals. Reguly travelled east of the Urals, as well, where he managed to make contact with an informant from along the Lozva River, from whom he collected extremely important material. After Reguly, August Ahlqvist (1826–89) made three trips to the Mansi region, but managed to bring back relatively little material.

Reguly died young. It fell to his contemporary, Pál Hunfalvy (1810–91), to work up the texts Reguly had collected, something he did with only limited success. It was not until Bernát Munkácsi (1860–1937) that Mansi studies were put on a firm footing. Munkácsi sorted out Reguly's material, and in a year of his own fieldwork (1888–9) collected further material from all Mansi dialects. The longest stretch of fieldwork was carried out by Artturi Kannisto (1874–1943), who spent nearly six years (1901–6) among the Mansi, and visited every area where Mansi was spoken.

After the 1917 Revolution, foreign access to the Mansi was effectively shut off; between the two world wars and after, the only foreigner permitted to enter the region was Wolfgang Steinitz (1905–67). Fortunately, Soviet linguists, as well, visited the area, among them V.I. Chernetsov and A.N. Balandin. 'Western' investigators – among whom the most important is Béla Kálmán – were allowed to travel no further than St Petersburg, where they were able to collect fresh material from Mansi, studying at the Herzen Institute. Other investigators fortunate enough to carry out such fieldwork with native speakers include György Lakó and the present author.

The first researcher to venture beyond St Petersburg after the Second World War was Éva Schmidt, who reached the Mansi lands by dint of persistence in the face of natural adversity and bureaucratic obstacles. Since the beginning of the 1990s it has become possible once again for researchers from the West to do Mansi fieldwork.

Among native-speaker researchers of Mansi, M.P. Vakhrusheva, A.I. Sainakhova and E.I. Rombandeeva deserve special mention. At the end of the twentieth century a new brigade of indigenous Mansi language scholars is beginning to test its wings.

Mansi has always enjoyed a favoured position among Finno-Ugric scholars. This is evidenced in the first instance by the attention paid it by scholars in Hungary (in the nineteenth century: Móric Szilasi and Zoltán Trócsányi; in the first half of the twentieth century: Olivér Hazay, Ödön Beke, Dávid Fokos, Zoltán Gombocz, Manó Kertész, Antal Klemm, Dezső Szabó, Magda Kövesi; in the second half of the twentieth century: Magdolna Kispál, Éva Sal, Ödön Lavotha, Károly Rédei, János Gulya, László Honti, Éva Schmidt and László Keresztes). But in Finland, too, prominent scholars have devoted their attention to this language which, for them, is only a distant relative (Matti Liimola, Kaisa Häkkinen, Vuokko Eiras, Ulla-Maija Kulonen).

The work of Wolfgang Steinitz stands out among that done by scholars whose native language was not a Finno-Ugrian one. Besides Steinitz, one should also mention the names of Wolfgang Veenker, Robert Austerlitz, and Giuliano Pirotti.

Mansi Linguistic Sources
Great caution must be used in exploiting the wordlists from eighteenth-century expeditions. It was these early perceptions, however, which led the first dedicated linguistic investigators to the Mansi regions. They returned with extensive folkloristic texts. The chain of scholarly collectors was unbroken, from Reguly to Hunfalvy (who made promising stabs at inter-pretation) to Bernát Munkácsi, who was the first to make a thorough analysis and to publish the data. Munkácsi also did his own fieldwork; he began to work up the texts he had collected and part of a commentary, and after his death Béla Kálmán finished the commentary. By this time Kálmán had already been collecting texts himself: he published these, and worked their lexical material into the corpus of the Mansi dialect dictionary based on Munkácsi's notes.

Another important, albeit smaller, source for Mansi is the nineteenth-century material collected by August Ahlqvist. The material collected by Kannisto has been edited and published, for the most part, by Matti Liimola. The most extensive Mansi dialect dictionary is still in preparation, under the direction of Vuokko Eiras.

E.I. Rombandeeva's monographs (1976, 1979) offer ample storehouses of examples for investigators. She is currently working on an edition of folklore texts and on a dictionary. School textbooks and university teaching materials produced during the Soviet era are also illuminating.

The Development of the Mansi Language and People

The Mansi – in their own language, *maan^j s^j i* – live chiefly along rivers in the area between the Urals and the left bank of the Ob'. With its closest congener, Ostyak, it forms the so-called ObUgrian branch of the Uralic language family. The term *Ugric* is used to refer to ObUgrian and Hungarian together.

After the speakers of proto-Hungarian broke away (roughly seventh to fifth century BCE), the linguistic ancestors of the Khanty and the Mansi remained in western Siberia, where they spoke a common language for some considerable time. Although linguistically they are the closest relatives to the Hungarians, in terms of physical anthropology they are quite distinct. This differentiation may be due to genetic admixture with other, unknown, groups.

The distinction, in name, of 'Mansi' from 'Khanty' is datable to no earlier than the fourteenth century. This is doubtless due to the great similarities in the physical and spiritual culture of the two groups. The linguistic split, however, must have been much earlier, perhaps as early as the first half of the first millenium CE. The period between the breakaway of Hungarian and the breakup of Khanty and Mansi is called the ObUgrian period, and the common language, proto-ObUgrian (Honti 1982a: 15).

During the ObUgrian period a significant number of speakers lived to the west of the Urals. The ethnonym *Vogul* is first attested in 1396: the Russians thus named the first *mansi* speakers with whom they came into contact, *mansi* who were then living along the Vogulka River. The name then spread to designate all the Mansi. The self-designation *maan^j s^j i* (western *maan^j s^j*, eastern *mœœn^j s^j*, southern *män^j c^j i*) is perhaps an Iranian loan meaning 'human', but it is also connected with the name of a Khanty/Mansi phratry (Mansi *moos^j*, Khanty Vakh *maan^j t^j*, Kazym *måås^j*) and with a Hungarian tribal name (*Megyer*) and with the self-designation of the Hungarians (*magyar*) as whole.

Between the tenth and fifteenth centuries CE the northern and western groups of Mansi speakers were subject to Komi, then Russian influence; southern and eastern groups experienced intensive contact with Siberian Tatar. The Russians took western Siberia from the Tatars in the sixteenth century; thereafter Russian colonization hit the Mansi population hard. In the eighteenth and nineteenth centuries there were new waves of Komi migration; these Komi settled between and among the Mansi, Khantak, and Samoyed population. During their entire history, the Mansi have been in contact with the Khanty, and northern groups of Mansi speakers have had contact with Nenets speakers, as well (Honti 1982a: 13–17; Kálmán 1988: 395–412).

Mansi Dialects

Mansi is spoken along the left-bank tributaries of the lower Ob', on the Siberian side of the Urals. The dialects are traditionally classified into Northern, Western, Eastern and Southern groups (Kálmán 1976: 10–11).

Northern Group

These dialects, upon which the literary standard is based, are spoken along the Sosva and Sygva Rivers, also formerly along the upper Lozva and in the Berezovo region (it is here that the Vogulka River is located). This grouping of dialects is characterized by strong Russian, Komi, and Nenets influence. The area is adjacent to that of northern Khanty, with which there has been intense contact. Phonological innovations include: the backing of certain vowels (e.g. *ä > a, *ää > aa); gemination of intervocalic consonants (upper Sosva); ŋx > x and k^w > k and k > t' before front vowels (Sygva); in Ob' subdialects, š' instead of s', and fricative laterals (ł, ł') instead of approximants (l, l') – this latter feature a result of northern Khanty influence. Throughout the Northern dialect area the accusative is unmarked, i.e. homophonous with the nominative. Dual forms of the direct object and of possessions are distinguished (Rombandeevea 1964: 51–8).

Western Group

These dialects were formerly spoken along the mid and lower reaches of the Lozva, also along the Vagilsk and Pelymka. In Reguly's day Western group dialects were spoken west of the Urals, as well (Chusovaya); they are now in the final stages of extinction. Russian and Komi influence was significant. They are characterized by a withering away of the dual, and, in common with dialects of the Eastern group, by the dipthongization of long vowels.

Eastern Group

Eastern group dialects are spoken by some 100–200 people along the Konda and Yukonda Rivers. There was close contact with Khanty speakers along the lower Konda; considerable Tatar influence is also present. Vowel harmony has been preserved. Word-initial š is more common in Yukonda subdialects. Corresponding to Northern aa and Southern ää is the characteristic æœ, which is frequently diphthongized.

Southern Group

These dialects were still spoken, along the Tavda River, at the beginning of the twentieth century. Vowel harmony and the greater part of the original vocalism are best preserved here; on the other hand the dual has disappeared. There is strong Tatar influence. The main stress is on the second syllable.

Table 13.1 provides an overview of the chief dialectal isoglosses for the Northern, Western, Eastern and Southern dialect groups (Honti 1982a).

There are differences in the morphology, as well (cf. Kálmán 1976: 12), as shown in Table 13.2.

Table 13.1 Illustrations of chief dialectal isoglosses

Gloss, Honti page no.	Northern	Western	Eastern	Southern
grandfather 123	aasʲ	—	œœsʲ	ääcʲi
daughter 123	aaɣi	åå	œœ	ääw
dog 126	aamp	ååmp	œœmp	äämp
pulls out 127	aaŋxʷ-	ëëŋkʷ-	aaŋxʷ-	aaŋk-
thin 130	sʲaaliɣ	sʲååliɣ	sʲœœli	cʲäälɘw
hill 131	saaŋkʷ	säx	säxʷ	sük
pours out 131	soos-	šooš-	šooš-	šaaš-
flea 133	sus	šuš	šonš	šoš
fog 133	seeŋkʷ	šeexʷ	šeeŋkʷ	šiikʷ
stone 147	kaw	käw	käw	küw
dies 149	xool-	kool-	xool-	kaal-
wave 150	xuump	kup	xop	kop
claw 152	kʷoss, kos	käš	kʷäš	künš
breast 163	maaɣɘl	maɣl	mœɣl	mäwl
wades 181	suus-	šuš-	šoš-	šooš-
cuts 183	saaɣr-	šaɣr-	sœɣr-	šäwr-
heart 184	sim	šim	šim	šäm
hundred 186	saat	šëët	šëët	šaat
god 190	toorɘm	tooräämt	toorɘm	taarɘm
fat 192	wooj	wooj	wooj	waaj
lives, exists 193	ool-	ool-	uul-	aal-

Table 13.2 Sample morphological differences

	Northern	Western	Eastern	Southern
Accusative	—	-m(ɘ)	-m	-mi ~ -më
Translative	-iɣ	-ä	-j	-o ~ -ü
Ablative	-nɘl	-nɘ	-nɘl	-naal ~ -nääl
Dual	-iɣ-	-a-	-åå- ~ -ɘj-	—
Conjunctive	[–]	[+]	[+]	[–]
Future	[–]	[–]	[–]	[+]
Infinitive	-ŋkʷe	-ux	-ɘx ~ -äx	-ŋ
Pres. part.	-ne	-nɘ	-p	-ni ~ -në

If alongside phonological and morphological differences we consider lexical ones, as well, it becomes obvious that interdialectal communication can become problematic (cf. Kálmán 1976: 12).

Table 13.3 Sample lexical differences

	Northern	Western	Eastern	Southern
[negator]	at	at	œœt	ää, äk
fire	naaj, uljᵃ	tååwt	tœœwt	täwət
small	maanʲ	wüsʲ	wisʲ	musʲ
bread	nʲaanʲ	nʲaanʲ	nʲœœnʲ	itʲmäx
cow	mis	säïr	sœɣər	sawər
reindeer	saali	kunna	xonəj	koŋka
wolf	saaliuj	šeeš	šaaš	cʲeesʲ

Phonology

Vowels

The vowel system of Northern (Literary) Mansi is summarized below (cf. Rombandeeva 1973: 17–28; Kálmán 1984: 73–6):

ii	i		u	uu
ee	e	ə	o	oo
		a	aa	

Here are the values of these symbols in some phonetic detail:

/u/: short back rounded high: *ut* 'something', *rusʲ* 'Russian', *laawuŋkʷe* 'to say'.

/uu/: long back rounded high: *uus* 'town', *suuj* 'forest'.

/i/: short front unrounded high: *iŋ* 'still', *kit* 'two', *toti-* 'brings'; retracted variants occur after x and before ɣ (*piɣ* [pïɣ] 'boy', *xili-* [xïli] 'digs').

/ii/: long front unrounded high: *iitʲi* 'at night', *jiiw* 'tree'; retracted before ɣ: *wiiɣ ər* [wïïɣər] 'red'.

/o/: short back rounded mid: *nʲol* 'nose', *joməs* 'good', *low* 'ten'.

/oo/: long back rounded low [åå]: *ooli-* 'is, lives', *poor* 'fish roe'. Often diphthongized as [oå].

/e/: short front unrounded mid [ɛ]. Occurs rarely in first syllable; example: *ness* 'only'. In non-first syllable it is more frequent, especially in absolute final position: *jaate* 'its river', *laawuŋkʷe* 'to say', *luwkʷel* 'with a little horse'. In non-first syllables and when non-final, the *e* phoneme is usually pronounced long. Velarized and diphongized variants also occur, e.g. *mineɣen* [mineeɣëën] 'you (plur) go', *taajen* [taajëën] '(you plur) eat! (imperative), *minimen* [minimeɛn] 'let's go!'.

/ee/: long front unrounded lower-mid [ɛ:]. Examples: *nee* 'woman', *keelp* 'blood', *seeməl* 'black'.

/a/: short back unrounded low: *aji-* 'drinks', *kan* 'space', *josa* 'ski'. Fronted variants occur after *j*, e.g. *janiɣ* [jänïɣ] 'big'.

/aa/: long back unrounded low: *aamp* 'dog', *taal* 'winter', *maa* 'earth', *saat* 'hundred'.

/ə/: A reduced vowel, occurring in the literary language only in unstressed syllables: *joxtəs* 's3 came'. Before *m p*, rounded variants occur, e.g. *toorəm* [to:rum] 'sky, god', *liltəp* [liltup] 'air'. In the environment of palatalized consonants [i]-like variants occur, e.g. *aakanʲəl* [a:kanʲil] 'with a doll'; in certain other environments [a]-like variants occur, e.g. *xansəŋ* [xansaŋ] 'many-coloured', *minəs* [minas] 's3 went'. These three phonetic variants of ə – [u], [i], and [a] – are indicated by the Cyrillic orthography, e.g. торум, лилтуп, аканил, хансанг, минас.

Oppositions among the Vowels
The most pervasive correlation in the vocalism is that of quantity. Witness the pairs: *sam* 'eye' – *saam* 'fish-scale; region', *xot* (perfectivizing coverb) – *xoot* 'six; where?', *tur* 'voice' – *tuur* 'lake'. Qualitative differences accompany the quantitative distinctions; for example, short *o* is higher than its long counterpart *oo*, and short *u* is higher than its long counterpart *uu*. The quantitative opposition is old; it is reconstructed for proto-Mansi and for proto-ObUgrian (cf. Steinitz 1955: 154; Honti 1982a: 26).

In all surviving Mansi dialects, the correlation front : back is irrelevant, i.e. [+/-] back can be considered a trivial byproduct of [+/–] labial.

Distribution of Vowels
The phonologically long vowels tend to occur in the first, stressed, syllable; contrast *e*, which tends to occur as (phonetically) long in non-first, non-final syllables. Short *u* and *o* are rare in unstressed syllables; in word-final position only *a e i* occur. The reduced vowel *ə* occurs only in unstressed syllables.

In descending order of textual frequency, the vowels are *a i ə o ee aa oo u e uu ii*. The proportion of back to front vowels has been measured as 66 to 34 (cf. Kálmán 1976: 36).

Consonants
The consonant system inventory of North (Literary) Mansi is summarized below (cf. Rombandeeva 1973: 28–37; Kálmán 1984: 76–9):

m	n	nʲ	ŋ	
p	t	tʲ	k	kʷ
	s	sʲ	x	
w		j	γ	
	l	lʲ		
	r			

Here are the values of these symbols in some phonetic detail:

/m/: voiced bilabial nasal: *maam* 'my land'.

/n/: voiced dental nasal: *naan* 'you (plur)'.

/nʲ/: voiced palatalized dental nasal: *nʲaanʲ* 'bread'

/ŋ/: voiced velar nasal stop: distinctive only word-internal and word-final, e.g. *sʲaŋsʲi* 'sparrow', *xuriŋ* 'good-looking'. Frequent, in all subdialects, before /k/ and /x/, e.g. *paaŋk* 'soot', *nooŋx* 'up'.

/p/: voiceless bilabial stop: *puut* 'pot', *tuup* 'oar'.

/t/: voiceless dental stop: *taal* 'winter', *tuur* 'lake'.

/tʲ/: voiceless palatalized dental stop: *waatʲi* 'short'.

/k/: voiceless velar stop: *kol* 'dwelling', *keer* 'iron'.

/kʷ/: voiceless labialized velar stop: *kʷonkʷaaluŋkʷe* 'to exit', *eekʷa* 'woman'. More frequent along the Sosva; along the Sygva, replaced by /k/, especially in initial position, e.g. *kol* 'dwelling', *kon* 'out'

/w/: voiced bilabial fricative or approximant: *wooj* 'fat', *jiw- ~ juw-* 'comes'. In some subdialects there is word-internal free variation of /w/ with /ɣ/, e.g. *puwi- ~ puɣi-* 'seizes'; in others, /w/ alternates freely with zero in word-initial position, e.g. Ob' *uɬʲa ~ wuɬʲa* 'fire'.

/j/: voiced palatal glide: *joxti-* 'arrives', *wooj* 'fat'.

/x/: voiceless velar fricative: *xanʲsʲi-* 'knows', *xum* 'man', *nox* 'up'; in some (idio)lects, also occurs labialized, e.g. *seeŋxʷ* (~ *seeŋkʷ*) 'fog'.

/ɣ/: voiced velar fricative: *janiɣ* 'big', *piɣ* 'boy'. Does not occur word-initially; cf. /w/. Along the Ob', frequently corresponds to /w/ in other areas, e.g. *paaɣəl* (other dialects: *paawəl*) 'village', *moɣinʲti- (mowinti-)* 'laughs'.

/s/: voiceless hissing sibilant: *saaw* 'many', *pos* 'light, shining'.

/š/: voiceless hushing shibilant: occurs only in recent Russian loanwords and in Ob' subdialects, e.g. *uuš* (other dialects: *uus*) 'town'.

/sʲ/: voiceless palatalized sibilant, varying subdialectally and idiolectally with a palatalized hushing sibilant [šʲ]: *sʲunʲ* 'wealth', *pasʲa* 'greeting'.

/l/: voiced dental lateral approximant: *lili* 'breath, life', *laawi-* 'says'. Along the Ob', as a result of Khanty influence, most words have a voiceless lateral fricative (ɬ).

/lʲ/: voiced palatalized dental lateral approximant: *lʲuulʲ* 'bad'; Along the Ob', as a result of Khanty influence, most words have the corresponding palatalized voiceless lateral fricative (ɬʲ), e.g. *ɬʲuuɬʲi-* 'stands'.

/r/: voiced strong apical trill: *rooŋxi-* 'shouts', *xuriŋ* 'good-looking'.

Oppositions among the Consonants

An important characteristic of the Mansi consonant system is the correlation of palatalization, which is relevant for all the consonants here classified as dental, e.g. *saaj* 'space behind', *sʲaaj* 'tea'; *sun* 'sled', *sʲunʲ* 'wealth'; *naan* 'you (plur)', *nʲaanʲ* 'bread'; *paal* 'side', *palʲ* 'ear'; *waati-* 'picks', *waatʲi* 'short time'. The palatalized stop /tʲ/ is rare, although a new *tʲ* is common in Sygva subdialects, where a change *ke, ki > tʲe, tʲi* has occurred, e.g. Sy (*kit*

>) $t^j it$ 'two', contrast *tit* 'here'. The sound sometimes transcribed as $\check{c}'$, which occurs in a few loanwords, is to be interpreted as a sequence of t^j plus s^j, e.g. $tut^j s^j aŋ$ 'sewing-bag made of reindeer hide' (cf. Honti 1977: 412).

No Mansi dialect knows a correlation of voice. The voiceless stops and sibilants generally lack voiced counterparts, and the sonorants and *j* lack voiceless ones. The only pair distinguished solely by the feature of voice are the velar fricatives /x/ : /γ/; the functional load is slight, however, since /γ/ never occurs word-initially and these phonemes do not appear to contrast word-internally, either.

Quantitative oppositions among the consonants are also few: geminates occur only at morpheme boundaries, e.g. *witt* 'in water' (*wit* 'water'), *xass əm* 'I wrote' (*xansi-* 'writes'), *laawwes əm* 'they said to me = I was told' (*laawi-* 'says').

The contemporary northern (and western) dialects preserve the proto-Mansi consonant system essentially unchanged, the only restructuring stemming from the disaffrication of pV $*c^j$ and the realignment of the sibilants (cf. Honti 1982a: 24–5 and Chapter 11 in this book).

Distribution of the Consonants
Most consonants occur in all positions, with the exception of γ and ŋ, which do not occur word-initially. Mansi also tends to avoid word-initial clusters; a limited number of word-final clusters are tolerated.

In descending order of textual frequency, the consonants of Northern Mansi are: $t, l, m, s, w, r, n, p, k, γ, x, j, s^j, l^j, n^j, ŋ, t^j$ (cf. Kálmán 1976: 36).

Morpho(no)logy

The Phonological Makeup of Morphemes

Free Morphemes (Stems)
The canonic Mansi word is bisyllabic, but monosyllabic and trisyllabic words are common as well. The most frequent types of stem morphemes are shown in Table 13.4.

Nominal stems end in vowels, consonants, and consonant clusters, but most verb stems have a final consonant(ism). There are just six verb stems, all monosyllabic (e.g. *wi-*, 'takes'), which have vowel-final forms before certain suffixes; but these, too, have consonant-final allomorphs.

Bound Morphemes (Suffixes)
The most common shapes of simple inflectional and derivational suffixes are shown in Table 13.5.

The Syllable
The number of syllables in a Mansi word-form is conditioned by the number of vowels present. Syllables begin with a consonant whenever possible, and

Table 13.4   Canonic shapes of stem morphemes

	Noun		*Verb*	
VC	ur	'mountain'	uur-	'waits'
CV	maa	'earth'	wi-	'takes'
CVC	tul	'cloud'	laaw-	'says'
VCV	ulja	'fire'	—	
VCC	oln	'money'	uunl-	'sits'
VCCV	oojka	'old man'	—	
CVCV	saali	'reindeer'	—	
CVCC	suunt	'opening'	rooŋx-	'shouts'
CVCCV	soornji	'gold'	—	

Table 13.5   Canonic shapes of inflectional and derivational suffixes

	Nominal suffixes	*Verbal suffixes*
V	-e (s3 px)	-i (s3 vx)
VC	-iɣ (dual)	-ew (p1 vx)
VCV	—	-awe (pass)
VCCV	—	-uŋkʷe (inf)
C	-t (loc)	-s (pret)
CV	-te (s3 px)	-te (s3 vx)
CVC	-nəl (abl)	-nuw (cond)

the last element in any word-internal cluster belongs to the subsequent syllable, e.g. *molwallaalli* 'laughs', *rooŋlxaxltelɣət* 'they shout'.

Morphonological Alternations

Stem Alternations
Nominal stems. Nominal stems which end in a vowel do not alternate: suffixes simply attach to the final vowel.

Consonant-final nominal stems, on the other hand, are augmented by the reduced vowel *ə* or, rarely, by *i* when certain suffixes are attached: contrast *kolə-t* 'dwellings' with *kol-t* 'in a/the dwelling' (*kol* 'dwelling'); *xumi-te* 'her husband' with *xum-nəl* 'from a man'.

When vowel-initial suffixes are attached, an analogous loss of *ə* and *i* in final syllables characterizes the syncopating class of stems, e.g. *xuurəm* 'three', *xuurm=it* 'third'; *soojəm* 'brook', *soojmə-t* 'brooks'; *eeriɣ* 'song', *eerɣ-e* 'song s3'; *laayəl* 'foot, leg', *laayl-e* 'foot/leg s3'.

The word *maa* 'earth' shows a unique alternation of *ɣ* with zero, e.g. the instrumental case form maaɣə-l.

Verbal stems. There are no non-alternating vowel-final verb stems. All consonant-final verb stems are characterized by the alternation of zero, ə, i, and a to the left of various suffixes, e.g. zero in *waar-s-əm* 'I made', *waar-nuw* 's3 would make', *waar-we-s* 's3 was made', and ə in *waarə-s* 's3 made', *waarə-s-te* 's3 made s3', i in *waari-ləm* 'I make s3', *waari-te* 's3 makes s3', and a in *waara-we* 's3 is made'.

In verbal stems ending in nasal plus homotopic obstruent (sibilant or x), the nasal goes to zero when consonant-initial suffixes are attached (denasalizing type): *l̡uunʲsʲi-* 'weeps', *l̡uusʲ-sə-m* 'I wept'; *sunsi-* 'looks', *sus-sə-m* 'I looked'; *xaaŋxi-* 'climbs', *xaax-sə-m* 'I climbed'.

Six verbal stems are characterized by alternations of final consonants (γ, w, j) with zero, and, in some cases, by vowel alternations as well. Table 13.6 sets out the stem variants of these verbs to the left of present, preterite, conditional, imperative, and passive suffixation.

Table 13.6   Stem variants

Present	Preterite, conditional	Imperative, passive	Gloss
miγ-	mi-	maj-	'gives'
liγ-	li-	laj-	'throws'
wiγ-	wi-	woj-	'takes'
teeγ-	tee-	taaj-	'eats'
waaγ-	waa-	waaj-	'sees'
juw- ~ jiw-	ju- ~ ji-	jaj-	'comes'

Suffix Alternations

Suffix allomorphy is dependent on whether the preceding segment is a consonant or a vowel (cf. Kálmán 1976: 40).

The third-person singular possessive suffix is *-te* after vowels, *-e* after consonants: *aayi-te* 'his/her daughter', *piγ-e* 'his/her son'. A homophonous pair is found in the third-person singular suffix of the definite conjugation: *waari-te* '(s)he makes it', *waari-jaγ-e* '(s)he makes them (dual)', *waari-jan-e* '(s)he makes them (plur)'.

The suffix of the instrumental is *-l* in the singular and plural, *-təl* in the dual: *puutə-l* 'with a pot', *puutə-tə-l* 'with pots', *puut-iγ-təl* 'with two pots'.

The distribution of the alternants of the diminutive suffix is unclear: *aayi=ke-m* 'my (little) girl', *aayi=kʷe* 'her/his little girl'.

Vowel Distribution and Vowel Harmony

The present-day dialects of Mansi have lost vowel harmony. The Southern (Tavda) dialect data collected at the turn of the last century show that this form of Mansi was archaic in this respect, e.g. Tavda *kül-nääl* 'from the/a house', *kaap-naal* 'from the/a boat'; *käät-tää* 'in the/a hand', *maa-taa* 'in the earth' (cf. Honti 1975: 122).

Stress

The primary stress falls on the first syllable. There is also a secondary, but considerable, stress on the third, but no stress falls on a final syllable. Examples: *lu"jyante 'yət* 'they chirp', *kaa"sala'sanəl* 'they noticed it/him/her'. The Tavda dialect deviated from this pattern: it had stress on the second syllable, apparently as a result of Tatar influence.

Verbs

Stem types
Mansi verb stems normally end in one or two consonants. Stem augmentation comes in the form of an additional *ə*, *i*, or *a*; the selection is conditioned by the suffix. Only six stems have vowel-final variants (see p. 397).

Conjugation
Active v. passive forms are distinguished. All forms encode tense/mood. In addition, passive forms encode the person and number of the experiencer, while active forms encode the person and number of the subject. Active forms further encode whether or not there is a definite object; if the object is definite, its number is also encoded. Number can be singular, dual, or plural (cf. Balandin–Vakhrusheva 1957: 111–39; Rombandeeva 1973: 111–45; Kálmán 1976: 56–64).

Indeterminate (Indefinite, Subjective) Conjugation
Three moods are distinguished: indicative, conditional, and imperative.

The *indicative* distinguishes two tenses: present and preterite. The indeterminate person-suffixes in the *present* tense are as follows:

	Singular	Dual	Plural
1	-eyəm	-imen	-ew
2	-eyən	-eyə/en	-eyə/en
3	-i	-ey	-eyət

The -ey- component of certain of the person suffixes was originally a present-tense morpheme (?pFU *-k-). The γ and w final in the ablauting stems appear to have always belonged to the stem, however.

Most of the first- and second-person suffixes derive from personal pronouns. The *-n* of the second person, which has pendants in Khanty, Permian, and Nenets, is attributed by some scholars to dialectal variation in proto-Uralic, by others to a sound change (*t > *n; cf. Hajdú 1966: 132–3, 142). In either event, the distribution seems to indicate an areal phenomenon. In general, second-person forms – particularly dual and plural ones – tend to syncretize in Mansi.

The third-person forms of the indeterminate conjugation are not of pronominal origin. The third-person singular -*i* is historically the suffix of a now non-productive imperfective/continuous participle (pFU *=j). The six ablauting verbs have zero in the third person singular. The dual and plural third-person forms consist of dual and plural suffixes (-γ, -*t*) added to the stem; this state of affairs is best preserved in the forms of the ablauting stems.

The first-person plural suffix -*w* is perhaps a continuation of a pFU pluralizer *-k.

Future time is indicated either by present-tense forms, often with the aid of a temporal adverb, or with the auxiliary verb *pati*-, e.g. *eerγ-e sujtuŋkʷ akʷ tox pati* 'his/her/its song will always (re)sound'.

Table 13.7   Present-tense indeterminate person suffixes *ooli*- 'is, lives', *waari*- 'makes', *xansi*- 'writes'

	Singular	*Dual*	*Plural*
1	ool-eγəm	ool-imen	ool-ew
2	ool-eγən	ool-eγə/en	ool-eγə/en
3	ool-i	ool-eγ	ool-eγət
1	waar-eγəm	waar-imen	waar-ew
2	waar-eγən	waar-eγə/en	waar-eγə/en
3	waar-i	waar-eγ	waar-eγət
1	xans-eγəm	xans-imen	xans-ew
2	xans-eγən	xans-eγə/en	xans-eγə/en
3	xans-i	xans-eγ	xans-eγət

Table 13.8   Present-tense forms of the six ablauting stems

	'gives'	*'throws'*	*'takes'*	*'eats'*	*'sees'*	*'comes'*
s1	miγ-əm	liγ-əm	wiγ-əm	teeγ-əm	waaγ-əm	juw-əm
s2	miγ-ən	liγ-ən	wiγ-ən	teeγ-ən	waaγ-ən	juw-ən
s3	miγ	liγ	wiγ	teeγ	waaγ	juw ~ jiw
d1	miγ-men	liγ-men	wiγ-men	teeγ-men	waaγ-men	juw-men
d2	miγ-en	liγ-en	wiγ-en	teeγ-en	waaγ-en	juw-en
d3	miγ-iγ	liγ-iγ	wiγ-iγ	teeγ-iγ	waaγ-iγ	juw-iγ
p1	miγ-uw	liγ-uw	wiγ-uw	teeγ-uw	waaγ-uw	juw-uw
p2	miγ-en	liγ-en	wiγ-en	teeγ-en	waaγ-en	juw-en
p3	miγ-ət	liγ-ət	wiγ-ət	teeγ-ət	waaγ-ət	juw-ət

Note: See Table 13.6 for ablauting stems.

The *preterite* forms are built with the suffix -*s* (< pU *-sʲ), which is added to the plain (unaugmented) stem in all forms save the third person singular, where either ə or (more rarely) *a* occurs. The person suffixes in the preterite are:

	Singular	Dual	Plural
1	-əm	-əmen	-uw
2	-ən	-en	-en
3	-∅	-iγ	-ət

The third-person singular suffix is always -∅ in the preterite; the dual and plural third-person forms are built with the dual and plural suffixes found in the nominal paradigm.

Dual and plural syncretize in the second person.

Table 13.9   Preterite-tense person suffixes: *ooli-* 'is, lives', *mini-* 'goes', *sunsi-* 'looks'

	Singular	*Dual*	*Plural*
1	ool-s-əm	ool-s-əmen	ool-s-uw
2	ool-s-ən	ool-s-en	ool-s-en
3	ool-(ə)s-∅	ool-s-iγ	ool-s-ət
1	mina-s-əm	mina-s-əmen	mina-s-uw
2	mina-s-ən	mina-s-en	mina-s-en
3	mina-s-∅	mina-s-iγ	mina-s-ət
1	sus-s-əm	sus-s-əmen	sus-s-uw
2	sus-s-ən	sus-s-en	sus-s-en
3	sunsə-s-∅	sus-s-iγ	sus-s-ət

Table 13.10   Preterite-tense forms of the six ablauting stems

	'gave'	*'threw'*	*'took'*	*'ate'*	*'saw'*	*'came'*
s1	mi-s-əm	li-s-əm	wi-s-əm	tee-səm	waa-s-əm	juw-əm
s2	mi-s-ən	li-s-ən	wi-s-ən	tee-s-ən	waa-s-ən	juw-ən
s3	mi-s-∅	li-s-∅	wi-s-∅	tee-s-∅	waa-s-∅	ji-s-∅
d1	mi-s-men	li-s-men	wi-s-men	tee-s-men	waa-s-men	juw-men
d2	mi-s-en	li-s-en	wi-s-en	tee-s-en	waa-s-en	juw-en
d3	mi-s-iγ	li-s-iγ	wi-s-iγ	tee-s-iγ	waa-s-iγ	juw-iγ
p1	mi-s-uw	li-s-uw	wi-s-uw	tee-s-uw	waa-s-uw	juw-uw
p2	mi-s-en	li-s-en	wi-s-en	tee-s-en	waa-s-en	juw-en
p3	mi-s-ət	li-s-ət	wi-s-ət	tee-s-ət	waa-s-ət	juw-ət

Conditional. The suffix of the conditional mood is *-nuw-* (< pFU *-nek). The person suffixes in the conditional are:

	Singular	Dual	Plural
1	-əm	-amen	-uw
2	-ən	-en	-en
3	-∅	-iγ	-ət

Table 13.11   Conditional mood person suffixes: *toti-* 'takes away, brings', *mini-* 'goes', *xanli-* 'glues', *miɣ-* 'gives'

	Singular	Dual	Plural
1	tot-nuw-əm	tot-nuw-amen	tot-nuw-uw
2	tot-nuw-ən	tot-nuw-en	tot-nuw-en
3	tot-nuw-Ø	tot-nuw-iɣ	tot-nuw-ət
1	min-nuw-əm	min-nuw-amen	min-nuw-uw
2	min-nuw-ən	min-nuw-en	min-nuw-en
3	min-nuw-Ø	min-nuw-iɣ	min-nuw-ət
1	xanlə-nuw-əm	xanlə-nuw-amen	xanlə-nuw-uw
2	xanlə-nuw-ɔn	xanlə-nuw-en	xanlə-nuw-en
3	xanlə-nuw-Ø	xanlə-nuw-iɣ	xanlə-nuw-ət
1	mi-nuw-əm	mi-nuw-amen	mi-nuw-uw
2	mi-nuw-ən	mi-nuw-en	mi-nuw-en
3	mi-nuw-Ø	mi-nuw-iɣ	mi-nuw-ət

i.e., identical with those of the preterite except for the initial vowel in the first person dual.

Some scholars (e.g. Kálmán 1976: 56) use the term 'conditional', others call this mood 'conjunctive' (e.g. Rombandeeva 1973: 128–9) or 'conditional–optative' (Riese 1984: 75).

Conditions may also be expressed by means of a particle *ke*, used with the indicative, e.g. *jolǝl ke mini* 'if (s)he/it goes up there' (cf. Rombandeeva 1973 129).

Imperative. The imperative is formed by direct suffixation of the second-person suffix to the stem, i.e. its suffix is zero. This may preserve an archaic (pU) state of affairs, or the imperative *-k- may have been lost through sound change (cf. Hajdú [2]1966: 136).

Examples: *waari-* 'makes', plus the ablauting verbs:

s2	waar-ən	maj-ən	laj-ən	woj-ən	taaj-ən	waaj-ən	ji/aj-ən
d2	waar-en	maj-en	laj-en	woj-en	taaj-en	waaj-en	ji/aj-en
p2	waar-en	maj-en	laj-en	woj-en	taaj-en	waaj-en	ji/aj-en

Imperatives for the other persons are constructed by means of a particle *(w)os* plus the present indicative, e.g. *(w)os ujj-eɣ ǝm* 'may I sink'.

Determinate (Definite, Objective) Conjugation
Forms of the determinate (definite, objective) conjugation encode not only the person and number of the subject but also the number of a direct object which is 'definite' (see p. 417).

The determinate conjugation has the same tenses and moods as the indeterminate. The person suffixes are shown in Table 13.12.

Table 13.12   Determinate conjugation person suffixes

	Definite object number Singular	Dual	Plural
s1	-ləm	-(j)aγəm	-(j)anəm
s2	-lən	-(j)aγən	-(j)an(ən)
s3	-te	-(j)aγe	-(j)ane
d1	-lamen	-(j)aγ(a)men	-(j)an(a)men
d2	-len	-(j)aγen	-(j)an(en)
d3	-ten	-(j)aγen	-(j)anen
p1	-luw	-(j)aγuw	-(j)anuw
p2	-len	-(j)aγen	-(j)an(en)
p3	-anəl	-(j)aγanəl	-(j)an(an)əl

Indicative forms of the determinate conjugation are shown in Table 13.13.
The paradigms of *xanli-* 'causes to adhere' and *miγ-* 'gives (away)' in Table 13.14 illustrate the preterite forms of the definite conjugation.

The person suffixes of the determinate conjugation are difficult to analyse from both descriptive and historical points of view. In forms which encode

Table 13.13   Determinate conjugation present-tense forms: *uunti-* 'occupies (a place)', *teeγ-* 'eats (up)'

	Singular Definite object	Dual Definite object	Plural Definite object
s1	uunti-ləm	uunti-jaγəm	uunti-janəm
s2	uunti-lən	uunti-jaγən	uunti-jan(ən)
s3	uunti-te	uunti-jaγe	uunti-jane
d1	uunti-lamen	uunti-jaγmen	uunti-janmen
d2	uunti-len	uunti-jaγen	uunti-jan(en)
d3	uunti-ten	uunti-jaγen	uunti-janen
p1	uunti-luw	uunti-jaγuw	uunti-januw
p2	uunti-len	uunti-jaγen	uunti-jan(en)
p3	uunti-lanəl	uunti-jaγanəl	uunti-jan(an)əl
s1	teeγ-ləm	teeγ-aγəm	teeγ-anəm
s2	teeγ-lən	teeγ-aγən	teeγ-an(ən)
s3	teeγ-te	teeγ-aγe	teeγ-ane
d1	teeγ-lamen	teeγ-aγmen	teeγ-anmen
d2	teeγ-len	teeγ-aγen	teeγ-an(en)
d3	teeγ-ten	teeγ-aγen	teeγ-anen
p1	teeγ-luw	teeγ-aγuw	teeγ-anuw
p2	teeγ-len	teeγ-aγen	teeγ-an(en)
p3	teeγ-lanəl	teeγ-aγanəl	teeγ-an(an)əl

Table 13.14   Determinate conjugation preterite forms: *xanli-* **'causes to adhere',** *miɣ-* **'gives (away)'**

	Singular Definite object	Dual Definite object	Plural Definite object
s1	xanlə-sləm	xanlə-saɣəm	xanlə-sanəm
s2	xanlə-slən	xanlə-saɣən	xanlə-san(ən)
s3	xanlə-ste	xanlə-saɣe	xanlə-sane
d1	xanlə-slamen	xanlə-saɣmen	xanlə-sanmen
d2	xanlə-slen	xanlə-saɣen	xanlə-san(en)
d3	xanlə-sten	xanlə-saɣen	xanlə-sanen
p1	xanlə-sluw	xanlə-saɣuw	xanlə-sanuw
p2	xanlə-slen	xanlə-saɣen	xanlə-san(en)
p3	xanlə-sanəl	xanlə-saɣanəl	xanlə-san(an)əl
s1	mi-sləm	mi-saɣəm	mi-sanəm
s2	mi-slən	mi-saɣən	mi-san(ən)
s3	mi-ste	mi-saɣe	mi-sane
d1	mi-slamen	mi-saɣmen	mi-sanmen
d2	mi-slen	mi-saɣen	mi-san(en)
d3	mi-sten	mi-saɣen	mi-sanen
p1	mi-sluw	mi-saɣuw	mi-sanuw
p2	mi-slen	mi-saɣen	mi-san(en)
p3	mi-sanəl	mi-saɣanəl	mi-san(an)əl

first- and second-person subjects, a singular definite object is generally indicated by the element *-l-*, which is of uncertain origin; in analogous forms with third-person subject-marking, a singular definite object is indicated by *-t-*, which descends from either pU *se, a personal, or pU *tä, a demonstrative, pronoun. Duality of the definite object is encoded by *-(j)aɣ-* (< pU *-ka-/kä-), and plurality by *-(j)an-* (< pU *-n*).

To the right of the element which encodes the number of the definite object come the (subject) person suffixes. Some of these – those of pronominal origin – are identical to those found in the indeterminate conjugation. Syncretisms, especially among second-person forms, are common here as well. Throughout the definite conjugation, third-person plural subject is encoded by the historically obscure suffix *-anəl*.

Passive

Forms of the passive conjugation are all built to a stem formed with the suffix *-(a)we-*, which continues a proto-Uralic reflexive-passive derivational suffix *=w. The person encoded in passive forms is the experiencer; there is no direct object and *a fortiori* no need to distinguish definite from indefinite objects. Passive forms may be built to both transitive and intransitive verbs.

Table 13.15   Conditional (present): *waari-* **'makes',** *liɣ-* **'hits by throwing, shoots (dead)'**

	Singular Definite object	Dual Definite object	Plural Definite object
s1	waar-nuwləm	waar-nuwaɣəm	waar-nuwanəm
s2	waar-nuwlən	waar-nuwaɣən	waar-nuwan(en)
s3	waar-nuwte	waar-nuwaɣe	waar-nuwane
d1	waar-nuwlamen	waar-nuwaɣamen	waar-nuwanamen
d2	waar-nuwlen	waar-nuwaɣen	waar-nuwan(en)
d3	waar-nuwten	waar-nuwaɣen	waar-nuwanen
p1	waar-nuwluw	waar-nuwaɣuw	waar-nuwanuw
p2	waar-nuwlen	waar-nuwaɣen	waar-nuwan(en)
p3	waar-nuwanəl	waar-nuwaɣanəl	waar-nuwanəl
s1	li-nuwləm	li-nuwaɣəm	lí-nuwanəm
s2	li-nuwlən	li-nuwaɣən	li-nuwan(en)
s3	li-nuwte	li-nuwaɣe	li-nuwane
d1	li-nuwlamen	li-nuwaɣamen	li-nuwanamen
d2	li-nuwlen	li-nuwaɣen	li-nuwan(en)
d3	li-nuwten	li-nuwaɣen	li-nuwanen
p1	li-nuwluw	li-nuwaɣuw	li-nuwanuw
p2	li-nuwlen	li-nuwaɣen	li-nuwan(en)
p3	li-nuwanəl	li-nuwaɣanəl	li-nuwanəl

In the *Present conditional* the *w*'s of the conditional and the passive suffixes merge (*-nuw-w-* > *-nuw-*).

Table 13.16   Imperatives: *toti-* **'takes away, brings',** *teeɣ-* **'eats (up)'**

	Singular Definite object	Dual Definite object	Plural Definite object
s2	tot-eln	tot-eɣən	tot-en
d2	tot-elen	tot-eɣen	tot-en
p2	tot-elen	tot-eɣen	tot-en
s2	taaj-eln	taaj-eɣən	taaj-en
d2	taaj-elen	taaj-eɣen	taaj-en
p2	taaj-elen	taaj-eɣen	taaj-en

Imperative. The *imperative passive* can be formed periphrastically: *(w)os* 'let!' + the indicative present passive – e.g. *naŋ wos alawen* 'may you be killed' (more literally: 'let + you.are.killed'), *taw wos alawe* 'may (s)he be killed' (more literally: 'let + [s]he.is.killed').

Table 13.17   Indicative passive, present tense: *keeti-* **'sends (away)',** *joxti-* **'arrives',** *waaγ-* **'knows'**

	keeti- 'sends (away)'	*joxti-* 'arrives'	*waaγ-* 'knows'
s1	keet-awem	joxt-awem	waa-wem
s2	keet-awen	joxt-awen	waa-wen
s3	keet-awe	joxt-awe	waa-we
d1	keet-awemen	joxt-awemen	waa-wemen
d2	keet-awen	joxt-awen	waa-wen
d3	keet-aweγ	joxt-aweγ	waa-weγ
p1	keet-awew	joxt-awew	waa-wew
p2	keet-awen	joxt-awen	waa-wen
p3	keet-awet	joxt-awet	waa-wet

Table 13.18   Indicative passive, preterite tense: *toti-* **'takes away, brings',** *alisʲli-* **'kills (game)',** *miγ-* **'gives'**

	toti- 'takes away, brings'	*alisʲli-* 'kills (game)'	*miγ-* 'gives'
s1	tot-wesəm	alisʲl-awesəm	maj-wesəm
s2	tot-wesən	alisʲl-awesən	maj-wesən
s3	tot-wes	alisʲl-awes	maj-wes
d1	tot-wesamen	alisʲl-awesamen	maj-wesamen
d2	tot-wesen	alisʲl-awesen	maj-wesen
d3	tot-wesiγ	alisʲl-awesiγ	maj-wesiγ
p1	tot-wesuw	alisʲl-awesuw	maj-wesuw
p2	tot-wesen	alisʲl-awesen	maj-wesen
p3	tot-wesət	alisʲl-awesət	maj-wesət

Occasionally simple forms in the second person singular are also found, e.g.

s2   miγ-wen   liγ-wen   wiγ-wen   teγ-wen   waaγ-wen

Narrative
Narrative verb forms express events not eyewitnessed by the speaker. Translations include 'allegedly', 'they say', 'it seems'.

The *indicative present* is built with personal suffixes from the continuous/non-perfective participle. Its suffix is *-ne-* (< pFU *-n, which formed nouns from verbs; cf. pp. 414–15). In transitive verbs, the active/passive opposition is neutralized: *tot-ne-m* can be either 'allegedly I bring' or 'allegedly I am brought/to me is brought'. The categories of the definite object can also be

Table 13.19   Present conditional, passive: *xaⁿⁱisⁱti-* **'teaches',** *miɣ-* **'gives'**

	xaⁿⁱisⁱti- 'teaches'	*miɣ-* 'gives'
s1	xaⁿⁱisⁱta-nuwem	miɣ-nuwem
s2	xaⁿⁱisⁱta-nuwen	miɣ-nuwen
s3	xaⁿⁱisⁱta-nuwe	miɣ-nuwe
d1	xaⁿⁱisⁱta-nuwemen	miɣ-nuwemen
d2	xaⁿⁱisⁱta-nuwen	miɣ-nuwen
d3	xaⁿⁱisⁱta-nuweɣ	miɣ-nuweɣ
p1	xaⁿⁱisⁱta-nuwew	miɣ-nuwew
p2	xaⁿⁱisⁱta-nuwen	miɣ-nuwen
p3	xaⁿⁱisⁱta-nuwet	miɣ-nuwet

Table 13.20   Indicative present, narrative form: *porɣi-* **'jumps',** *toti-* **'brings'**

			(Definite) sO	*(Definite) dO*	*(Definite) pO*
s1	porɣə-nem	tot-nem	tot-neləm	tot-neɣəm	tot-nenəm
s2	porɣə-nen	tot-nen	tot-nelən	tot-neɣən	tot-nen(ən)
s3	porɣə-nete	tot-nete	tot-nete	tot-neɣe	tot-nene
d1	porɣə-nemen	tot-nemen	tot-nelamen	tot-neɣamen	tot-nenamen
d2	porɣə-nen	tot-nen	tot-nelen	tot-neɣen	tot-nenen
d3	porɣə-neten	tot-neten	tot-neten	tot-neɣen	tot-nenen
p1	porɣə-new	tot-new	tot-neluw	tot-neɣuw	tot-nenuw
p2	porɣə-nen	tot-nen	tot-nelen	tot-neɣənen	tot-nenen
p3	porɣə-nenəl	tot-nenəl	tot-nenəl	tot-neɣanəl	tot-nen(an)əl

expressed, as in *tot-ne-l-əm* 'I bring him/her/it, allegedly'.

In the *preterite narrative*, the opposition of voice is not neutralized. The *active* indicative preterite is built with personal suffixes from the perfective participle. Its suffix is *-m-* (< pFU *=m, which formed nouns from verbs; cf. p. 415). There can be epenthesis, to the left of this suffix, of an *ə*, *u*, or *a*.

With person suffixes, the number of a definite direct object may also be expressed, as in the present.

The *passive* indicative narrative is formed with personal suffixes from the gerund, whose suffix is *-ima-* (cf. p. 415).

s1	tot-imam	'I was brought, allegedly'
s2	tot-iman	
s3	tot-ima	

d1	tot-imamen	
d2	tot-iman	
d3	tot-imaɣ	
p1	tot-imaw	
p2	tot-iman	
p3	tot-imat	

Table 13.21   Indicative preterite, narrative form: *ooli-* **'is, lives',** *ali-* **'kills'**

	ooli- 'is, lives'	*ali-* 'kills'
s1	ool-məm	ala-məm
s2	ool-mən	ala-mən
s3	ool-um	ala-m
d1	ool-mumen	ala-mamen
d2	ool-men	ala-men
d3	ool-miɣ	ala-miɣ
p1	ool-muw	ala-muw
p2	ool-men	ala-men
p3	ool-mət	ala-mət

Table 13.22   Person suffixes, narrative form: *toti-* **'brings'**

	sO	dO	pO
s1	tot-amləm	tot-maɣəm	tot-manəm
s2	tot-amlən	tot-maɣən	tot-manən
s3	tot-am(t)e	tot-maɣe	tot-mane
d1	tot-amlamen	tot-maɣamen	tot-manamen
d2	tot-amlen	tot-maɣen	tot-manen
d3	tot-am(t)en	tot-maɣen	tot-manen
p1	tot-amluw	tot-maɣuw	tot-manuw
p2	tot-amlen	tot-maɣen	tot-manen
p3	tot-amanəl	tot-maɣanəl	tot-man(an)əl

Precative

Although some grammars (e.g. Kálmán 1976: 56 61) treat the precative as a mood, it is more accurate, on formal grounds, to distinguish these interesting, affect-laden verb forms from the true moods (cf. Rombandeeva 1973: 176–8). Formally, the precative suffixes lie somewhere between inflection and derivation; they are coloured by positive affect (*-ke-*, *-kʷe-*; dialectally *-tʲe-*; e.g. *xaajtikʷe* '(s)he/it is running, the dear') or pity (*-risʲ-*). To the right of these suffixes may occur temporal or modal suffixes, or both; the passive occurs, as well (Honti 1977: 414–6).

Indicative present. Example: *xaajti-* 'runs'.

s1	xaajtikem	xaajtiris^jəm
s2	xaajtiken	xaajtiris^jən
s3	xaajtik^we	xaajtiris^j
d1	xaajtikemen	xaajtiris^jəmen
d2	xaajtiken	xaajtiris^jen
d3	xaajtikew	xaajtiris^jiγ
p1	xaajtikew	xaajtiris^juw
p2	xaajtiken	xaajtiris^jen
p3	xaajtiket	xaajtiris^jət

Further examples: *teeγt^jem* 'I, cute little thing, am eating'; *sunsiγt^jewes-men* 'we two dearies are being looked at'; *sunsiris^jlasəm* 'I looked around, poor me'; *sunsiγris^jawem* 'I, miserable thing, am being looked at'; *woje-ris^jlen* 'catch it, you wretch!'.

Verb Formation

Verbs may be formed from verbs or from nominals (Rombandeeva 1973: 148–76; Kálmán 1976: 55–6).

Table 13.23   Examples of deverbal verb derivation

Suffix	Function	Origin	Example	Gloss
=axt-	reflexive	< pFU *=kt	paajt=axti-	cooks (intr)
=xat-	reflexive	< pFU *=kt	lowt=xati-	washes (refl)
=aj-	momentaneous	< pFU *=k	por=aji-	flashes
=iγl(aal)-	frequentative		suns=iγl(aal)i-	looks around
=iγt-	frequentative		xaajt=iγti-	runs around
=l-	frequentative	< pFU *=l	peelə=li-	pokes at
	causative		xan=li-	causes X to adhere
=laal-	frequentative		laawi=laali-	keeps saying
=lt-	inchoative		jeek^wə=lti-	begins to dance
	causative		ojə=lti-	puts to sleep
	frequentative		laawə=lti-	mentions
=ltaxt-	reflexive/inchoative		rooŋxa=ltaxti-	(suddenly) shouts
=m-	momentaneous	< pFU *=m	muur=mi-	sinks
=mt-	momentaneous		puwə=mti-	seizes
=ml-	inchoative		xaajtə=mli-	starts running
=nt-	frequentative	< pFU *=nt	mina=nti-	goes along
=p-	momentaneous	< pFU *=pp	s^jalta=pi-	pops in
=s-	frequentative	< pFU *=s^j	jala=si-	goes around
=t-	causative	< pFU *=tt	jooŋx=ti-	turns (tr)

Table 13.24   Examples of denominal verb derivation

Suffix	Function	Example	Gloss
=m-	becomes X	janiɣmi-	grows (*janiɣ* big)
		kantmi-	grows angry (*kant* anger)
=t-	provides with X	ooxti-	tars (*oo(ŋ)x* resin, tar)
=l-	becomes X	sakʷali-	breaks (intr; *sakʷ* small piece)
		aaɣəmli-	becomes ill (*aaɣəm* sickness, pain)
	provides with X	xoramli-	decorates (*xoram* decoration)
		tinʲsʲaŋli-	lassoos
=ltt-	transitive act	saməltti-	notices (*sam* eye)
=j-	intransitive act	uulm=aji	dreams (*uuləm* dream)
		namaji-	names; offers (to gods) (*nam* name)
=laxt-	reciprocity	pasʲalaxti-	greets (*pasʲ* 'reciprocally')
		rumalaxti-	become friends (*ruma* friend)

Besides the more common derivational suffixes and suffix-sequences (such as *=iɣlaal-*) there are also numerous nonce-combinations, e.g. *jooŋxiɣpapti-* 'turns on heel', *jooŋxataxtiɣli-* 'turns round and round (intr)', *juuntsaxti-*, *noməlmati-* 'thinks, ponders', *teesʲənti-* 'keeps eating', etc.

Nominals

Nouns
The base form of nouns is the nominative singular. This can end in a consonant or a vowel; among the latter group, nouns ending in *i* form a special subclass. There is no grammatical gender.

Absolute declension. Three numbers are distinguished: singular, dual, and plural (Balandin–Vaxruševa 1957: 50–72; Rombandeeva 1973: 38–64; Kálmán 1976: 41–7).

Singular is unmarked. The suffix of the dual is -ɣ (< pU *-kA); that of the plural is *-t* (< pU *-t). Examples with a vowel-final stem: *eekʷaɣ* 'two women', *eekʷat* 'women'. Stems in final *i* show a hiatus-blocking *j* in the dual: *aaɣi* 'girl', *aaɣijiɣ* 'two girls'. Consonant-final stems are extended, e.g. *luw* 'horse', *luwiɣ* 'two horses', *luwət* 'horses'. Syncopating stems lose their stem-internal vowel, e.g. *sʲaxəl* 'pile, heap', *sʲaxliɣ* 'two heaps', *sʲaxlət* 'heaps'. In northern dialects, reduplicated forms are also attested.

Northern Mansi noun declension distinguishes six cases:

Nominative	-∅		(= Accusative, Genitive)
Locative	-(ə)t	< pFU *-ttA	
Lative	-(ə)n	< pUg *-nä-k/j	
Elative/ablative	-nəl	< pUg *-nä-l	
Instrumental	-(ə)l/-təl	< pUg *-l	
Translative/essive	-iɣ	< pU *-kA	

The translative/essive is not frequently used in the dual and plural. The -*t*- of the instrumental is the result of *fausse coupe* in the plural. Certain northern dialects also have a vocative in -*aa* (Liimola 1963: 24–131; Riese 1992: 379–88).

Possessive declension. Suffixes express the person and number of the possessor, and the number of the possession; see Table 13.26.

Consonant-final stems take the variants with initial *a* (or *e*); *i*-final stems take the *j*-initial variants, and stems ending in other vowels take the consonant-initial variants.

Personal suffixes precede case suffixes (example: *puut* 'pot'):

N/A/G	Gloss	Loc	Lat	Ela/Abl	Ins
puutəm	my pot	puutəmt	puutəmn	puutəmnəl	puutəmtəl
puutaɣəm	my 2 pots	puutaɣəmt	puutaɣəmn	puutaɣəmnəl	puutaɣəmtəl
puutanəm	my 3+ pots	puutanəmt	puutanəmn	puutanəmnəl	puutanəmtəl

Table 13.25   Noun declension: *ala* 'roof', *aawi* 'door', *puut* 'pot', *paart* 'board', *laaɣəl* 'foot, leg'

	ala 'roof'	*aawi* 'door'	*puut* 'pot'	*paart* 'board'	*laaɣəl* 'foot, leg'
Singular					
N/A/G	ala	aawi	puut	paart	laaɣəl
Loc	alat	aawit	puutt	paartət	laaɣəlt
Lat	alan	aawin	puutn	paartən	laaɣəln
Ela/Abl	alanəl	aawinəl	puutnəl	paartnəl	laaɣəlnəl
Ins	alal	aawil	puutəl	paartəl	laaɣləl
Trans/Ess	alaɣ	aawijiɣ	puutiɣ	paartiɣ	laaɣliɣ
Dual					
N/A/G	alaɣ	aawijiɣ	puutiɣ	paartiɣ	laaɣliɣ
Loc	alaɣt	aawijiɣt	puutiɣt	paartiɣt	laaɣliɣt
Lat	alaɣn	aawijiɣn	puutiɣn	paartiɣn	laaɣliɣn
Ela/Abl	alaɣnəl	aawijiɣnəl	puutiɣnəl	paartiɣnəl	laaɣliɣnəl
Ins	alaɣtəl	aawijiɣtəl	puutiɣtəl	paartiɣtəl	laaɣliɣtəl
Trans/Ess	—	—	—	—	—
Plural					
N/A/G	alat	aawit	puutət	paartət	laaɣlət
Loc	alatt	aawitt	puutətt	paartətt	laaɣlətt
Lat	alatn	aawitn	puutətn	paartətn	laaɣlətn
Ela/Abl	alatnəl	aawitnəl	puutətnəl	paartətnəl	laaɣlətnəl
Ins	alatəl	aawitəl	puutətəl	paartətəl	laaɣlətəl
Trans/Ess	—	—	—	—	—

Table 13.26 Possessive declension

	Possession in singular	Possession in dual	Possession in plural
s1	-(ə)m	-([j]a)ɣəm	-([j]a)nəm
s2	-(ə)n	-([j]a)ɣən	-([j]a)n
s3	-(t)e	-([j]a)ɣe	-([j]a)ne
d1	-men	-([j]a)ɣamen	-([j]a)namen
d2	-(e)n	-([j]a)ɣen	-([j]a)nen
d3	-(t)en	-([j]a)ɣen	-([j]a)nen
p1	-([j]u)w	-([j]a)ɣuw	-([j]a)nuw
p2	-(e)n	-([j]a)ɣen	-([j]a)nen
p3	-([j]a)nəl	-([j]a)ɣanəl	-([j]a)n(an)əl

Table 13.27 Possessive declension stem variants: *ula* 'bow', *aaɣi* 'girl'

	Possession in			Possession in		
	Singular	Dual	Plural	Singular	Dual	Plural
s1	ulam	ulaɣəm	ulanəm	aaɣim	aaɣijaɣəm	aaɣijanəm
s2	ulan	ulaɣən	ulanən	aaɣin	aaɣijaɣən	aaɣijanən
s3	ulate	ulaɣe	ulane	aaɣite	aaɣijaɣe	aaɣijane
d1	ulamen	ulaɣamen	ulanamen	aaɣimen	aaɣijaɣamen	aaɣijanamen
d2	ulan	ulaɣen	ulanen	aaɣin	aaɣijaɣen	aaɣijanen
d3	ulaten	ulaɣen	ulanen	aaɣiten	aaɣijaɣen	aaɣijanen
p1	ulaw	ulaɣuw	ulanuw	aaɣijuw	aaɣijaɣuw	aaɣijanuw
p2	ulan	ulaɣen	ulanen	aaɣin	aaɣijaɣen	aaɣijanen
p3	ulanəl	ulaɣanəl	ulan(an)əl	aaɣijanəl	aaɣijaɣanəl	aaɣijan(an)əl

In general, the personal suffixes are pronominal in origin; the dual and plural suffixes are also of FU or U origin (*-m -n -te* < pU *-me, *-te, *-se; dual -ɣ- < pU *-kA-, etc.).

The personal suffixes in the noun are similar to those of the definite conjugation of the verb; they are of a common origin (cf. p. 402; Liimola 1963: 202–41).

Adjectives
Adjectival declension. In attributive position, adjectives remain uninflected. In predicative position, adjectives agree with their subject in number, and thus take dual and plural suffixes, e.g. *towl-aɣ-əm osʲsʲa-ɣ* WING-dual-s1 THIN-dual 'my (two) wings are thin', *laaɣl-an-əm xosa-t* LEG-plur-s1 LONG-plur 'my legs are long'. The translative case is frequent, e.g. *xoopsim mosəŋ-iɣ jeemtəs* 'my lung became ill' (*mosəŋ* ill; Rombandeeva 1973: 82).

Comparative and superlative. There is a comparative suffix *-nuw*, e.g. *ta* *xum karəs-nuw* 'that man is taller', but in full-blown comparisons the plain form is at least as usual. The bested member of the comparison is then in the ablative, e.g. *naŋ aasʲ-əm-nəl janiɣ* PRO.s2 FATHER-s1-abl BIG 'you are bigger than my father' (cf. Kálmán 1976: 48). The superlative is rendered by particles, e.g. *am sʲar karəs* s1.PRO PARTIC TALL 'I am the tallest'.

Numerals
Cardinal numerals are as follows:

1	akʷ(a)	20	xus
2	kit(iɣ)	21	waat nopəl akʷa
3	xuurəm	30	waat
4	nʲila	40	naliman
5	at	50	atpan
6	xoot	60	xootpan
7	saat	70	saatlow
8	nʲololow	80	nʲolsaat
9	ontolow	90	ontərsaat
10	low	100	(janiɣ) saat
11	akʷxujplow	1000	sootər

The non-primary numerals are built either by compounding, e.g. '95' is *ontərsaat at*, '991' is *ontolowsaat ontərsaat akʷa*, or by 'adding' the smaller number to the larger. The larger numeral is then put into some form of lative, either the lative case, e.g. *waat-n akʷa* THIRTY-lat ONE '21 (i.e., one towards thirty)' or by means of the postposition *nopəl* 'towards', e.g. *naliman nopəl akʷa* FORTY TOWARDS ONE '31 (i.e. one towards thirty). Numerals occur most frequently in the nominative, translative, and instrumental (Rombandeeva 1973: 91–8; Kálmán 1976: 48–9). The numerals for 1–6, 10, 20, and 100 are FU in origin; '7', '8', and '1,000' date from the Ugric period, as do some of the now synchronically opaque decades.

Ordinal numerals. 'First' is *oowəl*, 'second' is *moot* or *kit=it*. All other ordinals are formed, like *kit=it*, from the corresponding cardinal with the suffix *=it*, e.g. *xuurm=it* 'third', *saat=it* 'seventh', *low=it* 'tenth'.

Pronouns
Table 13.28 attempts to capture the formal system of Mansi *personal pronouns* (Com = comitative).

There is also an intensivizing clitic, *-ki* (*-tʲi*), which is particular to the personal pronouns, e.g. *amki* 'I myself', *neenki* 'you two yourselves' (Rombandeeva 1973: 103–5).

The intensive forms of the personal pronouns are used as *reflexive pronouns*, e.g. accusative *amkinaam* 'myself', *takʷinaate* 'him/herself', dative *amki(naa)mn* 'to myself', *takʷi(naa)ten* 'to him/herself'. For the declension of these forms see Rombandeeva 1973: 103–4.

Table 13.28   Mansi personal pronouns

	Person First	Second	Third
Nom	am	naŋ	taw
Acc	aanəm	naŋən	tawe
Dat	aanəmn	naŋənn	tawen
Abl	aanəmnəl	naŋənnəl	tawenəl
Com	aanəmtəl	naŋəntəl	tawetəl
Dual			
Nom	meen	neen	teen
Acc	meen(a)men	neenan	teen(a)ten
Dat	meen(a)menn	neenann	teen(a)tenn
Abl	meen(a)mennəl	neenanənnəl	teen(a)tennəl
Com	meen(a)mentəl	neenantəl	teen(a)tentəl
Plural			
Nom	maan	naan	taan
Acc	maana(nu)w	naanan(en)	taanan(an)əl
Dat	maana(nu)wn	naanann	taanan(an)əln
Abl	maana(nu)wnəl	naanan(ən)nəl	taanan(an)əlnəl
Com	maana(nu)wtəl	naanan(ən)təl	taanan(an)əltəl

Demonstrative pronouns may be subdivided into proximal and distal sets, e.g. *tiji* 'this', *ta(ji)* 'that'; *akʷti* 'this same (one)', *akʷta* 'that same (one)'; *tamlʲe*, *tixurip* 'this kind of', *taxurip* 'that kind of' (Kámán 1976: 51).

Interrogative and relative pronouns may distinguish animate from inanimate, e.g. *xooŋxa* 'who?', *manər* 'what?' Others include *mana(x)* 'what kind of?', *mansaawit* 'how many?'. They decline like nouns, *xooŋxa-təl* 'with whom?', *manər-nəl* 'from what?' (Rombandeeeva 1973: 107–8; Kálmán 1976: 51). The interrogative pronouns are also used as *relative pronouns*.

Indefinite and negative pronouns include forms such as *xootpa* 'someone', *neemxootpa* 'no one', *xotixootpa* 'no matter who'; *matər* 'something', *neematər* 'nothing', *matərsirmat* 'some kind of', *neematərsir* 'of no kind', *mataxkem* 'somewhat'.

Nominal Formation
Examples of denominal derivation of nominals:

Noun-forming suffixes:

=it	abstracts	< pFU *=tt	xos=it	length
=k(ʷ)e	diminutive/affectionate	< pU *=kk	piγ=kʷe	little boy
=risʲ	diminutive/pejorative		piγ=risʲ	little boy

Certain roots occur so frequently as the second member of compounds that they begin to take on derivational status, e.g. *kol* 'house; place' in *pumkol* 'grassland' (*pum* grass), *ut* 'thing' in *teenut* 'food' (*teen* eating), *sak^w* 'small piece' in *jiwsak^w* 'splinter' (*jiw* tree, wood).

Adjective-forming suffixes:

=i	position	< pU *=j	*num=i*	upper
			jol=i	lower
=kapaj	augmentative	*kapaj* 'giant'	*mil=kapaj*	very deep
=k^we	diminutive	< pU *=kk	*ł'uuł'=k^we*	pretty bad
=tal	privative	< pFU =pt=	*waɣ=tal*	weak (waɣ strength)
			pał'=tal	deaf (*pał'* ear)
=ŋ	provided with X	< pU *=ŋ	*xuul=ŋ*	rich in fish
			wit=əŋ	wet, watery
=p(a)	bahuvrhi compounds	< pU *=p	*wit=əp*	-watered
			xuul=pa	-fished

Numeral-forming suffix:

| =it | ordinals | < ? pU *=mt | *n'il=it* | fourth |

Examples of deverbal derivation of nominals:

=m	abstract	= perf. participle	*mat=əm*	old age (*mat-* ages)
=p	*nomen instrumenti*	< pU *=p	*saaɣra=p*	axe (*saaɣri-* cuts)
=t	*nomen resultatis*	< pU *=tt	*nom=t*	thought (*nomi-* thinks)
=tal	privative	< pFU *=pt=	*joxt=tal*	inaccessible (*joxt-* arrives)

Verbal Nouns
Infinitive, participle, and gerund are distinguished in Mansi (Rombandeeva 1973: 145–7; Kálmán 1976: 62).

Infinitive
The suffix is *-(u/a)ŋk^we*. The initial vowel is *u* with verbs whose stem has an odd number of syllables, *a* with verbs whose stem has an even number of syllables. The consonant-initial variant, *-ŋk^we*, occurs only with the six unstable stems (see Table 13.6). Examples: *laaw-uŋk^we* 'to say', *potərt-aŋk^we* 'to speak', *tee-ŋk^we* 'to eat'.

Participles
The present (imperfective) participle suffix is *-ne* (< pU derivational *=n + ?*-k~*-j lative; the participial role is a Mansi innovation (Sz. Kispál 1966: 68,

185). This suffix attaches to the consonant-stem of all verbs save the unstable six, e.g. *laaw-ne* 'saying', *potərt-ne* 'speaking', *tee-ne* 'eating'. These forms are also used as nouns denoting actions, e.g. *laaw-ne* 'a(n instance of) saying'.

With personal suffixes, *-ne* forms the present narrative (see p. 406).

The older imperfective participle, built with =*i* (< pFU *=j or *=k, which made deverbal nouns, Sz. Kispál 1966: 28–9), now serves as the third-person singular ending in the finite paradigm (*laawi* '(s)he says'). In folkloristic texts, however, it may still be found in its original participial function, e.g. *teeli* '(child-)bearing'.

The privative suffix =*tal* may be thought of as a kind of negative participle, e.g. *sam+pos joxt=tal xɔsa woolj* EYE+LIGHT ARRIVE=priv LONG RIVER-STRETCH 'stretch of a river longer than the eye can see'.

The *perfective participle* suffix is *-m*, preceded, except when added to the six unstable stems, by one of the vowels *i ~ a ~ ə*, e.g. *laaw-əm* 'said', *potərt-am* 'spoken', *waar-im* 'made', *tee-m* 'eaten'. According to Sz. Kispál (1966: 193), this suffix dates back to pU *=m, which formed nominals from verbs.

With personal suffixes, *-m* forms the preterite narrative active (see p. 407).

The perfective participle can syncretize with variants of the gerund (Sz. Kispál 1966: 337).

Gerund

The suffix is *-im(a)* (< *-j + *-m, a combination of deverbal noun-forming suffixes, plus a lative ?*-k (cf. Sz. Kispál 1966: 336–7)). Examples: *juuns-im(a)* 'while sewing', *potərt-im(a)* 'while speaking', *taaj-im* 'while eating'.

With personal suffixes, *-im(a)* forms the preterite narrative passive (see p. 407).

Adverbs

This class may be defined to include forms built from interrogative and demonstrative stems, both productive and non-productive, by means of the addition of case and other suffixes. Meanings range from space through time and other abstracts (Rombandeeva 1973: 186–92; Kálmán 1976: 52). A few examples must suffice here.

Place: *xoot* 'where?', *xotəl* 'whence?', *xottalʲ* 'whither?', *tit* 'here', *tot* 'there', *tiɣl* 'hence', *tuwl* 'thence', *tiɣ(lʲe)* 'hither', *tuw(lʲe)* 'thither'.

Time: *xunʲ* 'when?', *tuwl* 'then', *akʷmateert(n)* 'once', *moolal* 'recently', *anʲ* 'now', *xoli* 'in the morning', *eetʲi* 'at night', *teeli* 'in winter'.

Manner: *xumus* 'how?', *tox* 'like that, thus', *maanʲsʲiŋisʲ* 'in Mansi', *molʲax* 'quickly', *jorəl* 'very; powerfully', *taakəsʲ* 'very'.

Cause: *manriɣ* 'why?'.

State: *xomi* 'prone', *sisi* 'supine'.

Quantitative: *manax* 'how many times?', *sʲos* '-fold' (*xuurəm sʲos* 'three times').

Preverbs

These were originally independent, concrete-spatial, adverbs. They gradually grew together with their verbs, first modifying them semantically, then aspectually; some among them have now become pure perfectivizers. The most frequent preverbs are: *xot* (perfectivizer), *eel* 'away', *jol* 'down', *juw* 'in/back', *k(ʷ)on* 'out', *lakʷa* 'asunder', *lap* 'down/away, shut', *nal* 'down/riverward', *no(ŋ)x* 'up', *paaɣ* 'out/riverward', *pal* 'apart'. (Kálmán 1976: 53–4.)

Postpositions

Some were originally (spatial) nouns with defective case paradigms. All Mansi postpositions follow the noun in the nominative. Among the most frequent are: *xalt* 'in between', *xalnəl* 'from between', *xaln* 'to between', *xoojtəl* 'in the manner of', *xolʲt* 'as', *jot* 'with', *kiwərn* 'into', *ľalʲt* 'against', *maaɣəs* 'because of', *muus* 'as far as', *muwəl, ontsəl* 'around', *nupəl* 'towards', *sist* 'behind', *sisnəl* 'from behind', *sisiɣ* 'to behind', *tarməl* 'on', *taara* 'through', *uultta* 'across'.

Fitted with personal suffixes, postpositions function as adverbial complements, e.g. *jotəm* 'with me' (Rombandeeva 1973: 193–5; Kálmán 1976: 54).

Particles

These express the speaker's attitude towards the utterance (Rombandeeva 1973: 196–8; Kálmán 1976: 53). Their chief functional categories are:

- interrogative: *-a* (signals yes/no questions); *aman* 'or, whether';
- assent and denial: *soolʲ* 'yes, indeed'; *atxunʲ* 'no way!';
- uncertainty: *tel* 'probably'; *jar* 'as if'; *tup* 'hardly'; *eerəŋ* 'perhaps';
- negation, prohibition: *aatʲi* 'no' *at* 'not'; *ul* 'don't!';
- command: *(w)os* 'let!';
- hypothesis: *ke, pəl* 'if'.

Some particles have become filler-elements without lexical meaning: *ti, ta, i, ja*, etc.

Conjunctions

The conjunctions tie together sentences and sentence-parts. They originate in part from independent words, in part from adverbs (Rombandeeva 1973: 198–200). The most frequent conjunctions are *os* 'and/also', *i* 'and', *xunʲ* 'when', *ke* 'if', *akʷtup* 'as if', *kos* 'although'.

Interjections

Alongside the greeting *pasʲa* 'hi' these include *kaaj* 'oh!', *axaa* 'aha', *ja ti* 'there you are!', *ananaa* 'alas!', *a-a* 'now you're talking'.

Syntax

The Simple Sentence

Predicative Construction: Subject–Predicate
The *subject* of a sentence is generally a noun, but it can also be another type of nominal, including infinitives and participles. There is no article. Definiteness and its opposite is implicit in the context, thus *nee juunt-i* out of context can be 'a woman is sewing' or 'the woman is sewing'. The suffix of the third person singular can serve to mark for definiteness, however: *nee-te juunt-i* 'the/his woman is sewing', *woot-e xoot* WIND-s3 WHERE 'where is the wind?', *eekʷa-te laaw-i* 'the woman says' (Kálmán 1976: 65; Rombandeeva 1979: 104–11).

Predicate: the most common type is the verbal predicate, e.g. *xootal kaatkʷe witkʷet joŋy-i* SUN BEAM WATER.dimin.loc PLAY-s3 'the sunbeam is playing on the water', but nominal predicates are also common (as in Hungarian), e.g. *nʲool-əm peelp* NOSE-s1 POINTED 'my nose is pointed'. Zero copula is used in all three persons (unlike Hungarian), e.g. *naŋ sʲar karəs* PRO.s2 SUPERL TALL 'you are the tallest' (Kálmán 1976: 65; Rombandeeva 1979: 9, 32–6, 87–98).

Direct Object Constructions
The *direct object* stands in the nominative if a noun, in the accusative if a pronoun, e.g. *xum xaap waar-i* MAN BOAT MAKE-s3 'the man is making a boat', *xaap wit-n jol+xarti-te* BOAT WATER-lat DOWN+DRAG-s3sO '(s)he drags the boat down to the water', *taw aanəm waay-te* PRO.s3 PRO.s1.acc see-s3sO '(s)he sees me'. Definiteness of the object may be implicit in the context, or may be encoded by a personal suffix on the noun and/or definite endings on the verb, e.g. *puki-te lap+juunt-əs-te* STOMACH-s3 COVERB+SEW-past-s3sO '(s)he sewed his/her/its stomach shut', *saali+ur=ne xum sʲar jomas saali-jay-e sun-n keer-s-ay-e* REINDEER WATCHES=pres.part MAN SUPERL GOOD REINDEER-dual-s3 SLEDGE-lat HARNESS-past-dO-s3DEF 'the reindeer herder harnessed his two best reindeer to the sledge'. Objects of first and second person can be definite, as well, e.g. *manriy at wiy-lan* 'why don't you take (me) away?', *eerapti-lam* 'I love (you)'.

Adverbials
Adverbial complements may consist of adverbs, nominals with case suffixes or postpositions, or verbal nouns, e.g. *aas waata-t lʲuulʲeyəm* 'I stand on the bank of the Ob'', *aayit eeryim jaleyət* 'the girls go a-singing'.
The following is a summary of the adverbial functions of the cases:
The *nominative* (-∅) expresses temporal relations, e.g. *eet-∅ xuml-awe-∅* NIGHT LIGHTNING-pass-s3 'there is lightning in the night'.
The *locative* (-t) refers to stationary location, e.g. *witkasʲ mil aayər-t ooli*

'the water-monster lives in a deep whirlpool' or to time, e.g. *am ta pora-t maans^j up=tal xaajtiɣta-s-əm* PRO.s1 THAT TIME-loc UNDERPANTS=priv RUNS.AROUND-past-s1 'at that time I ran around without underpants'.

The *lative* (*-n*) refers to motion to a place, e.g. *nee kol-n s^j alt-i* WOMAN HOUSE-lat ENTERS-s3 'the woman comes into the house'; it also functions as indirect object marker, e.g. *am ti xum-n oln miɣ-əm* PRO.s1 THIS MAN-lat MONEY GIVES-s1. In passive constructions, the lative marks the agent, e.g. *woot-n tot-we-s-Ø* WIND-lat BRING-pass-past-s3 'it was carried (away) by the wind', *aamp-ən joxt-we-s-Ø* DOG-lat ARRIVE-pass-past-s3 '(s)he was approached by a dog', *neemxotjut-n at puwa-we-m, neemxotjut-n at ala-we-m* NO.ONE-lat NOT SEIZE-pass-s1 NO.ONE-lat NOT KILL-pass-s1 'no one can catch me, no one can kill me'.

The *elative/ablative* refers to motion from a place, e.g. *n^j aawram-ət woornəl xaajt-eɣ ət* CHILD-plur FOREST-ela/abl RUNS-p3 'the children run out of the forest', or from a person, e.g. *am as^j-əm-nəl neepak-əl joxt-we-s-əm* PRO.s1 FATHER-s1-ela/abl LETTER-ins ARRIVE-pass-past-s1 'I got a letter from my father'. It also has a prolative function: *am suup-əm-nəl k^w aalən* 'come out through my mouth!'

The *instrumental* refers to both means and accompaniment. Examples: *man kasaj-əl jakt-ew* 'we cut with a knife', *n^j aawram aak^w eek^w a-l uunl-i* 'the child is sitting with the grandmother'. In passive constructions the instrumental encodes the direct object of the corresponding active, cf. *neepak-əl* 'letter' in the preceding paragraph.

The *translative/essive* refers to results and states into which things change, e.g. *am aas^j-iɣ jeemt-s-əm* 'I became a father', and to goals (*manr-iɣ* 'why?').

All of the cases participate in lexicalized verb rections, e.g. the elative/ablative with *pil-* 'fears', the translative/essive with *namtal-* 'names', the instrumental with *n^j ult-* 'swears (by)'.

Attributive Constructions

Any nominal (including the participles) may stand in attributive position; it then takes no agreement suffixes, e.g. *eerɣ=əŋ maake-m-n* SONG=FUL HOMELAND-s1-lat 'into my songful homeland', *xurmit klass-ət* THREE=ord CLASS-loc 'in the third class'.

In possessive constructions the possessor is similarly unmarked. The possession, on the other hand, may be marked with the third-person singular suffix, e.g. *eeləmxolas saat as-e* HUMAN SEVEN APERTURE-s3 'the seven openings of the human (head)', *waan^j ka maan^j xaap-e* VANYKA SMALL BOAT-s3 'Vanyka's little boat'. Zero marking of both possessor and possession is also possible, at least with inanimates, e.g. *poriɣpanek^w a ta tuur waata-t iŋ ooli* FROG THAT LAKE SHORE-loc STILL EXISTS-s3 'the frog still lives on the shore of the lake', (Kálmán 1976: 66).

Habeoconstruction
Unlike most Uralic languages (but like Khanty), Mansi has a verb which
means 'has': *taw saali, aamp oon^{j}s^j-i* '(s)he has a reindeer (and) a dog';
oojka=ŋ eeka tin at oon^{j}s^j-əs-Ø HUSBAND=adj WOMAN MONEY NOT
HAS-past-s3 'the married woman had no money'.

Agreement
Subject and predicate agree in number and person: *naŋ tin^{j}s^{j}aŋ-ay-ən kol
muwəl joxt-ey* PRO.s2 LASSO-dual-s2 HOUSE AROUND ARRIVE-d3
'your two lassos reach around the house'.

Within the noun phrase, the existence of a numeral triggers the singular:
waat xum TWENTY MAN 'twenty men'; the predicate to such a noun phrase
agrees with the sense rather than the form, viz. *waat xum saayr-ey ət*
TWENTY MAN CHOPS-p3 'twenty men are chopping'. Dvandva compounds decline in the dual, and their predicates agree with them in number,
e.g. *eek^{w}a-y&oojka-y xuu tot-ey* WIFE-dual&HUSBAND-dual FISH
BRING-d3 'the married couple bring (a/some) fish'.

If the verb is in the definite conjugation, it agrees with its direct object in
number, e.g. *laayl-ay-e eelal^j nar=iyta-s-ay-e* LEG-dual-s3 FORWARD
STRETCHES-past-dual-s3 '(s)he stretched his/her legs forward',
saayrapsup-an-e ta t^{j}iwt-uŋk^{w}e pat-s-an-e AXE-plur-s3 THEN HONES-inf
BEGINS-past-plur-s3 'then (s)he began to sharpen his/her axes' (Kálmán
1976: 66–7; Rombandeeva 1979: 17–21).

Modality
Non-singular first-person indicative forms are hortative in force, e.g.
tuujtiylaxt-imen PLAYS HIDE-AND-SEEK-d1 'let's (the two of us) play
hide-and-seek!', *min-ew* GO-p1 'let's (all) go!' (Rombandeeva 1979: 24).

The narrative mood refers to activities and states recounted by others, e.g.
xaaroojka al-am-e '(s)he killed, it seems, the reindeer-stag' (Rombandeeva
1973: 137–44).

The conditional mood refers to unreality: *tot-nuw-ən* 'you might bring/you
might have brought'. With the particle *ke* it may express hypothesis, e.g.
joms^{j}ak^w ke xuuntla-nuw-əm, pussən toryamta-nuw-ləm WELL IF LISTEN-
cond-s1 ENTIRELY UNDERSTAND-cond-slDEFsg 'if I had paid attention,
I would have understood everything'. Notice the neutralization of tense: any
temporal reference must be understood from the context (Riese 1984: 87).

The affectionate/commiserative moods reflect the speaker's affective
stance towards the utterance. Used with the imperative, the commiserative has
precative undertones, e.g. *wooje-ris^j-l-en, taaje-ris^j-en* TAKE-commis-
DEFsg-s2 EAT-commis-s2 'take it and eat (you miserable wretch)!'

Negation and Prohibition
The general negative particle is *at*: *at teey-əm* 'I'm not eating'. Prohibition is expressed by *ul*: *ul eessiɣxat-ən* 'don't boast!'

Negation of existence is expressed by predicative *aatʲim*, which agrees with its subject in number: *naŋ ooma-n tit aatʲim* PRO.s2 MOTHER-s2 HERE NON.EXIST 'your mother isn't here', *nʲaawram-iɣ neemxot aatʲim-iɣ* CHILD-dual NOWHERE NON.EXIST-dual 'the two children aren't anywhere'.

There is also a negation particle which is equivalent to a sentence: *aatʲi*. This is usually followed by a negated sentence, e.g. – *naŋ xuulʲteɣ ən? – aatʲi. at xuulʲteɣ əm* ' – are you staying? – no, I'm not staying'.

Aspect
As in the other Ugric langauges, perfective aspect is expressed in Mansi by means of coverbs, e.g. *jakti-* 'cuts', *xot+jakti-* 'cuts off, cuts completely'. The development of the individual coverbs from spatial adverbs seems to have occurred independently in each Ugric language.

Constituent Order
Mansi is basically SOV. An indicative predicate normally stands at the end of the sentence, e.g. *taaliɣ &tuwiɣ sis matəm woorajanxum sawsir uuj ti pisalʲ-əl aliɣla-s-Ø* WINTER&SUMMER TIME OLD HUNTER VARIOUS ANIMAL THIS RIFLE-ins KILLS-past-s3 'winter and summer, the old hunter killed all kinds of animals with this rifle' (Kálmán 1976: 65; Rombandeeva 1979: 52–67).

Constructions Involving Verbal Nominals
Embedded in the sentence, verbal nominals often replace subordinate clauses. Verbal nominals take the same complements as finite verbs. The most important types are listed here.

Infinitive
This can replace an object-clause in an analogue to the accusative and infinitive (indirect statement) construction: *akmateertn maataaprisʲ kʷonəl kʷaal-uŋkʷe noməlmata-s-Ø* SUDDENLY MOUSE OUT GOES-inf THINKS-past-s3 'suddenly, the mouse thought he would go out'. It can also replace goal-clauses and respect-clauses, either concrete, e.g. *am xuul alisʲ-aŋkʷe mina-s-əm* PRO.s1 FISH KILLS-inf GOES-past-s1 'I went fishing', or abstract: *uus-iɣ laaw-uŋkʷe maanʲ naaŋk-i* CITY-trans/ess SAYS-inf SMALL APPEARS-s3pres 'it seems (too) small to be called a city' (Kálmán 1976: 70).

Participle
This, too, can replace an object-clause, e.g. *anʲ xaap jii-ne ta kaasala-s-anəl* NOW BOAT COMES-pres.part THEN PERCEIVES-past-p3 'now they

noticed that a boat was coming', but it may also function as subject, e.g. *tʲiwtxa-ne-te sujt-i* SHARPENS-pres.part-s3 IS AUDIBLE-s3pres 'one can hear that he is sharpening (his teeth)'. But participles most commonly replace descriptive or determinative clauses, e.g. *piɣkʷe-t joom-ne xara nʲol* BOY-plur WANDERS-pres.part BARRENNESS 'a barren promontory where boys wander', *maasʲtər saaxi mas-əm aaɣi-t* EXCELLENT FUR.GARMENT DONS-perf.part GIRL-plur 'girls who have put on excellent furs'. The original imperfective participle, now the marker of the third person singular present (see p. 399), survives as a participle in archaicizing constructions such as *nʲeelm-e xul=i nʲeelm=əŋ uuj* TONGUE-s3 FALLS.OFF=imperf.part TONGUE=adj BIRD 'the tongued bird whose tongue perishes' (Kálmán 1976: 70–1; Rombandeeva 1979: 44).

Gerund

This replaces temporal clauses: *am ta sis waanʲka maanʲ xaap-e sunsiɣla-ma-m kaasala-s-əm* 'meanwhile, while (I was) watching Vanyka's little boat, I noticed ...'. The following sentence illustrates both the gerund and the perfective participle: *joomant=ima-te akʷmateertn aamp xil=əm wooŋxa-n raaɣat-i* RUSHES-ger-s3 SUDDENLY DOG DIGS=perf.part HOLE-lat FALLS-s3pres 'as (s)he rushes (along), (s)he falls in a hole dug by a dog'. The gerund also replaces clauses of manner and of state, e.g. *poriɣpaneekʷa nʲeelm-e jol+xanuwjane xurip=a, akʷtop eelʲm-əl sart=ima* FROG TONGUE-s3 DOWN+STICKING SURFACE=adj, AS.IF GLUE-ins SMEARS-ger 'the frog's tongue is sticky as if it had been smeared with glue', *pees jakti=m jiiw+aaŋkʷal tuujt-n pat=ima* LONG.AGO CUTS=perf.part TREE+STUMP SNOW-lat FALLS=ger 'the tree stump, cut long ago, has been covered by snow' (Kálmán 1976: 71).

Compound Sentences
Co-ordination

Co-ordination is usually effected by simple asyndetic concatenation, e.g. *laaɣl-e waaɣtal, kaat-e waaɣtal* 'his/her legs are weak, (and) hi/her hands are weak', *turpate taaɣlak šarəl toxrite, kosamtite, mossake astal uunli, tuwl oowəlti* '(s)he fills his/her pipe full of tobacco, lights it, sits for a while without speaking, then begins' (Rombandeeva 1979: 122–34).

There are native conjunctions (*os* 'and, also', *man* 'or'), but the majority are of Russian origin (*i* 'and', *a* 'but').

Subordination

Alongside the use of participles to express subordination (p. 420) Mansi also uses clauses with finite verbs, linked by conjunctions. These are derived from, or equivalent to, interrogative pronouns and adverbs, e.g. *xoot* 'where', *xomos* 'how'. Examples: *naŋ waaɣlən, xoot oln waarawe?* 'Do you know where money is made?' In sentences containing a hypothesis, the particle *ke* (*tʲe*) is used, e.g. *sⁱisⁱnaaj tⁱe teeɣ, asjəmaɣ jeemti* 'if the aurora borealis is burning, it will be cold' (Rombandeeva 1979: 135–40).

Lexicon

Etymological research has determined the origin of roughly 60 per cent of the Mansi lexicon. A significant portion of the base vocabulary is either inherited, i.e. Uralic, Finno-Ugric, or Ugric in origin, or has arisen internally by morphological means (derivation and compounding) or by sound-symbolism.

Inherited Vocabulary

The entries of the *UEW* demonstrate that a great part of the known Uralic and Finno-Ugric lexicon has been preserved in at least one of the Mansi dialects (cf. p. 390). Approximately 155 Mansi words may be seen as Ugric innovations; these have cognates only in Hungarian, Khanty, or both. Half are found in all three Ugric languages, e.g. *saat* 'seven', *nⁱololow* 'eight', *tur* 'throat', *jomas* 'good', *joxti-* 'arrives', *kʷon* 'out', *maanⁱsⁱi* 'Mansi', *posim* 'smoke', *mil* 'deep', *tawt* 'quiver', *aamp* 'dog', *luw* 'horse', *nⁱaɣir* 'saddle'; roughly one quarter are found only in Mansi and Hungarian, e.g. *jeekʷər* 'root', *puwi-* 'seizes', *koləs* 'grain (millet)', *mowinⁱt-* 'laughs' cf. Hungarian *gyökér, fog-, köles*, and *nevet-*.

Loan Words

We may reckon with Proto-Iranian (*saat* 'seven') and Proto-Turkic (*luw* 'horse') influence as early as the Ugric period. Both Iranian and Turkic influence continued after Hungarian broke away.

Iranian Loans

The influence of Old Iranian languages on ObUgrian is attested by a body of loanwords in diverse semantic fields. This vocabulary must have entered proto-ObUgrian no later than the fourth to sixth century CE. About a dozen survive in Mansi, e.g. *aarasⁱ* 'hearth', *waasiɣ* 'calf', *eeriɣ* 'song', *eesərma* 'shame', *ootər* 'chief, price', *puuŋ* 'wealth(y)', *sⁱak* '(sledge)hammer', *woot* 'wind', *waar-* 'makes', *tuujt-* 'hides' (Korenchy 1972: 46–84).

Tatar Loans

There is evidence for Siberian Tatar influence on Southern dialects of Mansi from the fourteenth century onwards. There are more than 500 Tatar loans, embracing most social and economic semantic spheres: alongside words pertinent to animal husbandry, agriculture, handicrafts, and commerce we also find vocabulary from the domains of clothing, food, medicine, and even Islamic religious life. The main current of Tatar influence was broken by the Russian conquest of western Siberia in the sixteenth century. Only about 5 per cent of the Tatar loans are found in all Mansi dialect areas, and only about 10 per cent reached the northern dialects. Among these latter loans are e.g. *xoosax*

'Cossack', *xoon* 'Khan', *japak* 'silk', *suuntax* 'box', *toor* 'piece of cloth', *eelak* 'sieve', *tolmas^j* 'interpreter', *aaməs^j* 'riddle', (Kannisto 1925: 1–264).

Russian Loans

There appears to have been sporadic Russian influence as early as the twelfth to the fifteenth century. With the conquest of western Siberia, however, Russian influence grew significantly; since then Russian loans have flowed into Mansi consistently and directly. Russian loans number over 600 in dialect texts collected in the last century; the number in the standard language as currently used is demonstrably greater. From the semantic point of view, Russian loans extend and elaborate the fields represented by Tatar loans; an important novelty are the terminologies of Russian central government and orthodox religion. Examples: *aarkəri* 'bishop', *l^jeekkar* 'physician', *mir* 'people', *is^jwes^js^ja* 'candle', *laampa* 'lamp', *turpa* '(tobacco) pipe', *puska* 'cannon', *peetər* 'pail', *tas* 'vessel', *ras* 'case, instance', *s^jaaj* 'tea', *kaalas^j* 'bun', *kurka* 'hen', *paan^ja* 'bath-house' (Kálmán 1960: 1–327).

Komi Loans

The earliest Komi merchants and settlers appeared in western Siberia in the tenth century, and we may date the first phase of Komi influence on Mansi to the period from the tenth to the fifteenth century, when commercial centres and towns arose. The second phase of Komi influence on Mansi occurred in the eighteenth and nineteenth centuries. In both phases, the greatest contact was in the northern Mansi linguistic area. Of the more than 300 Komi loans in Mansi, 85 per cent may be found in northern dialects. Only about 10 per cent pervaded to all Mansi dialects. Prominent among the Komi loans are words from the semantic domains of building, furnishings, foodstuffs, clothing and transport, e.g. *isnas* 'window', *kuur* 'oven', *ulas* 'chair', *pasan* 'table', *n^jaan^j* 'bread', *kaas^j* 'women's undergarment', *toos* 'cross-strut in boat'. Other examples include *moojt* 'tale', *pupak^we* 'bear', *s^jaarəs^j* 'sea', *kaasal-* 'notices', *sart-* 'smears', *turap* 'storm', *aakan^j* 'doll', *oojka* 'old man', *rus^j* 'Russian'.

It should be noted here that Udmurt loans penetrated the Chusovaya dialect of Mansi described by Reguly (Kálmán 1988: 411).

Samoyed Loans

Roughly thirty Nenets loanwords concerned with reindeer-breeding and life on the tundra have entered Northern Mansi. Such are *xalew* 'gull', *tin^js^jaŋ* 'lasso', *tut^js^jaŋ* 'sewing bag made of reindeer hide', *s^jowal* 'chuval' (Steinitz 1959: 426–53).

Khanty Loans

The Northern Mansi dialect groups are in contact with Obdorsk (now Salekhard) and Kazym Khanty speakers, and Eastern Mansi dialect groups were once in contact with the Konda Khanty. In the case of two closely related languages such as Mansi and Khanty it is of course difficult to determine whether in a given instance we have to deal with a cognate or a later borrowing; the entire question still awaits monographic treatment. It is beyond doubt, however, that there are many Khanty loans in many layers of the Mansi lexicon. This is especially true of the vocabulary of the bear ceremony: to this day the Khanty are the custodians of the world's most elaborate bear cult. Examples of probable Khanty loans in Mansi are: *nʲaawram* 'child', *aapsʲi* 'younger brother; nephew', *kur* 'leg', *laj* 'dark', *uunt* 'forest', *leeŋkər* 'mole', *luuli* 'wild duck', *luuɲi* 'dog', *maaɣ* 'honey', *ooxi* 'bear's head', *xos* 'bear's eyes' (Sz. Bakró-Nagy 1979: 23–59; Steinitz 1996–93 s.vv.).

Words of Internal Origin

There is much sound-symbolic vocabulary, e.g. *lʲatɣ-* '(fire) crackles', *mirɣ-* 'there is thunder'. The most productive form of word-formation, however, is regular derivation (cf. p. 408, 414). The oldest roots have the most extensive derivational profiles, e.g. *xuulʲ-* 'leaves behind', *xuulʲt-* 'remains', *xuulʲtiɣl-* 'keeps getting left behind', *xuulʲiɣl-* 'suddenly is there', *xuulʲiɣlant-* 'keeps cropping up'. But recent loans are also susceptible to derivational processes, e.g. *tumaj* 'thought', *tumajt-* 'thinks'.

The second most common type of word-formation is compounding, e.g. *aaɣi+piɣ* 'child (GIRL+BOY)', *maa+xum* 'people (EARTH+MAN)', *numi-+toorəm* 'god (UPPER+SKY)', *nʲuli+kis* 'rainbow (PITCHPINE+HOOP)', *woot+piɣ* 'storm (WIND+SON)'. For a time, efforts at centrally directed language reform created amalgams of compounding and derivation such as *xanʲisʲtan+xum* 'teacher (TEACH=ING+MAN)', *xanʲisʲta=n+kol* 'school (TEACH=ING+HOUSE)', *towl=əŋ+xaap* 'aeroplane (WING=ED+BOAT)'.

Words of Unknown Origin

A significant portion of the base vocabulary of Mansi consists of words with no known cognates. Such are *xanʲsʲ-* 'knows', *laaw-* 'says', *oonʲsʲ-* 'has', *pat-* 'falls', *raat-* 'strikes', *woow-* 'calls', *lʲapa* 'near', *oxsar* 'fox'.

Text

(For a slightly different version, in Cyrillic orthography, see Kálmán 1976: 92).

seer&moor	woor-t	sʲir&sʲir	towl=əŋ
DENSE&DENSE	FOREST-loc	VARIOUS&VARIOUS	WING=ED

uuj-ət	ool-eɣət.	ti-t	sʲopər	kisup
ANIMAL-plur	LIVE-p3pres	HERE	CAPERCAILLIE	HAZEL-GROUSE

kukuk   maaŋkʷla   xoont-uŋkʷe   weeɼm-eɣən.   uuj=risʲ-ət
CUCKOO   OWL   FIND-inf   IS.ABLE-s2pres   BIRD=sx-plur

sujəŋ=əsʲ   lujɣ-eɣət   eerɣ-eɣət.   jiiw+tow-ət
LOUD=adv   CHIRP-p3pres   SING-p3pres   TREE+BRANCH-plur

paal-t   nʲirsʲaxl-ət-t   uumi-t-t   taan
SURFACE-loc   BUSH-plur-loc   HOLLOW-plur-loc   PRO.p3

pitʲi   waar-eɣət   muuŋi-t   pin-eɣət
NEST   MAKE-p3pres   EGG-plur   LAY-p3plur

nʲaawram-ət   janmalt-eɣət.
CHICK-plur   RAISE-p3pres

'In the dense dark forest many kinds of birds live. Here you can find capercaillie, hazel-grouse, cuckoos, and owls. The little birds loudly chirp and sing. On tree-branches, in bushes, in hollows they build (their) nest(s), lay eggs, raise (their) young.'

References and Further Reading

Ahlqvist, A. (1891) *Wogulisches Wörterverzeichnis*, MSFOu 2, Helsingfors: Société Finno-Ougrienne.
Bakró-Nagy, Sz. Marianne (1979) *Die Sprache des Bärenkultes im Obugrischen*, Budapest: Akadémiai kiadó.
Balandin, A.N., and Vakhrusheva, M.P. (1957) Мансийский язык, Leningrad: Учпедгиз.
——— (1958) Мансийский-русский словарь. Leningrad: Учпедгиз.
Chernetsov, V.N. (1937) 'Мансийский (вогульский) язык', in Г.Н. Прокофьеь (ed.), Языки и письменность народов Севера. Часть, vol. I, Leningrad: Учпедгиз, pp. 163–92.
Collinder, B. (1957) *Survey of the Uralic Languages*, Stockholm: Almqvist & Wiksell, pp. 319–44.
Hajdú, P. (1966) *Bevezetés az uráli nyelvtudományba*, Budapest: Tankönyvkiadó.
Honti, L. (1975) *System der paradigmatischen Suffixmorpheme des wogulischen Dialektes an der Tawda*, Budapest: Akadémiai Kiadó.
——— (1977) review of Kálmán 1976.
——— (1980) 'Zur Phonemanalyse des Tavda-Wogulischen', *Finnisch-Ugrische Mitteilungen* 4: 61–8.
——— (1982a) *Geschichte des Obugrischen Vokalismus der ersten Silbe*, Budapest: Akadémiai Kiadó.
——— (1982b) 'Der Passiv in der Obugrischen Sprachen', *Acta Linguistica Hungarica* 32: 39–51.
——— (1984) 'Versuch einer Beschreibung des Phonembestandes im wogulischen Dialekt an der Pelymka', in P. Hajdú and L. Honti (eds), *Studien zur phonologischen Beschreibung uralischer Sprachen*, Budapest: Akadémiai Kiadó, pp. 87–102.
——— (1988) 'Die wogulische Sprache', in D. Sinor (ed.), *The Uralic Languages:*

Description, History and Foreign Influences, Handbuch des Orientalistik 8/1, Leiden: Brill, pp. 147–71.

Kálmán, B. (1961) *Die russischen Lehnwörter im Wogulischen*, Budapest: Akadémiai Kiadó.

—— (1965) *Vogul Chrestomathy*, Indiana University Uralic and Altaic Series 46, Bloomington–The Hague: Indiana University–Mouton.

—— (1975) *Chrestomathia Vogulica*, Budapest: Tankönyvkiadó.

—— (1976) *Wogulische Texte mit einem Glossar*, Budapest: Akadémiai Kiadó.

—— (1984) 'Das nordwogulische Phonemsystem', in P. Hajdú and L. Honti (eds), *Studien zur phonologischen Beschreibung uralischer Sprachen*, Budapest: Akadémiai Kiadó, pp. 73–9.

—— (1988) 'The history of Ob-Ugric languages', in D. Sinor (ed.), *The Uralic Languages: Description, History and Foreign Influences*, Handbuch der Orientatistik 8/1, Leiden: Brill, pp. 395–412.

Kannisto, A. (1919) *Zur Geschichte des Vokalismus der ersten Silbe im Wogulischen vom quantitativen Standpunkt*, MSFOu 46, Helsinki: Société Finno-Ougrienne.

—— (1925) *Die tatarischen Lehnwörter im Wogulischen*, FUF 17: 1–264.

Kannisto, A. and Liimola, M. (1951–63) *Wogulische Volksdichtung*, vols I–VI, MSFOu 101, 109, 111, 114, 116, 134, Helsinki: Société Finno-Ougrienne.

Kannisto, A., Liimola, M. and Eiras, V. (1982) *Wogulische Volksdichtung*, vol. VII, MSFOu 180, Helsinki: Société Finno-Ougrienne.

Keresztes, L. (1972) 'Über das Vokalsystem des Jukonda-Dialekts im Wogulischen', *FUF* 39: 277–94.

—— (1973) 'Vogulin Jukondan (Ala-Kondan) murteen konsonanttijärjestelmästä', *JSFOu* 72: 167–74.

Kispál Sz., M. (1966) *A vogul igenév mondattana*, Budapest: Akadémiai kiadó.

Korenchy, É. (1972) *Iranische Lehnwörter in den obugrischen Sprachen*, Budapest: Akadémiai kiadó.

Kövesi, M. (1933) 'Igemódok a vogulban', *Finnugor Értekezések* 1 Budapest: Kirélyi Magyar Egyetem Nyomda.

Kulonen, U.-M. (1989) *The Passive in Ob-Ugrian*, MSFOu 203, Helsinki: Société Finno-Ougrienne.

Lakó, G. (1957) *Nordmansische Sprachstudien*, Acta Linguistica Hungarica 6: 347–423.

Liimola, M. (1963) *Zur historischen Formenlehre des Wogulischen*, vol. I: *Flexion der Nomina*, MSFOu 127, Helsinki: Société Finno-Ougrienne.

Munkácsi, B. (1894) 'A vogul nyelvjárások szóragozásukban ismertetve', *Ugor Füzetek* 1.

Munkácsi, B. and Kálmán, B. (1952) *Manysi (vogul) népköltési gyüjtemény*, vol. III/2, Budapest: Akadémiai kiadó.

—— (1963) *Manysi (vogul) népköltési gyüjtemény*, vol. IV/2, Budapest: Akadémiai kiadó.

—— (1986) *Wogulisches Wörterbuch*, Budapest: Akadémiai kiadó.

Pirotti, G. (1972) *Grammatica vogula*, Mantu: Associazione culturale Italo-Ungherese Taddeo Ugoleto da Parma.

Rédei, K. (1970) *Die syrjänischen Lehnwörter im Wogulischen*, Budapest: Akadémiai kiadó.

Riese, T. (1984) *The Conditional Sentence in the Ugrian, Permian and Volgaic Languages*, Vienna: Institut für Finno-Ugristik de Universität Wien.

—— (1988) 'Zur Herkunft des Konditionalis im Südwogulischen', *FUF* 48: 51–61.

—— (1992) 'Zur Entwicklung des Kasussystems im Wogulischen', in P. Deréky et al. (eds), *Festschrift für Károly Rédei zum 60 Geburtstag*, Vienna–Budapest: Institut für Finno-Ugristik der Universität Wien–MTA Nyelvtudományi Intézet.

Rombandeeva, E.I. (1954) Русско-мансийский словарь, Leningrad: Учпедгиз.

——— (1964) Фонстические особенности в диалектах северных манси, in B.A. Serebrennikov (ed.), Вопросы Финно-угорского языкознания, Грамматика и дексикология, Moscow–Leningrad: Наука.

——— (1973) Мансийский (вогульский) язык, Moscow: Наука.

——— (1979) Синтаксис мансийского (вогульского) языка, Moscow: Наука.

——— (1993) История народа манси (вогулов) и его духовная культура (по данным фольклора и обрядов), Surgut: Сеьерный дом

Rombandeeva, E.I., and Kuzakova, E.A. (1982) Словарь мансийско-русский и русско-мансийский, Leningrad: Просвещение.

Steinitz, W. (1955) *Geschichte des wogulischen Vokalismus*, Berlin: Akademie-Verlag.

——— (1959) 'Zu den samojedischen Lehnwörtern im Ob-ugrischen', *UATb* 31: 426–53.

Steinitz, W. et al. (1993–96) *Dialektologisches und etymologisches Wörterbuch der ostjakischen Sprache* [= *DEWOS*], Berlin: Akademie Verlag.

Szabó, D. (1904) 'A vogul szóképzés', *Nyelvtudományi Közlemények* 34: 55–74, 217–34, 417–57.

Veenker, W. (1971) *Rückläufiges Wörterbuch der vogulischen Schriftsprache*, Wiesbaden: Otto Harrassowitz.

14 Hungarian

Daniel Abondolo

Hungarian is by far the most widely spoken Uralic language, with some thirteen million speakers in Hungary and adjacent countries and roughly another million scattered around the globe. The oldest continuous text dates from the end of the twelfth century, and from the fifteenth century a considerable philological record begins to accumulate.

Hungarian is traditionally assigned to the eastern, more commonly called Ugric, branch of Finno-Ugric; it broke away from this node between two-and-a-half and three-and-a-half millennia ago, leaving behind proto-ObUgrian, the ancestor of Khanty and Mansi.

Hungarian probably began as a core, rather than as a peripheral, dialect in proto-Uralic. Although typically Uralic in many respects (broadly agglutinating, with vowel harmony, postpositions, possessive suffixes, and minimal noun-phrase agreement), Hungarian is also strongly deviant in certain regards, in particular in the development of its vowels and in the details of its noun and verb finite paradigms. In terms of historical phonology, Hungarian is the only Finno-Ugric language to spirantize original initial *p-; in this it patterns, coincidentally, with the northernmost and southernmost Samoyedic idioms, Nganasan and Mator. Coincidental, too, are the independent spirantizations of initial *k before back vowels in Hungarian, Northern and Eastern Mansi, and Western Khanty. On the other hand sound changes such as *mp > *b, shared with Permian, and the (partial) marking of object person in the finite verb, shared with Mordva, point to *Sprachbund* convergences. In fact what is traditionally termed 'Ugric' may itself have been more a *Sprachbund* than a node in the Uralic family tree (see now Viitso 1996, who speculates along these lines on the basis of the development of the consonants).

Much has been written about Hungarian in the readily available linguistic literature of the past few decades. Accordingly, this chapter concentrates on some of the aspects which have tended to be neglected, with particular emphasis on the morphological typology and prehistory of Hungarian *qua* Uralic language.

Map 14.1   Hungarian Dialects

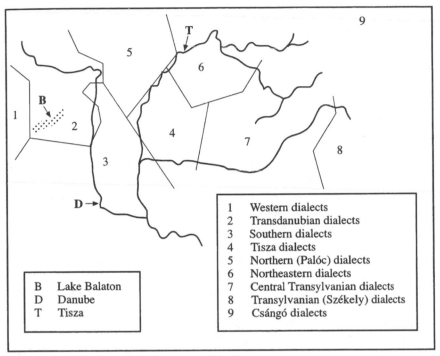

B	Lake Balaton
D	Danube
T	Tisza

1	Western dialects
2	Transdanubian dialects
3	Southern dialects
4	Tisza dialects
5	Northern (Palóc) dialects
6	Northeastern dialects
7	Central Transylvanian dialects
8	Transylvanian (Székely) dialects
9	Csángó dialects

Source: Simplified from Hajdú-Domokos 1987: 44.

Phonology

Primary word stress is assigned to the first syllable; sentence-stress rules then heighten, dampen, or delete this stress in accordance with syntactic, aspectual, and pragmatic variables. See Hetzron 1982 for a detailed exploration.

Vowels

Depending on the variety, there are two main vowel inventories, one with fourteen and one with fifteen vowels. Perhaps as many as two-thirds of speakers use the smaller inventory: this consists of seven short and seven long vowels. The inventory used by most of the remaining one-third of speakers has an additional short vowel, front mid unrounded *e*:

	Short Front		Back		Long Front		Back	
	-R	+R	-R	+R	-R	+R	-R	+R
High	i	ü		u	ii	üü		uu
Mid	(e)	ö		o	ee	öö		oo
Low	ä			å			aa	

In the standard orthography, both ä and e are written with <e>; in specialist contexts (linguistics, lyrics of folksong) e is differentiated by means of diaeresis, <ë>. In older specialist works, ä is sometimes written <ɛ>. Otherwise, the orthographic symbols are as given above, except that long vowels are written not double, as in both the phonetic and the phonological transcriptions used in this book, but with an acute diacritic, thus <á> <ó> <ú> <é>. The acute replaces the dot of <i>, viz. <í>, and a double acute replaces the diaeresis of <ü> and <ö>, viz. <ű> <ő>.

On the whole, the duration of the long vowels is from 50 to 60 per cent greater than that of the short vowels; the chief deviations from this distribution are å, whose duration often approaches that of a long vowel, and ee, whose duration usually is as low as that of a short vowel (for some recent figures see Gósy 1989: 80). From the point of view of phonetics these deviations are not unexpected, since å is quite open and ee is rather close. Distinctiveness of length among the high vowels is the least consistent; many speakers have it only in orthoëpic social contexts, or not at all.

Syllable structure has only restricted effects on vowel quantity; see on marginal phone(me)s, below. The effects of word stress on vowel quantity has not been adequately investigated (see, however, Nádasdy 1985: 229).

The long mid vowels ee öö oo are pronounced rather more close than their short counterparts (e) ö o. This is also true, though to a lesser degree, of the high vowels. The tongue-height of ä is often quite low, even for speakers who lack e. Of all the vowels, aa is pronounced the most open. Note also that although aa is here classified as 'back', it can be pronounced rather centrally or even somewhat front, especially by urban young women.

There are also several marginal vowel phones; we may group these into three types. One type is represented by a phone of external origin: it is a short central-to-front low unrounded a, occurring most frequently in the pronunciation of foreign items such as Weis(s) [vajs] and Arafat [arafat]. When followed by j, this a remains unchanged, but any a in words of the Arafat-type reverts to core å when the word is inflected, e.g. singular dative Weisnak [vajsnåk] but Arafatnak [åråfåtnåk].

The second type of marginal vowel phone involves the short low vowels ä and å. Frequently in the pronunciation of the deictics arra 'this way, thereabouts', erre 'this way, hereabouts' and merre '(by) which way? whereabouts?' the first vowel is pronounced long, i.e. we have [åår(r)å], [äär(r)ä], [määr(r)ä]. (The duration of the rhotic varies considerably in these forms and is non-distinctive; the length of the preceding vowel, however, is distinctive, cf. arra [årrå] 'onto that'.) This kind of pronunciation appears now to be spreading to acronyms, e.g. EK [ääkaa] 'E(uropean) C(ommunity)' and other quotative instances of letter-names. For a recent discussion of these two types of marginal vowel see Keresztes 1993.

The third, somewhat controversial, type of marginal vowel phone is the mirror image of the second type: it involves the relatively short duration of the pronunciation of phonologically long vowels when these are followed, within the morpheme, by homotopic clusters of resonant (particularly nasals) plus obstruents, e.g half-long [a·] in *bánt-* [ba·nt] 'harms, irritates' but fully long in *bán-t-Ø* [baant] 'treated, dealt with'.

To varying degrees and in various registers, any short vowel may be pronounced longer when to the left of a tautomorphemic resonant followed by an obstruent or pause, e.g. *bors* [bo·rš] 'pepper', *bor* [bo·r] 'wine', and any long vowel may be pronounced shorter in a closed syllable, particularly before non-geminate clusters.

One must also distinguish phenomena associated with affective pronunciation, in which any vowel may be rendered with (much) increased duration. Even in this type of durational deviation, tongue-height remains constant, e.g. the long vowel of *hooogy?* [hooodʲ] '*how*?!' (with a quick dip, followed by a slow rise, in pitch, and with optional creaky voice) has the same tongue-height as that of its non-affective pendant *hogy?*

At the phonological level, Hungarian vowels exhibit a range of alternations involving length, frontness/backness, the presence/absence of lip-rounding, and tongue-height. These are briefly presented under morphophonology, below.

Much is known about the history of the Hungarian vowels over the last millennium, because the philological record has been studied and well summarized (e.g. Bárczi 1958). On the prehistorical side, many of the details of the background of the Hungarian vowels have been worked out by the comparative method (e.g. Sammallahti 1988: 500–501, 513–15). Nevertheless the overall picture remains unclear, and the following must therefore be cursory. Labial low **å** was probably still a positional variant of unrounded *a in the thirteenth century. The long mid vowels **ee öö oo** are probably all secondary, the result of (1) contraction after the loss of glides, e.g. *ősz* [öös] 'autumn' < *öγös < pUgric *θükəs, << pFU *süksʲi; (2) monophthongization of diphthongs; or (3) compensatory lengthening after the loss of the vowel of the second syllable, e.g. *vér* [veer] 'blood' (<< *weri < pFU *wiri), or *kéz* [keez] 'hand'. On the other hand the length of the first-syllable high vowel in many words, at least in parts of their paradigm, may be a preservation from p(F)U, e.g. *húgy* [huudʲ] 'urine' < *kuunʲsʲï, *nyíl* [nʲiil] 'arrow' < pFU *nʲïïlï < pU *nʲïxlï. The low vowels (ä å aa) usually date back to p(F)U non-high vowels, as in *hal* [hå·l] 'fish' < pU *kala, *ház* [haaz] 'house' < pFU *kaata, *kéz* (accusative *keze-t* [käzät]) < pFU *käti, but in words which were built with derivational suffixes already in p(F)U, they are often from (short) non-lows, e.g. *egér*, accusative *egere-t* ([ägeer], [ägärät]) < pFU *šiŋiri (> Finnish *hiiri*, Komi *šïr*).

Vowel Oppositions and Alternations, and the Morphophonemic Code
From the morphophonological point of view, the vowel inventories as given above are extravagant. Productive or extensive morphophonemic vowel

alternations on the one hand, and numerous restrictions on the distribution of vowels on the other, enable the extraction of prosodic features such as length, frontness/backness, and lip-rounding. Such extractions, in turn, allow us to reduce the vowel inventories given above to five, written in this chapter in *code* (given in capital letters): I E A O U. The trivial readings for these abstract segments are **i e** (or, in varieties lacking this segment, **ä**) **å o u** when single, **ii ee aa oo uu** when double; in front-prosodic contexts (marked with prefixed # where necessary) the readings are **i e(/ä) ä ö ü** and **ii ee ee öö üü**. Note that the abstract description of the standard language, in which the merger of **e** and **ä** has been completed at the surface level, is best carried out with distinct underlying E (= **e**) and #A (= **ä**) units (cf. Szépe 1969; Abondolo 1988: 34; Kornai 1994: 14).

In bound morphemes, the short mid vowels **o ö e** (with **ä** counting as a mid vowel for those speakers who lack **e**) may in most cases be unambiguously recovered from a cover symbol, written here as **3**. Front prosody, indicated by # at the start of a root morpheme in the manner of a key signature before a sequence of tonal music, is necessary only if the morpheme contains one of the vowels A O U, i.e. those with dual surface prosodic readings, and with verb roots and themes whose sole vowel is I, which normally have back vocalism. Examples: BOR *bor* [bo·r] 'wine', #BOOR *bőr* [böör] 'skin, hide, leather', IRT-Ø-3K *irtok* 'I extirpate', #HINT-Ø-3K *hintek* 'I sprinkle'. In front-vowel roots, the symbol **3** may be used to indicate superabundant forms, e.g. #F3L *fel/föl* 'up(wards)'. The code renders transparent much of the phenomena which operate in the morphophonology, and will therefore be used here. The fact that this procedure accommodates many unassimilated foreign items awkwardly – e.g. *nüansz* [nüäns] would have to be written #NU^bANS, with change of prosody in mid-morpheme – is of interest to diachronists.

In terms of lexical frequency, the most pervasive vowel alternation is AA ~ A, i.e. **aa ~ å** and **ee ~ ä**; this alternation is most characteristic of, but not restricted to, nominal inflection and derivation, e.g. *utca* 'street' ~ *utcán* 'on (the) street', *feje* 'his/her/its head' ~ *fején* 'on his/her/its head', *szoba* 'room' ~ *háromszobás* 'three-roomed'. In all such cases, the short vowel is the result of reduction of stem-final AA, either in word-final position (as in *utca, feje, szoba*) or to the left of certain derivational suffixes, e.g. UTCAA = I *utcai* 'pertaining to the street', contrast UTCAA-I-NKÅ *utcáink* 'our streets'. The cancellation of the A in this last example is the most pervasive alternation in terms of textual frequency; such cancellation befalls every A when it is in final position in the non-compound word, and henceforth will not be indicated in the code.

In non-final position in large, but closed, sets of core nominal vocabulary, the peripheral vowels I U A alternate with their long pendants II UU AA, while A in morpheme-final position alternates with zero. Examples: non-final I is read as II (**ii**), and final A as zero, in N^JILA *nyíl* [n^jiil] 'arrow'; similarly, final A is read as zero, non-final U is read UU (here **üü** because of front prosody) in #TUZA *tűz* [tüüz] 'fire'; and final A is read as zero, but non-final A is read as AA, in MADARA *madár* [mådaar] 'bird'. Contrast the isochronic readings of these segments in the corresponding accusative forms NᴶILA-T *nyilat* [nʲilåt], #TUZA-T *tüzet* [tüzät], MADARA-T *madara-t* [mådåråt]. Many nominals (belonging to other large closed lexical sets) and many (mostly derived) verbs show epenthesis of a short mid vowel, **e** (**ä**), **o**, or **ö** (cover symbol: **3**) between the consonants of their stem-final cluster, e.g. AALM *álom* 'sleep; dream', TITK *titok* 'secret', IKR *iker* 'twin', #OKR *ökör* 'ox', MOZ=G-*mozog* [mozog] 'moves'. As these examples suggest, the quality of the epenthetic vowel depends on front/back prosody, [+/-] roundedness of the vowel of the preceding syllable, and the nature of the surrounding consonants (Abondolo 1988: 108–10, 205–9). A few words show both epenthesis and quantitative alternations, e.g. #LALKA *lélek* [leelek] 'soul'.

In many people's speech, the long high vowels II and UU alternate with their short pendants in subsystems of the derivational morphology of certain univocalic verbs, e.g. HUUZ- *húz-* [huuz] 'pulls, draws', HU*U*Z=AT *huzat* [huzåt] 'draught', BIIZ- *bíz-* [biiz] 'entrusts', BI*I*Z=ALMA *bizalom* [bizålom] 'confidence, trust'.

Consonants

The inventory of Hungarian consonants is set out in Table 14.1. The places of articulation are (1) bilabial, (2) labiodental, (3) apicodental (nasals and stops), lamino-alveolar (sibilants, and release portions of affricates), (4) palatals, (5) lamino-palatalveolar (hushing fricatives and affricates), (6) dorsovelar, and (7) glottal. The stops are unaspirated.

The orthographic representations given in Table 14.1 are the default spellings; numerous other spellings also occur because Hungarian

Table 14.1 Hungarian consonants and their main orthographic representations

	1	*2*	*3*	*4*	*5*	*6*	*7*	*Orthography*			
Nasals	m		n	nʲ			m		n	ny	
Stops	p		t	tʲ	k			p		t	ty	k
	b		d	dʲ	g			b		d	gy	g
Fricatives		f	s	(ç)	š	(x)	h	f	sz	ch s	ch h
		v	z		ž			v	z	zs	
Affricates			c		č			c	cs		
			dᶻ		dᶽ			dz	dzs		
Lateral			l					l			
Glide				j				j/ly			
Trill			r					r			

orthography is for the most part morphophonemic. Most notably, the output of all of the morphophonemic processes (1–5) outlined below is not normally reflected in writing.

The palatal glide **j** is written <j> or <ly> on historical grounds (the shift from *ļʲ to **j** was not completed until the nineteenth century, when the orthography had begun to jell). Long consonants are written double, but in digraphs only the first member is written twice, e.g. <ggy> for **dʲdʲ**. In a few foreign words, the digraph <ch> is used to write the segments çç (in front-vowel environments) and **xx** (elsewhere), e.g. *pech* [pe/äçç] 'hard luck' and *krach* [kråxx] 'financial collapse'. These phones (and their voiced pendants, which arise in sandhi; see below) are marginal, occur most typically in slang/foreign vocabulary, and are long insofar as the environment permits (see below). Certain instances of ç are derived from I, e.g. LOP-IA-Ø *lopj* [lopç] 'steal!' Otherwise, ç and **x** may be derived morphophonemically from geminate sequences of an abstract fricative H, which when single is the source of **h** (Abondolo 1988: 67–9). Similarly, the glide **j** may be derived from the short vowel I. The voiced labiodental fricative **v**, on the other hand, is more firmly rooted and must have its own abstract segment V.

In general, consonant length is distinctive intervocalically and between the last vowel of a word and pause. Long consonants occur most frequently astride morpheme boundaries, e.g. KANALA *kanál* [kånaal] 'spoon', KAN-NAAL *kannál* [kånnaal] 'than a male (animal)', MEN-IA-Ø *menj!* [menʲnʲ] 'go!', but are also quite frequent root-final, particularly in recently acquired vocabulary, e.g. SᴴOKK *sokk* [šokk] 'shock', cf. SᴴOKA *sok* [šok] 'much, many'. Length in affricates is realized in the stop component: LAZAC-VAL *lazaccal* [låzåttˢål] 'with salmon'. There seem to be no instances of long **vv** or **žž** in prepausal position; on the other hand, **dž** and **dᶻ** occur short only where length is disallowed. Consonants which are long at the morphophonemic level are shortened wherever their occurrence is precluded, e.g. #FUSᴴT-TOOL *füsttől* [füštööl] 'from smoke'.

If we minimalize the redundancies in the matrix given above we arrive at an abstract consonantal inventory with twenty-five members (plus **j**, which impinges from the realm of the vowels, see Table 14.2).

The main oppositions are thus (1) [+/-] voiced and, among the core consonants, the oppositions (2) [-/+] palatalized for the stops and (3) hissing : hushing for the fricatives and affricates. The most important synchronic consonant alternations involve neutralizations of these oppositions in various forms of sandhi. These are as follows (note that none is reflected in the orthography).

1   *Obstruent voice assimilation*, in which an obstruent assimilates in voice to an obstruent to its right, e.g. HAT-BAN *hatban* [hådbån] 'in six'; excluded is **v**, to the left of which obstruents do not assimilate in voice, e.g. HAT=VAN *hatvan* [håtvån] sixty'.

2   *Adaffrication*, in which any sequence of core stop or affricate plus core

Table 14.2   Hungarian abstract consonants

Peripheral		core	
		a	*b*
		L	L^J
M		N	N^J
P	K	T	T^J
B	G	D	D^J
F	H	S	S^H
V		Z	Z^H
		C	C^H
		X	X^H
		R	**j**

fricative yields a geminate affricate, e.g. HAT-S3R hatszor [håccor] 'six times'; with obstruent voice assimilation: NEED^J=S3R *négyszer* [neet^{j}t^{js}er] or [neeccer] 'four times'.

3   *Adpalatalization*, in which [- palatal] consonants (column *a* in Table 14.2) are replaced by their palatal equivalents when to the left of palatals (column b) or **j**, e.g. **t** is replaced by **t^j** to the left of **n^j** in $^\#$OT N^{J}ULA *öt nyúl* 'five hares'. Adpalatalization is most consistent in the case of the oral and nasal stops; its application in sequences whose first member is **l**, or whose second member is **j**, or both, is more complicated, mostly because other processes compete; see Kiefer 258 ff.

4   *j-Assimilation*: when the input of adpalatalization involves **j** as second member, impermissable sequences such as **n^{j}j are the output. These sequences, as well as all sequences consisting of a core fricative or affricate plus **j**, are automatically fed into *j-assimilation*, which converts them into geminates of the first consonant, e.g. **n^{j}j > n^{j}n^j, **sj > ss. Examples: AD-IA-NAK *adjanak* [åd^{j}d^{j}ånåk] 'let them give; they should give', RAAZ-Ø-IAA *rázza* [raazzå] '(s)he shakes it'.

5   *Hissing-to-hushing assimilation*, parallel to adpalatalization, involves the assimilation of a fricative in column *a* to a following fricative from column *b*, e.g. OLAS $^\#$S^{H}OR *olasz sör* [olåššö·r] 'Italian beer'.

There are also morphophonemic operations which apply only to specific morphemes, such as (6) complete assimilation of the **v** initial in the instrumental and translative suffixes to a consonant to their left, e.g. VAS^H-VAL *vassal* [våššå·l] 'with iron', $^\#$TOK-VAL *tökkel* [tökkä·l] 'with pumpkin' and (7) complete assimilation of the **z** final in the demonstrative prounouns *az* 'that' and *ez* [äz] 'this' to a consonant initial in a morpheme attached to its right, e.g. *effajta* [äffåjtå] 'this kind of'. As the examples indicate, the output of complete assimilation is normally indicated in the orthography.

See also the subjunctive, under verb morphology, p. 449.

The historical background of the Hungarian consonants is complex but for the most part clear. The best survey is Kálmán 1965; see also Lakó (1965) and Sammallahti (1988: 490–94, 501–2, 510–11, 515–20).

The correlation of palatalization among the consonants is built upon the proto-Uralic state of affairs. Distinctive voice on the other hand is an innovation, and must have developed after Hungarian broke away from the rest of Ugric. We may outline the most characteristically Hungarian developments as follows:

1 The voiced palatal stop **dʲ** comes from *j in initial position (*gyalog* 'on foot'), but root-internally it can come not only from *-j- (*fagyal* 'privet') but also from a variety of palatalized consonantisms including *-ðʲ- (*hagy-* 'leaves behind'), *-cʲ- (*vigyáz-* 'watches closely') *-nʲcʲ- (*magyar* 'Hungarian') and *-lʲ- (*meggy* [medʲdʲ] 'morello cherry').

2 The remaining voiced stops (**b d g**) stem from clusters of nasal plus homotopic stop, e.g. *eb* 'hound' = Trj (= Tremjugan) Khanty *äämp* 'dog', *had* 'army, host' = Trj Khanty *kant=əγ* 'Khanty', *szeg-* 'slices (bread); hems' = Trj Khanty *säŋʷkʷ-* 'strikes'. There was also some voicing of initial stops, particularly in roots containing such medial clusters, e.g. *dug-* 'inserts' = Finnish *tunke-*. Voiced stops later became common in initial position in affective vocabulary (*búb* 'crown, crest', *baba* 'doll', *báb* 'puppet') after the example of first Turkic, then Slavonic loans. Hungarian *z* is of parallel origin, viz., orginally from p(F)U intervocalic *-t- (*ház* 'house'), then spreading to initial position in Slavonic loans such as *zálog* 'pledge'.

3 p(F)U initial *p- gave Hungarian **f-** (*fagyal*) and *k- gave **h-** to the left of originally back vowels (*had*; *híz-* 'grows fat' = Vach Khanty *kaat= əγt-*). Of the p(F)U initial stops, only *t- persists uniformly into Hungarian (*tél*, oblique stem *tele-* 'winter' = Sosva Mansi *taal*).

4 The non-palatalized s(h)ibilants p(F)U *s- and pFU *š- fell together, presumably in Ugric, although Samoyedic shows no clear evidence for an *s/*š distinction, either. In any event the two s(h)ibilants have both been lost in Hungarian. Thus we have zero initial in e.g. *ín* (oblique stem *ina-*) 'sinew' = Trj Khanty *łåån* = Komi *sën*, and *egér* (oblique stem *egere-*) = Trj Khanty *łäŋʷkʷər* = Komi *šir*. Present-day Hungarian **s** reflects *sʲ in p(F)U vocabulary (*szem* [sem] 'eye'), while **š** comes primarily from the p(F)U affricates *č- (*sovány* 'thin'), *-č- (*kés* 'knife'), and *-cʲ- (*ős* 'ancestor'). The asymmetry of the pU s(h)ibilant/affricate system, *s :: *sʲ : *cʲ :: *č, is perhaps reflected in two kinds of Hungarian doublets involving **š** which have been ascribed to internal borrowing: (a) those with **s-** ~ **š-**, such as *szöv-* 'weaves' ~ *sövény* 'hedge', or *szem* 'eye' ~ *sömör* 'herpes', and (b) those with **š-** ~ **č-**, such as *sajog-* ~ *csillog-* 'glitters, shines'.

5   From pU to pre-Hungarian, non-initial consonants tended to weaken. For single consonants this meant at least a decrease in the degree of constriction. Thus p(F)U intervocalic *-t- gives Hungarian **z**, and the regular development of p(F)U intervocalic *-m- is **v** (< earlier *w); non-initial **-m-** seems always to have had support from an adjacent consonant, as in *szem* [sem] 'eye' = Finnish *silmä*. In fact, most original consonant clusters preserve one member at the expense of the other, e.g. *köt-* 'ties, knits' = Finnish *kytke-*, *két* 'two'= Udmurt *kĭkt-*, *mos-* 'washes' = Estonian *mõske-*, *ősz* 'autumn' = North Saami *čakča*. The development of the clusters mentioned above at (2), and of the long consonants (6, below) may also be seen in this light.

6   Hungarian provides some fairly good evidence – better than that found in the ObUgrian languages – for a distinction between short and long medial stops. The latter mostly date from pFU; they are especially frequent in affective vocabulary (onomatopoeic verbs, kinship terms) such as *fak=ad-* 'bursts' < pFU *pakkV- (re-created in Hungarian *pukkan-* 'pops, explodes'), *ap=a* 'father' ~ (dialect) *ip=a* 'father-in-law' = Finnish *appi* (oblique stem *appe-*) 'father-in-law'.

7   Some of the morphophonemic properties characteristic of certain consonants may be traced to their phonological roles in earlier stages of the language. For example, **v**, although in present-day Hungarian an obstruent opposed in voice to **f**, does not induce obstruent voice assimilation. This is in keeping with the fact that in morpheme-initial position **v** has developed from non-distinctively voiced *w. With **h**, the reverse is true: this segment now has no voiced phonemic pendant, yet it induces obstruent voice assimilation. This morphophonemic behaviour reflects its earlier systemic status: **h** developed from *x, which in pre-Hungarian was opposed to *γ (< non-initial *w and *k).

Morphology

Stem Architectonics

Most Hungarian monomorphemic verbs are monosyllabic; all verbs are easily accommodated, in a synchronic analysis, as ending in a consonant. Nominals are more various. Several bisyllabic and even a few trisyllabic stems have cognates in ObUgrian or beyond, e.g. *fekete* 'black' = Vach Khanty *peγtə* < *p#VkkVttV.

The morphophonemic operations triggered by suffixation are largely predictable in terms of interaction between various kinds of stem-type and suffix type. The primary stem types are (A) stable v. (B) unstable, and within the latter, (B1) epenthesizing v. (B2) non-epenthesizing stems (see the section on vowel oppositions and alternations, p. 431–3). The greater formal diversity of nominal stems is enhanced by the presence of A-final stems, which have numerous, but complementarily distributed, subtypes (Abondolo 1988: 185).

In inflection, the sole morphological process is suffixation. Derivational morphology is also overwhelmingly suffixal, but there are also various kinds of compound and there is one prefix: see Pronouns and the deictic system, p. 443.

Inflection of Nominals

The word-class of nominals consists of nouns, adjectives, numerals, deictics, and pronouns. The inflection of all of these categories overlaps, but each has distinctive features; the inflection of the personal pronouns is the most deviant. Within the subcategory *noun*, *names* show distinct inflectional properties.

Person (= Possessive Suffixes)

A nominal may be marked for any of six person-number categories, or left unmarked for person (-∅-). The possessive suffixes are s1 -MA, s2 -DA, s3 -IAA, p1 -UNKA, p2 -T3KA, p3 -IUKA.

A few sample forms will illustrate the types of sandhi which occur when these suffixes are attached directly to the stem. As noted above, AA alternates with A, and A with zero, e.g. SOBAA-MA *szobám* [sobaam] 'my room', SOBAA-IAA *szobája* [sobaajå] 'his/her room'. Epenthesis of 3 occurs between consonants, e.g. ABLAK-MA *ablakom* [åblåkom] 'my window', #GOOG-DA *gőgöd* 'your arrogance'. Suffix-initial U cancels an A to its left, e.g. HAAZA-UNKA *házunk* [haazuŋk] 'our house', but is itself deleted by a preceding AA, e.g. SOBAA-UNKA *szobánk* [szoba·ŋk] 'our room'. The initial I of the third-person suffixes -IAA, -IUKA is deleted to the right of stem-final palatals and core fricatives and affricates, but persists to the surface (as **j**) to the right of all vowels save A, e.g. LAAN^J-IUKA *lányuk* [laanʲuk] 'their daughter', TANAAC^H-IAA *tanácsa* [tånaačå] 'his/her advice', ORVOS^H-IUKA *orvosuk* [orvošuk] 'their doctor', but KAAVEE-IAA *kávéja* [kaaveejå] 'his/her/its coffee'. In the sequence A–I, the destruction is mutual, e.g. HAAZA-IAA *háza* [haazå] 'his/her house'. Otherwise, whether this I is deleted or not is not entirely predictable from the shape of the stem (Papp 1975: 109–63, Abondolo 1988: 213–21).

In six kinship terms, stem-final AA is deleted before the I of the third-person suffixes, e.g. AN^JAA-IAA *anyja* [ånʲnʲå] 'mother s3'. This operation has analogues in Mari and Khanty, where the person distribution is the reverse.

Number

Plurality is specified by the suffixes -KA- or -I-. The latter suffix is used when possessive suffixes are also present. Examples: SOBAA-KA *szobák* [sobaak] 'rooms', SOBAA-I-MA *szobáim* [sobaajim] 'rooms s1', #AS^H=AT-KA *esetek* [äšätek] 'cases', #AS^H=AT.IA-I-IAA *esetei* [äšätäʲi] 'cases s3'. As the last example shows, certain sectors of the plural possessive paradigm resist agglutinating-analogue analysis. In the analysis offered here, the possessive plural morpheme is seen as intolerant both of vowels to its right (witness the wholesale cancellation of the entire bulk of the s3 suffix -IAA) and of consonants to its left. This latter intolerance requires the addition of the thematic sequence .IA to consonant-final stems whenever they are inflected with the plural possessive morpheme. This subsection of the Hungarian noun paradigm has been interpreted in several other ways in the descriptive literature, including the positing of a discontinuous morpheme, e.g. Melcsuk 1968.

The history of both of the plural number suffixes is disputed. The -KA- is either from a FU derivational suffix *=kkV which formed resultative and collective nouns from nouns, e.g. North Saami *čázet* 'summer footwear' (< *cʲaaccee* 'water' plus *=k), Finnish *punakka* 'rubicund' < *puna=* 'red=' plus *=kkA), or it is the same morpheme as that seen in the plural possessive suffixes, e.g. p1 -UNKA, as in *házunk* [haazuŋk] 'our house' < *kaata-mï-k HOUSE-1-plur. For the historical background of the possessive suffixes, see below.

The origin of the possessive plural suffix -I- is also disputed. According to one line of thinking, it is the same morpheme as that of the third person singular possessive, which does indeed have -i- allomorphs in a few areas of nominal inflection. The other view holds that this -i- is historically identical with the -i- which occurs in the oblique cases of Saamic, Fennic, and Samoyedic (Papp 1968: 136–8, Kulonen 1993: 56–7).

The possessive suffixes do not derive directly from proto-Uralic analogues. The set of Hungarian possessive suffixes is perhaps best reconstructed as the result of analogical levelling which favoured one or the other of two originally complementary sets of suffixes, one set marking singular, the other non-singular possessions (Kulonen 1993: 72). In one version of this theory, the proto-Uralic, or at least the proto-Finno-Ugric, noun paradigm is thought to have had a suffix *-n- which indicated non-singularity of the possession, with the result that there were opposing forms such as *kala-tï 'your (one) fish' : *kala-n-tï 'your (several) fish' (cf. Korhonen 1981: 234). In Hungarian, no trace of *kala-tï remains (but cf. North Saami *guollát*, Finnish *kalasi*), and the form *halad* 'your fish (one or several, indifferently)', which lacks reference to explicit plurality, is the direct and regular descendant of a form which was orginally explicitly non-singular. A parallel collapse occurred in Finnish, leading to syncretism: Finnish has distinct forms for 'a fish' and 'fishes' but only *kalasi* 'your fish(es)'. In Hungarian, on the other hand, the collapse of the original singular/plural distinction, based on *-Ø-/*-n-, was remedied by its replacement with the -i- plural mentioned above.

If this theory is correct, the levelling which occurred in Hungarian is in nearly perfect complementary distribution with the levelling thought to have occurred in Finnish. An example is provided by the second- and third-person singular forms:

pU	Finnish	Hungarian
*kala-tï	*kalasi*	
*kala-n-tï		*halad*
*kala-sa		*hala* (< *xaləjə)
*kala-n-sa	*kalansa*	

Case

The precise number and inventory of the case suffixes is a matter of dispute, but we will not err grossly in positing sixteen, of which ten (group B in Figure 14.1) are primarily spatial in meaning.

The categories and cells in Figure 14.1 have been arranged so as to highlight formal and functional correspondences and overlaps. The column-labels *Stasis*, *Source*, and *Goal* are thus somewhat exaggerated when taken to refer to the more grammatical, more abstract, suffixes of section A. The traditional names for the cases are (1) nominative, dative; (2) accusative, instrumental, translative; (3) causal/final; (4) inessive, elative, illative; (5) superessive, delative, sublative; (6) adessive, ablative, allative; and (7) terminative. There are also two other spatial suffixes with limited distribution, a locative -T(T) used only with certain toponyms and with deictics (e.g. *mögött* 'behind', *Vác-ott* 'at (the town of) Vác (in Pest county)', and a separative/locative -L found in postpositions and as a building block in composite case suffixes (e.g. *mögül* 'from behind'; for elative -BOOL, delative -ROOL, ablative -TOOL, see below).

In unguarded speech, the illative usually performs the functions of the inessive.

The morphophonemic operations triggered by the case suffixes vary in accordance with (1) phonological or (2) morphological (i.e., historical) conditions. Broadly speaking, all case suffixes (other than the exceptions discussed below) attach to a noun stem by means of operations identical to

Figure 14.1   Hungarian case suffixes

			Stasis	Source	Goal
A	1	gramm-1	-∅		-NAK
	2	gramm-2	-T	-VAL	-VAAH
	3	cause/aim		-EERT	

			Stasis	Source	Goal
B	4	interior	-BAN	-BOOL	-BAA
	5	surface	-N	-ROOL	-RAA
	6	proximity	-NAAL	-TOOL	-H3Z
	7	terminus			-IG

those seen in the nominative, e.g. S^HAATRA *sátor* [šaator] 'tent sN', S^HAATRA-BAN *sátorban* [šaatorbån] 'in a tent'. The exceptions are:

1 The accusative, which attaches in the manner of the possessive suffixes, e.g. S^HAATRA-MA *sátram* [šaatråm] 'my tent', S^HAATRA-T *sátrat* [šaatråt] 'tent sA', except that no epenthesis is required to the right of stem-final postvocalic core continuant consonants, e.g. BETON-T *betont* [bätont] 'concrete sA' but CITROM-T *citromot* [citromot] 'lemon sA';

2 The superessive, which selects the non-nominative shapes of epenthetic stems, e.g. TITK-N *titkon* [titkon] 'secret sSUP', and, in poetic language, of A-stems, e.g. #AGA-N *egen* [ägän], cf. standard *égen* [eegen] 'sky sSUP';

3 The instrumental and the translative, whose initial V assimilates to any preceding consonant, e.g. CITROM^H-VAL *citrommal* [citrommå·l] 'lemon sINST', VAS^HA-VAAH *vassá* [våššaa] 'iron sTRANS'.

As is suggested by their behaviour in the present-day language, the Hungarian case suffixes fall into two basic historical types, primary and secondary. The primary suffixes all derive from morphemes dating from at least the FU period. These are:

1 The accusative -T, which was originally an encliticized demonstrative pronoun, either proximal or, more likely, distal. Hungarian HALA-T *halat* [hålåt] 'fish sA' was thus originally something like *kala--tV FISH--THAT 'that fish', wherein 'that' had at least as much anaphoric as demonstrative force. The closest typological parallel is found in Mordva, where encliticized demonstratives have served as the building blocks of an entire definite paradigm, e.g. Erzya Mordva *kaľ--sʲ* 'fish sNdef', *kaľonʲ--tʲ* 'fish sGdef'.

2 The superessive -N, which continues pU *-nA, as in Finnish *koto-na* 'at home', North Saami *gōđi-i-n* 'tent pLoc', Selkup *ïïloo-qï.n* 'floor sLoc'.

3 The instrumental -VAL, which probably derives from an old locative/separative form of the FU root *wäki 'strength; people'. A form such as KEES^H-VAL *késsel* [keeššä·l] 'knife sINST' would then come from earlier (*) KNIFE + STRENGTH-loc, i.e. *küči + wäki-lV >> *keečəɣääl >> *keešɣäl > [keeššä·l].

4 The translative -VAAH, as in #KOVA-VAAH *kővé* [köövee] 'stone sTRANS', KEES^H-VAAH *késsé* [keeššee] 'knife sTRANS'. This suffix is usually explained as simply a continuation of the pU lative suffix *-j, with pendants scattered throughout the adverbial and deictic portions of the Hungarian lexicon, e.g. the *e/a* of *ide* 'hither', *oda* 'thither' and the *é* of *mögé* 'to behind'; see the sections on postpositions and deictics pp. 443 and 445. Its initial V has been explained as *fausse coupe* (Papp 1968: 155–6), but given the assimilatory behaviour of this V it seems

more likely that -VAAH is actually the sum of two latives, *-kI plus *-j, e.g. *küči-ki-j >> *keečǝɣǝj >> *keešɣej > [keeššee].

5   The terminative -IG. The origin of this suffix is unclear. On the one hand, its morphophonemic behaviour is characteristic of secondary suffixes; on the other hand, it lacks postpositional and person-inflected pendants, in the manner of primary suffixes. It may continue the lative suffixes mentioned in connection with the translative, but in the reverse order, or it may be the result of a strengthening of the pU lative *-ŋ. Neither explanation accounts adequately for the vowel. Parallel developments of *ŋ in deictics, e.g. Hungarian mög- < *müŋä 'behind', render the latter explanation slightly more credible.

The remaining case suffixes are all clearly secondary. The adessive -NAAL is a composite, made up of a pronominal base *na plus a locative/separative *-l (as seen in the instrumental suffix, above). This pronominal base may or may not be connected with *nä, a pronominal base which served as the initial component of the Hungarian dative (-NAK; cf. Selkup -nik/-niŋ) and was a building block for local cases in Common Ugric (Riese 1992; Mikola 1975: 164–170). The interior suffixes -BAN, -BOOL, -BAA are eroded and fossilized composites of a nominal base (cf. #BALA 'interior, gut') plus locative *-nA, locative/separative *-l, and lative *-j (Kulonen 1993: 84). The delative (-ROOL) and sublative (-RAA) are also thought to derive from a noun plus local suffixes, but the identity of this noun is disputed. It is most likely that the noun in question is found in Mansi (UEW 883; Kulonen 1993: 84) and in the Mordva superficial postposition laŋ-, e.g. Erzya Mordva laŋ-so 'on', laŋ-s 'on to'. The ablative has a parallel background: it continues a locative/separative form of FU *tüŋi '(area around the) base (of X)', cf. Eastern Mari tüŋ 'base (incl. of tree)' and the Komi postpositional din, as in pu din-iš̑ 'away from the tree'. The allative -H3Z is formed from a base which is identical with a Khanty spatial noun, seen in e.g. Tremjugan Khanty kuutʲ=ə̑ŋ 'adjacent space' and the Sherkal Khanty postposition xosʲ-aa (with an -aa lative); see Honti (1984: 81). Causal/final -EERT is presumed to be an old locative form of a noun with a spatial/local meaning, but no credible etymon has been put forward.

Personal forms of case morphemes: Of the sixteen productive case suffixes presented above, twelve have independent analogues which take person suffixes, thereby suppleting defective personal pronoun paradigms.

-NAK   -VAL   -EERT
#NAK-   #VALA-   #EERTA-

-BAN   -BOOL   -BAA
#BANNA-   #BALOOLA-   #BALAA-

-N	-ROOL	-RAA
RAITA-	ROOLA-	RAA-

-NAAL	-TOOL	-H3Z
NAALA-	#TOOLA	HOZZAA-

Note the stem RAITA- (< *raŋ-tV, with old locative *-t) suppletive to -N in the superessive. Examples: #TOOLA-MA *tőlem* [tööläm] 'from me', ROOLA-UNKA *rólunk* [rooluŋk] 'about us', HOZZAA-DA *hozzád* [hozzaad] 'towards you'. The dative #NAK- stands out as the only stem in this class to have a final consonant. It is probably not a coincidence that its third-person forms are deviant, e.g. #NAK-IAA *neki* [näki] 'to him/her/it' instead of expected (*neke [näkä]), but for another interpretation see Kulonen (1993: 56, 85–6).

Pronouns and the Deictic System

Hungarian has three articles, definite AZ (~ A before consonants), singulative EDᴶDᴶ *egy*, and zero. The definite article implies that its noun exists. Thus *a lány-om* is 'my daughter (who exists)', whereas *lány-om*, with zero article, leaves the question open, witness *Nincs lány-om* DOES.NOT.EXIST DAUGHTER-s1 'I have no daughter'. The singulative article individuates an instance of a member of a category not yet alluded to (Sherwood 1996: 26), e.g. *egy lányom* 'a daughter of mine'. The development of the definite article from the demonstrative AZ can be followed through the philological record. The singulative article is etymologically identical with the numeral EDᴶDᴶ *egy* 'one'.

Somewhere between inflection and derivation hovers the suffix =EE. This suffix descends from diphthongs arising from the combination of stem-final vowel with the lative case suffix *-j, but in the present-day language it converts any noun stem, with or without person suffixes, into a possessive pronoun, e.g. HAAZA-UNKA=EE *házunké* [haazuŋkee] 'that (e.g. the roof) of our house'. Such pronouns may then be fully inflected for case, e.g. TART=ALMA-IAA=EE-NAAL HOLDS=NdV-s3=EE-ade *tartalmáénál* [tårtålmaaeenaal] '(e.g. the impressiveness of its form is greater) than that of its content'. Iteration of =EE (*Péteréé* 'that of that of Peter'), and plurals built to it with both -I- and -KA (*Péteréi* 'those things of Peter', *Péterék* 'Peter and his associates') vary from variety to variety; see Lotz (1967) and, for a recent stab at an analysis, Kornai (1994: 124–6). The non-occurrence of this suffix in the philological record until the mid-fifteenth century is attributed to chance (Berrár 1957: 20).

The bases of the personal pronouns have only nominative and accusative forms, the rest of the paradigm being supplied by person-inflected stem-forms of the case suffixes (see above). The first- and second-person singular pronouns exhibit aberrant consonantal and vocalic alternations, and in all non-axis-of-discourse accusatives the appropriate person suffix is obligatory (while, at least in the singular, the case suffix may be omitted):

	Nominative		Accusative	
s1	#AAN	én	#ANG-MA(-T)	engem(et)
s2	TE	te	TEEG-DA(-T)	téged(et)
s3	#OVA	ő	#OVA-T	őt
p1	MI	mi	MI-UNKA-T	minket
p2	TI	ti	TI-T3KA-T	titeket
p3	#OVA-K	ők	#OVA-KA-T	őket

There are also corresponding possessive pronouns s1 #AN^{J}EEMA, s2 TIADA, s3 #OV=EE, p1 MIEENKA, p2 TIAT3KA, p3 #OVA=EE-KA; these occur always with the definite article, e.g. AZ #AN^{J}EEMA *az enyém* '(that which is) mine'. Note that the final sequence OVA of the third-person pronoun behaves in a manner which is the reverse of that seen in the noun, cf. #KOVA-T *követ* [kövät] 'stone (acc)', #KOVA=EE *kőé* [kööee] 'that of a stone'.

Demonstrative pronouns distinguish proximal #AZ from distal AZ; each of these may be intensified by the prefixation of AM--, viz. AM--#AZ *emez* [ämäz] 'this (one even closer than *ez*)', AM--AZ *amaz* [åmåz] 'that (one even further away than *az*)'. The Z final in these pronouns assimilates fully to the initial consonant of most case suffixes (and of six other morphemes, Szilágyi 1980: 115), e.g. AZ-BAN *abban* [åbbån] 'in that', #AZ-NAAL *ennél* [änneel] 'at this, than this', #AZ+KOR *ekkor* [äkkor] 'this time', AZ+FAJTAA *affajta* [åffåjtå] 'that kind (of)'. There is no such assimilation in the accusative or superessive, e.g. #AZ-N *ezen* [äzen] 'on this', AZ-T *azt* [åst] 'that (acc)'; the terminative exhibits the unique alternation Z ~ DD, viz. #AZ-IG *eddig* [äddig] 'up until this'.

The rest of the spatial deictic system consists of parallel proximal/distal pairs expressed by front/back pairs of forms, e.g. #AZ=N^{J}I : AZ=N^{J}I *ennyi* : *annyi* 'this much' : 'that much'; I-TT : O-TT *itt* : *ott* 'here' : 'there'; I=DAA : O=DAA *ide* : *oda* 'there' : 'thither'; I=L^J=AN : O=L^J=AN *ilyen* : *olyan* 'like this' : 'like that'; II=D^J : UU=D^J *így* : *úgy* 'in this way' : 'in that way'.

Interrogative pronouns are built to the bases KI, MI, and HO=, all from Uralic stems. They distinguish animate (*ki* 'who?') from inanimate (*mi* 'what?'), and countable from non-countable quantity (*mennyi* 'how much?', *hány* 'how many?'). There are interrogative pendants for all proximal/distal deictic pairs, usually but not always built with identical or similar suffixes, e.g. ME=N^{J}N^{J}I *mennyi* 'how much?', MI=L^{J}AN *milyen* 'what kind of?', HO= NNAN *honnan* 'whence?', HO=D^J *hogy* 'how?' (cf. *ennyi/annyi*, *ilyen/olyan*, *innen/onnan*, *így/úgy* above).

Relative, negative, indefinite, and indifferent pronouns are built to the same bases. Most relative pronouns consist of the appropriate interrogative base preceded by invariable A, e.g. A+KI aki [åki] 'who', A+ME=N^{J}N^{J}I *amennyi* [åmen^{j}n^{j}i] 'as much as'; negative pronouns have S^{H}E(N)+, e.g. S^{H}E+HOL *sehol* [šeho·l] 'nowhere', S^{H}EN+KI *senki* [šeŋki] 'no one'; indefinite forms have VALAA+, and indifferent forms have AKAAR+, e.g. VALAA+KI *valaki* [vålåki] 'someone', AKAAR+KI *akárki* [åkaarki] 'anyone (it doesn't matter who)'. The derivation of several paradigmatic members deviates from the agglutinating matrix just outlined, yielding forms which are synchronically more or less opaque, e.g. *soha* [šohå] 'never' (< *S^{H}EN 'not + HA 'if/when').

Postpositions, Coverbs, and Other Adverbials
There are about twenty-five widely used postpositions. Most are perhaps better classified as dependent adverbs (Lotz 1939: 101), for they occur only in combination with nouns or with person suffixes. There are also a few pure postpositions, i.e. forms which occur only with nouns and never with person suffixes, e.g. OOTA *óta* [ootå] 'since'.

A small subgroup of eight postpositions distinguishes three (or, sometimes, two) locational/directional modes by means of marginal case suffixes, e.g. ALA-TTA *alatt* '(located) under', AL*A*-OOLA *alól* 'from under', AL*A*-AAH *alá* 'to under'. The remaining postpositions have only one form each, e.g. D^{J}ANAANT *gyanánt* [d^{j}ånant] 'as a', or, if two forms are used, at least one of them has only abstract, non-spatial, reference, e.g. $^\#$VEEGA-IG *végig* 'along' : $^\#$VEEGA-TT *végett* 'with an aim to'.

Most postpositions occur with their lexical noun in the nominative, but a few govern the superessive, e.g. TUUL 'beyond', AAT 'across, through', $^\#$BALUL 'within', as in AZ VAAROS^H-N $^\#$BALUL *a városon belül* 'within the city'. In stylistically marked utterances, a subset of this group of postpositions can also occur before their noun, e.g. TUUL AZ FOL^{J}OO-N *túl a folyón* 'beyond the river'. One postposition, KEEPAS^{H}T 'compared with, considering', takes the allative, e.g. KOR-IAA-H3Z KEEPAS^{H}T *korához képest* 'for his/her age'. In older varieties of Hungarian, postpositions commonly entered into possessive constructions, e.g. *szeretet-nek miatt-a* instead of *szeretet miatt* 'on account of affection'; see **Syntax**, p. 450.

Coverbs are a special class of adverbial modifiers which form loose compounds with verbs. There are about forty coverbs; many share root morphemes with postpositions, e.g. $^\#$ALOO *elő* [älöö] 'to the fore', cf. postposition $^\#$ALOO-TT *előtt* [älöött] 'in front of, before'. The productive noun case suffixes -RAA, -IG and -BAA are evident in a few coverbs, e.g. $^\#$ALOO-RAA *előre* 'in advance', $^\#$KOZ-RAA *közre* 'public', e.g. $^\#$KOZ-RAA|AD- *közre|GIVES-* 'publishes', $^\#$VEEGA-IG|FUT *végigfut-* 'runs the length of', cf. the postposition *végig* 'along'. Other coverbs are (often shorter variants of) third-person forms of case morphemes, e.g. *neki* 'to it' in $^\#$NAK-

IAA|LAAT- *nekilát-* 'sees to', *rajta* 'on it' in RAITĄ-ĮAA|KAP- *rajtakap-* 'catches in the act'. Still others are deictic primitives, e.g. KI 'out(wards)', LE 'down(wards)', and MEG 'correctly; back (to correct place or state)', which functions most often as a perfectivizer.

Besides their semantic and aspectual functions within the lexicon, coverbs also play an aspectual role within syntax; see the section on constituent order, p.451.

In their semantic and aspectual functions Hungarian coverbs overlap with those of Mansi and Khanty, but there are few cognates. Aspectual parallels may be found in Estonian and Slavonic, and German verbal prefixes have often served as models in calquing, e.g. *fel|fog-* UP|GRASPS 'comprehends' (*auffassen*), *be|lát-* IN|SEES 'understands' (*einsehen*), *utána|néz-* AFTER| SEES 'checks (whether X is the case)' (*nachsehen*).

Adverb formation. Many textually frequent adverbs are synchronically monomorphemic, e.g. *ma* 'today', *most* 'now', *már* 'now/then (as opposed to before)', *még* 'now/then (as before)', *rég* 'long ago', *rögtön* 'immediately'. Most commonly, however, adverbs are derived by one of three suffixes. In decreasing order of frequency, these are as follows:

1   =AN, e.g. D^JORS^H=AN *gyorsan* [d^joršån] 'quickly', cf. *gyors* 'quick', SEEP=AN *szépen* 'nicely', cf. SEEP *szép* 'good-looking, nice'. This suffix is thought to have arisen through a split in the function of the old locative *-nA; cf. the superessive suffix of the noun case paradigm (and D^JORS^H-N *gyorson* [d^joršon] 'on a fast (train)'). There is a parallel in Permian: cf. Komi/Udmurt instrumental *-ën/-en*, inessive *-ïn*.

2   =UL, e.g. MAD^JAR=UL *magyarul* 'in Hungarian', FINN=UL *finnül* 'in Finnish', KONOK=UL *konokul* 'stubbornly'. As the examples suggest, ethnonyms and pejoratives predominate. This suffix is often classified as a noun case, with the meaning 'as a, *qua*', i.e. as an essive. Historically, it is probably from a suffix sequence *-kI-lV, i.e. LATIVE + LOCATIVE/SEPARATIVE. Example: TAARS^H-UL *társul* [taaršul] 'as a companion'.

3   =LAG, e.g. KI|ZAAR=OO=LAG OUT|CLOSES=pres.part=*LAG kizár-ólag* 'exclusively', VISON^J=LAG RELATION=*LAG viszonylag* 'relatively', *RAMEEL=HAT=OO=LAG HOPES=potential=pres.part= *LAG remélhetőleg* 'hopefully'. Adverbs formed with this suffix occasionally contrast minimally with adverbs made with =AN, e.g. *egyhangúan* [et^jhåŋguuån] 'monotonously', *egyhangúlag* [et^jhåŋguulåg] 'unanimously', cf. ED^JD^J 'one', HANG 'sound, voice'.

Verb Inflection

Non-composite finite forms of verbs in Contemporary Standard Hungarian can be inflected either for mood or for tense. The moods are subjunctive (-IA-) and conditional (-ANAA-), both neutral with regard to tense (=

universal tense). The tenses are past (-TTA-) and non-past (-Ø-, -S-), both neutral with regard to mood (= indicative).

Person suffixes are added to the right of the tense/mood suffix. It is traditional to speak of two conjugations in Hungarian, the difference residing in the type of direct object encoded. Here we shall simplify by saying that there are two sets of person suffixes, each of which encodes a different sort of relationship between subject and object person. Suffixes of one set, here termed centrifugal, are used when the person of the object is greater than that of the subject (e.g. first-person subject/second-person object: 'I see you', or second-person subject/third-person object: 'you see her'). Suffixes from the other set, termed centripetal, are used when the reverse relation obtains (e.g. 'she sees me', 'they see you'). Centripetal suffixes are also used when there is no object at all ('they stand') or when the object is indefinite ('he makes coffee'). This formulation is correct as far as it goes, but the selection of suffixal morphemes and the morphophonemic details involved in their realization are both more complex than a binary split would suggest. For example, the centripetal suffix for first-person subjects is -3K, but with two types of exception: (1) in the past tense, it is -3M, syncretizing with its centrifugal pendant, and (2) for a large set of verbs (the deponents, called *ikes igék* 'verbs with *ik* [in the third person singular non-past]' in Hungarian) it is -3M or -3K in both tenses and both moods, the choice being made on the basis of a complex interaction of sociolinguistic, lexical, and stylistic factors (Abondolo 1988: 97–101). Figure 14.2 sets out the two sets of suffixes in morphophonemic code, with neither phonological nor morphological operations carried out, and presents a simplified picture in that deponent suffixation is not indicated. The following sample forms will illustrate some of the complexities entailed in the production of actual forms' from these analogues: OLVAS^H-Ø-IAA *olvassa* [olvåššå] '(s)he/it reads it (s33)', NEEZ-Ø-IAA *nézi* [neezi] '(s)he/it beholds him/her/it (s33)', MEN-ANAA-EEK *mennék* [menneek] 'I would (fain) go (s1cond)', #VAT=IIT-ANAA-IUK *vetítenők* [vätiitänöök] 'we would project it (p13cond)', #VAT=IIT-IA-IUK *vetítsük* [vätiiččük] 'let's/we should project it (p13sj)', LEV-IA-ANAK *legyenek* [ledʲänäk] 'they should be (p3sj)', MEN-TTA-M *mentem* [mentäm] 'I was going'.

There are also composite verb forms. These are rare in the standard contemporary language, with one exception: the past conditional, which is formed by the addition of the fixed form *volna* to a finite past-tense form, e.g. MEN-TTA-M VOLNAA *mentem volna* 'I would have gone (but I didn't)'.

Suppletion occurs only in the verb 'to be', which is also unique in showing ablaut of its stem vowel: VAL- (~ past-tense and conditional stem VOL-) : subjunctive stem LEV-. The stem LEV- has a full paradigm with the meaning 'becomes'. Two other stems, MEN- 'goes' and #IOV- 'comes', also show a few irregularities.

Figure 14.2   Hungarian verb person suffixation: agglutinating analogue

s1	s2	s3

	s1		s2	s3

P	-3K -EEK -3M	-AS/-3L -∅
		        -3L
			-3N
			     - ∅

F	-3M	-3D	-IAA

ps	sj	cd	pt	ps	sj	cd	pt	ps	sj	cd	pt

P	-UNK	-T3K	-ANAK	-K
F	-UNK -IUK -IUK	-IAAT3K	-IAAK	

p1	p2	p3

Key: s1, s2, etc. = subject person; ps = present, sj = subjunctive, cd = conditional, pt = past, P = centripetal, F = centrifugal object marking.

Non-finite Verb Forms, History of Verb Inflection

These are three participles, two gerunds, and an infinitive. Of these, the future participle and the past gerund are stylistically marked and have a limited distribution. In modal constructions the infinitive can take person suffixes in agreement with the agent e.g. #NAM SABAD SEM-T HUN^J-NI-IAA NOT PERMITTED EYE-acc SHUTS-inf-s3 *nem szabad szemet hunynia* '(s)he must not close (his/her) eye(s)'.

The infinitive -NI appears to be an old formation consisting of a deverbal noun in *=nA inflected with a lative suffix *-j; there is an exact parallel in Permian (Kulonen 1993: 65). The gerunds =VAA, =VAAN are probably cognate with the Khanty gerund reconstructed as *=mAAn ~ *=mIIn (Honti 1984: 59). The present participle =OO probably descends from a verbal noun built with *=pA, with cognates in Fennic (e.g. -b in Estonian third person singular *kuuleb* '(s)he hears') and Saamic (e.g. -p in Arjeplog Saami first person plural *kulla-p* 'we hear'). The future participle =ANDOO is thought to derive from the present participle of stems derived with the suffix chain =AM3D-, which once formed inchoatives, e.g. *fut=amod-ik* 'begins to run'. For the past participle, see under tense, below.

The historical background of Hungarian verb inflection is not clear in all of its details; here we briefly summarize a few of the less controversial highlights. The past-tense suffix used in contemporary standard Hungarian (-TTA-) is an innovation; it is based on the inflection, with person suffixes, of the past participle =TTA. The past participle, in turn, descends from a proto-Uralic verbal noun, *=(n)tA. An older past tense has been all but lost: it survives only in ceremonial and jocular language, and is formed with the suffix -AA-, which is a continuation of diphthongs arising from the combination of the stem-final vowel plus a past-tense suffix *-i-, which seems to have evolved from a verbal noun (Janhunen 1982: 36). This *-i- has clear cognates in Permian and the languages to the west, but it has also been detected in the final vocalism of the Hungarian conditional suffix -ANAA-. The long unrounded vowel of this latter suffix probably derives from an *i*-final diphthong; the conditional would then be the result of a relatively late compounding of the Finno-Ugric *-ne- conditional/potential suffix with the past-tense morpheme (Kulonen 1993: 64). We thus have a double shift in function, from tense to mood and from participle to tense:

	Stage I	Stage II	Contemporary Hungarian
Mood suffix		*-ne-i conditional ⟶	mennél 'you would go'
Tense suffix	*-i- past	*-tta- past ⟶	mentél 'you were going'
Verbal noun	*=(n)tA		

The present-tense zero suffix -∅- has parallels in all Finno-Ugric languages. The present tense in -S-, which is used only with the seven textually frequent verbs TEV- 'does/makes', VEV- 'takes ([-] locomotion)', #VIV- 'takes away ([+] locomotion)', EV- 'eats', IV- 'drinks', #HIV- 'believes', and LEV- 'becomes', is the continuation of a p(F)U durative, or de-perfectivizing, derivational suffix *=s^j, and may also be concealed in the present-tense stems of MEN- *megy-* 'goes' (with *gy* < *n-s^j) and VAL- *vagy-* 'is' (with *gy* < *l-s^j).

The subjunctive (-IA-) descends from proto-Uralic *-k(A-); it triggers several morphophonemic processes, including the above-mentioned ad-palatalization and j-assimilation, but also processes which are unique to it. For example, to the left of the subjunctive suffix a verb-stem final T > C^H if preceded by a consonant or a long vowel, but > S^H if preceded by a short vowel, cf. #VAT=IIT-IA-IUK *vetítsük* [vätiiččük] 'we should project it', #VAT-IA-IUK *vessük* [vässük] 'we should cast it'. Another example: in six stems, final V melds with the initial I of the subjunctive suffix to form the segment **d^j**, e.g. LEV-IA-3N *legyen* [led^{j}en] '(s)he/it should be'.

Since Hungarian finite verb forms encode not only subject person but also features of the direct object, it is not surprising that many of the suffixes are innovations, and that some of them have no exact analogues elsewhere in Uralic. Oldest are the singular centrifugal suffixes -3M, -3D, and -IAA, all three of which are historically identical with the corresponding possessive suffixes. Thus the third-person centrifugal -IAA seen in, e.g., *adja* '(s)he gives it' in all likelihood continues a verb form with a third-person suffix *-sA, e.g. *ïmta-sa >> *adəjə > *adjə > [åd^{j}d^{j}å]. The suffix which encodes first-person singular subject and second-person object is clearly a relatively late composite made up of the (secondary) second-person marker -3L plus the first-person suffix -3K, for both of which see below. Mordva, which is the only Uralic language to have a paradigmatic slot corresponding to this suffix, encodes it with etymologically different material, but in analogous fashion, viz. Erzya Mordva *kat\t\an* = Hungarian *hagy\l\ak* LEAVES-s2-s1 'I'll leave you' (cf. Tálos 1975: 46). The plural centrifugal suffixes all appear to be secondary formations: the *-j-* element that has crept into them all probably did so by analogy from the third person singular, but the precise lines of descent for the remaining portions of these suffixes remain unclear (see, however, Honti 1984: 75–6 for a Ugric etymology of the first-person plural form).

The centripetal forms are for the most part straightforward. The unmarked second- and third-person forms, i.e. respectively the imperative and indicative, were marked with zero. The marked forms were built up later, in the second-person non-imperative by means of suffixes which were originally durative/deperfectivizing in function (-3L, -AS; see also derivation, p. 452), and in the third-person imperative by means of suffixation of the third-person pronoun *sVn, i.e. *ïmta-ka-sVn >> *adəɣəjən >> [åd^jd^jon] *adjon* '(s)he should give' (cf. Kulonen 1993: 92–3); the third person plural -ANAK is a later secondary pluralization of this form. The first and second persons plural appear to be continuations of the pluralized person suffixes *-mI and *-tI.

The first person singular -3K (along with its offspring, the K of s12 -ALAK), however, is an enigma. Kulonen lists three explanations, none of them convincing (1993: 89–90); a few more may be found in Papp (1968: 174–7).

Syntax

In its simplest form, the Hungarian noun phrase consists of a nominal head (with inflectional suffixes and/or postpositions, any or all of which may be zero) preceded by slots (any of which may be empty) for quantifiers (QN), counters (CN), qualifiers (QL), emphatic pronouns (PRO), articles (ART), and demonstratives (DEM). Some of the combinatory possibilities are illustrated below, where the English equivalents are (1) 'my key', (2) 'these three large keys of mine', (3) 'concerning these keys of mine', (4) 'concerning this rusty bunch of keys', (5) 'concerning these three large keys'.

	DEM	ART	PRO	QN	QL	CN	QL	N-sxx (PP)
1		az	én					kulcs-Ø-om-Ø
2	ez	a		három			nagy	kulcs-Ø-om-Ø
3	ez-ek-ről	a						kulcsa-i-m-ről
4	er-ről	a			rozsdás	csomó		kulcs-Ø-Ø-ről
5	er-ről	a		három			nagy	kulcs-Ø-Ø-ról

As these examples show, the only members to show agreement within the noun phrase are the demonstratives, which agree with the head noun in number and case (3); furthermore, the presence of a quantifier higher than *egy* 'one', or of a counter, precludes plural marking (2, 4, 5). As examples 2–5 suggest, occupancy of the demonstrative slot by AZ or #AZ forces the presence of the definite article in the following slot, but in stylistically marked registers there are other demonstrative forms which preclude the article, e.g. (2a) *e három nagy kulcsom*.

Noun phrases may be linked in a possessive relation by the suffixation of the s3 person suffix to the possessed, with or without suffixation of the dative to the possessor, e.g. *a kalap-om(-nak a) karimá-ja* D.A HAT-s1(-dat D.A) RIM-s3 'the rim of my hat'. The longer construction is obligatory in the expression of multiple possessive relations, e.g. *a rövid hangzó-k idő+tartam-á-nak arány-a* D.A SHORT VOWEL-plur TIME+DURATION-s3-dat PROPORTION-s3 'the ratio of the duration of long vowels' and when the possessed precedes the possessor (*húg-a az apá-m-nak* YOUNGER.SISTER-s3 D.A FATHER-s1-dat 'my father's younger sister') or is separated from the possessor by the predicate (*apá-m-nak meghalt a húg-a* FATHER-s1-dat DIED D.A YOUNGER.SISTER-s3 'my father's younger sister died'). Otherwise both constructions are possible, but with pragmatic and textual distinctions, some of which entail the anaphoric and global functions of the article.

Qualifiers in the noun phrase may be participles with their own adverbial and object complements, e.g. *a népi műveltség-ben mutatkoz=ó különbség-ek* D.A FOLK CULTURE-ine IS.EVIDENCED=pres.part DIFFERENCE-plur 'differences evidenced in folk culture', or they may be qualifiers derived by means of the suffix =I from postposition-final noun phrases, e.g. *a vacsora után-i órá-k-ban* D.A DINNER AFTER=adjsx HOUR-plur-ine 'in the hours after dinner'.

More sophisticated accounts of the noun phrase may be found in Kornai 1985 and Szabolcsi 1987, both with good bibliography; on counters see now Beckwith (1992).

Syntactic Roles, the Use of Case Suffixes and Constituent Orders

Subjects are normally marked with zero (-∅) and direct objects with -T, e.g. *a jel=z=ő-∅ meg\elő=z-∅-i a jel=z=ett szó-t* D.A SIGN=VdN=pres.part-N PERF\FORE=VdN-pres-s33 D.A SIGN=VdN=past.part WORD-acc '(the) modifier precedes the modified word'. A direct object which is inflected for first or second person singular, however, can also go into the nominative, e.g. *levele\d-∅ meg\kap-ta-m* LETTER-s2-N PERF\GETS-past-s13 'I got your letter'. Indirect objects are put in the dative (-NAK), e.g. *malac+sül=te-t ad-ott-∅ a fiú-k-nak* PIGLET+ROASTS=past.part-ACC GIVES-past-s3 D.A BOY-plur-dat '(s)he gave roast suckling pig to the boys'. The dative here acts like any other lative in that it is interchangeable with the accusative in parallel instrumental constructions, e.g. *meg\kínál-t-a a fiú-ka-t malac+súl=t-tel* PERF|OFFERS-past-s33 D.A BOY-plur-acc PIGLET+ROASTS=past.part-ins '(s)he offered the boys roast suckling pig'.

The dative is also used to mark higher participants in constructions with auxiliaries, e.g. *Kálmán-nak Budá-ra kell-Ø-Ø men-ni(-e)* KÁLMÁN-dat BUDA-subl IS.NECESSARY-pres-s3 GOES-inf(-s3) 'Kálmán has to go to Buda', and in sentences with non-personal verb forms such as *kövér-nek len-ni vidám dolog* FAT-dat IS-inf MERRY THING 'being fat is fun'.

The neutral order for major constituents is TOPIC(S) – FOCUS – FINITE VERB, e.g. *András grúzul tud ANDRÁS* GEORGIAN-adv KNOWS '(As for) Andrew, it's Georgian that he knows'. If the finite verb is the focus, it comes first, e.g. *Tud András grúzul* or *Tud grúzul András*. The rules applying to the order of (aspectual v. spatial) coverbs and of auxiliary verbs are of special interest and complexity; see Kálmán et al. (1990).

Lexicon

Derivation of four basic types is widespread, viz. (1a) denominal nominals (e.g. *sár* 'mud' : *sár=os* 'muddy', *sárga* 'yellow' : *sárgá=s* 'yellowish'), (1b) deverbal nominals (e.g. *ad-* 'gives' : *ad=ás* 'act of giving' : *ad=at* 'datum' : *ad=ag* 'portion' : *ad=ó* 'tax'), (2a) denominal verbs (e.g. *sárg=ul-* 'becomes yellow', *sárgás=od-ik* 'becomes yellowish', *ad=at=ol-* 'provides/backs up with data') and (2b) deverbal verbs. Space permits us only a brief glance at this last type.

A large and open set of affective, quasi-descriptive verbs are formed with the suffix =(3)G-, usually from themes, e.g. *kop=og-* 'knocks', *tip=eg-* waddles, toddles', *döc=ög-* 'trundles along'; most of these verbs refer to repeated activities or to activities which consist of numerous recurrences. Many have semelfactive analogues formed with =$AN- which refer to single events ($ is an operator which occurs only in derivation and which lengthens a preceding consonant, where possible), e.g. *kop=pan-* 'knocks (once)', *döc=cen-* 'jolts, jerks (once)'. Productive, also, is the detransitivizing =OOD-, e.g. *emel=őd-ik* 'rises (of its own accord)' alongside *emel=ked-ik* 'rises, climbs', both from *emel-* 'raises'.

Many verbs which are synchronically monomorphemic contain the relicts of older derivational suffixes, e.g. *néz-* 'beholds' from *näki=tä-, a durative/continuative derivate of *näki- 'sees', known from e.g. Finnish *näke-* 'sees'; *keres-* 'seeks', built with a detransitivizing/deperfectivizing suffix *=s^j ~ *=c^j, cf. *kér-* 'asks for' and Komi *kor* 'asks for', *kor=š^j-* 'seeks'. Reflexes of other Finno-Ugric suffixes with deperfectivizing, frequentative, or multiobjectival force are the =*sz-* found in *met=sz-* [mäcc] 'slices thinly', cf. *met=él=t* 'noodles' and the present-tense -S- suffix (see p. 447), as well as the =*d-* in *marad-* 'remains' (< *=ntV-).

Loanwords come from four major sources and may be grouped, in rough chronological order, into Iranian, Turkic, Slavonic, and Western European, although there is some overlap, e.g. early Turkic loans into pre-Hungarian, contemporaneous with the earliest Iranian layers, or the thin layer of sixteenth-century Turkish loans (see below), which postdate the early Slavonic items. Loans from Romanian and Romani are relatively few in number, but rich in semantic and stylistic content.

Iranian loans into Hungarian date back to the time immediately after the breakup of Ugric unity or contact. Early examples are #TIZA *tíz* 'ten', #TAHANA *tehén* 'cow', and #TAIA *tej* 'milk', in all of which pre-Hungarian has substituted its sole, voiceless, initial dental *t-* for the voiced sounds of the donor language; by the time Hungarian borrowed the Slavonic cognate of the last of these, viz. *dajka* 'wet nurse', it had acquired *d-* in initial position. Contact with Iranian idioms must have lasted well over a thousand years, culminating with loans such as *nád* 'reed', from a late Middle Iranian language of the southern Russian steppe.

The three layers of loans from Turkic languages are surveyed in Róna-Tas (1988: 751–60). These are (1) so-called pre-conquest loans, i.e. borrowed into Hungarian before its speakers arrived in Europe, (2) medieval loans, and (3) occupation loans. The first layer is particularly large and varied, and includes words which must have been borrowed from Turkic idioms of a Chuvash type, e.g. *borjú* 'calf', cf. Chuvash *pŏru* v. Turkish *buzağı*, *dél* 'midday; south', cf. Chuvash *tĕl* v. Common Turkic *'tüš'*. The second layer is made up primarily of words borrowed from the languages of the Pechenegs and the Cumanians, Turkic-speaking groups which settled in Hungary in the twelfth and thirteenth centuries; examples are *koboz* 'lute-like instrument', and *komondor* 'breed of dog'. The most recent layer entered Hungarian with the Turkish occupation (roughly 1526–1698). These words, of which only about twenty survive, are usually also well represented in the languages of the Balkans, through which the Turks had passed earlier on their way into the heart of Europe. Examples are *zseb* 'pocket', with pendants in Serbian, Albanian, Bulgarian, and Greek, and *tepsi* 'baking dish', with pendants in all those languages plus Romanian.

A conspicuous number of the items borrowed from or via Slavonic are religious or domestic/agrarian in content. For example, from Latin come both *pogány* 'pagan' (via South Slavonic) and its doublet *pohánka* 'buckwheat' (via Czech); note also *paradicsom* 'paradise'; [from 1856] 'tomato', borrowed direct from Latin, with the Latin neuter ending (*-um*) intact. Other Slavonic doublets: *vacsora* 'evening meal', *vecsernye* 'vespers'; *cölöp* 'peg', *oszlop* 'column'; *genny* 'purulent matter', *ganéj* 'manure'. Not only doublets, but also interdialectal synonyms have entered Hungarian from Slavonic, e.g. *bab* 'bean' and (dialect) *paszuly* 'bean' (via Slovene from Greek, which had it from Italian). Many items must, to judge from their meaning and form, be Slavonic, but their antecedents are as yet unknown, e.g. *poggyász* 'luggage', *drusza* 'namesake'.

Loans from German(ic) date from the first arrival of the Hungarians in

Europe, perhaps even earlier (Rot 1988: 697). Among the older loans are *példa* 'example' (Modern German *Bild*), *cérna* 'thread' (*Zwirn*), and *bognár* 'cartwright' (*Wagner*).

Until recently, western European loans entered primarily by way of German (e.g. *kozmosz* 'cosmos', *likőr* 'liqueur', *meteor* 'meteor', *nábob* 'nabob', and *púder* 'powder'), although there was also some direct borrowing from Italian and from French (there were Walloon merchants from at least the twelfth century in the larger Hungarian cities [Bárczi 1958: 111]). Examples of direct Italian borrowings, probably adopted during the Angevin period (1308–82) are *pajzs* 'shield' (Italian *pavese* 'of Pavia [famous for its shields])', *pálya* 'prize, contest, racetrack; career' (*palio*). Examples from French: *kilincs* 'latch' (*clenche*), *tárgy* 'object (earlier: type of shield; target)'.

Hungarian Text
From a letter written 1910 by Artúr Elek to Miksa Fenyő (Vezér 1975: 336).

A: orthography; B: phonological transcription; C: morphophonemic code, segmented; D: morpheme-by-morpheme gloss; E: loose translation of D; F: freer translation.

A1 Ezzel	a	levelemmel	egyidejűleg
B1 äz-zäl	å	lävälämmäl	ed^jd^jidäjü(ü)läg
C1 #AZ-VAL	AZ	#LAVALA-MA-VAL	ED^J+#IDAIA=IUU=LAG
D1 THIS-ins	D.A	LETTER-s1-ins	ONE+TIME=adjsx=adv
E1 with this	the	with my letter	simultaneously

postára	adom	a	Fogazzaro-fordítást
poštaarå	ådom	å	fogådd^zåroofordiitaašt
POS^HTAA-RAA	AD-Ø-3M	AZ	F+^FOR=D=IIT=AAS^H-T
POST-subl	GIVES-pres-s13	D.A	F.+TURN=vbsx=vbsx=NdV-acc
on to post	I give it	the	Fogazzaro-translation

A2 Nem	tudom	hogy	elég	lesz-e
B2 näm	tudom	hod^j	äleeg	lässe
C2 #NAM	TUD-Ø-3M	HOD^J	#ALAGA	LEV-S-Ø--E
D2 NOT	KNOWS-pres-s13	CJ	ENOUGH	BECOMES-pres-s3–I.Q
E2 not	I know it	that	enough	whether it will be

nem	is	hiszem	A3 Legjobb	lenne
näm	iš	hisem	B3 lägjobb	lennä
#NAM	IS^H	HIV-S-3M	C3 #LAG+IO=BBA	LEV-ANAA-Ø
NOT	PTL	BELIEVES-pres-s13	D3 SUP+GOOD=cfv	BECOMES-cond-s3
not	duly	I believe it	E3 best	it would be(come)

kiszedetni   hogy   megtudjam   esetleg
kisädätni   hod^j mektud^{j}d^{j}åm   äšätläg
KI|SED=AT=NI   HOD^J MEG|TUD-IA-M $^\#$AS^H=AT=LAG
OUT|SETS=caus=inf   PERF|KNOWS-sj-s13   FALLS=NdV=adv
to have (it) set   (so) that   I should find it out   if such is the case

mekkora   terjedelmű   másik   novellát
mäkkorå   tärjädälmü(ü)   maašik   novällaat
$^\#$MAK+KORAA $^\#$^TARI=AD=ALMA=IUU   MAAS^H=IK   NOVELLAA-T
HOW.BIG   ^EXTEND=vsx=NdV   OTHER=   NOVELLA-acc
               =adjsx   INDIV
how big   extensive   other   novella

fordítsak   hozzája.
fordiiččåk   hozzaajå
^FOR=D=IIT-IA-3K   HOZZAA-IAA
^TURN=vbsx=vbsx-sj-s1   TO-s3
I should translate   to (go with) it

F1 I'm posting the Fogazzaro translation at the same time as this letter (of
mine). F2 I don't know whether it'll be enough; I doubt it (in fact). F3 The
best thing would be to have it typeset so I can see whether I have to translate
another novella to go with it, and if so, how long it'll have to be.

References and Further Reading

Abondolo, D. (1988) *Hungarian Inflectional Morphology*, Bibliotheca Uralica 9,
    Budapest: Akadémiai kiadó.
Bárczi, G. (^{2}1958) *Magyar hangtörténet*, Budapest: Tankönyvkiadó.
Beckwith, C.I. (1992) 'Classifiers in Hungarian', in Kenesei et al., vol. IV,
    pp. 197–204.
Berrár, J. (1957) *Magyar történeti mondattan*, Budapest: Tankönyvkiadó.
Gósy, M. (1989) *Beszédészlelés*, Linguistica Series A, Studia et dissertationes 2.
    Budapest: A magyar tudományos akadémia nyelvtudományi intézete.
Hetzron, R. (1982) 'Non-applicability as a test for category definitions', in F. Kiefer
    (ed.), *Hungarian Linguistics*, Linguistic and Literary Studies in Eastern Europe 4,
    Amsterdam–Philadelphia: Benjamins, pp. 131–83.
Honti, L. (1984) *Chrestomathia ostiacica*, Budapest: Tankönyvkiadó.
Janhunen, J. (1982) 'On the structure of Proto-Uralic', *FUF* 44: 23–42.
Kálmán, B., (1965) 'A magyar mássalhangzó-rendszer kialakulása', *Magyar Nyelv*
    61, 285–398.
Kálmán, G.C. et al. (1990) 'A magyar segédigék rendszere', *Általános Nyelvészeti
    Tanulmányok* 17: 49–103.
Kenesei, I. et. al (eds) (1985–92) *Approaches to Hungarian* [= *ATH*], vol. I 1985, vol.
    II 1987, vol. IV 1992, Szeged: Attila József University.
Keresztes, László (1993) 'Új magánhangzó-fonémák a magyarban?', in *Hajdú Péter
    70 éves* [Festschrift for P. Hajdú], Linguistica Series A, Studia et dissertationes 15,
    ed. Sz. M. Bakró-Nagy and E. Szíj, Budapest: Linguistic Institute of the Hungarian
    Academy of Sciences.

Kiefer, F. (ed.) (1992) *Strukturális magyar nyelvtan*, vol. II: *Fonológia* [= SMN, 2], Budapest: Akadémiai kiadó.

Korhonen, M. (1981) *Johdatus lapin kielen historiaan*, Helsinki: Suomalaisen Kirjallisuuden Seura.

Kornai, A. (1985) 'The internal structure of noun phases', in Kenesei et al. vol. I, pp. 79–92.

—— (1994) *On Hungarian Morphology*, Linguistica Series A, Studia et dissertationes, Budapest: Linguistics Institute of the Hungarian Academy of Sciences.

Kulonen, Ulla-Maija (1993) *Johdatus unkarin kielen historiaan*, Suomi 170, Helsinki: Suomalaisen kirjallisuuden seura.

Lakó, G. (1965) *A magyar hangállomány finnugor előzményei*, Nyelvtudományi értekezések 47, Budapest: Akadémiai kiadó.

Lotz, J. (1939) *Das ungarische Sprachsystem*, (Old) Publication Series of the Hungarian Institute of Stockholm 3, reissued 1988 as Eurasian Language Archives 1, ed. G. Décsy, Bloomington: Eurolingua.

Lotz, J. (1967) 'Egy nyelvtani modell (Két fejezet a magyar nyelvtanból)', *Magyar Nyelv* 63: 394–408.

Melcsuk, I. (1968) 'A magyar főnévragozás egy újabb modellje', *Nyelvtudományi Értekezések* 58: 502–5.

Mikola, T. (1975) *Die alten Postpositionen des Nenzischen (Juraksamojedischen)*, Budapest: Akadémiai kiadó.

Nádasdy, A. (1985) 'Segmental Phonology and Morphophonology', in Kenesci et al., vol. I, pp. 225–46.

Papp, F. (1975) *A magyar főnév paradigmatikus rendszere*, Budapest: Akadémiai kiadó.

Papp, I. (1968) *Unkarin kielen historia*, Tietolipas 54, Helsinki: Suomalaisen kirjallisuuden seura.

Róna-Tas, A. (1988) 'Turkic influence on the Uralic languages' in D. Sinor (ed.), *The Uralic Languages: Description, History and Foreign Influences*, Handbuch der Orientalistik 8, Leiden: Brill, pp. 742–80.

Rot, S. (1988) 'Germanic influences on the Uralic languages', in D. Sinor (ed.), *The Uralic Languages: Description, History and Foreign Influences*, Handbuch der Orientalistik 8, Leiden: Brill, pp. 682–705.

Sammallahti, P. (1988) 'Historical phonology of the Uralic languages, with special reference to Samoyed, Ugric, and Permic', in D. Sinor (ed.), *The Uralic Languages: Description, History and Foreign Influences*, Handbuch der Orientalistik 8, Leiden: Brill, pp. 478–554.

Sherwood, P. (1996) *A Concise Introduction to Hungarian*, SSEES Occasional Papers no. 34, London: University of London.

Sima, F. (1971) *Magyar nyelvtörténet*, vol. I, Bratislava: Slovenské pedagogické nakladatel'stvo.

Szabolcsi, A. (1987) 'Functional categories in the noun phrase', in Kenesei et al. (eds) vol. II, pp. 167–89.

Szilágyi, S. N. (1980) *Magyar nyelvtan*, Bucharest: Editura didactică şi pedagogică.

Tálos, E. (1975) 'A magyar hang- és alaktan néhány kérdéséhez', *Uralica (Journal of the Uralic Society of Japan)* 3: 39–53.

Vezér, E. (1975) *Feljegyzések és levelek a Nyugatról*, Új magyar múzeum: irodalmi dokumentumok gyűjteménye 10, Budapest: Akadémiai kiadó.

Viitso, T.-R. (1996) 'On classifying the Finno-Ugric languages', *C8IFU* vol. IV: 261–6.

15 Samoyedic

Juha Janhunen

Geographically occupying the eastern periphery of the language family, Samoyedic is conventionally classified as one of the two principle branches of Uralic. After the breakup of proto-Uralic linguistic unity, the speakers of pre-proto-Samoyedic gradually came to be concentrated in the region located between the middle courses of the Ob' and Yenisei Rivers in southwest Siberia. Unlike the Finno-Ugric branch, which shows a high degree of internal diversity, Samoyedic has no surviving early sub-branches, the historically known Samoyedic languages forming a coherent group of relatively closely related idioms. In terms of absolute dating, proto-Samoyedic seems to have dissolved as recently as the last centuries BCE. Consecutive waves of ethnic and linguistic expansion then spread the various forms of Samoyedic both northwards, along the Ob' and Yenisei basins, and southwards, in the direction of the Altai and Sayan Mountains. It is reasonable to assume that in the course of this expansion several unidentified non-Samoyedic languages spoken earlier in the same regions became extinct due to linguistic assimilation. Most of the modern Samoyedic-speaking ethnic groups are therefore composed of two major ethnohistorical components: a local component corresponding to the earlier indigenous population, and an immigrant component responsible for the Samoyedic language.

The Samoyedic branch may rather uncontroversially be divided into six main entities or independent major languages: Nenets (Yurak), along the Arctic coast from the White Sea region to western Taimyr; Enets (Yenisei-Samoyed), in the lower Yenisei region; Nganasan (Tavgy), on the Taimyr Peninsula from the lower Yenisei in the west to the Khatanga Bay in the east; Selkup (Ostyak-Samoyed), in the region between the Ob' and Yenisei from the Taz and Turukhan in the north to the Chaya and Chulym in the south; Kamas (Kamassian), in the eastern part of the upper Yenisei region; and Mator (Motor), in the eastern Sayan Mountains from the upper Yenisei in the west to the Baikal region in the east. Considerable dialectal differences are present within Nenets (with Tundra Nenets and Forest Nenets), Enets (with Tundra or *Madu* Enets and Forest or *Bai* Enets), and Selkup (with a complex dialect continuum). In addition, a separate, transitional idiom, technically termed *Yurats*, once existed between Nenets and Enets. Both Kamas and Mator are historically known by a variety of alternative names, including

457

Taigi and *Karagas* for Mator, and *Koibal* for Kamas. These names are mainly of geographical and chronological interest; linguistically Kamas and Mator are two well-delimited entities with a minimum of internal dialectal differentiation. Some sources recognize a transitional idiom, technically termed *Abakan*, between Kamas and Mator, but this is better seen as a philological conglomeration of early Kamas and Mator lexical material.

In terms of their geographical environment, the speakers of the Samoyedic languages form three distinct ecological groups: the Tundra Samoyeds, the Taiga Samoyeds, and the Mountain Samoyeds. The Taiga Samoyeds are essentially identical with the speakers of Selkup, who up to the present day occupy a territory more or less coterminous with the original Samoyed habitat in the western Siberian forest zone. The Tundra Samoyeds comprise the major part of the speakers of Nenets, Enets, and Nganasan, who together occupy the whole of the Arctic tundra zone of European Russia and western Siberia. The Mountain Samoyeds comprise the speakers of Kamas and Mator, who used to inhabit the wooded highlands of southern Siberia. The ethnolinguistic development during the last few centuries has been least favourable for the Mountain Samoyeds, whose languages are now extinct, Mator since the first half of the nineteenth century and Kamas since the death of the last speaker in 1989. Extinction also threatens the Taiga Samoyeds, although Selkup (with under 2,000 speakers) still survives, albeit dialectally highly fragmented, as a living language. The Tundra Samoyeds have been generally less exposed to external threats, and Nenets (with some 25,000 speakers) has emerged (together with Northern Saami and Greenlandic) as one of the three principal Arctic languages of the world. Unfortunately, the expansion of Nenets in the lower Yenisei region has been at the expense of Enets, which (with fewer than 100 speakers remaining) is now facing imminent extinction. The Nenets expansion was also one of the factors that caused the disappearance of Yurats in the nineteenth century. Nganasan was never seriously affected by these developments, but the small size of the Nganasan community (with hardly more than 500 speakers) is becoming an obstacle to the survival of this language in the future.

Taxonomic Relationships

The conventional view holds that the ecological trichotomy of the Samoyedic-speaking populations correlates with a genetic division (cf. Figure 15.1), in that the Tundra Samoyeds are linguistically supposed to correspond to a separate Northern Samoyedic sub-branch, as opposed to a Southern Samoyedic sub-branch. Within the latter, the languages of the Mountain Samoyeds have been assumed to form a shallow-level sub-branch termed *Sayan Samoyedic*. This taxonomy has been questioned more and more often in recent years, as it has become evident that much of the internal coherence within each proposed sub-branch must be due to secondary mutual influences.

Figure 15.1 The conventional taxonomy of the Samoyedic languages

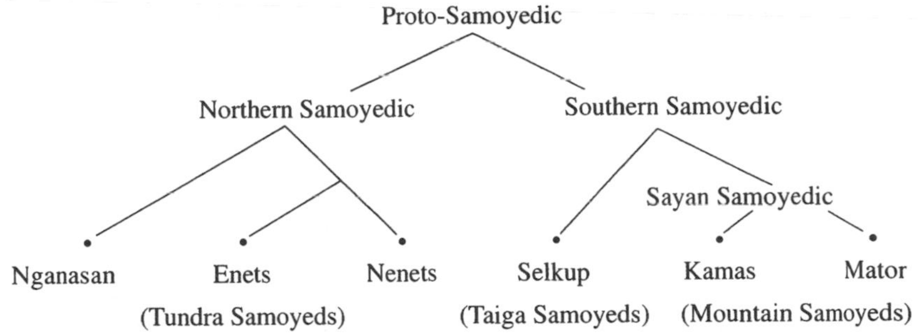

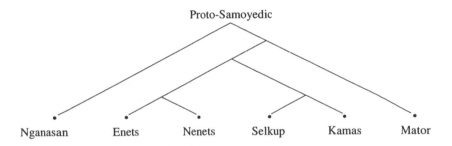

Figure 15.2 An alternative taxonomy of the Samoyedic languages

No conclusive new taxonomy has yet emerged, but there are indications that the first entity to have broken off from proto-Samoyedic unity may have been Nganasan, possibly followed by Mator (cf. Figure 15.2). This situation would correlate well with the geographical fact that Nganasan and Mator represent the northeastern and southeastern extremities in the geographical continuum of the Samoyedic languages. In this continuum, each language shares a number of diagnostic features with its immediate neighbour: Nganasan with Enets, Enets with Nenets, Nenets with Selkup, Selkup with Kamas, and Kamas with Mator. However, there are also features which, at least superficially, link the extremities with each other: Nganasan with Mator, and Northern Samoyedic with Sayan Samoyedic.

Documentation

Of the six Samoyedic languages, only Nenets may be regarded as well documented for both descriptive and comparative purposes, though a considerable amount of additional documentation will still be required for a detailed understanding of Nenets dialectology. Somewhat less information is available on Selkup, especially if only printed sources are taken into consideration. Additional material on both (Tundra) Nenets and (Northern) Selkup is provided by the modern literary languages, which have existed, with many vicissitudes, since the early 1930s. By contrast, Nganasan and Enets have until recently remained poorly documented at all levels of linguistic substance, the results of the latest field research being still unpublished. Nevertheless, the grammatical and lexical information now available on Nganasan and Enets is quite sufficient to allow these two languages to be seriously analysed in a comparative context. The same is true of Kamas, although the material collected from the last few generations of Kamas speakers reflects a somewhat rudimentary command of the language. For Mator, only lexical information was noted down in time, leaving the morphology and syntax of this language virtually unknown. In terms of absolute time, the available notes on Mator cover the period extending from the early eighteenth to the early nineteenth century, while Kamas material was collected from the early eighteenth century until the 1970s. The earliest notes on the other Samoyedic languages derive from the seventeenth century.

Diachronic Evaluation

The close cognateness of the Samoyedic languages allows us to reconstruct proto-Samoyedic as a rather uniform idiom with a relatively elaborate set of unambiguously established phonological and morphological characteristics. The conventional view has been that a feature which is present in both Northern Samoyedic and Southern Samoyedic is to be recognized as deriving from proto-Samoyedic, but this criterion will have to be reviewed if a different approach is adopted to the internal taxonomy of Samoyedic. Although there is no single Samoyedic language which would provide a simple key to proto-Samoyedic, a great deal of diachronic information can be drawn from Nenets by the method of internal reconstruction. In the comparative framework, an important place is occupied by Nganasan, which in some fundamental ways deviates from the patterns exhibited by the rest of the Samoyedic languages. At the opposite extreme, Mator would also be of great potential importance, were it not so poorly documented. Each Samoyedic language is characterized by a basically idiosyncratic set of archaisms and innovations, but there are indications that Nganasan and Mator are in certain ways particularly conservative, while the more centrally located languages are generally more innovatory. Nevertheless, even Selkup occasionally preserves diachronically relevant information which has been obscured in the rest of the Samoyedic languages.

Typological Variation

In the light of the available reconstructions, and possibly because of systematic distortions connected with the comparative method, proto-

Samoyedic appears to have been a language with an abundant system of word forms created by quasi-mechanical agglutination. A few morphophonological alternations can also be reconstructed, but morphophonology plays a considerably more important role in the modern Samoyedic languages. There is a clear tendency towards increasing morphophonological complexity towards the north and northeast, with Nganasan exhibiting an exceptionally large number of cumulative morphophonological phenomena, including consonant gradation in both stems and suffixes, stem-final vowel and consonant alternations, and vowel harmony of a highly idiosyncratic type. As far as the system of morphophonological categories is concerned, Northern Samoyedic seems to have preserved the original proto-Samoyedic state somewhat better than Southern Samoyedic has done, but variation is considerable between the individual languages. The same is true of the patterns of segmental structure, which differ greatly not only between adjacent languages, but even between the dialects of a single language. Areally and typologically relevant peculiarities of the segmental paradigm appear to be particularly numerous in Nenets and Selkup.

Proto-Samoyedic and Proto-Uralic

For a long time in the history of Uralic comparative studies, it was customary to approach proto-Uralic from the Finno-Ugric side alone. Insofar as Samoyedic is to be recognized as a branch parallel with Finno-Ugric, it is obvious that a definitive understanding of proto-Uralic will only be possible after binary comparison has been made between proto-Samoyedic and proto-Finno-Ugric. However, as there still seem to be considerable taxonomic and reconstructional problems to be solved for the eastern branches of Finno-Ugric, a simplified but very useful approximation of proto-Uralic can be obtained in the meantime by comparing proto-Samoyedic with proto-Baltic-Fennic, with additional information drawn, as required, from Saami and Mordva. On the historical map of the Uralic languages, proto-Samoyedic and proto-Baltic-Fennic are two roughly contemporaneous idioms, both of which are fairly uncontroversially reconstructable by a comparative analysis of their modern descendants. Also, as these two branches represent opposite geographical extremes of the Uralic language family, it may be assumed that any diachronic feature shared by proto-Samoyedic and proto-Baltic-Fennic is likely to derive from proto-Uralic. The number of such shared features is fairly high, especially as far as morphology is concerned, a situation which suggests that Samoyedic and Baltic-Fennic are in many important respects equally and similarly conservative. The eastern branches of Finno-Ugric obviously represent the more innovatory centre of the language family, and they may well prove to be of less relevance to the reconstruction of proto-Uralic than the two peripheries.

Further Reading

Classic introductory works on Samoyedic with good bibliographies are Hajdú (1963, 1968, and 1988). A general evaluation of the ethnohistorical position of the Samoyedic-speaking peoples is Xelimskij (1983). Problems of genetic taxonomy are dealt with in Xelimskij (1982a: 27–47) (Samoyedic in general), Xelimskij (1976) (the status of Yurats), Janhunen (1991) (the position of Nganasan). Dialectological treatments of the individual Samoyedic languages include Salminen (1990) (Nenets), Janurik (1985) (Nenets and Selkup), Xelimskij (1985a) (Enets), Janurik (1978) (Selkup), Künnap (1985) (Selkup and Kamas).

Phonology

Consonant Paradigm

There is a widespread consensus today that proto-Samoyedic possessed thirteen consonant phonemes, which represent four or five places of articulation and five to seven modes of articulation (cf. Figure 15.3). Four places of articulation (labial : dental : palatal : velar) are clearly present in the nasal series *m *n *ñ *ng, while the five obstruents *p *t *c *s *k may be defined either in terms of five separate places of articulation (labial : dental : cacuminal : palatal : velar) or, alternatively, by assuming distinctive modes of articulation for *s (continuant and/or sibilant) and *c (retroflex and/or affricated). The interpretation of *s as belonging to the palatal series is probably correct for pre-proto-Samoyedic, but by the proto-Samoyedic period this segment seems to have become more closely connected with the dental series. The segment *c is preserved only in part of the Selkup dialects, where its quality varies between a dental affricate and a retroflex stop, while in the rest of the Samoyedic idioms it has invariably merged with the dental stop *t. The two liquids *l *r may be characterized in terms of a complex distinction involving both place and mode of articulation (lateral : vibrant), but morphophonological evidence suggests that their primary phonological

Figure 15.3   The proto-Samoyedic consonant paradigm

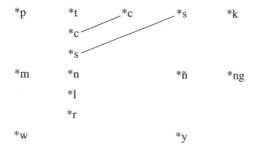

opposition may have concerned the feature of continuance (stop : continuant). The two glides *w *y correspond to two separate places of articulation (labial : palatal).

Vowel Paradigm

Proto-Samoyedic seems to have had a system of one reduced and ten full vowel phonemes (see paradigm below).

Full				
	*u	*ï	*ü	*i
	*o	*ë	*ö	*e
	*a			*ä

Reduced		*ø		

The reduced vowel *ø was probably the least marked member of the paradigm, distinguished from the full vowels by being quantitatively shorter and prosodically weaker. The full vowels represent three degrees of opening (high v. middle v. low) and four different combinations of lip-rounding with frontness/backness (rounded back v. unrounded back v. rounded front v. unrounded front). In pre-proto-Samoyedic these distinctions were probably fully employed only in the high series *i *u *ï *ü, while the mid series seems originally to have comprised only the three vowels *e *o *ë, the fourth mid vowel *ö appearing as a marginal new phoneme at the proto-Samoyedic level. The low series consisted of the two vowels *a *ä; these may have been distinguished phonetically either by lip-rounding (rounded back v. unrounded back) or by frontness/backness (unrounded back vs. unrounded front). The vowel *ä, in particular, may have been qualitatively unstable: its reflexes in the modern languages are variously either front vowels (in Nenets, Enets and Mator) or back vowels (elsewhere).

Vowel Sequences

An important characteristic of proto-Samoyedic vowel phonotaxis was the fact that in initial syllables any full vowel could be followed by the reduced vowel, in a sequence of the type *Vø. There is evidence that these vowel sequences were in proto-Samoyedic rhythmically equivalent to bisyllabic sequences of the type *VCø, but at the pre-proto-Samoyedic level they may be derived from monosyllabic units involving a syllable-final consonant. The consonant in question has been reconstructed as *x, and it is probably to be classified as a velar glide, paradigmatically parallel to the other two glides *w *y. The non-syllabic origin of the reduced vowel in vowel sequences explains the absence of any such sequences with a full vowel as the latter component. For related diachronic reasons it also seems that a sequence of two reduced vowels was not permitted in proto-Samoyedic. Among the modern languages, consistent traces of the vowel sequences are preserved only in Nganasan and Enets, the two idioms which synchronically permit the linear accumulation of two or more syllabic segments. Nganasan and Enets also possess secondary vowel sequences, sometimes analysed as 'long vowels' and 'diphthongs', which have arisen through the loss of an intervocalic consonant or glide. Somewhat similar secondary vowel sequences are present in Nenets, where original vowel sequences have generally merged with the paradigm of single vowels. In the other Samoyedic languages vowel sequences can only occasionally be traced in otherwise inexplicable qualitative developments.

Morpheme Structure

The structure of underived nominal and verbal stems in pre-proto-Samoyedic may be described by the general formula *(C)V(X)(C)(CV), where X stands for the glides *w *y *x. The same structural types were preserved in proto-Samoyedic, with the modification that by then *x was vocalized into *ø. Like Baltic-Fennic, proto-Samoyedic had many lexical items of the proto-Uralic bisyllabic type *(C)V(C)CV, as in *møna 'egg' (proto-Uralic *muna), *yentø 'sinew' (proto-Uralic *yänti). However, structurally innovative monosyllables of the type *(C)VC, as in *wit 'water' (proto-Uralic *weti), were also conspicuously abundant. An important new type of morpheme structure was *(C)V, which developed regularly in items containing a proto-Uralic intervocalic *x, as in *to 'lake' (proto-Uralic *toxï). The occurrence of vowel sequences in underived stems was primarily restricted to the type *(C)VXC, as in *kaøt 'fir' (proto-Uralic *kaxsï), but for reasons not yet explained there also appeared the type *(C)VX, as in *kaø- 'dies' (proto-Uralic *kax=lï-). Any more complicated structures, as in *kaøsa 'man' (< *kaø=sa 'mortal'), imply the presence of an etymological morpheme boundary. A morpheme boundary may also be assumed to have been originally present in any other cases in which a bisyllabic sequence is followed by an extension of the type *-C((C)V). It seems, however, that a few original complex stems had already been transformed into monomorphemic entities in proto-Samoyedic. This must have been the case in, for instance, *ïnø(=)pø 'parent-in-law' (proto-Uralic *ïna+ïppï).

Consonant Phonotaxis

The complete proto-Samoyedic paradigm of consonants is attested only intervocalically; other positions were subject to various phonotactic restrictions. A restriction of areal relevance, deriving from proto-Uralic and still valid for the modern Samoyedic languages, excluded the liquid *r* from word-initial position. In pre-proto-Samoyedic there seems to have been a tendency to extend this restriction to the other liquid *l*, as well, for most of the Uralic items with *l- show *y- in proto-Samoyedic, as in *yom- 'to snow' (proto-Uralic *lomï-). There are, however, a few instances in which *l- has been preserved intact, as in *lë 'bone' (proto-Uralic *lïxï), and in the post-proto-Uralic part of the proto-Samoyedic lexicon *l- is fully permitted.

Interestingly, the word-initial situation is echoed word-internally, in that only *l, and not *r, was permitted to occur as the latter component of a consonant cluster in proto-Samoyedic. Of the other consonants, only the velar nasal *ng was excluded from initial position, a phonotactic gap which has been filled in Northern Samoyedic by the introduction of a prothetic (*)ng- before all original initial vowels. In fact, it would be tempting to assume that *ng was on the way to becoming complementary with *ñ in proto-Samoyedic, for the possible word-internal and word-final occurrences of *ñ are difficult to distinguish from the sequence *yn, while *ng is well attested both word-internally and word-finally. On the basis of evidence from Selkup (and Finno-Ugric) it appears, nevertheless, reasonable to reconstruct an intervocalic *ñ in a few items, as in *ïñø 'tame' (proto-Uralic *ïñï). A stem-final *ñ is perhaps to be reconstructed in a few items which in Nenets exhibit an alternation of *n with *y, as in Nenets *toh: toy- 'blanket' < pSAM *toñ.

Vowel Phonotaxis

The maximal proto-Samoyedic paradigm of vowels has thus far been verified as valid only for the initial syllable; how many distinct vowel phonemes occurred in non-initial syllables is still a matter of controversy. In the lexical items inherited from proto-Uralic only the three vowels *a *ä *ø (and zero) are reliably attested in non-initial syllables, as in *yøka 'river' (proto-Uralic *yuka), *pitä 'nest' (proto-Uralic *pesä), *kunsø 'urine' (proto-Uralic *kunçï). In the post-proto-Uralic part of the proto-Samoyedic lexicon, however, there are undeniable examples of other vowels, notably *u and *i, as in *køru 'knife' > Enets køru v. Nenets *xør⁰ (formerly regarded, probably incorrectly, as a Uralic item), *wäpi 'luck' > Nganasan baxi : babi- 'wild reindeer' v. Nenets yab⁰ 'luck'. On the other hand, evidence from the internal reconstruction of Nenets and Enets suggests that many of the instances that would superficially suggest the reconstruction of vowels other than *a *ä *ø in non-initial syllables actually require the reconstruction of sequences containing *a *ä *ø in various combinations with the glides *w *y. Contracted vowels of various types and origins in non-initial syllables are also present in the other Samoyedic languages, although the diachronic details still remain to be worked out. The principal problem to be solved in the future concerns not so much the sequential origin of such vowels as the relative chronology of the contractive developments.

Vowel Harmony

Although vowel harmony as a productive process is attested only in Nganasan, related phenomena are present in Nenets and Enets. The combined evidence of these three languages suggests that proto-Samoyedic had a residual harmony of the palatovelar type, which affected the use of the low vowels *a *ä in suffixes. The structure of stem morphemes in themselves was not subject to any harmonic restrictions, for various innovations had introduced violations of vowel harmony even in items of proto-Uralic origin, as in proto-Samoyedic *kalä 'fish' (< proto-Uralic *kala). Suffixal harmony in proto-Samoyedic was conditioned by the quality of the vowel in the initial syllable of the stem morpheme. Thus stems containing any of the non-low front vowels *i *ü *e (and possibly *ö) in their initial syllable required a suffixal *ä, while stems containing any of the back vowels *u *ï *o *ë or the low vowels *a *ä in the initial syllable were combined with *a, as is still evident from modern examples such as Nenets *yik°nya* 'in the water' < *wit-kø-nä v. *myak°na* 'in the tent' < *mät-kø-na. It is of diachronic relevance to note that *ä in the initial syllable (a post-proto-Uralic innovation) behaved like a back vowel, while *ä in non-initial syllables (proto-Uralic *ä) was a front vowel. In other words, the two vowels were not diachronically identical, although they occupied an identical place in the paradigm. The reduced vowel *ø also seems to have been ambivalent, in that it was able to behave both as a back vowel and as a front vowel depending on the stem, as in *tø=ta- 'to bring' v. *tø-nä 'there'. Such examples suggest that pre-proto-Samoyedic may have had two separate reduced vowel phonemes.

Consonant Correspondences

The phonological correspondences among the Samoyedic languages are for the most part transparent to the professional eye, although a naïve native speaker of any single Samoyedic language would often find it impossible to recognize cognate items even in the immediately neighbouring language. The innovations responsible for the differences in the development of the consonants include, among others:

- the prothesis of (*)ng- in Northern Samoyedic, as in *opa 'glove' > Nganasan *nguxu* v. Kamas *uba*;
- the spirantization of *p into *x* in Nganasan and Mator, as in *päyma 'boot' > Nganasan *xåjmu* v. Nenets *pyíwa*;
- the development of *w into (*)k (> *k, q*) in Selkup, as in *wøta 'hook' > Selkup *kotø* v. Nenets *wøda*;
- the sporadic development of *y into (*)k (> *k, q*) in Selkup, as in *yorä 'deep' > Selkup *qorø* v. Nenets *yorya*;
- the neutralization of syllable-final obstruents into a glottal stop in Northern Samoyedic, as in *kät 'face' > Enets *seq* v. Selkup *qaat*;
- the simplification of all consonant clusters in Enets, as in *mir-wø 'weapon' > Enets *mimø* v. Nenets *myirw°*;
- the assimilation of *t (< *t and *c) after dental sonorants in Nenets, as in *sølcø 'stump' > Nenets *søl°* v. Nganasan *sëltë*;
- the translocation of palatality from any original front vowel on to the preceding consonant in Nenets, as in *pir=kä 'high' > Nenets *pyircya* v. Mator *xirge*.

An example of a less trivial set of correspondences is offered by the proto-

Table 15.1   Reflexes of proto-Samoyedic *k v. *s before different vowels

Nganasan	Enets	Nenets	Selkup	Kamas	Mator	Before:
s	ç	sy	ç v. s	ç v. s	k	*i *e
k v. s	ç	sy	ç v. s	ç v. s	k	*ü *ö
k v. s	s	sy	(*)k v. s	k v. s	k v. s	*ä
k v. s	k v. s	(*)k v. (*)s	(*)k v. s	k v. s	k v. s	others

Samoyedic opposition between initial *k and *s (cf. Table 15.1). It may be seen that, although *k has undergone assibilation in all the Samoyedic languages except Mator, the development shows three different contextual patterns: one for Nganasan (neutralizing assibilation before *i *e), another for Nenets and Enets (neutralizing assibilation before any front vowel, including *ä), and a third for Selkup and Kamas (non-neutralizing assibilation before any front vowel except *ä). The most curious situation is encountered in Mator, where *s has developed positionally into *k (neutralizing occlusivization before any front vowel except *ä).

Vowel Correspondences

The vowel distinctions originally present in the initial syllable are best preserved in Selkup, which dialectally still retains the proto-Samoyedic vowel paradigm almost intact. Apart from the effect of the translocation of palatality, Nenets normally also allows a reliable reconstruction of vowels in the initial syllable to be made, while the rest of the Samoyedic languages exhibit cases of complete paradigmatic neutralization. Nganasan, for instance, has merged *ë and *ä into a, *o and *ö into u, and *ï and *ü into i (which also represents original *i). Such neutralizations are often connected with major tendencies affecting the whole vowel system, such as the Nganasan 'vowel shift', which is also responsible for the developments *a > o and *u > ü. On the other hand, the history of individual lexical items occasionally reveals interesting minor phenomena, such as the qualitative levelling in *sïra 'snow' > Nganasan (eighteenth century) siru > (nineteenth century) sirü > (twentieth century) sürü v. Nenets sira. There are particularly many problems still connected with vowel sequences, as well as with sequences involving the palatal glide *y; in many cases these have reflexes different from those of the single vowels (cf. Table 15.2). Proto-Samoyedic also had syllable-final instances of the labial glide *w, as in *kaw 'ear', but such examples seem to have been so few in number that they had no relevance to the evolution of the modern vowel paradigms.

Further Reading

Some aspects of the phonological reconstruction of proto-Samoyedic are discussed in Janhunen (1976) (vowels of the initial syllable), Xelimskij

Table 15.2   Examples of Samoyedic vowel correspondences

	Nganasan	Enets	Nenets	Selkup	Kamas	Mator
*u	ü	u	u	u	u	u
*uy	uj	u	ú	ü:	ü	uj
*uø	uë	ua	ú	u:	u	u
*uøy	üë	ua	o	u:	ü	u

(1978) (vowels of the non-initial syllables), Janhunen (1986: 149–68) (syllable-final consonants), Janurik (1982) (consonant correspondences) Terentjev (1982) (various topics). A summary of the phonological developments from proto-Uralic down to the individual Samoyedic languages is presented in Sammallahti (1988: 484–6, 494–9).

Morphology

Morphophonology
Most of the morphophonological phenomena that can be dated back to proto-Samoyedic are peculiar to stems ending in a consonant. When followed by a suffix consisting of a single consonant, such stems require the insertion of the reduced vowel *-ø- as a connective segment, as in *nim 'name': (genitive) *nim-ø-n; it is, of course, a matter of interpretation whether this connective segment is viewed as belonging to the stem or to the suffix. On the other hand, if a stem-final consonant is followed by a suffix beginning with a consonant cluster, the initial segment of the suffix is deleted in order to avoid a sequence of three consonants, as in *op 'one': dative *op-tø(-ng) 'together' < pre-proto-Samoyedic *o(=)p-ntø(-ng). Also, according to the rules of consonant phonotaxis, a suffix-initial *r was replaced by *l after a stem-final consonant, as in *wën 'dog': *wën-lø 'your dog' < pre-proto-Samoyedic *wën-rø. All of these phenomena are preserved as synchronic processes in the modern Samoyedic languages. As far as stems ending in a vowel are concerned, the final *a and *ä of bisyllabic stems alternate morphophonologically with *ø. In the case of nouns, the altered stem seems to have been used as an accusative plural in proto-Samoyedic, as in Nenets tyon° (< *töntø), accusative plural of tyonya 'fox' (< *töntä). In the case of verbs, the stem alternation was perhaps primarily connected with the transitive/intransitive opposition, as in Nenets xaye- (< *kayä-) 'leaves (tr)' : xayo- (< *kayø=y=øy-) 'remains'. At the pre-proto-Samoyedic level, the stem alternants with *ø probably involved sequences of a final vowel plus the glide *y, but the diachronic details remain obscure. The entire phenomenon is preserved in Northern Samoyedic only, where it has been affected by various types of morphological restructuring.

Table 15.3   Case endings in proto-Samoyedic

	Spatial nouns	Ordinary nouns		
Nominative			*-Ø	
Accusative			*-m	
Genitive			*-n	
Dative	*-ng	*-kø-		*-ntø(-ng)
Locative	*-na²	*-kø-na²		*-ntø-na²
Ablative	*-t(ø)	*-kø-t(ø)		
Prosecutive	*-m-na²		*-mø-na²	

Note: ²The digital index stands for the variation connected with vowel harmony.

Case Declension

Proto-Samoyedic nominal declension seems to have had a system of one unmarked and six suffixally marked cases (cf. Table 15.3). With the exception of a few lacunae of documentation for Kamas and Mator, this system is preserved as the core of the case systems of all the modern Samoyedic languages. Three of the cases express general grammatical relationships and have proto-Samoyedic shapes deriving directly from proto-Uralic: the unmarked nominative (absolutive) in *-Ø, the genitive in *-n, and the accusative in *-m. The other four cases express local relationships and occur with two principal sets of endings, depending on whether they are attached to an ordinary noun or to a spatial noun used as an adverb or postposition. The declension of spatial nouns is structurally more simple and incorporates archaic endings deriving from proto-Uralic: *-ng for the dative/lative, *-na² for the locative, and *-t(ø) for the ablative. The declension of ordinary nouns, on the other hand, was based on the coaffixal use of the elements *-kø- and *-ntø(-), which function basically as dative/lative endings with a varying distribution in the modern languages. Nganasan is alone in using the locative complex *-ntø-na² as opposed to *-kø-na² elsewhere, a situation which suggests that the local case system was still being formed at the time when Nganasan broke off from the rest of proto-Samoyedic. The ending of the remaining local case, the prosecutive/prolative, may also have a coaffixal origin, in that it possibly contains a combination of the accusative *-m- with the locative *-na². The fact that the prosecutive complex appears as *-mø-na² in the declension of ordinary nouns may be explained as due to a rhythmic analogy with the locative complex *-kø-na².

Number

Apart from the unmarked singular (absolute) number of nominal declension, proto-Samoyedic retained the proto-Uralic markers for the dual and plural numbers. These were originally not combinable with the normal case endings; various types of plural paradigm were constructed secondarily out of the available elements (cf. Table 15.4). It is important to note that the plural was

Table 15.4   Patterns of the plural and dual declensions in Samoyedic

		Proto-Samoyedic	Nenets	Nganasan
Plural	nominative	*-t		
	accusative	*-y		
	genitive		*-y-q	
	dative	*-kø-q		*-ntø-y-q
	locative	*-kø-q-na²		*-ntø-y-(q-)na²
	ablative	*-kø-q-tø		*-kø-y-(q-)tø
	prosecutive		*-y-q-mø-na	
Dual		*-kø-ñ		

from the beginning marked by two different suffixes depending on the morphological context: *-t for the nominative (absolute) and *-y for the accusative (oblique). This difference is synchronically preserved in Northern Samoyedic, where the formation of the accusative plural, in particular, is connected with a multitude of morphophonological complications, including reflexes of the proto-Samoyedic stem-final alternation of *a and *ä with *ø. The accusative plural is also used as a base for several types of denominal verbs, such as the captatives in *=y=n- and the possessives in *=y=s-. The Northern Samoyedic genitive plural is formed by adding a glottal stop (-q) to the accusative plural. The form has been explained as a combination of the two plural markers *-y and *-t, but there is little actual evidence for the precise original identity of the latter component, which might just as well have been *-s or *-k. The genitive plural, in turn, is used to form the prosecutive plural, a circumstance which superficially would appear to suggest a postpositional origin of the prosecutive ending. However, in view of the secondary nature of the whole plural paradigm, the prosecutive plural is likely to be a recent structural innovation with no relevance to the origin of the prosecutive as a category.

Personal Endings
All the Samoyedic languages have at least two main types of personal endings: the predicative and the possessive suffixes. The predicative suffixes are used to express the actor of a finite verb (the subjective conjugation) or the subject of a predicatively used noun (the nominal conjugation), while the possessive suffixes express the possessor of a noun (the possessive declension) or the actor of a transitive verb with a definite object (the objective conjugation). The possessive suffixes are also used, together with a special marker, to express the recipient of a noun (the predestinative declension). The details vary from language to language, but there are indications that the highly differentiated system synchronically attested in Nenets most closely reflects the proto-Samoyedic state of affairs. In this system, the possessive suffixes appear in four different variants, depending on which other suffix, if

Table 15.5   The system of personal endings in pre-proto-Nenets

		Predicative	Possessive Nominative	Accusative	Oblique	Plural/dual	Reflexive
Singular	1	*-m	*-mø	*-Ø-mø	*-Ø-nø	*-nø	*-m-ø-q
	2	*-n(-tø)	*-rø	*-m-tø	*-n-tø	*-tø	
	3	*-Ø	*-ta^2	*-m-ta^2	*-n-ta^2	*-ta^2	*-Ø-q
Dual	1	*-mi-ñ	*-mi-ñ	*-Ø-mi-ñ	*-Ø-ni-ñ	*-ni-ñ	
	2	*-ti-ñ	*-ri-ñ	*-m-ti-ñ	*-n-ti-ñ	*-ti-ñ	
	3	*-kø-ñ	*-ti-ñ	*-m-ti-ñ	*-n-ti-ñ	*-ti-ñ	
Plural	1	*-ma-t^2	*-ma-t^2	*-Ø-ma-t^2	*-Ø-na-t^2	*-na-t^2	
	2	*-ta t^2	*-ra-t^2	*-m-ta-t^2	*-n-ta-t^2	*-ta-t^2	
	3	*-Ø-t	*-ton	*-m-ton	*-n-ton	*-ton	*-Ø-t-ø-q

any, precedes them (cf. Table 15.5). There is also a fragmentary set of endings used in a separate paradigm of reflexive finite forms (the reflexive conjugation). As for the material shapes of the personal endings in the different categories, many problems still await a definitive solution. From the proto-Uralic point of view, one of the most interesting features is that the second-person singular predicative ending seems to have been *-n in proto-Samoyedic, as opposed to *-t in most sub-branches of Finno-Ugric. The simple shape *-n is, however, preserved only in Nganasan, while the other Samoyedic languages have *-n-tø, possibly as a result of the influence of the corresponding possessive suffixes. In the possessive sets, the second-person endings for all the three numbers show a morphophonological alternation of *-t- with *-r-. In addition, the suffix-initial *-r- (used after stem-final vowels) participates in the normal alternation with *-l- (after stem-final consonants). The third-person endings in the predicative set are identical with the number markers of the nominal declension. The plural number marker *-t- also appears as a component of the third-person plural reflexive ending.

Finite Conjugation

One of the formal differences between verbs and nouns in Samoyedic is that a verbal stem is normally not combinable with the personal endings without an element of stem enlargement. In this respect, Samoyedic seems to be innovative, for it may be assumed that the use of an unmarked finite stem was possible in proto-Uralic, as it still is in Finno-Ugric, as in Finnish *mene-n* 'I go' (proto-Uralic *meni-m). Most types of stem enlargement in the modern Samoyedic languages may be traced back to non-finite derivational suffixes which have developed secondarily into temporal and modal markers of the finite conjugation. In other words, the origins of the various finite sub-paradigms in Samoyedic lie in the predicative conjugation of verbal nouns. There are considerable differences between the synchronic systems of the individual languages, suggesting that the functions of the morphological elements had not yet been fully crystallized at the proto-Samoyedic level. One of the few elements occurring in several languages in an essentially identical function is the past-tense marker *-sa²-, as in Selkup *ap-sa-p* 'I ate' of *am-* 'eats' (proto-Samoyedic *øm-). In Nenets and Enets, this element has been restructured into a modal marker (the interrogative mood), but it still retains a connotation corresponding to the earlier temporal function. As a verbal noun suffix, *=sa² is attested only in a few lexicalized relics, as in Selkup *apsø* 'meat' < 'food' < 'edible' (proto-Samoyedic *øm=sa).

Aorist Formation

A central role among the various finite sub-paradigms formed by stem-enlargement is played by the aorist, which may be defined as a temporally ambivalent category referring to either on-going or completed action depending on the intrinsic aspectual content of the verb, as in Nenets (third person singular) *yilye°* '([s]he) lives' v. *xa°* '([s]he) died'. In the functional sense, the aorist is an archaic feature preserved only in Northern Samoyedic, but the category has formal parallels in Southern Samoyedic. Aorist formation is another morphological feature by which Nganasan stands alone, opposed to the rest of the Samoyedic languages. The Nganasan aorist, as in (third person singular objective) *xån-u-q-a-tu* of *xån-* 'places' (proto-Samoyedic *pën-), is formed synchronically by suffixing a vowel (-*a-* or -*ë-*) to a stem showing material properties identical with those observed in the genitive plural of nominal declension. The material background of the Nganasan aorist remains obscure, but a verbal noun suffix containing the palatal glide *-y- is likely to have been involved. In the other Samoyedic languages, two types of aorist formation may be observed synchronically: stem-final consonants are normally combined with *-nga-, as in Nenets (third person singular) *nger-nga* of *nger-* 'to drink' (proto-Samoyedic *ër-), while stem-final vowels require a vocalic element, as in Nenets (third personal singular) *xada-°* : (objective) *xada-°-da* of *xada-* 'kills' (proto-Samoyedic *ka[=]ta-). A vocalic element, at least superficially identifiable with *-ø-, is also present in combination with the reflexive and plural possessive (objective) personal endings, which require the additional segment *-y- as a marker of reflexivity or plurality, as in Nenets (third person singular with plural object) *xada-y-°-da*. There have been suggestions that the vocalic element in question might also ultimately go back to *-nga-, but this identification seems to involve insurmountable phonological problems. The element *-nga-, however, is also attested in Nganasan, where it occurs in a modal function (the interrogative mood). There are indications that *-nga-, also, was once a verbal noun suffix, still preserved in relics, as in Nenets *yengø* 'river' < *wen=nga from *wen- 'flows'.

Periphrastic Conjugation

It cannot be ruled out that the formation of the aorist actually involves traces of an obscured periphrastic conjugation, in that the vocalic element of the aorist, as observed in both Nganasan and the other Samoyedic languages, might represent the stem of an originally independent auxiliary verb, perhaps identical with proto-Samoyedic *i- 'to be'. Whether or not this is so, Nenets and Enets exhibit a transparent case of periphrastic conjugation in the formation of their normal finite past-tense paradigm, which has the rather unusual formula of STEM + AORIST FORMATIVE + PERSONAL ENDING + PAST-TENSE SUFFIX, as in Nenets (second person singular) *yilye-°-nø-sy°* 'you lived'. Diachronically, this type of conjugation involves the suffixation of the past tense auxiliary form *+i-sä '(it) was' to a fully conjugated aorist form of the main verb. The appearance of the periphrastic past tense has, incidentally, diminished the formal difference between verbal and nominal inflection, in that it can also be formed from nouns used predicatively, as in Nenets *xasawa+sy°* 'he was a man'. Another possible example of the periphrastic conjugation is involved in the Sayan Samoyedic present/future tense paradigm, which is based on a Southern Samoyedic gerund suffix, as in Kamas *kal-la-m* 'I (will) go' < *kan=la+V-m (proto-Samoyedic *kan- 'goes').

Non-finite Forms
While many of the pre-proto-Samoyedic verbal noun suffixes were restructured into temporal and modal markers of the finite paradigm, there always existed a system of productive non-finite forms, as well. At the proto-Samoyedic level, three functional categories of such forms seem to have been distinguished: infinitives (verbal substantives), participles (verbal adjectives), and gerunds (verbal adverbs). It is difficult to reconstruct the proto-Samoyedic system because of cross-connected developments which have affected the functional distinctions. Proto-Samoyedic verbal noun types dating back as far as proto-Uralic comprise:

- the infinitive in *=ma², as in Nenets *to=wa* '(the act of) coming' < *toy=ma (proto-Samoyedic *toy- 'comes');
- the perfect participle in *=mø-, as in Nenets *to=wi* '(one who has) come' < *toy=mø=yø;
- the negative participle in *=mø=ta=ma²- (with the abessive element *=ta²- < proto-Uralic *=kta²-), as in Nenets *to=w°dawe=y°* '(one who has) not come' < *toy=mø=ta=ma=yø.

The proto-Uralic verbal noun formatives *=ta² and *=pa² survive in Samoyedic as *=n(=)ta(=) and *=m(=)pa(=), with an apparently secondary nasal element, as in the Selkup imperfect and perfect participles *ilø-ntø-lʲ* '(one who is) living' < *ilä=n(=)tä=yø v. *ilø-mpø-lʲ* '(one who has) lived' < *ilä=m(=)pä=yø. Among the gerunds, there are only two which can with reasonable certainty be considered as proto-Samoyedic: the co-ordinative (modal) gerund in *=ki(-), as in Nenets *yilye-sy°* '(by way of) living' <

*ilä=ki, and the subordinative (conditional) gerund in *=put-, as in Nganasan *tuj-xüq* '(under the condition of) coming' < *toy=put. In view of their phonological shapes (involving the vowels *i and *u), both seem to be post-proto-Uralic innovations. Both also share the characteristic of having a fragmentary nominal paradigm, suggesting that they may originally have functioned as verbal nouns. This is particularly obvious in the case of the subordinative gerund, which in combination with the possessive suffixes requires the presence of a local case ending (dative or locative) of the archaic simple type, as in Nenets (dative first person singular) *to=bøq-n°* 'under the condition that I come' < *toy=put-ng-nø and (locative) *to=b°q-na-n°* 'id.' < *toy=put-na-nø.

Imperative

In the Samoyedic systems of verbal conjugation, the imperative sub-paradigm occupies an exceptional position, in that it not only varies considerably from language to language, but it also shows a conspicuous lack of structural coherence within each individual language. There is no doubt that the imperative in pre-proto-Uralic originally existed as a special category for the second person, and in the modern Samoyedic languages to this day it remains somewhat unclear whether it is at all possible to regard the imperative sub-paradigm as comprising other persons; the third person is notably questionable. The only Samoyedic imperative form that can be unambiguously dated back to proto-Uralic is the second person singular in *-k, as in Nenets *nger-°-q* '(thou) drink!' < *ër-ø-k. The synchronic status of the element *-k and its reflexes in the modern languages provides an interesting object for synchronic morphological analysis, for it should perhaps not be considered a personal ending in the same sense as the ordinary personal endings of the finite paradigm. However, it contrasts with the true personal ending *-tø in the second-person singular imperative form with a definite object, as in Nenets *nger-t°* '(thou) drink it!' < *ër-tø. This form is also of structural interest, for it is a rare example of finite conjugation without a stem enlargement, a peculiarity shared only by the other Northern Samoyedic second-person singular imperative forms (reflexive and plural/dual objective). In contrast, the third-person forms contain the normal aorist enlargement in combination with special imperative markers. The imperative marker for the simple third-person singular and plural forms may have been *-ya in proto-Samoyedic, as in Nenets *nger-nga-ya* 'may he drink' < *ër-nga-ya. Curiously, an entirely different marker, reconstructable as *(-ø)-m-, appears before the possessive (objective) and reflexive personal endings, as in Nenets (third-person singular objective imperative) *nger-nga-m-da* < *ër-nga-m-ta. The original identity of both *-ya and *(-ø)-m- remains obscure.

Negation

With the exception of Selkup, all the modern Samoyedic languages preserve the proto-Uralic feature of expressing negation by means of a negative verb, probably to be reconstructed as proto-Samoyedic *i-. With some variation in the synchronic details of the system, the paradigm of the negative verb basically comprises all the normal morphological distinctions connected with the categories of personal conjugation, including tense and aspect, as well as the formation of verbal nouns and related forms. The main verb, which normally follows the conjugated negative verb, has the invariable connegative form in *-k, identical with the second-person singular imperative ending. However, synchronic evidence from the modern languages, particularly Nenets, suggests that the negation of verbal nouns in proto-Samoyedic took place by using the negative verb not in the connegative but in the corresponding verbal noun form, as in Nenets (imperfect participle) *nyi-nya yilye-nya* 'not living'.

Further Reading
Up-to-date literature on Samoyedic diachronic morphology is scarce, but a wealth of information on earlier research may be obtained from Künnap (1971 and 1978). Some useful material is also found in Mikola (1988: 236–59). Aspects of comparative morphosyntax are dealt with in Tereščenko (1973) (general syntax), Katschmann (1986) (expressions for 'to be'). The proto-Uralic background of Samoyedic morphology is discussed in Janhunen (1981b).

Lexicon

Common Uralic Vocabulary
In accordance with the assumption that Samoyedic forms one of the two principal branches of Uralic, the Samoyedic languages have relatively few lexical items that can uncontroversially be regarded as direct inheritances from proto-Uralic. Even by a very optimistic estimation, the number of proto-Uralic underived stems surviving in Samoyedic cannot possibly be much more than 150. Apart from pronouns and other auxiliaries, the common items are confined to basic terms for body parts and bodily functions, kinship terms, celestial objects, meteorological phenomena, and topographical concepts. Of some chronological and areal relevance are items pertaining to primitive technology, apparently reflecting the neolithic level of development, and terms for fauna and flora, pointing to the boreal forest environment of the Ural region.

Common Samoyedic Vocabulary
The number of stem morphemes attested in both Northern Samoyedic and Southern Samoyedic seems to be approximately 700. In addition, some 150 lexicalized derivatives with a similar distribution are known. If items shared by any two Samoyedic languages, including adjacent ones (such as Nenets and Enets, or Kamas and Mator), were also to be recognized as deriving from

the proto-language, the number of proto-Samoyedic stem morphemes would probably rise to over one thousand. This vocabulary covers a wide range of socio-technological concepts, many of which are connected with post-proto-Uralic cultural innovations. Important in the Northern Eurasian context are the proto-Samoyedic items relating to reindeer-breeding, such as *tëø 'reindeer' and *cørkø(=)y 'reindeer calf', as well as those relating to shamanistic beliefs, such as *cacä=pä 'shaman', *pe=n+kir 'shaman's drum', *sampø- 'to shamanize', *kaykø 'spirit'. Of ethnohistorical interest are also the two proto-Samoyedic hydronyms *yentø(=)si(=ng) 'the Yenisei' and *yäm 'sea, large river (?the Ob' ?Lake Baikal)', which define the main geographical dimensions of the proto-Samoyedic territory. As far as vocabulary pertaining to the details of natural environment and material culture is concerned, a massive semantic and material differentiation has taken place between the three ecological groups of the Samoyedic-speaking peoples. A case in point is proto-Samoyedic *møya 'land, terrain', which in the modern languages has meanings ranging from 'tundra' to 'taiga' to 'mountain'. Particularly many idiosyncratic items of cultural vocabulary seem to be present in Nganasan.

Numerals

Although the mutual relationships of the main sub-branches of Finno-Ugric are still a matter of discussion, it is of considerable taxonomic importance that the Finno-Ugric languages possess common basic numerals from 1 (or, at least, 2) to 6, of which only two have cognates in Samoyedic. Moreover, of these, only the item for '2' occurs in identical functions in Samoyedic and Finno-Ugric, while the cognate of the Finno-Ugric item for '5' appears in the function of '10' in Samoyedic. The rest of the Samoyedic basic numerals very probably represent post-proto-Uralic innovations (cf. the list of numerals, below).

1	*o(-)p	derivative of *o(-) '1'
2	*kitä	< proto-Uralic *kektä/*käktä
3	*näku(-)r	? derivative with unidentified elements
4	*tettø	
5	*sømpø-längkø	derivative of an otherwise unknown root
6˙	*møktu(-)t	? derivative with unidentified elements
7	*seytwø	< *seyptø < pre-proto-Tocharian
8	*kitä(-y-n)+tettø	'2×4', compositum of *kitä and *tettø
9	*ämäy-tumø	derivative of *ämäy 'other'
10	*wüøt	< proto-Uralic *wixti '5'
100	*yür	< proto-Bolgar-Turkic *yür

Among the numerals with no cognate in Finno-Ugric, only the item for '4' seems to consist of a single indivisible indigenous stem morpheme, while the other items are either composita, derivatives, or loanwords. The overall structure of the numeral system suggests that there was a time when the count extended only from 1 to 6, with the original item for '5' perhaps also functioning as '10'. After the borrowing of the item for '7', the expressions for '8' and '9' were created at such a late date that their representation in the modern languages is in fact not fully uniform. The expressions for '9', in particular, vary considerably, with the proto-Samoyedic item being reliably attested in only two languages (Nganasan and Kamas).

Foreign Contacts
After the break-up of proto-Uralic, the early stages of pre-proto-Samoyedic probably long continued to maintain an areal contact with Finno-Ugric, especially Ugric. As traces of this interaction, Samoyedic possesses a few lexical items which may be explained as early loanwords from Ugric or pre-Ugric, such as *num 'sky, god', *kalmä 'dead body, grave'. Another concretely identifiable linguistic entity in the neighbourhood of early pre-proto-Samoyedic seems to have been some kind of pre-proto-Tocharian, which also yielded a few loanwords, notably the numeral *seytwø '7'. Contacts with Indo-European then probably continued during the period of the early Iranian presence in southern Siberia in the second to first millennium BCE. During the ethnic movements of the subsequent 'Hunnic' period, just around the time of the break-up of proto-Samoyedic unity, Samoyedic received an important layer of proto-Bolgar Turkic loanwords, including items pertaining to animal husbandry, such as *yuntø 'horse' and *kaptø- 'castrates', as well as the numeral *yür '100'. It cannot be ruled out that proto-Samoyedic also had direct contacts with early forms of Mongolic, Tungusic, and Yeniseic, but the linguistic evidence of these contacts remains inconclusive. In any case, after the break-up of proto-Samoyedic, the individual Samoyedic languages have entered into contact with all the neighbouring languages, which include idioms of the Turkic (Khakas, Tuva, Dolgan), Mongolic (Buryat), Tungusic (Evenki), and Yeniseic (Ket, Kott, Arin) families, as well as of the Finno-Ugric branch (Khanty, Mansi, Komi). To some extent, this interaction extends beyond the limits of the lexicon. Particularly close areal bonds of typological interaction have been formed between Selkup and Yeniseic (Ket), as well as between Sayan Samoyedic and Turkic (Khakas, Tuva). As the most recent contact phenomenon, all Samoyedic languages have incorporated lexical elements from Russian. In addition to lexical impact, Russian influence is currently also penetrating into the syntactic and morphological systems of the surviving Samoyedic languages.

Further Reading
The lexical items shared by Northern Samoyedic and Southern Samoyedic are listed in Janhunen (1977a). The proto-Uralic items surviving in Samoyedic are discussed in Janhunen (1981a) and listed in Sammallahti (1988: 536–41).

Other studies pertaining to Samoyedic comparative lexicology include Xelimskij (1986 and 1992–3) (Mator etymologies), Joki (1975) (numerals). A pioneering work on foreign lexical elements in Samoyedic (Kamas and Mator) is Joki (1951). Recent discussions of the topic include Janhunen (1983) (contacts with Indo-European), Janhunen (1977b) (contacts with 'Altaic'), Róna-Tas (1980) (contacts with Turkic), Xelimskij (1982a) (parallels with Ugric), Xelimskij (1982b) (contacts with Yeniseic), Janhunen (1989) and Xelimskij (1991) (selected controversial issues). An attempt at an analysis of structural interaction (with Ugric) is Katz (1975).

References and Further Reading

Hajdú, P. (1963) *The Samoyedic Peoples and Languages*, Indiana University Uralic and Altaic Series 14, Bloomington–The Hague: Indiana University–Mouton.

—— (1968) *Chrestomathia Samoiedica*, Budapest: Tankönyvkiadó.

—— (1988) 'Die Samojedischen Sprachen', in D. Sinor (ed.), *The Uralic Languages: Description, History and Foreign Influences*, Handbuch der Orientalistik 8/1, Leiden: Brill, pp. 3–40.

Janhunen, J. (1976) 'Adalékok az északi-szamojéd hangtörténethez. Vokalizmus: az első szótagi magánhangzók', *Néprajz és nyelvtudomány* 19–20: 165–88.

—— (1977a) *Samojedischer Wortschatz. Gemeinsamojedische Etymologien*, Castrenianumin toimitteita 17, Helsinki: Société Finno-Ougrienne.

—— (1977b) 'Samoyed–Altaic Contacts: Present State of Research', in *Altaica*, MSFOu 158, Helsinki: Société Finno-Ougrienne, pp. 123–9.

—— (1981a) 'Uralilaisen kantakielen sanastosta', *JSFOu* 77: 219–74.

—— (1981b) 'On the structure of proto-Uralic', *FuF* 44: 23–42.

—— (1983) 'On early Indo-European–Samoyed contacts', in J. Janhunen et al. (eds), *Symposium Saeculare Societatis Fenno-Ugricae*, MSFOu 185, Helsinki: Société Finno-Ougrienne, pp. 115–27.

—— (1986) *Glottal Stop in Nenets*, MSFOu 196, Helsinki: Société Finno-Ougrienne.

—— (1989) 'On the interaction of Mator with Turkic, Mongolic, and Tungusic', *JSFOu* 82: 287–97.

—— (1991) 'Нганасаны и распад прасамодийской языковой общности', in *Seminar* «Проблемы происхождения народов уральской языковой семьи», Izhevsk, pp. 16–19.

Janurik, T. (1978) 'A szölkup nyelvjárások osztályozásához', *Nyelvtudományi Közlemények* 80: 77–104.

—— (1982) 'Szamojéd hangmegfelelések. I. Mássalhangzók', *Nyelvtudományi Közlemények* 84: 41–89.

—— (1985) 'Kriterien zur Klassifizierung der Dialekte der Samojedischen Sprachen', in W. Veenker (ed.), *Dialectologia Uralica*, Veröffentlichungen der Societas Uralo-Altaica 20, Wiesbaden: Harrassowitz, pp. 283–301.

Joki, A.J. (1951) *Die Lehnwörter des Sajansamojedischen*, MSFOu 103, Helsinki: Société Finno-Ougrienne.

—— (1975) 'Über einige Zahlwörter im Samojedischen', *C3IFU*, vol. I, pp. 729–32.

Katz, H. (1975) *Generative Phonologie und phonologische Sprachbünde des Ostjakischen und Samojedischen*, Finnisch-Ugrische Bibliothek 1, Munich: Wilhelm Fisk.

Katschmann, M. (1986) *Nominal- und Esse-Satz in den samojedischen Sprachen.*

Dargestellt anhand ausgewählten Belegmaterials, Fenno-Ugrica 9, Hamburg: Helmut Buske Verlag.

Künnap, A. (1971, 1978) *System und Ursprung der kamassischen Flexionsuffixe*. vol. I: *Numeruszeichen und Nominalflexion*; vol. II: *Verbalflexion und Verbalnomina*, MSFOu 147, 164, Helsinki: Société Finno-Ougrienne.

—— (1985) 'Zur Klassifizierung der Dialekte des Selkupischen und Kamassichen', *Dialectologia Uralica*, Veröffentlichungen der Societas Uralo-Altaica 20, Wiesbaden: Harrassowitz, 309–16.

Mikola, T. (1988) *Geschichte der samojedischen Sprachen*, in D. Sinor (ed.), *The Uralic Languages: Description, History and Foreign Influences*, Handbuch der Orientalistik 8/1, Leiden: Brill, pp. 219–63.

Róna-Tas, A. (1980) 'On the earliest Samoyed–Turkish contacts', *C5IFU*, vol. III, pp. 377–85.

Salminen, T. (1990) 'Phonological criteria in the classification of the Nenets dialects', *C7IFU*, vol. IIIC, pp. 344–99.

Sammallahti, P. (1988) 'Historical phonology of the Uralic languages, with special reference to Samoyed, Ugric and Permic', in D. Sinor (ed.), *The Uralic Languages: Description, History and Foreign Influences*, Handbuch der Orientalistik 8/1, Leiden: Brill, pp. 478–554.

Terentjev, V.A. (1982) 'К вопросу о реконструкции прасамодийского языка', *Sovetskoe finno-ugrovedenie* 18: 189–93.

Tereščenko, N.M. (1973) Синтаксис самодийских языков, Leningrad: Nauka.

Xelimskij, E.A. (1976) 'Об одном переходном северносамодийском диалекте (К исторической диалектологии ненецкого языка)', Происхождение абори-генов Сибири и их языков 3: 89–93.

—— (1978) 'Реконструкция прасеверносамодийских (PSS) лабиализованных гласных непервых слогов', in Конференция «Проблемы реконструкции», Moscow: Institut Yazykozhaniya, pp. 123–6.

—— (1982a) Древнейшие венгерско-самодийские языковые параллели, (Лингвистическая и этногенетическая интерпретация), Moscow: Nauka.

—— (1982b) 'Keto-Uralica', in Кетский сборник (3), антропология, этнография мифология, лингвистика, Leningrad: Nauka, pp. 238–50.

—— (1983) 'Ранние этапы этногенеза и этнической истории самодийцев в свете языковых данных', in Проблемы этногенеза и этнической истории самодийских народов, Omsk, pp. 5–10.

—— (1985a) 'Die Feststellung der dialektalen Zugehörigkeit der enzischen Materialien', in *Dialectologia Uralica*, Veröffentlichungen der Societas Uralo-Altaica 20, Wiesbaden: Harrassowitz, pp. 303–8.

—— (1985b) 'Самодийско-тунгусские лексические связи и их этноисторические импликации', in Урало-алтаистика. Археология, этнография, язык, Novosibirsk: Nauka, pp. 206–13.

—— (1986) 'Etymologica 1–48' *Nyelvtudományi Közlemények* 88, p. 119–43.

—— (1991) 'On the interaction of Mator with Turkic, Mongolic, and Tungusic: a rejoinder', *JSFOu* 83: 257–67.

—— (1992–3) 'Etymologica 49–79', Материалы по этимологии маторско-тайгийско-карагасского языка', *Nyelvtudományi Közlemények*, pp. 101–23, Budapest.

16 Nganasan

Eugene Helimski

The Nganasan language, known also as Tawgi or Tawgi-Samoyed, is spoken by the northernmost ethnic group in Eurasia. The Nganasan call themselves *Nya* (*nʲaa*, formally an adjective from *nʲa* 'mate'). The appellation 'Nganasan' is based on *ŋanasa* (plural *ŋanasanə?*) 'human being, person' (never used, however as a self-designation); the appellation 'Tawgi' is based on Nenets *tawi?* 'Nganasan'.

Until recently all Nganasans led the nomadic life of tundra dwellers – wild reindeer hunters, fishermen and domestic reindeer breeders – in the central and northern parts of the Taimyr Peninsula (excluding its coastal areas). Since the 1960s the majority of the population, which according to census data numbered about 900 persons in 1979 and about 1,300 persons in 1989, is concentrated mainly in three villages which lie to the south of the original ethnic territory – Ust-Avam, Volochanka, and Novaya. Only several dozens of Nganasan families continue to live as hunters on isolated spots on the tundra.

The transition to the settled way of life together with other rapid and dramatic social and economic changes – all carried out in a purely administrative way – broke the normal transmission of cultural values to subsequent generations and posed a mortal threat to the language and national heritage of Nganasans. The sociolinguistic situation around 1990 was as follows: people aged forty to fifty years and over were all perfectly fluent in their native language and often unable to communicate effectively in any other language, while among those under thirty, who had gone or were going through the experience of living in villages with an ethnically mixed population, and of studying in Russian-language boarding schools, only about one-third was able to understand Nganasan and hardly more than ten per cent were able to speak it. According to my own estimate (the official census data are in this respect heavily distorted), the total number of Nganasan native speakers was about 600 in 1990, a number which is permanently decreasing despite the remarkably high birth rate and natural growth.

The Nganasan language is used in traditional spheres of the economy and in families (within the limits determined by the lack of linguistic proficiency among younger age groups), but not in administration, culture, trade, or any other activities of village communities. Recently it began to be taught at primary schools (practically as a second language even for Nganasan

children). Native-language literacy remains the privilege of only a few
Nganasans, mainly graduates of teacher-training colleges.

Bilingualism

As the sociolinguistic data above show, Nganasan–Russian bilingualism (with
varying degrees of proficiency in the two languages) is at present especially
typical of middle-aged Nganasans (between thirty and sixty); this bilingualism is strictly unilateral: among the Russian-speaking population of
Taimyr (predominantly newcomers or temporary dwellers) there seems to be
not a single person who speaks Nganasan – this may, however, be at least
partly due to the extreme morphophonemic complexity of the language.

In all three villages mentioned above the Nganasans live together with the
Dolgans, an ethnic group of mixed (predominantly Tungusic) origin whose
language can be classified as a dialect of (Turkic) Yakut. Many Nganasans,
especially in the eastern part of Taimyr (Novaya), are able to understand or
even to speak Dolgan (but usually not vice versa).

The river basin of Pyasina (Western Taimyr) was for many generations an
area of Nganasan–Enets bilateral bilingualism (to some extent also of
trilingualism, with Nenets as the third language), but the transition to settled
life meant an end to these very close contacts (though there are still many
mixed Nganasan–Enets older married couples).

An important element of the ethnolinguistic situation in the area was the
creation and functioning of the so-called 'Govorka' – a Taimyr Pidgin
Russian with analytic grammar, which follows Ural-Altaic morphosyntactic
patterns (see Helimski 1987). Until the first half of our century it served as
an important means of interethnic communication in the area, but has now
largely been ousted by Standard Russian. Many elderly Nganasans, especially
males, still speak 'Govorka' fluently.

In earlier times, before the formation of the Dolgan ethnicum, there also
existed Nganasan–Evenki contacts, probably with a certain degree of
bilingualism.

Dialects

Nganasan is split into two very close dialects, Avam (spoken in the western
and central parts of the ethnic territory by c.75 per cent of all Nganasans) and
Vadey (spoken in its eastern part and under stronger Dolgan influence). Still
smaller are the differences between the two subdialects, Pyasina Avam (now
spoken in Ust-Avam and Volochanka) and Taimyra Avam (now mainly in
Volochanka).

The dialectal distinctions in phonetics are not structural and mostly are
restricted to the choice of preferred variants: Pyasina, Vadey δ : Taimyra $\underset{.}{d}$
(cacuminal d) or δ, depending on position; Avam d^j (idiolectally j): Vadey j
(idiolectally d^j); the reduced mid vowel ∂ is in Vadey more closed than in

Avam). Other dialectal distinctions have never been specially studied. It is known, however, that they do not go beyond very few lexical and morphological items (e.g. Vadey *torautu* 'works': Avam *ŋojbautu* 'works' versus *torautu* 'is good for, is useful'), and the Nganasan dialects are completely mutually intelligible.

The description below refers to the Pyasina Avam subdialect.

Historical Development

There are sufficient reasons to believe that an early form of the Nganasan language was spoken by reindeer-breeding Samoyeds who reached the Taimyr peninsula in the first millennium CE from the south, moving along the Yenisei River. They assimilated linguistically the local population of wild-reindeer hunters, adopting certain elements of material and spiritual culture from them.

Nganasan differs from all other Samoyedic languages, including also its Northern Samoyedic neighbours (Nenets and Enets), in at least two important points of morphology, namely the marking of the locative case (*-ntə-nå instead of *-kə-nå) and the formation of the present tense (see Janhunen 1991).

Of utmost importance for Uralic linguistics is the obvious and far-reaching similarity between Nganasan consonant gradation (see below) and the corresponding phenomenon in Baltic-Fennic and Saamic. The co-existence of two different mechanisms, syllabic gradation and rhythmic gradation (cf. so-called 'stem gradation' and 'suffixal gradation' in Baltic-Fennic) is particularly suggestive. In view of the absence of typological parallels in other languages of the world it seems highly improbable that these mechanisms could be separate and wholly independent developments on the western and the eastern periphery of the Uralic language-family tree. The similarity must be explained either by the parallel influence of a common unknown substratum, or – and this is much more likely – by the phonologization of a phonetic mechanism that already operated in the Uralic proto-language.

Otherwise Nganasan shows numerous innovations, both shared with Nenets and Enets (such as the rise of word-initial prothetic nasals before vowels, the development of glottal stop and its morphophonemic alternations, the wide usage of incorporated particles and modal markers) and individual. Unique to Nganasan is the relatively recent – partly already after the beginning of Russian–Nganasan linguistic contacts, i.e. not before the seventeenth century – vowel chain-shift *ü > *i*,*u > *ü*, *o > *u*, *å > *o* and also *e > *i̇*, with numerous special cases of retentions and deviations from this general scheme due to phonetic positions.

Table 16.1   Consonants and their Cyrillic graphic symbols

	Labials	Dentals	Palatals	Velars	Glottals
Voiceless stops	p <б>[1], <п>	t <т>	tʲ <ч>	k <к>	ʔ <">
Voiced stops	b <б>	d <д>	dʲ <д>[2]	g <г>	
Voiced fricatives		ð <з>	j <й>		
Voiceless fricatives		s <с>	sʲ <с>[2]	h <х>	
Nasals	m <м>	n <н>	nʲ <н>[2], <нь>[3]	ŋ <ӈ>	
Laterals		l <л>	lʲ <л>[2], <ль>[3]		
Vibrants		r <р>			

Note: 1 Before voiceless stops and fricatives. 2 Before the 'yotated' vowel letters – <e>, <ё>, <и>, <ᵘa>, <ю>, <ᶦᵒa>, <я>. 3 Before consonants.

Table 16.2   Vowels and their Cyrillic graphic symbols

	Front			Non-front		
	Unrounded		Rounded	Unrounded		Rounded
High	i	<i>[1], <и>	ü <ÿ>, <ю>[2]	ï	<ы>	u <у>
Mid	e	<e>				o <o>, <ё>[2]
				ə	<э>, <e>[2]	
Low	ᶦa	<ᶦa>[1], <ᵘa>		a	<a>, <я>[2]	ᵘa <ʸa>, <ᶦᵒa>[2]

Note: 1 Used after <д>, <с>, <н>, <л> to denote their dental (non-palatal) character. 2 Used after <д>, <с>, <н>, <л>, to denote their palatal character.

Phonology and Morphophonology

Phonemes and their Distribution

The phoneme inventory of Nganasan consists of twenty-one consonants, including three 'subphonemes' (phonetically distinct units, which are in complementary distribution with other units in genuine words and partly independent in borrowed words), and ten vowels. They are shown in Tables 16.1 and 16.2.

Consonants

In Nganasan, as well as in other Northern Samoyedic languages, there are systematic restrictions on the occurrence of consonants in different positions. The maximal differentiation is found in intervocalic position, less free is the distribution of consonants word-initially, word-finally, and in clusters (which occur only word-medially, and until very recently were regularly eliminated from the two other positions in borrowings, as well); see Table 16.3 for the

Table 16.3   Occurrence of consonants in diagnostic positions

	[p]	t	t^j	k	ʔ	s	s^j	h	b	d	[ð]	d^j	[j]	g	m	n	n^j	ŋ	l	l^j	r
#__V	(–)	+	+	+	–	+	+	+	+	(+)	–	+~+	(+)	+	+	+	+	+	+	(–)	
C__V	(–)	+	+	+	–	+	+	+	+	+	–	+	–	+	+	+	+	+	+	(–)	
V__V	(–)	+	+	+	+	+	+	+	+	(+)	+	+~+	+	+	+	+	+	+	+	+	
V__C	+	(–)	(–)	(–)	+	(+)	–	–	–	–	–	–	+	–	+	+	+	+	+	+	
V__#	–	–	–	–	+	–	–	–	–	–	–	–	+	–	+	–	–	+	–	–	+

Key: (+) occurs only in non-native words, including old and otherwise adapted borrowings.
(–) occurs only in recent borrowings. ~ in free alternation.

occurrence of consonants word-initially, syllable-initially after consonants, between two vowels, syllable-finally before consonants, and word-finally.

This table lists also the 'subphonemes' [p] [ð] [j] and thus allows for the possibility of treating [p] in genuine words as an allophone of *b* (or of *h*, which is less plausible phonetically, but historically adequate: Nganasan *h* < *p*), of treating [ð] in genuine words as an allophone of *d* (or vice versa), and of treating [j] as an allophone (partly in complementary distribution, and partly in free alternation) of d^j.

Which of the phonological interpretations of these 'subphonemes' is adopted is not crucial. As a matter of fact, it is questionable whether the phonological level itself (as a stage between deep morphophonemic and surface phonetic representations) is a psychological reality for the speakers of Nganasan, and whether phonology is a necessary part in the description of this language.

The other allophonic phenomena characteristic of the consonants are as follows:

t^j is in free variation with the palatal affricate [čj]; in fact, there is but slight phonetic difference between these two consonants in Nganasan pronunciation;

the glottal stop ʔ is realized word-medially usually as a break in articulation after a vowel; optionally even this break may be absent, so that a word-medial glottal stop is reduced to zero – this optional effect is especially frequent in the Taimyra Avam subdialect;

b between vowels is idiolectally pronounced as the corresponding voiced fricative [β];

in Taimyra Avam Nganasan, δ is usually pronounced as the corresponding voiced stop, cacuminal [ḍ] or postdental [d̪] (in M.A. Castrén's Nganasan records from the 1840s, δ was not distinguished from *d* at all);

the sibilants have relatively rare optional free alternants: [θ] (voiceless dental non-sibilant fricative) for *s*, and [šj] for s^j;

in archaic pronunciation, which is still fairly frequent among elderly women,

a labial fricative ([ɸ], [f]) or a labiovelar [hʷ] is used instead of *h* (Castrén's materials and even records from the beginning of the twentieth century have <f> in corresponding words); moreover, the consonant *h* is realized as a voiced velar fricative [ɣ] between two vowels;
all labials and velars, *δ*, and *r* are strongly palatalized before front vowels.

Vowels
The inventory of vowel phonemes includes eight short monophthongs and two diphthongoids with very short initial elements, *ⁱa* and *ᵘa*. The diphthongoids are more liable to positional and idiolectal variation than the other vowels. In particular, idiolectally in casual pronunciation they lose their initial element (and thus their contrast with *a*): *kəbtᵘasuə* ~ *kəbtasuə* '(it) faded', *küüʔa* ~ *küüʔa* '(s)he died'; in final syllables before a glottal stop they are monophthongized into *ä* and *å*: *kəbtᵘaʔ* [kəptå?] 'fade!', *küüʔaʔ* [küü?ä?] 'they died'. After labials, velars, *δ*, or *r* the vowel *ⁱa* is often pronounced as *a* or *ä* with a strong palatalization of the preceding consonant: *hⁱaŋ* [hʲaŋ], [hʲäŋ] 'palm'.
There are certain restrictions on the occurrence of vowels:

the phonemes *e* and *o* occur (in genuine or adapted words) only in the first syllable; the sounds [e] and [o] in non-first syllables are the phonetic manifestations of the phoneme *ə*;
the front vowels (*i*, *e*, *ⁱa*, *ü*) do not occur in the first syllable after dentals;
the vowels *ə*, *ï*, *u* do not occur in the first syllable (*ï* and *u* – also in other syllables) after palatals, being in this position neutralized with *e*, *i*, and *ü*, respectively;
the vowels *ə* and *o* are neutralized after labial consonants and *h*; the corresponding sequences have the phonetic shapes [bo], [mo] (before labial consonants and labialized vowels), [bə], [mə] (otherwise), [ho] (in the first syllable), [hö] (after a syllable with *ü*), [ho] or [hʷə] (otherwise in non-first syllables);
the vowels *a* and *ⁱa* are neutralized in favour of *a* after palatals.

The phonetic stock of Nganasan is very rich in long vowels and diphthongs, but (apart from the case of *ⁱa* and *ᵘa*, see above) it is reasonable to treat and to transcribe them as vocalic sequences. This approach is supported by abundant evidence from phonetics (normally a long vowel or a diphthong is approximately twice as long as a single vowel), accentology and metrics (a long vowel or a diphthong usually counts as two morae, as seen already by Hajdú (1964)), morphophonology (when necessary, the morphophonemic rules are applied separately to each part of long vowels and diphthongs), and morphology (very often the parts are divided by morpheme boundaries); see relevant examples in the following sections.
The diphthongs have *i*, *ü*, *u*, *a*, *ⁱa* and (only after high vowels) *ə* as their

second component. Contractions are not typical, but the reduced vowel *ə* is assimilated by first components into the corresponding mid vowel, and then optionally contracted with first components into the corresponding long mid vowel: *s^{j}iə* [s^{j}ie ~ s^{j}ee] 'hole'; *hüə* [h^{j}üö ~ h^{j}öö] 'year'; *honsïəðï* [honsïëðï ~ honsëëðï] '(he) had it'; *n^{j}omuə* [n^{j}omuo ~ n^{j}omoo] 'hare (attributive)' (derived from *n^{j}omu* 'hare'). This assimilation (and contraction) accounts for the presence of the vowels [ö], [ë] (and also of [e], [o] in non-first syllables) in the phonetic stock of Nganasan, though they do not belong to the phonemic system. The assimilation occurs also in *əu* [ou] and *əü* [öü].

The simple vowels *i, ü, ï, u, a, ə* participate also in the formation of long vowels: *hii* 'night'; *bəjküü?*, pG of *bəjkuə* 'old'; *hïïm-* 'to be frightened'; *tuu*, sG of *tuj* 'fire'; *n^{j}aa* 'Nganasan' (derived from *n^{j}a* 'mate'); *səə* 'heart'. Other long vowels, namely [ee] [öö] [ëë] and [oo], are phonetically secondary (see above).

Orthography

The graphic system of Nganasan (Tereščenko 1986, with modifications officially adopted in 1990), based on the Russian Cyrillic system, is presented in Tables 16.1 and 16.2. Its slightly modified version (e.g. with <?> instead of <">, <δ> instead of <з>, and without <ь>) is used in Helimski (ed.) (1994).

Because it has inherited the Russian orthographic tradition, which denotes 'hard' and 'soft' consonants with the same symbol, and distinguishes them by the use of different symbols for the following vowels, the graphic system of Nganasan is not phonological. Nevertheless, in principle it is automatically convertible into phonemic transcription, if both the conventions connected with the 'yotated' vowel letters and the above mentioned phonotactic restrictions are taken into account. For example, the Cyrillic <e> is used in the first syllable for *e*, and in non-first syllables, where *e* does not occur, it is used to indicate the vowel *ə* plus the palatal quality of the preceding consonant; thus <меньдяде> = *men^{j}d^{j}ad^{j}ə* 'new'.

Long vowels and diphthongs are written as sequences of graphemes (as in phonemic transcription). Beside the graphic symbols in Tables 16.1 and 16.2, other Cyrillic letters can be used to write borrowed words.

Accent and the Rhythmic Organization of Words

The main stress is normally placed on the penultimate vowel or on the vocalic sequence which includes the penultimate vowel: *ko̱ru?* 'house', *koruðə?* 'houses', *kümaa* [k^{j}üma̱a] 'knife', *baarbə* [ba̱arbə] 'master, chief', *bəlo̱ukə* [bəlo̱ukə] 'a kind of movable dwelling on runners'. This general principle is optionally violated by the retraction of stress from a high vowel or *ə* to the vowel (usually an open one) in the preceding syllable: *baru̱s^{j}i ~ ba̱rus^{j}i* 'devil'.

Longer words (with five syllables and more – such words are very common in Nganasan, cf. the text at the end of this chapter) are usually divided into two, three, or four – potentially even more – rhythmic groups. Each group typically contains two syllables (two phonological vowels), and the last group has two or three syllables. It is very common – especially for verbal forms – that the stem and the derivational suffix (or suffixes) are bisyllabic, so that the boundaries between groups in most cases coincide with the boundaries between morphemes, while the last group includes a cluster of inflectional suffixes (sometimes together with a monosyllabic derivational suffix).

The boundaries between rhythmic morphemic groups are very distinct: sometimes the break in articulation creates the acoustic impression of a glottal stop (which, as mentioned above, is also realized word-medially as a break). The last group has, according to the general rule, the main stress on its penultimate vowel, and all preceding groups receive additional stresses on their first vowels. In the following examples, rhythmic groups are separated by the symbol ' $_{($ '; secondary, group-initial stresses are indicated by a colon):

ko:ðu₍sʲüðün̄ʲə	'I will kill them'
ki:ntə₍lə:btï₍kutjiŋ	'you are smoking'
ki:ntə₍lə:btï₍kutʲinə	'I am smoking'
kə:rï₍gə:ɬi₍tini	'in marches'
kə:rï₍gə:ɬi₍tininə	'in my marches'
kə:rï₍gə:ɬi₍rï:a₍tininə	'only in my marches'.

The rhythmic organization of words plays an important role also in the morphophonology of Nganasan, regulating the phenomenon of rhythmic gradation; see below.

Morphophonology

Alternations and Morphophonemes
The abundance and complexity of productive morphophonological alternations place Nganasan in an exclusive position among the Uralic languages. This uniqueness is the result of the co-existence and cumulative effect of several relatively independent mechanisms, including glottal stop alternation, truncation, rhythmic gradation, syllabic gradation, nunation, stem alternation, vowel harmony and accommodation. Most of these mechanisms – syllabic gradation and vowel harmony in particular – have largely lost their synchronic phonetic motivation; this does not prevent them, however, from remaining regular and productive.

As a result of the above-listed processes, Nganasan exhibits great diversity of both radical and suffixal allomorphs; to serve as an illustration, Table 16.4 and Figure 16.1 account for the distribution and generation of ten allomorphs

Table 16.4 Allomorphy: suffix of the renarrative mood

	Features of the preceding stem (= sequence of morphemes)							
	Even number of vocalic morae				Odd number of vocalic morae			
	Vocalic		Consonantal		Vocalic		Consonantal	
	U-stem	Ï-stem	U-stem	Ï-stem	U-stem	Ï-stem	U-stem	Ï-stem
Second syllable of suffix is open	baŋhu	bïaŋhï	h^{u}aŋhu	h^{i}aŋhï	bahu	bïahï	h^{u}ahu	h^{i}ahï
Second syllable of suffix is closed	bambu	bïambï	h^{u}ambu	h^{i}ambï	bahu	bïahï	h^{u}ahu	h^{i}ahï

Table 16.5 Consonant morphonemes (and some morphoneme clusters), their transformations and phonemic realizations

	H	T	K	S	S^j	MH	NT	ŊK	NS	N^{j}S^j	^{c}H	^{c}T	^{c}T^j	^{c}K	^{c}S	^{c}S^j
Morphoneme(s)	H	T	K	S	S^j	MH	NT	ŊK	NS	N^{j}S^j	^{c}H	^{c}T	^{c}T^j	^{c}K	^{c}S	^{c}S^j
RhG, weak grade	b	ð	g	d^j	d^j	^{c}H	^{c}T	^{c}K	^{c}S	^{c}S^j						
SyG, weak grade	b	ð	g	d^j	d^j	mb	nd	ŋg	n^{j}d^j	n^{j}d^j						
Nunnation								ŋg								
Word-finally	?	?		?							ŋh	nt	n^{j}t^j	ŋk	ns	n^{j}d^j
Syllable-finally	(?)	(?)	(?)	(?)												
Otherwise (prior to accommodations)	h	t	k	s	s^j	mh	nt	ŋk	ns	n^{j}s^j	h	t	t^j	k	s	s^j

	T^j	B	D^j	J	M	N	N^j	Ŋ	L	L^j	R	^{c}
Morphoneme(s)	T^j	B	D^j	J	M	N	N^j	Ŋ	L	L^j	R	^{c}
Word-finally	ʔ			j		ŋ, Ø[1]	j					^{c}
Syllable-finally	(?)	p		j								
Between vowels			Ø									
Otherwise (prior to accommodations)	t^j	b	d^j	j	m	n	n^j	ŋ	l	l^j	r	Ø

An empty cell in this table means that the corresponding morphoneme undergoes no transformation in the corresponding position or does not occur there.

Note: 1 ŋ in monosyllabic words, Ø (sometimes ŋ ~ Ø) in longer words.

Figure 16.1   Generation of allophones: suffix of the renarrative mood

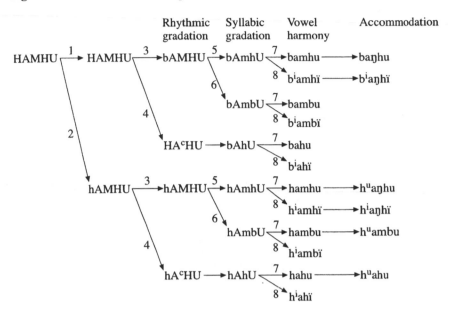

Key: 1 after vocalic stems. 2 after consonantal stems. 3 after stems with even number
of vocalic morae. 4 after stems with odd number of vocalic morae. 5 second syllable of
suffix is open. 6 second syllable of suffix is closed. 7 after stems of the first harmonic
class. 8 after stems of the second harmonic class.

of the renarrative mood suffix, allomorphs which range from -*hᵘambu*-, as in
kou-hᵘambu-? 'they are said to remain', to -*bⁱahï*-, as in *koliði-bⁱahï-?* 'they
are said to be fishing'. Other alternations, with their occasionally paradoxical-
seeming outcomes, are illustrated below, as well as by paradigmatic tables in
the section on morphology.

The character of Nganasan morphophonology makes it convenient to
describe the composition of morphemes in terms of morphophonemes. Below,
this approach is applied mainly to suffixes, but when necessary, parts of stems
can also be transcribed morphonemically. The morphophonemes, as distinct
from surface level phonemes, are written in capital letters; for example, the
generalized morphonemic shape of the above mentioned renarrative mood
suffix is written HAMHU.

It appears sufficient to distinguish, instead of the twenty-one surface-
level consonant phonemes and 'subphonemes' (Table 16.1), 18 deep-level
consonant morphonemes: H T Tᴶ K ? S Sᴶ B J Dᴶ M N Nᴶ ŋ L Lᴶ R ᶜ.
Perhaps at a still deeper level of description five of these (Tᴶ ? Sᴶ Dᴶ ᶜ)
could be eliminated – but at the expense of making the description more
artificial and complicated. Most of these consonant morphonemes, if they
are not affected by any regular and obligatory rules applied to

Table 16.6   Vowel harmony: phonemic realizations of vowel morphonemes in suffixes (prior to accommodations)

Morphoneme		A	A₁	A₀	U	U₀	Ü	Ü₀	Ï	I	ə	ᵘA	ⁱA
After U-stems (first class)	Preceding vowel is not i or ü	a	a	a	u	u	ü	ü	ï	i	ə	ᵘa	ⁱa
	Preceding vowel is i or ü	a	a	a	ü	u¹	ü	ü	ï	i	ə	ᵘa	ⁱa
After Ï-stems (second class)	Preceding vowel is not i or ü	ⁱa	ï	a	ï	u	i	ü	ï	i	ə	ᵘa	ⁱa
	Preceding vowel is i or ü	ⁱa	i	a	i	u¹	i	ü	ï	i	ə	ᵘa	ⁱa

Note: 1 In Taimyra Avam subdialect ü (at least in certain suffixes with U₀).

individual units and their strings, are rewritten in the corresponding non-capital letters. The morphoneme ᶜ ('zero-consonant') corresponds to a surface-level zero: it is used to denote a conventional unit which occurs syllable-finally after vowels and imparts to the (phonetically) open syllable the phonological properties of a closed one; it also participates in certain morphophonological rules. Like other morphonemes, ᶜ is a phonological reality from the viewpoint of proto-Nganasan (proto-Samoyedic) reconstruction. The most important transformations and surface level realizations of consonant morphonemes are indicated in Table 16.5.

The treatment of vowels in terms of morphonemes is connected almost exclusively with the phenomenon of vowel harmony, see pp. 493–40 and Table 16.6.

Rhythmic Gradation (RhG)

The grade alternation, or gradation, of word-medial consonants and clusters consists in the alternative appearance of two grades, strong and weak, depending on the (morpho)phonological environment.

In general, the strong grade of RhG surfaces after an odd number of vocalic morae (= phonological vowels) in the preceding part of a word, and its weak grade surfaces after an even number of vocalic morae. RhG affects five morphonemes (H T K S Sᴶ) and clusters of these with preceding nasals (MH NT ŋK NS NᴶSᴶ), see Table 16.5. RhG manifests itself very clearly in the allomorphy of suffixes, cf. *ni-ti, bïnï-ði, hïadʲə-ti, kərigəlʲi-ði* 'his wife, rope, thumb, march' (all with the s3 possessive suffix); *ni-rəgï, bïnï-rəki, hïadʲə-rəgï, kərigəlʲi-rəki* 'similar to a woman, rope, thumb, march' (all with the same similative suffix) etc., cf. also Table 16.4. Historically, the functioning of RhG is attested also in roots, cf. *hütəðə* 'trunk' from *putətə (= Nenets *pudăd*, Enets *puðoðo*).

The functioning of RhG is restricted by several additional rules:

1 Only the strong grade surfaces after consonants (including ^{C}), unless the resulting cluster itself participates in RhG: *tər-tu* 'his/her hair', *kaδar-tu* 'his/her light';

2 Only the weak grade comes out directly after vocalic sequences: *lataə-δu* 'his/her bone', *biriə-δï* 'his/her wound';

3 Only the weak grade of the cluster NT occurs before an open non-second syllable: *hütəδə-tənu* 'in the trunk' (with the locative suffix NTəNU). Closed non-second syllables preserve the strong grade of this cluster, which then undergoes syllabic gradation: *hütəδə-ndinü* 'in the trunks' (with NTI^{C}NU).

The number of vocalic morae is normally counted on the phonological level and may differ from the number of phonetic vowels and phonetic syllables. So for example the stems *h"aa* 'tree' or *b^{i}ai* 'target', both phonetic monosyllables, are treated from the viewpoint of RhG as having two morae: *h"aa-rəku, b^{i}ai-rəkï*, 'similar to a tree, to a target'. However, it is typical, perhaps even normal, for a word-medial (and non-first-syllable) vocalic sequence to be counted as only one vocalic mora: *lataə-rəku, biriə-rəkï* 'similar to a bone, wound'.

Syllabic Gradation (SyG)
In general, the strong grade of SyG surfaces before the vowel of an open syllable, and its weak grade surfaces before the vowel of a closed syllable. SyG affects the same morphonemes and clusters as RhG, but the weak grades of clusters resulting from SyG differs from those resulting from RhG; see Table 16.5. In terms of rule-ordering SyG follows RhG and is applied only to those units that are preserved in their strong grade by RhG (the weak grades of RhG, e.g. *δ* from T, or ^{C}T from NT, do not participate in SyG).

SyG functions in both nominal and verbal paradigms, cf. (sN : pN) *kuhu : kubu?* 'skin, hide', *basa : bad^{j}a?* 'iron', *kəntə : kəndə?* 'sledge', *kaδar : katarə?* 'light', *hen^{j}d^{j}ir : hensirə?* 'shaman's drum'; (verbal adverb : connegative) *kotud^{j}a : koδu?* 'kills', *d^{j}embi?s^{j}i : d^{j}eŋhid^{j}ə?* 'gets dressed'. For the functioning of SyG in suffixes (combined with that of RhG) see Table 16.4 and Figure 16.1.

Like RhG, SyG does not affect postconsonantal consonants, unless the cluster participates in SyG itself, cf. *ŋəmsu* 'meat', pN *ŋəmsu?*.

If the closed character of a syllable is determined by a deep level ^{C}, SyG may surface as an 'unconditioned' alternation: *kəntə* 'sledge', sG *kəndə* (with the sG case suffix -^{C}). It must also be noted that an intervocalic glottal stop always makes the preceding syllable closed.

The morphemes that end in ^{C} ('pseudo-vocalic' or 'quasi-consonantal') are twice abnormal from the viewpoint of SyG. Not only does the weak grade surface in phonetically open syllables, but also the strong grade is used in final syllables followed by a glottal stop or a second (suffixal) ^{C}, as well as in certain types of word-medial phonetically closed syllables: *koδu* 'snow-storm', sG *kotu*, pN *kotu?*; *dʲügusa* 'being lost', *dʲüku?* 'gets lost (con-negative)', *dʲüku?əm* 'I got lost' (stems: KOTU^C, DʲÜKU^C-). Probably this paradox is to be accounted for by a special rule that changes the zero-consonant ^{C} into the zero-vowel ^{V} in the relevant positions (^{C}?# > ^{V}?#, ^{CC}# > ^{VC}#, etc.)

Nunation

This morphophonological mechanism, known as 'Nunation' since M.A. Castrén (1854: 162), consists in the change of ^{C} into a nasal consonant when ^{C} is followed by H, T, Tʲ, K, S, or Sʲ and is preceded by a nasal, being separated from that preceding nasal only by a vowel or a vowel sequence; see Table 16.5. In terms of rule-ordering it follows both RhG and SyG. Thus, on the one hand, some deep level clusters are, after the application of RhG, 'restored' by nunation and, on the other hand, neither type of gradation is applied to the output of nunation. Therefore there are such forms as e.g. *mununtum* 'I say', in which the deep level cluster NT appears to be preserved in its strong grade contrary to the conditions of both RhG and SyG. The actual path that generates such forms looks as follows:

munu-NTU-M > *munu*-^{C}TU-M > *mununtum*
         (RhG)   (Nun)

The functioning of nunation is evident in pairs such as: *kundᵘasuə* '[s]he slept' : *tanᵘansuə* '[s]he was accustomed' (stems *kundᵘa^C-*, *tanᵘa^C-*), *nʲaaδu* 'his/her Nganasan' : *nʲantu* 'his/her mate' (stems *nʲaa* and *nʲa^C*; the suffix is -TU); *basu-tu* 'hunts' : *nïa-ntu* 'saves up' (the suffix is -NTU, transformed by RhG into ^{C}TU).

The rule of nunation is less obligatory (especially in derivation) than other morphophonological rules, and sometimes nunated and non-nunated forms coexist as variants: *kəməutə-* ~ *kəməuntə-* 'to wrestle', *ləŋintï* ~ *ləŋïtï* 'burns [intr]'.

Vowel Harmony (VH)

From the viewpoint of VH all mono- and bisyllabic stems are divided into two harmonic classes of approximately the same size. Historically, this division corresponds to the opposition 'front : back', and was determined by the last vowel or (if this vowel was harmonically neutral) by the first vowel. Today, however, this original principle is so overshadowed by secondary changes of vowel quality, that it is more convenient simply to ascribe to each stem its harmonic class, first ('U-stems') or second ('Ï-stems'), as a lexical morpho-phonological characteristic. The synchronic phonetic composition of stems is in many cases not sufficient to determine their harmonic class: e.g. *hon-* 'to plait' is a U-stem (*honsuəδu* '[s]he plaited it'), while *hon-* 'to have' is an Ï-stem (*honsïəδï* '[s]he had it'); cf. also *dʲintə* 'archer's bow', and *kəmə-* 'to catch' (U-stems) v. *kintǝ* 'smoke' and *kǝrǝ-* 'to moor' (Ï-stems).

Another way of dealing with VH would be to distinguish twice (or nearly twice) as many vowel morphonemes as there are vowel phonemes. In this presentation, however, the description in morphonemic terms will be applied only to the vocalism of suffixes, in order to account for the impact of VH on it (Table 16.6). The impact on suffixal vowels is also not systematic from the synchronic point of view. For example, the vowel *u* is in harmonic alternation with *ï* in some suffixes, but remains stable in others: *basu-gu-mu?* 'let us hunt' and *nʲilï-gu-mï?* 'let us live'. This means that *u* represents two different morphonemes, U_O in *-gu-* and U in *-mu?/-mï?* (and historically, that *u* results from a merger of two different vowels).

The situation is further complicated by a kind of 'secondary' VH, which is due to the fronting influence of *i* and *ü* on high vowels in the next syllable, so that each harmonic class becomes further divided into two subclasses (Table 16.6).

The assertion that 'there is no vowel harmony in Nganasan' (Tereščenko 1979: 48) is true in the sense that what is called VH here lacks synchronic motivation and does not create a real 'harmonic unity' of words. Besides, within bisyllabic primary stems and old derivatives the principles of VH can be violated.

Like other morphophonological norms, the principles of VH are sometimes disregarded, usually by younger and less capable native speakers. In such cases the prevailing direction of neutralization is in favour of the first harmonic class (U-stems).

Stem Alternation

While the alternations described above have phonetic motivation (synchronic or historical), the choice between stem variants can be determined by the morphological environment, as well. It is convenient to distinguish three variants of nominal and verbal stems:

S1, which occurs, in particular, in the nominative singular of nouns and in verbal adverbs, and can be considered the basic stem form;
S2, e.g. in the genitive singular and nominative plural of nouns, and in the connegative form of verbs;
S3, e.g. in the genitive plural of nouns, and in the present tense of perfective verbs.

Some types of relationship between stem variants are shown on p. 495. Nouns are cited in sN for S1, in sG for S2, in pG for S3. Verbs are cited in the forms of verbal adverb for S1, in connegative forms for S2, in the forms of indicative present s3 (suffix *?ǝ*) or of perfective verbal noun (suffix *?MUǝ*) for S3.

1 Vocalic basic stems:

ŋusï	ŋusï	ŋusï?	'work'	nənsudʲi	nənsu?	nənsu?ə	'stands up'
ŋuta	ŋuδa	ŋuδa?	'berry'	ŋonsïdʲi	ŋondʲi?	ŋondʲi?ə	'goes out'
kolï	kolï	kola?	'fish'	konïdʲi	konï?	kona?a	'goes'
məku	məgu	məga?	'back'	kontudʲa	kondu?	konda?a	'carries'
hüü	hüü	hia?	'tinder'	büüdʲa	bü?	bia?muə	'departs'
dʲakə	dʲagə	dʲagü?	'twin'	hotədʲa	hoδə?	hoδü?ə	'writes'
latəə	latəə	latəi?	'bone'	hursədʲi	hursə?	hursʲi?ə	'returns'

2 Consonantal basic stems:

bï?	bïδə	bïδï?	'water'	nəsa	nəδə?	nəδu?ə	'scours'
hiə?	hiədʲə	hiədʲi?	'fur overcoat'	dʲembi?sʲi	dʲeŋhidʲə?	dʲeŋhidʲi?ə	'dresses'
hʲadʲir	hʲasïrə	hʲasïrï?	'fishing-rod'	bïδïrsï	bïtïrə?	bïtïrï?mïə	'drinks'
tuj	tuu	tuu?	'fire'	tu(j)sʲa	tu?	tuu?ə	'comes'
ŋoj	ŋuə	ŋuə?	'foot'	me(j)sʲi	mï?	mïï?ə	'makes'

3 Pseudo-vocalic basic stems:

koδu	kotu	kotu?	'snowstorm'	dʲügusa	dʲüku?	dʲüku?ə	'get lost'

It is also possible to describe stem alternations as resulting from the application of special operators (vowel addition, vowel replacement, etc.) to a basic deep level stem form. For certain stems two alternants, or even all three of them, may syncretize.

Stem-medial consonants typically occur in strong grades of SyG in vocalic S1, and in its weak grades in S2 and in consonantal S1. In keeping with this general tendency, the secondary symbol S1′ is used to denote those morphological positions in which the opposite distribution obtains, i.e. where weak grades of SyG are used in vocalic S1, and similarly the symbol S2′ denotes positions where S2 has strong grades of SyG.

Within suffixal strings many suffixes (for example, mood and tense markers) undergo alternations which are essentially the same as stem alternations.

Other Morphophonological Rules

The rule of *truncation* operates even before RhG and SyG. Truncation works as follows: 1) $^C > ∅ /$ __CC; 2) $C > ∅ / C$__C. That is, (1) a suffix that begins in a consonant cluster ousts a final ^{C} in the preceding morpheme or (2) loses its first consonant, if the preceding morpheme ends in a non-zero consonant.

Table 16.5 reports the word- and syllable-final change of the morphonemes T, K (which does not occur word-finally), and S into a glottal stop, which can then be reduced phonetically to zero (this reduction is almost regular within rhythmic groups, optional at boundaries between these groups, and rare in word-final position). This results in alternations such as *ma?* 'house', sG *maδə*, sEla *makətə* (stem *maT*); *ŋəmsa?suə* '(s)he ate', *ŋəmsadʲə?* 'eat! (s2 imp)' (stem *ŋəmsaS-*). At a deeper level of description it is also possible to treat every word- and syllable-final glottal stop as T (or S), even when it does not participate in such alternations.

Numerous accommodative processes follow, in terms of rule-ordering, the above-described mechanisms, and are usually applied to the phonemic realizations of morphonemes (see Tables 16.5 and 16.6). They operate both within morphemes and across morphemic boundaries (internal sandhi). The most important rules of accommodation are listed below. Symbols: C = consonant, C^J = palatal consonant, [a b] = a and b correspondingly, {a b} = a or b, (a) = a may be present or absent, ~a = not a, (>) = the rule is optional or restricted to certain morphological positions. The rules are arranged so that those under (B) operate after those under (A) and before those under (C), while the rules under (D) appear to be neutral to rule ordering.

(A)

t (>) Ø /r___
[u ï] (>) [ü i] / {ü i}(C(C))___
[u ï] (>) [ü i] / ___ (C(C)){ü i}
[e o] > [ï u] / ___ə

(B)

r > l / {~i ~ü}C___
r > l^j / {i ü}C___
i (>) ü / ___(C(C))ü
i (>) ü / ü(C(C))___
[t s n l] > [t^j s^j n^j l^j] / j___
[s l] > [s^j l^j] / ___ {i ü ¹a}
[ï u ¹a] > [i ü a] / C^J___

(C)

{ʔ l n ŋ} > Ø / ___{l l^j}
j (>) Ø / ___C^J
[n l] > [n^j l^j] / ___C^J

(D)

[m n n^j ŋ] > Ø / ___[m n n^j ŋ]
{m n n^j ŋ} > Ø / {m ŋ}
{n n^j} > ŋ / ___{k h}
m (>) ŋ / ___h
ə > a / {a ^{u}a ¹a}(ʔ)___
a > ^{u}a / h___

Morphology

Nominal Categories and Nominal Inflection
The grammatical categories of nouns in Nganasan are as follows:

Number: singular, dual, and plural are distinguished. Plural forms occur more frequently than in many other Uralic languages, often rendering the general idea of abundance (*kamə?* 'bloods = a lot of blood') or collectivity (*n^{j}emin^{j}ə* 'my mothers = my mother and other female relatives'). Plural forms also may combine with numerals: *nakürə? basutuə?* 'three hunters, as many as three hunters'.

Case: nominative (= absolute form), genitive, accusative, lative (= dative or dative/lative), locative (= locative/instructive), elative (= ablative), prolative (= prosecutive), and comitative (= sociative) are distinguished. There are also several forms that stand on the borderline between case forms and postpositional constructions (the allative with the marker *-d'aa*, joined to the genitives singular and plural), between case forms and non-finite verbal constructions (the essive/translative with the marker *-is'a*, joined to the nominative singular), and between case forms and denominal adverbs (the caritive [= abessive], with the suffix -KAJ or -KA^{C}L^{J}I, joined to stem variant S1).

Possessivity: non-possessive (= absolutive) forms and possessive forms with the subcategories of possessor's number (singular, dual, plural) and person (first, second, third) are distinguished. The possessive forms of the second person singular are often used to specify nouns as definite and co-referent with their predecessors in the discourse (rather than implying collocutor's possession), and occasionally definiteness is expressed also by possessive forms of the third person singular.

Predicativity: with the subcategories of subject's number (singular, dual, plural) and person (first, second, third). Predicative forms are used as predicates without copulae or, if another grammatical meaning than that of indicative present must be expressed, with corresponding forms of the verb *ij-* 'to be': *mənə n'aam* 'I am Nganasan', *mənə n'aam is'üəm* 'I was Nganasan'.

Tables 16.7 and 16.8 show the morphonemic composition of suffixes for the above-listed grammatical categories, the structure of the paradigmatic forms, and an example of nominal declension. There are also special shorter

Table 16.7   Nominal personal endings

	Predicative	Possessive Px1 sN	Px3 sA	Px4 dpNGA	Px2 Other cases, adverbials
s1	M	Mə	Mə	Nə	Nə
s2	ŋ	Rə	MTə	Tə	NTə
s3	Ø	TU	MTU	TU	NTU
d1	MI^c	MI^c	MI^c	NI^c	NI^c
d2	RI^c	RI^c	MTI^c	TI^c	NTI^c
d3	KəJ	TI^c	MTI^c	TI^c	NTI^c
p1	MUʔ	MUʔ	MUʔ	NUʔ	NUʔ
p2	RUʔ	RUʔ	MTUʔ	TUʔ	NTUʔ
p3	ʔ	TUŋ	MTUŋ	TUŋ	NTUŋ

forms of local case suffixes which are used mainly in adverbials (local and temporal adverbs, postpositions, adverbial pronouns): lative -^{C}, locative -NU, elative -T∂.

The combinability of categorical meanings is partly restricted. The dual paradigm lacks local cases, these meanings being rendered by constructions with the dual genitive and corresponding case forms of the postposition *na-*: *kuhugi na* 'to two skins', *kuhugi nanu* 'in/with two skins', etc.). There are no possessive forms of the comitative case. The predicative forms have no case or possessive inflection. Further restrictions are found primarily in special categories of nominal words (pronouns, adverbials).

Some descriptions of Nganasan also reckon with a category of (pre)-destinativeness: *kuhuðəmə* 'skin for me', etc. (cf. Tereščenko 1979:102–7). It seems, however, more appropriate to treat the so-called (pre)destinative forms as possessive forms of substantives that have been built with the clitic -T∂, which shifts the temporal reference to the future: *kuhuðə* 'what is going to be a skin, future skin'; cf. the clitic -D^J$\partial\partial$ with the opposite temporal reference: *kuhudⁱ$\partial\partial$* 'what used to be a skin, former skin'.

Adjectives

The semantic difference between substantives and adjectives is supported derivationally (most adjectives contain special adjectival suffixes, e.g. -K$\partial\partial$ and -^{C}L^{J}I^{C}KU$_O$ in qualitative, and -∂ or -∂D^J∂ in relative words), but from syntactic and inflectional viewpoints they are identical. Like adjectives, substantives can be used attributively and then have a defective case paradigm with only three cases (see Syntax, p. 511), while in non-attributive position adjectives undergo complete substantivization and have all nominal inflectional forms.

A small group of qualitative adjectives has formally distinct attributive-positive, attributive-comparative and predicative forms: *tanəgəə* 'wide' : *tandudⁱə* 'wider (attrib)' and *tandᵘa* 'is wide', *kəəlⁱükü* 'short' : *kəimdⁱə* 'shorter (attrib)' : *kəim* 'is short'. The singular prolative and plural genitive case forms of qualitative adjectives are used as qualitative adverbs, e.g. *tantəgəəmənu, tantəgəi?* 'widely'.

Numerals

Primary cardinal numerals and corresponding ordinal numerals and numeral adverbs (answering the question 'how many times?') are listed in Table 16.9 (see p. 500). Other numerals are compounds, formed without any connecting elements additively (*bii? sⁱiti* '12'), multiplicatively (*sⁱiti bii?* '20'), or multiplicatively and additively (*sⁱiti bii? sⁱiti* '22').

Pronouns

Personal pronouns and related pronominal forms (Table 16.10, p. 500) have many formal peculiarities. Basic personal pronouns actually have no

Table 16.8 Nominal declension: deep structure of forms and the paradigm of *kuhu* 'skin, hide'

	Non-poss	Poss	s1	s2	s3	d1	d2	d3	p1	p2	p3
sN	S1 kuhu	S1-Px1	kuhumǝ	kuhurǝ	kuhuðu	kuhumi	kuhuri	kuhuði	kuhumuʔ	kuhuruʔ	kuhuðuŋ
sG	S2-ᶜ or S2-Ŋ[1] kubu(ŋ)	S1-Px2, S1´-Px2[2]	kuhunǝ	kubutǝ	kubutu	kuhuni		kubuti	kuhumuʔ	kubutuʔ	kubutuŋ
sA	S2-ᶜ or S2-M[1] kubu(m)	S1-Px3, S2-Px3[3]	kuhumǝ	kubumtǝ	kubumtu	kubumi		kubumti	kuhumuʔ	kubumtuʔ	kubumtuŋ
sLat	S1-NTƎ kubutǝ	S1´-NTƎ-Px2	kubutǝnǝ	kubutǝtǝ	kubutǝtu	kubutǝni		kubutǝndi	kubutǝnuʔ	kubutenduʔ	kubutenduŋ
sLoc	S1-ᵁNNƎTN kubutǝnu	S1´-NTNNU-Px2	kubutǝnunu	kubutenuntǝ	kubutǝnuntu	kubutǝnumi		kubutǝnunti	kubutǝnunuʔ	kubutenuntuʔ	kubutenuntuŋ
sEla	S1-ᵉLᵉᵉK-1S kuhugǝtǝ	S1-ᵉLᵉᵉK-ᵉᵉ-Px2	kuhugǝtǝnǝ	kuhugǝtǝtǝ	kuhugǝteŋ	kuhugǝtǝni		kuhugǝtǝti	kuhugǝtenuʔ	kuhugǝtetuʔ	kuhugeteŋ
sProl	S1-MǝNU kuhumǝmu	S1-MǝNU-Px2	kuhumǝnunu	kuhumǝnuntǝ	kuhumǝnuntu	kuhumǝnuni		kuhumǝnunti	kuhumǝnunuʔ	kuhumenuntuʔ	kuhumenuntuŋ
dN	S1-KǝJ kuhugǝj	S1-KǝJ-J-Px4	kuhugǝinʲǝ	kuhugǝtǝ	kuhugǝiteiŋ	kuhugǝinʲi		kuhugǝiti	kuhugǝinʲiʔ	kuhugǝitiʔ	kuhugǝitiŋ
dG	S1-KIᶜ kuhugi	S1-KǝJ-ʔ-Px4	kuhugǝinǝ	kuhugǝitǝ	kuhugǝitu	kuhugǝini		kuhugǝiti	kuhugǝinuʔ	kuhugǝituʔ	kuhugǝituŋ
dA	=dG	=dN									

	Deep structure								
pN	S2-ʔ kubuʔ	S3-J-Px4	kuban'ə	kubatˈü	kuban'i	kubatˈi	kuban'üʔ?	kubatˈüʔ?	kubatˈüŋ
pG	S3-ʔ kubaʔ	S3-ʔ-Px4 =pN	kubanə	kubatu	kubani	kubati	kubanuʔ?	kubatuʔ?	kubatuŋ
pA	S2-J kubuj								
pLat	S1ʹ-NTT^{c}[4] kubutiʔ	S1ʹ-NTT^{c} -Px2	kubutinə	kubutitü	kubutini	kubutindi	kubutinüʔ?	kubutindüʔ?	kubutindüŋ
pLoc	S1ʹ- $NTT^{F}NU$ kubutinü	S1ʹ- $NTT^{F}NU$ -Px2	kubutinünə	kubutinüntü	kubutinüni	kubutinünti	kubutinüntüʔ?	kubutinüntüʔ?	kubutinüntüŋ
pEla	S1-$K^{F}Tə^{s}$[5] kuhugitə	S1-$K^{F}TI$ -Px2[6]	kuhugitinə	kuhugititü	kuhugitini	kuhugititi	kuhugitinüʔ?	kuhugitütüʔ?	kuhugitütüŋ
pProl	S3-ʔ-MƏNU kubaʔmanu	S3-ʔ -MƏNU -Px2	kubaʔmanunə	kubaʔmanuntu	kubaʔmanuni	kubaʔmanunti	kubaʔmanunuʔ?	kubaʔmanunuʔ?	kubaʔmanuntuŋ
sCom	S2-NA kubuna	—							
dCom	S1-K^{F}-NA kuhugina	—							
PCom	S3-ʔ-NA kubaʔna	—							

Note: For the explanations of symbols used in presenting deep structures of forms (stems S1, S1ʹ, S2, S3; morphonemes) see 'Morphophonology' pp. 487–495. Px1–4 are different series of possessive suffixes, see Table 16.7.

1 The second variant is archaic and occurs mainly in the language of folklore.

2 S1-Px2 in possessive forms of first person, S1ʹ-Px2 in possessive forms of second and third persons.

3 S1-Px3 in possessive forms of first person, S2-Px3 in possessive forms of second and third persons. Cf. *bigaj* 'river': sA + Px1 *bigajma*, sA + Pxs3 *bikaamtu*.

4 There is an optional variant S3-NTIʔ for certain stems: *bigajHiʔ* or *bikautiʔ* 'to the rivers'.

5 Variants with less frequent optional forms of case suffix: S1-$KI^{c}TIʔ$, S1-$Kə^{c}TIʔ$ (*kuhugitiʔ*, *kuhugaiʔ*).

6 The deep structure can also be interpreted as S1-$K^{F}TI$-Px2 (or S1-$KƎTⁱ$-Px2).

Predicative forms are as follows:

s1 kubum	*d1* kuhumi	*p1* kuhumuʔ
s2 kubuŋ	*d2* kuhuri	*p2* kuhuruʔ
s3 kuhu	*d3* kuhugəj	*p3* kubuʔ

inflection: their nominatives, genitives, and accusatives formally coincide, and the roles of their local cases are played by the corresponding possessive case forms of the postposition *na-* (used also to supply surrogate case forms in the dual of nominal inflection).

Table 16.9   Numerals

Number	Cardinal numeral	Ordinal numeral	Numeral adverb [1]
1	ŋuʔəiʔ ~ ŋuʔəj	nʲerəðïtïə, nʲerəbtəə	ŋuʔəðuʔ
2	sʲiti	sʲiðimti(ə)	sʲiði?
3	nagür	nagəmtu(ə)	nakürü?
4	tʲetə	tʲetəmtï(ə)	tʲeti?
5	səŋhəlʲaŋkə	səmbəmtï(ə)	səŋhəlʲaŋgi?
6	mətüʔ	mətəmtï(ə)	mətüðü?
7	sʲajbə	sʲajbəmtï(ə)	sʲajbi?
8	sʲitiðətə	sʲitiðətəmtï(ə)	sʲitiðəti?
9	ŋamⁱatʲümə	ŋamⁱatʲüməmtï(ə)	ŋamⁱatʲümi?
10	bii?	biimti(ə)	biiði?
100	dʲir	dʲirəmtï(ə)	dʲiri?

Note: 1 Identical to the pG of cardinal numerals.

When combined with clitics (and such combinations are used very frequently), basic personal pronouns are replaced with bound pronominal stems: MÏN for sdp1, TÏN for sdp2, and SÏʔ for sdp3. These stems are then followed by a clitic (in Table 16.10 exemplified by RA_1A_O 'only') and Px2 (cf. Table 16.7).

The indeclinable personal emphatic pronouns ('myself' etc.) contain the bound stem *ŋonə-* and Px2. Both structurally and syntactically they are similar to personal forms of nominal adverbials.

In other categories, nominal pronouns are usually inflected like ordinary nouns (and distinguish all inflectional categories). These categories also include pronouns that are formally and functionally similar to adjectives, numerals, and adverbs.

Demonstrative pronouns distinguish deixis of proximate object (*əmtï*, *əm-* 'this', *əmənʲiə* 'this one', *əmə* 'here [lative]', *əmnï* 'here [locative]', *əmkətə* 'from here', *əmləðʲi* 'like this, such', *əmiʔïˀa* 'like this, so', etc.), deixis of distant object (*takəə* 'that', *taanʲiə* 'that one', *tabə* ~ *tabaʔa* 'there [lative]', *tamnu* 'there [locative]', *tabkətə* 'from there', etc.), and anaphoric (*təti* 'this/ that, it', *tənʲiə* 'this/that one', *təndə* and *tənʲi* 'there [lative]', *tənï* and *tənʲini* 'there [locative]', *təgətə* and *tənʲiðə* 'from there', *tərəðʲi* 'such', *tənʲiʔïˀa* 'so', etc.).

Interrogative pronouns include *maa* and *maaŋuna* 'what', *silï* and *silïŋuna*

Table 16.10   Personal pronouns and related pronominal forms

	N, G, A	Lative	Locative	Elative	Prolative	Personal pronouns + clitic ('only')	Personal emphatic pronouns
s1	mənə	nanə	nanunə	nagətənə	namənunə	mïlʲianə	ŋonənə
s2	tənə	nantə	nanuntə	nagətətə	namənuntə	tïlʲiatə	ŋonəntə
s3	sïtï	nantu	nanuntu	nagətətu	namənuntu	sïlʲiatï	ŋonəntu
d1	mi	nani	nanuni	nagətəni	namənuni	mïlʲiani	ŋonəni
d2	ti	nandi	nanunti	nagətəndi	namənundi	tïlʲiati	ŋonənti
d3	sïti	nandi	nanunti	nagətəndi	namənundi	sïlʲiati	ŋonənti
p1	mïŋ	nanu?	nanunu?	nagətənu?	namənunu?	mïlʲianï?	ŋonənu?
p2	tïŋ	nandu?	nanuntu?	nagətəndu?	namənundu?	tïlʲiatï?	ŋonəntu?
p3	sïtïŋ	nanduŋ	nanuntuŋ	nagətənduŋ	namənunduŋ	sïlʲiatïŋ	ŋonəntuŋ

'who', kuə 'what (attrib)', kanə 'how many', kanəmtu(ə) 'which (in order), das wievielte', kanü? 'how many times', kunʲiə 'what kind of', kundə and kunʲi 'where [lative]', kunu and kunʲini 'where [locative]', kunʲiδə 'from where', kurədʲi 'what, what kind of', kunʲiʔïʲa 'how', kaŋgə 'when', maadʲaa 'why', etc.

Negative pronouns (or rather emphatic interrogative pronouns, used in negative sentences) and indefinite pronouns are correlative with the interrogative ones and incorporate clitics: maagəlʲitʲə 'nothing, anything', kaŋkəgəlʲitʲə 'never, whenever'; maagüə, maatʲə, maatʲəküə 'something', kaŋkəgüə, kaŋgətʲə, kaŋgətʲəküə 'somewhere', etc.

Determinative pronouns include bənsə 'whole, all' (dN bənsəgəj 'both', pN bəndʲəʔ 'all'), ŋamʲaj 'another', ŋamʲadʲüm 'the other', hunsəə 'other', malamsə 'whatever, different', etc.

Adverbs and Syntactic Words (Adverbials)
The vast and heterogeneous class of adverbials comprises, from the syntactic viewpoint, adverbs proper (with the semantic subgroups of local, temporal, qualitative, modal, gradational adverbs, etc.), postpositions, and conjunctions. From a morphological viewpoint it is possible to single out the subclass of inflected nominal adverbials, which have personal and, to an extent, case forms as well. This subclass includes not only local and temporal adverbs and postpositions (cf. ŋilʲəni 'below', ŋilʲəδə 'from below', hʷaa ŋilʲəni 'under the tree', hʷaa ŋilʲəδə 'from under the tree', ŋilʲəninə 'under me', ŋilʲəninti 'under him/her', etc.), but also such words as kərutə- 'simply, just so', ŋïtə- 'still', ŋonəəδə 'once again', etc.: ŋïtənə 'I still', ŋïtətï '(s)he still'. The morphological subclass of indeclinable adverbials is the more numerous, however.

Verbs

Conjugation Type, Person, and Number

There are five conjugation types (voices) in Nganasan with five partly different sets of finite personal endings: (1) subjective, (2–3–4) objective with singular, dual, and plural object, and (5) objectless (or reflexive). Transitive verbs are conjugated in all five types: according to three objective types (if their object in the corresponding number is definite), to subjective type (if their object is indefinite and in some other situations), and to objectless type (if they render reflexive meaning). Intransitive verbs are divided into those conjugated according to objectless or, alternatively, subjective types (reflexive, reciprocal, passive, many inchoative and finitive verbs) and those conjugated only according to subjective type.

Verbal personal endings (Table 16.11) distinguish three persons and three numbers of the subject. In the subjective type they are similar to the nominal predicative paradigm, and in the objective types they resemble the possessive endings of nouns. The personal endings used in the imperative are partly different from the endings in other moods. Mood and tense suffixes that directly precede the endings of the objective-plural and objectless types undergo changes similar to those found in S3 as compared with S1 (see pp. 494–5).

Table 16.11   Verbal personal endings (Vx)

	Subjective conjugation	Objective conjugation with singular object	with dual object	with plural object	Objectless conjugation
s1	M	Mə	Kəl-J-Nə	J-Nə	Nə
s2	ŋ	Rə	Kəl-J-Tə	J-Tə	ŋ
s3	Ø	TU	Kəl-J-TU	J-TU	? or Təᶜ
d1	MIᶜ	MIᶜ	Kəl-J-NIᶜ	J-NIᶜ	NIᶜ
d2	RIᶜ	RIᶜ	Kəl-J-TIᶜ	J-TIᶜ	NTIᶜ
d3	Kəj	TIᶜ	Kəl-J-TIᶜ	J-TIᶜ	NTIᶜ
p1	MU?	MU?	Kəl-J-NU?	J-NU?	NU?
p2	RU?	RU?	Kəl-J-TU?	J-TU?	NTU?
p3	?	TUŋ	Kəl-J-TUŋ	J-TUŋ	NTə?
Imp pres s1	TəM	Mə	Kəl-J-Nə	J-Nə	Nə
Imp pres s2	?[1]	Tə[4]	Kəl-J-Nə[2]	J-Nə[3]	TIŋ[1]
Imp fut s2	Kəŋ or Kə[2]	KəᶜTə[2]	Kəl-J-Tə	J-Tə	KIŋ[2]

Note:
1 Joined directly to the second stem of the verb – S2.
2 Joined directly to the first stem of the verb – S1.
3 Joined directly to the third stem of the verb – S3.
4 Joined directly to the verbal stem: usually to s1, but in some verbs with consonantal S1 – to S2 or S3.
In other forms Vx are joined after mood and tense suffixes: see Table 16.12.

Aspect
The aspectual distinction between perfective and imperfective verbs is displayed formally in the indicative present, where perfective verbs take only the suffixes of the present perfect (and render the corresponding meaning), and where imperfective verbs take only the suffixes of the present continuous. In other verbal forms the [+/- perfective] distinction remains on the semantic level (this is easily rendered in Russian, but not in English translations). From many verbal roots both perfective and imperfective stems are derived (cf. from *kəmə-* 'catches': *kəmiʔəmə* 'I have caught [pres perf]' and *kəmüδütüm* 'I am catching [pres cont]'. There are also rare examples of biaspectual stems (*hʷaŋku-* : *hʷaŋkaʔam* 'I got drunk' and *hʷaŋkutum* 'I am drunk').

Mood and Tense
The system of moods includes indicative, imperative, interrogative (used in interrogative sentences and in relative clauses), inferential (or latentive, used for reporting events which the speaker did not witness directly), renarrative (mood of reported speech), irrealis (used to denote imaginary results of unfulfilled conditions), optative (used to denote desirable, but hypothetical events), admissive-cohortive (with several functions, including those of expressing gnomic constatation [with neutral intonation], doubt [with interrogative intonation], and polite recommendation [with exclamatory intonation]), debitive (or obligative, used to denote a future action which is considered proper), abessive (not-yet-accomplished action), prohibitive (warning against an action); this list is not exhaustive.

Tenses are distinguished in three moods:

*   in the indicative (present, with the complementarily distributed subcategorical meanings of present perfect and present continuous: see above; past, past perfect, future, and future-in-the-past – this last denotes an action that was supposed to be done);
*   in the imperative (present and future, with the meanings of, correspondingly, immediate and remote future);
*   in the interrogative (present, past, future).

Suffixes and selected forms of verbal inflection are given in Table 16.12.

Non-finite Forms
The main non-finite verbal forms are indicated in Table 16.12 (with translations and in some cases with the constructions in which they are used); the terms used and especially the distinctions made between verbal nouns and verbal adverbs are conventional and provisional. Like other nominals, most non-finite verbal forms take possessive suffixes with reference, in this case, to the subject of the verbal action. Verbal nouns also take case suffixes, and participles take number and case suffixes.

The *connegative* form is used in analytic constructions with the negative

Table 16.12   Verbal inflection: deep structure of forms and selected fragments of paradigms (*kotu-* [S2 *koδu-*, S3 *koδa-*] 'to kill; (in objectless conjugation) to ruin oneself', *koδutə-* 'to be [in the process of] killing, ruining oneself', *nʲi-* auxiliary negative verb)

	1	*2*	*3*	*4*	*5*
Indicative present perfect					
S3-*ʔə*-Vx and S3-*ʔī*-Vx[1]					
s1	koδaʔam	koδaʔamə	koδaʔakəinʲə	koδaʔinʲə	koδaʔinə
s2	koδaʔaŋ	koδaʔarə	koδaʔakəitʲə	koδaʔitʲə	koδaʔiŋ
s3	koδaʔa	koδaʔatu	koδaʔakəitʲü	koδaʔitʲü	koδaʔiδə ~ koδaʔi?
d1	koδaʔami	koδaʔami	koδaʔakəinʲi	koδaʔinʲi	koδaʔini
d2	koδaʔari	koδaʔari	koδaʔakəitʲi	koδaʔitʲi	koδaʔindi
d3	koδaʔagəj	koδaʔaδi	koδaʔakəitʲi	koδaʔitʲi	koδaʔindi
p1	koδaʔamu?	koδaʔamu?	koδaʔakəinʲü?	koδaʔinʲü?	koδaʔinü?
p2	koδaʔaru?	koδaʔaru?	koδaʔakəitʲü?	koδaʔitʲü?	koδaʔindü?
p3	koδaʔa?	koδaʔaδuŋ	koδaʔakəitʲüŋ	koδaʔitʲüŋ	koδaʔində?
Indicative present continuous					
S1-*NTU*-Vx and S1-*NTA₁*-Vx[1]					
s1	koδutəndum	koδutətumə	koδutətugəinʲə	koδutəndanʲə	koδutətanə
	nʲindïm	nʲintïmə	nʲintïgəinʲə	nʲindïnʲə	nʲintïnə
s2	koδutənduŋ	koδutəturə	koδutətugəitʲə	koδutəndatʲə	koδutəndaŋ
	nʲindïŋ	nʲintïrə	nʲintïgəitʲə	nʲindïtʲə	nʲindïŋ
s3	koδutətu	koδutətuδu	koδutətugəitʲü	koδutəndatʲü	koδutətaδə ~ koδutətanda?
	nʲintï	nʲintïδï	nʲintïgəitʲi	nʲindïtʲi	nʲintïδə ~ nʲindï?
d1	koδutətumi	koδutətumi	koδutətugəinʲi	koδutəndanʲi	koδutətani
	nʲintïmi	nʲintïmi	nʲintïgəinʲi	nʲindïnʲi	nʲintïni
d2	koδutəturi	koδutəturi	koδutətugəitʲi	koδutəndatʲi	koδutəndati
	nʲintïri	nʲintïri	nʲintïgəitʲi	nʲindïtʲi	nʲindïti
d3	koδutətugəj	koδutətuδi	koδutətugəitʲi	koδutəndatʲi	koδutəndati
	nʲintïgəj	nʲintïδi	nʲintïgəitʲi	nʲindïtʲi	nʲindïti
p1	koδutətumu?	koδutətumu?	koδutətugəinʲü?	koδutəndanʲü?	koδutətanu?
	nʲintïmï?	nʲintïmï?	nʲintïgəinʲi?	nʲindïnʲi?	nʲintïnï?
p3	koδutəturu?	koδutəturu?	koδutətugəitʲü?	koδutəndatʲü?	koδutəndatu?
	nʲintïrï?	nʲintïrï?	nʲintïgəitʲi?	nʲindïtʲi?	nʲindïtï?
p3	koδutəndu?	koδutətuδuŋ	koδutətugəitʲüŋ	koδutəndatʲüŋ	koδutəndatə?
	nʲindï?	nʲintïδïŋ	nʲintïgəitʲiŋ	nʲindïtʲiŋ	nʲindïtə?
Indicative past					
S1-*SUə*-Vx and S1-*SʲÜÜ*-Vx[1,2]					
s1	kotudʲüəm	kotudʲüəmə	kotudʲüəgəinʲə	kotudʲüünʲə	kotudʲüünə
	nʲisïəm	nʲisïəmə	nʲisïəgəinʲə	nʲisʲiinʲə	nʲisʲiinə
Indicative past perfect					
S1-*SUə-Dʲəə*-Vx and S1-*SUə-Dʲəi*-Vx[1]					
s1	kotudʲüədʲəəm	kotudʲüədʲəəmə	kotudʲüədʲəəgəinʲə	kotudʲüədʲəinʲə	kotudʲüədʲəinə
	nʲisïədʲəəm	nʲisïədʲəəmə	nʲisïədʲəəgəinʲə	nʲisïədʲəinʲə	nʲisïədʲəinə

Table 16.12   (Continued)

1	2	3	4	5

Indicative future
S1´-*ʔSUTƏ*-Vx and S1´-*ʔSʲÜTI*-Vx[1,2]

s1	koðuʔsuðəm	koðuʔsutəmə	koðuʔsutəgəinʲə	koðuʔsʲüðinʲə ~ koðuʔsʲüðünʲə	koðuʔsʲütinə ~ koðuʔsʲütünə
	nʲisïðəm	nʲisïðəmə	nʲisïðəkəinʲə	nʲisʲiðinʲə	nʲisʲiðinə

Indicative future-in-the-past
S1´-*ʔSUTƏ-Dʲ Əə*-Vx and S1´-*ʔSUTƏ-Dʲ Əl*-Vx[1]

s1	koðuʔsutə-dʲəəm	koðuʔsutə-dʲəəmə	koðuʔsutədʲəə-gəinʲə	koðuʔsutə-dʲəinʲə	koðuʔsutə-dʲəinə
	nʲisïðədʲəəm	nʲisïðədʲəəmə	nʲisïðədʲəəgəinʲə	nʲisïðədʲəinʲə	nʲisïðədʲəinə

Imperative present
s1/d1/pl: S1-*KUₒ*-Vx
d2/p2[3]: S1-*ŋU*-Vx and S1-*ŋAₗ*-Vx[1]
s3/d3/p3: S1-*ŋƏƏ*-Vx and S1-*ŋƏl*-Vx[1]

s1	kotuguðəm	kotugumə	kotugukəinʲə	kotugunʲə	kotugunə
	nʲikuðəm	nʲikumə	nʲikugəinʲə	nʲikunʲə	nʲikunə
s2	koðuʔ	kotuðə	kotugəinʲə	koðanʲə	kotuðiŋ
	nʲiʔ	nʲintə	nʲikəinʲə	nʲinʲə	nʲiðiŋ
s3	kotuŋəə	kotuŋəəðu	kotuŋəəgəitʲü	kotuŋəitʲü	kotuŋəiʔ ~ kotuŋəiðə
	nʲiŋəə	nʲiŋəəðï	nʲiŋəəgəitʲi	nʲiŋəitʲi	nʲiŋəiʔ ~ nʲiŋəiðə
d1	kotugumi	kotugumi	kotugukəinʲi	kotugunʲi	kotuguni
	nʲikumi	nʲikumi	nʲikugəinʲi	nʲikunʲi	nʲikuni
d2	kotuŋuri	kotuŋuri	kotuŋukəitʲi	kotuŋatʲi	kotuŋandi
	nʲiŋïri	nʲiŋïri	nʲiŋïgəitʲi	nʲiŋïtʲi	nʲiŋïnti
d3	kotuŋəəgəj	kotuŋəəði	kotuŋəəgəitʲi	kotuŋəitʲi	kotuŋəinti
	nʲiŋəəgəj	nʲiŋəəði	nʲiŋəəgəitʲi	nʲiŋəitʲi	nʲiŋəinti
p1	kotugumuʔ	kotugumuʔ	kotugukəinʲüʔ	kotugunʲüʔ	kotugunuʔ
	nʲikumïʔ	nʲikumïʔ	nʲikugəinʲiʔ	nʲikunʲiʔ	nʲikunïʔ
p2	kotuŋuruʔ	kotuŋuruʔ	kotuŋukəitʲüʔ	kotuŋatʲüʔ	kotuŋanduʔ
	nʲiŋïrïʔ	nʲiŋïrïʔ	nʲiŋïgəitʲiʔ	nʲiŋïtʲiʔ	nʲiŋïntïʔ
p3	kotuŋəəʔ	kotuŋəəðuŋ	kotuŋəəgəitʲüŋ	kotuŋəitʲüŋ	kotuŋəintəʔ
	nʲiŋəəʔ	nʲiŋəəðïŋ	nʲiŋəəgəitʲiŋ	nʲiŋəitʲiŋ	nʲiŋəintəʔ

Imperative future (excepting s2[4])
S1-*KUₒƏ*-Vx and S1-*KÜₒÜₒ*-Vx[1,2]

s1	kotuguəm	kotukuəmə	kotuguəgəinʲə	kotugüünʲə	kotugüünə
	nʲikuəm	nʲikuəmə	nʲikuəgəinʲə	nʲiküünʲə	nʲiküünə
s2	kotugə(ŋ)	kotugətə	kotuguəgəitʲə	kotugüütʲə	kotugiŋ
	nʲigə(ŋ)	nʲigətə	nʲikuəgəitʲə	nʲiküütʲə	nʲigiŋ

Interrogative present
S1-*ŋU*-Vx and S1-*ŋAₗ*-Vx[1]

s1	kotuŋum	kotuŋumə	kotuŋukəinʲə	kotuŋanʲə	kotuŋanə
	nʲiŋïm	nʲiŋïmə	nʲiŋïgəinʲə	nʲiŋïnʲə	nʲiŋïnə

Table 16.12   (Continued)

	1	2	3	4	5

Interrogative past
S1-*HU*-Vx and S1-*HA₁*-Vx[1]

| sl | kotubum | kotubumə | kotubukəinʲə | kotubanʲə | kotubanə |
| | nʲibïm | nʲihïmə | nʲihïgəinʲə | nʲibïnʲə | nʲihïnə |

Interrogative future
S1'-*NTƏ-ŊU*-Vx and S1'-*NTƏ-ŊA₁*-Vx[1]

| sl | kuðutəŋum | koðutəŋumə | koðutəŋugəinʲə | koðutəŋanʲə | koðutəŋanə |
| | nʲintəŋïm | nʲintəŋïmə | nʲintəŋïkəinʲə | nʲintəŋïnʲə | nʲintəŋïnə |

Inferential
S1-*HATU*-Vx and S1-*HATA₁*-Vx[1]

| sl | kotubaðum | kotubatumə | kotubatugəinʲə | kotubaðanʲə | kotubatanə |
| | nʲih¹aðïm | nʲih¹aðïmə | nʲih¹aðïkəinʲə | nʲih¹aðïnʲə | nʲih¹aðïnə |

Renarrative
S1-*HAMHU*-Vx and S1-*HAMHA₁*-Vx[1]

| sl | kotubambum | kotubaŋhumə | kotubaŋhugəinʲə | kotubambanʲə | kotubaŋhanə |
| | nʲib¹ahïm | nʲib¹ahïmə | nʲib¹ahïkəinʲə | nʲib¹ahïnʲə | nʲib¹ahïnə |

Irrealis
S1-*HA₁AₒTƏƏ*-Vx and S1-*HA₁AₒTƏI*-Vx[1, 2]

| sl | kotubaaðəəm | kotubaaðəəmə | kotubaaðəəgəinʲə | kotubaaðəinʲə | kotubaaðəinə |
| | nʲihïaðəəm | nʲihïaðəəmə | nʲihïaðəəgəinʲə | nʲihïaðəinʲə | nʲihïaðəinə |

Optative
S1-*HA₁Aₒ*-Vx and S1-*HA₁I*-Vx[1, 2]

| sl | kotubaam | kotubaamə | kotubaagəinʲə | kotubainʲə | kotubainə |
| | nʲihïam | nʲihïamə | nʲihïagəinʲə | nʲihiinʲə | nʲihiinə |

Admissive/cohortative
S1'-ᶜ*KƏƏ*-Vx and S1'-ᶜ*KƏI*-Vx[1]

| sl | koðukəəm | koðukəəmə | koðukəəgəinʲə | koðukəinʲə | koðukəinə |
| | nʲiŋkəəm | nʲiŋkəəmə | nʲiŋkəəgəinʲə | nʲiŋkəinʲə | nʲiŋkəinə |

Debitive
S1'-*BSUTƏ*-Vx and S1'-*BSʲÜTI*-Vx[1, 2]

| sl | koðupsuðəm | koðupsutəmə | koðupsutəgəinʲə | koðupsʲüðinʲə ~ koðupsʲüðünʲə | koðupsʲütinə ~ koðupsʲütünə |
| | nʲipsïðəm | nʲipsïðəmə | nʲipsïðəkəinʲə | nʲipsʲiðinʲə | nʲipsʲiðinə |

Abessive[5]
S1-*MƏTUMA₁ʔAₒ*-Vx and S1-*MƏTUMA₁ʔI*-Vx[1, 2]

| sl | kotumətumaʔam | kotumətuma-ʔamə | kotumətumaʔa-gəinʲə | kotumətuma-ʔinʲə | kotumətumaʔinə |

Prohibitive
S1-*LÏ*-Vx

| sl | kotulïm | kotulïmə | kotulïkəinʲə | kotulïnʲə | kotulïnə |
| | nʲilïm | nʲilïmə | nʲilïgəinʲə | nʲilïnʲə | nʲilïnə |

Table 16.12   (Continued)

Non-finite forms:

Imperfective verbal noun
S1-*MUN*(-Cx) (-Px)
        kotumu
sG   *kotumunə hirə* 'worth killing'
sLat   *hiïmsïəm kotumundə* 'I was afraid to kill'
sEla + s1   *kotumuŋgətənə* 'so that I do not kill', etc.

Perfective verbal noun
S3-*ʔMUə*(-Cx) (-Px) or S1'-*ʔMUə*(-Cx) (-Px)
        koðaʔmuə ~ koðuʔmuə
sLoc + s1   *koðaʔmuəntənunə* 'where I killed', etc.

Preterite verbal noun
S1'-*NTU*(-Cx) (-Px); the most commonly used form is sLat without or with Px
        koðutu
sLat   *koðutundə* 'when killed'
sLat + s1   *koðutundənə* 'when I killed', etc.

Supine
S1-*NAKə*(-Px2)
        kotunakə
s3   *kotunagətu* 'in order that he killed', etc.

Present participle
S1'-*NTUə*(-NCx) (-Px)
        koðutuə 'which has killed ~ which has been killed'

Preterite participle
S1-*SUə-Dʲəə*(-NCx) (-Px)
        kotudʲüədʲəə 'which killed ~ which was killed'

Future participle
S1'-*ʔSUTə*(-NCx) (-Px)
        koðuʔsutə 'which will kill ~ which will be killed'

Future-in-the-past participle
S1'-*ʔSUTə-Dʲəə*(-NCx) (-Px)
        koðuʔsutədʲəə 'which was to kill ~ which was to be killed'

Abessive participle
S1-*MəTUMA₁ʔA_O*(-NCx) (-Px)
        kotumətumaʔa 'which has not killed ~ which has not been killed'

Preterite abessive participle
S1-*MəTUMA₁ʔA_O-Dʲəə*(-NCx) (-Px)
        kotumətumaʔdʲəə 'which did not kill ~ which was not killed'

Passive participle
S1-*Məə*(-NCx) (-Px)
        kotuməə 'killed'

Preterite passive participle
S1-*Məə-Dʲəə*(-NCx) (-Px)
        kotuməədʲəə 'which was killed'

Verbal adverb
S1-*SA₁*
        kotudʲa 'having killed', *nʲisï kotudʲa* 'having not killed'

Verbal adverb of immediate precedence
S1-*KAJ-SA₁*.
        kotugasʲa 'having just killed'

Table 16.12   (Continued)

Conditional-temporal verbal adverb
S1-*HÜ?*(-Px4)
     kotubü? '(if ~ when) to kill', *kotubünə* 'if ~ when I kill', etc

Preterite temporal verbal adverb
S1-*HÜ?-ə*(-Cx) (-Px)
     kotubü?ə 'when killed', *kotubü?əmə* 'when I killed', etc.

Future conditional verbal adverb:
S1-*HÜ?-NÜ*-Px2
     kotubününə 'if I will kill', etc.

Connegative
S2-*?*
     koδu?

Key: 1–5 = conjugation types (subjective, objective with singular/dual/plural object, object-less); S1–3 = variants of stems; capital letters = morphonemes, see Morphophonology, p. 489; Vx = verbal personal endings (Table 16.11); Px (Px1, Px2, Px4) = nominal personal (possessive) endings (Table 16.7); Cx and NCx = nominal case and nominal number + case suffixes (Table 16.8).
Notes:
1 Among two patterns the first is used in 1–3, and the second in 4 and 5.
2 From the viewpoint of morphophonology it is possible to treat -*S^JÜə*- as -*SUI*-, -*?S^JÜTI*- as -*?SUTI*- -*KÜ_oÜ_o*- as -*KU_oJ*-, -*HA_IA_oTə(I)*- as -*HA_IəTə(I)*-, -*HA_IA_o*- as -*HA_Iə*-, -*BS^JÜTI*- as -*BSUTI*-, -*MəTUMA?A_o*- as -*MəTUMA_I?ə*-.
3 For the form of imperative present s2 see Table 16.11.
4 For the form of imperative future s2 see Table 16.11.
5 Negative forms of this mood are hardly used.

---

verb *n^ji*- (for paradigmatic forms see Table 16.12) and semantically related auxiliaries, which are also used to render emphatic affirmative meanings: *n^jisïə kuə?* '(s)he did not die' (cf. *kuəd^jüə* '(s)he died'), *kasad^jüə kuə?* '(s)he almost died', *kuə?n^jili* '(s)he must die' (with negative verb in the prohibitive), *ŋuəli kuə?* 'how can it be that (s)he will not die = (s)he will certainly die'.

Derivation

Clitics
Typical of Nganasan are the *clitics* with meanings which in other languages are usually expressed by particles or by attributes. Normally, Nganasan clitics are attached to S1 of both nouns and verbs, and occupy the position between stems and inflectional elements; they thus stand on the borderline between word-compounding and derivation. The most common universal (nominal and verbal) clitics are as follows:

-*RA_IA_O* 'only, still': *kolï-rïa-?* 'only fishes', *i-ł^jia-d^ja* 'only/still being' (from *ij*- 'to be');

-BTA 'or': *kuədʲümu nï-btʲa* 'man or woman', *basu-bta-buŋ nʲi-btʲa-bïŋ* 'are you hunting or not?';

-KəLʲITʲə 'even': *dʲintə-gəlʲitʲə-mə* 'even my archer's bow', *nʲisï ŋəmlu-gəlʲitʲə-?* 'even being not eaten';

-ŊALə 'also': *kurədʲi-ŋalə* 'any' (from *kurədʲi* 'what kind of'), *dʲorə-ŋalə-tu hidʲi-ŋʲalə-tï* 'both cries and laughs';

-KÜₒᶜMÜₒ 'but': *taagümü* 'but the reindeer', *nʲigümüntï tu?* 'but (s)he has not come';

-Tʲə 'at least': *bəðʲa-tʲə-bününə* 'if even/at least I will grow';

-KÜₒə (with emphatic oppositive meaning): *hirəgəəgüə* 'as for the high one' or 'high (s)he really is, but . . .'.

Several other clitics occur mainly or exclusively with nominals: -Tə (with reference to a future state), -Dʲəə (with reference to a former state), -RəKU (similative), -DʲÜₒM (selective).

Denominal Derivation
The following patterns of derivation and their suffixes are especially productive (some of them use as their bases of derivation almost any nominal, including even participles and other non-finite verbal forms, i.e. approach 100 per cent productivity):

diminutives (S2-A?KUₒ with the final vowel(s) of S2 truncated, in certain cases also S1´-KÜₒ and S2-AŊKU with truncation): *kuba?ku* 'little skin' (from *kuhu*), *nʲilitʲa?ku* 'the little living' (from the participle *nʲilitïə*);

augmentatives (S3-RBA₁?ə or -?ə after various stem modifications): *kubar-ba?a* 'big skin', *nʲilitʲa?a* 'the big living';

denominal adjectives (S3-?BALə) with the meaning 'abundant in X' (where 'X' is the base of derivation): *kuba?balə* 'abundant in skins';

desubstantival locative adjectives, correlative with locatives singular (S1´-NTəə) and plural (S1´-NTIᶜə): *koru?təə* 'which is in the house', *koru?tiʔə* 'which is in the houses';

denominal verbs with the basic meaning 'to acquire X' (S3-S-): *sïrajkuə kuba?-* 'gets white skin, becomes white-skinned';

denominal verbs with the basic meaning 'to have X' (S3-?Tə-): *kəndüʔtə-* 'goes by sledge' (from *kəntə* 'sledge');

denominal verbs with the basic meaning 'to become X' (S3-M-): *anika?im-* 'increases [intr]' (from *anika?a* 'big');

denominal verbs with the basic meaning 'to make X out of something' (S3-MTU-): *anika?imtü-* 'increases [tr]';

denominal verbs with the basic meaning 'to lose X' (S1-KAᶜLʲI-M-): *kuhugalʲim-* 'loses one's skin'.

Deverbal Nouns
At least four deverbal substantives can be derived from practically any verbal stem (except for some types of derived deverbal stems): *nomen agentis* (S2-ʔSʲI), *nomen amatoris* (S1-KUTə)*, nomen instrumenti* (S1′-BSAN), *nomen loci* (S1-RəMU). Examples: *basuʔsʲi* 'hunter', *basugutə* 'hunt-lover, fond of hunting', *basupsa* 'means/tools for hunting', *basurəmu* 'hunting area'. The productivity of other deverbal nominal suffixes (-Tə for *nomina actionis*, -HUə for adjectives) is restricted.

Intransitive and Transitive, Passive, Causative Verbs
In primary verbal stems the (in)transitivity remains unmarked, but in derived verbs the stem-forming suffixes often render, along with other lexical and grammatical meanings, the meaning of (in)transitivity. There are also regular patterns by which transitive verbs are derived from intransitive ones (with the suffix -BTU-: *nənsu-* 'stops [intr]', *nənsuptï-* 'stops [tr]') and of deriving intransitive, especially stative, verbs from transitive ones, e.g. *talə-* 'closes [tr]', *taĺüⁱᶜ-* 'is (in a) closed (state)', *bətu-* 'grows [tr]', *bəδ"aᶜ-* 'grows [intr]'.

Passive verbs are regularly derived from transitive bases (S1-RU-). They are perfective or imperfective (depending on the aspect of their bases) and are usually conjugated according to the subjectless type: *ŋuamə ŋanasandi? dʲarkəbtalurunda?* 'people are knocking at my door', literally 'my-door to-people is-knocked-at'. The high textual frequency of passive forms and constructions in Nganasan is determined by the stylistic rule which seeks to preserve the same grammatical subject in a sequence of sentences that form a discourse.

Causative verbs are regularly derived from both intransitive and transitive bases (S1-RU-BTU-, so that causatives can formally be viewed as transitive derivatives of passive derivatives). They are perfective if their base is perfective, and biaspectual if their base is imperfective: *nʲilï-riptï-ʔətï* 'has let him live', *nʲilï-riptï-tïtï* 'lets him live'.

Mode of Action (Aktionsart)
The most productive modes of action and their suffixes are as follows:

Iterative (imperfective verbs; S1-Kə-)*: kotugə-*'kills many times, repeatedly';
Habitual (imperfective verbs; S1-MUMHAᶜ-): *kotumumba-* 'kills usually';
Durative (imperfective verbs, derived mainly from non-primary transitive bases; S1-KU$_O$J-): *koturubtuguj-* 'continuously causes someone to kill';
Non-perfective, denoting that an action remained unfinished or is only planned (imperfective verbs, derived from perfective bases; S1′-NTə-): *koδutə-* 'is in the process of killing, is trying to kill';
Inchoative (perfective verbs; S1′-ʔKə-): *koδuʔkə-* 'starts killing';
Attenuative (derived from transitive bases; S1′-BTU-): *bʲarəptï-* 'opens a

little' (from *bʲarə-* 'opens');

Multisubjective, denoting a collective action (S1´-ʔNAR-): *büüʔnar-* '(of many persons) leave; disperse' (from *büü-* 'leaves, departs').

There are also two completely productive imperfective derivatives which can be viewed as modal modes of action: the volitive (S1-NANTU-) and the intentional (S2-ʔHAN- or S3-ʔHAN-), e.g. *kotunantu-* 'wants to kill', *koðuʔhʷan-* ~ *koðaʔhʷan-* 'is going to kill'.

Syntax

Noun Phrase
Within the noun phrase the attributes normally precede the head noun. Adjectives and participles (often with subordinate words of their own) can, however, be put into focus by placing them postpositively.

Adjectives (including adjectival pronouns and participles) agree with their head nouns in number; adjectives and numerals agree with their head in case. The case agreement of attributes is complete in three cases (nominative, genitive, accusative), but if the head noun is in another case the attribute has the appropriate (singular or plural) form of the genitive: sN *nəŋhə taa* 'bad reindeer', sG *nəmbə taa*, pA *nəmbəj taaj*, pG *nəmbuʔ taaʔ*, sLat *nəmbə taatə*, pLat *nəmbuʔ taatiʔ*.

The link between possessor and possessed is expressed by genitive constructions (with genitive only in preposition) or by attaching a possessive suffix to the possessed.

Simple Sentence
The dominating word order is SOV; other types of word orders are used for shifting the sentence focus, especially in emphatic speech.

The case of the logical subject is nominative, or genitive (in constructions with most non-finite verbal forms), or lative (with passive and causative verbs, when the nominative is reserved for the logical object, i.e. the causator), or locative (in constructions with passive participles in -Məə and -Məə-Dʲəə). The case of the direct object in non-passive sentences is accusative, but nominative in special cases (e.g. when the verb is in the imperative or when the direct object is non-focal and typical for the corresponding verb); for many words, including personal pronouns, there is no formal distinction between nominative, genitive, and accusative singular.

Within the verb complex the negative auxiliary verb normally precedes the main verb, which stands in the connegative form (but the negative auxiliary can be placed postpositively in emphatic affirmative constructions, see p. 508). In compound nominal and verbal predicates the conjugated auxiliary verb (usually *ij-* 'is') is placed postpositively.

Due to the existence of the interrogative mood, interrogative sentences can be both syntactically and intonationally similar to narrative sentences.

Sentence Combining

Co-ordination or subordination of sentences can be achieved both by parataxis and with conjunctions: *tujh"aδəəm (tə?), taanʲə dʲaŋgu?* 'I would have come, but my reindeers are absent (= I have no reindeers)'; the adversative conjunction *tə?* belongs intonationally to the first part, and is optional. The most typical method of sentence combining consists, however, in transforming subordinate clauses into constructions with non-finite verbal forms; for examples see two such constructions in the last sentence of the text on p. 514.

Lexicon

It can be said that the entire structure of Nganasan is dominated by a strong preference for rhythmically canonic trochaic word forms, in which the boundaries between bisyllabic (bivocalic) rhythmic groups tend to coincide with morpheme boundaries. This tendency is due to the following factors:

1   A prevalence of bisyllabic primary stems (= roots); in some cases such roots result from irregular lengthening of vowels in original monosyllabic roots (*bii?* 'ten' instead of *bi?* from Samoyedic *wüt) or from stem-final vocalic extensions (*mənə* 'I', *tənə* 'you' from Samoyedic *mən, *tən);

2   A prevalence of bisyllabic suffixes (or suffixal clusters) with derivational and non-syntactical inflectional meanings, as well as of bisyllabic incorporated clitics; there are instances of rhythmically motivated reduplication of suffixes and clitics (-^{C}Kə^{C}Kə- instead of -^{C}Kə- in inchoative verbs, -TəTə- instead of -Tə- for expressing temporal reference to the future in nouns) and of suffixal synonymy (-ə or -əD^{J}ə in relative adjectives).

This rhythmic preference is, on the other hand, also obviously related to the metrical requirements of the much-respected traditional versification system, and especially to the canonic metrical pattern of shamanistic incantations, which normally consisted of octosyllabic lines with four bisyllabic feet in each, with a caesura after the second foot and with no foot-medial word boundaries, cf.: *mənə nʲimə biðə taɲu / əmə dʲeriðibininə / ləptimʲaku baarbəmə / ŋanasanu? sʲüdʲamində / nʲaagəi? nʲiliʔsïðəŋ* 'My name is Water Eagle / If I have guessed it / O my master Laptimyaku / until the expiration of humans / you will live well'.

The paradigmatic and syntagmatic rules of Nganasan phonology are observed throughout the inherited vocabulary (with violations allowed in sound-imitative interjections) and, to a great extent, even in very recent borrowings from Russian. Cf. the phonetic adaptation in *kəlkuəsə* 'kolkhoz', *səbiəskə* 'Soviet (Russian советский')', *mətuərə* 'motor(-boat)', etc. Note, however, that initial voiced consonants are preserved even in older Russian loans: *gərədə* 'town (Russian го́род)', *dərəbatu-* 'greets (Russian здоро́ваться)'.

Several dozen Russian words were borrowed into Nganasan in the period from the beginning of the seventeenth century until the 1940s. Since then, the influx of loans has greatly increased.

Other foreign influences on the Nganasan lexicon have not been adequately studied. Their sources are Dolgan (*bulunʲə* 'bastard', cf. Yakut *bulunʲnʲa*); Tungusic (*turkutʲanə* 'sledge for transporting goods', cf. Evenki *turku*; see Futaky (1983, 1990), Katzschmann (1986)), Enets (*ukudʲarï* 'white-nosed loon', cf. Enets *uɲoseri*), Nenets (*meŋgʲa* 'depression in ground with water', cf. Nenets *mʲeŋgʲa*), and possibly even Ket (*biʲa* 'wind', cf. Ket *bei*) as well as unknown substratum language(s). The extralinguistic evidence suggests that the layer of Enets loans (together with words borrowed into Enets from Nganasan) must be the most significant, but it is often difficult or even impossible to distinguish such loans from the (Northern) Samoyedic heritage which is common to both Enets and Nganasan.

Nganasan Text

Source: Fieldwork.

A: morphophonemic transcription (stems are not transcribed morphophonemically, but have an index showing their harmonic class); B: phonemic transcription; C: morpheme-by-morpheme gloss; D: close translation; E: freer translation.

nidv = deverbal *nomen instrumenti*; vadv = verbal adverb; vadvcond = conditional/temporal verbal adverb; vidn = denominal intransitive verb; vnpret = preterite verbal noun; vtdn = denominal transitive verb.

A1 dʲesï²-Mə ŋadʲaʲ-KəJ-TU tə²+ijʲ-SUƏ-KəJ
B1 dʲesï-mə ŋadʲa-gəj-tʲü tə+i-sʲüə-gəj
C1 FATHER-s1 YOUNGER.SISTER-N-s3 THAT+BE-pret-d3
D1 my father two younger sisters they two were

A2 dʲakəʲ-KəJ ijʲ-SUƏ-KəJ sʲiti² nï² A3 ŋamʲajʲ
B2 dʲakə-gəj i-sʲüə-gəj sʲiti nï B3 ŋamʲaj
C2 TWIN-N BE-pret-d3 TWO WOMEN C3 OTHER
D2 two twins they two were two women D3 one

dʲakəʲ manuʲ=RʲAI? kuəʲ-SUƏ ijʲ-HAMHU ŋamʲajʲ
dʲakə manu=rʲai? kuə-dʲüə i-bahu ŋamʲaj
TWIN EARLY=adv DIE-pret(-s3) BE-renarr(-s3) OTHER
twin died _____early (so they say), the other

dʲakə¹   noku¹=RA₁A_O=NU   nʲilï²-SUə
dʲakə   noku=raa=nu   nʲilï-dʲiə
TWIN   NEAR=ONLY=loc.adv   LIVES-pret(-s3)
twin   only recently   was (still) alive

A4 tə²=NU=A₁ʔA_O+ijˡ-SA₁   nʲim²-TU   dʲakə¹=DʲЭЭ
B4 tə=nʲi=iʔⁱa+i-sʲa   nʲim-ti   dʲakə=dʲɘɘ
C4 THAT=loc.adv=lat.adv+BE=vadv   NAME-s3   TWIN=FORMER
D4 that being the case   her name   (was) 'Former Twin'

A5 kobtᵘaᶜ¹=MÜ-HÜʔ-ə-TU   dʲesï²-Nə   kəntə¹-ᶜ
B5 kobtᵘa=mü-büʔ-ə-tu   dʲesï-nə   kəndə
C5 GIRL=vidn-vadvcond-pret-s3   FATHER-s1sG   SLEDGE-sG
D5 when she was a girl   my father's   sledge's

tʲerə²=DʲЭЭ   matˡ-U=S=BSAN-U=ʔTə-NTU+dʲaaᶜ
tʲerə=dʲɘɘ   maδ-u=ʔ=sʲan-u=ʔtə-tu+dʲaa
LOAD=FORMER   TENT-S3=vtdn=nidv-S3-vtdn-vnpret+TO
former cargo   to (there being) a tent-festivity

biuˡ-HÜʔ-TU
büü-bü-tü
DEPART-vadvcond-s3
when he left

E1 As for my father, he had two younger sisters. E2 They were twins, two girls. E3 One of the twins died young, the other was still alive not long ago. E4 Therefore her name was Diakadiaa ('former[ly a] twin'). E5 When she was a girl, she used to be taken in my father's sledge, when he was going to celebrate tent-festivities ('Festivities of the Pure Tent').

References and Further Reading

Castrén, M.A. (1854) *Grammatik der samojedischen Sprachen*, St. Petersburg: Buchdruckerei der Kaiserlichen Akademie der Wissenschaften.

Futaky, I. (1983) 'Zur Frage der nganasanisch-tungusischen Sprachkontakte', in G. Bereczki and P. Domokos (eds), *Uralisztikai tanulmányok* (*Hajdú Péter 60. születésnapja tiszteletére*), vol. I, Budapest: ELTE, pp.155–62.

——(1990) 'Etymologische Beitrage zum Nganasanischen', *Specimina Sibirica* 3: 51–5.

Hajdú P. (1964) 'Samoiedica', *Nyelvtudományi Közlemények* 66: 397-405.

Helimski, E.A. (1987) 'Русский говорка место казать будем (Таймырский пиджин)', in *Возникновение и функционирование контактных языков*, Moscow: Nauka, pp. 84–93.

——— (in press) 'О морфологии нганасанского языка', paper read at the Fourth International Symposium 'Uralic Phonology' (Hamburg, 4–8 September, 1989).

—— (ed.) (1994) Таймырский этнолингвистический сборник, вып. 1: Материалы по нганасанскому шаманству и языку, Moscow: Rossijskij gosudarstvennyj gumanitarnyj universitet.

Janhunen, J. (1991) 'Нганасаны и распад прасамодийской языковой общности', in Семинар 'Проблемы происхождения народов уральской языковой семьи', Izhevsk, I pp. 16–19.

Katzschmann, M. (1986) 'Tunguso-Nganasanica', *Finnisch-Ugrische Mitteilungen* 10: 173–87.

—— (1990) *Vorläufiges Nganasanisches Wörterverzeichnis auf der Grundlage alter und neuer Quellen*, Teil 1: *Nganasanisch-fremdsprachig*, n.p. (private edition).

Mikola, T. (1970) 'Adalékok a nganaszan nyelv ismeretéhez', *Nyelvtudományi Közlemények* 72: 59–93.

—— (1986) 'Beitrage zum nganasanischen Sprachgeschichte', *Finnisch-Ugrische Mitteilungen* 10: 243–8.

Prokof'ev, G.N. (1937) 'Нганасанский (тавгийский) диалект', in *Языки и письменность народов Севера*, *Часть*, I Moscow–Leningrad : Učpedgiz, pp. 53–74.

Tereščenko, N.M. (1973) *Синтаксис самодийских языков*, Leningrad: Nauka.

—— (1979) *Нганасанский язык*, Leningrad: Nauka.

—— (1986) 'Алфавит нганасанского языка', in P.A. Skorik (ed.), *Палеоазиатские языки*, Leningrad: Nauka, pp. 45–7.

17 Nenets

Tapani Salminen

The traditional territory of the Tundra Nenets language extends along a vast tundra zone from the Kanin Peninsula in the west to the Yenisei River delta and the Yenisei Bay in the east. The northern boundary is formed by the Arctic Ocean, Tundra Nenets being also spoken on several of its islands. In the south, the language boundary extends just beyond the tree line. In terms of present administrative units of the Russian Federation, the area thus defined includes: (1) the whole Nenets district, including the Kolguev and Vaigach Islands, and part of the Mezen' county in the Arkhangelsk Province; (2) parts of the four northernmost counties in the Komi Republic; (3) practically all of the Yamal, Nadym, and Taz counties, about half of the Ural county, and minor parts of the remaining three counties of the Yamal Nenets district in the Tyumen' Province; (4) most of the Ust'-Yeniseisk county of the Taimyr district in the Krasnoyarsk region.

The dialects of Tundra Nenets exhibit relatively little diversity. There are no grave obstacles to mutual comprehension despite the geographical distance. This must be due to both the relatively recent occupation of much of the present territory and the great mobility typical of the nomadic way of life. Nevertheless, several phonological and lexical, and a few morphological isoglosses cross the language area.

Three dialect groups may be recognized, viz. Western (to the west of the Pechora, with the subdivisions of Far Western on the Kanin Peninsula, and Mid Western in the Malaya Zemlya); Central (from the Pechora to the Ural, i.e. in the Bol'shaya Zemlya); and Eastern (on the Siberian side, with the subdivisions of Mid Eastern, including the Ob' area and the Yamal Peninsula, and Far Eastern, to the east of the Ob' Bay). Phonologically, the main bifurcation is between the Western dialect group, which exhibits several peculiar innovations, and the Central–Eastern cluster, which, though less innovative, possesses a couple of common sound changes. By contrast, the Urals tend to divide morphological and lexical variants, so that it is often justified to talk about specifically European v. Siberian features of Tundra Nenets. The actual isoglosses, however, vary from one case to another. Unless stated otherwise, the material presented in this chapter is in accordance with the Central dialects.

The languages that historically border, and partly mingle in, the Tundra

Nenets country are Russian in the far west, Komi on most of the European side, Mansi to a limited extent in the Ural area, Khanty in the Ob' area, Forest Nenets in the Nadym and the Pur areas, Northern Selkup along the Taz after the historically attested arrival of the Selkups there, and Forest Enets, Tundra Enets, Evenki, Ket, Yakut (Dolgans), and Nganasan in the east, ever since the gradual expansion of Tundra Nenets to the Yenisei area. Komi and Northern Khanty are the two languages that are known to have had the most extensive contacts with Tundra Nenets for a lengthy period, while Russian influence has now by far surpassed their effects on Tundra Nenets.

The number of Tundra Nenets speakers has been growing throughout the historical era. Since the Tundra Nenets area has been mostly expanding until recently, both the growth of the national population and the absorption of members of other nations have contributed to an increase in the number of speakers. In recent decades, however, the number of speakers has remained fairly constant, because population growth is offset by linguistic assimilation. Currently, there are approx. 25,000 Tundra Nenets speakers. The official population figure for the Nenets people was 34,665 in the 1989 Soviet census, and the number of first language speakers among them was 26,730, i.e. 77 per cent, including approx. 2,000 Forest Nenets of whom maybe 1,500 spoke it as their first language. The average percentage of native language proficiency tells little of the real situation, as it varies enormously from one district to another.

The above-defined traditional Tundra Nenets territory comprises areas that are known to have been inhabited by other peoples in the beginning of the historical era. Firstly, the areas west of the Yenisei were formerly populated by speakers of Yurats. By now, the Yurats appear to have completely adopted the Tundra Nenets language and identity, and the recordings of their original vernacular are meagre. Secondly, seventeenth-century explorers reported that other, linguistically unrelated people had been living side by side with the Nenets in the westernmost areas of Kanin and Kolguev. Presumably, an extensive part of the modern Nenets area was inhabited by a more aboriginal population in not too remote prehistorical times. There is a Tundra Nenets word *syix°rtya* referring to the aborigines, vividly described in Nenets folklore, but there is no material evidence of their language or languages.

In more recent times, Tundra Nenets settlers have continued to expand by inhabiting further areas lying beyond the traditional territory as defined above. The islands of Novaya Zemlya in the Arkhangelsk Province received their first inhabitants only in the nineteenth-century, when the Russian government brought in Nenets families in order to strengthen its claim to sovereignty over the islands. Some Nenets also followed the Izhma Komi who emigrated to the Kola Peninsula in Murmansk Province, though it is not known to what extent Nenets rather than Komi was used by them. In the east, the Tundra Nenets-speaking area now extends across the Bay of Yenisei to larger parts of the Taimyr district, where a process of Nenetsization, similar to the completed absorption of Yurats, is underway among both groups of Enets.

While continuously expanding in the east, the Tundra Nenets area has lately been receding on the European side. Not only is the Russian presence most influential there, but a number of Izhma Komi have also immigrated to Nenets areas, often taking a leading position in economic spheres; this has led to many communities shifting to the use of Komi. Because of nuclear experiments beginning in the 1950s, the inhabitants of Novaya Zemlya were resettled in urban settlements on the continent, which effectively led to the loss of native language command among the Nenets in question. The net result is that while some of the local dialects in the vicinity of Komi areas have already become extinct, many if not all forms of European Nenets must be regarded as moribund. In the 1989 census, only 2,875, or 45 per cent, of the 6,423 ethnic Nenets in the Nenets district were first language speakers, a figure that cannot include very many adolescents, while 2,474 Nenets were listed as Russian speakers and 1,074 as speakers of another language, obviously Komi.

The survival forecast on the Siberian side is, as is to be expected, much brighter. In the Ob' area, the relative vigour of the aboriginal Tundra Nenets and Northern Khanty communities together with the diversity of Komi, Russian, and Tatar immigrant groups have traditionally favoured widespread multilingualism rather than the domination of a single language. In the more eastern areas, it is Tundra Nenets that has functioned as a lingua franca, gradually replacing other vernaculars. During the Soviet era, however, Russification policies and the massive influx of Russian-speaking colonizers nearly eliminated both the multilingual tradition and the interethnic use of Tundra Nenets, leaving only the home and the traditional economy, based on nomadic reindeer breeding, for the native language. The deliberate alienation of children from their native language and culture through the Soviet schooling system is, of course, deeply felt among the Siberian Nenets, as well, so that not even Nenets homes have avoided Russification. Nevertheless, the traditional Nenets way of life is still a competitive alternative to the adoption of Russian habits and, eventually, of the Russian language. Many younger Nenets seem to be devoted to the maintenance of their national culture, and to the Nenets language as its expression. According to the 1989 census, the rate of native language retention was a remarkable 94 per cent (19,713 of 20,917; the figures also include Forest Nenets) in the Yamal Nenets district, and a fair 81 per cent (1,990 of 2,446) in the Taimyr district.

Despite many positive indications, even the Siberian Tundra Nenets community is still very much threatened, and perhaps more so now that the heartlands of the Nenets country on the Yamal Peninsula are being invaded by oil and gas prospectors. Because of continuing Russian cultural oppression and economic exploitation, only a wide-scale national awakening, leading to a real ethnic autonomy with a strict control of the native territory, may secure the long-term existence of the Tundra Nenets people and their language.

Phonology

Syllable Structure

The basic syllable structure is CV(C), i.e. a syllable consists of an initial consonant, a medial vowel, and an optional final consonant, e.g. *ya* 'earth', *myaq* 'tent', *wada* 'word', *ngarka* 'big', *nyaxᵒr* 'three', *xampol* 'litter'.

There exist, however, vowel sequences, with the schwa ᵒ or the reduced vowel ø as the latter segment. Such sequences are best divided into separate syllables, which yields an additional, non-initial syllable structure ᵒ/ø(C), e.g. *xoᵒba* 'cradle', *nyaᵒra* 'inner part of hide', *ngøøbtᵒq* 'poison', *wíh* 'tundra' : sG *wíᵒh*, *to-* 'to come' : subj s1 *toødᵒm* : s2 *toønᵒ* : s3 *toᵒ*.

The basic syllable structure implies that word forms do not begin with a vowel. However, many dialects seem to contain a few words with an initial vowel. For instance, *ømke* 'what' is widely used instead of *ngømke*. By contrast, the Western dialects, because of the loss of initial *ng, possess a large number of initial vowels, and thus an initial syllable structure V(C), e.g. Western *arka* 'big' ~ Central–Eastern *ngarka*.

Monosyllabic word forms cannot end with a reduced vowel, so there are no word forms of the structure *Cø. In other respects, the basic syllable structure holds good for all dialects, i.e. there are no diphthongs or double vowels, no initial or final consonant clusters, and no medial consonant clusters with more than two consonants.

Stress Pattern and Vowel Reduction

Stress is predictable from syllable and segmental structure. It falls on an initial syllable, syllables preceding a syllable with a schwa, and non-final syllables preceded by an unstressed syllable. Stress does not fall on a final syllable, syllables with a schwa, and syllables following a stressed syllable unless they precede a syllable with a schwa. Most typically, the first syllable of each two-syllable string is stressed, or in other words, the stress falls on non-final odd syllables.

However, the predictability of stress holds good only if the opposition of the reduced vowel and the schwa is respected, because the stress relations which govern vowel reduction are partly lexical and morphological. Taking into account those complications, vowel reduction is an automatic phonological process where ø → ᵒ in unstressed positions. It yields alternations such as *xørᵒ* 'knife' : poss. sNs2 *xørørᵒ* : s3 *xørᵒda*, *xarødᵒ* 'house' : *xarᵒdørᵒ* : *xarᵒdøda*.

Under certain conditions, however, the unstressed schwa vowel appears in an odd syllable. Such cases include, in the first place, vowel sequences after a stressed syllable, unless they precede a syllable with a schwa, e.g. *xada-* 'to kill' : sOs3 *xada°da* : sOs2 with a clitic particle *xada°rø-wa* (instead of **xadaør°-wa*; cf. *xadaør°* without a clitic particle).

A number of sequences with a consonant, in most cases a suffix-initial glide, following a vowel, show a similar effect, e.g. *xada-* 'to kill' : pOs3 *xadey°da*, *tyenye-* 'to remember' : partic.fut *tyenyew°nta*, *søwa* 'good' : sPros *søwaw°na*, *yedey°* 'new' : sPros *yedey°wøna*, ⟹ *yedey°mta-* 'to renew', *tyorye-* 'to shout' : subord s3 *tyoryeb°ta*. In the last mentioned case, there is variation, and *tyoryebøta* is also attested. However, manifesting the morphological conditioning of the stress pattern, a similar sequence retains the reduced vowel in other morphological structures, e.g. *nyadayø-* 'to smell of lichen' : partic.impf *nyadayøda*, *tyenyewø-* 'to know' : partic.impf *tyenyewøna*.

Further, secondary vowel stems formed from liquid stems have the added vowel unstressed whenever possible, often yielding a schwa in the third syllable, e.g. *yayol-* 'to grow turbid' ⟹ iter *yayol°ngkø-*, *syibyel-* 'to turn pale and earthy' ⟹ *syibyel°ngkø-*, *poyol-* 'to get mixed up' ⟹ tr *poyol°ta-* 'to mix up'. Such cases contrast with primary vowel stems, e.g. *wenolø-* 'to get frightened (an animal)' ⟹ iter *wenoløngkø-*, *pyidyelø-* 'to become pliable' ⟹ *pyidyeløngkø-*. In other instances, though, it is the final vowel of primary vowel stems or the vowel preceding the stem-final consonant that undergoes reduction, e.g. *løkadø-* 'to snap (fingers)' ⟹ tr *løkad°ta-*, *nyancyaløm-* 'to become dumb' : s3 *nyancyal°ma*, ⟹ freq *nyancyal°wor-* 'to grow dumb', ⟹ tr *nyancyal°mtye-* 'to make dumb'.

In a few loanwords, a schwa may also appear in an initial syllable, e.g. *p°rasyin°* 'tarpaulin', *t°ronyi* 'peasant's sledge (for carrying wood)', *x°ryís°tya* 'club (playing card)'. The primary stress is then on the next syllable.

In compounds, each part has a separate stress pattern, e.g. *nye-nya* 'sister' : sLoc *nye-nyax°na* (rather than **nyenyaxøna*).

Vowels

The general system of Tundra Nenets vowel phonemes is shown below. (Distinct subsystems for plain and stretched vowels are justifiable mainly on historical grounds.)

Schwa	Reduced	Plain		Stretched	
		i	u	í	ú
		e	o		
o	ø		a		æ

Some of the Far Western dialects seem to lack **æ* (> *e*).

Pronunciation

1   Frontness/backness. All vowels except *æ* (**Cyæ* not existing) have two basic allophones, a front one when preceded by a palatal consonant, and

a back one when preceded by a non-palatal consonant. In other words, palatality is a property prevailing within the syllable as a whole.

2 Quantity. The schwa is pronounced either as an over-short vowel or not at all; nevertheless, it is always reflected in the phonetic substance. The reduced vowel is generally a relatively low and short vowel. The high plain vowels vary from half-long to short. The mid plain and all stretched vowels are pronounced long or half-long. In stressed positions *a* is long but subject to reduction when unstressed. The vowel sequences are invariably over-long or long vowels, with the possibility of two syllable peaks in their pronunciation.

3 Phonetic vowel reduction. When unstressed, *a* is pronounced short, or half-long at best, and more central, close to the quality but not the quantity of the mid vowels. (As a relic of the former view that the reduction of *a* should be regarded as phonemic, early publications by the author use the symbol *â* for the reduced *a*.)

4 Phonetic schwa. In sequences of qC^o, an over-short vowel is often pronounced between the glottal stop and the consonant.

5 Diphthongization. Most typically, and especially in the Eastern dialects, *æ* is pronounced as a slightly rising diphthong, while *e* and, after palatal consonants, *a*, can be slightly falling.

6 Vowel harmony. After *x* and, in the few existing cases, *q*, the quality of the following ^{o}, *ø* and, occasionally, *a* matches that of the preceding vowel. The quantitative oppositions remain, so that the phonemic distinctions are preserved. A phonetic metathesis occurs in unstressed sequences of Vx^o so that the pronunciation of the schwa is almost that of a full vowel while the preceding vowel is phonetically reduced. However, no neutralization takes place, so that pairs like *xorøx^oq* 'oven' pD and *xor^oxaq* 'birch' simulative pN are kept apart.

7 Especially in the Eastern dialects, unstressed *e* and *o* appear as relatively high vowels, quite close to the allophones of *i* and *u*. However, in most, if not all, dialects, the contrast is retained.

Orthography
The basic standard orthography recognizes only five vowel units, with a double number of vowel signs for indicating the palatality of the preceding consonant, i.e. *ø* & *a* = ‹а/я›, *e* & *æ* = ‹э/е›, *i* & *í* = ‹ы/и›, *o* = ‹о/ё›, *u* & *ú* = ‹у/ю›. The schwa usually has no overt marking, except after *x* and *q* where it is written according to (phonetic) vowel harmony, and, inconsistently, in other positions, such as between consonant clusters where it is written like *ø*. In dictionaries, a refined version of standard orthography is used. It could in principle distinguish all vowel phonemes, but fails to do so in practice. Most consistently, (back) *e* and *æ* are differentiated by a dot on the former, i.e. *e* = ‹З›, *æ* = ‹э›. The high stretched vowels are, by contrast, only rarely written with a macron, i.e. *í* = ‹ӣ›, *ú* = ‹ӯ›. As a further complication, the macron

is also used to indicate vowel sequences. The crucial distinction of ϕ v. *a* is more often than not rendered with a micron over the reduced vowel, i.e. ϕ = ‹ă/я̆›, *a* = ‹a/я›. Vowel harmony is indicated, e.g. *noxa* 'Arctic fox' = ‹нохо›, *nix^o* 'power' = ‹ныхы› (‹ныхы̆›), *pyix^{o}nya* 'night sLoc' = ‹пихиня› (‹пихйня›). The reduced vowel is written allophonically also before a pre-schwa labial glide, e.g. *padøw^o* 'bag sNs1' = ‹падув› (‹падў в›). The phonetic schwa between a glottal stop and a consonant preceding a schwa is reflected in the orthography, though inconsistently, e.g. *waqw^o* 'bed' = ‹ва"ав› (‹ва"ăв›), *myaqm^o* 'tent sNs1' = ‹мя"ам› (‹мя"ăм›).

Phonotactics
As explained in connection with the stress pattern, the schwa is practically absent in the first syllable, and there cannot be two schwa vowels in consecutive syllables. As the latter part of a vowel sequence, only the schwa or the reduced vowel, not mutually contrastive in that position, may appear. The stretched vowel *æ* does not appear after palatal consonants, and the reduced vowel ϕ not after labiopalatal consonants. The distribution of non-initial stretched vowels is not entirely clear: in the present description non-initial *æ* is restricted to the essive *-ngæ* and the high stretched vowels do not appear in non-initial syllables at all, with the possible exception of dialectal accusative plural forms.

Consonants
Palatal consonants are marked by *Cy* digraphs. Word-initially and post-vocalically, where no confusion with palatality marker is possible, the palatal glide is written *y* instead of *ÿ*. In the morphology section, p. 526, suffix-initial *y* always indicates the palatalization of the preceding consonant. The dual marking of the glottal stop as either *q* or *h* is explained below.

Historically, the Central–Eastern system has changed from the proto-system only by *wy → *by*. By contrast, the Western system has not only retained *wy*, but has also acquired four secondary consonants through

Table 17.1   Tundra Nenets consonant phonemes: the two main systems

		Central–Eastern					Western					
Nasals		m	my	n	ny	ng		m	my	n	ny	ng
Stops	strong	p	py	t	ty	k	q/h	p	py	t	ty	k	q/h
	weak	b	by	d	dy			b	by	d	dy	g	
Affricates	strong			c	cy					c	cy		
	weak									j	jy		
Fricatives				s	sy	x				s	sy	x	
Semivowels		w		ÿ				w	wy	z	ÿ		
Liquids	lateral			l	ly					l	ly		
	tremulant			r	ry					r	ry		

denasalization, i.e. *nt → *d* whereby *d → *z*, *nc → *j*, *ncy → *jy*, and *ngk → *g*; *mp, *mpy and *ndy have presumably merged with *b*, *by*, and *dy*, respectively. Two additional systems are also known to exist, viz. a Far Eastern one where *c → *s*, *cy → *ty*, and a Western one with *wy* but without denasalization, thus lacking *j*, *jy*, *g*, and *z*.

Pronunciation

1   Palatalization/velarization. While the palatal counterparts of dental consonants are also phonetically palatal, the labiopalatal consonants are palatalized. On the other hand, the non-palatal counterparts of palatal consonants are frequently velarized. Cf. frontness/backness of vowels, p. 520.

2   Postnasal obstruent weakening. Especially in the European dialects, obstruents are often voiced after a nasal. Furthermore, postnasal affricates may lose their closure, yielding phonetic voiced sibilants, which is also the usual pronunciation of the Western weak affricates *j jy*.

3   Fricativization. The Central–Eastern weak obstruent *d* and the historically identical Western *z* are typically pronounced as a fricative. Other weak obstruents are subject to slighter fricativization.

4   Gemination. All consonants except the weak obstruents (including the Western *z*) and *x* are half-long and often transcribed as short geminates in intervocalic positions; the same is true of obstruents when preceded by a liquid.

5   The added glottal stop. A glottal stop is pronounced after other consonants in final position, i.e. *b l m r*. The resulting phonetic sequences differ from sequences of a consonant followed by a schwa and a glottal stop, i.e. $C^o q$ ($C^o h$), mainly by the consonants being pronounced markedly longer in the latter case.

6   Most typically in the Far Eastern dialects, the palatal obstruents *sy* and *ty* (< *ty and *cy) are pronounced with a more hushing quality.

Orthography

Spelling of consonants is for the most part phonemic, but in a few cases it is phonetic. Postnasal obstruent weakening is reflected in standard orthography with ‹мб›, ‹мд›, ‹мз›, ‹мг›, ‹нд›, ‹нз›, ‹нг› for *mp*, *mt*, *mc*, *mk*, *nt*, *nc*, *ngk*. In normative orthography, the glottal stop is written with separate letters for the different sandhi variants, i.e. *q* = ‹"›, *h* = ‹'›, though many publications are content with a single letter. The added glottal stop is written with the same letters, so that *m* is followed by ‹'›, e.g. *num* ‹нум'› 'sky', and *b*, *l*, and *r* are followed by ‹"›, e.g. *ngob* ‹ӈоб"› 'one', *xampol* ‹хамьол"› 'litter', *yur* ‹юр"› 'hundred'. It is vital that the added glottal stop has an overt expression in the orthography, because from the phonemic point of view, it denotes the absence of the schwa in the final position.

Sandhi

Consonant sandhi is an automatic phonological process, valid irrespective of word boundaries. It includes the following interconnected subprocesses:

1   Postvocalic obstruent weakening: *p py t ty* → *b by d dy* → *-V*, e.g. *ya* 'earth' : sNs3 *yada* (cf. *yam* 'sea' : *yamta, yar* 'side' : *yarta*);
2   Postconsonantal continuant strengthening: *s sy x* → *c cy k* / C _, e.g. *yam* 'sea' : sLoc *yamk°na*, ⇒ com *yamcawey°*; *yar* 'side' : sLoc *yark°na*, ⇒ com *yarcawey°*; (cf. *ya* 'earth' : *yax°na*, ⇒ *yasawey°*);
3   Preobstruental loss of the non-nasalizable glottal stop: *q* → Ø / _ C[obstruent], e.g. *yaq* 'strand of hair' : sNs3 *yata*: sLoc *yak°na*, ⇒ com *yacawey°*;
4   Preobstruental nasalization of the nasalizable glottal stop: *h* → *m n ng* / _ C[obstruent], e.g. *yah* 'soot' : sNs3 *yanta*: sLoc *yangk°na*;
5   Presonorantal loss of the nasalizable glottal stop: *h* → Ø / _ C[sonorant], e.g. *yah* 'soot' : sNs2 *yal°* (cf. *yaq* 'strand of hair' : *yaql°*).

Phonotactics

On the basis of consonant sandhi, consonants are divided into primary and secondary consonants. The secondary consonants, *b by d dy c cy k* and the Western *j jy g z*, are in all instances derived from primary consonants, except the cases where *b* and *by* are due to the morphophonological palatalization of *w*.

Phonotactic distribution of Central–Eastern Tundra Nenets consonants is as follows:

#_V	m my n ny ng	p py	t ty		s sy	x	l ly		w ÿ
C_V	m my n ny ng	p py b by	t ty	c cy		k	l ly		w ÿ
V_V	m my n ny ng	p py b by	t ty d dy	c cy s sy	k x q	l ly r ry			w ÿ
V_C	m n ng	b			q	l	r	
V_#	m	h	b		q	l	r	

Restrictions on initial consonants are strictly observed in the present-day language, as seen in such Russian loanwords as Eur *pangkor* ~ Sib *pakor* 'gaff' (< *bagór*), *syas°* 'hour, watch' (< *čas*), *xos°ka* 'cat' (< *kóška*). The initial vibrants *r ry* are nowadays allowed in the European but not in the Siberian dialects, e.g. Eur *ryes°ka* ~ Sib *lyes°ka* 'unleavened flat cake, pie, (Sib also) dough'. Initial secondary consonants may also appear in recent loanwords but only in restricted areas, viz. *b by d dy g* in the Western dialects, and *c cy k* in the neighbourhood of Komi and Khanty dialects. Postconsonantal *by* appears only as a result of the morphophonological palatalization of *w*, as in *myirw°* 'weapon' : pA *myirbye*, *syíqw°* 'seven' ⇒ ord *syíqbyimtyey°* 'seventh'.

Vowel sequences cannot precede *x*. This is reflected in verbal morphology in connection with *x*-initial suffixes.

The intervocalic glottal stop is present only in a few cases, notably augmentative forms like *pøncyeq°* 'louse' and the (typically Eastern) adverbal stem *tyuqø-* 'up'.

Because of consonant sandhi, the glottal stop is excluded and the opposition of the non-labial nasals is neutralized before obstruents.

There are three interpretations of the glottal stop sound in final position according to its behaviour, but only the nasalizable and the non-nasalizable are phonologically significant, the added glottal stop being an automatic concomitant of a prepausal consonant. The nasalizable and the non-nasalizable glottal stop, transcribed *h* v. *q*, are to be understood as not phonemic but nonetheless phonological, their opposition being manifested by distinct sandhi patterns, e.g. *nyeh xøn°* = *nyeng_køn°* 'a woman's sledge' v. *nyeq xøn°* = *nyeng_køn°* 'a women's sledge', *toh war°* = *to_war°* 'a shore of a lake' v. *toq war°q* = *toq_war°q* 'shores of lakes'. The nasalizable glottal stop is, consequently, present only prepausally. In all likelihood, its pronunciation coincides with that of the non-nasalizable glottal stop. A reservation may be in order here because speakers are clearly aware of the dual phonological nature of the glottal stop, a circumstance that may give rise to some difference, real or pretended, in the pronunciation. In any case, the description obviously benefits by having distinct symbols for the two phonological glottal stops.

The number of consonant clusters is further restricted by morpho-phonological processes, as a residue of assimilative sound changes. In a few cases, there remains a possibility of analogical restorations, the extent of which varies from one dialect to another. The acceptable clusters include:

1   *q* + a sonorant. On the basis of Lehtisalo's recordings, it is often assumed that the glottal stop has been lost preconsonantally in the Siberian dialects but this does not hold true for all if any of them.
2   *m, b, l, r* + any consonant. Geminate type clusters, i.e. *mm(y)*, *bp(y)*, *ll(y)*, *rl(y)*, are, however, in principle excluded, though they may emerge analogically in some dialects. The clusters **mw*, **mby*, **bw*, **bby* are, by contrast, unattested, and probably unacceptable.
3   *n, ng* + a homorganic obstruent.
4   *n* + *ÿ*. This cluster appears to be of analogical origin. Dialectally, analogical *nl(y)* may also appear.

Across word boundaries, geminate type clusters excluded above as well as *m_w* and *b_w* occur freely when the first word ends in *m, b, l*, or *r*. By contrast, **n_ÿ*, **n_l*, **n_ly* are impossible. It is another issue whether the outcome of a nasalizable glottal stop plus an initial sonorant differs from a single consonant. While there may be some evidence that points to an affirmative answer, the question does not arise when words are spelled separately, the nasalizable glottal stop being consequently rendered with its own symbol, i.e. *h*.

Morphology

Within inflection, there is one word-form, the absolute nominative singular of nouns, where no morphological process is involved, so that the form is identical with the basic stem, disregarding morphophonological processes. For a few stem types, no morphological process takes place in the formation of the absolute accusative plural, either. In derivation, there are instances of noun–verb conversion. All other word forms and derivatives exhibit morphological processes, i.e. suffixation, modification, or (partial) suppletion. Suffixation is the most frequent of them, though modification is by no means uncommon. Partial suppletion, by contrast, is rare and confined to a number of irregular verbal forms.

Morphological Word Classes

The two major word classes are verbs and nouns. Alongside the nouns, there are minor classes which exhibit some nominal categories. These include the personal pronouns and various groups of adverbs and postpositions. Adjectives do not form a word class distinct from nouns on the basis of their inflection, though they may have derivational peculiarities. The same applies to numerals, i.e. *ngob* '1', *syidya* '2', *nyax°r* '3', *tyet°* '4', *sømp°lyangk°* (in European dialects *søm°lyangk°*) '5', *møt°q* '6', *syíqw°* '7', *syid°ntyet°* '8', *xasu-yúq* (Eastern *xasawa-yúq*) '9', *yúq* (Eastern also *lúca-yúq*) '10', *yur* '100', *yon°r* '1,000'. Non-personal pronouns also conform to normal nominal inflection, e.g. demonstrative *tyuku°* 'this', *taki°* 'that', *tyiki°* 'it', *tørcya* 'that kind', or interrogative *xíbya* 'who', *ngømke* 'what', *xurka* 'what kind'.

The residual morphological class is the particles, i.e. non-inflected words. In syntactic classification, they would mostly be included among the adverbs, as there are no true conjunctions in the language. Some particles are synchronically unanalysable, e.g. *tøryem* 'thus, so', *ngoq ~ ngod°q* 'also', but others have morphological structure, evident in derivation, e.g. *tyedah* 'now' ⇒ lim *tyedaryih* 'for a while', *xøn-cyer°q* 'how' ⇒ lim *xøn-cyelyiq* 'anyhow'.

Stem Types

The basic stem types are (1) vowel stems, (2) glide stems, (3) mixed stems, and (4) consonant stems, the major division being between vowel and consonant stems. The number of glide stems is very small, and they differ from vowel stems only because of the appearance of a glide when a suffix with an initial vowel is attached. Mixed stems, including all *o*- and some *ø*-stems of verbs, show, besides specific peculiarities, a mixture of properties of vowel and consonant stems; the remaining *ø*-stems as well as all monosyllabic, *a*- and *e*-stems of verbs belong to vowel stems. Two verbs, *xæ-* 'to depart' and *ngæ-* 'to be', may be characterized as irregular. The negative verb *nyi-* 'not' also exhibits idiosyncrasies.

Morphophonology

Morphophonological processes include morphophonological assimilations, alternations, and changes, vowel stem formation, truncation, and (de)palatalization. They differ from phonological processes, i.e. (primarily) consonant sandhi, in that they do not occur at word boundaries and that they are not valid stem-internally. Cf., for instance, *ngarkamør^{o}q* 'big town', and *nyema* 'sleep' or *xamada-* 'to understand' despite a morphophonological process m > w intervocalically. Analogical exceptions are also possible in certain cases.

Assimilations

1   r ry > *l ly* / C _, e.g. *nyum* 'name' : sNs2 *nyuml^o*, *syer* 'thing' : *syel^o* (cf. *nya* 'friend' : *nyar^o*).

2   t s > *q* / _ C or #, e.g. *myaq* 'tent' : sNs2 *myaql^o* : s3 *myata* (cf. sG *myad^{o}h*, pA *myado*), *møn^{o}q* 'lump' : *mønøql^o* : *møn^{o}ta* (cf. *mønøs^{o}h*, *møn^{o}so*).

3   n ng > *h* / _ C, except ÿ (and, dialectally, liquids) in most cases, or #, e.g. *peh-* 'to put' : modal gerund *pency^o* : s3 *penga* (cf. pOs3 *penÿ^{o}da*), *weh* 'dog' : dN *wengk^{o}h* : sNs2 *wel^o* (~ *wenl^o*) : sGs1 *wen^o* (cf. sG *wen^{o}h*, pA *weno* or odorative *wenÿø-*), *wíh* 'tundra' : sD *wínt^{o}h* : sNs2 *wíl^o* : sGs1 *wín^o* (cf. pA *wíngo*), *tideh* 'sembra pine'⇒ odorative *tideyø-* 'to smell of sembra pine'.

4   ng > *n* / _ ÿ in certain cases, e.g. *nyenecy^{o}h* 'person, human being' ⇒ pejor *nyenecyønÿe* 'poor man'.

5   ng > Ø / _ ø (in vowel stem formation), e.g. *wíh* 'tundra' : sG *wí^{o}h*.

6   m > *w* / V _ V, e.g. *ngum* 'grass' : pN *nguw^{o}q* : pA *nguwo*, *ngøm-* 'to eat' : conneg *ngøw^{o}q* : inf.perf *ngøwoqma*, *xo-* 'to find' : inf.impf *xowa* (cf. *xoq-* 'to fetch' : *xoqma*).

7   Degemination: m > Ø / _ m, e.g. *nyum* 'name' : poss sNs1 *nyum^o*; p → Ø / _ p, e.g. *ngob* 'one' ⇒ mod *ngopoy^o* 'the one'; l r → Ø / _ l or r, e.g. *ser* 'salt' : sNs2 *sel^o*. Dialectally, degemination may be suppressed by analogy.

8   a > *e* / _ ÿø in non-initial syllables under certain conditions, e.g. *xada-* 'to kill' : pOs3 *xadey^{o}da*, ord *nyax^{o}r* 'three' ⇒ *nyax^{o}romtey^o* 'third' v. *nyabyi* 'other' ⇒ *nyabyimtyey^o* 'second'.

9   ø → *u* / _ w in prosecutive singular, e.g. *xør^o* 'knife' : sPros *xøruw^{o}na*.

Alternations

1   *n~ÿ*-stems: *n* _ C, ÿ _ V, e.g. *toh* 'blanket' : pN *toy^{o}q* : sD *tont^{o}h* : sLoc *tongk^{o}na* : pA *toyo*, *peh-* 'to put' : partic.impf *penta* : s3 *penga* : pOs3 *penÿ^{o}da* : conneg *pey^{o}q* : inf. perf *peyoqma*.

2   *e~i-*, *e~iø-*, *o~uø-*, *Ø~ÿø*-stems: the latter in final syllables and optionally preceding the preterite suffix, e.g. *ti* 'reindeer' : sNs2 *ter^o* : pred pret s3 *tisy^o* (~ *tesy^o*), *me-* 'to be' : conneg *miq*; *pøni^o* 'dress' : sNs2 *pøner^o* : pred

pret s3 *pǿniǿsyº* (~ *pǿnesyº*); *tyukuº* 'this' : sD *tyukonºh*; *ngopoyº* 'the one' : sNs2 *ngoporº*.

3   Glide stems, with Ø ~ *w* or *ÿ*: the glides appear before a vowel, e.g. *xa* 'ear' : pA *xawo*, *yí* 'wits' : pA *yíbye*, *myí-* 'to prepare' : inf. perf *myíyeqma*.

4   Suffixes with initial *n* ~ *t*: the latter attaches to consonant and mixed stems, e.g. *lúca* 'Russian' : pred s2 *lúcanº* : sD *lúcanºh* v. *nyenecyºh* 'person, human being' : *nyenecyǿntº* : *nyenecyǿntºh*, *nú-* 'to stand' : partic.impf *núna* v. *myih-* 'to go' : *myinta* (~ *myintya*) v. *xonyo-* 'to sleep' : *xonyoda*.

Suffix-initial Change

In the formation of the general finite stem for *m*-stems, the *ng* of the suffix is lost: *ngǿm-* 'to eat' : s3 *ngǿma*. This is not a question of a simple assimilation, as *mng* generally remains intact, e.g. *ngum* 'grass' ⇒ ess *ngumngæ*.

Internal Changes

The few cases include the accusative plural stems of *xasawa* 'man, male' : pA *xasyewº*, *yǿxa* 'river' : *yesyi*, and the general finite stem and the connegative of the mixed stems *yoxo-* 'to disappear' : s3 *yuxu* : conneg *yuxuq*, *toxo-* 'to learn' : *tuxu* : *tuxuq*. As can be seen, internal vowel changes do not occur independently of a modification affecting the final vowel of the stem.

Vowel Stem Formation

Consonant stems have a secondary vowel stem used before certain suffixes, formed by adding *ǿ* to the final consonant. For *ng*-stems, removal of the final *ng* takes place simultaneously, which yields a vowel sequence. The suffixes in question include those consisting of a single consonant, viz. sA *-m*, sG *-h*, and pN *-q*, e.g. *myaq* 'tent' : pN *myadºq*, *syuh* 'navel' : *syuºq*, and conneg = imp s2 *-q*, e.g. *myiq-* 'to give' : *myisºq*. Other inflexional suffixes involved are the imp pOs2 *-n-ǿq*, e.g. *ngǿm-* 'to eat' : *ngǿwǿnºq*, and imp refl s2 *-t-ǿq*, e.g. *sǿl-* 'to return' : *sǿlǿdºq*. There are more cases within derivation, for instance the comparative *-rka*, e.g. *sǿngkowoq-* 'to be heavy' ⇒ *sǿngkowosºrka-* 'to be heavier'.

Truncation

Certain suffixes and suffix combinations with two initial consonants are subject to the process of truncation, whereby the first consonant is lost when attached to a stem with a final consonant. The cases include the second- and third-person accusative and genitive possessive suffix combinations, e.g. *myaq* 'tent' : poss sNs3 *myata* = sA = sG (contrast *ya* 'earth' : sN *yada* : sA *yamta* : sG *yanta*), and the necessitative and durative suffixes, e.g. *ngǿm-* 'to eat' : nec s3 *ngǿmcu* (cf. *pya-* 'to begin' : *pyabcu*), *myiq-* 'to give' ⇒ dur *myipǿ-* (cf. *xo-* to find' ⇒ *xompǿ-*).

Palatalization and Depalatalization
There are two processes which affect the palatality of a consonant. (1) *obligatory* palatalization or depalatalization of a consonant occurs in connection with certain morphological processes; (2) *optional* palatalization concerns the initial consonants of certain suffixes. In both cases, the non-palatal v. palatal pairs of consonants are *m* ↔ *my*, *n* ↔ *ny*, *ng* → *ÿ*, *p* ↔ *py*, *t* ↔ *ty*, *k* → *cy*, *b* → *by*, *d* ↔ *dy*, *c* ↔ *cy*, *s* ↔ *sy*, *x* → *sy*, *w* ↔ *by*, *r* ↔ *ry*, *l* ↔ *ly*; ↔ indicates both palatalization and depalatalization, → only palatalization. There is a tendency for palatality within the stem to favour palatalization, e.g. *nyum* 'name' : *nyubye* v. *ngum* 'grass' : *nguwo*, but there are counterexamples: *syer* 'thing' : *syero* or *tør* 'body-hair' : *tørye*. The two palatality processes do not necessarily conform, cf. *syer* : sPros *syerm°nya*.

Obligatory palatalization and depalatalization are met with in four contexts:

1   accusative plural stem formation, e.g. *nguda* 'hand' : pA *ngudyi*, *tyonya* 'fox' : *tyon°*, *myir* 'price' : *myirye*, and a number of derivational operations, e.g. *ngødyim-* 'to appear' ⇒ freq *ngødyibyer-*;
2   general finite stem formation for *m*-stems, e.g. *ngødyim-* 'to appear' : s3 *ngødyimya*;
3   mixed stem inflection, e.g. *xonyo-* 'to sleep' : s3 *xoni*;
4   the dual personal suffix, e.g. sNd2 *-r-yih* (cf. s2 *-r-°* and p2 *-r-aq*).

Optional palatalization yields suffixal variants with a palatal consonant. It occurs in conjunction with certain suffixes when attached to a number of stems, which require lexical marking. Examples of nominal forms include *yiq* 'water' : sLoc *yik°nya* : sPros *yiqm°nya* : poss sNs3 *yitya* : p3 *yityoh*, *syí* 'hole' : sLoc *syíx°nya* : sPros *syíw°nya*; ord *nyabyimtyey°* 'second' (cf. *nyax°-romtey°* 'third'). Examples of verbal forms involve mainly the imperfective participle, e.g. *yilye-* 'to live' : *yilyenya*, *myih-* 'to go' : *myintya*, *pæør-* 'to do' : *pæ°rtya*, *pæwø-* 'to be dark' : *pæw°dya*. A non-palatalized variant is always possible, though a few forms are so lexicalized that such variants are rare, e.g. *pøryidyenya* 'black', *yøngk°nya* 'excessive (used for the second ten numerals)', *tyírtya* 'flying; (Eur) bird'. At least the verb *xæ-* 'to depart' has forms like partic.fut *xæw°ntya* : inf. impf *xæbya* : inf. perf *xæqmya*. In the case of the negative verb *nyi-* 'not' there appear forms like subord s3 *nyib°tya* : ind sOs3 *nyídya* : interr s3 *nyisya* : obligative s1 *nyibcyaked°m*. Other verbs may occasionally have similar forms, e.g. *pyisyøh-* 'to laugh' : inf. impf *pyisy°mya*. Certain postpositions invariably have a palatal consonant in certain case suffixes, notably *nyi-* 'on' : loc *nyinya* : pros *nyimnya*, and *myu-* 'in' : loc *myunya* : pros *myumnya*.

Verbal Inflection

The finite inflectional categories are mood, tense, conjugation (subjective, objective, and reflexive), number of object in the objective conjugation, person of subject, and number of subject. There are also several non-finite forms.

Mood

According to the present count, there are sixteen moods. The formation of the indicative, imperative proper, and optative is based on various morphological substems and distinct sets of personal suffixes. The other moods have characteristic substems with suffixal markers, and the same personal suffixes as in the indicative. The moods, exemplified, where possible, by the third person singular of the verb *nú*- 'to stand', are:

1   The indicative, e.g. *nú°* '(s)he stands';
2   The imperative, comprised of three submoods, which are
   (a)   the hortative -xø in the first person, e.g. s1 *núxød°m* 'let me stand';
   (b)   the imperative proper in the second person, e.g. s2 *núq* 'stand!';
   (c)   the optative in the third person, e.g. s3 *nú°ya* 'let him/her stand';
3   The conjunctive -ÿi, e.g. *núyi* '(s)he will stand (request)';
4   The necessitative -psu, e.g. *núbcu* '(s)he shall stand (demand)';
5   The interrogative -sa, e.g. *núsa* 'did (s)he stand?';
6   The imperfective probabilitative -n~ta-qxe~iø, e.g. *núnaki°* '(s)he may stand';
7   The perfective probabilitative -me-qxe~iø, e.g. *núweki°* '(s)he may have stood';
8   The obligative -psa-qxe~iø, e.g. *núbcaki°* '(s)he should stand (expectation)';
9   The imperfective approximative -n~ta-røxa, e.g. *núnarøxa* '(s)he seems to stand';
10   The perfective approximative -me-røxa, e.g. *núwerøxa* '(s)he seems to have stood';
11   The futuritive approximative -mønta-røxa, e.g. *núw°ntar°xa* '(s)he seems to be going to stand';
12   The superprobabilitative -ma-n~tøh-xøbya, e.g. *núwan°ngkøbya* '(s)he probably stands';
13   The hyperprobabilitative -røxa-me~iø, e.g. *núr°xawi°* '(s)he must have stood';
14   The narrative -me~iø, e.g. *núwi°* '(s)he has stood';
15   The reputative -møna, e.g. *núw°na* '(s)he is supposed to stand';
16   The desiderative -røwa, e.g. *núr°wa* '(s)he is encouraged to stand'.

The mood system could of course be presented more hierarchically. Many moods have complex markers consisting of participial and derivational suffixes, and their morphological behaviour depends on the individual suffixes. For instance, the choice of the suffix-initial consonant in the imperfective probabilitative and approximative follows that of the imperfective participle. The superprobabilitative mood, in turn, consists of the dative of the imperfective infinitive and the noun *xøbya* 'sign; sense'. However, as long as the formations in question are, on the one hand, conjugated in all conjugations, and do not, on the other hand, possess non-finite forms, their status as moods is not in question. The habitive, regarded as a derivative in this description, may dialectally behave like a mood. There is also a peculiar construction with a postverbal negative verb plus a clitic particle that could be regarded as a compound mood, e.g. *ngæq nyí-w°h* 'it certainly is', *maq nyí-w°h* '(s)he certainly said' (also notice the difference from the connegative forms *ngaq* and *man°q*).

Tense
The inflectional category of tense comprises two tenses, the aorist and the preterite. While the aorist has no marking, the preterite is expressed by the suffixation of -syø after the personal suffixes, e.g. *nú-* 'to stand' : aor s1 *núød°m* : s2 *núøn°* : s3 *nú°* 'I : you : he stand(s)' : pret s1 *nú°dømcy°* : s2 *nú°nøsy°* : s3 *núøsy°* 'I : you : he stood'. Despite the morphotactic peculiarity of preterite suffixation, there is no doubt about its true inflectional status. While the category of tense exists in conjunction with the indicative, conjunctive, and narrative, it does not appear in the imperative, interrogative, or necessitative, and is marginal in the other moods.

All verbs are divided into two groups with regard to their temporal relations. For momentaneous verbs, the indicative aorist expresses immediate past, and the indicative preterite expresses more remote past. For continuous verbs, the indicative aorist expresses present, and the indicative preterite expresses simple past. In the conjunctive, the aorist expresses conditional future, and the preterite expresses conditional past. In the narrative, the opposition is basically perfect v. pluperfect.

The past expressed by the indicative preterite always refers to the speaker's personal experience of the action. For the expression of an action which was not observed but the results of which are still observable, the narrative mood is used.

For the expression of non-conditional futurity, a particular derivative is used, as explained below.

The future derivative co-occurs with inflectional tense, e.g. *ladø-* 'to beat' : fut sOs1 pret *lad°ngkuwøsy°* 'I was going to beat him'.

Conjugation
Verbs belong to one of four conjugational groups.

1   Intransitive verbs have only the subjective conjugation.
2   Transitive verbs have both the subjective and objective conjugation.

3   Reflexive verbs have only the reflexive conjugation.
4   Transitive/reflexive verbs have all three conjugations.

The category of conjugation is connected with four sets of personal suffixes.

1   The first set is used in the subjective conjugation.
2   The second set is used in the objective conjugation when the object is in the singular.
3   The third set is used in the objective conjugation when the object is in the dual or plural.
4   The fourth set is used in the reflexive conjugation.

Morphological Substems

General Finite Stem
1   The vowel stems, and the mixed and irregular stems in the optative of the subjective conjugation, add -ø, except before a suffix with an initial x, where -nga is added, e.g. *to-* 'to come' : s3 *to°* : d3 *tongax°h*, *yilye-* 'to live' : *yilye°* : *yilyengax°h*.
2   The mixed stems, except in the optative of the subjective conjugation, change their final vowel into *i* or *u*, occasionally accompanied by a change of palatality of the preceding consonant, e.g. *nyenø-* 'to be angry' : s3 *nyeni* : d3 *nyenix°h*, *pæwø-* 'to be dark' : s3 *pæbyi*, *ngødyø-* 'to be visible' : *ngødyi*, *yakø-* 'to itch' : *yaku*, *ngeso-* 'to camp' : *ngesi*, *xonyo-* 'to sleep' : *xoni*, *løbcyo-* 'to stick together' : *løbcyi*, *yangko-* 'to lack' : *yangku*, *pyiryencyo-* 'to do cooking' : *pyiryencyu* (notice *toxo-* 'to learn' : *tuxu*, *yoxo-* 'to disappear' : *yuxu*).
3   The consonant stems add -nga, e.g. *pæør-* 'to do' : sOs3 *pæ°rngada*. In *m*-stems, the ng of the suffix is lost, e.g. *ngøm-* 'to eat' : *ngømada*. The verb *mah-* 'to say' exhibits an irregular vowel stem, viz. s3 *ma*, but d3 *mangax°h* (~ *max°h*).
4   The irregular stems, except in the optative exhibit partial suppletion, viz. *xæ-* 'to depart' : s3 *xøya* : d3 *xøyax°h*, *ngæ-* 'to be' : *nga* : *ngax°h*. The negative verb is also exceptional, viz. *nyi-* 'not' : *nyí* : *nyíx°h*.

Dual Object Substems
The dual object substems are formed by adding -xøÿu to the basic stem in the imperative proper, the general finite stem in the indicative and optative, and the modal substems in other moods, e.g. *xada-* 'to kill' : imp dOs2 *xadaxøyun°q* : ind dOs3 *xadangax°yuda* : interr dOs3 *xadasax°yuda*, (a mixed stem) *tampø-* 'to be giving' : ind dOs3 *tampyixøyuda*.

Special Finite Stem

1   The ø-stems change their final vowel into *i* and add -ø, except before a suffix with an initial x (present, incidentally, only in the reflexive conjugation, so that this variant does not exist for transitive verbs), where -ÿø is added, e.g. *yurkø*- 'to stand up' : refl s3 *yurki°q* : d3 *yurk°yøx°h*.
2   The other vowel and all consonant stems simply add -ÿø, e.g. *peda*- 'to be tired' : refl s3 *pedeÿ°q*, *søl*- 'to return' : *sølÿ°q*.
3   For the mixed stems, the general finite stem is used instead, e.g. *tampø*- 'to be giving' : pOs2 *tampyid°* 'you are giving them' (cf. sO *tampyir°*).

Special Modal Substems

The special modal substems correspond to the special finite stem of the indicative and optative. They are formed from modal substems mostly by a final vowel change, as exemplified by the pOs2 forms of *xada*- 'to kill'.

1   The interrogative: a → ø ~ yø e.g. *xadasød°* ~ *xadasyød°* 'did you kill them?' (cf. sOs2 *xadasar°*).
2   In the objective conjugation the probabilitatives, obligative, hyper-probabilitative, and narrative: e~iø → iø, e.g. narr *xadawiød°* 'you have killed them' (cf. *xadawer°*).
3   The approximatives, superprobabilitative, reputative, and desiderative: a → *i*, e.g. approximative impf *xadanar°xid°* 'you appear to kill them' (cf. *xadanar°xar°*) : superprob *xadawan°ngkøbyid°* 'you probably kill them' (cf. *xadawan°ngkøbyar°*).
4   The hortative, conjunctive, and necessitative, and in the reflexive conjugation, the moods listed in (2): no change from the modal substem, e.g. conj pOs2 *xadayid°* 'you will kill them' (cf. sOs2 *xadayir°*), *søna*- 'to jump' narr refl s2 *sønawen°* : s3 *sønawi°q*.

Person and Number

Indicative

In the subjective conjugation, the first set of personal suffixes is attached to the general finite stem, e.g. (a transitive/reflexive verb) *yempøq*- 'to dress' : s1 (*xíbyaxøwam*) *yemp°qngad°m* 'I dressed (somebody)' : s2 *yemp°qngan°* : s3 *yemp°qnga* : d1 *yemp°qnganyih* : d2 *yemp°qngadyih* : d3 *yemp°qngax°h* : p1 *yemp°qngawaq* : p2 *yemp°qngadaq* : p3 *yemp°qngaq*.

In the objective conjugation, the second set of personal suffixes is attached to the general finite stem, e.g. sOs1 *yemp°qngaw°* 'I dressed him' : s2 *yemp°qngar°* : s3 *yemp°qngada* : d1 *yemp°qngamyih* : d2 *yemp°qngaryih* : d3 *yemp°qngadyih* : p1 *yemp°qngawaq* : p2 *yemp°qngaraq* : p3 *yemp°qngadoh*.

The third set, with a dual object, is attached to a dual object substem, e.g. dOs1 *yemp°qngax°yun°* 'I dressed them (two)' : s2 *yemp°qngax°yud°* : s3 *yemp°qngax°yuda* : d1 *yemp°qngax°yunyih* : d2 *yemp°qngax°yudyih* : d3 *yemp°qngax°yudyih* : p1 *yemp°qngax°yunaq* : p2 *yemp°qngax°yudaq* : p3 *yemp°qngax°yudoh.*

In the objective conjugation with a plural object, the third set and in the reflexive conjugation the fourth set of personal suffixes are attached to the special finite stem of the vowel and consonant stems, e.g. pOs1 *yemp°qÿøn°* 'I dressed them (many)' : s2 *yemp°qÿød°* : s3 *yemp°qÿøda* : d1 *yemp°qÿønyih* : d2 *yemp°qÿødyih* : d3 *yemp°qÿødyih* : p1 *yemp°qÿønaq* : p2 *yemp°qÿødaq* : p3 *yemp°qÿødoh* : refl.s1 *yemp°qÿøw°q* 'I got dressed' : s2 *yemp°qÿøn°* : s3 *yempøqÿ°q* : d1 *yemp°qÿønyih* : d2 *yemp°qÿødyih* : d3 *yemp°qÿøx°h* : p1 *yemp°qÿønaq* : p2 *yemp°qÿødaq* : p3 *yemp°qÿød°q,* and to the general finite stem of the mixed stems, for which no special finite stem exists.

Imperative Proper
The imp.s2 is identical with the connegative, e.g. *yempøq-* 'to dress' (*xíbyaxøwa*) *yempøs°q* 'dress (somebody)'. The other s2 forms exhibit peculiar suffixes, attached to the basic stem, viz. sO -tø, dpO -n-øq, and refl -t-øq (the latter two requiring vowel stem formation), e.g. sO *yempøt°* 'dress him' : dO *yemp°køyun°q* 'dress them (two)' : pO *yemp°søn°q* 'dress them (many)' : refl *yemp°sød°q* 'get dressed'. The d2 and p2 forms are replaced by the respective indicative forms. The indicative forms of the stem *nyo-* perform the imperative function of *nyi-* 'not', e.g. *nyon°* *tuq* 'do not come', *nyor°* *xadaq* 'do not kill it'.

Optative
There are peculiar optative sets of personal suffixes distinct from those used in the other moods. The first and second sets are usually attached to the

Table 17.2   Sets of personal suffixes in the indicative and most other moods

	Subjective	sO	dpO	Reflexive
s1	-t-øm	-m-ø	-n-ø	-m-øq
s2	-n~tø	-r-ø	-t-ø	-n~tø
s3	Ø	-t-a	-t-a	-q
d1	-n-yih	-m-yih	-n-yih	-n-yih
d2	-t-yih	-r-yih	-t-yih	-t-yih
d3	-xøh	-t-yih	-t-yih	-xøh
p1	-m-aq	-m-aq	-n-aq	-n-aq
p2	-t-aq	-r-aq	-t-aq	-t-aq
p3	-q	-t-oh	-t-oh	-t-øq

Note: (Morpho)phonological processes not executed.
The s1 suffix is -m-møh rather than -t-øm in the European dialects.

general finite stem, e.g. *yilye-* 'to live' : s3 *yilye°ya*, *pæør-* 'to do' : sOs3 *pæ°rngamta*; notice *mah-* 'to say' : s3 *mangaya* (cf. the irregular indicative *ma*). The exception are the mixed and irregular stems when the first set is attached: they appear as vowel stems presenting a similar variant of the general finite stem, e.g. *syur°mpø-* 'to run' : s3 *syur°mpø°ya* (cf. ind *syur°mpyi*), *xonyo-* 'to sleep' : s3 *xonyo°ya* (cf. ind *xoni*), *xæ-* 'to depart' : *xæ°ya* (cf. *xøya*), *ngæ-* 'to be' : *ngæ°ya* (cf. *nga*). The stem *nyo-* is used also in the negative optative, e.g. *nyo°ya tuq* 'let him not come'. The third and the fourth sets are attached as in the indicative.

The sets of personal suffixes in the optative are shown below; (morpho-) phonological processes are not executed.

	Subjective	sO	dpO	Reflexive
s3	-ÿa	-m-t-a	-tø-m-t-a	-m-t-øq
d3	-ÿa-xøh	-m-t-yih	-tø-m-t-yih	-xø-m-t-øq
p3	-ÿa-q	-m-t-oh	-tø-m-t-oh	-tø-m-t-øq

The dpO forms are not used in the Siberian dialects, the corresponding indicative forms being used instead.

Other Moods
The same sets of personal suffixes as in the indicative are attached to modal substems, exemplified in the list of moods.

Non-finite Forms
There are two infinitives (imperfective and perfective), four participles (imperfective, perfective, negative, futuritive), two gerunds (modal and final), three subordinates (the subordinative, the auditive, and the evasive), and a connegative. There are no verbal nouns of the *actio* or *actor* type, but the infinitives and participles fulfil their function as well. The infinitives and participles are, nevertheless, verbal inflectional forms rather than deverbal nominal derivatives, since they take normal verbal qualifiers such as accusative object. The infinitives and participles are inflected like nouns except that they lack predicative forms. The gerunds are not further declinable. The subordinates have an absolute form and possessive forms with the oblique singular co-affix -n; it seems that the auditive may be further inflected in tense.

Infinitives
The imperfective infinitive has the suffix *-ma*, e.g. *nú-* 'to stand' : *núwa*. The perfective infinitive has the suffix *-qma*, which for the vowel and mixed stems is simply added to the stem, e.g. *nú-* 'to stand' : *núqma*. For the consonant stems *-o* is added first, e.g. *pæør-* 'to do' : *pæ°roqma*. The unique

glide stem *myí-* 'to prepare' shows the suffix variant *-ye* before *-qma*, viz. *myíyeqma*.

Participles

The imperfective participle has the variable suffix -n~ta. The vowel stems use -na, e.g. *nú-* 'to stand' : *núna*, except *to-* 'to come' : *toda* (also *tona*). Both the consonant and the mixed stems have *-ta*, e.g. *pæør-* 'to do' : *pæºrtya*, *xonyo-* 'to sleep' : *xonyoda*. Of the irregular stems, *xæ-* 'to depart' prefers *xæna*, while *ngæ-* 'to be' shows *ngæda*. The negative verb *nyi-* 'not' always has *nyinya*.

The perfective participle has the suffix -me~iø, e.g. *nú-* 'to stand' : *núwiº*.

The negative participle has the suffix -møtawa(ÿø), e.g. *nú-* 'to stand' : *núwºdaweyº*.

The futuritive participle has the suffix -mønta, e.g. *nú-* 'to stand' : *núwºnta*.

Gerunds

The modal gerund has the suffix -syø for the consonant stems and monosyllabic vowel stems, e.g. *pæør-* 'to do' : *pæørcyº*, *nú-* 'to stand' : *núsyº*, and the suffix -ø for the polysyllabic vowel stems, including the mixed stems, e.g. *yilye-* 'to live' : *yilyeº*, *xonyo-* 'to sleep' : *xonyoº*. In the Western dialects, however, the suffix -syø is invariably used.

The final gerund has the suffix -mønsyø, e.g. *nú-* 'to stand' : *núwøncyº* 'in order to stand'.

Subordinates

The subordinative has either the suffix -pøq or the suffix combination -pøq-na, e.g. *nú-* 'to stand' : s3 *núbºta* or *núbºqnanta* 'if/when he stands'.

The auditive has the suffix variants -manoh and -moh, e.g. *ye-* 'to ache' : s3 *yewanonta ~ yewonta* 'it feels like it aches'.

The evasive has the suffix -moh followed by the ablative -xø-tø, e.g. *nú-* 'to stand' : s3 *núwongkødºnta* 'lest he stands'.

Connegative

The connegative, used with the negative verbs, notably *nyi-* 'not', has the suffix -q. The s2 imperative is formally identical.

1   Vowel stems generally do not require anything else, e.g. *yilye-* 'to live' : *yilyeq*, but notice the *e~i*-stem *me-* 'to be' : *miq*, and the irregular *to-* 'to come' : *tuq*.

2   Mixed stems have their final vowel changed into *u*, the preceding consonant being palatal if either or both of the basic stem and the general finite stem have a palatal consonant before the final vowel, e.g. *nyenø-* 'to be angry' : s3 *nyeni* : conneg. *nyenuq*, *pæwø-* 'to be dark' : *pæbyi* :

pæbyuq, ngeso- 'to camp' : *ngesi* : *ngesuq, xonyo-* 'to sleep' : *xoni* : *xonyuq* (notice also *toxo-* 'to learn' : *tuxuq, yoxo-* 'to disappear' : *yuxuq*).

3   The irregular stems exhibit decided irregularities, viz. *xæ-* 'to depart' : *xany°q, ngæ-* 'to be' : *ngaq*.

4   Consonant stems have the regular vowel stem formation, dictated by the shape of the suffix, as the only complication, e.g. *ngøm-* 'to eat' : *ngøw°q*.

Nominal Inflection

The nominal inflectional categories are number, case, declension (absolute, possessive, and predestinative), and, in the non-absolute declensions, person and number of possessor or predestinator. Besides nominal declension, there are also predicative forms of nouns, or the nominal conjugation.

Number and Case

There are three numbers, singular, dual, and plural. Of the seven cases, the grammatical cases (nominative, accusative, and genitive) combine with all three numbers, while the local cases (dative, locative, ablative, and prosecutive), appear only in singular and plural, the missing local dual forms being replaced by expressions with the corresponding case forms of the postposition *nya-* 'at'. No morphological process takes place in the nominative singular, e.g. *myaq* 'tent'. Some forms have simple suffixes, e.g. sA *myad°m* : sG *myad°h* : sPros *myaqm°na* : dN *myak°h* = dA = dG : pN *myad°q*. Most local forms exhibit a system of multiple suffixation, e.g. sD *myat°h* : sLoc *myak°na* : sAbl *myakød°* : pD *myak°q* : pLoc *myak°qna* : pAbl *myakøt°*. The accusative plural stem is used for the rest, e.g. pA *myado* : pG *myadoq* : pPros *myadoqmøna*. However, the prosecutive plural of monosyllabic vowel stems is based either invariably on the basic stem, e.g. *pya* 'tree' : *pyaqm°na* (not *pyíqm°na*), *li* 'bone' : *leqm°na* (not *líqm°na*), or variably on both stems, e.g. *ya* 'earth' : *yaqm°na* ~ *yoqm°na*.

Accusative Plural Stem

The vowel stems either require no morphological process or have their final vowel changed. Consonant and glide stems attach a vowel to the final consonant or glide.

The vowel stems requiring no change in the form of the accusative plural include (1) most monosyllabic stems, e.g. *to* 'lake' : *to, nyú* 'child' : *nyú*; (2) some ø-stems, e.g. *sæw°* 'eye' : *sæw°*; (3) *i-* and *u-*stems, e.g. *ngesi* 'camp' : *ngesi, súyu* 'calf' : *súyu*.

Other vowel stems show various vowel changes:

1   monosyllabic *a-* and *e~ i-*stems:
      a → o, ya → yí, e~i → í, e.g. *ya* 'earth' : *yo, nya* 'friend' : *nyí, ti* 'reindeer' : *tí* (: poss. sNs3 *teda* : pN *tída*);

2   some ø-stems:

Table 17.3   Case, number, and possessive suffixes

	Declension		Person of possessor		
	Absolute	Possessive	1	2	3
Singular					
Nominative	Ø	Ø-	→ -m-	-r-	-t-
Accusative	-m	Ø-	→ -m-	-m-t-	-m-t-
Genitive	-h	Ø-	→ -n-	-h-t-	-h-t-
Dative	-n~tø-h	-xø-	→ -n-	-h-t-	-h-t-
Locative	-xø-na	-xø-na-	→ -n-	-h-t-	-h-t-
Ablative	-xø-tø	-xø-tø-	→ -n-	-h-t-	-h-t-
Prosecutive	-møna	-møna-	→ -n-	-h-t-	-h-t-
Dual					
Nominative	-xøh	-xøyu-	→ -n-	-t-	-t-
Accusative	-xøh	-xøyu-	→ -n-	-t-	-t-
Genitive	-xøh	-xøyu-	→ -n-	-q-t-	-q-t-
Plural					
Nominative	-q	¥-	→ -n-	-t-	-t-
Accusative	¥	¥-	→ -n-	-t-	-t-
Genitive	¥-q	¥-q-	→ -n-	-q-t-	-q-t-
Dative	-xø-q	-xø-q-	→ -n-	-q-t-	-q-t-
Locative	-xø-q-na	-xø-q-na-	→ -n-	-q-t-	-q-t-
Ablative	-xø-q-tø	-xø-q-tø-	→ -n-	-q-t-	-q-t-
Prosecutive	(¥)-q-møna	(¥)-q-møna-	→ -n-	-q-t-	-q-t-
			↓	↓	↓
Number of possessor					
Singular			-ø	-ø	-a
Dual			-yih	-yih	-yih
Plural			-aq	-aq	-oh

Note: (Morpho)phonological processes not executed; preconsonantal h represents an archiphoneme for *n* and *ng*, i.e. -h-t- yields *nt* as -q-t- yields *t* and postvocalic -t-*d*; the formation of the accusative plural stem symbolized by ¥.

$ø \rightarrow o$, $yø \rightarrow yo$, $ø \rightarrow ye$, e.g. *xør°* 'knife' : *xøro, nyany°* 'bread' : *nyanyo, syun°* 'steam' : *syunye*;

3   some *a*- stems:

$a \rightarrow ø$, $ya \rightarrow ø$, $ya \rightarrow yø$, e.g. *xoba* 'fur' : *xob°* (notice *xasawa* 'man, male' : *xasyew°*), *tyonya* 'fox' : *tyon°*, *yesya* 'iron, money' : *yesy°*;

4   other *a*- stems:

$a \rightarrow i$, $a \rightarrow yi$, $ya \rightarrow yi$, (two words only) $ya \rightarrow e$, e.g. *ngaw°ka* 'pet reindeer' : *ngaw°ki, nguda* 'hand' : *ngudyi* (notice *yøxa* 'river' : *yesyi*), *ngodya* 'berry' : *ngodyi, xalya* 'fish' : *xale* (and *yalya* 'day' : *yale*);

5   *e*- and *o*- stems:
   $e \to i$, $o \to u$, e.g. *yake* 'smoke' : *yaki*, *ngøno* 'boat' : *ngønu*;
6   alternating stems:
   $e\sim i\emptyset \to i\emptyset$, $o\sim u\emptyset \to u\emptyset$, $\emptyset\sim\ddot{y}\emptyset \to \ddot{y}\emptyset$, e.g. *pøni^o* 'dress' : *pøni^o* (: poss sNs3
   pøneda : pNs3 *pøni^{o}da*), *tyuku^o* 'this' : *tyuku^o* (: *tyukoda* : *tyuku^{o}da*),
   ngopoy^o 'the one' : *ngopoy^o* (: *ngopoda* : *ngopoy^{o}da*).

Dialectally, *i*- and *u*-stems may also exhibit vowel change, yielding pA *ngesí, súyú*.

Consonant stems add *-o* or *-ye*, e.g. *myaq* 'tent' : *myado*, *nyum* 'name' : *nyubye*. Glide stems follow the consonant stems, viz. *xa* 'ear' : *xawo*, *yí* 'wits' : *yíbye*, *syo* 'throat' : *syoyo*, *xøbyí* 'Khanty; servant' : *xøbyiye*. Notice that the base used for *ngømke* 'what' is in this case *ngøm-*, yielding pA *ngøwo*. At least for most functions, the d1 possessive forms take over the s1 forms in the Siberian dialects.

Possessive Declension
There are forms for three persons and three numbers of the possessor for each absolute form. They are formed through complex suffixation, with number and case suffixes partly different from the absolute ones. The accusative plural stem is used in the nominative plural, too. For example: *ya* 'earth' : sNs1 *yaw^o* : s2 *yar^o* : s3 *yada* : d1 *yamyih* : d2 *yaryih* : d3 *yadyih* : p1 *yawaq* : p2 *yaraq* : p3 *yadoh*; sAs3 *yamta* : sG *yanta* : sD *yax^{o}nta* : sLoc *yax^{o}nanta* : sAbl *yax^{o}dønta* : sPros *yaw^{o}nanta* : nom.du *yax^{o}yuda* = dA : dG *yax^{o}yuta* : pN *yoda* = pA : gen.plur *yota* : pD *yax^{o}ta* : pLoc *yax^{o}qnata* : Sabl *yax^{o}tøta* : pPros *yaqm^{o}nata* ~ *yoqm^{o}nata*.

Predestinative Declension
There are forms for three persons and three numbers of the predestinator for each singular grammatical case form of the absolute declension. They are formed by suffixing -tø, followed by the respective possessive suffixes. For example, *xør^o* 'knife' : nom s3 *xør^{o}døda* : acc *xør^{o}dømta* : gen *xør^{o}dønta* 'a knife for him'.

Nominal Conjugation
When predicates, absolute forms are conjugated for person, and both absolute and possessive forms are conjugated for tense. In the aorist, the third-person forms of these predicative forms of nouns coincide with the corresponding nominative forms of declension. For example, *nye* 'woman' : predic aor s1 *nyed^{o}m* : s2 *nyen^o* : s3 *nye* 'I am : you are : she is a woman' : pret s1 *nyedømcy^o* : s2 *nyenøsy^o* : s3 *nyesy^o* 'I was : you were : she was a woman', *nya* 'friend' : poss s1 aor sg *nyaw^o* : pret *nyawøsy^o* 'he is : was my friend' : pl aor *nyín^o* : pret *nyínøsy^o* 'they are : were my friends'.

Table 17.4   The inflection of the personal pronouns

	1		*2*		*3*
Nominative					
s1	møny°	s2	pidør°	s3	pida
d1	mønyih	d2	pid°ryih	d3	pidyih
p1	mønyaq	p2	pid°raq	p3	pidoh
Accusative					
s1	syiqm°	s2	syit°	s3	syita (~ syitya)
d1	syid°nyih	d2	syid°dyih	d3	syid°dyih
p1	syid°naq	p2	syid°daq	p3	syid°doh
Genitive					
s1	syiqn°	s2	syit°	s3	syita (~ syitya)
d1	syid°qnyih	d2	syid°tyih	d3	syid°tyih
p1	syid°qnaq	p2	syid°taq	p3	syid°toh

Personal Pronouns

The s1 variants acc *syiqmyih* : gen *syiqnyih* are common especially in the Eastern dialects. The 2/3 N stem has an Eastern variant with *pø-* and a further Far Eastern variant with *pu-* instead of *pi-*. That the forms have inner morphological structure is seen in derivation, e.g. *møny°ryinaq* 'only we', *pid°ryidoh* 'only they'. The local case forms are taken over by the possessive forms of the postposition *nya-* 'at'. The nominative forms are used only for emphasis, and can in that role occur also before the accusative and genitive forms as well as the postpositional forms.

Adverbs and Postpositions with Partial Declension

There are several groups of adverbial stems, each with particular categories of nominal declension. For those with a local function, a special set of local case suffixes exists, viz. dat -h, loc -na, abl -tø, and pros -mna, e.g. *nyah* 'to' : *nyana* 'at' : *nyad°* 'from' : *nyamna* 'along, about', *nyih* 'on to' : *nyinya* 'on' : *nyid°* 'off' : *nyimnya* 'over'.

Local postpositions like *nya-* 'at', *nyi-* 'on', *myu-* 'in', *ngilø-* 'under', *tyaxø-* 'behind', *pú-* 'after', *yeq-* 'towards', *xi-* 'near', *yer-* 'in the middle of', *nyerø-* 'before' have both absolute case forms and a full possessive declension, formed with the same co-affix as the nominal singular local case forms, e.g. *nyamnanta* 'about it', *nyinyantoh* 'on them'.

A number of nominal stems occur in conjunction with *nya-*, e.g. *xæw°-nya-* 'beside'. Postpositional stems often have compound forms with *nya-*, e.g. *myu-nya-* 'inside'. There are also derived stems like *nyayuø-* and *nyaku-* from *nya-* 'at'.

Local adverbs have only absolute case forms, e.g. *tyuqø-* 'up' : *tyuq°h* : *tyuq°na* : *tyuqød°* : *tyuq°mna*, *tøsyi-* 'down' : *tøsyih* : *tøsyina* : *tøsyid°* :

tøsyimna. This group includes several compound forms with *nya-*, e.g. *tø-nya-* 'there', *xø-nya-* 'where', *syata-nya-* 'left', *møxa-nya-* 'right'.

Pronominal stems in their local case forms also render an adverbial meaning, e.g. *tyuku°* 'this' : *tyukoxøna* 'here'. Some nominal stems are lexicalized in their adverbial function, but they still exhibit normal nominal case inflection, occasionally even in the plural, e.g. *nga-* 'far' : *ngax°q* : *ngax°qna* : *ngaxøt°* : *ngaqm°na*.

Non-local postpositions have absolute and possessive forms but no case inflection, e.g. *xaw°na* 'except' : *xaw°nanta* 'except him' (a petrified nominal prosecutive).

There are also adverbs with only possessive forms, often fulfilling the function of conjunctions of other languages, e.g. *ngødy°bya-* 'because' : *ngødy°byanta* 'because of that'. From the morphological point of view, the reflexive pronoun *xørøq-* belongs here, e.g. *xør°ta* 'he himself'.

Derivation

Deverbal Nouns
1 Local nouns, e.g. *xanye-* 'to hunt' ⇒ *xanyeløwa* 'hunting ground', *yoør-* 'to fish' ⇒ *yo°løwa* 'fishing hamlet'.
2 Instrumental nouns, e.g. *ngædalyo-* 'to travel' ⇒ *ngædalyosy°h* 'travelling sledge', *pad°nø-* 'to be writing' ⇒ *pad°nøbcy°h* 'pen', *yenyer-* 'to shoot' ⇒ *yenyercy°h* 'gun'.
3 Potential nouns, usually in possessive forms, e.g. *xetø-* 'to tell' ⇒ *xet°yiq* 'possibility to tell', *yoq-* 'to lose' : poss.s3 *yoqÿita* 'the possibility of losing it'.
4 Potential adjectives, e.g. *tæwø-* 'to reach' : *tæw°nana* 'within reach'.
5 Inclinative adjectives, e.g. *pyínø-* 'to be afraid' ⇒ *pyín°xad°* 'coward'.
6 Other deverbal nouns, e.g. *pyirye-* 'to boil' ⇒ *pyiryebco* 'something boiled' ⇒ *pyiryebcod°* 'something to be boiled'; *yilye-* 'to live' ⇒ *yilyebc°* 'subsistence'; *xanye-* 'to hunt' ⇒ *xanyeya* 'hunting occupation', *yoør-* 'to fish' ⇒ *yo°rÿa* 'fishing occupation'.

Denominal Verbs
1 Possessive verbs, e.g. *søwa* 'cap' ⇒ *søbyiq-* 'to have a cap, to use as a cap'.
2 Translative verbs, e.g. *ngar°* 'largeness' ⇒ *ngarøm-* 'to become larger'.
3 Captative verbs, e.g. *noxa* 'Arctic fox' ⇒ *nosyih-* : conneg. *nosyiy°q* 'to hunt Arctic foxes'.
4 Caritive verbs, e.g. *myaq* 'tent' ⇒ *myacyø-* : s3 *myacyi* 'to be tentless'.
5 Odorative verbs, e.g. *xalya* 'fish' ⇒ *xalyayø-* : s3 *xalyayi* 'to smell of fish'.

Denominal Adverbs

1   Caritives, e.g. *myaq* 'tent' ⇒ *myacyiq* 'without a tent'.
2   Predestinatives, e.g. *ngøno* 'boat' ⇒ *ngønod°* 'a boat for someone'.
3   Essives, e.g. *li* 'bone' ⇒ *lengæ* 'as a bone, for a bone', *syidya* 'two' ⇒ *syidyangæ* 'both together'.
4   Other denominal adverbs, e.g. *sarmyik°* 'animal, wolf' ⇒ *sarmyikød°ryem* ~ *sarmyikød°ryew°h* 'like a wolf'; *tyet°* '4' ⇒ *tyet°lød°h* 'four at a time'; *yúq* '10' ⇒ *yúcyan°* 'about ten'.

Denominal Nouns

1   Comitative nouns, e.g. *nye* 'woman' ⇒ *nyesawey°* 'married (man)'.
2   Various adjectives, e.g. *war°* 'edge, shore' ⇒ *war°xi°* '(what is) on the shore'; *war°* ⇒ *wari°* 'outermost'; *limpød°* 'swamp' ⇒ *limp°dølyangk°* 'paludified'.
3   Ordinal numerals, e.g. *nyax°r* 'three' ⇒ *nyax°romtey°* 'third', *tyet°* 'four' ⇒ *tyetyimtyey°* 'fourth'.
4   Relational nouns, for semantic reasons not used in the singular, e.g. *nya* 'friend' ⇒ du *nyasøx°h* : pl *nyas°q* 'friends (to each other)'; *nyísya* 'father' ⇒ N p3 *nyísyanødoh* 'their (respective) fathers'.

Deverbal Verbs

1   Future verbs, with an incomplete paradigm, e.g. (vowel stems and mixed ø-stems) *me-* 'to be' ⇒ *mengko-* : s3 *mengku* 'is going to be', *nyenø-* 'to be angry' ⇒ *nyen°ngku-*; (mixed o-stems and consonant stems) *xonyo-* 'to sleep' ⇒ *xonyodø-*, *mah-* 'to say' ⇒ *mantø-*; notice *xæ-* 'to depart' ⇒ *xan°tø-* (but *ngæ-* 'to be' ⇒ *ngængko-*), *to-* 'to come' ⇒ *tútø-*, *ta-* 'to bring' ⇒ *tøtø-*.
2   Habitive verbs, also with an incomplete paradigm, e.g. *túr-* 'to come' freq ⇒ *túrcy°tø-* : s3 *túrcy°ti* 'is in the habit of coming' : conneg. *túrcy°tuq*.
3   Precative verbs, with a fragmentary paradigm, mainly used in the imperative, e.g. *to-* 'to come' ⇒ *toxør-* : imp s2 *toxør°q* 'please come'.
4   Intensive verbs, e.g. *tønya-* 'to exist' ⇒ *tønyaxøya-* 'to really exist'.
5   Intransitive verbs, e.g. *tola-* 'to read' ⇒ *tolangko-* 'to do reading', *pyirye-* 'to cook' ⇒ *pyiryencyo-* ~ *pyiryengko-* 'to do cooking', *peh-* 'to put' ⇒ *pentø-* 'to do loading'.
6   Transitive verbs, e.g. *nyeseyøm-* 'to change' ⇒ *nyesey°mta-* 'to change (tr)', *ngødyim-* 'to appear' ⇒ *ngødyimtye-* 'to bring forth', *tørpø-* 'to exit' ⇒ *tørp°ra-* 'to take out', *yøngkøm-* 'to separate' ⇒ *yøngk°mla-* 'to separate (tr)', *tira-* 'to dry' ⇒ *tirabta-* 'to dry (tr)'.
7   Imperfective verbs, e.g. *pyi-* 'to boil' ⇒ *pyinø-* 'to be boiling', *wadyo-* 'to grow' ⇒ (Western–Central) *wadyodønø-*, (Eastern) *wadyodø-* 'to be growing'.
8   Durative verbs, e.g. *myiq-* 'to give' ⇒ *myipø-* 'to keep giving' : s3 *myipyi* : conneg *myipyuq*, *xada-* 'to kill' ⇒ *xadabø-* 'to keep killing'.

9 Frequentative verbs, e.g. *ngøm-* 'to eat' ⇒ *ngøwor-* 'to have a meal', *xayo-* 'to stay' ⇒ *xayur-* 'to remain'.

10 Iterative verbs, e.g. *tyu-* 'to enter' ⇒ *tyungkø-* 'to enter frequently, regularly', *ngamtø-* 'to sit down' ⇒ *ngamtᵒngkø-* 'to sit regularly'.

11 Inchoative verbs, e.g. (vowel stems) *yilye-* 'to live' ⇒ *yilyel-* 'to start living'; (consonant and mixed stems) *pyisyøh-* 'to laugh' ⇒ *pyisyᵒlø-* 'to start laughing'.

12 Incompletive verbs, e.g. *nú-* 'to stand' ⇒ *núyᵒbtye-* 'to stand for a while', *ngøwor-* 'to have a meal' ⇒ *ngøworÿøbtye-* 'to have a snack'.

13 Momentative verbs, e.g. *tesø-* 'to drip' ⇒ *tesᵒxøl-* 'to drop'.

14 Passive verbs, e.g. *xada-* 'to kill' ⇒ *xadara-* refl 'to get killed'.

Omnibased Derivatives

1 Comparatives, e.g. *søwa* 'good' ⇒ *søwarka* 'better', *søngkowoq-* 'to be heavy' ⇒ *søngkowosᵒrka-* 'to be heavier'.

2 Moderatives, e.g. *ngarka* 'big' ⇒ *ngarkampoyᵒ* 'rather big'.

3 Augmentatives, e.g. *ngarka* 'big' ⇒ *ngarkaqÿa* 'very big'.

4 Diminutives, e.g. *søqla* 'moron' ⇒ *søqlako* 'fool', *tuq* 'animal fat' ⇒ *tudako* 'mushroom', *wada* 'word' ⇒ *wadako* 'tale'.

5 Pejoratives, e.g. *ti* 'reindeer' ⇒ *tekocya* 'poor little reindeer'; *nyenecyᵒh* 'person, human being' ⇒ *nyenecyønÿe* 'poor man'.

6 Limitatives ('only'), e.g. *ngømkeryi* 'whatever; thing'.

7 Simulatives ('as if'), e.g. *syunᵒrøxa* 'steam-like; blue'.

8 Concessives ('even'), e.g. *xíbyaxørtᵒ* 'anybody'.

9 Affirmatives ('indeed'), e.g. *xíbyaxøwa* 'somebody', *xadaxøwaᵒ* 'to kill indeed' modal gerund.

Syntax

Word Order

The word order is predicate-final. A regular transitive sentence appears as (*Time adverbial*) *Subject noun phrase* (*Place adverbial*) *Object noun phrase* (*Manner adverbial*) *Predicate verb*. Any focused constituent may be placed in preverbal position, but otherwise the order is quite rigid; only heavy emphasis may result in a postverbal constituent. Notably, question words do not cause changes in the word order. In negative sentences, the two final word-forms are, in this order, the negative auxiliary verb and the main verb in the connegative. Within noun phrases, the attribute always precedes its head.

Constituent Structure and Agreement

The head of a subject noun phrase is in the nominative. Subject personal pronouns are used only for emphasis, while the person is expressed by conjugation. Subjectless constructions include sentences with the second person imperative and impersonal sentences with the verbs *tara-* and *siør-* in the sense 'must'.

The subject of an embedded clause, the possessor attribute, and the head of a postposition are in the genitive. Personal pronouns in these functions are, however, in the nominative, and used only for emphasis, while person is expressed by possessive declension. The genitive of personal pronouns is used only in those rare instances which do not allow possessive declension of the main word.

The head of an object noun phrase is in the accusative, except if the verb is in the second person imperative, when the object is in the nominative. Personal pronouns are, however, invariably in the accusative.

Within a noun phrase, an attribute never agrees with its head in case, but agreement in number is possible, the choice depending on the particular focus relations. In a special form of agreement, an attribute may duplicate the possessive suffix of its head.

A predicate verb or noun agrees in person and number with the subject. A predicate verb also agrees in number with the object if it is in the objective conjugation. The choice of conjugation depends on the focus of the object. When introduced as new information, the object usually stands immediately before the verb, which is then in the subjective conjugation. When non-focused, the object may appear apart from the verb or be completely omitted, the verb being obligatorily in the objective conjugation.

A predicate noun is followed by a form of the copula *ngæ-* 'to be' if and only if the sentence is negative, non-indicative, future or habitive.

There are no conjunctions, but subordination is expressed by subordinate non-finite forms or infinitives and participles in local case forms and postpositional phrases. Simple parataxis often serves for co-ordination, but various connective adverbs are also available. Yes–no questions are expressed (1) by the interrogative mood, when referring to past time, or (2) by a special intonation, when referring to the present or future time. A few clitic particles are also used for special emphasis.

Nenets Text
Excerpted from Susoi 1990: 20.

A: transcription, with segmentation of suffixes; B: morphemological glosses, unmarked features not indicated; C: freer translation

A1 nyew°xi°   nyenecyøy-e-q   syo-q
B1 ANCIENT   PERSON-plur-G   song-pN

A2 xurka=ryi   lax°naku,   yarøbc°
B2 WHAT.KIND=lim   TALE.pA   *YARABTS*.pA

syud°bøbc° ngødyibyelye=wa-n-t-oh xaw°na
SYUDBABTS.pA PRESÈNTS=inf (impf)-sG-p3 BESIDES

nyenecyø°-q yilye=wa-n-t-oh yampø-n°-h
PERSON-pN LIVES=inf(impf)-sG-3-plur LONG-sD

xør°-toh yí-x°n-toh syoy-o syerta=bø=wi°-q
SELF-p3 MIND-sD-3-plur SONG pA MAKES=dur=narr-p3

A3 ya-h syar°-h nyi-nya ngoyak°-q
B3 EARTH-sG SURFACE-sG ON-loc RARE-pN

nyenecyø=lyi-q xør°-t-oh syerta=wi°
PERSON-lim-pN SELF-3-plur MAKES=partic(perf)

wadyi-d-oh syo-ngæ me=cy° nyí-doh
WORD.pA-3-plur SONG-ess PERFORMS=ger(mod) NEG=-pO-p3

pyirøs°-q tyiki°-q syo-m me=cy°
IS.ABLE-conneg IT-pN SONG-sA PERFORMS=ger(mod)

nyi=nya pyir°=ta-q xíbya-q
NEG=partic(impf) IS.ABLE=partic(impf)-pN WHO-pN

A4 tørcya nyenecy°h ngulyịq tyanyo
B4 SUCH PERSON VERY LITTLE

C1 Traditional folk songs.
C2 Besides presenting various kinds of tales (*lax°nako*), lament recitatives (*yarøbc°*), and heroic recitatives (*syud°bøbc°*), the people, in the course of their lives, have made songs in their own minds.
C3 On the surface of the earth, only few people cannot perform words made by themselves as a song – they are the ones unable to perform a song.
C4 Such people are very few.

References and Further Reading

Major introductions and grammatical treatments appear in Castrén (1854 [²1966]), Tereščenko (1947), Décsy (1966), and Hajdú (1968 [²1982]). Textbooks include Tereščenko (1959), Almazova (1961), Barmič and Kuprijanova (1979), and Kuprijanova and Barmič and Homič (1985). Tereščenko (1956) and Hajdú (1975) present wide selections of articles on various topics. Among dictionaries, Castrén (1855) is the earliest, Lehtisalo (1956) extensive, phonetic, and dialectological, and Tereščenko (1965) large and standard.

Pyrerka and Tereščenko (1948) is the only larger dictionary from another language to Nenets. Text collections focusing on folklore include Castrén (1940), Castrén and Lehtisalo (1960), Lehtisalo (1947), Kuprijanova (1965), Tereščenko (1990). For a literary history in Nenets see Susoj (1990). Large bibliographies have been published by Hajdú (1968 [²1982], 1988).

For the phonology, an early publication is Lehtisalo (1927). A major work in the spirit of generative phonology is Janhunen (1986), with an ample bibliography. Later articles include Helimski (1989), Janhunen (1993), Salminen (1990a, 1990b, 1993a, 1993b). Morphology is the focus of all Nenets grammars and textbooks. Honti and Zaicz (1970) is a reverse listing of suffixes and suffix combinations compiled on the basis of Hajdú (1968 [²1982]). Mikola (1975) is a thorough survey of the postposition system. Hajdú, Labádi, Labanauskas, Perfil'eva, Sebestyén, and Ščerbakova, among others, have been active in publishing articles, as seen in the the bibliography by Hajdú (1988). Salminen (1997a) is a reverse dictionary with a key to inflectional paradigms, and Salminen (1997b) a monograph on inflection. The only major publication on syntax is Tereščenko (1973).

Almazova, A.V. (1961) Самоучитель ненецкого языка, Leningrad: Učpedgiz.
Barmič, M. Ja. and Kuprijanova, Z. N. (1979) Практикум по ненецкому языку, Leningrad: Prosveščenie.
Castrén, M. A. (1854 [²1966]) *Grammatik der samojedischen Sprachen*, Hrsg. A. Schiefner, St Petersburg [Indiana University Uralic and Altaic Series 53, Bloomington: Indiana University–The Hague: Mouton].
—— (1855) *Wörterverzeichnisse aus den samojedischen Sprachen*, Hrsg. A. Schiefner, St Petersburg.
—— (1940) *Samojedische Volksdichtung*, ed. T. Lehtisalo, MSFOu 83, Helsinki: Société Finno-Ougrienne.
Castrén, M. A. and Lehtisalo, T. (1960) *Samojedische Sprachmaterialien*, in T. Lehtisalo (ed.), MSFOu 122, Helsinki: Société Finno-Ougrienne.
Décsy, G. (1966) *Yurak Chrestomathy*, Indiana University Uralic and Altaic Series 50, Bloomington: Indiana University–The Hague: Mouton.
Hajdú, P. (1968 [²1982]) *Chrestomathia Samoiedica*, Budapest: Tankönyvkiadó.
—— (1975) *Samojedologische Schriften*, Studia Uralo-Altaica 6, Szeged: József Attila Tudományegyetem.
—— (1988) 'Die samojedischen Sprachen', in D. Sinor (ed.), *The Uralic Languages: Description, History and Foreign Influences*, Handbuch der Orientalistik 8/1 Leiden: Brill, pp. 3–40.
Helimski, E. A. (1989) 'Глубинно-фонологический изосиллабизм ненецкого стиха', *JSFOu* 82, 223–68.
Honti, L. and Zaicz, G. (1970) 'Jurák à tergo toldaléktár', *Nyelvtudományi Közlemények* 72, 363–98.
Janhunen, J. (1986) *Glottal Stop in Nenets*, MSFOu 196, Helsinki: Société Finno-Ougrienne.
—— (1993) 'Options for Tundra Nenets vowel analysis', in M. Sz. Bakró-Nagy and E. Szíj (eds), *Hajdú Péter 70 éves*, Budapest: MTA Nyelvtudományi Intézet, pp. 143–7.
Kuprijanova, Z. N. (1965) Эпические песни ненцев, Moscow: Nauka.

Kuprijanova, Z. N., Barmič, M. Ja., and Homič, L. V. (1985) Ненецкий язык, Leningrad: Prosveščenie.

Lehtisalo, T. (1927) *Über den vokalismus der ersten silbe im juraksamojedischen*, MSFOu 56, Helsinki: Société Finno-Ougrienne.

—— (1947) *Juraksamojedische Volksdichtung*, MSFOu 90, Helsinki: Société Finno-Ougrienne.

—— (1956) *Juraksamojedisches Wörterbuch*, Lexica Societatis Fenno-Ugricae 13, Helsinki: Société Finno-Ougrienne.

Mikola, T. (1975) *Die alten Postpositionen des Nenzischen (Juraksamojedischen)*, Budapest: Akadémiai kiadó.

Pyrerka, A. P. and Tereščenko, N. M. (1948) Русско-ненецкий словарь, Moscow: Ogiz Gis.

Salminen, T. (1990a) 'Samoyedology in Finland 1985–1989: the glottal stop', in *Problems of Uralistics*, vol. I, Moscow: Institute of Scientific Information on Social Sciences, USSR Academy of Sciences, pp. 216–37.

—— (1990b) 'Phonological criteria in the classification of the Nenets dialects', in L. Keresztes et al. (eds), *C7IFU*, vol. IIIC, Debrecen, pp. 344–9.

—— (1993a) 'On identifying basic vowel distinctions in Tundra Nenets', *FUF* 51, pp. 177–87.

—— (1993b) 'A phonemization of Tundra Nenets long vowels', in M. Sz. Bakró-Nagy and E. Szíj (eds), *Hajdú Péter 70 éves*, Budapest, Nyelvtudományi Intézet, pp. 347–52.

—— (1997a) *A Morphological Dictionary of Tundra Nenets*, Lexica Societatis Fenno-Ugricae 26, Helsinki: Société Finno-Ougrienne.

—— (1997b) *Tundra Nenets Inflection*, MSFOu 227, Helsinki: Société Finno-Ougrienne.

Susoi, E. G. (1990) Ненэцие" литература, Leningrad: Prosveščenie.

Tereščenko, N.M. (1947) Очерк грамматики ненецкого (юрако-самоедского) языка, Leningrad: Učpedgiz.

—— (1956) Материалы и исследования по языку ненцев, Moscow–Leningrad: Akademija Nauk SSSR.

—— (1959) В помощь самостоятельно изучающим ненецкий язык, Leningrad: Učpedgiz.

—— (1965) Ненецко-русский словарь, Moscow: Sovetskaja Ènciklopedija.

—— (1973) Синтаксис самодийских языков: простое предложение, Leningrad: Nauka.

—— (1990) Ненецкий эпос, Leningrad: Nauka.

18 Selkup

Eugene Helimski

The Selkup language, formerly known also as Ostyak Samoyed(ic), is now spoken by *c.* 2,000 descendants of an indigenous population of a vast West Siberian taiga area located mainly between the Ob' and Yenisei rivers. The total number of Selkups according to the Soviet censuses of 1979 and 1989 was the same, about 3,600 persons, but the level of native-language retention, and the proficiency of its speakers, are both steadily decreasing due to linguistic assimilation: in almost all parts of their original ethnic territory the Selkups are now outnumbered by Russians. Beyond this territory, there are no sizeable groups of Selkup resettlers.

Selkup is used in family life and in traditional domains of the economy such as fishing and hunting, but not in administration or other official spheres. Several attempts to introduce it as the language of education in elementary schools and to develop Selkup literacy, made especially between the 1930s and 1950s, have never been supported by any systematic efforts. Having recently been reintroduced in several schools, Selkup found itself in the position of a second and foreign language as a result of low native-language proficiency among schoolchildren. The activity of the national cultural society *Qoltə Qup* ('Man of the [Ob'] River') since the late 1980s has been a help in preserving Selkup national identity (see Pusztay: 1992), but the chances for the retention of Selkup by coming generations are close to zero for Southern Selkups (in the Tomsk region) and not very high in the North (the Tyumen and Krasnoyarsk regions).

Bilingualism

Selkup–Russian bilingualism, with varying degrees of competence in the native and second languages, and, typically, with a transitory stage of semilingualism, in which the command of neither language is perfect, is universally spread among Selkup speakers in the South (where in younger generations most ethnic Selkups are Russian monolinguals) and at least among younger and middle-aged Northern Selkups (here there are still some Selkup monolinguals among older people, especially women).

While this type of bilingualism is unilateral and leads ultimately to Russification, there exists also, now mainly among the people connected with traditional occupations, bilateral bilingualism on both sides of the borderlines of the Selkup ethnic territory: Selkup–Khanty in the river basins of Vasyugan and Vakh, Selkup–Ket in the basin of Yelogui, a left tributary of the Yenisei River, Selkup–Tungus in the Krasnoyarsk region and the adjacent parts of the Taz river basin. The reindeer-breeding Selkups in the middle part of the Taz river basin usually speak both Selkup and Nenets, and there are cases of Selkup–Turkic (Chulym Turkic, Siberian Tatar) bilingualism in the South.

Up to the beginning of the twentieth century Selkup used to be spoken as a lingua franca, widely known by non-Selkups, in the northeastern parts of West Siberia, and this role, played through centuries, may have contributed to the relative simplicity of its grammatical system in comparison with the other Samoyedic languages.

Dialects

The dialects of Selkup form a chain, originally continuous, but now no longer unbroken. The differences between any adjacent idioms are minimal, but for example the Taz dialect (North) and the Middle Ob' dialect (South) are mutually incomprehensible, differing approximately as much as Russian and Polish or Udmurt and Komi.

The main dialect groups are:

1 *Northern* (*Taz*), with the dialects of Middle Taz, Upper Taz, Baikha-and-Turukhan, Karasino, Yelogui (the first two are spoken in the eastern part of the Yamal Nenets Autonomous district of the Tyumen region, and the last three along the tributaries of the Yenisei River in the Krasnoyarsk region). The dialects of Middle Taz and Baikha–Turukhan are very close and account for about one-half of today's native speakers of Selkup. They have served as the dialect base for all main attempts to promote Selkup literacy and for the publication of school textbooks (with the exception of the most recent ones, which lean towards the Upper Taz dialect). The description below refers, unless otherwise specified, to the Middle Taz dialect.

2 *Central*, in the northwestern parts of the Tomsk region, with the dialects of Tym (closer to the Northern group) and of Narym (closer to the Southern group). Central dialects are or were spoken also by minor Selkup groups in areas adjacent to those of the Khanty (Ostyaks), along the rivers Vasyugan, Parabel, Vakh, and their tributaries.

3 *Southern*, in the central part of the Tomsk region, with the dialects of Middle Ob' (spoken along the Ob' River between the towns Narym and Kolpashevo, and standing closer to the Central group), Upper Ob' (upriver from Kolpashevo), and the now extinct dialects of Chaya and Chulym (along the Ob' tributaries). The Middle Ob' and Chaya dialects

were used in several Selkup books published by Orthodox missionaries in the late nineteenth century.

The Selkup dialect spoken at one time still further to the southeast, in the vicinities of Tomsk, and ousted as early as in the eighteenth century, must probably be classified as representing a separate dialect group.

4   The Ket' group, in the northeastern part of the Tomsk region along the Ket' River, with the dialects of Middle Ket' (close to the Southern group) and Upper Ket' (Nat-Pumpokolsk dialect). These dialects are preserved relatively better and look more viable than other Selkup dialects in the Tomsk region.

The grouping set out above correlates closely with the distribution of Selkup self-designations. In the absence of any single autoethnonym for all territorial groups the Northern Selkups call themselves *šölʲqup*, *şölʲqup* (hence 'Selkup'), the Central ones, *čumǝl qup*, the Southern ones *süsöqǝ(j) qum* (but Chulym *tʲujqum*), and the Ket' Selkups *süs(s)ü qum*.

Historical Development

According to the opinion shared by specialists in archaeology and anthropology, at least the Southern Selkups continue to live in the area which belonged to the original Samoyedic proto-homeland two thousand years ago and more (see Helimski 1991). The present-day repartition of dialects is the result of the gradual penetration of Selkup speakers in the northwestern and northern directions. The Northern Selkups took over their present-day habitat (ousting or assimilating the previous Enets population of this area) as recently as the second half of the seventeenth century. Still, the earliest linguistic records from the beginning of the eighteenth century prove that all the main distinctive traits of all Selkup dialect groups were already present at that time (see Helimski: 1985a).

Structurally, Selkup looks in many respects closer to Ugrian languages than its Northern Samoyedic relatives; this may be at least partly due to secondary contacts between Selkup and ObUgrian.

In the domain of phonology both innovations and unique retentions can be found. Selkup has developed a secondary correlative opposition between short and long vowels, and has undergone an extensive process of qualitative vowel reduction in non-first syllables; a series of labialized plosives appeared, later to be lost in the Northern dialects. On the other hand, the vowels of the first syllable preserve, in the main, the quality of their Proto-Samoyedic monophthongal prototypes, and the dialects of the Tomsk region are the only Samoyedic idioms in which the distinction between *t and *č is preserved (these two consonants merged long ago in other Samoyedic languages, and, as late as the first half of the twentieth century, also in Northern Selkup).

The most characteristic innovations in Selkup morphology are the radical extension of the case system (mainly through the fusion of postpositional constructions), the loss of a conjugated negative verb, the development of preverbs (separable verbal prefixes), the development of the morphological means for mutual transformations of syntactic roles of nominal, adjectival, and verbal stems. Further developments in individual dialects pertain in most cases to inventory rather than to structure.

The original syntactic system, with extensive use of non-finite verbal forms, has been replaced in most non-Northern dialects (partly also in the North) by the use of subordinate clauses with conjunctions, patterned after Russian. Other domains of syntax, including word order, display stronger retentive properties.

Phonology

Phonemes and their Modifications

The phonemic inventory of Middle Taz Selkup includes forty-one segmental units, with the vowels far outnumbering the consonants (twenty-five against sixteen), see Table 18.1 and Figure 18.1.

This numerical superiority manifests itself only paradigmatically, i.e. in the phonemic system, while syntagmatically (i.e. in texts) the average ratio of phonemes is roughly 132 consonants to 100 vowels.

Consonants

From the viewpoint of phonology the sole affricate $\check{c}^j$, which has $[t^j]$ as its optional variant (occurring idiolectally in all positions), forms jointly with the stops a single series of plosives. Numerous empty cells in the system of consonants, especially in the fricative series and in the postvelar (uvular) zone, as well as the absence of distinctively voiced and palatalized consonants, open wide the possibilities for considerable allophonic variation.

The phonologically voiceless plosives and fricatives are usually realized as voiced or weak (half-voiced) between two vowels or after resonants, cf. *üt* 'water': sG *ütïn* [üDįn ~ üdįn]. At morphemic boundaries this voicing may often be absent, cf. *uukï* [-G- ~ -g-] 'tip', but *uukïtïl^j* [-k-] 'having no

Table 18.1 Middle Taz Selkup consonants

	Labials	*Dentals*	*Palatals*	*Velars*	*Postvelars*
Nasals	m	n	n^j	ŋ	
Stops	p	t		k	q
Affricates			č^j		
Fricatives		s	š^j		
Laterals		l	l^j		
Trills		r			
Glides	w		j		

Figure 18.1   Middle Taz Selkup vowels

	Front			Central (unrounded)	Back (rounded)	
	unrounded		rounded			
	tense	lax			tense	lax
High	i ii	I II	ü üü	ï ïï	u uu	
Mid	e ee	ɛ ɛɛ	ö öö	ë ëë	o oo	o͜ao͜a
Low	ä ää				a aa	

ptarmigan' (*uu* 'ptarmigan'); this phenomenon is better accounted for by differentiating morpheme-internal and morpheme-initial (like word-internal and word-initial) positions, rather than by ascribing phonemic status to voiced consonants. On the other hand, in Narym Selkup and some other Central and Southern dialects the loss of word-final reduced vowels and some other secondary phonetic developments have resulted in the rise of a phonemic contrast between voiceless and voiced sounds: Narym *pet* 'by night': *ped* 'nest', *qop* 'man': *qob* 'skin' (in Taz Selkup respectively *pit* : *pitï*, *qup* : *qopï*).

Most (non-palatal) consonants become palatalized when followed by front, especially front tense, vowels. The stops are optionally realized as implosives word-finally or before other stops. Also optional is the fricative pronunciation of stops, when they are followed by *s* or *šʲ*: *apsï* [-fs- ~ -ps-] 'food', *rakšʲa* [-xšʲ- ~ -kšʲ-] 'jingling pendant'.

Especially dispersed are the positional (obligatory or optional) allophones of the sole postvelar phoneme *q*. Beside voiced, half-voiced, palatalized, and implosive postvelar stops, as well as the postvelar fricative [x̌], their set includes the postvelar nasal [ŋ] (occurs before nasals) and the postvelar trill [ř] (occurs word-internally mainly in the vicinity of liquids: *qaqlï* [qařl̦ï] 'sledge').

Idiolectally *šʲ* is realized as a non-palatal alveolar [š], a cacuminal [ṣ̌] or [ṣ]; this last pronunciation is typical of the Upper Taz dialect. Still another case of optional variation is that between 'Russian' non-palatal [ł] and slightly palatalized [l], both representing the phoneme *l*.

Vowels

The richness of the phonemic inventory of vowels is due, in the main, to the vast scope of the quantitative opposition (unlike Northern Samoyedic, in Selkup long vowels can hardly be treated as phonemic sequences), and to the contrast, in five pairs, of tense and lax vowels: *i* : ɪ, *ii* : ɪɪ, *e* : ɛ, *ee* : ɛɛ, *oo* : *åå*. The rise of this last contrast appears to be a Northern Selkup innovation. The tense/lax contrast may originally have been restricted to the front vowels in sequences like *čʲi-* : *čʲ*ɪ (where [ɪ] was originally merely a manifestation of *ï*, due to the restriction on the occurrence of *ï* after palatals), but later the distribution of front lax vowels became more complicated (e.g., lax but not tense front vowels occur after dentals), and in a number of instances morphophonemic developments or borrowings led to the penetration of the opposition to other positions (cf. *merka* 'measure for gunpowder' (from Russian): *mɛrka* 'the wind is blowing'). The contrast between *oo* and *åå* is the result of the development *aa > *åå* (modern *aa* is of secondary origin).

Phonetically lax vowels differ from corresponding tense ones by a less strained articulation and by a concomitant shift towards the central zone (ɪ, ɪɪ, ɛ, ɛɛ) and/or lower tongue-height (ɛ, ɛɛ, *åå*).

Long front vowels and *oo* are optionally diphthongized in open syllables. In allegro speech, and especially in unstressed positions, long vowels are pronounced half-long or even almost short; this tendency towards the phonetic neutralization of the quantitative opposition is very typical of Central and Southern Selkup dialects.

The phonemic symbol *ï* in non-first syllables denotes a reduced vowel (common Selkup *ə); it is realized as [ɨ̂] or, more seldom, [ə̂], and, after palatals , [ɪ] or [ə]. While there is no vowel harmony in Selkup, non-Northern dialects tend to assimilate the reduced vowels in their phonetic quality to the vowel of the first syllable: Ket' *suurəm* [suurŭm] 'animal', Tym *eləgu* [elĕgu] 'to live', and this creates an effect similar to vowel harmony.

Stress

The dynamic stress in Selkup is mobile. Its placement in a word is determined by a combination of phonetic and morphological factors.

According to the most widespread phonetic rule of accentuation, stress is placed on the last long vowel; if there are no long vowels in non-first syllables it is placed on the first vowel: *pur̲qï* 'smoke', *uu̲čʲïqo* 'to work', *aqqå̲ålʲ* 'rein', *uu̲čʲå̲åmïт* 'we work', *å̲åtääqɪlɪɪ* 'your two reindeers'. Regular deviations from this rule are determined by the presence of inflectional and derivational suffixes of two accentologically specific types. One type of suffix contains vowels, which, although phonetically short, behave as though they were long and attract the stress (unless there are long vowels in following syllables): *koŋa̲ltïqo* 'to tell', *puuto̲ntï* '(to the) inside'. The other type of suffix creates the phenomenon of double stress within a single phonetic word: *tï̲ïlå̲å* 'closer here', *tɛ̲nïsï̲mïlʲ* 'clever'; each accentologically separate part is then governed by the basic phonetic rule of accentuation given on p. 533.

Differences in the morphemic composition of words account for the relatively rare examples of contrastive stress, such as *čʲεlʲčʲalqo* 'to stamp down': *čʲεlʲčʲalqo* 'to stamp (once)', *kikitilʲ* 'loving': *kikitilʲ* 'riverless'. It is possible that certain accentological relics are preserved by second-person singular imperative forms, in which there are such unusual contrastive pairs as e.g. *ürtäšʲ* 'make fat!': *ürtäšʲ* 'lose!'.

In non-Northern Selkup dialects there is often a strong tendency for the stress to migrate rightwards on to short low vowels of non-first syllables: Tym *kanak* 'dog', *äwä* 'mother'.

Distribution of Phonemes
Among the consonants, *ŋ* does not occur word-initially, *j* occurs in this position only in borrowings, and word-initial *r* occurs only in borrowings and onomatopoetic words. Word-finally *čʲ* and *w* do not occur at all (*w* is rare word-internally, as well), and *q* and *nʲ* are extremely rare. According to phonostatistic data, the most frequent consonants are (in descending order of frequency) *t, n, m, q, p, l, k*.

Consonant clusters (consisting of two, seldom of three phonemes) are normal only word-internally. Most common among them are the combinations of a nasal or a liquid plus a plosive, and particularly the homotopic clusters *mp, nt, nʲčʲ, ŋk, lt, lʲčʲ*, and the geminate clusters *tt, qq, mm, nn, ss, šʲšʲ*, etc. (these are the result of sandhi phenomena in many cases; see pp. 555–6). Other types of clusters are considerably less frequent.

All vowels can occur in the first syllable, though there are numerous restrictions on the occurrence of vowels after certain consonants. In non-first syllables long *uu* and *ïï*, and long and short *ë/ëë, ü/üü, ö/öö, e/ee* do not occur at all, while short *u* and long and short *i/ii* occur only in a few suffixes. In general, the reduced vowel *ï* and the short full vowel *a* are much more frequent than any of the other vowels; the relative frequencies of *ëë, aa, üü, ää*, and *e* are close to zero.

Vowel clusters are possible only at morpheme boundaries, but there are always optional variants with hiatus eliminated by contraction or the epenthesis of a glide: *kanaiilï ~ kanajiilï ~ kanεεlï* 'your (sg) dogs'. Very often the first of two adjacent vowels in word groups is apocopated: *soma εεŋa ~ som εεŋa* 'is good'.

Morphophonology

Nasal ~ Stop Alternation
Perhaps the most characteristic morphophonemic phenomenon of Selkup is the alternation of nasals with homotopic stops (*m ~ p, n ~ t, ŋ ~ k*), in some cases also with zero in word-final position, cf. *qontam ~ qontap* 'I'll find',

suurïm ~ suurïp ~ suurï 'animal', *karman ~ karmat* 'pocket', *somaŋ ~ somak* 'well', *ååŋ ~ ååk ~ åå* 'mouth', etc. Such variants are functionally equal and they are almost equally frequent, for example, in pre-pausal position. The alternation is not automatic: word-final nasals and stops may be also stable, e.g., *këm* 'blood', *toop* 'edge', *č'ësïn* 'snare', *köt* 'ten', *tååŋ* 'taiga', *tuk* 'beetle' etc. Depending on the presence/absence and the conditions of this alternation, several types of stems and suffixes can be distinguished; their morphophonological differences manifest themselves in both inflection and derivation, cf. sG *åå-n* 'of a mouth', *tååŋi-n* 'of taiga', *tukï-n* 'of a beetle'. In order to account for this difference, the following symbols will be used (**N** = nasal, **T** = stop):

	N_1	T_1	N_2	T_2	N_{2x}	N_3
Alternation in word-final position	none	none	N~T	N~T	N~T	N~T~Ø
Consonant typically preserved in inflection	N	T	N	T	(–)	Ø

(The morphophonemic N_{2x} does not occur in inflection.) We may therefore write the examples given above morphophonemically as *qontam$_2$*, *suurïm$_3$*, *karman$_2$*, *somaŋ$_{2x}$*, *ååŋ$_3$*, *këm$_1$*, *toop$_1$*, *č'ësïn$_1$*, *köt$_1$*, *tååŋ$_1$*, *tuk$_1$*.

Sandhi

The sandhi processes caused by the assimilative interaction of two consonants belonging to different morphemes (stem + suffix, suffix + suffix, compounds and fused word groups), are shown in Figure 18.2. It will be seen that the assimilation can be complete or partial, progressive, regressive, or even bilateral (as in the case of *š'-n > n'n'*). Sandhi is determined by morphological rather than purely phonetic factors: the same cluster may be 'tolerable' in nominal forms, but eliminated through sandhi in verbal ones (*purïš'tï* 'his torch', but *suurïč'č'ï* 'it turns out that he is hunting' from *suurïš-tï), or 'tolerable' in derivation, but not in inflection (cf. *këtsan* 'grandson' and the regular transformation *ts > ss* in both nominal and verbal inflection).

A special sandhi rule transforms the clusters **NP** (where **N** is a nasal and **P** is a plosive, not necessarily homotopic) into nasal clusters **NN$_p$** (where **N$_p$** is a nasal homotopic with **P**), if they are followed, after a vowel, by another cluster consisting of a nasal and a plosive: *qomtä* 'money': *qomnäntï* 'of his money', *soqïn'č'iqo* 'to ask': *soqïn'n'impa* 'he asked': *soqïn'n'immantï* 'you asked'. As the last example shows, this rule applies recursively from the beginning to the end of a word. The morpheme boundary (or boundaries) may be located at any place in the string **-NPVNP-**.

Some other sandhi phenomena are caused by phonetic processes which are no longer productive and regular (for example, the loss of initial *t* in certain

Figure 18.2   Sandhi in Middle Taz Selkup: assimilative interaction of the consonants C_1 and C_2 where C_1 and C_2 belong to different morphemes

C_1 \ C_2	k	t	q	s	šʲ	m	n	l
p						mm	mn	[βl]
t				ss	šʲ šʲ	nm	ŋn	ll
k			qq			ŋm	ŋn	[γl]
q	kk					ŋ̈m	ŋ̈n	[ïl]
s					šʲ šʲ			
sʲ		čʲ čʲ$^{(1)}$		šʲ šʲ			nʲ nʲ$^{(1)}$	lʲ lʲ$^{(1)}$
m_1								[βl]
n_1	ŋk			nʲ šʲ				ll
nʲ		nʲ čʲ					nʲ nʲ	
$ŋ_1$								[γl]
$m_{2,3}{}^{(2)}$	pk$^{(3)}$	pt$^{(3)}$	pq	ps	pšʲ			[βl]
$n_{2,3}{}^{(2)}$	tk$^{(3)}$	tt$^{(3)}$	tq	ss	šʲ šʲ			ll
$ŋ_{2,3}{}^{(2)}$	kk$^{(3)}$	kt$^{(3)}$	qq	ks	kšʲ			[γl]
lʲ		lʲčʲ						lʲ lʲ
j		jčʲ						

Notes: This figure accounts only for those output clusters which differ from the simple sum of their input components. If the output is phones rather than phonemes, these are given in square brackets (i.e. phonologically [βl] is equal to /pl/ or /ml/, [ŋ̈m] to /qm/, etc.).
    (1) This sandhi assimilation occurs only in verbal inflexion. (2) Final nasals in bound morphemes usually behave like N_3. (3) For N_2 this assimilation is optional.

verbal suffixes after verbal stems ending in *r*). They shall therefore be relegated to the domain of suffixal allomorphy.

Stem Variants
While the nominative singular serves as the main stem (first stem) of nouns, certain paradigmatic and derivational forms are based on its modified variant

(second stem). If the first stem ends in a vowel, the two stems are identical. If the first stem ends in a consonant, the second stem acquires an additional final vowel (*ï*), or loses its final consonant (usually **N₃**) and, in monosyllabic nouns, may contain a vowel quantitatively or qualitatively different from that of the first stem. In the following examples, the second stem is exemplified by plural nominatives (suffix *-t*): *qum* 'man' : *qumït*, *kanaŋ* 'dog' : *kanat*, *aqsïl* 'mushroom' : *aqsïlït*, *ruš^j* 'Russian' : *ruuš^{j}ït*, *sër* 'bog, marsh' : *sïïrït*, *nom* 'God, heaven' : *nuut*, *qoŋ* 'chief' : *qoot*.

The modification of verbal stems occurs mainly in derivation (paradigmatically it is found only in several monosyllabic verbal stems). Here the morphophonemic processes which produce stem variants are less regular and more diverse; they include lengthening or shortening of stem vowels, truncation, and gemination of intervocalic stem consonants, e.g. *č^{j}uurï-* 'to cry' : *č^{j}urqïl-* 'to start crying', *qo-* 'to find': *qooqïl-* 'to find many', *såårï-* 'to bind' : *sarrɛɛ-* 'to bind (already, intensively)'.

In both nominal and verbal stems the last vowel (usually *ï*) is often ousted, if the suffix that follows begins with a vowel: *utï* 'hand' : *utam* 'my hand', *ilï-* 'to live' : *ilɛntak* 'I'll live'.

Morphology

Parts of Speech and Category of Representation
The Selkup language, with its more or less banal set of parts of speech (substantives, adjectives, numerals, pronouns, verbs, adverbs with particles, postpositions, preverbs, interjections), has developed a system of morphological means for transforming the typical syntactic roles of parts of speech into one another. While for verbs such transformations (into verbal nouns, participles, and verbal adverbs) are a common phenomenon in the Uralic languages, there are in Selkup also special paradigmatic forms of substantives with the meanings and syntactic functions of adjectives, verbs, and adverbs, e.g. (*qum* 'man, person'): *qumååk* 'I am a human being', *qumïl^j* 'human', *qumïk* 'human(ly)', etc. The regularity and productivity of such formations makes it expedient to treat them as inflectional rather than derivational, and to use in the description of (at least) substantives, adjectives, and verbs the notion of category of representation, with four categorical meanings (substantival, adjectival, verbal, and adverbial representations).

Substantives
Number. The singular is unmarked. The dual has the suffix *-QI* (to the left of which reduced *ï* goes to *oo*, and other vowels are lengthened), in several words also *-ÄÄQI*, *-OOQI*, and (with reduplication) *-QÄÄQI*. The plural has the suffix *-T₂* (joined to the second stem), in the vocative case *-N*, in possessive forms *-lï-* (joined to the second stem). The collective form has *-L^{J}MÏ* (joined to the second stem), so that formally it is a combination of the

Table 18.2 Nominal declension, substantival representation: *nom* 'God, heaven'

	Singular	Dual	Plural	Collective
Non-possessive forms				
N	nom	nopqɪ	nuut	nuulʲmï
G	nuun	nopqɪn	nuutïn	nuulʲmïn
A	nuum	nopqɪm	nuutïm	nuulʲmïm
Ins	nopsä	nopqɪsä	nuussä	nuulʲmïsä
Car	nomkåålïk	nopqɪkåålïk	nuutkåålïk	nuulʲmïkåålïk
Trans	nuutqo	nopqɪtqo	nuutïtko	nuulʲmïtqo
Co-ord	nuušʲšʲak	nopqɪšʲšʲak	nuutïšʲšʲak	nuulʲmïšʲšʲak
Dat/All	nuunïk	nopqɪtkïnɪ	nuutïtkïnɪ	nuulʲmïnïk
Ill	nomtï	nopqɪtkïnɪ	nuutïtkïnɪ	nuulʲmïntï
Loc	nopqïn	nopqɪɪqïn	nuutqïn	nuulʲmïïqïn
Ela	nopqïnï	nopqɪɪqïnï	nuutqïnï	nuulʲmïïqïnï
Prol	nommïn	nopqɪɪmïn	nuunmïn	nuulʲmïïmïn
Voc	nomëë	nopqëë ~ nopqɪɪ	nuunëë	
s1 Possessive forms				
NA	nommï	nopqɪm(ï)	nuuiim(ï)	nuulʲmïmï
G	nomnï ~ nuunï	nopqɪnï	nuuiinï	nuulʲmïnï
Ins	nomnïsä ~ nuunïsä	nopqɪnïsä	nuuiinïsä	nuulʲmïnïsä
Car	nomnïkåålïk ~ nuunïkåålïk	nopqɪnïkåålïk	nuuiinïkåålïk	nuulʲmïnïkåålïk
Trans	nomnoo(qo) ~ nuunoo(qo)	nopqɪnoo(qo)	nuuiinoo(qo)	nuulʲmïnoo(qo)
Co-ord	nomnïsʲak ~ nuunïsʲak	nopqɪnïsʲak	nuuiinïsʲak	nuulʲmïnïsʲak
Dat/All	nomnïnïk ~ nuunïnïk	nopqɪnïkinɪ	nuuiinïkinɪ	nuulʲmïnïnïk
Ill/Loc/Ela	nopqäk	nopqɪɪqäk	nuuiiqäk	nuulʲmïïqäk
Prol	nommäk	nopqɪɪmäk	nuuiimäk	nuulʲmïïmäk
s2 and s3 Possessive forms				
N (s2)	nomlï	nopqɪlï	nuuiilï	nuulʲmïlï
(s3)	nomtï	nopqɪtï	nuuiitï	nuulʲmïtï
G	nomtï	nopqɪntï	nuuiintï	nuulʲmïntï
A	nomtï	nopqɪmtï	nuumtï	nuulʲmïmtï
Ins	nomtïsä	nopqɪntïsä	nuuiintïsä	nuulʲmïntïsä
Car	nomtïkåålïk	nopqɪntïkåålïk	niintïkåålïk	nuulʲmïntïkåålïk
Trans	nomtoo(qo)	nopqɪntoo(qo)	nuuiintoo(qo)	nuulʲmïntoo(qo)
Co-ord	nomtïšʲak	nopqɪntïšʲak	nuuiintïšʲak	nuulʲmïntïšʲak
Dat/All	nomtïnïk	nopqɪntïkinɪ	nuuiintïkinɪ	nuulʲmïntïnïk
Ill/Loc/Ela				
(s2)	nopqäntï	nopqɪɪqäntï	nuuiiqäntï	nuulʲmïïqäntï
(s3)	nopqïntï	nopqɪɪqïntï	nuuiiqïntï	nuulʲmïïqïntï
Prol (s2)	nommäntï	nopqɪɪmäntï	nuuiimäntï	nuulʲmïïmäntï
(s3)	nommïntï	nopqɪɪmïntï	nuuiimïntï	nuulʲmïïmïntï

d1 Possessive forms

NA	nommıı	nopqımıı	nuuiimıı	nuulʲmïmıı
G	nomnıı ~ nuunıı	nopqınıı	nuuiinıı	nuulʲmïnıı
Ins	nomnıısä ~ nuunıısä	nopqınıısä	nuuiinıısä	nuulʲmïnıısä
Car	nomnııkåålïk ~ nuunııkåålïk	nopqınııkåålïk	nuuiinııkåålïk	nuulʲmïnııkåålïk
Trans	nomnııqo ~ nuunııqo	nopqınııqo	nuuiinııqo	nuulʲmïnııqo
Co-ord	nomnııšʲak ~ nuunııšʲak	nopqınııšʲak	nuuiinııšʲak	nuulʲmïnııšʲak
Dat/All	nomnıınïk ~ nuunıınïk	nopqınııkinı	nuuiinııkinı	nuulʲmïnıınïk
Ill/Loc/Ela	nopqïnıı	nopqııqïnıı	nuuiiqïnıı	nuulʲmïïqïnıı
Prol	nommïnıı	nopqıımïnıı	nuuiimïnıı	nuulʲmïïmïnıı

d2 and d3 Possessive forms

N (d2)	nomlıı	nopqılıı	nuuiilıı	nuulʲmïlıı
(d3)	nomtıı	nopqıtıı	nuuiitıı	nuulʲmïtıı
G	nomtıı	nopqïntıı	nuuiintıı	nuulʲmïntıı
A	nomtıı	nopqïmtıı	nuuiimtıı	nuulʲmïmtıı
Ins	nomtıısä	nopqïntıısä	nuuiintıısä	nuulʲmïntıısä
Car	nomtııkåålïk	nopqïntııkåålïk	nuuiintııkåålïk	nuulʲmïntııkåålïk
Trans	nomtııqo	nopqïntııqo	nuuiintııqo	nuulʲmïntııqo
Co-ord	nomtııšʲak	nopqïntııšʲak	nuuiintııšʲak	nuulʲmïntııšʲak
Dat/All	nomtıınïk	nopqïntııkinı	nuuiintııkinı	nuulʲmïntıınïk
Ill/Loc/Ela	nopqïntıı	nopqııqïntıı	nuuiiqïntıı	nuulʲmïïqïntıı
Prol	nommïntıı	nopqıımïntıı	nuuiimïntıı	nuulʲmïïmïntıı

p1 Possessive forms

NA	nommït	nopqımït	nuuiimït	nuulʲmïmït
G	nomnït ~ nuunït	nopqınït	nuuiinït	nuulʲmïnït
Ins	nomnïssä ~ nuunïssä	nopqınïssä	nuuiinïssä	nuulʲmïnïssä
Car	nomnïtkåülïk ~ nuunïtkåålïk	nopqınïtkåålïk	nuuiinïtkåålïk	nuulʲmïnïtkåålïk
Trans	nomnïtqo ~ nuunïtqo	nopqınïtqo	nuuiinïtqo	nuulʲmïnïtqo
Co-ord	nomnïšʲšʲak ~ nuunïšʲšʲak	nopqınïšʲšʲak	nuuiinïšʲšʲak	nuulʲmïnïšʲšʲak
Dat/All	nomnïnnïk ~ nuunïnnïk	nopqınïtkinı	nuuiinïtkinı	nuulʲmïnïnnïk
Ill/Loc/Ela	nopqïnït	nopqııqïnït	nuuiiqïnït	nuulʲmïïqïnït
Prol	nommïnït	nopqıımïnït	nuuiimïnït	nuulʲmïïmïnït

p2 and p3 Possessive forms

N (d2)	nomlït	nopqılït	nuuiilït	nuulʲmïlït
(d3)	nomtït	nopqıtït	nuuiitït	nuulʲmïtït
G	nomtït	nopqıntït	nuuiintït	nuulʲmïntït
A	nomtït	nopqımtït	nuuiimtït	nuulʲmïmtït
Ins	nomtïssä	nopqıntïssä	nuuiintïssä	nuulʲmïntïssä
Car	nomtïtkåålïk	nopqıntïtkåålïk	nuuiintïtkåålïk	nuulʲmïntïtkåålïk
Trans	nomtïtqo	nopqıntïtqo	nuuiintïtqo	nuulʲmïntïtqo
Co-ord	nomtïšʲšʲak	nopqıntïšʲšʲak	nuuiintïšʲšʲak	nuulʲmïntïšʲšʲak
Dat/All	nomtïnnïk	nopqıntïtkinı	nuuiintïtkinı	nuulʲmïntïnnïk
Ill/Loc/Ela	nopqïntït	nopqııqïntït	nuuiiqïntït	nuulʲmïïqïntït
Prol	nommïntït	nopqıımïntït	nuuiimïntït	nuulʲmïïmïntït

Table 18.3   Nominal declension, adjectival, verbal, and adverbial representation: *nom* 'God, heaven'

	Relative adjectival form	Co-ordinative adjectival form	Locative adjectival form
Non-possessive	nuulʲ	nuušʲšʲalʲ	nopqïlʲ
Possessive			
s1	nuunïlʲ	nuunïšʲalʲ	nopqälʲ
s2	nomtïlʲ	nomtïšʲalʲ	nopqäntïlʲ
s3	nomtïlʲ	nomtïšʲalʲ	nopqïntïlʲ
d1	nuunтɪlʲ	nuunтɪšʲalʲ	nopqïnтɪlʲ
d2	nomtɪlʲ	nomtɪšʲalʲ	nopqïntɪlʲ
d3	nomtɪlʲ	nomtɪšʲalʲ	nopqïntɪlʲ
p1	nuunïtïlʲ	nuunïšʲšʲalʲ	nopqïnïtïlʲ
p2	nomtïtïlʲ	nomtïšʲšʲalʲ	nopqïntïtïlʲ
p3	nomtïtïlʲ	nomtïšʲšʲalʲ	nopqïntïtïlʲ

Verbal representation (predicative forms)

s1	nomååk	*d1*	nomïŋmɪɪ	*p1*	nomïŋmït
s2	nomääntï	*d2*	nomïŋlɪɪ	*p2*	nomïŋlït
s3	nom	*d3*	nopqɪ	*p3*	nuut

Adverbial representation
nuuk

relative adjectival form (see below) with the generic pronoun *MÏ* (the orthographic convention is to write collectives and other similar cases as two words, but the two components are inseparable).

The collective form, as distinct from the plural, renders the meaning of integral and often uncountable plurality: *pülʲmï* 'stones, heap of stones, stony place', cf. *püt* '(several) stones'; *qumilʲmï* 'people, crowd', cf. *qumït* 'men, human beings'. It is more common to use collective forms of inanimate, and plurals of animate nouns.

Suffixes of number always precede those of case and possession; see Tables 18.2 and 18.3.

In most non-Northern Selkup dialects there are no collective forms, and the plural suffix is *-LA*.

Case. The case system includes:

Nominative (unmarked, i.e. -∅);
Genitive (*-N₂*, joined to the second stem);
Accusative (*-M₂*, joined to the second stem);
Instrumental (*-SÄ*) , rendering both instrumental and sociative meanings;

Caritive (-*KÅÅLÏN`3*, or optionally -*KÅÅL*);

Translative (-*QO*, joined to the form of the genitive; in first, second, and third singular possesive forms the preceding reduced *i* changes to *oo*, and the suffix -*QO* itself may be then omitted) , denotes the state of the sentence subject or the destination of the sentence object;

Co-ordinative (-Š*j*AN`$_{2x}$, joined to the form of genitive) , denotes measure or point of reference;

Dative/allative (in the singular and the collective -*NÏN`3*, joined to the second stem, and in the dual and plural -*KÏNI*, with several variants such as -*KÏNÏ*, -*KÏNÏN`3*, -*KÏNTÏ*, joined to the form of the genitive);

Illative (in the singular and the collective -*NTÏ* after vowels and -*TÏ* after consonants; before -*NTÏ* reduced *i* goes to stressed short *o*, and other short vowels become stressed; in the dual and plural this case syncretizes with the dative/allative, and in possessive forms with the locative);

Locative (-*QÏN`$_2$*; to the left of this suffix reduced *i* goes to *oo*, and other vowels become lengthened);

Elative (in non-possessive forms -*QÏNÏ* with the same morphophonological properties as -*QÏN`$_2$*; in possessive forms syncretizes with the locative);

Prolative (-*MÏN`$_2$*, with the same morphophonological properties as -*QÏN`$_2$*);

Vocative (has only non-possessive forms of singular, dual, and plural, and is marked with a long, commonly pronounced overlong, final or added vowel, usually -*ËË*).

In adverbs, postpositions, and pronouns local cases are often marked with -*Ä* or zero (illative), -*N`$_2$* (locative), and -*NÏ* (elative).

Other Selkup dialects often lack some of the above-listed case forms (especially the co-ordinative and the elative) or have additional and alternative case forms of secondary origin (e.g., elative or adessive in -*NANÏ*, destinative in -*WLÄ*, etc.); see Becker (1978).

Nominals which designate animates lack locative and elative forms. This appears to be the only obligatory morphological distinction between animate and inanimate nouns in Middle Taz Selkup.

Possessivity. Possessive forms distinguish three persons and three numbers of possessors with the help of two series of possessive suffixes, one used with nominative forms and the other with all oblique cases:

	s1	s2	s3	d1	d2	d3	p1	p2	p3
Nominative	-MÏ, -(A)M$_2$	-LÏ, -(A)L	-TÏ	-MII	-LII	-TII	-MÏT$_2$	-LÏT$_2$	-TÏT$_2$
Oblique	-Ï	-TÏ	-TÏ	-II	-TII	-TII	-ÏT$_2$	-TÏT$_2$	-TÏT$_2$

In oblique cases, possessive suffixes either follow case suffixes or (in the instrumental, caritive, translative, co-ordinative, and dative/allative) precede it. Locative and prolative have special fused possessive forms of s1 and s2. Further details concerning the combinations of case and possessive suffixes can be extracted from the data in Table 18.2.

The possessive forms of the third person (and, in imperative sentences, of the second person) often render the meaning of definiteness rather than that of possession.

Non-substantive Representations

The marker of *adjectival* representation is -L^J. In relative adjectival forms it is joined to the second stem, in co-ordinative and locative adjectival forms it replaces the final consonants of the relevant case suffixes (-$\check{S}^J AN_{2x}$ > -$\check{S}^J AL^J$, -$Q\ddot{I}N_2$ > -$Q\ddot{I}L^J$): *alako* 'boat' > *alakoľ lapï* 'boat-oar', *alako$^{\check{s}j}\check{s}^j$aľ lapï* 'an oar good for a boat', *alakooqiľ lapï* 'an oar (which is) on the boat'. The structure of the noun phrase is preserved in adjectival forms: *soma alakomï* 'my good boat', *soma alakoniľ lapï* 'oar of my good boat' (and not *'good oar of my boat'), *soma alakooqäľ lapï* 'oar (which is) on my good boat', etc. As the two last examples show, adjectival forms can render possessive meanings.

The forms of *verbal* representation (usually treated in descriptive grammars as predicative forms of substantives) use in the axis-of-discourse person suffixes which are similar to the verb suffixes of the subjective conjugation (s1 -N_{2x}, s2 -$NT\ddot{I}$, d1 -MII, d2 -LII, p1 -$M\ddot{I}T_2$, p2 -$L\ddot{I}T_2$); they are preceded by a special marker of V[erbal] R[epresentation] (-$\mathring{A}\mathring{A}$- ~ -η- ~ $\mathring{A}\mathring{A}\eta$- ~ -$\eta\mathring{A}\mathring{A}$-). In the third person the singular, dual, and plural nominatives of substantival representation are employed.

The verbal forms of substantives are used as predicates: *tan kïpa iija-ŋåå-ntï* PRO.s2 LITTLE BOY-VR-s2 'you are a little boy'. When it is necessary to render meanings of mood and tense other than indicative present, the relevant forms of the verb *εε-* 'to be' are used, e.g. *tan kïpa iijaŋåånti εppïntï* PRO. s2 LITTLE BOY-VR-s2 BE-narrative-inferential-s2 'it turns out that you were a little boy'.

The suffix of *adverbial* representation is -N_{2x}, which is joined to the second stem. It functions most often as a replacement for relative adjectival forms in compound predicates, e.g. *tmolï* 'cloud' > *tmoliľ čʲeelï* 'cloudy day', *tmolïŋ εsïmpa* 'it became cloudy'.

Adjectives

Inasmuch as relative adjectival forms belong, in Selkup, to the paradigms of substantives, the class of adjectives comprises mainly words with qualitative meanings, both primary (*soma* 'good') and derived (and then usually ending in -L^J: *soopiľ* 'sharp'). When used attributively, adjectives are not inflected. When used non-attributively as independent substantives, they are declined like nouns (= substantival representation of adjectives).

The adverbial representation of adjectives is regularly formed by adding the suffix -N_{2x} or replacing -L^J with -N_{2x}: *somak* 'well', *soopik* 'sharply'. Combinations of these adverbial forms (or of truncated adjectival stems) with existential verbs are used as predicates and can be viewed as compound verbal representations of adjectives: *som(a) εεŋa* 'is good', *soopïŋ εεŋa* 'is (in a) sharp (state)'.

There are no morphological degrees of comparison. The meaning of the superlative degree is rendered with the help of the prepositive particle *poosï*: *poosï soma* 'best', *poosï soopïlʲ* 'sharpest'.

Numerals
The primary cardinal numerals are:

1	*ukkïr*	6	*muktït₂*
2	*šʲittï* (non-attributively: *šʲittääqı*)	7	*seelʲčʲï*
3	*nååkïr*	10	*köt₁*
4	*tɛɛttï*	100	*toon₂*
5	*sompïla*	1000	*tïšʲšʲa* (< Russian)

Other cardinal numerals are formed subtractively (*šʲittï čʲääŋkïtïlʲ köt* TWO LACKING TEN 'eight', *ukkïr čʲääŋkïtïlʲ köt* ONE LACKING TEN '9'), additively (*ukkïr këëlʲ köt* ONE EXTRA TEN '11'); (*toon ɛj köt* HUNDRED AND TEN '110'), multiplicatively (*šʲittï tɛɛsar* TWO FORTY '80'; *sompïla toon* '500'), by suffixation (*šʲittï-sar* '20'; *nas-sar* '30', with a reduction of the first component), or by combinations of these methods. Like adjectives, cardinal numerals are inflected (according to nominal patterns) only when they are used non-attributively.

Ordinal numerals (except *ukoolʲ*, *poos+ukoolʲ* 'first') are built with the suffix -*MTÄLÏLʲ* (joined to the second stem): *šʲittïmtälïlʲ* 'second', *köötïmtälïlʲ* 'tenth'. The suffix -*MTÄL* forms multiple numerals: *šʲittïmtäl* 'again, for the second time', *köötïmtäl* 'for the tenth time'.

Pronouns
The class of pronouns (or rather of 'prowords') can be viewed as comprising not only pronoun-substantives and pronoun-adjectives, but also pronoun-verbs (e.g. *qattıı-* 'to get where?') and pronoun-adverbs (e.g. *tïmtï* 'here'). Their relationship, however, is different from the relationships between the forms of different representations, because morphosyntactically different pronouns normally are built to different stems.

The *personal pronouns* (see Table 18.4) and the *emphatic reflexive personal pronouns* (see Table 18.5) have case paradigms with fewer distinctions than those of nouns, and often with irregular (partly suppletive) relationships between case forms, especially in the axis-of-discourse persons. Third-person pronouns are used only with reference to persons, the meaning 'it' being rendered by the demonstrative anaphoric pronoun *namï*.

Other pronoun-substantives are declined like ordinary nouns (and have, in particular, numerative and possessive forms, e.g. *tammääqımï* 'these two of mine', from *tammï* 'this', *kutiintïssä* 'with which persons of theirs', from *kutï*

Table 18.4 Declension of personal pronouns

	First person	Second person	Third person
sN	man	tan	tëp
sG	man	tan	tëpïn
sA	(ma)š^jım	(ta)š^jıntï	tëpïm
sIns	massä	tassä	tëpsä
sCar	matkåålïk	tatkåålïk	tëpkåålïk
sTrans	matqo	tatqo	tëpïtqo
sDat/All	mäkkä ~ matqäk	täntï ~ tatqäntï	tëpïnïk
dN	mee	tɛɛ	tëpääqı
dG	mee	tɛɛ	tëpääqın
dA	(mee)š^jımıı ~ (mee)š^jınıı	(tɛɛ)š^jıntıı	tëpääqım
dIns	meesä	tɛɛsä	tëpääqısä
dCar	meekåålïk	tɛɛkåålïk	tëpääqıkåålïk
dTrans	meeqo ~ meetqo	tɛɛqo ~ tɛɛtqo	tëpääqıtqo
dDat/All	meeqïn^jıı	tɛɛqïn^jč^jıı	tëpääqıtkını
pN	mee	tɛɛ	tëpït
pG	mee	tɛɛ	tëpïtïn
pA	(mee)š^jımït ~ (mee)š^jınït	(tɛɛ)š^jıntït	tëpïtïm
pIns	meesä	tɛɛsä	tëpïssä
pCar	meekåålïk	tɛɛkåålïk	tëpïtkåålïk
pTrans	meeqo ~ meetqo	tɛɛqo ~ tɛɛtqo	tëpïtïtqo
pDat/All	meeqïń^jït	tɛɛqïń^jč^jït	tëpïtkını

Table 18.5 Declension of emphatic/reflexive personal pronouns

	First person	Second person	Third person
sNG	onäk 'myself'	onäntï 'yourself (sg)'	ontï 'him/herself'
sA	onäqqoš^janoo(qo)	onäntïqoš^jantoo(qo)	ontïqoš^jïntoo(qo)
sIns	onäksä	onäntïsä	ontïsä
sDat/All	onäqqäk ~ onäqqoš^jaqäk	onäntïqäntï ~ onäntïqošaqäntï	ontïqïntï ~ ontïqoš^jooqïntï
dG	onıı 'ourselves (du)'	ontıı 'yourselves, themselves (du)'	
dA	onııqoš^jïnııqo	ontııqoš^jïntııqo	
dIns	onıısä	ontıısä	
dDat/All	onııqïnıı ~ onııqoš^jooqïnıı	ontııqïntıı ~ ontııqoš^jooqïntıı	
pNG	onït 'ourselves (pl)'	ontït 'yourselves, themselves (pl)'	
pA	onïtqoš^jïnïtqo	ontïtqoš^jïntïtqo	
pIns	onïssä	ontïssä	
pDat/All	onïtqïnït ~ onïtqoš^jooqïnït	ontïtqïntït ~ ontïtqoš^jooqïntït	

'who?'). Pronoun-verbs are conjugated; pronoun-adjectives and pronoun-adverbs are normally not inflected.

The demonstrative pronouns distinguish proximal and distal deixis:

tam 'this (attrib)', *tammï* 'this (non-attrib)', *tï* 'here (lat)', *tïmtï* 'here (loc)', *tïïnï* 'from here', etc.,

versus

toonna 'that (attrib)', *toonnamï* 'that (non-attrib), *too* 'there (lat)', *toonnimtï* 'there (lat)', *toonï* 'from there', etc.,

and anaphora

(*na* 'this/that (attrib)', *namï* 'this/that (non-attrib), it', *nïï* 'here/there [lat]', *nïmtï* 'here/there [loc]', *nïïnï* 'from here/there, afterwards', etc.).

Occasionally, first-person or second-person deixis is also expressed: *ilnam* 'this (of mine or near me, attrib)', *ilna* 'this (of yours or near you, attrib), Latin *iste*'.

Interrogative pronouns (which are also used as relative pronouns) include *qaj* 'what', *kutï* 'who', *qajiⁱʲ* 'what kind of', *kutiⁱʲ* 'whose', *qattıı-* 'to get to where?', *qatampï-* 'what? to happen', *qatamıı-* 'what? to have happened', *kučʲčʲä* 'where (lat)', *kun* 'where (loc)', *kuunï* 'from where', *kušʲšʲan* 'when'.

Negative pronouns are derived from interrogative ones with the prepositive particle *NʲI* or with the suffix -NƐJ: *nʲi qaj, qajnɛj* 'nothing', *nʲi kušʲšʲan* 'never' etc.

Indefinite pronouns are derived from interrogative ones with the particles *KOS* (pre- or postpositive), *ƐƐMÄ* (postpositive), *QAM$_2$* (postpositive). These particles render different shades of indefiniteness: *qaj kos, kos qaj* 'something', *qaj ɛɛmä* 'something, anything', *qaj qap* '(at least) something', etc.

The generic pronoun *mï* and its correlatives *miⁱʲ* (adjectival), *mi-* (verbal), *mik* (adverbial) function as surrogates, i.e. as universal indicators for the corresponding parts of speech. The pronoun *mï* occurs, for example, as a replacement for a missing or forgotten noun ('thingamy') and as a substantivizing element with adjectives and participles (*qëtpiⁱʲ mi* 'what is killed'). Its verbal correlate similarly replaces verbs in sentences such as *man mannï-mp-ap, tan ašʲšʲa mi-ŋ-al* PRO.s1 SEE-dur-s1obj PRO.s2 NEG DO-pres-s2obj 'I see it, you don't'.

Determinative pronouns include *muntik* 'all, entire(ly)' (functions as a substantive, or adjective, or adverb), *isï* 'every', *jarik* 'other'.

Pronoun-numerals belong to different morphosyntactic (adjectives, adverbs) and semantic (demonstrative, interrogative ...) categories: *našʲšʲaⁱʲ* 'so many', *našʲšʲak* 'so much', *kušʲšʲaⁱʲ* 'how many', *kušʲšʲak* 'how much', *kušʲšʲamtäliⁱʲ* 'which (in order), German *das wievielte*', etc.

Verbs

Category of aspect. Verbs in Selkup are perfective or imperfective (this distinction is more readily rendered in Russian: *laŋkalʲ-* 'крикнуть, 'to shout, to have shouted' : *laŋkiɣʲ-* 'кричать, 'to shout, to be shouting'. The same aspectual meaning is preserved throughout the paradigm of verbal forms derived from the same stem. In particular, it determines the temporal reference of the present tense (see below). On the formal plane, the paradigms of perfective verbs, as distinct from imperfective ones, lack present participles. Otherwise, perfective and imperfective verbs with primary (non-derived) stems do not differ formally, while verbal derivational suffixes usually render aspect unambiguously.

Categories of mood and tense. The system of moods includes:

Indicative (unmarked);

Inferential, or *latentive,* used for reporting events which the speaker did not witness directly (suffix *-NT-,* often in combination with the prepositive particle *NA*; the suffix surfaces as *-T-* after most consonantal stems and as zero after stems ending in *r*);

Auditive, used for reporting events which the speaker witnessed by hearing (suffix *-KUNÄ-*);

Conditional, used for indicating real conditions in present and future (suffix *-MMÄ-* after vocalic and *-MÄ-* after consonantal stems);

Subjunctive, used for indicating unreal conditions and consequences in the past (postpositive particle ƐNÄ, joined to slightly modified forms of the past indicative);

Debitive, used for qualifying future events as obligatory or enforced (suffix *-PSÅÅT-* after vocalic and *-SÅÅT-* after consonantal stems);

Optative, used for qualifying future events as desirable or appropriate (suffix *-LÄ-,* often in combination with the pre- or postpositive particle *SÄ*);

Imperative (with no special suffix, but with a set of finite suffixes for the second and third persons, which differ from the finite suffixes used in other moods).

Different *tenses* are distinguished only in the indicative (present, future, past, past narrative) and the inferential (present, future, past narrative).

The *present tense* renders the meaning of 'present perfect' with perfective verbs and that of 'present continuous' with imperfective ones: the verb *qo-* 'to find' is intrinsically (lexically) perfective, so *qoŋal* means 'you have found it (just now, and what has been found is at your disposal)' whereas the corresponding present-tense form of the intrinsically imperfective verb *pee-* 'to search for', *peeŋal*, means 'you are searching for it'. The present tense has no special suffix, but the finite suffixes in the present tense are separated from their stem with the elements (suffixes) *-N-* after consonantal stems and *-Nʲ-* after stems ending in non-reduced vowels (sometimes also after *i*-stems). The same elements occur also before the finite suffixes in the imperative.

The *future tense*, etymologically related to the non-perfective derivatives (see p. 573), has the suffixes or suffix clusters -*T*-, -*NT*-, -*ƐNT*-, -*TƐNT*- etc., depending on the phonetic structure of the stem to which it is attached. The suffix of the *past tense* is -*S*-, and that of the *past narrative tense* is -*MP*- after consonantal and -*P*- after vocalic stems. Tense suffixes always follow mood suffixes and precede finite ones; for further details see Tables 18.6–18.8.

Categories of person, number, and conjugation type. The finite suffixes indicate the person and number of the subject and form two (partly

Table 18.6   Verbal inflection: indicative, inferential (*qo*- 'to find, to see')

	Present	*Future*	*Past*	*(Past) Narrative*
Indicative				
s1	qoŋak	qontak	qoosak	qompak
s1obj	qoŋam	qontam	qoosam	qompam
s2	qoŋantï	qonnantï	qoosantï	qommantï
s2obj	qoŋal	qontal	qoosal	qompal
s3	qoŋa	qonta	qoosa	qompa
s3obj	qoŋïtï	qontïŋïtï	qoosïtï	qompatï
d1	qoŋïmɪɪ ~	qontïmɪɪ ~	qoosïmɪɪ ~	qompïmɪɪ ~
	qoŋɛj	qontɛj	qoosɛj	qompɛj
d2	qoŋïlɪɪ	qontïlɪɪ	qoosïlɪɪ	qompïlɪɪ
d3	qoŋååqɪ	qontååqɪ	qoosååqɪ	qompååqɪ
d3obj	qoŋïtɪɪ	qontïŋïtɪɪ	qoosïtɪɪ	qompatɪɪ
p1	qoŋïmït	qontïmït	qoosïmït	qompïmït
p2	qoŋïlït	qontïlït	qoosïlït	qompïlït
p3	qoŋååtït	qont-ååtït	qoosååtït	qompååtït
Inferential[1]				
s1	qontak	qonnïntak	—	qommïntak
s1obj	qontam	qonnïntakm	—	qommïntam
s2	qonnantï	qonnïnnantï	—	qommïntal
s2obj	qontal	qonnïntal	—	qommïnnantï
s3	qontï	qonnïntï	—	qommïntï
s3obj	qontïtï	qonnïntïtï	—	qommïntïtï
d1	qontïmɪɪ ~	qonnïntïmɪɪ ~	—	qommïntïmɪɪ ~
	qontɛj	qonnïntɛj		qommïntɛj
d2	qontïlɪɪ	qonnïntïlɪɪ	—	qommïntïlɪɪ
d3	qontååqɪ	qonnïntååqɪ	—	qommïntååqɪ
d3obj	qontïtɪɪ	qonnïntïtɪɪ	—	qommïntïtɪɪ
p1	qontïmït	qonnïntïmït	—	qommïntïmït
p2	qontïlït	qonnïntïlït	—	qommïntïlït
p3	qontååtït	qonnïntååtït	—	qommïntååtït

Note: 1 The inferential mood is often additionally marked with the prepositive particle *na*.

568   SELKUP

Table 18.7   Verbal inflection: auditive, conditional, subjunctive

	Auditive	Conditional	Subjunctive
s1	qokunäk	qommäk	qoosaŋ ɛnä
s1obj	qokunäm	qommäm	qoosam ɛnä
s2	qokunäntï	qommäntï	qoosant ɛnä
s2obj	qokunäl	qommä-l	qoosal ɛnä
s3	qokunä	qommä	qoosan ɛnä
s3obj	qokunätï	qommätï	qoosït ɛnä
d1	qokunämʊ	qommämʊ	qoosïmʊ ɛnä
	~ qokunɛj	~ qommɛj	~ qoosɛj ɛnä
d2	qokunälʊ	qommälʊ	qoosïlʊ ɛnä
d3	qokunääqɪ	qommääqɪ	qoosååqɪ ɛnä
d3obj	qokunätʊ	qommätʊ	qoosïtʊ ɛnä
p1	qokunämït	qommämït	qoosïmïn ɛnä
p2	qokunälït	qommälït	qoosïlïn ɛnä
p3	qokunäätït	qommäätït	qoosååtïn ɛnä

Table 18.8   Verbal inflection: debitive, optative, imperative

	Debitive	Optative [1]	Imperative
s1	qopsååtak	qoläk	—
s1obj	qopsååtam	qoläm	—
s2	qopsååtantï	qoläntï	qoŋäš(ïk) ~ qoŋïk
s2obj	qopsååtal	qoläl	qotï
s3	qopsååta	qolä	qoŋïjä
s3obj	qopsååtïtï	qolätï	qoŋimtïjä
d1	qopsååtïmʊ	qolämʊ	—
	~ qopsååtɛj	~ qolɛj	
d2	qopsååtïlʊ	qolälʊ	qoŋïlʊ
d3	qopsååtååqɪ	qolääqɪ	qoŋïjääqɪ
d3obj	qopsååtïtʊ	qolätʊ	qoŋimtïjääqɪ
p1	qopsååtïmït	qolämït	—
p2	qopsååtïlït	qolälït	qoŋït ~ qoŋïlït
p2obj	qopsååtïlït	qolälït	qoŋååtï ~ qoŋïlït
p3	qopsååtååtït	qoläätït	qoŋïjäätït
	qopsååtååtït	qoläätït	qoŋimtïjäätït

Note: 1 The optative mood is often additionally marked with the pre- or postpositive particle *sä*.

coinciding) series: the subjective and the objective conjugation. Intransitive verbs always take subjective suffixes, transitive verbs can take suffixes of either type (objective forms are used mainly if the sentence focus is the object,

Table 18.9   Verbal inflection, substantival representation: *nomen actionis* I[1]

	Nominative	Genitive	Translative	Locative
Non-possessive	qoptä	qoptän	qoptätqo	qoptääqïn
Possessive				
s1	qoptäm(ï)	qoptänï	qoptänoo(qo)	qoptääqäk
s2	qoptälï	qoptäntï	qoptäntoo(qo)	qoptääqäntï
s3	qoptätï	qoptäntï	qoptäntoo(qo)	qoptääqïntï
d1	qoptämɪɪ	qoptänɪɪ	qoptänɪɪqo	qoptääqïïnɪɪ
d2	qoptälɪɪ	qoptäntɪɪ	qoptäntɪɪqo	qoptääqïntɪɪ
d3	qoptätɪɪ	qoptäntɪɪ	qoptäntɪɪqo	qoptääqïntɪɪ
p1	qoptämït	qoptänït	qoptänïtqo	qoptääqïnït
p2	qoptälït	qoptäntït	qoptäntïtqo	qoptääqïntït
p3	qoptätït	qoptäntït	qoptäntïtqo	qoptääqïntït

Note: Only the commonly used case forms of *nomen actionis* are given here.

or in elliptical sentences with the object omitted). The suffixes of the subjective type (I) are similar to the predicative suffixes of nouns, those of the objective type (II) to the possessive suffixes of nouns:

	s1	s2	s3	d1	d2	d3	p1	p2	p3
I	$-(A)\eta_{2x}$	-(A)NTÏ	(-A)	-(ÅÅ)MII ~ ƐJ	-(ÅÅ)LII	-(ÅÅ)QI	-(ÅÅ)MÏT$_2$	-(ÅÅ)LÏT2	-(ÅÅ)TÏT$_2$
II	$-(A)M_2$	-(A)L	-(A)TÏ			-(AA)TII			

Special sets of both subjective and objective suffixes are used in the imperative; see Table 18.8.

Non-verbal Representations
As in the case of the finite verbal forms, the substantival forms of verbs distinguish the person and number of the subject with the help of suffixes which are formally similar to the possessive suffixes of nouns. This is so in the case of *nomina actionis* I (suffix *-PTÄ* after vocalic stems, *-TÄ* after most consonantal stems, *-Ä* after *r*-stems) and II (suffix *-KU*; the two *nomina actionis* occur in different constructions), and in the case of the infinitive (suffix *-QO*, in possessive forms *-QÏ . . . QO*).

The adjectival representation of verbs comprises five participles: present (suffix *-TÏL^J* or *-NTÏL^J*), past (*-PÏL^J* or *-MPÏL^J*), debitive *(-PSÅÅTÏL^J* after vocalic and *-SÅÅTÏL^J* after consonantal stems), destinative (denotes the destination of an object for a certain action; suffix *-PSO* after vocalic and *-SO* after consonantal stems), caritive (denotes non-realized action; suffix *-KUN^{J}Č^{J}ÏTÏL^J*). Participles of transitive verbs render, depending on the

Table 18.10   Verbal inflection, substantival representation: *nomen actionis* II[1], infinitive

	Nomen actionis II Genitive	Co-ordinative	Infinitive
Non-possessive	qokun	quokuš^jš^jak	qoqo
Possessive			
s1	qokunï	qokunïš^jak	qoqïnoo(qo)
s2, s3	qokuntï	qokuntïš^jak	qoqïntoo(qo)
d1	qokunп	qokunпš^jak	qoqïnпqo
d2, d3	qokuntп	qokuntпš^jak	qoqïntпqo
p1	qokunït	qokunïš^jš^jak	qoqïnïtqo
p2, p3	qokuntït	qokuntïš^jš^jak	qoqïntïtqo

Note: Only those case forms of the *nomina actionis* which are commonly used are indicated here. Potentially the paradigms of *nomina actionis* contain other forms, as well.

Adjectival representation is as follows:

Present participle	(*peentiɬ^j*, from *pee-* 'to search for')	(Perfective verbs [*qo-* among them] do not form present participles.)
Past participle	qopïɬ^j ~ qompïɬ^j	
Debitive participle	qopsåått^j	
Destinative participle	qopso	
Caritive participle	qokun^jč^jïtï^j	

Adverbial representation is as follows:

Present verbal adverb	qolä
Past verbal adverb	qolä puulä
Caritive verbal adverb	qokun^jč^jåålïk

constructions in which they are used, both active and passive meanings: *qorqï-m qo-piɬ^j ima* BEAR-acc FIND-past.part WOMAN 'the woman who found the bear', *qorqï-n qo-piɬ^j ima* BEAR-gen FIND-past.part WOMAN 'the woman who was found by the bear'.

The present verbal adverb (suffix *-LÄ*), like the present tense, denotes a simultaneous action with imperfective verbs and a directly preceding action with perfective verbs. When supplemented with the particle *PUULÄ*, it serves as the preterite verbal adverb and denotes a previous action.

While the verbal system principally and in most details is the same throughout the Selkup language territory, there are numerous dialectal peculiarities in the formation and usage of non-verbal representations. In particular, at least some Southern Selkup dialects use the pure verbal stem (which for Northern Selkup is a mere abstraction) as a verbal adverb in verbal compounds (see Helimski 1983: 46).

Adverbs and Syntactic Words
While many adverbial forms with qualitative meanings belong in Selkup to the paradigms of substantives and adjectives, the class of adverbs, which comprises indeclinable forms that serve as attributes of adjectives and verbs (*orsä* 'very, very much', *kënpïlä* 'quickly') or as modifiers of whole sentences (*qååtï* 'maybe, perhaps', *ïïrïk* 'still'), is frequently formally intermingled with classes of syntactic words.

Some local adverbs, especially (il)lative adverbs in -*Ä*, are employed also as *preverbs*, i.e. prepositive particles in phrasal verbs, e.g. *ıllä* 'down' in *ıllä mee-* 'to bury' (lit. 'to make down'). Preverbs can be separated from their main verbs by pronominal objects, negative and other grammatical particles, and in imperatives they are placed after the main verbs: *ıllä š^jintï meeläk* 'I will bury you', *meeŋimtïjä ıllä* 'let him bury'. An example of a non-adverbial preverb is *ļʲam* 'one another, each other': *ļʲam ora-* 'to wrestle', cf. *ora-* 'to seize, to catch'.

About twenty nominal stems, some of them bound, are employed in four local cases (illative, locative, elative, prolative) as local/temporal adverbs and postpositions, cf. the theme *ïl-* in *ïlqin* 'below', *poo-n ïlqin* 'under the tree', *ïlqïnï* 'from below', *poo-n ïlqïnï* 'from under the tree', etc. Like other nominals, such postpositions also have possessive forms, which are used with personal pronouns: *man ïl-qä-k* PRO.s1 UNDER-loc/ill/ela-s1 '(to) under me, from under me'. In addition, there are many non-adverbial (non-nominal) and indeclinable postpositions, e.g. *tarä* 'like, as', *č^jååtï* 'for, about'. Most postpositions occur with the genitive case of the preceding noun, cf. *-n* in *poo-n ïlqin* 'under the tree', cited above.

Derivation

Denominal Derivatives
The most productive – or, in some cases, maximally productive within a closed semantic group – patterns of denominal derivatives in Selkup and their suffixes are as follows:

1 Nouns:
  Diminutive nouns (=*L^JA*, joined mainly to the second stem): *iija=ļʲa* 'baby' (*iija* 'child'), *mååtï=ļʲa* 'little house' (*mååt₂* 'house'); diminutives are also derived with several other, less productive or non-productive, suffixes (usually containing the consonant *K*);
  Singulative nouns (=*LAKA*, lit. 'piece, lump'; for round objects =*SAJÏ*, lit. 'eye'; for oblong objects =*QU*, lit. 'stalk'; all these formations are derived mainly from adjectival forms of substantives and can be treated as compounds rather than suffixal derivatives): *ulqa-l=laka* 'ice-floe' (*ulqa* 'ice'), *ütï-ļʲ=sajï* 'drop' and *ütï-ļʲ=qu* 'jet of water' (*üt* 'water');
  Associative (connective/reciprocal) nouns, with the meaning 'X plus the

person(s) for whom he or she is X', where X is the base of derivation
(=SΪ, followed by dual or plural suffixes): *ima=sï-qääqı* 'married couple'
(*ima* 'woman, wife'), *ësï=sï-t* 'father with his children' (*ësï* 'father'). The
bases of derivation are mostly kinship terms;

Instructive nouns, with the meaning 'person who has X' (=SΪMA):
moolmï=sïma 'liar' (*moolmï* 'lie, deception');

Caritive nouns, with the meaning 'person who lacks X (=KΪTA):
ëëtï=kïta 'dumb person' (*ëëtï* 'word, language').

2   Adjectives:

Instructive adjectives, with the meaning 'having X' (=SΪMΪL^J): *tɛni=si-mïl^j* 'clever' (*tɛnï* 'mind, intellect');

Caritive adjectives with the meaning 'lacking X' (=KΪTΪL^J): *sajï=kïtïl^j*
'blind' (*sajï* 'eye');

Destinative adjectives (=TΪL^J): *pič^{j}ï=tïl^j* 'for making an axe' (*pič^{j}ï*
'axe').

3   Verbs:

Verbs with the basic (but not the only) meaning 'to become X' (=N^a or
=M-, added to the second stem; also used with adjectives): *åålïŋ-*
'becomes weak' (*åålï* 'weak'), *ira=m-* 'gets old (of males)' (*ira* 'old
man');

Verbs with the basic meaning 'to transform something into X' (=MTΪ-,
added to the second stem; also used with adjectives): *ååli=mtï-* 'makes
weak', * påårï=mtï-* 'arranges a feast' (*påårï* 'feast');

Verbs with the basic meaning 'to do/make with X' (=T- or =TTΪ-:
č^{j}mï=t- 'glues' (*č^{j}mï* 'glue'), *kekkï=ttï-* 'suffers' (*kekkï* 'trouble, tor-
ment');

Verbs with the meaning 'to search/hunt for X' ('captitives', =Š^J-, added
to the second stem): *qorqï=š^j-* 'hunts bear' (*qorqï* 'bear');

Verbs with the meaning 'to lose X' (=KΪLΪM-): *sajï=kïlïm-* 'loses one's
sight, goes blind' (*sajï* 'eye');

Verbs with the meaning 'to deprive of X' (=KΪLTΪ-): *olïkïltï-* 'beheads'
(*olï* 'head');

Verbs with the meaning 'to smell of X' ('olefactives', =N^{J}Ϊ, added to the
second stem): *kana=n^{j}i-* 'to smell of dog(s)' (*kanaŋ* 'dog').

4   Adverbs:

Instrumental adverbs (=N$_2$, added to the second stem; of limited
productivity): *topi=n* 'by foot' (*topï* 'foot'), *qëqqï=n* 'at a walk' (*qëqqï*
'step').

Deadjectival Derivatives

Beside the deadjectival verbs mentioned above, the derivatives with restrictive meaning are very productive, both adverbs (suffix =LÅÅQΪ) and
adjectives (=LÅÅQΪ=L^J): *soma=lååqï* 'rather well', *soma=lååqï=l^j* 'rather
good' (*soma* 'good'). Occasionally these suffixes are joined to adverbs and

even to verbal adverbs, as well: *ira=m-lä=låàqï* 'getting a little older' (*ira=m-lä* 'getting older', *ira=m-* 'gets older').

Intransitive and Transitive, Causative, Reflexive Verbs

The valence (+/– transitivity) in primary verb roots is unmarked, and occasionally the same verb can be used both as intransitive and as transitive: *iïtï-* 'is suspended; hangs (tr)'. In derived verbs, however, the derivational suffixes usually render unambiguously, often together with other grammatical meanings, the meanings of intransitivity or transitivity. There are several types of correlative derivatives. For example, intransitive perfective verbs built with the suffix =MÅÅT- systematically correlate with transitive perfective verbs built with the suffix =ALTÏ-: *n^jen^jn^jïmååt-* 'gets angry' : *n^jen^jn^jalti-* 'makes X angry', *tarqïmååt-* 'shakes (intr)' : *tarqalti-* 'shakes (tr)'. Many borrowed roots add =TTÏ- to form intransitive imperfective verbs, and add =N- to form transitive perfectives: *uč^jïtti-* 'studies, learns' : *uč^jïŋ-* 'teaches' (Russian учи/, ть, -ться).

The *causative* (curative) suffix clusters (=RALTÏ-, =TALTÏ-, =L^JL^JALTÏ-, =ALLALTÏ-) can be joined to most verb roots and to many derived verb stems. The causative verbs indicate that their subject (the causator, in the nominative) does not coincide with the subject of the action itself (the performer, usually in the dative/allative): *mat tïmn^ja-nï-nïk na alako-m iïtï=ralti-s-am on-äk č^jååti* PRO.s1 BROTHER-s1-dat/all THIS BOAT-acc TAKE=caus-past-s1obj SELF-s1gen FOR 'I made my brother take this boat for me'.

The *reflexive* verbs are derived from transitive (sometimes also from intransitive) verb stems with the suffixes =Ï-, =Č^JÏ- or (with additional intensive/perfective meaning) =Il-, =IL^JČ^JÏ-: *panal-ï-* 'breaks [intr]' (*panal-* 'breaks [tr]'), *tott=ïl^jč^jï-* 'brings self to vertical position' (*totti-* 'stands'). Many reflexive verbs with the same suffixes are derived directly from bound roots. There are certain peculiarities in the conjugation of reflexive verbs, cf. *ilï-s-a* '(he) lived', but *panal=ï-s-Ø* '(he) broke [intr]'.

Mode of Action (Aktionsart)

The most productive modes of action and their suffixes are as follows:

Iterative (imperfective verbs; =kïl^jol^jpï-, with numerous variants): *č^jatti=kïl^jol^jpï-* 'throws many times, repeatedly' (*č^jatti-* 'throws');

Habitual, often used in gnomic sentences (imperfective verbs; =KKÏ- after vocalic and =KÏ- after consonantal stems): *č^jatti=kki-* 'throws usually';

Durative (imperfective verbs; =MPÏ- after vocalic and =PÏ- after consonantal stems): *č^jatti=mpi-* 'is throwing'. With their logical object treated as syntactic subject, the durative derivatives of transitive verbs acquire (in the subjective conjugation) a passive meaning: *pü č^jatti=mp-a* 'the stone is thrown';

Non-perfective, denoting that an action remains unfinished (imperfective verbs; =TÏ-, =NTÏ-, =ƐNTÏ-, =TƐNTÏ-, etc., depending on the phonetic structure of the base stem): *čʲatt=εntï-* 'makes an attempt at throwing, is in act of throwing without finishing the movement'. The future tense of verbs is related to the non-perfective mode of action, but in modern Selkup the two forms are independent, as is proven by the existence of the future tense of non-perfective verbs: *čʲatt=εnn-εnt-a-m* 'I will make an attempt at throwing';

Intensive/perfective (perfective verbs; =*LʲČʲÏ-*, =*ΕΕ*, =*ΕLʲČʲÏ-*, =*II*, =*ILʲČʲÏ-*, depending on both phonetic and morphological factors): *čʲatt=εε-* 'has already thrown with an intensive effort';

Multiobjectival, denoting that an action is applied to many objects or to different parts of a single object (perfective or imperfective verbs, derived only from transitive bases; =*QÏL-* or =*QÏLÅÅL-*, =*ÄL-* or =*ÄLÅÅL-*, =*L-* or =*LÅÅL-*, depending on the phonetic structure of the base stem): *čʲatt=äl(åål)-* 'throws many things';

Multisubjectival, denoting that an action is performed simultaneously by a multitude of homogeneous subjects (perfective or imperfective verbs, derived only from intransitive bases; the same suffixes as from multi-objectival verbs, followed by the reflexive suffix =*Ï-*, then followed by the durative suffix =*MPÏ-* or an intensive/perfective suffix): *åålʲčʲ=äli=mpï-* 'falls in large quantities (e.g. of leaves in autumn)' (*åålʲčʲï-* 'falls');

Inchoative (perfective verbs, derived from imperfective bases; =*ALʲ-*, =*ÄLÏ-* and several other suffixes): *qüüt=äli-* 'falls ill' (*qüütï-* 'is ill');

Attenuative (mainly perfective verbs; =*ΕČʲÏ-* in intransitive and =*ÄPTÏ-* in transitive verbs): *qant=εčʲi-* 'gets slightly frozen' (*qantï-* 'becomes frozen'), *čʲatt=äptï-* 'throws slightly, to not far away'.

In many instances these suffixes are joined to themes, rather than existing verbs. The suffixes, and meanings, of different modes of action can be combined in clusters, as in *čʲatt=ält=tεntï=kiĺʲoĺʲpï-* THROW=multiobj=non-perf=iter 'makes numerous attempts at throwing many things'.

Other Deverbal Derivatives

There are several suffixes for forming deverbal nouns, for example, =*SAN₃* for *nomina instrumenti* (*mir=san* 'carpenter's plane' from *miir-* 'planes') or =*MO* for *nomina loci* (*minïr=mo* 'hunting area' *minïr-* 'hunts'), but none of them is productive in present-day Selkup. On the other hand, the combinations of participles with *qum* 'person' for *nomina agentis* (*suuričʲčʲiĺʲ qum* 'hunter') and with the generic pronoun *mï* for *nomina acti* (*tεεpiĺʲ mï* 'rot, rotten scrap') occur very frequently and transfunctionally approach suffixal derivatives.

The derivation of adjectives and adverbs from verbs, as well as any derivational processes with adverbs or syntactic words as their base, are only sporadic phenomena in Selkup.

Syntax

Noun Phrase

Within the noun phrase attributes (adjectives, numerals, pronoun-adjectives, subordinate nouns in the genitive, appositive nouns in the nominative, etc.) normally precede the head noun. Occasionally, however, attributes that have subordinate words of their own (participles and some other types of adjectival words) are placed postpositively: *tan wërqï tɨmnʲa-l, šʲittï poo-t kuntï čʲääŋŋï=mpï-tïlʲ, moqïnä tü-ŋ-a* PRO.s2 BIG BROTHER-s2 TWO YEAR-gen DURING BE.ABSENT-pres.part BACK COME-pres-s3 'your elder brother, who was absent for two years, has come home'. The names of units of measurement are treated as attributes to the names of substances, and placed prepositively: *počʲka üt* 'a cask of water', *počʲka ütï-m ii-s-ap* CASK WATER-acc TAKE-past-s1obj 'I took a cask of water'.

There is no agreement between adjectives (and other attributes) and head nouns. Normally there is also no agreement in number with attributive numerals: *ukkïr qum* 'one person', *šʲittï qum* 'two persons' (but also *šʲittï qumooqɪ*, in dual), *nååkïr qum* 'three persons'.

The link between possessor and possessed is expressed either by placing the possessor in the genitive prepositively or by attaching a possessive suffix to the possessed. The use of both markers within the same noun phrase occurs in non-Northern Selkup dialects, especially when the possessed is a term of kinship: (Lower Chaya) *era-n ii-dǝ* OLD.MAN-gen SON-s3 'the old man's son'.

Verb Complex

Within the verb complex, inflected verbal auxiliaries are normally placed postpositively. This statement holds for both compound predicates with substantival, adjectival, or adverbial first components (*ütqïn εεŋa* 'is in water', *sääq εsimpa* 'became black', *čʲasïq εεŋa* 'it is cold'; cf. also *puu-t čʲååtï εε-tïlʲ* AFTERWARDS-gen FOR BE-pres.part 'left for later need', and *puu-t čʲååtï εε-lä* AFTERWARDS-gen FOR IS-verb.adv 'for later need', and for numerous verbal analytic constructions with 'non-finite' first components (*quntïlä orïnʲnʲa* 'is dying', *ilïqo olapsak* 'I began to live', *qënqo εεŋa* 'it is necessary to go', *ütïr-qo εsïmp-ak* DRINK-inf BECOME-s1 'I am thirsty', etc.).

The same order of constituents also occurs in negative constructions with verbal nouns (*nomina actionis* I), where the conjugated component is actually the verbal noun with its possessive suffixes: *qo-ptä-mï čʲääŋk-a* FIND-verb.noun-s1 BE.ABSENT-s3 'I did not find', *qo-ptä-lï čʲääŋk-a* FIND-verb.noun-s2 BE.ABSENT-s3 'you did not find'. Such constructions are used when reporting real events in the past. In other situations the negation is expressed by the preverbal particles *ikï* (with optative and imperative forms) and *ašʲšʲa* (with forms of other moods); there is no negative verb in Selkup.

In interrogative sentences the verb often has the form of the inferential mood. With the prepositive unstressed particle *qaj* (cf. *qaj* 'what', which normally has sentence stress) the verb complex expresses general questions: *tëp koptooqïn qaj ippïntï* 'is it true that (s)he lies in bed? (cf. *koptooqïn qaj ippïntï* 'what lies in bed?', with a focal, sentence stress on *qaj*).

Simple Sentence

In syntactic terms, the dominant word order in Selkup is SOV. But as long as, in terms of discourse relations, the topic is placed sentence-initially and the focus is placed directly before the verb, other types of word order can also occur: OSV (with topicalization of the direct object), SVO (with the subject focalized). Typically, interrogative words (as subjects, objects, or circum-stantial modifiers in interrogative sentences) directly precede sentence predicates.

The case of the sentence subject is nominative, but genitive in construc-tions with non-verbal representations of verbs (see examples in the next section).

The choice of the case of the direct object depends on several morpho-syntactic factors. We may say with some simplification that the direct object is (1a) always in the nominative, if the verb is an imperative, and (1b) predominantly in the nominative, if the object is indefinite; but (2a) predominantly in the accusative, if the object is definite, and (2b) always in the accusative, if the object is a personal pronoun.

As mentioned on pp. 568–9, a significant role in shaping the topic/focus structure of the simple sentence is also played by the conjugation type (objective or subjective) of transitive verbs.

Sentence Combining

Typically in Selkup the co-ordination or subordination of sentences is achieved by parataxis, without conjunctions, but sometimes with the correl-ative use of verbal moods: *ima-tï moqïnä qal-a, ira-tï karrä qënn-ɛɛ-ja* OLD.WOMAN-s3 BACK REMAIN-s3 OLD.MAN-s3 TOWARDS.RIVER GO-perf.intensive-s3 'his (=the) wife remained at home, her (= the) husband went down to the water'; *apstäti, apsal ɛɛmmä* 'feed him, if you have food' (lit. '... your food is [conditional mood]'). Subordinating and co-ordinating conjunctions are partly borrowed from Russian, but partly result from secondary functions of native words (e.g., from employing interrogative pronouns in the role of relative ones); they occur in the present-day colloquial language more often than in traditional folklore texts, and still more often in non-Northern Selkup dialects, so sentence-combining by means of conjunc-tions must be attributed mainly to the influence of the Russian language.

Another method of sentence-combining consists in transforming the finite verb in the subordinate clause into a form of non-verbal representation: *qumïtït kït qantï tüptääqïn čʲasïq ɛsikka* 'when the people were approaching the river, it was getting cold', lit. 'people (pG) river to-bank in-coming (*nomen actionis* I) cold becomes-usually'; *tan n^jen^jn^jantï š^jütpïl^j porqal tokkaltätï* 'put on the fur-coat sewn by your sister', lit. 'you your-sister (sG) sewn your-fur-coat put-on'; *mat kuttar ilɛntak äsänï š^jıp pɛltïkun^jč^jåålïk?* 'how can I live without father's help?', lit. 'I how will-live my-father (sA) me (sG) not-helping (ger)'.

Lexicon

The canonic shape of primary (non-derived) stems is (C)V(C) for mono-syllabics and (C)VC(C)V(C) for bisyllabics, with the structures (C)VC(C)VC occurring in nominal, but not in verbal primary stems. There are no stem-initial or stem-final clusters, and all other phonotactic restrictions mentioned above (see Distribution of Phonemes, p. 554) are strictly observed. Deviations from this canonic shape are frequent in interjections and other affective words (*ksa* 'come on!', *aa?* 'yeah', *kïpïl^joo.oo* 'very-very little'), but they virtually never penetrate into non-affective lexical domains. Such deviations occur, however, in some recent Russian loans, such as *stado* 'herd' or *metr* 'meter', though there usually are (unless the word is a nonce-usage) parallel adapted forms (*istatï, metra*).

The older strata of borrowings in the lexicon of Selkup include:

Turkic loans, which are especially numerous in Southern and Ket' Selkup, but more than a dozen of which occur in Northern Selkup: *mååtïr* 'warrior, hero', *sïïrï* 'cow', *č^jåårïk* 'bifurcation, tributary', etc. This topic receives monographic treatment in Filippova (1991);

Ostyak loans, more typical of Central and Northern Selkup: *purqï* 'smoke', *kuras* 'view, exterior', *nurïk* 'straight', etc. (see Rédei 1972, and Uralic and Ostyak etymological dictionaries).

Several words of *Zyrian* origin must have reached Selkup by way of Ostyak: *n^jän^j* 'bread', *ruš^j* 'Russian [noun]', *mojtak ~ mon^jč^jak* 'soap'.

Ket (and other Yeniseic) loans. It is often difficult to distinguish these from Selkup loans in Ket: *kupak* 'fist', *qëq* 'pine forest', etc. (see Helimski 1982, with further bibliography).

Tungusic (Evenki) loans, more typical of Northern and Ket' Selkup: *ol^jqan* 'small wooded areas in tundra', *č^jååwïrï-* 'to step aside', *kuja* 'birch-bark box for beating down and gathering berries', etc. (see e.g. Helimski 1985b).

Early *Russian* loans, beginning in the sixteenth century: *qam* 'linen' (Old Russian хамъ), *sïpïn^jč^ja* 'pig', *sååqïr* 'sugar', etc.

There are also sporadic borrowings from Mansi (? *š^jäq* 'salt'), Mongolic (*torqï* 'receptacle'), Nenets (*waŋkïta* 'barren reindeer cow'), Enets (*Rååtta*, a place-name), as well as numerous words of unknown, possibly substrate, origin.

No systematic efforts to develop the vocabulary of Selkup by coining new terms for culture and technology have ever been made, and the speakers of Selkup apparently prefer direct borrowings from Russian to descriptive coinages.

Text

A: phonemic transcription, segmental; B: morpheme-by-morpheme gloss; C: free translation.

infrntl = inferential; inf = infinitive; vidv = derivational suffix making intransitive verbs from verbs; lat.adv = lative adverb; dn = denominal; dec = decade.

A1 nʲoma-łʲ   porqï   ira   karr=ä   na
B1 HARE-adj COAT OLD.MAN DOWN.TO.WATER=lat.adv infrntl

paɪ=šʲ-mï-nt-ï   kɪnʲnʲï-m-tï   mannï=mpï-qï-ntoo-qo.
COME.DOWN=vidv-narr-   FISHWEIR-acc-s3   LOOK=dur-inf-s3-inf
infrntl-s3

A2 na   čʲasïq-ïłʲ   čʲeelï-tï   na   εε-ppï-nt-ï.
B2 THIS COLD-adj   DAY-s3   infrntl BE-narr-infrntl-s3

A3 qo-ŋ-ïtï   takki=t   qoltï-t
B3 SEE-pres-s3obj NORTH/DOWNSTREAM=loc.adv   RIVER-gen

čʲiipï-qït purqï-sä   tååt-ïk   čʲiqqï=måått=εε-mp-a.
END-loc SMOKE-ins DIRECT-adv SMOKE=vidv=int-narr-s3

A4 seepï=la-k   ira   mannï=mpï-lä   tattï=raltï-mp-atï.
B4 ENOUGH=   OLD.MAN LOOKS=dur-   BRING=caus-
   dn-adv   verb adv   narr-s3obj

A5 na   qaj   nas=sar-ïłʲ   qälï-łʲ   mütï   tü-ŋ-ååtït.
B5 THIS WHAT THREE=dec-   NENETS- TROOP COME-pres-p3
                  adj   adj

C1 Old Hare Coat came down to the river to check his fishweir. C2 It was a cold day. C3 He saw that downstream, at the end of the (visible part of the) river, there was directly rising steam (from the mouths of reindeer). C4 The old man looked long enough to let (the newcomers) approach him. C5 That's it: thirty Nenets warriors have come.

References and Further Reading

Becker, E.G. (1978) Категория падежа в селькупском языке, Tomsk: Tomsk University Press.

Erdélyi, I. (1969) *Selkupisches Wörterverzeichnis (Tas-Dialekt)*, Budapest: Akadémiai kiadó.

Filippova, T.M. (1991) 'Тюркские заимствования в селькупском языке', Novosibirsk: unpublished manuscript (dissertation).

Helimski, E.A. (1982) 'Keto-Uralica', in E.A. Alekseenko et al. (eds), Кетский Сборник, Leningrad: Nauka, pp. 238–50.

—— (1983) *The Language of the First Selkup Books*, Szeged: József Attila University.

—— (1985a) 'К исторической диалектологии селькупского языка', in Лексика и грамматика языков Сибири, Barnaul: Altai University Press, pp. 42–58.

—— (1985b) 'Самодийско-тунгусские лексические связи и их этноисторические импликации', in Урало-алтаистика: Археология, этнография, язык, Novosibirsk: Nauka, pp. 206–13.

Irikov, S.V. (1988) Словарь селькупско-русский и русско-селькупский, Leningrad: Prosveščenie.

Janurik, T. (1978) 'A szölkup nyelvjárások osztályozása', Nyelvtudományi Közlemények 76/1: 77–104.

Katz, H. (1975–88) *Selcupica*, vols. I–IV, Munich: Finnisch-Ugrisches Seminar der Universität München.

—— (1979) *Selkupische Quellen: Ein Lesebuch*, Vienna: Verband der wissenschaftlichen Gesellschaften Österreichs.

Kazakevič, O.A. (1990) Использование ЭВМ для исследования бесписьменных и младописьменных языков (На материале селькупского языка), Moscow: University of Moscow Press.

Kuz'mina, A.I. (1974) Грамматика селькупского языка, pt. I, Novosibirsk: Novosibirsk University Press.

Kuznecova, A.I., Helimski, E.A. and Gruškina, E.V. (1980) Очерки по селькупскому языку: Тазовский диалект, pt. I, Moscow: Moscow University Press.

Kuznecova, A.I., Kazakevič, O.A., Ioffe, L. Ju., and Helimski, E.A. (1993) Очерки по селькупскому языку: Тазовский диалект, pt II, Moscow: Moscow University Press.

Prokof'ev, G.N. (1935) Селькупская (остяко-самоедская) грамматика, Leningrad: Izdatel'jstvo Instituta Narodov Severa CIK SSSR.

Pusztay, J. (1992) 'Lesz-e szölkup újjászületés?', in *Festschrift für Károly Rédei*, in P. Deréky et al. (eds), Vienna – Institut für Finno-Ugristik der Universität Wien – MTA Nyelvtudományi Intézet, pp. 367–70.

Rédei, K. (1972) 'Ostzják jövevényszavak a szelkupban', *Nyelvtudományi Közlemények* 74: 186–93.

19 Kamassian

Péter Simoncsics

Although Kamassian is no longer used – the last speaker, Klavdija Plotnikova, died on 20 September 1989 – it is perhaps one of the best documented among the Samoyedic languages thanks to the endeavours, perseverance, and hard work of its collectors: Mathias Alexander Castrén (1813–52) first of all, then Kai Donner and his meticulous editor, Aulis Joki (1888–1935), and last, but not least, Ago Künnap.

Kamassian, together with several other cognate and non-cognate languages of Russia, hove into the view of students of language in the eighteenth century when mapping and assessing this vast Eurasiatic empire became technically possible, economically necessary, and culturally desirable. The travellers, discoverers and, scholars who collected and/or published Kamassian material, most of them Russian subjects, are the following: G.F. Müller (1735), F. Adelung (1735), Johann Eberhard Fischer (1739–47), P.S. Pallas (1772/1776/1786–89, 1811), and J. von Klaproth (1823).

A Finn, Mathias Alexander Castrén, the founder of Samoyedology, made his records of Kamassian material (some 870 words) in November 1847. The bulk of his œuvre was published posthumously, by Anton Schiefner, in 1855.

On two occasions another Finnish scholar, Kai Donner, visited Abalakovo, a village north of the Sayan Mountains where Kamassian speakers lived. The first visit was in 1911; the second, longer, visit was in the summer of 1914, when he stayed for almost two months. Donner collected some 1,550 lexical items as well as texts. His collection was also published posthumously, by Aulis Joki, in 1944.

In 1926 a Russian scholar, A.J. Tugarinov, recorded and published some thirty Kamassian words in an article entitled 'Последние калмажи', i.e. 'The last Kamassians' (in Северная Азия 1926: 1:73–8).

It was only thirty-seven years later, in 1963, on a toponomastic expedition arranged by the Uralic State University in Sverdlovsk (formerly, and now once again, Ekaterinburg), that it became apparent that the Kamassian death notice had been premature: there were two elderly ladies still living who used Kamassian.

From 1964 to 1970 the Estonian scholar Ago Künnap worked with these last two speakers of Kamassian, Alexandra Žibjeva (born in the 1880s or 1890s) and Klavdja Plotnikova (born as Andžigatova in 1895), and was able to collect precious and linguistically unique material.

In the early 1950s two exemplary studies were published on Kamassian versification by J. Lotz, an American linguist of Hungarian origin.

There are sound recordings of Kamassian dating from the beginning of the twentieth century (Donner used the phonograph). The Uralic University expedition and Künnap both carried out extensive tape-recording during the 1960s.

Among the South Samoyedic or Sayan Samoyedic languages Kamassian seems to be more closely affiliated to Koibal than to the linguistic complex known as Mator-Taigi-Karagass-Soyot. All of these languages/dialects died out *ante* Kamassian, probably in the nineteenth century or even earlier.

The ethnonym Kamassian may well go back to a compound, *kama(?) + as* 'mountain + Az [an ancient Siberian ethnonym])'. Such a compound would fit in well with neighbouring ethnonyms such as Karagass (? *kara + as* 'black Az') and Hakass (*hak + as* 'white Az'). In another, equally justifiable interpretation the ethnonym Karagass comes from *kara + kaš* 'black Kaš', the latter member of the compound being another Siberian ethnonym meaning 'Tatar from the region of Minusinsk; Kača-Tatar' and deriving, perhaps, from a proto-Samoyedic word meaning 'human being, man' (Hajdú 1950: 95–6). Both of these interpretations receive some support from a third ethnonym of the area, *Kyzyl* (Turkic 'red'), which forms – together with the other two ethnonyms which contain colour terms – a tricolour of 'black–white–red'. Yet another interpretation is possible, one which derives the *kara* of Karagass not from Turkic *kara* 'black' but from another Kamassian stem (also of Turkic origin), namely *kara? ~ karad* 'steppe'. We would then have a correlative pair, Kamass/ Karagass 'mountain Az [people]/steppe Az [people]', cf. the entry *kardəj* in Donner's dictionary: 'Tatar in the village of Ugumakova; these people earlier lived in the steppe, as opposed to the Kamass, who lived in the taiga and in the mountains' (see also Joki 1952: 163). The etymon 'mountain people' may be echoed in the Latin term *Monticolae Sajanenses* of P.S. Pallas, one of the earliest references to this population (possibly dating from 1735). Spontaneous mixing of explanations and etymologies cannot be excluded either. Alongside an ethnic triad (perhaps Samoyeds–Tatars–Mongols), the tricolour white– black–red may well refer to the habitat of these speakers and cover a trio of topographic descriptors (snow-clad mountains, barren steppe, red-sand desert).

In the following pages a somewhat speculative description of the language as if it were still alive is attempted. The categories are traditional (phonology, morphology, syntax, stylistics), but the emphasis is on processes categorized as morphophonology.

Phonology

In its final phase Kamassian had nine vowels, eight full and one reduced. The reduced vowel ə seems to have alternated mostly with [+ high] vowels, and

Reduced		ə	

	high	i	ü	u
Full	mid	e	ö	o
	low	ä		a

was in all likelihood originally only a combinatory variant of these, even in
the middle of the nineteenth century: Castrén counted only eight vowels. In
sum, the phonemicization of ə is a recent process.

The alternation of ə with high vowels is certainly not independent of the
general reduction of the short, unstressed, high vowels of Hakassian, a
neighbouring Turkic language which influenced Kammassian and to which
most speakers of Kamassian finally switched.

Donner's data show that the full, back, low vowel a is more often than not
rounded [å].

Since vowel harmony dominates the language it seems unnecessary to
reckon with pairs such as i ~ ï, e ~ ë, and ə ~ ə̂. It is sufficient to consider the three
phonemes i, e, and ə as neutral with respect to vowel harmony (see below).

With respect to quantitative oppositions, in addition to the opposition
FULL : REDUCED mentioned above there is also a tendency for stem-final
syllables to be lengthened, e.g. bəraa-n 'sack (dative), amnoo-bi '[(s)he]
lived'. This non-phonological phenomenon is due to the influence of
neighbouring Turkic idioms.

Vowel Harmony

We may distinguish two types: tonal and serial. *Tonal* vowel harmony is based
upon the opposition of front and back vowels. In Kamassian the vowels fall
into three tonal-harmonic categories, back (u o a), front (ü ö ä), and neutral
(i e ə). The domain in which tonal vowel harmony operates is the non-
compound word (a stem followed by one or more suffixes, including zero).
Within this domain, back vowels co-occur only with back vowels, and front
vowels only with front, while neutral vowels co-occur with either as well as
with themselves. A neutral vowel has no intrinsic phonological value unless
it occurs in the company of another neutral vowel, when together they count
as front. Otherwise, neutral vowels obtain their value from the vocalism
occurring in the same domain. The following examples illustrate some of this
by means of suffixal allomorphy:

	Bisyllabic stem	Plural suffix allomorph	Tonal domain	Example
1	back + back	back	back	*tura-zaŋ* 'houses'
2	front + front	front	front	*üžü-zäŋ* 'caps'
3	back + neutral	back	back	*kaləš-(z)aŋ* 'swords'
4	neutral + front	front	front	*sirä-zäŋ* 'snows'

Neutral vowels occurring alone usually make front-tonal words:

5   neutral + neutral   front   front   *nere-ᵖä-m* 'I am
                                                                frightened'

Serial vowel harmony is doubtless due to Turkic influence. Its effects are more limited than those of tonal vowel harmony, in that it affects only the syllables occurring in certain subcategories of stem-suffix sandhi: serial harmony determines the [+/-] labial feature of these vowels in the singular non-third-person forms of the possessive paradigms of nouns.

Table 19.1   Serial vowel harmony: *num* 'thunder; God', *müt* 'liver', *kama?* 'mountain', *šärgät* 'elbow'

Singular Px1	Px2	Px3		Plural Px1	Px2	Px3
num-b T	*num-n* T	*num-d* T	v.	*num-b*⊥?	*num-n*⊥?	**num-d* Tn
müt-p T	*müt-l* T	*müt-t* T	v.	*müt-p*⊥?	*müt-l*⊥?	**müt-t* Tn
kama-b⊥	*kama-l*⊥	*kama-de*	v.	*kama-b*⊥?	*kama-l*⊥?	*kama-den*
šärgät-p⊥	*šärgät-l*⊥	*šärgät-t*⊥	v.	*šärgät-p*⊥?	*šärgät-l*⊥?	*šärgät-ten*

Key: T marks a high vowel which is governed both by tonal and serial harmony.
⊥ marks a low vowel which is governed only by tonal harmony.
* marks a form (P3) which is *not* ruled by serial harmony. Note, however, that the s3 form upon which it is based *is* so ruled.
– connects stem with relational suffix.

The coded forms above read as follows in a quasi-phonemic transcription:

> *numbu/numnu/numdu/numba ?/numna ?/numdun*
> *mütpü/mütlü/müttü/mütpä ?/mütlä ?/müttün*
> *kamaba/kamala/kamade/kamaba ?/kamala ?/kamaden*
> *šärgätpä/šärgätlä/šärgätte/šärgätpä ?/šärgätlä ?/šärgätten*

Consonants

The consonants are set out in Table 19.2:

The tense oral stops are strongly aspirated. The palatal(ized) (in Donner's terms: 'postdental') stops *tʲ* and *dʲ* are more often hushing affricates (*č*, *dž*) than hissing ones (*cʲ*, *dzʲ*).

The inventory given in Table 19.2 is a cautious one. With some morphophonemic trickery a tighter inventory of consonants is possible (Castrén, for example, assumed only twenty-four).

Table 19.2 Kamassian consonantism

	1	2	3	4	5	6
Nasals	*m*	*n*	*nʲ*		*ŋ*	
Tense stops	*p*	*t*	*tʲ*		*k*	*ʔ*
Lax stops	*b*	*d*	*dʲ*		*g*	
Glides	*w*		*j*			
Tense fricatives		*s*	*sʲ*	*šʲ*	*x*	
Lax fricatives		*z*	*zʲ*	*žʲ*	*γ*	
Laterals		*l*	*ʎ*			
Trill		*r*				

Note: Columns 1–6 contain bilabial, dental, palatal(ized), palatalized hushing, velar, and glottal consonants.

Glottal Stop in Kamassian

When it occurs in prepausal position, the glottal stop in Kamassian 'can best be compared with the non-nasalizable glottal stop of Tundra Nenets, for it alternates with obstruents only' (Janhunen 1986: 155). Elsewhere, the Kamassian glottal stop is the 'mirror image', as Janhunen puts it, of the so-called 'added' glottal stop of Nenets, inasmuch as it can precede the obstruent with which it paradigmatically alternates, e.g. *maʔ* ~ *maʔd* 'tent' (both sN). This and other, similar, occurrences indicate that the Kamassian glottal stop may have arisen from the implosion of obstruents (rather than their explosion, as in the case of Tundra Nenets). Since such implosion probably involved some staggering in the onset of the three closures (oral, velic, and glottal), it is probably not unconnected with the neutralization of word-final nasality in Selkup (Janhunen 1986: 167) and may also be related to the reduction of stem-final vowels as well. In this connection Janhunen refers to the 'pharyngealization' of Tuva and Tofa short vowels before a prepausal or a preconsonantal obstruent as an indication of specifically Kamassian, and generally Sayan-Samoyedic, influence on these neighbouring languages (Janhunen 1986: 168). It is possible that the etymology of the ethnonym Kamass(ian) itself reflects such staggered timing: if the root in question is the same as that seen in *kamaʔ* ~ *kawaʔ* 'high place, heap; edge of a ditch; height, hill, mountain' (from Turkic, where the forms have medial *-b-*), the neutralization of word-medial nasality is probably due to the imperfect synchronization of glottal and velic closure. The *-ŋ-* in the self-designation of the Kamassians, *kaŋmaažə*, is probably yet another, segmental, manifestation of this glottalic activity, although it it is the only known instance of nasalization of a glottal stop before *m*. For a parallel to the lenition *ʔb* > *w* one can cite *mənzᵊlleβᵊ* (Donner 1944: 85, 101) 'is cooking', in which the final *εβᵊ* represents the auxiliary verb *iʔbə* 'to lie'. This verb form is a composite, made up of the gerund *mənzə=lä* 'cooking' plus *iʔbə* 'lies' expressing continuity (i.e. *iʔbə* > *εβᵊ*).

Morphology

Nominal Inflection

Absolute Paradigm

Traditionally, grammars list seven cases for the absolute (non-possessed) singular nominal paradigm: N[ominative] -Ø, A[ccusative] -Ø/-m/-bV/-pV, G[enitive] -n, L[ative] -nə/-də/-tə, LO[cative] -ʔVn/-ɣən/-gən/-kən, Ab[lative] -ɣəʔ etc. and INS[trumental] -ze ʔ/-seʔ. The suffix variants are selected according to stem-type, which may be determined from the segments occurring final in the stem. Stems are either (V) vocalic or (C) consonantal, and if the latter, end either (C1) in glottal stop with or without a following lax consonant (usually d) or (C2) in all other consonants, which is always tense.

The case endings may be divided according to their relative age into three classes: (1) old (A, G, L), (2) more recent (LO, AB[lative]), and (3) most recent (INS). In the paradigm of nominal stem-type (C1), which is the most problematic and fairly recent, the three age-classes of case-ending also differ in the morphological processes which they undergo in inflection. Thus the accusative ending is attached to a C1-stem either by *deletion* of stem-final ʔ, e.g. sN maʔ, sA *maʔ-m > mam, or by the opposite process of extension of the suffix itself, viz. *syllabification*, e.g. -m > -ba in sA maʔdba. In this stem-type, deletion is also characteristic of the sG (man < *maʔ-n), while syllabification, together with simultaneous *denasalization*, characterizes the suffixation of the L morpheme (*maʔ-nə > maʔdə). Another process, akin to syllabification, is *reduplication*, characteristic of the LO forms of the C1 paradigm, in which the stem-vowel is repeated in the suffix, e.g. maʔ-an.

The superabundance of A forms for stem-class C1 may reflect the relative newness of this form class, but it may also be seen as reflecting a much older, areal tendency to neutralization and alternation of nasals and their

Table 19.3   Singular case endings by stem-type

		Vowel	Consonant − ʔ ~ ʔ + Lax consonant	Tense:-k, -t, -p, -s, -š
1	N	dʲaɣa 'river'	maʔ or maʔd 'house'	kürüp 'pit, hole'
	A	dʲaɣam	mam or maʔdba	kürübüm
	G	dʲaɣan	man	kürübün
	Lat	dʲaɣanə	maʔdə	kürüptə
2	LO	dʲaɣaɣən	maʔan	kürüpkün
	AB	dʲaɣaɣəʔ	maʔgəʔ	kürüpküʔ
3	INS	dʲaɣazeʔ	maʔzeʔ	kürüpseʔ

corresponding oral stops. The morphophonemics entailed in the short sA form *mam* parallel those of the sG (*man*), while the processes entailed in the long sA form *ma ʔdba* resemble those of the sLat (*ma ʔdə*).

Dual

Only one dual form, that of the nominative absolute, was recorded by Donner. The rest of the paradigm must have perished earlier, since no records of such forms exist in Castrén's or Künnap's materials. In a form such as *kaɣaazəgej* 'two brothers', the dual ending *-zəgej* consists of two elements: *-gej* is a dual marker of Samoyedic origin, and the preceding morpheme *-zə* is a connective-reciprocal suffix, also of Samoyedic origin.

Plural

Kamassian has two plural markers. In one of them *-zaŋ* (*-zäŋ* ~ *-saŋ* ~ *-säŋ*), the same connective/reciprocal suffix seen in the dual (*-zə*) serves as a base. The plural marker *-zaŋ* is used in both absolute and relative nominal inflection (see the next section). The other plural marker is *-ʔje ʔ* (or *-ʔi ʔ*) in final position and *-ʔi-* in non-final position. There appears to be a semantic complementarity in the use of the two plural markers, in that *-zaŋ* is used only with members of a nominal class that may be labelled [+HUMAN]: persons, parts of the body, and domesticated animals, while *-ʔje ʔ-* (and its variants) occurs with all nominals.

The plurals of two nouns, *essäŋ* 'children' (singular *eši*) and *kopsaŋ* 'daughters' (singular *ko ʔbdo*), are traditionally classified as irregular. As indicated above, a morphophonemic analysis of the Kamassian consonant paradigm which is rather more generous with rules but more parsimonious with underlying segments (e.g. only one bilabial oral stop and only one unpalatalized sibilant) would account for such forms descriptively while at the same time offering insights into the internal reconstruction of the language.

The Relative Paradigm

The semantic and morphological cohesion of the three grammatical cases N, A, and G is apparent also in the relative paradigm: here, these three cases

Table 19.4 Nominal paradigms of *dʲaɣa* 'river' with plural markers

	-zaŋ/-saŋ	*-ʔje ʔ*
N	*dʲaɣazaŋ*	*dʲaɣa ʔje ʔ*
A	*dʲaɣazaŋəm*	*dʲaɣa ʔim*
G	*dʲaɣazaŋən*	*dʲaɣa ʔin*
L	*dʲaɣazaŋdə*	*dʲaɣa ʔinə*
LO	*dʲaɣazaŋɣən*	*dʲaɣa ʔiɣən*
AB	*dʲaɣazaŋɣə ʔ*	*dʲaɣa ʔiɣə ʔ*
INS	*dʲaɣazaŋze ʔ*	*dʲaɣa ʔize ʔ*

Table 19.5   Relative paradigms

	Possessor		Possessed Singular	Plural
Syncretic forms of N/A/G				
	Singular	1	dʲaɣam	dʲaɣazaŋba
		2	dʲaɣal	dʲaɣzaŋna
		3	dʲaɣat	dʲaɣazaŋda
	Dual	1	dʲaɣawej	dʲaɣazaŋbij
		2	dʲaɣalej	dʲaɣazaŋnij
		3	dʲaɣaduj	dʲaɣazaŋduj
	Plural	1	dʲaɣawaʔ	dʲaɣazaŋbaʔ
		2	dʲaɣalaʔ	dʲaɣazaŋmaʔ
		3	dʲaɣaden	dʲaɣazaŋden
Syncretic forms of L/LO				
	Singular	1	dʲaɣanʲi	dʲaɣazaŋani
		2	dʲaɣanan	dʲaɣazaŋanan
		3	dʲaɣanda	dʲaɣazaŋanda
	Dual	1	dʲaɣanʲiwej	dʲaɣazaŋaniwej
		2	dʲaɣanʲilej	dʲaɣazaŋanilej
		3	dʲaɣandej	dʲaɣazaŋandej
	Plural	1	dʲaɣanʲiwaʔ	dʲaɣazaŋaniwaʔ
		2	dʲaɣanʲilaʔ	dʲaɣazaŋanilaʔ
		3	dʲaɣanden	dʲaɣazaŋanden
Syncretic forms of AB				
	Singular	1	dʲaɣatʲe	dʲaɣazaŋatʲi
		2	dʲaɣattan	dʲaɣazaŋattan
		3	dʲaɣatte	dʲaɣazaŋatte
	Dual	1	dʲaɣatʲiwej	dʲaɣazaŋatʲiwej
		2	dʲaɣatʲilej	dʲaɣazaŋatʲilej
		3	dʲaɣattej	dʲaɣazaŋattej
	Plural	1	dʲaɣatʲiwaʔ	dʲaɣazaŋatʲiwaʔ
		2	dʲaɣatʲlaʔ	dʲaɣazaŋatʲilaʔ
		3	dʲaɣatten	dʲaɣazaŋatten
Syncretic forms of INS ®				
	Singular	1	dʲaɣamzeʔ	
		2	dʲaɣalzeʔ	
		3	dʲaɣatʲsʲeʔ	

Note: The symbol ® indicates that the forms included in the table here differ in their morphological structure from the rest of the forms cited, as they are in fact postpositional phrases rather than suffixated nominal forms.

syncretize. The more covert affinity of the L and LO cases also manifests itself here, again as a formal syncretism. The AB and INS have distinct forms, the latter consisting of a postpositional phrase.

According to the available data the category of the dual appears in this paradigm only in connection with the possessor, and never with the possessed; contrast the personal pronouns, below.

Pronominal Inflection

Demonstratives
Kamassian has a more archaic, three-way, deictic system than the binary *this–that* type of most European languages such as English, Russian, and Hungarian. We may best describe the Kamassian system, borrowing Lotz's term, as a T-shaped structure:

dü 'this' ———┬——— *di* 'that'

še 'yonder'

This three-way demonstrative system is extended by two remonstratives, *düm* 'and this (even closer to speaker)' and *iidə* 'and that (even farther from speaker)'. The form *iidə* '... and that' may well be a compound of the Russian conjunction и 'and' plus the Kamassian demonstrative *di*. The initial long *ii-* may be due to the foreign origin of the morpheme or, what is more probable, by the characteristically deviant phonological behaviour of deictic systems.

Personal pronouns
Unlike nouns, Kamassian personal pronouns do have dual forms. The nominative forms are:

	s	d	p
1	man	mište	mi?
2	tan	šište	ši?
3	di	dišide	dizäŋ

We evidently have here another T-shaped structure, in which the third person is opposed to the tandem of first and second persons. Recall that the lone third-person form, *di* '(s)he; that', also participates in the demonstrative system.

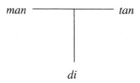

man ———┬——— *tan*

di

The axis-of-discourse forms build yet another T-structure: the singular first- and second-person forms (*ma-*/*ta-*) on the one hand, and the dual and plural forms on the other (*mi-*/*ši-*).

The forms of the s1, s2, and p1 personal pronouns are transparent. Of Uralic origin are the stems (*ma-*, *ta-*), the pronoun-forming suffix =*n*, and probably also the plural suffix -*ʔ* (< *-t). In the d2 form we have a suffixal element -*šte* (from the numeral *šide* 'two'); the base *ši-* of the d2 and p2 forms is thought to come from proto-Samoyedic *te, the non-singular base for second-person pronouns. Beside Kamassian, Koibal also has an initial sibilant in this pronoun (p2 *ce* 'you, your'); Mator does not.

The dual forms d1 *mište*, d2 *šište*, and d3 *dišide* clearly consist of the pronominal stems *mi-*, *ši-*, and *di-* plus the dual marker *šide* ~ *šte* mentioned above. The case forms of the singular axis-of-discourse pronouns are as follows:

	s1	s2
N/G	*man*	*tan*
A/L/LO	*mana*	*tanan*
AB	*manatʲeʔ*	*tanatan*
INS	*manzʲeʔ*	*tanzʲeʔ*

In the axis-of-discourse paradigm, the syncretism of the N and G is opposed to that of the A, L, LD, resulting in only a partial overlap with the relative paradigm of nominal inflection. In the pronominal paradigm, the A patterns with the oblique cases (LO and L) and is set against the unmarked N/A form; this contrasts sharply with the relative nominal paradigm, in which N/A/G is set against LO/L. It would appear that the markedness of the A is more important in axis-of-discourse contexts than it is at the more neutral level of substantives (grammatically: third person).

Whereas the paradigm of axis-of-discourse pronominals shows similarities with the relative nominal paradigm, the inflection of the s3 pronoun *di*, which is, at the same time, a demonstrative, is identical with the nominal absolute paradigm, i.e. there is no syncretism whatsoever:

	s3
Nominative	*di*
Genitive	*din*
Accusative	*dim*
Lative	*diʔne*
Locative	*diʔən*
Ablative	*diʔəʔ*
Instrumental	*dizʲeʔ*

Other Pronouns

The reflexive pronoun (s1 *bospə*, s2 *boslə*, s3 *bostə*, etc.) consists of the relative paradigm of a noun of Turkic origin (*bos* 'body'). Interrogative pronouns include *šimdə* 'who?', *əmbi* 'what?', *əmbi šer* 'what kind of?', *šombi* 'what (else)?', *gi ʔi ʔ* 'which (of the two)?', *mo(ʔ)* 'why?', *kajet* 'what kind of?', *kadə* 'how?', *kümen* 'how many?', *kamen* 'when?'.

Adverbials

These consist of adverbs proper and postpositions. Adverb-forming suffixes are *-i ~ -j*, as in *paardej* 'around' (cf. *paarlʲam* 'I turn [myself]'), *nʲeeri* 'by' (cf. *nʲeerəlʲem* 'I miss [when shooting]'), *pinzi* 'over', *šaməj* 'near, along'.

Most postpositions normally occur with their noun in the genitive, e.g. *dʲaŋa-n kunzu* RIVER-sG ALONG 'along the river', *pa-n sʲukut* FOREST-sG THROUGH 'through the forest', *kuza-n naamən* MAN-sG FOR 'for the man'. The accusative is required by the postposition *nʲeeri*, e.g. *koonu-m nʲeeri* BEAR-sA BY '(passing) by a bear'. Postpositions may also occur with their noun in the nominative, and may take case and person suffixes, as in *ki jil-gən-də* MOON UNDER-LO-s3 'under the moon'.

Verbal inflection

Alongside the categories of person and number, which they share with nominal and pronominal inflection, Kamassian verb stems also encode tense-and-mood and the category of the definite object. All four categories are represented at the morphological level, e.g. *iʔbe-m* LIES-s1 'I lie', *iʔbe-jeʔ* LIES-p3 'they lie', *iʔbe-ʔ* LIES-s2imp 'lie!', *paarga-t-θ* CUTS-dO-s2imp 'cut it!'

The category of aspect, on the other hand, is expressed by syntactic means, i.e. with the help of auxiliaries; this contrasts sharply with the situation in the other Samoyedic languages. Such aspectual syntagms are made up of the gerund of the lexical verb plus auxiliary verbs such as *iʔbe-* 'lies' (imperfective aspect) or *walʲa-* 'leaves, abandons ' (perfective). Examples: imperfective *kuja dʲemdəlaa ʔbə* 'the sun is shining' < *dʲemdə=laa iʔbə* SHINES=ger LIES-s3, perfective *ətʲerlaawalʲam* 'I have tied it (up) tight' < *ətʲer=llʲaa walʲa-m* TIES=ger LEAVES-s1.

This spillover of verbal semantics into the syntactic domain is perhaps the result of a functional push-chain: the tense markers for the present and past tense are themselves relatively recent intruders into the domain of verbal inflection, being of derivational origin (they are historically participles and gerunds), e.g. present tense *kallam* 'I go' < *kan=la-m* GOES-pres.part-s1, past tense *kambiam* 'I went' < *kan=bi-am* GOES-past.part-s1.

From a strictly morphological point of view there are only two modal/temporal formations of the Kamassian verb: the imperative and the adhortative. These two moods are in complementary distribution: the imperative has forms for the second and third person, and the adhortative has only first-person forms. Examples of imperatives: *kana-?* 'go! (s2)', *kaŋ-gə-j* 'may (s)he go', *kaŋ-gə-ləj* 'may they (both) go', *kaŋ-ga-ji?* 'may they (all) go'. Adhortative: *kan-ža-bəj* GOES-adhort-d1 'let's both go!'

The conditional, on the other hand, is a synthetic form consisting of the conjunctive morpheme *-na-* (~ *-nä-* ~ *-da-* ~ *-dä-* ~ *-ta-* ~ *-tä-*) plus a fossilized archaic preterite form *i-zä* from the verb *i-zet* 'is', e.g. *i?benämzä* 'if I lay' < *i?be-nä-m i-zä-∅* LIES-conj-s1 IS-pret-s3. The conjunctive suffix probably continues the Uralic conditional/potential modal suffix *-nV-.

As a result of the influence of neighbouring Turkic idioms, converbal phrases such as *məllaandəɣɑm* 'I go' (< *mən=la* + *xandə=ɣɑ-m* WANDERS=1st.ger + GOES=part-s1) occur quite frequently. The auxiliary verbs met with most often in such constructions are (cited in the first person singular) *kalam*, *xandəɣɑm*, (infinitive *kanzet*) 'I go', *i?bem* 'I lie', *amnam* 'I sit', *nuɣɑm* 'I stand', and *walʲam* 'I leave'; these are usually preceded by the lexical verb in its first gerund form, built with *=la*(~ *=lä*; see p. 592). As mentioned above these phrases also function as means of expressing aspectual distinctions.

The modal auxiliary *moolʲam* (~ *malʲam*) 'I am about to, wish to, would like to, am able to X' is also frequently used, e.g. *kamnəldə moolʲam* 'I am going to [cure with] smoke, I would like to [cure with] smoke', in which *kamnəl=də* is the participle of *kamnəl=lʲa-m* 'I smoke'. See also Affirmative Auxiliaries, pp. 593f.

Derivation

Aktionsart, *genus verbi*, and other Verbal Constellations

The complementary category to aspect, that of Aktionsart or *mode of action*, is expressed in a typically Uralic way, viz. by means of derivational suffixes. Thus the derivational suffix *=r* forms augmentative-frequentatives, as in *amo=r=la-m* 'I eat frequently' (cf. *am=nʲa-m* 'I eat'), and the suffix *=lu?* forms momentaneous-inchoatives, as in *dʲoor=lu?=lʲa-m* 'I begin to cry, burst into tears' (cf. *dʲoor=lʲa-m* 'I weep').

The category of *genus verbi* has the passive as its marked member. This is expressed by the suffix *=oo-*, as in *iinä saroona* 'the horse is tethered', in which *sar=oo=na* is the first participle of the passive pendant to *sar=lʲa-m* 'I tie'. Reflexivity is also expressed by this suffix, as in *amn=oo=lʲa-m* 'I seat myself, I sit (down)', cf. *amn=na-* 'sits'.

Other constellations of subject and object, such as causatives, are also expressed by means of derivation. Straightforward causatives are formed with *=də-*(~ *=tə-*), e.g. *dʲemdəlʲem* 'I heat X', cf. *dʲeem=nʲə-* 'X is warm'; an example of a more complex, quasi-causative relation is *tüšülʲlʲom* (< *tüšü=l=lʲo-m*) 'I teach [= I make X understand]', formed with the suffix *=l-*, cf. *tüšü=lʲe m* 'I understand, I learn'.

Modality is also expressed by means of derivation. For example, the desiderative, a mood roughly synonymous with constructions built with the modal auxiliary *mooʲa-* (above), is formed with the suffix =*nzə-* (~ =*zə-*), e.g. *kono=nza=ʲə-m* 'I would like to sleep', cf. *kuno=ʲa-m* 'I am sleeping'.

Gerunds and Participles
The distinction between the categories of gerund and participle is one of syntactic function rather than morphology: the term 'gerund' applies to deverbal adverbs, while 'participles' are deverbal nouns (and adjectives).

The most frequent gerundive suffixes are:

1 =*la(ʔ)* ~ =*lä(ʔ)*, after nasals: =*na(ʔ)* ~ =*nä(ʔ)*, which expresses either simultaneity, e.g. *nee kunoolamna* < *kunoo=la* + *am=na-Ø* 'the woman is sleeping' or finality, e.g. *ka=laʔ nerbe-ʔ* GOES=ger TELLS-s2imp 'go [= having gone] tell (him/her)';

2 =*bi* ~ =*pi*, followed by personal forms of the lative case, also expresses simultaneity, e.g. *man amor=bi=nʲi di šoo-bi-Ø* s1.PRO EATS=ger-s1lat s3.PRO COMES-pret-s3 'while I was eating, (s)he came';

3 =*bi* (~ =*pi*) plus =*za* (~ =*zä*) expresses anteriority, e.g. *di nʲi-m ku=bi=za tunoldə=la šoo-bi-Ø* THIS CHILD-A SEES=having RUNS=ger COMES-pret-s3 'having seen this child, (s)he came running'.

Suffixes (1) and (2) also function as markers of present and past tense, respectively. In the case of suffix (1), there is an additional fine point: palatalization of the lateral (*ʲ*) seems to mark present tense, while the plain, unpalatalized *l* indicates future, e.g. (1) FUTURE *nʲeʔ-le-m* 'I shall blow', (1[1]) PRESENT *nʲeʔ-ʲe-m* 'I blow', (2) PAST *šoo-bi-Ø* '(s)he came'.

The most frequently attested participial derivatives are

4 =*na* ~ =*nä*, after consonants: =*da* ~ =*dä*, which forms *nomina agentis*, e.g. *bü-ɣin nu=na pa* WATER-loc STANDS=part TREE 'a tree which stands in water';

5 =*ɣa* ~ =*ɣä*, after consonants: =*ga* ~ =*gä*, which forms present participles with active or passive meaning, e.g. *puʔdʲə=ɣa tüʔ* 'stinking bug', *tʲemd=gä maʔ* 'heated tent'.

Suffix (5) is also used as a present-tense marker, e.g. *nu=ɣa-m* 'I am standing'.

Syntax
The basic order is modifier before modified. Thus adjective precedes noun: *bilä kuza* 'poor man', and adverb precedes verb: *šojdʲoo-zeʔ suʔbtə-bi-Ø* BASKET-INS SCOOPS-pret-s3 '(s)he scooped (it) with a basket'. Object precedes verb: *šüjmü-bü ʒeer-bi-Ø* MARE-A TIES-pt-s3 '(s)he tied the

Table 19.6 A sample paradigm of verbal inflection: *ʔbəm* 'to lie', infinitive *i ʔbezet*, gerund *i ʔbelä ʔ*, '-ing' *i ʔbij*

		Singular	Dual	Plural
Indicative Present	1	*i ʔbəm*	*i ʔbebəj*	*i ʔbebää ʔ*
	2	*i ʔbəl*		
	3	*i ʔbə*		*i ʔbejə ʔ*
Preterite	1	*i ʔbebijäm*		
	2			
	3			*i ʔbebi*
Adhortative	1		*i ʔbežbəj*	
Imperative	2	*i ʔbə ʔ*	*i ʔbeguləj*	
	3	*i ʔbəgəj*		
Conditional	1	*i ʔbenämzä*		
	2			*i ʔbenälä ʔzä ʔ*
	3			

mare', as does the negative auxiliary: *ej surarga* '([s]he) doesn't ask'. Subject generally precedes predicate: *meŋgej to ʔbtoobi* 'the fox came', but the reverse order occurs in sentences with focalization, e.g. *axsa ʔ i-bi-∅ šejmü-t* LAME IS-pret-s3 MARE-s3 'lame was his mare'.

Certain features of the direct object may be encoded morphologically on the verb. This category is traditionally termed [+/-] definite, but the 'definiteness' of a Kamassian object is evidently dependent on semantic and pragmatic factors about which we have only limited information. Whatever its precise content, the formal distinction [+/-] definite obtains only if the object is in the third person (but objects of imperatives may be both definite and axis-of-discourse) and then only in forms with a third-person subject in the indicative present/future and conditional, and in second-person singular forms of the imperative. Definiteness of the direct object is indicated by the morpheme *-t* (~ *-d*, from the third-person pronominal stem *te), non-definiteness by its absence. So for example we have in the present tense *paarga-lʲa-∅-t* '(s)he cuts it' as opposed to *paarga-lʲa-∅* '(s)he cuts', and in the imperative *paarga-t* 'cut it!' versus *paarga- ʔ* 'cut!', but in the past tense there is only *paarga-bi- ʔ* '(s)he cut (it)'. The definiteness marker occurs between the two elements of the conditional complex (above), e.g. *paarga-na-t-sa* '(s)he would cut it' v. *paarga-na-za* '(s)he would cut'.

Three basic types of auxiliary verb may be distinguished: aspectual, affirmative, and negative. The first of these was discussed under Verbal Inflection, p. 590.

The primary *affirmative auxiliary* is *i-gä-* 'is'. This may be used as copula, e.g. *man tan kaŋa-l i-gä-m* 'I am your brother', with zero variant in the third person, e.g. *di ko ʔbdo* s3.PRO DAUGHTER 'she is a daughter/girl', but it is also used to express possession, e.g. *büz^jə-n naɣur ko ʔbdo-t i-bi-Ø* OLD.MAN-G THREE DAUGHTER-s3 IS-pret-s3 'the old man had three daughters'.

In either of its two roles the verb 'is' is normally situated at the end of the sentence, although various textual/pragmatic effects (focus, foregrounding) may be achieved by inversion, as in *to ʔbdži-t mana, müner-d mana, i-gä-Ø mana* 'strike me down, break me up, I still have. . .'.

We may also classify the verb *mool^ja-*, first mentioned above in connection with converbal phrases, as an affirmative auxiliary. The lexical verb then stands (1) in the infinitive, as in *man am=zət mool^ja-m* 'I would like to eat', (2) in the participle in *=na*, e.g. *samo=nu mool^ja-m* 'I am going to shamanize', or (3) in the gerund in *=la*, e.g. *o ʔblej* (< *o ʔb=la + ej*) *mool^ja-m* COLLECTS=ger NEG.PART AFFIRM.AUX-s1 'I can't collect'.

Negative auxiliaries are used to express negation. We know of two negative verbs in Kamassian: one is the inflectable pair *ä-/e-* (non-imperative) ~ *i-* (imperative, i.e. prohibitive), for general negation; the other is *naɣa-*, with a defective paradigm, used to negate existence and possession.

General negation is expressed in two ways. In the older construction, the negative auxiliary *ä-/e-* ~ *i-* is inflected for mood and tense, number and person; it also encodes the [+/-] definite distinction for direct objects. The lexical verb stands in the connegative, a form built with the suffix *-ʔ* and thus homophonous with the second-person singular (indefinite) imperative. As Kamassian became moribund, this construction began to be rivalled by one built from the invariable negative particle *ej* (itself historically from the negative auxiliary) plus the regularly inflected form of the lexical verb. In both constructions the negator normally precedes the lexical verb. Examples: *man e-m šo-ʔ* s1.PRO NEG.AUX-s1 COMES-conneg 'I don't come', *tan e-l-lə šü-ʔ* s2.PRO NEG.AUX-pres-s2 ENTERS-conneg 'you don't enter', *bos-tu ej di xam-bi-Ø* SELF-s3 NEG.PART s3.PRO GOES-pret-s3 '(s)he him/herself didn't go', *i(-ʔ) d^joora-ʔ* PROHIB.AUX(-s2imp) CRIES-conneg 'don't cry!'

The negative pendant to the verb 'is' (*i-*, above) is *naɣa-*, with a somewhat defective paradigm. It is used to negate predicates, as in *bilä kuza man naɣa-m* BAD MAN s1.PRO ISN'T-s1 'I am not a poor man', and to express non-possession, e.g. *ipäk di-n naɣa-Ø* BREAD s3.PRO-G ISN'T-s3 '(s)he doesn't have any bread'; notice also *di-zä-n am=zət naɣoʔ-bi-Ø* s3.PRO-plur-G EATS-inf ISN'T-pret-s3 'they didn't have anything to eat'.

Historically, the general auxiliary negative *ä-/e-* ~ *i-* may well be related to the verb 'is' (*i-*). On the synchronic plane, we would then have the opposition indicative v. prohibitive based upon a metonymic axis, *i-* 'is' occurring in sentence-final position, *i-* 'don't!' occurring non-final; while within the domain of negation, the opposition of negation v. prohibition is expressed by quite different means, namely the metaphorical axis of vowel alternation, *ä-/e-* v. *i-*. Examples: (sentence-final *i-*, existence) *di i-gä-Ø*

s3.PRO IS-pres-s3 '(s)he exists', (non-final, prohibition) *i šo-ʔ* 'don't come!';
(*e-*, negation) *e-m šo-ʔ* NEG.AUX-s1 COMES-conneg 'I'm not coming', (*i-*,
prohibition) *i(-ʔ) kuro-ʔ* PROHIB.AUX(-s2imp) IS.ANGRY-conneg 'don't
be angry!'

Stylistics

Thanks to the analyses of John Lotz we know Kamassian versification well:
parallelism of numerically defined phrases and/or lines is the central device
of the Kamassian versificator, who in this respect differs little from other
Siberian bards. Because of the relative scarcity of Kamassian linguistic and
folkloristic material we know little of the differences between the various uses
of the language: everyday v. ritual; if ritual, sung v. recited; if recited,
numerical or free; if free: everyday v. ... *e così via, da capo*. For the same
reason, we know next to nothing of the miniature devices which wordsmiths
(shamans, singers, storytellers) might have used for the purposes of enchant-
ment, entertainment, or deception. I have already cited an example of
emotionally motivated metathesis at the syntactic level in riddle 29 (*toʔbdžit
mana, münerd mana, igä mana* 'even if you strike me, even if you break me,
I still have ...', in which we see an atypical sort of *regens–rectum* word order.
Since the text is a folkloristic one, it is perhaps not too daring to propose that
breaking the basic word-order rule is part of the arsenal of artistic word-
arrangement, i.e. poetry. This is all the more true because this metathesis is,
at the same time, part of a parallelism which is built upon the syncretic
pronominal form *mana* 'me (A)' = 'to me (L)' as *rectum* and the preceding
verbal forms as *regens*. In the first two phrases the sequence modifier–
modified is justified by the universal rule according to which a verb in the
imperative always comes first, but in the third phrase the verb is in the
indicative, so the metathesis must be explained by something else. In this
instance stylistic/poetical reasons underlie. The syntactic manipulation of
linguistic material for poetic ends is frequent in the folk-poetry of the other
Samoyedic peoples, as well.

As a further illustration, we shall now examine another type of manipulation of linguistic material common in the folklore of the Samoyedic peoples.
The hero of the tale chosen as our sample text is called *tarčaabərdžä*.
Mentioning this name is part of the tale's opening formula: 'There was a poor
man. His name was ~'. Perhaps not unexpectedly, it is part of the closing
formula, as well. At the end of the tale, the antagonist *kaan* (the Emperor)
surrenders, and addresses our hero as follows: '*tartʲaa-bartʲa, pol bartʲa*'.
This somewhat distorted variant of the name is embedded in a parallelism of
which the frame is the mysterious sequence *tʲa*:

tar tʲaa	*bar tʲa*
pol	*bar tʲa*

We can identify the element t^j in the sequence t^ja as the third-person singular possessive suffix of the syncretic forms N/G/A and L/LO/AB. The former also occurs in the form t^j, the latter in the form $t^jə$, according to Künnap (1971: 157, 159). On the other hand the final a cannot be identified with any grammatical element: it is an inetymological element which functions as the nucleus of an expletive syllable which, at the same time, indicates the end of a grammatical morpheme or stem.

Having identified the frame of the parallelism, we may now turn to its content. The stem *bar* 'all' is repeated: this repetition constitutes the bearing pillars of the parallelism, i.e. the identical elements. The differing elements (the parallel elements) occupy the slots preceding the identical elements. The first of these parallel words is possibly to be identified with *tar* 'hair; feather'. As for the second, there are several candidates. In Donner's (1944) dictionary we find (1) *рол* 'ground, floor' (from Russian пол), (2) *ролиʔl^jɛm* 'to dive', and (3) *poʔl^jam* 'to bathe, to dip, to swim, to run (water); to be on heat'. Considering the hero's final trick, by which he compels the *kaan* and all his people to surrender by drenching them with water poured from a sack, thus washing them away, we can exclude item (1). We are thus left with items (2) and (3). Perhaps it is not too far-fetched to suppose that these two verbs have in common a root *pol-*, with the meaning 'is immersed into a stream; is overcome by water/sexual desire'. A more literal translation of our parallel lines would then be:

FEATHER/HAIR-s3   ALL-s3
OVERCOME   ALL-s3

or, in paraphrase: 'One who is covered all over in feathers/hair is swept away by passion', or: 'The feathered man/hairy man is in a trance'.

Obviously both of these interpretations refer to, and are appropriate descriptions of, the shaman. The parallel arrangement of the constituents in this miniature couplet are reminiscent of a technique in Nenets verbal art, whereby the words are cut up into their constituent syllables/morphemes with the help of expletives, thereby filling out the metrical scheme and creating a pattern in which the original message is woven in and out of a quasi-syllabic texture, like inlaid-work:

tar-		bar-	
	t^jaa-		t^ja
pol		bar-	
	■		t^ja

i.e. schematically:

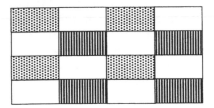

    Seen in this framework, the first variant of the name, *tarčaabərdžä*, is even more interesting. Unlike the variant examined above, here the two halves of the name are set against one another as velar and palatal (back and front) constituents, i.e. opposite poles in tonal vowel harmony; this contrast in vowel colour is accompanied by the opposition unvoiced : voiced in the variants of the third-person possessive suffix, -*tʲa(a)*: it appears as -*čaa* and -*džä*. Let us now set aside these constants (disguised as variables) in order to concentrate on the real variables in the parallelism: *tar* and *bər*. Even if the first of these (*tar*) is the same morpheme as in the other variant of the name, the second one, *bər*, is certainly not: it is a palatal word, as its suffix -*džä* plainly shows. The interpretations given above will not work here, then. If on the other hand we revert to our original procedure, and strip away the pseudo-possessive suffixe(/)expletives to expose the real variables, we arrive at the constellation:

tar-   bər-
       čaa-   džä

in which we have not the compound *tar+bar* 'hair/feather all over', as in the earlier variant of the name, but rather *tar-bər*. This sequence seems to be a cover for the word *taarbə* 'shaman'. If we try to force *taarbə* into the frame, the final -*r* is assigned to the following pseudo-possessive suffix, but for the formal parallelism to remain, the final -*r* of the first half must be re-assigned, as well:

ta-   bə-
      rčaa-   rdžä

Although the formal parallelism is maintained, the semantic transparency is blurred once again, since this time the final -*r* of *tar* has slipped away in spite of the fact that it belongs to the etymological material of the word. The result is an acoustic hide-and-seek similar to certain kinds of optical illusion based on the complementarity of black-and-white patterns which one can only identify one at a time: when you focus on one, the other is blurred, and vice versa.

The parallelism *tart^{j}aa-bart^{j}a/pol bart^{j}a* and the variant of its first part, *tarčaabərdžä*, both refer to the same denotatum, but they do it in different ways. The first parallelism tells a story while describing its topic; the second tries to utter and, at the same time, to conceal a word. Yet both do the same: poetry, since neither speaks directly. In addition to manipulations at the syntactic level, Kamassian poetic speech also relies on transformations at the level of morphology (break-up of the word by expletives, splitting words into constituent morphs and intermixing them with inetymological phonic material, etc.) just as do the northern Samoyedic traditions, Nenets and Nganasan.

Sample Kamassian Text
Adapted from *Märchen* no. 2, pp. 88–90, in Donner 1944.

numak	Tale
bilä kuza amnoo-bi-Ø	There was a poor man,
nəm-də tarčaa+bərdžä	his name [was] *Tarčabərdžä*.
bilä šejmü-bü džaab-pi	He took a poor mare,
axsaʔi-bi-Ø šejmü-t	lame was his mare.
konzan=de-bi-Ø	He equipped [it]:
saaγər bəraa-ba saar-bi-Ø	[a] black sack [he] tied [to its saddle],
šojd^{j}oo-ba saar-bi-Ø	[a] birchbark basket he tied [to it].
məl=le oʔbtə-bi-Ø	Going he started (= he set off).
urγaba toʔbtoo-bi-Ø	'Grandpa' (= bear) came [along].
mana ji-t hälaa=s-tə	'Me take as a companion,
pada-ʔ saγər bəraa-nə!	put [me] into [the] black sack!'
pada-bi saaγən bəraa- nə	He put [the bear] into [the] black sack
məl=le oʔbtə-bi-Ø	Going he started,
meŋgej toʔbtoo-bi-Ø	[a] fox came [along].
mana ji-t hälaa=ʒə-tə	'Me take as a companion,
pada-ʔ saaγər bəraa-nə!	put [me] into [the] black sack!'
pada-bi-Ø saaγər bəraa-nə	He put [the fox] into [the] black sack
di-γiʔ-ti kuš toʔdoo-bi-Ø	Then a wolf came [along].
mana ji-t hälaa-zə-t	'Me take as a companion,
pada-ʔ saaγər bəraa-nə!	put [me] into [the] black sack!'
di-γit-ti bü toʔktoo-bi-Ø	Then water came [along].
də bü-m suʔlej-bi-Ø saaγər bəraa-ndə	This water he scooped into his black sack,
šojd^{j}oo-zeʔ suʔbtə-bi-Ø	with a basket he scooped [it],
šejme-ndə sar=lawaʔ-bi-Ø	to his mare he tied [it].
ku=bi-ndə	He sees:
talaj-ndə toʔ-ondə jada nu-γa-Ø	on the sea's shore [a] village stands.

jadaa-nə ej tu-ɣa-Ø	Into [the] village he does not go.
üzü-bi-Ø	He got off [the horse],
šü [h]äm-bi-Ø	[a] fire he made,
šüjmü-bü ǯeer-bi-Ø	[the] mare he tied,
am-na-Ø	he sits [down to wait].
kaan nʲiʔnen məl=leʔ-bi-Ø	The Tsar was walking outside,
ku=laʔwa-bi-Ø	[and] saw:
šindi di-ɣin am-na-Ø	'Who is sitting there,
inä-bə ǯeer=lawa-bi-Ø	[who] tied [the] horse,
man kük noo-ba toonolaʔ bi-Ø	[who] trod my grccn/bluc/golden grass
ej surar=ga	not asking [for permission]
toʔ-ondə məndənʲä-bi-Ø	on the side/road passed [his day]
əʔlə-bi-Ø	[and] let [it] go [by]?
kal=la suraar-də	Going, ask it!'
šindi dərgit ii-gä-l	'What kind of man are you,
ej suraar=ga kaan-əm	[who] without asking the Tsar
kaan-ən noʔb-to tooʔna-bi-Ø	trod the grass of the Tsar?
əmbi tan-an karä?	What do you want?'
kam-bi-Ø suraar=laʔ-bi-Ø	[The servant] went [and] asked:
kajət kuza i-gə-l	'What kind of man are you?
əmbii-m pi=läʔ məŋ-gə-l	What are you looking for, wandering?'
kaan-ən koʔbtoo-bi ii-zit šoo-bija-m	'I came to take the Tsar's daughter.'
də kuza paar-bi-Ø	This man (= the servant) returned [to the Tsar],
kaan-də neerbü-bi-Ø	to [the] Tsar he answered:
kaan-ən koʔbtoo-bo ii-šit šoo-bija-m	'I came to take the Tsar's daughter.'
kala-ʔ, neerbä-ʔ	'Go, tell [him]:
jakšə-l-zi paara-ʔ	'Of your [own] good [will], go back!'
ə-m paara	'I won't go back.'
jakšə-zə ej mə=bi-ndə	'If he doesn't go back willingly,
biläʔ-z ii-li-m	I shall take [it] with bad [feelings].
eeli-t kaazər askər-i-m	Release the wild horses,
šəjmə-t-sʲi taləj-din	with your mare they will knock you down,
	they will tear you apart.'
nʲeʔle-din	He let their wild horscs run,
uʔdulu-bi-Ø kaazər askər-za dən	[When] wild horses are running
askər-ieʔ tunoo=la χandə-ɣa-i?	he opened [the] black sack
saaɣər bəraa-bo čikə-bi-Ø	he let out the black bear.
saaɣər koonə-m uʔtullu-bi-Ø	'Grandpa', following the horses,
urɣaaba askər-iji-m pjaŋdəl=laʔ	chased them away.
kuna-mbi	

Ɂbtul-gu-t buga-Ɂi-m, kaazər-iji-m 'Release the bulls [and] horses to
šejmü-tʲ-sʲe tjüɣa mülä trample [him] to death with his
mare!'

saaɣər boraa-bə tʲikə-bi-Ø [The] black sack he opened,
kuš-tu əɁ-lä mə-bi-Ø his wolf he released.
kuš buɣa-ji-m paɳdə=la Ɂ ku-mbi [The] wolf, chasing the bulls,
pa-məɳgən pursued them in[to] the forest.
kaan maala kojoo-bi-Ø [The] Tsar, remaining, stayed,
iil obtə-bi-Ø paardəj [his] people gathered around [him]:
i-š-päɁ də-m 'Let's take him!'
paarəldluɁ-bi-Ɂji They surrounded [him],
dʲabə=nə malʲa-Ɂji wanted to grab [him].
saaɣər boraa-bə tʲike i-bi-Ø, nʲeptə- [The] black sack he opened, pulled,
bi-Ø
bü-bü ko Ɂmnəj ba Ɂptə-bi-Ø shaking [the] water poured [it onto
them].

iilii-m bü kundə-ɣa-t χaɳdə-ɣa-t [The] water chases the folk away.
tartʲä&bartʲa, pol bartʲa 'tartʲä&bartʲa, pol bartʲa,
piil mal-bə mə-lʲi-m half of my cattle I shall give [you],
piil baj-bu mə-lʲi-m half of my empire I shall give [you],
ko Ɂbdoo-m mə-lʲi-m my daughter I shall give [you].'
ej karä mana tan mal-lə 'I don't need/want your cattle,
ej karä tan baj-lə I don't need/want your empire,
tolʲko abakaj ko Ɂbdo-l karä mana only your princess daughter I do
need/want.'

i Ɂ-bi-Ø šojdʲoo-bo He took [the] basket,
bü-bü su Ɂgda-bi-Ø poured [out the] water.
kaan ko Ɂbdoo-bə mə-bi-Ø The Tsar gave [him his] daughter.
aχsa šəjmə-ndə šiltə-bi-Ø He sat [her] on to the lame mare,
boku-Ɂla u Ɂbtə-bi-Ø fastening, he mounted,
ma Ɂ-andə kunna aam-bi-Ø to his tent he took [her].

References and Further Reading

Note: all examples cited in this chapter are taken from Donner 1944.

Castrén, M.A. (1854) *Grammatik der samojedischen Sprachen*, St. Petersburg. (Re-issued 1966, with a foreword by P. Hajdú, as volume 53 of the Indiana University Uralic and Altaic Series, Bloomington: Indiana University).
Donner, K. (1944) *Kamassisches Wörterbuch nebst Sprachproben und Hauptzügen der Grammatik*, bearbeitet und herausgegeben von A. Joki, Helsinki, Lexica Societatis Finno-Ugricae 8, Helsinki: Société Finno Ougrienne.
Hajdú, P. (1950) 'Die Benennungen der Samoyeden', *JSFOu* 54/1: 1–112.
——— (1963) *The Samoyed Peoples and Languages*, Bloomington: Indiana University; The Hague: Mouton.
——— (1968, ²1982) *Chrestomathia Samoiedica*, Budapest: Tankönyvkiadó.

——— (1975) 'Über die Herkunft des kamassischen Pluralsuffixes -saŋ', *UAJb* 47: 85–8.

Janhunen, J. (1977) *Samojedischer Wortschatz, Gemeinsamojedische Etymologien,* Castrenianumin toimitteita 17, Helsinki: Castrenianum.

——— (1986) *Glottal Stop in Nenets, MSFOu* 196, Helsinki: Société Finno-Ougrienne.

Joki, A. (1952) *Die Lehnwörter der Sajansamojedischen, MSFOu* 103, Helsinki: Société Finno-Ougrienne.

Künnap, A. (1971) *System und Ursprung der Flexionkamassischensuffixe,* vol. I: Numeruszeichen und Nominalflexion, *MSFOu* 147, Helsinki: Société Finno-Ougrienne.

——— (1978) *System und Ursprung der kamassischemn Flexionsuffixe,* vol. II: *Verbalflexion und Verbalnomina, MSFOu* 164, Helsinki: Société Finno-Ougrienne.

——— (1993) Камасинский язык in: Уральские языки, Moscow.

Lotz, J. (1953) *Structural Presentation of the Kamassian Lament,* Stockholm: Thesis Instituti Hungarici Universitatis Holmiensis.

——— (1954) 'Kamassian verse', *Journal of American Folklore* 67: 369–77.

Simoncsics, P. (1986) *Aenigma Camassica,* Pomaz: Editio propria. 7 pp.

——— (1988) 'Rejtélyes liliom', in: *Studia in honorem P. Fábián, F. Rácz, I. Szathumán oblata a collegiis et discipulis* Budapest: n.p., pp. 125–32.

——— (1993a) 'Szibériai delikatesz' [= 'A Siberian delicacy. Yet another Kamassian riddle analysed'], *Nyelvtudományi közlemények* 91: 195–202.

——— (1993b) 'Kamassz világ – ahogy a találóskérdések mutatják' [= 'The World of the Kamassian – as it is seen through riddles'], in M.Sz. Bakró-Nagy and E. Szíj (eds), *Hajdú Péter 70 éves,* Linguistica Series A, Studia et dissertationes 15, Budapest: MTA Nyelvtudományi Intézet, pp. 371–82.

Index